An introduction to
Positive Economics

sixth edition

An introduction to

Positive
Economics

Richard G. Lipsey

Sir Edward Peacock Professor
of Economics, Queen's University,
Kingston, Ontario

Weidenfeld and Nicolson London

© 1963 by Richard G. Lipsey
First printed October 1963

Second edition October 1966
Reprinted August 1967
Reprinted May 1968
Reprinted March 1969
Reprinted September 1970
Reprinted November 1970

Third edition August 1971
Reprinted March 1972

PAPERBACK EDITION
first published 1972
Reprinted September 1973
Reprinted May 1974

Fourth edition July 1975
Reprinted 1976

Fifth edition 1979
Reprinted 1980 (twice)
Reprinted 1982

Sixth edition 1983
Reprinted 1985

Part of this sixth edition appeared
in the United States in *Economics*
by Richard G. Lipsey and
Peter O. Steiner, © 1981,
published by Harper and Row.

Weidenfeld and Nicolson
91 Clapham High St, London SW4

ISBN 0 297 78264 9 cased
ISBN 0 297 78265 7 paperback

Printed in Great Britain by
Butler & Tanner Ltd
Frome and London

To Diana

Contents

Fact and theory in economics

'. . . Einstein started from facts – the Morley Michelson measurements of light, the movements of the planet Mercury, the unexplained aberrancies of the moon from its predicted place. Einstein went back to facts or told others where they should go, to confirm or to reject his theory – by observation of stellar positions during a total eclipse.

'. . . It is not necessary, of course, for the verification of a new theory to be done personally by its propounder. Theoretical reasoning from facts is as essential a part of economic science as of other sciences, and in a wise division of labour there is room, in economics, as elsewhere, for the theoretician pure and simple, for one who leaves the technical business of verification to those who have acquired a special technique of observation. No one demanded of Einstein that he should visit the South Seas in person, and look through a telescope; but he told others what he expected them to see, if they looked, and he was prepared to stand or fall by the result. It is the duty of the propounder of every new theory, if he has not himself the equipment for observation, to indicate where verification of his theory is to be sought in facts – what may be expected to happen or to have happened if his theory is true, what will not happen if it is false.

'[Now consider by way of contrast the behaviour of the participants in a current controversy in economics.] . . . None of them takes the point that the truth or falsehood of . . . [a] . . . theory cannot be established except by an appeal to the facts; none of them tests it by facts himself. The distinguishing mark of economic science as illustrated by this debate is that it is a science in which verification of generalizations by reference to facts is neglected as irrelevant. . . . I do not see how . . . [members of the public who survey the controversy] . . . can avoid the conclusion that economics is not a science concerned with phenomena, but a survival of medieval logic, and that economists are persons who earn their livings by taking in one another's definitions for mangling.

'. . . I know that in speaking thus I make enemies. I challenge a tradition of a hundred years of political economy, in which facts have been treated not as controls of theory, but as illustrations. I shall be told that in the Social Sciences verification can never be clean enough to be decisive. I may be told that, in these sciences, observation has been tried and has failed, has led to shapeless accumulations of facts which themselves lead nowhere. I do not believe for a moment that this charge of barrenness of past enquiries can be sustained; to make it is to ignore many achievements of the past and to decry much solid work that is being done at this School and elsewhere. But if the charge of barrenness of realistic economics in the past were justified completely, that would not be a reason for giving up observation and verification. It would only be a reason for making our observations more exact and more numerous. If, in the Social Sciences, we cannot yet run or fly, we ought to be content to walk, or to creep on all fours as infants. ... For economic and political theorizing not based on facts and not controlled by facts assuredly does lead nowhere.

'There can be no science of society till the facts about society are available. Till 130 years ago we had no census, no knowledge even of the numbers and growth of the people; till fifteen years ago we had no comprehensive records about unemployment even in this country, and other countries are still where we were a generation or more ago; social statistics of every kind – about trade, wages, consumption – are everywhere in their infancy.

'... From Copernicus to Newton is 150 years. Today, 150 years from the *Wealth of Nations*, we have not found, and should not expect to find, the Newton of economics. If we have travelled as far as Tycho Brahe we may be content. Tycho was both a theorist and an observer. As a theorist, he believed to his last day in the year 1601 that the planets went round the sun and that the sun and the stars went round the earth as the fixed centre of the universe. As an observer, he made with infinite patience and integrity thousands of records of the stars and planets; upon these records Kepler, in due course, based his laws and brought the truth to light. If we will take Tycho Brahe for our example, we may find encouragement also. It matters little how wrong we are with our existing theories, if we are honest and careful with our observations.'

Extracts from Lord Beveridge's farewell address as Director of
the London School of Economics, 24 June 1937. Published in *Politica*, September 1937.

The use of this book

This is an introductory textbook in economics, starting at an elementary stage and progressing, in some places, to an intermediate level. It is designed to be read as a first book in economics. I hope, on the other hand, that the book will not be without interest for someone who has already studied one of the many existing basic textbooks written at a first-year university standard. The details of the complete revision which this latest edition has received are given in the 'Notes on the Sixth Edition' which follow this preface.

The book had its beginnings when I was asked to give the basic economic theory lectures for the revised B.Sc.(Econ.) degree introduced at the London School of Economics in October 1961. I started to write my first few lectures and, almost before I knew it, a book was well under way. Had I appreciated at the outset what was involved in carrying such a project through to completion, I would never have begun it, but that is probably true of a great many enterprises in all fields.

There are three major themes of this textbook which should be mentioned here: first, an attempt to explain what economic theory is about and how one can go about criticizing it effectively and hence improving it; second, an attempt to elaborate, in so far as is possible within the confines of an introduction to economic theory, the relation between theory and real-world observations; and third, a consideration of the relation between economic theory and economic policy.

The first major theme of this book is how one can go about being intelligently and constructively critical of the existing body of economic theory. I have tried to address myself throughout to the intelligent student of honours-school quality. I have assumed that the student was interested in the subject and that he or she wished to know, at every stage, what was going on and why. There is a tradition of trying to sneak quite complex bits of analysis past students without telling them what is happening. This may be the best thing to do if the object is to get through an examination a large mass of people who have neither interest nor ability in economics, and who are hostile to the basic idea of a Social Science. I am not interested in reaching such a public. I have assumed that I am addressing an intelligent set of students, who may or may not be honours students and intending specialists, but who want to learn and who do not have closed minds. One of the troubles with the traditional approach of sneaking analysis past the student is that, when the intelligent reader feels that there is something wrong with what has been taught, he or she does not know how to go about being critical of it in an effective way. I have made a point of telling the student what is going on, to say 'now we are doing comparative-static equilibrium analysis' or whatever it might be, and I have devoted considerable space to an analysis of both sensible and silly criticisms of the theories described. I do not accept the idea that the possibility of criticizing what has been learned should not be mentioned because, if it is, the student will be led to make hasty and confused criticisms. A good student will always attempt criticisms and evaluations of what he or she has been taught. It seems to me that criticisms are much more likely to be informed and relevant ones if students are given both practice and instruction in how to set about effectively challenging what they have been taught than if they meet a conspiracy of silence on this topic.

The second major theme is the relation between economic theory and observation. All too often economic theory is taught merely as logical analysis, and is, at best, only vaguely related to the world, while applied economics becomes description unenlightened by any theoretical framework. Economic theory is meant to be about the real world. We seek, by the use of theory, to explain, understand and predict phenomena in the real world, and our theory must therefore be related to, and tested by, empirical observations. The student of economic theory needs to ask at every stage what are the relevant empirical magnitudes and quantities. This is the theme set by the quotation from Beveridge that opens this book.[1]

The third major theme is the relation between economic theory and economic policy. The distinction between positive and normative statements is well known to professional economists, but all too often we fail to communicate its significance to our students. Even the best American textbooks often manage to convey the idea that economic theory justifies the private-enterprise market economies found in most Western countries. The experience of interviewing, for admission to the London School of Economics and later to the University of Essex, students who had done A-level economics at school made it painfully obvious that from somewhere – I am never sure from where – students get such ideas as the ones that the 'Law' of Comparative Advantage proves that nations *ought* to specialize in the production of certain goods, or that economics has proved that rent and price controls are wicked and ought not to be used. The student who can think of good reasons why, under some circumstances, price and rent controls and tariffs might be desirable, reacts by dismissing economics as medieval Scholasticism, or as a fraud perpetrated by whichever political party he happens not to support; and so he should do if economics did purport to prove such propositions. Economic theory cannot, of course, ever show us what we ought to do, but only what will happen if we do do certain things. The uses and the limitations of economic theory in dealing with matters of public policy is a theme which recurs throughout the book.

The study of economics can be both interesting and rewarding. To students not intending to specialize in economics it can give some understanding of the functioning of the economy, and some appreciation of the issues involved in current controversies over economic policy. It may also give him some idea of the methods which have been applied with some modest success in one Social Science. To would-be economics specialists, the study of an introductory book, such as this one, can be the beginning of a real adventure. The scope of your chosen science opens up before you. At first you encounter theories which add to your understanding of the world, but very soon you begin to encounter problems: observations for which there are no satisfactory explanations, and theories which are generally agreed to be unsatisfactory, but which have not been adequately tested. Both of these constitute a challenge, in the first case for the development of new theories and in the second

---

[1] I take it that in the last sentence quoted, Beveridge is saying that it does not matter how wrong present theories may be as long as we make careful observations of the facts on which these theories stand or fall, and then discard or amend theories when they are found to be inconsistent with the facts.

for the making of a careful set of observations to test an existing theory. One of the interesting things about economics today is that the frontiers of knowledge in terms of unsolved problems can be reached very quickly, even though, as the reader of this book will soon learn, it may take a very long time to reach the frontiers of knowledge in terms of techniques available for the handling of problems.

Economics is a subject quite unlike some other subjects studied at school. Economic theory has a logical structure; it tends to build on itself from stage to stage. Thus the student who only imperfectly understands some concept or theory will run into increasing difficulty when, in subsequent developments, this concept or theory is taken for granted and built upon. Because of its logical structure, quite long chains of reasoning are encountered: if A then B, if B then C, if C then D, and if D then E. Each step in the argument may seem simple enough, but the cumulative effect of several steps, one on top of the other, may be bewildering on first encounter. Thus when, having followed the argument step by step, the reader encounters the statement 'now obviously if A then E', it may not seem obvious at all. This is a problem which almost everyone encounters with chains of reasoning. The only way to deal with it is to follow the argument through several times. Eventually, as one becomes familiar with the argument, it will become obvious that, *if A then E.*

Another problem is posed by the fact that economics has a large technical language or jargon. At first students feel that all they are being asked to do is to put complicated names to common-sense ideas. To some extent this is true. At the beginning, economics consists largely of making explicit ideas which appeal strongly to common sense and which one has already held in a vague sort of way. This is a necessary step, because loose thinking about vaguely formed ideas is a quick route to error in economics. Furthermore, the jargon, the single word or phrase given to the common-sense idea, becomes necessary in the interests of brevity of expression as the subject is built up. You should try the exercise of removing every technical term from the argument of one of the later chapters in this book and replacing these terms with the full verbal description of the ideas expressed. The argument would then become too cumbersome. If we are going to put several ideas together to see what follows from them, then the single clearly defined word or phrase to refer to these ideas becomes a necessary part of our equipment.

It follows from all of this that you should use this book in quite a different way than you would use a book on many other subjects. A book on economics is to be worked at, and understood step by step, and not to be read like a novel. It is usually a good idea to read a chapter quickly in order to see the general run of the argument and then to re-read it carefully, making sure that the argument is understood step by step. You should be prepared at this stage to spend a very long time on difficult sections. You should not be discouraged if, occasionally, you find yourself spending an hour on only two or three pages. A paper and pencil is a necessary piece of equipment in your reading. Difficult arguments should be followed by building up one's own diagram while the argument unfolds, rather than by relying on the printed diagram which is, perforce, complete from the beginning. Numerical examples should be invented to illustrate general propositions. At various stages you are asked to put the book down and think out the answer to some problem for yourself before you read on: *you should never read on without attempting to do what is asked.* You should also make your own glossary of technical terms, committing the definitions to memory. The first time a technical term is introduced, it is printed in capital letters so that it may easily be recognized as such.

After the book has been read in this detailed manner, it should be re-read fairly quickly from cover to cover; it is often difficult to understand why certain things are done until one knows the end product, and, on a second reading, much that seemed strange and incomprehensible will be seen to have an obvious place in the analysis.

In short, the technical vocabulary aside, one must seek to understand economics, not to memorize it. Memorization is the royal road to disaster in economics; theories, principles and concepts are always turning up in slightly unfamiliar guises. To one who has understood his or her economics, this poses no problem; to one who has merely memorized it, this spells disaster. *The required approach is not more difficult than, but it is different from, that encountered in many other subjects.*

This is a book about economic theory. Although I have tried to relate the theory to the real world and although where the theory is inextricably bound up with institutions, as in the money supply, I have described British institutions, I have not tried to fill in details of the institutions or structure of any one economy in *Positive Economics*. Instead I have joined forces with Professor Colin Harbury of City University, London, to write a descriptive companion to *Positive Economics*. This book, *An Introduction to the UK Economy: A Companion to Positive Economics* (Pitman, 1983), is designed to give the institutional and factual background needed for an application of economic theory to the UK economy. We have tried not to clutter our *Companion* with unnecessary details but rather to give our readers a feel for the economy's essential features and basic orders of magnitude. Of course there are many other valuable books on the UK economy, although some are in our view too detailed while others are not detailed enough. For myself, however, I can do no better than to recommend the book that Professor Harbury and I wrote at what we hoped was the right level to accompany the study of *Positive Economics*.

One major aid that is available to you is the *Workbook* prepared by Rosemary Clarke, John Stilwell and myself. It is very easy to think you understand a verbal presentation, only to discover that you do not when you come to use what you have tried to learn. The *Workbook* is designed to test your comprehension at every stage and to send you back to the relevant part of the text when your comprehension is faulty. Without using a workbook or doing its equivalent in class exercises, most readers will get much less than they could out of this book.

Students who would like to see a more formal treatment of some of the theories and those who would like an introduction to the necessary mathematics should consult *An Introduction to a Mathematical Treatment of Economics* (3rd edition, Weidenfeld and Nicolson, 1977) by G.C. Archibald and myself.

You should seek to master completely one textbook, but, generally, you should not confine yourself exclusively to this one book; you should read sections in other texts, particularly those sections dealing with ideas that you find difficult. There are many first-class books to which you can refer, and unfortunately there is an even larger number of not-very-good books and you should seek expert advice before adopting a book for major study.

The first chapter of this book is a general essay on scientific method, particularly as it applies to the Social Sciences. None of the ideas is unduly difficult but each may seem rather abstract and 'up in the air' to someone unable to relate it to a detailed knowledge of some social science. The ideas are, however, of critical importance. You should read the chapter carefully to get the general drift of the argument. You should refer back to it at times when the issues raised turn up in the contexts of particular bits of economics and, finally, when you have finished the whole book you should re-read Chapter 1, making sure that you follow the argument fully.

Chapter 2 deals with the economists' tools of analysis. It is not necessary to be a mathematician to learn economics, but it is necessary to have a mastery of the equivalent of O-Level mathematics. There is not room in an economics textbook to teach the elementary mathematics that is assumed in economics. The Appendix to Chapter 2 does, however, outline some of the most important techniques that are commonly used. Readers who are unsure of any of the points outlined must go back to an elementary mathematics textbook and review these.

Finally I should like to say a word of thanks to all those people who have made this book possible. In so far as the ideas and viewpoints expressed here are novel, they are the common property of all my colleagues who in the late 1950s and early 1960s were members of the L.S.E. *Staff Seminar on Methodology, Measurement and Testing in Economics*. All that I did in the first edition was to give a slightly personal expression to this general viewpoint. Mr K. Klappholz read the manuscript of the first edition, removing countless blemishes, and contributed greatly to some of the novel ideas expressed therein. Mr R. Cassen read the proofs and contributed many last-minute improvements. Professor G. C. Archibald and John Black gave detailed scrutiny of the proofs of the second and third editions respectively and their penetrating criticisms led to many improvements. Ms Claire Rubin contributed greatly to the fifth edition. Major help on the sixth edition came from Professor Douglas Purvis. Traces of his ideas can be found everywhere. In particular, however, he has contributed heavily to the integration of open-economy aspects into the macro part of the book. Major thanks also go to Mr Bryan Hurl, Mr Somnath Sen and Mr David Tash for contributing a series of comments and suggestions that have had an important influence particularly on the microeconomic part of the book. The largest single debt of all I owe to Professor P. O. Steiner, who co-authored with me the American textbook *Economics*. To Professor Steiner, who was everywhere my severe critic and often my teacher, I and the substance of the present book owe a very great debt.

The executor of Lord Beveridge's estate has kindly granted permission to quote extracts from Beveridge's farewell address at the London School of Economics. Thanks are also due to Macmillan and McGraw-Hill for permission to quote from Lord Robbins' *Essay on the Nature and Significance of Economic Science* and *The British Economy* respectively. Harper and Row has also been generous in giving their permission to quote at length from material first prepared for the American textbook *Economics*, written by Professor P. O. Steiner and myself.

I am also extremely grateful to the many users, students and teachers, who have taken the trouble to write to me pointing out errors, making comments and suggestions. Economics is a subject in which one never stops learning and it is always gratifying to realize that one can still learn from one's students. I hope that the readers of this book will continue to teach me with as many further comments and criticisms as they have in the past. At one time or another valuable research assistance has been provided by M. V. Blandon, June Wickins, P. Geary, J. Stilwell, A. Popoff, D. Gilchrist, and T. Whitehead. Mrs S. Craig, Mrs Evelyn Dean, Miss Tina Brown, Mrs Joanne Marlieb, Mrs Marlene Rego, Miss Laura Elston and Miss Cynthia Price have shown unlimited patience in dealing with manuscripts. Thing I, George, Chekov, Pushkin, and Tiger Lilly have sat on my manuscript, chewed my pen and otherwise offered invaluable feline assistance through successive editions. The usual disclaimer of course holds here: for all shortcomings and mistakes remaining I am solely to blame.

R. G. LIPSEY
Sir Edward Peacock Professor of Economics
at Queen's University, Ontario

Notes on the sixth edition

The sixth edition has had the most thorough rewriting of any edition since the second. I have sought to create a book that is as relevant to the 1980s as the first edition was to the 1960s. I hope that the book will continue to prove valuable as an introduction to economics to beginners who are serious about their subject, but I also hope that, even more than in the recent past, I have provided a book that students will find useful as an overview throughout their undergraduate studies. It used to be said of Samuelson's great textbook that students who failed their American Ph.D. comprehensive examinations failed because they had not really understood something that was in Samuelson. I hope it is still true that successful students at the BA level in Britain are still working to understand some of the ideas presented in Lipsey. The major points concerning the sixth edition are presented under three headings: the open economy, microeconomics and macroeconomics.

The open economy

One of the major changes in this edition is a long-overdue integration of the open economy into the entire treatment. All previous editions followed the old Keynesian tradition of dealing with closed economies throughout the bulk of the book and then introducing the complications of foreign trade and finance almost as an afterthought. In the sixth edition I have sought to integrate open-economy considerations wherever they are relevant and in particular into the discussion of macroeconomic policy. The gains from trade and exchange rates are introduced, in a wholly new Chapter 11, as illustrations of the use of production-possibility curves and demand-supply models. Part 6, near the end of micro, deals with real trade problems. Chapter 30 on the gains from trade and the theory of commercial policy is based on the old Chapters 42 and 43. Chapter 31 on less developed economies is the old Chapter 47 reordered and somewhat updated.

In the basic macro model the effect of foreign trade in reducing the multiplier is shown in Chapter 36. Chapter 37 then goes on to introduce the absorption approach and such concepts as 'expenditure changing' and 'expenditure switching' as well as other basic open-economy issues that arise in the theory of income determination. Finally, Chapter 45 discusses the complications raised by the openness of the economy for issues of economic policy. The first part covers fixed and flexible exchange rates and is based on material from the old Chapters 43 and 45. The second part is wholly new. It considers the limitations of monetary and fiscal policy caused by the openness of the economy. It goes on to deal with problems, such as exchange-rate overshooting, which were raised by recent international experiments with monetarist doctrines.

Microeconomics

I have reworked all of the microeconomic chapters but have made no change in their structure, other than the integration of the material on international trade. Most chapters have new material, such as that on the pricing policies of nationalized industries which has been added to Chapter 23.

A major change is to introduce more analysis relevant to the micro underpinnings of standard Keynesian macroeconomic models. As the profession rightly becomes more concerned with these micro underpinnings, the American tradition of teaching macro before micro becomes increasingly outdated. This tradition, which is a now-conservative attachment to Samuelson's revolutionary approach of the early 1950s, shows how easy it is for today's liberating revolutions to become tomorrow's inhibiting orthodoxies. I have added to the chapter on oligopoly a major section which derives from my 1981 presidential address to the Canadian Economics Association[1] explaining how Keynesian macro models (which all of us teach) are rooted in a particular theory of short-run oligopolistic pricing (which not all of us teach). My embarrassment that earlier editions did not include this section is only mitigated by my discovery, on doing research for the address, of just how little explicit elaboration of these links exists anywhere in the literature. Nonetheless, this theory – of short-run oligopolistic pricing – underlies Keynesian macro models where quantities are demand-determined and goods markets can come to a state of rest where firms would like to sell more at prevailing prices but there is no significant tendency for these prices to fall. I have also added a section at the end of Chapter 27 on labour, giving the outlines of a general version of implicit contract theory. I do not believe that this is the final answer to problems of labour-market behaviour but I understand the theory to reveal the basic issue that underlies the factor-market underpinnings of Keynesian macro models: why do labour markets come to rest in situations in which more people would like to work at the going wage rate than can find jobs while there is no significant pressure for wage rates to fall? Without an understanding of these issues of micro underpinnings, one cannot sensibly assess current criticisms of orthodox Keynesian macro models.

I have also added quite a bit on optimality. This is mainly in response to teachers who say they wish to discuss the issue. As one of the authors of 'The General Theory of Second Best'[2], however, I cannot repeat optimality considerations in a totally uncritical fashion. Instead Chapter 32 outlines the strong *intuitive* case for relying heavily on the price mechanism but also assesses the problems arising out of the *formal* case for relying on the price system when this case is based on the optimality of perfect competition.

Macroeconomics

The most thorough revisions of this edition have been reserved for macroeconomics. The details of the changes are discussed below. To users at an elementary level there are two major problems in the new treatment. First, I have used some elementary algebra. This looks formidable on the printed page but the mathematics involved is simple and *well* inside of the frontiers reached by O-level mathematics. Second, I have gone beyond the old-fashioned introduction based on the aggregate

---

[1] R. G. Lipsey, 'The Understanding and Control of Inflation: Is There a Crisis in Macroeconomics?', *Canadian Journal of Economics*, XIV, November 1981.

[2] R. G. Lipsey and K. J. Lancaster, 'The General Theory of Second Best', *Review of Economic Studies*, XXVII, March 1957.

expenditure function and the 45° line. It seems to me that none of today's issues can be discussed without, first, the integration of money and interest rates that is accomplished by the *IS-LM* model and, second, the separation of demand and supply shocks that is accomplished by the aggregate-demand/aggregate-supply model. I believe that a book which wishes to touch on modern macro-policy issues and controversies cannot any longer stop short of these models. Chapters 47 and 48 go further to a model of continuous inflation and a discussion of some current policy controversies. These may be omitted by anyone seeking to stop short of the full treatment of this book. Below is a more detailed consideration of some of the major changes made to the macro part of the book.

(1) I have finally come to the view that it is wrong to avoid the use of school algebra in the macro section of the text. Accordingly I have used linear algebra to lay out the models formally and to manipulate them. All of the mathematics used is well within the capabilities of anyone who has passed O-level mathematics. The use of algebra in the text does, however, pose problems for two quite different types of student. *To those who had difficulty with O-level mathematics, some of the algebra may seem formidable. It is not. It is in fact intellectually simpler than some of the issues in the micro part of the book that are expressed through words and graphs. With some practice to breed familiarity, no one who is capable of understanding the ideas expressed throughout this book is incapable of handling the very elementary algebra that I use.* There is a different problem for students who know mathematics, say at an A-level standard. The algebra used will for them be so simple that there is a danger they will conclude that the economics comprehended by the algebra is trivial. This is not so. Indeed some very subtle economic ideas can be expressed by some very simple mathematics. For example, the law on comparative advantage can be expressed, in its linear version, in a few lines of algebra. Yet a full understanding of its implications continues to evade many policy-makers, and not a few economists, a century and a half after it was first stated. The subtlety in the economics that can be expressed in elementary mathematics is in the economic behaviour that lies behind, and gives rise to, the expressions written down mathematically. Because of this I have not relied exclusively, or even mainly, on the algebra. On all points I have used words and geometry as well. This should help readers to begin to learn how to relate verbal and geometrical discussions to their algebraic counterparts. Once one does get used to it, the algebra provides a simplicity and a finality to theoretical arguments that often seem both complex and uncertain when expressed in verbal and geometric terms alone.

Some readers of the manuscript have asked 'why mathematics in the macro part but not in the micro part?' The answer is that microeconomics, being based on relations that are essentially non-linear, is involved with calculus almost from the outset and, being based on maximizing models, soon requires the techniques of constrained maximization. Not only are these techniques beyond the O-level syllabus, some of them are beyond A-level. In contrast macro models, not being maximizing models (at least until we get to the theory of policy), do not need constrained maximizing techniques. Even more important, there is nothing fundamentally non-linear about the relations. We can, therefore, linearize all behavioural relations at the outset, as I do, and use very elementary algebra.[1]

---

[1] We could if we prefer use general functional forms for all our behavioural relations. The models are then solved by substituting definitional and behavioural equations into the equilibrium conditions, totally differentiating these, setting the results up in matrix form and solving using Cramers' rule. Although dropping the assumptions of linearity may be good practice for more advanced theorizing, it produces no new insights since all of the results are the same, only with partial derivatives replacing the parameters of the linearized version.

(2) The introductory macro chapter, Chapter 34, is wholly new. The first part considers the major macro variables as objects of policy, and the second part is a new introduction to national-income accounting that avoids my use of the four increasingly complex models that seemed unnecessary at this point.

(3) The macro model has been greatly extended beyond what can be found in any earlier edition of *IPE*. Basically there is only a single macro model of the demand side of the economy. But simpler versions of it arise by treating as exogenous some variables that are endogenous in the full model. Part 8 takes the rate of interest and the price level as exogenous and so produces the standard Keynesian 'diagonal cross model' with the aggregate expenditure function and the $E = Y$ 45° line. This model carried the burden of the formal analysis in previous editions. It is no longer an adequate framework for even an introductory discussion of most current policy issues. To talk about policy issues today we need two further developments. First, money must be formally integrated, which is achieved by treating the interest rate as an endogenous variable thus giving rise to the *IS-LM* model. Second, we need to make the price level endogenous, which creates the aggregate-demand/aggregate-supply version of the model. This allows us to separate out demand and supply shocks, and to explain the phenomenon of stagflation that seemed such a mystery only a decade ago.

When I first decided to go beyond the $E = Y$ model, I thought I would follow the emerging American tradition (which Professor Steiner and I helped to establish) of going straight from that simple version of the macro model to the full aggregate-demand/aggregate-supply version. This tends, however, to make the aggregate-demand curve a major mystery – and I do not wish to teach economics in such a way that it must seem a mystery even to those who try to understand rather than memorize it. The aggregate-demand curve is the locus of price-level (P) and real-income (Y) combinations where Y is the solution to the *IS-LM* version of the model and P is treated as an exogenous variable. To get this across in any meaningful way to a student, it seems to me that one has to go through the *IS-LM* model first. This takes the mystery out of the aggregate-demand curve and also has the advantage that monetary and fiscal policy can be put in their proper perspectives as alternative methods for shifting the aggregate-demand curve, one policy working through the *LM* curve and the other through the *IS* curve.

One concern I have about the increasing use of aggregate-demand/aggregate-supply models, particularly in American introductory texts, is that their formal analysis deals with once-and-for-all changes in the price level but the interpretative verbal discussion deals with varying inflation rates. I worry that we may be raising a generation of students who are seriously confused over the price level and its first time-derivative, the rate of inflation. In my treatment, I have tried very hard to match the interpretive words to the formal analysis, making it clear when we were dealing with once-and-for-all shocks to the price level and when we were dealing with variations in the rate of inflation.

The final part, 11, deals with some current issues in theory and policy. The first chapter, 46, can be read by anyone. Chapter 47 treads on some more difficult ground by introducing a model of continuous inflation. The model uses a Phillips curve relating inflation to the gap between actual and potential output to describe the effect of demand on inflation. It then adds core and shock inflation, leaving open the question of an exogenous wage-cost push due to such forces as competing demands for income shares. It is surprising how many economists whose econometric training should make them know better are prepared to draw a scatter diagram between unemployment and the percentage change in the RPI and dismiss by inspection any relation between demand forces and inflation. The Keynesian model of oligopoly pricing makes demand inflation work first through factor prices and only then onto goods prices. So many other forces such as supply shocks and inertias affect goods prices that only a carefully specified econometric model can detect the effect of current demand pressures on inflation rates. Most econometric studies do show such an effect, although it is only a small part of the total explanation of price changes. Many modern controversies turn on the strength and the timing of the influence of demand on inflation rates. The model of Chapter 47 is set up to handle these issues. This is the hardest of the analytical macro chapters, and students should not be too concerned if they find it difficult. Not a few professional economists are still confused on some of the issues discussed in this chapter.

The last chapter surveys some current controversies among Keynesians, traditional monetarists and new-Classicists. Some of these issues are very complex and are still being debated at the frontiers of the subject. The treatment is therefore impressionistic and should be read as such. I have used references in a way that I have not done in the rest of the book. Many are not suitable for beginners. They are there to show that I am not just expounding personal and possibly eccentric views, and to give suggestions for further readings for those who are not beginners but who may not be expert in this particular branch of the subject. I am alarmed at the spread in popularity of the new-Classicism among graduate students, particularly in the US where the bulk of English-language post-graduate training goes on. Personally I have no doubt that the beauty and precision of the new-Classicism's theoretical constructs is fully matched by their empirical irrelevance. I find it hard to take seriously a model where the tens of millions of people currently unemployed in the world survey the current rate of increase of the money supply, form an (incorrect) anticipation of the rate of inflation and then *voluntarily* withhold their labour because they estimate that the real wage will be too low to make work worthwhile. Nonetheless, I have tried to outline the core of its model faithfully. But readers who want to see the new-Classicism given a sympathetic treatment by someone who believes in its power to help us understand reality must go elsewhere.

A note on definitions

Definitions should be our tools not our masters. There is no right or wrong about definitions, but there are customary usages. Problems arise when, as is often the case, different definitions are customary in different branches of our subject. Confusion can then occur when various people are unknowingly using different definitions of the same term and, therefore, talking past each other. In this note I refer to some of the most common terminological problems.

Algebraic versus absolute values   If we compare two negative numbers such as -10 and -2, the one with the largest absolute value $(10 > 2)$ is algebraically smaller than the one with the smaller absolute value $(-10 < -2)$. Being unclear whether one is talking about absolute or algebraic values is an endless source of confusion. Here are two illustrations.

Elasticity of demand: The natural definition of elasticity of demand makes it a negative number. In this usage, the more responsive of two demands has the lower algebraic elasticity. Economists invariably speak of sensitive demands as having high elasticities and are therefore referring to absolute values. To conform to this linguistic custom, I define elasticity as a positive number by multiplying it by -1. This conforms with common language but not with much literature, where the negative sign remains and verbal descriptions refer to absolute values. Either approach will do if followed consistently, but students should be prepared to meet elasticities treated both in their natural form as negative numbers or transformed into positive numbers by the use of the multiplicative constant -1 in the definition (or just written as positive numbers out of sheer carelessness).

Marginal rate of substitution: Since both indifference curves and isoquants are downward sloping, their slopes, which are called the marginal rates of substitution, are negative. J. R. Hicks, who gave us our terminology for these curves, referred, however, to their flattening (as one moves downwards to the right along them) as the *diminishing marginal rate of substitution*. Here he was clearly referring to the absolute not the algebraic values of the slopes. To be algebraically correct, one should speak of increasing marginal rates of substitution, but we follow Hicks and refer to absolute values.

Relative prices Let the prices of goods A and B be symbolized by p_A and p_B. We can define their relative price as either p_A/p_B or p_B/p_A. For example, if A costs £4 while B costs £2, the first definition gives us 2 as the relative price, while the second definition gives us $\frac{1}{2}$. Both definitions convey the same information and students should not be encouraged to think that one is right and the other wrong – although one definition may be customary in certain circles (and the other customary in other circles). Here are two illustrations.

The exchange rate: It is standard practice in the theoretical literature of international economics to define the exchange rate as 'the number of units of domestic currency needed to buy one unit of foreign currency'. This treats foreign currency like any ordinary commodity where the price is quoted as how many units of domestic currency are needed to buy a unit of the commodity, and not how many units of the commodity can be bought by one unit of domestic currency (£1). On this usage, from Britain's point of view, the sterling-dollar exchange rate in March 1983 was about £0·68 to US$1.

Since I am writing a textbook on economic theory, I have followed this customary practice. Unfortunately, it is common in British financial circles to define the exchange rate the other way around, making its value £1 = US$1·47 in March 1983. The advantage of this usage is that when sterling depreciates in value, the exchange rate falls, while in the standard theoretical usage when sterling depreciates, the exchange rate rises.

Students should be flexible enough to use either definition and to realize that both convey identical information. Confusion can be avoided, however, by never talking about the exchange rate appreciating or depreciating but concentrating instead on the value of sterling. In either usage a change from the exchange rate quoted above to a rate of £0·80 = $1, i.e. £1 = $1·25, means a *fall or depreciation in the value of sterling*.

The terms of trade: To make contact with the theoretical concepts of opportunity cost, I have defined the terms of trade as the number of units of domestic commodities that must be exported to obtain a unit of imports: p_m/p_x. It is customary in official government publications to define the terms of trade the other way around, p_x/p_m. Again students should be willing, indeed encouraged, to look at any relative price both ways round – since it takes a lot of practice to feel at home reasoning with relative prices.

Investment goods There is an important distinction between the stock of capital, and the flow of gross investment by which the stock of capital is maintained and augmented. National accounts focus on the flow of investment and therefore identify plant and equipment, inventories and new housing as investment goods. This, of course, does not refer to the stocks of these goods but to the flows of current production of each, which is investment.

The aggregate demand function For a very long time the function $E = C + I + G + (X - M)$ was the mainstay of macro models and was referred to interchangeably as the 'aggregate expenditure' or the 'aggregate demand' function (or curve, when graphed). The first person to my knowledge to popularize the use of the relation between the price level and real national income was the American economist, William Branson, in an advanced macro textbook that was popular in the early 1970s. He called it *the economy's demand curve* to distinguish it from the E function which was then still commonly called the aggregate demand function. With the solution to the mystery of stagflation, aggregate supply analysis became important in the late 1970s. The key tools of macro analysis then became the two functions relating aggregate supply and aggregate demand to the price level. By the early 1980s the term aggregate demand curve was firmly established as the name for the latter function, and the term aggregate expenditure function was reserved for the E function. This terminology, which is the one now used in this book, has become standard in the advanced literature, common in intermediate texts and is just entering usage in elementary texts. It will be a long time, however, before the usage becomes universal. People educated in the earlier tradition and not doing research at the frontiers of macroeconomics may be expected to use the term aggregate demand to refer to $E = C + I + G + (X - M)$ for a long time to come. Readers should be warned of possible confusions that may arise from this evolution of terminology.

Part one

Scope and method

1

Introduction

Why has the history of most capitalist countries been one of several years of boom and plenty followed by several years of depression and unemployment with consequent poverty for a great many citizens? Why, during the 1930s in most capitalist countries, was up to one person in four unemployed while factories lay idle and raw materials went unused; why, in short, was everything available to produce urgently needed goods and yet nothing happened? Have we now learned, thanks to the theories propounded by many British and Continental scholars and then synthesized and further developed by an English academic economist writing over forty years ago from King's College, Cambridge, how to avoid for ever such devastating situations? Why, then, in the 1980s, did unemployment in Britain, the United States and several other countries reach the highest levels ever attained since the Great Depression of the 1930s? Is it really true that while the Great Depression of the 1930s overwhelmed unwitting and powerless governments, the great slump of the 1980s was deliberately engineered by governments who knew full well what they were doing?

What determines exchange rates and why do they change? Why was one British pound sterling worth 4·86 US dollars in 1930, 2·80 in 1950, 2·39 in 1970, 1·80 in 1976, 2·33 in 1980 and 1·65 at the beginning of 1983? What is the point of international trade and would Britain be better off if it reduced its dependence on trade? Are tariffs needed to protect home industries from unfair competition, particularly from low-wage countries?

What determines the level of wages and what influences do unions have on the share of national income going to labour? What functions do unions fulfil in today's world? Is it possible that having fully achieved the purpose of putting labour on an equal footing with management they have outlived their usefulness?

Must all modern economies make use of money? Could money be eliminated in a truly socialist state? How is it that new money can be created by ordinary commercial banks within broad limits, and by governments without limits? If money is valuable, why do economists insist that countries with large supplies of it are no richer than countries with small supplies?

Why did inflation accelerate so dramatically in most countries in the mid-1970s? Why did inflation peak at over 25 per cent in Britain and only 11 per cent in the United States? Are the group of economists called monetarists right in arguing that the primary cause of British inflation is the mismanagement of the British monetary system by that famous old institution, the Bank of England?

What influence does government have on people's welfare? What are the effects of a government's taxation policies? What are the effects of public expenditure? How important to our welfare is the size of our national debt?

These are the types of questions with which economists concern themselves, and on which the theories of economics are designed to shed some light. Such a list may give you a better idea of the scope of economics than could be obtained at this stage from an enumeration of the common textbook definitions.

When you begin this book you are setting out on a study of positive economics or, to use a slightly more accurate phrase, POSITIVE ECONOMIC SCIENCE. From the questions listed above you now have some idea of the scope of *economics*. Next we must consider in some detail what is meant by the terms *positive* and *science*. After that we will ask whether or not it is really possible to conduct a scientific study of anything that is basically concerned with human behaviour. Economics is generally regarded as a social science, but can any study of human behaviour ever hope to be 'scientific'? Economists claim to be able to understand and to predict certain aspects of human behaviour. To anyone who wishes to be able to evaluate these claims this introductory discussion is critical, because the questions 'What can we hope to learn?' and 'How can we go about it?' are basic to the whole subject. These are also questions over which there is some disagreement among professionals and a vast amount of misunderstanding and even superstition among the general public.

Positive and normative statements

The success of modern science rests partly on the ability of scientists to separate their views on *what does happen* from their views on *what they would like to happen*. For example, until the nineteenth century virtually all Christians, Jews and Mohammedans believed that the earth was only a few thousand years old. About two hundred years ago, evidence began to accumulate that some existing rocks were millions of years old, possibly even thousands of millions. Most people found this hard to accept; it would force them to rethink their religious beliefs and abandon those that were based on a literal reading of the Bible. Many wanted the evidence to be wrong; they wanted rocks to be only a few thousand years old. Nevertheless, the evidence continued to accumulate until today virtually everyone accepts that the earth is neither thousands, nor millions, but four or five thousand million years old. This advance in our knowledge came because the question 'How old are observable rocks?' could be separated from the feelings of scientists (many of them devoutly religious) about the age they would have liked the rocks to be.

Definitions and illustrations

Distinguishing what is from what we would like, or what we feel ought, to be,[1] depends partly on knowing the difference between *positive* and *normative* statements.

---

[1] This word 'ought' has two distinct meanings: the 'logical ought' and the 'ethical ought'. The logical ought refers to the consequences of certain things: e.g., 'you ought to leave now if you don't want to be late'. The ethical ought refers to the desirability of certain things: e.g., 'you ought to leave now because it is impolite to stay too long'. The text obviously refers to the ethical ought.

Positive statements are about what is, was or will be; they assert alleged facts about the universe in which we live. Normative statements are about what ought to be. They depend on our judgements about what is good or bad, and they are thus inextricably bound up with our philosophical, cultural and religious positions.

We say that normative statements depend on our VALUE JUDGEMENTS.

Let us consider some assertions, questions and hypotheses that can be classified as positive or normative. The statement 'It is impossible to break up atoms' is a positive one that can quite definitely be (and of course has been) refuted by empirical observations, while the statement 'Scientists ought not to break up atoms' is a normative statement that involves ethical judgements, and cannot be proved right or wrong by any amount of evidence. In economics the questions 'What policies will reduce unemployment?' and 'What policies will prevent inflation?' are positive ones, while the question 'Ought we to be more concerned about unemployment than about inflation?' is a normative one. The statement 'An increase in government spending will reduce unemployment and increase inflation' is a positive hypothesis. The statement 'Unemployment is a more serious social problem than inflation' is normative.

As an example of the importance of this distinction in the social sciences, consider the question 'Has the payment of generous unemployment benefits increased the amount of unemployment?' This positive question can be turned into a testable hypothesis by asserting something like: 'The higher are the benefits paid to the unemployed, the higher will be the total amount of unemployment.' If we are not careful, however, our attitudes and value judgements may get in the way of our study of this hypothesis. Some people are opposed to the welfare state and believe in an individualist, self-help ethic. They may hope that the hypothesis will be found correct because its truth could then be used as an argument against welfare measures in general. Others feel that the welfare state is a good thing, reducing misery and contributing to human dignity. They may hope that the hypothesis is wrong because they do not want welfare measures to produce results of which people disapprove. In spite of different value judgements and social attitudes, however, evidence is accumulating on this particular hypothesis. As a result, we have much more knowledge than we had ten years ago of why, where and by how much (if at all) unemployment benefits increase unemployment. This evidence could never have been accumulated or accepted if investigators had not been able to distinguish their feelings on how they wanted the answer to turn out from their assessment of evidence on how people actually behaved.

Positive statements such as the one just considered assert things about the world. If it is possible for a statement to be proved wrong by empirical evidence, we call it a TESTABLE STATEMENT. Many positive statements are testable, and disagreements over them are appropriately handled by an appeal to the facts.

In contrast to positive statements, which are often testable, normative statements are never testable. Disagreements over such normative statements as 'It is wrong to steal' or 'It is immoral to have sexual relations out of wedlock', cannot be settled by an appeal to empirical observations. Thus, for a rational consideration of normative questions, different techniques are needed to those used for a rational consideration of positive questions. Because of this, it is convenient to separate normative and positive enquiries. We do this not because we think the former are less important than the latter, but merely because they must be handled in different ways.

Some points of possible confusion

Having made this distinction between positive and normative, a number of related points require mention. Although we deal with them only briefly, any óne of them could be the subject of extended discussion.

The classification is not exhaustive The classifications 'positive' and 'normative' do not cover all statements that can be made. For example, there is an important class, called *analytic statements*, whose truth or falsehood depends only on the rules of logic. Consider the single sentence: 'If every X has the characteristic Y, and if this item Z is in fact an X, then it has the characteristic Y.' This sentence is true by the rules of logic, and its truth is independent of what particular items we substitute for X, Y, and Z. Thus the sentence '*If* all men are immortal *and if* you are a man, *then* you are immortal' is a true analytic statement. It tells us that *if* two things are true *then* a third thing must be true. The truth of this *statement* is not dependent on whether or not its individual parts are in fact true. Indeed the sentence 'All men are immortal' is a positive statement which has been refuted by myriad deaths. Yet no amount of empirical evidence on the mortality of men can upset the truth of the sentence '*If* all men are immortal *and if* you are a man, *then* you are immortal.'

Not all positive statements are testable A positive statement asserts something about the universe. It may be empirically true or false in the sense that what it asserts may or may not be true of the universe. If it is true, it adds to our knowledge of what can and cannot happen. Many positive statements are refutable: if they are wrong this can be ascertained (within a margin for error of observation) by checking them against data. For example, the positive statement that the earth is less than five thousand years old was tested and refuted by a mass of evidence which had been accumulated in the nineteenth century. The statement 'Angels exist and frequently visit the earth in visible form' is, however, also a positive statement. It asserts something about the universe. But we could never refute this statement with evidence because, no matter how hard we searched, believers could argue that we did not look in the right places or in the right way, or that angels won't reveal themselves to non-believers, or any one of a host of other alibis. Thus statements that could conceivably be refuted by evidence if they are wrong are a subclass of positive statements; other positive statements are irrefutable.

The distinction is not unerringly applied Because the positive-normative distinction helps the advancement of knowledge, it does not follow that all scientists automatically and unerringly apply it. Scientists are human beings. Many have strongly held values and they may let their value judgements get in the way of their assessment of evidence. For example, many scientists are not even prepared to consider evidence that there may be differences in intelligence among races because as good liberals they feel that all races ought to be equal. Nonetheless, the desire to separate *what is* from *what we would like to be* is a guiding light, an ideal, of science. The ability to do so, albeit imperfectly, is attested to by the acceptance, first by scientists and then by the general public, of many ideas that were initially extremely unpalatable – ideas such as the extreme age of the earth and the evolution of man from other animal species.

Ideals can be important even though they are not universally applied. Consider an analogy. (1) Many people try to be good (according to their own lights). (2) Most people do not live up to their own standards of goodness all of the time. (3) Ideas of goodness are an important force in motivating human behaviour. All three of these statements are probably true: the truth of (1) does not preclude the truth of (2) and the truth of (2) does not preclude the truth of (3). In an analogous way all three of the following statements might be true. (1) Positive and normative statements can be distinguished. (2) Not all scientists do, or even could, maintain the distinction all of the time. (3) The distinction has been a potent force in the advancement of knowledge and in the separation of knowledge from prejudice. Statement (1) does not preclude (2) and (2) does not preclude (3).[1]

Economists do not need to confine their discussions merely to positive statements Some critics have mistakenly assumed that economists must try to deal only in statements that are positive and testable. In fact the positive economist must spend time worrying about the correctness of analytic statements: 'Is a certain prediction actually implied by a certain set of assumptions?' He must also be prepared to have any number of non-testable assumptions in his theory as long as some testable predictions can be deduced from it. Also, he should not shrink from discussing value judgements, as long as he knows what he is doing. From the fact that positive economics does not include normative questions (because its tools are inappropriate to them) it does *not* follow that the student of positive economics must stop his inquiry as soon as someone says the word ought. The pursuit of what appears to be a normative statement will often turn up positive hypotheses on which our *ought* conclusion depends. For example, although many people wax quite emotional for or against government control of industry, probably few of them believe that government control is good or bad in itself. Their advocacy or opposition will be based on certain beliefs about relations which can be stated as positive rather than normative hypotheses. For example: 'Government control reduces (increases) efficiency, changes (does not change) the distribution of income, leads (does not lead) to an increase of state control in other spheres.' A careful study of this emotive subject will reveal an agenda for positive economic inquiry that could keep a research team of economists occupied for a decade.

The nature of positive economics

Positive economics is concerned with the development of knowledge about the behaviour of people and things in the world. This means that its practitioners are concerned with developing propositions that fall into the positive, testable class. This does not mean, however, that every single statement and hypothesis to be found in positive economics will actually be positive and testable. Some time ago a philosophy of knowledge called *logical positivism* was popular. It held that every single statement in the theory had to be positive and testable. This proved to be a harmful and unnecessary strait-jacket.

> **All that the positive economist asks is that something that is positive and testable should emerge from his theories somewhere – for if it does not, his theories will have no relation to the world around him.**

---

[1] Many critics of the idea of positive science have argued otherwise. They feel that because no person can ever be perfectly objective about other people, the idea of an objective, fact-guided science of human behaviour is a contradiction. Fortunately, science based on the testing of positive hypotheses is possible even though no one individual can be relied on completely and always to separate his judgement of facts from his desires on what he would like the facts to be.

The positive economist seeks ways of answering positive testable questions such as those listed at the outset of this chapter. His approach to these questions can, in a general way, be described as scientific. We must now consider in more detail just what the scientific approach is, and how scientific theories are developed and used.

The scientific approach

Very roughly speaking, the scientific approach consists in relating questions to evidence. This approach to a problem is what sets scientific inquiries off from other kinds of inquiries.[1]

In some fields, the scientist is able to generate observations that will provide evidence concerning any hypothesis that he wishes to test. Experimental sciences, such as chemistry and some branches of psychology, have an advantage because it is possible to produce relevant evidence through controlled laboratory experiments. Other sciences, such as astronomy and economics, cannot do this. They must wait for time to throw up observations that may be used to test hypotheses.

The ease or difficulty with which one can collect evidence does not determine whether or not a subject is scientific, although many people have thought otherwise.[2] The procedure of scientific inquiry does, however, differ radically between fields in which laboratory experiment is possible and those in which it is not. Here we consider general problems more or less common to all sciences. In Chapter 3 we deal with problems peculiar to the non-experimental sciences, which must accept those observations that the world of actual experience provides.

It is often said that we live in a scientific age. Over the last several hundred years the citizens of most Western countries have enjoyed the fruits of innumerable scientific discoveries. But the scientific advances that have so profoundly affected the average citizen have been made by an extremely small minority of the population. Most people have accepted these advances without the slightest idea either of the technical nature of the discoveries involved, or of the attitude of mind that made them possible. If we take as a measure of the influence of science the degree of dissemination of the fruits of science, then we live in a profoundly scientific age; but if we take as our measure the degree to which the general public understands and practises the scientific approach, then we are definitely in a pre-scientific era. Indeed, the scientific method of answering questions by appealing to a carefully collected and co-ordinated body of facts is a method that is seldom adopted by the public.

Consider, for example, the argument about capital punishment that continues even in many of the countries that have abolished the death penalty. It is possible to advocate capital punishment as an act of pure vengeance, or because we believe that morally a person who kills *ought* himself to be killed. If we argue about capital punishment on these grounds, we are involved in normative questions depending upon value judgements. The great majority of arguments for capital punish-

---

[1] Other approaches might be to appeal to authority, for example, to Aristotle or the Scriptures, to appeal by introspection to some inner experience (to start off 'all reasonable men will surely agree'), or to proceed by way of definitions to the 'true' nature of the problem or concepts under consideration.

[2] It is often thought that scientific procedure consists of grinding out answers by following blind rules of calculation, and that only in the arts is exercise of real imagination required. This view is misguided. What the scientific method gives is an impersonal set of criteria for answering some questions. What questions to ask, exactly how to ask them and how to obtain the evidence are difficult problems for which there are no rules. They require, upon occasion, great feats of imagination and ingenuity.

ment, however, are not of this type. Instead, they depend on predictions about observable behaviour, and thus belong to the field of science. These are usually variants of the general argument that capital punishment is a deterrent to murder.

It is truly amazing how people can become committed to agreeing or disagreeing with this proposition without considering the available evidence. How many people involved in these debates know anything, for example, of the mass evidence on murder rates before and after the abolition of capital punishment in the large number of jurisdictions where it has been abolished and in those few where it has been reimposed? Indeed most popular arguments for and against capital punishment involve a maximum of empirical questions and a minimum of empirical evidence used to arrive at the answers given. If we really believed in a scientific inquiry into human behaviour, we would try to state the arguments about capital punishment in terms of a specific set of propositions, and then set out systematically to gather evidence relating to each one.

We may conclude that many hotly debated issues of public policy involve positive, not normative, questions, but that the scientific approach to them is very often avoided.

A science of human behaviour?

The preceding discussion raises the question of whether or not it is possible to have a scientific study in the field of human behaviour.

Behaviour in various kinds of sciences

It is often argued that natural sciences deal with inanimate matter that is subject to natural 'laws', while the social sciences deal with man, who has free will and cannot, therefore, be made the subject of such (inexorable) laws. Such an argument, however, concentrates on the physical sciences; it omits biology and the other life sciences which deal successfully with animate matter. When this point is granted, it may then be argued that the life sciences deal with simple living material, while only the social sciences deal with human beings who are the ultimate in complexity and who alone possess free will. Today, when we are increasingly aware of our common heritage with apes in particular, and primates in general, an argument that man's behaviour is totally different from the behaviour of other animals finds few adherents among informed students of animal behaviour.

Human behaviour

Nonetheless, many social observers, while accepting the success of the natural and the life sciences, hold that there cannot be a successful social science. Stated carefully, this view implies that inanimate and non-human animate matter will show stable responses to certain stimuli, while humans will not. For example, if you put a match to a dry piece of paper the paper will burn, while if you try to extract vital information from unwilling human beings by torture, some will yield it and others will not, and, more confusingly, the same individual reacts differently at different times. Whether human behaviour does or does not show sufficiently stable responses to factors influencing it as to be predictable within an acceptable margin of error is a positive question that can only be settled by an appeal to evidence and not by *a priori* speculation.[1]

---

[1] *A priori* is a phrase commonly used by economists. It may be defined as that which is prior to actual experience, or as that which is innate or based on innate ideas.

In fact, it is a matter of simple observation that when we consider a group of individuals they do not behave in a totally capricious way, but do display stable responses to various stimuli. The warmer the weather, for example, the higher the number of people visiting the beaches and the higher the sales of ice-cream. It may be hard to say when or why one individual will buy an ice-cream, but we can observe a stable response pattern from a large group of individuals: the higher the temperature the greater the sales of ice-cream.

Many other examples will come to mind where, because we can say what the individual will probably do – without being certain of what he will do – we can say with quite remarkable accuracy what a large group of individuals will do. No social scientist could predict, for example, when an apparently healthy individual is going to die, but death rates for large groups are stable enough to make life insurance a profitable business. It could not be so if group behaviour were capricious. Also, no social scientist can predict what particular individuals will be killed in car accidents next holiday, but we can come very close to knowing how many in total will die, and the more objectively measurable data we have concerning, for example, the state of the weather on the day, and the increase in car sales over the last year, the closer we will be able to predict the total of deaths.

If group human behaviour were in fact random and capricious, existence would be impossible. Neither law, nor justice, nor airline timetables would be more reliable than a roulette wheel; a kind remark could as easily provoke fury as sympathy; one's landlady might put one out tomorrow or forgive one the rent. One cannot really imagine a society of human beings that could possibly work like this. Indeed a major part of brainwashing techniques is to mix up rewards and punishments until the victim genuinely does not know 'where he is': unpredictable pressures drive human beings mad. In fact, we live in a world which is some sort of mixture of the predictable, or average, or 'most of the people most of the time,' and of the haphazard, contrary, and random.

When we try to analyse our world, and apply our orderly models to it, we need help from specialists in probability – statisticians – but we have not yet found that we need the advice of experts in the behaviour of systems in states of total chaos.

The 'law' of large numbers

We may now ask how it is that we can predict group behaviour when we are never certain what a single individual will do. As a first step, we must distinguish between *deterministic* and *statistical* hypotheses. Deterministic hypotheses admit of no exceptions. An example would be the statement: 'If you torture any man over this period of time with these methods he will *always* break down.' Statistical hypotheses, however, admit of exceptions and purport to predict the probability of certain occurrences. An example would be: 'If you torture a man over this period of time with these methods he will *very probably* break down; in fact if you torture a large number of men under the stated circumstances about 95 per cent of them will break down.' Such an hypothesis does not predict what an individual will certainly do, but only what he will probably do. This does allow us, however, to predict within a determinable margin of error what a large group of individuals will do.

Successful predictions about the behaviour of large groups are made possible by the statistical 'law' of large numbers. Very roughly, this 'law' asserts that random movements of a large number of items tend to offset one another. The law is based on one of the most beautiful constants of behaviour in the whole of science, and yet the law can be derived from the fact that human beings make errors! This constant is the *normal curve of error* which you will encounter in elementary statistics.

Let us consider what is implied by the law of large numbers. Ask one person to measure the length of a room and it will be almost impossible to predict in advance what sort of error of measurement he will make. Thousands of things will affect the accuracy of his measurements. Furthermore, he may make one error today and quite a different one tomorrow. But ask one thousand people to measure the length of the same room and we can predict with a high degree of accuracy how this *group* will make its errors! We can assert with confidence that more people will make small errors than will make large errors, that the larger the error the fewer will be the number of people making it, that the same number of people will overestimate as will underestimate the distance, and that the average error of all the individuals will be zero.[1] Here then is a truly remarkable constant pattern of human behaviour; a constant on which much of the theory of statistical inference is based.

If a common cause should act on all members of the group we can successfully predict their average behaviour, even though any one member of the group may act in a surprising fashion. If, for example, we give all our thousand individuals a tape measure which understates 'actual' distances, we can predict that, on the average, the group will now understate the length of the room. It is, of course, quite possible that one member who had in the past been consistently undermeasuring distance because he was depressed will now overestimate the distance because the state of his health has changed; but something else may happen to some other individual that will turn him from an overmeasurer into an undermeasurer. Individuals may do peculiar things which, as far as we can see, are inexplicable, but the group's behaviour, when the inaccurate tape measure is substituted for the accurate one, will nonetheless be predictable, *precisely because the odd things that one individual does will tend to cancel out the odd things some other individual does.*

The nature of scientific theories

So far we have seen that there is real evidence that human behaviour does show stable response patterns. Theories grow up in answer to the question 'Why?' Some sequence of events, some regularity between two or more things is observed in the real world and someone asks why this should be so. A theory attempts to explain why. One of the main practical consequences of a theory is that it enables us to predict as yet unobserved events. For example, national income theory predicts that a cut in tax rates will reduce the amount of unemployment. The simple theory of market behaviour predicts that, if there is a partial failure of the potato crop, the total income earned by potato farmers will increase!

The construction of theories

A theory consists of a set of definitions, stating clearly what is meant by various terms, and a set of

---

[1] For purposes of measuring the error we define the 'true' distance to be that measured by the most precise instruments of scientific measurement (whose range of error will be very small relative to the range of error of our one thousand laymen all wielding tape measures). Those familiar with statistical theory will realize that the predictions in the text assume that all the necessary conditions, such as the existence of a large number of independent factors causing individuals to make errors, are fulfilled. The purpose of the discussion in the text is not to give readers a full appreciation of the subtleties of statistical theory, but to persuade them that anyone is misguided who holds the common view that free will and the absence of deterministic certainty about human behaviour makes a scientific study of such behaviour impossible.

assumptions about the way in which the world behaves. Students often worry about what appears to them to be the unrealistic assumptions that they encounter in economics. *It is important to remember, however, that all theory is an abstraction from reality.* If we did not abstract we would merely duplicate the world camera-style, and would add nothing to our understanding of it.

A good theory abstracts from reality in a useful way; a bad theory does not.

But how do we know if the abstractions of a particular theory are useful or not? To do this we must take the next step in the construction of theories: we follow a process of logical deduction to discover what is implied by the assumptions of the theory. For example, if we assume that businessmen always try to make as much profit as is possible, and if we make assumptions about how taxes affect their profits, we can derive implications about how they will behave when taxes change. These implications are the predictions of our theory. If the theory is useful, its predictions will pass empirical tests. For example, when taxes are next changed, businessmen will react in the way predicted by the theory.

Scientific predictions

We have seen above that a successful theory enables us to predict events. What is the nature of a scientific prediction, and is it the same thing as a prophecy about the future course of events?

A scientific prediction is a conditional statement having the form '*if* you do this *then* such and such will follow.'

If you mix hydrogen and oxygen under specified conditions, *then* water will be the result. *If* the government has a large budget deficit, *then* unemployment will be reduced. It is most important to notice that this prediction is very different from the statement: 'I prophesy that in two years' time there will be a large increase in employment because I believe the government will decide to have a large budget deficit.' The government's decision to have a budget deficit or surplus in two years' time will be the outcome of many complex factors, emotions, objective circumstances and chance occurrences, most of which cannot be predicted. If the economist's prophecy about the level of employment turns out to be wrong, because in two years' time the government does not have a large deficit, then all we have learned is that the economist is not a good guesser about the behaviour of the government; we will not have found evidence that conflicts with any economic theory. However, *if* the government does have a large deficit (in two years' time or at any other time) and *then* unemployment does not fall, we have found evidence conflicting with a (conditional) scientific prediction in the field of economics.[1]

---

[1] It is very important not to treat economic forecasting as synonymous with economic prediction. Forecasting is a type of conditional prediction which attempts to predict the future by discovering relations between economic variables of the sort that the value of Y at some future date depends on the value of X today, in which case future Y can be predicted by observing present X. Many conditional predictions are not of this form; those which relate the Y today to the value of X today provide significant and useful relations that allow us to predict 'if you do this to X you will do that to Y', without allowing us to forecast the future. The analogy often drawn between economics and weather forecasting relates to economic forecasting rather than to the wider class of scientific economic predictions.

The testing of scientific predictions

If we wish to test any theory we confront its predictions with evidence. We seek to discover if certain events have the consequences predicted by the theory. Some of the difficult problems involved in this task are the subject of Chapter 3. In the meantime we should notice that as with most other sciences it is never possible to prove or to refute any theory in economics with 100 per cent certainty.

Proof and refutation Consider the simple economic theory that predicts: 'If a sales tax is levied on the product of a competitive industry, *then* the price of the product will rise but by less than the amount of the tax.' It is not claimed that this prediction holds only for the years 1970–95, or only in odd-numbered years, nor is it supposed to hold in the USA and Germany but not in France and Paraguay. The theory simply says that this result will hold *whenever a sales tax is levied in an industry that is competitive*. We may say that the theory is unbounded both in time and in space. But since we can make only a limited number of observations, we can never prove conclusively that the theory is true. Even if we have made a thousand observations which agree with the prediction, it is always possible that in the future we will make observations which conflict with the theory. Since this possibility can never be ruled out completely (no matter how unlikely we might think it to be), we can never regard any theory as conclusively proved.

It is also impossible to refute any theory conclusively. This matter is considered in some detail in Chapter 3. Suffice it to say now that, since human beings make the tests, and since human beings are fallible, it is always possible that a piece of apparently conflicting evidence arose because we made a mistake in our observations. One conflicting observation does not worry us very much, but as a mass of them accumulate we become more and more worried about our theory and will regard it as less and less likely to be true. Eventually we shall abandon it, even though we can never be 100 per cent certain we are not making an error in doing so.

When is a theory abandoned? As a generalization we can say that our theories tend to be abandoned when they are no longer useful, and that they cease to be useful when they cannot predict the consequences of actions in which we are interested better than the next best alternative. When this happens the theory is abandoned and replaced by the superior alternative. In the process of upsetting existing theories we learn new, surprising facts.

Any developing science will continually be having some of its theories rejected; it will also be cataloguing observations that cannot be fitted into (explained by) any existing theory. These observations indicate the direction required for the development of new theories or for the extension of existing ones.[1] On the other hand, there will be many implications of existing theories that have not yet been tested, either because no one has yet figured out how to test them, or merely because no one has got around to testing them. These untested hypotheses provide agenda for new empirical studies.

---

[1] The development of a new theory to account for existing observations is often the result of real creative genius of an almost inspired nature. This step in the development of science is the exact opposite of the popular conception of the scientist as an automatic rule-follower. One could argue for a long time whether there was more original creative genius embodied in a first-class symphony or a new theory of astronomy. Fascinating studies of the creative process may be found in A. Koestler, *The Sleep Walkers* (Hutchinson, 1959), especially the section on Kepler, and J.D. Watson, *The Double Helix* (Wiedenfeld and Nicolson, 1968).

The state of economics

Economics provides no exception to the comments made in the previous paragraph. On the one hand, there are many observations for which no fully satisfactory theoretical explanation exists. On the other hand, there are many predictions which no one has yet satisfactorily tested. Thus serious students of economics must not expect to find a set of answers to all possible questions as they progress in their study. They must expect very often to encounter nothing more than a set of problems for further theoretical or empirical research. Even when they do find answers to problems, they should accept these answers as tentative and ask, even of the most time-honoured theory: 'What observations might we make that would be in conflict with this theory?' Economics is still a very young science and many problems in it are almost untouched. Those of you who venture further in this book may well, only a few years from now, publish a theory to account for some of the problems mentioned herein, or else you may make a set of observations which will upset some time-honoured theory described within these pages.

Having counselled disrespect for the authority of accepted theory, it is necessary to warn against adopting an approach that is too cavalier. No respect attaches to the person who merely says: 'This theory is for the birds; it is *obviously* wrong.' This is too cheap. To criticize a theory on logical grounds (economists sometimes say 'on theoretical grounds'), one must show that its alleged predictions do not follow from its assumptions. To criticize a theory effectively on empirical grounds, one must demonstrate by a carefully made set of observations that some aspect of the theory is contradicted by the facts. These tasks are seldom easily or lightly accomplished.

Figure 1.1 provides a summary of the discussion of theories. It shows a closed circuit, because theory and observation are in continuous interaction with each other. Starting at the top left (because we must start somewhere), we find the definitions of terms and assumptions of a theory. The theorist then deduces by logical analysis everything that is implied by the assumptions. These implications are the predictions of the theory. The theory is then tested by confronting its predictions with evidence. Tests may be made for the direct purpose of testing a theory, but they are also made incidentally whenever an applied economist uses the theory in a real-world context. If the theory is in conflict with facts, it will most likely be amended to make it consistent with the new facts (and thus make it a better theory); in extreme cases it will be discarded in place of a superior alternative. The process then begins again as the new or amended theory is subjected first to logical analysis and then to empirical testing.

Scientific crises

Sciences often appear to evolve through a series of stages. At first, an existing theory seems to be working well and the main scientific tasks are to extend it in various directions. Then, gradually, observations begin to accumulate that conflict with the theory. For a long time these exceptions are explained away on an ad hoc basis, but eventually the weight of conflicting evidence causes a crisis for the theory. Finally a breakthrough occurs, and some genius develops a new theory that comprehends both what still seems right in the older theory *and* the observations that were not accounted for. Once the new theory is accepted, often after an interlude of uncertainty and heated controversy, another period of consolidation and extension occurs until new conflicts between theory and observation emerge.

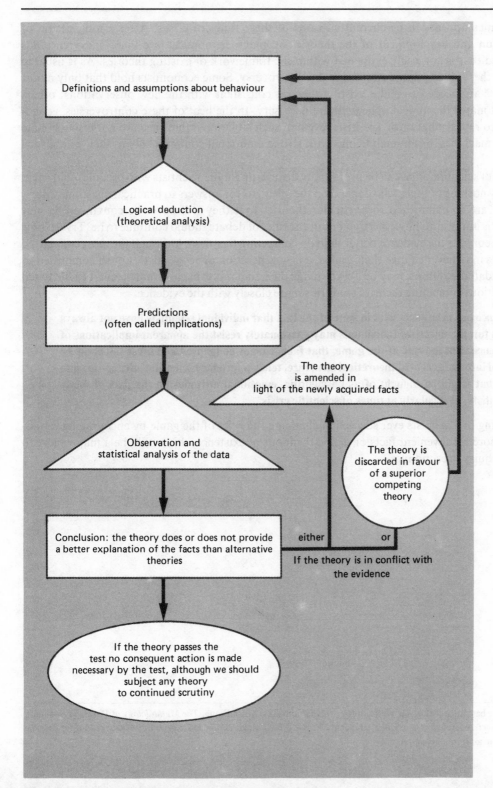

Fig. 1.1 The interaction of deduction and measurement in theorizing

Economics appears to be currently in one of these times of crises. After a long period of consolidation and development of the theories of 'macroeconomics' (see Part 7), evidence has accumulated that is not easily explained within the framework of existing theories. As is usual in such times, there is substantial confusion and controversy. Some economists hold that only minor amendments are needed to make existing theories consistent with the new observations; others believe that major theoretical upheavals are necessary. In the heat of these controversies, economists tend to reveal what most scientists reveal in such situations: that they are not dispassionate calculating machines, but human beings with strong emotional commitments to their established positions.

Periods of scientific crisis can be profoundly disturbing for the scientists who become involved in them, to say nothing of those who depend on the scientists for answers to practical questions. Many economists are so committed to particular theories that they will never be convinced by new evidence. It is important, however, that one of the rules of debate should continue to be 'Try to show that your theory fits the evidence better than do competing theories'. Although the most committed protagonists may never change their minds, a new generation of economists, not so committed to old and outdated positions, may be able to judge the issues more dispassionately and be able to tell which of various competing theories conforms more closely with the evidence.

> **Science has been successful in spite of the fact that individual scientists have not always been totally objective. Individuals may passionately resist the apparent implications of evidence. But the rule of the game, that facts cannot be ignored and must somehow be fitted into the accepted theoretical structure, tends to produce scientific advance in spite of what might be thought of as unscientific, emotional attitudes on the part of many scientists, particularly at times of scientific crisis.**

But if existing protagonists ever succeed in changing the rules of the game by encouraging economists to ignore inconvenient facts or define them out of existence, this would be a major blow to scientific enquiry in economics.[1]

---

[1] One of the best introductions to methodology for economists is Mark Blaug, *The Methodology of Positive Economics: Or How Economists Explain* (Cambridge University Press, 1980), which is, however, probably better read after one has studied a certain amount of economics.

2

The tools of theoretical analysis

If you look at the left-hand side of Figure 1.1 on page 15, you will see two triangles. The first stands for the movement from the assumptions to the implications, or predictions, of theories. To make this move the economist uses the tools of logic, which allow him to deduce the implications of his assumptions. The second triangle stands for the testing of implications against empirical evidence. To do this the economist uses the tools of statistical analysis. This chapter is devoted to the tools of logical deduction or, as they are often called, the tools of theoretical analysis. The tools of statistical analysis are considered in Chapter 3.

Expressing hypotheses

We have already noted that an economic theory consists of definitions and assumptions about the behaviour of people and things. The assumptions of economic theory may be described in words, formulated mathematically or illustrated graphically. Once they are expressed in a precise way, their implications may also be derived by verbal, mathematical or geometrical analysis.[1] To a great extent all of these methods are interchangeable; any piece of logical reasoning that can be done verbally or geometrically can also be done mathematically. Some things that are done in mathematics, however, cannot be done rigorously in verbal or in geometrical analysis. Where various methods can be used, the choice among them will be dictated by considerations of convenience, economy, the techniques at the command of the practitioner and the audience at which he is aiming.

The concept of a functional relationship

The idea that one thing depends on another is one of the basic notions behind all science. The gravitational attraction of two bodies depends on their total mass and on the distance separating them; this attraction increases with size and diminishes with distance. The number of murders in a country is thought to depend on, among other things, the severity of the penalties for murder; the amount of a commodity that people will buy is observed to depend on, among other things, the price of the commodity. When mathematicians wish to say that one thing depends on another, they say

---

[1] Geometry is, of course, a branch of mathematics, but it is convenient to distinguish between 'geometrical' and 'mathematical' methods – meaning by the latter term, mathematical other than the geometrical.

that one is a *function* of the other. Thus gravitational attraction is a function of the mass of the two bodies concerned and the distance between them; the incidence of murder is a function of the severity of the punishment for it; and the quantity of a product demanded is a function of the price of the product.

There are two steps in giving compact symbolic expressions to the relations we have just described. First, we give each concept a symbol; second, we designate a symbol to express the idea of one factor's dependence on another. Thus, if we let g stand for gravitational attraction, M stand for the mass of two bodies, and d stand for the distance between two bodies, we may write

$$g = f(M, d),$$

where f is read 'is a function of' and means 'depends upon'. The whole equation defines an hypothesis and is read 'Gravitational attraction is a function of the mass of the two bodies and the distance between them.' This is the same as the verbal statement with which we began.

The second hypothesis, that the number of murders depends on the severity of punishment for murder, may be expressed as

$$K = f(S),$$

where K is a measure of the frequency of murders and S is a measure of the severity of punishment for being convicted of murder. The final hypothesis, that the quantity demanded depends on the price of the product, is written

$$q = f(p),$$

where q is the quantity demanded of some commodity, and p is the price of the commodity.

The expression

$$Y = f(X)$$

says that Y is a function of X. It means that Y depends upon or varies with X, whatever Y and X may be. The quantities X and Y in this functional relation are called *variables*. The notation often looks frightening to students, especially those who did not get on well with their school mathematics. However, once one becomes familiar with it, this notation is extremely helpful, and since the functional concept is basic to all science, the notation is well worth mastering.

The expression $Y = f(X)$ states that Y is related to X; it says nothing about the form that this relation takes. Does Y increase as X increases? Does Y decrease as X increases? Or is the relation more complicated? Take a simple example: Y is the length of a board in feet, and X is the length of the same board in yards. Clearly, $Y = f(X)$. Further, in this case we know the exact form of the function, for length in feet (Y) is merely 3 times the length in yards (X); so we may write $Y = 3X$.

This example is not typical of all functional relationships because it is true by definition. It merely states in functional form the relation between the definitions of a foot and a yard. It is nonetheless useful to have a way of writing down relationships that are definitionally true.

Now consider a second example. Let C equal the total spending of a household on all consumption goods in one year, and Y equal the household's income. Now state the hypothesis

$$C = f(Y), \tag{1}$$

and, more specifically,

$$C = 0.8Y. \tag{2}$$

Equation (1) expresses the general hypothesis that a household's consumption depends upon its income. Equation (2) expresses the more specific hypothesis that expenditure on consumption will be four-fifths as large as the household's income. There is no reason why either of these hypotheses *must* be true; indeed, neither may be consistent with the facts. But those are matters for testing. What we do have in each equation is a concise statement of a particular hypothesis.

Thus the existence of some relation between two variables, Y and X, is denoted by $Y = f(X)$, whereas any precise relation may be expressed by a particular equation such as $Y = 2X$, $Y = 4X^2$, or $Y = X + 2X^2 + 0.5X^3$.

If Y increases as X increases (e.g., $Y = 10 + 2X$), we say that Y in an INCREASING FUNCTION of X or that Y and X are POSITIVELY RELATED to each other. If Y decreases as X increases (e.g. $Y = 10 - 2X$), we say that Y is a DECREASING FUNCTION of X or that Y and X are NEGATIVELY RELATED to each other.

> **Economic theory is based on relations among various magnitudes. Because all such relations can be expressed mathematically, mathematical analysis is important in economics. Once hypotheses have been written down as algebraic expressions, mathematical manipulation can be used to discover their implications.**

The error term

The examples of functional relations considered above were all *deterministic*, in the sense that they were expressed as if they held exactly: given the value of X, we knew the value of Y exactly. The relations considered in economic theory are seldom of this sort, except where definitions are being expressed. When an economist says that the world behaves so that $Y = f(X)$, he does not expect that knowing X will tell him *exactly* what Y will be, but only that it will tell him what Y will be *within some margin of error*.

The error in predicting Y from a knowledge of X arises for two quite distinct reasons. First, there may be other variables that also affect Y. Although we may say that the quantity of butter demanded is a function of the price of butter, $q_b = f(p_b)$, we know that other factors will also influence this demand. A change in the price of margarine will certainly affect the demand for butter, even though the price of butter does not change. Thus we do not expect to find a perfect relation between q_b and p_b that will allow us to predict q_b exactly, from a knowledge of p_b. Second, we can never measure our variables exactly, so that, even if X is the only cause of Y, our measurements will give various Ys corresponding to the same X. In the case of the demand for butter, our errors of measurement might not be large. In other cases, errors might be substantial. In the case of a relation between total spending on consumption goods and total income earned in the nation ($C = f(Y)$), our measurements of both C and Y may be subject to quite wide margins of error. We may thus observe various values of C associated with the same measured value of Y, not because C is varying independently of Y, but because our error of measurement is itself varying from period to period.

If all the factors other than X that affect the measured value of Y are summarized into an error term, ε, we write

$$Y = f(X, \varepsilon).$$

This says that the observed value of Y is related to the observed value of X as well as to a lot of other things, both observational errors and other causal factors, all of which will be lumped together and called ε (the Greek letter epsilon). In economic theory this error term is almost always suppressed, and we proceed as if our functional relations were deterministic. (When we come to test our theories, however, some very serious problems arise precisely because we do not expect our functional relations to hold exactly.)

> **It is extremely important to remember, both when interpreting a theory in terms of the real world and when testing a theory formally against empirical observations, that the deterministic formulation is a simplification. The error term is really present in all the functional relations with which we deal in economics.**

Alternative methods of representing functional relations

A functional relation can be expressed in words, in graphs or in mathematical equations. As a simple example let us consider a hypothetical relation between the annual expenditure of a household on all the goods and services that it consumes (C) and its annual disposable income (Y). The assumed relation may be expressed in three ways.

(1) VERBAL STATEMENT: When income is zero the household will spend £800 a year (either by borrowing the money or by consuming past savings), and for every pound of income that the household obtains net of taxes (called *disposable income*) it will increase its expenditure by £0·80.

(2) MATHEMATICAL (ALGEBRAIC) STATEMENT: $C = 800 + 0\cdot8\,Y$.

(3) GEOMETRICAL (GRAPHICAL) STATEMENT:

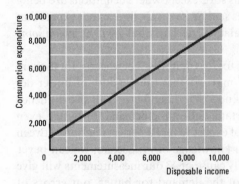

Fig. 2.1 A relation between a household's expenditure and its income

The graphical representation of functional relations

Since we shall make much use of the graphical representation of functional relations, it may be helpful to consider graphical techniques in a little more detail. In the previous section we considered a relation between annual expenditure and annual disposable income for a single hypothetical household:

$$C = 800 + 0\cdot8\,Y. \qquad (3)$$

We may refer to this as the household's CONSUMPTION FUNCTION. For any specified value of Y, we can use the consumption function in (3) to determine the corresponding value of C. Let us start by taking five different levels of income, £0, £2,500, £5,000, £7,500 and £10,000, and calculating the level of consumption expenditure that would be associated with each. Table 2.1 shows these values and for further reference assigns a letter to each pair of values.

Table 2.1 Selected values of the function
$C = 800 + 0.8Y$

Y(£s)	C(£s)	Reference letter
0	800	A
2,500	2,800	B
5,000	4,800	C
7,500	6,800	D
10,000	8,800	E

We can, if we wish, show the data of Table 2.1 on a graph. To do this, we take each pair of values, i.e. a value of Y and the corresponding value of C, and plot them as a point on a co-ordinate grid, which we do in Figure 2.2(i). In part (ii) of the figure we have plotted not only these five points but a line relating C to every value of Y in the range covered by the graph. You should take the equation $C = 800 + 0.8Y$ and plot as many points as necessary to satisfy yourself that they all lie on the straight line that we have drawn in Figure 2.2(ii).

Once we have plotted this line, which *is* the function $C = 800 + 0.8Y$ in the interval from $Y = 0$ to $Y = 10,000$, we have no further need for the co-ordinate grid, and the figure will be less cluttered if we suppress it, as in Figure 2.2(iii). For some purposes we do not really care about the specific numerical values of the function; we are content merely to represent it as an upward-sloping straight line. This is done in Figure 2.2(iv). We have replaced the specific numerical values of the variables C and Y with the letters C_1, C_2, Y_1 and Y_2 to indicate specific points. Figure 2.2(iv) tells us, for example, that if we increase the quantity of disposable income from OY_1 to OY_2, consumption expenditure will increase from OC_1 to OC_2.[1]

The beginning student may feel that we have lost ground by omitting so much, but it is in the form of (iv) that most diagrams appear in economics texts. The great advantage of illustrating functional relations graphically is that we can easily compare different relations without specifying them in precise numerical form.

Suppose, for example, that we wish to compare and contrast three households, R, S, and T, whose behaviour is described by the following general assumptions. (1) All three have the same amount of consumption expenditure when their disposable income is zero. The amount is greater than zero, which implies that they must be either consuming past savings or going into debt. (2) In response to an increase in disposable income of £1, household R increases its consumption expenditure by more than does household S, and household S increases its consumption by more than

---

[1] In speaking of the quantity of Y as OY_1 or OY_2 we are following good geometric practice and recognizing that a *value* of Y is a *distance* on the Y axis. For brevity, we will usually use a shorter notation and speak of the quantity of Y as Y_1 or Y_2. This is somewhat less cumbrous, but it is important to remember that *any point on the axis represents the distance from the origin to that point* (e.g., Y_1 stands for the distance from O to Y_1).

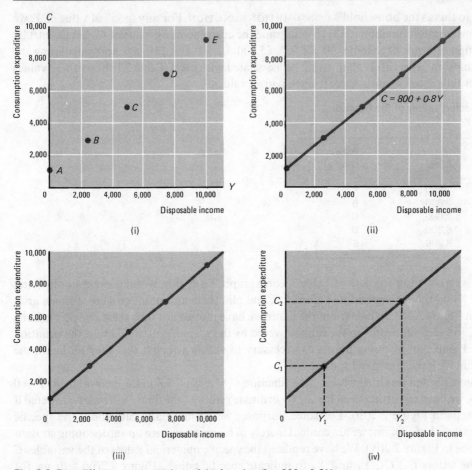

Fig. 2.2 Four different representations of the function $C = 800 + 0.8Y$

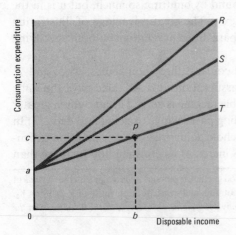

Fig. 2.3 Consumption functions for three hypothetical households

does household T. (3) The response of each household's consumption expenditure to a change of £1 in its own disposable income is the same whatever its existing level of disposable income. These assumptions are cumbersome to state in words, but they are easily illustrated graphically.

Figure 2.3 shows the postulated relations for the three households. The fact that the consumption lines all intersect the vertical axis at the same point expresses the assumption that all three households spend the same amount, Oa (or simply a), when their disposable income is zero. The third assumption is shown by the fact that for each household the relationship between C and Y is a straight line. This means that the change in C for a unit change in Y will be the same wherever we measure it on any one of the lines. The second assumption is shown by the fact that R's line is steeper than S's line, which in turn is steeper than T's line. The steeper the line, the larger the change in C for a given change in Y.[1]

When we are dealing with hypotheses that are not specified quantitatively, we normally suppress most of the co-ordinate grid to prevent the figures from being cluttered up with irrelevant details. The grid is always understood to be there, of course, and, when required, we draw in the necessary grid lines. For instance, the co-ordinates of point p in Figure 2.3 are Ob and Oc, and the grid lines bp and cp are drawn in because they are needed. If you find this at all difficult, you should redraw all of the graphs studied so far on graph paper until you feel at home with graphical analysis.

Deriving implications from functional relationships

When the economist has laid out the functional relations that describe the assumptions of his theory, his next task is to discover what they imply. In the process of making logical deductions from his theories, he may again employ verbal, geometrical or mathematical forms of reasoning. His main concerns will be to ensure that his reasoning processes are correct, so that the things he discovers are actually implied by his theory, and are efficient, so that he discovers everything that is implied by his theory.

The use of mathematics in theoretical reasoning

Many people – not just beginning students – are disturbed by the use of mathematics in economic reasoning. 'Surely,' they argue, 'human behaviour is too subtle and complex to be reduced to mathematical formulae.' At least four issues can be distinguished here.

First, we might wonder if we can ever understand enough about human behaviour to be able to build useful theories about it. This has to do with our ability to understand, not with the language we should use to express what we do understand. To construct any economic theory, whatever the language it is ultimately to be expressed in, we must begin by assuming that coherent assumptions about relevant human behaviour can be stated. (That we can make coherent assumptions about

---

[1] The same general relations can also be specified algebraically. We have

$$C_r = a + bY_r$$
$$C_s = c + dY_s$$
$$C_t = e + fY_t$$

where the subscripts r, s and t tell us whose income and consumption we are referring to. Assumption (1) means that $a = c = e$. Assumption (2) means that $b > d > f$. Assumption (3) means that the equations are all linear.

human behaviour is beyond question, since economic theory is full of them; whether or not they are relevant to the real world is an empirical question that will come up frequently in this book.)

Second, we might wonder if it is possible to express assumptions about human behaviour in mathematical terms. If such assumptions can be stated at all, they can be stated mathematically, since mathematics is just another language like English or Polish – albeit more precise than any of the languages of common speech. Any hypothesis about how two or more things are related can be expressed mathematically.

Third, we might wonder if the subtlety and complexity of human behaviour make mathematics *less appropriate* than a verbal language such as English for expressing our assumptions. Verbally, it is always possible to mask fuzziness in our concepts and assumptions. Verbal expression may sometimes be so vague as to *hide* our ignorance, but verbal expression can never *overcome* our ignorance. Mathematical expression is more precise than verbal expression. Not only can a relation between two or more things be stated mathematically, but any qualifications to that relation can also be stated mathematically, *if it is clearly understood*. The language of mathematics turns out to be amazingly subtle; anything that we do understand clearly can be expressed most precisely by its terminology. It is an advantage, not a disability, of mathematical formulation that it exposes what is being said and what is left unsaid, and that it makes it hard to employ imprecise qualifications.

Fourth, we might worry about the application of long chains of mechanical mathematical deductions to our theories. This worry is the source of some very serious confusions. Once the assumptions of a theory have been fully stated, all that remains for the theorist is to discover their implications. This stage simply requires logical deduction. It is not a criticism to say that a technique is mechanical if by mechanical we mean that it allows us to discover efficiently and accurately what is or is not implied by our assumptions. It is never an advantage to use a technique that leaves us in doubt on this. If we accept the view that, somehow, verbal analysis (or 'judgement') can solve problems, even though we are unable to state clearly how we have reached the solutions, then we are involved not in a science but in a medieval mystery, in which the main problem is to be able to distinguish between the true and the false prophet.

Mathematics is neither the maker nor the destroyer of good economic theory. It is merely a precise and compact means of expression and an efficient tool for deriving implications from assumptions. Irrelevant or factually incorrect assumptions will yield irrelevant or factually incorrect implications, whatever logical tools are used to derive them.

Examples of theoretical reasoning

In later chapters you will encounter many interesting examples of the process of logical deduction in economics. In the meantime we can illustrate the procedure with some very simple manipulation of the household's consumption function $C = 800 + 0 \cdot 8Y$, first introduced on page 20. What can we discover about the behaviour of a household which has such a consumption function? First, it is clear that when its income is zero, the household is using up past savings or going into debt at the rate of £800 per year. Second, it is clear that an increase in income of £1 leads to an increase in consumption of 80p. Third, there will be a level of income at which the household is neither running into debt nor saving any of its income. This is called the *break-even level* of income, and it is easily discovered by finding the level of Y such that C and Y are equal.

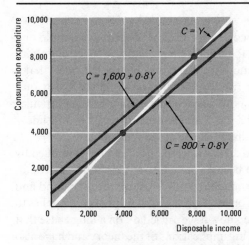

Fig. 2.4 The determination of the break-even level of income

To discover the break-even level algebraically, we need to solve the two simultaneous equations $C = 800 + 0 \cdot 8 Y$ and $C = Y$. The first tells us how the household's consumption expenditure varies with its income, and the second imposes the condition that consumption expenditure should equal disposable income. If you solve these two equations, you will discover that the break-even level of income for this household is £4,000. A little further experimentation will show that at any level of income less than £4,000, expenditure exceeds income, while at any income level over £4,000, expenditure is less than income. The graphical determination of the break-even level of income is shown in Figure 2.4.

As a final example of elementary theoretical reasoning, let us ask by how much the break-even level of income will increase if the household's behaviour changes so that, at each level of income, consumption expenditure is £800 higher than before. The changed behaviour is described by the new equation: $C = 1,600 + 0 \cdot 8 Y$. To find the new break-even level of income, we solve this simultaneously with $C = Y$ and find the solution to be £8,000. Thus, when consumption is increased by £800 at each level of income, the break-even level of income rises by £4,000. This result, which is illustrated in Figure 2.4, is perhaps a little less obvious than the previous ones.

Is this an accident depending upon the numbers chosen or is there some more general relation being illustrated by this particular example? A bit of experimentation with the algebra or geometry of this case should allow you to prove that, with the consumption function $C = a + bY$, any change in the constant a by an amount Δa will change the break-even level of income by $\Delta a/(1-b)$. This is a general result that holds for all straight-line consumption functions.[1]

---

[1] This last result can be proved with simple algebra using the delta notations for changes explained in more detail in the Appendix to this chapter on page 30. We have two equations; the first expresses the consumption function, and the second expresses the condition for the break-even level, that consumption should equal income: $C = a + bY$; and $C = Y$. Solving these simultaneously yields:

$$Y = a/(1-b).$$

Now let a increase by Δa, and denote the resulting increase in Y by ΔY. We can then write

$$Y + \Delta Y = (a + \Delta a)/(1-b) = a/(1-b) + \Delta a/(1-b).$$

Subtracting the equation for Y from that for $Y + \Delta Y$ yields

$$\Delta Y = \Delta a/(1-b).$$

Notice how far we have come. We began with a very simple economic hypothesis relating two variables, consumption expenditure and disposable income. We took a numerical example and expressed it algebraically and geometrically. We then made certain simple logical deductions about what was implied by the hypothesis. At first these deductions were obvious, but the last one – that if £800 more is spent at each level of income, break-even Y rises by £4,000 – was not quite so obvious. We then wondered if this not-quite-so-obvious result was an accident depending on the particular numbers we chose. Experimentation showed that there was a single general result for all linear consumption functions: break-even Y rises by $1/(1-b)$ times the rise in the constant a.

All of this illustrates how the tools of logical analysis do allow us to discover what is implied by our assumptions. It also shows how theorizing tends to become cumulative: we obtain one result, possibly quite an obvious one, and this suggests another possible result to us; we check this and find that it is true and this suggests something else. Then we wonder if what we have discovered applies to cases other than the one we are analysing, and before we know it we are led off on a long chase that ends only when we think we have found all of the interesting implications of the theory and have also found out how generally they apply outside the specific case we began by analysing. Of course, when we say the chase ends, we mean it ends for the particular investigator, for he is usually wrong when he thinks he has found all the implications of a complex theory. Some new and ingenious investigator is likely to discover new implications or generalizations, and so the chase begins again.

The quantitative relation between variables

The *magnitude* of the change that occurs in one variable in response to changes in another variable is extremely important in economics. We expect the quantity of any commodity that people wish to purchase (which we call 'quantity demanded' and symbolize by q^d) to vary with its own price, $q^d = D(p)$, and we are interested in *how much q^d changes for a given change in price*. We expect the amount of a commodity produced and offered for sale (called 'quantity supplied' and symbolized by q^s) to vary with its own price, $q^s = S(p)$, and again it is important to know *by how much q^s will change for a given change in price*.[1]

There is a precise mathematical method of handling problems arising from the question of how one variable changes as another variable on which it depends changes. The branch of mathematics which deals with these problems is called *differential calculus*. A knowledge of the calculus is not necessary in order to read this book. In fact one can usually obtain a first degree in economics without such knowledge, but those who do have some idea of the calculus will find it a great help.[2] The number of people obtaining a first degree in economics while remaining ignorant of mathematics is diminishing rapidly with the passage of time, and the serious student of economics is well advised to learn some mathematics.

---

[1] Here we have two variables both related to price. To distinguish the two we use two letters, D and S, in the place of the f already used, to indicate the functional relationships. This is discussed further on pages 27–8.

[2] An introduction to the ideas of the differential calculus plus a review of very elementary arithmetic, algebra and geometry can be found in W.W. Sawyer's excellent little book *Mathematician's Delight* (Penguin); a somewhat more advanced treatment may be found in J. Parry Lewis, *An Introduction to Mathematics for Students of Economics* (Macmillan, 2nd edn., 1969). A more rigorous treatment can be found in R.G.D. Allen's classic *Mathematical Analysis for Economists* (Macmillan, 1938). All these books are devoted mainly to mathematics with only passing references to economic applications. An introduction to mathematics with detailed applications to economics can be found in G.C. Archibald and R.G. Lipsey, *An Introduction to a Mathematical Treatment of Economics* (Weidenfeld and Nicolson, 3rd edn., 1977).

Appendix to chapter 2

Some common techniques for theoretical analysis

Certain graphical and mathematical concepts are frequently encountered in economic analysis. In this appendix we deal briefly with the ones most frequently used in this book. Only the barest outlines are possible, and the student who wants a fuller treatment of the ideas expressed here should read the appropriate references listed in footnote 2, page 26.

Every student needs to master the elementary techniques described in this appendix before completing his or her study of introductory economics. Those who find they can manage it at this stage should study the appendix carefully now. Those who had difficulty with simple mathematics at school should read carefully as far as the beginning of the section entitled *Straight lines and slopes*. Up to that point there is no algebraic manipulation. They should then skim through the rest of the material, making a list of the concepts discussed. When these concepts are encountered later in the text they should be reviewed again carefully here.

(1) The function as a rule

If X and Y are related to each other, we say they are functions of each other.[1] We write this, $Y = f(X)$, and we read it, 'Y is a function of X'. The letter 'f' stands for a rule which we use to go from a value of X to a value of Y. The rule tells us how to operate on X to get Y. Consider for example, the specific function

$$Y = 5X - 3.$$

The rule here is 'take X, multiply it by 5 and subtract 3'; this then yields the value of Y. In another case we may have

$$Y = X^2/2 + 6.$$

This rule says 'take X, square it, divide the result by 2, then add 6'; again, the result is the value of Y. If, for example, X has a value of 2, then the first rule yields $Y = 7$, while the second rule yields $Y = 8$.

The equations displayed above describe two different rules. We may confuse these if we denote both by the same letter. To keep them separate we can write

$$Y = f(X)$$

for the first and

$$Y = g(X)$$

for the second.

Since the choice of symbols to designate different rules *is* arbitrary, we can use any symbols that are convenient. In the above examples we had $Y = 5X - 3$ and $Y = X^2/2 + 6$ and we chose to indicate these rules by 'f' and 'g'. If we wanted to indicate that these were rules for yielding Y we could use that letter, and then use subscripts to indicate that there were two different rules. Thus we would write

$$Y = Y_1(X)$$

and

$$Y = Y_2(X),$$

where Y_1 and Y_2 stand for two different rules for deriving Y from any given value of X.

Suppose now that we have two different variables Y and Z both related to X. A specific example would

---

[1] Modern mathematicians distinguish between a correspondence and a function. There is a *correspondence* between Y and X if each value of X is associated with one or more values of Y. Y is a *function* of X if there is *one and only one* value of Y associated with each value of X. Mathematicians of an older generation described both relations as functions and then distinguished between single-valued functions (in modern language, functional relations) and multi-valued functions (in modern language, relations of correspondence). In the text we adopt the older, more embracing usage of the term *functional relation*.

be

$$Y = 3 + 10X$$

and

$$Z = 28 - 2X.$$

Again we have two different rules for operating on X; the first rule yields Y and the second rule yields Z. We could denote these rules $f(X)$ and $g(X)$ but, since the choice of a letter to denote each rule is arbitrary, we could also write

$$Y = Y(X)$$

and

$$Z = Z(X).$$

In this case the choice of letters is a memory device which reminds us that the first rule, $3 + 10X$, yields Y, while the second rule, $28 - 2X$, yields Z.

(2) Some conventions in functional notation

Assume we are talking about some sequence of numbers, say, 1, 2, 3, 4, 5, ... If we wished to talk about one particular term in this series without indicating which one, we could talk about the ith term, which might be the 5th or the 50th. If we now want to indicate terms adjacent to the ith term, whatever it might be, we talk about the $(i-1)$th and the $(i+1)$th terms.

By the same token we can talk about a series of time periods, say, the years 1900, 1901 and 1902. If we wish to refer to three adjacent years in any series without indicating which three years, we can talk about the years $(t-1)$, t and $(t+1)$.

Consider a functional relation, between the quantity produced by a factory and the number of workers employed. In general, we can write $Q = Q(W)$, where Q is the amount of production and W is the number of workers. If we wished to refer to the quantity of output where ten workers were employed, we could write $Q_{10} = Q(W_{10})$, whereas, if we wished to refer to output when some particular, but unspecified, number were employed, we would write $Q_i = Q(W_i)$. Finally, if we wished to refer to output when the number of workers was increased by one above the previous level, we could write $Q_{i+1} = Q(W_{i+1})$. This use of subscripts to refer to particular values of the variables is a useful notion, and one that we shall use at various points in this book.

We may use time subscripts to date variables. If, for example, the value of X depends on the value of Y three months ago, we write this as $X_t = f(Y_{t-3})$. Another convention is the use of ... to save space in

functions of many variables. For example, $f(X_1, \ldots, X_n)$ indicates a function containing n (some unspecified number of) variables.

(3) Exogenous and endogenous variables

In economic theories it is convenient to distinguish between EXOGENOUS and ENDOGENOUS VARIABLES. Endogenous variables are ones that are explained *within* a theory; exogenous variables are ones that influence the variables but are themselves determined by factors outside the theory. Assume, for example, that we have a theory of what determines the price of apples from day to day in London. The price of apples in this case is an endogenous variable – something determined within the framework of the theory. The state of the weather, on the other hand, is an exogenous variable. It will influence apple prices but will be uninfluenced by these prices. The state of the weather will not be explained by our theory; it is something that happens from without, so to speak, but it nonetheless influences our endogenous variable, apple prices, because it affects the demand for apples. Exogenous variables are sometimes referred to as AUTONOMOUS VARIABLES.

(4) Identities and equations

A DEFINITIONAL IDENTITY is true for all values of the variables; no values can be found that would contradict it. An example of such an identity is

$$1 \text{ Yard} \equiv 3 \text{ Feet.}$$

It should be noted that identities are often written with a three-bar sign and that the expression $y \equiv x$ is read 'y is identical to x'.

EQUATIONS are relations that are true only for some values of the variables but that can be contradicted by other values. Thus the expression $y = 10 + 2x$ is an equation. It is written with a two-bar or equals sign and is read y is equal to ten plus two x. This expression is true, for example, for $x = 2$ and $y = 14$, but not for $x = 2$ and $y = 4$. Definitional identities can be used to state definitions in economic theories, but they do not state behavioural hypotheses. Thus a theory that consisted only of definitional identities would tell us nothing about the real world. Equations can be used to state testable hypotheses, since they make statements that are true for some states of the universe but false for others. A theory that has empirical content will usually contain some definitional identities, but it must also contain some equations that express behavioural assumptions and that are not true merely by the way we use words.[1]

(5) Stocks and flows

Some of the most serious confusions in economics have arisen from a failure to distinguish between STOCKS and FLOWS. Imagine a bathtub half full of water with the tap turned on and the plug removed; you have in mind a model similar to many simple economic theories. The level of water in the bath is a stock – an amount that is just there. We could express it as so many gallons of water. The amount of water entering through the tap and the amount leaving through the drain are both flows. We could express them as so many gallons *per minute* or *per hour*. A flow necessarily has a time dimension – there is so much flow *per period of time*. A stock does not have a time dimension – it is just so many tons or gallons or heads.

The amount of wheat produced is a flow, so much per month or per year. The amount of wheat sold is also a flow. The amount of wheat stored (produced but unsold) in the granaries of the world is a stock; it is just so many millions of tons of wheat. The distinction between stocks and flows will arise many times throughout this book.

(6) Necessary conditions and sufficient conditions

It is common in popular discussion to confuse necessary and sufficient conditions. Many futile arguments have been caused by one person arguing that a condition was sufficient for a result and another arguing that it was not necessary, each thinking he was contradicting the other when, in fact, both were correct. Consider, for example, a club that normally admits only males who are graduates of Oxford, but that is also willing to admit all male MPs, whatever their background. Being a male MP is thus sufficient to admit you to the club, but it is not necessary to be one. Being a male is a necessary condition for admission (since no females are

admitted on any terms), but it is not a sufficient condition. Being a graduate of Oxford is by itself neither necessary (since non-Oxford graduates who are MPs can be admitted) nor sufficient (since female graduates of Oxford are not admitted). We may summarize the conditions for admission as follows:

> To be male is necessary but not sufficient.
> To be a male MP is sufficient but not necessary.
> To be both a male and an Oxford graduate is sufficient but not necessary.
> To be an Oxford graduate is neither necessary nor sufficient.
> To be an MP is neither necessary nor sufficient.
> To be *either* a male graduate of Oxford *or* a male MP is necessary and sufficient.

In general, a NECESSARY CONDITION is something that must be present but by itself may not guarantee the result. A SUFFICIENT CONDITION is something that, if present, does guarantee the result but that need not be there for the result to occur. A condition (or set of conditions) that is necessary *and* sufficient must be there and, if there, is enouth to guarantee the result.

In this club, the necessary and sufficient condition for entry is a compound either-or condition: to be either a male graduate of Oxford or a male MP. If, however, another club were set up that was open to all former members of the House of Commons and to no one else, then a simple condition – to have been an MP – would be both necessary and sufficient for admission.

(7) Graphing functions

A co-ordinate graph divides space into four quadrants, as shown in Figure 2.5. The upper right-hand quadrant, which is the one in which both *X* and *Y* are positive, is usually called the *positive quadrant*. Very often in economics we are concerned only with the positive values of our variables, and in such cases we confine our graph to the positive quadrant. Whenever we want one or both of our variables to be allowed to take on negative values we must include some or all of the other quadrants. For example, one of the functions in Figure 2.6(ii) is extended into the quadrant in which *X* is positive and *Y* is negative, while the remaining two functions are not extended beyond the positive quadrant.

(8) Straight lines and slopes

Consider the following functional relations:

$$Y = \cdot 5X,$$

---

[1] Confusion between equations and definitional identities is a source of error in economics. One of the most perplexing habits of economists is to warn students about the nature of identities and then to introduce national-income theory with several pages of definitional identities claimed to be the foundation of the theory. A criticism of this practice, and reference to places where it is used, is given in K. Klappholz and E.J. Mishan, 'Identities in Economic Models', *Economica*, May 1962, and R.G. Lipsey in *Essays in Honour of Lord Robbins*, ed. M. Peston and B. Corry (Weidenfeld & Nicolson, 1971).

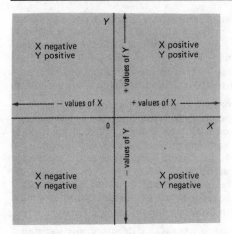

Fig. 2.5 A co-ordinate graph divides space into quadrants

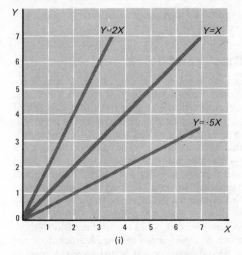

(i)

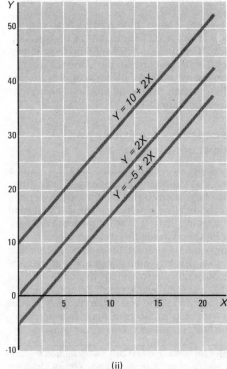

(ii)

Fig. 2.6 Some linear functions

$$Y = X,$$
$$Y = 2X.$$

These are graphed in Figure 2.6(i). You will see that they all pass through the origin. This is also obvious from the fact that if we let $X = 0$ in each of the above relations, Y also becomes 0. In the first equation, Y goes up half a unit every time X goes up by one unit; in the second equation, Y goes up one unit every time X goes up one unit; and in the third equation, Y goes up two units every time X goes up one unit.

We now introduce the symbol Δ to indicate a change in a variable. Thus ΔX means the value of the change in X and ΔY means the value of the change in Y. In the first equation if $X = 10$ then Y is 5 and if X goes up to 16, Y goes up to 8. Thus, in this exercise, $\Delta X = 6$ and $\Delta Y = 3$.

Next consider the ratio $\Delta Y/\Delta X$. In the above example it is equal to ·5. In general, it will be noted that, for any change we make in X in the first equation, $\Delta Y/\Delta X$ is always ·5. In the second $\Delta Y/\Delta X$ is unity and in the third the ratio is always 2. In general, if we write $Y = bX$, then, as is proved below, the ratio $\Delta Y/\Delta X$ is always equal to b.

We now define the slope, or gradient, of a straight line to be the ratio of the distance moved up the Y axis to the distance moved along the X axis. We start at the point (X_1, Y_1) and then move to the point (X_2, Y_2). The change in X is $X_2 - X_1$ or ΔX. The change in Y is $Y_2 - Y_1$ or ΔY. Thus the ratio $\Delta Y/\Delta X$ is the slope of the straight line. This slope tells us the ratio of a change in Y to a change in X.

In trigonometry the tangent of an angle is defined as $\Delta Y/\Delta X$; thus the slope of the line is equal to the tangent of the angle between the line and any line parallel to the X axis. In general, the larger the ratio $\Delta Y/\Delta X$, the steeper the graph of the relation. Figure 2.6(i) shows three lines corresponding to $\Delta Y/\Delta X = 0\cdot5$, 1 and 2. Clearly, the steeper the line the larger the change in Y for any given change in X.

Now consider the following equations,

$$Y = 2X$$
$$Y = 10 + 2X$$
$$Y = -5 + 2X,$$

which are graphed in Figure 2.6(ii). All three lines are parallel. In other words, they have the same slope. In all three $\Delta Y/\Delta X$ is equal to 2. Clearly, the addition of a (positive or negative) constant does not affect the slope of the line. This slope is influenced only by the number attached to X.

(9) First differencing linear equations

In national-income theory we make much use of linear equations. A typical equation relates consumption expenditure, C, to income, Y:

$$C = a + cY,$$

where a is any positive constant and c is positive but less than unity.

We can now first difference this equation to get an expression relating changes in C to changes in Y. To do this let Y take on some specific value, Y_1, multiply it by c and add a to obtain C_1:

$$C_1 = a + cY_1.$$

Now do the same thing for a second value of Y called Y_2:

$$C_2 = a + cY_2.$$

Next, subtract the second equation from the first to obtain

$$C_1 - C_2 = a - a + cY_1 - cY_2$$
$$= c(Y_1 - Y_2).$$

Now use the delta notation for changes to write

$$\Delta C = c\Delta Y.$$

The constant a disappears and we see that the change in C is c times the change in Y, and also that the ratio of the changes is c, i.e.

$$\Delta C/\Delta Y = c.$$

Thus whenever we have a linear equation in any number of variables, i.e.,

$$Y = a_0 - a_1X_1 + a_2X_2 + \dots a_nX_n,$$

we can immediately first difference it to obtain

$$\Delta Y = a_1\Delta X_1 + a_2\Delta X_2 + \dots + a_n\Delta X_n.$$

Of course where the constant coefficient is a fraction:

$$Y = a_0 + (1/a_1)X = a_0 + X/a_1,$$

then first differencing produces a fraction:

$$\Delta Y = (1/a_1)\Delta X = \Delta X/a_1.$$

(10) Nonlinear functions

All of the examples used so far in this appendix and most of the examples in the text of Chapter 2 concern *linear relations* between two variables. A linear relation is described graphically by a straight line, and algebraically by the equation $Y = a + bX$. It is characteristic of a linear relation that the effect on Y of a given change in X is the same everywhere on the relation.

Many of the relations encountered in economics are *nonlinear*. In these cases the relation will be expressed graphically by a curved line and algebraically by some expression more complex than the one for a straight line. Two common examples are:

$$Y = a + bX + cX^2$$

and

$$Y = a/X^b$$

The first example is a *parabola*. It takes up various positions and shapes depending on the signs and magnitudes of a, b and c. Two examples of parabolas are given in Figures 2.7 and 2.8. The second example

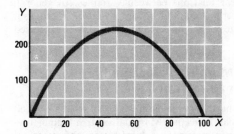

Fig. 2.7 A parabola with a maximum value of Y

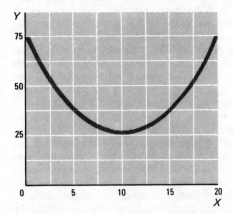

Fig. 2.8 A parabola with minimum value of Y

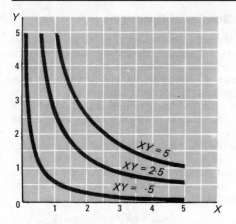

Fig. 2.9 Three rectangular hyperbolae

becomes a rectangular hyperbola if we let $b = 1$, and then the position is determined by the value of a. Three examples where $a = 0.5$, 2.5 and 5 are shown in Figure 2.9.

There are, of course, many other examples of nonlinear relations between variables. In general, whatever the relation between X and Y, as long as it can be expressed on a graph it can also be expressed by means of an algebraic equation.

(11) Marginal values and incremental ratios

Economic theory makes much use of what are called 'marginal' concepts. Marginal cost, marginal revenue, marginal rate of substitution and marginal propensity to consume are a few examples. Marginal means on the margin or border and the concept refers to what would happen if there were a small change from the present position.

Marginals refer to functional relations: the independent variable X is determining the dependent variable Y and we wish to know what would be the change in Y if X changed by a small amount from its present value. The answer is referred to as the marginal value of Y and is given various names depending on what economic variables X and Y stand for.

There are two ways of measuring the marginal value of Y. One is exact and the other is an approximation. Because the exact measure uses differential calculus, introductory texts in economics usually use the approximation which depends only on simple algebra. Students are often justifiably confused because the language of economic theory refers to the exact measure while introductory

examples use the approximation. For this reason it is worth explaining each at this time.

Consider the example shown in Figure 2.10 in which a firm's output, Q, is measured on the X axis and the total revenue earned by selling this output, R, is measured on the Y axis. Thus we have the function $R = R(Q)$. (We shall see later that the graph corresponds to the shape of a monopolist's revenue function, but right now we may take its shape as given.)

The marginal concept that corresponds to this function is *marginal revenue*. It refers to the change in the firm's revenue when sales are altered slightly from their present level. But what do we mean by 'altered slightly'? There are two answers depending on which marginal concept we use.

The approximation to marginal revenue is called

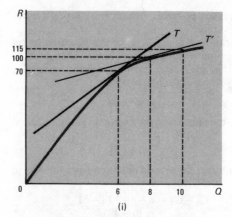

Fig. 2.10(i) The revenue function of a firm

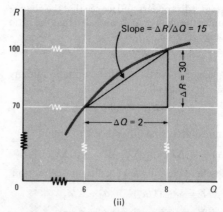

Fig. 2.10(ii) An enlargement of a section of the firm's revenue function

the INCREMENTAL RATIO. Let sales in Figure 2.10(i) be 6, with a corresponding revenue of £70. Now increase sales to 8, so that revenue rises to £100. The increase in sales is 2 and the increase in revenue is £30. Using the Δ notation for changes, we can write this as

$$\Delta R/\Delta Q = £30/2 = £15.$$

Thus incremental revenue is £15 when sales change from 6 to 8. This means that sales are increasing at an average rate of £15 *per unit of commodity sold* over the range from 6 to 8 units. We may call this the marginal revenue at 6 units of output but, as we shall see, it is only an approximation to the true marginal revenue at that output.

Graphically, incremental revenue is the slope of the line joining the two points in question. In this case they are the two points on the revenue function corresponding to outputs of 6 and 8. This is shown in Figure 2.10(ii), which is an enlargement of the relevant section of the function graphed in 2.10(i). Look at the small triangle created by these points. Its base is 2 units long and its vertical side is 30 units in height. The slope of the hypotenuse of the triangle is 30/2 = 15, which is the incremental revenue. Visually it is clear that this slope tells us the gradient or steepness of the revenue function over the range from $Q = 6$ to $Q = 8$. It thus tells us how fast revenue is changing as output changes over that range of Q.

Incremental revenue will be different at different points on the function. For example, when output goes from 8 to 10, revenue goes from 100 to 115 and this gives us an incremental revenue of

$$\Delta R/\Delta Q = £15/2 = £7{\cdot}50.$$

This calculation confirms what visual inspection of the figure suggests: the larger is output (at least over the ranges graphed in the figure), the less is the response of revenue to further increases in output.

The incremental ratio is an approximation to the true marginal concept which is based on the derivative of differential calculus. The derivative is symbolized in general by dY/dX, and in the case of the function $R = R(Q)$, by dR/dQ. It measures the tendency for R to change as Q changes *at a precise point on the curve.* (Whereas the incremental ratio measures the average tendency *over a range of the curve.*) The value of the derivative is given by the slope of the tangent at the point on the function in which we are interested. Thus 'true' marginal revenue at 6 units of output is given by the slope of the tangent, T, to the curve at that point. This slope measures the tendency for R to change *per unit change in Q* at the precise value at which it is

evaluated (i.e., the point on the function at which the tangent is drawn).[1]

We saw in the example of Figure 2.10 that the incremental ratio declined as we measured it from larger and larger values of Q. It should be visually obvious that this is also true for marginal revenue: the slope of the tangent to the function will be smaller the larger is the value of Q at which the tangent is taken. Two examples are shown in Figure 2.10(i); one, T, for $Q = 6$ and the other, T', for $Q = 8$.

Now try measuring the incremental ratio starting at 6 units of output but for smaller and smaller changes in output. Instead of going from 6 to 8, go, for example, from 6 to 7. This brings the two points in question closer together and, in the present case, it steepens the slope of the line joining them. It is visually clear in the present example that as ΔQ is made smaller and smaller, the slope of the line corresponding to the incremental ratio starting from $Q = 6$ gets closer and closer to the slope of the tangent corresponding to the true marginal value evaluated at $Q = 6$.

Let us now state our conclusions in general for the function $Y = Y(X)$.

(1) The marginal value of Y at some initial value of X is the rate of change of Y per unit change in X as X changes from its initial value.

(2) The marginal value is given by the slope of the tangent to the curve graphing the function at the point corresponding to the initial value of X.

(3) The incremental ratio $\Delta Y/\Delta X$ measures the average change in Y per unit change in X over a range of the function starting from the initial value of X.

(4) As the range of measurement of the incremental ratio is reduced (i.e., as ΔX gets smaller and smaller), the value of the incremental ratio eventually approaches the true marginal value of Y. Thus the incremental ratio may be regarded as an approximation to the true marginal value, the degree of approximation improving as ΔX gets very small.[2]

---

[1] The text discussion refers to functions of a single variable. Where Y is a function of more than one variable, $X_1, \ldots, X_n$, then the marginal concept refers to a *partial* derivative: $\partial Y/\partial X_1$ etc. There is then a marginal value of Y with respect to variations in *each* of the independent variables, $X_1, \ldots, X_n$.

[2] This footnote need only concern those who already know some calculus. We must be careful how we state conclusion (4) since on a wavy function the degree of approximation may alternately improve and worsen as ΔX gets smaller, but, providing the conditions for a derivative to exist are met, there *must* be a small neighbourhood around the point in question within which the degree of approximation improves as ΔX gets smaller, with the 'error' going to zero as ΔX goes to zero.

(12) Maximum and minimum values

Consider the function

$$Y = 10X - 0.1X^2,$$

which is plotted in Figure 2.7. Y at first increases as X increases, but after a while Y begins to fall as X goes on rising. We say that Y rises to a *maximum*, which is reached in this case when $X = 50$. Until $X = 50$, Y is rising as X rises, but after $X = 50$, Y is falling as X rises. Thus Y reaches a maximum value of 250 when X is 50.

A great deal of economic theory is based on the idea of finding a maximum (or a minimum) value. Since Y is a function of X, we speak of *maximizing the value of the function*, and by this we mean that we wish to find the value of X (50 in this case) for which the value of Y is at a maximum (250 in this case).

Now consider the function

$$Y = 75 - 10X + 0.5X^2,$$

which is graphed in Figure 2.8. In this case, the value of Y falls at first while X increases, reaches a *minimum*, and then rises as X goes on increasing. In this case, Y reaches a minimum value of 25 when X is 10. Here we speak of *minimizing the value of the function*, by which we mean finding the value of X for which the value of Y is at a minimum.

(13) Functions of more than one variable

In most of the examples used so far Y has been a function of only one variable, X. In many cases, however, the dependent variable is a function of more than one independent variable. The demand for a good might depend, for example, on the price of that good, on the prices of a number of competing products, on the prices of products used in conjunction with the product with which we are concerned, and on consumers' incomes.

When we wish to denote the dependence of Y on several variables, say, V, W and X, we write $Y = Y(V, W, X)$, which is read Y is a function of V, W and X.

In mathematics and in economics we often wish to discover what happens to Y as X varies, assuming meanwhile that the other factors that influence X are held constant at some stated level. The result is often phrased 'Y varies in such and such a way with X *other things being equal*' or 'Y varies with X in such and such a way *ceteris paribus*'.

Students who do not know mathematics are often disturbed by the frequent use in economics of arguments that depend on the qualification 'other things being equal' (for which we often use the Latin phrase *ceteris paribus*). Such arguments are not peculiar to economics. They are used successfully in all branches of science and there is an elaborate set of mathematical techniques available to handle them.

When mathematicians wish to know how Y is changing as X changes when other factors that influence Y are held constant, they calculate what is called the *partial derivative of Y with respect to X*. This is written symbolically as $\partial Y/\partial X$. We cannot enter here into a discussion of how this expression is calculated. We only wish to note that finding $\partial Y/\partial X$ is a well-recognized and very common mathematical operation, and the answer tells us approximately how Y is affected by small variations in X *when all other relevant factors are held constant*.

3

The tools of statistical analysis

Look once again at Figure 1.1 on page 15 and notice that the second of the two triangles indicates the process of statistical analysis. This is used for two related purposes: first, to test the predictions of our theories against evidence, and, second, to estimate the magnitude of relations among variables. For example, statistical analysis has been used repeatedly to test the prediction that when the price of any product falls people will wish to buy more of it. Statistical analysis has also been used to measure the quantitative relations between the prices of particular products and the amounts bought. This allows economists to reach such conclusions as 'A 1 per cent fall in the price of wheat will lead to an increase in purchases of $\frac{1}{4}$ of 1 per cent, while a 1 per cent fall in the price of dairy cream will lead to a 2 per cent increase in purchases.' In the first case we see statistical analysis being used to test a general prediction of theory; in the second case we see statistics providing numerical estimates of *how much* one variable changes in response to changes in a related variable.

An understanding of the intricacies of statistical analysis when used for either of these purposes can be gained only from a detailed study of statistical theory. In this chapter we take a brief look at how statistical analysis is used in economics. Because this is a book about economic theory, we concentrate on the use of statistics in testing theories. Later, however, we shall often refer to quantitative statistical estimates of the relations among economic variables.

Kinds of sciences

In order to determine whether or not their predictions are correct within some acceptable margin of error, we must test our theories against the evidence. This is not a task that is easily accomplished (or briefly described). As a first step in discussing the testing of theories, we must distinguish between laboratory and non-laboratory methods.

Laboratory sciences

In some sciences, it is possible to obtain all necessary observations from controlled experiments made under laboratory conditions. In such experiments, we hold constant all the factors that are thought to affect the outcome of the process being studied. Then we vary these factors one by one while we observe the influence that each variation appears to have on the outcome of the experiment.

Suppose, for example, we have a theory that predicts that the rate at which a substance burns is a function of the chemical properties of that substance and the rate at which oxygen is made available during the process of combustion. To test this theory, we can take a number of identical pieces of some substances and burn them, varying the amount of oxygen made available in each case. This allows us to see how combustion varies with the quantity of oxygen used. We can then take a number of substances with different chemical compositions and burn them, using identical amounts of oxygen. This allows us to see how combustion varies with chemical composition. In such an experiment, we never have to use data that are generated when both chemical composition and the quantity of oxygen are varying simultaneously. Laboratory conditions are used to hold other things constant and to produce data for situations in which factors are varied one at a time.

Non-laboratory sciences

In some sciences we cannot isolate factors one at a time in laboratory experiments. In these sciences observations are still used to establish relationships and to test theories, but such observations appear in a relatively complex form, because several things are usually varying at the same time.

Consider, for example, the hypothesis that one's health as an adult depends upon one's diet as a child. Clearly, all sorts of other factors affect the health of adults: heredity, conditions of childhood other than nutrition, and various aspects of adult environment. There is no possible way to examine this hypothesis in the manner of a controlled experiment, for we are unlikely to be able to find a group of adults whose diet as children varied but for whom all other influences affecting health were the same. Should we conclude that the hypothesis cannot be tested because other facts cannot be held constant? If we did, we would be denying the possibility of many advances in medicine, biology and other sciences concerned with humans that have actually been made during the last hundred years. Testing is harder when one cannot use laboratory methods, but, fortunately, it is still possible.

In a situation in which many things are varying at once, we must be careful in our use of data. If we study only two people and find that the one with the better diet during his youth has the poorer adult health record, this would not disprove the hypothesis that a good diet is a factor leading to better health. It might well be that some other factor exerted an overwhelming influence on these two individuals. Clearly, a single exception does not disprove the hypothesis of a relation between two things as long as we admit that other factors can also influence the outcome.[1]

It is rarely, if ever, possible to conduct controlled experiments with the economy. Thus economics must be a non-laboratory science. A mass of data is, however, being generated continually by the economy. Every day, for example, consumers are comparing prices and deciding what to buy; firms are comparing prices and deciding what to produce and offer for sale; and governments are intervening with taxes, subsidies and direct controls. All of these acts can be observed and recorded. These data then provide the empirical observations against which economic theories can

---

[1] Note how often in ordinary conversation a person advances a possible relation (e.g., between education and some facet of character), while someone else will 'refute' this theory by citing a single counter-example (e.g., 'my friend went to that school and did not turn out like that'). It is a commonplace in everyday conversation to dismiss an hypothesis with some such remark as 'Oh, that's just a generalization.' All interesting hypotheses are generalizations and it will always be possible to notice some real or apparent exceptions. What we need to know is whether or not the mass of evidence supports the hypothesis as a statement of a general tendency for two or more things to be related to each other. This issue can never be settled one way or the other by the casual quoting of a few bits of evidence that just happen to be readily available.

be tested. Given the complexity of data generated under non-experimental conditions, casual observation is not likely to be sufficient for testing economic hypotheses. Modern statistical analysis was developed to test hypotheses rigorously in situations in which many things were varying at once. Its early development was mainly concerned with experiments in biology and agriculture. Later, however, ECONOMETRICS grew up as a special branch of statistics, concerned to develop techniques that would allow rigorous testing of hypotheses against data generated in the circumstances in which economic events typically occur.

> **Although economics must be a non-laboratory science, the masses of data produced by the economy under continually changing circumstances do provide evidence against which economic theories may be tested.**

An example of the statistical testing of economic theories

Consider the hypothesis that one of the important factors influencing the purchase of each commodity is the incomes of consumers. We shall examine one test of this hypothesis that was actually made some years ago in the United States – relating incomes and the demand for beef. To conduct the test the US Department of Agriculture gathered data for households, that is, a group of individuals who live under the same roof and make joint consumption decisions.

Let us imagine ourselves in the place of the investigators setting out to make this test. We realize that we need to know each household's income and the amount of beef that is purchased. In this case it is obvious that it would be prohibitively expensive to enumerate all the individual households in the American population, so we must take a smaller number of observations (called a *sample*) and hope that it is typical of all US households.[1]

Table 3.1 Beef consumption and income for three US households

Household	Annual household income (dollars)	Average weekly beef consumption (pounds)
1	4,500	5·10
2	5,500	5·05
3	6,500	4·93

The sample

We start by observing the three households whose data are recorded in Table 3.1. These data may lead us to wonder if the hypothesis is wrong, but, before we jump to that conclusion, we should consider the possibility that we may have selected three households that are not typical of all the households in the country. The expenditure on food is undoubtedly influenced by factors other than income and possibly these other factors just happen to be dominant in the three cases selected.

So we select a large number of households in order to reduce the chances of consistently picking

[1] The data for this example are adapted from Daniel B. Suits, *Statistics: An Introduction to Quantitative Economic Research* (Rand McNally, 1963), p. 169.

up untypical ones. Suppose someone does this by taking 100 households from friends and acquaintances. A statistician points out, however, that our new group is a very *biased sample*, for it contains households from only a limited geographical area, probably with only a limited occupational range, and possibly with very similar incomes. It is unlikely that this sample of households will be representative of all households we wish to study.

The statistician suggests taking a *random sample* of households. A random sample is one chosen according to a rigidly defined set of conditions that guarantees, among other things, that every household in which we are interested has an equal chance of being selected. Choosing our sample in a random fashion has an important consequence. It allows us to calculate the probability that our sample is unrepresentative in any given aspect by any stated amount. The reason is that our sample was chosen by chance, and chance events are predictable.

That chance events are predictable may sound surprising. But if you pick a card blindly from a deck of ordinary playing cards, how likely is it that you will pick a heart? an ace? an ace of hearts? You play a game in which you pick a card and win if it is a heart and lose if it is anything else; a friend offers you £5 if you win against £1 if you lose. Who will make money if the game is played a large number of times? The same game is played again, but you get £3 if you win and pay £1 if you lose. Now who will make money over a large number of draws? If you know the answers to these questions, you know that chance events are in some sense predictable.

How does this measurability of chance events apply to our present problem? If we select our households by pure chance we can know the probability of selecting an unrepresentative sample. If, for example, the average income of all American households is $15,000, the most likely single result is that the average income of our random sample will also be $15,000, but we should not be very surprised if it were $14,950 or even $16,000. The further away is the average income of our sample from the true value for all households, the more unrepresentative is our sample.

> **The predictability of chance events allows us to calculate the probability that the average value of a variable in a random sample will differ by any stated amount from the true average value of the same variable in the whole population. In general, the bigger the deviation the less likely it is to occur in a truly random sample.**

The analysis of the data

Having chosen our random sample – in this case it was 4,827 households – we collect information from each household on its income and its beef purchases. Then we plot the data so that we can inspect it visually. To do this we use a SCATTER DIAGRAM.[1] We measure household income along the horizontal axis and expenditure on beef along the vertical axis. For each household we place a dot on the graph indicating its annual income and the amount of beef it purchases per week. A scatter diagram with 4,827 dots would, however, be unintelligible when reduced to the size of a printed page. We have, therefore, drawn the diagram in Figure 3.1 by taking a 5 per cent random sample of the 4,827 households. Each of these 241 dots in the Figure is to be thought of as representing 20 of the households in our original sample.

---

[1] The two major techniques for graphing economic data, scatter diagrams and time-series charts, are further discussed in the Appendix to this chapter.

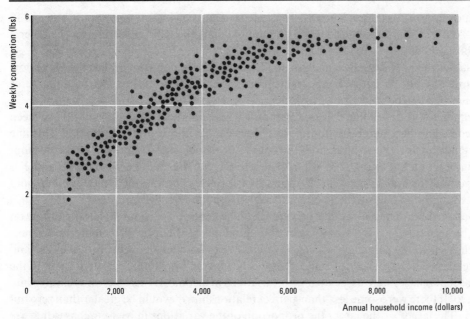

Fig. 3.1 A scatter diagram showing income and expenditure on beef of a random sample of American households.

The scatter diagram suggests a tendency: the higher a household's income, the greater its purchase of beef. In the language of Chapter 2 (page 19), beef purchases are an increasing function of household income. The relationship is not deterministic, however, for there is considerable variation in beef purchases that cannot be associated with variations in incomes. These 'unexplained variations' occur for two main reasons: first, there are factors other than income that influence beef purchases; second, there will be some errors in our measurements (e.g., a household might have incorrectly recorded its beef purchases).

To make the data somewhat more manageable, we gather them into groups. To obtain Table 3.2, the households are divided into 10 groups according to income, and the average beef consump-

Table 3.2 Beef consumption and income for a sample of US households

Average household income ($)	Average weekly beef consumption (lbs)	Number of families
0–999	2·13	532
1,000–1,999	2·82	647
2,000–2,999	3·70	692
3,000–3,999	4·25	867
4,000–4,999	4·86	865
5,000–5,999	5·16	513
6,000–6,999	5·20	371
7,000–7,999	5·30	159
8,000–8,999	5·52	121
9,000–9,999	5·90	60

tion for each income group is then calculated. This reduces a mass of 4,827 observations to a mere 10 observations. At the loss of some considerable amount of detail, the table makes clearer the general tendency for beef purchases to rise with income.

The next step is to apply statistical analysis to all of the data in our sample. The details of how this is done must be left to courses in statistics and econometrics, but we can mention three important things that can be done.

First, we can fit to the data a line that represents the best estimate of the actual relation between household income and beef purchases for all 4,827 households in our original sample.[1] This line describes the tendency for higher household incomes to be associated with greater beef consumption. (The equation of a line is $B = 2{\cdot}35 + 0{\cdot}47Y$, where B is purchases of beef in pounds and Y is income in thousands of dollars per year. It shows that for every increase of \$1,000 in household income, beef consumption tends to increase by about half a pound per week.)

Second, we can obtain a measure of the percentage of the variations in household expenditure on beef that can be accounted for by variations in household income. This is the commonly encountered r^2, which is called the *coefficient of determination*. r^2 can take on any value between zero and unity. If the relationship were deterministic, r^2 would be unity. This would indicate that all of the variations in beef purchases were associated with variations in income. If there were no relationship, r^2 would be zero. If there were some less-than-perfect relationship, r^2 would be greater than zero but less than unity. The larger r^2, the larger the proportion of the variations in beef purchases that are associated with variations in income. Loosely speaking, r^2 is a measure of the degree of scatter of the individual observations around the line that describes the average relation between beef purchases and income: if all points lie on the line, r^2 is unity, while the more diffuse the scatter of points around the line, the weaker the relation and the closer to zero the value of r^2.

Third, we can apply a 'significance test'. This allows us to discover the chances that the relation we have discovered has arisen only because our sample is not representative of all households in the United States. In the present case, there is less than one chance in one million that we could have made the observations that we did if, in fact, there were no positive relation between income and beef purchases for all US households. Thus we can have a great deal of confidence in the hypothesis that these two variables, beef purchases and household income, are in fact positively related in the United States.

The influence of additional variables

It is clear from the scatter diagram that we cannot account for *all* of the variation in households' purchases of beef by observed variations in household income. We may wish to look for some other factor that might also exert a systematic influence on beef expenditure. What could make one household with an income of \$6,000 buy 20 per cent more beef than another household with the same income? One possible factor is that households in different parts of the country faced different prices of beef. Of course, there will be many other factors, such as size of family and religion, but we shall select price as our second factor for the purpose of illustration. Assume that the survey also

---

[1] Before we fit the line, we must decide if the relation is best described by a straight line or a curve. Fortunately there are tests that allow us to tell if we made an error in thinking that the relation was linear when it really was curvilinear. In the example considered here, the correct relation is slightly curvilinear, but a straight line is a reasonable approximation to the correct relation over the range of most of the data.

collected data on the prices of various cuts of beef in each city or town from which a household in the sample bought its meat. These data were then used to calculate the average price of beef facing households in each area.

We now have three observations for each one of our 4,827 households – their annual income, their weekly purchases of beef, and the average price of the beef that they purchase. How should we handle these data? Unfortunately, our scatter-diagram technique has now let us down, since we cannot easily show the relation among three things on a two-dimensional graph. We can, however, *cross-classify* the data. To do this we first classify households into five income groups, each with a spread of $2,000.[1] We then subdivide the households in each income group according to the price they paid for their beef. This gives us twenty groups of households. For each we calculate the average purchases of beef and enter it in the appropriate cell of Table 3.3. For example, households that had an income between $6,000 and $7,999 and who faced a price of beef between $0·80 and $0·99 a pound bought an average of 5·35 pounds of beef a week, while those households in the same income group who faced a price between $1·40 and $1·59 bought an average of only 5·07 pounds per week.

Table 3.3 Average household purchases of beef in pounds per week, classified by household income and the average purchase price of beef

Annual household income ($)	Average price of beef per pound			
	$0·80–0·99	$1·00–1·19	$1·20–1·39	$1·40–1·59
0–1,999	2·65	2·59	2·51	2·43
2,000–3,999	4·14	4·05	3·94	3·88
4,000–5,999	5·11	5·00	4·97	4·84
6,000–7,999	5·35	5·29	5·19	5·07
8,000–9,999	5·79	5·77	5·60	5·53

Each row of this table exhibits the effect of *price* on the purchases of beef for a given level of income. Reading across the second row, for example, we see that households with incomes between $2,000 and $3,999 bought an average of 4·14 pounds of beef when the price was between 80 and 99¢ per pound, 4·05 pounds when the price was between $1 and $1·19, and so on. Each column of the table shows the effect of *income* on purchases of beef in a given price range. For instance, the last column shows how beef purchases varied with income for those households that were subject to a very high average price of beef. When these prices were faced, purchases ranged from 2·43 pounds for the group with the lowest income to 5·53 for the one with the highest income.

This device of cross-classification manages to catch observationally much of the idea of *holding other things constant* that is sometimes thought to be possible only in laboratory sciences.[2] Reading across any row, we are holding income constant within a specified range while varying price; reading down any column, we are holding price constant within a specified range while varying income.

---

[1] To prevent the table from becoming too large, we have grouped households into income groups of $2,000 rather than $1,000, as was done in Table 3.2; but this is only a matter of convenience, and the classification can be made as detailed as is required for any particular purpose.

[2] See the discussion on page 34, 'Functions of More than One Variable'.

If we wish to go further than this, we need to apply once again the rigorous tools of statistical analysis. When, as in the present case, we have more than one explanatory variable, we use a technique called *multiple regression analysis*. Just as in the case of one explanatory variable, we can do three important things with this tool. First, we can estimate the numerical relation between weekly beef purchases, on the one hand, and price and income, on the other. Second, we can measure the proportion of the total variation in beef purchases that can be explained by associating it with variations both in income and in price. Finally, we can estimate the probability that the relations we have found in our sample are the result of chance because by bad luck we had chosen an unrepresentative sample of households.

Testing and measurement

Statistical techniques help us to judge the probability that any particular theory is false. This is an extremely valuable thing to be able to do. What statistical techniques cannot do is *prove with certainty* that an hypothesis is either true or false. We have already discussed this matter in Chapter 1. We now summarize the earlier discussion and then take it a step further.

Can we prove that an hypothesis is true?

Most hypotheses in economics are what may be called universal hypotheses. They say that, whenever certain specified conditions are fulfilled, cause X will always produce effect Y. We have already pointed out that universal hypotheses cannot be proved to be correct because we can never rule out the possibility that we shall in the future make observations that conflict with the theory. (See page 13.)

Can we prove that an hypothesis is false?

By the same token, we cannot get a categorical disproof of an hypothesis. Consider the hypothesis '*Most* crows are black'. We observe 50 crows; 49 are grey and only one is black. Have we disproved the hypothesis? The answer is no, for it is *possible* that this was just bad luck and if we could observe all the crows in the world it would indeed prove to be the case that most are black.

What, then, is required if we are to be able to refute any hypothesis? First, the hypothesis must admit of no exceptions: it must say, for example, '*All* crows are black.' Using the language introduced in Chapter 1, it must be a deterministic, not a statistical hypothesis. (Recall that a deterministic hypothesis admits of no exceptions while a statistical hypothesis deals in general tendencies.) Second, we must be certain that any apparently refuting observations are not mistaken. The observation of 49 black crows and one grey refutes the hypothesis that *all* crows are black only if we are sure that we genuinely saw a grey crow. But are we sure that the odd bird really was a crow? Are we sure that what looked like a grey crow was not a dusty black crow?[1] Errors in observation may always be present. For this reason, an hypothesis cannot be refuted on the basis of a single

---

[1] Even if we satisfy ourselves that we saw a grey crow, future generations may not accept our evidence unless they go on observing the occasional grey crow. After all we no longer accept the mass of well-documented evidence accumulated several centuries ago on the existence and power of witches, even though it fully satisfied most contemporary observers. Clearly the existence of observational errors on a vast scale has been shown to be possible even though it may not be frequent.

conflicting observation, and indeed it can never be categorically refuted, no matter how many conflicting observations we make. If we observe 49 grey crows and only one black one, our faith in the hypothesis that all crows are black may well be shaken and as a practical measure we may choose to abandon the hypothesis (see below). We can never be certain, however, that all 49 cases were not due to errors of observation and had we persisted we might have ended up with 999,951 black crows and 49 grey ones. (This would make the hypothesis look pretty good, since a measurement error on 0·005 per cent of our cases might not seem at all improbable.)

Rules for decision-taking

We have seen that in general we can neither prove nor refute an hypothesis conclusively, no matter how many oberservations we make.[1]   Nonetheless, we have to make decisions and act as if some hypotheses were refuted (i.e., we have to reject them) and we have to act as if some hypotheses were proved (i.e., we have to accept them). Such decisions are always subject to error, but by using statistical analysis we can control the possibility of making errors even if we cannot eliminate it.

Consider an example. When studying beef purchases our hypothesis might have been that the expenditure on beef of US households *falls* as their income rises. We would then ask what the chances were of making the observations shown in Figure 3.1 if the hypothesis were correct. There is always some chance that our sample was untypical of all US households or that the relationship appears as it is because of measurement errors. If we calculate (using the tools taught in courses on statistics) that there is *less* than one chance in 100 of making the observations in Figure 3.1, if the hypothesized relation that beef purchases fall as income rises actually holds for all US households, then we would abandon the hypothesis and for practical purposes regard it as refuted.

It is important, however, to understand, first, that we can never be certain that we are right in rejecting a statistical hypothesis and, second, that there is nothing magical about our arbitrary cut-off points. The cut-off point (less than one chance in 100 of being wrong in this case) is used because some decision has to be made. Notice also that decisions can always be reversed should new evidence come to light.

Judging among hypotheses

Older statistical methodology tended to emphasize the testing of theories one at a time. As it has become clearer that theories in economics could be neither confirmed nor refuted with finality, the newer methodology has tended to emphasize the use of statistical analysis to choose among two or more competing theories. Although we can never be absolutely sure that one is right and the other is wrong, we can hope to show that the data favours one over the other in the sense that there is a greater chance that we would have observed what we did observe if the causal forces were those described by theory A rather than those described by theory B. To make such tests we must first find

[1] This is because I take all hypotheses about observable events to be statistical ones due to unavoidable errors of observation. We do of course make arbitrary decisions to reject statistical hypotheses but so also do we make arbitrary decisions to accept them. These rules of thumb for practical decision-taking have nothing to do with the methodological questions of whether any hypothesis can be conclusively refuted and whether any hypothesis can be conclusively proved. My answer to both questions is no. Those who are not convinced by my arguments may proceed with the text as long as they are prepared to accept that most hypotheses in economics are statistical hypotheses.

out where theories A and B make predictions that conflict with each other. Theory A might for example predict a close relation between variables X and Y because, according to it, X causes Y; theory B might predict no strong relation between the two variables because, according to it, X has no effect on Y one way or the other. The empirical relation between X and Y can then be studied and conclusions reached about the probability that what we saw could have happened if theory A were correct or if theory B were correct.

Quantitative measurement of economic relations

So far we have asked if certain observations support certain general hypotheses. The actual data do, for example, support the hypothesis that households' expenditures on beef increase as their incomes increase. This, however, is not enough. It is important to quantify such qualitative statements. We should like to be able to say that American household expenditure on beef increases by some definite amount for every $1·00 that household income increases.

Economic theories are seldom of much use until we are able to give quantitative magnitudes to our relations. For estimating such magnitudes, our common sense and intuitions do not get us very far. Common sense might well have suggested that expenditure on beef would rise rather than fall as income rose, but only careful observation is going to help us to decide *by how much* it typically rises. One of the major uses of statistical analysis is to quantify the general relations suggested by theory. In practice, we can use actual observations both to test the hypothesis that two things are related and to estimate the numerical values of the relations that do exist.

Sometimes a statistical test of an hypothesis suggests a new hypothesis that 'fits the facts' better than the previous one. You should look back to Figure 1.1 on page 15 once again, this time to see where such new hypotheses enter the picture.[1]

> **Although there can never be absolute finality in the testing of economic hypotheses, statistical analysis can be used first to establish the probability that we would have seen what we did see if one theory of the operative causal forces was correct; secondly to establish the balance of probabilities between two competing theories; and thirdly to measure the quantitative relations between variables that theory suggests are related.**

Words of warning

In the first three chapters of this book I have made a case that economics can be a scientific enquiry. Some words of caution are now in order.

There are major differences among the various sciences. Because of these, methods that work well in one science may not be suitable in another. In particular, what works in physics, the queen of sciences, may not work well in a social science such as economics. What unites all sciences, however, is the explanation and prediction of observed phenomena. The successes and failures of all sciences are judged by their abilities to further these objectives.

Because this is not a textbook in economic statistics, the problems involved in collecting reliable observations, of 'facts', against which to judge our theories, are not stressed.[2] Such problems can be

---

[1] Hypotheses that originate from data are sometimes called *inductive* hypotheses in contrast to *deductive* ones. But in any science, the sequence of theory and testing is continuous. The question of which came first, theory or observation, is analogous to the debate over the chicken and the egg.

[2] Although I have not stressed it, the question of the reliability of observation is either explicit or implicit in the discussion on pages 10–11, 13, 19 and 42–3.

formidable, and there is always the danger of rejecting a theory on the basis of mistaken observations. Unreliable observations are all too frequently encountered. It is important to note, however, that if, on the one hand, we think all our observations are totally unreliable, then we have nothing to explain and, hence, no need for any economic theory. If, on the other hand, we believe that we do have observations reliable enough to require explanation, then we must also believe that we have observations reliable enough to provide tests for the predictive powers of our theories.

I have been concerned in this chapter to dispel the common view that economists cannot be scientific in their use of data because they cannot make controlled experiments. The statistical tasks described in this chapter are often difficult to perform, and the pitfalls ready to trap the unwary user of inappropriate statistical procedures are too numerous to mention. Indeed a whole new subject, econometrics, has grown up to amend statistical techniques that were developed for the natural sciences and to develop new ones able to handle the special data problems that occur in economics and other social sciences. To launch into a career in economic or social research without a full knowledge of the field of statistical analysis would be foolhardy in the extreme.

Appendix to chapter 3

Graphs and index numbers

The popular saying 'The facts speak for themselves' is almost always wrong when there are many facts. Theories are needed to explain how facts are linked together, and summary measures are needed to assist in sorting out what it is that facts do show in relation to theories. The simplest means of providing compact summaries of a large number of observations is through the use of tables and graphs. Graphs play important roles in economics by representing geometrically both observed data and economic theories, and they are the subject of the first part of this Appendix. Index numbers, which are commonly used to compress a mass of data into a few summary statistics, are the subject of the second part of the Appendix.

Graphs

The scatter diagram

The SCATTER DIAGRAM provides a method of graphing any number of observations made on two variables; one variable is measured on each axis and any point on the diagram refers simultaneously to a particular value of each of the variables. It is useful because if there is a simple relation between the two variables, this will be apparent to the eye once the data are plotted. Thus in Figure 3.1 (see page 39) meat purchases clearly tend to rise as income rises. It is also apparent that this relation is only approximately linear since, as income rises above $5,000 a year, beef purchases seem to rise less and less with further equal increases in income. The diagram also gives some idea of the strength of the relation: if income were the only determinant of beef purchases, all of the dots would lie on a single line; as it is, the points are somewhat scattered and particular incomes are often represented by several households, each with different quantities of beef purchased. The data used in this example are CROSS-SECTIONAL DATA. The incomes and beef purchases of different

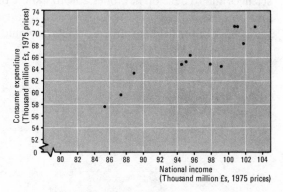

Fig. 3.2 A scatter diagram relating consumers' expenditure to National Income (GDP)

households are compared over a single period of time.

Scatter diagrams may also be drawn of a number of observations taken on two variables at successive periods of time. Thus, if one wanted to know if there had been any simple relation between national income and total consumers' expenditure in the UK between 1970 and 1981, data would be collected for these years, as is shown in Table 3.4. This information could be plotted on a scatter diagram with income on the X axis and consumption on the Y axis to discover any systematic relation between the two variables. The data are plotted in Figure 3.2 and do indeed suggest a general tendency for consumers' expenditure to be positively related to national income. In this exercise a scatter diagram of observations taken over successive periods of time has been used. Such data are called TIME-SERIES DATA and plotting them on a scatter diagram involves no new technique: when cross-sectional data are plotted, each point gives the values of two variables for a particular unit (say a household);

46

Table 3.4 Consumers' expenditure and national income (GDP) in the UK 1970–81, in constant (1975) prices

	Consumers' expenditure (£ millions)	National income (GDP, £ millions)
1970	57,814	85,402
1971	59,724	87,654
1972	63,270	88,815
1973	66,332	95,635
1974	65,113	94,905
1975	64,749	94,475
1976	64,815	97,948
1977	64,583	99,240
1978	68,222	101,869
1979	71,485	102,901
1980	71,477	100,729
1981	71,467	101,021

Source: *National Institute Economic Review*, May 1982

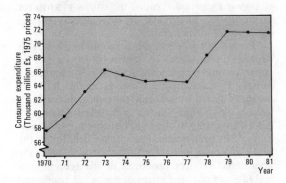

Fig. 3.3 A time series of consumers' expenditure, 1970–1981

when time-series data are plotted, each point tells the values of two variables for a particular year.

Time-series graphs

Instead of studying the relation between income and consumption suggested in the previous paragraph, a study of the pattern of the changes in either one of these variables over time could be made. In Figure 3.3 this information is shown for consumers' expenditure. In the figure, time is one variable, consumers' expenditure the other. But time is a very special variable: the order in which successive events happen is important. The year 1975 followed 1974; but they were not two independent and unrelated years. (By way of contrast, two randomly selected households are independent and unrelated.) For this reason it is customary to draw in the line segments connecting the successive points. A chart such as this figure is called a TIME-SERIES DIAGRAM or, more simply, a time-series: it plots the values of a single variable at successive periods of time. This kind of graph makes it easy to see if the variable being considered has varied in a systematic way over the years or if its behaviour has been more or less erratic.

Ratio (logarithmic) scales

Often *proportionate* rather than absolute changes in variables are important. In such cases it is more revealing to use a ratio scale rather than a natural scale. On a NATURAL SCALE the distance between numbers is proportionate to the absolute difference between those numbers. Thus 200 is placed halfway between 100 and 300. On a RATIO SCALE the distance between numbers is proportionate to the absolute difference between their logarithms. Equal distances anywhere on a ratio scale represent equal percentage changes rather than equal absolute changes. On a ratio scale the distance between 100 and 200 is the same as the distance between 200 and 400, between 1,000 and 2,000, and between any two numbers that stand in the ratio 1:2 to each other. For obvious reasons a ratio scale is also called a LOGARITHMIC SCALE.

Table 3.5 Two series

Time period	Series A	Series B
0	£10	£10
1	18	20
2	26	40
3	34	80
4	42	160

Table 3.5 shows two series, one growing at a constant absolute amount of 8 units per period and the other growing at a constant rate of 100 per cent per period. In Figure 3.4 the series are plotted first on a natural scale and then on a ratio scale. Series A, which grows at a constant absolute amount, is a straight line on a natural scale but a curve of ever-decreasing slope on a ratio scale, because the same absolute growth is decreasing percentage growth. Series B, which grows at a rising absolute but a constant percentage rate, is upward-bending on a natural scale but is a straight line on a ratio scale. The

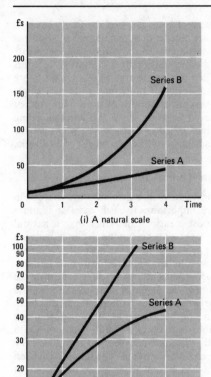

(i) A natural scale

(ii) A ratio scale

Fig. 3.4 The difference between natural and ratio scales

natural scale makes it easy for the eye to judge absolute variations, and the logarithmic scale makes it easy for the eye to judge proportionate variations.[1]

Index numbers

Economists frequently seek simple answers to questions such as 'How much have prices risen this year?' or 'Has the quantity of industrial production increased this year, and if so, by how much?' There is no perfectly satisfactory answer to the first question

[1] Graphs with a ratio scale on one axis and a natural scale on the other are frequently encountered in economics. In the cases just illustrated there is a ratio scale on the vertical axis and a natural scale on the horizontal (or time) axis. Such graphs are often called *semi-log* graphs. In scientific work graphs with ratio scales on both axes are frequently encountered. Such graphs are often referred to as *double-log* graphs.

because all prices do not move together, nor to the second because one cannot simpy add up tons of steel, pieces of furniture and gallons of oil to get a meaningful total. Yet these are not foolish questions. There *are* trends in prices and production, and thus there are real phenomena to describe.

Index numbers are statistical measures that are used to give a concise summary answer to the complex questions of the kind just suggested. An INDEX NUMBER measures for some broad average the percentage change that has occurred since some base period. As such it points to overall tendencies or general drifts, not to specific single facts. The two most important kinds of index numbers are price indices and quantity indices.

Index numbers of prices

A PRICE INDEX shows the average percentage change that has occurred in some group of prices over some period of time. The point in time from which the change is measured is called the BASE PERIOD (or base year), while the point in time to which the change is measured is called the GIVEN PERIOD (or given year). There are several aspects to the definition of index numbers.

First, what group of prices should be used? This depends on the index. The INDEX OF RETAIL PRICES (RPI) covers prices of commodities commonly bought by households. Changes in the RPI are meant to measure changes in the typical household's 'cost of living'. The Wholesale Price Index measures a different group of commodities commonly bought and sold by wholesalers. The 'implied deflator for the GDP' is a price index that covers virtually all of the goods and services produced in the economy; it includes not only the prices of consumer goods and services bought by households but the prices of capital goods such as plants and machinery bought by firms.

Second, what kind of average should be used? If all prices were to change in the same proportion, this would not be an important question. A 10 per cent rise in each and every price covered means an average rise of 10 per cent no matter how much importance we give to each price change when calculating the average. But what if – as is almost always the case – different prices change differently? Now it does matter how much importance we give to each price change. A rise of 50 per cent in the price of caviar is surely much less important to the average consumer than a rise of 40 per cent in the price of bread, and this in turn is surely less important than a rise of 30 per cent in the cost of housing. Why? The reason is that the typical household spends less on caviar than

Table 3.6 The calculation of a price index covering three commodities

Commodity	Quantity in fixed bundle	Base year 1983		Given year 1984	
		Price in 1983	Value in 1983	Price in 1984	Value in 1984
A	500 units	£1·00	£ 500	£2·00	£1,000
B	200 units	5·00	1,000	7·00	1,400
C	50 units	2·00	100	9·60	480
			1,600		2,880

Index value 1983 $= \dfrac{1600}{1600} \times 100 = 100$

Index value 1984 $= \dfrac{2880}{1600} \times 100 = 180$

on bread and less on bread than on housing.

In calculating any price index, statisticians seek to weight each price according to its importance. Let us see how this is done for the RPI. Government statisticians periodically survey a group of households to discover how they spend their incomes. The average bundle of goods bought is calculated, and the quantities in this bundle become the weights attached to the prices. In this way the average price change heavily weights commodities on which consumers spend a lot and lightly weights commodities on which consumers spend only a little. The procedure is illustrated in Table 3.6.

Finally, how is the average change calculated? This is done by comparing the costs of purchasing the typical bundle of commodities in the base period and in the given year. The given-year cost is expressed as a percentage of the base-period cost, and this figure is the index number of the new period. For example, in Table 3.6 the index for year 1984 is the cost of purchasing that bundle in 1984 expressed as a percentage of the cost of purchasing the same bundle in the base year (which is 1983 in this example). The price index is thus always 100 in the base year. The index of 180 means that prices have risen on average by 80 per cent between the base year and the year in question.

> **A price index number with base-year weights is the ratio of the cost of purchasing a bundle of commodities in the given year to the cost of purchasing the same bundle in the base year multiplied by 100.**

The percentage *change* in the cost of purchasing the bundle is thus the index number minus 100. An index number of 110 indicates a percentage increase in prices of 10 per cent over those ruling in the base year.

Some difficulties An index number is meant to reflect the broad trend in prices rather than the details. This means that although the information it gives may be extremely valuable, it must be interpreted with care. Here are three of the many reasons why care is required.

First, the weights in the index refer to an average bundle of goods. This average, although 'typical' of what is consumed in the nation, will not necessarily be typical of what each household does. The rich, the poor, the young, the old, the single, the married, the urban and the rural households typically consume bundles that differ from one another. An increase in air fares, for example, will raise the cost of living of a middle-income traveller while leaving that of a poor stay-at-home unaffected. In the example of Table 3.6, the cost of living would have risen by 100 per cent, 40 per cent and 380 per cent respectively for three different families, one of whom consumed only commodity *A*, one only commodity *B*, and one only commodity *C*. The index in the table shows, however, that the cost of living went up by 80 per cent for a family that consumed all three goods in the relative quantities indicated.

> **The more an individual household's consumption pattern diverges from that of the typical pattern used to weight prices in the price index, the less well the price index will reflect the average change in prices relevant to that household.**

Second, households usually alter their consumption patterns in response to price changes. A price index that shows changes in the cost of purchasing a fixed bundle of goods does not allow for this. For example, a typical cost-of-living index for middle-income families at the turn of the century would have given heavy weight to the cost of maids and children's nurses. A doubling of servants' wages in 1900 would have greatly increased the middle-class cost of living. Today it would have little effect, for the rising cost of labour has long since caused most middle-income families to cease to employ full-time servants. A household that greatly reduces its consumption of a commodity whose price is rising rapidly does not have its cost of living rise as fast as a household that continues to consume that commodity in an undiminished quantity.

A fixed-weight price index tends to overstate cost-of-living changes because it does not allow for changes in consumption patterns that shift expenditure away from commodities whose prices rise most and toward those whose prices rise least.

Third, as time goes by, new commodities enter the typical consumption bundle and old ones leave. A cost-of-living index in 1890 would have had a large item for horse-drawn carriages and horse feed but no allowance at all for motorcars and petrol.

A fixed-weight index makes no allowance for the rise of new products nor for the declining importance of old ones in the typical household's consumption bundle.

The longer the period of time that passes, the less some fixed consumption bundle will be typical of current consumption patterns. For this reason the government makes periodic surveys of household expenditure patterns and revises the weights. The base period is then usually changed to conform to the year in which the new set of commodity weights was calculated.

Index numbers of physical outputs

There are many output indices. Like the price indices discussed above, they are averages of the changes in thousands of individual items. It is not hard to measure the change in production of tons of steel from month to month or year to year, nor that of tyres or television sets. It is somewhat harder to measure the quantity of printing, furniture or aircraft because the unit of output is less well defined; but these too can be approximated.

Table 3.7 illustrates in simplified form the required computation for a two-industry example. The increase in quantity in each industry is shown in the 'quantity relative' column, Q_1/Q_0. Industry A was more important in the base year than industry B, as is shown by V_0, the values of outputs in 1983. Thus industry A gets greater weight in computing the quantity index. The total value of output in 1983 was £12 billion. The last column shows the increase in value of output caused by the increase in quantity, *assuming that prices and relative importance of the two commodities did not change*. This computed value is £15·5 billion for 1984. The index for 1984 is $15·5/12·0 \times 100 = 129·2$. Thus the index has increased by 29·2 per cent between 1983 and 1984. This is the weighted average of the 25 per cent increase in production of industry A and the 50 per cent increase in industry B. Nothing tangible increased by 29·2 per cent. Yet this average reflects the fact that both industries expanded output and that industry A was in the aggregate five times as important as industry B. The procedure used in Table 3.7 can be extended to include thousands of commodities, and this leads to an overall index of physical production. Compilers of index numbers of physical output face many practical problems – which products to include, how to adjust for changes in quality of product, and which values to use as weights.

Table 3.7 The calculation of a quantity index

	Output		Quantity relative	Value of 1983 output (billion £s)	
	1983 (Q_0)	1984 (Q_1)	Q_1/Q_0	V_0	$\dfrac{Q_1}{Q_0} \times V_0$
Industry A	40,000 tons	50,000 tons	1·25	£10	£12·5
Industry B	200,000 yards	300,000 yards	1·50	2	3·0
Total				12	15·5
Index value (1983 = 100)				100	129·2

4

The problems of economic theory

We are now ready to begin our study of economics. This chapter explains the main divisions of the subject which we shall study in subsequent chapters. Theory is meant to relate to problems. If you cannot think of a set of problems to which the theory you are studying might help to provide answers, then either you or the theory has failed. You are advised to refer back to this chapter whenever in your subsequent studies you feel that you have lost sight of the problems to which a particular part of economic theory is directed.

The source of economic problems

Resources and scarcity

The resources of a society consist not only of the free gifts of nature, such as land, forests and minerals, but also of human capacity, both mental and physical, and of all sorts of man-made aids to further production, such as tools,.machinery and buildings. It is sometimes useful to divide those resources into three main groups: (1) all those free gifts of nature, such as land, forests, minerals, etc., commonly called *natural resources* and known to economists as LAND; (2) all human resources, mental and physical, both inherited and acquired, which economists call LABOUR; and (3) all those man-made aids to further production, such as tools, machinery, plant and equipment, including everything man-made which is not consumed for its own sake but is used in the process of making other goods and services, which economists call CAPITAL. These resources are called FACTORS OF PRODUCTION because they are used in the process of production. Often a fourth factor, ENTREPRENEURSHIP (from the French word *entrepreneur*, meaning the one who undertakes tasks), is distinguished. The entrepreneur is the one who takes risks by introducing both new products and new ways of making old products. He organizes the other factors of production and directs them along new lines. (When it is not distinguished as a fourth factor, entrepreneurship is included under labour.)

The things that are produced by the factors of production are called COMMODITIES. Commodities may be divided into goods and services: GOODS are tangible, as are cars or shoes; SERVICES are intangible, as are haircuts or education. This distinction, however, should not be exaggerated: goods are valued because of the services they confer on their owners. A car, for example, is valued because of the transportation that it provides – and possibly also for the flow of satisfaction the owner gets from displaying it as a status symbol. The total output of all commodities in one country over some period, usually taken as a year, is called GROSS NATIONAL PRODUCT, or often just NATIONAL PRODUCT.

The division of resources into land, labour and capital, and the division of consumption commodities into goods and services, are matters of definition. Definitions are to be judged not as matters of fact but on the grounds of usefulness and convenience. The question 'Is this division likely to be a useful one?' can be discussed fruitfully. Useless arguments about which of many definitions is the correct one are so common that they have been given a name, *essentialist arguments*. An essentialist argument takes place whenever we have no disagreement about the facts of the case but we argue about what name to use to indicate the agreed facts. Essentialist arguments are usually a waste of our time.

In most societies goods and services are not regarded as desirable in themselves; no great virtue is attached to piling them up endlessly in warehouses, never to be consumed.[1] Usually the end or goal that is desired is that individuals should have at least some of their wants satisfied. Goods and services are thus regarded as *means* by which the *goal* of the satisfaction of wants may be reached. The act of making goods and services is called PRODUCTION, and the act of using these goods and services to satisfy wants is called CONSUMPTION. Anyone who helps to produce goods or services is called a PRODUCER, and anyone who consumes them to satisfy his or her wants is called a CONSUMER.

The wants that can be satisfied by consuming goods and services may be regarded, for all practical purposes in today's world, as insatiable.[2] In relation to the known desires of individuals for such commodities as better food, clothing, housing, schooling, holidays, hospital care and entertainment, the existing supply of resources is woefully inadequate. It can produce only a small fraction of the goods and services that people desire. This gives rise to one of the basic economic problems: the problem of SCARCITY.

> **Every nation's resources are insufficient to produce the quantities of goods and services that would be required to satisfy all of its citizens' wants.**

Most of the problems of economics arise out of the use of scarce resources to satisfy human wants.

Choice and opportunity cost

Choices are necessary because resources are scarce. Because we cannot produce everything we would like to consume, there must exist some mechanism to decide what will be done and what left undone; what goods will be produced and what left unproduced; what quantity of each good will be produced; and whose wants will be satisfied and whose left unsatisfied. In most societies many different people and organizations either make or influence these choices. Individual consumers, business organizations, labour unions and government officials all exert some influence. One of the differences among various economies such as those of the United States, the United Kingdom, India

---

[1] This is a positive statement about what is, not a normative statement about what ought to be.

[2] Whether or not it would ever be possible to produce enough goods and services to satisfy all human wants is a question we need not consider here. It would take a vast increase in production, a percentage increase in the thousands to raise all citizens of any country to the standard at present enjoyed by its richer citizens. It is doubtful that, even if this could be done, all of them would find their wants fully satisfied so that there would then be no one who would desire more commodities.

and the Soviet Union is the amount of influence that different groups have upon these choices.

If you choose to have more of one thing, then, where there is an effective choice, you must have less of something else. Think of a man with a certain income who considers buying bread. We could say that the cost of this extra bread is so many pence per loaf. A more revealing way of looking at the cost, however, is in terms of what other consumption he must forgo in order to obtain his bread. Say that he decides to give up some cinema attendances. If the price of a loaf is one fifth of the price of a cinema seat, then the cost of five more loaves of bread is one cinema attendance forgone or, put the other way around, the cost of one more cinema attendance is five loaves of bread forgone.

Now consider the same problem at the level of a whole society. If the government elects to build more roads, and finds the required money by cutting down on its school construction programme, then the cost of the new roads can be expressed as so many schools per mile of road. If the government decides that more resources must be devoted to arms production, then less will be available to produce civilian goods and a choice will have to be made between 'guns and butter'. The cost of one will be expressible in terms of the amount of the other forgone. The economist's term for expressing costs in terms of forgone alternatives is OPPORTUNITY COST.

Our discussion may now be summarized briefly. Most of the problems of economics arise out of the use of scarce resources to satisfy human wants. Resources are employed to produce goods and services, which are then used by consumers to satisfy their wants. The problem of choice arises because resources are scarce in relation to the virtually unlimited wants they could be used to satisfy.

> **The concept of opportunity cost emphasizes the problem of choice by measuring the cost of obtaining a quantity of one commodity in terms of the quantity of other commodities that could have been obtained instead.**

Basic economic problems

Most of the specific questions posed at the beginning of Chapter 1 (and many other questions as well) may be regarded as aspects of seven more general questions that must be faced in all economies, whether they be capitalist, socialist or communist.

Seven questions faced by all economies

(1) What commodities are being produced and in what quantities? This question arises directly out of the scarcity of resources. It concerns *the allocation of scarce resources among alternative uses* (a shorter phrase, *resource allocation*, will often be used). The questions 'What determines the allocation of resources in various societies?' and 'What are the consequences of conscious attempts to change resource allocation?' have occupied economists since the earliest days of the subject. In free-market economies, most decisions concerning the allocation of resources are made through the price system. The study of how this system works is the major topic in the THEORY OF PRICE.

(2) By what methods are these commodities produced? This question arises because there is almost always more than one technically possible way in which goods and services can be produced. Agricultural goods, for example, can be produced by farming a small quantity of land very intensively, using large quantities of fertilizer, labour and machinery, or by farming a large quantity of land extensively, using only small quantities of fertilizer, labour and machinery. Both methods can be used to produce the same quantity of some good; one method is frugal with land but uses larger quantities of other resources, whereas the other method uses large quantities of land but is frugal in its use of other resources. The same is true of manufactured goods; it is usually possible to produce the same output by several different techniques, ranging from ones using a large quantity of labour and only a few simple machines to ones using a large quantity of highly automated machines and only a very small number of workers. Questions about why one method of production is used rather than another, and the consequences of these choices about production methods, are topics in the THEORY OF PRODUCTION.

(3) How is society's output of goods and services divided among its members? Why can some individuals and groups consume a large share of the national output while other individuals and groups can consume only a small share? The superficial answer is because the former earn large incomes while the latter earn small incomes. But this only pushes the question one stage back. Why do some individuals and groups earn large incomes while others earn only small incomes? The basic question concerns the division of the total national product among individuals and groups. Economists wish to know why any particular division occurs in a free-market society and what forces, including government intervention, can cause it to change.

Such questions have been of great concern to economists since the beginning of the subject, and interest in them is as active today as it was almost two centuries ago when Adam Smith and David Ricardo made their path-breaking attempts to solve them. These questions are the subject of the THEORY OF DISTRIBUTION. When they speak of the division of the national product among any set of groups in the society, economists speak of THE DISTRIBUTION OF INCOME.[1]

(4) How efficient is the society's production and distribution? These questions quite naturally arise out of questions 1, 2 and 3. Having asked what quantities of goods are produced, how they are produced and to whom they are distributed, it is natural to go on to ask whether the production and distribution decisions are efficient.

The concept of efficiency is quite distinct from the concept of justice. The latter is a normative concept, and a just distribution of the national product would be one that our value judgements told us was a good or a desirable distribution. Efficiency and inefficiency are positive concepts. Production is said to be inefficient if it would be possible to produce more of at least one commodity – without simultaneously producing less of any other – by merely reallocating resources. The commodities that are produced are said to be inefficiently distributed if it would be possible to redistribute them among the individuals in the society and make at least one person better off without simultaneously making anyone worse off. Questions about the efficiency of production and allocation belong to the branch of economic theory called WELFARE ECONOMICS.

---

[1] In the eighteenth century, when the theory of distribution was first developed, the three great social classes were workers, capitalists and landowners, and the problem of distribution was to explain how the national product was split up among these classes. (This was why early economists split up factors of production into three groups, labour, capital and land.) Modern economists do not confine their interest to these three groups, but seek rather to study distribution among numerous different groups in the society.

Questions 1 to 4 are related to the allocation of resources and the distribution of income and are intimately connected, in a market economy, to the way in which the price system works. They are sometimes grouped under the general heading of MICROECONOMICS.

(5) Are the country's resources being fully utilized, or are some of them lying idle? We have already noted that the existing resources of any country are not sufficient to satisfy even the most pressing needs of all the individual consumers. It may seem strange, therefore, that we must ask this question at all. Surely if resources are so scarce that there are not enough of them to produce all of those commodities which are urgently required, there can be no question of leaving idle any of the resources that are available. Yet one of the most disturbing characteristics of free-market economies is that such waste sometimes occurs. When this happens the resources are said to be involuntarily unemployed (or, more simply, unemployed). Unemployed workers would like to have jobs, the factories in which they could work are available, the managers and owners would like to be able to operate their factories, raw materials are available in abundance, and the goods that could be produced by these resources are urgently required by individuals in the community. Yet, for some reason, nothing happens: the workers stay unemployed, the factories lie idle and the raw materials remain unused. The cost of such periods of unemployment is felt both in terms of the goods and services that could have been produced by the idle resources, and in terms of the effects on people who are unable to find work for prolonged periods of time.

Why do market societies experience such periods of involuntary unemployment *which are unwanted by virtually everyone in the society*, and can such unemployment be prevented from occurring in the future? These questions have long concerned economists, and have been studied under the heading TRADE CYCLE THEORY. Their study was given renewed significance by the Great Depression of the 1930s. In the USA and the United Kingdom, for example, this unemployment was never less than one worker in ten, and it rose to a maximum of approximately one worker in four. This meant that, during the worst part of the depression, one quarter of these countries' resources were lying involuntarily idle. A great advance was made in the study of these phenomena with the publication in 1936 of the *General Theory of Employment, Interest and Money*, by J. M. Keynes. This book, and the whole branch of economic theory that grew out of it, has greatly widened the scope of economic theory and greatly added to our knowledge of the problems of unemployed resources. This branch of economics is called MACROECONOMICS.

Since the mid-1970s high unemployment has once again beset Western economies. Unemployment rates, although not nearly as high as in the 1930s, have reached the highest levels since that time. In the UK, for example, the unemployment rate fluctuated between 1·0 and 3·4 per cent of the labour force between 1945 and 1970 and between a low of 3·1 and a high of 13·5 between 1970 and 1983.

(6) Is the purchasing power of money and savings constant, or is it being eroded because of inflation? The world's economies have often experienced periods of prolonged and rapid changes in price levels. Over the long swing of history, price levels have sometimes risen and sometimes fallen. In recent decades, however, the course of prices has almost always been upward. The 1970s saw a period of accelerating inflation in Europe, the United States and in most of the world.

Inflation reduces the purchasing power of money and savings. It is closely related to the amount of money in the economy. Money is the invention of human beings, not of nature, and the amount in existence can be controlled by them. Economists ask many questions about the causes and consequences of changes in the quantity of money and the effects of such changes on the price level. They also ask about other causes of inflation.

(7) Is the economy's capacity to produce goods and services growing from year to year or is it remaining static? The misery and poverty described in the England of a century and a half ago by Charles Dickens is no longer with us as a mass phenomenon; and this is largely due to the fact that the capacity to produce goods and services has grown about 2 per cent per year faster than population since Dickens' time. Why the capacity to produce grows rapidly in some economies, slowly in others, and not at all in yet others is a critical problem which has exercised the minds of some of the best economists since the time of Adam Smith. Although a certain amount is now known in this field, a great deal remains to be discovered. Problems of this type are topics in the THEORY OF ECONOMIC GROWTH.

There are, of course, other questions that arise, but these seven are the major ones common to all types of market economies. Most of the rest of this book is devoted to a detailed study of these questions. We shall study among other things how decisions on these questions are made in free-market societies, the (often unexpected) consequences of settling these questions through the price system, and why and how governments sometimes intervene in an attempt to alter the decisions.

The questions distinguished diagrammatically

Four of the above questions that are most easily confused can be distinguished by introducing a simple diagram. Consider the choice that faces all economies today, between producing armaments and producing goods for civilian use. This is a problem in the allocation of resources: how many resources to devote to producing 'guns for defence' and how many to devote to producing goods for all other purposes. We illustrate this choice in Figure 4.1. On one axis we measure the quantity of military goods produced and on the other axis the quantity of all other goods, which we call *civilian goods*. Next we plot all those combinations of military and civilian goods that can be produced if all resources are fully employed. We join up these points and call the resulting line a PRODUCTION-POSSIBILITY BOUNDARY. Points inside the boundary such as c show the combinations of military and civilian goods that can be obtained given the society's present supplies of resources. Points outside the boundary such as d show combinations that cannot be obtained because there are not enough resources to produce them. Points on the boundary such as a and b are just obtainable; they are the combinations that can just be produced using all the available supplies of resources.

The downward slope of the boundary indicates that there is an opportunity cost of producing more of one type of commodity, cost being measured in terms of the quantity forgone of the other type of commodity. Thus if we move from point a to point b we are reallocating resources out of civilian production and into military production. The amount of military goods produced increases from q to s, while the quantity of civilian production falls from p to r. Thus the opportunity cost of getting $s-q$ more arms produced is $p-r$ civilian goods sacrificed. When we talk about moving between points a and b we are talking of the allocation of resources discussed in question 1.

If the economy could be at point b, then it could also be at point c, producing less of both military and civilian goods than at b, or indeed at any point inside the boundary. The reader can easily check that, when the economy is located at a point inside the boundary, production of both types of

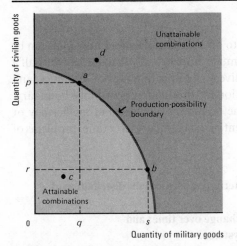

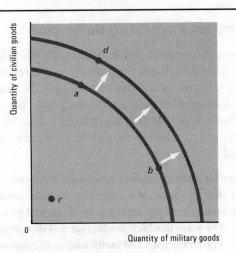

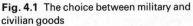

Fig. 4.1 The choice between military and
civilian goods

Fig. 4.2 The outward shifting of the
production-possibility boundary by economic
growth

commodity is less than it would be if some points on the boundary were attained. An economy can
be producing at some point, such as *c*, inside its production-possibility boundary, either because
some of its resources are lying idle (question 5), or because its resources are being used inefficiently in
production (question 4).

Let us now ask: 'How can an economy produce more military goods?' Clearly we must know
whether the present position is on the boundary or inside it. If the economy is on the boundary, then,
assuming for the moment that the boundary cannot be shifted, the answer is: more arms can be
obtained only at the cost of producing less civilian goods (e.g., by moving from point *a* to point *b*).
If, however, the economy is at some point, such as *c*, inside the boundary, then more of both goods
can be produced simultaneously. If the economy is inside the boundary because there is unemployment, then the measures which succeed in reducing unemployment will allow the economy to have
more of both goods. If, on the other hand, the economy is inside the boundary because, although
existing resources are fully employed, they are being used inefficiently, then measures which increase
the efficiency of resource utilization will allow more of both goods to be produced.

Now consider economic growth (question 7). If the economy's capacity to produce goods is
increasing through time, then the production-possibility boundary is pushed outwards over time as
illustrated in Figure 4.2. If the economy then remains on the possibility boundary, more of all goods
can be produced moving the economy, for example, from point *a* to point *d*.

Thus in order to increase the production of *all* goods simultaneously, it is necessary to do one of
two things. If production is at a point inside the production-possibility boundary, then it may be
moved to a point closer to, or actually on, the boundary, from *c* to *b* in Figure 4.1, for example. If the
economy is already on the boundary, then it is necessary to move the boundary outwards so that
production can expand, for example from *a* to *d* in Figure 4.2. It is very important to distinguish
between two sorts of movements: (i) a movement from a point within, to a point on, the boundary,
and (ii) a movement of the actual boundary. A policy that would succeed in increasing total output if
the object were to move from a point within the boundary to a point on the boundary would be a
failure if what was necessary was to increase output by moving the actual boundary.

Economics: a working definition

Our purpose in listing the problem areas of economics is to outline its scope more fully than can be done with short definitions. Economics today is regarded much more broadly than it was even half a century ago. Earlier definitions stressed only the alternative and competing uses of resources, and focused on choices between alternative points on a stationary production-possibility boundary. Other important problems concern failure to achieve the boundary (problems of inefficiency or underemployment of resources) and the outward movement of the boundary over time (problems of growth and development).

> **Broadly defined, modern economics concerns:**
> (1) **The allocation of a society's resources among alternative uses and the distribution of the society's output among individuals and groups;**
> (2) **The ways in which production and distribution change over time; and**
> (3) **The efficiencies and inefficiencies of economic systems.**

5

A general view of the price system

The evolution of market economies

The great seventeenth-century political philosopher Thomas Hobbes described life in a state of nature as 'nasty, brutish and short'. Modern study of the several surviving food-gathering societies suggests that Hobbes' ideas were wide of the mark. In fact societies in the pre-agricultural stage are characterized by a

relative simplicity of the material culture (only 94 items exist among Kung bushmen); the lack of accumulation of individual wealth [and mobility]. . . . Subsistence requirements are satisfied by only a modest effort – perhaps two or three days work a week by each adult; they do not have to struggle over food resources; the attitudes toward ownership are flexible and their living groups open. Such features set hunters and gatherers apart from more technologically developed societies whose very survival depends upon their ability to maintain order and to control property.

Most of the characteristic problems of economics do not arise in these primitive societies. Indeed the economic problem as we know it today has been with us only ten thousand or so years – little more than an instant compared to the tens of millions of years that hominid creatures have been on earth. It began with the original agricultural revolution, dated between 6000 and 8000 BC, when people first found it possible to stay in one place and survive. Gradually abandoning the old nomadic life of food gathering, people settled down to tend crops that they themselves had learned to plant and animals that they had learned to domesticate. All societies since that time have faced an all-pervading problem of choice under conditions of scarcity.

Specialization, surplus and trade

Along with permanent settlement, the agricultural revolution brought surplus production: farmers could produce substantially more than they needed to survive. The agricultural surplus led to the appearance of new occupations such as artisans, soldiers, priests and government officials. Freed from having to grow their own food, these people turned to producing specialized services and goods other than food. They too produced more than they themselves needed, so they traded the excess to obtain whatever else they required.

Economists call this allocation of different jobs to different people SPECIALIZATION OF LABOUR. Specialization has proved extraordinarily efficient compared to universal self-sufficiency, for at least two reasons. First, individual abilities differ, and specialization allows each person to do the thing he or she can do relatively best, while leaving everything else to be done by others. People not only do their own thing; they do their own best thing. Second, a person who concentrates on one activity becomes better at it than could a jack-of-all-trades.

Probably the exchange of goods and services in early societies took place by simple, mutual agreement among neighbours. In the course of time, however, trading became centred in particular gathering places called markets. Today we use the term MARKET ECONOMY to refer to a society in which people specialize in productive activities and meet most of their material wants through exchanges voluntarily agreed upon by the contracting parties.

> **Specialization must be accompanied by trade. People who produce only one thing must trade most of it to obtain all of the other things they require.**

Early free-market economies used BARTER, the trading of goods directly for other goods. But barter is costly in time spent searching out satisfactory exchanges. If a farmer has wheat and wants a hammer, he must find someone who has a hammer and wants wheat. A successful barter transaction thus requires what is called a DOUBLE COINCIDENCE OF WANTS. Money eliminates the cumbrousness of barter by separating transactions. If a farmer has wheat and wants a hammer, he does not have to find someone who has a hammer and wants wheat. He merely has to find someone who wants wheat. The farmer takes money in exchange, then finds another person who wishes to trade a hammer, and gives up the money for the hammer.

> **By eliminating the cumbrousness of barter, money greatly facilitates trade and specialization.**

Factor services and the division of labour

Market transactions in early economies involved mostly goods and services for consumption. Producers specialized in making some commodity and then traded it for the other products they needed. The labour services required to make the product would usually be provided by the makers themselves, by apprentices who were learning to become craftsmen, or by slaves. Over the last several hundred years many technical advances in methods of production have made it efficient to organize agriculture and industry on a very large scale. These technical developments have made use of what is called the DIVISION OF LABOUR. This term refers to specialization within the production process of a particular commodity. The labour involved is divided into repetitive tasks, and each individual does one task that may be a minute fraction of those necessary to produce the commodity. Indeed, it is possible today for an individual to spend years doing a production-line job without knowing what commodity emerges at the end of the line!

To gain the advantages of the division of labour it became necessary to organize production in large and expensive factories. With this development workers lost their status as craftsmen (or peasants) and became members of the proletariat, wholly dependent on their ability to sell their labour to factory (or farm) owners and without any plot of land to fall back on for subsistence in times of need.

> **The day of small craftsmen who made and sold commodities themselves is over. Today's typical workers do not earn their incomes by selling commodities they themselves have**

produced; rather they sell their labour services to firms and receive money wages in return.

The allocation of resources

The term ALLOCATION OF RESOURCES refers to the way in which the available factors of production are allocated among the various uses to which they might be put. This allocation of resources helps to determine how much of the various goods and services will actually be produced. In a market economy, millions of consumers decide what commodities to buy and in what quantities; a vast number of firms produce those commodities and buy the factor services that are needed to make them; and millions of factor owners decide to whom they will sell these services. These individual decisions collectively determine the economy's allocation of resources.

> In a market economy, the allocation of resources is the outcome of millions of independent decisions made by consumers and producers, all acting through the medium of markets.

How market economies work

Early economists observed the market economy with wonder. They saw that although most commodities were made by a large number of independent producers, they were made in approximately the quantities that people wanted to purchase. Natural disasters aside, there were neither vast surpluses nor severe shortages. These economists also saw that most labourers were able to sell their services to employers most of the time, in spite of the fact that the kinds of products made, the techniques used to make them, and the places in which they were made changed over time.

How does the market produce this order without conscious direction by some central co-ordinating body? It is one thing to have the same commodities produced year in and year out when people's wants and incomes do not change; it is quite another to have production adjusting continually to changing wants, incomes and techniques of production. Yet this *relatively* smooth adjustment is accomplished by the market – albeit with occasional, and sometimes serious, interruptions. It happens because individuals take their private decisions in response to publicly known signals such as prices, while these signals respond to the collective actions entailed by the sum of all individual decisions. Because of the importance of prices in market economies, we say that they employ a PRICE SYSTEM. This term refers to the role that prices play in determining the allocation of resources and the distribution of national product.

> The great discovery of the eighteenth-century economists was that the price system is a social-control mechanism.

In 1776 Adam Smith published his classic *The Wealth of Nations*, the culmination of the early attempts to understand the workings of market economies. Smith spoke of the price system as 'the invisible hand' because it co-ordinated decision-taking that was decentralized among millions of individual producers and consumers.

We may now study two illustrations designed to give some intuitive understanding of how the price system works in market economies.

A change in demand

First consider how the market reacts to a change in the tastes of individual consumers. Let us say, for example, that consumers experience a greatly increased desire for Brussels sprouts and a diminished desire for carrots. It might, for example, be the result of some new discovery about the nutritive powers of the vegetables. The cause, however, is unimportant; all that matters is that consumers desire more sprouts and fewer carrots.

What will be the effects of this change? First, consumers will buy more Brussels sprouts and fewer carrots. With production unchanged, a shortage of Brussels sprouts and a glut of carrots will develop. In order to unload their surplus stocks of carrots, merchants will reduce carrot prices on the principle that it is better to sell them at a reduced price than not to sell them at all. On the other hand, merchants will find that they cannot keep Brussels sprouts on their shelves. Sprouts will become a scarce commodity and the merchants will raise their price. As the price rises, fewer sprouts will be bought. Thus the consumers' demand will be limited to the available supply by the means of making the commodity more expensive.

Farmers will now observe that the price of sprouts is rising while the price of carrots is falling. Brussels sprout production will be more profitable than in the past, for the costs of producing them will be unchanged, while their market price will have risen. Carrot production will be less profitable than it was because costs will be unchanged but prices will have fallen. Thus the change in consumers' tastes, working through the price system, causes the allocation of resources to change in such a way that less resources are devoted to carrot production and more to sprout production. Economists use the term REALLOCATION OF RESOURCES to refer to a change in the use of the economy's resources.

As the production of carrots declines, the glut on the market will diminish, and carrot prices will begin to rise. On the other hand, the expansion in Brussels sprout production will reduce the shortage and the price will fall. These price movements will continue until it no longer pays farmers to reduce carrot production and to increase the production of sprouts.

Let us review this last point. When the price of carrots was very low and the price of sprouts very high, carrot production was unprofitable and sprout production was very profitable. Therefore more sprouts and fewer carrots were produced. These changes in production caused sprout prices to fall, and carrot prices to rise. Once the prices of these goods became such that it no longer paid farmers to transfer out of carrots into sprouts, production settled down and price movement ceased.

We can now see how the reallocation of resources takes place. Carrot producers will be reducing their production, and they will therefore be laying off workers and generally demanding fewer factors of production. On the other hand, Brussels sprout producers will be expanding production by hiring workers and generally increasing their demands for factors of production. Labour can probably switch from carrot to sprout production without much difficulty. If, however, there are certain resources, in this case say certain areas of land, which are much better suited for sprout-growing than for carrot-growing, and other resources, say other areas of land, which are much better suited for carrot-growing than sprout-growing, then their prices will be affected. Since farmers are trying to increase sprout production, they will be increasing their demand for factors which are especially suited for this activity. This will create a shortage and cause the prices of these factors to rise. On the other hand, carrot production will be falling, and hence the demand for resources especially suited for carrot-growing will be reduced. There will thus be a surplus of these resources and their prices will be forced down.

The changes in factor prices in turn influence the distribution of income. Factors particularly suited to sprout production will be earning more than previously, and they will obtain a higher share of total national income than before. Factors particularly suited for carrot production, on the other hand, will be earning less than before and so will obtain a smaller share of the total national product than before.

These changes may now be summarized.

(1) A change in consumers' tastes causes a change in purchases, which causes a shortage or a surplus to appear. This in turn causes market prices to rise in the case of a shortage and to fall in the case of a surplus.

(2) The variations in market price affect the profitability of producing goods, profitability varying directly with price. Producers will shift their production out of less profitable lines and into more profitable ones.

(3) The attempt to change the pattern of production will cause variations in the demand for factors of production. Factors especially suited for the production of commodities for which the demand is increasing will be heavily demanded and their prices will rise. Changes in factor prices cause changes in the incomes earned by factors, and this changes the distribution of the national product.

Thus the change of consumers' tastes sets off a series of market changes which causes a reallocation of resources in the required direction and in the process causes changes in the distribution of total national income among the various factors of production. We shall study changes of this kind more fully later. For now the important thing to notice is how a change initiated in consumers' tastes causes a reallocation of resources in the direction required to cater to the new set of tastes.

A change in supply

For a second example, consider a change originating with producers. Begin as before, by imagining a situation in which farmers find it equally profitable to produce sprouts and carrots, and consumers are willing to buy, at prevailing market prices, the quantities of these two commodities that are being produced. Now imagine that, with no change in prices, farmers become more willing to produce sprouts than in the past and less willing to produce carrots. This shift might, for example, be caused by a rise in carrot costs and a fall in sprout costs which raises the profitability of sprout production relative to that of carrot production.

What will happen now? For a short time, nothing at all; the existing supplies of sprouts and carrots are the results of decisions taken by farmers some time in the past. But farmers will now plant fewer carrots and more sprouts, and soon the quantities coming on to the market will change. The amounts available for sale will rise in the case of sprouts and fall in the case of carrots. A shortage of carrots and a glut of sprouts will result. The price of carrots will rise and the price of sprouts will fall. As carrots become more expensive and sprouts become cheaper, fewer carrots and more sprouts will be bought by consumers. On the other hand, the rise in carrot prices and the fall in sprout prices will act as an incentive for farmers to move back into carrot production and out of sprout production. We started from a position in which there was a shortage of carrots which caused carrot prices to rise. The rise in carrot prices removed the shortage in two ways: first by reducing the demand for the increasingly expensive carrots, and second by increasing the output of carrots which became increasingly profitable. We also started from a position in which there was a surplus of Brussels sprouts, which caused their price to fall. The fall in price removed the surplus in two ways: first by encouraging the consumers to buy more of this commodity as it became less and less expensive, and second by discouraging the production of this commodity, as it became less and less profitable.

Who controls the free market?

These examples illustrate several features of the price system. First, the market responds to the collective decisions of either consumers or producers, even though the decision of any one of them would go unnoticed. There are millions of purchasers of carrots and Brussels sprouts, and a change in the tastes of a single purchaser will have a negligible effect on market prices and resource allocation. But if many consumers change their tastes, the effect will be significant. The situation is similar for producers. There are thousands of farmers, and the effect on market prices and resource allocation of the change in the behaviour of a single one of them is negligible. But if many farmers alter their behaviour, the effect on prices will be significant and there will be changes in the allocation of resources.

The second point to notice is that systematic adaptations to changes in demand and supply take place without being consciously co-ordinated by anyone. When shortages develop, prices rise and profit-seeking farmers are led to produce more of the good in short supply. When surpluses occur, prices fall and production is voluntarily contracted. The price system provides a series of automatic signals so that a large number of independent decision-taking units do react in a co-ordinated way.

We have seen that although no single individual may be able to exert any significant control over a free market, the decisions of two groups, producers and consumers, do determine what is produced and sold. Thus the decisions of both groups influence the allocation of resources. A change in either consumers' demand or producers' supply will affect the allocation of resources and thus also the pattern of production and consumption.

> **It is often remarked that in a free-market society the consumer is king. Such a maxim reveals only half the truth. Prices are determined by supply as well as demand. A free-market society gives sovereignty to two groups, producers and consumers, and the decisions of both groups affect the allocation of resources.**

Under certain conditions, known as PERFECT COMPETITION, the producer loses his sovereignty and becomes a mere automaton responding to the will of consumers. These very special conditions are described in Chapter 19. Aside from this special case, however, the producer has at his command, and actually does exercise, considerable power in the allocation of the economy's resources.

There is a great deal of empirical evidence showing that, for many agricultural commodities and industrial raw materials, the price system works very much as described above. In any retail or wholesale produce market, prices can be observed to react to the state of demand and supply, rising when there is a shortage and falling when there is a surplus. Even the most casual observation of agriculture will show farmers varying their production of different crops as market prices vary. Is it valid, however, to extend this view of the price system to cover all commodities including agricultural goods, manufactured goods and services? This is a much more difficult question and it must be postponed until after the theory of price has been developed more fully.

Part two

The elementary theory of price

6

Basic concepts of price theory[1]

In Part 2 we are going to construct a formal theory of the price system whose behaviour was intuitively sketched in Chapter 5. We begin in this chapter by outlining some basic theoretical concepts. In Chapter 7 we develop the theory of demand, which concerns the behaviour of consumers, and the theory of supply, which concerns the behaviour of producers. After that we combine these two theories to develop in Chapter 8 a theory of how individual markets work. This is called the THEORY OF PRICE or, sometimes, the THEORY OF MARKET BEHAVIOUR. Finally, in Chapter 10, we are able to use this theory to predict the behaviour of actual markets under a variety of interesting circumstances.

The decision-takers

We first introduce some of the concepts and assumptions that form the basis of a theory of market behaviour. Many of these have already been used in Chapter 5. There we could be satisfied with rather rough and ready notions. To build a formal theory, however, we now need more precise concepts.

Economics is about the behaviour of people. Much that we observe in the world, and that we assume in our theories, can be traced back to decisions taken by individuals. There are millions of individuals in most economies. To make our systematic study of their behaviour more manageable, we consolidate them into three important groups: households, firms and central authorities. These are the *dramatis personae* of economic theory, and the stage on which their play is enacted is the market.

Households

We have used the term consumer to mean anyone who consumes commodities to satisfy his or her wants. To develop a theory that can be applied empirically we replace the concept of the consumer with that of the household. A HOUSEHOLD is defined as all the people who live under one roof and

[1] No one should begin Part Two without having already studied Chapters 4 and 5, which contain material that is basic to everything that follows. UK material giving factual background to many of the concepts used in this chapter can be found in C. Harbury and R.G. Lipsey, *An Introduction to the UK Economy: A Companion to Positive Economics* (Pitman, 1983), Chapter 1.

who take, or are subject to others taking for them, joint financial decisions. In our theory we give households a number of attributes.

First, we assume that each household takes consistent decisions as if it were composed of a single individual. Thus we ignore many interesting problems of how the household reaches its decisions. It may be by paternal dictatorship or democratic voting – that does not matter to us. Intra-family conflicts and the moral and legal problems concerning parental control over minors are dealt with by other social sciences.[1] These problems are avoided in economics by the assumption that the household is the basic decision-taking atom of consumption behaviour.

Second, we assume that each household seeks to maximize *satisfaction* or *well-being* or *utility*, as it is variously called. This it tries to do within the limitations of the resources available to it. The concept of satisfaction or utility maximization can be tricky, and it is considered in some detail in Part 3.

Third, we assume that households are the principal owners of factors of production. They sell the services of these factors to producers and receive their incomes in return. It is obvious that labour is 'owned' by those individuals who sell their labour and receive wages and salaries in return. Most capital equipment is owned by firms; but firms are in turn owned by households. Joint stock companies, for example, are owned by the households that hold those companies' stocks. These households provide the firms with the money needed to purchase capital goods and they receive the firm's profits as their income. Land is owned by households and firms – which are in turn owned by households. A household may use its land itself or it may make it available to some other user in return for rent which becomes the household's income.[2] In making all these decisions on how much to sell and to whom to sell it, we again assume that households seek to maximize their utility.

Firms

In Chapter 5 we used the term producer to mean someone who makes commodities. The terms *producer* and *firm* are used interchangeably and we define the FIRM to be the unit that employs factors of production to produce commodities that it sells to other firms, to households or to the central authorities (defined below). Firms have a number of attributes.

First, we assume that each firm takes consistent decisions as if it were composed of a single individual. Thus we ignore the internal problems of who reaches particular decisions and how they are reached. In doing this, we assume that the firm's internal organization is irrelevant to its decisions. This allows us to treat the firm as our atom of behaviour on the production or supply side of commodity markets, just as the household is treated as the atom of behaviour on the consumption or demand side.

Second, we assume that the firm takes its decisions with respect to a single goal: to make as much *profit* as it possibly can. This goal of profit maximization is analogous to the household's goal of

---

[1] In academic work, as well as elsewhere, a division of labour is useful. It is important to remember, however, that when economists speak of *the* consumer or *the* individual they are in fact referring to the group of individuals composing the household. Thus, for example, the commonly-heard phrase *consumer sovereignty* really means *household sovereignty*. These two concepts are, however, quite distinct: it is one thing to say that individuals should be free to decide their own fate, and quite another thing to say that the head of the household should be free to decide the fate of its members.

[2] The only organization which owns capital and land without itself being a household, or being owned by a household, is the government. Thus all factors of production are owned either by households or by the government.

utility maximization. There is a difference, however: although household satisfaction cannot be directly measured, a firm's profits can be. The assumption of profit maximization has, as we shall see later, come under serious criticism, and there are several competing theories of the motivation of firms. We shall consider some of these in Chapter 24, but for now, we can go quite a long way using the simple assumption of profit maximization.

Third, we assume that firms are the principal users of the services of factors of production. In markets where factor services are bought and sold, the roles of firms and households are thus reversed from what they are in commodity markets: in factor markets firms do the buying and households do the selling.

Central authorities

The comprehensive term CENTRAL AUTHORITIES includes all public agencies, government bodies and other organizations belonging to or owing their existence to the government. It includes such institutions as the central bank, the civil service, commissions and regulatory agencies, the cabinet, the police force, the judiciary and all other authorities that can exercise control over the behaviour of firms and households. It is not important to draw up a comprehensive list of all central authorities; just keep in mind the general idea of a group of organizations that exist at the centre of legal and political power and exert some control over the rest of us. Economists often use the simpler, though less accurate, term *government* to refer to the central authorities.

It is *not* a basic assumption of economics that the central authorities always act in a consistent fashion as if they were a single individual. Indeed, conflict among different central-authority agencies is often an important component in theories that analyse government intervention in the economy.

> **The decision-taking units in economic theory are households for demand, firms for supply, and central authorities for government regulation and control. Given the resources at their command, each household is assumed to act consistently to maximize its satisfaction, and each firm is assumed to act consistently to maximize its profit.**

The concept of markets

Markets are basic concepts in economics and we must consider them in some detail.

An individual market

Originally the word *market* designated a place where items were bought and sold. Once developed, however, theories of market behaviour were easily extended to cover commodities such as wheat, which can be purchased anywhere in the world and the price of which tends to be uniform the world over. Clearly when we talk about 'the wheat market', we have extended our concept of a market well beyond the idea of a single place to which the householder goes to buy something. For our present purposes, we define a MARKET as an area over which buyers and sellers negotiate the exchange of a well-defined commodity. For a single market to exist, it must be possible for buyers and sellers to communicate with each other and to make meaningful deals over the whole market.

The separation of individual markets

Markets are separated from each other by the commodity sold, by natural economic barriers, and by barriers created by the central authorities. To illustrate, consider one example of each type of separation. First, the market for men's shirts is different from the market for refrigerators because they are different commodities. Second, the market for cement in Britain is distinct from the market for cement in the eastern United States, since transport costs are so high that British purchasers would not buy US cement even if its US price were very much lower than the British price of cement. Third, the market for textiles is separated among many countries since textiles are often the subject of heavy tariffs and restrictive quotas that make it difficult or impossible for firms in one country to sell to households in another.

The interlinking of individual markets

Although all markets are to some extent separated, most are also interrelated. Consider again the three causes of market separation: different commodities, spatial separation and government intervention. First, the markets for different kinds of commodities are interrelated because all commodities compete for consumers' income. Thus if more is spent in one market, less will be available to spend in other markets. Second, the geographical separation of markets for similar commodities depends on transport costs. Commodities with high transport costs per ton relative to their production cost per ton tend to be produced and sold in geographically distinct markets, while commodities with low transport costs are sold in what amounts to a single world market. But whatever the transport costs, there will be some price differential at which it will pay someone to buy in the low-priced market and ship to the high-priced one. Thus, there is some potential link between geographically distinct markets, even when shipping costs are high. Third, markets are often separated by policy-induced barriers, such as tariffs. Although high tariffs tend to separate markets, they do leave some link because, if price differences become large enough, it will pay buyers in the high-priced market to switch to the low-priced one and sellers in the low-priced one to switch to the high-priced one, even though they have to pay the tariff as well as the market price.

> **Individual markets are separated from each other either because different commodities are sold in each, or because barriers to the movement of commodities among markets such as transport costs (a natural barrier) and tariffs (a policy-induced barrier) exist. In spite of a substantial degree of separation, most individual markets are more or less interlinked.**

Differences among markets

Competitiveness   Individual markets may differ from each other according to the degree of competition among the various buyers and sellers in each market. Throughout Part 2 we shall confine ourselves to markets in which the number of buyers and sellers is large enough so that no one of them has any appreciable influence on price. This is a very rough definition of what economists call COMPETITIVE MARKETS. In Part 4 we shall consider the behaviour of markets that do not meet this competitive requirement.

Goods and factor markets We distinguish two different types of markets. GOODS MARKETS are those where goods and services are traded.[1] The sellers in such markets are usually firms; the buyers may be households, other firms or the central authorities. FACTOR MARKETS are those where factor services are bought and sold. The sellers in such markets are the owners of factors of production (usually households); the buyers are usually firms and the central authorities.

Free and controlled markets A FREE MARKET is one over which the central authorities exert no direct control. Buyers and sellers are free to arrive at any agreements on quantities to be traded and on prices at which trade will occur. A CONTROLLED MARKET is one over which the central authorities exert some substantial, direct control. This can be done in many ways: by licensing buyers and sellers in the market; by setting legal minimum or maximum (or both) prices at which trade can take place; or by setting a quota of minimum or maximum amounts that individual buyers and sellers may trade in the market.

The national product

In Chapter 4 we noted that a country's total output of goods and services is called its national product. Some, but not all, of the national product passes through markets and some, but not all, is produced by private firms. It is useful at this point to subdivide a country's productive activity in a number of ways.

Market and non-market sectors

There are two basic ways in which commodities may pass from those who make them to those who use them. First, commodities may be sold by producers and bought by consumers in markets. When this happens the producers must cover their costs by the revenues they obtain from the sale of the product. We call this production *marketed production* and we refer to this part of the country's activity as belonging to the MARKET SECTOR. Second, the product may be given away. In this case the costs of production must be covered by some means other than sales revenues. We call this production *non-marketed production*, and we refer to this part of the country's activity as belonging to the NON-MARKET SECTOR. In the case of private charities, the money required to pay for factor services may be raised from the public by voluntary subscriptions. In the case of production by the state – which accounts for the great bulk of non-marketed production – the money is provided from government revenue, which in turn comes mainly from taxes levied on firms and households.

Whenever a state enterprise *sells* its output, this is in the market sector. Much state output is, however, in the non-market sector. Some is there by the very nature of the product. One could not imagine, for example, the criminal paying the judge for providing him with the service of criminal justice. Some products are in the non-market sector because the state has decided to remove them from the market sector. In some countries, for example, firms producing medical and hospital

---

[1] Since these markets include both goods and services, it might seem better to refer to them as *commodity markets*. Unfortunately, this term is in common use in the business world to refer to markets where basic commodities, such as rubber, tin and jute, are sold. To avoid confusion, economists speak of *goods markets* where, in their own terminology, commodity markets would be better.

services are in the market sector and their products are sold to consumers for a price that must cover their costs. In other countries, such as Britain, however, the production of these services is in the non-market sector; they are provided at little or no cost to users, and costs are covered by the state.

Production falls clearly into one sector or the other when either all, or none, of its costs are covered by selling the products to users. In some cases, however, production falls partly into one sector and partly into the other. If 10 per cent of costs are covered by small charges made to users and 90 per cent by the government, then the production is 10 per cent in the market sector and 90 per cent in the non-market sector. If private firms get a subsidy from the government to cover 10 per cent of their costs, but meet the rest out of sales revenue, then their production is 10 per cent in the non-market sector and 90 per cent in the market sector.

All of the country's national product is produced in either the market or the non-market sector of the economy.

The public and private sectors

The productive activity of a country is often subdivided in a different way to obtain the private and the public sectors. The PRIVATE SECTOR refers to all production that is in private hands; the PUBLIC SECTOR refers to all production that is in public hands. The distinction between the two sectors depends on the legal distinction of ownership. In the private sector, the organization that does the producing is owned by households or other firms; in the public sector, it is owned by the state. The public sector includes all production of goods and services by central authorities plus all production by nationalized industries that is sold to consumers through ordinary markets.

> **The distinction between the marketed and non-marketed sectors is an economic one: it depends on whether or not the costs of producing commodities are recovered by selling them to their users. The distinction between the private and the public sectors is a legal one: it depends on whether the firms are owned privately or publicly.**

The concept of an economy

An ECONOMY is a rather loosely defined term for any specified collection of interrelated marketed and non-marketed productive activity. It may refer to productive activity in a region of one country, such as *the economy of Eastern Canada*; it may refer to one country, such as *the UK economy*, or it may refer to a group of countries, such as *the economy of Western Europe*.

The economies of all countries contain market and non-market sectors. A FREE-MARKET ECONOMY is one in which most production is in the market sector, and these markets are relatively free from control by the central authorities. In such an economy the allocation of resources is determined by production, sales and purchase decisions taken mainly by firms and households. How these decisions influence the allocation of resources was discussed in Chapter 5.

At the opposite extreme from a free-market economy is a CENTRALLY-CONTROLLED ECONOMY or, as it is sometimes called, a COMMAND ECONOMY. Here all the decisions about the allocation of resources are taken by the central authorities, so that firms and households produce and consume only as they are ordered. In such an economy most production will be in the non-market sector.

Neither the completely free-market economy nor the completely controlled economy has ever existed in recent history. In practice, all economies are MIXED ECONOMIES in the sense that some decisions are taken by firms and households, and some by the central authorities. The emphasis varies, however. In some economies, the influence of the central authorities is substantially less than in others. Not only may the average amount of central control vary among economies, it may also vary among markets within one economy. Thus, in Britain, the day-to-day behaviour of the stock market is relatively free from central control, while the market for rented housing is heavily controlled by the central authorities.

The theory that we will develop applies specifically to the behaviour of free markets, but it can also deal with many types of central control commonly found in Western economies. We shall use the phrase 'free-market economy' to indicate economies in which the decisions of individual households and firms exert a substantial influence over the allocation of resources. The dividing line is an arbitrary one. We must always remember that every possible mixture of centralized and decentralized control exists, and that the economies of Poland and the Soviet Union differ from those of France and the UK only in the *degree* to which the central authorities exert an influence over the markets of each economy.

Free-market economies are sometimes called capitalist economies. Capitalist means that the factor of production, capital, is owned by private individuals rather than by the state. The legal distinction of ownership is, however, less important than the economic distinction of control, so we shall not usually use the term capitalist.

An economy refers to an interrelated set of marketed and non-marketed productive activities. The behaviour of free-market economies is primarily determined by individual firms and households; the behaviour of command economies is primarily determined by the central authorities.

7

The elementary theory of demand and supply

The elementary theory of demand

We saw in Chapter 5 that households' purchases of carrots and Brussels sprouts influenced the markets for these commodities. As the next step in building our theory of market behaviour, we outline a simple theory of the determinants of such purchases. It is called the theory of demand. In this part we develop only the minimum that we need. In Part 3 we study demand in more detail.

The nature of demand

The amount of a commodity that households wish to purchase is called the QUANTITY DEMANDED of that commodity. Notice two important things about quantity demanded. First, it is a *desired* quantity. It is how much households *wish* to purchase, not necessarily how much they actually succeed in purchasing. For example, if a sufficient quantity is not available, the amount households wish to purchase may exceed the amount that they do purchase. We use phrases such as QUANTITY ACTUALLY PURCHASED or QUANTITY ACTUALLY BOUGHT AND SOLD to distinguish actual purchases from quantity demanded. Second, note that quantity demanded is a *flow*. (See page 29.) We are concerned not with a single isolated purchase, but with a continuous flow of purchases, and we must therefore express demand as so much per period of time – one million oranges *per day*, say, or seven million oranges *per week*, or 365 million *per year*.

The concept of demand as a flow appears to raise difficulties when we deal with the purchases of durable consumer goods that are bought only occasionally. It makes obvious sense to talk about consuming oranges at the rate of thirty per month, but what can we say of someone who buys a new television set every five years or a new car every two? This apparent difficulty disappears if we measure the demand for the *services* of the consumer durable. Thus, at the rate of a new set every five years, the television purchaser is using the services of television sets at the rate of $\frac{1}{60}$ of a set per month. If a fall in the price of television sets makes him discard his old set every four years instead of every five, we say that his consumption of the services of television sets has gone up from $\frac{1}{60}$ to $\frac{1}{48}$ of a set per month.

The determinants of quantity demanded: the demand function

We now introduce five hypotheses about what determines the quantity of a commodity demanded by an individual household.

(1) Quantity demanded is influenced by the price of the commodity.
(2) Quantity demanded is influenced by the prices of other commodities.
(3) Quantity demanded is influenced by the size of the household's income and wealth.
(4) Quantity demanded is influenced by various 'sociological' factors.
(5) Quantity demanded is influenced by the household's tastes.

This list of factors influencing the household's demand may conveniently be summarized using the notation developed in Chapter 2. What we have said is that the amount of a commodity a household is prepared to purchase is a function of (i.e., depends upon) the price of the good in question, the prices of all other goods, the household's income and its tastes. This statement may be expressed in symbols by writing down what is called a DEMAND FUNCTION:

$$q_n^d = D(p_n, p_1, \ldots, p_{n-1}, Y, \varepsilon),$$

where q_n^d is the quantity that the household demands of some commodity, labelled 'commodity n', where p_n is the price of this commodity, where $p_1, \ldots, p_{n-1}$ is a shorthand notation for the prices of all other commodities, where Y is the household's income, ε stands for a host of sociological factors and the form of the function, D, is determined by the tastes of the members of the household.[1]

This is quite a complicated functional relationship, and we shall not succeed in developing a simple theory if we consider what happens to the quantity demanded when these things – prices, income and tastes – all change at once. To avoid doing this, we use a device that is very frequently employed in economic theory. We assume that all except one of the terms in the right-hand side of the above expression are held constant; we then allow this one factor, say p_n, to vary, and consider how the quantity demanded (q_n^d) varies with it, *assuming that all other things remain unchanged*, or, as the economist is fond of putting it, *ceteris paribus*. We then allow some other term, say income (Y), to vary, and consider how, *ceteris paribus*, quantity demanded varies as income varies. We can now consider the relation between quantity demanded and each of the variables on the right-hand side of the demand function, taking them one at a time.[2]

The price of the commodity   In the case of almost all commodities, the quantity demanded increases as the price of the commodity falls, income, tastes and all other prices remaining constant. As its price falls, a commodity becomes cheaper relative to its substitutes, and it is therefore easier for it to compete against these substitutes for the household's attention. If, for example, carrots become very cheap, the household will be induced, up to a point, to buy more carrots and less of other vegetables whose prices are now high relative to the price of carrots.

To illustrate the relation between the quantity of a commodity demanded and its price, we shall take imaginary data for the prices and quantities of carrots. Table 7.1 is an example of what is called a DEMAND SCHEDULE. It shows the quantity of carrots that a household would demand at six selected prices. For example, at a price of £40 per ton, the quantity demanded is 10·25 lbs per month. Each of the price-quantity combinations in the table is given a letter for easy reference.

We can now plot the data from Table 7.1 on a graph, with price on the vertical axis and quantity

---

[1] This functional notation is merely a shorthand notation; it is not of itself mathematics. If you still find this troublesome you should read pages 17–19 and 27–8 of Chapter 2 and its Appendix now.

[2] This technique is discussed further on page 34, section 13.

on the horizontal one.[1] In figure 7.1 we have plotted the six points corresponding to the price-quantity combinations shown in Table 7.1. Point *n* on the graph shows the same information as the first row of the table: at £20 a ton, 14 lbs of carrots will be demanded by the household each month. Point *t* shows the same information as the last row of the table: when the price is £120 a ton, the quantity demanded will be only 2·5 lbs per month.

We now draw a smooth curve through these points. This curve is called the DEMAND CURVE for carrots. It shows the quantity of carrots that the household would like to buy at every possible price; its downward slope indicates that the quantity demanded increases as the price falls.

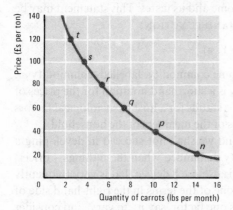

Fig. 7.1 A household's demand curve for carrots

Table 7.1 A household's demand schedule of carrots

	Price (£s per ton)	Quantity demanded (lbs per month)
n	20	14·0
p	40	10·25
q	60	7·5
r	80	5·25
s	100	3·5
t	120	2·5

A single point on the demand curve indicates a single price-quantity relation. *The whole demand curve shows the complete functional relation between quantity demanded and price.* Economists often speak of the conditions of demand in a particular market as given or as known. When they do so they are not referring just to the particular quantity that is being demanded at the moment (i.e., not just to a particular point on the demand curve). They are referring rather to the whole demand curve, to the complete functional relation whereby desired purchases are related to all possible alternative prices of the commodity.

> **The demand curve for a commodity shows the relation between its price and the quantity a household wishes to purchase per period of time. It is drawn on the assumption that income, tastes and all other prices remain constant, and its downward slope indicates that the lower the price of the commodity, the more the household will desire to purchase.**

[1] Readers trained in other disciplines often wonder why economists plot demand curves with price on the vertical axis. The normal convention is to put the independent variable (the variable that does the explaining) on the *X* axis and the dependent variable (the variable that is explained) on the *Y* axis. This would lead us to plot price on the horizontal axis and quantity on the vertical axis. The axis reversal – now enshrined by nearly a century of usage – arose as follows. The analysis of the competitive market that we use today stems from Leon Walras, in whose theory quantity was the dependent variable. Graphical analysis in economics, however, was popularized by Alfred Marshall, in whose theory price was the dependent variable. Economists continue to use Walras' theory and Marshall's graphical representation and thus draw the diagram with the independent and dependent variables reversed – to the everlasting confusion of readers trained in other disciplines. In virtually every other graph in economics the axes are labelled conventionally, with the dependent variable on the vertical axis. (See, for example, Figure 7.3.)

The prices of other commodities   There are three possible relations between the demand for one commodity and the prices of other commodities: a fall in the price of one commodity may lower the quantity demanded of another, it may raise it, or it may leave it unchanged.

If a fall in the price of Y causes a fall in the quantity demanded of X, the two commodities, X and Y, are said to be SUBSTITUTES. When the price of one commodity falls, the household buys more of it and less of commodities that are substitutes for it: thus the quantity demanded of a commodity varies directly with the price of its substitutes. This relation is illustrated for our imaginary carrot example in Figure 7.2(i). The curve slopes upwards, indicating that as the price of a substitute rises, the quantity demanded of carrots rises, while when the price of a substitute falls, the quantity demanded of carrots falls. Examples of commodities which are substitutes are butter and margarine, carrots and cabbage, cinema tickets and theatre tickets, bus rides and taxi rides.

If a fall in the price of one commodity raises the quantity demanded of another commodity, the two are said to be COMPLEMENTS. When the price of one commodity falls, more of it is consumed and more of those commodities that are complementary to it are consumed also. This relation will occur between commodities that tend to be consumed together: motorcars and petrol, cups and saucers, bread and butter, trips to Austria and skis. This is illustrated for our carrot example in Figure 7.2(ii). The curve slopes downwards, indicating that when the price of a complement falls there is a rise in the quantity of carrots demanded.[1]

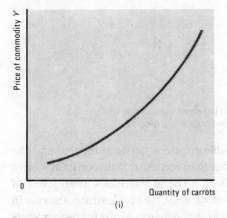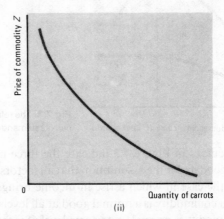

Fig. 7.2 (i) The relations between the quantity of carrots demanded and the price of a substitute (Y)
  (ii) The relation between the quantity of carrots demanded and the price of a complement (Z)

If two commodities are unrelated, then a change in the price of one will have no effect one way or the other on the quantity demanded of the other.

The size of the household's income   Ordinarily we would expect a rise in income to be associated with a rise in the quantity of a good demanded. Commodities that obey this rule are called NORMAL GOODS.

---

[1] Readers familiar with more advanced texts will realize that the definitions used here are those of *gross substitutes* and *gross complements*, rather than those of net substitutes and net complements which are more commonly used in advanced theoretical work.

Two possible exceptions need to be noted. In some cases, a change in income might leave the quantity demanded completely unaffected. This will be the case with goods for which the desire is completely satisfied after a level of income is obtained. Beyond this level, variations in income will have no effect on the quantity demanded. This is possibly the case with many of the more inexpensive foodstuffs. It is unlikely, for example, that the demand for salt would be affected by either an increase in a household's income from £8,000 to £8,100 per annum, or by a decrease in its income from £8,000 to £7,900 (although salt purchases might be influenced by income changes if income were as low as, say, £500 per annum). In the case of other commodities, it is possible for a rise in income beyond a certain level to lead to a fall in the quantity that the household demands. Such a relation is likely to occur when one commodity is a cheap but inferior substitute for some other commodity. In many countries beer, potatoes, margarine and black bread provide examples. If the demand for a commodity falls as income rises, it is called an INFERIOR GOOD.

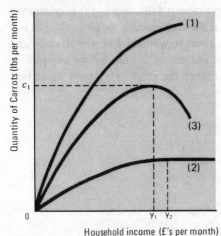

Fig 7.3 The relation between the quantity of carrots demanded and household income

The three curves in Figure 7.3 indicate the three possible relations between income and the demand for a good under the assumption that all factors other than income remain constant. Curve (1) illustrates the case in which a rise in income brings about a rise in purchases at all levels of income. Such a commodity is a normal good at all levels of income. Curve (2) illustrates the case in which the commodity is normal up to some level of income (y_2 in the figure), while for higher levels of income quantity demanded does not respond to changes in income. Curve (3) illustrates the case in which the commodity is a normal good up to some level of income but then becomes an inferior good at higher levels. In this case quantity demanded rises with income up to y_1 and then falls as income rises beyond y_1. Every actual commodity has its own characteristic curve: many will have a curve similar to (1), with quantity demanded continuing to rise indefinitely with income; some will have curves similar to (2), with a saturation point being reached after which increases in income leave demand unaffected; a few will have curves similar to (3), with demand increasing with income over the range of income variation, and then falling as income rises over a higher range of income variation. (By now you should have no trouble explaining why a commodity cannot be inferior over the entire range of income variation starting from zero.)

As well as its income, a household's wealth may affect its consumption. *Ceteris paribus*, the higher the household's wealth, the higher will be its consumption of all normal goods.

Sociological factors Household's purchases are influenced by such 'sociological' factors as class background, education, marital status, age and place of residence – particularly urban or rural.

The household's tastes If it becomes fashionable among middle-class households to have a second car, the flow of expenditure on cars will increase. This does not mean that everybody will buy a second car, but that some people will, and quantity demanded will rise. When there is change in tastes in favour of a commodity, more of that commodity will be demanded even though its price, the prices of all other commodities and household income have not changed. When there is a change in tastes away from a commodity, less of it will be demanded even though all of the other factors that influence quantity demanded are unchanged.

Some changes in tastes are passing fads, like punk rock and skateboards. Others are permanent, or at least long lasting, such as the switch to filter cigarettes and ball-point pens.

The market demand curve

So far we have discussed how the quantity of a commodity demanded by one household depends on such things as prices and income. To explain market behaviour, however, we need to know the total demand for some commodity on the part of all households. To obtain a market demand schedule from the demand schedules for individual households, we merely sum the quantities demanded by all households at a particular price to obtain the total quantity demanded at that price; we repeat the process for each price to obtain a schedule of a total or market demand at all possible prices. A graph of this schedule is called the MARKET DEMAND CURVE.

The relation between the individual demand curves of households and the market demand curve is illustrated in Figure 7.4, where, for simplicity, we deal with a market containing only two households. We assume that we know the complete demand curve for each household and we show these in Figures 7.4(i) and (ii). From these individual demand curves we have derived the market demand curve (iii), which merely shows how much will be demanded at each price by both households. Geometrically, the market demand curve in (iii) is derived by a horizontal summation of the two individual curves in (i) and (ii). At a price of £40, for example, household (i) demands 10·25 lbs of carrots and household (ii) demands 10 lbs; the total demand is 20·25 lbs, which quantity is plotted in Figure 7.4(iii) against the price of £40. At a price of £100 household (i) demands 3·5 lbs while household (ii) demands 6·25 lbs, and total demand is 9·75 lbs. Thus the market demand curve is the horizontal sum of the demand curves of all the households in the market.[1]

---

[1] When summing curves, students sometimes become confused between vertical and horizontal summation. Such a confusion can only result from the application of memory rather than common sense to one's economics. *Consider what would be meant by vertical summation*: measure off equal quantities, say 7·5 lbs in Figure 7.4(i) and (ii). Now add the price to which this quantity corresponds on each household's demand curve. This gives £60 + £72 = £132. If we now plot the point corresponding to £132 and 7·5 lbs in Figure (iii) we have related a given quantity of the commodity to the sum of the prices which households (i) and (ii) are separately prepared to pay for this commodity. Clearly, this information is of no interest to us in the present context. *Every graphical operation can be translated into words.* The advantage of graphs is that they make proofs easier; the disadvantage is that they make it possible to make silly errors. To avoid these, you should always translate into words any graphical operation you have performed and ask yourself: 'Does this make sense and is this what I meant to do?' For example, a market demand curve is meant to tell us total purchases at each price, and hence it is obtained from individual curves by adding up the *quantities* demanded by each consumer at given prices, not by adding the *prices* which each consumer would pay for some given quantity.

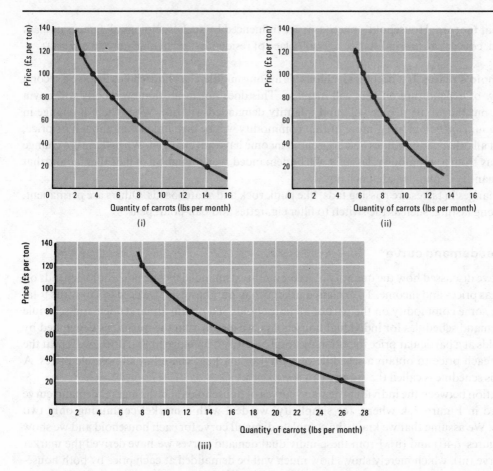

Fig. 7.4 Aggregation of individual demand curves to obtain a market demand curve: (i) first household's demand curve; (ii) second household's demand curve; (iii) total demand curve for the two households

We have illustrated the market demand curve by summing the demands for only two households. An actual market demand curve will represent the demands of all the households located in the area that makes up the market for a commodity. We shall now assume that we have gathered data for the total market demand for carrots in a particular market. These data are given in Table 7.2 and are shown by the curve D_1 in Figure 7.5.

In practice, we seldom obtain market demand curves by summing the demand curves of individual households. Our knowledge of market curves is usually derived by observing total quantities directly. The derivation of market demand curves by summing individual curves is a theoretical operation. We do it here because we wish to understand the relation between curves for individual households and market curves.

When we go from the individual household's demand curve to the market demand curve, we must reconsider item (3) in our list of the determinants of demand. 'Household income' now refers to *the total income of all households*. If, for example, the population increases due to immigration and each new immigrant has an income, the demands for most commodities will rise even though existing households have no changes either in their incomes or in the prices that they face.

Once we take our income variable to be the total income of all households, we must recognize that demand for many products will also depend on how much of this total income is earned by each of the households in the economy. This means that we must add another factor to the major determinants of demand.

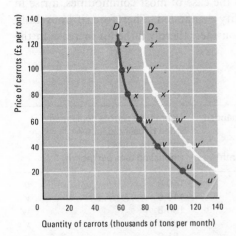

Fig. 7.5 Two market demand curves for carrots

Table 7.2 A market demand schedule for carrots

Price £s per ton	Quantity demanded (thousands of tons per month)
u	20	110·0
v	40	90·0
w	60	77·5
x	80	67·5
y	100	62·5
z	120	60·0

A sixth determinant: income distribution among households Consider two societies with the same total income. In one society there are quite a few very rich households, many very poor ones, but hardly anyone is in the middle-income range. In the second society most of the households have incomes that do not differ much from the average income for all households. Even if all other variables that influence demand are the same, the two societies will have quite different patterns of demand. In the first there will be a large demand for Mercedes-Benz and Rolls-Royce cars and also for black bread and potatoes. In the second, there will be a small demand for these products, but a large demand for television sets, medium-sized cars and other middle-class consumption goods. Clearly, the distribution of income is a major determinant of market demand.

> **The total quantity demanded in any market depends on the price of the commodity being sold, on the prices of all other commodities, on the total income of all the households buying in that market, on the distribution of that income among the households, and on tastes.**

To obtain the market demand curve, we hold constant all the factors that influence demand, including total income and its distribution among households.

> **The market demand curve relates the total quantity demanded of a commodity to its own price on the assumption that all other prices, total household income, its distribution among households, and tastes are held constant.**

Causes of shifts in the market demand curve

We must now consider the effect on the market demand curve of a change in each of the other factors that were held constant when we drew the curve. These effects are, of course, implicit in what has already been said about the relation between the quantity demanded of any commodity and each of these other factors.

Changes in income It has already been argued that, in the case of most commodities, a rise in income will, *ceteris paribus*, cause an increase in quantity demanded. Therefore, if household income rises, we shall find that whatever the price we consider, there will be an increase in the quantity demanded at that price.

Table 7.3 Two alternative demand schedules for carrots

	Price of carrots (£s per ton)	Quantity of carrots demanded at original level of household income (thousand tons per month)	Quantity of carrots demanded when household income rises to new level (thousand tons per month)	
u	20	110·0	140·0	u'
v	40	90·0	116·0	v'
w	60	77·5	100·8	w'
x	80	67·5	87·5	x'
y	100	62·5	81·3	y'
z	120	60·0	78·0	z'

Table 7.3 shows, for our hypothetical example of carrots, the possible effect of an increase in the income of each household that purchases carrots. These new data are shown by the white curve, D_2, in Figure 7.5.[1] The original demand curve is also shown and is labelled D_1. We say that the demand curve has *shifted* (in this case it has shifted to the right). The shift from D_1 to D_2 indicates an increase in the desire to purchase carrots at each possible price. At the price of £40 a ton, for example, 116,000 tons are demanded, whereas only 90,000 were demanded at the lower income.[2] A rise in income thus shifts the demand curve to the right, whereas a fall will have the opposite effect, of shifting the curve

[1] The convention used throughout this book for shifts in curves is as follows. The initial position of the curve is indicated by the subscript 1, the position after the first shift by 2, after the second shift by 3, and so on. The equilibrium price and quantity associated with the initial curve are indicated by p_1 and q_1, those associated with the curve after one shift by p_2 and q_2 and so on. When there is no curve shift, and hence no room for ambiguity, the subscripts are often dropped. Thus, for example, there are no subscripts on Figures 7.1 to 7.4, but on Figure 7.5, the initial curve is labelled D_1 and the shifted curve D_2.

Where we wish to indicate two alternative curves rather than a shift of a curve, we use prime ($'$) marks. Thus, for example, D_1 and D_2 refer to the curve that starts at D_1 and shifts to D_2 while D' and D'' refer to two alternative curves, only one of which will actually exist.

[2] Thus a righward shift in the demand curve indicates an increase in demand in the sense that more is demanded at a given price, and that a higher price would be paid for the original quantity. It is, of course, true that the amount demanded at point y' on D_2 is less than the amount demanded at point u on D_1. This comparison merely shows that, in spite of the increased desire to purchase the good, a sufficiently large rise in price can reduce the quantity actually demanded to an amount lower than it was originally.

to the left. In the case of an inferior good, a rise in income will cause a reduction in the quantity demanded at each market price and the whole demand curve will shift to the left.

Changes in the price of other goods Here the effect depends on whether the good whose price changes is a complement or a substitute. Consider, for example, the effect on the demand curve for electric cookers of a rise in the price of electricity. Electricity and electric cookers are complementary commodities and the rise in the price of electricity makes cooking with electricity more expensive than previously. Some households will switch to gas when they come to replace their existing cookers and some newly formed households will buy a gas, rather than an electric, cooker when they are setting up their household. Thus the rise in the price of electricity leads to a fall in the demand for electric cookers. Now consider the effect of a rise in the price of gas cookers. Gas and electric cookers are substitutes for each other and when gas cookers rise in price some households will buy electric rather than gas cookers, and the demand for electric cookers will thus rise.

For a general statement we may refer to commodity X rather than to electric cookers. A rise in the price of a commodity complementary to X will shift the demand curve for X to the left, indicating that less X will be demanded at each price. A rise in the price of a commodity that is a substitute for X will shift the demand curve for X to the right, indicating that more X will be demanded at each price.

Changes in tastes A change in tastes in favour of a commodity will simply mean that at each price more will be demanded than previously, so that the whole demand curve will shift to the right. On the other hand, a change in tastes away from a commodity will mean that at each price less will be demanded than previously, so that the whole demand curve will shift to the left.

Figure 7.6 summarizes the discussion of the effects on the demand curve of changes in the other

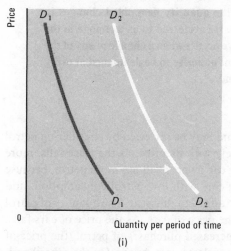
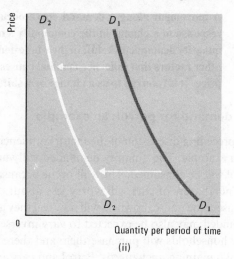

Fig. 7.6 Shifts in demand curves
(i) A rise in demand – the demand curve shifts to the right, indicating a larger quantity is demanded at each price. This can be caused by (1) a rise in income, (2) a rise in the price of a substitute, (3) a fall in the price of a complement, (4) a change in tastes in favour of this commodity
(ii) A fall in demand – the demand curve shifts to the left, indicating a smaller quantity is demanded at each price. This can be caused by (1) a fall in income, (2) a fall in the price of a substitute, (3) a rise in the price of a complement, (4) a change in tastes away from this commodity

things which are assumed constant when the curve is drawn. It is, of course, possible to do the same thing for the curves illustrated in Figures 7.2 and 7.3, and you should check that you understand the analysis by showing what shifts in these curves would be caused by variations in the factors that were assumed to be constant when the particular curve was constructed. (For example, what will happen to the curves in Figure 7.3 if there is a fall in the price of carrots?)

Movements along demand curves versus shifts

It is most important to distinguish between a *movement along* a demand curve and a *shift* of the whole curve. A movement along a demand curve indicates that a different quantity is being demanded *because* the price of that commodity has changed. A shift of a demand curve indicates that a different quantity will be demanded at each possible price because something else, either incomes, tastes, or the price of some other commodity, has changed. There is no generally accepted terminology to distinguish between these two quite different occurrences – a movement along one curve and a shift of the whole curve. When economists speak of an increase or a decrease of demand, however, they are usually referring to a shift of the whole curve, because they are more concerned with the whole functional relation between demand and price than with the particular quantity that happens to be demanded at any one moment. We shall follow this usage, and when we speak of *an increase or a decrease in demand* we shall be referring to a *shift* in the whole curve – to a change in the quantity that will be demanded at each possible price. When we refer to a movement along a curve, we shall call it a change in the *quantity demanded*; specifically, an increase in the quantity demanded will indicate a movement down the curve because of a fall in price, a decrease in the quantity demanded will indicate a movement up the curve because of a rise in price.[1]

> **A movement along a demand curve occurs when the quantity demanded changes in response to a change in the commodity's own price. It is referred to as a change in the quantity demanded. A shift in the whole demand curve occurs when a change in any of the other factors that influence demand causes a different quantity to be demanded at every price. It is referred to as a change or a shift in demand.**

The demand for petrol: an example

The preceding discussion of the factors influencing demand may be reviewed by considering petrol as an example. The quantity demanded will vary inversely with its price: as the price falls, more petrol will be consumed. This will occur because existing car owners will use more petrol, because new purchasers of cars will worry less about obtaining cars with low petrol consumption, and because some non-car owners will now feel they are able to afford to run a car. The quantity of petrol demanded may also be expected to vary inversely with the price of cars. As the price of cars falls, more households will purchase them and there will be increased purchases of petrol (the price of petrol remaining unchanged). Petrol and cars are thus complementary goods. On the other hand, the demand for petrol can be expected to vary directly with the price of public transport – a fall in the

[1] Sometimes a movement along a demand curve is referred to as an *expansion* or a *contraction of demand*: an expansion referring to what we have called an increase in the quantity demanded and a contraction to a decrease in the quantity demanded.

price of public transport leading to a fall in the demand for petrol, and a rise in the price of public transport leading to a rise in the demand for petrol. If the price of public transport rises, car owners can be expected to use their own vehicles more frequently, and public transport less frequently, and it is possible that some non-car owners will be induced to buy cars because public transport is now more expensive. Public transport and petrol are thus substitutes for one another. The demand for petrol will vary directly with household incomes, a rise in total income leading to a rise in petrol consumption. This will occur because car owners will use their existing cars more frequently, because some households will switch to more expensive cars, which generally use more petrol per mile than do the less expensive ones, and because some non-car owners will now purchase cars as their incomes rise. Finally, the demand for petrol will vary with the distribution of income. If income is redistributed from those who are well enough off to be car owners to those who are not and remain too poor to own cars, then the demand for petrol will fall. If, however, income is redistributed from the very rich to those who are thereby made well enough off to buy cars, then the demand for petrol will rise.

The elementary theory of supply

We saw in Chapter 5 that the amount of carrots and Brussels sprouts that farmers produced and offered for sale had an important influence on the markets for these commodities. Our next task is to outline a simple theory of the determinants of this behaviour. It is called the theory of supply.

The nature of supply

The amount of a commodity that firms are able and willing to offer for sale is called the QUANTITY SUPPLIED of a commodity. Like demand, supply is a desired flow: it measures how much firms would like to sell, not how much they actually sell, and it measures it as so much per period of time.

We shall make a very superficial study of supply in this chapter, establishing only what is necessary for a simple theory of price. In Part 4 we shall devote considerable attention to the theory of production, which is the branch of economics concerned with determination of supply. In Part 4 we will start with the behaviour of individual firms and then aggregate to obtain the behaviour of market supply. For our elementary theory it is sufficient to go directly to market supply, the collective behaviour of all the firms in a particular market.

The determinants of quantity supplied: the supply function

We now introduce four hypotheses about what determines the quantity of a commodity that will be supplied by all the firms in a particular market.
(1) Quantity supplied is influenced by the price of the commodity.
(2) Quantity supplied is influenced by the prices of factors of production.
(3) Quantity supplied is influenced by the goals of producing firms.
(4) Quantity supplied is influenced by the state of technology.

This list of factors influencing supply may be conveniently summarized using functional notation by writing out what is called a SUPPLY FUNCTION.

$$q^s_n = S(p_n, F_1, \ldots, F_m)$$

where q^s_n is the quantity supplied of commodity n, p_n is the price of that commodity, $F_1, \ldots, F_m$ is shorthand for the prices of all factors of production, and where the goals of producers and the state of technology determine the form of the function S.

Let us now briefly consider the nature of each of these influences.

The price of the commodity   *Ceteris paribus*, the higher the price of any commodity, the more profitable will it be to make it. We expect, therefore, that the higher the price, the greater will be the quantity supplied.

The prices of factors of production   *Ceteris paribus*, the higher the price of any factor used in the production of a commodity, the less profitable will it be to make it. We expect, therefore, that the higher the price, the lower will be the quantity supplied. (It is important to notice the qualification *ceteris paribus* in the above two points. If, as happens in an inflation, the price of a commodity and the price of the factors used to make it rise together, their effects may cancel each other out leaving production unaffected.)

The goals of firms   If producers of some commodity want to sell as much as possible, even if it costs them some profits to do so, more will be offered for sale than if they wanted to make maximum profits. If producers are reluctant to take risks, we would expect smaller production of any good whose production was risky.

In elementary economic theory we assume that the goal of the firm is to make as much profit as possible. The full implications of this hypothesis, the implications of alternative hypotheses and the consequences of rejecting the 'profit-maximizing hypothesis' are considered in detail in Part 4.

The state of technology   The enormous increase in production per worker that has been going on in industrial societies over the last two hundred years is very largely due to improved methods of production. These in turn have been heavily influenced by the advance of science. Discoveries in chemistry have led to lower costs of production of well-established products, such as paints, and to a large variety of new products made of plastics and synthetic fibres. The new electronics industry rests upon transistors and other tiny devices that are revolutionizing production in television, high-fidelity equipment, computers and guidance-control systems. Atomic energy may one day be used to extract fresh water from the sea. At any time, what is produced, and how it is produced, depend on what is known. Over time, knowledge changes, and so do supplies of individual commodities.

Market supply

For a simple theory of price we need only to know how the quantity supplied of a commodity varies with its own price, all other things being held constant. We are only concerned, therefore, with the *ceteris paribus* relation, $q^s = S(p)$, where p is the commodity's own price. There is much to be said about the relation between quantity supplied and price. For the moment we shall content ourselves with the hypothesis that, *ceteris paribus*, the quantity of any commodity that an individual firm will produce and offer for sale will vary directly with the commodity's price, rising when price rises and falling when price falls, because the higher the price of the commodity, the greater the profits that can be earned, and thus the greater the incentive to produce the commodity and offer it for sale. This hypothesis is known to be correct in a large number of cases, and for the next few chapters we shall proceed assuming it to be generally correct. The exceptions and their implications will be studied in Part 4.

As with demand, we can imagine discovering the quantity supplied by each firm in the market at any given price and then aggregating over all firms to discover the market supply at that price. Repeating this procedure for each price would yield a relation between price and the total quantity supplied by all firms in the market. The procedure is the same as that already discussed for the demand curve.

We now extend the numerical example of the carrot market to include the quantity of carrots supplied. The SUPPLY SCHEDULE given in Table 7.4 is analogous to the demand schedule in Table 7.2, but it records the quantities producers wish to sell at a number of alternative prices rather than the quantities consumers wish to buy. At a price of £80 per ton, for example, 100,000 tons of carrots would come onto the market each month; at a price of £40 per ton, only 46,000 would be forthcoming.

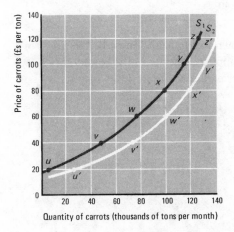

Fig. 7.7 Two supply curves for carrots

Table 7.4 A market supply schedule for carrots

	Price of carrots (£s per ton)	Quantity supplied (thousand tons per month)
u	20	5·0
v	40	46·0
w	60	77·5
x	80	100·0
y	100	115·0
z	120	122·5

We can now plot the data from Table 7.4 onto a graph similar to the demand curve. In Figure 7.7 price is plotted against the vertical axis and quantity against the horizontal one, and the six points corresponding to each price–quantity combination shown in the table are plotted. The point labelled u, for example, gives the same information that is on the first row of the table: when the price of carrots is £20 a ton, 5,000 tons will be produced and offered for sale each month.

Now we draw a smooth curve through the six points. This is the SUPPLY CURVE for carrots. It shows the quantity produced and offered for sale at each price.

> **The supply curve for a commodity shows the relation between its price and the quantity producers wish to sell per period of time. It is drawn on the assumption that all other factors that influence quantity supplied remain constant, and its upward slope indicates that the higher the price, the more producers will wish to sell.**

Shifts in the supply curve

A shift in the supply curve means that, at each price, a different quantity will be supplied than previously. An increase in the quantity supplied at each price is illustrated in Table 7.5 and plotted as the white curve, S_2, in Figure 7.7. This change appears as a rightward shift in the supply curve for carrots, for example from S_1 to S_2. A decrease in the quantity supplied at each price would appear as a leftward shift, for example from S_2 to S_1.

Table 7.5 Two alternative supply schedules for carrots

	Price of carrots (£s per ton)	Original quantity supplied (tons per month)	New quantity supplied (tons per month)	
u	20	5	28	u'
v	40	46	76	v'
w	60	77·5	102	w'
x	80	100	120	x'
y	100	115	132	y'
z	120	122·5	140	z'

A bodily shift in the supply curve such as the one shown in Figure 7.7 must be the result of a change in one of the factors that influence the quantity supplied other than the commodity's own price. The major possible causes of such shifts are summarized under Figure 7.8.

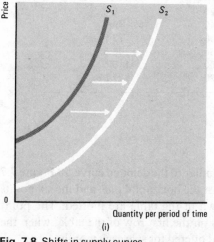
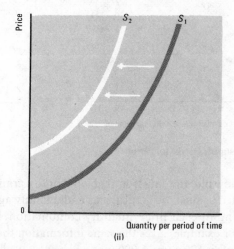

Fig. 7.8 Shifts in supply curves
(i) A rise in supply – the supply curve shifts to the right, indicating that producers wish to make and sell more at each price. This can be caused by (1) improvements in technology, (2) decreases in the prices of other commodities, (3) decreases in the prices of factors of production used in making this commodity, (4) some kinds of changes in the goals of producers
(ii) A fall in the supply – the supply curve shifts to the left, indicating that producers wish to make and sell less at each price. This can be caused by (1) loss of technical knowledge (unlikely), (2) increases in the prices of other commodities, (3) increases in the prices of factors of production used in making this commodity, (4) some kinds of changes in the goals of producers

Movements along supply curves versus shifts

As with demand, it is essential to distinguish between a movement along the supply curve (caused by a change in the commodity's own price) and a bodily shift in the curve (caused by a change in something other than the commodity's own price). We adopt the same terminology as with demand: SUPPLY refers to the whole relation between price and quantity supplied, and QUANTITY SUPPLIED refers to a particular quantity actually supplied at a particular price of the commodity. Thus, when we speak of *an increase or a decrease in supply*, we are referring to shifts in the supply curve such as the ones illustrated in Figures 7.7 and 7.8. When we speak of *a change in the quantity supplied*, we mean a movement from one point on the supply curve to another point on the same curve – for example, a movement from *w* to *y* in Figure 7.7, where quantity changes from 77,500 to 115,000 tons per year in response to a rise in price from £60 to £100 per ton.[1]

Now that we have studied the basic concepts of demand and supply, we can go on, in the next chapter, to study the theory of the determination of market prices by the interaction of these two forces.

---

[1] As with demand, an alternative terminology refers to an increase in the quantity supplied as an *expansion of supply* and a reduction in the quantity supplied as a *contraction of supply*.

8

The theory of the behaviour of individual competitive markets

We can now get some pay-off for the work we did in the previous chapter. We combine our theories of demand and supply to develop a theory of the behaviour of a competitive market. This allows us to derive the famous 'laws' of supply and demand.

The determination of the equilibrium price

It is convenient to continue with the example of carrots. Table 8.1 brings together the market demand and supply schedules for carrots from Tables 7.2 and 7.4. The table defines twelve points. Figure 8.1 shows both the demand and the supply curves on a single graph; the six points on the demand curve are labelled with upper-case letters, while the six points on the supply curve are labelled with lower-case letters, each letter referring to a common price on both curves.

Table 8.1 Demand, supply and excess demand schedules for carrots (thousand tons per month)

Price per ton (£s)	Quantity demanded	Quantity supplied	Excess demand (quantity demanded minus quantity supplied)
20	110·0	5·0	+105·0
40	90·0	46·0	44·0
60	77·5	77·5	0·0
80	67·5	100·0	− 32·5
100	62·5	115·0	− 52·5
120	60·0	122·5	− 62·5

The relation between quantity supplied and quantity demanded at various prices

Consider first the point at which the two curves in Figure 8.1 intersect: the market price is £60; the quantity demanded is 77·5 thousand tons and the quantity supplied is the same. Thus at the price of £60, consumers wish to buy exactly the same amount as producers wish to sell. Provided that the demand curve slopes downwards and the supply curve slopes upwards throughout their entire ranges, there will be no other price at which the quantity demanded equals the quantity supplied.

Now consider any price higher than £60, say £100. At this price consumers wish to buy 62·5 thousand tons, while producers wish to sell 115 thousand tons; thus quantity supplied exceeds quantity demanded by 52·5 thousand tons. It is easily seen, and you should check a few examples, that for any price above £60, quantity supplied exceeds quantity demanded. Furthermore, the higher the price, the larger the excess of the one over the other. The amount by which the quantity firms wish to sell exceeds the quantity households wish to buy is called the EXCESS SUPPLY.

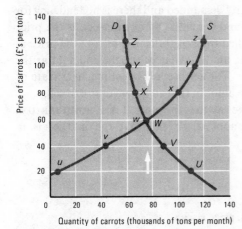

Fig. 8.1 The determination of the equilibrium price of carrots

Finally, consider a price below £60, say £40. At this price, consumers' desired purchases of 90 thousand tons far exceed the producers' desired sales of 46 thousand tons. There is an excess demand of 44 thousand tons. It is easily seen, and you should again check one or two examples, that at all prices below £60 the quantity demanded exceeds the quantity supplied. Furthermore, the lower the price, the larger the excess of the one over the other. The amount by which the quantity demanded exceeds the quantity supplied is called the EXCESS DEMAND.

Changes in price when there is either excess demand or excess supply

When there is excess demand, households will be unable to buy all they wish to buy; when there is excess supply, firms will be unable to sell all they wish to sell. In both cases some people will not be able to do what they would like to do, and we might expect some action to be taken as a result.

To develop a theory about how the market does behave in the face of excess demand or excess supply, we now make two further assumptions. First we assume that when there is excess supply, the market price will fall. Producers, unable to sell some of their goods, may begin to ask lower prices for them; purchasers, observing the glut of unsold output, may begin to offer lower prices. For either or both of these reasons, the price will fall. This hypothesis is illustrated in Figure 8.1 by the arrow indicating a downward pressure on price at all prices above £60.

Second, we assume that when there is excess demand, market price will rise. Individual households, unable to buy as much as they would like to buy, may offer higher prices in an effort to get more of the available goods for themselves; suppliers, who could sell more than their total production, may begin to ask higher prices for the quantities that they have produced. For either or both of these reasons, prices will rise. This hypothesis is illustrated in Figure 8.1 by the arrow indicating an upward pressure on price for all prices below £60.

The equilibrium price

For any price above £60, according to our theory, the price tends to fall; for any price below £60, the price tends to rise. At a price of £60, there is neither excess demand creating a shortage, nor excess supply creating a glut; quantity supplied is equal to quantity demanded and there is no tendency for the price to change. The price of £60, where the supply and demand curves intersect, is the price towards which the actual market price will tend. It is called the EQUILIBRIUM PRICE: the price at which quantity demanded equals quantity supplied. The amount that is bought and sold at the equilibrium price is called the EQUILIBRIUM QUANTITY. The term *equilibrium* means a state of balance; it occurs when demanders desire to buy the same amount that suppliers desire to sell.

When quantity demanded equals quantity supplied we say that the market is in EQUILIBRIUM. When quantity demanded does not equal quantity supplied we say that the market is in DISEQUILIBRIUM. We may now summarize our theory.

> **Hypotheses concerning a competitive market:**
> **(1) demand curves slope downward continuously;**
> **(2) supply curves slope upward continuously;**
> **(3) if quantity demanded exceeds quantity supplied, price rises;**
> **(4) if quantity supplied exceeds quantity demanded, price falls.**
> **Implications:**
> **(1) there is no more than one price at which quantity demanded equals quantity supplied: equilibrium is unique;**
> **(2) only at the equilibrium price will market price be constant;**
> **(3) if either the demand or the supply curve shifts, the equilibrium price and quantity will change.**

The actual changes are considered below.[1]

Shifts in demand and supply

In Chapter 7 we studied shifts in demand and supply curves. Recall that a rightward shift in the relevant curve means that more is demanded or supplied *at each market price*, while a leftward shift means that less is demanded or supplied *at each market price*. How does a shift in either curve affect price and quantity?

We start by considering an increase in demand. In Figure 8.2 the original demand curve is D_1 and the supply curve is S. The original equilibrium price and quantity are p_1 and q_1. Now assume that the demand curve shifts to D_2. This shift means that a larger quantity is demanded *at each*

---

[1] For a long time it was thought that the following inference could be drawn from these hypotheses: the market will be *stable* in the sense that, if the price is moved away from its equilibrium level, it will move back towards it and will eventually return to it. This inference cannot be drawn from the theory as presently formulated. This is discussed further in the Appendix to Chapter 10.

possible market price. As a result, excess demand develops because at the original price of p_1, the quantity demanded is now q_3, whereas the quantity supplied remains at q_1. Because of the excess quantity demanded $(q_3 - q_1)$, price rises towards the new equilibrium price of p_2. When this price is attained, the quantity demanded once again equals the quantity supplied. The new equilibrium quantity bought and sold is q_2: the rise in price from p_1 to p_2 reduces the quantity demanded from q_3 to q_2, whereas it increases the quantity supplied from q_1 to q_2. This analysis establishes our first implication.

(1) **A rise in the demand for a commodity (a rightward shift of the demand curve) causes an increase in both the equilibrium price and the equilibrium quantity bought and sold.**

The effect of a decrease in demand can also be seen in Figure 8.2 by letting the demand curve shift from D_2 to D_1. The initial equilibrium price and quantity are p_2 and q_2. When the demand curve shifts to D_1, excess supply develops at price p_2 and price falls. The new equilibrium price and quantity are p_1 and q_1. This gives us our second implication.

(2) **A fall in the demand for a commodity (a leftward shift of the demand curve) causes a decrease in both the equilibrium price and the equilibrium quantity bought and sold.**

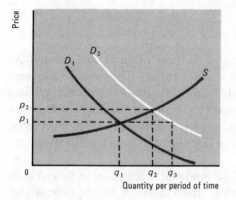

Fig. 8.2 The effects of shifts in the demand curve

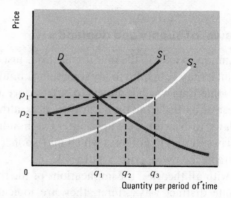

Fig. 8.3 The effects of shifts in the supply curve

The effect of a rise in supply is shown in Figure 8.3. The shift in the supply curve to the right, from S_1 to S_2, indicates an increase in supply: at each price more is now offered for sale than was previously offered. This time, however, the shift of the curve causes a glut to develop at the old equilibrium price. When the curve shifts, the quantity offered for sale increases from q_1 to q_3 but the quantity demanded remains unchanged at q_1. The excess supply causes price to fall. As the price comes down, the quantity supplied diminishes and the quantity demanded increases. The new equilibrium price is p_2, where the quantity supplied and the quantity demanded equal q_2. This gives us our third implication.

(3) **A rise in the supply of a commodity (a rightward shift of the supply curve) causes a decrease in the equilibrium price and an increase in the equilibrium quantity bought and sold.**

The effect of a decrease in supply can also be seen in Figure 8.3 by assuming a shift in the supply curve from S_2 to S_1. The leftward shift in the supply curve causes excess demand to develop at the original equilibrium price, p_2. Price rises and, as a result, quantity demanded diminishes, while quantity supplied increases. The new equilibrium price, at which quantity demanded again equals quantity supplied, is p_1. As a result of the fall in supply, equilibrium price increases from p_2 to p_1, and the equilibrium quantity bought and sold decreases from q_2 to q_1.

> **(4) A fall in the supply of a commodity (a leftward shift in the supply curve) causes an increase in the equilibrium price and a decrease in the equilibrium quantity bought and sold.**

In Figures 7.6 and 7.8 we summarized the many factors that cause demand or supply curves to shift. If we combine this analysis with the four implications just worked out, we can link the many events that cause demand or supply curves to shift, to consequent changes in market prices and quantities bought and sold. To take one example, a rise in the price of butter will lead to an increase in both the price and the quantity bought and sold of margarine (because a rise in the price of one commodity causes a rightward shift in the demand curves for its substitutes).

The theory of the determination of price by demand and supply is beautiful in its simplicity and yet, as we shall see, powerful in its wide range of applications.

The 'laws' of supply and demand

It is common to refer to the four implications just developed as the 'laws' of supply and demand. At this point it may be helpful to say something about the idea of scientific *laws*. The notion of a natural law, as something which is proven to be true once and for all, is an eighteenth-century concept. It has long been discarded from the natural sciences, although traces of it still linger on elsewhere. Even the great 'laws' of Newton were upset after two hundred years, and scientific theories are now accepted not as laws, but as hypotheses which may sooner or later be discovered to be in conflict with facts and be replaced by superior hypotheses.

As with all theories, the implications of the theory of demand and supply may be looked at in two quite distinct ways. First, they are logical deductions from a set of assumptions about behaviour. When we consider the truth of the implications we are concerned with whether or not they are logically correct deductions. If we discovered that we made mistakes in our reasoning process, then we would conclude that the alleged implications are false in the sense that they do not follow from the assumptions of the theory. Second, the implications are predictions about real-world events. When we consider the truth of the implications, we are concerned with whether or not they are empirically correct. If one or more of our assumptions do not correctly describe what happens in the real world, the implications of those assumptions will also *not* correctly describe the real-world behaviour. In this case we would conclude that the implications are false in the sense that they are empirically incorrect, i.e., they are contradicted by certain real-world observations.

Consider an example. The sentence '*If* the demand curve for motorcars slopes downwards and *if* the supply curve slopes upwards, *then* an increase in demand for cars will raise their equilibrium price,' is logically correct in the sense that the 'then' statement follows logically from the two 'if' statements. The single sentence 'A rise in the demand for motorcars will increase the price of motorcars,' is one that may or may not be empirically true. If any one of the assumptions is not empirically correct for motorcars, the statement may be empirically false even though it is a correct logical implication of the theory of competitive market behaviour. If, for example, the market for cars does not respond to excess demand with a rise in price, the statement may be empirically false: even though a rise in demand for motorcars does create excess demand, market price will not rise.

> **Economists are concerned with developing implications that are correct in both senses – that they follow logically from the assumptions of theories, and that they are not contradicted by the evidence of the real world.**

The use of the term 'laws' in the popular phrase 'the laws of supply and demand' implies that the four implications have been shown to be true in the empirical sense. We must remember, however, that these 'laws' are nothing more than predictions that follow from price theory and that, as such, they are always open to testing. There is considerable evidence that the predictions are consistent with the facts in many markets. In other markets, especially those for durable consumers' goods such as cars and TV sets, it is not so clear that they are completely consistent with empirical observations. In general, however, we should not speak of 'laws'; we should speak rather of predictions that appear to be empirically at least somewhere near the mark in a considerable number of cases.

An example: sprouts and carrots again

In Chapter 5 we discussed the effects of various changes in the demand for and supply of Brussels sprouts and carrots. We can now formalize part of that discussion to gain practice by using our new tools of demand and supply curves in the context of an already familiar problem.

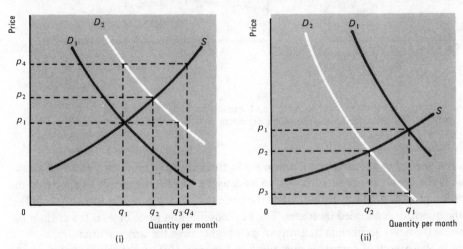

Fig. 8.4 The effects of shifts in the demand curves for carrots and Brussels sprouts: (i) a rise in the demand for sprouts; (ii) a fall in the demand for carrots

A rise in the demand for sprouts and a fall in the demand for carrots The market for sprouts is illustrated in Figure 8.4(i). The original demand and supply curves are D_1 and S, so that the original equilibrium price is p_1 and quantity is q_1. The demand curve then shifts to D_2. At the original price of p_1, there is an excess of quantity demanded over quantity supplied of $q_3 - q_1$. If, for the time being, the supply of sprouts is fixed at q_1, then the price will rise to p_4, which equates the original quantity supplied with the increased demand. Equilibrium is obtained at first solely by choking off demand through price increases. However, at the price p_4 producers would like to grow and sell the quantity q_4. Production will begin to increase and, as the increased flow comes onto the market, the price will fall, for no more than q_1 can be sold at the price p_4. The new equilibrium price is p_2, where the quantities demanded and supplied are both q_2.

The effects on carrots, which are shown in Figure 8.4(ii), are the reverse of the effects on sprouts. The leftward shift in demand causes price to fall to p_3 as long as the quantity supplied remains at its original level of q_1. The fall in price, however, causes a contraction in output and then a rise in price to its new equilibrium level of p_2. The fall in demand thus causes both the new equilibrium price and quantity to be lower than their original levels.

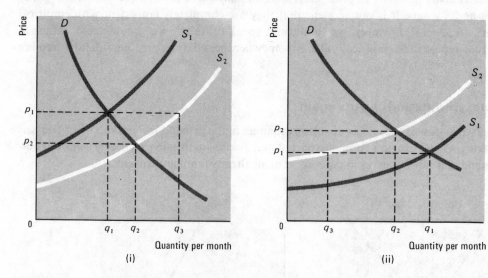

Fig. 8.5 The effects of shifts in the supply curves for carrots and Brussels sprouts: (i) an increase in the supply of Brussels sprouts; (ii) a decrease in the supply of carrots

An increase in the supply of sprouts and a decrease in the supply of carrots Figure 8.5 shows that the increase in the supply of sprouts from S_1 to S_2 causes a surplus of sprouts to appear at the original equilibrium price of p_1. The surplus causes the price to fall; as it falls, the quantity supplied decreases and the quantity demanded increases. The new equilibrium price of p_2 is lower than the original price, while the new equilibrium quantity of q_2 is higher than the original quantity.

The decrease in the supply of carrots is illustrated in Figure 8.5(ii) by the leftward shift in the supply curve from S_1 to S_2. At the original price of p_1 there is now a shortage of $q_1 - q_3$, because the quantity supplied has fallen from q_1 to q_3, while the quantity demanded has remained unchanged. As a result of the shortage, the price rises. This rise in price reduces the quantity demanded and increases the quantity supplied. The new equilibrium price is p_2, which is higher than the original price by $p_2 - p_1$. The new equilibrium quantity is q_2, which is lower than the original equilibrium quantity by $q_1 - q_2$.

9

Elasticity of demand and supply

When flood damage recently led to a major destruction of the onion crop, onion prices rose across the country. Not surprisingly, onion consumption fell. Very often it is not enough to know merely that quantity rises or falls in response to a change in price; it is also important to know by how much. In this case, the press reported that many consumers stopped using onions altogether, substituting onion salt, leeks, cabbage, and other food products. Others still bought onions, but in reduced quantities. Overall consumption was sharply reduced. Was the aggregate value of onion sales (price *times* quantity) higher or lower? The data above do not tell, but the answer may matter a good deal. A government concerned with the effect of a partial crop failure on farm income will not be satisfied with being told that food prices will rise and, as a result, quantities consumed will fall; to assess the effect on farmers it will need to know approximately by how much they will rise and fall.

Price elasticity of demand

Policy relevance

Suppose there is a rise in the supply of a farm crop. The two parts of Figure 9.1 show the same rightward shift in the supply curve. In part (i) of the figure, the demand curve is very flat and the increase in supply from S_1 to S_2 causes a large increase in the quantity bought and sold, from q_1 to q_2, while price falls only a bit, from p_1 to p_2. In part (ii) the demand curve is much steeper, and the same shift in supply from S_1 to S_2 causes only a small increase in quantity bought and sold but a large decrease in price. Why are the two cases so different? In both the rightward shift in the supply curve causes excess supply to develop at the initial equilibrium price of p_1. This causes price to fall. In case (i) demand is very responsive to price and only a small fall in price is sufficient to increase the quantity demanded to the point where it is equal to quantity supplied. In case (ii) demand is not very responsive to price and the fall in price mainly reduces the quantity supplied while it only slightly increases the quantity demanded. Price falls a great deal, and at the new equilibrium most of the extra quantity that was supplied at the old price of p_1 has been choked off by the fall in price. Thus quantity supplied ends up only a little higher than it was before the supply curve shifted.

The difference between these two cases may be significant for policy. Consider what will happen, for example, if the government pays a subsidy for each bushel of carrots grown. This will shift the supply curve of carrots to the right because more will be produced at each price. If the demand for carrots is as shown in part (i) of the figure, the effect of the government's policy will be to reduce carrot prices slightly while greatly increasing the quantity grown and consumed. If, however, the demand is as shown in (ii), the effect of the policy will be to reduce carrot prices greatly but to increase carrot production and consumption by only a small amount.

In comparing the two parts of Figure 9.1, it can be seen that in both cases the government's policy has exactly the same effectiveness as far as farmers' willingness to supply the commodity is concerned (the supply curve shifts are identical). But the effects on the equilibrium price and quantity are very different because of the different degrees to which quantity demanded by consumers responds to price changes. If the purpose of the policy is to increase the quantity that is produced and consumed, then the policy will be a great success when the demand curve is similar to the one shown in Figure 9.1(i), but a failure when the demand curve is similar to that shown in Figure 9.1(ii). If, however, the main purpose of the policy is to achieve a large reduction in the price of carrots, the policy will be a failure when demand is as shown in (i) but a great success when demand is as shown in (ii).

Shifts in supply have very different effects, depending on the shape of the demand curve.

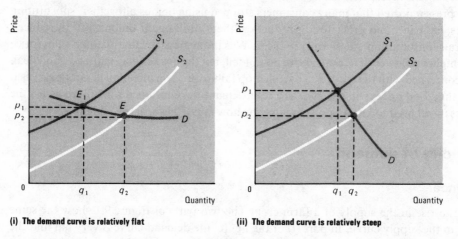

(i) The demand curve is relatively flat   (ii) The demand curve is relatively steep

Fig. 9.1 The shape of the demand curve influences the outcome of a change in supply

Measuring the responsiveness of demand to price

Sometimes we wish to know how the responsiveness of demand for one product changes over time, or to compare this responsiveness for several products. We may wish to make statements such as the following: 'The demand for carrots was more responsive to price changes ten years ago than it is today', or 'The demand for meat responds more to price changes than does the demand for green vegetables.' In Figure 9.1 we were able to compare the responsiveness of quantity demanded along the two demand curves because they were drawn on the same scale. But you should not try to compare two curves without making sure that the scales are the same. Also, you must not leap to conclusions about responsiveness of quantity demanded on the basis of the apparent steepness of a single curve. To illustrate the hazards, look at the demand curve in Figure 9.2 (i). Five points on this curve are singled out and labelled a to e for purposes of comparison. The curve appears rather flat,

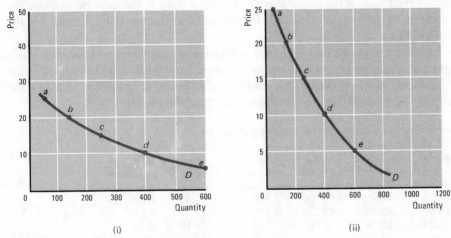

Fig. 9.2 A single demand curve drawn on two different scales

Table 9.1 Changes in prices and quantities for three commodities

Commodity	Reduction in price	Increase in quantity demanded
Sausages	£0·10 per pound	7,500 lbs
Men's shirts	£0·15 per shirt	4,500 shirts
Radios	£0·05 per radio	20 radios

but by a mere change in scale in Figure 9.2 (ii) we can draw a rather steep demand curve *showing the identical information.*

Rather than look at geometrical shape as we just did, we might concentrate on actual quantities. Assume, for illustration, that we have the information shown in Table 9.1. Does this tell us enough to make meaningful comparisons? Can we conclude, for example, that the demand for shirts is less responsive to price changes than the demand for sausages because a 10 pence cut in the price of sausages gives a large increase in its demand, while a larger cut in the price of shirts has a smaller effect on their demand?

There are two problems here. First, a reduction of 10 pence will be a large price cut for a low-priced commodity, but an insignificant price cut for a high-priced commodity. It is more revealing for purposes of comparison to know the percentage change in the prices of the various commodities. Second, by an analogous argument, the quantity by which demand changes is not very revealing, unless we also know the level of demand. An increase of 10,000 tons is quite a significant reaction of demand if the quantity formerly bought was, say, 15,000 tons, while it is but a drop in a very large bucket if the quantity formerly demanded was 10,000,000 tons.

The first columns of Table 9.2 record the original levels of price and quantity as well as the changes in them. From it we can derive what we really need to know: how large is the decrease in price, expressed as a percentage of the original price, and how large is the increase in quantity, expressed as a percentage of the quantity originally being sold? This information is recorded in the last two columns of the Table.

It is now seen that quite a large percentage change in the price of sausages brought about a much smaller percentage change in quantity purchased. On the other hand, although the increase in the number of radios purchased was only twenty, this is seen to be quite a large percentage change in the quantity *in comparison to the percentage change in price that brought it about.*

Table 9.2 Relevant price and quantity data for three commodities

Commodity	Original price	Change in price	Original quantity	Change in quantity	% Change in price	% Change in quantity
Sausages (lbs)	£0·80	−£0·10	108,750	7,500	−12·50	6·90
Men's shirts	£4·98	−£0·15	144,750	4,500	− 3·01	3·11
Radios	£50·00	−£0·05	9,980	20	− 0·10	0·20

A formal definition

The above example leads us to the concept of the PRICE ELASTICITY OF DEMAND, which is defined as the percentage change in quantity demanded *divided by* the percentage change in price that brought it about, the result being expressed as a positive number. This elasticity is usually symbolized by the Greek letter eta, η:

$$\eta = (-1)\frac{\text{percentage change in quantity demanded}}{\text{percentage change in price}}$$

Many different elasticities are used in economics. To distinguish η from the others, the full term *price elasticity of demand* can be used. Since η is by far the most commonly used elasticity, economists often drop the adjective *price* and refer to it merely as *elasticity of demand*, or sometimes just as *elasticity*. Where more than one kind of elasticity might be meant, however, η should be given its full title.

When the above formula is used to calculate η, two problems commonly arise. First, when we deal with a percentage change, we must define the change as a percentage of something. Should it be the original amount? This is simple but has the disadvantage of making the percentage change, and hence the elasticity, depend on the direction of the movement. Thus if we define the percentage change in price as the change from the original price, a movement from £1·00 to £1·20 is a 20 per cent change (price increased by $\frac{1}{5}$), while a movement from £1·20 to £1·00 is only a $16\frac{2}{3}$ per cent change (price decreased by $\frac{1}{6}$). If, however, we take the percentage change to be the change in price divided by the average price (£1·10), both the change from £1·00 to £1·20 and the change from £1·20 to £1·00 give a percentage change of 18·18 per cent. Since we want the elasticity between two points on a demand curve to be a single value, independent of the direction of movement between the two points, we shall take all percentage changes to be the change in price or quantity divided by the average of the original and the new prices or quantities.

The second problem in calculating elasticity arises from the fact that every change has a sign attached to it; it is either an increase (+) or a decrease (−). Since demand curves slope downwards, the change in quantity has the opposite sign to the change in price, which means that the number expressing elasticity will always be negative. The minus sign in the formula for elasticity is there simply to make elasticity of demand a positive number. This is a matter of convenience; it allows us to equate 'more elastic' with 'more responsive'. Consider an example in which commodities X and Y have elasticities of $+10$ and $+0\cdot5$ (calculated according to the above formula). The demand for commodity X is more responsive to price changes than is the demand for commodity Y, and X has the larger measured elasticity ($+10 > +0\cdot5$). But if we did not multiply by (-1) the two elasticities would be -10 and $-0\cdot5$ so that the commodity with the more responsive demand, X, would have a smaller elasticity than $Y(-10 < -0\cdot5)$. (The Note on Definitions, p. xxiii, is relevant here.)

Having dealt with these two problems we may calculate the elasticities in Table 9.2. The calculations are shown in Table 9.3.

Table 9.3 Calculation of elasticities of demand for sausages, men's shirts and radios from the data given in Table 9.2

	Old amount	New amount	Change in amount	Average amount	Percentage change	Elasticity
Sausages						
price (£s)	0·80	0·70	−0·10	0·750	$\dfrac{-0\cdot10}{0\cdot750}100 = -13\cdot33$	$\eta = -\dfrac{+6\cdot67}{-13\cdot33} = +0\cdot5$
quantity (lbs)	108,750	116,250	7,500	112,500	$\dfrac{7,500}{112,500}100 = +6\cdot67$	
Men's shirts						
price (£s)	4·98	4·83	−0·15	4·905	$\dfrac{-0\cdot15}{4\cdot905}100 = -3\cdot06$	$\eta = -\dfrac{+3\cdot06}{-3\cdot06} = +1\cdot0$
quantity	144,750	149,250	4,500	147,000	$\dfrac{4,500}{147,000}100 = +3\cdot06$	
Radios						
price (£s)	50·00	49·95	−0·05	49·975	$\dfrac{-0\cdot05}{49\cdot975}100 = -0\cdot10$	$\eta = -\dfrac{+0\cdot20}{-0\cdot10} = +2\cdot0$
quantity	9,980	10,000	20	9,990·	$\dfrac{20}{9,990}100 = +0\cdot20$	

We now have a precise measure of elasticity. According to this measure, the demand for radios in the above example is more responsive to a price change than the demand for sausages and men's shirts. The percentage change in the quantity of radios demanded is twice as large as the percentage change in price that brought it about ($\eta = 2$); the percentage change in the quantity of men's shirts demanded is the same as the price change that brought it about ($\eta = 1$); but the percentage change in the quantity of sausages demanded is only half as large as the price change that brought it about ($\eta = 0\cdot5$).[1]

---

[1] The measure of elasticity defined in the text is called *arc elasticity*. In theoretical work the elasticity is defined not between two points on a curve but at each point. This measure is called *point elasticity* and it makes use of derivatives. The relation between arc and point elasticity is further considered in the appendix to this chapter.

Interpreting demand elasticity

The value of elasticity of demand ranges from zero to infinity. It is zero if there is no change in quantity demanded when price changes, i.e., when quantity demanded does not respond to a price change. A demand curve of zero elasticity is shown in Figure 9.3(i). It is said to be *perfectly* or *completely inelastic*.

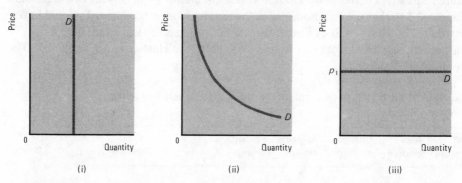

Fig. 9.3 (i) A demand curve of zero elasticity; (ii) a demand curve of unit elasticity; (iii) a demand curve of infinite elasticity

As long as there is some positive response of quantity demanded to a fall in price, elasticity will exceed zero. The larger the elasticity, the larger the percentage change in quantity demanded for a given percentage change in price. As long as the elasticity of demand has a value of less than one, however, the percentage change in quantity is less than the percentage change in price.

When elasticity is equal to one, the two percentage changes are then equal to each other. This is the important boundary case of unit elasticity. A demand curve having this elasticity over its whole range is shown in Figure 9.3(ii).[1]

When the percentage change in quantity demanded exceeds the percentage change in price, then the elasticity of demand is greater than one. The more responsive the quantity demanded becomes to a given change in price, the higher the elasticity of demand. In the limiting case, quantity becomes infinitely responsive. This means that there exists some small price reduction that will raise demand from zero to infinity. Above the critical price, consumers will buy nothing. At the critical price, they will buy all that they can obtain (an infinite amount, if it were available). The graph of a demand curve having infinite price elasticity is shown in Figure 9.3(iii). Quantity demanded (and hence elasticity) is zero at all prices above p_1, but at price p_1 quantity demanded is infinite. Such a demand curve is said to be *perfectly* or *completely elastic*. (This very unlikely-looking case will turn out to be

---

[1] The curve is a rectangular hyperbola having the formula: price *times* quantity equals a constant ($pq = C$). Beginners are often confused by the fact that any demand curve having a constant elasticity other than zero or infinity is a curve and *not* a straight line. In Figure 9.3(ii), as we move down on the price axis, equal *absolute* changes in price (say continuous price cuts of 10p) represent larger and larger *percentage* changes. But as we move outwards on the quantity axis, equal *absolute changes* represent smaller and smaller *percentage changes* in quantity, because the quantity from which we start is becoming larger and larger. If the ratio *percentage change in quantity/percentage change in price* is to be kept constant, equal absolute price cuts must be met with larger and larger absolute increases in quantity. Thus, geometrically, the curve must get flatter and flatter as price becomes lower and lower. This increasing flatness of the demand curve, of course, indicates an increasing responsiveness of the absolute quantity demanded to any given changes in price.

very important later when we study the demand for the output of a single firm with many competitors.)

When the percentage change in quantity is less that the percentage change in price (elasticity less than one), the demand is said to be INELASTIC. When the percentage change in quantity is greater than the percentage change in price (elasticity greater than one), the demand is said to be ELASTIC. Table 9.4 on page 107 summarizes the discussion. The terminology in the table is important, and you should become familiar with it.

Demand elasticity and total expenditure

Money spent by purchasers of a commodity is received by the sellers. The total amount spent by purchasers is thus the gross revenue of the sellers. Often we are interested in how total expenditure by purchasers of a commodity, or total gross receipts of sellers of the commodity, reacts when the price is changed.

If the price of a product falls, there will be an increase in quantity sold; what happens to total revenue depends on the amount by which sales rise in response to a given price cut. The simplest example is sufficient to convince us that total revenue may either rise or fall in response. One hundred units of a commodity are being sold at a price of £1·00; the price is then cut to 90 pence. If the quantity sold rises to 101, the total revenue of the sellers falls (from £100 to £90·90), but if quantity sold rises to 120, total revenue rises (from £100 to £108).

You should now take the earlier example of radios, shirts and beefsteak, and calculate what happened to total revenue when price fell in each case. When you have done this, you will see that in the case of beefsteak, where the demand was inelastic, a cut in price lowered the revenue of sellers; in the case of the radios, where the demand was elastic, a cut in price raised the revenue earned by sellers. The borderline case is provided by men's shirts; here the demand elasticity was unity, and the cut in price left total revenue unchanged. These relations are no accident. Total consumer expenditure is related to elasticity in the following way: if the demand is inelastic, a change in price causes a less than proportionate change in the quantity demanded, so that total revenue falls when price falls and rises when price rises. If the demand is elastic, a change in price causes a more than proportionate change in quantity demanded, so that total revenue rises when price falls and falls when price rises. When the elasticity of demand is unity, a change in price is met by an exactly proportionate (and therefore exactly offsetting) change in quantity demanded, and hence total revenue remains constant when price changes.[1] In summary:

> **(1) If elasticity of demand exceeds unity (demand elastic), a fall in price increases total consumer expenditure and a rise in price reduces it.**
> **(2) If elasticity is less than unity (demand inelastic), a fall in price reduces total expenditure and a rise in price increases it.**
> **(3) If elasticity of demand is unity, a rise or a fall in price leaves total expenditure unaffected.**

---

[1] Algebraically, total revenue is price *times* quantity. If, for example, the equilibrium price and quantity are p_1 and q_1, then total revenue is p_1q_1. On a demand curve diagram, price is given by a vertical distance and quantity by a horizontal distance. It follows that on such a diagram total revenue is given by the *area* of a rectangle, the length of whose sides represent price and quantity.

What determines demand elasticity?

The importance of substitutes   One of the most important determinants of elasticity is undoubtedly the degree of availability of close substitutes. Some commodities, like margarine,
cabbage, pork and Ford cars, have quite close substitutes – butter, spinach, beef and Renault cars. A
change in the price of these commodities, *the prices of the substitutes remaining constant*, will cause
quite substantial substitution – a fall in price leading consumers to buy more of the commodity in
question and a rise in price leading consumers to buy more of the substitute. Other commodities,
such as salt, housing and all vegetables taken together, have few, if any, satisfactory substitutes. A
rise in their prices will cause a smaller fall in quantities demanded than if close substitutes were
available.

The false dichotomy between necessities and luxuries   The following hypothesis about elasticity of demand is commonly found in popular writing: commodities can be divided into two sets;
commodities in the first set are called necessities and have highly inelastic demands; commodities in
the second set are called luxuries and have highly elastic demands. The argument for necessities is
that they are, as their name implies, necessary to life and that when their prices rise, consumers have
no choice but to cut back expenditures on other products and to go on buying the necessities. The
argument for luxuries is that they are dispensable and when their prices rise, people will in fact
dispense with them: thus they have highly elastic demands.

There is nothing logically wrong with this hypothesis; it is quite easy to imagine a world that
behaves like this. The only problem is that the hypothesis does not describe *our* world; it is
contradicted by the facts. In all the demand studies that have been made, there is no observable
tendency for commodities to fall into two groups, one with very low elasticities and one with very
high elasticities. There seem to be goods with all possible elasticities. A few are very low, a few are
very high and the remainder are spread out in between. It is true, of course, that food is a necessity in
the sense that life cannot go on without some minimum quantity of it, and it is probably true that
food as a whole has an inelastic demand. It does not follow from this, however, that any one food,
for example white bread or cornflakes, is a necessity in the same sense, since individual foods have
many close substitutes. Thus the quantities demanded of many individual food products fall greatly
as a result of rises in their own prices.

> To a great extent demand elasticity depends on how widely or narrowly a commodity is
> defined.

Other demand elasticities

The concept of demand elasticity can be broadened to measure the response of quantity demanded
to changes in *any* of the factors that influence demand. Besides the commodity's own price, it is
important to know how changes in income and the prices of other commodities can affect quantity
demanded.

Income elasticity

The reaction of demand to changes in income is extremely important. In many economies, economic growth is doubling real national income every 20 or 30 years. This rise in income is shared more or less equally by all the households in the economy. As they find their incomes increasing, households increase their demands for many commodities,. In the richer countries the demand for food and basic clothing does not increase with income nearly so much as does the demand for many other commodities. In all but the richest of the developed countries it is the demand for such durable goods as cars, refrigerators and washing machines that is currently increasing most rapidly as household incomes rise. In the very richest of the Western countries it is the demand for services that is rising most rapidly.

The responsiveness of demand for a commodity to changes in income is termed INCOME ELASTICITY OF DEMAND, and is defined as

$$\eta_Y = \frac{\text{percentage change in quantity demanded}}{\text{percentage change in income}}.$$

For most commodities, increases in income lead to increases in demand, and income elasticity is therefore positive. For these we have the same subdivisions of income elasticity as for price elasticity. Consider a given percentage change in income. If the resulting percentage change in quantity demanded is larger, η_Y will exceed unity and the commodity is said to be INCOME ELASTIC. If the percentage change in quantity demanded is smaller than the change in income, η_Y will be less than unity and the commodity is said to be INCOME INELASTIC. In the boundary case, the percentage changes in income and quantity demanded are equal; η_Y is unity and the commodity is said to have a *unit income elasticity of demand*.

Virtually all commodities have positive price elasticities. Both positive and negative income elasticities, however, are commonly found.

Goods with positive income elasticities are called normal goods (see page 77). Goods with negative income elasticities are called inferior goods; for them, a rise in income is accompanied by a fall in quantity demanded. Normal goods are much more common than inferior goods. The boundary case between normal and inferior goods occurs when a rise in income leaves quantity demanded unchanged so that income elasticity is zero.

If you look back now to Figure 7.3 on page 78, you will see several curves relating demand to income. Whenever such a curve is rising, income elasticity is positive. When demand is unaffected by the level of income, as in the right-hand portion of the curve labelled (2), income elasticity is zero. When the curve declines, as in the right-hand portion of (3), income elasticity is negative.

The important terminology of income elasticity is summarized in Figure 9.4 and Table 9.4 on pages 106 and 107. You should spend time studying the terminology and committing it to memory.

Cross-elasticity

The responsiveness of quantity demanded of one commodity to changes in the prices of other commodities is often of considerable interest. Producers of beans and other meat substitutes find the demands for their products rising when cattle shortages force the price of beef up. Sellers of large cars find their custom falling off when OPEC (the Organization of Petroleum Exporting Countries) forces up the price of oil.

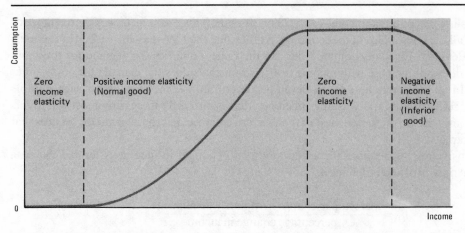

Fig. 9.4 A relation between expenditure on a single commodity and household income

The responsiveness of demand for one commodity to changes in the price of another commodity is called CROSS-ELASTICITY OF DEMAND. It is defined as

$$\eta_c = \frac{\text{percentage change in quantity demanded of commodity } X}{\text{percentage change in price of commodity } Y}.$$

Cross-elasticity can vary from minus infinity to plus infinity. Complementary goods have negative cross-elasticities and substitute goods have positive cross-elasticities.

Bread and butter, for example, are complements: a fall in the price of butter causes an increase in the consumption of both commodities. Changes in the price of butter and the quantity of bread demanded as a result will therefore have opposite signs. Butter and margarine, on the other hand, are substitutes: a fall in the price of butter increases the quantity of butter demanded but reduces the quantity of margarine demanded. Changes in the price of butter and in the quantity of margarine demanded will, therefore, have the same sign.

The closer the relation of substitutability or complementarity, the larger the quantitative reaction to any given price change and thus the larger the absolute value of the cross-elasticity. If the two goods bear little relation to each other, we may expect their cross-elasticities to be close to zero. The terminology of cross-elasticity is also summarized in Table 9.4.

Elasticity of supply

The concept of elasticity may now be expanded to cover supply. Just as elasticity of demand measures the response of quantity demanded to changes in any of the factors that influence it, so elasticity of supply measures the response of quantity supplied to changes in any of the factors that influence it. Because we are focusing mainly on the commodity's own price as a factor influencing supply, we shall be concerned mainly with *price elasticity of supply*. We shall follow the usual practice of dropping the adjective 'price' and referring simply to 'elasticity of supply' whenever there is no ambiguity in this usage.

Supply elasticities are very important in economics. The brevity of our treatment here reflects two main facts: first, that much of the technique of demand elasticity carries over to the case of supply and does not need repeating, and, second, that we will have more to say about the determinants of supply elasticity in Part 4.

Table 9.4 The terminology of elasticity

Terminology	Numerical measure of elasticity	Verbal description
Price elasticity of demand (supply)		
Perfectly, or completely inelastic	Zero	Quantity demanded (supplied) does not change as price changes
Inelastic	Greater than zero, but less than one	Quantity demanded (supplied) changes by a smaller percentage than does price
Unit elasticity	One	Quantity demanded (supplied) changes by exactly the same percentage as does price
Elastic	Greater than one, but less than infinity	Quantity demanded (supplied) changes by a larger percentage than does price
Perfectly, or completely or infinitely, elastic	Infinity	Purchasers (sellers) are prepared to buy (sell) all they can at some price and none at all at an even slightly higher (lower) price
Income elasticity of demand		
Inferior Good	Negative	Quantity demanded decreases as income increases
Normal Good	Positive	Quantity demanded increases as income increases:
Income inelastic	Greater than zero, but less than one	less than in proportion to income increase
Income elastic	Greater than one	more than in proportion to income increase
Cross-elasticity of demand		
Substitute	Positive	Price increase of a substitute leads to an increase in quantity demanded of this good (and also less of substitute)
Complement	Negative	Price increase of a complement leads to a decrease in quantity demanded of this good (and also less of the complement)

A formal definition

The ELASTICITY OF SUPPLY is defined as the percentage change in quantity supplied divided by the percentage change in price that brought it about. Letting the Greek letter epsilon, ε, stand for this measure, its formula is

$$\varepsilon = \frac{\text{percentage change in quantity supplied}}{\text{percentage change in price}}.$$

Supply elasticity is a measure of the degree of responsiveness of quantity supplied to changes in the commodity's own price.

Since supply curves normally slope upwards, indicating that an increase in price calls forth an increase in the quantity supplied, supply elasticity, as defined by the above formula, will normally be positive. As with demand elasticity, it is best to calculate percentage changes on the average of the new and old prices and the new and the old quantities when applying the above formula.

Interpreting supply elasticity

Figure 9.5 illustrates three cases of supply elasticity. The case of zero elasticity is one in which the quantity supplied does not change as price changes. This would be the case, for example, if suppliers persisted in producing a given quantity, q_1 in Figure 9.5 (i), and dumping it on the market for whatever it would bring. Infinite elasticity is illustrated in Figure 9.5 (ii). The supply elasticity is infinite at the price p_1, because nothing at all is supplied at lower prices, but a small increase in price to p_1 causes supply to rise from zero to an infinitely large amount, indicating that producers would supply any amount demanded at that price. The case of unit elasticity of supply is illustrated in Figure 9.5 (iii). Any straight-line supply curve drawn through the origin has, in fact, an elasticity of unity. For a proof of this, see proposition (4) on page 110 of the Appendix to this chapter.

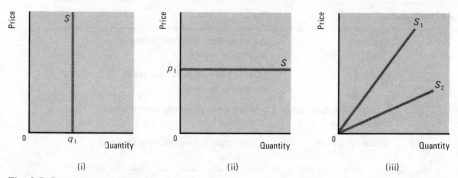

Fig. 9.5 Supply curves of (i) zero, (ii) infinite and (iii) unit elasticity

The case of unit supply elasticity illustrates that the warning given earlier for demand applies equally to supply: do not confuse geometric steepness of supply curves with elasticity. Since *any* straight line supply curve that passes through the origin has an elasticity of unity, it follows that there is no direct simple correspondence between geometrical steepness and supply elasticity. The reason is that varying steepness (when the scales are constant) refers to varying *absolute* reactions, while elasticity refers to *proportionate* reactions. The terminology of supply elasticity is also summarized in Table 9.4.

Appendix to chapter 9

A formal analysis of elasticity

Arc elasticity of demand is defined as the ratio of the percentage change in the quantity demanded to the percentage change in price. In Chapter 9, we defined elasticity of demand as the negative of this amount so that it would be a positive number. It is convenient in this appendix to maintain this simplification.

In Chapter 9 we also took price and quantity to be the average of the prices and quantities before and after the change being considered; for the more formal treatment in this appendix it is more satisfactory to take price and quantity to be the ones ruling before the change being considered. The difference between taking p and q as original or as average amounts diminishes as the magnitude of the change being considered diminishes.

The elasticity measure commonly used in theoretical treatments is called POINT ELASTICITY. Arc elasticity, described in Chapter 9, may be regarded as an approximation to it.

We shall consider arc and then point elasticity, but first we must define some symbols:

$q \equiv$ the original quantity;
$\Delta q \equiv$ the change in quantity;
$p \equiv$ the original price;
$\Delta p \equiv$ the change in price.

We can now express the definition of arc elasticity of demand in symbols:

$$\eta \equiv -\frac{\Delta q/q}{\Delta p/p}.$$

By inverting the denominator and multiplying, we get

$$\eta \equiv -\frac{\Delta q}{q} \cdot \frac{p}{\Delta p}.$$

Since it does not matter in which order we do our multiplication (i.e., $q.\Delta p \equiv \Delta p.q$), we may reverse the order of the two terms in the denominator and write

$$\eta = -\frac{\Delta q}{\Delta p}\frac{p}{q}. \qquad (1)$$

We have now split elasticity into two parts: $\Delta q/\Delta p$, the ratio of the change in quantity to the change in price, which is related to the slope of the demand curve, and p/q, which is related to the place on the curve at which we made our measurement.

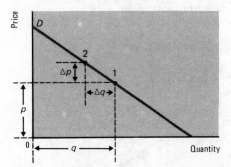

Fig. 9.6 A straight-line demand curve

Figure 9.6 shows a straight-line demand curve by way of illustration. If we wish to measure the elasticity at point 1, we take our p and q at the point and consider a price change, taking us, say, to point 2, and measure our Δp and Δq as indicated. The slope of the straight line joining points 1 and 2 is $\Delta p/\Delta q$ (if you have forgotten this, refer to the appendix to Chapter 2, pp. 29–30), and the term in equation (1) is $\Delta q/\Delta p$, which is the reciprocal of $\Delta p/\Delta q$. We conclude, therefore, that the first term in our elasticity formula is the reciprocal of the slope of the straight line joining the two price-quantity positions under consideration.

We may now develop a number of theorems relating to the elasticity of demand and supply.

(1) *The elasticity of a downward-sloping straight-line demand curve varies from infinity (∞) at the price axis*

109

to zero at the quantity axis. We first notice that a straight line has a constant slope so that the ratio $\Delta p/\Delta q$ is the same anywhere on the line. Therefore, its reciprocal, $\Delta q/\Delta p$, must also be constant. We can now infer the changes in η by inspecting the ratio p/q. At the price axis $q = 0$ and p/q is undefined, but as we let q *approach* zero, without ever quite reaching it, the ratio p/q increases without limit. Thus $\eta \rightarrow \infty$ as $q \rightarrow 0$. As we move down the line, p falls and q rises steadily; thus p/q is falling steadily so that η is also falling. At the q axis the price is zero, so the ratio p/q is zero. Thus $\eta = 0$.

(2) *Comparing two straight-line demand curves of the same slope, the one farther from the origin is less elastic at each price that the one closer to the origin.* Figure 9.7 shows two parallel straight-line demand functions. Pick any price, say p, and compare the elasticities of the two curves at that price. Since the curves are parallel, the ratio $\Delta q/\Delta p$ is the same on both curves. Since we are comparing elasticities at the same price on both curves, p is the same, and the only factor left to vary is q. On the curve farther from the origin, quantity is larger (i.e., $q_2 > q_1$), and hence p/q is smaller; thus η is smaller.

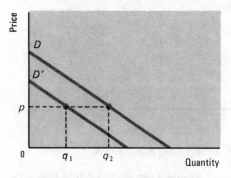

Fig. 9.7 Two parallel straight-line demand curves have unequal price elasticities at p

It follows from Theorem 2 that a parallel shift of a straight-line demand curve lowers elasticity (at each price) if the line shifts outward, and raises elasticity if the line shifts inward.

(3) *The elasticities of two intersecting straight-line demand curves can be compared at the point of intersection merely by comparing slopes, the steeper curve being the less elastic.* In Figure 9.8 we have two intersecting curves. At the point of intersection p and q are common to both curves, and hence the ratio p/q is the same. Therefore η varies only with $\Delta q/\Delta p$. On the steeper curve $-\Delta p/\Delta q$ is larger than on the flatter curve; thus the ratio $-\Delta q/\Delta p$ is smaller on the

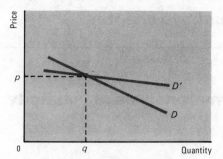

Fig. 9.8 Two intersecting straight-line demand curves have different elasticities at the point where they cross

steeper curve than on the flatter curve, so that elasticity is lower.

(4) *Any straight-line supply curve through the origin has an elasticity of one.* Such a supply curve is shown in Figure 9.9. Consider the two triangles with the sides p, q, and the S curve, and Δp, Δq, and the S curve. Clearly these are similar triangles. Therefore the ratios of their sides are equal, i.e.,

$$\frac{p}{q} = \frac{\Delta p}{\Delta q}. \tag{2}$$

Elasticity of supply is defined as

$$\varepsilon = \frac{\Delta q}{\Delta p} \cdot \frac{p}{q}, \tag{3}$$

which, by substitution from (2), gives

$$\varepsilon = \frac{q}{p} \cdot \frac{p}{q} \equiv 1. \tag{4}$$

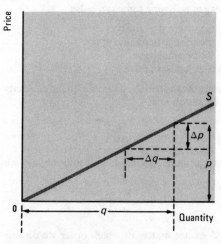

Fig. 9.9 A straight-line supply curve through the origin has an elasticity of one

(5) *With a straight-line demand curve, the elasticity measured from any point (p, q), according to equation (1) above, is independent of the direction and magnitude of the change in price and quantity.* This follows immediately from the fact that the slope of a straight line is a constant. If we start from some point (p, q) and then change price, the ratio $\Delta q/\Delta p$ will be the same whatever the direction or the size of the change in p.

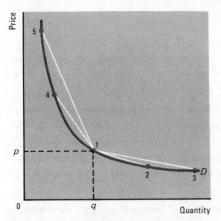

Fig. 9.10 Arc elasticity measured from a particular point (1) on a demand curve that is not a straight line

(6) *The elasticity measured from any point (p, q), according to equation (1) above, is in general dependent on the direction and magnitude of the change in price and quantity.* Except for a straight-line demand curve (for which the slope does not change) the ratio $\Delta q/\Delta p$ will not be the same at different points on a demand curve. Figure 9.10 shows a demand curve that is not a straight line. We desire to measure the elasticity from point 1. The figure makes it apparent that the ratio $\Delta q/\Delta p$, and hence the elasticity, will vary according to the size and the direction of the price change. This result is very inconvenient. It happens because we are averaging the reaction of Δq to Δp over a section of the demand curve, and, depending on the range that we take, the *average reaction* will be different.

If we wish to measure the elasticity at a point, we need to know the reaction of quantity to a change in price at that point, not over a whole range. We call the reaction of quantity to price change at a point

dq/dp, and we define this to be the reciprocal of the slope of the straight line (i.e., $\Delta q/\Delta p$) tangent to the demand curve at the point in question. In Figure 9.11 the point elasticity of demand at a is the ratio p/q (as it has been in all previous measures) now multiplied by the ratio of $\Delta q/\Delta p$ measured along the straight-line tangent to the curve at a. This definition may now be written as

$$\eta = -\frac{dq}{dp}\cdot\frac{p}{q}. \qquad (5)$$

The ratio dq/dp, as we have defined it, is in fact the differential-calculus concept of the derivative of quantity with respect to price.

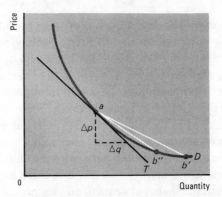

Fig. 9.11 Point elasticity of demand measured from a particular point (a) on the demand curve

This elasticity is the one normally used in economic theory. Equation (1) may be regarded as an approximation to this expression. It is obvious by inspecting Figure 9.11 that the elasticity measured from (1) will come closer and closer to that measured from (5) the smaller the price change used to calculate the value of (1). From (1), change the price so that we move from a to some point b'; the ratio $\Delta q/\Delta p$ is the reciprocal of the slope of the straight line joining a and b'. The smaller the price change that we make, the closer the point comes to point a and the closer the slope of the line joining the points comes to the slope of the line tangential to the curve at a. If the slopes of these two lines get closer together, so also do the reciprocals of the slopes and, thus, so do the elasticities as measured by equations (1) and (5). Thus, if we consider (1) as an approximation to (5), the error will diminish as the size of Δp diminishes.

10

Applications of the theory of price: price controls and agriculture

The theory of the determination of price by supply and demand is an extremely powerful tool, allowing us to explain and to predict behaviour in markets that are competitive (in the sense discussed on page 94) and in those that would be in the absence of government intervention. Before applying the theory, a few words need to be said about the method of analysis. The theory explains, first, the determination of the equilibrium price and quantity, and, second, the effects of various shifts in the demand and supply curves. These 'effects' are the theory's implications or predictions. As mentioned in Chapter 8, we are interested in their correctness in two senses. First, are they logically correct in the sense that they follow from our assumptions? Second, are they empirically correct in the sense that they agree with the facts? In order to use our theory to develop predictions about real-world markets, we advance three hypotheses: (1) that the assumptions of our theory (e.g., about the shapes of demand and supply curves) adequately describe relations that exist in the real world; (2) that once the actual price is equal to the equilibrium price, the actual price will not change unless the equilibrium price changes; and (3) that if there is a change in the equilibrium price, the actual price will move fairly quickly towards the new equilibrium price. *If* these hypotheses are correct, *then* the propositions of our theory will provide useful predictions about how prices and quantities will actually behave; if not, the predictions of our theory will frequently be contradicted by the evidence.

The cases studied in this chapter and in the next, are examples chosen both to illustrate the use of price theory and to give you practice in using it. Particular examples need not be commited to memory. Working through these examples should develop your own facility with the theory, so that you will be able to use it yourself to analyse new problems when they arise.

Price control

Quantity exchanged at non-equilibrium prices

In competitive markets, price tends to change whenever quantity supplied does not equal quantity demanded. Thus price tends towards its equilibrium value at which there are neither unsatisfied suppliers nor unsatisfied demanders. Price controls, however, create the possibility that price may be held indefinitely at a disequilibrium value. When this happens, what determines the quantity actually traded on the market? Any voluntary market transaction requires both a willing buyer and a willing seller. This means that if quantity demanded is less than quantity supplied, the former will determine the amount actually exchanged and the rest of the quantity supplied will remain in the hands of the unsuccessful sellers. On the other hand, if quantity demanded exceeds quantity supplied, the latter will determine the amount actually traded and the rest of the quantity demanded will represent desired purchases of unsuccessful buyers.

At any disequilibrium price, quantity exchanged is determined by the lesser of quantity demanded or quantity supplied.

This is shown graphically in Figure 10.1. At p_1 the market is in equilibrium with quantity demanded equal to quantity supplied at q_1. For prices below p_1, the quantity exchanged will be determined by the supply curve. For example, the quantity q_3 will be exchanged at the disequilibrium price p_2 in spite of the excess demand of q_2-q_3. For prices above p_1, the quantity exchanged will be given by the demand curve. For example, the quantity exchanged will be only q_3 at the price p_3 in spite of the excess supply of q_4-q_3. Thus the heavy black line shows the whole set of actual quantities exchanged, at different prices.

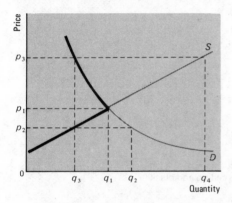

Fig. 10.1 The determination of quantity exchanged in disequilibrium

This result is often summarized in the maxim: *in disequilibrium the short side of the market dominates* (i.e., determines what is bought and sold).

Maximum-price legislation

Since the dawn of history, governments have passed laws regulating the prices at which some commodities have been sold. In this section we shall concentrate on laws setting *maximum* permissible prices, which are often called 'price ceilings'. Such laws have had many purposes. Often they were an attempt to hold down the prices of foodstuffs during severe temporary shortages caused by crop failures. Medieval city governments often sought to protect their citizens from the consequences of failures of the wheat crop by regulating the maximum price of bread. Modern governments in several countries, including the UK, have employed rent controls in an attempt to make housing available at a price that could be afforded by lower-income groups. Whatever the motivation of the policy, the theory of the determination of price by demand and supply makes some quite general predictions about the consequences of price controls. Before reading on, it would be a good exercise to ask yourself what you would expect to be the consequences of fixing some prices by law rather than allowing them to be determined by demand and supply.

The effects on price and quantity Figure 10.2 shows the demand and supply curves for some commodity. The equilibrium price is p_1 and the equilibrium quantity is q_1. If the central authorities enforced a maximum price above the equilibrium price, the intervention would have no effect. The equilibrium price would still be attainable and the market equilibrium would not be inconsistent with the maximum-price law. On the other hand, if the maximum price is set at a level below equilibrium, the equilibrium price is no longer legally obtainable. If, for example, a price ceiling is set at p_2 the quantity demanded will rise to q_2 while the quantity supplied falls to q_3. Quantity actually exchanged will be q_3. Although excess demand is q_2–q_3, price may not legally rise to restore equilibrium.

> **The setting of a maximum price either will have no effect (maximum price set at or above the equilibrium) or will cause a shortage of the commodity (maximum price set below the equilibrium), reducing the quantity actually bought and sold below its equilibrium value.**

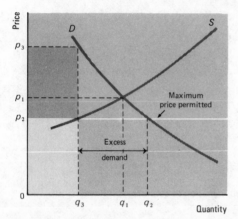

Fig. 10.2 A price ceiling and black market pricing

Allocation of available supply In the case of an effective price ceiling, production will not be sufficient to satisfy everyone who wishes to buy the commodity, and price will not be allowed to change so as to allocate the available supply among the would-be purchasers. It follows, then, that some other method of allocation will have to be adopted. Our theory does not predict what this other method will be, but experience has shown a number of alternatives that may arise.

If shops sell their available supplies to the first customers who arrive, then people are likely to rush to those stores that are rumoured to have any stocks of the scarce commodity. Long queues will develop, and allocation will be on the basis of luck, or to those knowing enough to gain from the principle of 'first-come-first-served'. This is a system commonly found in the command economies of Eastern Europe. Another system may develop if shopkeepers themselves decide who will get the scarce commodities and who will not. They might keep commodities under the counter and sell them only to regular customers, or only to people of a certain colour or religion. When commodities are allocated according to such criteria we refer to it as ALLOCATION BY SELLERS' PREFERENCES.

If the central authorities dislike the somewhat arbitrary system of allocation that grows up as the result of price ceilings, they can ration the goods, giving out ration coupons sufficient to purchase the quantity q_3 in Figure 10.2. The authorities can then determine, as a conscious act of policy, how the available supply is to be allocated. The coupons might be distributed equally, or on the basis of age, sex, marital status, number of dependents or any other criterion. Thus we are led to make another prediction.

Where there is a feeling against allocation on the basis of first-come-first-served or sellers' preferences, effective price ceilings will give rise to strong pressure for a centrally administered system of rationing.

Black markets Under certain circumstances, price control with or without rationing is likely to give rise to a BLACK MARKET, a market in which goods are sold illegally at prices that violate the legal restrictions. For many products, there are only a few manufacturers but many retailers. Although it is easy to police the producers, it is difficult even to locate all those who are, or could be, retailing the product, much less police them. Although the central authorities may be able to control the price that producers get, they may not be able to control the price at which retailers sell to the public. If this were the case with the commodity represented in Figure 10.2, what would you predict would happen?

First, the amount produced will remain unchanged at q_3, because producers will continue to receive the controlled price for their product. At the retail level, however, a black market will arise, because purchasers will be willing to pay more than the controlled price for the limited amounts of the commodity available. If the whole quantity were sold on the black market, it would fetch a price of p_3 per unit. The total amount paid by consumers would be p_3 *times* q_3 which in the figure is the two (light and dark) shaded rectangles. The total amount of the illegal receipts of black marketeers would be the dark-shaded rectangle while the light-shaded area would be the receipts of producers.

The theory predicts that the potential for a profitable black market will exist whenever effective price ceilings are imposed. The actual growth of such a market depends on there being a few people willing to risk heavy penalties by running a black-market supply organization and a reasonably large number of persons prepared to purchase goods illegally on such a market. It is an interesting comment on the strengths of various human motives that there has never been a case documented where effective price ceilings were not accompanied by the growth of a black market.

It is unlikely that all goods will be sold on the black market – both because there are some honest people in every society and because the central authorities always have some power to enforce their price laws. Thus we would normally expect not the extreme result given above, but rather that some of the limited supplies would be sold at the controlled price and some would be sold at the black-market price.

An economist's evaluation of a black-market situation can be made only when it is known what objectives the central authorities were hoping to achieve with their price-control policy. If they are mainly concerned with an equitable distribution of a scarce product, it is very likely that effective price control on manufacturers plus a largely uncontrolled black market at the retail level produces the worst possible results. If, however, they are mainly interested in restricting production in order to release resources for other more urgent needs, such as war production, the policy works effectively, if somewhat unfairly. Where the purpose is to keep prices down, the policy is a failure to the extent that black marketeers succeed in raising prices, and a success to the extent that transactions at controlled prices actually take place.

Empirical evidence There is much evidence confirming predictions which we have shown to follow from our simple theory of price. Practically all belligerent countries in both the First and Second World Wars set ceilings on many prices well below free-market, equilibrium levels. The legislation of maximum prices was always followed by shortages, then by either the introduction of rationing or the growth of some private method of allocation such as sellers' preferences, and finally by the rise of some sort of black market. The ceilings were more effective in limiting consumption than in controlling prices, although they did restrain price increases to some extent.

The theory of maximum prices applied to rent controls[1]

Rent controls are just a special case of maximum prices. Controls are usually imposed to freeze rents at their current levels at times when equilibrium rents are rising either because demand is shifting rightward (due to forces such as rising population and income) or because supply is shifting leftward (due to forces such as rising costs). The result is that soon rents are being held below the free-market equilibrium level and excess demand appears. The following predictions about rent controls are simply applications to housing of the results that apply to any commodity subject to binding ceiling prices.

(1) There will be a housing shortage; quantity demanded will exceed quantity supplied.

(2) The quantity of accommodation occupied will be less than if free-market rents had been charged.

(3) The shortage will lead to alternative allocation schemes. Landlords may allocate by sellers' preferences, or the government may intervene. In the housing market, government intervention usually takes the form of security-of-tenure laws, which protect the tenant from eviction and thus give existing tenants priority over potential new tenants.

(4) Black markets will appear. Landlords may require large lump-sum entrance fees from new tenants. In general, the larger the housing shortage, the bigger the sum required. In the absence of security-of-tenure laws, landlords may evict tenants in order to extract a large entrance fee from new occupants.

Special aspects of the housing market Housing has unusual attributes that make the analysis of rent controls somewhat special. The most important is the nature of the commodity itself. So far in this book we have mainly considered markets for commodities that are consumed soon after they are purchased. But housing is an example of a DURABLE GOOD, a good that yields its services only gradually over an extended period of time. Once built, a block of flats lasts for decades or even centuries, yielding its valuable services continuously over that time. Thus the supply of rental accommodation depends on the *stock* of rental housing available, and in any year it is composed mainly of buildings built in prior years. The stock is added to by conversions of housing from other uses and construction of new buildings, and it is diminished by conversions to other uses and demolition or abandonment of existing buildings whose economic life is over. The stock usually changes slowly from year to year.

These considerations mean we can draw more than one supply curve for rental accommodation, depending on how much time is allowed for reactions to occur to any given level of rents. We shall distinguish just two such curves. The *long-run supply curve* relates rents to the quantity of rental

---

[1] For a discussion of rent controls in Britain, see Harbury and Lipsey, op. cit., Chapter 6.

accommodation that will be supplied after sufficient time has passed for all adjustments to be made. The *short-run supply curve* relates rents to quantity supplied when only a short time – say, a few months – is allowed for immediate adjustments to be made in response to a change in rents. In the short run very few new conversions and very little new construction can occur.

The long-run supply curve Among the many suppliers of rental accommodation are large investment companies and individuals with modest savings invested in one or two small houses. There is a large potential source of supply, for it is relatively easy to build a new block of flats or to convert an existing house and offer its units for rent. If the expected return from investing in new rental units rises significantly above the return on comparable other investments, there will be a flow of investment funds into the building of new flats. If the return from rental accommodation falls significantly below that obtainable on comparable investments, funds will go elsewhere. The construction of new accommodation will fall off and possibly stop altogether. Old flats will not be replaced as they wear out, so the quantity available will fall drastically. Therefore the long-run supply curve of rental accommodation is highly *elastic*.

> **Because of the ease of entry there is a long-run tendency for the rate of profit on rental accommodation to be pushed to the rate that can be earned on similar investments elsewhere in the economy.**

In the short term there can be large profits or losses, but in the long term the tendency is for any large profits or losses to be eliminated.

Now consider the supply response over a few months. What if rents rise? Even though it immediately becomes profitable to invest in new blocks of flats, it may well take years for land to be obtained, plans drawn up, and construction completed. Thus a long time may pass between the decision to create more flats in response to changes in market signals and their occupancy by tenants. Of course some existing housing can be more quickly converted to rental uses, but in many cases even this is likely to take more than a few months.

What if rents fall? New construction will fall off, and this will surely decrease the supply at some time in the future. It will, however, pay the owners of existing accommodation with no attractive alternative use for their rental units to rent them for whatever they will earn, providing that the rentals at least cover current out-of-pocket costs such as taxes and heating. Some rental housing can be abandoned or converted to other uses, but, again, this will not usually happen very quickly. Thus the short-run supply curve that relates rentals to the quantity supplied tends to be quite *inelastic* at the level of the quantity currently supplied.

Supply response to changes in rents If rents rise, what will the supply response be? In the short run, the quantity will remain more or less the same because the short-run supply curve is inelastic. For a while existing landlords will make WINDFALL PROFITS, profits that bear no relation to current or historical costs. Yet these profits are the spur to the long-run allocation of resources. In a rush to gain some of the profits, new construction will begin. After a year or two new rental units will begin to come onto the market. The quantity will continue to expand until the housing stock is fully adjusted to the new, higher rents. At that time, a new point on the long-run supply curve will have been attained.

If rents decrease, the quantity supplied will remain more or less unchanged because of the inelastic short-run supply curve. But the profitability of supplying rental accommodation will fall, and new construction will be curtailed as a result. The time required for the current stock of housing to shrink to its new, lower equilibrium level – to its new point on the long-run supply curve – depends on the type of adjustment that leads to the long-run shrinkage in the quantity supplied. Because houses are durable, they will not quickly disappear. But owners of rental properties can speed the shrinkage in various ways.

Many rental units have alternative uses. Some can be withdrawn from the rental market and sold to owner-occupiers more or less on an 'as is' basis. Others can be converted for owner-occupancy. As soon as leases on rental units expire, conversions of this sort can begin. Even small reductions in rents may be sufficient to cause a withdrawal from the market of those flats that are suitable for conversion. Other flats occupy land with valuable alternative uses. If rents fall far enough, it will pay to demolish those buildings and use the land for something else, but it requires a substantial and long-lasting fall in rents before demolition costs are worth incurring.

Many existing blocks of flats and other rental accommodation have no real alternative uses and will continue to be rented until they are abandoned as useless. Yet the useful life of a building depends on how well it is maintained. In general, the less spent on maintenance and repairs, the shorter the structure's effective life. How much it pays landlords to spend on maintenance and repairs depends on the level of rents. The lower the rents, the less will it pay to spend on upkeep and thus the faster will the building 'wear out'.

If rental revenues fall below the minimum costs of operation (which include rates and heating), the owner may simply abandon the buildings. Blocks of flats once abandoned fall quickly to total disrepair. Although this may sound extreme, it has happened repeatedly in both America and Europe. When it happens, a stock of housing that might have lasted decades or even centuries is dissipated within a few years.

The special features of the housing market lead to an important additional prediction about rent controls.

> **Because the long-run supply curve of rental housing is highly elastic, rent controls that hold rents below their free-market levels for an extended period will inevitably lead to a large reduction in the quantity of rental housing available.**

This prediction is illustrated in Figure 10.3. The controlled rent, r_c, is below the equilibrium rent, r_1. The short-run supply of housing is the inelastic curve S_s. Thus quantity supplied remains at q_1 in the short run, and the housing shortage is $q_2 - q_1$. Over time the quantity supplied shrinks, as shown by the long-run supply curve S_L. In the long run there are only q_3 units of rental accommodation, far fewer than when controls were instituted. Since the long-run supply is quite elastic, the housing shortage of $q_2 - q_3$, that occurs after supply has fully adjusted, ends up being much larger than the initial shortage of $q_2 - q_1$.

The demand for rental accommodation There are many reasons to expect the demand for rental accommodation to be quite elastic. As rents rise, each of the following will occur:
(1) some people will stop renting and will buy instead;
(2) some will move to where rental accommodation is cheaper;
(3) some will economize on the amount of housing they consume by renting smaller, cheaper accommodation (or renting out a room or two in their present accommodation);

(4) some will double up and others will not 'undouble' (for example, young adults will not move out of parental homes as quickly as they might otherwise have done).

Such behaviour contributes to a substantial elasticity of the demand for rental housing: increases in rents will significantly decrease the quantity demanded.

Rent controls prevent such increases in rents from occurring. Thus, even while the supply of rental housing is shrinking for the reasons discussed above, the signal to economize on rental accommodation is *not* given through rising rents. The housing shortage grows as the stock of rental accommodation shrinks while nothing decreases the demand for it.

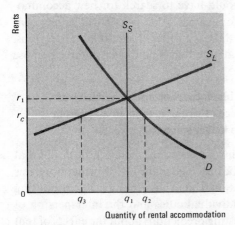

Fig. 10.3 Effects of rent control in the short and long run

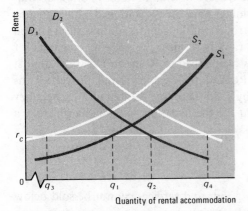

Fig. 10.4 An ever-growing housing shortage

Inflation in housing costs Rent controls are often introduced to protect tenants from rent increases in an inflationary world. Inflation raises both the costs of construction of new housing and the costs of operating and maintaining existing housing. As we saw in Chapter 7, a rise in costs shifts the supply curve upward and to the left.

Fixed-rent controls in an economy that is experiencing a steady inflation will produce a housing shortage that grows over time. If inflation is combined with growth in demand, the growth in the housing shortage becomes very large.

This is shown in Figure 10.4. The rise in everyone's income consequent on the inflation means that people are prepared to pay more to buy the same quantity of each commodity: the demand curve shifts rightward. But the supply curve is continually shifting leftward because construction, maintenance and operating costs are rising. Such shifts when combined with rent controls cause the housing shortage to grow over time. For example, when the curves are D_1 and S_1, rent control at r_c is accompanied by a housing shortage of q_2-q_1. When the curves have shifted to D_2 and S_2, however, the same controlled rent causes an overall housing shortage of q_4-q_3.

The growing housing shortage then puts pressure on the state to build the accommodation that private investors will not supply at controlled rents. The shortage will also make people who do have rent-controlled housing reluctant to move, since they would have to search for new accommodation under conditions of severe shortage. This means, for example, that people will be reluctant to move from areas of high unemployment to areas where there is a better chance of obtaining jobs, and that people will be reluctant to move out of accommodation that is no longer suitable because families have grown up and moved away.

Effective rent control leads to housing shortages, black-market prices, security-of-tenure laws, pressure for public housing and reluctance of sitting tenants to move from their present accommodations even when these are no longer suitable.

Although there is debate on the desirability of rent-control legislation, there is little doubt that the above are among its major consequences. They can all be observed in the UK. Furthermore, it is well established that areas with effective rent control legislation tend to have the most severe housing shortages. In the US, rent control is in the hands of individual cities and the interspersing of controlled and uncontrolled markets for housing makes testing predictions about the effects of rent control relatively easy. For example, rent control in the Queens borough of New York is accompanied by severe housing shortages; whole blocks of buildings have been abandoned, although they would probably have lasted centuries with care. Uncontrolled markets in the southwestern United States, on the other hand, have seen supplies increase rapidly to meet the growing demands for housing as population moved there. Rent control was introduced in Rome in 1978 and almost immediately increased the shortage of accommodation. Rent control over lower-rent properties was introduced in many Canadian provinces in 1975, and by 1980 there was enough of a discrepancy between the free-market and the controlled prices that for the first time in Canadian history a persistent housing shortage developed.

Minimum-price legislation

Governments sometimes pass laws stating that certain goods and services cannot be sold below some stated minimum price. In many Western countries today there are minimum-wage laws specifying 'floors' for the wages to be paid to different kinds of labour. Resale price maintenance, which exists in many countries, gives the manufacturer power to prevent the retailer from selling below prices set by the manufacturer. Before reading on, see if you can work out for yourself what our theory predicts about the effects of minimum-price laws.

The effects on price and quantity   The case of a commodity subject to minimum-price legislation is illustrated in Figure 10.5. The free-market equilibrium price is p_1, and the equilibrium quantity traded is q_1. If the minimum price is set below the equilibrium price, it has no effect on the market.

The attainment of the free-market equilibrium and the fulfilment of the minimum-price law are perfectly compatible. On the other hand, if the minimum price is set above the equilibrium, say at p_2, the free-market equilibrium will be legally unobtainable. At price p_2 there will be an excess of quantity supplied over quantity demanded. Suppliers would like to sell q_3, but purchasers are only willing to buy q_2. The actual amount bought and sold will thus be q_2 and there will be excess supply of $q_3 - q_2$. This leads to our first prediction about minimum prices:

The setting of minimum prices either will have no effect (minimum prices set at or below the equilibrium) or will cause a surplus of the commodity (minimum price set above the equilibrium), reducing the quantity actually bought and sold below its equilibrium value.

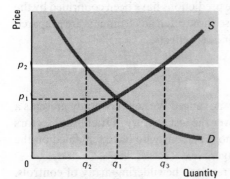

Fig. 10.5 Minimum-price controls

No alternative allocation systems and no black markets In this case there is, at the legally enforced price, no scarcity of the controlled commodity. Therefore we do not predict that alternate allocative systems will grow up. There will, however, be a shortage of purchasers, and potential suppliers may compete in various ways for the available customers. Methods of price cutting will be searched for; some will find loopholes in the law and some will merely flout it. For example, travel clubs and other organizations grew up rapidly in the early 1970s in order to take advantage of cheap group rates which the scheduled airlines are not legally allowed to offer individual passengers.

There will be no opportunity for black-market operators to take over the distribution of the product, since they would lose money by buying at the controlled price and selling at the free-market price. There will, however, be an incentive for an individual producer to sell his product at less than the controlled price as long as his only alternative is not to sell it at all. Thus we predict:

Effective minimum-price laws will not give rise to alternative allocation systems or to organized black markets, but will be accompanied by some clandestine selling by individual producers at prices below the legal minimum.

Empirical evidence In the next section of this chapter we shall see that the setting of minimum prices in the agricultural sector of the economy has led, just as the theory predicts, to an excess of quantity supplied over quantity demanded. Governments responsible for these minimum prices have found embarrassing surpluses of unsold agricultural goods piling up in their warehouses, surpluses that cannot be sold at the legislated minimum prices.

In Chapter 33 we extend the analysis to cover minimum-wage legislation. There we find that the predicted surpluses take the form of unemployed labour that cannot find employment at the minimum wage and that is prevented by law from accepting employment at a lower wage that would eliminate the excess supply.

In other cases such as government-sanctioned producers' associations that set minimum prices above the competitive level, the surplus is prevented from developing by assigning each producer a quota. In this way the association seeks to limit quantity supplied to no more than the quantity demanded at the controlled minimum price. OPEC functions in this way and IATA is not too dissimilar from this model. Such producers' associations are further discussed in Chapter 22.

Conclusion It is remarkable how many predictions our simple theory yields about the effects of minimum and maximum price controls, and how often these predictions have been confirmed by the evidence. It is also interesting, and not a little depressing, to see how often governments are prepared to pass price-control laws without appearing to foresee their likely effects.

The problems of agriculture[1]

To the casual observer, the agricultural sector of almost any advanced Western economy presents a series of paradoxes. Food is a basic necessity of life. Yet, over the last century, agricultural sectors have been declining in relative importance, and many of those persons who have remained on the land have been receiving incomes well below national averages.

Governments have felt it necessary to intervene. As a result, a bewildering array of controls, supports and subsidies has been built into agricultural markets. Subsidies and price floors have led to the accumulation of vast government surpluses which have sometimes rotted in their storage bins and sometimes been sold abroad at prices well below their costs of production. All of this has gone on against a backdrop of endemic malnutrition and occasional outbursts of famine in the 'Third World'. Why has agriculture so often been a problem industry in the past? Is it possible that it may cease to be one in the near future?

Short-term fluctuations in prices and incomes

Agricultural production is subject to large variations due to factors completely beyond human control: lack of rainfall, invasion of pests, floods and other natural events are all capable of reducing output to a level well below that planned by farmers, while exceptionally favourable conditions can cause production to be well above the planned level. We may now ask what our theory of price predicts about the effect of these unplanned fluctuations.

A supply curve is meant to show desired output and sales at each market price. If there are unplanned variations in output, then actual output and sales will diverge from their planned level. The supply curve drawn in Figure 10.6 shows the total quantity farmers desire to produce and offer for sale at various prices. Two demand curves are drawn in Figure 10.6, one is relatively elastic (D_e) and the other is relatively inelastic (D_i) over the quantity range from q_2 to q_3. In a world in which plans were always fulfilled, price would settle at the equilibrium level of p_1 with output q_1. But unplanned fluctuations in output will cause the actual price to fluctuate. If, for example, the crop is

_____
[1] For a discussion of British agricultural policy, see Harbury and Lipsey, op. cit., Chapters 1 and 6.

poor so that the actual production is q_2, then a shortage will develop; prices will rise to p_2 in the case of demand curve D_i, and p'_2 in the case of curve D_e. In each case the quantity demanded will be reduced to a point at which it is equal to the available supply. If, on the other hand, growing conditions are particularly favourable, actual production will exceed planned production, a surplus will occur and price will fall. For example, when production is q_3, price will fall to p_3 in the case of curve D_i and to p'_3 in the case of curve D_e. In each case the fall in price will increase the quantity demanded sufficiently to absorb the extra unplanned supply, but the fall in price will be larger when the demand curve is D_i than when it is D_e.

We have now derived the following prediction:

Unplanned fluctuations in output will cause price variations in the opposite direction (the higher the output, the lower the price); for given output fluctuations, the smaller the elasticity of demand for the product, the larger the price variations.

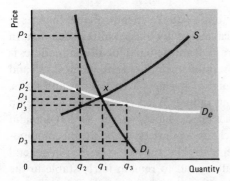

Fig. 10.6 Fluctuations in price caused by unplanned fluctuations in supply operating on elastic and inelastic demand curves

Now consider the effects on the revenues received by farmers from the sale of their crops.[1] Here the relations are a bit more complex, but they all follow immediately from the results established on page 103. If the good in question has an elasticity of demand greater than unity, then unplanned increases in supply raise farmers' revenues while unplanned decreases lower them. If, on the other hand, the good has an inelastic demand, consumers' total expenditure on the product, and thus farmers' revenues, will rise when price rises and fall when price falls. Thus, good harvests will bring reductions in total farm revenues, while bad harvests will bring increases in farm revenues![2] If the elasticity happens to be unity, then farmers' revenues will not vary as output and prices vary because every change in output will be met by an exactly compensating change in price so that total expenditure remains constant.

Unplanned variations in output will cause producers' sales revenue:
(1) to vary in the same direction as output varies whenever demand for the product is elastic;

---

[1] While we can only make predictions in this section about the revenues, such receipts are closely related to the incomes of farmers. We can, therefore, without risk of serious error, extend these predictions to incomes.

[2] It does not follow that every individual farmer's income must rise (after all, some farmers may have nothing to harvest); it follows only that the aggregate revenue earned by *all* farmers must rise.

(2) to vary in the opposite direction as output varies whenever demand for the product is inelastic;

(3) to fluctuate more the further does the elasticity of demand diverge from unity in either direction.

Unplanned fluctuations in output occur frequently in agriculture. Where the prices of the products are left to be determined by the free market, large price fluctuations do result. In the case of many agricultural goods, the demand is quite inelastic. In these cases we find very large price fluctuations together with the surprising situation that when nature is unexpectedly kind and produces a bumper crop, farmers see their incomes dwindling, while when nature is moderately unkind so that supplies fall unexpectedly, farmers' incomes rise. The interests of the farmer and those of the consumer then appear to be exactly opposed.

Cyclical fluctuations in prices and incomes

Agricultural markets are subject not only to short-run instabilities due to uncontrollable changes in output, but also, like most raw materials markets, to cyclical instability due to shifts in demand. In periods of prosperity, full employment prevails, incomes are high and demand for all commodities is high. In periods of depressed business activity, there is substantial unemployment, incomes fall and demand for most commodities falls as a result. As the pulse of business activity ebbs and flows, we thus find demand curves for all commodities rising and falling. What effect will this have on commodity prices? Industrial products typically have rather elastic supply curves, so that demand shifts cause fairly large changes in outputs but only small changes in prices. Agricultural commodities tend to have rather inelastic supplies. Thus, when demand falls due to a recession in general business activity, prices tend to fall drastically in agriculture but to remain fairly stable in the manufacturing sector. In both cases revenues fluctuate cyclically. When demand falls and the supply is very inelastic, revenue falls because *price* falls a great deal; when demand falls and the supply is very elastic, revenue falls because *quantity* falls a great deal.

Agricultural stabilization programmes

In free-market economies, agricultural incomes often tend to fluctuate around a low *average* level. Agricultural stabilization programmes have two goals: to reduce the fluctuations and to raise the average level of farm incomes. The two goals, stable incomes and reasonably high incomes, as we shall see, often conflict. We shall illustrate the working of stabilization schemes to lessen the effects of unplanned fluctuations in supply. A similar analysis could be carried out for policies to lessen the effects of cyclical fluctuations in demand.

Market fluctuations due to unplanned fluctuations in output Figure 10.7 duplicates the planned supply curve and the demand curve D_i from Figure 10.6. When plans are fulfilled, equilibrium price and quantity are p_1 and q_1. But unplanned fluctuations in output between q_2 and q_3 cause price to vary over the range from p_2 to p_3. In this analysis we shall make the simplifying assumption that planned production remains at q_1 and actual output varies only because of unplanned fluctuations. In the Appendix to Chapter 10 we shall reconsider this example, allowing planned production to change in response to changes in market price.

Market stabilization by a producers' association   One method of preventing fluctuations in prices and incomes is for the individual farmers to form a producers' association which tries to even out the supply actually coming on to the market, in spite of variations in production. Since one firm's output is a very insignificant part of total production, it would be futile for an individual firm to hold some of its production off the market in an effort to force up the price. This behaviour would only reduce the firm's own income without having any appreciable effect on price. But if many firms get together and agree to vary the supply coming on to the market, then collectively they can have a major effect on price.

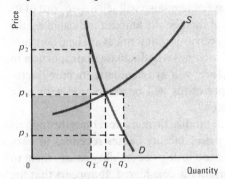

Fig. 10.7 Policies designed to stabilize price in the face of unplanned fluctuations in supply

Under the conditions illustrated by Figure 10.7, a producers' association might be quite successful in keeping the price at p_1 and incomes at the level indicated by the dark and light shaded areas indicating a revenue of p_1 times q_1. Any excess of production over q_1 would have to be stored away unsold. If, for example, production for one year were q_3, then $q_3 - q_1$ would have to be added to the association's stocks while q_1 was sold at price p_1. Any deficiency of production below q_1, on the other hand, would have to be made good by sales out of the association's stocks. If production were q_2, for example, then $q_1 - q_2$ would be sold out of stocks, making total sales again equal to q_1 at a price of p_1. In this way the producers' association could keep sales, price and incomes stabilized at q_1, p_1 and q_1p_1 respectively, in spite of fluctuations in production.

Provided that the level of sales to be maintained (q_1 in Figure 10.7) was equal to average production, the policy could be carried on indefinitely. If, however, the producers attempted to keep the price too high, so that sales were continually less than average production, then, taken over a number of years, additions to stocks would exceed sales from stocks, and the stocks held by the association would tend to increase.

Market stabilization by government sales and purchases   What will happen if a producers' association is not formed, but the government attempts to stabilize the incomes of farmers by entering the market itself, buying and adding to its own stocks when there is a surplus, and selling from its stocks when there is a shortage? If the government wishes to stabilize farmers' incomes, what policy should it adopt? Should it aim, like the producers' association, at keeping prices constant at all times?

Before reading further, attempt to work out for yourself the consequences of a government policy designed to keep price fixed at level p_1 in Figure 10.7 by buying goods when production is in excess of q_1 and selling goods when production falls short of q_1. The government is assumed not to consume any of the commodity but only to hold stocks.

If the average level of production around which the year-to-year figure fluctuates is q_1, then there is no reason why the government should not successfully stabilize the price at p_1 indefinitely. This policy will not, however, have the result of stabilizing farmers' incomes. Farmers will now be faced with an infinitely elastic demand at price p_1: whatever the total quantity produced, they will be able to sell it at price p_1; if the public will not buy all the production, then the government will purchase what is left over. If total production is q_3, then q_1 will be bought by the public and $q_3 - q_1$ by the government. Total farm income in this case will be the amount indicated by the two shaded areas and the white area (the quantity q_3 multiplied by the price p_1). If total production in another year is only q_2, then this quantity will be sold by farmers and the government also will sell $q_1 - q_2$ out of its stocks so that price will remain at p_1. Total farm income will then be the amount indicated by the dark shaded area (quantity q_2 multiplied by the price p_1). It is obvious that if prices are held constant and farmers sell their whole production each year, farmers' incomes will fluctuate in proportion to fluctuations in production. This government policy, therefore, will not eliminate income fluctuations but will simply reverse their direction. Now bumper crops will be associated with high incomes, while small crops will be associated with low incomes.

What, then, must a government's policy be if it wishes to stabilize farmers' revenues through its own purchases and sales in the open market? Too much price stability causes revenues to vary directly with production, as in the case just considered, while too little price stability causes them to vary inversely with production, as in the free-market case originally considered. It appears that the government should aim at some intermediate degree of price stability. In fact, if it allows prices to vary in inverse proportion to variations in production, revenues will be stabilized. A 10 per cent rise in production should be met by a 10 per cent fall in price, and a 10 per cent fall in production by a 10 per cent rise in price.

Each year farmers sell their whole crop. When production unexpectedly exceeds normal output, the government enters the market and buys enough to prevent price from tumbling. Instead it allows price to fall only by the same proportion that production has increased above normal. When production unexpectedly falls short of normal output, the government enters the market and sells enough to prevent price from soaring. Instead, it allows price to rise only by the same proportion that production has fallen below normal. Thus as farmers encounter unplanned fluctuations in their output, they encounter exactly offsetting fluctuations in prices so that their revenues are stabilized.

If this policy is successful, it will have the following results. First, there will be smaller fluctuations in the price of this product than if price were determined on a completely free market. Second, total revenues of the producers will be stabilized in the face of fluctuations in production. Finally, the government scheme should be self-financing. In fact, if we ignore costs of storage, the scheme will show a profit, for the government will be buying at low prices (below p_1) – the lower the price the more it buys – and selling at high prices (above p_1) – the higher the price, the more it sells. This scheme has a financial advantage over the previous one in which the government completely stabilized prices. In that case there would necessarily be a loss, for all purchases and sales would be made at the same price, p_1, and there would be no trading profit to set against the costs of storage.

Problems with stabilization policies

The above analysis illustrates some of the many types of stabilization schemes and shows how the theory of price can be used to predict their consequences. If such schemes have all of the advantages outlined above, why is it that there is so much trouble with most actual stabilization programmes?

Choosing the proper price   One of the major problems arises from uncertainty, combined with political pressure applied by farmers. Demand and supply curves are never known exactly, so the central authorities do not know what the average production will be over a number of years at each possible price. They do not know, therefore, exactly what level of income they can try to achieve while also keeping sales from stocks equal to purchases for stocks on average over a large number of years. Since farmers have votes, there is strong pressure on any government to be over-generous. If the price, and hence the level of income, is fixed too high, then the central authorities will have to buy unsold crops in most years. Thus, stocks will build up more or less continuously and, sooner or later, they will have to be destroyed, given away, or dumped on the market for what they will bring, thus forcing the market price down, defeating the purpose for which the crops were originally purchased.

The authorities' plan will now show a deficit, for goods will have been purchased which cannot be sold at all. This deficit will have to be covered by taxation, which means that people in cities will be paying farmers for producing goods which are never consumed. The next step is often to try to limit the production of each farmer. Quotas may be assigned to individual farmers and penalties imposed for exceeding them, or bonuses may be paid for leaving land idle. Such measures attempt to get around the problem that too many resources are allocated to the agricultural sector by preventing these resources from producing all that they could.

> **Government policies that stabilize prices at too high a level will cause excess supply, a rising level of unsold stocks, and pressure for further government intervention to restrict output.**

The long-term problem of resource reallocation   Even if the temptation to set too high a price is avoided, there is still a formidable problem facing the managers of agricultural-stabilization programmes. It results from the fact that the productive capacity of almost all economies is growing over time. Owing to better health, better working conditions, and more and better capital equipment, each worker can produce more than he or she previously did. In the United Kingdom, the increase in *per capita* production has averaged almost 2 per cent a year over the last hundred years. If the allocation of resources were to remain unchanged, there would be an increase in the output of each commodity in proportion to the increase in productivity in that industry.

The real incomes of the population will also increase, on average at a rate equal to the production increase. How will the people wish to consume their extra income? The relevant measure in this case is the income elasticity of demand, which measures the effect of increases in income on the demands for various commodities. Only if all commodities had unit income elasticities of demand would the proportions in which commodities are demanded not change as income changed: in this special case an *x* per cent rise in income would lead to an *x* per cent rise in the demand for every commodity.

Assume that productivity expands more or less uniformly in all industries. The demand for commodities with low income elasticities will be expanding slower than the supplies; excess supplies will develop, prices and profits will be depressed, and it will be necessary for resources to move out of these industries. Exactly the reverse will happen for commodities with high income elasticities: demand will expand faster than supply, prices and profits will tend to rise, and resources will move

Table 10.1 Surpluses and shortages resulting from uniform increases in productivity and differing income elasticities of demand

	Agriculture	Manufacturing
Production originally was	50·0	50·0
Production after productivity change, if there were no reallocation of resources, would be	100·0	100·0
Income elasticity of demand is	0·50	1·5
Therefore quantity demanded after rise in income is	75·0	125·0
Therefore surplus or shortage is	25·0 (surplus)	25·0 (shortage)

into those industries. Table 10.1 illustrates this. It gives a simple numerical example of an economy divided into an agricultural and a manufacturing sector. Originally, resources are divided equally between the two. Productivity then doubles in both sectors. The incomes of all consumers double and the income elasticity of demand for manufactured goods is higher than the income elasticity of demand for agricultural goods. The rise in productivity causes a surplus equal to one-quarter of the agricultural production, and a shortage equal to one-quarter of the manufactured-goods production. With continuous productivity increases, there will be a *continuous tendency* toward excess supply of agricultural goods and excess demand for manufactured goods. Thus a continuous movement of resources out of agriculture and into the manufacturing industries will be needed.

In a free-market economy, this reallocation will take place under the incentives of low prices, wages and incomes in the declining sector, and high prices, wages and incomes in the expanding sector. Look at Table 10.1 again. Because there is excess supply in the agricultural sector, prices will fall and incomes of producers will fall. There will be a decline in the demand for farm labour and the other factors of production used in agriculture, and the earnings of these factors will decline. At the same time, exactly the opposite tendencies will be observed in manufacturing. Here demand is expanding faster than supply; prices will rise; incomes and profits of producers will be rising. There will be a large demand for the factors of production used in manufacturing industries, so that the price of these factors, and consequently the incomes that they earn, will be bid upward. In short, manufacturing will be a buoyant, expanding industry and agriculture will be a depressed, contracting industry.

> **In a free-market society, the mechanism for a continued reallocation of resources out of low-income-elasticity industries and into high-income-elasticity ones is a continued depressing tendency of prices and incomes in contracting industries, and a continued buoyant tendency of prices and incomes in expanding industries.**

Stablization schemes that guarantee a 'reasonable' income to farmers provide no incentives for resources to transfer out of the agricultural sector. Unless some other means is found to persuade resourcess to transfer, a larger and larger proportion of the resources in agriculture will become redundant since productivity growth will be raising quantity supplied faster than income growth is raising quantity demanded. If, however, the government does not intervene at all, leaving the price mechanism to accomplish the resource reallocation, it will be faced with the problem of a more or less permanently depressed sector of the community.

Economics cannot prove that governments ought or ought not to interfere with the price mechanism. Such a conclusion cannot be *proved*; it is a *judgement*, which depends on a valuation of the risks of such intervention. Positive economics, by providing some insight into the workings of the price mechanism, can be used to predict some of the gains and losses, and to point out problems that must be solved if intervention is to be successful.

> **If the problem of reallocating resources out of the rural sector is not solved, intervention to secure high and stable levels of farm incomes will be unccessful over any long period of time. It will give rise to a characteristic, and predictable, set of problems that will eventually defeat the original purposes of the schemes.**

A better future for agriculture?

Throughout the 1950s and 1960s the agricultural sectors of Western European and North American economies showed ample behaviour confirming the predictions developed above. Subsidies and price supports led to over-production and ever-growing surpluses that strained government warehouses everywhere to overflowing. Then, however, came a very significant change. Throughout the 1970s, the demands for many of the agricultural products produced by advanced Western countries have soared. A few of the most important reasons may be mentioned.

First, the world population explosion has reached dramatic proportions, adding in a matter of decades thousands of millions of new mouths to feed. Second, agricultural production, particularly of grains, has been disappointingly low in the USSR and other countries of the Eastern bloc. A major cause has been a failure of their system of collectivized agriculture to produce anything like the rate of growth of output that the farmers of Western countries have achieved. As a result, the 1970s and 1980s have seen massive sales of Western output to Eastern countries. Third, although the income elasticities of demand for many foodstuffs are low in advanced Western countries, they remain quite high for meat in general, and for beef in particular.[1]

For these and other reasons, the chronic excess supply and rising stocks of unsold output that characterized Western agriculture in the 1950s and 1960s are much abated. The United States, the leading supplier of food exports for the rest of the world, had stopped its payments to farmers for keeping land out of production, and has brought nearly all of its idle crop land back into production. For that nation, then, three decades of agricultural surpluses, which grew to seemingly unmanageable proportions, have given way to several years of excess demand.

The rising world demand has certainly helped European agriculture but it has not yet allowed it to exist in its present form without major subsidies. The subsidization programme at a high level of income not only inhibits the transfer of resources out of agriculture (as analysed above), it also protects high-cost, small-scale farming which, since the abandonment of American farm supports, has given way in the USA to lower-cost, large-scale farming. As a result, the EEC common agricultural policy still involves very large transfers of income from urban taxpayers to subsidized

---

[1] Meat is a technically inefficient way of turning grain into calories for human consumption. Grain may be used as food directly, by making it into such commodities as bread and breakfast cereal, or it may be used indirectly by feeding it to cattle that are then consumed as meat. The indirect method requires several times as much grain as the direct method to produce a calorie consumed by a human being. This means that even if the total calories consumed per person does not rise with income, the switch from farinaceous products to meat that commonly accompanies a rise in income produces a very large rise in the demand for grains.

farmers. Because the UK is the most urbanized of the EEC countries the inter-sectoral transfers become in its case an international transfer. British taxpayers pay large sums to subsidize farmers in continental Europe. This source of serious EEC conflict in the 1980s was easily predicted by price theory well before the UK entered the Common Market.

Whether its predictions are gloomy or cheerful, welcome or unwelcome, it is clear that the theory of price in competitive markets is a remarkable tool for explaining much of what we see in the world around us and for predicting in advance the effects of many changes, whether natural or policy induced.[1]

---

[1] For a discussion of EEC agricultural policy, see Harbury and Lipsey, op. cit., Chapter 5.

Appendix to chapter 10

The elementary dynamic theory of price

Statics and dynamics

All the predictions derived in previous chapters have one characteristic in common. They are derived by comparing the new equilibrium position with the original equilibrium position. A moment's reflection will show that this has been the method of analysis used throughout all of the previous chapters. To form a hypothesis about the effect of some change in the data – for example, the introduction of a tax or a change in the conditions of demand – we start from a position of equilibrium and then introduce the change to be studied. The new equilibrium position is determined and compared with the original one; we therefore know that the differences between the two are due to the change that was introduced. This kind of analysis, based on a comparison of two positions of equilibrium, is called COMPARATIVE STATIC EQUILIBRIUM ANALYSIS – a rather cumbersome expression usually abbreviated to COMPARATIVE STATICS.

Comparative statics is useful but it cannot be used to handle two important classes of problems. It cannot predict the path followed from one equilibrium to another, and it cannot predict whether or not a given equilibrium will ever be attained. In many cases we are not interested so much in the position of equilibrium as in how the market behaves when it is out of equilibrium. For these purposes we require DYNAMIC ANALYSIS, which may be defined as the study of the behaviour of systems (single markets or whole economies) in states of disequilibrium.

Agricultural price fluctuations

In the previous chapter, we applied comparative statics to a simple case of agricultural price fluctuations. In that example planned production was constant and price fluctuations were caused by unplanned changes in supply. After each change there was time for the price to settle at its new equilibrium level, well before supply was subject to another unplanned change. The price fluctuations could thus be viewed as a series of movements between successive equilibrium positions, each one equating the current supply with demand.

Many agricultural markets exhibit regular oscillations in price which cannot be accounted for by unplanned shifts in supply. In such markets there is definite evidence that the fluctuations in price result from *planned* fluctuations in farmers' output that follow a definite cyclical pattern. This phenomenon requires explanation, and the explanation lies, as we shall see, in the observation that all decisions take some time to implement, and some decisions take a very long time.

Supply lags

The supply curve relates the price of the commodity to the quantity producers wish to sell. If price changes, they will want to sell a different quantity. But a change in price causes a *desired* change in quantity supplied. Only after sufficient time has elapsed to give effect to decisions to change supply, will there be a change in actual quantity supplied. The delay between the decision to do something and its actually being done is called a TIME LAG. The delay between the decision to change quantity supplied and its actually being changed is called a SUPPLY LAG.

> **Output currently coming onto the market is the result of production decisions taken in the past, while current production decisions will not have their effect on quantity supplied until some time in the future.**

Time lags are of two sorts. In one, the full adjustment occurs instantaneously but only after a lapse of time. For instance, the decision to double output may take a year to implement, but at the end of the year production may suddenly be doubled. In such a case we refer to a DISCRETE LAG. In the other kind of time lag the adjustment is spread over time. For instance, the decision to double output may give rise to a 10 per cent increase in output for each subsequent month until the rate is finally doubled ten months later. In this case we refer to a DISTRIBUTED LAG.

Every commodity has its own characteristic supply lag, and many are quite complex. Consider an example. An increase in the demand for raw milk can be met to some extent almost immediately by diverting milk from other uses; to a greater extent within 27 months by not slaughtering calves at birth but allowing them to reach maturity; and to an ever-increasing extent over the long term by allowing the larger population of adult cows to give birth to a larger number of calves. This gives rise to a complex distributed lag.

Often in agriculture the time interval between successive crops is the major factor determining the supply lag. A simple lag occurs when this year's price has no effect whatsoever on this year's supply. Farmers look to the existing market price when deciding what crops to plant, and thus *next year's* supply depends on *this year's* price, while this year's supply depends on last year's price. This gives a discrete time lag of one year in the adjustment of quantity supplied to a change in price.[1]

> **When supply lags are unimportant, comparative statics will successfully predict market behaviour. When supply lags exert an important influence, many aspects of market behaviour will require dynamics for their analysis.**

Agricultural markets tend to have rather long supply lags. Comparative statics is nonetheless useful in analysing the long-term behaviour of such markets. For example, the secular upward trend in the amount of beef production and in the amount of land devoted to growing grain for cattlefeed can be understood in comparative static terms. Each decade income is higher than in the previous decade. Given the high income elasticity of demand of beef, the demand curves for beef and for feed-grain can be seen as shifting rightwards decade by decade. Thus we would expect the quantities of beef and grain and their prices (relative to other prices) to be rising

decade by decade. This is what has in fact been happening.

Large cyclical ups and downs in cattle prices and production have, however, been superimposed on this upward secular trend. These cyclical movements, particularly when they take prices temporarily to unusually high levels, loom large in newspaper reports and popular discussion. To understand them, we need to take account of supply lags and use at least some elementary dynamic theory.

The cobweb theory

We shall now introduce an elementary dynamic theory. We assume that producers' output plans are fulfilled, but with a time lag, and then show how *planned* changes in supply can give rise to oscillations. We shall consider only the simplest possible time lag: this year's price has no effect whatsoever on this year's supply, the full adjustment to this year's price being made all at once next year. We have already seen that such lags are typical of many agricultural products that give one crop annually, such as wheat, oats and barley.

Markets subject to simple one-year time lags are illustrated in Figures 10.8 and 10.9. Look first at Figure 10.8. The demand curve shows the relation

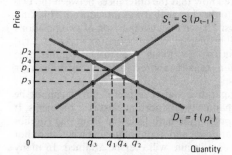

Fig. 10.8 A stable cobweb

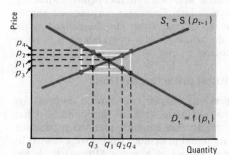

Fig. 10.9 An unstable cobweb

---

[1] In the terminology of the Appendix to Chapter 2 (page 28) we may write $S_t = S(p_{t-1})$, which reads: supply at time period t depends on (i.e., is a function of) the price ruling in the previous time period, $t-1$, where time periods are measured in years.

between the price ruling in any year and the quantity that will be demanded in the same year; the supply curve shows the relation between the price ruling in any year and the quantity that will be supplied to the market in the following year. The price that equates demand and supply is p_1. At this price q_1 units will be produced and sold.

What will happen if this equilibrium is disturbed by, for example, a temporary fluctuation in either of the curves? If in one year, year t, the price is p_2, farmers will plan to produce q_2 in the following year. In that year, 'year $t+1$', q_2 will come on the market, and, in order that q_2 may be sold, the price will have to fall to p_3. The price of p_3 will induce farmers to produce the quantity q_3. When this quantity comes on the market in the following year, 'year $t+2$', the price will rise to p_4. This price will call forth a supply of q_4 the next year 'year $t+3$', and this will depress the price below p_4. It is clear from this that, in the market described in Figure 10.8, the price and quantity will oscillate around their equilibrium values in a series of diminishing fluctuations, so that, if nothing further disturbs the market, price and quantity will eventually approach their equilibrium values, p_1 and q_1.

Now consider the case illustrated in Figure 10.9. Exactly the same argument as in the previous paragraph applies here, and the text of that paragraph should be re-read to describe the process in this market. Notice that here, however, the last sentence of the previous paragraph does *not* apply: this time the oscillations get larger so that the equilibrium is never restored.

The market in Figure 10.8 has an adjustment mechanism which is *stable*, while Figure 10.9 has one which is *unstable*. A STABLE ADJUSTMENT MECHANISM is one which will take the market to its equilibrium; the actual price and quantity will tend towards their equilibrium values. An UNSTABLE ADJUSTMENT MECHANISM is one which will not take the market to its equilibrium; the actual price and quantity will tend away from equilibrium values. What makes one of these markets stable and the other unstable?

Given the simple supply lag that we are considering, the difference between the stable and unstable markets is in the relative slopes of the demand and supply curves. In Figure 10.8 the demand curve is flatter than the supply curve. As price changes, the absolute quantity demanded changes more than the absolute quantity supplied. Excess demand or supply can be eliminated with only a small price change, and the price change in turn causes only a very small change in supply in the following year. Hence the supply change has only a small effect on next year's

price. In Figure 10.9 the supply curve is flatter than the demand curve; the quantity supplied responds more to price changes than the quantity demanded. When there is excess supply, a large price fall is necessary to call forth the required demand. This price fall causes a large reduction in the next year's supply (because supply is very responsive to price). Next year there is a large shortage, and a very big price increase is necessary to reduce quantity demanded to the level of the available supply. This price rise causes a very large increase in quantity supplied the following year, and so it goes, in a series of alternating periods of ever-increasing surplus and shortage.

In the unstable case the oscillations increase steadily. In practice, however, the oscillations will tend to reach limits. A full theory of such a market would require an analysis of the limits, but this is beyond the scope of this book. We have, however, established the following:

Although the price system does allocate resources, it does not always cause adjustments to occur in a smooth fashion. Where supply lags are long and delayed reactions are large, fluctuations around equilibrium are possible with alternatively too much and too little being produced.

The cobweb model is a very simple theory, and more complicated lags on demand and supply are easy to imagine. Most such complications cannot, however, be handled without the help of mathematical analysis.[1] The study of the simplest cobweb model does, however, serve to introduce dynamic theory, and to illustrate its value by providing a reasonably satisfactory explanation of an interesting real-world phenomenon: the tendency toward oscillations in many agricultural markets with periods of shortages and high prices alternating with periods of surpluses and low prices for reasons that cannot be blamed on such uncontrollable factors as the weather. It also shows in a fairly dramatic way that even very simple competitive markets can show oscillatory behaviour, and may therefore require dynamic analysis rather than simply comparative statics.

---

[1] See, e.g., R.D.G. Allen, *Mathematical Economics* (Macmillan, 1966), Ch. 1.

11

Applications of price theory: international trade[1]

In this chapter we study some problems concerned with international trade and the exchange rate. We do this both for further practice in using price theory and for an introduction to some important international aspects of the economy.

An economy that engages in international trade is called an OPEN ECONOMY. One that does not is called a CLOSED ECONOMY and a situation with no international trade is called AUTARKY. In this chapter we examine the simple case of A SMALL OPEN ECONOMY, which is an economy that can exert no influence on the world prices of traded goods. The quantities that it exports and imports are small in relation to the total volume of world trade, and, therefore, changes in these quantities do not influence the prices established in world markets. For many countries and commodities, this is an empirically applicable assumption.

Because a small open economy cannot by its own actions significantly influence the prices of world traded commodities, it cannot influence the terms on which it can exchange exports for imports on the international market. These terms are called THE TERMS OF TRADE and they are defined as the quantity of domestically produced goods that must be exported in order to obtain a unit of imports. Thus the terms of trade are nothing more than the opportunity cost of obtaining goods through international trade rather than producing them at home. The terms of trade may be measured by the relation *price of imports/price of exports*. Thus if, for example, exports sell for £1·50 a unit while imports sell for £3, the terms of trade are *two*, indicating that two units of domestically produced goods had to be exported to pay for each unit of imports.[2]

The advantages of trade

In the first section of this chapter we use the production-possibility boundaries, first introduced in Chapter 4, to discuss the general nature of the gains from trade, a topic to which we return in more detail in Chapter 30.

In Chapter 5 we found that efficiency gains arise from specialization and that specialization must be accompanied by trade. This applies as much to international situations as it does within a

---

[1] For a discussion of British trading patterns and exchange-rate behaviour, see Harbury and Lipsey, *op.cit.*, Chapter 5.

[2] When there is only one export and one import, as in the illustrations used in this chapter, the measurement is simple. When there are many exports and many imports, price indices need to be used. The Note on Definitions, p. xxiii, is relevant at this point.

country. To make this idea more precise we need to define a few terms. A BUNDLE of goods is a specific amount of each of a number of goods, say, 10 apples, 5 oranges and 3 cars for one bundle and 6 apples, 9 oranges and 4 cars for a second bundle. The PRODUCTION-POSSIBILITY SET is the set of bundles of goods that could be produced by the nation's resources. Its graphical expression is the production-possibility boundary of Chapter 4. Finally the CONSUMPTION POSSIBILITY SET is the set of all possible bundles of goods that could be consumed within the country.

The key proposition about the gains from trade is that *trade expands a country's consumption-possibility set.* In autarky an economy consumes those goods, and only those goods, that it produces. By allowing the goods consumed by a nation to differ from the goods it produces, international trade actually increases the consumption possibilities open to the nation. What happens can be seen in two distinct stages.

Expansion in consumption opportunities with given production

The first stage is straightforward and is shown in part (i) of Figure 11.1, which gives a country's production-possibility boundary. In autarky the consumption-possibility set coincides with the production-possibility set. The economy must consume the same bundle of goods that it produces.

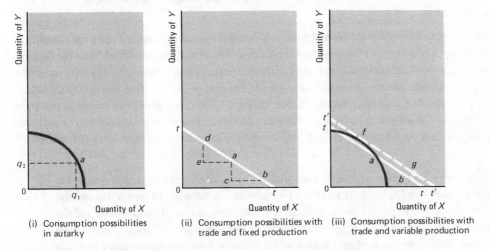

(i) Consumption possibilities in autarky

(ii) Consumption possibilities with trade and fixed production

(iii) Consumption possibilities with trade and variable production

Fig. 11.1 The effects of international trade on the consumption possibility set

For example, if production is at point *a*, consumption must also be at *a*. The bundle of goods consumed is then q_1 of good *X* and q_2 of good *Y*. When trade is allowed, a wide variety of consumption combinations is possible, *including the no-trade option*. In part (ii) of the figure, production remains fixed at point *a* but now the possibility of international trade means that consumption need not be at point *a*. Good *Y* can be exchanged for good *X* in the international market. The consumption-possibility set is now shown by the line *tt* drawn through *a*. The slope of this line indicates the world terms of trade expressed as the *price of good X/price of good Y*. This tells us the quantity of *Y* that exchanges for (i.e. has the same value as) a unit of *X* on the international market.

Although production is fixed at *a*, consumption can now be anywhere on the line *tt*. For example, the consumption point could be taken to b by exporting ac units of Y and importing cb units of X. Consumption could also be taken to point d by importing ed units of Y and exporting ae units of X.

Expansion in consumption opportunities with variable production

So far we have held production constant at a. The second reason for the expansion of the consumption-possibility set is that, with trade, the production bundle may be altered in response to international prices. This is illustrated in part (iii) of the figure. The consumption possibility set is shifted to the line $t't'$ by changing production from a to f and thereby increasing the country's degree of specialization in good Y. For any point on the original consumption-possibility set, tt, there are points on the new set, $t't'$, which allow more consumption of both goods. Compare, for example, points b and g. Notice also that, except at the zero-trade point f, the new consumption-possibility set lies everywhere above the production-possibility curve. Consumption bundles that cannot be produced domestically are made available by trade.

Summary of sources of expansion of consumption possibilities through international trade

We have just seen that international trade leads to an expansion of the set of goods that could be consumed in the economy by (1) allowing the bundle of goods consumed to differ from the bundle produced, and (2) permitting a profitable change in the pattern of production. The key to these gains is that international trade allows the separation of production decisions from consumption decisions. Without the possibility of international trade, the choice of which bundle of goods to produce is the same thing as the choice of which bundle to consume. With the possibility of trade, the production bundle can be altered to reflect the relative value placed on goods by international markets.

> **For a country with a given production-possibility curve, international trade expands the consumption-possibility set beyond that which prevails in autarky. In an open economy, the consumption of imported goods exceeds domestic production of those goods and the production of exported goods exceeds domestic consumption of those goods. The expansion of consumption opportunities arises directly from the opportunity to trade and indirectly from the opportunity to specialize in production.**

In Figure 11.1 the movement from (i) to (ii) corresponds to the direct gain and the movement from (ii) to (iii) corresponds to the indirect gain.[1]

The indirect gain arises from appropriate specialization in production. In our example, the economy expands its consumption opportunities by increasing the production of good Y and decreasing the production of good X, taking production from point a to point f in part (iii). Economists often refer to such production changes as exploiting the country's comparative ad-

---

[1] In Figure 11.1 we consider only situations of *balanced trade* – where the value of goods imported is exactly matched by the value of goods exported. (Later, we consider situations of unbalanced trade, where differences between the value of exports and imports gives rise to a transfer of a financial claim on one economy to the other.)

vantage. The benefits that arise in moving from the autarky position at point *a* in Figure 11.1(i) to the trading position in part (iii) are called the GAINS FROM TRADE. These topics are taken up in more detail in Chapter 30.

The determination of imports and exports

In the second section of this chapter we use demand and supply analysis to show how the quantities of imports and exports are determined. We first divide all goods into two types. TRADEABLES are goods and services that enter into international trade. For a small open economy the prices of tradeables, whether the economy imports or exports them, are given, since they are set on international markets. NON-TRADEABLES are goods and services that are produced and sold domestically but do not enter into international trade. Their prices are set on domestic markets by domestic supply and demand and they are unaffected by market conditions for the same products in other countries.

Exports

In Figure 11.2, D_1 and S_1 give the domestic demand and supply curves for a typical exported commodity. In autarky the price will be p_a, with q_a produced and consumed at home. For a small open economy the world price is given and the country can buy or sell all that it wishes at that price. We show the world price in the figure by the white line p_w. Because the world price is higher than the autarky price, trade raises the price of this commodity. Quantity supplied increases while quantity demanded decreases, and the surplus is exported. In equilibrium at the world price of p_w, q_2 is produced, q_1 is consumed and the difference, $q_2 - q_1$, is exported.

Notice that trade raises the price of the exported good above its autarky level. Notice also that the equilibrium is no longer where quantity demanded domestically equals quantity supplied domestically; instead, the equilibrium price is the given world price and the excess of domestic quantity supplied over domestic quantity demanded is exported.

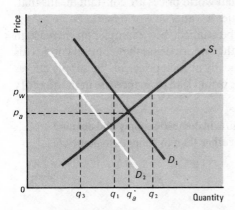

Fig. 11.2 The domestic supply and demand for a typical exported good

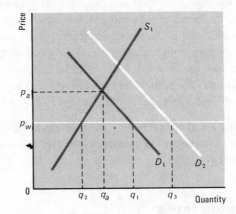

Fig. 11.3 The domestic supply and demand for a typical imported good

Imports

In Figure 11.3, D_1 and S_1 give the domestic demand and supply curves for a typical imported commodity. In autarky, the price is once again p_a with q_a being produced and consumed at home. This time, however, the world price of p_w is below the autarky price. Since the country's citizens can buy or sell all that they wish at that price no one will buy at a higher price. The introduction of foreign trade, therefore, lowers price to p_w; domestic output falls to q_2, while quantity demanded expands to q_1 with the difference, q_1-q_2, being imported.

Notice that trade lowers the price of the imported good below its autarky level. Notice also that the equilibrium is once again not where quantity demanded domestically equals quantity supplied domestically; price is given by the world price and the excess of domestic quantity demanded over domestic quantity supplied is met by imports.

> **For an open economy, equilibrium in particular markets is consistent with domestic demand for that product being different from domestic supply. If at the world price quantity demanded domestically exceeds quantity supplied domestically, the good will be imported; if quantity supplied domestically exceeds quantity demanded domestically, the good will be exported.**

Effects of changes in domestic supply and demand

Suppose that domestic residents experience a change in tastes. At the same prices, and values of other variables that influence quantity demanded, they decide to consume less of their exported good and more of their imported good. This decision is illustrated in Figure 11.2 where the demand for the exported good shifts to the left to D_2 and in Figure 11.3 where the demand for imported goods shifts to the right to D_2. At the prevailing world prices, these shifts lead to an increase in the quantity of the good that is exported and also to an increase in the quantity of the good that is imported. Exports rise to q_2-q_3 in Figure 11.2, while imports rise to q_3-q_2 in Figure 11.3.

Since the economy we are studying is assumed to be small relative to the whole world, these changes do not have a noticeable effect on world prices. The result of the shifts in demand is a change in the *quantities* of imports and exports. The assumption that world prices are constant means that, in effect, the domestic economy can buy or sell any quantities it wants on world markets.

The effects of a change in domestic supply can also be studied. For example, an increase in domestic wages would increase the cost of producing both the imported and the exported good. This would reduce the quantity that would be supplied domestically at each price, i.e. the supply curves shift upwards. The reader can verify that *ceteris paribus* this would lead to an increase in the quantity of imports and a decrease in the quantity of exports.

> **In a small open economy, other things being equal, shifts in domestic supply and demand lead to changes in quantities imported and exported rather than to changes in domestic prices.**

Exchange rates

In the final part of this chapter we deal with exchange rates. One of the major differences between international trade and trade within one country is that while different regions of the same country use the same money, different nations do not. The currency of one country is generally acceptable within the bounds of that country, but usually it will not be accepted by households and firms in another country. When a British producer sells his products he requires payment in sterling. He must meet his wage bill, pay for his raw materials, and reinvest or distribute his profits. If he sells his goods to British purchasers there is no problem, since they will pay in sterling. If, however, he sells his goods to an Indian importer, either he must accept rupees or the Indian must exchange his rupees for sterling to pay for the goods. The British producer will accept rupees only if he knows that he can exchange them for the sterling that he requires. The same is true for producers in all countries; each must eventually receive payment in the currency of his own country for the goods that he sells.

In general, trade between nations can occur only if it is possible to exchange the currency of one nation for that of another.

FOREIGN EXCHANGE refers to the actual foreign currency, or various claims on it such as cheques and promises to pay, that are traded for each other. The EXCHANGE RATE is the price at which purchases and sales of foreign currency, or claims on it, take place; it is the amount of one currency that must be paid in order to obtain one unit of another currency. For example, in the early 1980s the exchange rate between pounds sterling and American dollars was approximately £1 = $2·00, or, what is the same thing, £0·50 = $1·00. Thus one pound exchanged for two dollars, and one dollar exchanged for £0·50.

The exchange of currencies

What is the mechanism for exchanging currencies? International payments that require the exchange of one national currency for another can be made in a bewildering variety of ways, but in essence they involve the exchange of currencies between people who have one currency and require another.

Suppose an American dealer wishes to purchase a British antique to sell in the United States. The British manufacturer requires payment in sterling. If the antique is priced at, say, £2000, the American importer can go to his bank, purchase a cheque for £2,000 and send it to the British seller. Given an exchange rate of $2·00 to £1, the US importer would write a cheque on his own account for $4,000 in payment of his £2,000 sterling cheque or 'draft'. The British producer would deposit the cheque in his own bank. When all this was done, the banking system would have exchanged obligations to Americans for obligations to the residents of the UK. The deposits of the American purchaser, which are liabilities of his bank, would be reduced by $4,000 and the deposits of the British seller, which are liabilities of the British bank, would be increased by £2,000. The banking system, as a whole, makes a profit by charging a small commission for effecting such transactions.

Now consider a second transaction. Assume that a British wholesaler wishes to purchase ten American refrigerators for sale in Britain. If the refrigerators are priced at $400 each, the American seller will require a total payment of $4,000. To pay it, the British importer goes to his bank, writes a cheque on his account for £2,000 and receives a cheque drawn on a US bank for $4,000. This reduces the deposit liabilities of the British bank by £2,000. When the American seller deposits this cheque, his deposits, which are liabilities of the US banking system, are increased by $4,000. Thus the banking system as a whole has merely switched liabilities, this time from the UK to the US.

These two transactions cancel each other out, and there is no net change in international liabilities. The balance sheets of the British and the American banks will show the changes in Table 11.1. No money need flow between the banks; each merely increases the deposits of one domestic customer and lowers those of another. Indeed, as long as the flows of payments between the two countries are equal, so that Americans are paying as much to UK residents as UK residents are paying to Americans, all payments can be managed as in this example and there is no need for a net payment between the two countries.

When the flow of payments is not the same in both directions, the difference is referred to as the BALANCE OF TRADE. When exports exceed imports, a country has a TRADE SURPLUS; when imports exceed exports, it has a TRADE DEFICIT. In a later chapter we consider the problems that arise when trade is not in balance.

Table 11.1 Changes in the balance sheets of two banks

UK Bank			US Bank		
Liabilities		Assets	Liabilities		Assets
Deposits of antique exporter	+£2,000	No change	Deposits of antique importer	−$4,000	No change
Deposits of refrigerator importer	−£2,000		Deposits of refrigerator exporter	+$4,000	

The terminology of exchange rates The exchange rates between two currencies can be expressed in either of two ways. First, the number of units of domestic currency required to buy one unit of foreign currency and, second, the number of units of foreign currency required to buy one unit of domestic currency. Thus if £2 currently exchanges for $4, the exchange rate is £0·50 = $1·00 expressed the first way and £1 = $2 expressed the second way.

When a change in the exchange rate raises the value of one currency, that currency is said to have APPRECIATED; when a change in the exchange rate lowers the value of one currency, that currency is said to have DEPRECIATED. If sterling appreciates against the dollar it becomes more valuable. It will thus take less sterling to buy a US dollar or, what is the same thing, more US dollars to buy a pound sterling. Say, for example, £1 used to exchange for $2 but now it exchanges for $3; sterling has appreciated and the dollar has depreciated. Whereas before it took 50p to buy a dollar and $2 to buy a pound sterling, it now takes only 33⅓p to buy a dollar and $3 to buy a pound sterling. Clearly sterling has become more valuable. (The Note on Definitions, p. xxiii, is relevant here.)

Exchange rates and the domestic prices of traded goods As far as a small open economy is concerned, internationally traded goods have prices that are fixed in foreign currency. The exchange rate translates these into domestic prices. If, for example, the price of wheat is $4 a bushel on international wheat markets, its sterling price in Britain depends on the exchange rate. When the rate is 50p to the dollar, the British domestic price of wheat is £2. This is because £2 must be recovered from domestic sales in order to buy on the foreign-exchange market the $4 needed to buy a bushel of wheat on the international wheat market.

In Figures 11.2 and 11.3 we plotted the domestic demand and supply curves for British imports and exports. We also plotted the world price of these goods in terms of the domestic currency, sterling. To do this we needed, although we did not say so at the time, an exchange rate so that we could convert world prices into local currency. *We express the exchange rate, e, as the number of units of domestic currency needed to buy one unit of foreign currency.* The *domestic* price of traded goods, p_d, is then the *world* price expressed in foreign currency, p_f, multiplied by the exchange rate:

$$p_d = (e)(p_f).$$

For example: when the international price of wheat is \$4 per bushel and the exchange rate is £0·50 = \$1·00, the sterling price of wheat is (4)(0·50) = £2·00 per bushel.

It is now a simple matter to see the important effect of a change in the exchange rate on the domestic prices of traded goods. Say, for example, that sterling appreciates in value so that it only takes £0·33 to buy a US dollar. The sterling price of a bushel of wheat that costs US \$4 is now only £1·33 since £1⅓ is sufficient to buy \$4. Now say, for a second example, that sterling depreciates in value from 50p to 75p for one US dollar. Now the sterling price of wheat rises to £3 since it takes £3 to buy \$4. (Our formula $(e)(p_f) = p_d$ gives the correct answer since $(0·75)(4) = 3$.)

> **An appreciation of the value of domestic currency lowers the domestic prices of traded goods while a depreciation raises these prices.**

The influence of exchange rates on imports and exports

Say that sterling depreciates so that it takes more sterling to buy a US dollar. This, as we have seen, raises the domestic price of tradeables. In Figures 11.4 and 11.5 the sterling price of imported and exported goods rises from p_w to p_w'. In Figure 11.4 this raises the quantity of the good that is exported from $q_2 - q_1$ to $q_2' - q_1'$. In Figure 11.5 the rise in the sterling price of imports lowers the quantity imported from $q_1 - q_2$ to $q_1' - q_2'$.

> **For a small country, a depreciation of the domestic currency causes the domestic prices of traded goods to rise, thereby increasing the quantity supplied and reducing the quantity demanded domestically. Therefore, the quantity of exports increases while the quantity of imports falls.**

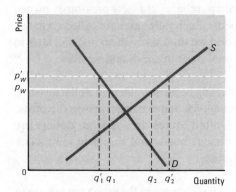

Fig. 11.4 The effects of an increase in the domestic-currency price of an exported good

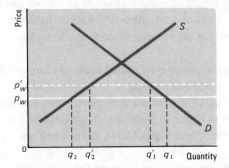

Fig. 11.5 The effects of an increase in the domestic-currency price of an imported good

Now consider an appreciation of sterling. This means that it takes less sterling to buy a unit of foreign currency, so the sterling price of tradeable goods falls. This can be shown by a fall in Figures 11.4 and 11.5 of the sterling price of tradeables from p'_w to p_w. The effects are then easily seen from the diagram to be a reduction in the quantity of exports and an increase in the quantity of imports.

> **For a small country, an appreciation of the domestic currency causes the domestic prices of traded goods to fall, thereby reducing the quantity supplied and increasing the quantity demanded domestically. Therefore, the quantity of exports falls and the quantity of imports rises.**

The determination of exchange rates

The theory that we develop here applies to all exchange rates, but for convenience we shall continue to deal with the example of trade between America and Britain and with the determination of the rate of exchange between their two currencies, dollars and pounds sterling.

> **Because one currency is traded for another on the foreign exchange market, it follows that to desire (demand) dollars implies a willingness to offer (supply) pounds, while an offer (supply) of dollars implies a desire (demand) for pounds.**

If at an exchange rate of £0·50 = $1·00 British importers demand $6·00, they must be offering £3; if American importers offer $6·00, they must be demanding £3. For this reason, the theory can deal either with the demand for, and the supply of, dollars, or with the demand for, and the supply of, pounds sterling; both need not be considered. Because we are interested in buying and selling *foreign* exchange, we shall conduct the argument in terms of the supply, demand and price of dollars (quoted in pounds) which is foreign exchange from the point of view of Britain.

In our two-country model of the foreign-exchange market there are only two groups of private traders: people who have sterling and who want dollars, and people who have dollars and who want sterling. We shall assume for the moment that the Bank of England does not intervene in the market.

The demand for dollars The demand for dollars arises because holders of sterling wish to make payments in dollars; it thus arises from imports of American goods and services into the UK. In addition to the purchase of imports studied before, there are purchases of assets previously owned or newly issued by Americans (and the American government). Such purchases are called CAPITAL FLOWS. They play an important role in exchange markets, and we shall study them in detail later in the book; for the present we continue to focus on international trade in goods and services.

The supply of dollars Dollars are offered in exchange for sterling because holders of dollars wish to make payments in sterling. The supply of dollars on the foreign-exchange market arises, therefore, because of British exports of goods and services to the United States. In addition, dollars are supplied in order to purchase British assets such as government bonds and shares in joint stock companies. These capital flows are ignored until a later chapter.

The demand and supply curves for dollars Now consider what changes in the exchange rate do to the demand for and the supply of dollars. As the price of dollars falls the dollar is depreciating and sterling is appreciating. The appreciation of sterling lowers the sterling price of internationally traded goods. This, as we have seen, lowers Britain's exports and raises its imports. The dollar prices of these goods are, however, unchanged. So the demand for dollars must rise since more imports are being bought at the same dollar price. British exports fall and, given their constant dollar price, the dollar value of these exports must fall, therefore the quantity of dollars offered to obtain sterling to pay for these goods falls.

> **A small open economy's demand curve for foreign exchange is downward-sloping while its supply curve of foreign exchange is upward-sloping plotted against the domestic price of a unit of foreign exchange.**

The exchange rate determined graphically

Figure 11.6 plots the sterling price of a dollar on the vertical axis and the quantity of dollars on the horizontal axis. Assume that the current price of dollars is too low, say 33p to the dollar. At this exchange rate the demand for dollars exceeds the supply. Some people who require dollars to make payments to America will be unable to obtain them, and the price of dollars will be bid up. The value of the dollar *vis-à-vis* the pound will appreciate or, what is the same thing, the value of the pound *vis-à-vis* the dollar will depreciate. This rise in the price of the dollar reduces the quantity demanded and increases the quantity supplied. Where the two curves intersect, quantity demanded equals quantity supplied, and the exchange rate is in equilibrium. In Figure 11.6 the equilibrium exchange rate is at $1 = 50p$, which is £1 = $2.

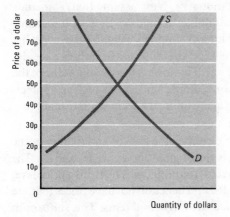
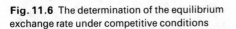
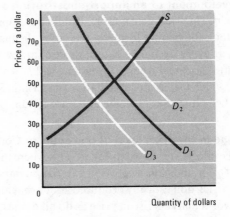

Fig. 11.6 The determination of the equilibrium exchange rate under competitive conditions

Fig. 11.7 The effects of shifts in demand for dollars on the equilibrium exchange rate

Now let us see what will happen if the price of dollars is too high. In this case the demand for dollars will fall short of the supply; the dollar will be in excess supply, so that some people who wish to convert dollars into pounds will be unable to do so. The price of dollars will fall, fewer dollars will be supplied, more will be demanded and an equilibrium will be re-established.

Some comparative static results

We may now use the theory just developed to generate predictions about the effect of several important changes in which we are interested.

A rise in the world price of imports First consider the effect of a rise in the world price of some important imports from the US. This lowers the quantity imported but lowers the demand for dollars only if the fall in the quantity is more than proportionate to the rise in the price. If, for example, the world price of wheat rises 10 per cent from \$4 to \$4·40 and British demand falls 20 per cent from 10 to 8 million bushels per period, the demand for dollars to import wheat falls from \$40 million to \$36·2 million per period. Assuming the quantity response to be large enough, the rise in the price of imports lowers the quantity of dollars demanded. The demand curve in Figure 11.7 shifts left from D_1 to D_3 depreciating the dollar from 50p to 40p, which is the same thing as an appreciation of sterling from £1 = \$2 to £1 = \$2·50.

Now assume, however, that the demand response is less than in proportion to the price rise. Say, for example, the price of oil rises by 20 per cent while the quantity imported only falls by 10 per cent. Now more foreign exchange is needed. The demand curve for dollars shifts right from D_1 to D_2 in Figure 11.7. The price of dollars appreciates from 50p to 60p, which is the same thing as a depreciation of the pound from \$2 to \$1·67. An example was the 1970s experience of oil-importing countries with the OPEC cartel. The large rise in the price of oil initiated by OPEC caused depreciations in the exchange rates of major oil-importing countries including the UK.

The development of an import-substituting domestic industry Now assume that, sometime after the rise in price of an import, Britain develops a low-cost domestic industry that captures some of the domestic market formerly served by the high-priced import. Imports will fall off drastically, so that at every exchange rate fewer dollars will be demanded (because fewer imports are demanded). The demand curve for dollars will now shift to the left. This lowers the sterling value of the dollars, which means an appreciation of sterling. Sterling, for example, underwent such an appreciation when North Sea oil came into production, largely replacing imported oil in the UK market.

A change in the price level of one country Consider, for example, the case of an inflation in the UK. The effects are shown in Figure 11.8 where in both parts the original curves are D_1 and S_1. The amount q_1–q_2 indicates exports in part (i) and imports in part (ii) of the figure. The British price level then rises, i.e. domestically produced goods that are not traded and hence do not have prices that are set on world markets rise in price as do all domestic costs such as wages and rents. This shifts both supply curves to S_2, indicating a higher money price is necessary to call forth any given quantity supplied because of the rise in costs. The demand curves shift to D_2, indicating that the higher money incomes caused by the inflation allow consumers to pay a higher price for any given quantity while the higher price of non-traded goods encourages the shift to goods whose prices are set on international markets. As a result of these shifts, the quantity of imports rises while exports fall. In both parts of the figure the new quantities are indicated by q_3–q_4.

A local British inflation raises the quantity of imports and lowers the quantity of exports.

Since international prices are unaffected by the localized British inflation, the demand for dollars, to

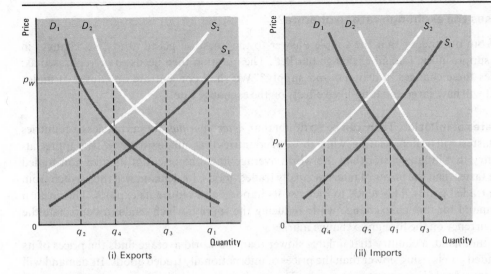

Fig. 11.8 The effect of a local inflation: (i) exports fall; (ii) imports rise

buy increased imports at a given dollar price, must rise. Similarly the supply of dollars, to buy fewer British exports at an unchanged dollar price, must fall. The demand curve for dollars will shift to the right while the supply curve shifts to the left, so that the equilibrium price of dollars must rise.

> **A local British inflation will lead to a depreciation of the exchange value of the pound (an appreciation of the value of the dollar).**

An equal percentage change in the price level in both countries   Now the demand and supply curves in Figure 11.8 shift upwards by 10 per cent as before but so does the world price of imports and exports. (The upward shift in p_w is not shown in the figure.) These shifts are exactly offsetting so there is no change in imports or exports. The equal inflation in Britain and abroad leaves the relative prices of goods from Britain and from the rest of the world unchanged and hence has no effects on the patterns of trade. There is no reason to expect any change in either country's demand for imports at the original exchange rate and hence in the demands and supplies of foreign exchange. The inflations in the two countries leave the equilibrium exchange rate unchanged.

> **Offsetting inflations in two countries will leave the incentive to import and to export unchanged, and thus will cause no change in their exchange rates.**

Consideration of the last two cases, of changes in price levels, shows that what matters is the relative rates of inflation between two trading countries. Differences in the inflation rates will cause changes in imports and exports and hence changes·in quantities demanded and supplied on the foreign-exchange market. Thus the exchange rate between the two currencies will change. The general conclusion that follows from a simple extension of the two cases just studied is:

> **If the price level of one country is rising faster (falling slower) than that of another country, the equilibrium value of the first country's currency will be falling relative to that of the second country.**

What causes the exchange rate to change?

It follows from our theory that the simple answer to the question posed above is: 'changes in demand or supply in the foreign-exchange market'. The question then needs to be rephrased as: 'What causes these changes in demand and supply?' We shall concentrate on causes of major changes that will have large and long-lived effects on the exchange rate.

Differing rates of inflation There can be no doubt that, *ceteris paribus*, the currencies of countries that inflate fastest will be depreciating, while those of countries that inflate slowest will be appreciating. A country that inflates faster than the world average finds the prices of its own non-traded goods rising faster than the prices of internationally traded goods. Its demand will thus switch from domestic to traded goods. This tends to increase its imports and reduce its exports. This in turn raises its demand for foreign exchange while reducing the supply, which tends to depreciate the value of its currency on the foreign-exchange market.

On the other hand, a country that inflates slower than the world average finds the prices of its own non-traded goods rising slower than the prices of internationally traded goods. Its demand will thus switch from traded to non-traded goods. This tends to decrease its imports and increase its exports. This in turn lowers its demand for foreign exchange while increasing the supply of foreign exchange (offered to buy its exports). This tends to appreciate the value of its currency on the foreign-exchange market.

Structural changes At the existing price levels, an economy can undergo structural changes that affect the exchange rate. 'Structural change' is an omnibus term for changes in cost structures, the invention of new products or anything else that affects the patterns of international competitiveness. For example, a country might be less dynamic than its competitors, so that at the initial set of prices consumers' demand shifts slowly away from the home-country products towards those of foreign countries. This would cause a slow trend depreciation in the home country's exchange rate.

Dramatic changes, such as major shifts in OPEC pricing policies, will have similar effects, except that they may occur suddenly over a space of months rather than gradually over a space of years. Big events such as the beginning or the end of the production of North Sea oil will also cause major changes in equilibrium exchange rates.

> **Long-term changes in exchange rates can be accounted for mainly by the relative inflation rates and structural changes.**

12

Postscripts and previews

Some postscripts on the price system

In Part 2 we have developed a theory of the behaviour of individual competitive markets. Although there are great insights to be gained from this theory, it is important to realize that the markets of the economy do not function in isolation from each other. Our first postscript, therefore, concerns the interrelationship of markets.

The interrelationship of markets

The economy is an interlocking system in which anything happening in one market has profound effects on many others and could, potentially, influence all of them. Thus our study of the behaviour of individual markets is only the first step towards understanding the behaviour of a whole economy. We also need a theory of how the individual markets are linked together and of how they act and react on each other. We shall consider this, albeit very briefly, in Part 7. In the meantime let us try to assemble an intuitive picture of the interactions within a market economy.

Consider, for example, the effects of a rise in the demand for some product. Fairly soon it will be met by a rise in production. If the rise in demand is considerable, and judged to be permanent, there will also be a planned increase in productive capacity in the industry. Employment will rise and producers may try to attract labour from other industries by offering higher wages. Thus, one of the first impacts on other markets will be a loss of labour and possibly a need to raise wages in order to compete effectively with the expanding industry for that labour. This will cause profits to fall in these other industries.

The increased employment in the expanding industry may occasion some geographical movement of labour. There will then be a rise in the demand for housing in the expanding centres and a corresponding fall in demand elsewhere. New housing construction will lead to a rise in the demand for construction workers and materials. Quarries and brickworks may have to take on additional labour and expand output.

Further, there will be a rise in the demand for materials used in the expanding industry. Firms making component parts elsewhere in the country and raw material producers on the other side of the world may be affected. If new investment in plant and equipment takes place, there will be a rise in the demand for many capital goods; shortages and bottlenecks may develop, and other industries which use these capital goods may find that their costs go up and they may have trouble meeting delivery dates. There will also be a change in consumers' expenditure because some people's earnings will be increased and other people's reduced. Imports and exports will change and as a result the exchange rate may be affected. If sterling is appreciated this will encourage imports of other commodities and discourage exports. If sterling is depreciated this will discourage imports and encourage exports. Thus the effects of a change in one market will spread through the economy rather like the ripples which spread out over the smooth surface of a pond after a pebble has been dropped into it.

The price system is a control mechanism

The example considered above illustrates two very important points. First, the various markets of the economy are interrelated: a single initial change in demand has numerous repercussions throughout the economy. Second, adaptations to the initial shift take place without anyone's conscious co-ordination.

This second point leads us to our second postscript: the price system co-ordinates economic activity without the need for the intervention of co-ordinating decisions by the central authorities.

When shortages develop in a market economy, prices rise and profit-seeking entrepreneurs want to produce more of the commodities in short supply. When surpluses occur, prices fall and producers voluntarily contract the supply. It was the great discovery of the eighteenth-century economists that a competitive price system produces a co-ordination of effort in which – by seeking their own private gains and responding to such public signals as prices, costs and profit rates – individuals automatically react in orderly fashion to changes in demand and supply.

> **The price system was not consciously created. It does not require that anyone consciously foresee and co-ordinate the necessary changes; adjustments occur automatically as a result of the separate decisions taken by a large number of individuals, all seeking their own best interests, but all responding to the same changes in demands and prices.**

Efficient and inefficient control mechanisms Having grasped the idea that the price system is an automatic control mechanism, beware of jumping to the conclusion that it has been shown to be the *best* system of regulating the economy. The word 'automatic', which we have used, is not equivalent to the phrase 'perfectly functioning', which we have not used. It is easy enough to control the heat in your house by means of an automatic thermostatic control, but it is equally easy to have such a badly designed or imperfectly functioning system that you actually achieve worse temperature control than you would have done by 'stoking up' and 'damping down' by hand. To say that the price system functions automatically, i.e., without conscious centralized co-ordination, is not to say how *well* it functions. We have seen, for example in the case of the 'cobweb' in the Appendix to Chapter 10, that the automatic working of the price system can produce oscillations in price and output.

The reader who believes that behaviour in a free-market economy is unplanned and unco-ordinated must abandon this notion. The existence of a co-ordinating mechanism – the price system – is beyond dispute. There is a strong case that no practical alternative comes anywhere near to working as well as the price system, but this case is still disputed by advocates of a mixed system of free markets plus substantial government intervention to improve the workings of the markets.[1] Thus the question of how well it works in comparison with practical, alternative co-ordinating systems has been a matter of dispute for two hundred years and is still a great unsettled social question. We consider this issue in more detail in Chapter 32.

Some lessons about resource allocation

Our study of the operation of free markets, and of intervention into such markets by central authorities, has suggested a number of general lessons. Here we mention four of the most important of these.

Free-market prices and profits encourage economical use of resources   Prices and profits in a market economy provide signals to both demanders and suppliers. Prices that are high and rising (relative to other prices) provide an incentive to purchasers to economize on the commodity. They may choose to satisfy the want in question with substitutes whose prices have not risen so much (because they are less costly to provide) or to satisfy less of that want by shifting expenditure to the satisfaction of other wants. There is substantial scope for such economizing reactions even for commodities as 'necessary' as housing: *some* housing is necessary, but a particular quantity or quality is not.

On the supply side, rising prices tend to produce rising profits. High profits attract further resources into production. Short-term windfall profits (i.e., profits that bear no relation to current costs) repeatedly occur in market economies; they induce resources to move into those industries until the return on investment falls to levels that can be earned elsewhere in the economy.

Falling prices and falling profits provide the opposite motivations. Purchasers are inclined to buy more; sellers are inclined to produce less and move resources out of the industry into more profitable undertakings.

The pattern we have described may be summarized:

> **Free-market prices and profits are signals to producers and consumers. Changing relative prices and profits signal a need for change to which consumers and producers respond.**

Controls inhibit the allocative mechanism   Some controls prevent prices from rising (in response, say, to an increase in demand). If the price is held down, the signal is never given to consumers to economize on a commodity that is in short supply. On the supply side, when prices and profits are prevented from rising (on the grounds, for example, that no more than a 'fair' return should be earned at all times), the profit signals that would attract new resources into the industry are never given. The shortage continues, and the movements of demand and supply that would remove it are not set in motion.

In the opposite case, where there is excess supply, an appropriate response would be some increase in quantity purchased and some decrease in production, accompanied by a shift of

---

[1] Few still believe that a complete command economy could work better than a mixed market economy in producing goods and fulfilling accepted canons of justice. The experience of contemporary command economies has convinced most people whose minds are open to evidence.

resources to production of other, more valued commodities. Falling prices and profits would motivate such shifts. When prices are prevented from falling in the face of temporary surpluses (on the grounds, for example, that producers of an essential product must have a 'fair' return guaranteed to them), the signals that would increase purchases or push resources out of an industry are never given.

Controls require alternative allocative mechanisms If the price system with its profit incentives is not used to allocate resources, alternative methods will necessarily appear. Temporary fluctuations in demand and supply will give rise to shortages and surpluses. During times of shortages, allocation will be by sellers' preferences unless the state imposes rationing. During periods of surplus, there will be unsold supplies or illegal price cutting unless the state buys and stores the surpluses. Long-run changes in demand and costs will not induce resource reallocations through private decisions. As a result, the state will be put under strong, long-run pressure to step in. It will have to force or order resources out of industries where prices are held above their free-market level – as with agriculture. It will also have to force or order resources into industries where prices are held below their free-market level.

Any specific alternative scheme of allocation that is imposed is costly in a number of additional ways. First, the allocation itself usually requires the use of resources for administering and enforcing the rules. Second, since centralized bureaucratic systems tend to be less flexible and adaptive than decentralized decision-taking systems, flexibility in adapting to long-term changes is usually sacrificed. Third, the freedom of some individuals to act in what they consider their own best interest is reduced. Sometimes the benefits of the policies will be judged to justify the costs, sometimes they will not. Justified or not, the costs are always present and need to be taken into account when balancing the pros and cons of any particular policy.

Costs may be shifted, but they cannot be avoided Production, whether in response to free-market signals or to government controls, uses resources; thus it involves cost to members of society. If it takes 5 per cent of the nation's resources to provide housing to some stated average standard, then those resources will not be available to produce other commodities. For society as a whole there is no such thing as free housing. The average standard of living depends on the amounts of resources available to the economy and the efficiency with which these resources are used. *It follows that costs of producing goods and services are real and are incurred no matter who provides these to consumers.* Rent controls, housing subsidies or public provision of housing can change the share of the costs of housing paid by particular individuals or groups, lowering the share for some, raising the share for others. But such policies cannot make the costs go away.

Different ways of *allocating* the costs may also affect the total amount of resources used, and thus the amount of costs incurred. Controls that keep prices and profits of some commodities below free-market levels will lead to increased quantities demanded and to decreased quantities supplied. Unless the central authorities step in to provide additional supplies, fewer resources will be allocated to producing these commodities. If the authorities choose to supply all the demand at the controlled prices, more resources will be allocated to producing for it, which means fewer resources will be devoted to producing other kinds of goods and services. *The opportunity cost of more housing is less of something else.*

The opportunity cost of more of *any* commodity is less of *some other* commodity.

A preview of demand and supply

In developing a theory of the behaviour of competitive markets – markets in which no single buyer or seller is important enough to exert any significant influence on prices – we first introduced a theory of households' demand and a theory of firms' supply (Chapter 7). We must now consider in much more detail the theory of demand (Part 3) and the theory of supply (Part 4). The theory of demand will occupy us for only three chapters because we never need to depart from our competitive assumption that each household is a price-taker, totally unable to influence by any action of its own the market prices of the commodities it purchases.

The theory of supply will require much more space. This is because a large proportion of production is carried on by firms in non-competitive situations – in the sense that each *is* able to exert a significant influence on market price. Serious complications arise as a result. Therefore, although we do not need to alter any of the hypotheses about demand introduced in Chapter 7, it becomes necessary, as a result of the existence of these non-competitive situations, to abandon the hypothesis that there *always* exists a simple relation between market price and firms' supply. Moreover, many interesting issues of economic policy are encountered in the theory of supply. But first we must turn our attention to the theory of demand.

Part three

The intermediate theory of demand

13

Effects of changes in prices and incomes

Is a household's consumption affected differently if its money income falls than if the prices of commodities rise? Does an increase in the level of all prices hurt everybody? Does it hurt anybody? Can we predict the effect of price changes on a household's behaviour? To answer these and similar questions, we must look in more detail at the behaviour of the millions of independent decision units whose aggregate behaviour is summarized in the market demand curve.

In this chapter we shall study the effects on a household's consumption of changes in relative prices, absolute prices and incomes. In the following chapter we shall show some alternative methods of deriving from assumptions about household behaviour the basic prediction that the demand curve for a commodity slopes downwards. We have already discussed in Chapter 6 the general assumptions made about the household, which is the basic decision unit on the side of demand, and you should now review pages 67–8 of that chapter.

Choices facing the household

We shall study a single household allocating the whole of its money income between two goods, food and clothing.[1] We start with numerical examples, but later go on to state the argument in general terms. In Figure 13.1 the quantity of food is measured on the horizontal axis and the quantity of clothing on the vertical one. Any point on the graph represents a combination of the two goods. Point m, for example, represents 40 units of food and 60 units of clothing.

The budget line

We now construct the household's BUDGET LINE, which shows all those combinations of the goods that are just obtainable, given the household's income and the prices of the two commodities.[2]

---

[1] These assumptions are not as restrictive as they at first seem. Two goods are used so that the analysis can be handled geometrically; the argument can easily be generalized to any number of commodities with the use of mathematics. Savings are ignored because we are interested in the allocation of expenditure between commodities for current consumption. The possibilities of saving or borrowing (or using up past savings) can be allowed for, but they affect none of the results in which we are interested here.

[2] This budget line is analogous to the production-possibility boundary shown in Figure 4.1 on page 57. The budget line shows the combinations of commodities available to one household given its income and prices, while the production-possibility curve shows the combinations of commodities available to the whole society given its techniques of production and supplies of resources.

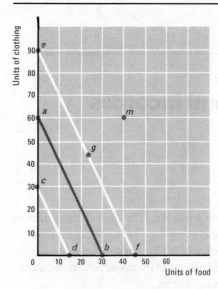

Fig. 13.1 Shifts in the budget line caused by changes in household income

Assume, for example, that the household's income is £120 per month, that the price of clothing is £2 per unit, and the price of food is £4 per unit. What combinations of the two are open to the household? First, it could spend all its money on clothing, obtaining each month 60 units of clothing and no food (this combination is indicated by point *a* on Figure 13.1). It could also buy 30 units of food and no clothing (point *b*). Other combinations open to it are 58 units of clothing and 1 unit of food, 56 units of clothing and 2 units of food, 54 units of clothing and 3 units of food, and so on.

All the possible combinations of food and clothing obtainable by the household are shown by the straight line *ab* in Figure 13.1. Points between *ab* and the origin do not use all the household's income, and points above *ab* require more than the household's income. Points on *ab* are just attainable in the sense that they require all the household's income and no more.

Changes in income

What happens to the budget line when the household's income changes? If, for example, income is halved from £120 to £60 per month, prices being unchanged, then the amount of goods the household can buy will also be halved. If the household spends all of its income on clothing, it will now get only 30 units of clothing and no food (point *c*); if it spends all of its income on food, it will get just 15 units of food and no clothing (point *d*). All combinations now open to the household appear on budget line *cd*. Note that this line is parallel to budget line *ab*, but closer to the origin.

If the household's income rises to £180, it will be able to buy more of both commodities than it could previously. If it buys only clothing, it can have 90 units (point *e*); if it buys only food, it can have 45 units (point *f*); if it spends equal amounts on the two, it gets 45 units of clothing and $22\frac{1}{2}$ units of food (point *g*). All the combinations available to the household appear on budget line *ef*.

We conclude that variations in the household's income, with prices constant, shift the budget line in a parallel fashion inward towards the origin when income falls, and outward away from the origin when income rises. For practice you might draw budget lines for incomes of £100 and £40 per month, with the same prices for food and clothing that were used in the above example.

Proportional changes in all prices

Let us start with the budget line *ab* in Figure 13.1, which corresponds to an income of £120 and prices of £2 and £4 respectively for clothing and food. If we now double both prices, we will halve the amount of both goods that the household can purchase. The budget line becomes *cd*, because the income of £120 will now buy 30 units of clothing and no food, 15 units of food and no clothing, or any combination of food and clothing on the straight line joining these two points.

Now let us go back to line *ab* and reduce both prices by one third so that clothing costs £1·33⅓ while food costs £2·66⅔. The household can now have 50 per cent more of both goods, and the budget line moves outward to *ef*. Notice that changing both prices in the same proportion shifts the budget line parallel to itself in the same way that a change in income shifted it.

Offsetting changes in prices and income

The results obtained in the last two sections suggest that we can have offsetting changes in money prices and money income. Consider the budget line *ab* in Figure 13.1. This budget line was originally obtained from an income of £120, with prices of £4 and £2 for food and clothing respectively. What will happen if the household's income doubles to £240? The budget line will shift outward, since the household can buy twice as many units of both goods as it could previously. But what if both prices double as well? This cuts the household's consumption possibilities in half, and the budget line is back to *ab*. A rise in money income and a proportionate rise in the money prices of both goods leave the position of the budget line unchanged.

Opportunity cost, relative prices and the slope of the budget line

Why does changing either income or both prices in the same proportion shift the budget line to a parallel position? The reason is that the slope of the budget line indicates the opportunity cost of one commodity in terms of the other, and either a change in income with prices unchanged or a proportionate change in both prices leaves this opportunity cost unaffected.[1]

Consider an example. If clothing costs £2 and food costs £4, then 2 units of clothing must be forgone in order to be able to purchase 1 unit of food; if clothing costs £4 and food costs £8 it is still necessary to forgo 2 units of clothing to be able to purchase one more unit of food. In fact, as long as the price of food is twice the price of clothing, it will be necessary to forgo two units of clothing in order to be able to purchase one more unit of food. More generally, the amount of clothing that must be given up to obtain another unit of food depends only on *the relation between the price of clothing and the price of food*. If we take the money price of food and divide it by the money price of clothing, we have the opportunity cost of food in terms of clothing (the quantity of clothing that must be forgone in order to be able to purchase one more unit of food). This may be written:

$$\frac{p_f}{p_c} = \text{opportunity cost of food in terms of clothing,}$$

where p_f and p_c are the money prices of food and clothing. It is apparent that changing income

---

[1] See Chapter 4, pp. 52–3, for a general discussion of the concept of opportunity cost.

and/or changing both prices in the same proportion leaves the ratio p_f/p_c unchanged.[1]

In economics, any price expressed as a ratio of another price is called a RELATIVE PRICE. The relative price must be distinguished from the MONEY PRICE of a single commodity, which is also called its ABSOLUTE PRICE. These concepts can prove tricky and the reader is urged to experiment with some examples.[2]

Changes in relative prices

A change in the relative price p_f/p_c may be accomplished either by changing both money prices but in a different proportion or by holding one money price constant and changing the other. It is useful for illustrative purposes to do the latter.

Figure 13.2 repeats the budget line *ab* from Figure 13.1, which corresponds to an income of £120 and prices of £2 and £4 respectively for clothing and food. On the one hand, a fall in the price of food to £2 doubles the quantity of it that can be purchased along with any given quantity of clothing. This has the effect of pivoting the budget line to the position *ag*. On the other hand, a rise in the price of food from £4 to £8 halves the quantity of food that can be purchased along with any given quantity of clothing. This pivots the budget line to *ah*. Thus a change in the relative price changes the slope of the budget line; the higher the price of food relative to the price of clothing, the steeper the budget line.

Implications and predictions

We have now derived a number of implications about the effects on the budget line of changes in prices and incomes. These are summarized below.

(1) **A change in money income, with money prices (and thus, necessarily, relative prices) constant, shifts the budget line parallel to itself, inward towards the origin when income falls, and outward away from the origin when income rises.**

(2) **An equal percentage change in all absolute prices leaves relative prices unchanged. If money income remains unchanged the budget line shifts parallel to itself, inward towards the origin when prices rise, and outward away from the origin when prices fall.**

(3) **Multiplying all money prices by the same constant, λ, while holding money income constant, has exactly the same effect on the budget line as multiplying money income by $1/\lambda$ while holding money prices constant. For example, doubling all money prices has the same effect on the budget line as halving money income.**

(4) **A change in relative prices causes the budget line to change its slope.**

(5) **Equal percentage changes in all absolute prices and in money income leaves the budget line unaffected.**

---

[1] Those who prefer an algebraic derivation may refer now to the proof of this proposition on page 162 of the Appendix to this chapter.

[2] For example, if the prices of food and clothing are £2 and £6 respectively, what are the values of: (i) the relative price of food, (ii) the relative price of clothing, (iii) the opportunity cost of food measured in units of clothing, (iv) the opportunity cost of clothing measured in units of food and (v) the slope of the budget line drawn with food on the horizontal and clothing on the vertical axis?

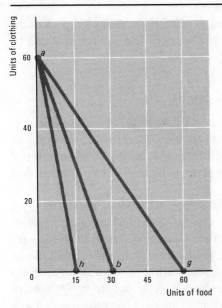

Fig. 13.2 Shifts in the budget line caused by changes in the price of food

The five implications listed above are matters of logic. The effects on the budget line of changes in prices and incomes are incontrovertible. In order to translate these implications into predictions about household behaviour, we advance the hypothesis that a household's market behaviour depends solely on the tastes of the members of the household and the location of the household's budget line. This behavioural hypothesis, along with the five propositions above, will allow us to make testable predictions about the behaviour of households. The following are two important examples.[1]

> **The change in a household's market behaviour will be the same if either its income changes by λ or all money prices change by 1/λ.**
> **A household's market behaviour will be unaffected if its money income and all money prices change simultaneously by λ.**

Further predictions will be derived in Chapter 14 after we have developed a theory of the household's tastes.

Real and money income

We may now make an important distinction between two concepts of income. MONEY INCOME measures a household's income in terms of some monetary unit; for example, so many pounds sterling or so many dollars. REAL INCOME measures the purchasing power of the household's money income. A rise in money income of x per cent combined with an x per cent rise in all money prices

---

[1] Strictly speaking, these predictions apply only to households that do not have any significant quantities of bonds, cash or other assets whose value is fixed in money units and whose real value thus changes when money prices change. (For example, the real value of a cash hoard would be halved by a doubling of the price level.) The predictions apply to those households for whom income is the main determinant of current expenditure.

leaves a household's purchasing power, and hence its real income, unchanged. When we speak of the real value of a certain amount of money, we are referring to the goods and services that can be bought with the money; that is, to the purchasing power of the money.

Allocation of resources: the importance of relative prices

Price theory predicts that the allocation of resources depends on the structure of relative prices. If the money value of all prices, incomes, debts and credits were doubled, there would, according to our theory, be little noticeable effect. The economy would function as before. The same set of relative prices and real incomes would exist, and there would be no incentive for any reallocation of resources.

This prediction is an implication of the theories of the behaviour of households and firms. We have already seen that doubling all money prices and money income leaves the household's budget line unchanged and so, according to the theory of household behaviour, gives it no incentive to vary the quantity of each commodity that it purchases. As far as producers are concerned, if all prices, both of final goods and of factors of production, double, then the relative profitability of different lines of production will be unaffected, as indeed will the real level of profits in all lines of production.[1] Thus producers will have no incentive to alter production rates so as to produce more of some things and less of others.

If *relative* prices change, however, then our theory predicts that resources will be reallocated. Households will buy more of the cheaper commodities and less of the expensive ones, and producers will expand production of those commodities whose prices have risen relatively and contract production of those whose prices have fallen relatively (since the latter will be relatively less profitable lines of production).

The theory of price and resource allocation is a theory of relative, not absolute, prices.

Inflation and deflation: the importance of absolute prices

The average level of all money prices is called the PRICE LEVEL. If all money prices double, we say that the price level has doubled. An increase in the price level is called an INFLATION, a decrease is called a DEFLATION. If a rise in all money prices and incomes has little or no effect on the allocation of resources, it may seem surprising that so much concern is expressed over inflation. Clearly, a person who spends all of his income, and whose money income goes up at the same rate as money prices, loses nothing from inflation. His real income is unaffected.

Inflation, while having no effect on a household whose income rises at the same rate as prices, does nonetheless have serious consequences. These are studied in detail in the latter half of this book, along with theories of the causes of and possible cures for inflation.[2]

Until we reach Part 8 *we shall assume that the price level is constant*. A change in one money price is then necessarily a change in that price *relative* to the average of all other prices in the economy.

---

[1] Since all prices will have doubled, money profits will have doubled, but since all costs will also have doubled, the purchasing power of these profits will be just what it was before.

[2] Anyone who wishes to understand now why inflation is important in spite of the propositions demonstrated in this chapter, can read pages 504–7.

The theory can easily be extended to situations in which the price level is changing. Then every time shifts in demand or supply required a change in a commodity's relative price, its price would change *faster* (its relative price rising) or *slower* (its relative price falling) than the general price level. Explaining this each time can be cumbersome. It is, therefore, simpler to deal with relative prices in a theoretical setting in which the price level is constant. It is important to realize, however, that even though we develop the theory in this way, it is not limited to such situations. The propositions we develop can be applied to changing price levels merely by making explicit what is always implicit: that in the theory of relative prices 'rise' or 'fall' *always* means rise or fall *relative to the average of all other prices*.

Appendix to chapter 13

A formal analysis of the budget line

In this appendix we shall use simple algebra to prove the propositions asserted in the chapter.

Let the household's money income be M. Let p_x and p_y be the prices of food and clothing, and let X and Y be the quantities of food and clothing purchased by the household. Total expenditure is thus $p_x X + p_y Y$. If we assume, as we did in the text, that the household spends all of its income on these two goods, we have the following equation:

$$p_x X + p_y Y = M. \tag{1}$$

Rearrangement of terms yields the equation of the budget line as it is plotted in Figures 13.1 and 13.2. To do this, we subtract $p_x X$ from both sides, and then divide through by p_y to obtain:

$$Y = \frac{M}{p_y} - \frac{p_x}{p_y} X. \tag{2}$$

Equation (1) is a linear equation of the form

$$Y = a - bX, \tag{3}$$

where $a = M/p_y$ and $b = p_x/p_y$. The intercept a is the number of units of Y that can be purchased by spending all of M on Y, i.e., money income divided by the price of Y. The slope b depends on the relation between p_x and p_y.

We first prove that the opportunity cost, the slope of the budget line and the relative price are identical. If we take first differences representing changes in quantities, with prices constant, we get from (1):

$$p_x \Delta X + p_y \Delta Y = \Delta M.$$

This says that the sum of any changes in the value of purchases of X and the value of purchases of Y must be equal to the change in income (since income determines the total value of purchases).

Along a budget line expenditure is constant, so we can write

$$p_x \Delta X + p_y \Delta Y = 0,$$

which says that if income does not change, the change in the total value of purchases must be zero. Simple manipulation of the above equation yields:

$$p_x/p_y = -\Delta Y/\Delta X. \tag{4}$$

Now $-\Delta Y/\Delta X$ is the change in Y per unit change in X. It is thus the opportunity cost of X measured in units of Y: the amount of Y sacrificed (gained) per unit of X gained (sacrificed). From (4) this is equal to the relative price of X, which, from (2), is the slope of the budget line.

We may now prove the five propositions on page 158 of the text.

PROPOSITION (1): A change in money income, with money prices (and thus, necessarily, relative prices) constant, shifts the budget line parallel to itself, inward towards the origin when income falls, and outward away from the origin when income rises.

PROOF: If we change the value of M in (2), we change the value of a in (3) in the same direction: $\Delta a = \Delta M/p_y$, but b is unaffected since M does not appear in that term; thus changing M shifts the budget line inwards ($\Delta M < 0$) or outwards ($\Delta M > 0$) but leaves the slope unaffected.

PROPOSITION (2): An equal percentage change in all absolute prices leaves relative prices unchanged. If money income remains unchanged, it will shift the budget line parallel to itself, inward towards the origin when prices rise, and outward away from the origin when prices fall.

PROOF: Multiplying both prices in equation (2) by the same constant λ gives

$$Y = \frac{M}{\lambda p_y} - \frac{\lambda p_x}{\lambda p_y} X.$$

Since the λs cancel out of the slope term, b is unaffected; the a term however is changed. If $\lambda > 1$, then a is diminished, while if $\lambda < 1$ then a is increased.

PROPOSITION (3): Multiplying all money prices by the same constant, λ, while holding money income constant, has exactly the same effect on the budget line as multiplying money income by $1/\lambda$ while holding money prices constant.

PROOF: Multiply both money prices in (2) by λ:

$$Y = \frac{M}{\lambda p_y} - \frac{\lambda p_x}{\lambda p_y} X.$$

Cancelling the λs from the slope term gives:

$$Y = \frac{M}{\lambda p_y} - \frac{p_x}{p_y} X.$$

Finally bringing the λ from the denominator to the numerator of the constant term gives:

$$Y = \frac{(1/\lambda)M}{p_y} - \frac{p_x}{p_y} X.$$

PROPOSITION (4): A change in relative prices causes the budget line to change its slope.

PROOF: The relative price p_x/p_y in (2) is the slope term, b, in (3). Thus changing the relative price is necessary and sufficient for changing the slope of the budget line.

Note that to pivot the budget line, keeping its Y intercept (and money income) constant as in Figure 13.2, it is necessary to change the relative price by changing p_x only. This can be seen algebraically by inspection of (2), since p_x does not appear in the constant term. If the relative price change is accomplished solely, or partly, by changing p_y, then both the slope and the Y intercept change. This is because in (2) p_y appears in both the a and the b term. The common sense of these results is that the Y intercept measures the quantity of Y that can be consumed by buying only Y and this obviously depends on money income and the price of Y.

We conclude that any change in the relative price necessarily changes the slope of the budget line; while with money income constant, a change in p_y changes the Y intercept and (by analogous reasoning) a change in p_x changes the X intercept of the budget line.

PROPOSITION (5): Equal percentage changes in all absolute prices and in money income leaves the budget line unaffected.

PROOF: Multiply M and both prices in equation (2) by λ:

$$Y = \frac{\lambda M}{\lambda p_y} - \frac{\lambda p_x}{\lambda p_y} X.$$

Cancel out the λs from the intercept and the slope terms to obtain:

$$Y = \frac{M}{p_y} - \frac{p_x}{p_y} X$$

which is equation (2) once again.

14

Theories of household demand

The early economists, struggling with the problem of what determines the relative prices of commodities, encountered what they came to call the PARADOX OF VALUE: many necessary commodities, such as water, had prices that were low compared to the prices of many luxury commodities, such as diamonds. Writing some two hundred years ago, these early economists argued in the following manner. Water is necessary to our very existence, whereas diamonds are a luxury that could disappear tomorrow without causing any real upset. Does it not seem odd, therefore, that water is so cheap and diamonds so expensive? It took a long time for economists to resolve this apparent paradox. Thus it is not surprising that even today the confusion persists and clouds many policy discussions.

We have already encountered one key to the paradox of value: it is supply and demand, not 'necessity' or 'luxury', that determines price, and the price that equates supply and demand is relatively low for water and relatively high for diamonds. But why is the demand for a necessity not enough to assure that its price is high? After all, it is necessary to life itself. To address this more fundamental question we must go behind the market demand curve, which is the aggregate of all households' desired purchases at each possible price, and look at the motivation of individual households. In this chapter two theories of household demand are studied. They provide alternative rather than competing explanations, since they lead to almost the same set of basic predictions.

The utility theory of household behaviour

The first half of the chapter covers utility theory. This is the older theory, but it is still worth studying because the distinction it makes between marginal and total utility has widespread significance for practical policy.

Marginal and total utility

The satisfaction a household receives from consuming commodities is called *utility*. The total utility obtained from consuming some commodity can be distinguished from the marginal utility of consuming one unit more or one unit less of it.

The concepts defined TOTAL UTILITY refers to the total satisfaction gained from consuming some commodity. MARGINAL UTILITY refers to the change in satisfaction resulting from consuming a little more or a little less of that commodity. Thus, for example, the total utility of consuming ten units of some commodity is the total satisfaction that those ten units provide. The marginal utility of the tenth unit consumed is the satisfaction gained by consuming that unit – or, in other words, the difference in total utility between consuming nine units and consuming ten units.[1]

This distinction can be illustrated by asking two questions. (1) If you had to give up one of the following commodities completely, which would you choose: water or TV? (2) If you had to give up one of the following, which would you choose: 35 gallons of water a month (the amount required for an average bath) or one hour of TV viewing per month?

In the first choice you are comparing the *total utility* of your water consumption with the *total utility* of your TV watching. Of course everyone would answer question (1) in the same way, revealing that the total utility derived from consuming water exceeds the total utility derived from watching TV.

In the second choice you are comparing the value you place on a small reduction in your water consumption with the value you place on a small reduction in your TV viewing. You are comparing your *marginal utility* of water with your *marginal utility* of TV viewing. The response to question (2) is far less predictable than the response to choice (1). Some people might elect to reduce their TV viewing while others might elect to cut their water consumption. Furthermore, their choice would depend on whether water was plentiful at the time, so that they had more or less all they wanted (marginal utility of water, *low*), or whether water was scarce, so that a little more of it would be very desirable (marginal utility of water, *high*).

Choices of type (1) are encountered much less commonly than choices of type (2). If our income rises a little, we have to decide to have more of one thing or another. If our income falls, we have to decide what to cut down on.

Whenever real choices concern a little more or a little less, they are influenced by marginal utilities not by total utilities.

The hypothesis of diminishing marginal utility   The basic hypothesis of utility theory is sometimes called the 'law of diminishing marginal utility'.

The utility that any household derives from successive units of a particular commodity will diminish as total consumption of that commodity increases, the consumption of all other commodities being held constant.

Consider further the case of water. Some minimum quantity of drinking water is necessary to sustain life, and a household would, if necessary, give up all of its income to obtain that quantity. The marginal utility of that quantity is extremely high. Much more than this bare minimum can be drunk, but the marginal utility of successive glasses of water drunk over some time period will decline steadily. Evidence for this hypothesis will be considered later, but you can convince yourself

---

[1] In elementary economics it is common to use interchangeably two concepts that mathematicians distinguish. Technically, *incremental* utility is measured over a discrete interval, such as from nine to ten, whereas marginal utility is a rate of change measured at one point, say 9. The difference between incremental and marginal values is discussed further in Section 11, p. 32, of the Appendix to Chapter 2. This is an important discussion and it should be read, or reread, at this time.

Readers who are familiar with elementary calculus may imagine a function relating utility to the quantity of goods X, Y, ... consumed: $U = U(X, Y, ...)$. Incremental utility of X is then $\Delta U / \Delta X$, while marginal utility of X is $\partial U / \partial X$.

that it is at least reasonable by asking yourself some questions. How much money would induce you to cut your consumption of water by one glass per week? The amount would not be large. How much would induce you to cut it by a second glass? By a third glass? and so on back to one glass. The fewer glasses you are consuming already, the higher the marginal utility to you of one glass.

Water has many uses other than for drinking. A fairly high marginal utility will be attached to some minimum quantity for bathing, but much more than this minimum will be used for frequent baths and for having a water level in the bath higher than is absolutely necessary. The last weekly gallon used for bathing is likely to have quite a low marginal utility. Again, some small quantity of water is necessary for brushing one's teeth, but many people leave the water running while brushing, and the water so consumed between wetting and rinsing the brush will not have a high utility. When all of the modern uses of water are considered, it is certain that the marginal utility of the last units consumed is very low, even though the total utility of *all* the units consumed is extremely high.

Utility schedules and graphs   Let us assume for purposes of illustration that utility can be measured. The schedule in Table 14.1 is hypothetical and is intended only to illustrate the assumptions that have been made about utility. It shows total utility rising as the number of hours spent watching TV per week rises. Everything else being equal, the household gets more satisfaction, the more TV it watches – at least over the range shown in the table. But the marginal utility of each hour of TV per week is less than that of the previous one (even though each adds something to the household's satisfaction); thus the marginal utility schedule shows a declining value as hours watched rises. These same data are shown graphically in Figure 14.1.

Can marginal utility ever reach zero? With many commodities there is some maximum consumption after which additional units would confer no additional utility. Cigarettes provide an obvious example. There is some maximum number of cigarettes that most people would smoke per day, even if they did not have to worry about the cost. Additional cigarettes smoked would begin to subtract from utility; that is, additional cigarettes would have a negative marginal utility or, as it is sometimes called, a marginal *disutility*. The same is undoubtedly true of many other commodities such as food, alcoholic beverages and most games. (Although we know one economist who would

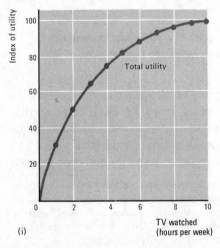

(i)

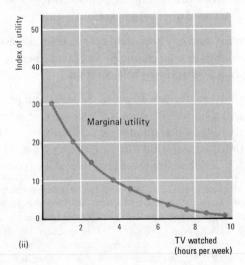

(ii)

Fig. 14.1 Total and marginal utility curves

Table 14.1 Total and marginal utility schedules

Number of hours of TV watched per week	Total utility	Marginal* utility
0	0	
		30
1	30	
		20
2	50	
		15
3	65	
		10
4	75	
		8
5	83	
		6
6	89	
		4
7	93	
		3
8	96	
		2
9	98	
		1
10	99	

* The marginal utility of 20, shown as the second entry in the last column, arises because total utility increased from 30 to 50 – a difference of 20 – with the second hour watched. Technically, this is 'incremental utility' over the interval from 1 to 2 units. When plotting marginal utility on a graph, this value is plotted at the mid-point of the interval over which it is computed.

be happy to play golf from sunrise to sunset seven days a week for the rest of his life, most people would not.)

Maximizing utility

A basic assumption of the utility theory of household behaviour is that

The members of a household seek to maximize their total utility.

This is just another way of saying that they try to make themselves as well off as they possibly can in the circumstances in which they find themselves. This assumption is sometimes taken to mean that households are assumed to be narrowly selfish and devoid of any altruistic motives. On the contrary, if a household derives satisfaction from giving its money away to others, this can be incorporated into the analysis, and the marginal utility that it gets from £1 given away can be compared with the marginal utility that it gets from £1 spent on itself.

The equilibrium of a household   How can a household adjust its expenditure so as to maximize the total utility of its members? Should it go to the point at which the marginal utility of each commodity is the same – i.e., the point at which it values equally the last unit of each commodity consumed? This would make sense only if all commodities had the same price per unit. But if a household must spend £3 to buy an additional unit of one commodity and only £1 for a unit of another, the first commodity would represent a poor use of its money if the marginal utilities of both were equal: the household would be spending £3 to get satisfaction that it could have acquired for only £1.

What the household needs to consider is not the utility of the last unit of each commodity consumed, but the utility of the last penny spent on each commodity. To illustrate, imagine a household whose utility from the last penny it spent on carrots is three times the utility it gets from the last penny it spent on Brussels sprouts. The household's total utility could clearly be increased by switching a penny of expenditure from sprouts to carrots and gaining the difference between the utility obtained from a penny spent on each.

The utility-maximizing household will continue to switch its expenditure from sprouts to carrots as long as a penny spent on carrots yields more utility than a penny spent on sprouts. But this switching reduces the quantity of sprouts being consumed and, given the law of diminishing marginal utility, raises the marginal utility of sprouts: at the same time, it increases the quantity of carrots consumed, and thereby lowers the marginal utility of carrots. Eventually the marginal utilities will have changed enough so that the utility yielded by a penny spent on carrots is just equal to the utility yielded by a penny spent on sprouts. At this point, there is nothing to be gained by a further switch of expenditure from sprouts to carrots. If the household did persist in reallocating its expenditure, it would further reduce the marginal utility of carrots (by consuming more of them) and raise the marginal utility of sprouts (by consuming less of them). Further reallocation would then lower total utility, because the utility of a penny spent on sprouts would now exceed the utility of a penny spent on carrots.

> **The household maximizing its utility will allocate its expenditure among commodities so that the utility of the last penny spent on each is equal.**

Let us now leave carrots and sprouts and deal with commodities in general. Denote the marginal utility of the last unit of one commodity, X, by M_x and its price by p_x. Let M_y and p_y refer to the marginal utility and the price of a second commodity, Y. The marginal utility per penny spent on X will be M_x/p_x. For example, if the last unit of X adds 30 units to utility and costs 2p, then its marginal utility *per penny* is $30/2 = 15$.

The condition required for a household to maximize its utility is, for all pairs of commodities, X and Y,

$$\frac{M_x}{p_x} = \frac{M_y}{p_y}.$$ (1)

This is just another way of saying that the household allocates its expenditure so that the utility gained from the last penny spent on each commodity is equal.

This is the fundamental equation of the utility theory of demand. Each household demands each commodity up to the point at which the marginal utility of a penny spent on it is the same as the marginal utility of a penny spent on every other commodity. When this condition is met, the household cannot increase its total utility by shifting a penny of expenditure from one commodity to another.

An alternative interpretation of household equilibrium   Multiplying both sides of equation (1) by p_x/M_y produces the following:

$$\frac{M_x}{M_y} = \frac{p_x}{p_y}.$$ (2)

The right-hand side of this equation is the *relative* price of the two commodities. It is outside the control of the individual household, which reacts to market prices but is powerless to change them. The left-hand side concerns the ability of the commodities to add to the household's satisfaction and is within the control of the household. By determining the quantities of different commodities it buys, the household also determines their marginal utilities.

If the two sides of equation (2) are not equal, the household can increase its total satisfaction by rearranging its purchases. Assume, for example, that the price of a unit of X is twice the price of a unit of Y, $(p_x/p_y = 2)$, while the marginal utility of a unit of X is three times that of a unit of Y, $(M_x/M_y = 3)$. It will now pay the household to buy more X and less Y. If, for example, it reduces its purchases of Y by two units, it will free enough purchasing power to buy a unit of X. Since one new unit of X bought yields 1.5 times the satisfaction of two units of Y forgone, this switch is worth making. What about a further switch of X for Y? As the household buys more X and less Y, the marginal utility of X will fall and the marginal utility of Y will rise. The household will carry on rearranging its purchases – reducing Y consumption and increasing X consumption – until, in this example, the marginal utility of X, like its price, is only twice that of Y. At this point total utility cannot be increased further by rearranging purchases between the two commodities.

The household is faced with a set of prices that it cannot change. It responds to these prices, and maximizes its satisfaction, by adjusting the things it can change, the quantities of the various goods it purchases, until equation (2) is satisfied for all pairs of commodities. This type of equation occurs frequently in economics. One side represents the choices the outside world presents to decision-takers and the other side represents the effect of their decisions on themselves. The equation expresses the equilibrium position reached when decision-takers have made the best adjustment they can to the external conditions that limit their choices.

When all households are fully adjusted to a given set of market prices, all households will have identical ratios of their marginal utilities for each pair of goods. This is because each household faces the same set of market prices. Of course, a rich household may consume more of each commodity than a poor household. The rich and the poor households (and every other household) will, however, adjust their *relative* purchases of each commodity so that the relative marginal utilities are the same set of market prices. Of course, a rich household may consume more of each commodity purchase X and Y to the point at which the household's marginal utility of X is twice its marginal utility of Y.

The derivation of the household's demand curve

To derive the household's demand curve for a commodity, we ask what happens when there is a change in the price of that commodity. To do this for carrots, let X stand for carrots and Y for all other commodities in equation (2).

Now assume that carrots involve such a small proportion of the household's total expenditure that the marginal utilities of all *other goods* are unaffected when it spends a little more or a little less on carrots. Consider an example. If total expenditure on carrots rises from £1 to £2 a month in response to a 10 per cent fall in the price of carrots, this is a large increase in carrot consumption and the marginal utility of carrots will fall. But the extra pound spent on carrots may mean only 1p less spent on each of a hundred commodities. The reduction in the consumption of each is so small that it will have a negligible effect on their marginal utilities.

The slope of the demand curve What will happen if, with all other prices constant, the price of carrots rises? The household that started from a position of equilibrium will now find itself in a situation in which[1]

$$\frac{MU \, of \, carrots}{MU \, of \, Y} < \frac{price \, of \, carrots}{price \, of \, Y}. \tag{3}$$

To restore equilibrium, it must buy less carrots, thereby raising their marginal utility until once again equation (2) is satisfied (where X is carrots). The common sense of this is that the marginal utility of carrots *per penny* falls when its price rises. If the household began with the utility of the last penny spent on carrots equal to the utility of the last penny spent on all other goods, the rise in carrot prices makes this no longer true. The household must buy fewer carrots (and more of other goods) until the marginal utility of carrots has risen enough that the utility of a penny spent on carrots is the same as it was before. Thus, if carrot prices double, the quantity purchased is reduced until the marginal utility of carrots doubles.

This analysis leads to the basic prediction of demand theory.

> **A rise in the price of a commodity (with income and the prices of all other commodities held constant) will lead to a decrease in the quantity of the commodity demanded by each household.**

If this prediction is valid for each household, it is also valid for all households taken together. Thus the theory predicts a downward-sloping market demand curve.

Elasticity of demand

When the price of carrots rises, will the household cut its purchases a lot or a little? If the price doubles, we have already predicted that the household will reduce its purchases until the marginal utility has doubled, but we do not yet know if this will be accomplished by a large or a small reduction in purchases. Figure 14.2 shows two possibilities. If carrots have a marginal utility curve

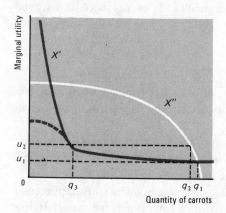

Fig. 14.2 Two alternative marginal utility schedules for carrots

---

[1] The inequality sign ($<$) always points to the smaller of two magnitudes. Since the price of carrots rose, the right-hand side of equation (2) increased and the left-hand side stayed the same. Thus equation (2) was replaced by the inequality shown in (3).

such as X', which is flat over the relevant range, consumption is cut from q_1 to q_3 before the marginal utility is doubled from u_1 to u_2. If carrots have a steep marginal utility curve over the relevant range, such as X'', only a slight reduction in purchases from q_1 to q_2 suffices to double their marginal utility. In both cases the household reaches an equilibrium that satisfies equation (2), but in one case purchases fall by a large amount, whereas in the other case they fall only a little.

Curve X' is shown in two forms in Figure 14.2. The solid version has a higher total utility than X'' because the utility of the first units consumed is very high. The dashed version has a much lower total utility than X''. Notice that the reactions to the rise in price are independent of the shape of the curve outside the relevant range. Curve X' could be as shown by the solid line or it could be shown by the broken line, and the result would be the same when the household cuts consumption to raise marginal utility from u_1 to u_2. This leads to the following important conclusion.

The magnitude of the response of quantity demanded to a change in price (i.e., the elasticity of demand) depends on the marginal utility over the relevant range and has no necessary relation to total utility.

Confusion between total and marginal utilities: some examples

The paradox of value This apparent paradox, which was discussed at the beginning of this chapter, arises because an intuitively appealing hypothesis is obviously refuted by any number of day-to-day observations. Early economists believed that commodities with high total utilities should be expensive because people valued them highly, while commodities with low total utilities should be cheap because people did not value them highly. They were thus arguing that market values should be related to total utilities. These economists referred to market values as *exchange values* and to total utilities as *use values*. They posed their problem by saying that use values should be, but were observed not to be, related to exchange values.

The hypothesis compares the total market value of two commodities with their total utilities.[1] A precise statement of it would be:

$$\frac{p \times q \text{ of diamonds}}{p \times q \text{ of water}} = \frac{\text{total utility of diamonds}}{\text{total utility of water}}. \tag{4}$$

This relation does not hold in the real world since the total utility of diamonds is always less than the total utility of water, while at many times and places the total market value of diamonds traded exceeds the total market value of water.

We have seen already that we should not expect market behaviour to be related to total utility. When the price of carrots doubles in Figure 14.2, for example, the reaction of quantity demanded is the same with the broken black marginal utility curve as with the solid black curve. Yet these two curves imply very different total utilities. The paradox of value is explained because relation (4) is not a valid deduction from household utility maximization. Maximizing utility requires relating market prices to marginal utility (equation 2), not relating total market values of purchases to total utilities (equation 4).

---

[1] We cannot relate the total utilities of two commodities simply to their relative market *prices*, since we can make the latter be anything we want by choosing our units appropriately. For example, a bushel of diamonds is expensive relative to a gallon of water, but a small industrial diamond is cheap relative to a million gallons of water.

To see this intuitively, remember that water is cheap because there is so much of it that people consume it until its *marginal* utility is very low, so they are unwilling to pay a high price for a little more of it. Diamonds are very expensive because they are scarce (the owners of diamond mines keep diamonds scarce by limiting output), so people have to stop consuming them at a point where marginal utility is still high. Thus consumers are prepared to pay a high price for an additional diamond.

Necessities, luxuries and total utility   On page 104 we discussed the common tendency to divide commodities into two groups: necessities, having very low price elasticities of demand, and luxuries, having very high elasticities. The reasoning behind this division can be re-stated using the language of utility theory. There are commodities, called luxuries, that have low total utilities. Since they can easily be dispensed with, they have highly elastic demands: when their prices rise, consumers stop purchasing them. There are other commodities, called necessities, that have high total utilities. These commodities have almost completely inelastic demands because when their prices rise, the consumer has no choice but to continue to buy them. Many goods fall into one or the other of these classes, entertainment being an example of a luxury and food an example of a necessity.

Earlier we pointed out that the facts do not support this hypothesis. We can now see *why* this is so. This hypothesis tries to predict elasticity, which is the reaction of the quantity demanded to a small change in price, from a knowledge of total utilities. But as we saw above, elasticity is related to marginal, not total, utility. Those who predict relative demand elasticities on the basis solely of relative total utilities can thus expect to be wrong as often as they are right, since we do not expect elasticities and total utilities to be related one way or the other.

Pricing policies related to total utilities   There is very little doubt that the emotional reaction of people to goods is in response to their total rather than to their marginal utilities. We often hear an argument such as the following: 'Water is a necessity of life, and it would be wrong to make people pay for it.' Such views often produce curious results. If, for example, water is provided free instead of at a modest price, the additional consumption that will occur will be on account of the many uses that yield a relatively low utility (such as letting the water run while cleaning one's teeth). The relevant question when deciding between a zero and a modest price for water is not 'Is water so necessary that we would not want to deprive anyone of *all* of it?' but rather 'Are the marginal uses of water which our policy will encourage so necessary that we want to encourage them in spite of the fact that it is costly to provide the water for these uses?' Clearly, these two questions can be given different answers.

Evidence about the consumption of water at various prices suggests that the marginal utility curve for water is shaped somewhat like the curve labelled X' in Figure 14.2, so that much more water is consumed at a zero price than at a modest positive price. This additional water has an opportunity cost, since its provision requires resources. If the utility of the commodities forgone is higher than the utility of the extra water consumed, then people are worse off as a result of receiving water free. A charge for water would release resources from water production to produce goods that yield a higher utility. (Against this, of course, would have to be set the cost of metering water consumption and collecting accounts.)

The belief that some minimum quantity of water is so important that no one should be deprived of it is quite irrelevant to the policy decision about whether to provide water free or at a modest price. One might wish to provide some minimum of water free, but this is not the primary effect of making water generally free.

The measurement of total utilities by attitude surveys Attitude surveys often ask people which of several alternatives they prefer. Such questions *measure total rather than marginal utilities*.[1] Where the behaviour being predicted involves an either-or decision, such as to vote for the Socialist or the Conservative candidate, the total utility that is attached to each party or candidate will indeed be what matters, because the voter must choose one and reject the other. Where the decision is a marginal one regarding a little more or a little less, however, total utility is not what will determine behaviour. If one attempts to predict behaviour in these cases from a knowledge of total utilities, even if the information is correct, one will be hopelessly in error.

Here is an example of how such surveys can be misleading. A political party made a survey to determine what types of public expenditure people thought most valuable. Unemployment benefits rated very high. The party was subsequently astonished when it aroused great voter hostility by increasing unemployment benefits. Although the party was surprised, there was nothing inconsistent or irrational in the voters' feeling that protection of the unemployed was a very good thing, providing a high total utility, while additional payments were unnecessary and therefore had a low marginal utility.

Consumers' surplus

Diminishing marginal utility gives rise to a concept that has been extremely influential, that of consumers' surplus. A precise definition will follow later. Let us now see how the 'surplus' arises from the fact that the market places the same value on each unit of a commodity that the household purchases, while the household places a different value on each unit.

To illustrate, we first conduct an imaginary experiment with consumer A and product Z. We start by asking A, 'If you are consuming no Z at all, how much would you be willing to pay to obtain one unit of Z per week?' Assume he replies £3. We then ask, if he was already consuming one unit, how much would he pay for a second unit per week? After a bit of thought, he answers £1·50. Adding one unit per week with each question, we discover that he would be willing to pay £1 to get a third unit per week and 80p, 60p, 50p, 40p, 30p, 25p and 20p for successive units from the fourth to the tenth units per week. The information is summarized in column (2) of Table 14.2. It shows that he puts progressively lower valuations on each additional unit of Z, and this illustrates the general concept of diminishing marginal utility.

Of course the consumer does not have to pay a different price for each unit of Z he consumes each week. Instead, he finds that he can buy all the Z he wants at the prevailing market price. Suppose the price is 30p. He will buy eight units per week because he values the eighth unit at exactly the market price while valuing all earlier units at higher amounts. Because he values the first unit at £3 but he gets it for 30p, he makes a 'profit' of £2·70 on that unit. Between his £1·50 valuation of the second unit and what he has to pay for it, he clears a 'profit' of £1·20. He clears 70p on the third unit, and so on. These 'profit' amounts are called his consumers' surpluses on each unit. They are shown in column (3) of Table 14.2.

---

[1] I am indebted to Professor G.C. Archibald for making this penetrating point when we were discussing the practical value of a particular attitude survey.

Table 14.2 Consumers' surplus on consumption of commodity Z by household A

(1) Units of Z consumed per week	(2) Amount A would pay to get this unit of Z	(3) Consumers' surplus if Z costs 30 pence per unit
First	£3·00	£2·70
Second	1·50	1·20
Third	1·00	0·70
Fourth	0·80	0·50
Fifth	0·60	0·30
Sixth	0·50	0·20
Seventh	0·40	0·10
Eighth	0·30	0·00
Ninth	0·25	—
Tenth	0·20	—

If we sum the surpluses gained on each unit of Z consumed, the total consumers' surplus is found to be £5·70. Note that instead of summing his consumers' surplus on each unit, we could arrive at the same total in a different way. First, add up the valuation he places on each of the eight units consumed. This total value is £8·10. Then determine what he actually paid: $8 \times £0·30 = £2·40$. Subtract £2·40 from £8·10 to obtain the consumers' surplus of £5·70.

While other consumers would put different numerical values into Table 14.2, diminishing marginal utility implies that the figures in column (2) would decline for each consumer. Since a consumer will go on buying further units until the value he places on the last unit equals the market price, it follows that there will be a consumers' surplus on every unit consumed except the last one.

In general, CONSUMERS' SURPLUS is the difference between the total value consumers place on all the units consumed of some commodity and the payment they must make to purchase the same amount of that commodity. The total value placed by each consumer on the total consumption of some commodity can be estimated in at least two ways: the valuation that the consumer places on each successive unit may be summed; or the consumer may be asked how much he or she would pay to consume the amount in question if the alternative were to have none of the commodity.

This derivation of consumers' surplus yields only an approximation that ignores the 'income effect' of the amount spent on commodity Z. Basically it assumes, as does the derivation of the demand curve on page 170, that commodity Z accounts for a negligible proportion of the consumer's total purchases. Thus the marginal utilities of consumption of all other goods are not affected by variations in the amount of money spent on Z (and hence variations in the amount spent on everything else). In some circumstances the approximation may be a very poor one. But no required correction will upset the general result that, when consumers can buy all units they require at a single market price, they pay much less for the quantity consumed than they would be willing to pay if faced with the choice between that amount and nothing.

The data in columns (1) and (2) of Table 14.2 give A's demand curve for Z. It is his demand curve because he will go on buying units of Z as long as he values each unit at least as much as the market price he must pay for it. When the market price is £3 per unit, he will buy only one unit; when it is £1·50, he will buy two units – and so on.

The data in the Table are graphed in Figure 14.3. The total valuation that A places on the eight units of Z he consumes is given by the areas of the eight rectangles, each of which gives the valuation attached to the unit in question. But because A gets each unit at a price of 30p, the total amount spent is given by the dark shaded area (8 units *times* 30p). Hence the consumers' surplus is the light shaded area, the area between the demand 'curve' and the line indicating the market price.

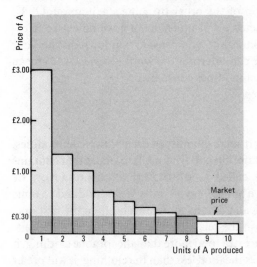

Fig. 14.3 Consumers' surplus for an individual

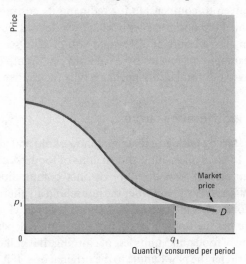

Fig. 14.4 Consumers' surplus for the market

Figure 14.4 illustrates a smooth market demand curve for commodity Z. It shows how total purchases of Z by all households vary with its market price. As with a single consumer, the area under the demand curve shows the total value that consumers place on a given quantity. This is the maximum amount that they would pay in order to consume that quantity rather than have none at all. It is also the amount they would pay if forced to buy the commodity a unit at a time, paying for each unit the full value that they placed on it. For example, the total value that consumers place on q_1 units is the entire shaded area under the demand curve up to q_1. At a market price of p_1 the amount paid for q_1 units is the dark shaded area. Hence consumers' surplus is the light shaded area.

> **Consumers' surplus is a measure of the difference between the value that consumers place on their total consumption of some commodity and the amount they must pay for it. A utility-maximizing household will consume any commodity up to the point where its consumers' surplus on the last unit purchased is zero.**

We shall find many uses for the concept of consumers' surplus later in this book.

Indifference theory

The utility theory of household behaviour came first historically and is still valued because of the great insights provided by the concept of marginal utility. With the publication in 1939 of Sir John

R. Hicks's classic *Value and Capital*, an alternative approach, called *indifference-preference analysis*, or just *indifference theory* for short, became popular in English-language economics. This is not a competing theory, but a slightly different way of looking at choices made by households. Its major innovation was that it did not assume utility to be measurable.

In utility theory, we start by asking what happens to the household's satisfactions if it consumes more or less of one commodity. In indifference theory, we start by asking a different, but closely related, question: 'If the household is consuming two commodities, how much more of one must it be given to compensate for reducing its consumption of the other by some small amount?' To parallel the questions with which we opened our discussion of utility theory, we now ask: 'How many extra hours of TV would you need to see per month to compensate you for reducing your consumption of water by 35 gallons per month?' We can interpret the word *compensate* to mean 'leave your total utility unchanged by the change in commodities consumed'.

An indifference curve

We start by taking an imaginary household and giving it some quantity of each of two commodities, say 18 units of clothing and 10 units of food. (A consumption pattern for a household that contains quantities of two or more distinct commodities is called a BUNDLE or a COMBINATION OF COMMODITIES.) Now offer the household an alternative bundle, say 13 units of clothing and 15 units of food. This alternative has 5 units fewer of clothing and 5 units more of food than the first one. Whether the household prefers this bundle depends on the relative value that it places on 5 units more of food and 5 units less of clothing. If it values the extra food more than the forgone clothing, it will prefer the new bundle to the original one. If it values the food less than the clothing, it will prefer the original bundle. There is a third alternative: if the household values the extra food the same as it values the forgone clothing, it would gain equal satisfaction from the two alternative bundles. In this case the household is said to be *indifferent* between the two bundles.

Assume that we have identified the bundles shown in Table 14.3, each of which gives equal satisfaction. There will, of course, be other bundles that yield the same level of satisfaction. All of these are shown in Figure 14.5 by the smooth curve that passes through the points plotted from the table. This curve is an indifference curve. In general, an INDIFFERENCE CURVE shows all combinations of commodities that yield the same satisfaction to the household. A household is *indifferent* between the combinations indicated by any two points on one indifference curve.

Table 14.3 Alternative bundles of food and clothing giving equal satisfaction to a household

Bundle	Clothing	Food
a	30	5
b	18	10
c	13	15
d	10	20
e	8	25
f	7	30

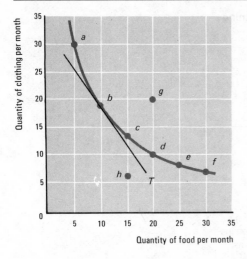

Fig. 14.5 An indifference curve

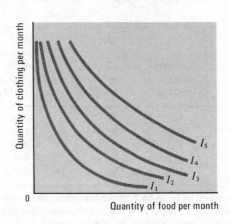

Fig. 14.6 An indifference map for a household

Any points above and to the right of the curve show combinations of food and clothing that the household would prefer to combinations indicated by points on the curve. Consider, for example, the combination of 20 food and 20 clothing, which is represented by point *g* in the figure. Although it might not be obvious that this bundle must be preferred to bundle *a* (which has more clothing but less food), it is obvious that it will be preferred to bundle *c*, because there is both less clothing and less food represented at *c* than at *g*. Inspection of the graph shows that *any* point above the curve will be obviously superior to *some* points on the curve in the sense that it will contain both more food and more clothing than those points on the curve. But since all points on the curve are equal in the household's eyes, the point above the curve must thus be superior to *all* points on the curve. By a similar argument, points such as *h*, which are below and to the left of the curve, represent bundles of goods that are inferior to bundles represented by points on the curve.

The hypothesis of a diminishing marginal rate of substitution

The basic postulate in utility theory is diminishing marginal utility: the more of a commodity already consumed by the household, the lower the utility of a bit more of it. The analogous postulate in indifference theory is DIMINISHING MARGINAL RATE OF SUBSTITUTION:

> **The less of one commodity presently being consumed by a household, the more unwilling will it be to give up a unit of that commodity to obtain an additional unit of a second commodity.**

This hypothesis is illustrated in Table 14.4 which is based on the example of food and clothing shown in Table 14.3. When, for example, the household moves from consumption bundle *a* to bundle *b*, it is sacrificing 12 units of clothing while gaining 5 units of food, making a rate of substitution of -2.4. This means that the household is prepared to give up 2·4 units of clothing for every extra unit of food obtained. As we move down the table through points *b* to *f*, the household is consuming bundles with less and less clothing and more and more food. In accordance with the

Table 14.4 The marginal rate of substitution between clothing and food*

Movement	(1) Change in clothing	(2) Change in food	(3) Marginal rate of substitution (1) ÷ (2)
From *a* to *b*	−12	5	−2·4
From *b* to *c*	−5	5	−1·0
From *c* to *d*	−3	5	−0·6
From *d* to *e*	−2	5	−0·4
From *e* to *f*	−1	5	−0·2

* This table is based on Table 14.2. When the household moves from *a* to *b*, it gives up 12 units of clothing and gains 5 units of food; it remains at the same level of overall satisfaction. The household at point *a* was prepared to sacrifice 12 clothing for 5 food (i.e., 12/5 = 2·4 units of clothing per unit of food obtained). When the household moves from *b* to *c*, it sacrifices 5 clothing for 5 food (a rate of substitution of 1 unit of clothing for each unit of food).

hypothesis of diminishing marginal rate of substitution, the rate at which the household is willing to give up further clothing to get more food diminishes. When the household moves from *c* to *d*, for example, it is only prepared to give up 6/10 of a unit of clothing to get a further unit of food, while when it moves from *e* to *f*, it will only give up 2/10 of a unit. These calculations illustrate the hypothesis: the less clothing and the more food does the household already consume, the smaller the further marginal sacrifice in clothing the household will be willing to make to get a further unit of food.

The geometrical expression of this hypothesis is found in the shape of the indifference curve. Look closely, for example, at the slope of the curve in Figure 14.5. Its downward slope indicates that, if the household is to have less of one commodity, it must have more of the other to compensate. Diminishing marginal rate of substitution is shown by the fact that the curve is convex viewed from the origin: moving down the curve to the right, its slope gets flatter and flatter. The slope of the curve is the marginal rate of substitution, the rate at which one commodity must be substituted for the other in order to keep total utility constant. Geometrically the slope of the indifference curve at any point is indicated by the slope of the tangent to the curve at that point. The slope of tangent *T* drawn to the curve at point *b* shows the marginal rate of substitution at that point. It is visually obvious that moving down the curve to the right, the slope of the tangent, and hence the marginal rate of substitution at that point, gets flatter and flatter.[1] (The Note on Definitions, p. xxiii, is relevant at this point.)

---

[1] Table 14.3 calculates the rate of substitution between distinct points on the indifference curve. Strictly speaking these are the incremental rates of substitution between the two points. Geometrically this incremental rate is given by the slope of the chord joining the two points. The marginal rate refers to the slope of the curve at a single point and is given by the slope of the tangent to the curve at the point. For a discussion of the relation between marginal and incremental rates, see page 32.

The indifference map

So far we have constructed only a single indifference curve. There must, however, be a similar curve through other points in Figure 14.5. Starting at any point, such as g, there will be other combinations that will yield equal satisfaction to the household and, if the points indicating all of *these* combinations are connected, they will form another indifference curve. This exercise can be repeated as many times as we wish, generating a new indifference curve each time.

In the previous section points g and h were compared to the indifference curve in Figure 14.5. It follows from this discussion that the farther away any indifference curve is from the origin, the higher is the level of satisfaction given by the combinations of goods indicated by it.

A set of indifference curves is called an INDIFFERENCE MAP. An example is shown in Figure 14.6. It specifies the household's tastes by showing its rate of substitution between the two commodities for every level of consumption of these commodities. When economists say that a household's tastes are *given*, they do not mean merely that the household's current consumption pattern is given; rather, they mean that the household's entire indifference map is given.

The equilibrium of the household

The indifference map describes the preferences or tastes of a household. In a sense, it tells us what the household would like to do: move to higher and higher indifference curves. To find out what the household will actually do, we must know what it can do. This information is supplied by the budget line we derived in Chapter 13. Figure 14.7 brings together the household's tastes, as shown by its indifference curves, and the possibilities actually open to it, as shown by its budget line. The particular budget line assumes a household income of £75 a month and prices of £2·50 per unit for clothing and £3·00 per unit for food. Any point on the budget line can be attained. Which one will the household actually choose?

Suppose that it starts at point a in Figure 14.7, where it is on indifference curve I_1. If it moves to point b, it is still just on its budget line, but it has moved to a preferred position, i.e., to a combination of goods on a higher indifference curve. The household can continue this process, moving down the budget line through point c and attaining higher curves, until it reaches point d. If it moves further, however, to points e, f, and g, it will begin to move to lower indifference curves.

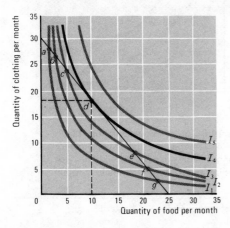

Fig. 14.7 The equilibrium of a household

If we start the household at a point to the right of *d*, say at *g*, the same argument applies: the household can attain higher curves by moving up its budget line until it reaches *d*, but if it persists beyond *d*, it moves to lower curves. This leads to the following conclusion.

Satisfaction is maximized at the point where an indifference curve is tangent to a budget line. At that point the slope of the indifference curve (the marginal rate of substitution of the goods in the household's preferences) is equal to the slope of the budget line (the opportunity cost of one good in terms of the other as determined by market prices).[1]

The common sense of this result is that, if the household values commodities at a different rate than does the market, there is room for profitable exchange. The household can give up the commodity it values less than the market does and take in return the commodity it values more than the market does. When the household is prepared to swap commodities at the same rate as they can be traded on the market, there is no further opportunity for it to raise its utility by substituting one commodity for the other.

Notice that this conclusion is very similar to the one we reached with marginal utility theory. The household is presented with market information (prices) that it cannot change. It adjusts to these prices by choosing a bundle of goods such that, at the margin, its own subjective relative evaluation of the two commodities conforms with the objective relative evaluations given by market prices.

When the household has chosen the consumption bundle that maximizes its satisfactions, it will go on consuming the goods in the proportions indicated unless something changes. The household is thus in equilibrium.

A change in income   Changes in income lead to parallel shifts of the budget line (see page 156). For each level of income there will, of course, be an equilibrium position at which an indifference curve is tangent to the relevant budget line. Each such equilibrium position means that the household is doing as well as it possibly can for that level of income. An example is shown in Figure 14.8. As the

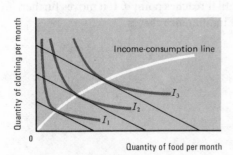

Fig. 14.8 The income-consumption line showing the reaction of the household to changes in its money income with money prices constant

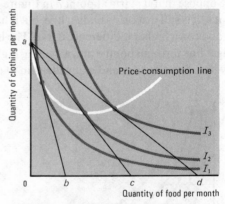

Fig. 14.9 The price-consumption line showing the reaction of the household to changes in the price of food with the price of clothing and money income held constant

---

[1] See the discussion of relative prices, opportunity costs and the slope of the budget line in Chapter 13.

household's income is twice increased, the budget line moves outwards from a tangency with indifference curve I_1 to I_2 to I_3. If we move the budget line through all possible levels of income, and join up all the points of equilibrium, we will trace what is called an INCOME-CONSUMPTION LINE. This line shows how consumption bundles change as income changes, with relative prices held constant.[1]

A change in price We saw in Chapter 13 that a change in the relative prices of the two commodities changed the slope of the budget line. Assume now that the money price of food falls, the money price of clothing being held constant. This is illustrated in Figure 14.9 in which the fall in the price of food pivots the budget line from *ab* to *ac* to *ad*. Equilibrium points of tangency are successively with indifference curves I_1, I_2 and I_3. If we now vary the price of food continuously, we will find an equilibrium position for each price. By connecting these, we trace out a PRICE-CONSUMPTION LINE. This line shows how consumption of the two commodities varies as the price of one changes, the price of the other and the household's money income being held constant. An illustration is shown by the white line in Figure 14.9.

The household's demand curve

To derive the household's demand curve for any commodity, we need to depart from our world of two commodities. We are now interested in what happens to the household's demand for some commodity, say carrots, as the price of that commodity changes, *all other prices being held constant* (see pp. 75–6). We plot a new indifference map in Figure 14.10 in which we represent the quantity of carrots on the horizontal axis and the value of all other commodities consumed on the vertical axis. The indifference curves tell us the rate at which the household is prepared to swap carrots for money (which allows it to buy all other goods) at each level of consumption of carrots and of other goods.

We now plot the household's income on the money axis. In Figure 14.10 the household has £*a* of income per month and is thus able to consume £*a* worth of all other goods, if it consumes no carrots. Given the money price of carrots and the household's income, we obtain a budget line showing all those combinations that the household can consume. We now change the money price of carrots (thus changing the slope of the budget line through *a*). By joining the points of equilibrium, we trace out a price-consumption line between carrots and all other commodities in just the same way as we traced out such a line for food and clothing in Figure 14.9.

Note that Figure 14.10 is very similar to Figure 14.9. The axes are labelled differently and the price-consumption line in Figure 14.10 is crowded into the upper part of the diagram, indicating that whatever the price of carrots, the household does not spend a large proportion of its income on them.

Every point on the price-consumption line corresponds to one money price of carrots and one quantity of carrots demanded. To derive the household's demand curve we plot these pairs of values on a new figure with price on one axis and quantity on the other. In Figure 14.10 the quantity of carrots consumed increases as the price of carrots falls, so the demand curve has a downward slope.

---

[1] We can use this income-consumption line to derive the curve relating consumption of one commodity to income that we first introduced on pp. 77–8. To do this, we merely take the quantity of either good consumed at the equilibrium position on a given budget line and plot it against the level of money income that determined the position of the particular budget line. By repeating this for each level of income, we produce the required curve.

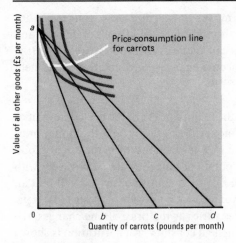

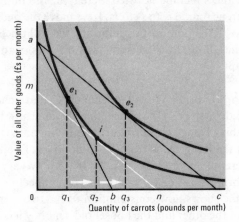

Fig. 14.10 The derivation of a household's demand curve for carrots

Fig. 14.11 The income and substitution effects of a fall in the price of carrots

Can the household's demand curve ever slope upward? The income and substitution effect[1]
The demand curve that we derived above has a downward slope: a fall in the price of carrots increases the quantity demanded. Is this a necessary result or merely a consequence of the way in which we happened to draw the indifference curves? To answer this question we must distinguish between the income and substitution effects.

A fall in the price of carrots has an effect similar to that of a rise in income since it makes it possible for the household to have more of all goods. In Figure 14.10 a fall in the price of carrots takes the budget line from ac to ad. Wherever the household was located on ac, it clearly can, if it wishes, move to ad by going upwards to the right thus consuming more carrots *and* more of everything else.

We can imagine removing this INCOME EFFECT of a price change by insisting that the household remain on its original indifference curve in spite of any change in price. A change in relative prices changes the slope of the budget line, but, if the household is to remain on its original indifference curve, money income must be changed just enough – so that the budget line slides around the same curve, always remaining tangent to it.

Assume for example, that the price of carrots is cut in half, so that the slope of the budget line becomes only half as steep, the actual line pivoting from ab to ac in Figure 14.11. The household was initially in equilibrium at point e_1 on Figure 14.11. If we adjust the position of the budget line after the price fall so as to keep the household on its initial indifference curve, the new position of equilibrium is at i. (The line mn is parallel to ac, and thus its slope is given by the new set of relative prices.) The increase in the consumption of carrots from q_1 to q_2 is the SUBSTITUTION EFFECT, the effect on carrot consumption of a fall in the price of carrots, household *utility* held constant. Because the indifference curve slopes downward to the right, a fall in the price of carrots necessarily raises the

---

[1] This section deals with a topic that is often left for intermediate courses and it may be omitted without loss of continuity.

quantity bought, if the level of utility is held constant. The substitution effect is thus negative: a change in price leads quantity demanded to change in the opposite direction.

We have said that halving the price of carrots will cause the household to move from e_1 to i on the *same* indifference curve. But this, of course, is not what happens when the price of carrots falls in the real world. No economic dictator reduces everyone's money income to remove any increases in utility they might otherwise get from the change. The budget line actually pivots through a, indicating that the household could obtain more of all goods if it wished. In Figure 14.11 the new budget line is ac and the new equilibrium position is e_2. Thus, when the price falls, carrot consumption rises from q_1 to q_3. This movement can, however, be broken up conceptually into a substitution effect from q_1 to q_2, between the points e_1 and i, which is the result of a change in relative prices, and the increase from q_2 to q_3, between points i and e_2, which is called the *income effect*. This income effect is equivalent to the increase in consumption that would have occurred owing to an outward shift in the budget line, relative prices being held constant at their new level.

In indifference theory the substitution effect is the change in consumption that would occur if relative price changes but the household is held on its original indifference curve. The income effect is the change in consumption as a result of the movement between the original indifference curve and the new indifference curve when the relative price is held constant at its new value.

This distinction permits a concise statement of the conditions under which the demand curve slopes downward. The change in demand for one commodity in response to a change in its price can be thought of as a composite of the income and the substitution effects. The theory predicts that the substitution effect is negative. Thus a fall in the relative price of a commodity, with the level of utility held constant, leads to a rise in the demand for that commodity. For all normal goods, therefore, where a rise in income (a parallel outward shift of the budget line) leads to a rise in demand, the theory gives the unambiguous prediction that more of the commodity will be demanded when its price falls.

A normal good must have a downward-sloping demand curve. A decrease in its price will lead to an increase in quantity demanded owing to both the substitution and the income effects.

In the case of an inferior good, we cannot obtain a definite prediction about what will happen. The income effect of a fall in price leads to a tendency for a decrease in the consumption of the good. But the substitution effect still works for an increase in the quantity demanded. Thus the final result depends on the relative strengths of the two effects. Two cases of a negative income effect are shown in Figures 14.12 and 14.13. The original equilibrium is at e_1, with q_1 pounds of carrots consumed per month. The price of carrots falls, and the pure substitution effect would move the household to i (with $q_2 - q_1$ *more* carrots consumed each month). The income effect is negative, but if it moves the household only to e_2' in Figure 14.12, the net effect is for household consumption to rise from q_1 to q_3. In the case shown in Figure 14.13, the negative income effect is stronger, and the final equilibrium is at e_2'' with the consumption of carrots falling by $q_1 - q_4$ per month as a result of the fall in their price.

A commodity whose price and quantity vary in the same direction is called a GIFFEN GOOD, after the Victorian economist alleged to have observed such a case. It must be an inferior commodity

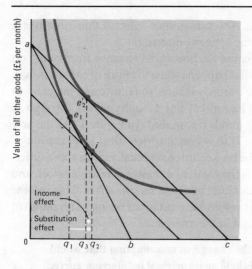

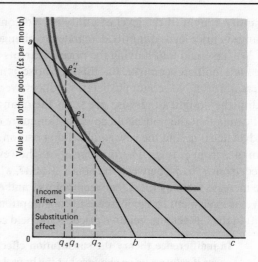

Fig. 14.12 A negative income effect that does not swamp the substitution effect

Fig. 14.13 A negative income effect that swamps the substitution effect to produce a Giffen Good

whose income effect outweighs its normal substitution effect. Such a commodity appears to be a rarely observed, but theoretically possible, exception to the 'law' that all demand curves slope downwards.[1]

We conclude than an upward-sloping demand curve for a product is a theoretical possibility. It requires that the commodity be an inferior good and that the change in price have a large enough negative income effect to offset the substitution effect. We do not expect such a combination of circumstances to occur often, therefore we expect an upward-sloping market demand curve to be a rare exception to the general prediction that demand curves slope downward. We shall examine this exception further in Chapter 15.

---

[1] Indeed there now seems to be some doubt if Giffen actually made and documented the famous alleged observations that upset the apparent universal applicability of the law of demand.

15

The theory of demand: measurements and tests

Much of what economists do to earn a living involves the use of demand measurements. The London Electricity Board asks economists to estimate the demand for electric power over the next decade; the United States National Parks Service asks economists to review its procedures for selling grazing rights and timber stands to private firms. Will a fare increase help to ease the deficit of the London Transport underground and bus system or of the Panama Canal? These are questions that cannot be answered reliably without knowledge of price elasticity of demand. When the United Nations Food and Agricultural Organization (FAO), or a producers' co-op, projects quantities of different foods demanded it needs to know income and price elasticities of demand. Today many industries need to know their products' cross-elasticities of demand with petroleum in order to estimate the effects of sharply changing petroleum prices. To deal effectively with many applied problems, knowledge of relevant demand conditions is indispensable. Fortunately, a great deal of this demand information is either already available or can be obtained without great cost or difficulty. The methods for doing so have been carefully worked out. Solutions to two of the most troubling problems concerning demand measurement are discussed in the second part of this chapter.

Critics of demand theory do not quarrel with the *need* for demand information, or even with the usefulness of applied economics. Some, however, have argued that the theory of demand is wrong, in the sense that its predictions are in conflict with empirical evidence; others have argued that it is empty, in the sense that all it tells us is that 'anything can happen'. In the final part of this chapter we shall consider these criticisms.

Demand measures

The solution of the statistical problems associated with demand measurement has led to a large accumulation of data on demand elasticities. The value of these data to the applied economist shows the usefulness of demand theory.

Price elasticities

Much of the early work on demand measurement concentrated on the agricultural sector. Large fluctuations in agricultural prices provided both the incentive to study this sector and the empirical observations on which to base estimates of price elasticities of demand. Professors Richard Stone, in the UK, and Henry Schultz, in the US, did much of the pioneering work. Many agricultural research centres extended their work, and even today make new estimates of the price elasticities of food-stuffs. The resulting data mostly confirm the general belief in low price elasticities for food products as a whole as well as for many individual products. The policy payoff of this knowledge in terms of understanding agricultural problems has been enormous; it represents an early triumph of empirical work in economics. (See the discussion in Chapter 10.)

Although agricultural commodities often have inelastic demands, the demand for some commodities, such as beef in the United States and domestically produced lamb and mutton in the United Kingdom, are measured to be elastic. The reason for this is that these products have close substitutes. For example, British households can choose between locally produced lamb and mutton and imported varieties (which typically have a somewhat lower quality and price). Similarly, American households can choose among beef, pork and chicken on the basis of price. The data also support the generalization that the broader the category of related products, the lower the observed price elasticity of demand.

Although the importance of the agricultural problem led early investigators to concentrate on the demand for foodstuffs, modern studies have expanded to include virtually the whole range of commodities on which the household spends its income. Particular interest has been attached to the demand for consumers' durables such as cars, radios, refrigerators, television sets and houses. Demands for these types of goods are particularly interesting because they constitute a large fraction of total demand and because they can vary markedly from one year to the next. A durable commodity can usually be made to last for another year; thus purchases can be postponed with greater ease than can purchases of non-durables such as food and services. If enough households decide simultaneously to postpone purchases of durables for even six months, the effect on the economy can be enormous.

Durables as a whole have an inelastic demand, while many individual durables have elastic demands. This is another example of the general proposition that the broader the category, the lower the elasticity because the fewer the close substitutes. Indeed, whether durable or non-durable, most specific manufactured goods have close substitutes, and studies show that they tend to have price-elastic demands. Millinery, for example, has been estimated to have a demand elasticity of 3·0. In contrast, the demand for all clothing tends to be inelastic. The accumulated data on price elasticity confirm this generalization.

> **Any one of a group of close substitutes will tend to have an elastic demand, even though the demand for the group as a whole may be inelastic.**

Income elasticities

A vast amount of data is available on income elasticities. Because changes in income exert a major effect on quantities demanded over time, the FAO has found it useful to estimate income elasticities for dozens of agricultural products, country by country. The data tend to show that the more basic, or staple, a commodity, the lower its income elasticity: food as a whole has an income elasticity of 0·2 in the UK, while in the US pork and such starchy roots as potatoes are inferior goods so that their quantity consumed falls as income rises.

The data show low income elasticities of most foodstuffs in high-income countries. It may seem odd at first sight, therefore, that restaurant meals are shown to have a high income elasticity. The explanation is, however, fairly straightforward. Restaurant meals are almost always more expensive, calorie for calorie, than meals prepared at home: they are thus regarded as an expensive luxury at lower ranges of income, and the demand for them expands substantially as households become better off. Does this mean that the market demand for the foodstuffs that appear on restaurant menus will also have high income elasticities? Generally the answer is No. When a household eats out rather than at home, the main difference is not in what is eaten but in who prepares it. The additional expenditure on food goes mainly to pay the wages of cooks and waiters and to yield a return on the restaurateur's capital. Thus, when a household expands its expenditure on restaurant food by 2·4 per cent in response to a 1 per cent rise in its income, most of this represents an increased demand for a service to replace the housewife's unpaid work, rather than an increased demand for food. We have here a striking example of the general tendency for households to spend a higher proportion of their income on services as their income rises.

Empirical studies tend to confirm that, as income rises, household expenditures follow broadly similar paths in different countries. Summarizing recent studies, Robert Ferber wrote that they tend to bear out earlier findings on income elasticity yielding low elasticities for food and housing, elasticities close to unity for clothing and education, and higher elasticities for various types of recreation, personal care, home operation and other services. Of course there are exceptions to country-wide uniformity. If a commodity plays a very different role in the consumption patterns of different groups, it may be expected to have different demand characteristics, even at comparable levels of income. Wine is a basic part of the French consumption bundle, and its consumption in France is little affected by changes in level of income. Wine in Canada and the United States is evidently a luxury good rather than a necessity at lower levels of income. The difference in income elasticity of demand for poultry between the United Kingdom and Ceylon is a matter of the level of average income as well as of differences in taste.

The accumulated data on income elasticity confirm this generalization:

The more basic an item is in the consumption pattern of households, the lower its income elasticity will be.

Cross-elasticities of demand

In many countries monopoly is illegal. Measurement of cross-elasticities have helped courts to decide on the allegation that a monopoly exists. To illustrate, assume that the government brings suit against a company for buying up all of the firms making aluminium cable, claiming the company has created a monopoly of the product. The company replies that it needs to own all of the firms in order to compete efficiently against the several firms producing copper cable. It argues that these two products are such close substitutes that the firms producing each are in intense competition, so that the only producer of aluminium cable cannot be said to have an effective monopoly over the whole market for cable. Measurement of cross-elasticity can be decisive in such a case. A cross-elasticity of 10, for example, would support the company by showing that the two products were such close substitutes that a monopoly of either was not an effective monopoly of the cable market. A cross-elasticity of 0·5, on the other hand, would support the government's contention that the monopoly of aluminium cable was a monopoly over a complete market.

Other variables

Modern studies show that demand is often influenced by a wide variety of socio-economic factors – family size, age, geographical location, type of employment, wealth and income expectations – not included in the traditional theory of demand. Although significant, the total contribution of all these factors to changes in demand tends to be small. Typically, less than 30 per cent of the variations in demand are accounted for by these 'novel' factors and a much higher proportion is explained by the traditional variables of prices and current incomes.

Problems of demand measurement

We have observed here just the tip of the iceberg of accumulated knowledge about the determinants of specific demand elasticities. The data are so plentiful that any economist who wishes to make an applied study of a particular market is likely to have some established evidence on which to draw. This relatively recent explosion of knowledge came about when econometricians overcame major problems in measuring demand relationships. A full discussion must be left to a course in econometrics, but some aspects of such measurements are sufficiently troubling to most students to make them worth mentioning.

Everything is changing at once

Since in a market economy all kinds of things are happening at once, how can they be sorted out into the neat theoretical categories we have created? When market demand changes over time, it is usually because *all* of the influences that affect demand have been changing.

What, for example, is to be made of the observation that the quantity of butter consumed per capita rose by 10 per cent over a period in which average household income rose by 5 per cent, the price of butter fell by 3 per cent and the price of margarine rose by 4 per cent? How much of the change is due to income elasticity of demand, how much to price elasticity and how much to the cross-elasticity between butter and margarine? If there is only this one observation, the question cannot be answered. If, however, there is a large number of observations showing, say, quantity demanded, income, price of butter and price of margarine every month for four or five years, it is possible, as we saw in Chapter 3, to discover the separate influence of each of the variables.

Separating the influences of demand and supply

A second set of problems concerns using data on price and quantity actually bought and sold to estimate demand and supply curves. We do not observe directly what people wish to buy and what producers wish to sell. Rather, we see what they do buy and what they do sell. The problem of how to estimate both demand and supply curves from observed market data on prices and quantities actually traded is called the IDENTIFICATION PROBLEM.

The nature of the problem can be illustrated simply. We start by assuming that all situations observed in the real world are equilibrium ones, in the sense that they are produced by the intersection of demand and supply curves. If, as in Figure 15.1 (i), the demand curve stays put while the supply curve shifts, possibly because of crop variations in some agricultural commodity, then the

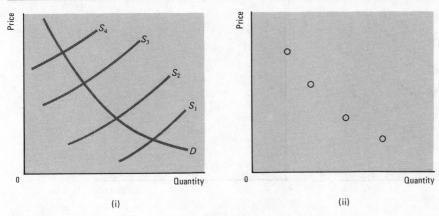

Fig. 15.1 (i) A shifting supply curve and a fixed demand curve; (ii) observations generated by (i)

price-quantity observations illustrated in Figure 15.1 (ii) will be generated. If we draw a line through these observed points, we will trace out the demand curve of Figure 15.1 (i).

Now assume, as illustrated in Figure 15.2 (i), that the supply curve stays put while the demand curve shifts, owing perhaps to changes in the number of consumers or in their incomes. The price-quantity relations that will be observed are those given in Figure 15.2 (ii). If we draw a curve through these points, it will trace out the supply curve in Figure 15.2 (i).

But what if both curves shift? Assume for example that the demand and supply curves in Figure 15.3 (i) shift randomly among the three positions shown. At any one time there is only one demand and one supply curve, but over time every one of the nine possible combinations of one of the demand curves and one of the supply curves shown will exist. As this happens, the series of market observations shown in Figure 15.3 (ii) will be obtained. These trace out neither the demand nor the supply curves that generated them.

The identification problem is surmountable. The key to identifying the demand and supply curves separately is to bring in variables other than price, and then to relate demand to one set and supply to *some other* set. For example, supply of the commodity might be related not only to the

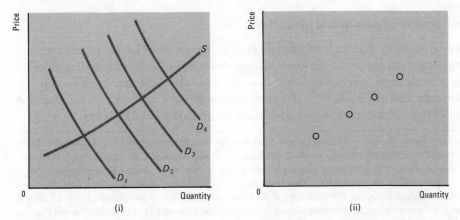

Fig. 15.2 (i) A shifting demand curve and a fixed supply curve; (ii) observations generated by (i)

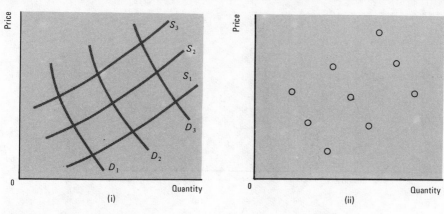

Fig. 15.3 (i) Shifting demand and supply curve; (ii) observations generated by (i)

price of the commodity but also to its cost of production, and demand might be related not only to the price of the commodity but also to consumers' incomes. Provided that both of these other variables vary sufficiently, it is possible to determine the relation between quantity supplied and price as well as the relation between quantity demanded and price. The details of how this is done will be found in a course on econometrics.

In serious applied work, concern is usually given to the identification problem. Sometimes, however, the problem is ignored. Whenever you see an argument such as the following: 'Last year the price of whisky rose by 10 per cent and whisky exports hardly fell at all, so we know that the foreign elasticity of demand must be very low', you should ask if the author has really identified the demand curve. If the rise in price was due to a rise in foreign demand for whisky, we may actually have discovered that the short-run *supply curve* of whisky is very inelastic (since whisky takes several years to manufacture). The general proposition to keep in mind is:

> **Unless we know that one curve has shifted while the other has not, price and quantity data alone are insufficient to reveal anything about the shape of either the demand or the supply curve.**

Why the measurement of demand is important

The work on demand elasticity that we have just surveyed is of great value because it provides our theory of price with empirical content. If we knew *nothing* about demand elasticities, then all of the exercises we have gone through in previous chapters would have very little application to the real world. Some economists hold a different view of the importance of empirical measures of demand. A classical statement of this alternative view was made many years ago by Lord Robbins:[1]

---

[1] L. Robbins, *An Essay on the Nature and Significance of Economic Science* (Macmillan, 1932), pages 98–101. Every economics specialist should read this provocative work. It contains the classic statements of many views still held by economists. It also states a view on the nature of economic theory and its relation to empirical observations that is contradictory to the one presented in this book. Many other economists of Lord Robbins' time shared this view. We quote from him because his is such a clear statement. For a similar one see L. von Mises, *Human Action* (Hodge, 1949), Chapter 2. For a view much closer to the one presented in the earlier parts of this chapter, however, see L. Robbins, 'The Present Position of Economics', *Rivista Di Economica*, September 1959.

Our deductions do not provide any justification for saying that caviare is an economic good and carrion a disutility. Still less do they inform us concerning the intensity of the demand for caviare or the demand to be rid of carrion. ... But is it not desirable to transcend such limitations? Ought we not to wish to be in a position to give numerical values to the scales of valuation, to establish quantitative laws of demand and supply? ... No doubt such knowledge would be useful. But a moment's reflection should make it plain that we are here entering upon a field of investigation *where there is no reason to suppose that uniformities are to be discovered....*

A simple illustration should make this quite clear. ... Suppose we are confronted with an order fixing the price of herrings at a point below the price hitherto ruling in the market. Suppose we are in a position to say, 'According to the researches of Blank (1907–1908) the elasticity of demand for common herring (*Clupea harengus*) is 1·3; the present price-fixing order therefore may be expected to leave an excess of demand over supply of two million barrels.'

But can we hope to attain such an enviable position? Let us assume that in 1907–1908 Blank had succeeded in ascertaining that, with a given price change in that year, the elasticity of demand was 1·3. ... But what reason is there to suppose that he was unearthing a constant law? ... Is it possible reasonably to suppose that coefficients derived from the observation of a particular herring market at a particular time and place have any *permanent* significance – save as Economic History?

The above argument runs somewhat as follows: 'I can think of no reasons why the relationship in question (e.g., the relation between demand and price) should be a stable one; I can in fact think of several reasons why it should not be stable; I conclude, therefore, that in the real world the relationship will not be stable, and attempts to *observe* whether or not it is stable can be ruled out on *a priori* grounds as a waste of time.'

Several criticisms can be made of Robbins' argument. First, *a priori* arguments, although they may strongly suggest the hypothesis that certain relationships will not be stable ones, can never establish this. Even if the *a priori* arguments turn out to be correct most of the time, there always exists the possibility that in a few cases they will be wrong. Only empirical observation is capable of discovering the cases in which the *a priori* argument is wrong.

The second major criticism is that it is extremely important to *economic theory* to know just how variable any given relationship is. If, for example, tastes are so variable that demand curves shift violently from day to day, then all of the comparative static equilibrium analysis of the previous chapters would be useless, for only by accident would any market be near its equilibrium, and this would occur only momentarily. If, on the other hand, tastes and other factors change extremely slowly, then we might do very well to regard the relation between demand and price as constant for purposes of all predictions of, say, up to twenty years. Even if we could show, on *a priori* grounds, that every relation between two or more variables used in economic theory was necessarily not a stable one, it would be critical for purposes of theory to know the quantitative amount of the lack of stability. Only empirical observations can show this, and such observations are thus important for economic theory as well as for economic history.

Let us consider an example of this point. Say that the relation between the demand for herrings and their price was so variable that the elasticity of demand was 1·37 in 1903, 0·01 in 1905, 8·73 in 1907 and 41·2 in 1908. If demand for all goods varied in such a capricious way, price theory would be of very little use, for we would be unable to predict the effects of the sort of shifts in costs, taxes, etc., that we have been considering. If, on the other hand, all the measures of the elasticity of demand for herrings over a period of twenty years lay between 1·2 and 1·45, then we could predict the effects of various changes in the herring market with a close degree of accuracy and with a high degree of confidence. We would be astounded, and indeed we would suspect a fraud, if a large number of measures of the elasticity of herring demand, made in several places and over a large number of years, all produced the value of, say, 1·347. What we want to know, however, is *how much* spatial and temporal variation there is in the demand for herrings. Only empirical observations can settle this question.

The third criticism is that even if we find substantial variations in our relations, we want to know if these variations appear capricious or if they display a systematic pattern that might lead us to suspect that herring demand is related to other factors. We might, for example, find a strong but sometimes interrupted tendency for the elasticity of demand for herrings to fall over time. We might then find that this systematic variation in price elasticity could be accounted for by income variations (as the population gets richer its demand for herrings is less and less affected by price variations and so the demand becomes more and more inelastic). We might now find that a high proportion of the changes in herring demand could be accounted for by assuming a *stable relation* between demand on the one hand, and price *and* income on the other. In general, what looked like a very unstable relation between two variables might turn out to be only part of a more stable relation between three or more variables. All of this leads us to the following conclusion.

> **Empirical measurements are critical to economics. Without some quantitative evidence of the magnitude and the stability of particular relations we cannot use economic theory to make useful predictions about the real world.**

Since the time when Lord Robbins made his criticism, modern research has gone a long way in establishing quantitative demand relations. As time goes by, further evidence accumulates, and economists are far beyond merely wondering if demand curves slope downward. Many methodological problems have been resolved and techniques sharpened. Not only do we now know the approximate shape of many demand curves, we also have information about how demand curves shift. Our knowledge of demand relations increases significantly every year.

Criticisms of demand theory

Students often find demand theory excessively abstract and feel that it is unrealistic. Some very senior critics have often felt more or less the same way. Here we shall take up the question of whether demand theory is obviously unrealistic.

Is demand theory in conflict with everyday experience?

It is easy to prove that people do not always behave in the rational manner assumed by demand theory. Does that make the theory inapplicable? The answer depends on what we want demand theory to accomplish. Three uses may be distinguished. First, we may be interested in the aggregate behaviour of all households as shown by the market demand curve for a product. Second, we may want to make probabilistic statements about the actions of individual households. Third, we may want to make statements about what *all* households *always* do.

The aggregate use of the theory of demand is the most common one in economics. All of the predictions developed in Chapter 10 depend on having some knowledge of the shape of the relevant market demand curves, yet they do not require that we be able to predict the behaviour of each individual household. The second use, though much less common than the first, is important; we do sometimes want to be able to say what a single household will probably do. The third use of demand theory is by far the least important of the three. Rarely do we wish to make categorical statements about what all households will always do.

Fortunately, the criticism cited at the beginning of this section applies only to this third use of demand theory. The observation that households sometimes behave in ways not predicted by demand theory would, if carefully documented, refute the assertion that the theory's predictions *always* applied to *all* households.

Neither the existence of a relatively stable downward-sloping market demand curve, nor our ability to predict what a single household will probably do requires that all households invariably behave in the manner assumed by the theory. Such fully consistent behaviour on the part of everyone at all times is sufficient but not necessary for a stable market demand curve. Consider two other possibilities. First, some households may always behave in a manner contrary to the theory. Households whose members are mental defectives or are emotionally disturbed are obvious possibilities. The erratic behaviour of such households will not cause market demand curves for normal goods to depart from their downward slope, provided that they account for a small part of purchases of any product. Their behaviour will be swamped by the normal behaviour of the majority of households. Second, an occasional irrationality on the part of every household will not upset the downward slope of the market demand curve for a normal good. As long as these are unrelated across households, occurring now in one and now in another, their effect will be swamped by the normal behaviour of most households most of the time.[1]

> **The downward slope of the demand curve requires only that at any moment of time most households are behaving as is predicted by the theory. This is quite compatible with behaviour contrary to the theory by some households all of the time and by all households some of the time. Thus we cannot test the theory of market demand by observing the behaviour of isolated households.**

Is demand theory just an elaborate way of saying that anything can happen?

Many critics of demand theory argue that the theory has little substantive content. They argue that, with respect to the commodity's own price, the theory says nothing more than that most demand curves slope downwards most of the time. They also argue that, with respect to such other variables as income and the prices of other commodities, the theory says nothing more than that when any of these changes, quantity demanded may go up, go down or stay the same. If all we can say is that anything can happen, we hardly need to base this agnostic position on an elaborate theory. According to these critics, demand theory is a lot of sound and fury signifying (almost) nothing. To weigh their claims, we must consider the relation between quantity demanded and the various factors that influence it.

Demand and tastes The proposition that demand and tastes are related is not really testable unless we have some way of measuring a change in tastes. Since we do not have an independent measure of taste changes, what we usually do is infer them from the data for demand. We make such statements as: 'In spite of the rise in price, quantity purchased increased, so there must have been a change in

---

[1] See the discussion of the 'law of large numbers' on page 10 of Chapter 1.

tastes in favour of this commodity.' More generally, we are likely to use prices and incomes to account for all of the changes in demand that we can, and then assert that the rest must be due to changes in tastes (and to errors of measurement). This does not concern us unduly because we are not particularly interested in establishing precise relations between tastes and demand.

The fact that we cannot identify those changes in demand that are due to changes in tastes does, however, cause trouble when we come to consider the relation between demand and other factors. Whenever we see something happening that does not agree with our theory it is always possible that a change in tastes accounts for it. Say, for example, *incomes and other prices were known to be constant*, while the price of some commodity rose and, at the same time, more of it was observed to

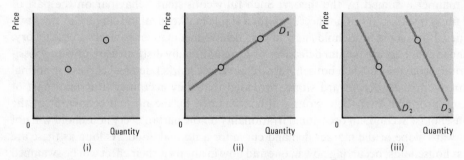

Fig. 15.4 Alternative interpretations of two price-quantity observations: either the demand curve slopes upwards or it has shifted

be bought. This gives us observations such as the two illustrated in Figure 15.4(i). It may be that the demand curve for the product has a shape similar to that shown by the line D_1 in Figure 15.4(ii), but it may also be that the rise in price coincided with a change in tastes, so that the demand curve shifted from D_2 to D_3 in Figure 15.4(iii). With only two observations, we are unable to distinguish between these two possibilities since we have no independent way of telling whether or not tastes changed. If, however, we have many observations, we can get some idea of where the balance of probabilities lies between the two explanations. If *after removing the effects estimated to be due to changes in income and other prices*[1] we have the 26 observations (say the commodity's own price changed each week over a period of six months) illustrated in Figure 15.5, we will be hard pressed to avoid the conclusion that the evidence conflicts with the hypothesis of a downward-sloping demand curve.

Of course, we can always explain away these observations by saying that tastes must have changed in favour of this commodity each time its price rose and against the commodity each time its price fell. This 'alibi' can certainly be used with effect to explain away a single conflicting observation, but we would be uncomfortable using the same alibi 26 times in six months. Indeed we should begin to suspect a fault in the hypothesis that demand and price vary inversely with each other.

We now have a problem in statistical testing of the sort described in Chapter 3. We are not prepared to throw away a theory after only one or two conflicting observations, but we are prepared to abandon it once we accumulate a mass of conflicting observations that were very unlikely to have

---

[1] This can be done through multiple regression analysis or other more sophisticated statistical techniques in the manner alluded to in Chapter 3.

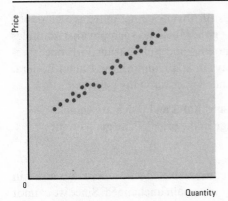

Fig. 15.5 Twenty-six price quantity observations

occurred if the theory was correct[1]. Thus, statistically, the theory is testable. Fortunately, there is, as we have seen, a great deal of evidence that most demand curves do slope downward. The predictions of the theory have, with a few possible exceptions, been found to be in agreement with the facts.

Demand and the prices of other commodities   In Chapter 7, we made a distinction between commodities that are complements to one another and those that are substitutes. Consider the demand for commodity X. This demand will *vary inversely* with the price of a complement (when the price of a complement falls, demand for X will rise), and will *vary directly* with the price of a substitute (when the price of a substitute falls, demand for X will fall). There may also be a group of commodities for which price variations leave demand for X unchanged. These commodities lie on the boundary dividing substitutes for X from complements to X.

These three reactions – demand for X rises, falls or remains unchanged when the price of some other good varies – cover all conceivable possibilities. So far we merely have a set of labels to attach to all possibilities. We do not have a useful theory unless we have a way of *deciding in advance* which goods are substitutable for and which are complementary to X. Fortunately, we can sometimes decide this from technical knowledge alone. To do so is particularly easy when we are considering the demands for inputs in production. Steel plates, electric welders and welder operators are complementary. Thus, we can predict that a fall in the price of any one will lead to an increase in the demand for all three. Cranes and crane operators, steam shovels and lorries, trains and rails, roads and fences, any piece of equipment and its human operator are all examples of pairs of commodities that are complements to each other. You will be able to expand this list more or less indefinitely. A similar list can be drawn up for inputs that are substitutes. It would include such things as wood, bricks and concrete in construction; manure and artificial fertilizers; and a building full of statistical clerks with desk calculators and a computer.

There are also many consumer goods for which we can predict complementarity or substitutability. Complementarity exists, for example, between electric razors and pre-shave lotion; ordinary razors, razor blades and shaving cream; golf clubs and golf balls; grass seed and lawn mowers;

---

[1] If changes in tastes are not related to changes in price, we can easily calculate the odds that the observations in Figure 15.5 are consistent with a downward-sloping but continually-shifting demand curve. If tastes changed randomly each week, there is a 50-50 chance that tastes changed in a direction to offset the first week's price change. In the second week there is also a 50-50 chance. The chances that they changed the 'right' way in both weeks are $(1/2)(1/2) = 1/4$ and the chance that they changed the right way for 25 successive weeks is $(1/2)^{25} = 1/33,554,432$!

electric stoves and electricity; and marriage and services of obstetricians, marriage guidance counsellors and divorce court judges.[1] The list of substitute goods includes such obvious examples as various green vegetables, beef and pork, private automobiles and public transport, open fire-places and central heating, gas and electric cookers, holidays in Spain and on the Italian Riviera, skiing in Switzerland and Austria – such a list could be extended to cover many pages.

> **Whenever the technical data tell us which goods are substitutes and which are complements, we can predict in advance the effect of a change in the price of one good on the demand for another.**

Demand and income A change in income can have any conceivable effect on demand: a rise in income may cause the demand for a product to rise, to fall or to remain unchanged. Since we cannot rule out any possibility, the theory is of no use to us unless we have a way of knowing in advance what the reaction will be to a change of income in the case of a particular commodity – otherwise we can predict nothing and can only classify changes after they have occurred.

In this situation two facts help to give content to the theory. First, *we observe that income elasticities are fairly stable over time*. If, over the last 20 years, the income elasticity of demand for some agricultural product has been observed to fall from 0·70 to 0·40, we are reasonably safe in predicting that a rise in income next year will be met by a less than proportionate rise in the demand for that product. If, on the other hand, the income elasticity of demand for cars and electricity are both observed to have been above unity for several years and also to be rising, it is fairly safe to predict that rises in income in the next few years will be met by more than proportionate rises in the demand for cars and electricity. Because these elasticities are observed not to change rapidly or capriciously we can predict into the near future from a knowledge of the level and direction of change of existing income elasticities.

The second observation that helps give empirical content to the theory is that *all households throughout the Western world tend to behave in a broadly similar fashion*. (Indeed it is not even clear that the qualification Western is necessary.) At low levels of income food tends to have a fairly high income elasticity of demand, but as the level of income rises, the income elasticity of demand for food tends to fall well below unity, so that very little of any additional amount of income is spent on food. This phenomenon has been observed in every growing country that has approached the levels of income currently enjoyed by the countries of Western Europe. Thus we can confidently predict (1) that as long as productivity growth continues in agriculture the long-run drift from the land will continue in Western countries (unless they have a large export market for their agricultural goods), and (2) that when other countries of the world achieve sustained positive rates of growth they will soon encounter the problem of a declining agricultural sector.

> **Incomes in Western countries have been doubling every thirty years or so. Over such periods of time, changes in income exert a major influence on changes in demand. Knowledge of what income elasticities are, and what they are likely to be, is one of the economist's most potent tools for predicting the future behaviour of the economy.**

---

[1] A somewhat high-minded reader once objected to this passage. Her objection illustrates the difference between positive and normative economics. Whatever we may think of the ethics of divorce, if we know that a stable or rising fraction of marriages end in divorce, we can predict with some confidence that an increase in marriages now will lead in the future to an increase in the demands for the factors of production that produce the commodity divorce.

Demand for the commodity and the commodity's own price The marginal utility theory of demand predicts that all demand curves will always slope downward (see p. 170). This prediction has long been known as the law of demand: the price of a product and the amount demanded always vary inversely with each other.

Giffen goods: Great interest was attached to a refutation of the law of demand, supposedly made by the Victorian economist Sir Robert Giffen. Giffen was reputed to have observed that an increase in the price of wheat led to an increase in the consumption of bread by nineteenth-century English peasants. If this observation is correct, it does refute the hypothesis that all demand curves always slope downwards. Does it refute the modern theory of demand? The answer is 'No', because that is just the type of rare exception to the normal case that is envisaged by the modern indifference-preference theory.[1]

Thus the modern theory of demand makes an unequivocal prediction only when we have extraneous information about income elasticities of demand. Since incomes change continuously as a result of economic growth, we are fortunate enough to have such information about most commodities. When we know that the income effect is positive (income elasticity of demand exceeds zero), as it is for most commodities, we can predict in advance that the quantity demanded will vary inversely with its price. When we know the income effect is negative (i.e., the good is inferior), we cannot be sure of the result. The only thing we can then say is that the smaller the proportion of total expenditure accounted for by this commodity, the less important the income effect and the more likely we are to get the normal result of price and quantity varying inversely with each other. Finally, if we have no knowledge about the income effect we can still hazard a probabilistic statement. The great weight of existing evidence suggests that if we had to guess with no prior knowledge whether the demand curve for some commodity X was downward or upward sloping, the former choice would be the odds-on favourite.

Alternative theories of the source of household utility: Some very different exceptions to the 'law of demand' were suggested by some theories of demand popular a few decades ago. The only exception to the law of demand admitted within indifference-preference theory is the Giffen good. These other exceptions all arise from making assumptions that contradict those of indifference theory. In particular, a household's utility is assumed to depend on variables other than the goods and services it consumes for its direct satisfaction.

Assume, for example, that a household's satisfaction also depends on the price it has to pay for some of the commodities. The household may, for example, buy diamonds not because its members particularly like diamonds *per se*, but because they wish to show off their wealth in an ostentatious but socially acceptable way. The household values diamonds precisely because they are expensive; thus, a fall in their price might lead it to stop buying them and switch to a more satisfactory object of ostentatious display. Such households will have upward-sloping demand curves for diamonds: the

---

[1] Students who have read the optional section on page 182 will understand the following explanations. The rest must take the text statement on trust. The possible explanation is in terms of a negative income effect swamping a normal substitution effect. Wheat accounted for a very large fraction of the total expenditure of the households affected by the price change. If wheat is an inferior good, so that the income effect is negative, it is possible that the large negative income effect overcame the normal substitution effect when the price of wheat rose.

lower the price, the fewer they will buy. If enough households act similarly, the market demand curve for diamonds could slope upwards as well.

But an upward-sloping market demand curve for diamonds and other similar products has never been observed. Why? A moment's thought about the industrial uses of diamonds, and the masses of lower-income consumers who would buy diamonds only if they were sufficiently inexpensive, suggests that upward-sloping demand curves for some individual households are much more likely than an upward-sloping market demand curve for the same commodity. Recall the discussion on page 192 about the ability of the theory of the downward-sloping demand curve to accommodate odd behaviour on the part of a small group of households (this time the 'odd' group is the rich, rather than the mentally defective or the emotionally disturbed).

Conclusion

Today we not only do believe that most demand curves slope downward, we also have a good idea of the elasticity in many cases. Reasonably precise knowledge about demand curves is needed if we are to make real-world applications of price theory. If we knew nothing at all empirically about these curves, the theory would be devoid of real-world applications. Since we do have this knowledge, we can predict in advance the effects of changes in many factors such as taxes, costs, the amount of competition in a particular market, and so forth. The more accurate our knowledge of the shape of demand curves, the smaller will be the margin of error in such predictions. Fortunately, as we have seen in this chapter, economists have accumulated a great store of the requisite empirical knowledge.[1]

---

[1] For an interesting discussion of the issues discussed in this chapter, see T. W. Hutchison, *Knowledge and Ignorance in Economics* (Oxford, Basil Blackwell, 1977), especially Chapter 2. Hutchison distinguishes between universal predictions and extrapolations of existing regulations and says I am concerned only with the latter in this chapter. In the first edition of this book I looked only for universal predictions and criticized demand theory for being almost empty of these. Later, when I contemplated how much economists did that was useful, I came to look beyond universal predictions. I noted many applications – including the triumph of the understanding of the agricultural problem which before econometric measurement had seemed a mystery – that rested on the ability to understand economic events by using theory plus empirical elasticities based on a knowledge of the past. Such studies have been fantastically successful, compared especially with the lack of equivalent success in other social sciences. I am not sure how to interpret these successes in terms of abstract scientific methodology. I suspect, however, that we need further methodological insights before we can understand these and place them outside Hutchison's simple dichotomy of generalized predictions and simple extrapolations.

Part four

The intermediate theory of supply

16

Background to the theory of supply

In Part 2 we assumed the existence of a supply curve relating the price of a commodity to the quantity firms would be willing to produce and offer for sale. Now we go behind this supply curve and explain it by the decisions of individual producers. Thus Part 4 does for the supply curve what Part 3 did for the demand curve. There is an apparently bewildering series of theories built on other theories relating to supply. For the moment we shall distinguish between the THEORY OF THE FIRM, which deals with the behaviour of individual firms, and the THEORY OF THE INDUSTRY or the THEORY OF SUPPLY, which deals with collective behaviour of all the firms producing a single product.

The theory helps us to trace aggregate behaviour back to the decisions taken by the individual units that comprise the aggregate. It is also a first step towards dealing with a host of interesting policy questions, of which the following are a few examples. What is the effect of various forms of competition or monopoly on the efficiency and level of production in an industry? Why do firms combine? Is there a tendency for monopoly to replace competition as the dominant form of production? What are the causes and consequences of take-over bids? Will taxing the domestic consumption of a good encourage its export?

In an introductory textbook we can do little more than outline the basic theory and show a few applications. This chapter presents some background material. A formal theory is constructed in subsequent chapters.

The firm in practice

First we shall say something about the structure of actual firms. This will show what organizational features are being abstracted from and set the stage for subsequent consideration of the argument that a successful theory cannot be built on such abstractions.

Forms of business organization[1]

There are three major forms of private business organization: the single proprietorship, the partnership and the joint-stock company (which in North America is called the corporation). In the

---

[1] For a detailed discussion of the types of business organization, their finance and other related issues, see Harbury and Lipsey, op. cit., Chapter 2.

SINGLE PROPRIETORSHIP there is one owner who is personally responsible for everything done by the firm. In the PARTNERSHIP there are two or more joint owners, each of whom is personally responsible. A JOINT-STOCK COMPANY is a firm regarded in law as having an identity of its own; its owners are not personally responsible for anything that is done in the name of the firm.

In most Western countries it is necessary to add two other forms of organizing production: nationalized industries, and the provision of goods and services by the state without direct charge to consumers. Nationalized industries are owned by the state but are usually under the direction of a more or less independent, state-appointed board. Although their ownership differs, the organization and legal status of these firms is very similar to that of the joint-stock company and they are usually very large firms. Their activity is also similar, in the sense that they gain their revenue by selling their output. The fifth method of organizing production differs from all the others in that the output is provided to consumers free (or at a nominal price), while costs of production are paid from the government's general tax revenue. Important examples found in all countries are agencies providing defence, roads and education. In the UK we must also add the National Health Service. In countries without nationalized medical services, hospitals and doctors behave just as other firms do: they purchase factors of production on the open market and gain revenue by selling their services to people who wish to, and can afford to, purchase them.

The financing of firms

The most important sources of funds for modern firms are (1) selling *equities* either by private or public sale; (2) borrowing by the sale of *debentures*; (3) borrowing from banks and other financial institutions; and (4) reinvesting the firm's profits.

Owners' capital The first source of funds is from the firm's owners. In individual proprietorships and partnerships one or more owners will put up some or all of the funds required by the firm. A joint-stock company acquires funds from its owners by selling STOCKS, SHARES or EQUITIES (as they are variously called) to them. These are basically ownership certificates. The money goes to the company and the purchasers become owners of the firm, risking the loss of their money and gaining the right to share in the firm's profits.

Debentures Holders of debentures are the firm's creditors, not its owners. They have loaned it money in return for a DEBENTURE, which is a promise both to pay a stated sum each year, and to repay the loan at some stated time in the future (say, five, ten or twenty years hence). The amount that is paid each year is called the INTEREST, while the amount of the loan that will be repaid at the stated date in the future is called the PRINCIPAL. The time at which the principal is repaid is called the REDEMPTION DATE of the debenture. It is the firm's legal obligation to make periodic interest payments and to repay the principal on the redemption date.

In economic theory we use the term BOND for any piece of paper that provides evidence of a debt carrying a legal obligation to pay interest and repay the principal at some stated future time. Hereafter we refer to debentures, as well as other similar debt instruments, as *bonds*.

Other borrowing Many short-term needs and some long-term ones are met by borrowing from banks. 'Term' (i.e., short-term) borrowing tends to be expensive for firms, so they usually prefer other methods of raising money for long-term purposes. Some companies are forced to seek funds from other financial institutions, at yet higher rates of interest. Many small businesses which are not well-established cannot sell stocks to the public and must borrow from banks and other financial institutions to finance their activities.

Reinvested profits For the established firm, as distinct from the new one, an additional and very important means of obtaining funds is by reinvesting, or ploughing back, its own profits. One of the easiest ways for the controllers of the firm to raise money is to retain some current profits rather than paying them out to shareholders. Financing investment from *undistributed profits* has become an important source of funds in modern times.

> **The modern firm finances itself by obtaining money from its owners, by borrowing from the public and from financial institutions, and by reinvesting its own undistributed profits.**

The firm in economic theory

In Chapter 6 we defined the firm as the unit that takes decisions with respect to the production and sale of commodities. This single concept of the firm covers a variety of business organizations, from the single proprietorship to the joint-stock company, and a variety of business sizes, from the single inventor operating in his garage and financed by whatever he can extract from a reluctant bank manager, to vast undertakings with many thousands of shareholders and creditors. We know that in large firms decisions are actually taken by many different individuals. We can, nonetheless, regard the firm as a single consistent decision-taking unit because of the assumption that all decisions are taken in order to achieve the common goal of maximizing profits. This assumption is critical to the whole traditional theory of the firm and we may state it formally as follows:

> **We assume that the same principles underlie each decision taken within a firm and that the decision is uninfluenced by who takes it. Thus the theory abstracts from the peculiarities of the persons taking the decisions and from the organizational structure in which they work.**

Whether a decision is taken by a small independent proprietor, a plant manager, or the board of directors, as far as the theory is concerned that person or group *is* the firm for the purposes of that decision. This is a truly heroic assumption. It amounts to saying that for purposes of predicting their behaviour, at least in those aspects that interest us, we can treat the farm, the corner greengrocer, the large department store, the small engineering firm, the giant chemical combine, and that largest of all business organizations, the Exxon Corporation, all under the umbrella of a single theory of the behaviour of the firm. Even if this turns out to be only partially correct it will represent an enormously valuable simplification which will show the power of theory in revealing some unity of behaviour where to the casual observer there is only a bewildering diversity.[1]

---

[1] Do not be surprised if at first encounter the theory seems rather abstract and out of touch with reality. Because it does generalize over such a wide variety of behaviour, it must ignore those features with which we are most familiar and which in our eyes distinguish the farmer and the grocer from Royal Dutch Shell. Any theory that generalizes over a wide variety of apparently diverse behaviour necessarily has this characteristic, because it ignores those factors that are most obvious to us and which create in our minds the appearance of diversity.

Criticisms of the theory for ignoring the importance both of decision-takers and of the institutional structure within which decisions are taken, are discussed in Chapter 24. Some competing hypotheses about actual business behaviour will also be discussed at that time. The final test of whether or not such factors can be legitimately ignored is an empirical one: if the theory that we develop by ignoring these factors is successful in predicting the outcome of the kind of events in which we are interested, then we can conclude that we were correct in assuming that these factors could be safely ignored.

The motivation of the firm

The assumption of profit-maximization enables us to predict the behaviour of the firm with regard to the various choices open to it. We do this by studying the effect that each of the choices would have on the firm's profits. We then predict that the firm will select alternatives that produce the largest profits.

> **We assume that the firm takes decisions in such a way that its profits will be as large as possible; we say that it maximizes its profits.**

At this point you might wonder if we are justified in building an elaborate theory based on such a crude assumption. It is well known that some businessmen are inspired some of the time by motives other than an overwhelming desire to make as much money as possible. Cases in which they have gone after political influence, and others in which decisions have been influenced by philanthropic motives, are not difficult to document. Should we not, therefore, say that the assumption that firms seek to maximize profits is refuted by empirical evidence?

The real world is complex. A theory picks on certain factors, and deals with them on the assumption that they are the important ones, while those that are ignored are relatively unimportant. If it is true that the key factors have been included, then the theory will be successful in predicting what will happen under specified circumstances. It follows that it is not an important criticism to point out that a theory ignores some factors known to be present in the world; this tells us nothing more than that the theory is a theory and not just a photographic reproduction of reality in its full complexity. If the theory has ignored some really important factors, then its predictions will be contradicted by the evidence, at least in those situations where the factor ignored is quantitatively important.

How does this discussion relate to the theory of profit-maximizing? First, the theory does not require that profit is the only factor that ever influences the firm. It is believed only that profits are an important consideration, important enough that a theory assuming profit-maximization to be the sole motive will produce predictions that are substantially correct. It follows that to point out that businessmen are sometimes motivated by considerations other than profits does not constitute a relevant criticism. It may well be that the theory is substantially wrong, but if so, the way to demonstrate this is to show that its predictions are in conflict with the facts. We cannot, of course, even consider such a possibility until we know what the theory does and does not predict. Accordingly, we shall press on to develop the theory. When we have completed this task we shall ask how it might be tested against empirical evidence. Finally, in Chapter 24, we shall consider several alternative theories of the firm's motivation.

Nationalized industries

Do we need a separate theory of the behaviour of nationalized industries? Usually they are run by boards that are appointed by the state but given considerable autonomy within the framework of broad directives on what goals to pursue. If the nationalized industries seek to maximize their profits, then their behaviour will be indistinguishable from that of private firms. If, however, they are given other goals, such as just to cover all their costs so as to make neither profits nor losses, then their behaviour may differ from that of the private sector. Once we know the objectives of these industries we shall be able to predict their response to changes in market signals. In the next few chapters we shall confine ourselves to the behaviour of privately owned firms, but in Chapters 23 and 33 we shall return to the question of nationally owned ones.

A preview of the theory of supply

We are interested in the behaviour of profits because we assume firms seek to maximize their profits.[1] Profits (π) are the difference between revenues derived from the sale of commodities (R) and the cost of producing these commodities (C):

$$\pi = R - C.$$

Thus, the behaviour of profits depends on the behaviour of revenues and costs.

In developing the theory of supply, we first explain the special meaning that economists give to the concept of costs and then develop a theory of how costs vary with output. This theory is common to all firms. We then consider how revenues vary with output and find that it is necessary to deal separately with firms in competitive and in monopolistic situations. Once this has been done, costs and revenues are combined to determine the profit-maximizing behaviour for firms in various competitive and monopolistic situations. When the firm has maximized its profits it is said to be in a position of equilibrium.

Once the theory of the equilibrium of the firm (and groups of firms that compose industries) has been developed, it can be used to predict the outcome of changes in such things as demand, costs, taxes and subsidies. These predictions can then be tested against observations. It is the steps of deriving predictions and testing them in which we are really interested, and towards which all previous steps are directed. We must be prepared, however, for some quite hard work before these last steps can be taken. The necessary theory is built up over the next few chapters.

---

[1] Economists often speak of the 'behaviour' of such inanimate things as profits. The term *behaviour of profits* refers to how profits vary as the factors that influence them vary.

17

The theory of costs

Profit, we have seen, is the difference between revenue and cost. Any rate of output will have a set of inputs associated with it. In order to arrive at the cost of producing this output we need to be able to put a value on each of the separate inputs used. The assignment of monetary values to physical quantities of inputs is easy in some cases and difficult in others. Furthermore, different people or different groups may assign different values to the same input.

Economists study the production behaviour of firms for a variety of reasons:

(1) to predict how the behaviour of firms will respond to specified changes in the conditions they face;

(2) to help firms make the best decisions they can in achieving their goals; and

(3) to evaluate from society's point of view how well firms use scarce resources.

The same measure of cost need not be correct for all of these purposes. For example, if the firm happens to be misinformed about the value of a resource, it will behave according to that misinformation. In predicting the firm's behaviour, economists should use the same information the firm does, even if they know it to be incorrect. But in *guiding* firm behaviour, in helping firms to achieve their goals, economists should substitute the correct information. Economists know exactly how to define costs for purposes (2) and (3) above. If we assume that businessmen use the same concept, the economist's definition will also be appropriate for purpose (1). We shall assume for this moment that it is; the consequences of being in error are discussed in Chapter 24.

The measurement of the firm's opportunity cost

All economic costing is governed by a common principle that is sometimes called user cost but is more commonly called opportunity cost, since it is an application of the concept that we first studied on pages 52–3.

> **The cost of using something in a particular venture is the benefit forgone by (or opportunity cost of) not using it in its best alternative use.**

In principle, measuring opportunity cost is easy. The firm must assign to each factor of production it uses a monetary value equal to what it sacrifices in order to have the use of that factor.

Assigning costs is straightforward when the firm buys a factor on a competitive market and uses up the entire quantity purchased during the period of production. Materials purchased by the firm fall into this category. If the firm pays £80 per ton for coal delivered to its factory, it has sacrificed its claims to whatever else £80 can buy, and thus the purchase price is a reasonable measure of the opportunity cost of using one ton of coal.

The situation is the same for hired factors of production. Most labour services are hired, but typically the cost is more than the wages paid because employers have to contribute to such things as national insurance and pension funds. The cost of these must be added to the direct wage in determining the opportunity cost of labour.

A cost must also be assigned to factors of production that the firm neither purchases nor hires because it already owns them. The costs of using such factors are called IMPUTED COSTS. They are reckoned at values reflecting what the firm could earn if it shifted these factors to their next best use. Important imputed costs arise from the use of owners' money, the depreciation of capital equipment, the need to compensate risk-taking, and the need to value any special advantages (such as franchises or patents) that the firm may possess. Correct cost imputation is needed if the firm is to discover the most profitable lines of production.

The cost of money Consider a firm that uses £100,000 of its own money that could have been loaned out to someone else at 15 per cent interest per year. Thus £15,000 (at least) should be deducted from the firm's revenue as the cost of funds used in production. If the firm makes only £14,000 over all other costs, then it should not calculate that it made a profit of £14,000 by producing, but rather that it lost £1,000. This is because if the firm closed down completely and merely loaned its money to someone else, it could earn £15,000.[1]

Special advantages Suppose a firm owns a valuable patent or a highly desirable location, or produces a product with a popular brand-name such as Coca Cola, Triumph or Player's. Each of these involves an opportunity cost to the firm in production (even if it was acquired free) because if the firm did not choose to use the special advantage itself, *it could sell or lease it to others*. Typically, the value of these things will differ from the cost at which the firm originally acquired them. This last cost is called the HISTORIC COST and must be sharply distinguished from the current opportunity cost.

Depreciation of existing equipment The cost of using capital equipment the firm owns, such as buildings and machinery, consists of the loss in the value of the asset, called DEPRECIATION, caused by its use in production. Accountants use various conventional methods of calculating depreciation based on the price originally paid for the asset. While such historical costs are often useful approximations, they may, in some cases, seriously differ from the depreciation required by the opportunity-cost principle. Two examples of the possible error involved follow.

---

[1] The cost of money may be higher than this if the best alternative use of the firm's own money could yield more than the market interest rate. Many firms cannot borrow nearly as much money as they would wish. If a firm is rationed in the amount of funds it can borrow, it will place a high value on the funds that it does have. In these circumstances, the firm must look at the other ventures it might have undertaken in order to assign opportunity cost because its inability to raise all the money it wants means that it will be unable to do all the things it wants. Many business firms operate with 'cut-off rates of return' that approximate the opportunity cost of money to the firm. They are chosen to approximate the return on projects that the firm cannot undertake because it lacks sufficient funds. The return on projects that the firm is just able to undertake is called the firm's internal rate of return. Empirical studies of manufacturing industries suggest that the opportunity cost of money is often substantially in excess of the rate of interest on bonds. An accurate figure may well be as high as 25 per cent. The fact that it is so high helps explain why many firms are anxious to retain a major portion of their profits and why many stockholders (who do not have similar personal investment opportunities) are willing to have corporations pay dividends that are substantially less than earnings and reinvest the remainder to earn their internal rate of return.

Example 1. The owner of a firm buys a £6,000 automobile that she intends to use for six years for business purposes and then discard. She may think this will cost her £1,000 per year. But if after one year the value of her car on the used-car market is £4,500, it has cost her £1,500 to use the car during the first year. Why should she charge herself £1,500 depreciation during the first year? After all, she does not intend to sell the car for six years. The answer is that one of the purchaser's alternatives was to buy a one-year-old car and operate it for five years. Indeed, that is the very position she is in after the first year. Whether she likes it or not, she has paid £1,500 for the use of the car during the first year of its life. If the market had valued her car at £5,800 after one year (instead of £4,500), the correct depreciation charge would have been only £200.

Example 2. A firm has just purchased a set of machines for £100,000. They have an expected lifetime of 10 years and the firm's accountant calculates the 'depreciation cost' of these machines at £10,000 per year. The machines can be used to make only one product and since they are installed in the firm's factory, they can be leased to no one else and have a negligible secondhand or scrap value. Assume that if the machines are used to produce the firm's product, the cost of all other factors utilized will amount to £25,000 per year. Immediately after purchasing the machines the firm finds that the price of the product in question has unexpectedly fallen, so that the output can now only be sold for £29,000 per year instead of the £35,000 that had originally been expected. What should the firm do?

If in calculating its costs the firm adds in the historically determined 'depreciation costs' of £10,000 a year, the total cost of operation comes to £35,000; with the revenue at £29,000 this makes a loss of £6,000 per year. It appears that the commodity should not be made! But this is not correct. Since the machines have no alternative use whatsoever, their imputed opportunity cost to the firm (which is determined by what else the firm could do with them) is zero. The total cost of producing the output is thus only £25,000 per year, and the whole current operation shows a return over cost of £4,000 per year rather than a loss of £6,000. (If the firm did not produce the goods, in order to avoid expected losses, it would be worse off by £4,000 per year more than if it carried on with production.)

Of course, the firm would not have bought the machines had it known that the price of the product was going to fall, but once it has bought them, the cost of using them is zero, and it is profitable to use them as long as they yield any net revenue whatsoever over all other costs.

The principle illustrated by both of these examples may be stated in terms of an important general maxim:

> **Bygones are bygones and should have no influence in deciding what is currently the most profitable thing to do.**[1]

---

[1] This is an important principle that extends well beyond economics and is often ignored in these other areas as well. In many poker games, for example, the cards are dealt a round at a time and betting proceeds after each player's hand has been augmented by one card. Players who bet heavily on early rounds because their hands looked promising often stay in through later rounds on indifferent hands because they 'already have such a stake in the pot'. The professional player knows that, after each round of cards, his bet should be made on the probabilities that the hand he currently holds will turn into a winner when all the cards have been dealt. If the probabilities look poor after the fourth card has been dealt (five usually constitutes a complete hand), he should abandon the hand whether he has put 5p or £5 into the pot already. The amateur who bases his current decisions on what he has put into the pot in earlier rounds of betting will be a long-term loser if he plays in rational company. In poker, war and economics bygones *are* bygones, and to take account of them in current decisions is to court disaster!

New capital equipment Once capital equipment is installed it may, as Example 2 showed, have little or no opportunity cost. In this case, it will be operated as long as it lasts, provided only that all other costs of production can be covered. But capital equipment wears out over time and has to be replaced. Over an extended period of time, the firm must earn a return to its capital equal to what an equivalent investment could earn in other industries. If it does not, the owners will be able to do better by transferring their capital elsewhere, which they can do by not replacing old machinery as it wears out and by investing in other industries the funds that could have been used for replacement.

From cost to profit

It is helpful to divide the return to capital into a pure return, a risk premium and pure profit. The PURE RETURN is what the capital could earn in a riskless investment. The RISK PREMIUM is what capital must earn to compensate the owners for the risk of losing it which accompanies *any* business venture in a world of less than perfect certainty. The riskier a particular use of capital, the higher the risk premium. Both of these elements are costs when viewed over a period of time long enough for capital equipment to be replaced. If the firm does not produce a return on its capital sufficient to cover the return on a riskless investment *and* sufficient to compensate for the riskiness involved, the owners of the capital are not covering their opportunity costs.

PROFIT is any excess of revenue over all opportunity costs including those of capital. To discover whether such profit exists, take the revenue of the firm and deduct the costs of all factors of production other than capital. Then deduct the pure return on capital and any risk premium necessary to compensate the owners of capital for the risks associated with its use in this firm and industry. Anything that remains is pure profit. It belongs to the owners of the firm and therefore may be regarded as an additional return on their capital. Profit in the sense just defined is variously called pure profit, economic profit or, where there is no room for ambiguity, just profit.

The production function

We have now seen how to calculate the cost and profit associated with any particular output. To discover which of its possible levels of output is the most profitable, the firm needs to know how costs and revenues vary with output. This tells it, by subtraction, how profit varies with output. It is then a simple matter to select the profit-maximizing output. In this chapter we shall confine our attention to costs; in subsequent chapters we shall study revenues.

To discover how costs (the value of inputs used) vary with output we first study how output varies with inputs of factors of production. We then place a value on the inputs used according to the principles already established and this tells us how costs (the value of inputs used) vary with output.

The PRODUCTION FUNCTION describes the purely technological relation between what is fed into the productive apparatus by way of inputs of factor services and what is turned out by way of product. In stating this relation it must not be forgotten that production is a flow: it is not just so many units; it is so many units *per period of time*. If we speak of raising the level of monthly production from, say, 100 to 101 units, we do not mean producing 100 units this month and one unit next month, but going from a rate of production of 100 units each month to a rate of 101 units each month.

The production function is written simply as:

$$q = q(f_1, \ldots, f_m), \tag{1}$$

where q is the quantity of output and $f_1, \ldots, f_m$ are the quantities of m different factors used in production, all expressed as rates per period of time.

For the rest of this chapter we shall consider a very simple example of some industrial product. We ignore land as being relatively unimportant and divide all the other inputs into the two categories – labour, L, and capital, K. We then have the simple production function:

$$q = q(L, K), \tag{2}$$

where q is tons of output per day, L is labour days employed, and K is units of capital services (e.g., machine days) used. This will make our task easier while still getting at the essential aspects of our problem.

Suppose now that the firm wishes to increase its rate of output. To do so it must increase the inputs of one or both factors of production. But the firm cannot vary all of its factors with the same degree of ease. It can take on or lay off labour on fairly short notice (a week or a month), but a long time is needed to install more capital.

To capture the fact that different kinds of inputs can be varied with different speeds we think of the firm as making three distinct types of decisions: (1) how best to employ its existing plant and equipment; (2) what new plant and equipment and production processes to select, within the framework of existing technology; and (3) what to do about encouraging the development of new techniques. These decisions are logically distinct although they abstract from the more complicated nature of real decisions. The first set of decisions is said to be made over the short run; the second, over the long run; the third, over the very long run.

The short run

The SHORT RUN is defined as the period of time over which the inputs of some factors, called FIXED FACTORS, cannot be varied. The factor that is fixed in the short run is usually an element of capital (such as plant and equipment), but it might be land, or the services of management, or even the supply of skilled, salaried labour. What matters is that at least one significant factor is fixed. Let us say that in the production function in (2) above, it is capital that is fixed in the short run.

In the short run, production must be varied by changing the quantities used of those inputs that can be varied; these are called VARIABLE FACTORS. In our simple example the variable factor is labour services. Thus, in the short run, q is varied by varying L, with K held fixed.

It is worth noting that the short run does not correspond to a fixed time period. In the electric-power industry, for example, where it takes three or more years to acquire and install a steam-turbine generator, an unforeseen increase in demand will involve a long period during which the extra demand must be met as well as possible with the existing capital equipment. At the other end of the scale, a machine shop can acquire new equipment (or sell existing equipment) in a few weeks, and thus the short run is correspondingly short. The length of the short run is influenced by technological considerations such as how quickly equipment can be manufactured and installed. But these things may be influenced to some extent by the price the firm is willing to pay.

The long run

The LONG RUN is defined as the period long enough for the inputs of all factors of production to be varied, but not so long that the basic technology of production changes. In our simple two-factor example, the firm varies q in the long run by varying L and K, using a given production function. Again, the long run is not a specific period of time, but varies among industries.

The special importance of the long run in production theory is that it corresponds to the situation facing the firm when it is *planning* to go into business, or to expand or contract the scale of its operations. The planning decisions of the firm are characteristically made with fixed technical possibilities but with freedom to choose whatever factor inputs seem most desirable. Once these planning decisions are carried out – once a plant is built, equipment purchased and installed, and so on – the firm has fixed factors and makes operating decisions in the short run.

The very long run

Unlike the short and the long run, the VERY LONG RUN is concerned with situations in which the technological possibilities open to the firm are subject to change, leading to new and improved products and new methods of production. The firm may bring about some of these changes itself, particularly through its own research and development. In the long run the production function itself changes so that in (2) above the same inputs of K and L are associated with a different output.

In the very long run the production function itself changes: the same quantity of inputs will yield a higher rate of output.

We shall now make an extended study of the firm's production possibilities and its costs under each of these 'runs'.

The short run

In the theory of the short run we are concerned with what happens to output and costs as more or less of the variable factor is applied to given quantities of the fixed factors. To illustrate we use the simplified production function of (2) above, and assume that capital is fixed and labour is variable.

Short-run variations in output

Assume that a firm starts with a fixed amount of capital (say 10 units) and contemplates applying various amounts of labour to it. Table 17.1 shows three different ways of looking at how output varies with the quantity of the variable factor. As a preliminary step, some terms must be defined.

(1) TOTAL PRODUCT (TP) means just what it says: the total amount produced during some period of time by all the factors of production employed. If the inputs of all but one factor are held constant, total product will change as more or less of the variable factor is used. This variation is shown in column (2) of Table 17.1, which gives a total product schedule. Figure 17.1 (i) shows such a schedule graphically. (The shape of the curve will be discussed shortly.)

Table 17.1 Variation of output (one fixed, one variable factor), with capital fixed at 10 units

(1) Quantity of labour L	(2) Total product TP	(3) Average product AP	(4) Marginal product* MP
1	43	43	43
2	160	80	117
3	351	117	191
4	600	150	249
5	875	175	275
6	1,152	192	277
7	1,372	196	220
8	1,536	192	164
9	1,656	184	120
10	1,750	175	94
11	1,815	165	65
12	1,860	155	45

* Marginal product shows what happens when the variable input changes from one value to another. It should thus be viewed as occurring in the interval *between* these two values of the variable input. In the table the marginal values occur *between* the units in question, and on a graph they should also be plotted between these units. Thus, for example, the marginal product of 117 refers to the interval $L = 1$ and $L = 2$, and should be plotted graphically at $L = 1·5$.

(2) AVERAGE PRODUCT (AP) is merely the total product per unit of the variable factor, which is labour in the present illustration:

$$AP = TP/L.$$

Average product is shown in column (3) of Table 17.1. Notice that as more of the variable factor is used, average product first rises and then falls. The point where average product reaches a maximum is called the POINT OF DIMINISHING AVERAGE PRODUCTIVITY. In the table, average product reaches a maximum when 7 units of labour are employed.

(3) MARGINAL PRODUCT (MP) is the change in total product resulting from the use of one more (or one less) unit of the variable factor:[1]

$$MP = \Delta TP/\Delta L,$$

---

[1] Strictly, the text defines what is called incremental product, the rate of change of output associated with a discrete change in an input. Strictly, marginal product refers to the rate at which output is tending to vary as input varies at a particular output. Students familiar with elementary calculus will recognize the marginal product as the partial derivative of the total product with respect to the variable factor. In symbols: $MP = \partial q/\partial L$. In the text we refer only to finite changes, but the phrase 'a change of one unit' should read 'a very small change'. At this time it would be helpful to read, or reread, the discussion of the marginal concept given on pages 32–3.

where ΔTP stands for the change in the total product and ΔL stands for the change in labour input that caused TP to change. In everything that follows in this chapter we assume that output is varied in the short run by combining different amounts of the variable factor with a given quantity of the fixed factor. As we shall see in Chapter 21 this is not a necessary short-run phenomenon *since some of the fixed factor can be left unemployed*. Dropping the assumption that all of the fixed factor is always employed in the short run has, as we shall see in that chapter, profound effects for the short-run behaviour of the economy.

Computed values of the marginal product appear in column (4) of Table 17.1. For example, the MP corresponding to 4 units of labour is given as 249 bushels. This reflects the fact that the increase in labour from 3 to 4 units ($\Delta L = 1$) increases output from 351 to 600 ($\Delta TP = 249$). MP in the example reaches a maximum between $L = 5$ and $L = 6$ and thereafter declines. The level of output where marginal product reaches a maximum is called the POINT OF DIMINISHING MARGINAL RETURNS.

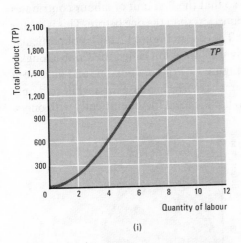
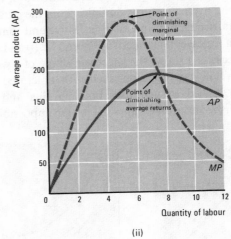

Fig. 17.1 (i) Total product from Table 17.1 ($K = 10$)
(ii) Average and marginal product curves plotted from data in Table 17.1

Figure 17.1 (ii) shows the average and marginal product curves plotted from the data in Table 17.1. Notice (1) that MP reaches its maximum at a lower level of L than does AP, and (2) that $MP = AP$ when AP is a maximum. These relations are discussed below.

Finally, bear in mind that the schedules of Table 17.1 and the curves of Figure 17.1 all assume a specified quantity of the fixed factor. If the quantity of capital had been, say, 6 or 14 instead of the 10 units that were assumed, there would be a different set of total, average, and marginal product curves. The reason is that if any specified amount of labour has more capital to work with, it can produce more output: its total product will be greater.

The hypothesis of diminishing returns The variations in output that result from applying more or less of a variable factor to a given quantity of a fixed factor are the subject of a famous hypothesis called the LAW OF DIMINISHING RETURNS.

The Law of Diminishing Returns states that if increasing quantities of a variable factor

are applied to a given quantity of a fixed factor, the marginal product and the average product of the variable factor will eventually decrease.

Empirical evidence in favour of the hypothesis of diminishing returns is strong in many fields. Indeed, were the hypothesis incorrect, there would be no need to fear that the present population explosion will cause a food crisis. If the marginal product of additional workers applied to a fixed quantity of land were constant, then world food production could be expanded in proportion to the increase in population merely by keeping the same proportion of the population on farms. As it is, diminishing returns means an inexorable decline in the marginal product of each additional labourer as an expanding population is applied, with static techniques, to a fixed world supply of agricultural land. Thus, unless there is a continual and rapidly accelerating improvement in the techniques of production, the population explosion must bring with it declining living standards over much of the world.

The law of diminishing returns is illustrated in Figure 17.2. It is consistent with the law that marginal and average returns diminish from the outset, so that the first unit of labour contributes most to total production and each successive unit contributes less than the one before. This is so, for example, in the cases illustrated in Figure 17.2 (i) and (ii). The case in Figure 17.2 (ii) is of particular interest, because it shows the short-run shape of a widely used function called the Cobb-Douglas production function. Situations such as that pictured in Figure 17.2 (iii) are possible and have been extensively studied. In such cases, both marginal and average returns increase for a while and only later diminish. This would happen if it were impossible to use the fixed factor efficiently with only a

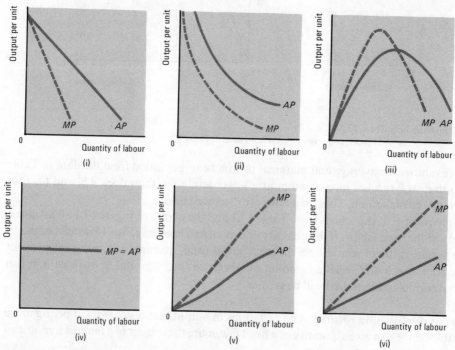

Fig. 17.2 The hypotheses of eventually diminishing productivity admit the possibility of (i) (ii) and (iii) but not, indefinitely, (iv) (v) and (vi)

small quantity of the variable factor (if, say, one man were trying to farm 1,000 acres). In this case increasing the quantity of the variable factor makes possible more efficient division of labour, so that the addition of another unit of the variable factor would make all units more productive than they were previously. According to the hypothesis of diminishing returns, the scope for such economies must eventually disappear, and sooner or later the marginal and average product of additional workers must decline.

> **The law of diminishing returns is also called *the law of variable proportions* because it predicts the consequences of varying the proportions in which factors of production are used.**

The relation between marginal and average product curves Notice that in Figure 17.2 (iii) the *MP* curve cuts the *AP* curve at the latter's maximum point. It is important to understand why. The key is that the average product curve slopes upward as long as the marginal product curve is above it; it makes no difference whether the marginal curve is itself sloping upward or downward. The common sense of this relation is that if an additional worker is to raise the average product of all workers, it is necessary and sufficient that a worker's output be greater than the average output of all other workers. It is immaterial whether his contribution to output is greater or less than the contribution of the worker hired immediately before him; all that matters is that his contribution to output exceeds the average output of *all* the workers hired before him.[1] Since *AP* slopes upwards or downwards depending on whether *MP* is above or below *AP*, it follows that *MP* must equal *AP* at the highest point on the *AP* curve.[2]

Short-run variations in cost

We now know how, according to economic theory, output varies with factor inputs in the short run and we know how to value the firm's inputs. By combining these two things, we can discover how a firm's output is related to its cost of production. For the time being we consider firms that are not in a position to influence the prices of the factors of production they employ. These firms must pay the going market price for factors.

The following brief definitions of several cost concepts are closely related to the product concepts defined earlier in this chapter.

(1) TOTAL COST (*TC*) means just what it says: the total cost of producing any given rate of output. Total cost is divided into two parts, total fixed costs (*TFC*) and total variable costs (*TVC*). FIXED COSTS are those costs that do not vary with output; they will be the same if output is 1 unit or 1

---

[1] To check your understanding, try an example in which five workers produce 50 units of output. In the first case a sixth worker adds 16 and a seventh worker adds 14 to total output. In the second case, the sixth worker adds 14 and the seventh worker adds 16 to total output. When you do the calculations you will find that *AP* is rising in both cases, although *MP* is declining in the first case and rising in the second.

[2] This is easily proved for those who know elementary calculus. Our definitions are: $TP = q(n)$, $AP = q(n)/n$, and $MP = q'(n)$, where the single prime mark indicates the first derivative and n is the quantity of the variable factor employed. A necessary condition for the maximum of the *AP* curve is that its first derivative, $[nq'(n) - q(n)]/n^2$, be equal to zero. Setting the above expression equal to zero, adding $q(n)/n^2$ to both sides and multiplying through by n yields: $q'(n) = q(n)/n$, which is to say $MP = AP$.

million units. These costs are also often referred to as 'overhead costs' or 'unavoidable costs'. All of those costs that vary directly with output, rising as more is produced and falling as less is produced, are called VARIABLE COSTS. In the previous example, since labour was the variable factor of production, the wage bill would be a variable cost. Variable costs are often referred to as 'direct costs' or 'avoidable costs'.[1]

(2) AVERAGE TOTAL COST (ATC) is the total cost of producing any given output divided by the number of units produced, or the cost per unit. ATC may be divided into AVERAGE FIXED COSTS (AFC) and AVERAGE VARIABLE COSTS (AVC) in just the same way as total costs were divided.

Although average *variable* costs may rise or fall as production is increased (depending on whether output rises more rapidly or more slowly than total variable costs), it is clear that average fixed costs decline continuously as output increases. A doubling of output always leads to a halving of fixed costs per unit of output. This is a process popularly known as 'spreading one's overheads'.

(3) MARGINAL COST (MC) is the increase in total cost resulting from raising the rate of production by one unit.[2] The marginal cost of the 10th unit, for example, is the change in total cost when production rises from the rate of nine to ten units per period.[3] Because fixed costs do not vary with output, marginal fixed costs are always zero. Therefore marginal costs are necessarily marginal variable costs, and a change in fixed costs will leave marginal costs unaffected. For example, the marginal cost of producing a few more potatoes by farming a given amount of land more intensively is the same whatever the rent paid for the fixed amount of land.[4]

These three measures of cost are merely different ways of looking at a single phenomenon, and they are mathematically interrelated. Sometimes it is convenient to use one, and sometimes another.

Short-run cost curves Let us take the production relationships in Table 17.1 and assume that the price of labour is £20 per unit and the price of capital is £10 per unit. In Table 17.2, we present the cost schedules computed for these values. (It is important that you see where the numbers come from; if you do not, review Table 17.1 and the definitions of cost just given.) Figure 17.3 (i) shows the total cost curves; Figure 17.3 (ii) plots the marginal and average cost curves.

---

[1] In symbols we may write

$$TC = TFC + TVC$$
$$TFC = K$$
$$TVC = wL$$

where K is some constant amount, L is the quantity of the variable factor used, and w is the price per unit of this factor. Since fixed costs are constant and since variable costs necessarily rise as output rises, total costs rise with output or, to put the point more formally, TC is a function of total product and varies directly with it: $TC = f(q)$.

[2] In symbols: $MC = \Delta TC/\Delta q$. Strictly, this is incremental cost for a discrete change in output. Strictly, marginal cost refers to the rate of change of costs at a particular output, i.e., $MC = dTC/dq$.

[3] For a one-unit change, $MC_n = TC_n - TC_{n-1}$, i.e., the marginal cost of the nth unit of output is the total cost of producing n units minus the total cost of producing $n-1$ (i.e., one less) units of output. If we are producing a number of identical units of output, we cannot, of course, ascribe a separate (and different) cost to each unit. When we speak, therefore, of the marginal cost of the nth unit we mean nothing more than the change in total costs when the rate of production is increased from $n-1$ units to n units per period of time.

[4] Students of calculus will realize that fixed cost, like any other constant, disappears in the process of differentiation. If $TC = c(q) + F$, where $c(q)$ is variable cost and F fixed cost, then marginal cost, dTC/dq, is independent of the size of F.

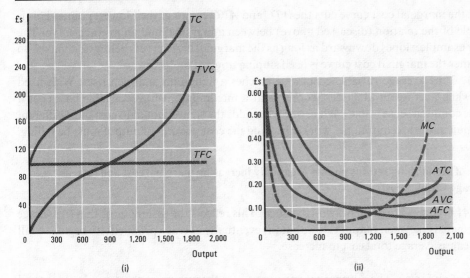

Fig. 17.3 (i) Three short-run total cost curves (ii) Marginal and average cost curves

Table 17.2 Cost schedules for data in Table 17.1 (price of labour, £20 per unit; price of capital, £10 per unit)

(1) Labour	(2) Output	Total cost			Average cost			Marginal cost*
		(3) Fixed	(4) Variable	(5) Total	(6) Fixed	(7) Variable	(8) Total	
L	q	TFC	TVC	TC	AFC	AVC	ATC	MC
1	43	£100	£ 20	£120	£2·326	£·465	£2·791	£·465
2	160	100	40	140	·625	·250	·875	·171
3	351	100	60	160	·285	·171	·456	·105
4	600	100	80	180	·167	·133	·300	·080
5	875	100	100	200	·114	·114	·229	·073
6	1,152	100	120	220	·087	·104	·191	·072
7	1,372	100	140	240	·073	·102	·175	·091
8	1,536	100	160	260	·065	·104	·169	·122
9	1,656	100	180	280	·060	·109	·169	·167
10	1,750	100	200	300	·057	·114	·171	·213
11	1,815	100	220	320	·055	·121	·176	·308
12	1,860	100	240	340	·054	·129	·183	·444

*'Marginal' cost is really 'incremental' cost, $MC = \Delta TC/\Delta q$, for intervals indicated in the table. Thus the MC of ·171 in line 2 is (£140–£120)/(160–43) = ·171. For graphical purposes this should be plotted at the level of output halfway between 43 and 160.

Notice that the marginal cost curve cuts the *ATC* and *AVC* curves at their lowest points. This is another example of the relation (discussed above) between a marginal and an average curve. The *ATC* curve, for example, slopes downward as long as the marginal cost curve is below it; it makes no difference whether the marginal cost curve is itself sloping upward or downward.

In Figure 17.3 the average variable cost curve reaches a minimum and then rises. With fixed factor prices, when average product per worker is at a maximum, average variable cost is at a minimum.[1] The common sense is that each new worker adds the same amount to cost but a different amount to output, and when output per worker is rising the cost per unit of output must be falling, and vice versa.

The law of diminishing returns implies eventually increasing marginal cost and increasing average variable cost.

Short-run *AVC* curves are often drawn U-shaped. This reflects the assumptions that (i) average productivity is increasing when output is low, but (ii) eventually average productivity begins to fall fast enough to cause average total cost to increase.[2]

The definition of capacity The output that corresponds to the minimum short-run average total cost is often called PLANT CAPACITY. Capacity in this sense is not an upper limit on what can be produced, as you can see by looking again at Table 17.2. In the example, capacity output is between 1,536 and 1,656 units, but higher outputs can be achieved. A firm producing *with excess capacity* is producing at a rate of output below the point of minimum average total cost. A firm producing *above capacity* is producing above this point, and is thus incurring costs higher than the minimum achievable.

A family of short-run cost curves A short-run cost curve shows how costs vary with output for a given quantity of the fixed factor – say a given size of plant.

There is a different short-run cost curve for each quantity of the fixed factor.

A small plant for manufacturing nuts and bolts will have its own short-run cost curve. A medium-size and a very large-size plant will each have its own short-run cost curve. If a firm expands by replacing its small plant with a medium-size plant, it will move from one short-run cost curve to another. This change from one size of plant to another is a long-run change. We now turn to a study of how short-run cost curves of different size plants are related to each other.

---

[1] The law of diminishing returns implies only that average costs will *eventually* rise. 'Eventually' may not mean whenever output is increased. The empirical evidence does show rising costs, but often the shape of the curve is very flat – more like a saucer than a cup – in the relevant range of outputs.

[2] This point is easily seen if a little algebra is used and the symbols are the same as those used in previous footnotes. By definition $AVC = TVC/q$. But $TVC = L \cdot w$, and $q = AP \cdot L$ (since $AP = q/L$). Therefore

$$AVC = (L \cdot w)/(AP \cdot L)$$
$$= w/AP.$$

In other words, average variable cost equals the price of the variable factor divided by the average product of the variable factor. Since w is constant, it follows that AVC and AP vary inversely with each other, and when AP is at its maximum value AVC must be at its minimum value.

The long run

In the short run, with only one factor variable, there is only one way to produce a given output: by adjusting the input of the variable factor until the desired level of output is achieved. Thus, in the short run, the firm must make a decision about its output, but once it has decided on a rate of output there is only one technically possible way of achieving it. In the long run, all factors are variable. If a firm decides on some rate of output, it has an additional decision to make: by which of the many technically possible methods will the output be produced? Should the firm adopt a technique that uses a great deal of capital and only a small amount of labour, or should it adopt one that uses less capital but more labour?

Since there are almost always many ways of achieving the same total output, the firm needs some method of choosing among them. The hypothesis of profit-maximization provides a simple rule for this choice: any firm that is trying to maximize its profits will select the method of producing a given output that incurs the lowest possible cost. We call this the implication of cost-minimization. Cost-minimization is not a separate hypothesis from profit-maximization. It is an implication of profit-maximization, since a firm that is not minimizing its costs is not maximizing its profits. Indeed cost-minimization follows from other assumptions as well. As long as the firm is trying to maximize anything that uses economic resources, it will wish to minimize the costs it incurs to produce any given level of output.

> **For any specific output, the firm chooses the least costly method of production from the alternatives open to it.**

If there is a known stable required rate of output, and if the costs of factors are known, this is all there is to it.

Long-run planning decisions are important because today's variable factors are tomorrow's fixed ones. A firm deciding on a new, fully equipped plant will have many alternatives to choose from, but once installed, the new equipment is fixed for a long time. If the firm errs now, its very survival may be threatened; if it estimates shrewdly and its rivals don't, it may reward its owners and its far-sighted managers with large profits and bonuses.[1]

Conditions for cost-minimization

Whenever the firm can substitute one factor for another in such a way as to keep its output constant while reducing its total cost, it has not succeeded in minimizing costs. Thus:

> **The firm will substitute one factor for another factor as long as the marginal product of the one factor per penny expended on it is greater than the marginal product of the other factor per penny expended on it.**

The firm has not minimized its costs as long as these two magnitudes are unequal. This leads to the

---

[1] Long-run decisions are among the most difficult and most important the firm makes. They are difficult because the firm must anticipate what methods of production will be efficient not only today but in the years ahead when costs of labour and raw materials may have changed. They are difficult because the firm must estimate its desired future output. Is the industry growing or declining? Is the firm's share of the market going to increase or decrease? Will new products emerge to render its own products less useful than an extrapolation of past sales might suggest?

following condition of cost-minimization (using K to represent capital, L labour, and p the price to the firm of a unit of the factor):[1]

$$\frac{MP_K}{p_K} = \frac{MP_L}{p_L} \; . \tag{3}$$

To see why this condition needs to be fulfilled if costs of production are to be minimized, suppose the left-hand side was equal to 10, showing that the last pound spent on capital produced 10 units of output, while the right-hand side was equal to 4, showing that the last pound spent on labour added only 4 units to output. In such a case, the firm by using £2·50 less of labour would reduce output by approximately 10 units. But it could regain that lost output by spending approximately £1 more on capital.[2] Making such a substitution of capital for labour would leave output unchanged and reduce cost by £1·50. Thus the original position was not cost-minimizing. Whenever the two sides of (3) are not equal, there are factor substitutions that will reduce costs.

By rearranging the terms in (3) we can look at the cost-minimizing condition in a slightly different way:

$$\frac{MP_K}{MP_L} = \frac{p_K}{p_L} \; . \tag{4}$$

The ratio of the marginal products on the left-hand side compares the contribution to output of the last unit of capital and the last unit of labour. If, for example, the ratio is 4, this means 1 unit more of capital will add 4 times as much to output as 1 unit more of labour. The right-hand side shows how the cost of 1 unit more of capital compares to the cost of 1 unit more of labour. If it is also 4, the firm can gain nothing by substituting capital for labour or vice versa. But suppose the right-hand side is 2. Capital, although twice as expensive, is 4 times as productive, and it will pay the firm to switch to a method of production that uses more capital and less labour. If, however, the right-hand side is 6 (or *any* number more than 4), it will pay to substitute labour for capital.

This formulation shows how the firm can adjust the things over which it has control (the quantities of factors used, and thus the marginal products of the factors) to the things that are typically given to it by the market (the prices of the factors). An analogous adjustment process was involved in households adjusting their consumption of goods to the market prices of those goods.

The principle of substitution

Suppose that a firm is producing where the cost-minimizing conditions shown in (3) or (4) are met, but that the cost of labour increases while the cost of capital remains unchanged. As we have just seen, the least-cost method of producing any output will now use less labour and more capital than was required to produce that same output before the factor prices changed. This prediction, called the PRINCIPLE OF SUBSTITUTION, follows from the cost-minimizing behaviour of firms.

---

[1] This condition is directly analogous to the condition for the utility-maximizing household, given on page 168, in which the household equated the marginal utility per penny spent on each of the two goods. Later in this chapter the condition is given a graphic analysis similar to that given for household behaviour in the second half of Chapter 14.

[2] The argument in the previous two sentences assumes that the marginal products do not change very much when expenditure is changed by a few pounds. If they did not change at all the 'approximatelys' could be eliminated.

Methods of production will change if the relative prices of factors change; relatively more of the cheaper factor and relatively less of the more expensive one will be used.

This proposition is central to the theory of the allocation of resources because it predicts how firms respond to changes in relative factor prices. Such changes are caused by the changing relative scarcities of factors in the whole economy. Individual firms thus use less of factors that have become scarcer in overall supply.

Cost curves in the long run

There is a best (least-cost) method of producing each rate of output when all factors are free to be varied. If factor prices are given, a minimum cost can be found for each possible level of output and, if this minimum achievable cost is expressed as an amount per unit of output, we obtain the long-run average cost of producing each level of output. When this information is plotted on a graph, the result is the LONG-RUN AVERAGE TOTAL COST ($LRATC$) CURVE, shown in Figure 17.4.

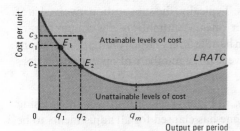

Fig. 17.4 A long-run average total cost curve

The long-run average total cost curve provides a boundary between attainable and unattainable levels of cost. If the firm wishes to produce output q_1 in Figure 17.4, the lowest attainable cost is c_1 per unit. Thus point E_1 is on the $LRATC$ curve. E_2 represents the least-cost method of producing q_2. Suppose, however, that a firm is producing at E_1 and desires to increase output to q_2. In the short run the firm will not be able to vary all factors, and thus costs above c_2, say c_3, must be accepted. In the long run, a plant optimal for output q_2 can be built and a cost of c_2 can be attained.

The $LRATC$ curve is determined by the technology of the industry (which is assumed to be fixed) and by the prices of the factors of production. It is a 'boundary' in the sense that points below the curve are unattainable, points on the curve are attainable if sufficient time elapses for all factors to be adjusted, and points above the curve are also attainable. Indeed, points above the $LRATC$ curve may represent the best that can be done in the short run when all factors are not freely variable.

The $LRATC$ curve divides the cost levels that are attainable with known technology and given factor prices from those that are unattainable.

The shape of the long-run average total cost curve

The long-run average cost curve in Figure 17.4 is shown as falling at first and then rising. This curve is often described as being U-shaped.

Decreasing costs Over the range of output from zero to q_m the firm has falling long-run average total costs. An expansion of output results in a reduction of costs per unit of output once enough time has elapsed to allow adjustments in capital as well as labour. Since the prices of factors are assumed to be constant, the reason for the decline in costs per unit must be that output increases faster than inputs as the scale of the firm's production expands. Over this range the firm encounters long-run INCREASING RETURNS, also called ECONOMIES OF SCALE.[1] Increasing returns may arise from increased opportunities for specialization of tasks made possible by the division of labour even with no substitution of one factor of production for another. Or they may arise because of factor substitution. Even the most casual observation of the differences in production technique used in large-size and small-size plants shows the existence of the differences in factor proportions. These differences arise because large, specialized machinery and equipment are useful only when the volume of output that the firm can sell justifies its employment.

For example, the use of the assembly-line technique, body-stamping machinery, and multiple-boring engine-block machines in car production is economically efficient only if individual operations are to be repeated thousands of times. The use of elaborate harvesting equipment (which combines many individual tasks that could be done by hand and by tractor) provides the least-cost method of production on a big farm but not on a few acres. Typically, the substitution involved is of capital for labour and of complex machines for simpler ones. Automation is a contemporary example of this kind of substitution. Electronic devices can handle a very large volume of operations very quickly, but unless the level of production requires very large numbers of operations, it does not make sense to use these techniques.

Increasing costs Over the range of outputs greater than q_m in Figure 17.4 the firm encounters rising costs. An expansion in production, even after sufficient time has elapsed for all adjustments to be made, is accompanied by a rise in average costs per unit of output. If the prices of factors of production are constant, this rise in costs must be the result of an expansion in output which is proportionately less than the expansion in inputs. Such a firm is said to suffer long-run DECREASING RETURNS or DISECONOMIES OF SCALE.[2] As the firm's scale of operations increases, diseconomies – of management or otherwise – are encountered. These increase the quantity of factors that must be used per unit of output produced.

Minimum costs At the output q_m in Figure 17.4 the firm has reached its lowest possible long-run costs per unit of output. If the firm produces at that output it is producing efficiently in the sense that the costs per unit of output are as low as they possibly could be (for given technology and factor prices). We shall see in Chapter 19 that under certain conditions (called those of perfect competition) each firm will, in equilibrium, produce at the minimum point on its *LRATC* curve.

Constant costs The firm's long-run average costs are shown in Figure 17.4 as falling to output q_m and rising thereafter. Another possibility should be noted: the firm's *LRATC* curve might be flat

---

[1] Economists often shift back and forth between speaking in physical output terms and cost terms. Thus a firm with increasing (physical) returns to scale (output rises more than in proportion to input in the long run) is also spoken of as a firm with decreasing long-run costs (costs rise less than in proportion to output in the long run).

[2] Long-run decreasing returns differ from the short-run diminishing returns that we encountered earlier. In the short run at least one factor is fixed and the law of diminishing returns ensures that returns to the variable factor will eventually diminish. In the long run all factors are variable and it is possible that physically diminishing returns would never be encountered – at least as long as it was genuinely possible to increase inputs of all factors.

over some range of output around q_m. When such a flat portion exists, the firm is said to encounter constant costs over the relevant range of output. This would mean that the firm's average cost per unit of output was not changing as its output changed. If factor prices are assumed to be fixed, this must mean that the firm's output is increasing exactly as fast as its inputs are increasing. Such a firm would be said to be encountering CONSTANT RETURNS.

The relation between long-run and short-run costs

The various short-run cost curves derived earlier in this chapter and the long-run cost curve just studied are all derived from the same production function, and each assumes given prices for all factor inputs. In the long run, all factors can be varied; in the short run, some must remain fixed. The long-run average total cost ($LRATC$) curve shows the lowest cost of producing any output when all factors are variable. The short-run average total cost ($SRATC$) curve shows the lowest cost of producing any output when one or more factors is not free to vary.

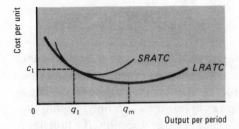

Fig. 17.5 Long-run and short-run average total cost curves

The short-run cost curve cannot fall below the long-run curve because the latter curve represents the *lowest* attainable costs for every output. It might be the same curve, but the law of variable proportions predicts that as output is changed, a different-sized plant would be required to achieve the lowest attainable cost. This is illustrated in Figure 17.5. Note that the short-run cost curve is tangent to (touches) the long-run curve at the level of output for which the quantity of the fixed factor is optimal and lies above it for all other levels of output. If output varies around q_1 units, with plant and equipment fixed at the optimal level for producing q_1, costs will follow the short-run cost curve. If some output other than q_1 is to be sustained, costs can be reduced to the level of the long-run curve when sufficient time has elapsed to adjust all factor inputs. While $SRATC$ and $LRATC$ are at the same level for output q_1 – since the fixed plant is optimal for that output – for all other outputs there is either too little or too much of the fixed factor and $SRATC$ lies above $LRATC$.

We saw earlier in this chapter that an $SRATC$ curve, such as the one shown in Figure 17.5, is but one of many such short-run curves. Each one shows how costs vary as output is varied from a base output, holding some factors fixed at the quantities most appropriate to the base output. This is illustrated in Figure 17.6. There is an associated short-run cost curve tangent to every point on the long-run cost curve. Each short-run curve shows how costs vary if output varies, with the fixed factor held constant at the level that is optimal for the output at the point of tangency. The long-run curve is sometimes called an ENVELOPE CURVE that encloses the whole family of short-run curves.[1]

---

[1] Each short-run curve touches the long-run curve at one point and lies above it everywhere else. This leads to a subtle consequence. Two curves that are tangent at a point have the same slope at that point. If $LRATC$ is decreasing where it is tangent to $SRATC$, then $SRATC$ must also be decreasing. What this tells us is that the best way to produce any output q_0 where economies of scale are not exhausted is to build a plant whose minimum $SRATC$ exceeds q_0 and then underutilize it.

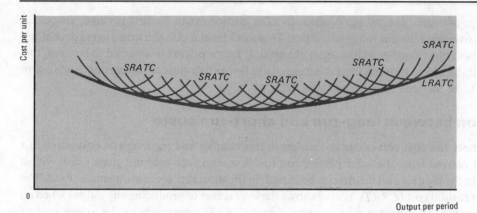

Fig. 17.6 The envelope relation between the long-run average total cost curve and all the short-run average total cost curves

Shifts in cost curves

The cost curves we have derived so far show how cost varies with output, given constant factor prices and fixed technology. Changes in either technological knowledge or factor prices will cause the whole family of short- and long-run cost curves to shift. Loss of existing technological knowledge is a rare thing, so technological change normally works in one direction only, to shift cost curves downward. Factor prices can, however, exert an influence in either direction. If a firm has to pay more for any factor that it uses, the cost of producing each level of output will rise; if the firm has to pay less, costs fall.

> **A rise in factor prices shifts the whole family of short- and long-run cost curves upwards.**
> **A fall in factor prices or a technological advance shifts the whole family of cost curves downwards.**

Isoquants: an alternative analysis of the firm's long-run input decisions[1]

The production function and the long-run choices open to the firm can be given a graphical representation using the concept of an isoquant.

A single isoquant

Table 17.3 gives a hypothetical illustration of those combinations of two inputs (labour and capital) that will each serve to produce a given quantity of output. The table lists some of the methods indicated by a production function as being available to produce 6 units of output. The first combination uses a great deal of capital (K) and very little labour (L). Moving down the table, labour is substituted for capital in such a way as to keep output constant. Finally, at the bottom of the table, most of the capital has been replaced by labour. The rate of substitution between the two

---

[1] The material in this section can be omitted without a loss of continuity.

Table 17.3 Alternative ways of producing 6 units of output

K	L	ΔK	ΔL	Rate of substitution ΔK/ΔL
18	2			
		−6	1	−6·0
12	3			
		−3	1	−3·0
9	4			
		−3	2	−1·5
6	6			
		−2	3	−0·67
4	9			
		−1	3	−0·33
3	12			
		−1	6	−0·17
2	18			

factors is calculated in the last three columns of the table. Note that as we move down the table, the absolute value of the rate of substitution declines.

The data from Table 17.3 are plotted in Figure 17.7. Points *a* to *d* refer to the first four points in the table. A smooth curve is drawn through the points to indicate that there are additional ways, not listed in the table, of producing 6 units. This curve is called an ISOQUANT. It shows the set of technologically efficient possibilities for producing a given level of output – 6 units in this example. It is analogous to an indifference curve that shows all combinations of commodities that yield a given utility.

The convex shape of the isoquant reflects a diminishing marginal rate of substitution. Starting from point *a*, which uses relatively little labour and much capital, and moving to point *b*, 1 additional unit of labour can substitute for 6 units of capital (while holding production constant). But from *b* to *c*, 1 unit of labour substitutes for only 3 units of capital. To replace the next 3 units of capital (to move from *c* to *d*) requires adding 2 units of labour. Capital is becoming scarcer. In order

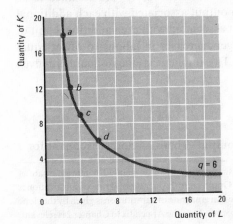

Fig. 17.7 An isoquant for output of six units

to keep production constant, moving from a to b to c to d, larger and larger quantities of labour must be added to compensate for equal reductions in the quantity of capital. The geometrical expression of this is that moving along the isoquant to the right, the slope of the isoquant becomes flatter.

As we move from one point on an isoquant to another we are *substituting one factor for another* while holding output constant. If we move from point b to point c, we are substituting 1 unit of labour for 3 units of capital. The MARGINAL RATE OF SUBSTITUTION measures the rate at which one factor is substituted for another with output held constant. Graphically the marginal rate of substitution is measured by the slope of the isoquant at a particular point. Table 17.3 shows the calculation of some rates of substitution between various points of the isoquant.[1]

The marginal rate of substitution is related to the marginal products of the factors of production. To see how, consider an example. Assume that at the present level of inputs of labour and capital the marginal product of a unit of labour is 2 units of output while the marginal product of capital is 1 unit of output. If the firm reduces its use of capital and increases its use of labour so as to keep output constant, it needs to add only one half unit of labour for one unit of capital given up. If, at another point on the isoquant with more labour and less capital, the marginal products are 2 for capital and 1 for labour, then the firm will have to add two units of labour for every unit of capital it gives up. The general proposition that this example illustrates is:

The marginal rate of substitution between two factors of production is equal to the ratios of their marginal products.

Isoquants are downward-sloping and are convex viewed from the origin. What is the economic meaning of each of these conditions?

We assume that the factor of production has a positive marginal product. If the input of one factor is reduced and that of the other is held constant, output must therefore be reduced. Thus, if one input is decreased, production can only be held constant if the other input is increased. This gives the marginal rate of substitution a negative value: decreases in one factor must be balanced by increases in the other factor if output is to be held constant.

Now consider what happens as the firm moves along the isoquant of Figure 17.7 downward and to the right. This movement means that labour is being added and capital reduced so as to keep output constant. If labour is added in successive increments of exactly one unit, how much capital may be dispensed with each time? The key to the answer is that both factors are assumed to be subject to the law of diminishing returns. Thus the gain in output associated with each additional unit of labour added is *diminishing*, while the loss of output associated with each additional unit of capital forgone is *increasing*. It therefore takes ever-larger increases in labour to offset equal reductions in capital in order to hold production constant. This implies that the isoquant is convex viewed from the origin.

An isoquant map

The isoquant drawn in Figure 17.7 referred to 6 units of output. There is another isoquant for 7

---

[1] The table calculates the incremental rate of substitution between distinct points on an isoquant. The marginal rate of substitution refers to substitutability at a particular point on the isoquant. Graphically the incremental rate of substitution is related to the slope of the chord joining the two points in question, while the marginal rate of substitution is given by the slope of the tangent to the curve at one particular point. Again the discussion of section 11 of the Appendix to Chapter 2 is relevant.

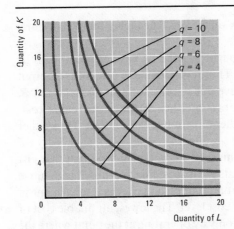

Fig. 17.8 An isoquant map

units, another for 7,000 units, and another for every other rate of output. Each isoquant refers to a specific output and connects alternative combinations of factors that are technologically efficient methods of achieving that output. If we plot a representative set of these isoquants on a single graph, we obtain an ISOQUANT MAP. Such a map is shown in Figure 17.8. The higher the level of output along a particular isoquant, the further away from the origin it will be.

Isoquants and the conditions for cost minimization

Finding the efficient way of producing any output requires finding the least-cost factor combination. To find this combination when both factors are variable, factor prices need to be known. Suppose, to continue the example, that capital is priced at £4 per unit and labour at £1. In Chapter 13, a budget line was used to show the alternative combinations of goods a household could buy; now an ISOCOST LINE is used to show alternative combinations of factors a firm can buy for a given outlay. Four different isocost lines are shown in Figure 17.9. The graph shows the four isocost lines that result when labour costs £1 a unit and capital £4 a unit and expenditure is held constant at rates of £12, £24, £36 and £48, respectively. The line labelled $TC = £12$ represents all combinations of the two factors that the firm could buy for £12. Point a represents 2 units of K and 4 units of L. The slope of the isocost line depends upon *relative* commodity prices. For given factor prices, a series of

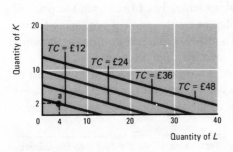

Fig. 17.9 Isocost lines

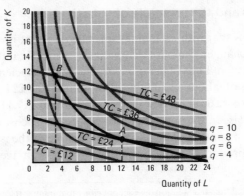

Fig. 17.10 The determination of the least-cost method of output

parallel isocost lines reflects alternative levels of expenditure on factors. The higher the expenditure, the farther from the origin is the isocost line.

In Figure 17.10 the isoquant and isocost maps are brought together. Consider point A in the figure. It is on the 6-unit isoquant and the £24 isocost line. Thus it is possible to achieve the output $q = 6$ for a total cost of £24. There are other ways to achieve this output, for example, at point B, where $TC = £48$. Moving along the isoquant from point A in either direction increases cost. Similarly, moving along the isocost line from point A in either direction lowers output. Thus either move would raise cost per unit.

The economically most efficient method of production must be a point on an isoquant that just touches (i.e., is tangent to) an isocost line. If the isoquant cuts the isocost line, it is possible to move along the isoquant and reach a lower level of cost. Only at a point of tangency is a movement in either direction along the isoquant a movement to a higher cost level. The lowest attainable cost of producing 6 units is £24, and this cost level can be achieved only by operating at the point where the £24 isocost line is tangent to the 6-unit isoquant. The lowest average cost of producing 6 units is thus £24/6 = £4 per unit of output.

> **The least-cost position is given graphically by the point of tangency between the isoquant and the isocost lines.**

Notice that point A in Figure 17.10 indicates not only the lowest level of cost for 6 units of output but also the highest level of output for £24 of cost.[1]

The slope of the isocost line is given by the ratio of the prices of the two factors of production. The slope of the isoquant is given by the ratio of their marginal products. When the firm reaches its least-cost position, it has equated the price ratio (which is given to it by the market prices) with the ratio of marginal products (which it can adjust by varying the proportions in which it hires the factors). In symbols,

$$\frac{MP_K}{MP_L} = \frac{p_K}{p_L} .$$

This is equation (4) on page 220. We have now derived this result by use of the isoquant analysis of the firm's decisions.

Isoquants and the principle of substitution

Suppose now that with technology unchanged – that is, with the isoquant map fixed – the price of one factor changes. Suppose that with the price of capital unchanged at £4 per unit, the price of labour rises from £1 to £4 per unit. Originally, the efficient factor combination of producing 6 units was 12 units of labour and 3 units of capital. It cost £24. To produce that same output in the same way would cost £60 at the new factor prices. Figure 17.11 shows why that is not efficient.

An increase in the price of labour pivots the isocost line inward and thus increases the cost of producing any output. It also changes the slope of the isocost line and thus changes the least-cost method of production. The steeper isocost line is tangent to the isoquant at C, not A in Figure

---

[1] Thus we find the same solution if we set out *either* to minimize the cost of producing 6 units of output *or* to maximize the output that can be obtained for £24. One problem is said to be the 'dual' of the other.

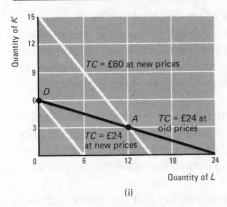
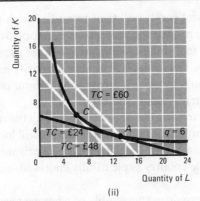

Fig. 17.11 The effects of a change in factor prices on costs and factor proportions: (i) the effect on the isocost line of an increase in the price of labour; (ii) substitution of capital for labour due to an increase in the price of labour

17.11 (ii). Costs at C are higher than they were before the price increase, but not as high as if the factor substitution had not occurred. The slope of the isocost line has changed making it efficient to substitute the now relatively cheaper capital for the relatively more expensive labour.

This result illustrates the principle of substitution.

> **Changes in relative factor prices will cause a partial replacement of factors that have become relatively more expensive by factors that have become relatively cheaper.**

Of course, substitution of capital for labour cannot fully offset the effects of a rise in the cost of labour, as Figure 17.11 (i) shows. Consider the output attainable for £24. In the figure there are two isocost lines representing £24 of outlay – at the old and new price of labour. The new isocost line for £24 lies everywhere inside the old one (except where no labour is used). The isocost line must therefore be tangent to a lower isoquant. This means that if production is to be held constant, higher costs must be accepted – but because of substitution it is not necessary to accept costs as high as would accompany an unchanged factor proportion. In the example 6 units can be produced for £48 rather than the £60 that would have been required if no change in factor proportions had been made (i.e., if inputs were held at A rather than changed to C).

This leads to the prediction that:

> **A rise in the price of one factor with all other factor prices constant will (1) shift upward the cost curves of commodities that use that factor, and (2) lead to a substitution of factors that are now relatively cheaper for the factor whose price has risen.**

Both of these predictions were stated in the first part of this chapter; they have now been derived formally using the isoquant technique.

The significance of the principle of substitution for the economy as a whole

The relative prices of factors of production in an economy will tend to reflect their relative scarcities. In a country with a great deal of land and a small population, for example, the price of land will be low while, because labour is in short supply, the wage rate will be high. In such circumstances firms producing agricultural goods will tend to make lavish use of (cheap) land and to economize on (expensive) labour; a production process will be adopted that is labour-extensive and land-intensive. On the other hand, in a small country with a large population, the demand for land will be high relative to its supply. Thus, land will be very expensive and firms producing agricultural goods will tend to economize on it by using a great deal of labour per unit of land. In this case production will tend to be labour-intensive and land-extensive.

Thus we see that relative factor prices will reflect the relative scarcities (in relation to demand) of different factors of production: abundant factors will have prices that are low relative to the prices of factors that are scarce. Firms seeking their own private profit will be led to use much of the factors with which the whole country is plentifully endowed, and to economize on the factors that are in scarce supply.

This discussion provides an example of what we mean when we say that the price system is an automatic control system. No single firm need be aware of national factor surpluses and scarcities. Prices determined on the competitive market tend to reflect these, and individual firms that never look beyond their own private profit are nonetheless led to economize on factors that are scarce in the nation as a whole. We should not be surprised, therefore, to discover that methods of producing the same commodity differ in different countries. In the United States, where labour is highly skilled and very expensive, a steel company may use very elaborate machinery to economize on labour. In China, where labour is abundant and capital very scarce, a much less mechanized method of production may be appropriate. The Western engineer who feels that the Chinese are way behind because they are using methods abandoned in the West as inefficient long ago may be missing the truth about economic efficiency in use of resources.

In spite of the price system's ability to induce profit-maximizing firms to take account of the nation's relative factor scarcities when choosing among possible methods of production, one must avoid jumping to the conclusion that whatever productive processes are adopted are the best possible ones and should never be interfered with. There is, however, a strong common-sense appeal in the idea that:

> **Any society interested in getting the most out of its resources should take account of their relative scarcities in deciding what productive processes to adopt, which is what the price system leads individual firms to do.**

The very long run

In the long run, when technology and hence the production function are given, a certain quantity of inputs produces a certain output. In the very long run, technology may change: the same quantities of inputs may then produce a different quantity of output than before.

Changes in supply over the very long run are strongly influenced by changes in the techniques of production, by changes in the goods being produced, and by changes in the quality of factor inputs. Much economic theory focuses attention on short- and long-run decisions taken within the context of given factor supplies, given products, and known techniques of production. These decisions are important but, if we are interested in the performance of the economic system over long time periods, questions concerning the causes and consequences of very-long-run changes cannot be ignored. In this section we shall confine ourselves to the question of how the economic system will respond in the very long run to changes in demands, prices and costs such as we considered in the short and long run. In doing this we shall concentrate on changes in *productivity*. Many of the wider aspects of very-long-run changes must be postponed until Chapter 46, which deals with the whole problem of long-term economic growth.

Productivity

Over the last few decades the material standard of living of the typical family has increased enormously in all of the world's industrialized countries. Much of this increase has been due to the invention of new, improved ways of making products. This causes an increase in PRODUCTIVITY, which is output per unit of input employed.

The magnitude of increases in productivity deserves some attention.

The apparently modest rate of increase of output per man-hour of labour of 2·0 per cent per year leads to a doubling of output per man-hour every 34 years.

Productivity in the United Kingdom has increased at approximately this rate over the last 100 years.

Between 1945 and 1970 productivity growth in the UK was closer to 3 per cent per year (which doubles output every 23¼ years), while in other countries it was much higher. In Japan, for example, it was increasing at about 10 per cent per year, a rate which doubles output per man-hour approximately every seven years. In the last few years the rate of productivity increase has greatly slackened in all industrial countries, creating fears that the steady increase in living standards to which people had become accustomed might cease.

Productivity changes and the theory of supply There is no doubt that productivity changes affect the supplies of commodities. What is in doubt is the extent to which productivity changes themselves are an endogenous response to economic signals and incentives, and the extent to which they are an exogenous consequence of the spontaneous creative activity of scientists, inventors and many other researchers. The answer to the question will greatly influence our judgement of the ability of the economy to adjust to various disturbances that impinge on it.

Sources of productivity increases Long-run and very-long-run productivity increases are due to scale effects, increases in the quality of the inputs, changes in the known techniques and improvements in products. Mere population growth, other things equal, will permit higher productivity if most products are subject to increasing returns to scale. Substitution of capital for labour as the level of production expands is likely to lead to greater productivity. Better raw materials, better trained or educated labour, or better machines will increase productivity even if no changes in factor quantities or proportions take place. Better organization of production alone can account for increases in productivity. New ideas can raise efficiency by being applied to new products: imagination can design a better mousetrap, with no change in the quantity, quality or proportions of factors.

Inventions and innovations

An INVENTION is defined as the discovery of something new, such as a new production technique or a new product. An INNOVATION is defined as the introduction of an invention into use.

It is generally accepted that innovation responds to economic incentives. New products and methods will not be introduced unless it appears profitable to do so, and a change in economic incentives can change the apparent profitabilities of various possible innovations.

But innovation can occur only when there has already been an invention. If there is a dramatic rise in labour costs, firms may now decide to take up some labour-saving process that hitherto has been ignored since its invention, but they cannot do so if the invention has not yet been made. If we are concerned with the response of the economy to such economic signals as changes in the relative prices both of consumer goods and of inputs, then we need to know the extent to which invention responds to such incentives. A number of hypotheses about the sources of invention have been put forward.

(1) Invention is a random process Some people are by nature both curious and clever. Thousands of attempts will be made to invent better ways of doing things. Many will fail, and they remain nameless, but a few succeed. The successful inventions become a pool of potential innovations, and, when the climate is right, they are introduced into production.

(2) Invention is a response to the institutional framework Things like the patent laws, the tax structure, or the organization of business enterprise stimulate or retard the process of invention. Invention, in this view, is not exogenous to society, but it does not respond primarily to economic variables, and it certainly is exogenous to the individual *firm*.

(3) Invention and innovation are the product of the inherent logic and momentum of science Science has a logic and momentum of its own. There was a time for the discovery of the steam-engine, the aeroplane, hybrid corn, the electron tube and the rocket. Particular men are the instruments, not the causes, of scientific discovery. Had Edison never been born we would still have had, at about the same time, both the lightbulb and the gramophone. According to this view, the present is the electronic age, and automation is its industrial application.

(4) Necessity is the mother of invention Ignorance is only skin deep. With enough expenditure of funds, people can do anything – split the atom, conquer cancer, fly to Mars or cultivate the desert. The impetus for invention may come from the firm or governments may set priorities and do the research that leads to major discoveries and innovations. Atomic energy, for example, is the result of the United Kingdom's, and later the United States', desire to develop superweapons during the Second World War.

(5) Profits are the spur The profit motive not only leads individuals and firms to seize the best methods known, but to develop new ways to meet both old and new wants. A firm for which a certain factor is becoming scarce will discover ways to economize on it, or will develop a more plentiful substitute for it. (For example, the scarcity of high-grade iron ore led to the development of ways of using low-grade ores.) In this view, automation is a response to expensive labour.

These hypotheses are not mutually exclusive and the evidence for one cannot be regarded as disproving the others. The fact that some firms spend millions of pounds on research and development to overcome specific problems or invent new products does not change the fact that many discoveries are made in university laboratories by men who have little knowledge of, or interest in, current prices and scarcities. The fact that many patentable discoveries are given to the world does not prove that others are not motivated by the prospect of huge personal gain. And so on.

We have asked whether the direction of invention responds to economic incentives. We are also interested in the volume of invention. Even if its direction does not exactly respond to current market signals, it is still a potent source of increases in living standards. Inventions that reduce the quantities of all inputs required to gain a given output are absolutely efficient and will raise living standards even if they save just as much on plentiful as on scarce resources.

Invention and economic incentives

Does it matter how invention is determined? Consider a single example to illustrate why it does.
Hypothesis 1: This hypothesis accepts the third view of invention listed above. This is the age of electronics and automation, and scientists just go on inventing methods that replace unskilled labour with capital, thereby creating unemployment among the unskilled. The normal corrective of the price system is for the relative price of unskilled labour to fall, thus inducing a substitution in favour of unskilled labour until the unemployment is eliminated. But, according to this hypothesis, scientists are uninfluenced by the incentives of relative factor prices. Now assume that each new technique invented is *absolutely* more efficient than its predecessors in the sense that it uses less of *all* factors than its predecessors – but it also uses less unskilled labour *relative to* other inputs. Firms will now be motivated to adopt the absolutely more efficient new techniques, but in so doing they will adopt a factor combination that increases the unemployment amongst the unskilled.
Hypothesis 2: This hypothesis accepts the fifth view of invention given above. If unemployment amongst the unskilled is allowed to drive down their relative wage, firms will be led to select from amongst existing techniques those that are more intensive in the use of unskilled labour. If there is still unemployment amongst the unskilled, their factor services will remain cheap and there will be a profit incentive to develop *new* techniques that substitute cheap unskilled labour for the more expensive factors of production.

Thus, in hypothesis 1, the long-term effects of invention and innovation are to increase the problem of 'structural unemployment' of the unskilled, while in hypothesis 2 the effect of the same inventive activity is to reduce this unemployment. Under hypothesis 1, allowing the relative wage of the unskilled to fall will only worsen their plight, while under hypothesis 2 it will cause a burst of inventive and innovative activity that will reduce their unemployment. Clearly it matters whether in the long run invention proceeds more or less autonomously or under the influence of such economic incentives as relative factor prices.

Summary of the basic theory of costs

This concludes our study of the theory of costs. A number of the subjects covered, although important, are digressions from the point of view of developing a theory of the behaviour of the firm. We shall now summarize the basic points that you should know before proceeding to the next few chapters on the theory of supply. Anyone who is not clear about the following points should review his or her understanding of them by re-reading the relevant parts of the preceding two chapters.

(1) We hypothesize that firms strive to maximize their profits, and, since profits are the difference between the costs and revenues of the firm, it is necessary to consider what we mean by costs and how these vary as output varies.

(2) The cost to the firm of any input that it uses is given by what the firm must sacrifice to have the use of the input.

(3) In the case of any factor service that the firm hires from outside, the cost to the firm is adequately measured by the price paid, since that sum of money cannot be used for other purposes.

(4) In the case of factors owned by the firm, the cost is measured by what the factor could be leased out (or sold) for on the open market. This cost may bear little relation to the cost originally paid to purchase these factors.

(5) Points (2)–(4) summarize an opportunity-cost principle of input valuation: the cost of using an input is the cost of the alternatives that are forgone by so doing.

(6) So far we have seen how to value inputs. To see how costs vary as production varies we need to see how inputs vary as production varies. This relation is described by the production function. When we have costed the inputs we can derive a cost function showing how costs vary as production varies.

(7) In the short run, some factors are fixed and some are variable. The variations in output that accompany variations in the input are described by the hypothesis of diminishing returns. Given the price of the variable factor, we can move directly from returns curves to cost curves. The short-run marginal and average cost curves are assumed to be U-shaped with the MC curve cutting the AC curve at its lowest point.

(8)   In the long run, all factors are variable and the long-run average total cost curve shows the lowest attainable average cost for each level of output, on the assumption that the proportion in which inputs are used is adjusted so as to minimize costs.

(9) Each short-run cost curve touches the long-run cost curve at one point and elsewhere lies above it.

(10) The principle of substitution says that the long-run effect of a change in factor prices is to cause a substitution of the relatively less expensive factors for the relatively more expensive ones. Thus a change in price induces an economizing of factors whose prices rise and a more lavish use of factors whose prices fall.

(11) In the very long run, technological knowledge changes, and the question of how costs change as output changes depends on the question of how invention and innovation respond to changes in economic incentives.

18

The equilibrium of a profit-maximizing firm

In Chapter 16 we hypothesized that firms maximize their profits, which are the difference between the total revenue derived from selling their product and the total cost of making it. In Chapter 17 we developed a theory of *the variation of cost with output* that applies to all firms. We cannot, however, develop a single theory of *the variation of revenue with output* that is applicable to all firms. In subsequent chapters we shall develop separate theories of revenue for firms in different market situations. In the meantime, we shall confine ourselves to what can be said about the rules for profit-maximizing behaviour as they apply to all firms.

Various revenue concepts

The revenues of a firm are the receipts that it obtains from selling its products. We can look at these as totals, averages or marginal quantities, exactly as we looked at costs in the previous chapter.

(1) TOTAL REVENUE (TR) refers to the total amount of money that the firm receives from the sale of its products. This will vary with a firm's sales, so we may write, using functional notation:

$$TR = R(q),$$

where TR is total revenue and, as in the last chapter, q is total production over some period of time.[1] Total revenue is obviously equal to the quantity sold multiplied by the selling price of the commodity, i.e.,

$$TR = pq,$$

where p is the price per unit. The unqualified term *revenue* is often used to refer to total revenue and whenever we speak of revenue or use the symbol R we shall mean total revenue.

(2) AVERAGE REVENUE (AR) is total revenue divided by the number of units sold (pq/q). Quite obviously, average revenue is the price of the commodity:

$$AR = p.$$

---

[1] Since we are not concerned with the holding of stocks, we can equate production with sales.

It follows from this that the curve which relates average revenue to output is the same thing as the demand curve that relates price to output.

(3) MARGINAL REVENUE (MR) is the change in total revenue resulting from an increase of one unit in the rate of sales per period of time (say per annum). The marginal revenue resulting from the sale of the nth unit of a commodity is thus the total revenue resulting from the sale of n units per annum minus the total revenue that would have been earned if only $n-1$ (i.e., one less) units had been sold per annum. Do not think that $n-1$ units are sold at some time and an extra unit at some later time. Marginal revenue refers to alternative sales policies *at the same period of time*. Thus, to find the marginal revenue of the 100th unit we compare the total revenue resulting when 100 units are sold over some period of time, with the total revenue that would have resulted if 99 units had been sold over the same period of time. In general we may write[1]:

$$MR_n = TR_n - TR_{n-1}.$$

Behavioural rules for profit-maximizing

We now translate the assumption of profit-maximization into several formal rules for a firm's behaviour. We do not suppose that firms consciously follow these rules, but as long as they succeed somehow in maximizing their profits the rules will allow us to predict firm behaviour.

A rule to decide whether or not to produce

A firm always has the option of producing nothing, in which case it will have an operating loss equal to its fixed costs. If production adds less to revenue than to costs, production will increase the loss suffered by the firm. If production adds more to revenue than to costs, production will reduce the firm's losses (or increase its profits). From this follows our first rule:

> **Rule 1. In the short run a firm should produce if and only if total revenue is equal to or greater than total variable cost.**

Another way of stating this rule is that the firm should produce output only if average revenue (price) is equal to or greater than average variable cost.

A rule to ensure that profits are either at a maximum or at a minimum[2]

If the firm is going to produce at all according to Rule 1, it will have to decide how much it should produce. If, on the one hand, the firm finds that at its present level of production the cost of making another unit (marginal cost) is less than the revenue that would be gained by selling that unit (marginal revenue), total profit could clearly be increased by producing another unit of output.

---

[1] Once again the definition invokes finite changes and therefore strictly refers to incremental revenue. Students familiar with the calculus will realize that true marginal revenue refers to $MR = dTR/dq$. In the text we do not distinguish the two concepts although their relation is further pursued in section 11 of the Appendix for Chapter 2.

[2] Advanced students will realize that the possibility of a stationary point of inflexion in the profit function is ignored in this treatment.

Thus whenever a firm finds that at the current level of output marginal revenue exceeds marginal cost, it can increase its profit by producing more. If, on the other hand, the firm finds that at the present level of production the cost of making the last unit exceeds the revenue gained by selling it, total profit could clearly be increased by not producing the last unit. Thus, whenever the firm finds that marginal cost exceeds marginal revenue it can increase its total profit by reducing its output.

Now we have the result that the firm should change its output whenever marginal cost does not equal marginal revenue, raising output if $MR > MC$ and lowering output if $MC > MR$. Rule 2 follows from this.

> **Rule 2. A necessary condition for the firm to be producing its profit-maximizing output is that marginal revenue should equal marginal cost.**

At the profit-maximizing output the last unit produced should add just as much to revenue as it adds to cost.

A rule to ensure that profits are maximized rather than minimized

It is possible to fulfil Rule 2 and have profits at a minimum rather than a maximum. Figure 18.1 illustrates. The firm has a short-run marginal cost curve similar to the ones derived in Chapter 17. The firm is assumed to be able to sell all its output at the going market price, so that the market price is the firm's marginal revenue. (If all units can be sold at the prevailing market price then each unit adds that price to the firm's total revenue.)

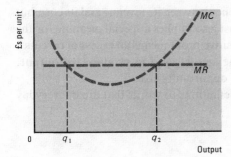

Fig. 18.1 Marginal cost = marginal revenue is a necessary but not a sufficient condition for a profit maximum

In the figure there are two outputs, q_1 and q_2, where marginal cost equals marginal revenue. Output q_1, however, is a minimum-profit position because a change of output in either direction would increase profit: for outputs below q_1 marginal cost exceeds marginal revenue and profits can be increased by *reducing* output, while for outputs above q_1 marginal revenue exceeds marginal cost and profits can be increased by *increasing* output.

Output q_2, however, is a maximum-profit position since at outputs just below it marginal revenue exceeds marginal cost and profit can be increased by *increasing* output towards q_2, while at outputs just above it marginal cost exceeds marginal revenue and profit can be increased by *reducing* output towards q_2.

Rule 3 is needed to distinguish minimum-profit positions such as q_1 from maximum-profit positions such as q_2.

Rule 3. For an output where marginal cost equals marginal revenue to be profit-maximizing rather than profit-minimizing, it is sufficient that marginal cost be less than marginal revenue at slightly lower outputs and that marginal cost exceed marginal revenue at slightly higher outputs.

The geometric statement of this condition is that, at the profit-maximizing output, the marginal cost curve should intersect the marginal revenue curve from below. This ensures that $MC < MR$ to the left of, and $MC > MR$ to the right of, the profit-maximizing output.[1]

The profit-maximizing output

The above three rules determine the output that will be chosen by any firm that maximizes its profits: (i) if the output is positive, total revenue is equal to or exceeds total variable cost; (ii) marginal cost equals marginal revenue; and (iii) if output were reduced slightly, marginal cost would be less than marginal revenue, while if output were increased slightly, marginal cost would exceed marginal revenue.

When the firm has chosen the output that maximizes its profits, we say that the firm is in equilibrium. In this position there are no forces acting on the firm to cause it to change its output. Output will thus remain constant unless either the revenues or the costs associated with various levels of output change.

The meaning and significance of profits

We assume the firm maximizes its profit, which is the difference between its revenue and its cost, but the special meaning that we have given to the concept of cost also implies a special meaning for the concept of profit. (This was first discussed on page 209). Positive profit means an excess of revenues from the sale of output over the opportunity costs of the factors used to produce the output; negative profit, i.e., a loss, means that revenues fall short of opportunity cost.

This use of the words *profit* and *loss* gives specialized definitions to words that are in everyday use. They are, therefore, a potential source of confusion.

Other definitions of profits

The businessman defines profits as the excess of revenues over the costs with which his accountant provides him. The major differences are that, since the accountant does not include charges for risk-taking and use of the owner's own capital as costs, these items are recorded by the businessman as part of his profits. When the businessman says he *needs* profits of such and such an amount in order to stay in business, he is making sense within his definition, for his 'profits' must be large enough to pay for those factors of production that he uses but does not account for as costs. The economist would express the same notion by saying that the businessman needs to cover *all* of his costs, including those not included by accounting conventions. If the firm is covering all its costs (in the sense that we have defined costs), then it follows that it could not do better by using its resources in

---

[1] Those students who are familiar with elementary calculus can follow the formal derivations of these three rules given in the Appendix to this chapter.

any other line of activity than the one currently being followed. Thus a situation in which revenues equal costs (profits of zero) is a satisfactory one – because all factors, hidden as well as visible, are being rewarded at least as well as in their *best* alternative uses[1].

The income-tax authorities have yet another definition of profits, which is implicit in the thousands of rules about what may be (and what may not be) included as a deduction from revenue in arriving at taxable income. In some cases, the taxing authorities allow more for cost than the accountant recommends; in other cases they allow less.

It is important to be clear about different meanings of the term *profits* to avoid fruitless semantic arguments. The economist's definition of profits is for many purposes the most useful, but if we wish to apply it to business behaviour or to tax policy, we must be prepared to make the appropriate adjustments. Also if we wish to use accounting or tax data to test particular economic theories, we must be prepared to rectify the data.

Profits and resource allocation

When resources are valued by the opportunity-cost principle, we have seen that the amounts assigned show how much these resources might earn if used in their best alternative uses. If there is some industry in which revenues typically exceed opportunity costs, the firms in that industry will be earning profits. Profit-maximizing firms will want to move resources into this industry because the earnings potentially available there are greater than in alternative uses of the resources. If, in some other industry, firms are incurring losses, some or all of this industry's resources are more highly valued in other uses, and profit-maximizing firms will want to reallocate some of the resources at their command.

> **Profits in some activity are the signal that resources can profitably be moved into that activity. Losses are the signal that they can profitably be moved elsewhere. Profits and losses thus play a crucial role in the workings of a free-market system. Only if they are zero (revenues equal to opportunity costs) is there no incentive for resources to move.**

The next step

Revenue is a function of (i.e., varies with) the firm's output. The firm is in equilibrium when it chooses the profit-maximizing output – the output for which marginal revenue equals marginal cost. In Chapter 17 we saw how cost varied with output. In subsequent chapters we shall study how revenue varies with output. The key to the behaviour of revenue is the competitive situation in which the firm finds itself.

---

[1] In some books the pure return to capital and the risk premium are not called costs. These returns are included in profits, and profits are divided between normal profits and super-normal profits. Normal profits are what must be earned to induce a firm to remain in an industry and they are thus the same thing as the returns to capital and risk-taking. Super-normal profits are anything in excess of normal profits and are thus the same thing as our profits. The difference is purely semantic. To say that an industry is in equilibrium when its firms are just earning normal profits, where such profits include returns to capital and risk-taking, is the same thing as saying that an industry is in equilibrium when its firms are earning neither profits nor losses when costs include returns to capital and risk-taking.

Appendix to chapter 18

A mathematical derivation of the rules of profit-maximization

In this brief appendix we provide formal derivations of the three rules for profit-maximization. The first derivation uses only algebra and can be read by anyone. The second and third use elementary calculus and should not be attempted by those who are unfamiliar with simple derivatives.

Condition 1: Profits, π, are defined as follows:

$$\pi = R - (F + V),$$

where R is total revenue, F is total fixed cost and V is total variable cost. Now let subscript n stand for a state where there is no production and p for one where there is production. It pays the firm to produce if there is at least one level of production for which

$$\pi_p \geq \pi_n.$$

When the firm does not produce, R and V are zero, so the above condition becomes

$$R - F - V \geq -F$$

or

$$R \geq V.$$

Dividing both sides by output, Q, we get: price $\geq AVC$.

Condition 2:

$$\pi = R - C,$$

where C is total cost $(F + V)$. Both revenues and costs vary with output, i.e., $R = R(Q)$ and $C = C(Q)$. Thus we may write

$$\pi = R(Q) - C(Q).$$

A necessary condition for the maximization of profits is[1]

$$\frac{d\pi}{dQ} = R'(Q) - C'(Q) = 0$$

or

$$R'(Q) = C'(Q).$$

But these derivatives define marginal revenue and marginal cost, so we have

$$MR = MC.$$

Condition 3: To ensure that we have a maximum and not a minimum for profits, we require

$$\frac{d^2\pi}{dQ^2} = R''(Q) - C''(Q) = \frac{dMR}{dQ} - \frac{dMC}{dQ} < 0$$

or

$$\frac{dMR}{dQ} < \frac{dMC}{dQ},$$

which means that the algebraic value of the slope of the marginal cost curve must exceed, at the point of intersection, the algebraic value of the slope of the marginal revenue curve. This translates into the geometric statement that the marginal cost curve should cut the marginal revenue curve from below.

---

[1] Note the convenient use of a prime for a derivative. Thus for the function $F(X)$, the two notations d/dX and $F'(X)$ mean the same thing and d^2/dX^2 and $F''(X)$ mean the same thing.

19

The theory of perfect competition

Is Saxone in competition with Dolcis? Does Selfridge's compete with Marks & Spencer's? Is a Yorkshire farmer in competition with a Somerset farmer? In the ordinary sense of competition the answers to the first two of these questions are plainly yes, and the answer to the third question is probably no. Saxone and Dolcis both advertise extensively to persuade the same group of buyers to buy *their* products. Everyone knows that many shoppers check the respective prices and qualities offered by two nearby department stores such as Selfridge's and Marks & Spencer's. But there is nothing that the Yorkshire farmer can do that will affect the sales or the profits of the Somerset farmer.

Firm behaviour and market structure

To decide who is competing with whom and in what sense they compete, it is necessary to distinguish between the behaviour of individual firms and the type of market in which the firms operate. Economists use the term *market structure* to refer to the latter concept. The concept of competitive behaviour is quite distinct from the concept of competitive market structure. The degree of *competitive behaviour* refers to the degree to which individual firms indulge in active competition with one another. The degree of *competitiveness of the market structure* refers to the degree to which individual firms have power over that market – power to influence the price or other terms on which their product is sold. In everyday use the term 'competition' usually refers only to competitive behaviour. Economists, however, are interested both in the behaviour of individual firms and in market structures.

Saxone and Dolcis certainly engage in competitive (i.e., rivalrous) behaviour. It is also true that both individually and together they have some power over the market. Either firm could raise its prices and still continue to sell its product, each has the power to decide – within limits set by buyers' tastes and the prices of competing products – what price consumers will pay for its own product.

The Yorkshire and the Somerset farmers do not engage in active competitive behaviour with each other. They operate, however, in a market over which they have no power. Neither one has significant power to change the market price for its product by altering his own behaviour.

To get to one extreme of competitive market structures, economists use a model in which no one firm has any market power. There are so many firms that each must accept the price set by the forces of market demand and supply. In this theory of the perfectly competitive market structure there is no need for individual firms to behave competitively with respect to one another since none has any power over the market and one firm's ability to sell its product is uninfluenced by the behaviour of any other single firm. The apparent paradox that inter-firm competition does not occur in perfectly competitive markets is resolved when we recognize the distinction between inter-firm competitive behaviour and the competitive *structure* of the market in which the firms operate.

The theory of the perfectly competitive market structure applies directly to a number of real-world markets, particularly agricultural goods and industrial raw materials. It also provides a benchmark for comparison with other market structures in which firms do have significant market power.

For a household, the MARKET consists of those firms from which it can buy a well-defined product; for a firm, the market consists of those buyers to whom it can sell a well-defined product. A group of firms that sells a well-defined product, or a closely related set of products, is said to constitute an INDUSTRY. The market demand curve is the demand curve for the industry's product.

Consider a firm that produces a specific product for sale in a particular market and competes for customers with other firms in the same industry. If a profit-maximizing firm knows precisely the demand curve it faces, it knows the price it could charge for each rate of sales, and thus it knows its potential revenues. If it also knows its costs, it can readily discover the profits that would be associated with any rate of output, and it can choose the rate that maximizes its profits. But what if the firm knows its costs and only the *market* demand curve for its product? It does not know what its own sales would be. In other words, it does not know its *own* demand curve. In order to determine what fraction of the total market demand will be met by sellers other than itself, it needs to know how other firms will respond if it changes its price. If it reduces its price by 10 per cent, will other sellers leave their prices unchanged or will they also reduce them? If they reduce their prices, will they do so by less than 10 per cent, by exactly 10 per cent, or by more than 10 per cent? Obviously, each of the possible outcomes will have a different effect on the firm's sales and thus on its revenues and profits.

The answers to questions about the relation of a firm's demand curve to the market demand curve depend on such things as the number of sellers in the market and the similarity of their products. For example, if there are only two large firms in an industry, each may be expected to meet most of the other's price cuts, but if there are 500 small firms, a price cut by one may go unmatched. For another example, if two firms are producing identical products, they may be expected to behave differently with respect to each other than if they are producing similar but not identical products. These are aspects of what is called MARKET STRUCTURE or MARKET FORM, which is defined as the characteristics of market organization that are likely to affect a firm's behaviour and performance.

There are many other aspects of market structure including the ease of entering the industry, the nature and size of the purchasers of the firm's products, and the firm's ability to influence demand by advertising. To reduce these aspects to manageable proportions, economists have focused on a few theoretical market structures that are intended to represent structures in actual market societies. In this chapter and the next two, we shall look at four of these: perfect competition, monopoly, monopolistic competition, and oligopoly.

In this chapter we shall study the theory of perfect competition. First we introduce the critical assumptions, then we derive the firm's demand curve and examine the equilibrium, and finally we examine the equilibrium of the competitive *industry* in both the short run and the long run.

The assumptions of perfect competition

The theory of PERFECT COMPETITION is built on two critical assumptions, one about the behaviour of the individual firm and one about the nature of the industry in which it operates.

The *firm* is assumed to be a PRICE-TAKER. This means that the firm is assumed to act as if it can alter its rate of production and sales within any feasible range without its actions having any significant effect on the price of the product it sells. Thus the firm must passively accept whatever price happens to be ruling on the market.

The *industry* is characterized by FREEDOM OF ENTRY AND EXIT. This means that any new firm is free to set up production if it so wishes and that any existing firm is free to cease production and leave the industry if it so wishes. Existing firms cannot bar the entry of new firms and there are no legal prohibitions on entry or exit.

The ultimate test of the theory based on these assumptions will be the usefulness of its predictions, but because students are often bothered by the first assumption, we examine it more closely. To see what is involved in the assumption of price-taking, contrast the demands for the products of a car manufacturer and a wheat farmer.

A car manufacturer

The Ford Motor Company is aware of the fact that it has some market power. If it substantially increases the price of one of its cars, sales will fall off; if it lowers the price substantially, it will be able to sell more. If Ford contemplates a large increase in production of one car that is not a response to some known or anticipated rise in demand, it knows that it will have to reduce prices in order to sell the extra output. The car manufacturing firm is *not* a price-taker. The quantity that it is able to sell will depend on the price it charges, but it does not have to accept passively whatever price is set by the market. In other words, the firm is faced with a downward-sloping demand curve and it may select any price-quantity combination consistent with that demand curve.

A wheat farmer

There are many contrasts between a car manufacturer and a wheat farmer. Three will be sufficient to explain the underpinnings of price-taking behaviour.

A homogeneous product   Every type of car Ford produces is distinct from every other type of Ford car and from every car produced by Ford's competitors. We say that car firms sell a DIFFERENTIATED PRODUCT. Each car has characteristics that appeal to particular customers, so Ford can raise the price of one of its cars without instantly losing all of its sales as customers switch *eñ masse* to other cars. In contrast, one farmer's No. 1 winter wheat is indistinguishable from any other farmer's No. 1 winter wheat. We say that wheat farmers sell a HOMOGENEOUS PRODUCT. Thus there is no reason why well-informed buyers would buy from anyone but the lowest-price supplier of No. 1 winter wheat. Since anyone who charges more than this minimum can expect to sell nothing, every supplier must sell at the same price.

Price-taking behaviour requires that firms sell a homogeneous product.

Well-informed buyers The argument just given assumes that buyers know when one firm is asking a higher price than other firms. A necessary condition for price-taking is that buyers are well enough informed that any firm that raises the price of its homogeneous product above the prices of other firms will lose all of its customers. If instead some customers are ignorant of prices charged by other firms, their supplier may be able to raise his price without losing all their custom.

> **For price-taking behaviour, buyers must be well enough informed so that they do not unknowingly pay more than is necessary for their purchases.**

Perfect knowledge among buyers is clearly sufficient for this result but it is not necessary since many markets function under price-taking conditions in spite of some ignorance of some purchasers.

Many sellers A key distinction between the car and the wheat industries is in the number of sellers. Any one wheat farmer's contribution to the total production of wheat is a very small drop in an extremely large bucket. Ordinarily a farmer will assume that he has no effect on price and will think of his own demand curve as being horizontal. Of course he can have *some* effect on price, but a straightforward calculation will demonstrate that the effect is small enough that he can justifiably neglect it.

The market elasticity of demand for wheat is approximately 0·25. This means that if the quantity of wheat supplied in the world increased by 1 per cent, the price would have to fall by 4 per cent to induce the world's wheat buyers to purchase the whole crop. Even a very large farmer produces a very small fraction of the total crop. In a recent year an extremely large Canadian wheat farm produced about 50,000 tons, only about 1/4,000 of the world production of 200 million tons. Suppose that a large wheat farm increased its production by 20,000 tons, say from 40,000 to 60,000 tons, a very large percentage increase in its own production but an increase of only 1/100 of 1 per cent in world production. Table 19.1 shows that this increase would lead to a decrease in the world

Table 19.1 The calculation of a firm's elasticity of demand (η_E) from market electricity of demand (η_M)

Given $\eta_M = 0\cdot25$

  World output $= 200$ million tons

  Firm's output increases from 40,000 to 60,000 tons, a 40% increase over the average quantity of 50,000 tons

Step 1. Find the percentage change in world price

$$\eta_M = -\frac{\text{percentage change in world output}}{\text{percentage change in world price}}$$

$$\text{Percentage change in world price} = -\frac{\text{percentage change in world output}}{\eta_M}$$

$$= -\frac{1/100 \text{ of } 1\%}{0\cdot25}$$

$$= -4/100 \text{ of } 1\%$$

Step 2. Compute the firm's elasticity of demand:

$$\eta_F = -\frac{\text{percentage change in firm's output}}{\text{percentage change in world price}}$$

$$= -\frac{+40\%}{-4/100 \text{ of } 1\%} = +1000$$

price of 4/100 of 1 per cent (4p in £100) and give the firm an elasticity of demand of 1,000! This is a very high elasticity of demand; the farm would have to increase its output 1,000 per cent to bring about a 1 per cent decrease in the price of wheat. Because the farm's output cannot be varied this much, it is not surprising that the firm regards the price of wheat as being unaffected by any changes in output that it could conceivably make.[1]

It is only a slight simplification of reality to say that the firm is unable to influence the world price of wheat and that it is able to sell all that it can produce at the going world price. In other words, the firm is faced with a perfectly elastic demand curve for its product – it is a price-taker.

The difference between firms producing wheat and firms producing cars is one of degree of market power. The wheat firm, as an insignificant part of the whole market, has no power to influence the world price of wheat. But the car firm does have power to influence the price of cars because its own production represents a significant part of the total supply of cars.

Demand and revenue curves for the perfectly competitive firm

In perfect competition the individual firm faces a perfectly elastic demand curve for its product. Since the market price is unaffected by variations in the firm's output, it follows that the marginal revenue resulting from an increase in the volume of sales by one unit is constant and is equal to the price of the product. If, for example, a farmer faces a perfectly elastic demand for wheat at a market price of £3 a bushel, it follows that each additional unit sold will bring in that amount, i.e., the marginal revenue is £3, and the average revenue (equals total revenue/number of units sold) is also £3. The demand curve facing the firm is thus identical with both the average and the marginal revenue curve. All three of these curves coincide in the same straight line, showing that $p = AR = MR$; all remain constant as output varies. Total revenue does, of course, vary with output; since price is constant, it follows that total revenue rises in direct proportion to output.

Calculations of these revenue concepts for a price-taking firm are illustrated in Table 19.2. The table shows that as long as the firm's output does not affect the price of the product it sells, both average and marginal revenue will be equal to price at all levels of output. Thus, graphically (as shown in Figure 19.1), average revenue and marginal revenue are both horizontal lines at the level of market price. Since the firm can sell any quantity it wishes at this price, the same horizontal line is also the *firm's* demand curve.

If the market price is unaffected by variations in the firm's output, the firm's demand curve, the average revenue curve and the marginal revenue curve coincide in the same horizontal line.

Short-run equilibrium: firm and industry

Equilibrium output of a firm in perfect competition

The firm in perfect competition (being a price-taker) can adjust to differing market conditions only

---

[1] This table relies on the concept of arc elasticity of demand developed on pp. 100–1. Step 1 shows that a 40 per cent increase in the firm's output leads to only a tiny decrease in the world's price. Thus, as step 2 shows, the firm's elasticity of demand is very high: 1,000. The arithmetic is not important, but understanding why the firm will be a price taker in these circumstances is vital.

Table 19.2 Revenue concepts for a price-taking firm*

Quantity sold (units) q	Price p	$TR = p \cdot q$	$AR = TR/q$	$MR = \Delta TR/\Delta q$
10	£3·00	£30·00	£3·00	
11	3·00	33·00	3·00	£3·00
12	3·00	36·00	3·00	3·00
13	3·00	39·00	3·00	3·00

* Marginal revenue is shown between the lines because it represents the change in total revenue (e.g., from £33 to £36) in response to a change in quantity (from 11 to 12 units).

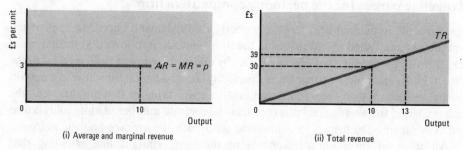

Fig. 19.1 Revenue curves for a price-taking firm (numerical values correspond to those shown in Table 19.2, but the shapes of the curves are general to all firms in perfect competition)

by changing its output. In the short run it has fixed factors, and the only way it can vary its output is by altering its variable inputs. Thus the firm's short-run cost curves are relevant to its output decisions.

We saw earlier that any profit-maximizing firm will seek to produce at a level of output where marginal cost equals marginal revenue. We saw in the immediately preceding section that a perfectly competitive firm's demand and marginal revenue curves coincide in the same horizontal line whose height represents the price of the product. Thus price equals marginal revenue, and it follows immediately that a perfectly competitive firm will equate its marginal cost of production to the market price of its product (as long as price exceeds average variable cost).

The market determines the price at which the firm can sell its product. The firm then picks the quantity of output that maximizes its profits. This is the output for which $p = MC$. Unless prices or costs change, the firm will continue producing this output because it is doing as well as it can do, given the situation it faces. The firm is then said to be in SHORT-RUN EQUILIBRIUM. The short-run equilibrium of a firm in perfect competition is illustrated in Figure 19.2. When $p = MC$ (and MC cuts the price line from below), as at q_E, the firm would decrease its profits if it either increased or decreased its output. At any point left of q_E, say q_1, price is greater than the marginal cost, and it pays to increase output. At any point to the right of q_E, say q_2, price is less than the marginal cost, and it pays to reduce output. The equilibrium output for the firm is q_E.

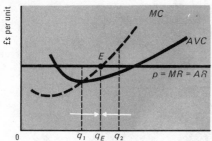

Fig. 19.2 The equilibrium of a competitive firm

The competitive firm is a mere quantity adjuster. It pursues its goal of profit-maximization by increasing or decreasing quantity until it equates its short-run marginal cost with the prevailing price of its product – a price that is given to it by the market.

The market price to which the perfectly competitive firm responds is set by the forces of demand and supply. The individual firm, by adjusting its quantity produced to whatever price is ruling on the market, helps to determine market supply. The link between the behaviour of the firm and the behaviour of the competitive market is provided by the market supply curve.

Short-run supply curves

The supply curve shows the relation between quantity supplied and price. For any given price we need to ask what quantity will be supplied. This question may be answered by supposing that a price is specified and then determining how much each firm will choose to supply. Next a different price is specified and quantity supplied is again determined – and so on, until all possible prices have been considered.

The supply curve of one firm

Figure 19.3 (i) shows a firm's marginal cost curve with four alternative demand curves. The firm's marginal cost curve gives the marginal cost corresponding to each level of output. From this we wish to derive a supply curve that gives the quantity the firm will supply at every price. For prices below AVC, the firm will supply zero units (Rule 1 in Chapter 18). For prices above AVC, the firm will equate price and marginal cost (Rule 2, modified by the proposition that $MR = p$ in perfect competition). As price rises in the figure from 2 to 3 to 4 to 5, the firm wishes to increase its production from q_1 to q_2 to q_3 to q_4. For prices below £2, output would be zero because the firm is better off if it shuts down. The point E_1, where price equals AVC, is called the shutdown point. The firm's supply curve is shown in (ii).

From this it follows that:

> **In perfect competition the segment of the firm's marginal cost curve that is above the AVC curve has the same shape as the firm's supply curve.**

This proposition is so obvious that it sometimes causes difficulty to the reader who is looking for

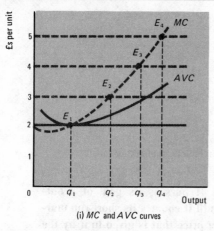
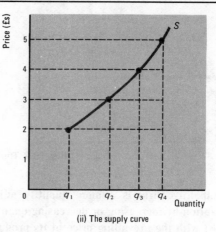

Fig. 19.3 Deriving the supply curve for a price-taking firm

something difficult and profound. If you are not certain that you understand it, construct the firm's supply curve for yourself. Given perfect competition, profit-maximization, and the cost curves of Figure 19.3 (i), you can discover the output of the firm corresponding to any given market price. You can then plot the firm's supply curve on a graph of your own by relating market price to quantity produced by the firm. Once you have done this, you will see that the supply curve you have constructed is identical in shape to the marginal cost curve above AVC. (See Figure 19.3(ii).)

The supply curve of an industry

Figure 19.4 illustrates the derivation of an industry supply curve for an example of only two firms. At a price of £3 firm A would supply 4 units and firm B would supply 3 units. Together, as shown in (iii), they would supply 7 units. If there are hundreds of firms, the process is the same: each firm's supply curve (which is derived in the manner shown in Figure 19.3) shows what the firm will produce at any given price p. The industry supply curve relates the price p to the sum of the quantities produced by all firms. Thus we have the following result:

> **The supply curve for a competitive industry is the horizontal sum of the marginal cost curves of all the individual firms in the industry.**

This supply curve, based as it is on the short-run marginal cost curves of the firms in the industry, is the industry's SHORT-RUN SUPPLY CURVE. In Part 2 we used short-run industry supply curves as part of our theory of price. We have now derived these curves for a competitive industry, and we have seen how they are related to the behaviour of individual, profit-maximizing firms.

The determination of short-run equilibrium price

The short-run supply curve and the demand curve for the industry's product together determine the market price (Chapter 8). Although no one firm can influence market price significantly, the collective actions of all firms in the industry (as shown by the industry supply curve) and the

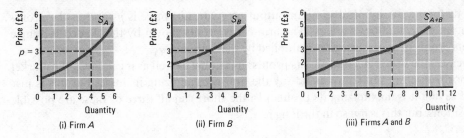

Fig. 19.4 The derivation of a supply curve for a group of firms

collective actions of households (as shown by the industry's demand curve) together determine market price.

> **At the equilibrium market price each firm is producing and selling a quantity for which its marginal cost equals the market price and no firm is motivated to change its output in the short run. Since total quantity demanded equals total quantity supplied, there is no reason for market price to change in the short run; the market and all the firms in the industry are in short-run equilibrium.**

Short-run profitability of the firm

Although we know that when the industry is in short-run equilibrium the competitive firm is maximizing its profits, we do not know *how large* these profits are. It is one thing to know that a firm is doing as well as it can in particular circumstances; it is another thing to know how well it is doing.

Figure 19.5 shows three possible positions for a firm in short-run equilibrium. The diagrams show a firm with given costs faced with three alternative prices p_1, p_2, p_3. In each part of the diagram, E is the point at which $MC = MR = $ price. Since in all three cases price exceeds short-run average variable cost, the firm is in short-run equilibrium at E. (The $SRAVC$ curve is only shown in (i) since in (ii) and (iii) p must exceed $SRAVC$ at E.) In (i) price is p_1 and at the profit-maximizing output of q_1 unit costs are c_1. The firm earns the losses shown by the shaded rectangle which represents the loss of $c_1 - p_1$ per unit multiplied by the quantity q_1. In (ii) price is p_2 and the firm

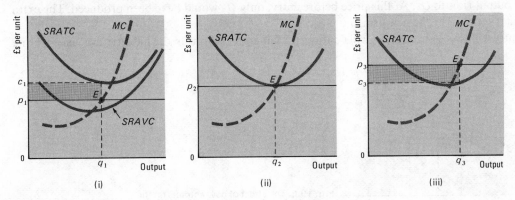

Fig. 19.5 Alternative short-run equilibrium positions of a competitive firm

can just cover its total costs by producing an output of q_2. In (iii) price is p_3 and at the profit-maximizing output of q_3 unit costs are c_3. The firm earns profits shown by the shaded rectangle which represents profits of $p_3 - c_3$ per unit multiplied by the output of q_3.

In all three cases, the firm is maximizing its profits; it is doing as well as it can given the market price and its short-run costs. (In (i) we could say the firm is minimizing its losses but this is just another way of saying it is maximizing its profits.) In the short run all three of these are possible equilibrium positions, but this is *not* so in the long run.

Long-run equilibrium

The long run in outline

The key to long-run equilibrium under perfect competition is entry and exit. We have seen that when firms are in *short-run* equilibrium they may be making profits or losses or they may be just breaking even. Since costs include the opportunity cost of capital, firms that are just breaking even are doing as well as they could if they invested their capital elsewhere. Thus there will be no incentive for existing firms to leave the industry; neither will there be an incentive for new firms to enter the industry, because capital can earn the same return elsewhere in the economy. If, however, existing firms are earning profits over all costs, including the opportunity cost of capital, new capital will enter the industry to share in these profits. If existing firms are making losses, capital will leave the industry because a better return can be obtained elsewhere in the economy. Let us consider the process in more detail.

If all firms in the competitive industry are in the position of the firm in Figure 19.5 (iii) new firms will enter the industry, attracted by the existing profits. Suppose that in response to high profits for 100 existing firms, 20 new firms enter. The market supply curve that formerly added up the outputs of 100 firms now must add up the outputs of 120 firms. At any price, more will be supplied because there are more suppliers. This shift in the short-run supply curve, with an unchanged market demand curve, means that the previous equilibrium price will no longer prevail. The shift in supply will cause the equilibrium price to fall, and both new and old firms will have to adjust their outputs to this new price. This is illustrated in Figure 19.6. The initial equilibrium is at the intersection of D and S_1. If the supply curve shifts to S_2 by virtue of new entry, the equilibrium price must fall to p_2 while output rises to Q_2. At this price before entry, only Q_3 would have been produced. The extra output is supplied by the new firms.

Entry will proceed and price will continue to fall until all firms in the industry are just covering

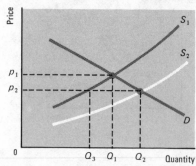

Fig. 19.6 The effect of new entrants on the supply curve

their total costs. Firms will then be in the position of the firm in Figure 19.5 (ii), which is called a *zero-profit equilibrium*.

> **Profits in a competitive industry are a signal for the entry of new capital; the industry will expand, forcing price down until the profits earned by firms, old and new, fall to zero.**

If the firms in the industry are in the position of the firm in Figure 19.5 (i), they are suffering losses. They are covering their variable costs, but the return on their capital is less than the opportunity cost of this capital; the firms are not covering their total costs. This is a signal for exit of capital. As plant and equipment wears out it will not be replaced. As a result, the industry's short-run supply curve shifts left and market price rises. Capital continues to exit and price continues to rise until the remaining firms can cover their total costs – that is, until they are all in the zero-profit equilibrium illustrated in Figure 19.5 (ii). Exit then ceases.

> **Losses in a competitive industry are a signal for the exit of capital; the industry will contract, driving price up until the remaining firms are covering their total costs.**

In all of this we see profits fulfilling their function of allocating resources among the industries of the economy. For many purposes this is as far as we need to go with the analysis of the long run.

Marginal and intramarginal firms When considering possible exit from an industry it is sometimes useful to distinguish marginal from intramarginal firms. The marginal firm is just covering its full costs and would exit if price fell by even a small amount. The intramarginal firm is earning profits and would require a larger fall in price to persuade it to exit. In the pure abstract model of perfect competition, however, all firms are marginal firms in long-run equilibrium. All firms have access to the same technology and all, therefore, have identical cost curves. In long-run industry equilibrium all firms are thus in position (ii) in Figure 19.5. If price falls below p_2 in that figure all firms wish to withdraw. Exit must then be by some contrived process, such as random lot, since there is nothing in the theory to explain who will exit first.

In real situations firms are not identical, since technology changes continually and different firms have different histories. The details of each practical case will then determine the identity of the marginal firm who will exit first when price falls a bit. For one example, assume that all firms have identical costs and differ only in the date at which they entered the industry. In this case, the firm whose capital comes up for replacement first will be the marginal firm. It will exit first because it will be the one that first has to make a long-run decision about replacing its capital in a situation where no firms are covering long-run opportunity costs. For a second example, assume that firms differ only in the quality of their managements. In this case the marginal firm will be the best managed one because that firm has the highest opportunity costs elsewhere in the economy. A slight fall in price may cause that firm to exit, leaving behind the less well managed firms whose opportunity costs are lower and who thus require a larger fall in price to drive them out of the industry. (This is a situation often found in declining regions where it is the most alert and best managed firms who leave first so that, as the decline continues, the remaining firms become less and less efficient on average.)

The response of a perfectly competitive industry to a change in technology

As an illustration of the use of long-run analysis we consider the effects of technological progress on a competitive industry. Initially the industry is in long-run equilibrium where each firm is earning zero profits. Now assume that some technological development lowers the cost curves of newly built plants. The technology cannot be used by old plants because it must be *embodied* in new plants and equipment. Since price is just equal to the average total cost for the old plants, new plants will now be able to earn profits and they will be built immediately. But this expansion in capacity shifts the short-run supply curve to the right and drives price down. The expansion in capacity and the fall in price will continue until price is equal to the *ATC* of the *new* plants. At this price old plants will not be covering their long-run costs. As long as price exceeds their average variable cost, however, such plants will continue in production. As the outmoded plants wear out they will gradually disappear. Eventually a new long-run equilibrium will be established in which all plants use the new technology.

What happens in a competitive industry in which this type of technological change occurs not as a single isolated event but more or less continuously? Plants built in any one year will tend to have lower costs than plants built in any previous year. Figure 19.7 illustrates such an industry. Plant 3 is the newest plant, with the lowest costs. Price will be determined by the average total costs of plants of this type, since entry will continue as long as the owners of the newest plants expect to earn profits from them. Plant 1 is the oldest plant in operation; it is just covering its *AVC* and if the price falls any further it will be closed down. Plant 2 is a plant of intermediate age. It is covering its variable costs

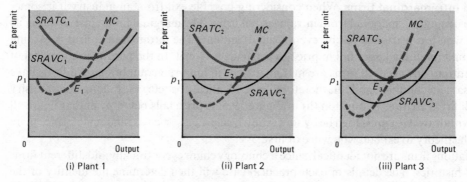

Fig. 19.7 Plants of different ages in an industry with continuing technical progress

and earning some return on its capital. The return will shrink over time as entry of new plants with lower and lower costs drives prices lower and lower. Real-world industries like this, with continual technological changes, have a number of interesting characteristics.

One is that plants of different ages and different levels of efficiency will exist side by side. This is dramatically illustrated by the variety of vintages of steam turbine generators found in any long-established electricity industry. Critics who observe the continued use of older, less efficient plants and urge that 'something be done to eliminate these wasteful practices' miss the point of economic efficiency. If the plant is already there, the plant can be profitably operated as long as it can do anything more than cover its variable costs. As long as a plant can produce goods that are valued by consumers at an amount above the value of the resources currently used up by its operation (variable costs), the value of society's total output is increased by producing these goods.

A second characteristic of such an industry is that price will be governed by the minimum *ATC* of the most efficient plants. Entry will continue until plants of the latest vintage are just expected to earn normal profits over their lifetimes. The benefits of the new technology are passed on to consumers because all units of the commodity, whether produced by new or old plants, are sold at a price that is related solely to the *ATC*s of the new plants. Owners of older plants find their returns over variable costs falling steadily as increasingly efficient plants drive the price down.

A third characteristic is that old plants will be discarded when the price falls below their *AVC*. This may occur well before the plants are physically worn out. In industries with continuous technical progress, capital is usually discarded because it is economically obsolete, not because it has physically worn out. This illustrates the economic meaning of obsolete: old capital is obsolete when its average variable cost exceeds the average total cost of new capital.

A more detailed analysis of the long run[1]

For some purposes it is important to understand some complications omitted from the foregoing broad treatment. The rest of this chapter will be devoted to a more detailed examination of the long-run behaviour of a perfectly competitive industry.

Consider the position of the firm and the industry when long-run equilibrium obtains. There is no change that the firm could make, over the short or the long run, that would increase its profits. This requirement can be stated as three distinct conditons.

1. *No firm will want to vary the output of its existing plants:* short-run marginal cost (*SRMC*) must equal price.

2. *Profits earned by existing plants must be zero.* This implies that short-run *ATC* must equal price – that is, firms must be in the position of the firms in Figure 19.5 (ii).

3. *No firm can earn profits by building a plant of a different size.* This implies that each existing firm must be producing at the lowest point on its long-run average cost curve.

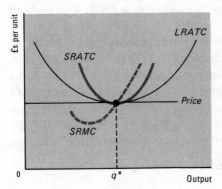

Fig. 19.8 The equilibrium of a firm when the industry is in long-run equilibrium

Taken together, these conditions mean that all firms in the industry should be in the position illustrated in Figure 19.8.[2] The firm is operating at the minimum point of its long-run cost curve and

---

[1] The remainder of this chapter may be omitted without loss of continuity.

[2] The text discussion implies that all existing firms and all new entrants face identical *LRATC* curves. This merely means that all firms face the same set of factor prices and have the same technology available to them. Do not forget that we are in the long run where technological knowledge is given and constant, and all firms have had a chance to adjust their capital to the best that is available.

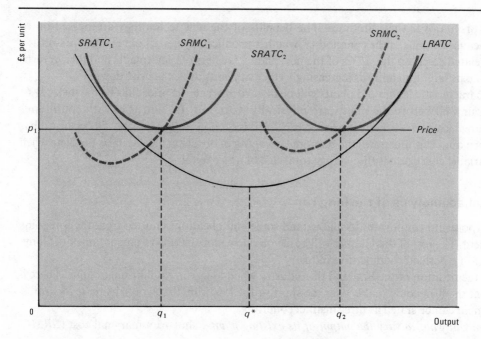

Fig. 19.9 Short-run versus long-run equilibrium of a competitive firm

thus also at the minimum point on the short-run plant cost curve associated with its present plant.

We have already seen why the first two conditions must hold. Now let us look at the third condition. Figure 19.9 shows two firms that have identical $LRATC$ curves, but one firm has too small a plant, with costs of $SRATC_1$, while the other firm has too large a plant, with costs of $SRATC_2$. Both firms are in short-run equilibrium at price $p_1 = MC = ATC$ with outputs of q_1 and q_2 respectively. Neither firm, however, is in long-run equilibrium. Firm 1 can increase its profits by building a larger plant (thereby moving downward to the right along its $LRATC$ curve). Firm 2 can increase its profits by building a smaller plant (thereby moving downward to the left along its $LRATC$ curve). Each of these firms can, therefore, increase its profits by discarding its present plant when it wears out and building a plant of different size. The smaller firm should increase its plant size, thereby lowering its average total costs. The larger firm should build a smaller plant, thereby also lowering its ATC. Since each firm is a price-taker, each of these changes will increase its profits.

> **A price-taking firm is in long-run equilibrium only when it is producing at the minimum point on its LRATC curve.**

The firm must be producing at the point labelled q^* in Figures 19.8 and 19.9.

An industry is nothing more than a collection of firms; for an industry to be in long-run equilibrium, each firm must be in long-run equilibrium. It follows that when a perfectly competitive industry is in long-run equilibrium, all firms in the industry will be selling at a price equal to minimum $SRATC$ – that is, they must be in zero-profit equilibrium, as in Figure 19.5 (ii). It follows that the short-run industry supply curve – which tells us how much all existing firms will supply at each market price – must intersect the market demand curve at that particular price.

The long-run response of a perfectly competitive industry to a change in demand

Now suppose that the demand for the product increases. Price will rise to equate demand with the industry's short-run supply. Each firm will expand output until its short-run marginal cost once again equals price. Each firm will earn profits as a result of the rise in price, and the profits will induce new firms to enter the industry. This will shift the short-run supply curve to the right and force down the price. Entry will continue until all firms are once again just covering average total costs. To recapitulate: the short-run effects of the rise in demand will be a rise in price and output; the long-run effects will be a further rise in output and a fall in price.

Now consider a fall in demand. The industry starts with firms in long-run equilibrium as shown in Figure 19.8 and the market demand curve shifts left and price falls. There are two possible consequences.

First, the decline in demand forces price below *ATC* but leaves it above *AVC*. Firms are then in the position shown in Figure 19.5 (i). They can cover their variable costs and earn some return on their capital, so they remain in production for as long as their existing plant and equipment lasts. But it is not worth replacing capital as it wears out. Exit will occur as old capital wears out and is not replaced. As firms exit, the short-run supply curve shifts left and market price rises. This continues until the remaining firms in the industry can cover their total costs. At this point it will pay to replace capital as it wears out, and the decline in the size of the industry will be brought to a halt. In this case the adjustment may take a very long time, for the industry shrinks in size only as existing plant and equipment wears out.

The second possibility occurs if the decline in demand is so large that price is forced below the level of *AVC*. Now firms cannot even cover their variable costs and some will shut down immediately.[1] Reduction in capital devoted to production in the industry occurs rapidly because some existing capacity is scrapped or sold for other uses. Once sufficient capital has been withdrawn so that price rises to a level that allows the remaining firms to cover their *AVC*s, the rapid withdrawal of capital ceases. Further exit occurs more slowly, as described in the previous paragraph.

> **Entry of new capital into a profitable industry occurs at the speed at which new plants can be built and new equipment installed. Exit of existing capital from an industry with losses may occur very quickly if price is less than average variable cost but only at the rate at which old plant and equipment wears out if price exceeds average variable cost.**

This adjustment process is examined in greater detail in the following section.

The long-run industry supply curve

Possible adjustments of the industry to the kinds of changes in demand just discussed are shown by the LONG-RUN INDUSTRY SUPPLY (LRS) CURVE. This curve shows the relation between equilibrium price and the output firms will be willing to supply after all desired entry or exit has occurred.

> **The long-run supply curve connects positions of long-run equilibrium after all demand-induced changes have occurred.**

---

[1] If the capital has no alternative use it may not be scrapped; instead it may be 'mothballed' in case of future need. As far as its influence on current production and price is concerned, however, it has withdrawn from the industry.

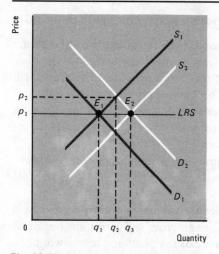
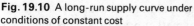

Fig. 19.10 A long-run supply curve under conditions of constant cost

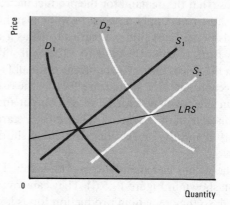

Fig. 19.11 A rising long-run supply curve

When induced changes in factor prices are considered, it is possible for *LRS* to rise, fall, or remain constant. The various cases are illustrated in Figures 19.10 to 19.12.

In Figure 19.10 the shift in demand from D_1 to D_2 first raises the price to p_2 as industry output expands along the short-run supply curve. Firms earn profits and entry thus occurs. This induces a shift in the short-run supply curve from S_1 to S_2. In the case illustrated the increase in supply is just sufficient to keep the price at p_1. Thus output is increased along *LRS* at constant cost in the long run.

The long-run supply curve in Figure 19.10 is horizontal. This indicates that the industry will, given time, adjust its size to provide whatever quantity may be demanded at a constant price. Such conditions obtain if factor prices do not change as the output of the whole industry expands or contracts. An industry with a horizontal long-run supply curve is said to be a CONSTANT-COST INDUSTRY. While conditions of constant *LRS* may exist, such conditions are not necessary. Other possibilities are considered below.

Changing factor prices and rising long-run supply curves   When an industry expands its output, it needs more inputs. The increase in demand for these inputs may bid up their prices. If costs rise with increasing levels of industry output, so too must the price at which the producers are able to cover their costs. As the industry expands, the short-run supply curve shifts outwards but the firms' *ATC* curves shift upwards because of rising factor prices. The expansion of the industry comes to a halt when price is equal to minimum *LRATC* for existing firms. This must occur at a higher price than ruled before the expansion began, as illustrated in Figure 19.11.

Rising *LRS* – RISING SUPPLY PRICE, as it is sometimes called – is often a characteristic of sharp and rapid growth. A competitive industry with rising long-run supply prices is often called a RISING-COST INDUSTRY.

Can the long-run supply curve decline?   So far we have suggested that the long-run supply curve may be constant or rising. Could it ever decline, thereby indicating that higher outputs were associated with lower prices in long-run equilibrium?

It is tempting to answer yes, because of the opportunities of more efficient scales of operation using greater mechanization and more effective specialization of labour. But this answer would not be correct for perfectly competitive industries, because each firm in long-run equilibrium must already be at the lowest point on its $LRATC$ curve. If a firm could lower its costs by building a larger, more mechanized plant, it would be profitable to do so without waiting for an increase in demand. Since any single firm can sell all it wishes at the going market price, it will be profitable to expand the scale of its operations as long as its $LRATC$ is falling.

There is a reason, however, why the long-run supply curve might slope downward: the expansion of an industry might lead to a fall in the prices of some of its inputs. If this occurs, the firms will find their cost curves shifting downward as they expand their outputs.

As an illustration of how the expansion of one industry could cause the prices of some of its inputs to fall, consider the early stages of the growth of the car industry. As the output of cars increased, the industry's demand for tyres grew greatly. This, as suggested earlier, would have increased the demand for rubber and tended to raise its price, but it also provided the opportunity for tyre manufacturers to build large modern plants and reap the benefits of increasing returns in tyre production. At first these economies were large enough to offset any factor price increases and tyre prices charged to car manufacturers fell. Thus car costs fell, because of lower prices of an important input.[1]

To see the effect of a fall in input prices caused by the expansion of an industry, suppose that the demand for the industry's product increases. Price and profits will rise and new entry will occur as a result. But when expansion of the industry has gone far enough to bring price back to its initial level, cost curves will be lower than they were initially because of the fall in input prices. Firms will thus still be earning profits. A further expansion will then occur until price falls to the level of the minimum points on each firm's new, lower $LRATC$ curve.[1]

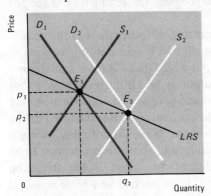

Fig. 19.12 A declining long-run supply curve

This case is illustrated in Figure 19.12. From an original equilibrium at E_1, an increase in demand to D_2 leads to an increase in supply to S_2 and a new equilibrium at E_2. Price p_2 is below the original price p_1 because lower factor prices allow firms to cover their total costs at the lower price. An industry that has a declining long-run supply curve is often called a FALLING-COST INDUSTRY.

[1] Notice that this argument requires that the supplying industry not be perfectly competitive. If it were, all of its scale economies would already have been exploited. So the case requires a perfectly competitive industry such as agriculture that requires input produced by a non-perfectly competitive industry such as agricultural implements whose own scale economies have not yet been fully exploited because demand is insufficient.

Does a long-run competitive equilibrium exist?[1]

A necessary condition for a long-run competitive equilibrium is that any economies of scale that are available to a firm should be exhausted at a level of output that is small relative to the whole industry's output. We have seen that a competitive firm will never be in equilibrium on the falling part of its *LRATC* – if price is given and costs can be reduced by expanding scale, profits can also be increased by doing so. Thus firms will grow in size at least until all scale economies are exhausted. Provided that the output that yields the minimum *LRATC* for each firm is small relative to the industry's total output, the industry will contain a large number of firms and will remain competitive. If, however, reaching the minimum *LRATC* makes firms so large that each one has significant market power, they will cease to be price-takers and perfect competition will cease to exist. Indeed if scale economies exist over such a large range that one firm's *LRATC* would still be falling if it served the entire market, a single firm may come to monopolize the market. This is what the classical economists called the case of *natural* monopoly; it is considered further in Chapter 23.

Only if the firm's *LRATC* curve is U-shaped will there be a determinate size of the firm in a competitive industry. To see why, assume instead that *LRATC* falls to a minimum at some level of output and then remains constant for all larger outputs. All firms will have to be at least the minimum size, but they can be just that size or much larger, since price will equal *LRATC* for any output above the minimum efficient size. In other words, there will then be no unique size for the firm.

There are very good reasons why the *LRATC* curve for a single plant may be U-shaped. Modern technology often results in lower average costs for large, automated factories compared with smaller factories in which a few workers use relatively unsophisticated capital equipment. As a single plant becomes too large, however, costs rise because of the sheer difficulty of planning for, and controlling the behaviour of, a vast integrated operation. Thus we have no problem accounting for a U-shaped cost curve for the *plant*.

What of the U-shaped cost curve for the *firm*? A declining portion will occur for the same reason that the *LRATC* for one plant declines when the firm is so small that it operates only one plant. Now, however, let the firm be operating one plant at the output where its *LRATC* is a minimum. (Call that output q^*.) What if the firm decides to double its output to $2q^*$? If it tries to build a vast plant with twice the output of the optimal size plant, the firm's average total cost of production may rise (because the vast plant has higher costs than a plant of the optimal size). But the firm has the option of *replicating* its first plant in a physically separate location. If the firm obtains a second parcel of land, builds an identical second plant, staffs it identically, and allows its production to be managed independently, there seems no reason why the second plant's minimum *LRATC* should be different from that of the first plant. *Because the firm can replicate plants and have them managed independently, there seems no reason why any firm faced with constant factor prices should not face constant LRATCs at least for intiger multiples[2] of the output for which one plant achieves the lowest plant LRATC.*

---

[1] This section deals with a difficult point that is often postponed until intermediate or even advanced courses. It may be omitted without loss of continuity.

[2] This means multiplying the output by any whole number, i.e., building and fully utilizing any number of complete new plants. It rules out multiplying it by some fractional number such as 7/2 which would mean only partially utilizing one plant.

In the modern theory of perfect competition, a U-shaped *firm* cost curve is merely assumed. Without it – although a competitive equilibrium may exist for an arbitrary number of firms – there is nothing to determine the equilibrium size of the firm and hence the number of firms in the industry when price equals each firm's *LRATC* (and when, therefore, there is incentive for neither entry nor exit).

20

The theory of monopoly

The market structure of MONOPOLY is at the opposite extreme from that of perfect competition. It exists whenever an industry is in the hands of a single producer. In the case of perfect competition there are so many individual producers that no one of them has any power whatsoever over the market; any one firm can increase or diminish its production without affecting the market price significantly. A monopoly, on the other hand, has power to influence the market price. By reducing its output it can force the price up, and by increasing its output it can force the price down. In the first half of this chapter we study monopolies that must charge a single price for the goods that they sell; in the second half we study monopolies that can sell their goods at different prices either to different classes of customers or in different geographical markets.

A monopoly that sells its product at a single market price

You should now review the section on total, average and marginal revenue on pages 235–6. Since the monopoly firm is the only producer of its product, the demand curve that it faces *is* the market demand curve. Also, since a 10 per cent variation in the firm's output *is* a 10 per cent variation in the industry's output, it follows that the firm's elasticity of demand is the same as the market elasticity of demand.

In perfect competition the price is unaffected by variations in the firm's output, and it follows that the addition to revenue resulting from increasing the level of sales by one more unit is the market price of that unit. Thus the marginal and average revenue curves coincide in the same horizontal straight line. With a monopoly, however, the average revenue curve, which is the same as the market demand curve, is *downward* sloping. Furthermore, the marginal revenue curve does not coincide with the demand curve: since the sale of an extra unit forces down the price at which *all* units can be sold, the sale of an extra unit results in a net addition to revenue of an amount less than its own selling price.

The relation between a monopolist's average and marginal revenue

Consider first the simple example illustrated in Table 20.1. We assume that the monopoly is selling 100 units each year at a price of £2, yielding a total revenue of £200. The firm then steps up its rate of sales to 101 units per year, but, as a consequence of the downward-sloping demand curve this drives

Table 20.1 Alternative price and sales combinations for a monopolist, together with the corresponding marginal revenues

	Price	Rate of sales per year	Total revenue	Average revenue (= price)	Marginal revenue
Situation 1.	£2·00	100	£200	£2·00	
					£0·99
Situation 2.	£1·99	101	£200·99	£1·99	
					−£0·05
Situation 3.	£1·97	102	£200·94	£1·97	

the price down to, say, £1·99. The firm's total revenue is now £200·99. Thus, the increase in revenue resulting from the sale of an additional unit per year is only £0·99, even though the extra unit sells for £1·99. A moment's thought will show that there is no mystery about the fact that the marginal revenue (£0·99) is less than the price (£1·99) at which the extra unit is sold. One hundred units per year could have been sold for £2, but in order to sell the extra unit, the firm reduces the price *on all units* by 1p. Thus, there is a loss of 1p per unit on each of the 100 units. This makes a total loss of £1·00, which must be deducted from the extra revenue of £1·99 obtained from the sale of the 101st unit. Thus, the net increase in revenue associated with the sale of the 101st unit is only £0·99. This numerical example illustrates the proposition that:

> **Whenever the demand curve slopes downward, the marginal revenue associated with an increase in the rate of sales by one unit per period will be less than the price at which that unit is sold.**[1]

Since the monopolist's demand curve is the market demand curve, the monopoly faces the same relation between elasticity of the demand curve and total revenue as we discussed on page 103.

> **If the market demand curve is elastic, a cut in price and a rise in sales will cause the monopolist's total revenue to increase; if the market demand curve is inelastic, a cut in price and a rise in sales will cause the monopolist's total revenue to decrease.**

If total revenue falls when price is cut, marginal revenue is negative. This is illustrated by the move from Situation 2 to 3 in Table 20.1.

Figure 20.1 (i) shows a numerical example of a demand curve for a monopoly. The corresponding marginal and total revenue curves are shown in parts (i) and (ii) of the figure. The demand curve

---

[1] It is easy to prove algebraically that, if the demand curve slopes downwards, marginal revenue is always less than price. Let subscripts n and $n+1$ indicate the revenue and price associated with the sale of n and $(n+1)$ units, so that, e.g., TR_n is the total revenue associated with the sale of n units per period.

$$\begin{aligned} MR_{n+1} &= TR_{n+1} - TR_n \\ &= (n+1)P_{n+1} - nP_n \\ &= nP_{n+1} + P_{n+1} - nP_n \\ &= n(P_{n+1} - P_n) + P_{n+1}. \end{aligned}$$

Since the demand curve slopes downwards, P_{n+1}, which is the price that rules when $n+1$ units are sold, is less than P_n, the price that rules when n units are sold. Thus the term $n(P_{n+1} - P_n)$ is negative, so that the MR of the $n+1$ unit is less than P_{n+1}.

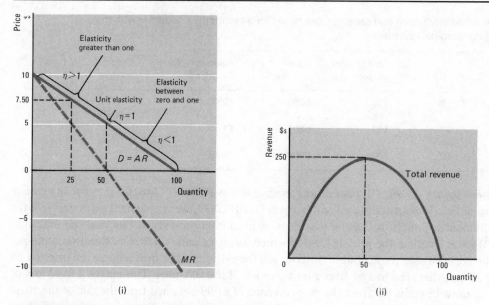

Fig. 20.1 The relation of total, average and marginal revenue to elasticity of demand (η)

shows the price corresponding to any given rate of sales, and the MR curve shows the change in total revenue that is brought about by increasing the rate of sales by one unit per period. For example, for $q = 25$ units the price is £7·50, but the MR is £5, which means that the 25th unit adds £5 to total revenue. When $q = 50$, price is £5, but MR is zero. To sell the last unit costs as much in lost revenue (because of the necessary price reduction) as the price it commands. For quantities greater than 50 units MR is negative, meaning that total receipts are decreased by additional sales.

The equilibrium of a monopolist

To describe the profit-maximizing position of a monopoly, we need only bring together information about the firm's revenues and costs and apply the rules developed in Chapter 18. This is done graphically in Figure 20.2. The technological facts of life are the same for the monopoly as for a competitive firm, so that the short-run cost curves have the same shape in both cases. (The monopoly's curves are assumed to be AVC, ATC and MC – the curve ATC' relates to a later argument.) The difference lies in the demand conditions. The perfectly competitive firm is faced with a perfectly elastic demand for its product, while the monopoly firm is faced with a downward-sloping demand curve. The equilibrium level of output is q_1 where marginal revenue equals marginal cost. The equilibrium price of p_1, the market price at which q_1 can be sold, is determined from the demand curve.

The monopolist's equilibrium at quantity q_1 and price p_1 meets the several conditions for profit-maximizing behaviour described in Chapter 18. Remember that output is determined from the MR and MC curves, while price is determined from the D curve.

> **When the monopoly is in equilibrium, marginal cost equals marginal revenue; marginal cost cuts marginal revenue from below; and price is greater than average variable cost.**

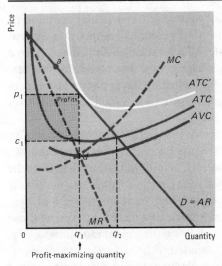

Fig. 20.2 The equilibrium of a monopolist

The aggregate amount of profits is represented by the shaded rectangle, which represents the output, q_1, multiplied by the gap between average revenue, p_1, and average total cost, c_1.

Two common misconceptions about monopoly profits need to be cleared up at this point. First, nothing guarantees that a monopoly will make profits in the short run. If you shift the ATC curve upward but leave all other curves unchanged, you will see that profits shrink as the curve moves up. When the curve gets as high as ATC', which is tangent to the demand curve, the monopoly earns zero profits at output q_1 (and losses anywhere else). All that the condition $MC = MR$ tells us is that the monopoly does better at that output than at other levels of output. It is possible for the firm to continue producing in the short run even if its ATC curve lies everywhere above D, as long as its AVC curve lies somewhere below D. In these circumstances the firm can set a price in excess of its AVC and lose less by producing than by letting its fixed factors stand idle.

The second common misconception about monopoly profits is that a monopoly that is not maximizing its profits must be making losses. This is, of course, not correct. At output q_1, where $MC = MR$, total profits are as large as possible. If output is increased beyond q_1, $MC > MR$, so that any additional units sold are *reducing* total profits, but *total* profits are still positive. In fact total profits remain positive until output reaches q_2 units. At that level, average total cost equals average revenue so that total cost equals total revenue. Should output be increased beyond q_2, total profits would finally become negative.

Firm and industry, short run and long run

A monopoly is the only producer in an industry. There is, thus, no need to have a separate theory of the firm and the industry. The monopoly firm *is* the industry. In a monopolized industry, as in a perfectly competitive one, profits provide an incentive for new firms to enter. If a profitable monopoly is to persist in the long run, other firms must not enter the industry. Circumstances that protect the monopolist by discouraging entry even when the monopolist is earning profits are called BARRIERS TO ENTRY. These barriers may take several forms. Patent laws may create and perpetuate monopolies by conferring on the patent holder the sole right to produce a particular commodity. The government may grant a firm a charter or a franchise that prohibits competition by law. Monopolies may also arise because of economies of scale. The established firm may retain a monopoly through a cost advantage because it can produce at a lower cost than could any new, and necessarily smaller, competitor. A monopoly may also be perpetuated by force: potential competitors can be intimidated by threats ranging from sabotage to a price war which the established monopoly has sufficient financial resources to win.

Because there is no entry into a monopolistic industry, profits may persist over time. In perfect competition, the long run differs from the short run because the process of entry forces profits down to zero in the long run. There is no such tendency under monopoly, and the long run differs from the short run only in terms of the cost curve on which the monopolist is operating. Consider a monopoly fully adjusted to a given demand curve: the appropriate sized plant has been constructed and *long-run marginal cost* has been equated to marginal revenue. Now assume that there is a permanent rise in demand. The best the firm can do in the short run is to work its existing plant more intensively, expanding output until the short-run marginal cost curve associated with the fixed plant intersects the marginal revenue curve. In the long run, however, a larger plant could be built, and any other relevant adjustments made to 'fixed' factors until the monopoly is again in a position at which long-run marginal cost equals marginal revenue.

Absence of a supply curve under monopoly

Now consider the relation between the price of the product and the quantity supplied under monopoly. In the case of perfect competition we were able to discover a unique relation between price and quantity supplied. This gave rise to a supply curve for each firm and, by aggregation, to a supply curve for the industry.

In monopoly, there is no unique relation between market price and quantity supplied.

As with all profit-maximizing firms, the monopolist equates marginal cost to marginal revenue; but marginal revenue does not equal price. Hence the monopoly does *not* equate marginal cost to price. In order to know the amount produced at any given price, we need to know the demand curve as well as the marginal cost curve. Under these circumstances it is possible for different demand conditions to give rise to the same output but to differing prices.

The proposition that when a firm faces a downward-sloping demand curve there is no unique relation between price and output is illustrated in Figures 20.3 and 20.4. In Figure 20.3 two different demand curves both result in the same output, q_2, but in different prices. When demand is D_1 marginal revenue equals marginal cost at output q_2 and price is p_1. When demand is D_2 marginal cost again equals marginal revenue at output q_2 but price is at p_2. Figure 20.4 illustrates the same general point by showing a case in which the same price is associated with two different quantities. When demand is D_3 marginal revenue equals marginal cost at output q_3 and the resulting price is p_3. When demand is D_4 marginal revenue equals marginal cost at output q_4 but price is again p_3.

A monopoly that can price discriminate

So far in this chapter we have assumed that the monopolist charges the same price for every unit of

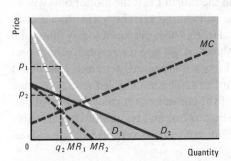

Fig. 20.3 Two different prices associated with the same output

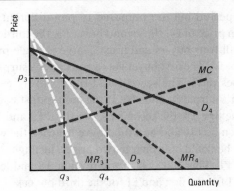

Fig. 20.4 Two different outputs associated with the same price

his product no matter to whom, or where, he sells it. But other situations are possible. Milk is often sold at one price if it is for drinking, but at a lower price if it is to be used to make ice-cream or cheese. Doctors in private practice, solicitors and business consultants sometimes vary their fees according to the incomes of their clients. Cinemas charge lower admission prices for children. In many countries railways charge different rates per ton mile for different kinds of loads. Firms often sell their products cheaper abroad than at home. Electrical companies in many countries sell electricity more cheaply for industrial use than for home use. All of these are examples of PRICE DISCRIMINATION. In general we may say that price discrimination occurs when a producer sells different units of his commodity at different prices *for reasons not associated with differences in costs*.

Why price discrimination pays

A formal analysis of price discrimination is given in the Appendix to this chapter. Here we shall discuss the common sense of price discrimination only intuitively. The basic point about price discrimination is that it allows sellers to capture some of the *consumer's surplus* that would otherwise go to buyers. This can be captured by two types of discrimination, one among units sold to individual buyers, the other among buyers. (You should now review the discussion of consumer's surplus given on pages 173–5.)

Discrimination among units sold to one buyer Look back to Table 14.2 on page 174. If the seller could sell each unit separately, he could extract all of the consumer's surplus. In the example he would sell the first unit for £3·00, the second for £1·50, the third for £1·00 and so on until the eighth was sold for £0·30. This would yield a total revenue of £8·10, rather than a mere £2·40 when all eight units are sold at a common price of £0·30.

Now assume that the seller cannot charge a separate price for each unit that he sells to the consumer, but he can charge two prices. If he sells the first four units at £0·80 and the second four at £0·30 he earns £4·40. This is less than he gets when he charges a separate price on each unit, but substantially more than the revenue of £2·40 that he gets by selling all eight units at a single price.

Discrimination among buyers Consider a simple example where four buyers each wish to buy one unit per period but are prepared to pay different prices. The first buyer is prepared to pay a maximum price of £4, the second buyer £3, the third £2, and the fourth £1. If the monopolist wishes to serve all four buyers and must charge a single price, he will charge £1. This yields him a total revenue of £4. The first buyer gets a consumer's surplus of £3 (the £4 he is prepared to pay minus the £1 he does pay). The second and third buyers get surpluses of £2 and £1 respectively. Total consumer's surplus is thus £6. If the monopolist could sell to each individual separately, he could charge the first £4, the second £3, the third £2 and the fourth £1. The monopolist's total revenue would then be £10 and he would have usurped the whole of the consumer's surplus for himself. If, however, he could only charge two prices, he might charge buyers one and two £3 and buyers three and four £1. This makes his total revenue £8 and leaves £2 of consumer's surplus in the hands of buyers (£1 for the first and £1 for the third buyer).

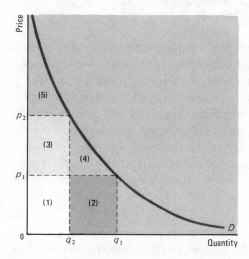

Fig. 20.5 Firm's total revenue and consumer's surplus under alternative pricing schemes

Price discrimination more generally Consider the demand curve shown in Figure 20.5. If the monopolist firm charges the single price of p_1, it sells q_1 and earns revenues ($p_1 q_1$), given by the two areas numbered (1) and (2). Now assume that it can charge two prices. If it sells the first q_2 units at a price of p_2 it earns the revenues ($p_2 q_2$) indicated by the areas (1) and (3). If it sells the next $q_1 - q_2$ units at p_1, it earns the revenue indicated by the shaded area labled (2). This price discrimination has allowed the firm to increase its revenue by the shaded area (3) over what it earns with the single price of p_1. It has gained that much of the consumer's surplus for itself while leaving the amounts indicated by the areas (4) and (5) still in the hands of buyers.

All of the above examples illustrate a general proposition:

> **For any given level of output there always exists some system of discriminatory prices that will provide a higher total revenue than will any given single price.**

Thus whenever it is possible, price discrimination will always pay because it can be used to increase the revenue associated with any level of output.

Not only does price discrimination increase a monopoly's total revenue for any given output, it will also encourage the firm to raise its output. The intuitive sense of this proposition concerns marginal revenue under single and discriminatory pricing systems. The monopoly that much charge a single price produces less than the perfectly competitive industry, because it is aware that by producing and selling more it drives down the price against itself. Price discrimination allows the firm to avoid this disincentive. To the extent that it can sell its output in separate blocks, it can sell another block without spoiling the market for the block already being sold.

In the case of *perfect* price discrimination, where every unit of output is sold at a different price, the monopoly output would be the same as the output of a perfectly competitive industry. This is easily seen as follows. If each unit can be sold at a separate price, the seller does nothing to spoil the market for previous units by selling an additional unit. The marginal revenue of selling an additional unit is the price of that unit. Thus the demand curve becomes the marginal revenue curve, and the monopolist reaches equilibrium at a point where the price (in this case, marginal revenue) equals marginal cost. This is also the point of competitive equilibrium.

When is price discrimination possible?

We have seen that price discrimination always pays if it is possible. But when is it possible? *Discrimination among units of output sold to the same buyer requires that the seller be able to keep track of the units a buyer consumes each period.* Thus the tenth unit purchased by a given buyer in a given month can be sold at a different price than the fifth unit *only* if the seller can keep track of who buys what. This can be done by the seller of electricity through his meter readings, or by the magazine publisher who can distinguish between renewals and new subscriptions. This may also be done by service establishments such as car washes by giving a certificate for a reduced-price car wash within a stated time from the first wash. It is also done by sellers of goods when they include coupons in a good bought at full price valued for a reduced-price purchase of the same good within a given period. A similar result is obtained when firms advertise sales: 'buy one for full price and get a second for only half price'.

Discrimination among buyers requires that the goods cannot be resold by the buyer who faces the low price to the buyer who faces the high price. Often such resale cannot be prevented. However much the local butcher would like to charge the banker's wife twice as much for a lamb chop as he charges the street sweeper, he cannot succeed in doing so. The banker's wife can always go into a supermarket where her husband's occupation is not known. Even if the butcher and the supermarket agreed to charge her twice as much, she could hire the street sweeper to do her shopping for her. On the other hand, the surgeon in private practice may succeed in discriminating (if all others will do the same) because it will not do the banker much good to hire the street sweeper to have his operations for him. The ability to prevent resale tends to be associated with the character of the product, or the ability to classify buyers into readily identifiable groups. Services are less easily resold than goods, and those goods requiring installation by the manufacturer (such as heavy equipment) are less easily resold than are movable commodities (such as household appliances). Transportation costs, tariff barriers or import quotas serve to separate classes of buyers geographically and may make discrimination possible.

For price discrimination to be possible the seller must be able to distinguish individual units bought by a single buyer or to separate buyers into classes where resale among classes is impossible.

The normative aspects of price discrimination

Price discrimination often has a bad reputation. The very word *discrimination* has undesirable connotations. Whether an individual judges price discrimination to be good or bad is likely to depend upon the details of the case, as well as upon his own personal value judgements. Certainly there is nothing in economic theory to suggest that price discrimination is always in some sense worse than non-discrimination. The following examples should serve to illustrate the varying aspects of price discrimination.

Example 1   Some years ago British Rail was not allowed to discriminate among passengers in different regions. To prevent discrimination, a fixed fare per passenger mile was laid down and had to be charged on all lines whatever the density of their passenger traffic and whatever the elasticity of demand for their services. In the interests of economy, branch lines which could not cover costs were often closed down. This meant that some lines closed even though the users preferred rail transport to any of the available alternatives and the strength of their preference was such that they would voluntarily have paid a price sufficient for the line to have covered its costs. The lines were nonetheless closed because it was thought inequitable to charge the passengers on their line more than the passengers on other lines. More recently, British Rail has been allowed to charge prices that take some account of market conditions. This seems to have increased profits.

Example 2   A very large oil refiner agrees to ship his product to a market on a given railway, but only if the railway gives his company a secret rebate on the transportation cost and does not give a similar concession to rival refiners. The railway agrees, and is thus charging discriminatory prices. This rebate gives the oil company a cost advantage that it uses to drive its rivals out of business or to force them into a merger on dictated terms. (John D. Rockefeller is alleged to have used such tactics in forming the original Standard Oil Trust in the US in the late nineteenth century.)

Example 3   Doctors in countries without National Health systems usually charge discriminatory prices for their services. When they are accused of behaving unfairly they point out that if they had to charge a uniform fee for all patients, it would have to be so high – if the doctor were to obtain a reasonable income – as to price their services out of reach of the lower-income groups. The discriminatory price system, they argue, is what allows them to make their services available to all income groups while still securing a high enough income to ensure a continued supply of doctors.

Example 4   A product that a number of people want has cost and demand curves such that there is no single price at which costs can be covered (i.e., the average cost curve lies everywhere above the demand curve). However, if a monopoly is allowed to charge discriminatory prices, it will make a profit. (Some nationalized industries are thought to operate under these conditions.)

Each of these examples, as well as those at the beginning of this chapter, involves price discrimination. Few readers would regard them all as equally good or bad situations. There are two points to be stressed. First, the consequences of price discrimination can differ in many ways from case to case; second, no matter what their values, most people will evaluate each individual case differently.

Appendix to chapter 20

A formal analysis of price discrimination among buyers

Consider a monopoly firm that sells a single product in two distinct markets, A and B, whose demands and marginal curves are shown in Figure 20.6. Resale among customers is impossible and a single price must be charged in each market.

What is the best price for the firm to charge in each market? The simplest way to discover this is to imagine the firm deciding how best to allocate any given total output Q^*, between two markets. Since output is fixed arbitrarily at Q^*, there is nothing the monopolist can do about costs. The best thing it can do, therefore, is to maximize the revenue that it gets by selling Q^* in the two markets. *To do this it will allocate its sales between the markets until the marginal revenues are the same in each market.* Consider what would happen if the marginal revenue in market A exceeded the marginal revenue in market B. The firm could keep its overall output constant at Q^* but reallocate a unit of sales from B to A, gaining

a net addition in revenue equal to the difference between the marginal revenues in the two markets. Thus it will always pay a monopoly firm to reallocate a given total quantity between its markets as long as marginal revenues are not equal in the two markets.

If we assume that marginal cost is constant, we can determine the profit-maximizing course of action from Figure 20.6. The MC curve in both figures shows the constant marginal cost. The firm's total profits are maximized by equating MR in each market to its constant MC, thus selling q_A at p_A in market A and q_B at p_B in market B. Marginal revenue is the same in each market ($c_A = c_B$) so that the firm has its total output correctly allocated between the two markets and marginal costs equals marginal revenue, showing that the firm would lose profits if it produced more or less total output.

Next assume that marginal cost varies with output, being given by MC' in Figure 20.7 (iii). Now

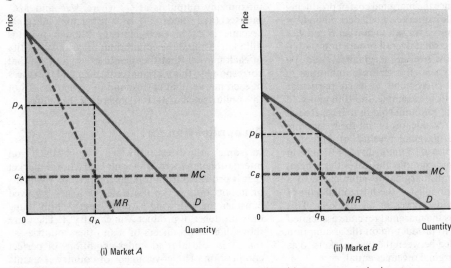

(i) Market A

(ii) Market B

Fig. 20.6 Equilibrium of a price-discriminating monopolist with constant marginal costs

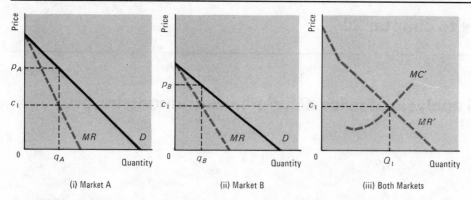

Fig. 20.7 Equilibrium of a price-discriminating monopolist with variable marginal costs

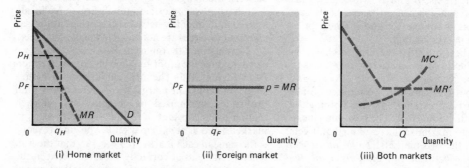

Fig. 20.8 Equilibrium of a firm with a monopoly in the home market but selling under perfectly competitive conditions abroad

we cannot just put the MC curve onto the diagram for each market, since the marginal cost of producing another unit for sale in market A will depend on how much is being produced for sale in market B and vice versa. To determine what overall production should be, we need to know overall marginal revenue. To find this we merely sum the separate quantities in each market that correspond to each particular marginal revenue. If, for example, the 10th unit sold in market A and the 15th unit sold in market B each have a marginal revenue of £1 in their separate markets, then the marginal revenue of £1 corresponds to overall sales of 25 units (divided 10 units in A and 15 in B). This example illustrates the general principle: the overall marginal revenue curve to a discriminating monopolist is the horizontal sum of the marginal revenue curves in all markets. This overall curve shows the marginal revenue associated with an increment to production on the assumption that sales are divided between the two markets so as to keep the two marginal revenues equal.

This overall MR curve is shown in Figure 20.7

(iii) and is labelled MR'. The firm's total profit-maximizing output is at Q_1 where MR' and MC' intersect (at a value of c_1). By construction, marginal revenue is c_1 in each market although price is different. To find the equilibrium price and quantity in each market, find the quantities, q_A and q_B, that correspond to this marginal cost; then find the prices in each market that correspond to q_A and q_B. All of this is illustrated in parts (i) and (ii) of the figure.

An application

In some industries firms sell competitively on international markets while enjoying a home market that is protected from foreign competition by tariffs or import quotas. To illustrate the issues involved consider the following extreme case. A firm is the only producer of product X in country A. There are thousands of producers of X in other countries so that X is sold abroad under conditions of perfect competition. The government of country A grants the firm a monopoly in the home market by prohibiting imports of X. The firm is now faced with a downward-sloping demand curve at home and a perfectly elastic demand curve abroad at the prevailing world price of X.

What will it do? To maximize profits the firm will divide its sales between the foreign and the home markets so as to equate marginal revenues in the two. On the world market its average and marginal revenues are equal to the world price. Thus the firm will equate marginal revenue in the home market with the world price, and since price exceeds marginal revenue at home (because the demand curve slopes downward), price at home must exceed price abroad.

The argument is illustrated in Figure 20.8. The home market is shown in (i), the foreign market in (ii) and the sum of the two marginal revenue curves in (iii). Provided that the marginal cost curve cuts the marginal revenue curve to the right of the kink (i.e., MC does not exceed the world price when only the home market is served), both markets will be served at prices of p_H at home and p_F abroad. The total quantity sold will be Q, of which q_H is allocated to the home market and the rest $(q_F = Q - q_H)$ is sold abroad.[1]

---

[1] It is an interesting exercise to consider the effect on the firm's exports of a tax on the sale of X in the home market.

21

Theories of imperfect competition

The two extreme market structures of perfect competition and monopoly do not cover all of the economic activity that we see today. In particular, most firms involved in the production, distribution and retailing of consumer goods and services, and also of capital goods, come under intermediate market structures. They are not monopolies because, with few exceptions, there is more than one firm in the industry, and these firms often engage in rivalrous behaviour. Residents even of small towns will find more than one chemist, garage, barber and ironmonger competing for their custom. Manufacturers of cars, refrigerators, TV sets, breakfast cereals, and just about any other consumer goods, are in industries where there are several close rivals (often foreign as well as domestic). Neither, however, are these firms in perfectly competitive markets. Usually there are only a few rival firms in an industry, but even when there are many, *they are not price-takers*. Basic raw materials and foodstuffs such as nickel and wheat are sold on world auction markets where prices change continually to equate quantity demanded with quantity supplied. But virtually all consumer goods are differentiated commodities. Any one firm will have several lines of a product that differ more or less from each other, and from competing lines produced by other firms. It is inconceivable therefore that any good such as refrigerators or TV sets could have an impersonal auction market set a single price that equated overall demand to overall supply and a price to which producers then reacted by setting their outputs. Instead, it is in the nature of such products that *sellers must state a price at which they are willing to sell*. (Of course, a certain amount of 'haggling' is possible, particularly at the retail level, but this is usually within well-defined limits set by the price initially quoted by the seller.)

Pricing under alternative market forms

In perfect competition firms sell a homogeneous product, face a market price that they are quite unable to influence, and adjust their quantities to that price. When market conditions change, the signal that the firm sees is a change in the market price of the commodity that it sells.

> **In perfect competition firms are price-takers and quantity adjusters. Changes in market conditions are signalled to firms by changes in the market prices that they face.**

In all other market structures, firms sell DIFFERENTIATED PRODUCTS. Each firm may have several lines of the one general product, and no two firms have products that are identical. Although the products produced by various firms in an industry may be close substitutes for each other, they are not perfect substitutes as in perfect competition. In such situations firms have control over their prices; they must decide on a price to quote for each of their product lines. If they are unsatisfied with their price–output position they can change their quote, but quote a price they must. In such circumstances we say that the firm administers its price. The term ADMINISTERED PRICES refers to prices that are set by the decisions of individual firms rather than by impersonal market forces.

When a firm sets its price, the amount that it sells is determined by its demand curve. Changes in market conditions will be signalled to the firm by changes in demand – by changes, that is, in the amount that can be sold at its administered price. The changed conditions may or may not lead the firm to change the price that it charges.

> **With market forms other than perfect competition, firms set their prices and must let demand determine their sales. Changes in market conditions are signalled to the firm by changes in the quantity the firm can sell at its administered price.**[1]

Imperfect competition among the many: monopolistically competitive market structure

Before the 1930s economists mainly studied the two polar market structures of perfect competition and monopoly. Then in the 1930s dissatisfaction with these two extremes led to the development of a theory of a new market structure called MONOPOLISTIC COMPETITION. The theory was developed in two classic books, one by the British economist Joan Robinson, the other by the American economist Edward Chamberlin.

The market envisaged in the then-new theory was similar to perfect competition in that there were many firms with freedom of entry and exit. But it differed in one important respect: each firm had some power over price because each sold a product that was differentiated significantly from those of its competitors. This phenomenon of product differentiation implied that each firm had a degree of local monopoly power over its own product. This was the 'monopolistic' part of the theory. The monopoly power was severely restricted, however, by the presence of similar products sold by many competing firms. This was the 'competition' part of the theory.

The major difference between monopolistic and perfect competition lies in the assumptions of homogeneous and differentiated products. Firms in perfect competition sell a homogeneous product, which from a practical point of view means a product similar enough across the industry so that buyers cannot distinguish physically among the products sold by different firms in the industry. They thus regard these products as perfect substitutes for each other. Firms in monopolistic competition sell a differentiated product, which from a practical point of view means a group of commodities similar enough to be called a product but dissimilar enough so that buyers can and do distinguish among the products sold by different firms in the industry. Because consumers regard the various products as close but not perfect substitutes, the producer of each has some power over its own price.

---

[1] Of course, given a demand curve, a firm could determine price, which implies a quantity of sales, or determine quantity of sales which implies a price. But in practice there is no impersonal auction market to set price so the firm *must* quote a price at which it is prepared to sell. If it has a quantity target, it can vary its price until it meets that target, but even then it cannot produce a quantity and accept an impersonal determination of its price. It must at each point in time decide on, and set, the price at which it is prepared to sell each of its differentiated products.

The theory of monopolistic competition was extremely important as a step in the development of models of intermediate market structures. Its main prediction is outlined below, and a more detailed discussion is given in the appendix to this chapter.

The excess capacity theorem

The major characteristics of monopolistic competition[1] are two. First, because each firm has a monopoly over its own product, each is not a price-taker. Instead each firm faces a downward-sloping demand curve. But the curve is rather elastic because similar products sold by other firms provide many close substitutes. The downward slope of the demand curve provides the potential for monopoly profits in the short run.

Second, freedom of entry and exit forces profits to zero in the long run. If profits are being earned by existing firms in the industry, new firms will enter. Their entry will mean that the demand for the product must be shared among more brands. Thus the demand curve for any one firm's brand will shift left. Entry continues until profits fall to zero.

The absence of positive profits requires that each firm's demand curve (its average revenue curve) be nowhere above its long-run average cost curve. The absence of losses (losses would cause exit) requires that each firm be able to cover its costs. Thus average revenue must equal average cost at some level of output. Together these requirements imply that when a monopolistically competitive industry is in long-run equilibrium, each firm will be producing where its demand curve is tangent to (i.e., just touching at one point) its average total cost curve.

Two curves that are tangent at a point have the same slope at that point. If a downward-sloping

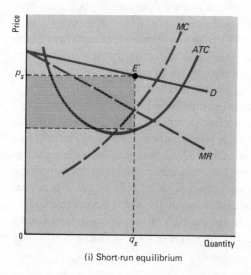

(i) Short-run equilibrium

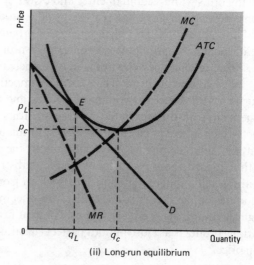

(ii) Long-run equilibrium

Fig. 21.1 Equilibrium of a firm in monopolistic competition

---

[1] The text refers to large-group monopolistic competition which exercised economists' imaginations in the decades after Chamberlin's and Robinson's writings. Small-group monopolistic competition is discussed in the next section on oligopoly.

demand curve is to be tangent to the *LRATC* curve, the latter must also be downward-sloping at the point of tangency. In such a situation each firm is producing an output less than the one for which its *LRATC* reaches its minimum point. This is the famous EXCESS CAPACITY THEOREM of monopolistic competition. Productive efficiency is not achieved under monopolistic competition because firms do not produce at their lowest attainable cost (see page 310).

This prediction, over which a seemingly endless controversy raged for decades, is illustrated graphically in Figure 21.1. Part (i) shows the short-run equilibrium of a firm in monopolistic competition. The result is similar to a monopoly. Equating marginal cost with marginal revenue leads to output q_s at price p_s with profits equal to the shaded rectangle. Attracted by the profits, new firms enter the industry. Their entry shifts the demand curve of each existing firm to the left as its market share is reduced. This goes on until the typical firm in the industry is in the tangency solution shown in part (ii) of the figure. Now marginal cost equals marginal revenue at output q_L leading to price p_L. Here the firm is just covering its total costs so there is no further incentive for entry. A competitive firm would produce at capacity output q_c where *ATC* is at its minimum value and sell at p_c. Thus in long-run zero-profit equilibrium the monopolistically competitive firm has excess capacity ($q_c - q_L$ in the figure) and sells at a higher price than would a perfectly competitive firm.

Short-run equilibrium of a monopolistically competitive firm is the same as for a monopolist. In the long run a monopolistically competitive industry has zero profits and excess capacity.

The excess-capacity theorem aroused passionate debate because it seemed to say that industries that sell differentiated products are inefficient in that they have excess capacity in long-run equilibrium and thus higher costs than are necessary.

The debate's resolution, which is largely due to the work of Kelvin Lancaster, formerly of the London School of Economics and now of Columbia University in New York, has only come in recent years. It is that the 'excess capacity' of monopolistic competition does not necessarily indicate inefficiency. The key point is that with differentiated products there is a choice concerning how many products to produce. Clearly, people have different tastes; some prefer one differentiated product and some prefer another. For example, each brand of breakfast food, or hi-fi set or watch has its sincere devotees. This creates a trade-off between producing more products to better satisfy diverse tastes and producing any given set of products at the lowest possible cost. The larger the number of differentiated products in existence, the further to the left of the least-cost level of output will be the production of each existing product, but the more will it be possible to satisfy diverse tastes. Under these conditions, consumers' satisfactions are not maximized by increasing production of each product until each is produced at its least-cost point. Instead the number of differentiated products must be increased until the gain from adding one more equals the loss from having to produce each existing product at a higher cost (because less of each is produced). For this reason, among others, the charge that large-group monopolistic competition would lead to a waste of resources is no longer accepted as necessarily, or even probably, true.

Large-group monopolistic competition produced a revolution in economists' attitudes. There was, however, a long debate over the theory's predictions and their empirical relevance. Today the debate has subsided somewhat, with the realization that – at least in manufacturing – product differentiation occurs mainly where a small group rather than a large group of firms compete with each other.

The empirical irrelevance of large-group monopolistic competition

Perhaps the major blow that the theories of Robinson and Chamberlin suffered was the slow realization that monopolistically competitive industries were rarely if ever found in the economy. At first sight this claim may sound surprising. A visit to any department store or supermarket will reveal that there are many industries in which a large number of slightly differentiated products compete for the buyers' attention. In most such cases, however, the industries contain only a few firms, each of which sells a large number of products. Thus it is the small-group case of 'differentiated oligopoly' rather than the large-group case of monopolistic competition that seems relevant today.[1] Indeed, over the last decade there has been a great outburst of theorizing about all aspects of product differentiation. Interestingly, the theory that studies market structures where a small number of firms compete to sell a large number of differentiated products has taken the name *monopolistic competition*. The term now refers to any industry containing more than one firm, all of whom sell differentiated products.

This modern theory is the direct descendant of the earlier theories of monopolistic competition. The focus remains on product differentiation and on industrial structures thought to describe the nature of the modern economy. The new theory is consistent with the famous propositions of Robinson and Chamberlin that it pays firms to differentiate their products, to advertise heavily, and to engage in many forms of non-price competition. These are characteristics to be found in the world but not in perfect competition. Most of the modern theory of product differentiation relates to situations where each firm has only a small number of competitors. This is the theory of oligopoly that we shall discuss in the next section.

Imperfect competition among the few: oligopoly

We now consider the market structure of oligopoly in which a few firms compete with each other. Each firm has enough market power so that it cannot be a price-taker, but it is subject to enough inter-firm rivalry that it cannot consider the market demand curve as its own. This is probably the dominant market structure outside of agriculture and basic industrial materials.

The short-term theory of the firm under oligopoly

Much empirical work has gone into studying short-term firm behaviour under oligopolistic conditions. The basic thrust of this work may now be outlined.

Short-run cost curves are flat   Ever since economists began measuring firms' costs, they reported very flat short-run variable cost curves. By now the evidence is overwhelming that in manufacturing, and some other industries, cost curves have the shape shown in Figure 21.2 with a long flat middle

---

[1] At first sight retailing may appear to be closer to the conditions of monopolistic competition than is manufacturing. Certainly every city has a very large number of retailers selling any one commodity. The problem is that they are differentiated from each other mainly by their geographical location, each firm having only a few close neighbours. Thus a model of interlocking oligopolies, with every firm in close competition with only a few neighbours, seems to be a better model for retailing than the large-group monopolistic competition model, in which every firm competes directly and equally with all other firms in the industry. These and other related matters are further discussed in the Appendix.

portion and sharply rising sections at each end. Over the flat range from q_1 to q_3 marginal and average variable costs coincide. At low outputs below q_1, AVC is declining so MC is below it, while at high outputs above q_3, AVC is rising so MC is above AVC. This 'saucer shape' is to be compared with the traditional U-shaped cost curve shown in Figure 19.5 on page 249.

Note two important points on the AVC curve in Figure 21.2. First, the level of output q_3 where the AVC curve starts to turn upwards is called FULL CAPACITY OUTPUT, or often just CAPACITY OUTPUT. Second, there is a level of output that the firm hopes to maintain on average. This is called NORMAL CAPACITY OUTPUT and is indicated by q_2 on the figure. The margin $q_3 - q_2$ is available to meet cyclical peaks in demand. The firm expects to use it in periods of peak demand but not in periods of average or slack demand.

The reason why As evidence accumulated on this shape for the short-run cost curve, a controversy broke out: does the saucer-shaped $SRAVC$ curve violate the law of variable proportions (the law of diminishing returns)? This law says that short-run returns and hence costs should vary whenever differing amounts of a variable factor are applied to a given amount of a fixed factor. It thus appears to deny the possibility of a horizontal range for the short-run cost curve.

The resolution of the debate is that there is no contradiction, only different circumstances from that envisioned by the law of variable proportions. This law, as expounded for example on pages 216–18 above, envisages applying a variable amount of one factor, say labour, to a fixed amount of a second factor, say capital. Thus as output is varied, factor proportions are necessarily varied. Note, however, that the argument for a declining portion of the MC curve (see pages 212–14) rests on having too low a ratio of the variable factor to the fixed factor. As production is increased, more of the variable factor is used and a more efficient combination with the fixed factor achieved. This clearly implies that all of the fixed factor must be used, i.e., that the fixed factor be *indivisible*.

Using technical language,

> **The constraint on the fixed factor that lies behind the U-shaped cost curve is $K_e = \bar{K}$, where K_e is the amount actually used in the short run and $\bar{K}$ is the amount actually available.**

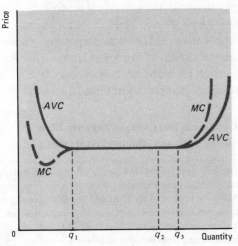

Fig. 21.2 Saucer-shaped average variable and marginal cost curves

In manufacturing and services, the important fixed factor in the short run is capital. The firm's plant and equipment is fixed while labour (plus materials) are varied in the short run. In the long run the firm's capital/labour ratio can be varied continuously by building slightly larger or smaller plants, slightly more or less integrated production processes and slightly more or less elaborate labour-saving machines. Once they are constructed, however, plant and equipment have a fairly rigid capital/labour ratio built into them. When production is reduced below full capacity, less labour *and* less capital is employed.

In formal language, the constraint on the fixed factor that lies behind the saucer-shaped cost curve is $K_e \leqslant \bar{K}$.

This means that the fixed factor is *divisible*. Since some of it may go unemployed, there is now no need, as production is decreased, to depart from the optimum ratio of the actual employed quantity of the fixed to the employed quantity of the variable factor. Thus, the average cost will be constant up to the point at which all of the fixed factor is used. Beyond this point, production can only be increased by combining more of the variable factor with the constant (total) amount of the fixed factor. Under these circumstances costs will be rising.

Consider as a simple example a 'factory' that consists of 10 sewing machines in a shed, each with a productive capacity of 20 units per day when operated for 8 hours by one operator. If 200 units per day are required, then all 10 machines are operated on a normal shift. If demand falls to 180, then one operator is laid off. But there is no need to have the 9 remaining operators dashing about trying to work 10 machines. Clearly one machine can be 'laid off' as well, and the ratio of *employed* labour to *employed* machines held constant. Clearly, production can go from 1 to 200 without any change in factor proportions. In this case we would expect the factory to have constant marginal costs up to 200 units, and only then to encounter rising costs, as production must be expanded by overtime and other means of combining more labour with the fixed supply of 10 machines.

For cost curves to be flat up to capacity output it is critical that the fixed factor be divisible in the sense that not all of it needs to be employed. The employment of the fixed factor is then subject to the 'inequality constraint', $K_e \leqslant \bar{K}$. If the fixed factor is indivisible in the sense that all of it must always be used, i.e., its use is subject to the 'equality constraint', $K_e = \bar{K}$, then variable proportions and diminishing returns are technologically dictated in the short run. In the real world much short-run capital *is* physically divisible, as in the rag-trade example given above, while almost all capital is divisible over time in the sense that it and its associated labour can be used fewer hours per day or fewer days per week, thus reducing K_e to hold the ratio of employed capital to employed labour constant.

This situation occurs, for example, when a refrigerator or TV manufacturer chooses to cut his output by closing one of several parallel plants or by putting one plant on short time. In each of these cases the firm is electing to unemploy labour and capital.

Short-run costs in manufacturing tend to be flat up to capacity output because both labour and capital inputs are varied so as to maintain the optimum labour/capital ratio.[1]

---

[1] The cost curve in Figure 21.2 can now be explained more fully. The falling part of the AVC to the left of q_1 implies that there is some minimum indivisible amount of capital $K^* < \bar{K}$ that must be used. As production is increased up to q_1 the ratio of employed capital to employed labour changes as more and more labour is applied to the fixed amount K^*. Once production reaches q_1 the ratio of employed factors is optimal. From q_1 to q_3 output is increased by taking on more labour and employing more of the available fixed stock of capital. At output q_3 all of the fixed capital stock is employed. Output can only be increased beyond q_3 by adding more labour to the fixed capital, thus departing from the optimal labour/capital ratio and thereby raising costs according to the law of variable proportions.

Demand conditions and pricing policy In perfect competition, firms are price-takers. They face a perfectly elastic demand curve indicating that they can sell all that they wish at the going price. In manufacturing, services, retailing, and wherever a differentiated product is sold, firms face downward-sloping demand curves. They can raise their prices and not lose all of their sales, and they can lower their prices without attracting all of the customers of other firms. In deciding on their marketing policies they must affix prices to their commodities indicating the terms on which they are willing to sell. This raises the key problem of pricing decisions.

If the amount of work that has gone into studying costs is voluminous, the amount that has gone into studying oligopolistic price policy is doubly so. The basic empirical finding is as follows:

> **Oligopolistic firms do not alter their prices every time demand shifts. Instead they fix prices and let sales do the adjusting in the short term.**

This phenomenon is often referred to as the *stickiness* of oligopolistic prices.

In what sense are oligopolistic prices sticky? First consider ways in which oligopoly prices are not sticky. Such prices usually change when there are major changes in input prices. Rises in costs are passed on fairly quickly in rises in prices.[1] Also major reductions in costs, as when a new product such as the home computer is being developed, are usually followed by reductions in prices. This is because of the rivalrous behaviour among oligopolistic firms: if one firm doesn't cut price when costs fall, another firm will do so, seeking thereby to increase its market share.

Also, major unexpected shifts in demand may lead to price adjustments in oligopoly prices. If an industry finds itself faced with an apparently permanent and unexpected downward shift in demand, it may cut its prices in an attempt to retain its market until longer-term adjustments can be made. A classic example occurred when the American car industry was faced with declining demand in the early 1980s due to its slowness in developing small, fuel-efficient cars that were competitive with imported cars. It slashed prices to levels that could not be maintained in the long run.

The rigidity of oligopoly prices lies not in the situations considered above. Instead it is mainly in respect to *predictable*, *cyclical* shifts in demand. The ebb and flow of business activity between slump and boom that is called the trade cycle is well known to firms, even if its precise course cannot be predicted in advance. Oligopolistic firms hold their prices fairly constant in the face of 'normal' cyclical fluctuations in demand. These fluctuations thus cause output to vary while prices stay relatively stable. The evidence for such oligopolistic price rigidity is overwhelming. Controversy only exists over its interpretation.

Full-cost pricing An early interpretation stems from the pioneering work of two Oxford economists, Robert Hall and Charles Hitch. Their view was that businessmen were conventional creatures of habit who were clearly not profit-maximizers. Businessmen calculated their full costs at normal capacity and then added a conventional markup to determine price. They then sold whatever they could at that price, so that demand fluctuations caused quantity rather than price fluctuations. This

---

[1] Oligopolistic pricing may, however, convert continuous changes in input prices into discrete changes in output prices. Say that inflation is continuously raising the prices of industrial raw materials as determined in perfectly competitive markets. Firms find it expensive to change list prices every day so they will make discrete jumps in their output prices, first getting output prices ahead of input prices then slowly falling behind until a further adjustment of output prices is necessary.

view of the conventional markup was successful in explaining the observed oligopolistic price stickiness, but was unsuccessful in explaining the observed fact that markups did vary from time to time.

Profit-maximization with costly price changes Another theory is based on the costs of changing prices. Firms that sell many differentiated products find it prohibitively costly to change their prices every time demand changes. Furthermore, their customers would find it difficult to cope with such changes and would shift to suppliers whose prices could be relied on not to change with such disturbing frequency. Profit-maximizing firms do not therefore change prices in response to every small shift in demand; the extra revenue *would be less* than the cost of making such price changes.

According to this theory, firms' decisions are made in stages.

(1) Firms estimate their *normal demand curve* which is the average of what they can expect to sell at each price over booms and slumps.

(2) Firms then determine their size such that long-run marginal cost equals marginal revenue at normal capacity output.

(3) Having built a plant whose normal capacity is the profit-maximizing output determined in (2), firms fix price at the profit-maximizing level. This is shown in Figure 21.3 where D_n is the normal demand curve, q_n is normal capacity and p_1 is the profit-maximizing price.

(4) With price fixed at p_1 and expressed as a mark up $p_1 - c_n$ over average variable cost at normal capacity output, q_n, short-run cyclical variations in demand are then met by quantity variations as shown in Figure 21.4. Normal demand results in output q_n, while the demands $- D_S$ in times of slump and D_B in times of economic boom – result in outputs q_S and q_B respectively.

(5) Changes in input costs shift the firm's cost curves and change its profit-maximizing price at normal capacity output. Thus changes in input prices do lead to changes in output prices.

The behaviour just described is profit-maximizing behaviour; since the cost of changing prices is

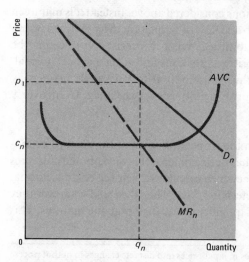

Fig. 21.3 Determination of the profit-maximizing price given normal demand

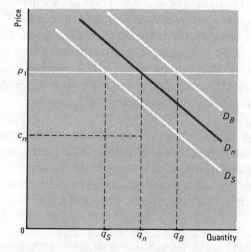

Fig. 21.4 Variations in output caused by variations in demand, with price fixed at the profit-maximizing level for normal demand

high, the best thing to do is to set the price that maximizes profits for average demand and then adjust output rather than price as demand varies over the cycle.

Implications of short-term price stickiness This theory of short-run oligopolistic behaviour turns out to be very important when we study some current controversies in macroeconomics. In the meantime, we shall content ourselves with outlining the theory's major implications.

(1) Cyclical fluctuations in demand are met by quantity rather than price adjustments.

(2) Cost changes in either an upward or a downward direction are passed on through price changes (although possibly with a lag because oligopolistic firms find it costly to make continuous price changes).

(3) Oligopolistic firms receive signals from the economy just as perfectly competitive firms do. But the form of the signals is different: any market change is signalled to perfect competitors by a price change. Oligopolies, however, receive their signals about changes in market conditions for their outputs from a change in their sales.

An alternative explanation of price stickiness: the kinked oligopoly demand curve[1]

An earlier explanation of oligopolistic price stickiness was developed in the 1930s by the economist Paul Sweezy. This theory predicts price stickiness in the face of significant shifts both in demand and in costs.

In Figure 21.5 the oligopolistic firm is assumed to be selling q_1 units at a price of p_1. It then considers altering its price and it makes two key assumptions. First it assumes that if it cuts its price, all of its competitors will match its price cut. Its demand will then expand along the relatively steep curve below a, which indicates the effect of the firm's price cut when its share of the market is

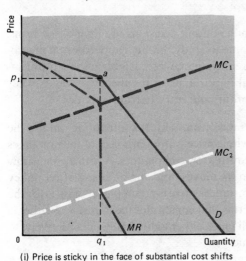

(i) Price is sticky in the face of substantial cost shifts

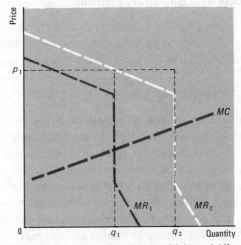

(ii) Price is sticky in the face of substantial demand shifts

Fig. 21.5 The theory of kinked oligopoly demand curves

[1] This section can be omitted without loss of continuity.

unchanged. Second, it assumes that if it raises its price, none of its competitors will raise theirs. Its demand for prices above p_1 thus contracts along the relatively flat curve indicating the effects of raising prices with a declining market share.

Because the demand curve is kinked at the current price-output combination, the marginal revenue curve is discontinuous. As price is raised above p_1, the firm's market share shrinks, so its loss in revenue (i.e., its marginal revenue) is quite large. As price is lowered below p_1 its market share is constant, so the gain in revenue (marginal revenue) is much less.

Figure 21.5 (i) shows the insensitivity of price to shifts in costs in this model. Any shift in marginal cost between a high of MC_1 and a low of MC_2 leaves price and output unchanged. Figure 21.5 (ii) shows the insensitivity of price to shifts in demand. To stop the figure from becoming unmanageably cluttered, only the marginal curves are shown in part (ii). The firm is originally setting price p_1 and selling quantity q_1. Demand then increases, taking sales to q_2 at the administered price of p_1. (Thus there is a demand curve through the point $p_1 q_2$ but it is not shown.) The firm then asks if it should raise or lower its price. The same assumptions about its competitors' reactions that were made earlier now produce a demand curve kinked at q_2 and the white marginal revenue curve shown in the figure. In the case of the relatively flat MC curve shown in the figure, the oligopolist raises output to q_2 but leaves price unchanged at p_1.

If the evidence supporting the explanation of price stickiness based on the normal-capacity pricing theory outlined in the previous section is voluminous, the evidence supporting the kinked demand curve explanation is almost non-existent. The theories clearly differ in predictions since although the kinked demand curve theory correctly predicts price stickiness in the face of demand shifts, it incorrectly predicts price stickiness in the face of cost shifts. The hold that Sweezy's theory still has on the profession in general and textbook writers in particular is possibly explained by its being relatively easy to teach.

Longer-run oligopoly problems

The above discussion concentrated on the short-run price-output decisions of oligopolistic firms. We shall return to the issues just discussed when we come to study the current debates on macro-economics later in this book. In the next part of the present chapter, we shall look at some problems in oligopoly behaviour that are of more fundamental importance to the theory of value. They concern longer-term behaviour with respect to prices, profits and entry-barring activities.

Competition among oligopolistic firms   When we move from perfect competition among the many to oligopolistic competition among the few, the whole price-output problem of the firm takes on a new dimension, that of the possible reaction of the firm's few competitors. A firm's policy now depends on how it *thinks* its competitors will react to its moves, and the outcome of its policy depends on how they *do* in fact react. Under these circumstances there is no simple set of rules for the equilibrium either of the firm or of the small group of firms that constitutes the industry. Neither is there a set of simple predictions about how the firms will react, either individually or collectively, to changes in such things as taxes, costs and market demand.[1]

---

[1] It is often said that, under these circumstances, price and output are *indeterminate*. Such a statement is misleading since the price and output do, of course, get determined somehow. What is meant, however, is that, under oligopoly, price and output are not determined by the same factors as in large-group cases. In small-group cases an additional set of factors – competitors' real and imagined reactions to each other's behaviour – contributes to the determination of price and output.

Theoretical approaches to oligopolistic behaviour: homogeneous products   The pathbreaking attack on the oligopoly problem occurred as long ago as 1838, in the work of the French economist A. A. Cournot. He dealt with the special case of an industry containing only two firms, called a DUOPOLY. The two firms sold an identical product. Each chose its profit-maximizing output on the assumption that the other firm would hold its own output constant. Cournot then showed that if each firm in turn adjusted to the last move made by its competitor (on the assumption that the competitor would make no further move), a stable equilibrium would be reached in which the market was divided between the two firms in a definite way. Each firm would charge the same price as the other, and that price would be higher than the perfectly competitive price but lower than the price a monopolist would charge. This finding established oligopoly as a truly intermediate case between perfect competition and monopoly.

Firms in the situation analysed by Cournot will raise price and lower output when costs rise, and they will usually raise price and raise output when demand increases. Thus changes in price and quantity are in the same direction as under perfect competition, though the magnitude of the changes will be different.

The equilibrium Cournot analysed has survived in modern theorizing. It is now called the Nash, or Cournot–Nash, equilibrium. It is the equilibrium that results when each firm makes its decisions on the assumption that all other firms' behaviour will be unchanged. Nash equilibria can be determined for many oligopolistic situations. Their properties can be compared with the equilibria that would result from perfect competition and from monopoly (usually, higher prices and lower output than under perfect competition; lower prices and higher output than under monopoly). The price-quantity differences can also be studied when equilibrium changes under the impact of shifts in input costs or demand for the industry's output.

Unfortunately the Cournot-Nash assumption, that each firm takes its rivals' behaviour as given, seems inapplicable to many small-group situations. The Ford Motor Company knows (or quickly learns) that if it slashes the prices of some of its cars, other firms will react by adjusting their prices on comparable cars. Similar considerations apply when Kelloggs considers changing the advertising for one of its breakfast cereals or Unilever the prices of its soaps. Thus not only must an oligopolistic firm be concerned with how *buyers* of its products will react to changes it makes, it must anticipate how each of a few identified rival *sellers* will react. Economists have sometimes tackled this problem of interactions by assuming that each firm makes its decisions subject to what are called *conjectural variations*. A firm making, say, a price decision conjectures how variations in its price would induce its rivals to vary their prices. Of course a wide range of conjectural variations is possible. For example, firm *A* might assume that whatever price it sets, its rivals will set the same price. Equilibrium can be shown to exist for many conjectural variations, and the properties of these equilibria can be compared with the equilibria that would result if the industry were either perfectly competitive or fully monopolized.

The problem with this approach is that it is difficult to state conjectural variations that are anything other than mechanical rules (although current work on 'consistent conjectural variations' is trying to do just that). Any mechanical rules ignore subtle considerations of strategy such as bluff and counterbluff that may be relevant in real situations of small-group competition. More importantly perhaps, they neglect the learning and adaptation that characterize most real oligopolistic situations.

Differentiated products: Cournot's analysis dealt with oligopolists selling homogeneous products. Most real-world oligopolistic firms sell differentiated products. For example, one brand of cigarettes sold by the Imperial Tobacco Company differs not only from all the brands sold by other companies but from other brands sold by itself. With differentiated products, each product is distinct from every other product; they may be close substitutes but they are not perfect substitutes.

Empirically based approaches to oligopolistic behaviour   Because the oligopoly problem is so complex, some economists have sought to build theories from observations of the actual behaviour of oligopolistic firms. These economists believe that we need to begin with detailed knowledge of the actual behaviour of such firms. The knowledge is then used to narrow the range of theoretically possible cases by selecting those that actually occur. This approach is associated with the names of many somewhat unorthodox economists. The most famous of these is, no doubt, that of Nobel Prize winner Herbert Simon who received his award for the type of work reported below.

In this section we shall (1) describe one major empirically based hypothesis about oligopoly behaviour, (2) describe briefly a number of subsidiary hypotheses concerning forces that pull in opposite directions, and (3) discuss at greater length one or two hypotheses that seem to shed some light on real oligopolistic behaviour.

The hypothesis of qualified joint profit-maximization: While explicit collusion is illegal in most countries, why cannot a small group of firms that recognize their interdependence simply act in a common manner? Such tacit collusion has been called 'quasi-agreement' by Professor William Fellner. If all firms behave as though they were branches of a single firm, they can achieve the ends of a monopolist by adopting price and output policies that will maximize their *collective profits*, often called *joint profits*. Every firm is interested, however, in *its own* profits, not the industry's profits, and it may pay one firm to depart from the joint profit-maximizing position if, by so doing, it can increase its share of the profits.

The hypothesis of qualified joint profit-maximization thus rests on the notion that a firm in an oligopolistic industry is responsive to *two* sets of influences.

> **Any oligopolistic firm wants to co-operate with its rivals to maximize their joint profits; it also wants to compete with its rivals in order to gain as large a share of these profits as possible.**

Consider the conflicting pressures on an oligopolistic firm when it chooses its price. First, if firms in a group recognize that they are *interdependent* and face a downward-sloping demand curve, they will recognize that their joint profits depend on the price that each of them charges. This pulls each firm to co-operate with its rivals in charging the same price that a single firm would charge if it monopolized the industry. Second, despite this pull, an aggressive seller may hope to gain more than its rivals by being the first to cut price below the monopoly level. But if it does this, other firms may follow and the total profits earned in the industry will then be pushed below their joint profit-maximizing level. A firm that initiates such a price-cutting strategy must balance what it expects to gain by securing a larger *share* of the profits against what it expects to lose because there will be a smaller total of profits to go around. The hypothesis of qualified joint profit-maximization is that the relative strength of the two tendencies (toward and away from joint profit-maximization) varies from industry to industry in a systematic way that can be associated with observable characteristics of firms, markets and products. Let us consider some examples.

1. *The tendency toward joint profit-maximization is greater for small numbers of sellers than for larger numbers.* Here the argument concerns both ability and motivation. When there are few firms, each will know that there is no chance of gaining sales without inducing retaliation by their rivals. At the same time, a smaller number of firms can tacitly co-ordinate their policies with less difficulty than can a larger number.

2. *The tendency toward joint profit-maximization is greater for producers of very similar products than for producers of sharply differentiated products.* The argument here is that the more nearly identical the products of sellers, the closer will be the direct rivalry for customers and the less the ability of one firm to gain a decisive advantage over its rivals. Thus, other things being equal, such sellers will prefer joint efforts to achieve a larger pie to individual attempts to take customers away from each other.

3. *The tendency toward joint profit-maximization is greater in a growing than in a contracting industry.* The argument here is that when demand is growing, firms can utilize their capacity fully without resorting to attempts to 'steal' their rivals' customers. In contrast, when firms have excess capacity, they are tempted to give discounts or secret price concessions in order to pick up customers. Eventually their rivals will retaliate, and large price cuts may become general. (This prediction has been borne out by recent OPEC behaviour.)

4. *The tendency towards joint profit-maximization is greater when the industry contains a dominant firm rather than a set of more or less equal competitors.* A dominant firm may become a PRICE LEADER, which is a firm that sets the industry's price while all other firms fall into line. If a dominant firm knows it really is a price leader it can set the monopoly price, confident that all other firms will follow it. Indeed the dominant firm may be able to gain a disproportionate share of the industry's profits by setting an output which all other firms accept as given. This technique was examined early in the century by the German economist von Stackelburg, who showed that a quantity leader could gain more than half the profits in a duopoly situation by fixing output and letting the other firm do the best it could do while taking the leader's output as given.

5. *Tacit price fixing to maximize joint profits will cause non-price competition that will take the industry away from its joint profit-maximizing position.* The argument here is that when firms seek to suppress their basic rivalry by agreeing, tacitly or explicitly, not to engage in price competition, rivalry will break out in other forms. Firms then seek to maintain or increase their market shares through heavy advertising, quality changes, the establishment of new products, bonuses, giveaways, and a host of other schemes for gaining at the expense of their rivals while leaving the list prices of products unchanged. Such rivalry is called NON-PRICE COMPETITION and it includes all methods of inter-firm competition other than price cutting. Non-price competition is one of the major features of modern inter-firm rivalry.

6. *The tendency toward joint profit-maximizing is greater, the greater are the barriers to entry of new firms.* The high profits of existing firms will attract new entrants who will drive down price and reduce profits. Less of this will occur the greater are the barriers to entry. Thus the greater the entry barriers, the closer the profits of existing firms can be to their joint profit-maximizing level.

Barriers to entry

Suppose firms in an oligopolistic industry succeed in raising prices above long-run average total costs so that profits are earned. Why do these profits not cause further firms to enter the industry? Why does entry not continue until the extra output forces prices down to the level where only the opportunity cost of capital is being earned (i.e., profits become zero)? The answer lies in *barriers to entry*, which are anything that puts new firms that wish to enter an industry at a significant competitive disadvantage relative to existing firms in the industry. Barriers are of three sorts: natural barriers, barriers created by the firms already in the industry, and barriers created by government policy. We discuss the first two in this chapter.

Natural barriers Natural barriers to entry may result from an interaction between market size – as shown by the market demand curve – and economies of scale, as shown by the firm's long-run average total cost curve.

One type of natural barrier depends on the shape of the *LRATC* curve and in particular on what is called MINIMUM EFFICIENT SCALE (*MES*). This term refers to the smallest size of firm that can reap all the available economies of large scale. Suppose, for example, that the technology of an industry is such that a typical firm's *MES* is 10,000 units a week at an *ATC* of £10 per unit and that at a price of £10 the total quantity demanded is 30,000 units per week. Clearly there is room for no more than three plants of efficient size – and hence three firms at most will serve this market. The industry will tend to be naturally oligopolistic.

Now say that demand expands to 35,000 units at a price of £10. There is still not room for a fourth plant operating at *MES*, but the existing firms can raise their prices above £10 a unit and earn a profit above total costs.

> **Natural barriers to entry occur when the output at which *MES* is achieved is large relative to total demand. Under these circumstances a small number of existing firms may earn profits without inducing a further firm to enter the market.**

A second type of natural cost barrier occurs when there are ABSOLUTE COST ADVANTAGES. This means that existing firms have average cost curves that are significantly lower over their entire range than those of potential new entrants. Among possible sources of such advantages are control of crucial patents or resources, knowledge that comes only from 'learning by doing' in the industry, and established credit ratings that permit advantageous purchasing and borrowing. Each of these may be regarded as only a temporary disadvantage of new firms, which, given time, might develop their own know-how, patents, and satisfactory credit ratings. But even a temporary disadvantage can inhibit entry if it causes sufficient losses at first to more than offset the profits to be earned later.

Firm-created barriers to entry If natural entry barriers do not exist, oligopolistic firms can earn long-run profits only if they can create barriers that prevent their profits from attracting new entrants into the industry.

Predatory pricing: One way of doing this is to create a situation that threatens a new entrant with losses in spite of the fact that existing firms are earning profits. For example, prices may be cut to or below cost whenever entry occurs, then raised after the new entrant has given up.

There is much controversy concerning predatory pricing. Some economists argue that pricing policies that appear to be predatory can be explained by other motives, and that existing firms only hurt themselves when they engage in such practices instead of reaching an accommodation with new entrants. Others argue that predatory pricing seems to have been observed and that it is in the long-run interests of existing firms to punish new entrants even when it is costly to do so in the short run.

Pre-emptive expansion in an expanding market: Say the market is growing (demand curve shifting outward) to an extent that there will be room for each of three existing firms to open one more plant operating at *MES* every four years beginning in 1984. If the firms were not worried about entry, each would build a new plant in 1984, 1988, 1992, and so on. But faced with this strategy, a new firm could build three plants in 1983, 1987, 1991 and so on – and thus be in possession of the market when the new plant became profitable a year later. The investment in fixed capital represents a commitment to the market. The first three plants that get in will have pre-empted the new part of the market, and it will not pay anyone else to build yet another plant because four new plants would all lose money.

In order to prevent this from happening, existing firms will be tempted to build their new plants some time before the demand expands enough for them to be operated at a profit. Once the plant is built, it will not pay a new firm to build a further plant, and the existing firms will remain in possession of the market when demand expands sufficiently to allow the new plant to cover its costs. Existing firms may well be in a stronger position to expand in anticipation of future demand than potential new entrants. This type of entry-preventing strategy – building new capacity to serve an expanding market before it is needed – has been alleged to occur in several oligopolistic and monopolistic situations.

Advertising: A policy that may be adopted by an industry that faces potential entrants owing to a low *MES* is to attempt to shift the cost curves (of itself *and* of potential entrants) upward and to the right by advertising. If there is much brand-image advertising, then a new firm will have to spend a great deal on advertising its product in order to bring it to the public's attention. If the firm's sales are small, advertising costs *per unit sold* will be very large. Thus, heavy advertising expenditures in an industry without economies of scale in production have the effect of changing total cost curves in such a way as to raise *MES* and thus make entry on a small scale more difficult.

This proposition is illustrated in Figure 21.6. The curve labelled *ATC (production)* shows a case in which economies of scale are all exhausted at a quite modest level of output, with constant long-run average costs beyond that level. Such an industry is easy to enter. We now add a fixed level of advertising costs necessary to establish a new brand against the heavy advertising of existing brands. When we divide this fixed cost by the number of units produced, we obtain the curve labelled *ATC (advertising)*, which shows how advertising cost per unit sold declines as output is raised, thus spreading the fixed cost over more and more units. If we add these two curves, we obtain the curve labelled *ATC (production plus advertising)*, which shows how *all* long-run costs vary as output varies. The curves are drawn to scale, and it is clear from inspection that there are substantial economies of large size up to a much higher level of output than when advertising was not a component of costs. A small new entrant will now be at a substantial cost disadvantage when competing against a large, established firm.

Brand proliferation: Many products have several characteristics, each of which can be varied over a wide range. Thus there is room for a large number of similar products, each with a somewhat different mix of characteristics. Consider the many different kinds of breakfast cereals or cars. The multiplicity of brands is in part a response to consumers' tastes. If you doubt this, try to persuade a

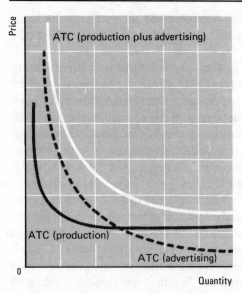

Fig. 21.6 Average total cost curves allowing for both production and advertising costs

sportscar addict to switch to a standard four-door saloon, or try to get a lover of Cornflakes to switch to Weetabix, or try to make all the members of one family select the same watch or tie when they go to the local shops.

Let us now consider, however, how product proliferation can also serve as a barrier to entry. Because there is a *MES* for producing every differentiated product, an infinite variety cannot be provided. Even though a small group of consumers could be found who would prefer each of 10,000 different breakfast cereals, their demands would not be large enough to cover the costs of production. Thus there is room in the market for perhaps only 50 or 60 brands rather than a few thousand. By producing many kinds of cars, cereals or soaps, and adding new ones whenever demand either increases or shifts toward a different mix of characteristics, existing firms can make it more difficult for new firms selling a differentiated product to enter the industry.

Having many differentiated products confers other advantages on existing firms. If the product is one in which consumers switch brands frequently, then increasing the number of brands sold by existing firms will reduce the expected sales of a new entrant. Say, for example, that an industry contains three large firms, each selling one brand of cigarettes, and say that 30 per cent of all smokers change brands in a random fashion each year. If a new firm enters the industry, it can expect to pick up 25 per cent of these smokers (it has one brand out of a total of four available brands). This would give it 7·5 per cent (25 per cent of 30 per cent) of the total market the first year merely as a result of picking up its share of the random switchers, and it would keep increasing its share year by year thereafter. (Because it is smaller than its rivals, it will lose fewer customers to them by random switching than it will gain from them.) If, however, the existing three firms have five brands each, there would be fifteen brands already available and a new small firm selling one new brand could expect to pick up only one-sixteenth of the brand-switchers, giving it less than 2 per cent of the total market in the first year, and its gains in subsequent years would also be less.

Applications of the theory of entry barriers   The hypothesis that non-price competition can create barriers to entry helps to clarify two apparently paradoxical aspects of everyday industrial life: that one firm may sell many different brands of the same product, and that each firm spends considerable sums on advertising, competing against its own products as well as those of rival firms. The soap and cigarette industries provide classic examples of this behaviour; both industries contain only a few firms that sell a large number of differentiated products that compete fiercely against each other.

Part of the reason surely lies in differences among consumers' tastes. Yet another part of the reason may lie in the creation of entry barriers. Here the explanation is that technological barriers to entry are weak in these industries; a small plant can produce at an average total cost just about as low as that of a large plant.

> **Product differentiation and brand-image advertising can be used to create substantial barriers to entry where natural barriers are weak.**

To the extent that these practices raise entry barriers, they allow existing firms to move in the direction of joint profit-maximization without fear of a flood of new entrants attracted by high profits.

Oligopoly and resource allocation

Behaviour under oligopoly is much more complex than is behaviour under perfect competition or under monopoly. If oligopolists made simplistic Cournot-Nash assumptions, behaviour would be relatively easy to predict. As it is, interactions are obvious and oligopolistic firms must – and plainly do – take account of them. The equilibrium reached will then depend on each firm's conjectural variations. There can be little doubt, therefore, that oligopoly is genuinely different from either perfect competition or monopoly.

Firms in oligopolistic markets (as well as monopolies) administer their prices. The market signalling system works slightly differently when prices are determined by the market than when they are administered. Changes in the market conditions for both inputs and outputs are signalled to the perfectly competitive firm by changes in the *prices* of its inputs and its outputs. Changes in the market conditions for inputs are signalled to the oligopolist by changes in the prices of its inputs. Changes in the market conditions for the oligopolist's outputs are signalled, however, by a change in sales at the administered price.

> **The oligopolist that administers its price gets a signal when the demand for its product changes, the signal taking the form of a variation in its sales. The perfectly competitive firm receives a signal of the same change in demand through a change in the market price that it faces.**

Rises in costs of inputs will shift cost curves upward, and oligopolistic firms will be led – if the shift is not reversed – to raise price and lower output. Rises in demand will raise the sales of oligopolistic firms. Firms will then respond by increasing output, thereby increasing the quantities of society's resources that are allocated to producing that commodity.

> **The market system reallocates resources in response to changes in demand and costs in roughly the same way under oligopoly as it does under perfect competition.**

Although the market system allocates resources under oligopoly in a manner that is qualitatively similar to what happens under perfect competition, the actual allocation is not likely to be the same. Generally, oligopolistic industries will earn profits and will charge prices that exceed marginal cost (because the firms face downward-sloping demand curves and will equate marginal cost to marginal revenue, not to price). In this respect oligopoly is similar to monopoly.

There is a wide range of possible oligopolistic behaviour. Some oligopolies succeed in coming close to the joint profit-maximization that would characterize monopoly. Others compete so intensely among themselves that they approximate to competitive prices and outputs. The allocative consequences vary accordingly.

In some respects, oligopolistic industries differ from either perfect competition or monopoly; they may exhibit more price rigidity, more advertising, and more product differentiation. There *may* also be some tendency for more non-price competition than consumers want.

Oligopoly is an important market structure in today's economy because there are many industries where the *MES* is simply too large to support a perfectly competitive market. Oligopoly will not, in general, achieve the optimal allocative efficiency of perfect competition. Rivalrous oligopoly, however, may produce more satisfactory results than monopoly. The defence of oligopoly as a market form is that it may be the best of the available alternatives where the *MES* is large. The challenge to public policy is to keep oligopolists competing. Public policies having this objective are discussed in Chapter 23.

Appendix to chapter 21

The rise and fall of the theory of large-group monopolistic competition

The theory of monopolistic competition recognized that manufacturing firms typically sell differentiated products. Indeed, an impressive array of differentiated products, no one precisely the same as another, greets the buyer on any shelf of any supermarket or in any part of a large department store. Product differentiation is a fact of life. It means that every firm has some control over the price of each of its products and that it cannot sell an unlimited amount of each at its current price: the firm faces downward-sloping demand curves, not a perfectly elastic one. This is the 'monopolistic' part of monopolistic competition.

Both Chamberlin and Robinson chose to analyse a market that had freedom of entry and that contained a large group of sellers rather than a small group. This is the 'competition' part of monopolistic competition. Indeed, they maintained all the assumptions of perfect competition except the one that all firms sell a homogeneous product. In other words, they let otherwise perfectly competitive firms sell a slightly differentiated product. This little change had enormous consequences; it produced what came to be called the monopolistic competition revolution.[1]

The theory

Product differentiation means that each firm does not face a perfectly elastic demand curve for its product because some people will prefer that product

---

[1] Chamberlin devoted some space to product differentiation in markets with a few firms and to both free and blockaded entry. Yet the main thrust of the monopolistic competition revolution was in the direction of the large-group case. In the words of the historian of economic thought, Mark Blaug, 'the 12 pages in *The Theory of Monopolistic Competition* on "mutual interdependence recognized" constituted a then original contribution to the theory of oligopoly, but this was not the core of Chamberlin's book.' (*Economic Theory in Retrospect*, 3rd edn, Cambridge University Press, 1978, p. 415.)

to other products even though it is somewhat more expensive. Thus the firm will be faced with a downward-sloping but quite elastic demand curve for its product. Generally, the less differentiated the product is from its competitors, the more elastic this curve will be.

The short-run equilibrium of the firm in monopolistic competition, shown in Figure 21.1 on page 274, is the same as that of monopoly. The firm may be making profits or losses or just covering costs. Assume that the firm earns profits in the short run. What then about the long-run equilibrium of the industry? There will be an incentive for new firms to enter the industry. As more firms enter, the total demand for the product must be shared among the larger number of firms, so each can expect to have a smaller share of the market. At any given price, each firm can expect to sell less than it could before the influx of new firms. At this point Chamberlin makes the absolutely critical *assumption of symmetry*: that *the entry of one new firm will shift the demand curve for each of the firms already in the industry by the same (small) amount to the left*.

This movement will continue as long as there are profits. At equilibrium, the monopolistically competitive firm is in the zero-profit tangency solution with excess capacity of $q_c - q_L$ shown in Figure 21.1.

A zero-profit equilibrium is possible under conditions of monopolistic competition, in spite of the fact that the individual firm is faced with a downward-sloping demand curve. Each firm is forced into a position in which it has *excess capacity*. That is, it is producing a lower quantity than its capacity level. The firm in Figure 21.1(ii) could expand its output and reduce average costs, but does not make use of this productive capacity because to do so would be to reduce average revenue even more than average costs. The reason for this is that it would have to lower its price to sell the extra output, and the resulting loss of revenue would more than offset the lower cost of production.

Modern developments

A major theoretical criticism of the large-group case began with Nicholas Kaldor in the 1930s but was fully articulated only with the work by Kelvin Lancaster on the 'New Theory of Demand' in the 1970s.

Differentiated products have several characteristics, and each product can be thought of as being located in its 'characteristics space'. This can be represented by a graph in which amounts of one characteristic are measured on each axis. A new product must occupy some point in characteristic space – that is, the product must have quantities of each characteristic. Thus a new product will have some closely competing products (those whose characteristics are very similar), more less close competitors, and even more further distant competitors. Consequently the new entrant will not affect the demand curves for all the industry's products to the same degree. Closely similar products will have their demands shifted a lot, less similar products less so, and so on. *Chamberlin's symmetry assumption does not apply to products differentiated in characteristics space.*

A similar argument applies to geographic differentiation. A large city may have hundreds of chemists' shops that are only slightly differentiated from each other in all non-geographic characteristics. But each has a specific location and thus a different level of convenience to each buyer. When a new shop enters the industry at one specific location, its arrival will have a major impact on the demand curves facing chemists in nearby locations, a smaller effect on chemists further away and virtually no effect on chemists located at the other end of the city. Consequently a new shop entering such a market will not shift the demand curves of existing shops to the same degree. Nearby shops will be affected a lot, more distant shops less so, and so on. *Chamberlin's symmetry assumption does not apply to firms differentiated in geographic space.*

The above shows why Chamberlin's large-group case, where, because of the symmetry assumption, each product or shop is *equally* in competition with every other product or shop, seems hard to justify empirically. A model in which the many firms in an industry are in intense competition with only a relatively few close neighbours seems a better fit to the world of experience.[1]

[1] We have discussed these matters in more detail elsewhere in a paper that is accessible only to more advanced students. See G.C. Archibald, B.C. Eaton and R.G. Lipsey, *Address Models of Value Theory*, Papers and Proceedings of the IEA Conference on Monopolistic Competition, Ottawa, May 1982.

The above arguments would hold even if each shop or product were owned by a separate firm. Empirically, a further shortcoming of the large-group case (as observed in the text of Chapter 21) is that a large number of differentiated *products* is much more common than is a large number of differentiated *firms*. In soap or cigarettes for example there is a large number of products but each firm produces many products, so there is only a small number of firms. Also chains such as Trust Houses Forte or Boots are common in spatially differentiated industries so that although many shops is the typical case, few firms is also often typical. Thus when we look at firms, which are the decision units, rather than products, we find once again that small-group is much more common than large-group monopolistic competition in the real world. As Mark Blaug puts it (*op. cit.*, p. 415): 'The most damaging criticism that can be made against the theory of monopolistic competition is not that some of its assumptions are unrealistic but that most of the product markets that appear at first glance to conform to the requirements of the Chamberlinian tangency solution turn out on closer examination to involve the "conjectural interdependence" characteristic of oligopoly: product differentiation takes place typically in a market environment of "competition among the few".'

Consequently, the main thrust of the development of the modern theory of product differentiation has been in the small-group case: a small number of firms compete, each selling its own range of differentiated products. Indeed in modern terminology monopolistic competition has come to mean product differentiation (the monopolistic aspect) rather than large numbers (the competitive aspect), so most modern work on what is called monopolistic competition is work on the case of differentiated oligopoly (a small group of firms selling a number of differentiated products).

The modern theory has suggested its own form of the excess-capacity theorem: that firms may sometimes create more capital than they need for their own current production, the excess being a barrier to the entry of new firms. There is a difference, however. In the older theory, firms were forced into excess capacity by the impersonal market forces of entry; in the new theory, existing firms may consciously create excess capacity as a barrier to entry. This proposition, still a subject of controversy, takes us to the very frontier of current research.

Conclusion

Looking back, we see that the original theory of

monopolistic competition contributed at least two important things to the development of economics. At the time that it was first developed, perfect competition was under attack for the lack of realism of its assumptions. The theory of monopolistic competition allowed for the facts of product differentiation, of the ability of firms to influence prices and of advertising. The incorporation of these into a new theory encouraged economists to consider the question of their effects on the operation of the price system.

A second major contribution of the theory is that many economists have been profoundly influenced by it. It rekindled economists' interest in such important things as how and when firms took each other's reactions into account, what made for easy or restricted entry, and the significance to competition of different products that were roughly similar to one another.

22

Competition, oligopoly and monopoly: some comparative-static predictions

In this chapter we use comparative-static analysis to derive some implications of the theories of competition, oligopoly and monopoly. These can be viewed in two different ways. First, they are logical implications. When we derive them, we are engaged in a purely logical process of discovering what is implied by the theory's assumptions. From this point of view the truth of a certain proposition is a matter of right or wrong: the proposition either is or is not implied by the theory. This is a matter on which we can come to a definite conclusion, and the probability that errors in logic still remain in this well-worked field is quite small. Second, these implications may be regarded as empirical hypotheses. Whether or not these hypotheses are consistent with the facts is a matter for testing and, in the absence of strong empirical evidence, it is not necessary to accept the propositions as true in the empirical sense.

> **Whether or not a given proposition is implied by, or follows from, some theory, is a purely logical question that can be settled definitely without reference to facts; but whether or not a given proposition (which follows from a theory) fits the facts or is inconsistent with them can be settled only by an appeal to real-world observations.**

In the present chapter we consider the logical problem of deriving propositions from theories. In subsequent chapters we look at some problems of empirical testing. We begin by re-examining those problems of perfectly competitive industries that we first illustrated in Chapter 10. There we considered producers' co-operatives that were designed to iron out year-to-year fluctuations in incomes.

The drive to monopolize perfectly competitive industries

Cocoa producers in West Africa, wheat producers in the United States, coffee growers in Brazil, oil producers in the OPEC countries, taxi drivers in many cities and labour unions throughout the world have all sought to obtain, through collective action, some of the benefits of departing from perfect competition.

The motivation behind this drive for monopoly power is not hard to understand. The equilibrium of a perfectly competitive industry is *invariably* one in which a restriction of output and a consequent increase in price would raise the profits of all producers. At any competitive equilibrium, each firm is producing where marginal cost equals price (see page 249). But as long as the demand curve slopes downward, marginal revenue for the industry is less than price and thus also less than marginal cost. Thus, in competitive equilibrium the last unit sold necessarily contributes less to the industry's revenue than to its costs. From this we derive the basic prediction:

> **It always pays the producers in a perfectly competitive industry to enter into an output-restricting agreement.**

We shall call a producer's association formed for such a purpose a co-op.

Once an output-restricting agreement has been concluded, there is a force tending to break down the producers' co-operative behaviour. Clearly, any one firm can raise its ouput without affecting the market price. Since this firm's actions would not affect the price, its income would rise because it could sell its pre-co-op output at the post-co-op prices. Thus, unless the co-op is very carefully policed and has the power to enforce its quota restrictions on everyone's output, there will be a tendency for member firms to violate quotas once prices have been raised. Furthermore, the co-op must have power over all producers, not merely over its members; otherwise a firm could avoid the quota restrictions on its output merely by leaving the co-op.

These two tendencies are illustrated graphically in Figure 22.1. Figure 22.1 (i) represents the market conditions of supply and demand; Figure 22.1 (ii) represents the conditions of demand and cost for an individual firm. Suppose that before the co-op is formed the market is in competitive equilibrium at price p_1 and output Q_1 (where the demand curve intersects the supply curve); the individual firm is producing output q_1 and just covering costs. The co-op is formed in order to allow producers to exert a monopolistic influence on the market. By making each firm reduce its output appropriately, market output is reduced to Q_2 (where the marginal revenue curve intersects the supply curve, which is also the industry's marginal cost curve) and the price p_2 is achieved. The firm in Figure 22.1 (ii) has a quota of q_2 ($q_1/q_2 = Q_1/Q_2$), but, even though it has reduced its output, it

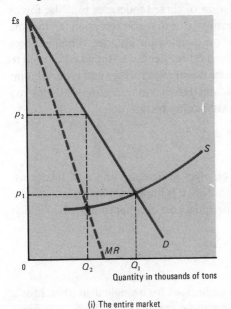

Quantity in thousands of tons

(i) The entire market

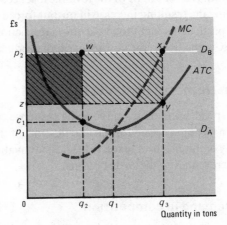

Quantity in tons

(ii) An individual producer

Fig. 22.1 The effect of output-restriction schemes

has improved its position. It is now earning profits of the amount shown by the darker section of the shaded area. This leads to our first prediction, that every firm will be better off if a co-op is formed and succeeds in raising price to p_2, than if no co-op is formed and price remains at p_1.

Once price is raised to p_2, the individual firm will want to increase its output because price is greater than its marginal cost. At q_2, price (and thus marginal revenue) exceeds marginal cost, and it follows that, left to itself, the firm will want to increase its output. It will want to move to output q_3 where marginal cost equals its marginal revenue and where it will earn the profits shown by the shaded area p_2xyz in Figure 22.1 (ii). But if everyone produces q_3 then output in Figure 22.1 (i) exceeds Q_1, price falls below p_1 and everyone makes losses. This leads to our second prediction, that each co-op member can increase its profits by violating its output quota, provided that the other members do not violate theirs.

These two predictions highlight the dilemma of the producer's co-op whether it be OPEC or a local dairy association. Each firm is better off if the co-op is formed and is effective. But each is even better off if everyone else co-operates and it does not. Yet if all cheat, all will be worse off.

> **Producers' co-ops formed to raise prices by restricting output in competitive industries will be able to raise producers' incomes, provided that they are able to enforce quotas on the outputs of all firms. Such co-ops will, however, exhibit unstable tendencies, for it will always be in the interest of any single member firm to raise its output. If many firms do so, the co-op will collapse and all firms will lose.**

The history of schemes to raise farm incomes by limiting crops bears testimony to the empirical applicability of these predictions. Crop restriction often breaks down, and prices fall as individuals exceed their quotas. The great bitterness and occasional violence that is sometimes exhibited by members of output-restriction schemes against cheaters and non-members is readily understandable. In 1983 OPEC itself was suffering from a combination of these tendencies plus the forces described in prediction 3 on page 285. As demand for oil declined due to world recession (an income effect), individual OPEC producers were tempted to cheat on their output quotas. If one country could cheat it would restore some of the revenue lost because of falling demand. But when all tried to do the same thing the resulting increase in output forced price down even further and reduced joint profits. Iran in particular sought to avoid quota restrictions, and its behaviour threatened to destroy the whole OPEC structure to the detriment of all producers including Iran.

Changes in demand and costs

We must now spend some time studying the response to changes in demand and cost functions. Although the analysis may seem formal and abstract at the outset, it is important because it sets the stage for a study of the effects of taxes, subsidies, innovations and a host of other things, all of which affect either the revenues or the costs of firms.

Changes in demand in competition

A rise in demand Figure 22.2 shows the cost and demand conditions for a single firm (i) and for a whole industry (ii) under perfect competition. When the demand curve is D_1, both the individual firm and the industry are in equilibrium at price p_1. (If you have any doubts about this, you should

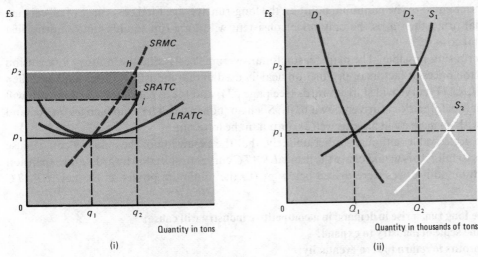

Fig. 22.2 The effects of an increase in demand under perfect competition: (i) equilibrium of a single firm; (ii) equilibrium of the industry

review Chapter 19 now.) There is no incentive for any firm to change its output, nor is there incentive for entry or exit of firms.

Now assume that the market demand curve in Figure 22.2 (ii) shifts from D_1 to D_2. This causes a shortage to develop. The shortage causes a rise in price, which in turn causes firms to increase their output. In the short run, the market price rises to p_2, total industry production rises to Q_2, and the individual firm that we are considering produces q_2. The firm will be making profits on each unit equal to the difference between the price per unit and its short-run average total cost ($q_2 h - q_2 i = hi$). Thus the firm's total profit is equal to the area of the shaded rectangle in Figure 22.2 (i).

> **In the short run, a rise in demand in a competitive industry will cause:**
> **(1) price to rise;**
> **(2) an increase in the quantity supplied by each firm and hence by the industry;**
> **(3) each firm to earn profits.**

The long-run effects follow from the third prediction. Since firms are now making profits, this industry will attract new investment. The entry of new firms will cause an increase in supply that will force the price below the previously established short-run equilibrium price p_2. Since in perfect competition all firms have access to the same technology, all firms have the same costs. Thus each new firm that enters the industry will have costs identical to those of the firm shown in Figure 22.2 (i). Thus new firms as well as old ones will be able to earn profits as long as price exceeds p_1. The process of entry will stop when price is driven back to p_1 and each original firm is producing its original quantity q_1, but the whole industry's output has expanded because there are more firms in the industry. When the expansion has come to a halt the new short-run supply curve in Figure 22.2 (ii) will be S_2, which is the sum of the marginal cost curves of the new larger number of firms in the industry. The total industry output is Q_2, which is divided between Q_1 produced by old firms and $Q_2 - Q_1$ produced by the new ones.

This leads in the long run to an expansion of output at a constant price. The argument is simple:

if p_1 is the price equal to the minimum point on the long-run average total cost curve of all existing and potential firms, then p_1 is the only price consistent with long-run equilibrium (all firms just covering total costs).

Are other results possible? The main reason for answering 'Yes' is that the industry's expansion may bid up the prices of factors of production heavily used in that industry.[1] If this happens, then each firm's $LRATC$ curve will shift upwards (see page 224) and the expansion of the industry will come to a halt before price is driven down to p_1. Such an industry will have an increase in demand associated with an increase in price as well as output in the long run.

It is also conceivable, although rather unlikely, that the expansion of the industry could cause factor prices to fall.[2] This would cause the firm's $LRATC$ curves to shift downwards, and expansion would continue until prices were driven below p_1 (to the minimum points on the new $LRATC$ curves).

In the long run, a rise in demand in a competitive industry will cause:

(1) the scale of industry to expand;

(2) profits to return to zero eventually;

(3) the new equilibrium price to be above, below or equal to the original price; but (i) constant factor prices and (ii) identical cost curves for new and old firms are sufficient to ensure that price returns to its original level.

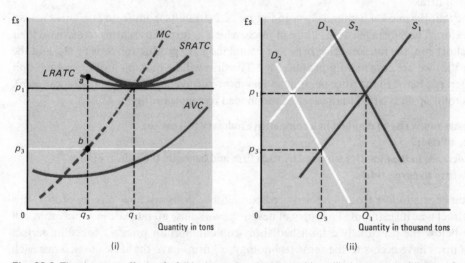

Fig. 22.3 The short-run effects of a fall in demand under competition: (i) short-run equilibrium of a firm in perfect competition; (ii) short-run equilibrium of a perfectly competitive industry

---

[1] It is also possible that costs could rise if there were real diseconomies of scale external to the firm so that with *factor prices constant* the expansion of the industry caused existing firms' $LRATC$ curves to shift upwards. This possible, but rather unlikely, case can be left for more advanced treatments that need to cover all logical possibilities.

[2] It is a well-known result in more advanced theory that if all industries have constant returns to scale (the location of minimum point on a firm's $LRATC$ curve is independent of the size of the industry) and if different industries use factors of production in different proportions, the production-possibility surface will be concave to the origin, which means that all industries will find their costs and long-run equilibrium prices rising because their factor costs rise as they expand.

A fall in demand Next consider a fall in demand. Figure 22.3 shows the firm and industry in their initial long-run equilibrium with price at p_1. When demand falls to D_2, a glut of the commodity is created; supply exceeds demand at the original price p_1; price then falls to p_3. At price p_1, the individual firm was just covering all opportunity costs. At the new price, p_3, the firm will produce q_3, the output for which marginal cost equals marginal revenue.

Individual firms will now be suffering losses. Average total cost is q_3a, and average revenue is q_3b $(= p_3)$; losses per unit are ba. Would it not be worth while to close down its operations altogether, instead of running at a loss? The answer to this is 'No'. We have already seen, on page 236, that the profit-maximizing firm should continue producing in the short run as long as price exceeds average variable costs.

We conclude, therefore, that if price falls below average total cost but exceeds average variable cost, the firm will make losses, but will stay in production at least in the short run. Only if price falls below average variable cost will the firm exit.

> **In the short run, a fall in demand in a competitive industry will cause:**
> **(1) price to fall;**
> **(2) a decrease in the quantity supplied by each firm and hence by the industry;**
> **(3) each firm to make losses;**
> **(4) firms to cease production immediately if they are unable to cover their variable costs of production.**

The long-run effects follow from the third prediction. Since firms in the industry are not covering all costs, the industry is not an attractive place in which to invest. No new capital will enter the industry; as old plant and equipment wear out, it will not be replaced. Thus the industry will contract. The short-run supply curve, showing how production varies with price, capital equipment held constant, shifts to the left. But as the supply diminishes, the price of the product rises. This price rise will continue until the firms remaining in the industry can cover their total costs.

The analysis for a rise in demand applies in the long run with only minor changes. If factor prices remain constant, then price must return to p_1 before the remaining firms can reach the minimum points on their $LRATC$ curves. If, however, the contraction of the industry causes a fall in the prices of factors of production used especially heavily by the industry, the cost curves of the remaining firms will shift down and price need not rise as far as p_1 before costs can be covered, thus stopping further contraction. In the unlikely event that the contraction causes the industry's heavily used factors to rise in price, cost curves rise and price must rise above p_1 before the remaining firms can cover their costs.

> **In the long run, a fall in demand in a competitive industry will cause:**
> **(1) the scale of the industry to contract;**
> **(2) losses to be eliminated eventually;**
> **(3) price to be above, below or equal to its original level; but (i) constant factor prices and (ii) identical cost curves for all firms are sufficient to ensure that price returns to its original level.**

Changes in demand in oligopoly

Once we leave perfect competition it is necessary to distinguish short-run cyclical fluctuations in demand from changes that are perceived to be more long lasting. We saw in Chapter 21 that oligopolies tend to adjust quantity rather than price when demand fluctuates in the short term. Thus cyclical fluctuations in demand cause output to change at a (more or less) constant price in oligopolistic industries.

Long-term changes in demand lead to more familiar adjustments. Permanent decreases in demand will cause exit of capital from the industry and a rise or a fall in price depending on what happens to the costs of the remaining firms and their degree of competition. Permanent increases in demand will cause an entry of capital to the industry and a rise or a fall in price depending on what happens to firms' costs and to the degree of competition.

Changes in demand in monopoly

Short-term cyclical fluctuations have the same effect as in oligopoly and for the same reasons: it does not pay the monopolist to vary price as demand varies cyclically.

Now consider a shift in demand that is assumed to be of a more permanent nature. On page 264, in the section on the absence of a supply curve under monopoly, we saw that we cannot predict that a rise in demand will always cause an increase in both the price and output of a monopolist, even in the short run. It is possible, provided that the elasticity of demand changes sufficiently, for a rise in demand to cause a fall either in price or in output.

At this level of generality, we are left with the implication that a rise in demand for a monopoly can cause both its price and its output to rise, but that either price or output might fall. This may seem a disappointingly vague conclusion, but it is all that the theory implies. In order to get a more specific prediction we need to know more about the demand curve than that it merely slopes downwards. If, for example, we know the slopes of the demand curves before and after the shift, we can make a definite prediction.

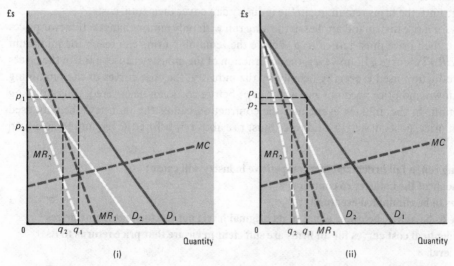

Fig. 22.4 (i) A parallel shift in the monopolist's demand curve changes the price and quantity in the same direction as the change in demand; (ii) a pivoting of the monopolist's demand curve through the price intercept changes the price and quantity in the same direction as the change in demand

There are some cases in which predictions are possible: (1) every point on the demand curve shifts by the same amount and (2) the demand curve pivots through its point of intersection on the price axis. In both of these cases price and quantity rise when demand rises, and fall when demand falls. These cases are important because they can be adapted to study the effects of a per-unit and an *ad valorem* tax or subsidy on the monopolist's output. The second case also arises if the market expands because of the addition of new customers with the same tastes as those initially in the market. They are illustrated in Figure 22.4 (i) and (ii).

Changes in costs

Competition Consider a case in which marginal costs are reduced by a given amount at all levels of output for all firms. This is shown by a downward shift in the marginal cost curves. In a competitive industry the short-run supply curve will shift downwards by the amount of the downward shift in the firm's marginal cost curves, and this will lead to a greater output at a lower price. But the price will fall by less than the vertical downward shift in the marginal cost curve, while profits will now be earned because of the lower costs of production.

> **In the short run under perfect competition, a fall in variable cost causes price to fall but by less than the reduction in marginal cost. The benefit of the reduction in cost is thus shared between the consumers, in terms of lower prices, and the producers, in terms of higher profits.**

In the long run, however, profits cannot persist in an industry having freedom of entry. New firms will enter the industry, and this influx will increase output and drive price down until all profits are eliminated.

> **In the long run under perfect competition, all of the benefits of lower costs are passed on to consumers in terms of higher output and lower prices.**

The case of a rise in costs is just the reverse, and in the short run the effects will be shared between consumers, in terms of higher prices, and producers, in terms of losses. In the long run, however, firms will leave the industry until those remaining can cover all their costs. Therefore, the effects of higher costs are borne fully by consumers in terms of lower output and higher prices in the long run.

Oligopoly In oligopoly a fall in costs yields a fall in the profit-maximizing price at normal capacity output. Therefore price will fall and output will rise. Also profits will rise so that once again pressure may occur for entry. A battle may then ensue between firms desiring entry and existing firms pursuing entry-barring strategies.

Monopoly In a monopoly, a fall in marginal costs will cause a reduction in price and an increase in output. (You should draw a graph to illustrate this for yourself.) Thus, the direction of the change in price and output in response to a change in cost is the same in monopoly as in perfect competition. But the magnitude of the change will be less in monopoly than in competition. Since a monopolist necessarily has barriers to entry (or he wouldn't be a monopolist), the higher profit that he earns as a result of a fall in his costs does *not* attract new entrants whose competition will drive profits to their original level.

> **In monopoly the effects of rising or falling costs are shared between the consumers, in terms of price and output variations, and the producers, in terms of profit variations both in the short run and in the long run.**

We now have a powerful tool at our command: once we can relate anything in which we are interested to a change in either costs or revenues, we have a series of predictions already worked out. We shall see examples of how this can be done in the next section of this chapter and in the following chapter.

The effect of taxes on price and output

There are many kinds of taxes which affect the costs of firms. We shall consider only three of them here: a tax that is a fixed amount per unit produced; a tax that is a fixed amount; and a tax that is a fixed percentage of profits. The first is called a per-unit tax, the second a lump-sum tax and the third a profits tax.

Per-unit tax   A per-unit tax increases the cost of producing each unit by the amount of the tax. The marginal cost curve of every firm shifts vertically upwards by the amount of the tax. In perfect competition, this means that the industry supply curve shifts upward by the amount of the tax. Now all we need is to refer to the results of the previous section in order to derive the required predictions.

> **The effects of a per-unit tax on the output of a competitive industry are:**
> **(1) in the short run, the price will rise but by less than the amount of the tax, so that the burden will be shared by consumers and producers;**
> **(2) in the long run, the industry will contract, profits will return to normal and the whole burden will fall on consumers;**
> **(3) if cost curves of firms remaining in the industry are unaffected by the contraction in the size of the industry, price will rise in the long run by the full amount of the tax.**

The second of the above predictions is an example of a most important general prediction: in an industry with freedom of entry or exit, profits (as the term is defined in economics) must be forced to zero in the long run. Thus, any temporary advantage or disadvantage given to the industry by government policy, by private conniving or by anything else, must be dissipated in the long run, since free entry and exit will ensure that surviving firms earn zero profits.

> **Government intervention in an industry with freedom of entry and exit can influence the size of the industry, the total volume of its sales, and the price at which its goods are sold; but intervention cannot influence the long-run profitability of the firms that remain in the industry.**

Many a government policy has started out to raise the profitability of a particular industry and only ended up increasing the number of firms operating at an unchanged level of profits.

Although the monopolist has no supply curve, the tax does shift his marginal cost curve. The analysis given in the chapter allows us to state the following:

> **In the short run and in the long run, the burden of a tax per unit on a monopoly will be shared between consumers, in terms of lower output and higher prices, and the producer, in terms of lower profits.**

Lump-sum tax Lump-sum taxes increase the fixed costs of the firm but do not increase marginal costs. The short-run effects on price and output of a change in fixed costs is zero, for firms in any market structure. Since both marginal costs and marginal revenues remain unchanged, the profit-maximizing level of output cannot be affected. Hence we deduce the implication:

> **A lump-sum tax leaves price and output unchanged in the short run unless the tax is so high that it causes firms simply to abandon production at once.**

The long-run effects of a lump-sum tax differ between monopolistic and competitive industries. Consider monopoly first. Assuming that the firm was previously making profits, the tax merely reduces the level of these profits. But, since the monopolist was making as much money as he possibly could before the tax, there is nothing that he can do to shift any of the tax burden onto his customers.

> **In the long run, the lump-sum tax has no effect on a monopolist's price and output.**

(Of course, if the tax is so large that, even at the profit-maximizing output, profits become negative, the monopolist will cease production in the long run.)

In perfect competition, the lump-sum tax will have a long-run effect. If the industry was in equilibrium with zero profits before the tax was instituted, then the tax will cause losses. Although nothing will happen in the short run to price and output, equipment will not be replaced as it wears out. Thus, in the long run, the industry will contract, and price will rise until the *whole tax* has been passed on to consumers and the firms remaining in the industry are again covering total costs.

> **A lump-sum tax will have no effect on a competitive industry in the short run, but in the long run it will cause the exit of firms; output will fall and price will rise until the whole of the tax is borne by consumers.**

Profits tax A famous prediction is that a tax on profits (in the economist's sense) will have no effect on price and output. Let us first see how the prediction is derived and then consider its application to real-world situations.

In perfect competition there are no profits in long-run equilibrium. Since profits taxes would not be paid by a perfectly competitive firm when it was in long-run equilibrium, it follows that the existence of the tax would not affect the firm's long-run behaviour. A monopoly firm usually earns profits in the long run and therefore would pay the profits tax. The tax would reduce its profits but would not cause the firm to alter its quantity produced nor (hence) its price. This is illustrated in Figure 22.5, in which profits are shown as varying with the quantity the monopolist sells. (Since the

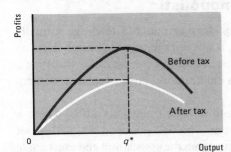

Fig. 22.5 A tax on pure profits will affect neither price nor output

firm faces a downward-sloping demand curve, every quantity implies a particular price.) Before the profits tax, the firm maximized profits by selling the quantity q^*. Now assume that a 20 per cent profits tax is imposed. Since every level of output is associated with 20 per cent less profit than before, the level of output, q^*, that produced the highest profits before the tax would still do so after the tax was imposed. Since q^* would remain the profit-maximizing output, the monopolist's price would not change.

A tax on profit, as it is defined in economics, affects neither price nor output in perfect competition and in monopoly. Hence it has no effect on the allocation of resources.

Does this prediction apply to real-world 'profit taxes'? The answer is an emphatic 'No' because profits as they are defined in tax law are very different from profits as defined in economics. In particular the tax-law definition includes earnings of the factor of production, capital, and the reward for risk-taking. To economists these are costs but for tax purposes they are profits.

Consider some of the consequences of such 'profits' taxes. First, perfectly competitive firms will pay 'profits' taxes even in long-run equilibrium, since they use capital and must earn enough money to pay a return on it. Second, the tax will affect costs differently in different industries. Assume that one industry is very labour-intensive, so that 90 per cent of its costs of production go to wages and only 10 per cent to capital and other factors, while another industry is very capital-intensive, so that fully 50 per cent of its costs (in the economist's sense) are a return to capital. The 'profits' tax will take a small bite of the total earnings of the first industry and a large bite of those of the second industry. If the industries were equally profitable (in the economist's sense) before the 'profits' tax, they would not be afterwards, and producers would be attracted into the first industry and out of the second one. This would cause prices to change until both industries became equally profitable, after which no further movement would occur.

A tax on profit as it is defined in tax law does not leave the allocation of resources unaffected.

Many further ways in which real-world taxes on profits influence the allocation of resources could be mentioned, but enough has been said to suggest that those who fail to make the distinction between taxes levied on what the economist means by profits and taxes levied on what the tax inspector means by profits will make predictions about the real world that do not in fact follow from their own theory. Clearly, great care must be taken when the same term is given one meaning by economists and another meaning by the general public or by government officials.

A competitive industry that becomes monopolistic

As well as yielding certain testable predictions based on the minimal amount of knowledge normally assumed, the theory of the firm and industry provides a framework into which more detailed knowledge can be fitted. In this section we shall consider one example of the use of the theory in a specific context. This example, although hypothetical, is not unlike many actual situations, particularly those in the retail trades.

Assume that in a particular city the barbers all belong to a single trade association. There is freedom of entry into the industry in the sense that anyone who has obtained a stated set of qualifications can set up as a barber. All barbers, however, must join the association and must abide by its rules. The association sets the price of haircuts and strictly enforces this single price.

Periodically the association raises the fixed price of haircuts in an attempt to raise the incomes of its members. The association is strong enough to prevent any illicit price-cutting and to resist all attempts to secede. The question is: will the barbers succeed in raising their incomes by raising the price of haircuts? If you were a consulting economist called in to advise the barbers' association, what would you predict to be the consequences of this price rise? Try to develop these predictions for yourself before you read on.

Clearly we need to distinguish between the short- and the long-run effects of this increase in the price of haircuts. In the short run the number of barbers is fixed. Thus in the short run the answer is simple enough: it all depends on the elasticity of the demand for haircuts. If the demand elasticity is less than one, total expenditure on haircuts will rise and so, therefore, will the income of barbers; if demand elasticity exceeds one, the barbers' incomes will fall. The problem in the short run amounts to that of getting some empirical knowledge about the elasticity of demand for haircuts. If you were actually advising the barbers' organization you might be lucky enough to be able to refer to a full-scale econometric study of demand. In the case of haircuts this is unlikely and you would probably have to try to gain some idea of demand elasticity by studying the effects of changes in haircut prices either at other times or in other places. We cannot go into this matter except to mention that you should not fall into the trap of reasoning as follows: 'Haircuts are a necessity, for no one goes without one. Therefore the demand for haircuts will be almost perfectly inelastic.' You should easily spot the fallacy in this argument. There are many reasons why the demand for haircuts is not perfectly inelastic. For example, the time between haircuts is by no means a constant. An increase in the average period between haircuts from three to four weeks would cause a 28·5 per cent decline in demand; if this change in habits were occasioned by a 15 per cent rise in price, then the demand elasticity over this price range would be 1·9! (We use here the procedure recommended on page 100 where the percentage change is taken as the actual change over the *average* of the new and the old prices.) Furthermore, habits can change drastically, as the change in fashion in the 1960s in favour of long hair shows. Sometimes such changes may be caused by non-economic factors, but they can also occur in response to a price change.

Assume, however, that, on the basis of the best available evidence, you estimate the elasticity of demand *over the relevant price range* to be 0·3. You then predict that the barbers will be successful in the short run; a 20 per cent rise in price will be met by a 6 per cent fall in custom, so that total barbers' revenue will rise by about 15 per cent. In predicting the consequences you would also need to estimate the length of the short run for this industry (a couple of years?).

Now what about the long run? If barbers were just covering all costs before the price change, they will now be earning profits. Barbering will become an attractive trade relative to others requiring equal skill and training, and there will be an inflow of barbers into the industry. As the number of barbers rises, the same amount of business must be shared among more firms, so that a typical barber will find a steady decrease in the amount of trade that he does. His profits will thus decrease. Profits may also be squeezed from another direction. Faced with increasing excess capacity – a typical barber could handle much more business than does in fact come his way – barbers may compete against each other for the limited number of customers. Since they are unable to compete through price cuts, they can only compete in service. They may redecorate their shops and buy expensive magazines. In these ways competition will raise costs. Thus, the profits of the individual barber will be attacked from two directions: falling revenues and rising costs. This movement will continue until barbers are once again just covering all costs. After which there will be no further attraction to new entrants. The industry will settle down in a new position of long-run equilibrium in which individual barbers are just covering all of their opportunity costs. There will be more barbers than in the original situation, but each barber will be working a lower fraction of the day and will be idle for a larger fraction (i.e., there will be excess capacity); the total number of haircuts given by each will be diminished, and possibly the level of costs and service will have increased. Thus your report would say 'You may succeed in the short run (if demand is sufficiently inelastic) but the policy is bound to be self-defeating in the long run.'

The general moral of the story is now familiar:

> **If you cannot control entry, you cannot succeed in earning profits in the long run. If price competition is ruled out, then profits will be driven down by the creation of excess capacity. Producers' associations that maintain positive profits must succeed in restricting entry.**

The predictions of the theory of the firm and industry

In this chapter we have developed a number of quite general predictions of the theory of the firm and industry, and we have also illustrated the use of the theory in yielding predictions after certain specific information has been added to its general assumptions. It is currently fashionable to emphasize the inadequacies and the failures of the traditional theory of the firm. Such shortcomings, real though they are, should not obscure the fact that this theory is an outstanding intellectual achievement. The theory of perfect competition shows in a quite general way how a large number of separate profit-maximizing firms can, with no conscious co-ordination, produce an equilibrium which depends only on the 'technical data' of demand and costs. Individual attitudes of producers, and a host of other factors, are successfully ignored, and an equilibrium is shown to follow solely from the conditions of costs and demand. The analysis extends *mutatis mutandis* to the cases of monopolistic competition and monopoly. It does not extend so easily, however, to oligopoly. In the case of competition among the few, it is no longer true that the solution depends only on the 'objective' factors of costs and market demand. The attitudes of each competitor to the stratagems of his few opponents becomes important, and, for the same costs and market demand, the equilibrium of the industry will vary considerably as the psychology of the competitors varies. It is here that the traditional theory has had the least success. A great burst of recent theorizing on small-group monopolistic competition (i.e., oligopolies with differentiated products) may hopefully yield some real advances in this area.

The consumer goods with which the ordinary citizen is most familiar – motorcars, radios, TV sets, washing machines, cookers etc. – are mostly produced by oligopolistic industries. For this reason we must beware of reaching the false conclusion that the perfectly competitive model is inapplicable to all real markets. This is emphatically not so. Markets where buyers and sellers adjust quantities to a given price that they cannot change by their own individual efforts abound in the economy. Foreign-exchange markets, markets for raw materials, markets for many agricultural commodities, real estate, most futures markets, the markets for gold and other precious metals and securities markets are but a few whose behaviour is comprehensible with, but makes no sense without, the basic model of perfect competition (possibly augmented by one or two specific additional assumptions to catch the key institutional details of each case).

Manufactured consumer goods are, as already mentioned, dominated by oligopolistic industries. Retail trades and many service industries were once thought to come close to the conditions of monopolistic competition in that there is free entry, a large number of competing firms and product differentiation (the person who provides the service matters, and each person is different). When consideration is given to their spatial differentiation, a model of overlapping oligopolies seems closer to the mark, however, than does that of large-group monopolistic competition.

Clearly, the whole armoury of market forms is relevant to our economy. Happily, as illustrated in this chapter, existing theories do make many important predictions about how our economy behaves. Unhappily, however, there are all too many situations for which current theory does not provide clear predictions.

23

Competition, oligopoly and monopoly: some predictions about performance

Monopoly has been regarded with suspicion for a very long time. Is the hostility towards monopoly justified? In this chapter we shall first consider the case for choosing between the two polar forms of monopoly and perfect competition. We shall then go on to consider policy problems that relate to the market forms in between these two extremes.

The case for preferring perfect competition to monopoly

The classical anti-monopoly case is based first on establishing the differences in behaviour between a competitive and a monopolized industry, and second on the argument that there are clear reasons for preferring the results of perfect competition to those of monopoly. This case is based on the static theory of resource allocation *within the context of a given technology*. It is based, in other words, on comparative-static analysis of long-run situations. We shall see in the second part of this chapter that serious doubts about the validity of the case arise when it is transferred to the very long run.

Price and output under monopoly and perfect competition

The comparison that we need here was first made in the first section of Chapter 22, so that only a brief rehearsal is given now. Equilibrium under perfect competition occurs where supply equals

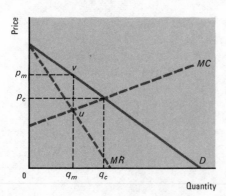

Fig. 23.1 The effect on price and output of the monopolization of a perfectly competitive industry

demand. Since the supply curve is the sum of the marginal cost curves, it follows that in equilibrium, marginal cost equals price. This is illustrated in Figure 23.1. The competitive supply curve is labelled *MC* to remind us that it is the sum of the marginal cost curves of the individual firms; the competitive output is q_c and the competitive price is p_c.

Now assume that this industry is monopolized when a single firm buys out all the individual producers. Further assume that each plant's cost curve is unaffected by this change. In other words, assume that there are neither economies nor diseconomies resulting from the co-ordinated planning of production by a single unit. This means that the marginal cost will be the same to the monopolist as to the competitive industry: the competitive industry's supply curve will be the marginal cost curve to the monopolist. But the monopolist who seeks to maximize profits will equate marginal cost to marginal revenue , not to price. The output of the industry falls from q_c to q_m, while the price rises from p_c to p_m.

> **A monopolist facing the same costs and market demand as a competitive industry will have a lower output and a higher price than the competitive industry.**

Are we justified in saying that a lower-price, higher-output situation is in any sense better than the reverse? We cannot go into this inquiry in any detail here, and we shall have to satisfy ourselves with a rather intuitive statement of why the allocation of resources resulting from perfect competition can be regarded as superior to that resulting from monopoly.

The efficiency of perfect competition

Because resources are scarce, wasted resources imply that households' consumption is not as high as it might be. The most obvious way to waste resources is not to use them at all. When labour is unemployed and factories lie idle, as occurs in serious recessions, their potential current output is lost. If these resources could be re-employed, total output would be increased and hence everyone could be made better off.

But full employment of resources by itself is not enough to ensure the resources are not wasted. Even when resources are fully employed, they may be used inefficiently. Consider two possible sources of inefficiency. First, if the industry's output is not produced at its lowest possible cost, then resources are being wasted. Less costly methods could be adopted, and the resources saved could then be used to produce other goods. If, for example, an industry achieves its monthly production of 30,000 pairs of shoes at a resource cost of £400,000 when it could have been achieved at a cost of only £350,000, resources are being used inefficiently. If the lower-cost method had been used, £50,000 worth of other commodities could have been produced each month by transferring the resources saved to their best alternative uses.

Second, if too much of one product and too little of another is produced, resources are also being used inefficiently. To take an extreme example, say that so many shoes are produced that their *marginal* utility reaches zero, while the marginal utility of coats remains positive at the current level of output. Since no one places any value on the last pair of shoes produced, while everyone places a positive value on an additional coat, no consumer will be made worse off by reducing the output of shoes; yet some consumers will be made better off by using the resources to increase the production of coats.

These examples suggest that we must refine our ideas of the waste of resources beyond the simple notion of ensuring that all resources are used. Economists have a precise definition of efficiency and inefficiency in resource use:

> **Resources are said to be used *inefficiently* when it would be *possible* by using them differently to make at least one household better off without making any household worse off. Conversely, resources are said to be used *efficiently* when it is *impossible* by using them differently to make any one household better off without making at least one other household worse off.**

Inefficiency implies that we could help someone without hurting someone else. Efficiency implies that we cannot. When resources are already being used efficiently, we can only make one household better off at the cost of making another household worse off. Efficiency in the use of resources is often called PARETO-EFFICIENCY or PARETO-OPTIMALITY, in honour of the great Italian economist Vilfredo Pareto (1848–1923), who pioneered the study of efficiency.

Productive efficiency This obtains when the industry's output is produced at the lowest possible cost. If this does not hold, more resources are being used in producing the output than is necessary. Achieving productive efficiency requires fulfilling two conditions. The first is that whatever output the *firm* selects must be produced at the lowest possible cost of producing that level of output. Otherwise more resources will be used for this output than are necessary. This condition will be fulfilled by *any* profit-maximizing firm. A firm is obviously not maximizing its profits when it produces its desired output at a higher cost than is necessary.

The second condition is that the costs of producing the *industry* output should be as low as possible. This condition is fulfilled when every firm in the industry has the same (rising) marginal cost. If this were not so, costs could be reduced by reducing production of the firm with the highest marginal cost and increasing production of the firm with the lowest marginal cost. This condition is automatically fulfilled under perfect competition because, as we saw on page 250, when a perfectly competitive industry is in long-run equilibrium, every firm is producing at the minimum point on its long-run average total cost curve, at which point every firm's marginal cost is equal to the price of the product.

Allocative efficiency This concerns the appropriate bundle of commodities to be produced in the whole economy. Resources are obviously not being used efficiently when they are being used to produce products that no one wants. ALLOCATIVE EFFICIENCY refers to the allocation of resources among the economy's various industries; it obtains when it is *impossible* to change that allocation in such a way as to make someone better off without making someone else worse off.

What is the right bundle? How many shoes and how many coats should be produced for allocative efficiency? The answer is that (under certain conditions that we shall specify later) the allocation of resources to any one commodity is efficient when its price is equal to its marginal cost of production, that is, $p = MC$. This rather subtle condition has been one of the most influential ideas in the whole of economics. To understand it, we need to remind ourselves of two points established earlier: first, the price of any commodity indicates the value that each household places on the last unit of the commodity that it consumes per period; second, marginal cost indicates the value that the resources used to produce the marginal unit of output would have in their best alternative uses.

The first proposition follows directly from marginal utility theory (see pp. 167–8). A household will go on increasing its rate of consumption of a commodity until the *marginal* valuation that it puts on the commodity is equal to its price. The household gets a consumers' surplus on all but the marginal unit because it values them more than the price it has to pay. On the marginal unit, however, it only 'breaks even' because the valuation placed on it is just equal to its price.

The second proposition follows from the nature of opportunity cost. The marginal cost of producing some commodity is the opportunity cost of the resources used. Opportunity cost means the value of the resources in their best alternative uses.

To see how these propositions fit together, assume that shoes sell for £30 a pair but have a marginal production cost of £40. If one less pair of shoes were produced, the value that households place on the pair of shoes not produced would be £30. But by the meaning of opportunity cost, the resources that would have been used to produce that pair of shoes could instead produce other goods (say a coat) valued at £40. If society can give up something its members value at £30 and get in return something its members value at £40, the original allocation of resources is inefficient in the sense that someone can be made better off, and no one need be worse off. This is easy to see when the same household gives up the shoes and gets the coat. But it follows even when different households are involved, for the gaining household could compensate the losing household and still come out ahead.[1]

Assume next that shoe production is cut back until the price of a pair of shoes rises from £30 to £35 while its marginal cost falls from £40 to £35. The efficiency condition is now fulfilled in shoe production because $p = MC$ ($= £35$). Now if one less pair of shoes were produced, £35 worth of shoes would be sacrificed while at most £35 worth of other commodities could be produced with the freed resources. In this situation, the allocation of resources to shoe production is efficient because it is not possible to change it and make someone better off without necessarily making someone else worse off. If one household were to sacrifice the pair of shoes, it would give up goods worth £35 and would then have to get all of the new production of the alternative commodity produced just to break even. The household cannot gain without making another household worse off. The same argument can be repeated for every commodity, and it leads to this conclusion:

The allocation of resources among commodities is efficient when, for each commodity, price equals marginal cost.

Allocative efficiency is thus satisfied when $p = MC$ in all industries. Since $p = MC$ in equilibrium for every industry in perfect competition, it follows that:

universal perfect competition fulfils the condition for allocative efficiency by ensuring that price equals marginal cost in every industry.

A graphic interpretation of allocative efficiency   Consider a competitive industry where forces of demand and supply establish a competitive price. Because the industry supply curve represents the sum of the marginal cost curves of the firms in the industry, the market-clearing price is the one at which $p = MC$. In Figure 23.2, such a price is shown as p^*, and the corresponding output is q^*.

---

[1] Efficiency thus relates to potential welfare: a move towards efficiency makes it possible, if compensation were paid, to make someone better off and no one worse off. If compensation is not paid, a move towards efficiency may make some better off and others worse off.

For every unit produced up to this output, the value consumers would be willing to pay, as shown by the demand curve, is greater that the opportunity cost of the resources used to produce it, as shown by the $S = MC$ curve.

The two shaded areas represent the excess of consumer valuation over opportunity cost. The equilibrium price p^* divides the total shaded area into two parts. The dark shaded area above p^* is the consumers' surplus that we have already encountered. The light shaded area below p^* but above MC is a new, but analogous concept called PRODUCERS' SURPLUS. It is the excess of producers' receipts over the minimum that would have to be paid to persuade them to produce a given quantity. Since a firm will produce any unit that will at least cover its marginal cost, all that needs to be paid to call forth q^* units of production is the area below the marginal cost curve. Since actual receipts are the whole area p^* *times* q^*, the producers' surplus is the light shaded area between the MC curve and the price p^*.

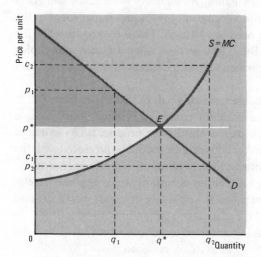

Fig. 23.2 The allocative efficiency of perfect competition   **Fig. 23.3** The allocative inefficiency of monopoly

The two shaded areas together represent the *sum* of consumers' surplus and producers' surplus. *Allocative efficiency* is achieved when the sum of the surpluses is maximized. This occurs at the output q^*, where $p = MC$. For any output less than q^*, such as q_1, a slight increase in output toward q^* would lead to an addition to both consumers' and producers' surplus. This is because at the level of output q_1, consumers' valuation of the commodity, p_1, exceeds the opportunity cost of producing it, c_1. For any output greater than q^* this is not the case. At q_2 for example, the last unit costs c_2 to produce but consumers only value it at p_2. Producing units beyond q^* would subtract from the sum of producers' and consumers' surpluses.

Thus:

> **producers' plus consumers' surplus is maximized *only* at output q^*. If some authority were to instruct producers to 'maximize the sum of producers' and consumers' surpluses', producers would produce every unit up to q^*. The perfectly competitive market price, p^*, provides exactly that signal.**

The inefficiency of monopoly

The other side of the coin to the allocative efficiency of perfect competition is the allocative inefficiency of monopoly. Let us look first, however, at the productive efficiency of monopoly.

Productive efficiency A profit-maximizing monopoly will meet the first condition of productive efficiency: whatever output it chooses, will be produced at the lowest possible cost. A monopoly that does not minimize its costs of producing its given output cannot be maximizing its profits. The second condition, that all firms in the industry should have the same long-run marginal costs, does not apply since there is only one firm under monopoly. Thus all profit-maximizing monopolies will achieve productive efficiency.

Allocative inefficiency Allocative efficiency requires that price equals marginal cost so that consumers pay for the last unit purchased an amount just equal to the opportunity cost of producing that unit. But at the monopoly output, price is greater than marginal cost. Thus consumers pay for the last unit an amount that exceeds the opportunity cost of producing it.

In Figure 23.3, for example, the monopolist's profit-maximizing output of q_M is produced at a marginal cost of c_M and sold for the much higher price of p_M (yielding, however, a marginal revenue of c_M). At that output, consumers put a value of p_M on the last unit produced, but the resources used to produce that last unit have a lower value, c_M, in their best alternative uses. Every unit between q_M and q^* would cost less to produce than the value consumers place on it. Output q_M is thus allocatively inefficient. The dark shaded area shows the gain in consumers' *plus* producers' surpluses that would occur if price were reduced to p^* and production increased to q^*. It is sometimes described as the deadweight loss due to the allocative inefficiency of monopoly.

The allocative inefficiency of oligopoly

Note that the argument for allocative inefficiency applies to oligopolies and all other markets where firms face downward-sloping demand curves. In all such situations marginal revenue will be less than price and when MR is equated with marginal cost this will leave MC less than price as well. This implies allocative inefficiency.

Requirements for an optimum allocation of resources to be achieved

Achieving an optimum allocation of resources requires, among other things, that the following conditions be met.

(1) *For an optimal allocation of resources under perfect competition, there should be no divergence between private and social cost anywhere in the economy.* From society's point of view it pays to produce a good up to the point at which the revenue gained from the last unit equals the opportunity cost of making it, only if the firms' private costs reflect the opportunity costs to society of using the resources elsewhere, and if the firms' private revenues reflect the gains to society of having an extra unit of this good produced. We shall see in Chapter 32 that social and private costs often diverge. This critical condition is therefore by no means always fulfilled.

(2) *For an optimal allocation of resources, there should be perfect competition in all sectors of the economy, therefore ensuring that marginal cost will equal price everywhere.* This is sometimes called

pluperfect competition. If it does not exist, we have no idea what the effect will be of making marginal cost equal marginal revenue somewhere in the economy. Specifically, if in a world of mixed market structures, we break up one monopoly and make it into a competitive industry, we have no general presumption even in a theoretical model that this will move us closer to an optimum position.[1]

(3) *For an optimal allocation of resources under perfect competition, there should be no external economies or diseconomies of scale.* An external economy or diseconomy is beyond the influence of a single firm and thus does not enter into the firm's calculations, even though it may be important for society.

It is clear that these conditions for an optimal allocation of resources are not fulfilled in any modern economy. In particular, perfect competition does not prevail everywhere, since many firms face downward-sloping demand curves. These firms will not take production to the point where marginal cost equals price.

The theory of the optimal allocation of resources under perfect competition provides very little firm guidance to practical policy concerning market intervention by the central authorities. Economic theory does *not* predict that in our societies of mixed market structures any increase in the degree of competitiveness will necessarily increase the efficiency of resource allocation. To evaluate current policy we need to know the effect on the efficiency of resource allocation of intervention to produce a little more or a little less competition in a few sectors of the economy. Unfortunately this is just what we cannot do in general, and every case must be studied and evaluated in terms of its own specific circumstances.

The political appeal of perfect competition

To someone who believes in the individual and fears all power groups,[2] the perfectly competitive model is almost too good to be true. In the perfectly competitive world, no single firm and no single consumer has any power over the market whatsoever. Both individual consumers and individual producers are members of a group of many similar consumers and producers, and no single one of them can affect the market. Individually they are passive quantity adjustors. If we add to this the assumption that firms are profit-maximizers, all firms become passive responders to market signals, always doing what is most desirable from the society's point of view. The great impersonal force of the market produces an appropriate response to every important change. If, for example, tastes change, prices will change and the allocation of resources will move in the appropriate direction. But throughout the whole process, no one will have any power over anyone else. Millions of firms are reacting to the same price changes. If one refuses to react, there will be countless other profit-maximizing firms eager to make the appropriate changes. If one firm refuses to take coloured employees or takes any other decision based on prejudice, there will be millions of other firms that

---

[1] This important proposition upsets much of the basis of piecemeal welfare economics. We know how to identify the best of all possible worlds (from the limited point of view of the optimum we are discussing), but we have little clear idea how to order two states of the very imperfect world in which we live. If this were not so economists could not disagree as much as they do about specific policy measures. More advanced students may wish to consult one of the early demonstrations of this proposition given in R. G. Lipsey and K. J. Lancaster, 'The General Theory of Second Best', *The Review of Economic Studies*, Vol. XXIV, No. 63, 1956–7.

[2] As Lord Acton put it a long time ago, 'power tends to corrupt and absolute power corrupts absolutely.'

will recognize that profit-maximization is not consistent with discrimination on the basis of race, colour or creed or anything other than how hard a man is prepared to work.

It is a noble model: no one has power over anyone, and yet the system behaves in a systematic and purposeful way. Many will feel that it is a pity that it corresponds so imperfectly to reality as we know it today. Not surprisingly, some people still cling tenaciously to the belief that the perfectly competitive model describes the world in which we live; so many problems would disappear if only it did.

Unsettled questions concerning alternative market structures

The classical condemnation of non-competitive forms of behaviour was based on the belief that the alternative to monopoly was perfect competition. Today we realize that very often the effective choice is not between monopoly and perfect competition, but between more or less oligopoly, so that we are not sure what effects a specific intervention will have on price and output. Thus, even if we accept the perfectly competitive result as being more desirable than a completely monopolistic one, this does not in itself tell us much about the real decisions that face us. In this section we shall talk about competitive and monopolistic situations in general terms. We do this because we wish to study and evaluate the effects of encouraging a little more or less competition than we now have.

The importance of the given-cost assumption

The classical predictions about monopoly depend critically on the assumption that costs are unaffected when an industry is monopolized. If any savings are effected by combining numerous competing groups into a single integrated operation, then the costs of producing any given level of output will be lower than they were previously. If this cost reduction does occur, then it is possible for output to be raised and price to be lowered as a result of the monopolization of a perfectly competitive industry.

Such a situation is illustrated in Figure 23.4. The competitive equilibrium price is p_c and quantity is q_c. If the industry were monopolized and costs were unaffected, production would fall to q_m and price would rise to p_m. If, however, the integration of the industry into a single unit causes some increase in the efficiency of organization and thereby reduces costs, then the marginal cost curve will shift downward. If it shifts to MC_m, then production will rise to q'_m and price will fall to p'_m.

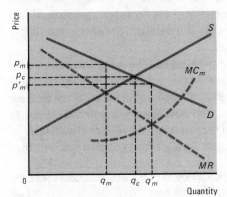

Fig. 23.4 Possible effects on price and output of a monopoly that is more efficient than a large number of competing firms

The monopolization of an industry, combined with a sufficiently large consequent increase in efficiency, can result in a fall in price and a rise in quantity produced, as compared to the competitive industry.[1]

Of course, the monopolization of an industry might reduce the efficiency of production and so shift the marginal cost curve upward. In this case, monopolization will, *a fortiori*, raise price and lower output as compared to the competitive industry. You should draw your own diagram, showing the effects of a monopolization that caused costs to rise above those ruling under competition.

We cannot predict the effects on price and output of monopolizing a competitive industry unless we know the effect of this change on the industry's costs. On the one hand, it is sometimes argued that monopolization will lower costs because wasteful duplication will be eliminated, and because one co-ordinated management body for the industry will be established. On the other hand, it is sometimes argued that competition forces the individual firm to be efficient because it will not survive unless it keeps its costs as low as its competitors', whereas although monopolistic inefficiency reduces profits, it need not drive the monopolistic firm out of business. Our theory can predict what empirical magnitudes are important, but until we have some evidence of the effects of monopolization on an industry's cost structure, we cannot predict the effect that it will have on price and output.

The effect of market structure on innovation: the very long run

The classical case against monopoly concerns the allocation of resources within the context of a fixed technology. We are now going to consider the very long run, where the production function is changing due to the discovery of lower-cost methods of producing old products and the introduction of new and improved products. We shall ask if market organization affects the rate of innovation. Before reading on it would be helpful to refresh your memory of the discussion of invention and innovation by re-reading pages 230–33.

The incentive to introduce cost-saving innovations   Both the monopolist and the perfect competitor have a profit incentive to introduce cost-reducing innovations. A monopoly can always increase its profits if it can reduce its costs. We saw in Chapter 22 (page 301) that a cost reduction will cause the monopoly to produce more, to sell at a lower price, and thus to increase its profits. Furthermore, since it is able to prevent the entry of new firms into the industry, these additional profits will persist into the long run. Thus, from the standpoint of maximizing profits, a monopoly has both a short- and a long-run incentive to reduce its costs.

The firm in perfect competition or in monopolistic competition has the same incentive in the short run, but not in the long run. In the short run, a reduction in costs will allow a firm that was just covering costs to earn profits. In the long run, other firms will be attracted into the industry by these profits. Existing firms will copy the cost-saving innovation, and new firms will enter the industry using the new techniques. This will go on until the profits of the innovator have been eliminated.

The effectiveness of profits as an incentive to reduce costs for a firm in competition will thus

---

[1] You should be able to show for yourself that if the elasticity of demand were less than one at the competitive price, the monopolist would reduce output and raise price, no matter how large the reduction in his costs.

depend on the magnitude of the extra profits and on how long they persist. If, for example, it only takes a few months for existing firms and new entrants to copy and install the new invention, then the original innovating firm will earn profits for only a few months. These may not be sufficient to compensate for the risks and the costs of developing the innovation. In such cases, the incentive to innovate will be absent from a competitive industry. On the other hand, if it takes several years for other firms to copy and install the cost-saving innovation, then the profits earned over these years by the innovating firm may be more than sufficient to compensate for all costs and risks. In this case, the incentive to innovate is present in a competitive industry.

> **Monopolies have both a short- and a long-run incentive to innovate; competitive firms have only a short-run incentive.**

Funds for research and development So far we have considered the profit incentive to introduce new innovations. Another consideration is the availability of the resources needed to finance research to invent new methods and new products. It is often held that the large profits available to monopolistic firms provide a ready fund out of which research and development will be financed. The typical, perfectly competitive firm, according to this argument, is only earning enough money to cover all its costs, and it will have few funds to spare for research and development. Supporters of this view can point to much illustrative evidence. They note, for example, that few of the innovations that have vastly raised agricultural productivity over the last century were developed by the typical competitive farming unit; they were developed, rather, by a few oligopolistic or monopolistic manufacturers of farm equipment and by researchers in universities and in government-financed research institutions.

Penalties for not innovating A further argument is that competitive firms *must* innovate or they will lose out to their competitors, while, although monopolists have an incentive to innovate, they do not need to do so because they are insulated from potential competitors by their barriers to entry. There is lack of agreement on the importance of this argument. Opponents of it would argue, first, that it is wrong to think a monopolist or oligopolist is shielded from all competition. It is always possible that some new firm will be able to break into the market by developing some new, similar, but superior product that evades existing patents and other barriers to entry. Furthermore, the larger the monopoly profits of the existing firm(s), the larger the incentive for new firms to break into the market. Thus, it is argued, all monopoly and oligopolistic firms are in potential competition with possible new entrants, and the firm that sits back and does not innovate will not long remain profitable. The second argument that opponents would advance is that the penalty for not innovating is not always high in perfect competition. If innovations are hard to copy, then there *is* a strong incentive for a competitive firm to innovate and a big penalty for firms who do not innovate because a long time will be needed before other firms can copy and catch up with the innovator. On the other hand, if innovations are easy to copy, there is a smaller incentive for the competitive firm to innovate and a smaller penalty for the firm that fails to innovate, since it is easy for it to copy and catch up with the innovator. The above discussion may be summarized as follows:

> **All firms have an incentive to innovate since they can increase their profits with a successful innovation. The greater the barriers to entry and the harder it is for other firms already in the industry to copy the innovation, the longer will the profits of**

innovating persist and, thus, the larger will be the incentive to innovate. In competitive industries without barriers to entry, there will be little incentive to make innovations that are very easily copied, since both the profits of innovating and the losses from not innovating ahead of other firms will be very short-lived.

Schumpeter's defence of oligopoly and monopoly   The greatest opponent of the classical position on monopoly was the distinguished Austrian (and later American) economist, Joseph A. Schumpeter.[1] Schumpeter's theory relies on many of the forces just discussed. His basic argument has two main parts. The first is that innovations that lower costs of production – by increasing output per head and creating economic growth – have a much larger effect on living standards than any 'miscallocation' of resources causing too much production of one kind of commodity and too little of another at any one time. The second part is based on his theory that innovation is functionally related to market forms in such a way that there is likely to be much more innovation under monopoly and oligopoly than under monopolistic and perfect competition. Let us look at each of these points in turn.

According to the classical case, monopoly results in a misallocation of resources with too few resources devoted to producing goods in the monopolistic sector and too many in the competitive sector. Schumpeter believed that the losses due to this misallocation were small relative to the gains and losses due to variations in the rate of economic growth. Modern measures made since Schumpeter wrote have tended to support him in this contention. It appears very unlikely that the losses due to monopolistic and oligopolistic misallocations have amounted to more than 2 or 3 per cent of a country's national income.[2] But the national income of most countries was for many years growing at that rate each year, and a growth rate of 3 per cent per year doubles material living standards in under 25 years.

The second part of Schumpeter's argument is that monopolistic and oligopolistic market forms are more conducive to growth than perfect competition. He claimed that only the incentive of profits leads people to take the great risks of innovation, and that monopoly power is much more important than competition in providing the climate under which innovation occurs. The large short-run profits of the monopolist provide the incentive for others to try to usurp some of these for themselves. If a frontal attack on the monopolist's barriers to entry is not possible, then the barriers will be circumvented by such dodges as the development of similar products against which the monopolist will not have entry protection. Schumpeter called the replacing of one monopoly by another through the invention of new products or new production techniques the *process of creative destruction*.

Since, in Schumpeter's theory, monopoly and oligopoly are more conducive to growth-creating innovations than perfect competition, it follows that the 'worse' the allocation of resources at any moment of time, i.e., the greater the amount of monopolization, the more rapid the rate of innovation and the resulting long-run rise in living standards. This important hypothesis cannot be handled with normal long-run theory, because long-run theory *assumes* constant technology.

Schumpeter put part of his argument in the following words:

---

[1] His most famous book is *The Theory of Economic Development* (English edn: Harvard University Press, 1934). The beginning student is referred to the lucid but less technical *Capitalism, Socialism and Democracy* (5th edn: Allen & Unwin, 1977). Both works are available in paperback.

[2] In one of the most famous of these studies Professor Harberger of the University of Chicago puts the figure at about $\frac{1}{10}$ of 1 per cent of the US national income!

What we have got to accept is that it [monopoly and oligopoly] has come to be the most powerful engine of progress and in particular of the long-run expansion of total output not only in spite of, but to a considerable extent through, this strategy [of creating monopolies] which looks so restrictive when viewed in the individual case and from the individual point of time. In this respect, perfect competition is not only impossible but inferior, and has no title to being set up as a model of ideal efficiency. It is hence a mistake to base the theory of government regulation of industry on the principle that big business should be made to work as the respective industry would work in perfect competition.[1]

> **Schumpeter's theory leads to the policy conclusion that attempting to break up monopolies and oligopolies and trying to make the economy behave as if it were perfectly competitive is undesirable, since it will reduce rather than raise the rate of growth of living standards.**

Consider an illustrative example. Let there be two countries, each with a national income of 100 that is growing at 3 per cent per annum. Country A breaks up its monopolies and thereby achieves an immediate rise of national income to 105 but a fall in its growth rate to 2 per cent. Country B lives with its monopolies and continues to have a 3 per cent growth rate. The arithmetic of growth then tells us that country B will catch up country A in five years' time, and in 50 years' time country B will have an income of just over 1·5 times that of country A. Clearly, given these figures, the long-term *losses* caused by breaking up A's monopolies are very large indeed.

The effect of alternative market forms on the process of innovation and economic growth is an extremely important question. Unfortunately it is one on which existing theory and empirical studies shed all too little light.

Ballpoint pens: an example of Schumpeterian creative destruction Much of the previous discussion can be illustrated by the rather spectacular case of the behaviour of the economy in response to the introduction of a revolutionary new technique for writing, the ballpoint pen. In 1945, Milton Reynolds acquired a patent on a new type of pen that used a ball-bearing in place of a conventional point. He formed the Reynolds International Pen Company, capitalized at $26,000 and began production on 6 October 1945.

The Reynolds pen was first introduced with a good deal of fanfare by the New York department store, Gimbels, which guaranteed that the pen would write for two years without refilling. The price was set at $12·50. Gimbels sold 10,000 pens on 29 October 1945, the first day they were on sale. In the early stages of production, the cost of production was estimated to be around $0·80 per pen.

The Reynolds International Pen Company quickly expanded production. By early 1946, it employed more than 800 people and was producing 30,000 pens per day. By March 1946 it had $3 million in the bank. Demand was intense. Macy's, Gimbels' traditional department-store rival, introduced an imported ballpoint pen from South America. Its price was $19·98 (production costs unknown).

The heavy sales quickly elicited a response from other pen manufacturers. Eversharp introduced its first model in April, at $15·00. In July 1946, the business magazine *Fortune* reported that Schaeffer was planning to put out a pen at $15·00, and Eversharp announced its plans to produce a 'retractable' model priced at $25·00. Reynolds introduced a new model, but kept the price at $12·50. Costs were then estimated at $0·60 per pen.

[1] *Capitalism, Socialism and Democracy* (3rd edn: Harper & Row, 1950), p. 106.

The first signs of trouble emerged. The Ball-point Pen Company of Hollywood (disregarding a patent infringement suit) put a $9·95 model on the market, and a manufacturer named David Kahn announced plans to introduce a pen selling for less than $3·00. *Fortune* reported fear of a price war in view of the growing number of manufacturers and the low cost of production. In October, Reynolds introduced a new model, priced at $3·85, production cost about $0·30.

By Christmas 1946, approximately 100 manufacturers were in production, some of them selling pens for as little as $2·98. By February 1947, Gimbels was selling a ballpoint pen made by the Continental Pen Company for $0·98. Reynolds introduced a new model priced to sell at $1.69, but Gimbels sold it for $0·88 in a price war with Macy's. Reynolds felt betrayed by Gimbels and introduced a new model listed at $0·98. By this time ballpoint pens had become economy items rather than luxury items, but were still highly profitable.

In mid-1948, ballpoint pens were selling for as little as $0·39, and costing about $0·10 to produce. In 1951, prices of $0·25 were common. Today there is a wide variety of models and prices, ranging from $0·25 to $25·00, and the market appears stable, orderly and only moderately profitable. Ballpoint pens were no passing fad, as every reader of this book knows. Their introduction has fundamentally changed the writing-implement industry throughout the world.

The ballpoint pen example has interested observers in many fields.

> **From the point of view of economic theory, the ballpoint pen case illustrates several things:**
>
> **(1) that a monopoly (in this case a patent monopoly) can in the short run charge prices not remotely related to costs and earn enormous profits;**
>
> **(2) that entry of new firms (even in the face of obstacles) will often occur in response to high profits;**
>
> **(3) that where it does occur, entry will in time drive prices down to a level more nearly equal to the costs of production and distribution;**
>
> **(4) that the lag between an original monopoly and its subsequent erosion by entry may nevertheless be long enough that the profits to the innovator, as well as to some of the early imitators, may be very large indeed.**

(It is estimated that Reynolds earned profits as high as $500,000 *in a single month* – or about 20 times its original investment.)

Pocket calculators   Although a spectacular case, the ballpoint pen is not an isolated illustration of the process of innovation in a market economy. Pocket calculators provide one of many more recent examples. When they were first introduced in the early 1970s their capacities were limited, prices were high and so were the profits on each calculator sold. Customer acceptance was, however, immediate. As a result, many firms producing other products, and many new firms, rushed into production. Technological advance was rapid. While the capacities of the machines expanded, competition forced prices down. Today consumers can choose from a vast array of calculators and the prices paid are closely related to costs, so that producing firms find these lines only moderately profitable.

The effect of market structure on consumer's range of choice

It is sometimes argued that one of the virtues of competition among several producers is that it presents the consumer with a wide range of differentiated commodities, while complete monopoly with only one producer tends towards uniformity of product. We shall not ask here to what extent a variety of products is desirable, but we shall ask if we would in fact expect competition to produce more diversity of product than monopoly. This is a very-long-run problem because we are concerned with changing the number of products to be produced.

An example from radio and television A very interesting case, in which competition tends to produce a nearly uniform product while monopoly tends to produce widely differentiated ones, is the case of radio and television.[1] Consider a case in which there are two potential radio audiences: one group, comprising 80 per cent of the total audience, wishes to hear pop music; the other group, comprising 20 per cent, wishes to listen to a concert of chamber music. Each individual radio station seeks to maximize its own listening audience.

If there is only the one station, it will produce pop music. If a second competing station is now opened up, its most profitable policy will be to produce a similar pop-music programme because half of the large audience is better than all of the small one. A third station would also prefer a third of the large audience to all of the small one. Indeed five stations would be needed before it would be profitable for any one station to produce a programme of chamber music. Thus competition between two or three stations would tend to produce two or three almost identical pop-music programmes, each competing for its share of the large audience.

A monopoly controlling two stations would not, however, pursue this policy. To maximize its total listening audience it would produce pop music on one station and chamber music on the other. The monopoly might spend more money on preparing the programme for the larger audience, but it would not spend money to produce a similar programme on its second station – the optimal policy for its second station is to go after the other 20 per cent of potential listeners so that, between the two channels, the monopoly would have the maximum audience.

In both cases, of monopoly and competition, each individual firm tries to maximize its own listening audience, but two competing stations will both go after the same large audience, ignoring the minority group, while two stations owned by one monopoly will go after both audiences, one for each station. Under these circumstances, competition produces a uniformity of product which ignores the desires of the minority, while monopoly produces a varied product catering to the desires of both the majority and the minority group.

At the time the case was studied, British radio was a three-station monopoly, and British television was based on competition between two stations, each taking as its criterion of success its own listening audience. It was found that the three stations of the monopolized radio produced very little similarity between the products offered at any one time, while the two competing stations of British television produced almost identical products a great deal of the time. Thus at a randomly selected time of the day the radio listener was likely to have two or three varied possibilities, while the television viewer was often forced to choose between two quite similar programmes.

The principle of minimum differentiation In some ways this radio example is a special case. We may now consider the problem in somewhat more general and abstract terms, as it was first laid out by Harold Hotelling.

---

[1] P. O. Steiner, 'Monopoly and competition in TV: some policy issues', *The Manchester School* (1961); and 'Program Patterns and Preferences and the Workability of Competition in Radio Broadcasting', *Quarterly Journal of Economics*, May 1952.

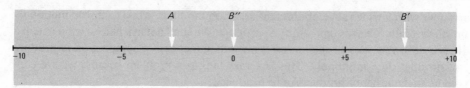

Fig. 23.5 The differentiation of a product with one independent characteristic

Consider a product with only one independent characteristic which we can measure on a scale from −10 to +10. This is illustrated in Figure 23.5. The product might, for example, be soap powder in which hardness was associated with cleansing power and mildness with lack of it. A rating of +10 might indicate a soap which had great cleansing power but removed the skin from the unfortunate user's hands, and −10 a soap which was positively beneficial to the hands but would not remove the merest speck of grease.[1] Let us assume that firm A has settled its product on the scale at −2. If firm B now wishes to produce a competing product, what will be its optimal policy? It might go to an extreme, producing a soap which had strong cleansing power but was also rather harsh on the hands, going out as far as, say, +8 on the scale (indicated by B′ in the figure). Consumers whose tastes lead them to prefer something *between* the two products would, presumably, choose the product which came closest to satisfying their tastes. Firm A would get all customers who preferred a product ranging from −10 to +3, while B would get all those who preferred a product in the range +3 to +10. Now let us assume that, having decided to make a product with more cleansing power and more harshness than the competitor's product, firm B goes only a little way in this direction, just enough to make the difference noticeable but not enough to cause a major difference between the two products. Let us say it goes to zero on our scale (see B″ in the figure). Now firm B should get all customers who would like a product rating between −1 and +10. Clearly firm B does better placing its product at B″ rather than at B′, and equally clearly the best policy is to locate the product just enough to the right of A on the scale for the difference to be noticeable. That the optimal policy is often to make your product different enough from your competitor's product for the difference to be noticeable but no more so, is sometimes referred to as the PRINCIPLE OF MINIMUM DIFFERENTIATION.[2]

---

[1] This product has two characteristics, cleansing power and effect on skin, but they are not independent of each other; we have assumed that they vary directly with each other.

[2] The principle of minimum differentiation has applicability well beyond the scope of economics. It goes a long way, for example, in explaining why in a two-party political system, both parties tend to gravitate towards a middle-of-the-road position that minimizes the real choice given to voters. The principle does not, however, generalize to more than two firms. The observed clustering of many firms must be explained by forces not covered by this principle. Two other forces are, first, that for many durable goods, customers engage in comparison shopping: they visit several shops to compare prices and qualities before making their purchase, and second, that consumers can economize on shopping costs by making multi-purpose shopping trips. The clustering of two firms in Hotelling's model *is not* in consumers' interests, it denies them a range of choices they would like to have available; the clustering of two or more firms in response to comparison and multi-purpose shopping *is* in consumers' interests since it facilitates the making of desired comparisons. (Intermediate and advanced students who wish to see these issues considered further can consult B. C. Eaton and R. G. Lipsey, 'Comparison Shopping and the Clustering of Homogeneous Firms', *Journal of Regional Science* (1979), 19, 421–35, and 'An Economic Theory of Central Places', *Economics Journal*, (1982), 92, 56–72.)

The nature and extent of monopoly power

There are certain conceptual difficulties with the theoretical concept of monopoly. Some firms which have fairly close competitors will face quite elastic demand curves; other firms with fewer close competitors will face less elastic demand curves.

It is impossible for a firm to be without any significant competition. It may have a complete monopoly of a particular product, but every product has some substitutes that can provide more or less the same services.

Some products have fairly close substitutes, and even a single seller producing such a product will have close rivals for his customers' expenditure. Not only will his demand be relatively elastic, but new entrants into closely allied fields may affect his sales. If other firms in other industries influence the monopolist's behaviour, they must do so by shifting his demand curve. The less the influence of other firms on the monopolist, the less their actions will cause shifts in his demand curve and the more insulated (i.e., the more monopolistic) he will be. Thus, it is useful to think of monopoly as a variable rather than as an absolute. In general, the extent of monopoly power will be greater, the smaller shifts in demand caused by the reactions of sellers of other products, and the smaller the shifts in demand caused by the entry of new sellers.

Our theory predicts that behaviour in monopolistic markets will differ from behaviour in perfectly competitive markets. We have also seen that it is more realistic to regard monopoly power as a variable than as an absolute. Thus if we are to apply the theory of monopoly we must be able to measure the extent of monopoly power in various markets. Ideally, one would like to compare the prices, outputs and profits of firms in any industry with what prices, outputs and profits would be if all firms were under unified (monopoly) control and were fully insulated from entry. But this hypothetical comparison does not lend itself to measurement. In practice, two alternative measures are widely used.

Concentration ratios This measure is the CONCENTRATION RATIO. A concentration ratio shows the fraction of total market sales controlled by the largest group of sellers. Common types of concentration ratios cite the share of total industry sales of the largest four or eight firms. The inclusion in concentration ratios of the market shares of several firms rests upon the possibility that large firms will adopt a common price-output policy that is no different from the one they would adopt if they were in fact under unified management. But of course they may not. Thus high concentration ratios are necessary for the exercise of monopoly power, but they are not sufficient. It is nevertheless interesting to know where potential monopoly power exists.

Profits as a measure of monopoly power Many economists, following the lead of American Professor J.S. Bain, use profit rates as a measure of monopoly power. By 'high' profits the economist means returns sufficiently in excess of all opportunity costs to motivate potential new entrants into the industry. If profits are *and remain* high, so goes the logic of this measure, it is evidence that neither rivalry among sellers nor entry of new firms prevents existing firms from pricing monopolistically.

Using profits in this way requires care, because, as we have seen, the profits reported in firms' income statements are not pure profits over opportunity cost. In particular, allowance must be made for differences in risk and in required payments for the use of the owners' capital.

While neither concentration ratios nor profit rates are ideal measures of the degree of market power that a firm, or group of firms, actually exercise, both are of some value and both are widely used. In fact, concentration ratios and high profit rates are themselves correlated. Because of this, alternative classifications of industries according to their degree of monopoly power, measured in these two ways, are often quite close to one another.

Policy issues[1]

MERGERS, which are the uniting of two or more formerly independent firms into a single unit, are a way in which monopoly power can grow. There are, however, several different types of merger and they do not all have the same consequences for market power. The type we think of most usually is called HORIZONTAL MERGER where firms at the same stage of production unite. Since these firms are selling the same commodities, horizontal mergers usually represent an increase in market power. If they proceed to the point that there is only one remaining firm, the market will be completely monopolized, and even before that point they may confer enough market power to permit the participating firms to raise their profits.

VERTICAL MERGERS occur when firms at different stages of production unite. Usually one merging firm's output is the other merging firm's input. The motive for such mergers is not to gain more power over one market, since the merged firms sell their products in different markets. The motive could be to obtain a secure supply of some raw material or a secure set of outlets for one's products (as when brewery firms buy up public houses).

The third form of merger, the so-called CONGLOMERATE MERGER, occurs when firms selling quite unrelated products merge. Again the motive is not to gain more power over any single market. The motive is more usually one of risk reduction. Firms in declining industries may seek to gain a share of expanding industries and so avoid being permanently depressed. Firms selling products that are very sensitive to trade-cycle fluctuations may seek to expand into industries that are less cyclically sensitive. Firms selling many products may feel better insulated from unforseen and unforseeable events that can depress the market for one particular product. Generally, conglomerate mergers have more to do with reducing risk than increasing market power. Conglomerates can, however, engage in certain anti-competitive actions. They can, for example, cross-subsidize various activities, with profits in a market insulated against entry being used to subsidize losses suffered because of predatory price behaviour in a market subject to entry.

Policy-makers who are concerned to control market power, the power to earn large profits by raising price well above marginal cost, will regard different types of mergers differently. Some types of mergers do much more to increase the market power of the participants than do others.

Control of natural monopolies

We saw in Chapter 19 that perfect competition can exist only in industries in which the output at which the *LRATC* curve reaches its minimum is small in relation to the total market demand. In this

---

[1] For the factual background to these issues and a discussion of UK anti-monopoly policies, see Harbury and Lipsey, Chapters 2, 3 and 6.

case the total necessary output can be produced by many competing firms, all producing at minimum average total costs. If, on the other hand, the output at which the $LRATC$ curve reaches a minimum is large in relation to the market demand, then perfect competition is impossible and firms will expand under the incentive of falling long-run costs, until the market is dominated by a few large producers, or possibly by only one. Such industries were regarded as NATURAL MONOPOLIES or NATURAL OLIGOPOLIES since competition among many firms would quickly give way to monopoly or oligopoly. The advantage of having one or a few large firms producing at a lower cost than could be achieved by many small firms is evident. In order to prevent higher price and lower output than was necessary to cover opportunity cost, however, some intervention was needed. The central authorities were advised to regulate prices so that the industry would earn only the competitive rate of return on its capital. Thus costs would be lowered by the monopolization, but the price would be held to its competitive level by the state intervention. This can be achieved either by leaving the natural monopoly in private hands and regulating its prices or by nationalizing it.

Pricing policies Whether the state nationalizes, or merely regulates, privately owned natural monopolies, the industry's pricing policy is a matter for determination by the state. Generally some policy other than profit-maximizing is imposed on the industry.

Marginal cost pricing: Sometimes the state dictates that the natural monopoly should try to set price equal to marginal cost in an effort to maximize consumers' plus producers' surpluses in that industry. This policy is called MARGINAL COST PRICING. But there are problems here. The natural monopoly may still have unexploited economies of scale and hence be operating on the falling portion of its ATC curve. In this case MC will be less than ATC and pricing at marginal cost will lead to losses. This is shown in part (i) of Figure 23.6 where output q_1 equates marginal cost to price at p_1; but with average cost of c_1, the result is losses equal to the shaded rectangle.

A falling-cost, natural monopoly directed to price at marginal cost will suffer losses.

If, however, demand is sufficient to allow the firm to exploit all its scale economies, it may be

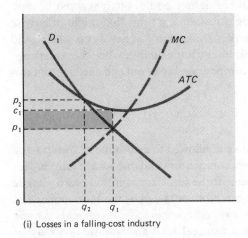

(i) Losses in a falling-cost industry

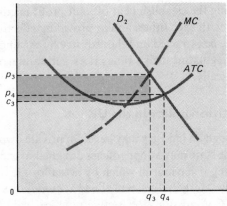

(ii) Profits in a rising-cost industry

Fig. 23.6 Marginal cost pricing

producing on the rising portion of its ATC curve. MC will then exceed ATC and profits will be earned if the firm is directed to equate MC to price. This is shown in part (ii) of the figure where output q_3 equates marginal cost to price at p_3, but with average costs at c_3, there are profits equal to the shaded rectangle.

A rising-cost, natural monopoly directed to price at marginal cost will earn profits.

Average cost pricing: Sometimes natural monopolies are directed to produce the output that will just cover total costs, thus earning neither profits nor losses. This means the firm produces to the point where average revenue equals average total cost, which is where the demand curve cuts the average total cost curve. Part (i) of Figure 23.6 illustrates that, for a falling-cost firm, this pricing policy requires an output (q_2) less than the one for which marginal cost equals price, and hence it does not maximize consumers' surplus. Part (ii) illustrates that in a rising-cost firm, the policy requires that output (q_4) exceeds that for which marginal cost equals price and so, once again, the sum of producers' and consumers' surplus is not maximized.

Generally, average cost pricing will not result in allocative efficiency.

In practice the policy of AVERAGE COST PRICING runs into difficulty in seeking to define the cost of capital. This cost, which represents what capital would earn in another comparably risky industry, is not easy to determine and regulated natural monopolies naturally seek to persuade the regulators that the true cost of their capital is quite high.

Persuading the regulators may not be as difficult as it might at first seem because a strong case has been made, particularly by American economists who have studied them, that regulatory bodies often work to the benefit of the firms they are supposed to control and to the detriment of consumers, whose interests they are supposed to protect. One of the major reasons set forth is that regulatory bodies must be staffed by experts in the relevant industry. The most obvious experts to select are persons with management experience in that industry. These people are often sympathetic to the industry, and work to protect its profits rather than to force price down to the level of costs.

The evidence from many studies also suggests that regulatory bodies often succeed both in supervising the establishment of joint profit-maximizing prices among firms that might otherwise compete with each other, and in providing effective barriers to the entry of new firms who would otherwise be attracted into the industry by existing profit levels. For example, when the Americans stopped regulating their airline prices, substantial price competition broke out and effective air fares fell drastically.

Competition policy in the UK

Even though an industry may be left in private ownership and allowed to determine its own pricing policy, the state may adopt policies designed to encourage competition and discourage joint profit-maximizing behaviour in which by actual or tacit agreement the firms act as if they were a single monopoly. Mergers that seem aimed at monopolization can be investigated by the Monopolies and Mergers Commission. Restrictive practices, which are explicit co-operative agreements among independent firms, must be registered with the Director General for Fair Trading and may be referred to the Restrictive Practices Court. The presumption is that agreements on prices, qualities and market shares are presumed to be illegal unless they can be justified on a number of special grounds. Resale price maintenance, whereby manufacturers could restrict competition among retailers by forcing them to sell their products at fixed prices, is now illegal in most industries. Also any practices thought to encourage non-competitive behaviour may be investigated by the Office of Fair Trading and then referred if necessary to the Monopolies and Mergers Commission.

Policy incentives to innovation

The above policy issues concern pricing and profits in the context of a given production function. But also important is their behaviour in the very long run when production functions change because of invention and innovation.

Patents Economists who believe that competitive market structures best serve consumers by assuring them low prices, but who worry about the possible lack of incentives to innovate under competition, believe that other institutions, such as the patent laws, can provide the necessary incentives. Patent laws confer a temporary monopoly on the use of an invention. They represent an attempt to lengthen the short-run period during which whoever controls the invention can earn profits as a reward for inventing it. Once the patent expires, and sometimes even before, as we saw in the case of ballpoint pens, other firms can copy the innovation. If there are no other barriers to entry, production will expand until profits fall to normal. Because patented items *can* be imitated, the real advantage of patents to the competitive firm should not be exaggerated. Some economists have argued that patents may be of even greater advantage to a monopolistic than to a competitive firm. A monopolist, so goes the argument, has the resources to develop, patent, and 'keep on the shelf' processes that might enable a potential competitor to challenge its position.

Reduction of entry barriers Those who accept Schumpeter's theory hold that anti-monopoly and public utility regulation policies are unnecessary as policies to influence behaviour in the very long run. They feel that the state may intervene positively to reduce existing entry barriers but they worry more that state intervention may inadvertently create entry barriers that will help to protect the profits of existing firms. They hold, therefore, that the state's main task is to avoid erecting barriers to entry that protect existing firms from the process of creative destruction. Otherwise they feel that the state should not attempt to control or regulate monopolies.

Nationalization Those who reject Schumpeter's argument often support anti-monopoly and public utility regulation policies as a means of preventing monopolies from earning large profits at the expense of consumers. Nationalized industries must face the pricing problem just discussed for regulated natural monopolies. A common policy is to direct them just to cover their costs, i.e., to adopt average-cost pricing. Some nationalized industries in some countries have been directed to use marginal-cost pricing. In falling-cost cases the state must then subsidize the industry's losses.

Supporters of Schumpeter's theory argue that nationalization, and public regulation, will defeat its own purpose. They argue that even if the nationalized or regulated industry works to the short-term advantage of consumers by keeping prices down to the level of the industry's costs, it will work to their long-term disadvantage by frustrating the process of creative destruction. A government monopoly is the ultimate in barriers to entry. To the extent that progress in new products, and new ways of producing old products, comes through new firms entering to attack the entrenched position of existing, sometimes sleepy and over-confident firms, this progress may be inhibited by the legal and fully enforceable monopoly created by the nationalisation of an industry. Supporters of this view point to the USSR's evident desire to buy technology from the US and argue that the rapid development of new products and processes in the oligopolistic and monopolistic industries in such countries as West Germany, Japan and the USA gives some support to Schumpeter's view.

A short-term, long-term trade-off? Economists who accept both the force of the argument that monopolistic firms can earn large exploitive profits in the short term *and* Schumpeter's argument about the very long run face a policy dilemma. In the short term, firms who gain monopoly power may earn very large profits at the expense of consumers. In the long term, however, attempts to control these monopolies may inhibit the creative destruction process that makes us all better off through productivity growth.

> **For these economists the policy world is not a simple place and policies that achieve desired goals over one time-span must be constantly scrutinized to see if they are producing undesired results over other time-spans.**

A conclusion

We have been concerned in this chapter with what could be said about monopoly, oligopoly and perfect competition on the basis of positive economic theory. On many crucial points, theory has not been adequately tested. It is obviously necessary to keep an open mind on the subject and to admit that, on the basis of existing theory, it is impossible to make out an overwhelming case either for or against monopoly and oligopoly as compared with competition. Everyone will have his or her own guess, hunch or prejudice on the subject, often based on bits of personal experience. But from the point of view of economic science we are interested in carefully documented, objective evidence, and on these grounds much still remains to be discovered about the comparison on the effects of monopoly, oligopoly and pure competition.

24

Criticisms and tests of the theory of supply

In previous chapters we have derived a number of testable implications from the theory of supply. The theory itself is tested every time one of these implications is confronted with facts in such a way that a conflict between theory and observation is possible. In many cases, if a particular implication is in conflict with the facts, this necessitates only a minor change in the basic theory. In other cases, however, empirical observations have been alleged that strike at the very core of the theory. If these conflicting observations were substantiated, it would be necessary either to make very drastic amendments to existing theory or to abandon it completely.

In this chapter we shall first discuss some general approaches to testing the theory and then consider a number of criticisms that have been raised against it. The final criticism relates to the work of Professor J. K. Galbraith, who has attacked some of the most fundamental aspects of the theory and suggested that its apparent policy implications are profoundly misleading.

Approaches to testing the theory

Over the last several chapters we have developed an elaborate theory of the behaviour of firms and industries. Although it does not cover all questions in which we might be interested, it does, as we have seen, provide predictions about many interesting situations. But is the theory right? Are we not being misled by accepting its predictions? How can we assess such worries? The answer to this last question is fundamental to an assessment of the practical value of economics. Several approaches to providing the answer have been used from time to time, and we shall now consider three of them.

Formulate an alternative theory that makes different predictions

Given alternative theories, one can eliminate their conflicting predictions and choose to accept the one that comes closer to predicting what actually is observed to happen. We might hypothesize, for example, that firms choose to maximize their sales rather than their profits, and we would then have two competing theories. We could then derive their predictions. Next we would select those that conflict with each other, and confront them with the evidence. This is a satisfactory way of choosing between two theories.

See if decision-takers behave as the theory predicts

We might observe, for example, how a certain executive takes a decision: what records he consults, what questions he asks, and so on. Or we might create a laboratory situation and give 'subjects' a chance to take decisions, then record and analyse their decisions.

This approach does not by itself provide a test of an existing theory, since it does not tell us whether the procedure actually employed by the decision-taker really makes any difference in his decision. If, for example, an executive systematically discusses proposed price changes with his sales manager and his solicitor, but rarely with his cost accountant, it may suggest the hypothesis that demand and anti-monopoly considerations loom larger in his mind than cost conditions, but it does not demonstrate that these things play a more important role than cost. Other explanations are possible. For example, the executive might be an expert on cost conditions, or he might need less time to acquaint himself with cost data than with demand data, or his cost accountant may provide him with lucid memos, whereas his sales manager can only communicate orally.

The approach may, however, suggest fruitful new theories. If we find that firms habitually follow certain procedures that seem to lead them away from profit-maximization, we can formulate a new theory in which these procedures play a prominent role. We would then have two conflicting theories, and we could proceed to test between them in the manner discussed in the previous section.

Ask decision-takers how they take decisions

Another approach to testing the theory of profit-maximization is to ask businessmen: 'Do you seek to maximize profits?' This approach has from time to time been tried and it will not surprise you to learn that, when asked if their sole motive were to make as much money as possible, businessmen replied that it was not, and that they sought to charge a 'fair price', to make only a reasonable profit and generally to conduct their affairs in a manner conducive to the social good. Asking people what they do and why they do it can provide some interesting hunches and suggest hypotheses about behaviour for further testing. For example if you have always taken it for granted that people do a certain thing and inquiry shows that everyone denies it, then this may make you suspicious and lead you to check your theories further. But consider what the denials might mean: (i) the people were lying; (ii) the people told what they thought was the truth, but they were not aware of their own motives and actions; (iii) the denials were true.

How are we to judge which of these possibilities is correct? One needs only a nodding acquaintance with elementary psychology to realize that we are not likely to discover very much about human motivation by asking a person what motivates him. Generally he or she will have either no idea at all, or else only a pleasantly acceptable rationalization.

Direct questioning at best (assuming the subject tries to be scrupulously honest) tells us what the person questioned thinks he is doing. Such information can never refute an hypothesis about what the person actually is doing. To challenge such an hypothesis, we must observe what he does, not ask him what he thinks he does.

We shall now consider several major criticisms of the theory of profit-maximization.

Who controls the modern firm? : alternative maximizing theories[1]

The first set of criticisms under this general heading centre around the question of who actually

---

[1] These and related matters are discussed in greater detail in Harbury and Lipsey, Chapter 2.

controls the firm. The owners of the firm are its shareholders, and they are the ones who, presumably, have most to gain from a policy of profit-maximization. Perhaps the great bulk of ordinary shareholders are not able to exercise any significant control over the firm's behaviour. Many investigators have forcefully advocated the view that groups other than the majority of ordinary shareholders exert the determining influence on firms' behaviour. For this to matter to positive economics, the controlling group must wish to pursue goals other than profit-maximization so that its behaviour will be different from that desired by the majority of ordinary shareholders.

The hypothesis of minority control

This hypothesis runs as follows: *Because of the widespread distribution of shares, the owners of a minority of the stock are usually able to control a majority of the voting shares and thus to exercise effective control over the decisions of the company.*

This possibility arises because not all shares are actually voted. Each share of common stock has one vote. Shares must be voted at the annual meeting of stockholders, either in person or by assigning a *proxy* to someone attending. Any individual or group controlling 51 per cent of the stock clearly controls a majority of the votes. But suppose one group owns 30 per cent of the stock, with the remaining 70 per cent distributed so widely that few of the dispersed group even bother to vote; in this event, 30 per cent may be the overwhelming majority of the shares *actually voted*. In general, a very small fraction (sometimes as little as 5 per cent) of the shares actively voted may exercise dominant influence at meetings of stockholders.

Dispersed ownership and minority control are common. But the hypothesis requires more than that a minority control the voting shares; it requires that stockholders be able to exert a significant influence on the firm's behaviour *and* that the controlling minority have interests and motives different from the holders of the majority of the firm's stock. If all stockholders are mainly interested in having the firm maximize its profits, then it does not matter, as far as market behaviour is concerned, which set of stockholders actually influences the firm's policy. There is no accepted evidence to show that controlling groups of stockholders generally seek objectives different from those sought by the holders of the majority of the firm's stock. Of course, disagreements between stockholder groups sometimes arise. A colourful phenomenon is the proxy fight, in which competing factions of stockholders (or management) attempt to collect the voting rights of the dispersed and often disinterested stockholders.

The hypothesis of inter-corporate control groups

The hypothesis runs as follows: *Whole sectors of the economy are effectively controlled by small groups of people through the mechanism of interlocking directorships.*

If each member of a small group holds directorships in several companies, the group can control the boards of directors of many different companies without being so obvious as to have the identical set of persons on each and every board. By controlling the boards of directors, this group can exert effective and relatively unostentatious control over the companies themselves. The factual basis of this hypothesis is that many individuals are directors of many companies. These 'interlocking directorships' have been widely studied.

There is no law against a particular individual being a director of many companies. Some individuals are wanted by many companies for the prestige that their names convey. Certain bank officers appear on many different boards of directors to represent their banks' interests in companies to which they have loaned money. The hypothesis of inter-corporate control groups is important to positive economics only if boards of directors are able to control the policies of companies in ways that would not be approved by managers or shareholders. Indeed, there does not seem to be any evidence that the common directors exert any significant influence altering the firms' behaviour from what it would be if no such interlocking existed.

The hypothesis of the separation of ownership from control

Because of diversified ownership and the difficulty of assembling shareholders or gathering proxies, the managers rather than the shareholders exercise effective control over the decisions of the company.

The argument offered in support of this hypothesis is as follows. Shareholders elect directors who appoint managers. Directors are supposed to represent shareholders' interests and to determine broad policies that the managers merely carry out. In order to conduct the complicated business of running a large firm, however, a full-time professional management group *must* be given broad powers of decision. Although managerial decisions can be reviewed from time to time, they cannot be supervised in detail. In fact, the links are typically weak enough so that top management often does truly control the destiny of the company over long periods of time. As long as directors have confidence in the managerial group, they accept and ratify their proposals, and shareholders characteristically elect and re-elect directors who are proposed to them. If the managerial group behaves badly, it may later be replaced, but this is a drastic and disruptive action that is infrequently employed. Within very wide limits, then, effective control of the company's activities does reside with the managers, who need not even be shareholders. But again, what is the significance of this fact?

For the hypothesis of the separation of ownership and control to be important, it is necessary not only that the managers should be able to exert effective control over business decisions, but also that they should wish to act differently from the way the shareholders and directors wish to act. If the managers are motivated by a desire to maximize the firm's profits – either because it is in their own interests to do so or because they voluntarily choose to reflect the shareholders' interests – then it does not matter that they have effective control over decisions. If the managers wish to pursue goals different from those of the owners, the behaviour of the firm will be different according to whether the managers or the owners exercise effective control.

This is a genuinely competing hypothesis to that of profit-maximization, but before we go on to consider it in detail we should notice that it is also in conflict with the two hypotheses outlined previously. Clearly one cannot hold simultaneously that managers take the effective decisions, ignoring the interests of shareholders and directors, and that directors take the effective decisions, ignoring the interests of managers and shareholders, and that a minority of shareholders take effective decisions, ignoring the interests of the other groups.

The sales-maximization hypothesis

Another maximizing theory, first offered by Professor William Baumol, is that firms seek to maximize not their profits but their sales revenue. Firms, it is assumed, wish to be as large as possible and, faced with a choice between profits and sales, would choose to increase their sales rather than their profits.

This hypothesis starts from the separation of management and ownership. In the giant corporation, the managers need to make some minimum level of profits to keep the shareholders satisfied; after that they are free to seek growth unhampered by profit considerations. This is a sensible policy on the part of management, so the argument runs, because salary, power and prestige all vary with the size of a firm as well as with its profits; the manager of a large, normally profitable corporation may well earn a salary considerably higher than that earned by the manager of a small but highly profitable corporation.

The sales-maximization hypothesis says that managers of firms seek to maximize their sales revenue, subject to a profit constraint.

Sales-maximization subject to a profit constraint leads to the prediction that firms will sacrifice some profits by setting price below, and output above, their profit-maximizing levels. This is demonstrated in Figure 24.1, which shows the profits associated with each rate of output. A profit-maximizing firm produces output q_m. A sales-maximizing firm, with a minimum profit constraint of π_c, produces the output q_2. Thus sales-maximization predicts a higher output than does profit-maximizing.

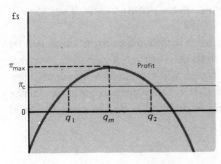

Quantity of output

Fig. 24.1 Output of the firm under satisficing, profit-maximizing and sales-maximizing

Sales-maximizing behaviour is constrained by outside forces. If the present management departs too far from profit-maximizing behaviour, it leaves its firm vulnerable to a take-over bid by a new owner who does intend to maximize profits. This is discussed further below.

The long-run profit-maximization hypothesis

In order to take account of various criticisms of the assumption of profit-maximization, some economists modify profit-maximization to mean long-run profit-maximization. For example, sales-maximization might be interpreted as long-run profit-maximization because sales are the key to growth and growth is the key to future profits. This eliminates any conflict between sales and profit-maximization. In much the same way, the 'long-run' approach can be used to account for other facts that appear to contradict predictions based on short-run profit-maximization. For one example, consumer goodwill gained by not taking advantage of temporary shortages may be worthwhile in terms of long-run profits. For another example, a firm may be right to avoid risky ventures, even if they promise large short-run profits, because the surest way to long-run profits is to survive in the short run. Long-run profitability requires survival and survival may require caution.

It is, however, exceptionally difficult to give such a long-run theory any testable content. If we are not careful, whenever we find a firm not maximizing profits, we may find ourselves rationalizing by saying that it was the firm maximizing over *some time period other than* the one we were considering. Unless we include in our theory a means of identifying the long-run period over which profits are supposed to be maximized, our theory becomes consistent with absolutely any business behaviour and as a result becomes totally uninteresting.

It is not unreasonable, however, to regard profit-maximizing as occurring over a realistic time horizon, such as one or two years, rather than day by day. Nor is it unreasonable to construct a testable theory of a firm attempting to maximize the 'present value' of future profits. In either of these ways long-run maximization can be brought into a profit-maximizing model.

Do firms maximize anything? : non-maximizing theories of the firm

Many students of large and complex organizations have been critical of economic theory for regarding modern corporations as 'simple profit-maximizing computers'. They believe that firms are profit-oriented in the sense that, *ceteris paribus*, they prefer more profits to less. They do not believe, however, that firms are profit-maximizers.

Maximization has two aspects. A firm is a *local maximizer* if it maximizes profits that can be earned with its present range of commodities and its present markets. A firm is a *global maximizer* if it surveys and chooses from all possible courses of action, which will include new products, new markets, and radically new sales and production techniques. It is fairly easy to gather evidence showing that most firms are not global maximizers; it is more difficult to do the same for local maximization.

Non-maximization due to ignorance

One group of critics say that profit-maximizing theory is inadequate because firms, however hard they may try, cannot reach decisions in the way the theory predicts. This criticism has several aspects, some crude and some quite sophisticated.

Businessmen do not understand marginal concepts One of the crudest criticisms is based on the observation that businessmen do not calculate in the manner assumed by the theory. Sometimes businessmen are interviewed and it is discovered (apparently to the surprise of the interviewer) that they have never heard of the concepts of marginal cost and marginal revenue. It is then argued that: (i) the theory assumes businessmen equate marginal cost to marginal revenue; (ii) empirical observations show that businessmen have not heard of marginal cost and marginal revenue; (iii) therefore the theory is refuted, because businessmen cannot be employing concepts of which they are unaware.

This observation, assuming it to be correct, does refute the theory that firms take decisions by calculating marginal values and consciously equating them. But it does not refute the theory that firms maximize profits. The mathematical concepts of marginal cost and marginal revenue (these are just the *first derivatives* of the total cost and total revenue functions by another name) are used by economic theorists to discover what will happen as long as, by one means or another – be it guess, hunch, clairvoyance, luck or good judgement – the firms do approximately succeed in maximizing their profits. The constructs of the theory of the firm are logical tools used to discover the consequences of certain behaviour. They are not meant to be descriptions of *how* firms reach their decisions. If firms are maximizing their profits, then the tools of economic theory allow us to predict how they will react to certain changes – e.g., the introduction of a tax – and this prediction is independent of the thought process by which firms actually reach their decisions.

Business calculations are cruder than assumed by profit-maximizing theory A similar argument stems from the observation that firms do not calculate down to single units with such a nice degree of accuracy as is assumed in profit-maximizing theory. In the verbal presentation of the theory of the firm, it is usually stated that firms will increase production until the cost of producing the very last unit is just equal to the revenue gained from its sale. This is merely a verbal statement of the mathematical conditions for the maximization of the profit function. The observation that firms do not calculate down to single units is not of itself relevant as a test of the theory. The marginal analysis allows us to predict how firms will respond to certain changes in the data; if they are maximizing their profits they will be observed to respond in this way even though they calculate in a much cruder fashion than mathematicians do.

Firms have inadequate information More sophisticated critics point out that the information available to decision-takers is simply not adequate to permit them to reach the decisions that economists predict they will reach. This argument generally takes one of three forms: that firms are the victims of their accountants, and base their decisions on accounting concepts, which differ from economic ones; that the natural lag between accumulating and processing data is such that important decisions must be made on fragmentary and partially out-of-date information; or, that firms cannot afford to acquire as much information as economists assume them to have.

Non-maximization by choice

Alternatives to profit-maximization are usually based on observations of actual firms. The observations and the theories all have in common the implication that firms *choose* not to be profit-maximizers.

Full-cost pricing Most manufacturing firms are price setters: they must quote a price for their products rather than accept a price set on some impersonal competitive market. Simple profit-maximizing theory predicts that these firms will change their prices in response to every change in demand and costs that they experience. Yet students of large firms have long alleged that this much price flexibility is not observed. In the short run, prices of manufactured goods do not appear to vary in response to every shift in the firm's demand. Instead they appear to change rather sluggishly.

This short-run behaviour is consistent with the hypothesis of FULL-COST PRICING, which was originally advanced in the 1930s by Robert Hall, a British economist, and Charles Hitch, an American, following a series of detailed case studies of actual pricing decisions made in Oxford. Case studies in the intervening decades have continued to reveal the widespread use of full-cost pricing procedures.

The full-cost pricer, instead of equating marginal revenue with marginal cost, sets price equal to average cost at normal-capacity output, plus a conventional markup.

The firm changes its prices when its average costs change substantially (as a result of such events as a new union contract or a sharp change in the prices of key raw materials), and it may occasionally change its markup. However, its short-run pricing behaviour is rather conventional and is not characterized even by local profit-maximization.

Modern supporters of profit-maximizing theory accept the full-cost evidence but argue that it reveals only the administrative procedure by which prices are set from day to day. They hold that management makes frequent changes in markups in an attempt to maximize profits. Thus they believe that, while firms may be full-cost pricers from day to day, they are profit-maximizers with respect to their average experience over, say, a year.

Modern critics of profit-maximizing theory accept the evidence that full-cost prices are sometimes changed in the profit-maximizing direction. They hold, however, that the prevalence of conventional full-cost practices shows that prices are typically not at their profit-maximizing level. They also hold that the prevalence of full-cost pricing shows that firms are creatures of custom that make fairly small, profit-oriented changes at fairly infrequent intervals.

We have seen in Chapter 21 that the short-term stickiness of oligopolistic prices can be accounted for under profit-maximizing theory by the fact that it is costly for a multi-product firm to change its list prices. The possible conflict between full-cost and profit-maximizing theory then concerns only the setting of the markup that relates prices to costs. If markups are conventional and only rarely revised then there is a conflict. If, however, the markup is the profit-maximizing one for normal capacity output, then full-cost pricing can be consistent with profit-maximization where it is costly to change prices.

Organization theory   According to profit-maximizing theory, firms constantly scan available alternatives and choose the most profitable ones. A common criticism of this theory is that behaviour is influenced seriously by the organizational structure of the firm. ORGANIZATION THEORY argues that in big firms decisions are made after much discussion by groups and committees and that the structure of the process affects the substance of the decisions.

The central prediction of organization theory is that different decisions will result from different kinds of organizations, even when all else is unchanged.

One proposition that follows from this theory is that large and diffuse organizations find it necessary to develop standard operating procedures to help them in making decisions. These decision rules arise as compromises among competing points of view and, once adopted, are changed only reluctantly. An important prediction following from this hypothesis is that the compromises will persist for long periods of time despite changes in conditions affecting the firm. Even if a particular compromise were the profit-maximizing strategy in the first place, it would not remain so when conditions changed. Thus profits will not usually be maximized.

Another prediction is that decision by compromise will lead firms to adopt conservative policies that avoid large risks. Smaller firms not faced with the necessity of compromising competing views will take bigger risks than larger firms.

Organization theorists have suggested an alternative to profit-maximization that they call SATISFICING. Satisficing theory was first suggested by Professor Herbert Simon of Carnegie-Mellon

University, who in 1978 was awarded the Nobel Prize in economics for his work on firm behaviour. Speaking of his theory, he wrote, 'We must expect the firm's goals to be not maximizing profits but attaining a certain level or rate of profit, holding a certain share of the market or a certain level of sales.'

According to the satisficing hypothesis, firms will strive to achieve certain target levels of profits, but having achieved them, they will not strive to improve their profit position further. This means that the firm could produce any one of a range of outputs that yield at least the target level of profits rather than the unique output that maximizes profits.

In Figure 24.1 on page 333 the satisficing firm would be content with any output between q_1 and q_2, assuming π_c was its satisficing level of profits. Thus

Satisficing theory predicts not a unique equilibrium output but a range of possible outputs that includes the profit-maximizing output somewhere within it and the sales-maximizing output at the upper limit.

Evolutionary theories The modern evolutionary theories advanced by such economists as Richard Nelson and Sidney Winter of Yale University build on the earlier theories of full-cost pricing and satisficing. Nelson and Winter argue that firms do not – indeed, could not – behave as profit-maximizing theory predicts. They accept that firms desire profits and even strive for profits; what they deny is that firms maximize profits globally or even locally.

Evolutionary theorists have gathered much evidence to show that tradition seems to be paramount in firms' planning. The basic effort at the early stages of planning is directed, they argue, toward the problem of performing reasonably well in established markets and maintaining established market shares. They quote evidence to show that suggestions, made by planners in preliminary planning documents, to do something entirely new in some areas, even on a 10-year horizon, are usually weeded out in the reviewing process. They believe that most firms spend very little effort on *planning* to enter entirely new markets, and still less on direct efforts to leave or even reduce their share in long-established markets.

These attitudes were illustrated by one firm which, although faced with obviously changing circumstances, reported that 'We have been producing on the basis of these raw materials for more than 50 years with success, and we have made it a policy to continue to do so.'

The evolutionary theory of the firm draws many analogies with the biological theory of evolution. Here are two of the most important.

The genes: In biological theory, behaviour patterns are transmitted over time by genes. Rules of behaviour fulfil the same function in the evolutionary theory of the firm. In Sidney Winter's words: 'That a great deal of firm decision behaviour is routinized ... is a "stylized fact" about the realities of firm decision process. Routinized ... decision procedures ... cover decision situations from pricing practices in retail stores to such "strategic" decisions as advertising or R and D effort, or the question of whether or not to invest abroad.' Winter talks of firms 'remembering by doing' according to repetitive routines. He adds that government policymakers tend to have unrealistic expectations about firms' flexibility and responsiveness to changes in market incentives. These expectations arise from the maximizing model, whose fatal flaw, Winter alleges, is to underestimate the importance and difficulty 'of the task of merely continuing the routine performance, i.e., of preventing undesired deviations'.

The mutations: In the theory of biological evolution, mutations are the vehicle of change. In the evolutionary theory of the firm this role is played by innovations. Some innovations are similar to those discussed in Chapter 17, the introduction of new products and new production techniques. However, a further important class of innovations in evolutionary theory is the introduction of new rules of behaviour. Sometimes innovations are thrust on the firm; at other times the firm consciously plans for and creates innovations.

According to maximizing theory, innovations are the result of incentives – the 'carrot' of new profit opportunities. In evolutionary theory, the firm is much more of a satisficer, and it usually innovates only under the incentive of the 'stick' either of unacceptably low profits or some form of external prodding. Firms change routines when they get into trouble, not when they see a chance to improve an already satisfactory performance. For example, in the growing markets of the 1960s many firms continued all sorts of wasteful practices that they shed fairly easily when their profits were threatened in the more difficult economic climate of the 1970s.

The significance of non-maximizing theories

An impressive array of evidence can be gathered in apparent support of various non-maximizing theories. What would be the implications if they were accepted as being better theories of the behaviour of the economy than profit-maximization?

If non-maximizing theories are correct, the economic system does not perform with the delicate precision that follows from profit-maximization. But the system described by evolutionary theory *does* function. Firms sell more when demand goes up and less when it goes down. They also alter their prices and their input mixes when hit with the 'stick' of sufficiently large changes in input prices.

> **Evolutionary theory does not upset the broad case for the price system: that it produces a co-ordinated response from decentralized decision-makers to changes in tastes and costs.**

But profit-oriented non-maximizing firms will also exhibit a great deal of inertia. They will not respond quickly and precisely to small changes in market signals from either the private sector or government policy. Neither are they likely to make radical changes in their behaviour even when the profit incentives to do so are large. This casts doubt over the efficacy of government policies that make relatively small changes in incentives hoping that firms will respond to these as profit-maximizers.

> **Non-maximizing models imply sensitivity of the price system to large but not to small changes in signals caused by changes in demand, costs, or public policy.**

Can firms control their own markets?: the Galbraith thesis

A very different hypothesis from the ones considered so far is advocated by John Kenneth Galbraith of Harvard University. Galbraith's theory has two major aspects. First it is *not* consumers' basic wants that create the market signals that in turn provide the profit opportunities that motivate business behaviour. Instead large corporations create and manipulate demand. Second, because the profitability of the enormous investments that large firms must make is threatened by the unpredictability of future events, firms render the future less unpredictable, in order to protect their investments, by actively manipulating market demand and by co-opting government agencies that are supposed to control their activities.

Although this theory was commonly advanced in the UK over the 1950s and 1960s, its second aspect became incredible in the 1970s. By that time it had become difficult to ascribe the required degree of power and influence to UK firms who were clearly being forced by governments and by unions into behaviour they thought profoundly undesirable. Because it is superficially more plausible in the US than in the UK, the theory has been subject to more empirical testing there. *For this reason, we shall discuss it in the light of US rather than UK experience.*

Manipulation of demand

The most important source of unpredictable events that may jeopardize corporate investments is unexpected shifts in market demand curves. To guard against the effects of unexpected declines in demand, companies spend vast amounts on advertising that allows them to sell what they want to produce rather than what consumers want to buy. At the same time, companies hold off the market products that consumers would like to buy. One way to do this is by buying up patents on new goods and then doing nothing with them. This reduces the risks inherent in investing in wholly new and untried products, and avoids the possibility that successful new products might spoil the market for existing products.

According to this hypothesis, consumers are the victims of firms; they are pushed around at whim, persuaded to buy things they do not want, and denied products they would like. In short, they are brainwashed ciphers with artificially created wants, exercising little real autonomy with respect to their own consumption. This aspect of the Galbraith thesis could be applied as well to the UK as to the US.

Corruption of public authorities

A second threat to the long-range plans and investments of firms comes from uncontrollable and often unpredictable changes in the nature of government interference. This political threat is met by co-opting or corrupting legislators, who pass laws affecting companies and the government agencies that are supposed to be regulating them. Company managers, according to the theory, indirectly subvert public institutions (from universities to regulatory agencies). Government, instead of regulating firms and protecting the public interest, has become the servant of the company. It supplies the company sector with such essential inputs into its productive process as educated, trained, healthy and socially secure workers. Government also serves the giant joint stock companies through policies concerning tariffs, import quotas, tax rules, subsidies, and research and development. These policies protect and insulate the industrial establishment from competitive pressures and reinforce its dominance and its profitability. This aspect is mainly concerned with the US, where public policy appears much more pro-business than it does in the UK.

Corruption of social values

These tasks, and the requirements of production, create a class of managers – a techno-structure – that exerts the dominant influence in the company. The managers have great power. The companies they manage earn large profits that can be reinvested to further the achievement of the values of the ruling techno-structure – values that emphasize industrial production, rapid growth, and highly materialistic aspirations at the expense of the better things of life (such as cultural and aesthetic values) and the quality of the environment.

More importantly, the industrial managerial group joins with the military in a military-industrial complex that utilizes, trains and elevates the technicians to positions of power and prestige not only in industry but in the army, the defence establishment and the highest positions of government. In so doing, the companies and their managers threaten to dominate if not subvert foreign as well as domestic policies.

The New Industrial State

The foregoing is an outline of what Galbraith calls the New Industrial State.[1] If Galbraith's theories of the behaviour of modern companies were substantially correct, we would have to make major revisions in our ideas of how free-market economies work.

> **According to the concept of the New Industrial State, the largest companies (i) tend to dominate the economy; (ii) largely control market demand rather than being controlled by it; (iii) co-opt government processes instead of being constrained by them; and (iv) utilize their discretionary power in ways that go against the interests of society.**

The evidence for the hypothesis

Superficially at least, many of the facts of Western economies in general and the American economy in particular lend support to Galbraith's hypothesis. Joint stock companies do account for approximately two-thirds of all business done in the United States today, and large firms dominate the company sector. Of nearly 200,000 American manufacturing companies, roughly 1 per cent of them have $10 million or more in assets. These large companies hold approximately 85 per cent of manufacturing assets. The 200 to 250 largest companies – one-tenth of 1 per cent of all manufacturing companies – control approximately 50 per cent of the total assets of manufacturing.

Many of the giant companies are highly profitable, and most are so widely owned that management, rather than shareholders, exercises effective control. If power comes with size, a 'few' people – several thousand strategically placed executives of a few hundred leading corporations – have great power over economic affairs. Moreover, these people are primarily white, male, wealthy, and politically conservative. As for political influence, individual companies and trade associations have lobbyists and exercise whatever persuasion they can. Executives of many of these companies serve on public commissions and frequently take important government positions. Executives often make large contributions to political campaigns. Political influence is exercised at all levels of government; indeed there have been cases where entire city governments have been effectively in the pockets of local companies.

---

[1] These views did not, however, originate with the publication in 1967 of Galbraith's book by that title. Much earlier, James Burnham wrote *The Managerial Revolution* and Robert Brady sounded an alarm in *Business as a System of Power*. Thorstein Veblen had predicted the technocratic take-over of society in *The Engineers and the Price System* in 1921, and Karl Marx predicted the subversion of the government bureaucrat by the businessman over a century ago.

The political activities of corporations are not confined to the home markets. In the 1970s the Lockheed Aircraft Corporation was implicated in scandals involving million-dollar bribes to secure foreign orders. The list of persons alleged to be involved included (among many others) a former Japanese prime minister, the husband of the ruling Queen of the Netherlands, and several former Italian Christian Democrat cabinet ministers. There is no longer any doubt that companies have succeeded in corrupting government at the highest levels (or at least in harnessing the corruption that was already there) and through political channels have achieved results that they might never have achieved in the market place.

The great firms, along with many smaller ones, spend vast amounts on advertising – as the hypothesis predicts. The total advertising expenditure of US companies is about 2·5 per cent of the contribution of the private sector to total American output. These expenditures are obviously designed to influence consumers' demand, and there is little doubt that if firms such as Lever Brothers (soap), Gulf Oil (petroleum products), Schlitz (beer) and General Motors (cars), cut their advertising, they would lose sales to their competitors.

Doubts about the hypothesis

Sensitivity to the market pressures Even the largest and most powerful industries are not immune to market pressures. The failure of the Edsel, a car once produced by the Ford Motor Company in the US and marketed with a vast advertising campaign, was a classic example of market rejection of a product. The penetration of small foreign cars into the American market forced the US automobile industry into producing small cars. But in spite of all the advertising, so many American customers still prefer the foreign imports to the local products that the industry remains in deep trouble. The decline of railroading as a mode of passenger travel is manifest in many ways, as the financial history of once great railroading corporations shows. The Pullman Company, maker of railway sleeping cars, was America's tenth largest firm in 1909; today it is not even in the top 300. The rise of air and motor travel and the decline of railroading were accompanied by a rise in the use of oil and a decline in the use of coal. More recently, the surge in demand for electric power and the shortage of oil have revitalized the coal industry.

Changes in demands and in tastes are sometimes sudden and dramatic, but in the main they are gradual and less noticeable month by month than decade by decade. On average about two new firms enter the top 100 every year, and, as a consequence, two others leave. This means a significant change over a decade. Turnover in the leading American companies is continuous and revealing. Only two, US Steel and Exxon (Standard Oil of New Jersey), were in the top 10 both in 1910 and a half-century later. Consider these giants of 1910, none of them among the largest 250 today: International Mercantile Marine (today United States Lines), United States Cotton Oil, American Hide and Leather, American Ice, Baldwin Locomotive, Cudahy, International Salt and United Shoe Machinery. They have slipped or disappeared largely because of the relative decline in the demand for their products. Today's giants include automobile, oil and airline companies, and electric power producers – for the obvious reason that demand for these products is strong.

Are these shifts in demand explained by manipulation of consumers' tastes through advertising or by more basic changes? Advertising has two major aspects: it seeks to inform consumers of the characteristics of the available products and it seeks to influence consumers by altering their demands. The first aspect, informative advertising, plays an important part in the efficient operation of any free-market system; the second aspect is one through which firms seek to control the market rather than being controlled by it.

Clearly, advertising does influence consumers' demand. We have observed that if General Motors stopped advertising, it would surely lose sales to Ford and Chrysler, but it is hard to believe that the automotive society was conjured up by the advertising industry or that when an American is persuaded to fly on United Airlines his real alternative is to use a covered wagon, a bicycle or even a Greyhound bus – more likely he is forgoing American, Eastern or Northwest Airlines. Careful promotion can influence the success of one new wave rock group over another, but could it sell the waltz to today's youth? Advertising – taste making – unquestionably plays a role in shaping demand, but so too do more basic human attitudes, psychological needs, technological opportunities and many fads and fashions stemming from sources other than advertising.

Certainly advertising shifts demands among very similar products. It is hard to believe, however, that the economy, or the average citizen's system of values, would be fundamentally changed if there were available one more or one less make of automobile or TV set or brand of shoes. A look at those products that have brought basic changes to the economy – and perhaps to value systems – suggests that these products succeeded *because consumers wanted them*, not because the advertising industry brainwashed people into buying them. Consider a few of the major examples.

The automobile transformed society and is now in demand everywhere in the world, even in Communist countries where only informative advertising exists. The Hollywood movie had an enormous influence in shaping society and in changing values; it was – and still is – eagerly attended everywhere in the world, whether or not it is accompanied by a bally-hoo of advertising. The aeroplane – and the jet in particular – has shrunk the size of the world: it has allowed major league sports to expand beyond the confines of the Northeastern and Midwestern United States (i.e., those cities which could be reached by an overnight bus or rail journey); it has made the international conference a commonplace among professionals; it has made European, Hawaiian and Caribbean vacations a reality for the many rather than a luxury for the very few. For better or worse, the revolution in behaviour caused by the birth control pill is still being worked out. TV has changed the activities of children (and adults) in fundamental ways and has brought to viewers a sense of immediacy about distant events that newspapers could never achieve. It also provided news coverage that both caused and partially compensated for the decline in the number of newspapers in many cities.

Many factors, including advertising and salesmanship, affect consumers' purchasing patterns. However, the new products that have really influenced the allocation of resources and the pattern of society – such as those mentioned in the previous paragraph – have succeeded because consumers wanted them; most of those that failed did so because they were not wanted – at least not at prices that would cover their costs of production.

> **The evidence suggests that the allocation of resources in any market economy owes more to the tastes and values of consumers than it does to advertising and related activities.**

Thus the Galbraithian view that companies are able to create the demand for their products seems less consistent with the evidence than the conventional view that consumers are a major force in determining the economy's allocation of resources.

Who controls the government?   Is the American government subservient to big business?

Lobbying is a legal, large-scale activity employed by many groups. Big business has its influence, but so too do farmers, labour unions and small business groups. Some American companies have certainly exercised illegal and improper influence on both domestic and foreign governments. Cases of corrupt behaviour have been documented at all levels of government; it does not follow from this, however, that government is subservient to the companies and that decisions taken by the former are *dominated* by the wishes of the latter. It is easy to assert that 'everyone knows that the oil lobby dominates the US Congress', but such assertions do not resolve empirical questions. Lobbying and influence may well help to explain why for years the United States imposed quotas on foreign oil imports, but lobbying by the oil companies did not prevent a delay of the Alaska pipeline for many years, the reduction in special tax reliefs or restrictions imposed on offshore oil drilling. Relaxation of many anti-pollution restrictions came because of the oil shortages of the 1970s, not political pressure. Government contracts bolster the aerospace industry, but Boeing and Lockheed have been in deep financial trouble, partly as a result of government decisions. Tobacco companies have seen government agencies first publicize the hazards of their principal product and then restrict their advertising.

Thus, while business often succeeds in its attempts to protect its commercial interests through political activity, it does so within limits. Where the truth lies between the extremes of 'no influence' and 'no limits' is a matter now being subjected to substantial research. It is a matter that will be clarified by further research, not by mere assertion. In the meantime we can safely say, first, 'firms have a lot of political influence' and, second, 'there are some serious constraints on the ability of firms to exert political influence over all levels of American government'.

Neglect of the public interest? A receptive American public has acclaimed one aspect of the Galbraithian critique: the apparent disregard by large companies for the adverse effects of productive activities on the environment. The problems of pollution arise from activities of both small and large companies, and from activities of government units and citizens as well. Do such polluting activities represent in a significant degree irresponsible behaviour by companies that can be countered by such things as Campaign GM – 'a campaign to make General Motors responsible'?

What has come to be known as the 'consumerist' view, or 'consumerism', is that companies ought on their own volition to serve the general public's interest, not merely the interests of their shareholders. Thus, for example, General Motors' directors must be made to recognize that automobiles both pollute and cause accidents, and General Motors' abundant resources should be invested in developing and installing both safety and anti-pollution devices. This, consumerists argue, is proper use of General Motors' profits, even if General Motors' shareholders do not see it that way and even if automobile purchasers do not want to pay the cost of the extra safety and anti-pollution devices.

The main arguments *for* this view are that only the company can know the potentially adverse effect of its actions and that by virtue of holding a corporate charter, the company assumes the responsibility to protect the general welfare while pursuing private profits.

The main argument *against* the consumerist view is that managers of companies have neither the knowledge nor the ability to represent the general public interest; they are largely selected, judged and promoted according to their ability to run a profit-oriented enterprise, and the assumption that they are especially competent to decide broader *public* questions is unjustified. Moral (as distinct from economic) decisions – such as whether to make or use nerve gas, to make or use internal combustion engines, to manufacture or smoke cigarettes and to manufacture or utilize DDT or aerosol sprays – cannot properly be delegated to individual companies or their executives. Some of them are individual decisions; others require either the expertise or the authority of a public regulatory agency. Whoever makes decisions on behalf of the public must be politically responsible to the public.

Those who oppose the consumerist view hold that most required changes in company behaviour should be accomplished not by exhorting business leaders to behave responsibly, nor by placing consumer representatives on the company's board of directors, but by regulations or incentives that force or induce the desired firm behaviour. Let companies pursue their profits – subject to public laws. For example, the government can require all cars to have seat belts, or require car manufacturers to install anti-pollution valves or to meet specific standards of emission levels. Another alternative is to open the way for law-suits against companies that either enjoin certain behaviour or force corporations to pay for the damages their products cause.

The controversy over policy alternatives is important, and much of the credit for its existence is due to Galbraith. It is essential to recognize that the policy issues at stake – whether and how to change the behaviour of companies – can arise whether companies are primarily responding to market signals or whether they are impervious to them. If citizens do not approve of the results of company behaviour, they will want to control the behaviour, whatever the cause, provided that the costs – including undesirable side-effects – do not exceed the benefits.

Some final words

The importance of profits

Economics is a continually developing subject; its theories are under constant scrutiny and even attack. Some of the major debates concerning the profit-maximizing theory of the firm have been reviewed in this chapter. On the one hand, the Galbraithian view that firms create their own market conditions seems difficult to maintain in the face of the evidence. On the other hand, it seems unlikely that simple profit-maximizing theory will be rich enough to capture all aspects of firm behaviour. Thus it may benefit by expansion to include elements of such theories as satisficing, sales-maximization, and evolutionary behaviour.

Profits, however, are unmistakably a potent force in the life – and death – of firms. The resilience of profit-maximizing theory and its ability to predict how the economy will react to some major changes (such as the recent dramatic increases in energy prices) suggests that firms are at least strongly motivated by the pursuit of profits and that, other things being equal, they prefer more profits to less profits.

If *profit-maximizing* theory should eventually give way to some more organizationally dominated theory, the new theory will still be a *profit-oriented* theory. The search for profits and the avoidance of losses is a powerful force that drives the economy even when firms do not turn out to be continual profit-maximizers.

How far can firms depart from profit-maximizing behaviour?

Many of the criticisms that we have just considered assume that firms seek to do things other than maximize their profits. If the present management elects not to maximize its profits, this implies that some other management could make more money by operating the firm. Major restraints on existing managements are the threats of a shareholder revolt or of a take-over bid. As we shall see in some detail in Chapter 28, the maximum amount one can afford to pay for any asset depends on how much it is expected to earn. If I can make an asset produce more than you, I can rationally outbid you for it.

A management that fails to come close to achieving the profit potential of the assets it controls becomes a natural target for acquisition by a firm that specializes in taking over inefficiently run firms. The management of the acquiring firm makes a TENDER OFFER (or a TAKE-OVER BID as it is sometimes called) to the shareholders of the target firm, offering them what amounts to a premium for their shares, a premium it can pay because it expects to increase the firm's profits. Managers who wish to avoid take-over bids cannot let the profits of their firm slip far from the profit-maximizing level – because their unrealized profits provide the incentives for take-overs. Some, though by no means all, of the so-called conglomerate firms have specialized in this kind of merger. The pressure of the threat of take-overs must be regarded as limiting the discretion of corporate management to pursue goals other than profit-maximization.

The general demand and supply theory of a market economy

In Chapter 5 we noted that there was evidence that markets for agricultural goods and other primary products did function as assumed in the theory of demand and supply. We also stated that the generalization of this demand-and-supply theory to a theory of the whole economy was a rather speculative leap in the dark. We have now studied the theory of production sufficiently to realize that we cannot in fact apply our simple demand-and-supply theory to the whole economy. This theory is a theory of *competitive* markets, markets in which there is a large number of buyers and sellers. Most manufactured goods, however, are produced under conditions of oligopoly in which there are a very few firms. These firms may or may not compete actively with each other, and in cases in which they do compete they are quite likely to change their prices only occasionally and to compete from day to day by adjusting such things as service, delivery dates, quality and special features of the product.

How important is it that the manufacturing sector is primarily oligopolistic? Does this fact undermine our ability to use economic theory as a successful predictive device? At least two things seem fairly clear.

First, we do have difficulty predicting the detailed effects on the manufacturing industries of changes in such things as tax rates, the number of firms in an industry, demands, costs and government regulations. In administered-price situations there is considerable non-price competition. Since we do not have a single well-tested theory of non-price competition, it is often, although by no means always, unclear what will be the effects of changes such as those just listed.

Second, if we wish to predict general long-term trends our theory is more helpful. There is substantial empirical evidence to support each of the following statements. The prices of most primary products are set on competitive markets and these prices do fluctuate in response to shifts in demands and supplies. Large changes in the relative prices of inputs do cause firms to change the proportions in which they use factors, since *whatever* the firm's objectives, they can usually be better served by minimizing costs rather than by wasting money unnecessarily. Continual changes in the prices of inputs sooner or later lead firms to change the prices of their outputs. (Even a non-profit-maximizing monopoly cannot afford to let its profits become significantly negative.) This means that, over the long term, relative prices of manufactured commodities do change to reflect major changes in the relative costs of producing these commodities. When relative commodity prices change, consumers react, and many long-term changes in consumption patterns that are often casually ascribed to changes in tastes, fashions and habits, are actually responses to changes in relative prices. Observers who predict the broad reactions to such major changes as the increases in the price of oil over the last decade make disastrous errors when they ignore this general long-term adaptability of the economy which makes it behave in broad outline as would a perfectly competitive economy.

This assessment would probably command general, although by no means universal, acceptance among economists. But just *how* bad is our ability to predict in detail (especially in the oligopolistic part of the economy), and just *how* good is our ability to predict long-term trend reactions to major events? (Do not forget that we are not trying to foretell the future, but to make conditional predictions about the reactions of the economy to given events.) Because it is hard to assemble the mass of available evidence so as to focus it on this issue, economists are left to their personal assessments of the balance between success and failure, and debate goes on among those who assess it differently. About all that it seems safe to say is that, when judged by its ability to predict the outcome of events in which we are interested, the theory of the allocation of resources reveals many substantial successes and some major failures.

Part five

The theory of distribution

25

The demand for and supply of factors of production

Are the poor getting poorer and the rich richer, as Karl Marx thought they would? Are the rich getting relatively poorer and the poor relatively richer, as Alfred Marshall hoped they would? Is the inequality of income a social constant, determined by forces possibly beyond man's understanding and probably beyond his control, as Vilfredo Pareto thought they were? These questions concern what is called *the size distribution of income.*

The great classical economists, Adam Smith, David Ricardo and Karl Marx, were concerned with the *functional distribution of income*: how income was shared among the three great social classes of their day – workers, capitalists and landowners. They defined three basic factors of production; labour, capital and land, according to the functions that they fulfilled in production. The return to each of these factors was the income of each of the three classes.

The functional and the size distribution of income[1]

Income takes many forms: wages and salaries, rental income from property, interest and profits, to name the major ones. When we classify income in this way we are interested in the FUNCTIONAL DISTRIBUTION OF INCOME, i.e., the amounts of income paid to the various factors of production rather than the amounts paid to various individuals or households. A single individual may receive income from several different factors of production. A man may get income for his own labour services, from renting property that he owns, and from his holdings of shares in various joint-stock companies. When we classify income according to the size of income received by each household irrespective of the sources of that income, we are dealing with the SIZE DISTRIBUTION of income. Many economic policies are designed to modify the size distribution of income.

Factor prices and factor incomes

It is tempting to give superficial explanations of differences in income: 'People are paid what they are worth.' But the economist must ask: Worth what to whom? What gives them value? Sometimes it is said that people earn according to their ability. But note that incomes are distributed in a very much

---

[1] For the factual background concerning various aspects of the distribution of income, see Harbury and Lipsey, Chapter 4.

more unequal fashion than any measured index of ability such as IQ or physical strength. In what sense is Cleo Laine 20 times as able as the promising new pop singer? She earns 20 times as much. In what sense is a lorry driver more able than a schoolteacher? In what sense is a football player more able than a wrestler? If answers couched in terms of worth and ability seem superficial, so are answers such as 'It's all a matter of luck' or 'It's just the system'. We are concerned now with discovering whether or not the theories of economics provide explanations of the distribution of income that are more satisfactory than the ones mentioned above. The traditional or *neo-Classical* theory states that the distribution of income is simply a special case of price theory. The income of any factor of production (and hence the amount of the national product that it is able to command) depends on the price that is paid for the factor and the amount that is used. If we wish to build a theory of distribution, we need a theory of factor prices. Such a theory involves little that is not already familiar.

The free-market price of any commodity is determined by demand and supply. In Figure 25.1 the original curves for some factor of production are D_1 and S. The equilibrium price and quantity are p_1 and q_1. The total income earned by the factor is the shaded area.

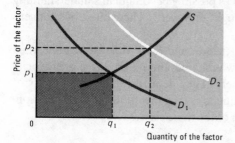

Fig. 25.1 The determination of the price, quantity and income of a factor of production

We assume that the price of all other factors of production, the prices of all goods, and the level of national income are given and constant.[1] Fluctuations in the equilibrium price and quantity will now cause fluctuations in the money earnings of the factor, in its relative earnings (compared to other factors) and in the share of national income going to the factor. Assume, for example, that the demand curve for the factor in question rises from D_1 to D_2. Now the money price of the factor rises from p_1 to p_2, and the relative price rises from p_1/F to p_2/F where F is the given average price of *all* other factors. The total earnings rise from p_1q_1 to p_2q_2 and, if the total income in the whole economy remains constant at γ, then the share of income going to this factor rises from p_1q_1/γ to p_2q_2/γ. This gives us the free-market determination of a factor's price and its share of national income. Onto this theory we can then, if necessary, superimpose the effects of any government interventions (as we did in Chapter 10) or any monopolistic elements (as we did in Chapter 20).

> **According to neo-Classical theory, the problem of distribution in a free-market society can be reduced to the question of the determinants of the demand and supply of factors of production, plus the problem of determining the effect of the departures from a free market caused by such forces as monopolistic organizations, government action, and unions.**

[1] We make these assumptions because we are concerned with a factor's relative share of total national income. As we observed in the last paragraph of page 160, these assumptions are a simplifying device for our analysis, but they do not restrict its applicability to inflationary situations.

The demand for factors

Firms require land, labour, raw materials, machines and other inputs to produce the goods and services that they sell. The demand for any input therefore depends on the existence of a demand for the goods that it helps to make. We say that the demand is a DERIVED DEMAND.

Obvious examples of derived demand abound. The demand for computer programmers is growing as industry turns increasingly to electronic computers. The demand for university teachers varies directly with the number of students going to university. The demand for coal miners and coal-digging equipment declines as the demand for coal declines. Typically, of course, one factor will be used in making many goods, not just one. Steel is used in dozens of industries, as are the services of carpenters. The total demand for a factor will be the sum of its derived demands in all of its productive activities.

In this section we are mainly concerned with deducing the prediction that the demand curve for a factor is downward sloping. We do this because derived demand provides a link between the pricing of factors and the pricing of products. This allows us to connect our theory of the behaviour of the firm to our theory of distribution.

The quantity of a factor demanded in equilibrium

We first derive a famous relation that will hold in equilibrium for every factor employed by a wide class of firms. Recall that in Part 4 we established a set of conditions necessary for the maximization of profits in the short run. Some factor was fixed (usually capital) and some other factor was allowed to vary, and we saw that the profit-maximizing firm would increase its output to the level at which the last unit produced added just as much to cost as it did to revenue or, in technical language, until marginal cost equalled marginal revenue. Another way of stating exactly the same thing is to say that *the profit-maximizing firm will increase production up to the point at which the last unit of the variable factor employed adds just as much to revenue as it does to cost.*

Just as it is true that all profit-maximizing firms, whether they are selling under conditions of perfect competition, monopolistic competition or monopoly, produce to the point at which marginal cost equals marginal revenue, so it is true that all profit-maximizing firms will hire units of the variable factor up to the point at which the marginal cost of the factor (i.e., the addition to the total cost resulting from the employment of one more unit) equals the marginal revenue produced by the factor. Since we have already used the term *marginal revenue* to refer to the change in revenue resulting from the sale of an additional unit of product, we shall use another term, MARGINAL REVENUE PRODUCT, to mean the addition to revenue resulting from the sale of the product contributed by an additional unit of the variable factor. It is true, therefore, of *all* profit-maximizing firms that are in equilibrium:

$$\text{marginal cost of the variable factor} = \text{marginal revenue product of that factor.} \tag{1}$$

If there were a single factor for which (1) did not hold, the firm could increase its profits by varying the employment of that factor. Thus (1) is a relation that must hold in equilibrium for *all* profit-maximizing firms with respect to all variable factors of production.

Now let us consider all those firms that are unable to influence the prices of the factors that they purchase (i.e., firms that are price-takers in factor markets). In this case the marginal cost of a factor is merely its price. The cost, for example, of obtaining an extra person on the payroll is the wage that must be paid to that person. For firms that take factor prices as given, condition (1) becomes:

$$\text{price of the factor} = \text{marginal revenue product of the factor.} \tag{2}$$

The firm's demand curve for a factor[1]

Conditions (1) and (2) describe relations that hold in equilibrium. We now wish to derive the demand curve for a factor of production. We shall do this assuming that the firm is unable to influence the price of the factor. (We shall drop this assumption in Chapter 27.) For the moment we shall also assume that there is only a single variable factor of production. This allows us to use condition (2) to derive the firm's demand for factor as soon as we have its marginal revenue product curve.

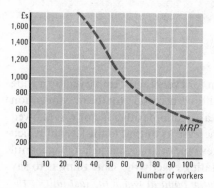

Fig. 25.2 A marginal revenue product curve for a factor

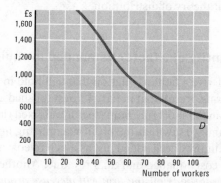

Fig. 25.3 A firm's demand curve for a factor of production when only one factor can be varied is the marginal revenue product curve of that factor

The derivation of the demand curve from the marginal revenue product curve   Figure 25.2 shows a marginal revenue product for some factor.[2] This shows how much would be added to revenue by employing one more unit of the factor for each level of total employment of the factor. Condition (2) states that the profit-maximizing firm will employ additional units of the factor up to the point at which the marginal revenue product equals the price of the factor. If, for example, the price were £1,200 per year, then it would be most profitable to employ 50 workers. (There is no point in employing a fifty-first, since that would add just less than £1,200 to revenue but £1,200 to costs, and hence would *reduce* total profits.)

The curve in Figure 25.3 shows the quantity of labour employed at each price of labour. Such a

---

[1] The following sections are difficult and may be omitted without loss of continuity by skipping directly to the summary that begins on page 357.

[2] We avoid a long chain of reasoning without any immediate payoff by first showing how to derive a demand curve *given* a marginal revenue product curve and then showing how to derive the marginal revenue product curve itself. A more straight-forward but less immediately appealing development of the argument would be to derive the *MRP* curve first and then the demand curve.

curve can be derived from Figure 25.2 by picking various prices of the variable factor, and reading off the amount used from the marginal revenue product curve in just the way described above for the price of £1,200.

Note that the curve in Figure 25.3 is identical with the marginal revenue product curve in Figure 25.2. The curve in Figure 25.3 relates the price of the variable factor to the quantity employed. Hence, it is the demand curve for the variable factor.

The marginal revenue product curve of a factor has the same shape as the firm's demand curve for that factor.

The derivation of the marginal revenue product curve We have related the firm's demand for a single variable factor to the marginal revenue product curve. Next we inquire into the derivation of that curve. The marginal revenue product of the factor is defined as the addition to total revenue resulting from the use of an additional unit. This may be broken up into a physical and a value component, and we now consider how each of these varies as the quantity of the factor varies.

The physical component: We have assumed that we have only one variable factor of production. As we vary the quantity of this factor, output will vary. The hypothesis of diminishing returns that we developed in Chapter 17 predicts that, as we go on adding more and more units of the variable factor to the given quantity of the fixed factor, the extra output produced by successive increments of the variable factor will decline. This extra output is called the marginal physical product (MPP) of the variable factor and its behaviour is shown in Figure 25.4.

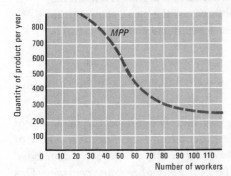

Fig. 25.4 The marginal physical product curve

The value component: Now to convert the marginal physical product curve of Figure 25.4 into a marginal revenue product curve, we need to know the value of the extra physical product. The marginal physical product depends solely on the technical conditions of production, but the value to the firm of this extra product depends on the price of the product. There are two cases to consider. If the firm sells its product in a perfectly competitive market, the price is given, and it accurately measures the value to the firm of an additional unit. Thus, in the case of perfect competition, the marginal revenue product is given by:

$$\text{marginal physical product multiplied by price of the product.} \tag{3}$$

If, on the other hand, the firm faces a downward-sloping demand curve for its product, the value to the firm of an extra unit of output will be less than its price, because to sell the extra unit it will have to reduce the price on all other units to be sold. In this case the marginal revenue due to an extra unit of output is less than its price. Thus, where any firm faces a downward-sloping demand curve for its product, the marginal revenue product is given by:

> marginal physical product multiplied by marginal revenue
> associated with the sale of the extra unit. (4)

In both cases the firm is interested in the gain in revenue. The only difference is that in (3) the marginal revenue is the price, while in (4) it is less than price (because the firm faces a downward-sloping demand curve for its product). We have avoided unnecessary terminology by referring to both (3) and (4) as marginal revenue product. Sometimes, however, when it is desirable to distinguish between the two, (3) is called *the value of the marginal product*, while the term *marginal revenue product* is reserved for (4).

Summary All of this no doubt sounds very forbidding at first reading. It is an example of a chain of reasoning, referred to in the Introduction, where each step is simple enough, but the cumulative effects of several steps can seem complex. And there are more steps to come! Perhaps it would be a good idea, before going on, to summarize the argument so far:

> **Any profit-maximizing firm will hire a variable factor up to the point at which the last unit adds as much to revenue as to costs. The addition to costs is the price of the factor (if the firm buys factors in a competitive market). The addition to revenue is the marginal physical product multiplied by the price of the product if the firm sells in a perfectly competitive market, and marginal physical product multiplied by marginal revenue if the firm faces a downward-sloping demand curve. In both cases, the curve showing the addition to revenue resulting from the employment of each additional unit of the factor is the firm's demand curve for the factor.**

The industry's demand for the factor

When we derived the market demand for a commodity, we merely summed the demands of individual households. We cannot rely on such a simple procedure in the case of a factor of production. The individual firm's demand curve shows how the quantity of the factor demanded varies with the factor's price, *assuming that the price of the firm's output remains constant*. This assumption is valid only if all other firms keep their outputs fixed. If the price of the variable factor changes, however, we should expect all firms to vary their production. If, for example, the price of the factor falls, then all firms will hire more of the variable factor and the resulting rise in output will cause a fall in the market price of the commodity. This fall in price will cause the marginal revenue product of the factor – the amount added to total revenue by the employment of one more unit of the factor – to be less than if the price of the product had remained unchanged. We may now derive a demand curve on the assumption that when factor prices change, all firms in the industry will vary their outputs in order to maximize their profits. We assume that we know the marginal physical product curves for all firms in the industry, and also the demand curve for the product produced by the industry, and we proceed in the following manner.

(1) Assume some particular price of the factor and find the equilibrium price for the product. This is

done in the manner described in Chapter 19: once the factor price is known, the marginal physical product curves can be translated into marginal cost curves; these cost curves are then summed, giving an industry supply curve which, together with the demand curve, determines the equilibrium price of the product.

(2) Next, take the marginal physical product curve of the firm in which we are interested, and multiply each quantity by the market price determined in (1) above. This gives a marginal revenue product curve on the assumption that market price remains constant as output is varied. This is the curve MRP_1 shown in Figure 25.5. Locate the point A in Figure 25.5, corresponding to the existing price of the factor and the quantity actually being employed. *This curve, MRP_1, is the firm's demand curve for the variable factor, on the assumption that the price of the commodity is fixed; its slope depends solely on the technical conditions of production, i.e. on the slope of the marginal physical product curve.*

(3) Now consider a lower price of the factor, say p_2, instead of p_1. Our firm, in an effort to maximize profits, will hire more labour and increase its output. But so will all other firms and, as a result, the price of the product will fall. This causes the curve showing marginal physical product (MPP) multiplied by existing market price to *shift inwards towards the origin* – to MRP_2 in the Figure. Thus the firm moves towards equilibrium in two ways: by hiring more labour and by having its curve showing marginal physical product *times* market price shift inwards. A possible equilibrium is illustrated by point B. The lower price of the product gives rise to a new curve showing MPP *times* market price and the new quantity of labour hired is q_2 instead of q_1. We repeat the procedure for each possible price of labour and generate a set of points such as A and B. We then join up these points and obtain a demand curve for labour allowing for the price changes in the final product. This curve, which is shown by the white line in Figure 25.5, is steeper than any of the fixed price demand

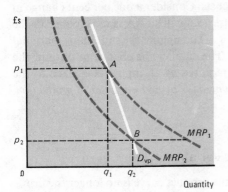

Fig. 25.5 Derivation of the firm's demand curve for a factor on the assumption that all firms change their output so that the price of a product changes when the price of the factor changes

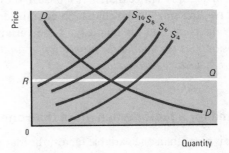

Fig. 25.6 Derivation of the demand curve for a factor by perfectly competitive industry

curves. How much steeper depends upon how much the price of the product falls as all firms expand output, i.e., on the elasticity of the market demand for the product. In order to derive the industry's demand curve for the factor, we merely aggregate the demand curves we have developed.

An alternative derivation of the industry's demand curve

Alternatively, we can derive the industry demand curve for a factor in the following way. Take the MPP curve for each firm. Assume some specific price of the variable factor. Derive a marginal cost curve for each firm by the means used in Chapter 17. Sum these to obtain an industry supply curve. Now repeat the process for each possible price of the variable factor. This gives rise to a whole family of short-run industry supply curves, each corresponding to a particular price of the variable factor. Such a family of curves is illustrated in Figure 25.6 (S_{10} corresponding to a factor price of £10 a day, S_8 to a factor price of £8, etc.). Assume a particular factor price, say £6. By using the market demand curve and the supply curve S_6, the equilibrium price and quantity can be derived. Now draw a horizontal line, RQ, through the point of intersection of S_6 and D. The points of intersection of RQ and the various supply curves tell how production would vary as factor prices varied, *if the market price did not change*. The points of intersection of the actual demand curve, D, and the various supply curves show how production varies when market prices vary. Since we now know the amount of production corresponding to each particular price of the variable factor, we know the amount of the variable factor that must be employed. Plotting this amount against its price gives the industry demand curve for the factor. Clearly, for given changes in factor prices, the variations in production, and hence the elasticity of demand for the variable factor, are less when the commodity's price varies than when it is assumed to be constant. Now draw for yourself a diagram similar to Figure 25.6, but with a much steeper demand curve than the one in the printed figure. You will then be able to show yourself that *the lower the elasticity of demand for the product, the lower the elasticity of demand for a factor*.

One other important relation can be derived from this analysis. Consider two factors of production: expenditure on factor A accounts for two per cent of the total costs of production; expenditure on factor B accounts for fifty per cent of total costs. Consider a one per cent change in the price of each factor. Clearly, the supply curves in Figure 25.6 will shift less in response to the change in factor A's price than in response to the change in B's. The smaller the shift in the marginal cost curve, the smaller the change in equilibrium output. The smaller the change in output, the smaller the change in the quantity of the variable factor required as an input. This leads to the conclusion that *the smaller the proportion of total cost accounted for by a given factor of production, the more inelastic its demand*.[1]

Demand for a factor when more than one factor is variable

If there is more than one variable factor, the marginal revenue product curve is no longer the firm's demand curve for the factor. This curve shows what happens to revenues as the quantity of the factor employed is varied *while all other factors are held constant*. If there is more than one variable

---

[1] This is necessarily true when we have only one variable factor of production, but care must be taken when there are many variable factors. The elasticity of demand depends in such cases both on the proportion of costs accounted for by the factor, and on the ease with which other factors can be substituted for it. Thus, we would not expect there to be an inelastic demand on British building sites for Irish labourers from the city of Cork because, although they account for a low proportion of total costs, other labourers are perfect substitutes for them. On the other hand, we would expect there to be an inelastic demand for door handles because, not only are they a small proportion of the total cost of building a house, it is very hard to build a satisfactory house without them.

factor, a change in the price of one factor will lead to a substitution between the variable factors; more of the now cheaper factor will be bought *even if the firm's output is unchanged*. Thus, the firm's demand curve for a factor will be more elastic than the marginal revenue product curve of the factor, the amount of additional elasticity depending on the ease with which one factor can be substituted for another.

How easy it is to substitute one factor for another depends on the technical conditions of production. It is very easy to underestimate the degree of substitutability. It is fairly obvious that a bushel of wheat can be produced by combining land either with a lot of labour and a little capital or with a little labour and a lot of capital. It is common, however, to think in terms of using inputs in fixed proportions in manufacturing. A bit of casual observation of any manufacturing industry over time will show that factor proportions can be varied to produce a given product. There is, for example, the case in which glass and steel turn out to be very good substitutes for each other. One would never guess this by considering their physical qualities in general, but in the case of car manufacture one can be substituted for the other over a wide range merely by varying the dimensions of the windows.

We have looked at some alternative ways of deriving the demand curve for a factor. However we do this, or whether we do it at all, the following will always hold:

Any profit-maximizing firm in equilibrium will always be equating the marginal cost of each of its variable factors with the marginal revenue product of that factor.

Summary of the theory of the demand for a factor

Our discussion of the demand for a factor of production leads to the conclusion that the elasticity of the demand for a factor depends on both the technical conditions of production and the market demand for the commodity that the factor produces. The main influences may be summarized as follows:

An industry's demand for a factor will be more elastic:
(1) the more elastic is the demand for the industry's output;
(2) the larger is the proportion of total cost accounted for by payments to the factor;
(3) the easier it is to substitute other factors for the one in question.

As well as predicting the forces that influence elasticity of demand, the theory shows certain relations that must hold in equilibrium for any firm that is unable to influence the prices of the factors that it purchases:

(1) If the firm sells its product in a perfect market, the price paid to a factor will be equal to the value of that factor's marginal product, i.e., marginal physical product multiplied by the price of the product.
(2) If the firm faces a downward-sloping demand curve for its product, the price of a factor will be equated in equilibrium with the marginal revenue product of the factor, i.e., marginal physical product multiplied by the marginal revenue resulting from the sale of the extra product. This amount is necessarily less than the value of the marginal physical product multiplied by the price of the product.

Finally, we note that although the above relations hold in all equilibrium situations, it does *not* follow from our theory that the sum of the firms' marginal revenue product curves is the industry's demand curve for the factor.

The supply of factors of production

We first make a distinction between the total supply of a factor to the whole economy and the supply to some small part of the economy, say to one industry or to one firm. We shall deal first with the total supply of factors to the economy.

The total supply of factors

At first glance it may seem plausible to assume that the total supply of most factors is fixed. After all, there is only so much land in the world, or in England, or in London. There is an upper limit to the number of workers. There is only so much coal, oil, copper and iron ore in the earth. These considerations do indeed put absolute maxima upon the supplies of factors. But in virtually every case we are not near the upper limits, and the determinants of changes in the total *effective* supply of land, labour, natural resources or capital need to be considered.

Labour   The number of people willing to work is called the LABOUR FORCE; the total number of hours they are willing to work is called the SUPPLY OF EFFORT or, more simply, THE SUPPLY OF LABOUR.

> **The supply of effort is a function of three things: the size of the population, the proportion of the population willing to work and the number of hours worked by each individual.**

Population: Populations vary in size, and these variations are influenced to some extent by economic factors. There is some evidence that the birth rate is higher in good times than in bad. Much of the variation in population is, however, explained by factors outside of economics.

The labour force: The labour force varies considerably in response to variations in the demand for labour. Generally, a rise in the demand for labour, and an accompanying rise in earnings, will lead to an increase in the proportion of the population willing to work. More married women and elderly people enter the labour force when the demand for labour is high.

Hours worked: Workers are in the position of trading their leisure for goods; by giving up leisure (by working), they obtain money and, hence, goods. A rise in the wage rate means that there is a change in the relative price of goods and leisure. Goods become cheaper relative to leisure, since each hour worked results in more goods than before, and each hour of leisure consumed is at the cost of more goods forgone. This is illustrated in Figure 25.7. Leisure is measured on the vertical axis and the money value of goods consumed on the horizontal axis. Each individual starts with 24 hours of his own time. If the wage rate is 50 pence per hour, he can have 24 hours of leisure and no goods, or £12 worth of goods and no leisure (much less any sleep), or any combination of goods and leisure indicated by points on budget line *A*. Assume, first, that he chooses the position indicated by point *x*, so that he consumes 14 hours of leisure and trades the other 10 (at 50 pence per hour) for £5 worth of goods. Now assume that the wage rate rises to, say, £1 per hour. He can now have any combination of goods and leisure indicated by points on budget line *B*. If he continues to work for 10 hours per day, he moves to point *z* and now gets £10 worth of goods, but there is nothing to stop him from moving to a point above and to the right of *x*, in which case he can have more goods *and* more leisure. If, for example, he moves to the position indicated by *y*, he will have an extra two hours of leisure and an extra £3 worth of goods. On the other hand, the extra income that can be obtained *per unit of leisure sacrificed* might make him more willing to give up leisure to get goods, He might, for example, move to point *w* and work one more hour, getting £11 worth of goods.[1]

The above analysis leads to the following conclusion:

Standard theory makes no prediction about the effect of an increase in wage rates on the overall supply of effort, which may rise, fall or remain unchanged.

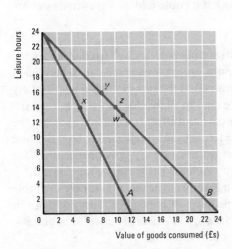

Fig. 25.7 The choice between income and leisure

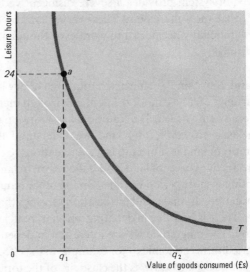

Fig. 25.8 The disincentive effects of work-related welfare payments

Much of the long-run evidence tends to show that as real earnings per hour rise, people wish to reduce the number of hours they work. This evidence is, of course, concerned with the supply of effort to the whole economy; there is also evidence to suggest that a rise in earnings in one industry will increase the supply of effort to that industry by attracting workers from other industries.

Work-related welfare schemes Throughout the world many welfare payments depend on the

---

[1] The movement from his original position on *A* to his new position on *B* is due to an income effect and a substitution effect. When the wage rate rises, the substitution effect works to increase the supply of labour, because giving up leisure to get goods is now a more profitable occupation than before. The income effect works to decrease the supply of labour (increase the consumption of leisure), because the person can consume more of everything including leisure. Whether the rise in wages causes a rise or a fall in the number of hours people will wish to work depends on the relative strengths of these two effects.

household not working. Sometimes the welfare payments are reduced pound for pound of income the household earns. In even more extreme cases the payments cease altogether if the household earns any income. In either case these operate a severe disincentive to work and we can hardly be surprised if households respond rationally to these market signals.

Figure 25.8 illustrates a case where welfare payments are reduced for every pound of income earned. If the household is totally unemployed it can achieve point a on the Figure: it has 24 hours of leisure to consume and q_1 of goods, where q_1 is its welfare receipts. The wage rate in the market presents the household with a trade-off between leisure and goods indicated, in the absence of welfare payments, by the slope of the budget line from 24 to q_2. But if the household begins at a and starts to work it loses a pound of welfare for every pound of income it earns. It thus moves down the vertical line a to b, giving up leisure and gaining no net increase in income. Only after b when welfare payments are zero will the household gain at the margin for working more. The household's budget line thus starts at a, falls vertically to b and then follows the 'normal' budget line to q_2.[1] This type of system provides a severe disincentive to work. Any household whose indifference curve through the welfare point a lies everywhere above the budget line (such as the curve T on the figure) will rationally decide not to work even though it would work if it could add its wages to its welfare earnings.

Land If by 'land' we mean the total area of dry land, then its supply is pretty well fixed. A rise in the earnings of land cannot result in much of an increase in supply, except where land can be reclaimed from swamp or sea. The traditional assumption in economics is that the supply of land is absolutely inelastic. However, if by 'land' we understand all the fertile land available for cultivation, then the supply of land is subject to large fluctuations. Considerable care and effort is required to sustain the productive power of land, and if the return to land is low, its fertility may be allowed to be exhausted within a short period of time. On the other hand, a high return to land may provide incentives for irrigation, drainage and fertilization schemes that can greatly increase the supply of arable land.[2]

There is no value in debating which is 'real' land, the total land area or the total supply of arable land. The magnitude we are interested in depends on the problem at hand. For most problems in agricultural economics – for example, in the effect of land taxes on the prices of agricultural goods – what we need to know is the elasticity of the total supply of cultivable land.

> **The total supply of cultivable land is not perfectly inelastic. It can be expanded greatly by irrigation and reclamation, and it can be contracted drastically and rapidly – as many farmers have found to their sorrow – through failure to observe the principles of soil conservation.**

Land is usually defined to include the natural resources found in or on it. The quantity of a given natural resource existing in the world is of course limited. But the problem of actual exhaustion does not arise as frequently as one might think. Often a large undiscovered or unexploited quantity exists,

---

[1] You can draw for yourself diagrams to show the disincentives of intermediate cases where each pound of income causes some reduction of less than a pound in welfare payments.

[2] It used to be common practice, following David Ricardo, a British economist of the early nineteenth century, to define land as the *original and inexhaustible powers of the soil*. Ricardo wrote before the phenomenon of dust bowls, which turn large tracts of land into barren deserts, was widely known, and before we were aware that the deserts of North Africa had once been fertile areas.

and a shortage of the resource that raises its price encourages exploration and the development of previously unprofitable sources. The world's proven and exploitable supply of any natural resource thus usually varies considerably with the price of the resource. This is certainly true today of both petroleum and natural gas, the worry about the 'energy crisis' not withstanding. Of course there is an upper limit, and resources can be totally exhausted. Worse, they can be polluted or otherwise despoiled so that they are rendered useless long before they have been consumed.

Capital Capital is a man-made factor of production. The supply of capital in a country consists of the existing machines, plant, equipment, etc. and it is called the CAPITAL STOCK. This capital is used up in the course of production, and the supply is thus diminished by the amount that wears out or is otherwise destroyed each year. On the other hand, new capital goods are produced each year. New machines and new buildings replace ones that wear out (although they will rarely be identical with the capital they are 'replacing'). The total amount of capital goods produced is called GROSS INVESTMENT. Capital goods that are not replacing worn-out equipment, and therefore represent net additions to the capital stock, are called NET INVESTMENT. Expenditure on capital goods is called INVESTMENT EXPENDITURE. To distinguish the two types of investment we talk of GROSS and NET INVESTMENT EXPENDITURE.

The supply of capital has increased considerably over time in all modern countries. The volume of net investment determines the rate of increase of the capital stock. Net additions to the stock of capital vary considerably over the trade cycle, being low in periods of slump and high in periods of boom.

> **Taking the long view and ignoring cyclical fluctuations, there has been a fairly steady tendency for the stock of capital to increase over a very long period of time.**

The theory of investment, which we shall develop in subsequent sections of this book, is thus a theory of changes in the stock of capital.

The supply of factors to particular uses

Even if all factors had only one use, it would still be necessary to allocate them among competing firms in the same industry. As it is, factors have many uses. A given price of land can, for example, be used to grow a variety of crops, and it can also be subdivided for a housing development. A machinist from Coventry can work in a variety of automobile plants, or in a dozen other industries, or even in the physics laboratories at Cambridge. Factors must be allocated among different industries and among different firms in the same industry.

If the owners of factors are mainly concerned with making as much money as they can, they will move their factors to that use in which they earn the most. This movement of factors out of the one use into another will continue until the earnings of any one factor in all of its various possible uses are the same. Owners of factors take other things besides money into account, including, for example, risk, convenience and a good climate. Factors will, therefore, be moved among uses until there is no net advantage in further movement, allowing for both the monetary and non-monetary advantages. We may now restate this discussion as the HYPOTHESIS OF EQUAL NET ADVANTAGE:

> **Owners will choose that use of their factors that provides them with the greatest net advantage. Net advantage includes both monetary and non-monetary elements.**

This hypothesis plays the same role in the theory of distribution that the profit-maximization hypothesis plays in the theory of production. It leads to the prediction that factors of production will be allocated among various uses in such a way that they receive the same net return in each use.

The influence of non-monetary advantages Difficulties arise unless we can measure non-monetary advantages. Suppose we observe that a mechanic is working in London for £500 a year less than he could make in Newcastle. Is this evidence against the hypothesis, or does it merely mean that the non-monetary benefits of living in London (or of *not* living in Newcastle) are £500? A moment's thought will make it clear that any conceivable observation could be rationalized to fit the hypothesis as long as we do not have an independent measure of non-monetary advantages. To make the hypothesis useful we must do one of two things: either we must define in a measurable way the non-monetary benefits that we believe are important to choices, or we must make an assumption about the relative stability of monetary and non-monetary advantages. The first alternative is generally regarded as impossible unless we assume that the hypothesis is correct, in which case whatever monetary difference occurs between the earnings of a factor in two uses is assumed to measure the extent of the difference in non-monetary advantages. The second alternative, to make an assumption about the relative stability of monetary and non-monetary advantages, is more promising. If, for example, we assume that the difference in non-monetary advantages between two uses remains constant, we can predict that variations in monetary advantages will cause variations in net advantage, and that some resources will flow in response to the change.

It is not necessary, however, to make the very strong assumption that non-monetary advantages are constant. We can assume instead that they change, but more slowly than monetary ones. In this case, we can still extract predictions about behaviour. This weaker assumption leads us to the following important prediction:

> **Any change in the relative price paid to a factor in two uses will lead owners of the factor to increase the quantity they supply to the use in which the relative price has increased, and decrease the quantity they supply to the use in which it has decreased.**

This prediction implies a rising supply curve for a factor in any particular use. Such a supply curve (like all supply curves) can shift in response to changes in other variables. One of these is the size of the non-monetary benefits.

Factor mobility How fast will factors move among uses when net advantages vary? FACTOR MOBILITY refers to the readiness of factors to respond to signals that indicate where factors are wanted. If a factor is highly mobile in the sense that owners will quickly shift from use A to use B in response to a small change in the relative factor price, then supply will be highly elastic. If, on the other hand, factor owners are 'locked in' to some use and will not, or cannot, respond quickly, the supply will tend to be inelastic. In Part 4 we discussed factor mobility with respect to capital and also the barriers that impede that mobility. We will now generalize that discussion to include all factors.

Mobility of land: Consider agricultural land. Many crops can be harvested within a year and a totally different crop planted. A farm on the outskirts of a growing city can be sold for subdivision and development on very short notice. Once land is built upon, as urban land usually is, its mobility is much reduced. One can convert a hotel site into an office-building site, but it takes a very large differential in the value of land use to make tearing down the hotel worthwhile.

> **Land, which is physically the least mobile of all factors, is one of the most mobile in an economic sense.**

Although the land is highly mobile among alternative uses, it is completely immobile as far as location is concerned. There is only so much land within the borders of any given city, and no increase in the price offered can induce more land to relocate within the city. This locational immobility has, as we shall see, important consequences.

Mobility of capital: Most capital equipment, once constructed, is immobile. A great deal of machinery is specific: it must either be used for the purpose for which it was designed, or not be used at all. This is, of course, not true of all pieces of capital equipment – a shed, for example, may be used for a large number of purposes. It is the immobility of most capital equipment that makes exit of firms from declining industries a slow and difficult process.

During the life of a piece of capital, the firm may make allowances for depreciation so that capital goods can be replaced when they wear out. If conditions of demand and cost have not changed, the firm may spend money to replace the worn-out piece of equipment with an identical one. It may also do other things with its funds: buy a newly designed machine to produce the same goods, buy machines to produce different goods, or lend money to another firm. In this way, the long-run allocation of a country's stock of capital among various uses changes.

> **Physical capital is often immobile in the short run, but in the long run the processes of depreciation and replacement mean that the capital stock can change greatly in its composition and allocation among users.**

In popular discussion, money is often referred to as 'capital'. Money provides a claim on resources. A firm or a household that has saved money can spend it on anything that it desires. For example it can choose to buy beer or machines; by doing so, it will direct the nation's resources to the production of beer or machinery. Also, the firm or household can lend its money to other firms or households and thereby allow the borrowers to determine what the nation's resources will be used to produce.

Mobility of labour: Labour is unique as a factor of production in that the supply of the service implies the physical presence of the owner of the source of the service. Landlords may live in the place of their choice while obtaining income from renting out land located in remote parts of the world. Investors can shift their capital from one firm to another so that their income is earned from activities throughout the world while they themselves never leave New York or Tokyo or London. But if a worker employed by a firm in Coventry decides to offer his labour services to a firm in south London, he must physically travel to south London to do so. If a capitalist decides to invest in steel mills, he need never visit one; if a labourer decides to work in a steel mill, he must be on the premises. This is, of course, all quite obvious, but it has one important consequence: non-monetary factors are much more important in the allocation of labour than in the allocation of other factors of production. If the rate of return is even slightly higher in steel mills than elsewhere, other things being equal, capital will move into steel. But the wage paid in steel mills can be substantially above that in other industries without inducing an analogous flow of labour, if people find working in steel mills unpleasant.

An important variable affecting labour mobility is *time*. In the short term, it is difficult for people to change occupations. It is not difficult for a file clerk to move from one company to another, or to take a job in London instead of in Colchester, but it will be difficult for her to become an editor or an advertising executive in a short period of time. There are two considerations here: ability and training. Lack of either will stratify some people and make certain kinds of mobility difficult.

Over long periods, labour mobility among occupations is very great indeed. In assessing this mobility, it is important to remember that the labour force is not static. At one end, young people enter from school, and, at the other end, older persons exit through retirement or death. The turnover due to these causes would make it possible to reallocate three or four per cent of the labour force annually merely by directing new entrants to jobs other than the ones left vacant by persons leaving the labour force. Over a period of twenty years, a totally different occupational distribution could appear without a single individual ever changing his or her job.

Studies have been made to determine the amount of mobility displayed by labour in moving from job to job and from place to place. There appears to be some evidence that in periods of more or less full employment, differentials in wages among areas and occupations do reflect relative scarcities, and that to some extent, labour does tend to move from low-wage sectors of the economy to high-wage ones. There seems to be even stronger evidence, however, that labour is attracted more by the chance of obtaining a job than by the wage rate actually paid for that job. By way of contrast, studies of labour mobility over the generations, or *social stratification*, as the sociologists call it, indicate impressive mobility. The data show very substantial movement, both up and down the scales of education, skill, training and social status, over the course of two or three generations.

Labour is much more mobile in the long run that in the short run. Over a given time period, it is more mobile among jobs in the same location and occupation than among locations (where movements of the family is a deterrent) or among occupations (where lack of skills is a deterrent).

Man-made barriers to labour mobility: Many organizations, private and public, adopt policies that influence labour mobility. Seniority rights not only protect older employees from being laid off in a cutback of production, but they also make them very reluctant to change jobs. Likewise, if a firm provides employees with a non-transferable pension plan, they may not want to forfeit this benefit by changing jobs. Licensing is required in dozens of trades and professions. Barbers, electricians, solicitors and, in some places, even pedlars must have licences. There is, of course, a generally acceptable reason for requiring licences when the public must be protected against incompetents, quacks or nuisances. But licensing can also have the effect of limiting supply. The fact that, in countries without national health services, medicine is often one of the highest paid occupations, while doctors are still in short supply, is a result of the difficulty of getting into medical schools, the long internship and residency requirements, the rules concerning certification, and so forth. It is possible that in these countries doctors' earnings are high because the barriers to entry into the profession prevent even long-run increases in the proportion of the population being admitted to medical practice. Such barriers exist partly to protect the standards of the profession and partly to keep the supply limited (and the earnings high).

Trade unions often impose similar barriers to mobility. The 'closed shop', for example, which requires all employees of a plant or a trade to be members of a particular union, also gives unions the power to limit the supply of labour that they represent. They can, therefore, raise the earnings of their members while being protected against the flood of new entrants their policy would generate in the absence of entry barriers. Racial prejudice, discrimination against women and other similar attitudes also limit the mobility of labour.

26

The pricing of factors in competitive markets

The theory of factor prices is quite general. If one is concerned with labour, one should interpret factor prices to mean wages; if one is thinking about land, factor prices should be interpreted to mean rent, and so on. In this chapter we assume that factors are bought and sold on competitive markets. In Chapter 27, we shall introduce monopolistic elements into factor markets.[1]

> **Given that factor prices are free to vary, they will move to a level at which quantity demanded equals quantity supplied.**

Furthermore, shifts in either the demand for or the supply of factors will have the effects on prices, quantities and factor incomes predicted by normal price theory.

Relative factor prices under competitive conditions

Conditions for every unit of one factor to be paid the same price If there were only one factor of production, if all units were identical, and if non-monetary advantages were the same in all uses, then the prices of all units would tend towards equality. Units of the factor would move from occupations in which prices were low, and the resulting shortage would tend to force the price up. Units would move into occupations in which prices were high, and the resulting surplus would force the price down. The movements would continue until there was no further incentive to transfer, i.e., until the price paid to the factor was the same in all its uses.

Conditions for different units of the same factor to be paid different prices We observe in the world that units of one factor are paid different prices in different uses. Why is this so? Causes of differences in the prices paid to different units of one particular factor are of two sorts, dynamic or disequilibrium, and static or equilibrium, causes. The differences may themselves be called dynamic and static differences. DYNAMIC DIFFERENCES are associated with changing circumstances, such as the rise of one industry and the decline of another. Such differences set up movements in factors that will act to remove the differences. The differences in prices may persist for a long time, but there is a

---

[1] We continue to make the simplifying assumption (first introduced on p. 350) that total income and all other prices remain constant so that a variation in the money price of a factor causes a simultaneous variation both in its relative price and in the share of the national income going to the factor.

tendency for them to be reduced, and in equilibrium they will be eliminated. STATIC or EQUILIBRIUM DIFFERENCES, on the other hand, are differences that persist in a state of equilibrium; there is no tendency for them to be removed by the competitive forces of the market. They are associated with such things as differences among various units of one factor and differences among the non-monetary compensations available in the uses to which that factor may be put.

Dynamic differentials and factor mobility First consider dynamic differentials. If there were a rise in the demand for product A and a fall in the demand for product B, there would be an increase in the (derived) demand for factors in industry A and a decrease in the (derived) demand for factors in industry B. Factor prices would go up in A and down in B. This is an example of a dynamic change in relative prices, for the changes themselves will cause factors to move from industry B to industry A, and this movement will cause the price differentials to lessen and eventually to disappear. How long this process takes depends on factor mobility. Labour may in particular circumstances be relatively immobile in the short run so that dynamic differentials often last for a long time in the labour market. The factors that affect labour mobility and thus determine the duration of dynamic differentials were discussed in Chapter 25.

Equilibrium differentials One cause of equilibrium differentials in factor prices is different non-monetary advantages. *Ceteris paribus*, a job with high non-monetary rewards will have a lower equilibrium wage rate than a job with low non-monetary rewards. For example, people in academic and research jobs are often willing to accept less than they would be able to earn in the world of commerce and industry, because there are substantial non-monetary advantages associated with university employment. If labour were paid the same in both jobs, then it would move out of industry and into academic employment. Excess demand for labour in industry and excess supply in universities would then cause industrial wages to rise relative to academic ones until the movement of labour ceased.

A second cause of equilibrium differentials is differences among different units of one factor. Thus the high pay of skilled workers relative to unskilled workers reflects the fact that there is a shortage of skilled workers relative to the demand for them. No movement from unskilled to skilled jobs eliminates this differential, because it is difficult for most adult unskilled workers to become skilled ones. It is important to realize that the high pay of the skilled person relative to the unskilled one merely reflects demand and supply conditions for these two types of labour. There is nothing in the nature of competitive markets that ensures that skilled workers always get higher pay just because they are skilled. If, on the one hand, the demand for skilled workers fell off so much that, even though the supply was small, there was a glut of such workers, their wages would come down. If, on the other hand, there was a change in education so that unskilled workers could acquire skills more easily, the wages of skilled workers would fall relative to those of unskilled workers. Indeed history is replete with examples of particular groups of skilled workers who have lost their privileged positions when there was a change in the demand for their services.

> **Dynamic differentials are disequilibrium phenomena which set up forces causing their elimination. Equilibrium differentials can persist indefinitely, and are associated with differences among various units of one factor and among non-monetary rewards in the various uses of one factor.**

Transfer earnings and economic rent

To study equilibrium differentials in factor prices further, we divide a factor's equilibrium earnings into two components. TRANSFER EARNINGS are the amount that any unit of a factor must earn in order to prevent it from transferring to another use. Thus transfer earnings are the minimum that must be paid to a unit of any factor to hold it in its present use. ECONOMIC RENT is any excess over transfer earnings that a unit of the factor actually earns: economic rent equals the factor's actual earnings *minus* its transfer earnings.

The development of the distinction

The term just defined uses 'rent' very differently from its ordinary usage as a payment for the hire of land and buildings. To understand this technical usage of 'rent' it may help to see how it arose.

The history of the concept   Early in the nineteenth century, when British economics was in its infancy, there was a controversy about the high price of 'corn' (the generic term for all grains). One group held that corn had a high price because the landlords were charging high rents to the farmers, and in order to meet these, farmers had to charge a high price for their product. Thus, it was argued, the price of corn was high because the rents of agricultural land were high. The second group, which included David Ricardo, one of the great figures of British classical economics, held that the reverse was true. The price of corn was high because there was a shortage caused by the Napoleonic Wars. Because corn had a high price there was keen competition among farmers to obtain land, and this competition bid up the rents of corn land. If the price of corn were to fall so that corn growing became less profitable, then the demand for land would fall, and the rent paid for the use of land would fall as well. Thus, this group held that the rent of corn land was high because the price of corn was high and not vice versa.

The modern student of economics will recognize in the Ricardian argument the idea of *derived demand*. Landlords, Ricardo was saying, cannot just charge any price they want for their land; the price they get will depend on demand and supply. The supply of land is pretty well fixed, and the demand depends on the price of corn. The higher the price of corn, the more profitable corn growing will be, the higher the demand for corn land will be, and the higher the price that will be paid for its use.

The argument was elaborated by making the assumption that land had only one use, the growing of corn. The supply of land was given and virtually unchangeable, i.e., land was in perfectly inelastic supply and landowners would prefer to rent out their land for some return rather than leave it idle. Nothing had to be paid to prevent land from transferring to uses other than growing corn, because it had none. Therefore, all of the payment to land was a surplus over and above what was necessary to keep it in its present use. *Given the fixed supply of land*, the price depended on the demand for land, which was itself a function of the price of corn.

Rent, which originally referred to the payment for the use of land, thus became the term for a surplus payment to a factor over and above what was necessary to keep it in its present use. Subsequently two facts emerged. First, it was realized that factors of production other than land often earn a surplus over and above what is necessary to keep them in their present use. Film stars, for example, are in very short and pretty well fixed supply, and their potential earnings in other occupations are often low. Because there is a huge demand for their services in the film industry, they may receive payments greatly in excess of what is needed to keep them from transferring to other occupations. Second, it was realized that land itself often has many alternative uses, so that *from the point of view of any one use*, part of the payment made to land would be a *necessary* inducement to keep the land in its present employment. Thus all factors of production were pretty much the same in these respects: part of the payment made to them is necessary to keep them from transferring to other uses, and part is a surplus over and above that amount. This surplus came to be called economic rent, whatever the factor of production that earned it.

Two meanings of the term 'rent' The term 'economic rent' is a most unfortunate one. The adjective 'economic' is often dropped and the economist often speaks of rent when he means economic rent, causing a confusion between the concept described above and the payment made to landlords for the hiring of land and buildings. When a tenant speaks of his 'rent', he is referring to what he pays his landlord, much of which is a transfer earning. When the economist speaks of the same tenant's 'rent', he may be referring to what the tenant pays in excess of transfer earnings. It is important to guard against confusing the two uses of 'rent'.

The modern distinction between transfer earnings and economic rent In most cases the actual earnings of a factor of production will be a composite of transfer earnings and economic rent. It is possible, however, to imagine limiting cases in which all earnings are either one or the other. Consider some individual firm or some industry faced with a perfectly elastic supply curve of a factor of production; it will be able to obtain all that it wants at the going price but, if it does not pay this price, it will be unable to obtain any of the factor. In such a case, which is illustrated in Figure 26.1, the whole price paid to the factor represents transfer earnings.

Now consider the case of a factor that is fixed in supply and has only one use. Assume that this factor is put on the market by its owners and sold for whatever it will fetch, on the grounds that some income is better than none. The whole supply is owned by thousands of different owners, so

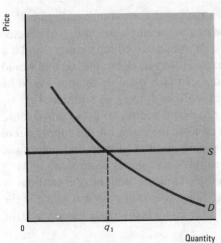

Fig. 26.1 All of the income earned by the factor is transfer earnings

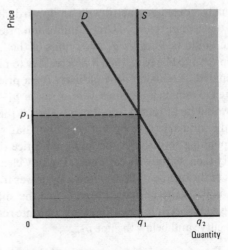

Fig. 26.2 All of the income earned by the factor is an economic rent

there is no point in any one of them withholding his own (small) supply from the market in an effort to raise the price. Such a factor will be in perfectly inelastic supply: the amount offered for sale will be the same whatever the price. This case is illustrated in Figure 26.2. The whole of the price that is paid to the factor is economic rent because even if a lower price were paid, the factor would not transfer to an alternative use. It might be thought that in such a case the factor would not command any price, but this is not so. The price is determined by demand and supply. The fixed quantity available is the amount q_1 in Figure 26.2; if the price were zero, the amount demanded would be q_2. Thus at a price of zero, competition among buyers would force the price upwards until it reached p_1. The income the factor would then earn is indicated by the area of the shaded rectangle.

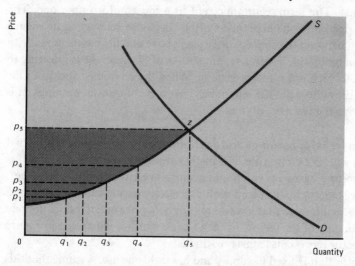

Fig. 26.3 Some of the income earned by the factor is a transfer earning and the remainder is economic rent

Finally, consider a factor with an upward-sloping curve such as the one shown in Figure 26.3. Given the demand curve, D, the equilibrium price would be p_5 and the employment q_5; total factor income would be p_5 *times* q_5. If q_5 units of the factor are to be attracted into the industry, and if a single price must be paid, then it is necessary to pay the price p_5. However, all but the last unit would be prepared to remain in the industry for a price less than p_5. In fact, q_1 of these units would be prepared to remain if the price were as low as p_1. If the price rose from p_1 to p_2, an additional $q_2 - q_1$ units would be attracted into the industry; if the price rose to p_3, an additional $q_3 - q_2$ units would enter the industry. Clearly, for any unit that we care to choose, the point on the supply curve corresponding to it shows the minimum price that must be paid in order to keep that unit in the industry (i.e., its transfer earnings). Equally clearly, if the supply curve slopes upward, all units to the left of the one being considered have lower transfer earnings. Thus the total transfer earnings of the q_5 units is the unshaded area *below* the supply curve. Since the total payment made is the rectangle $0p_5zq_5$, it follows that the economic rent earned by the factor is the shaded area *above* the supply curve and below the line p_5z.

Transfer earnings are shown by the area below a factor's supply curve. Economic rent is shown by the area above the supply curve and below the factor's market price.

The following example illustrates why a rising supply curve involves rents: if universities increase the salaries paid to economists in order to attract additional economists away from industry and government, those who are persuaded to make the switch will be receiving only transfer earnings. But those economists who were already content to be university teachers will find that their salaries have increased as well, and for them this increase will be economic rent.

Figures 26.1, 26.2 and 26.3 suggest the following important conclusion:

The more elastic the supply curve, the less the amount of the payment to factors that is rent and the more that is transfer earnings.

Kinds of transfers

How much of a given payment to a factor is economic rent and how much is transfer earnings depends on what sort of transfer we are considering. Consider first the transfer of a factor from one firm to another within a single industry. The supply of the factor to one firm is highly elastic since factors can easily move among firms in the same industry. Thus almost all of the factor's earnings will be transfer earnings. If the firm in question did not pay the factor the going price, then it would transfer to another firm in the same industry. Secondly consider the transfer of a factor from one industry to another. Mobility among industries will be less than mobility among firms in one industry. Thus the supply curve of a factor to one industry will be less elastic than the supply curve to one firm. Thus from the point of view of the industry, part of the payment is transfer earnings and part economic rent. The moral is that we cannot point to a given factor and assert that, of its income of £8,000, £6,000 is transfer earnings and £2,000 rent, for it all depends on what transfer we are considering.

Economic rent and transfer earnings in the payment to labour   Some labour is always able to move from job to job, and something must be paid to keep a given unit of labour in its present use. This amount is transfer earnings. How much has to be paid to keep labour in its present use depends upon what the use is.

Consider first the movement among firms in one industry. Assume, for example, that carpenters receive £24 for working a normal eight-hour day. Then a single small construction firm will have to pay £24 per day or it will not obtain the services of any carpenter. To that one firm the whole £24 is a transfer payment; if it were not paid, carpenters would not remain with that firm.

Secondly, consider movement among industries. Consider, for example, what would happen if as a result of a decline in demand for buildings all construction firms reduced the wages offered to carpenters. Now carpenters could not move to other construction firms to get more money. If they did not like the wages offered, they would have to move to another industry. If the best they could do elsewhere was £18 per day, then they would not begin to leave the construction industry until wages in that industry fell below £18. In this case the transfer earnings of carpenters in construction would be £18. When they were receiving £24 (presumably because there was a heavy demand for their services), the additional £6 was an economic rent from the point of view of the construction industry.

Thirdly, consider movement among occupations. Assume that there is a decline in the demand for carpenters in all industries. The only thing to do, if one does not like the wages, is to move to another occupation. If no one was induced to do this until the wage fell to £15, then £15 would be the transfer earnings for carpenters in general. The wage of £15 has to be paid to persuade people to be carpenters.

Some very highly specialized types of labour are in inelastic supply. Some singers and actors, for example, have a special style and talent which cannot be duplicated, whatever the training. The earnings that such persons receive are mostly economic rents: they enjoy their occupations and would pursue them for very much less than the high remuneration they actually receive. Their high rewards occur because they are in *very scarce supply relative to the demand for their services*. When the demand for their services rises, their earnings rise permanently; when the demand falls, their earnings fall permanently.

Rent and transfer earnings in the return to capital If a piece of capital equipment has several uses, then the analysis of the last section can be repeated. Much equipment however, has only one use. In this case, any income that is made from its operation is rent. Assume, for example, that when some machine was installed it was expected to earn £5,000 per annum in excess of all its operating costs. If the demand for the product now falls off so that the machine can earn only £2,000, it will still pay to keep it in operation rather than scrap it. Indeed it will pay to do so as long as it yields any return at all over its operating costs.[1] Thus, all of the return earned by the installed machine is economic rent because it would still have been allocated to its present use – it has no other – as long as it yielded even £1 above its operating costs. Thus, *once the machine has been installed*, any net income that it earns is rent.

The machine will, however, wear out eventually, and it will not be replaced unless it is expected to earn a return over its lifetime sufficient to make it a good investment for its owner. Thus, over the long run, some of the revenue earned by the machine is transfer earnings; if the revenue is not earned, a machine will not continue to be allocated to that use in the long run.

In the case just considered, whether a payment made to a factor is economic rent or a transfer earning depends on the time-span under consideration. In the short run all of the income of a machine with a specific use is a rent, while in the long run some (possibly all) of it is a transfer earning. Factor payments which are economic rent in the short run and transfer earnings in the long run are called QUASI-RENTS.

Economic rent and transfer earnings in the payment to land The formal analysis for land is identical to that given in the case of labour. How much of the payment made to a given piece of land is a transfer payment depends upon the nature of the transfer.

Consider, first, the case of an individual wheat farmer. He must pay the going price of land in order to prevent the land from being transferred to the use of other wheat farmers. From his point of view, therefore, the whole of the payment that he makes is transfer earnings to land.

Second, consider a particular agricultural industry that uses land. In order to secure land for, say, wheat production, it will be necessary to offer at least as much as the land could earn when put to other uses. From the point of view of the wheat industry, that part of the payment made for land which is equal to what it could earn in its next most remunerative use is transfer earnings. If that much is not paid, the land will be transferred to the alternative use. If, however, land particularly

---

[1] This is just another way of stating the proposition given in Chapter 18, page 236, that it pays a firm to continue in operation in the short run as long as it can cover its variable costs of production.

suitable for wheat growing is scarce relative to the demand for it, then the actual payment for the use of this land may be above the transfer earnings; any additional payment is an economic rent.

Next consider movement between agricultural and urban uses. Land is very mobile between agricultural uses because its location is usually of little importance. In the case of urban uses, however, location of the land is critical and, from this point of view, land is of course completely immobile. If there is a shortage of land in central London, such land as is available will command a high price, but no matter what the price paid, the land in rural areas will not move into central London. The very high payments made to urban land are economic rents. The land is scarce relative to demand for it, and it commands a price very much above what it could earn in agricultural uses. The payment that it receives is thus well in excess of what is necessary to prevent it from transferring from urban back to agricultural uses.

From the point of view of one particular type of urban use, however, high rents are transfer earnings. Cinemas, for example, account for but a small portion of the total demand for land in central London; if there were no cinemas at all, rentals of land would be about what they are now. Thus the cinema industry faces a perfectly elastic supply of land in central London, and the whole of the price that it pays for its land is a transfer payment which must be paid to keep the land from transferring to other urban uses.[1]

Some implications of the distinction between transfer earnings and rent

Increasing the supply of a factor Consider the effect of wage increases on the quantity of labour supplied. For example, if the central authorities want more physicists, should they subsidize physicists' salaries? As we have seen, such a policy may well have an effect on supply. It may influence schoolchildren uncertain about whether to become engineers or physicists to become physicists. But it will also mean that a great deal of money will have to be spent on extra payments to people who are already physicists. These payments will be economic rents, since existing physicists have demonstrated that they are prepared to be physicists at their old salaries. Although some may have been considering transferring to another occupation, such movements are not common.[2] An alternative policy, which may produce more physicists per pound spent, is to subsidize scholarships and fellowships for students who will train to become physicists. The policy tends to operate at the margin on persons just deciding whether or not to enter the occupation. It avoids the payment of additional rents to persons already in the occupation. Graphically, it is shown by a rightward shift in the supply curve because there will now be *more* persons in the occupation at each price of the factor.

> **If the supply curve is quite inelastic, an increase in the quantity supplied may be achieved more easily and at less cost by shifting the supply curve to the right rather than by moving along it.**

---

[1] Thus the old examination question 'Is it correct to say that the price of cinema seats is high in central London because the price of land is high?' should be answered in the affirmative, not in the negative, as examiners often seemed to expect. The view that the prices of *all* goods and services in central London are high because rents are high can, however, be denied.

[2] International mobility, it is clear, is another matter. One of the reasons for the considerable migration of trained professionals of all ages from Britain to the United States is the higher monetary rewards to be earned in the United States compared with the United Kingdom. When British professionals are being paid less than their international transfer earnings the result is steady emigration.

Urban land values and land taxes The high payments made to urban land are largely economic rents. The land is scarce relative to the demand for it, and it commands a price very much above what it could earn in agricultural uses. The payment it receives is thus well in excess of what is necessary to prevent it from transferring from urban back to agricultural uses. A society with rising population and rising per capita real income tends also to have steadily rising urban land prices. This fact has created a special interest in taxes on land values.

Who ultimately pays taxes on the value of land? If the same tax rate is applied to land in all uses, the relative profitability of different uses will be unaffected, and thus a landlord will not be tempted to change the allocation of his land. Land will not be forced out of use, because land that is very unprofitable will command little rent and so pay little tax. Thus there will be no change in the supply of goods that are produced with the aid of land, and, since there is no change in supply, there can be no change in their prices. Thus farmers will be willing to pay exactly as much as they would have offered previously for the use of land. Because the prices of agricultural goods and the prices paid by tenants for land will be unchanged, the whole of the tax will be borne by the landlord. The incomes earned by landlords will fall by the full amount of the tax, and land values will fall correspondingly (because land is now a less attractive investment than it was previously).

The single-tax movement Taxation of land values has had enormous appeal in the past. The peak of its appeal occurred about 100 years ago, when the 'single-tax movement' led by the American economist Henry George commanded great popularity. George's book *Progress and Poverty* is – as books on economic issues go – an all-time best seller. It pointed out that the fixed supply of land, combined with a rapidly rising demand for it, allowed the owners of land to gain from the natural progress of society without contributing anything. Along with many others, George was incensed at this 'unearned increment' from which huge fortunes accrued to landlords. He calculated that most of government expenditure could be financed by a single tax that did nothing more than remove the landlords' unearned increment. A further appeal of taxes on land values arises from the fact that economic rent can be taxed away without affecting the allocation of resources. Thus, for someone who does not wish to interfere with the allocation resulting from the free play of the market, the taxation of economic rent is attractive. But two problems arise with any attempt to tax economic rent. First, the theoretical statement refers to *economic rent*, not to the payment actually made by tenants to landlords. What is called rent in the world is partly an economic rent and partly a return on capital invested by the landowner. The policy implications of taxing rent depends on being able in practice to identify *economic rent*. At best, this is difficult; at worst, it is impossible.

The second problem is a normative one. If, in the interests of justice, we want to treat all recipients of economic rent similarly, we will encounter insurmountable difficulties because economic rent also accrues to factors other than land. It accrues to the owners of any factor that is in fixed supply and faces a rising demand. If there is, for example, a fixed supply of opera singers in the country, they gain economic rent as the society becomes richer and the demand for opera increases, without there being any corresponding increase in the supply of singers. No one has yet devised a scheme that will tax the economic rent but not the transfer earnings of such divergent factors as land, patents, football players and High Court judges.

When George died he left the huge royalties from his book to finance schools of 'economic science' which were to propagate his theories and policy recommendations. These schools are maintained throughout the world even today. The appeal of a single tax has, however, receded. This is partly because of the difficulties mentioned above and partly because, with the great increase in the size of the government, even an effective tax on economic rent would finance only a tiny portion of government expenditures. The hostility towards unearned increments of landowners still survives in various forms of taxes in many modern countries. In Britain the most obvious example is in the land development tax, which seeks to tax away most of the profit made by developing rural land for urban uses.[1]

---

[1] This tax and other relevant issues are discussed in Harbury and Lipsey, Chapter 6.

27

The income of labour

The last chapter referred to the pricing of all types of factors in competitive markets. In this and the next chapter we shall discuss the specific cases of labour and capital. The analysis of the previous chapter requires substantial amendment when it is applied to labour, because labour is often sold in non-competitive markets. In this chapter we shall extend the theory to cover cases in which labour markets are dominated by monopolistic buyers and/or sellers.[1]

The determination of wages without unions

We first look at the determination of wages in an individual labour market when labour is supplied competitively. We assume, therefore, that there are many individual workers each one of whom must take the existing wage rate as given and needs only to decide on how much, if any, labour services to supply at that wage. Each worker has a supply curve showing how much effort he will supply at each wage (see pp. 358–9). The sum of these curves yields a market supply curve showing the total supply of effort to this market as a function of the real wage rate. The determination of wages under competitive supply now falls into two cases depending on whether or not labour is demanded under competitive conditions.

Case 1: labour is supplied and demanded competitively

We first assume that there are so many purchasers of labour services that no one of them can influence the going wage rate. Instead each merely decides how much labour to hire at the going rate. Since both demanders and suppliers are price-takers and quantity adjusters, this labour market is perfectly competitive. As we saw in Chapter 26, the wage rate and volume of employment in such a market is determined at the intersection of the demand and supply curves. Although the demand curve is *not* the marginal revenue product curve, it is true that in equilibrium the wage rate will be *equal to* the value of the marginal product of labour. This is illustrated in Figure 27.1, where the equilibrium wage and the marginal value product are w_c, and quantity of employment is q_c.

---

[1] The descriptive and institutional background for this chapter is outlined in Harbury and Lipsey, Chapter 4.

Case 2: labour is supplied competitively but demanded monopsonistically

We now consider a labour market containing so few firms that each one realizes it can influence the wage rate by varying the amount that it purchases. The demanders are *not* price-takers in this labour market. For simplicity, we deal with a case in which the few purchasers form an employers' association and act as a single decision-taking unit in the labour market.

The sole purchaser in any market is called a MONOPSONIST, and we now speak of labour being purchased monopsonistically. The monopsonist purchasing labour can offer any wage rate it chooses and workers must either work for that wage or move to other markets (i.e., change occupation or location). For any given quantity that is purchased, the labour supply curve shows the price per unit that must be paid; to the monopsonist, this is the average cost curve. For example, if 100 units are employed at £2 per hour, then total cost is £200 and average cost per unit is £2. If 101 units are employed and the factor price is driven up to £2·05, then total cost becomes £207·05; the average cost per labourer is £2·05, but the total cost has increased by £7·05 as a result of hiring one more labourer.

> Whenever the labour supply curve is upward-sloping, the marginal cost to a monopsonist of obtaining an extra labourer will exceed the wage paid, because the increased wage rate necessary to attract the labourer must also be paid to all those already employed.

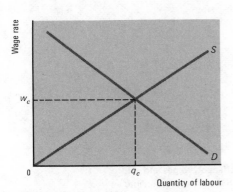

Fig. 27.1 The determination of wages in a competitive market

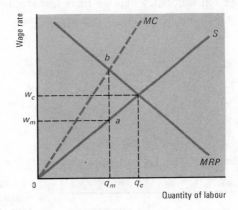

Fig. 27.2 The determination of wages when labour is sold competitively but bought monopsonistically

Thus, in Figure 27.2 we can draw a marginal cost curve for labour that will lie above the average cost curve. The profit-maximizing monopsonist will equate the marginal cost of labour with its marginal revenue product. In other words, it will go on hiring labour until the last unit hired increases total cost by as much as it increases total revenue.

Thus, in equilibrium, marginal cost, and not the wage rate, will be equated with the marginal revenue product of labour. Since marginal cost exceeds the wage rate, it follows that the wage rate will be less than the marginal revenue product. Also, since the supply curve of labour is upward-sloping, the volume of employment must be less than it would be if the market were perfectly competitive.

This is shown in Figure 27.2, in which w_c and q_c are the competitive wage and the volume of employment, while w_m and q_m are the corresponding values under monopsony. Since the monopsonist wishes to employ a quantity of labour equal only to q_m it need pay a wage of only w_m to call forth that quantity.

> **Monopsony results in a lower level of employment and a lower wage rate than when labour is purchased competitively.**

The reason is that the monopsonistic purchaser is aware that, by trying to purchase more of the factor, it is driving up the price against itself. It will, therefore, stop short of the point that is reached when the factor is purchased by many different firms, none of which can exert an influence on its price.

The determination of wages with unions

One major reason for the rise, and continued existence, of unions is to offset the power that monopsonistic employers have to force wages and employment below their competitive levels. Unions provide a monopoly of sellers of labour that can offset any monopsony of buyers of labour. Of course labour is interested not only in wages, but in all of the conditions of work. Let us first see, however, how a union that has the power to set the wage of its own workers can change the wage-employment outcomes that we have just studied. The union is assumed to set the wage while employers decide how much to hire at that wage.

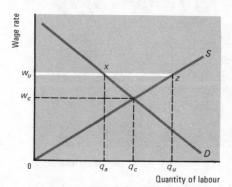

Fig. 27.3 The effect on wages and employment of the entry of a union into a competitive labour market

Case 3: labour is supplied monopolistically but purchased competitively

Say that a union enters the competitive labour market shown in Figure 27.1 and raises the wage above its competitive level. In Figure 27.3, for example, the union raises the wage from w_c to w_u. This creates a perfectly elastic supply of labour up to the quantity q_u (since this is the quantity of labour supplied at the union wage). The supply curve now becomes $w_u z S$ and equilibrium is at x, where the demand curve cuts the new supply curve. The union succeeds in raising the wage rate above its competitive level, but employment falls from q_c to q_a.

Notice also that there are would-be workers who cannot find employment (excess supply equals $q_u - q_a$ or $z - x$). Some of them would even be prepared to work for a wage *less than* w_u. It is clearly to the employers' advantage to hire some of these workers at less than the going wage and, given the chance, they will do so. This implies that only if it can strictly enforce the wage it sets, resisting wage-cutting pressure from unemployed workers, can a union succeed in raising the wage rate against a perfectly competitive set of demanders of labour.

> **A union entering a perfectly competitive labour market can raise the wage above the free-market level, but only at the cost of lowering the amount of employment. The new wage will create an excess supply of labour at the going rate and consequent pressure for wage-cutting, which the union must be powerful enough to resist if it is to be successful in holding wages up.**

Case 4: labour is supplied monopolistically and demanded monopsonistically

We now consider the effects of introducing a union into the monopsonistic labour market illustrated in Figure 27.2. We shall arrive at the surprising result that in this market the union can raise wages by a substantial margin and at the same time raise the volume of employment! We start in Figure 27.4 with the same labour supply curve, S, and marginal cost curve, MC, as shown in Figure 27.2. The analysis now becomes a little tricky and we shall take it in two steps.

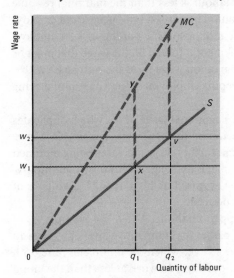

Fig. 27.4 The effect of a union-determined wage on the average and marginal cost curves of labour

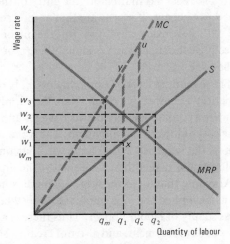

Fig. 27.5 The effect on wages and employment of the entry of a union into a monopsonistic labour market

First, consider the effect on the supply curve (i.e., the average cost curve) and on the marginal cost curve of labour when the union enforces some given wage. This creates a perfectly elastic supply curve up to the point at which the union wage cuts the supply curve. If the union wage is w_1, the supply curve for labour in Figure 27.4 now becomes $w_1 x S$.[1] Up to an employment level of q_1, the marginal cost curve is also $w_1 x$ (since the wage rate is constant, the marginal cost of the extra worker

---

[1] Note that this form of expression identifies a line to which the points or labels are attached. It is *not* a product of separate numbers.

is only the wage that must be paid to him). If the employer wants more than q_1 of labour, however, he can obtain it by paying everyone more than the union wage – to which the union will have no objection. The marginal cost of labour then jumps from x to y (i.e., it has a discontinuity at q_1) and thereafter becomes yMC. This is easily seen by the fact that once the employer is operating on the segment xS of the supply curve, the existence of the union minimum wage w_1 is irrelevant to him (because he is already paying more than that), and so his situation is exactly the same as if no union existed: S is the supply curve of labour that he now faces, and MC is its marginal cost curve. If, to take one more example, the union negotiates a new minimum wage of w_2, the supply curve becomes w_2vS and the marginal cost curve becomes w_2vzMC, with a discontinuous jump at an employment level of q_2.[1]

The second step in the analysis is to study the effects on employment when the union sets various alternative wage rates. In Figure 27.5 the curves S, MC and MRP are reproduced from Figure 27.2. The wage and employment levels without a union are w_m and q_m. Now assume that the union negotiates a wage of w_1. This creates the kinked supply curve w_1xS and a marginal cost curve w_1xyMC. The monopsonistic purchaser of labour will now be in equilibrium at employment q_1, since up to that level of employment the marginal cost of labour is less than the marginal revenue product, while for levels above q_1 the reverse is true. The union has raised both wages and employment! The reason is that before the entry of the union, the monopsonistic purchaser kept employment down because it was aware that as it increased employment it forced up the wage that must be paid to those already employed. But the introduction of the union wage faces the purchaser with a perfectly elastic supply curve, so that there is no point in keeping employment low for fear of driving up the wage.

The maximum level of employment, q_c, is reached at a negotiated wage of w_c, which duplicates the perfectly competitive result. Here the supply curve is w_ctS and the MC curve is w_ctuMC. Above this wage a conflict emerges between wages and employment, further wage increases being obtained at the cost of lowered employment. The wage w_2, for example, is associated with the same employment as the wage w_1. Note, however, that until the wage is raised as high as w_3 the volume of employment is higher than it was before the union was introduced.

Also note that up to the wage w_c, there is no excess supply of labour. At w_1, for example, q_1 of labour is supplied and q_1 is employed. Only when the wage passes the competitive level of w_c does an excess supply of labour appear. Thus there is a range w_m to w_c over which the union can raise both wages and employment, and also not create a surplus of labour eager to work at less than the union rate. There is a further range, w_c to w_3, over which both wages and employment can be raised above what they were in the absence of the union, but over which an excess supply of labour occurs, forcing the union to resist a downward pressure on wages exerted by the unemployed group. For example, at a wage w_2, the excess supply is $q_2 - q_1$.

A union entering a monopsonistic market will have a range over which it can raise wages and employment without creating a surplus of labourers eager to work at the going rate. There will be a further range over which it can raise both wages and employment above their pre-union levels but at the cost of creating an excess supply of labour.

---

[1] Students trained in the calculus will realize that the kink in the average cost curve (i.e., the supply curve) at v means a similar kink in the total cost curve, which is thus non-differentiable at the associated quantity. This means that MC is not uniquely defined at that point.

The rise of unions

One reason for the rise of unions was to turn Case 2 above into Case 4. Another was to provide the many workers with a collective, and hence effective, voice in dealing with the few employers on such other conditions of work as safety, hours, holidays and non-wage benefits.

Early in the history of unions their organizers perceived that ten or a hundred men acting together had more influence than one acting alone. The union was the organization that would provide a basis for confronting the monopsony power of employers with the collective (i.e., monopoly) power of the workers. But it was easier to see the solution than to achieve it. Employers did not accept organizations of workers passively. Agitators who tried to organize other workers were often dismissed and blacklisted; in some cases they were physically assaulted or even murdered. In order to realize the ambition of creating some effective power over the labour market, it was necessary to gain control of the supply of labour and to have the financial resources necessary to outlast employers. There was no 'right to organize', and a union usually had to force hostile employers to negotiate with it. Since early unions did not have large resources, employers had to be attacked where they were weakest.

This helps to explain why it was the unions of the highly skilled and the specialist types of labour that first met with success. The previous discussion provides two main reasons for this. First, it was easier to control the supply of skilled workers than that of unskilled workers. Organize the unskilled or the semi-skilled and the employer could find replacements for them. But the skilled workers – the coopers, the bootmakers, the shipwrights – were another matter. There were few of them, and they controlled the access to their trade by controlling the conditions of apprenticeship. The second main reason was that a union of a small number of highly skilled specialists could attack the employer where he was most likely to give in, and thus would need fewer resources to withstand employer resistance than would be needed by unions of the unskilled. In Chapter 25 (page 357) we discussed the determinants of the elasticity of demand for a factor. A particular skilled occupation is very difficult to dispense with in an industrial process, so that other factors cannot easily be substituted for it. Also, labour in a particular skilled occupation is likely to account for a relatively low proportion of total costs, so that the relative cost to the employers of giving in to a demand for, say, a twenty per cent wage increase, would be much less than the cost of giving in to an equivalent demand from the very numerous unskilled workers. Thus a low ability to substitute other factors plus a small contribution to total costs combined to give the unions of skilled workers an advantage in fighting the employer.

Today, unions are successful over all of the modern industrialized world. They have won the right to bargain with employers over wages and working conditions, and to use their ultimate weapon, the STRIKE, which is the concerted refusal of the members of a union to work. PICKET LINES are made up of striking workers who parade before the entrance to their plant or firm. Members of other unions will often not 'cross' a picket line. This means, for example, that if bricklayers strike against a construction firm, carpenters may not work on the project even though they themselves have no grievance against the firm and lorry drivers may not deliver supplies to a picketed site. Pickets therefore represent an enormous increase in the negotiating power of a small union.

Modern unions are organized throughout the world along two main principles. In TRADE (or

CRAFT) UNIONS, workers with a common set of skills are joined in a common association, no matter where or for whom they work. In INDUSTRIAL UNIONS, all workers in a given plant or a given industry are collected into a single union, whatever their skills.

Industrial unions became common in the United States with the rise in the 1930s of the Congress of Industrial Organizations (CIO). The existence of these unions means that the great automobile companies, for example, deal with one union, and so do the steel companies. A single agreement over wages, working conditions or union practices is sufficient to change the situation throughout the entire industry.

A single union covering an entire industry is uncommon in the UK (and in many other countries) because the main basis of organization is the trade union. As a result a typical employer has to deal with many unions – twenty or more within a single firm is not uncommon in the UK. Under these circumstances agreement between labour and management can be hard to reach. DEMARCATION DISPUTES often break out over which union is to be responsible for which jobs. Of course, such demarcation disputes may merely reflect power struggles between the managements of various unions. They do, however, have at least one substantial economic cause. In situations in which unions are holding the wage above its competitive level, we have seen that there will be an excess supply of labour at the going wage rate. Since more people would like to work in the occupation than can do so, both the union leaders and the rank and file will be acutely aware of the trade-off between wages and unemployment, and of the possibility that some workers who are currently employed may find themselves without work. (This does not mean, of course, that they must become permanently unemployed but only that they must move to less remunerative occupations.) In terms of Figure 27.3, if the union loses a demarcation dispute, the demand curve for its members shifts to the left and the excess supply rises, while, if the union wins the dispute, the demand curve shifts to the right and the excess supply diminishes. Such problems could not arise if the wage were set so that quantity demanded equalled quantity supplied, but:

> **Whenever the wage is such that excess supply develops, then the outcome of jurisdictional disputes genuinely affects employment opportunities and the amount of downward pressure on the wage rate exerted by unsatisfied suppliers of labour in a particular occupation.**

Clearly, however undesirable the consequences of such disputes might be, the caricature of them as squabbles about trivia is wide of the mark.

Union behaviour

Unions do many things designed to influence the wages and conditions of work of their members. What they are able to accomplish depends partly on the institutional setting within which they operate.

Institutions

Modern unions bargain under two basic types of arrangements, the open shop and the closed shop. In an OPEN SHOP a union represents its members, but does not have exclusive negotiating rights for all the workers of one kind. Membership in the union is not a condition of getting or keeping a job. Unions usually oppose such an arrangement and it is easy to see why. Consider an open-shop negotiating situation. If, on the one hand, employers accede to union demands, the non-members achieve the benefits of the union without paying dues or sharing the risks. If, on the other hand, employers choose to fight the union, they can run their plants with the non-union members, thus weakening the power of the union in the fight.

Now consider what will happen if the union does succeed in obtaining a wage above the competitive level in an open-shop industry. We have already seen that when wages exceed the competitive level, there arises an excess supply of labour *willing to work at less than the union wage*. With an open shop there is nothing to prevent these workers from accepting work below the union wage, undermining the union's power to maintain high wages. If, however, all workers must join the union, then the union can prevent its members from accepting lower wages, and can thus maintain high wages in spite of the existence of excess supply.

The desire to avoid the open shop leads to other union arrangements. In a CLOSED SHOP, only union members can be employed. (Closed shops may be either 'pre-entry' where the worker must be a member of the union before being employed, or 'post-entry' where the worker must join the union on becoming employed.)

Wages

One of the most important things over which unions bargain is the wage rate. One important difference between actual union wage bargaining and the theoretical analysis with which we began this chapter is that in collective bargaining both sides must agree to the wage, while in our analysis we assumed that the union set a wage and the employer decided how much labour to employ at that wage. In collective bargaining there is always a substantial range for compromise. In particular cases the actual range will depend on the goals of the two negotiating parties. Thus economic theory does not predict a precise outcome to the collective-bargaining process. By analysing the effects on unions and management it can, however, isolate some of the economic factors that will influence the final bargain. Just as in oligopolistic competition between firms, the outcome will be significantly influenced by such political and psychological factors as skill in bargaining, ability to bluff, and one side's assessment of the other side's reactions to its own moves. For example, the employers will ask, 'How much can we resist without provoking the unions into calling a costly strike?' and the union will ask, 'Will the employers force us to strike only for a token period so they can tell their shareholders they *tried* to resist, or do they think this is a really serious matter so that they intend to hold out to the bitter end against any strike that we might call?' It is because monopoly *versus* monopsony allows more than one acceptable economic solution that these non-economic factors become so important.

Supply restriction

When a union faces a competitive demand for its product, it can, as we saw in Case 2 above, set a wage above the competitive level and then accept the unemployment that results. An alternative is to reduce the supply of labour and then let the wage be that which equates demand and supply. This is illustrated in Figure 27.6, which shows a labour market that would be perfectly competitive in the absence of the union. The union can raise its wage above the perfectly competitive level, w_c, by two alternative policies. First, as already analysed, it can negotiate a wage of w_u, let the volume of employment fall from q_c to q_a and allow an excess supply of labour of $q_u - q_a$ to develop. The second policy is to restrict entry into the occupation by methods such as lengthening apprenticeship periods and rationing places for trainees. Such tactics will make it more expensive, or otherwise more difficult, to enter the occupation. Thus, at any given wage rate, the quantity supplied will be reduced; the supply curve shifts to the left. If it shifts to S_2, the wage w_u is set in the competitive market without the union having to intervene in the process of wage setting. Furthermore, there is no excess supply at w_u since the supply curve has been shifted. Thus, there is no wage-reducing pressure from unemployed job-seekers.

Supply restriction raises wages without creating a pool of unemployed.

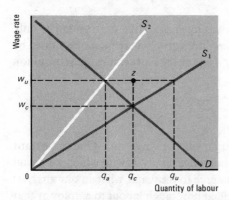

Fig. 27.6 An increase in wages caused by an entry restriction into a particular labour market

Which of the two tactics will appeal to a particular union will depend on many factors, such as the ease with which supply can be restricted, the ease with which union wages can be negotiated, and the public's reaction to these two tactics in particular situations. As an example of the force of the last point, consider doctors in countries such as the United States, where medical services are not nationalized. It is unlikely that either the public or the central authorities would accept a situation in which doctors raised the price of their services above the competitive level by collective agreement and then allowed an unemployed surplus of doctors to develop. So many people could clearly use more medical services than they receive that the existence of any substantial amount of unemployed medical talent would not be tolerated. Thus, doctors are forced back on the second alternative, which produces the same result but by more socially acceptable methods. They raise training periods and training costs and restrict entry into medical schools. By these and other tactics they shift the supply curve of qualified doctors to the left. If they shift it to S_2 in Figure 27.6, they give themselves the same wage as if they had left the supply curve at S_1 and regulated the wage at w_u, but they avoid what would be a very embarrassing surplus of unemployed doctors. In both cases the actual supply of doctors to the public is less (by $q_c - q_a$) than it would have been under competitive conditions.[1]

---

[1] Of course, some of the high standards for entry into the medical profession are needed to protect the public from incompetent doctors. Most investigations have concluded, however, that restrictions on entry are much greater than they need to be. Thus they partly serve the function analysed in the text.

A combination of these two policies of price fixing and supply restraint is available to unions that have a closed shop and can rigidly control the size of their membership. This is to fix the wage at the desired level and then to restrict membership to remove any excess supply that would otherwise develop. In terms of Figure 27.3 the union would fix the wage, say at w_u, and then restrict its membership to q_a. Such tactics are similar to those employed by medieval guilds and they are not unknown today.

Wages versus employment

We have already seen that in many situations the union faces a trade-off between wages and employment: an increase in wages can be obtained only at the cost of lowered employment.

In some cases it is possible to avoid the conflict between wages and unemployment by bargaining with the employer about *both* wages and employment.

This can be accomplished by manning agreements forcing employers to use more labour than they need for a given level of output; such agreements are very common in the UK.

The result is illustrated by point z in Figure 27.6. The demand curve shows for each wage rate the amount of labour the firm would like to hire. But it may prefer to hire some other amount rather than to go without labour altogether. When wages are w_c and employment is q_c the union might offer firms the alternative of employing q_c at a wage of w_u or facing a strike. If the firm accepts the former alternative, it will move to point z, which is off its demand curve. The union thus raises the wage rate and the total real income of its members without causing any reduction in employment. The union's success in pursuing such a policy will depend partly on the size of the profits in the industry (i.e., on the extent to which the industry departs from the perfectly competitive equilibrium), and partly on the state of the market, which will determine the relation between the losses resulting from hiring more than the desired quantity of labour at the agreed wage rate, and the expected losses resulting from a strike. If there are no pure profits, the union may succeed in the short run but lose in the long run when firms exit from the industry because their total costs now exceed their total revenues.

Wages versus job security

Unions vary greatly in the extent to which they adopt a defensive or an offensive attitude to the labour market. Until recently the leaderships of unions, management and government were dominated by people who were in their twenties during the Great Depression of the 1930s. Not surprisingly, the labouring members of this age-group have been strongly conditioned to a defensive attitude towards jobs. They lived through a period when unemployment never fell below twenty per cent of the labour force as a national average, and when it was over fifty per cent in many of the hardest-hit areas. They saw people grow up, marry and raise children on the dole. They saw young men, who were eager to work but were unable to find any form of employment, slowly have their spirits broken as they had to confess their failure to wives and children. They suffered the humiliation of being read lessons on hard work, thrift, and patience by a London-based, middle-class bureaucracy that had not itself experienced unemployment. When occasionally the unemployed rose up, as in the General Strike or the Hunger March, the troops were called out against them.

In those days of mass unemployment, the installation of a new machine in a factory condemned the worker it replaced to an indefinite future on the dole. It is little wonder that labour-saving machines were opposed bitterly, and that job-saving restrictive practices were adhered to with tenacity. The defensive attitude which was so understandable in the 1930s survived in the UK into the post-war period, when circumstances were very different. This was a time of full employment. New jobs were available to replace old ones that had been destroyed by technological change. In such a world the determination to preserve existing jobs at all costs made much less sense than in the 1930s.

Sustained economic growth means change, and change means that old jobs will be destroyed and new jobs created. The defensive attitude to old jobs persisted more in the UK than either in Europe, where the old order had been more disrupted by the Second World War, or in the US, where unions were never as strong as in the UK. The net effect was that the process of changing the structure of employment, which must accompany growth, was slowed. Studies of comparable factories in Britain, France and Germany often show up to twice as many workers used to produce the same output in Britain as on the Continent. Thus UK growth and hence the rise in living standards of the average person were slower than in Europe and in North America. Although particular jobs were saved in the UK, there is no evidence that the overall level of unemployment has been lower in the UK over the decades than in those countries where unions have been less defensive about preserving existing jobs.

> **Protecting existing jobs may be a successful way to protect the living standards of the average worker in the short term, but over the long term it lowers living standards below what they would be if the structure of jobs were allowed to change according to the requirements of a growing, changing economy.**

Once again in the early 1980s the spectre of mass unemployment haunts Britain. Once again workers can argue with some justification that growth creating technological change may mean an indefinite future of unemployment for the persons displaced by new techniques. This is an unfortunate situation since without the new techniques, productivity increases that are the engine for increasing living standards will be inhibited.

Unions and the structure of relative wages

So far we have considered the influence of one particular union, operating in a small section of the total labour market, on the wages of its members. Our theory predicts that a powerful union can in such circumstances raise the wages earned by its members, possibly at the expense of lowering the volume of employment. This prediction seems to be supported by substantial empirical evidence that all unions do influence the structure of relative wages by raising wages in some industries and occupations where they are particularly strong, without a corresponding rise in wages elsewhere.

Research suggests that British unions have been able to raise wages on average around 10 per cent above what they would have been if the occupation had not been unionized. It is not obvious where this extra return comes from, but clearly if one group gets a larger share of total national income some other groups must get less. A substantial amount of the extra earnings of unionized labour appears to be at the expense of lower wages for some groups of unorganized workers, as well as lower incomes for others who are unemployed but would otherwise have a job if wages were not raised above their competitive levels.

Unions and the functional distribution of income

Are unions able to influence the share of total national income going to labour in general? This question does not concern the power of one small union to raise the wages of its members, possibly at the expense of workers in less powerful situations. It concerns, rather, the ability of unions to raise the earnings of labour in general at the expense of the earnings of land and capital. Many of the efforts of the early classical economists were directed towards developing theories that would explain the functional distribution of income. A great deal of the concern of early trade unionists was over increasing the share of total national income going to labour – helping one group of labourers at the expense of other groups would not have had nearly the general appeal as helping all the workers at the expense of the capitalists and the landowners. It may seem surprising that in spite of all this early, and continued, interest, we cannot say very much about this question even now.

We have seen that we do have a well-developed micro-market theory that allows us to predict the effect on relative wages of a particular intervention of a union, an employers' organization, or the central authorities in any one market. We do not, however, have an accepted theory of the overall distribution of national income that allows us to predict the consequences of a particular intervention, such as the growth of trade unions, for the functional distribution of income.

To illustrate this problem, let us consider what effect trade union intervention may have in raising wages above their competitive level in all industries. The predictions for one industry are illustrated in Figure 27.3: the wage rate rises but employment falls. But if this occurs simultaneously in *all* industries we cannot apply the same analysis. The analysis of Figure 27.3 was based on demand curves, which are in turn based on assumptions of other things being equal. If unions raise the wage rate of even a significant part of the labour force, they will cause incomes to change significantly; this will cause demand curves for consumers' goods to *shift*; this will cause outputs to vary; and this, in turn, will cause shifts in the derived demand curves for labour. Unless we have a theory of how each of these changes is quantitatively related to the other, we cannot attempt to answer this question. In fact, there is no generally accepted, well-worked-out theory which would allow us to deal with it. There is no doubt that unions are extremely powerful organizations, particularly in the UK, and that they have important effects on the economy. Just how much they succeed in changing the functional distribution in labour's favour, however, remains an unsettled question.

For many years the share of total national income accounted for by wage income remained remarkably constant in the UK, and this caused a certain amount of scepticism concerning the claim that unions had significantly altered the functional distribution of income in favour of labour. In the last two decades, however, labour's share has risen significantly while the share going to profits has fallen. This occurred at a time when many observers felt that unions were becoming more powerful both in terms of membership and their ability to influence the labour market. This is at least consistent with the view that modern British unions have altered the functional distribution of income in favour of wages at the expense of profits over the last two decades.

Alternative theories of wage determination

Finally in this chapter we will take a quick look at some of the new theories of the labour market that are being developed to explain observations that are hard to understand in terms of the traditional theory. We first summarize the relevant parts of the traditional, or neo-Classical, theory that we have studied so far in this chapter.

The neo-Classical theory

In neo-Classical theory the wage rate adjusts to equate the demand for and supply of labour unless monopoly or monopsony elements intervene. In Figure 27.7 we show the demand and supply of labour as a function of the real wage rate (since the price level is assumed constant – see pages 160 and 350 – we need only plot the money wage rate). The supply curve is drawn to illustrate the empirical evidence that it is rather steeply sloped over the relevant range and that there is some maximum quantity of labour, q_m in the Figure, that will be supplied under free-market conditions.

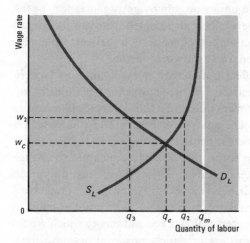

Fig. 27.7 A neo-Classical labour market

If the wage rate fluctuates freely so as to clear the labour market, the wage will be w_c while employment will be q_c. At this wage there is no involuntary unemployment. Everyone who wishes to work at w_c has a job. It is true that employment is $q_m - q_c$ below its maximum possible level. But the quantity of $q_m - q_c$ is *voluntarily* unemployed, and would only be supplied if the wage rate exceeded w_c.

It follows that persistent involuntary unemployment can occur in this world only if the real wage is held above its competitive equilibrium level. If, for example, the wage is w_2 in Figure 27.7, there will be $q_2 - q_3$ units of labour involuntarily unemployed: they would like to work at the going wage rate but there is no demand for their services. Thus the remedy for involuntary unemployment in the neo-Classical world is to reduce the wage rate: there can be no involunatry unemployment at the competitive equilibrium wage rate.

> **In the neo-Classical model the wage fluctuates (unless interfered with by monopoly or monopsony elements) so as to equate current demand for and supply of labour; involuntary unemployment can occur only if the wage is held above its equilibrium value.**

Non-market theories

Economists have long sought to understand the problem of involuntary unemployment. For a long time economists were satisfied with the explanation offered by early Keynesian economists: workers would stubbornly resist a downward movement in their money wage rate. Thus when the real wage rate was too high, competitive forces would not reduce it by forcing money wages down because workers would stubbornly resist such a fall.

Recently economists have sought better explanations of persistent unemployment by re-examining the determination of wages. As a result a new set of theories has arisen. These theories deny that forces exist to cause wages to fluctuate so as to continuously equate the current demands for and supplies of labour. These theories start with the obvious observation that labour markets are not auction markets where prices always respond to excess demand or excess supply. When unemployed workers are looking for jobs, employers do not go around to their existing workers and knock down their wages until there is no one looking for a job; instead they hang out a sign saying 'no help wanted'. This suggests something is wrong with the neo-Classical theory that views the labour market as a market where, in the absence of monopolies or monopsonies, excess supply quickly forces wages down.

A key aspect of the new theories is the observation that many workers hold their jobs for quite long periods of time so that many employers and employees have long-term relations with each other. Under these circumstances wages become insensitive to current economic conditions because they are in effect regular payments on the employer's obligation to transfer a certain amount of wealth to the employee over the duration of the employment relation. Given this situation:

> **The tendency is for employers to 'smooth' the income of employees by paying a steady wage, letting profits fluctuate to absorb the effects of temporary increases and decreases in demand for the firm's product.**

To see what is involved, consider a simple example in which an employee is obligated by an unbreakable contract to work for an employer for seven years. Scheme 1 for paying the worker would be to give him a lump sum at the outset, leaving him to invest the money and spread its use for consumption over the seven years. Scheme 2 would give him a (larger) lump sum at the end of the seven years, leaving him to borrow against that payment so as to spread its use for consumption over the seven years. Scheme 3 would be to give him equal payments at regular intervals over the seven years.[1] This last arrangement makes it unnecessary for workers to engage in large capital transactions (of investing as in scheme 1 or borrowing as in scheme 2).

In the real world, however, the worker's obligation to stay in his job for seven years would be unenforceable. He may quit. Also, the employer may dismiss him before the seven years are up. Thus where long-term arrangements depend only on unenforceable understandings, it is undesirable that either side be heavily in debt to the other at any point in the contract. Under scheme 1 the employee has an incentive to quit at any early date since he is in debt to his employer for the remaining years of work for which he has already been paid. Under scheme 2 the employer has an incentive to dismiss the worker at an early date since he is increasingly in debt to the employee until

---

[1] After studying the concept of present value in Chapter 28 you will see that the sums could be set so as to make the present value of entering into the seven-year contract the same to the employee under each of these payment schemes.

the end of the contract. Hence there is good reason for compensation to be paid as a steady stream of income so that neither side is too heavily in debt to the other at any point in time.

Where there are fluctuations in demand for the firm's products, and hence fluctuations in the marginal revenue product of a stable work force, paying a steady compensation to employees does mean that indebtedness will arise on one side or the other from time to time. For such arrangements to work there must be some adhesive that prevents workers from quitting when they are ahead of the game and from being dismissed when they are behind.

One institution by which the employee tends to be held to the firm is the pay-by-age tradition. Generally, the marginal product of workers rises as they gain experience, reaches a peak, and then falls off as their age advances. The pay pattern, however, is often one that rises steadily with age and seniority. Thus experienced workers will get less than the value of their marginal product at earlier ages and more at later ages. This tends to hold workers to their firms.[1] But what stops the employer from dismissing workers once the value of their current marginal product begins to fall below their current wages? Here union contracts requiring that least-senior employees be laid off first does the job. Between the two, rising wages with age, and dismissal in ascending order of seniority, employers and employees are held to each other allowing payment of a steady wage in the face of fluctuating economic circumstances.

In such labour markets the wage rate does not fluctuate so as to clear the market. Wages are written over what has been called the 'economic climate' rather than the 'economic weather'. Because wages are thus insulated from short-term fluctuations in demand, any market clearing that does occur is through fluctuations in the volume of employment rather than in the wage.[2]

These new theories of non-market clearing apply mainly to stable labour forces in established industries and less to markets where turnover is very high and long-term attachment of employees to firms rare. In the words of economist Robert E. Hall: 'There is no point any longer in pretending that the labour market is an auction market cleared by the observed average hourly wage. In an extreme case, wages are just instalment payments on a long-term debt and reveal essentially nothing about the current state of the market.'[3]

The basic message of these new theories is that freely functioning labour markets, even those completely free from monopoly and monopsony elements, cannot be relied on to minimize involuntary unemployment by equating current demand for labour with current supply.

Further important implications of these theories for the causes of, and cures for, persistent unemployment are discussed in detail in the macroeconomic Parts of this book.

---

[1] Mandatory retirement is an essential feature of this arrangement since without it workers could decide to stay on the job for an unpredictable amount of time when their current wage was more than the value of their marginal product.

[2] Of course wages must respond to permanent shocks to a market, such as, for example, the permanent and unexpected decline in the demand for the output of a particular industry.

[3] Robert E. Hall, 'Employment Fluctuations and Wage Rigidity,' *Brookings Economic Papers*, Tenth Anniversary Issue, 1980, p. 120. This whole section draws heavily on Hall's excellent survey paper.

28

The income of capital

To many Marxists the capitalist is a villain. To many socialists he is at best a dispensable drone. To many liberals he is an important part of the productive process, as necessary as the providers of land and labour. To many conservatives he is a heroic figure captaining the economy along the risky channels leading to ever-higher living standards.

A capitalist is someone who owns capital, which we have defined as all man-made aids to further production. A key characteristic of capital is that it is durable. This means that it has two prices associated with it. The first is the price at which ownership of the capital good may be purchased. This is called the purchase price of capital. The second is the price at which its services may be hired for a period of time. This is called the rental price of capital. Capitalists own the capital goods and receive the rental earned by them. Individuals are capitalists as a result of past saving, either their own or that of the persons from whom they inherited their capital goods.

In this chapter we shall study the determinants of capital's share in the functional distribution of income. Capital theory, however, is one of the most difficult branches of economics and we can do little more than examine its outer surface in an introductory book.

At the outset let us clear up three possible misconceptions. *First, is capital itself either a villain or a dispensable drone in the productive process?* None but the most extreme and unrealistic members of the back-to-nature school would say 'Yes'. A primitive society in which there are no capital goods – not a spear, a lever, a washing tub nor a stone axe – is almost impossible to imagine.

Second, is a charge for the use of capital necessary? Early communist societies thought not. Such charges were officially barred during the early years after the Russian revolution of 1917. The trouble with doing this, however, is that capital is scarce; all producers would like to have more of it than they now have. If it does not have a price, how is the available supply to be allocated among the virtually limitless demands for it? Of course the state could allocate it. But how? Any state that is interested in maximizing production will want to allocate its scarce capital to its most productive uses. For this reason, virtually all communist states today assign a price to capital, and allow firms to use more of it only if the capital will earn enough to cover its cost. Furthermore, the planners in these societies worry about setting the right price of capital. This problem has also much concerned those responsible for investment in British nationalized industries (see Harbury and Lipsey, pp. 40–41). The answer to the second question is therefore 'Yes'.

Third, does capital need to be in private hands so that the price of capital becomes an income for its private owners? This time the answer is clearly 'No'. In many communist countries capital is owned by the state and the payments made for its use go to the state rather than to private 'capitalists'. The advantages of private versus public ownership of the 'means of production' (the term often used in socialist and communist literature to describe capital) is still hotly debated.

Capital is indispensable, and its efficient use requires that it be priced. When capital is privately owned, its price becomes the income of its owners; when it is publicly owned its price goes to the state.

The productivity or efficiency of capital

Capital is productive, but in what sense? Rarely, if ever, do we make any consumers' good[1] directly with the aid of such simple tools as nature provides. Productive effort goes first into the manufacture of capital – tools, machines and other goods that are desired not in themselves but only as aids to making other commodities. The capital goods are then used to make consumers' goods. The use of capital renders production processes *roundabout*. Instead of making what is wanted directly, producers engage in the indirect process of first making capital goods that are then used to make consumers' goods.

In many cases, production is very roundabout indeed. For example, a worker may be employed in a factory making machines that are used in mining coal; the coal may be burned by a power plant to make electricity; the electricity may provide power for a factory that makes machine tools; the tools may be used to make a tractor; the tractor may be used by a potato farmer to help in the production of potatoes; and the potatoes may be eaten by a consumer. This kind of indirect production is worthwhile *if* the farmer, using his tractor, can produce more potatoes than could be produced by applying all the factors of production involved in the chain directly to the production of potatoes (using only such tools as were provided by nature). In fact, the capital-using, round-about method of production usually leads to more output than the direct method. The difference between the flows of output that would result from the two methods is called either the PRODUCTIVITY OF CAPITAL or the EFFICIENCY OF CAPITAL.

The extra output, however, is not achieved without cost, usually in the form of reduction of current consumption while the capital goods are being made.

A decision to increase the amount of capital available usually entails a present sacrifice and a future gain.

The present sacrifice occurs because resources are diverted from producing consumption goods to producing capital goods. The future gain occurs because in the long run production will be higher with the new capital than without it (even after allowing for maintenance and replacement of capital goods).

The rate of return on capital

Whenever capital is productive its use yields a return over all other costs of production. How is this

---

[1] In capital theory the term 'consumers' goods' refers to all goods and services consumed because of the direct utility they yield to households; the term 'producers' goods' is a synonym for capital goods. In modern terminology 'commodity' would be better, but 'good' is enshrined by over a century of usage.

return determined? Take the receipts from the sale of the goods produced by a firm and subtract the appropriate costs for purchased goods and materials, for labour, for land and for the manager's own contributed talents. Subtract from this an allowance for the taxes the firm will have to pay, and what is left may be called the GROSS RETURN ON CAPITAL.

It is convenient to divide this gross return into four components.

(1) DEPRECIATION is an allowance for the decrease in the value of a capital good as a result of using it in production.

(2) The PURE RETURN ON CAPITAL is the amount that capital could earn in a riskless investment in equilibrium.

(3) The RISK PREMIUM compensates the owners for the actual risks of the enterprise.

(4) ECONOMIC PROFIT is the residual after all other deductions have been made from the gross return. It may be positive, negative, or zero.

The productivity of capital is its gross return minus its depreciation. This is also called the net return on capital and it is composed of items (2), (3), and (4) in the list.

In a market economy, positive and negative economic profits are a signal that resources should be reallocated because earnings exceed opportunity costs in some lines of production and fall short of them in other lines. Profits, defined in this way, are thus a phenomenon of disequilibrium. In equilibrium, profits will be zero and the opportunity cost of capital will thus be composed of the first three items.

In order to study the return to capital in its simplest form, we consider an economy that is in equilibrium with respect to the allocation of existing factors of production among all their possible uses. Thus economic profits are zero in every productive activity. This does not mean that the owners of capital get nothing; it means rather that the gross return to capital does not now include a profit element that signals the need to reallocate resources.

To further simplify things at the outset, let us deal with a world of perfect certainty: everyone knows for sure what the productivity of an existing new unit of capital will be in any of its possible uses. We shall return to uncertainty later. If there is no risk, then the gross return to capital does not include a risk premium.

We have now simplified to the point where the net return to capital is all pure return (item (2) on the previous list), while the gross return is pure return plus depreciation (items (1) and (2)). What determines the size of the pure return on capital? Why is it high in some time periods and low in others? What causes it to change?

In discussing such questions, it is usual to deal with a rate of return *per pound (£)* of capital. This concept requires placing a money value on a unit of capital (the 'price of capital goods') and a money value on the stream of earnings resulting from the productivity of capital. If we let X stand for the annual value of the gross return on a unit of capital, and P for the price of a unit of capital, the ratio X/P may be defined as the rate of return on capital. As a preliminary to understanding the determinants of the RATE OF RETURN ON CAPITAL we must define two key concepts: marginal efficiency of capital and present value.

The marginal efficiency of capital

It is convenient to think of society as having a quantity of capital that can be measured in physical units. The term CAPITAL STOCK refers to this total quantity of capital. As with any other factor of production, there is an average and a marginal product of capital. The marginal product of capital is the contribution to output of the last unit of capital added to a fixed quantity of other factors.

Marginal product is a physical measure, the amount of output per unit of capital. To obtain a value measure we value the output and the capital at their market prices and express one as a ratio of the other. This gives the monetary return on the marginal dollar's worth of capital and it is called the MARGINAL EFFICIENCY OF CAPITAL (MEC).[1] A schedule that relates the rate of return on each additional dollar of capital stock to the size of the capital stock is called the MARGINAL EFFICIENCY OF CAPITAL SCHEDULE. The MEC schedule is constructed on the assumptions that the society's population is fixed and that *technology is unchanging*. These assumptions are made in order to focus on changes in the quantity of capital, other things remaining equal. As more and more capital is accumulated, with unchanging technical knowledge and population, the ratio of capital to labour increases. This is called CAPITAL DEEPENING. To see why it occurs, consider the difference between a single firm and the whole economy.

When a single firm wants to expand output, it can buy another piece of land, build a factory identical to the one it now has, and hire new labour to operate the new plant. In this way, the firm can replicate what it already has. Since each worker in the new factory can be given the same amount of capital to work with as each worker in the old factory, output per worker and per unit of capital can remain unchanged as output rises. Increasing the quantity of capital without changing the proportions of factors used is called CAPITAL WIDENING.

For the economy as a whole, capital widening is possible only as long as there are unemployed quantities of labour and other factors of production. Additional workers, for example, must be drawn from somewhere. In a fully employed economy, what one small firm can do the whole economy cannot do. If the size of the capital stock is to increase while the total employed labour force remains constant, the amount of capital per employed worker must increase. In other words, capital deepening rather than capital widening must occur.

What is the effect of capital deepening on the marginal efficiency of capital? Because capital is subject to diminishing returns, as are all other factors of production, the amount of output per unit of capital will fall as capital deepening occurs. Each unit of capital has, as it were, fewer units of labour to work with than previously. As more and more capital deepening occurs, the marginal return to capital declines. The MEC schedule when plotted graphically is thus downward-sloping (see Figure 28.1).

A recapitulation of terminology

The theory of capital can seem quite bewildering on first encounter because there are so many terms that mean almost the same thing. It may be useful at this point, therefore, to review the standard terminology. The *productivity of capital* is measured by the *return on capital*. This return is usually measured as an amount per dollar's worth of capital, which makes it a *rate of return on capital*. This

---

[1] Like the other *marginal* concepts that we have encountered, the MEC is a calculus concept. It is the derivative of the returns (or efficiency-of-capital) function with respect to the quantity of capital. For a non-calculus treatment, we use the ratio of two numbers. In this case, it is the change in the return of capital divided by the (small) change in the capital stock that brought it about.

may be calculated as an average over all capital, in which case it is called the *average efficiency of capital* (or *average rate of return*); or it may be calculated on the last unit of capital, in which case it is called the *marginal efficiency of capital* (or *marginal rate of return*). The MEC schedule relates the rate of return on the marginal unit of capital to the total capital stock. It shows that as the total stock grows, the marginal return on each additional unit declines.

The present value of future returns

The efficiency of capital takes the form of producing a stream of output extending into the future that, as it is sold, yields a stream of gross returns to the firm. How is the price of capital related to the efficiency of capital? To know what price a firm would be willing to pay for a piece of capital, we must be able to put a present value on the stream of gross returns that the capital will yield to the firm.

We assume first that the price level is constant; later we consider the effects of inflation.

The value of a single future payment For purposes of illustration, let us assume that the rate of interest on a perfectly safe loan is 5 per cent and then ask three separate questions.

(1) *How much money would you have to invest today if you wished to have £100 in one year's time?* Letting X stand for the answer, we have: $X(1 \cdot 05) = £100$. Or $X = £100/1 \cdot 05 = £95 \cdot 24$. What this tells us is that, if you lend out £95.24 today at 5 per cent interest, you will receive £100 a year from now (£95·24 as repayment of the principal of the loan and £4·76 as interest).

(2) *What is the maximum amount you would be prepared to pay now to acquire the right to £100 in cash in one year's time?* Surely this is £95·24. If you paid more you would be losing money, since you can loan out £95·24 at 5 per cent and receive £100 in a year's time. If you could buy the right to £100 cash for anything less than £95·24 it would be profitable to do so, since you could borrow £95·24 now in return for your promise to repay £100 one year from now.[1]

(3) *What is the most you could borrow today in return for your promise to repay £100 a year from now?* If lenders were perfectly certain you would meet your promise, they would lend you £95·24. No one would lend you any more since the lender has the option of lending his or her money elsewhere at 5 per cent. If you offered to take less (say £90) then everyone would rush to lend you money since lending to you would yield more than the going rate of return on safe loans of 5 per cent.

The present value of a single future payment These three questions can be reduced to one question: 'How much money now is equivalent to £100 payable for certain a year from now when the interest rate on perfectly safe loans is 5 per cent?' This sum is called the present value of £100 a year from now at a 5 per cent interest rate. In general, PRESENT VALUE (PV) refers to the value now of payments to be received in the future. When a future sum is turned into its equivalent present value, we say that sum is DISCOUNTED.

Because discounting must take place at some particular rate of interest, present value depends on the rate of interest that is used in the calculation. Thus the numerical example given above

---

[1] Suppose, for example, you were offered the right to £100 a year from now for £90 now. If the market rate of interest is 5 per cent, you could borrow £95·24 now, buy the right to £100 next year for £90 and pocket £5·24 as your profit. Next year you claim the £100, which is just enough to repay the loan of £95·24 plus interest (at 5 per cent) of £4·76.

depended on the 5 per cent interest rate that was chosen to illustrate the calculations. If the interest rate is 7 per cent, the present value of the £100 receivable next year is £100/1·07 = £93·45. In general, the present value of £X one year hence, at an interest rate of i per cent per year,[1] is

$$PV = \frac{X}{(1+i)}.$$

Now consider what would happen if the payment date is further away than one year. If we lend £X at 5 per cent for one year we will be paid £(1·05)X. But if we immediately relend that whole amount, we would get back at the end of the second year an amount equal to 1·05 *times* the amount lent out, i.e. £(1·05)(1·05)X. Thus £100 payable two years hence has a present value (at 5 per cent) of

$$\frac{£100·00}{(1·05)(1·05)} = £90·70.$$

The amount of £90·70 lent out now, with the interest that is paid at the end of the first year lent out for the second year, would yield £100 in two years.[2] In general, the present value of £X after t years at i per cent is

$$PV = \frac{X}{(1+i)^t}.$$

Inspection of the above expression shows that as either i or t is increased, the denominator increases and hence PV decreases. This leads to the following conclusion:

The farther away the payment date and the higher the rate of interest, the smaller the present value of a given sum payable in the future.

The present value of an infinite stream of payments So much for a single sum payable in the future; now consider the present value of a stream of income that continues indefinitely. While at first glance that might seem very high, since as time passes the total received grows without reaching any limit, considerations of the previous section suggest that one will not value highly the far distant payments. To find the present value of £100 a year, payable for ever, we need only ask how much money would have to be invested now at an interest rate of i per cent per year to obtain £100 each year. This is simply $i \times X = £100$, where i is the interest rate and X the sum required. This tells us that the present value of the stream of £100 a year for ever is

$$PV = \frac{£100}{i}.$$

If the interest rate were 10 per cent, the present value would be £1,000, which merely says that £1,000 invested at 10 per cent would yield £100 per year, for ever. Notice that here, as above, PV is *inversely* related to the rate of interest: the higher the interest rate, the less the (present) value of distant payments.

---

[1] In all these calculations the interest rate is expressed as a ratio of interest divided by principal, so that a rate of 100 per cent is written 1, while 10 per cent is written as 0·1 and so on.

[2] Readers familiar with this type of calculation will realize that the argument in the text is based on an annual compounding of interest.

The present value of a finite stream of income   It is also possible to obtain the present value of some finite stream of income and then convert it into an equivalent infinite stream. This is of considerable theoretical value, since it allows us always to deal with the equivalent infinite stream, even if the problem we are considering concerns a finite and irregular stream. Consider, for example a machine that yields the following stream of gross returns: £100 now, £275 in one year, £242 in 2 years, £133·10 in 3 years, £87·84 in four years, and nothing thereafter. The present value of this flow of income, when the market rate of interest is 10 per cent (and hence $1 + i = 1·1$), is

$$PV = £100 + \frac{£275}{1·1} + \frac{£242}{(1·1)^2} + \frac{£133·10}{(1·1)^3} + \frac{£87·84}{(1·1)^4}$$

$$= £100 + £250 + £200 + £100 + £60$$

$$= £710.$$

But £710 invested at 10 per cent interest will yield a flow of £71 per annum in perpetuity. Thus the irregular finite flow listed above is equivalent to (i.e., has the same present value as) the smooth flow of £71 for ever. Thus, in any practical problem concerning an irregular flow we can substitute the equivalent regular flow, which can be handled with much greater ease.

Calculating the productivity or efficiency of capital

So far we have seen how to calculate the present value of a piece of capital that yields a flow of gross returns in the future. We do this by discounting the flow at the current rate of interest.

> **We can obtain a measure of the productivity or efficiency of capital by finding the rate of discount, e, that will just make the present value of the flow of receipts equal to the purchase price of the capital.**

If we take the case of a constant flow for ever, we can show this easily. Find e such that

$$P = X/e$$

where P is the purchase price of the piece of capital, X is its constant flow of gross returns and e is the unknown value of the productivity or efficiency of capital. In this simple case we can solve for e as:

$$e = X/P .$$

When the flow is irregular, or does not continue indefinitely, the procedure is the same, although the calculations are more tedious. We must find e such that

$$P = \frac{X_1}{1+e} + \frac{X_2}{(1+e)^2} + \ldots + \frac{X_n}{(1+e)^n}$$

where $X_1, \ldots, X_n$ is the gross return produced for each of n years and P is again the purchase price of the piece of capital. If we think of a firm having an array of capital equipment and making a marginal decision to install one more bit of capital, we may call the e associated with this marginal increment that firm's marginal efficiency of capital. Thus e is the efficiency of *any* unit of capital and *mec* is the efficiency of the *marginal* unit. (We use lower-case *mec* to refer to one firm and upper-case *MEC* to refer to the whole economy.)

The demand for capital

We can now use this analysis of the efficiency of capital to determine the demand for capital goods. We first consider a single firm and then the whole economy.

The firm's demand for capital

What is the significance of calculating e such that the present value of the flow of gross receipts is equal to the purchase price of the capital? The answer is that the value to the firm now of the flow of its gross receipts is its present value, while the purchase price is the cost to the firm now of the capital. The former is the addition to revenue of a unit of capital; the latter value is its addition to cost. We know already that the profit-maximizing firm will go on adding units of any factor of production as long as its marginal revenue product exceeds its marginal cost. Thus the profit-maximizing firm will go on adding capital as long as the present value of the flow of gross receipts from the marginal unit exceeds its purchase price.

The value of e is the rate of discount at which these two are just equal. But present value is calculated from the market rate of interest, i. Thus when *mec* equals i, the present value of the returns to the marginal unit of capital equals its price. Thus the firm's capital would be of equilibrium size: it would not pay the firm to add more.

This is an important and subtle point. It may thus be worth going over it again using a slightly different argument. How does the firm decide whether or not to buy a piece of capital? One way is to use the market rate of interest to calculate the present value of the gross return and then compare it with the purchase price. Suppose, for example, that for £8,000 a firm can purchase a machine that yields £1,000 a year net of all non-capital costs *into the indefinite future*. Also suppose that the firm can borrow (and lend) money at an interest rate of 10 per cent. The present value of the stream of income produced by the machine (the capitalized value of the machine) is £1,000/0.10 = £10,000; the present value of £8,000 now is (of course) £8,000. Clearly, the firm can increase its value if it purchases for £8,000 something that is worth £10,000 to itself. Another way to see this is to suppose that the only uses a firm has for its money are to buy the machine or to lend out its £8,000 at 10 per cent interest. Buying the machine is the superior alternative since this yields £1,000 per annum while lending out the £8,000 purchase price yields only £800 per annum.

In general, a profit-maximizing firm will purchase a capital good if

$$\frac{X}{i} > P$$

where X is the flow of gross returns expressed as an infinite stream of payments. The term X/i is the present value of the stream of gross returns produced by the capital good or, in other words, the capitalized value of the asset.

It pays to purchase a capital good whenever the present value of its future stream of gross returns exceeds the purchase price of the capital good.

This same relationship can be looked at in another way, by rearranging the terms in the algebraic inequality above:

$$\frac{X}{P} > i \ .$$

But X/P is the marginal efficiency of capital. Thus we have the rule:

It pays to purchase a further unit of capital whenever its marginal efficiency exceeds the rate of interest.

Looked at in this way, *mec* is a measure of the return on a marginal unit of capital to the firm, while i is a measure of the opportunity cost of capital (always assuming that the firm can borrow and lend at the going rate of interest).

We now assume that capital is subject to the law of diminishing marginal returns within the firm. Every further investment in capital equipment that the firm makes yields a lower return than previous investments. The rule outlined above now implies the following equilibrium condition:

A profit-maximizing firm will be in equilibrium with respect to the size of its capital stock when its marginal efficiency of capital is equal to the interest rate ($mec = i$).

The market demand for capital

Consider increasing the quantity of capital throughout the entire economy. It is convenient now to think of society as having a total quantity of capital, called the CAPITAL STOCK, and measured by a single number.[1] When more capital is accumulated under conditions of fixed technology and constant supplies of land and labour, diminishing returns implies that the marginal efficiency of capital will fall. The economy's marginal efficiency of capital (MEC) schedule relates the size of the capital stock to the return on the marginal unit of capital. It is downward-sloping and an illustration is shown in Figure 28.1 by the curve labelled MEC.

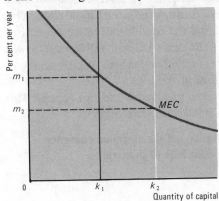

Fig. 28.1 In equilibrium the rate of interest is equal to the marginal efficiency of capital

A simple theory of the determination of the interest rate

Since each firm in the economy is in equilibrium with respect to its capital stock when its *mec* is equated with i, this will also be true of the economy. It follows that:

---

[1] The idea of a stock of capital being measured by a single number is a simplification. Society's stock of capital goods is made up of a diverse bundle of factories, machines, bridges, roads and other man-made aids to further production. For expository purposes, it is useful to make the heroic assumption that all of these can be reduced to some common unit and summed to obtain a measure of the society's *physical* stock of capital.

> **The *MEC* schedule is the economy's demand schedule for capital with respect to the rate of interest.**

A fixed stock of capital

The existing stock of capital can be changed only very slowly. Thus we may take the stock of capital as fixed over shortish time periods. If we assume that the present capital stock is k_1 in Figure 28.1, then the equilibrium rate of interest will be m_1.

How is this rate established? To answer this question assume that some other rate rules temporarily. First, assume that the rate is m_2. With the stock of capital k_1, the *MEC* of m_1 exceeds the interest rate of m_2. Investment will now look profitable to all firms and there will be a rush to borrow funds to invest in new capital equipment. The shortage of investment funds will bid up the rate of interest until it approaches m_1. Second, assume that the rate exceeds m_1. Now no firms will wish to borrow money for investment purposes and the glut of funds will bring the interest rate down.

> **Over short periods of time the capital stock, and hence the *MEC*, is given, so that the interest rate moves towards the *MEC*.**

A growing stock of capital

Over time, firms and households save and invest in new capital equipment, causing the capital stock to grow. This is shown by a slow rightward shifting of the line indicating the given capital stock. This has the effect of reducing the marginal efficiency of capital and the equilibrium interest rate. For example, if the stock grows from k_1 to k_2 in Figure 28.1, the *MEC* and i will both fall from m_1 to m_2. Thus in an economy with static technology and fixed supplies of land and labour, capital accumulation will lower the marginal efficiency of capital and the rate of interest.

The growth of technical knowledge, however, provides new productive uses for capital. This tends to push the *MEC* schedule outwards and *ceteris paribus* will raise *MEC* and i.

> **The accumulation of capital tends to lower the interest rate and the marginal efficiency of capital. The growth of technical knowledge tends to raise both of these rates.**

The pure and the market rates of interest

The simple theory outlined above takes the stock of capital as exogenous (constant over a short period and growing slowly over a long period) and determines simultaneously the pure return on capital, called the marginal efficiency of capital, and the rate of interest. The rate of interest so determined is called the PURE RATE OF INTEREST because it is the rate on a riskless loan to purchase capital (see the assumptions on page 393). According to this theory the marginal efficiency of capital must in equilibrium be equal to the pure rate of interest.

To obtain a theory of the actual rate of interest that rules in the market, which is called the MARKET RATE OF INTEREST (or sometimes simply 'the' rate of interest), we must allow for a number of complications. These will cause the market rate of interest to diverge from the pure rate.

Uncertainty So far we have discussed the present value of a *certain* future stream of gross returns. In reality, uncertainty will be attached to (i) the physical stream of goods the capital will produce; (ii) the value of the stream of goods (i.e., the gross monetary returns) the capital will produce; and (iii) the ability of a person who borrows money to repay the loan. Generally one can be fairly clear on the flow of goods one expects to gain from a piece of capital equipment. In these days of shortages of many raw materials and the possible outright exhaustion of others, however, there must be some uncertainty about the flow of goods that capital will produce. Even if everyone were perfectly certain about the physical productivity of capital, great uncertainty would inevitably attach to the expected value of the stream of gross returns associated with the capital goods. Even in the world of full employment, the prices of outputs and inputs fluctuate greatly. A favourable combination of changes – output prices up and input prices down – can greatly increase the value of the return to capital produced by the capital goods. An unfavourable combination can reduce this value or even eliminate it completely. In times of major depressions, demand for consumers' goods declines drastically as unemployment rises. Even if capital is physically productive, it will produce a zero stream of gross-value returns if the goods that it produces cannot be sold.

All of these uncertainties vary among firms and among industries. People investing their own money (e.g., by buying equities) in firms that are in high-risk industries will only do so if they expect a high yield from the capital that their money will be used to purchase. People lending their money to firms in high-risk industries (e.g. by purchasing their bonds) will only do so if they are offered a high rate of interest in return. For these reasons the return on capital and the rate of interest paid on borrowed money will differ among firms and industries.

The rate of interest will also differ systematically with the TERM (i.e. the duration) of the loan, for reasons that are ultimately related to uncertainty. Borrowers are usually willing to pay more for long-term loans than for short-term loans because they are certain of having use of the money for a longer period. Lenders usually require a higher rate of interest the longer the term of the loan, because the risk element is greater. (Will the borrower be able to repay? What will happen to the price level?) Thus, other things being equal, the shorter the term of a loan, the lower the interest rate.

All of these considerations affect the risk premium which is a part of the gross return to capital in addition to its pure return.

Inflationary expectations So far we have implicitly assumed a constant price level. In a world in which the purchasing power of money is constantly changing, it is necessary to distinguish between the real rate and the money rate of interest. The MONEY RATE OF INTEREST is measured simply in money paid. If you pay me £8 interest for a £100 loan for one year, the money rate is 8 per cent. The REAL RATE OF INTEREST concerns the ratio of the *purchasing power* of the money returned to the *purchasing power* of the money borrowed, and it may be different from the money rate.

Consider further my £100 loan to you at 8 per cent. The real rate that I earn depends on what happens to the overall level of prices in the economy. If the price level remains constant over the year, then the real rate that I earn is also 8 per cent. This is because I can buy 8 per cent more real goods and services with the £108 that you repay me than with the £100 I lent you. If, however, the price level were to rise by 8 per cent, the real rate would be nil because the £108 you repay me will buy the same quantity of real goods as the £100 I gave up. If I were unlucky enough to have lent money at

8 per cent in a year in which prices rose by 10 per cent, the real rate would be minus 2 per cent. This example illustrates the general proposition that the real rate of interest is the difference between the money rate of interest and the rate of change of the general price level.

In discussing the relation between the real and the money rates of interest, it is important to distinguish between an inflation that is fully anticipated by everyone (as might be the case when say a steady 5 per cent inflation has been going on for a long time) and an inflation that is unanticipated (as might be the case when the rate of inflation suddenly accelerates). Consider first the case of a fully anticipated inflation. The relation between real and money rates of interest often leads to much misunderstanding during times of anticipated inflation. Say, for example, that the equilibrium value of the real rate of interest is a modest 3 per cent and that the rate of inflation is now, and is expected to continue, at 5 per cent. The money rate should then be 8 per cent. Now assume that the rate of inflation accelerates to 15 per cent per year and is expected to remain at that figure. The money rate should now rise to 18 per cent. The 18 per cent money rate combined with a 15 per cent inflation rate represents the same real burden on borrowers as did the 8 per cent money rate combined with a 5 per cent rate of inflation. Yet when such changes occur it is common for the public to become very concerned at the 'crushing' burden of the rising interest rates on those with mortgages and other debts. But consider what would happen if in response to this worry the government legislated maximum interest rates of say 12 per cent in the face of the 15 per cent inflation. Now the real rate of interest would be negative: in real terms *lenders* would be paying for the privilege of being able to lend their money to the *borrowers*! This seems counter-intuitive to many people, but consider the example of a person who borrows £100 and repays £112 one year hence in the face of a 15 per cent inflation. The purchasing power of the £112 returned is less than the purchasing power of the £100 borrowed so that the real rate of interest has in fact proved negative in spite of the seemingly high money rate paid on the loan.

The real rate of interest is the money rate minus the rate of change of the general price level. A constant real rate of interest requires that the money rate increase by the same amount as any increase that occurs in the inflation rate.

If an inflation is fully expected, the money rate can be set to give any desired real rate of interest. Problems arise, however, when the inflation rate changes unexpectedly. Consider, for example, a loan that is supposed to carry a 3 per cent real rate of interest. If a 7 per cent inflation rate is expected, the money rate will be set at 10 per cent. But what if the inflationary expectations turn out to be wrong? If the inflation rate is only 4 per cent, the real rate of interest will be 6 per cent. If, on the other hand, the inflation rate is 12 per cent, the real rate of interest will be -2 per cent; the lender, even after paying the interest on the loan, will give back less purchasing power at the end of the period than he or she borrowed at the beginning.

Unexpected changes in the rate of inflation cause the real rate of interest on contracts already drawn up to vary in unexpected ways. An unexpected fall in the inflation rate is beneficial to lenders; an unexpected rise is beneficial to borrowers.

Uncertainty about the rate of inflation is an added complication, because people are uncertain about what the real rate of interest will be. If the rate of inflation accelerates unexpectedly borrowers gain; if it decelerates unexpectedly lenders gain. The effect on the current money rate of interest depends on how both borrowers and lenders react to uncertainty about the real rate of interest.

Other demands to borrow money So far we have considered only the purchase of new capital as a reason to borrow money. While capital equipment is a major source of the demand for funds, it is not the only source. Households borrow money to buy goods. The central authorities at all levels are major borrowers. Shifts in the demand to borrow money on the part of households or central authorities can cause the market rate of interest to change with no immediate change in the marginal efficiency of capital.

The influence of the central bank Central banks often intervene in the market for bonds in an attempt to influence the yield of these bonds. The central bank is a large enough potential buyer and seller of bonds to be able to do just this, and the exact way in which it is accomplished is analysed in Chapter 44.

Bank administration of interest rates The rate of interest does not fluctuate in response to every minor fluctuation in the demand to borrow money. Banks, for example, consider many factors when they fix the rate of interest that they charge on loans. They are reluctant to change these rates every time changes occur in the demand to borrow money. If there is an excess demand for loanable funds (because the *MEC* is greater than *i*), rather than raising the rate of interest, banks often ration the available supply of funds among their customers according to such criteria as the borrower's credit rating, how long the banker has known him and the amount of business he does. Credit rationing is commonly found in lending institutions in most Western countries. When the market rate of interest is below the pure return on capital, money will appear 'tight' – difficult to borrow – to the typical businessman.

Differences in the cost of administering credit There is great variation in the costs of different kinds of credit transactions. It is almost as cheap (in actual numbers of pounds) for a bank to lend £1 million to an industrial firm that agrees to pay the money back with interest after one year as it is for the same bank to lend you £4,000 to buy a new car on a loan that you agree to pay back over two years in 24 equal instalments. The difference in the cost *per pound* of each loan is considerable. The bank may very well make less profit per pound on a £4,000 loan at 18 per cent per year than on a £1 million loan at 8 per cent per year. In general, the bigger the loan and the fewer payments, the less the cost per pound of servicing the loan. Why, then, do banks usually insist that you repay the loan in frequent instalments? They worry that, if you do not pay regularly, you will not have the money when the loan comes due.

Many rates of interest In the real world there are many different rates of interest, not just a single one. Speaking in terms of the rate can, however, be a valid simplification for many purposes because the whole set of rates does *tend* to move upward or downward together. Concentrating on one 'typical' rate as 'the' rate of interest in such cases is quite acceptable. For some purposes, however, it is important to take into account the multiplicity of interest rates.

At the time that you receive an interest rate of 6 or 7 per cent on deposits at a building society, you may have to pay 10 or 11 per cent on a loan from the same building society to buy a house. Interest rates on hire-purchase credit of 16 per cent and 20 per cent are common. A small firm pays a higher interest rate than a giant corporation on funds it borrows from banks. Different government bonds pay different rates of interest, depending on the length of the period for which the bond runs.

Corporation bonds tend to pay interest at a higher rate than government bonds, and there is much variation among bonds of different companies. These differences persist because they reflect such things as differences in risk, term and cost of administration among different loans.

Recapitulation

(1) Capital is productive in that it provides a flow of gross returns over and above all non-capital costs of production.

(2) It will pay a firm to buy any piece of capital as long as the present value of its flow of gross returns exceeds its purchase price.

(3) The efficiency of capital is measured by the rate of discount that makes the present value of the flow of gross returns equal to its purchase price. It pays a firm to buy any piece of capital where efficiency exceeds the rate of interest.

(4) Capital is assumed to be subject to diminishing marginal returns so that the marginal efficiency of capital to each firm and to the economy as a whole declines as the capital stock rises.

(5) If the *MEC* exceeds the pure rate of interest, everyone will wish to borrow money and buy capital equipment. If the *MEC* is less than the pure rate of interest, no one will wish to borrow money to buy capital equipment. Thus in equilibrium the pure rate of interest tends to equal the marginal efficiency of capital.

(6) The income earned by an owner of capital, whether he uses it himself and gains the marginal efficiency of capital or lends it to someone and earns the pure rate of interest, is thus determined by the marginal efficiency of capital.

(7) The total return to capital includes, in addition to the pure return on capital, a risk premium and pure profits. If there are no barriers to entry, pure profits are a disequilibrium phenomenon which exists only until new capital enters the industry, expanding output and reducing prices so that the pure profits disappear (if there are barriers to entry the pure profits may persist in the long run).

(8) Actual interest rates differ from the pure rate of interest for a number of identifiable reasons such as risk and term of the loan.

The price of an income-producing asset

The analysis of this chapter allows us to understand the determination of the market price of *any* asset that produces a stream of income over time. The asset might be a piece of land, a machine, a football player's contract or a block of flats. It will produce a stream of output and the market conditions of demand and supply will determine the price of this output. This allows us to convert the stream of output into a stream of money. Now that we know how to calculate the present value of a stream of money, it only remains to make the obvious point that the equilibrium market price of the asset will be equal to the present value of the stream of money associated with it.

Thus the present value of a productive asset that produces the equivalent of £100 a year *net* income indefinitely is £2,000 if the appropriate rate of interest is 5 per cent, because £2,000 invested at 5 per cent per year would yield £100 a year. It would pay an investor to buy the equipment for any price up to and including £2,000. (Of course, the equipment will not produce income indefinitely, but we are making use of the result that for any finite, and possibly irregular, stream of income actually produced by the machine there will be an equivalent constant, infinite stream.) If the price were less than £2,000 everyone would be eager to buy the equipment and its price would rise. If the price were more than £2,000 it would not pay anyone to buy it. If, for example, the price were £2,500 and the equipment was bought with borrowed money, the purchaser would have to pay £125 a year to borrow the money necessary to purchase an asset that would yield only £100. If it were bought with the purchaser's own money, the purchaser could have lent the £2,500 out at the going rate of interest and earned £125 a year rather than buying the equipment and getting only £100. Thus no one would be willing to buy it and its price would fall. The only price at which people would be prepared to both buy and sell the piece of equipment is £2,000.

In general, if the market price of any asset is greater than the present value of the income stream it produces, no one will want to buy it, while if the market price is below its present value, everyone will want to buy it.

In a competitive market the equilibrium price of any asset will be the present value of the income stream it produces.

We have already noted that when we obtain the present value of any asset that yields a stream of future income, we speak of *discounting the future income stream* to get the CAPITALIZED VALUE of the asset. This is nothing other than the present value of the stream of income that the asset is expected to yield.[1]

A most important application of these general considerations concerns the relationship between the rate of interest and the price of bonds.

Consols A CONSOL, or *perpetuity*, is a bond that pays a fixed sum of money each year forever. It has no redemption date. The price of a consol promising to pay, for example, £100 per year, is £2,000 when the interest rate is 5 per cent and £1,000 when the rate is 10 per cent. *The price of a consol varies inversely with the rate of interest.*

Now consider a world in which consols are the only interest-earning asset, and assume that many people have excess money balances that they wish to invest. If everyone tries to buy consols their price will be bid up. If the price of consols paying £500 a year rises from say, £5,000 to £10,000, this means that the interest rate that lenders are prepared to accept has fallen from 10 per cent to 5 per cent. (If existing consols sell at £10,000 any new borrower can also sell a newly issued consol for £10,000.)

Any action of investors that causes the price of consols to change also causes the rate of interest to change in the opposite direction: a rise in the price of consols is the same thing as a fall in the rate of interest.

Redeemable bonds Most bonds are not consols. Instead they pay a fixed sum of money in interest each year but also have a redemption date on which the principal of the loan will be repaid. A bond

---

[1] A major problem in arriving at the present value of a future stream of money income is deciding on the appropriate interest rate to use in discounting the future stream. If the firm can borrow as much money as it wants at i per cent per year, it should discount at i per cent per year. If the firm cannot borrow all that it wishes, its internal rate of return on an extra pound invested may be substantially above the market rate of interest. In this case the firm should discount at its own opportunity cost of capital. The general principle is that the rate of discount should reflect the genuine opportunity cost of capital to the firm.

with a redemption value of £1,000 payable ten years hence and yielding £100 a year in the interim, would be worth the present value of a ten-year stream of £100 per year *plus* the present value of £1,000 payable in ten years. It is obvious that the same principles apply to redeemable bonds as to consols:

(i) The price of bonds and the rate of interest vary inversely with each other; (ii) Any action of investors that bids up the market price of existing bonds means that the rate of interest lenders are prepared to accept has fallen.

A redeemable bond differs from a consol, however, in that the present value of the former becomes increasingly dominated by the fixed redemption value as the redemption date approaches. Consider, for example, a bond that pays £100 interest in one year from now and a further £100 plus the principal of £900 two years from now. At a rate of interest of 5 per cent the price of that bond (its *PV*) is £1,002·27, while at a rate of 10 per cent it is £917·36.[1] Thus a doubling of the rate of interest only reduces the value of that two-year bond to 91·5 per cent of its former value while it reduces the value of the consol to half its former value. Taking an even more extreme case, if a bond is to be redeemed for £1,000 in a week's time, its present value will be very close to £1,000 and will hardly change if the rate of interest goes from 5 to 10 per cent.

The closer to the present the redemption date of a bond, the less its value changes with a change in the rate of interest.

---

[1] The bond yields two payments: £100 and £1,000 in one and two years' time respectively. The present value at 5 per cent is $100/1\cdot05 + 1,000/(1\cdot05)^2 = 1,002\cdot27$, and at 10 per cent is $100/1\cdot10 + 1,000/(1\cdot10)^2 = 9.17\cdot36$. The ratio of these two *PV*s is $917\cdot36/1,002\cdot27 = 0\cdot915$.

29

Criticisms and tests of the theory of distribution

In Part 5 we have developed the traditional theory of distribution in several contexts. Repeating what is basically the same analysis in a number of different guises helps to develop a 'feel' for the workings of the price system that is very important to the economist. It has the disadvantage, however, of making the theory appear to have much more content than it actually has. In fact, the whole of distribution theory depends on a very few basic hypotheses about the behaviour of factor owners and firms. Before going on to consider various criticisms and tests of the theory, it may be useful to lay out its underlying structure.

The theory restated

The traditional theory of distribution maintains that factor prices can be explained by demand and supply. The theory of factor supply is based on the assumption that factors will move among occupations, industries and places in search of the highest net advantage, taking both monetary and non-monetary rewards into account. Factors will move in such a way as to equalize the net advantages their owners could gain from using those factors in any of their possible uses. Because there are impediments to the mobility of factors, there may be lags in their response to changes in prices. The elasticity of supply will depend on what factor is being discussed and what time horizon is being considered.

The demand for a factor is a derived demand, depending for its existence on the demand for the commodity produced by the factor. The elasticity of an industry's demand curve for a factor will vary directly with (i) the elasticity of demand for the product produced by the industry; (ii) the proportion of total production costs accounted for by the factor; and (iii) the extent to which it is technically possible to substitute other factors for the one in question.

In equilibrium *all* profit-making firms will employ *all* variable factors up to the point at which the marginal unit of each type of factor adds as much to revenue as to costs. All profit-maximizing firms that are price-takers in the factor market will employ factors up to the point at which the price paid for the last unit equals the increase in revenue caused by its employment. For firms selling goods in competitive markets, the increase in revenue is the marginal physical product *times* the price; for firms facing downward-sloping demand curves for their products, the increase in revenue is marginal physical product *times* marginal revenue.

These equilibrium relations necessarily apply to all firms that are successfully maximizing their profits. On the one hand, the firm that is not equating the marginal revenue product of each of its factors with that factor's price is not maximizing its profits. On the other hand, a firm that is maximizing its profits is necessarily equating each factor's price to its marginal revenue product. The theory thus stands or falls with the theory of profit-maximization. It is merely an implication of profit-maximization, and the only reason for spelling it out in detail is that this helps us to develop interesting and useful hypotheses about the effects of various changes in the economy on the markets for factors of production.

When one thinks of all the heated arguments over the traditional theory of distribution, and of all the passionate denunciations and defences that it has occasioned, it is surprising to observe how few predictions it makes, and how uncontroversial most of them are. For example, the theory predicts that demand for a factor depends on, and varies with, the demand for the products made by the factor. This was undoubtedly a great discovery when it was first put forward; now, however, it is almost a platitude. The theory also predicts that (assuming the supply curve does not shift) changes in the factor price must reflect changes in the demand for the commodities made by the factor. On the supply side, the theory predicts that movement of resources will occur in response to changes in factor prices. It is hard to quarrel with these predictions, which are supported by much evidence. They are important since they frequently apply to practical issues of policy.

Criticisms of the theory

We have seen that marginal productivity theory relates to the demand for factors of production. It constitutes half of the traditional theory of distribution; the other half is the theory of supply, the theory of factor movement in search of the highest net advantage. It is the marginal productivity half of the theory that has been most criticized and about which so many misconceptions exist. We first discuss four common misconceptions, all of which have been drawn from real sources.

(1) *The theory assumes perfect competition in all markets (which is sometimes called pluperfect competition)*. This is just not correct. The relationship between the marginal physical product and the marginal revenue product will be altered if the degree of competition alters, but the marginal revenue product will be equated with the price of the factor in perfect competition, imperfect competition, oligopoly and monopoly, provided only that firms are price-takers in the factor market.

(2) *The theory assumes that the amount and value of the marginal product of a factor are known to the firm*. The theory assumes no such thing! Critics argue that the firm will not pay any factor the value of its marginal product because the firm will generally have no idea what that marginal product is and would be unable to calculate this magnitude even if it tried. What firms do or do not know about marginal products is irrelevant. It has already been pointed out that payment according to marginal revenue product occurs *automatically* whenever the firm is maximizing its profits. It does not matter *how* the firm succeeds in doing this – by guess, luck, skill or by calculating marginal quantities. As long as profits are maximized, factors will be getting the values of their marginal products. The theory does not purport to describe how firms calculate; it merely predicts how they will react to various situations on the assumption that they are maximizing profits.

(3) *The theory is inhuman because it treats labour in the same way as it treats an acre of land or a wagonload of fertilizer*. One must be careful to distinguish one's emotional reaction to a procedure that treats human and non-human factors alike from one's evaluation of it in terms of positive economics. Those who accept this criticism must explain carefully why separate theories of the

pricing of human and non-human factors are needed. They must also show that their 'human' theory makes predictions that differ from those made by marginal productivity theory. Marginal productivity theory is only a theory of the *demand* for a factor. It predicts that firms' desired purchases of labour (and all other factors) depend on the price of the factor in question, the technical conditions of production and the demand for the product made by labour. No evidence has yet been gathered to indicate that it is necessary to have separate theories of the *demand* for human and non-human factors of production. *Supply* conditions will differ between human and non-human factors, but these differences are accommodated within the theory. Indeed, one of the important insights from the theory of net advantage is that non-monetary considerations are more important in allocating labour than other factors because the owner of labour must be physically present to supply his factor's services, while the owner of land and capital need not be.

(4) *When all factors are paid according to their marginal products, the resulting distribution of income will be a just distribution.* Some supporters of the theory of marginal productivity have held not only that the theory was correct, but that it described a functional distribution of income that was a *just* one because factors were rewarded according to the value of their contributions to the national product. Many critics of the low level of wages prevailing in the nineteenth century reacted with passion against a theory that was claimed to justify these rates of pay.

It is beyond the scope of a book on positive economics to enter into normative questions of what constitutes a just distribution of income. It is, however, worth getting the facts straight. According to marginal productivity theory, each labourer (or each unit of any other factor) does *not* receive the value of what he or she personally contributes to production. Each labourer, instead, receives the value of what the last labourer employed would add to production *if all other factors of production were held constant*. If one million identical labourers are employed, then each of the one million receives as a wage an amount equal to the extra product that would have been contributed by the millionth labourer if he had been hired while capital, etc., had remained unchanged. Whatever the justice of the matter, it is not correct to say that each factor receives the value of *its own* contribution to production. Indeed, where many factors co-operate in production, it is generally impossible to divide up the *total production* into amounts contributed by each.

So much for crude misinterpretations. We must now consider more basic criticisms. It is often alleged that the theory does not explain factor allocation – and thus will not, for example, be able to predict the effect on factor allocation of the vast number of specific government interventions into factor markets. To make this general case, one of two things must be established: *either* the theory does not explain relative factor earnings, *or* factors do not move in response to relative earnings. Conversely, if the theory is to stand up to these criticisms, *both* of these allegations must be shown to be wrong. We shall consider them in turn.

Do market conditions determine factor earnings?

Factors other than labour

Most non-human factors are sold on competitive markets. The overwhelming preponderance of evidence supports the hypothesis that changes in the earnings of these factors are associated with changes in market conditions. Consider just a few examples.

Raw materials The prices of copper, tin, rubber and hundreds of other materials fluctuate daily in response to changes in the demand and supply of these products. Current shortages of certain key raw materials are almost always signalled by price increases. Materials prices also show a strong cyclical component. They rise on the upswing of the trade cycle when their (derived) demand rises, and fall on the downswing when their (derived) demand falls.

> **There is little question that the theory of factor pricing in competitive markets provides a good explanation of raw material prices and of the incomes earned by their producers.**

Of course if monopoly elements arise, the theories of factor pricing under monopoly or monopsony need to be applied. OPEC's escalation of prices in the 1970s, for example, led to a large rise in the price of the petroleum inputs to many production processes and to the owners of oil fields.

Land values Values of land in the hearts of growing cities rise in response to increasing demand. Often it is even worthwhile to destroy buildings to convert land to more profitable uses. The New York and London skylines are monuments to the high value of urban land. The increase in the price of land on the periphery of every growing city is another visible example of the workings of the market.

Agricultural land appears at first glance to provide counter-evidence. The classical economists predicted 150 years ago that, as population and the demand for agricultural products grew, the price of the fixed supply of land would rise enormously. The price of agricultural land, however, has *not* skyrocketed. Although the demand for agricultural produce did expand in the predicted fashion because of the rise in population, the productivity of agricultural land has increased in quite unexpected ways with the invention of the vast range of machines and techniques that characterize modern agriculture. The prediction was falsified, not because the price of agricultural land is not determined by market forces, but because some of the market forces were incorrectly foreseen.

Legal right to produce In many instances the right to produce is restricted by regulations enforced either by governments or private organizations. Many governments faced with agricultural surpluses due to over-generous price supports restrict output by issuing production quotas. The number of taxis operating in most North American cities is restricted by the local authorities who issue a fixed number of licences to operate. Sometimes the ability to produce a revenue requires admission to a professional society whose membership is controlled by quota. Also when a product or production process is controlled by patent, its use requires ownership of the patent or a licensing by its owners.

In these and similar cases the quota, licence or patent are factors of production: without them, production is impossible. Often the right to produce is saleable. In this case the market value of the right becomes exactly the capitalized present value of the monopoly profits that accrue because of the restriction on output. Suppose, for example, each unit of a good that is produced under quota restriction earns £1,000 of pure profit, i.e., £1,000 of revenue in excess of what it would have to earn to persuade firms to go on producing it. Anyone who obtains a quota to produce a unit of the product can thus make £1,000 per year more than he could by producing in some other industry where freedom of entry and exit forces profits to zero. The quota will thus sell in the open market for the present value of a flow of £1,000 per year, $1,000/i$, which for example is £10,000 at a 10 per cent rate of interest. As the demand for the product fluctuates and the supply restriction is held constant, the profits, and hence the present value of the quota, will fluctuate.

Various forms of such output restrictions are found throughout the world and the evidence amply supports the theory of the market determination of their values.

> **Where output restrictions create monopoly profits the market value of the instrument that confers the right to produce a unit of output will equal the capitalized present value of the flow of monopoly profits earned by a unit of output.**

Labour

When we apply our theory to labour, we encounter two important sets of complications: first, labour markets are a mixture of competitive and non-competitive elements, the proportions of the mixture differing from market to market; second, labour being the human factor of production, non-monetary considerations loom large in its incentive patterns. These complications help to make labour economics one of the most difficult – and interesting – fields of economics. Monopolistic elements and non-monetary rewards, both of which are difficult to measure, require careful specification if the theory that labour earnings respond to market prices is to be made testable. Nevertheless, we do have a mass of evidence to go on. We do have cases in which a strong union – one able to bargain effectively and to restrict entry of labour into the field – has caused wages to rise well above the competitive level. Unions can and do succeed in raising wages and incomes when they operate in small sections of the whole economy; the high earnings do attract others to enter the occupation or industry; and the privileged position can be maintained only if entry can be effectively restricted. Closed-shop laws are one obvious way of doing this.

Not only can monopoly elements raise incomes above their competitive levels, they can also prevent incomes from falling and reflecting decreases in demand. Of course, if demand disappears more or less overnight (as it did for silent-movie stars and carriage-makers), there is nothing any union can do to maintain incomes. But the story may be different if, as is more usual, demand shrinks slowly over a few decades. In this case, unions *that are powerful enough virtually to prohibit new entry of labour into the industry* can often hold wages up in the face of declining demand. The industry's labour force thus declines, through death and retirement, in spite of the relatively high wage being paid to the employees who remain.

Wages also respond to fluctuations in competitive conditions of demand and supply. Consider some examples. With the advent of the motorcar, many skilled carriage-makers found the demand for their services declining rapidly. Earnings fell, and many craftsmen who were forced to leave the industry found that they had been earning substantial rents for their scarce, but highly specific, skills. They were forced to suffer large income cuts when they moved to other industries. Many silent-screen actors whose voices were unsuitable for the talkies suffered disastrous cuts in income and fell into oblivion when the demand for silent films disappeared. Much earlier, the same fate had met those music-hall stars whose talents did not project onto the flat, flickering screen of the early silent films. A similar fate hit many radio personalities who were unable to make the transition to television and had to compete in a greatly reduced market for radio talent. How soon will television entertainers who have enormous incomes due to the high demand for their services, go the same way when a yet newer mass entertainment medium sweeps away the present one? When in a competitive, changing society you hear the bell toll for some once-wealthy and powerful group, always remember that someday it could be tolling for you!

These variations in factor earnings are caused by changes in market conditions, not by changes in our notions of the intrinsic merit of various activities. To illustrate, ask yourself why, if you have the talent, you can make a lot of money writing copy for a London advertising agency, whereas even if you have great talent you are unlikely to make a lot of money writing books of poetry. This is not because any economic dictator or group of philosophers has decided that advertising is more valuable than poetry, but because there is a large demand for advertising and only a tiny demand for poetry. A full citing of all such evidence would cover many pages, and it would point to the following conclusion.

> Earnings of labour do respond to changes in market forces. Some factor markets are competitive and some are monopolistic, and the evidence seems to suggest that the theory of competitive and monopolistic market behaviour helps to explain factor incomes.

Do factors move in response to changes in earnings?

In the previous section we saw that earnings do tend to change in response to the conditions of demand and supply. Changes in earnings are signals that attract resources into those lines of production in which more are needed and out of lines in which less are needed. But do changes in factor prices produce the supply responses predicted by the theory?

Land

In the case of land, there is strong evidence that the theory is able to predict the actual course of events quite accurately. Land is transferred from one crop to another in response to changes in the relative profitabilities of the crops. Land on the edge of town is transferred from rural to urban uses as soon as it can earn substantially more as a building site than as a corn field. Although physically immobile, land is constantly transferred among its possible uses as the relative profitabilities of these uses change. Little more needs to be said here; the most casual observation will show the allocative system working with respect to land much as described by the theory.

Capital

The location of, and products produced by, the nation's factories have changed greatly over the last two centuries. Over a period of, say, fifty years the change is dramatic; from one year to the next, it is small. Most plant and machinery is relatively specific. Once installed, it will be used for the purpose for which it was designed as long as the variable costs of production can be covered. But if full, long-run opportunity costs are not covered, the capital will not be replaced as it wears out. Investment will take place in other industries instead.

> Long-run movements in the allocation of capital clearly occur in response to market signals.

The mechanism will work easily as long as there is freedom of entry and exit. Exit is difficult to prevent (other than by government legislation and subsidy), but monopolies and oligopolies, government regulations, and nationalized industries do erect barriers to entry. Profits in a monopolized industry where entry is blocked do not induce flows of new investment, and they therefore serve no apparent long-run allocative function.

Although monopoly profits do not cause capital to move when entry is blocked in the long run, we cannot be so sure in the very long run. These profits may cause other firms to develop competing products and innovate in other ways so as to attack the sitting monopoly in a process of what Schumpeter called creative destruction (see p. 318). If so, then monopoly profits do infuence the allocation of capital in the very long run.

Labour

Countless studies of labour mobility do show conclusively that labour moves in response to monetary incentives. High relative wages do attract and hold labour in such unattractive parts of the world as the Canadian North, Siberia and the Amazon jungles, while occupations with much leisure and pleasant working conditions tend to pay much lower wages. There is a supply as well as a demand element at work here. Unpleasant but unskilled jobs are often poorly paid because anyone can do them, but even so, dustmen in the frozen Canadian North are paid more than dustmen in Montreal because otherwise they would not stay in the unattractive climate.

At the risk of grossly oversimplifying a complex situation, it may be said that the following hypotheses are consistent with the evidence.

(1) There exists a fairly mobile component of labour in any group. It tends to consist of the youngest, the most adaptable and often the most intelligent members of the group.

(2) This mobile group can be attracted from one area, occupation, or industry to another by relatively small changes in economic incentives.

(3) Provided that the pattern of demand for resources does not shift too fast, most of the necessary reallocation can be accomplished by movements of this mobile group. Of course, the same individual need not move over and over again. The group is constantly replaced by new entrants into the labour force.

(4) As we go beyond these very mobile persons, we get into ranges of lower and lower mobility until, at the very bottom, we find those who are completely immobile. The most immobile are the very old, those with capital sunk in non-marketable assets, the timid, the weak and those who receive high rents in their present occupation or location. It is difficult for them to move; in extreme cases, even the threat of starvation may not be enough since some people believe, rightly or wrongly, that they will starve even if they do move.

Thus, shifts in earnings may create substantial inflows of workers into an expanding occupation, industry or area and an outflow of workers from a depressed occupation, industry or area. Over long periods of time, outflows have been observed from depressed areas such as Appalachia and parts of New England in the US, the Maritime Provinces of Canada, Sicily and southern Italy, the Highlands of Scotland, declining areas of northeastern England and rural parts of central France. Although *some* out-migration occurs readily, it is difficult for large transfers to take place in short periods of time. When demand falls rapidly, pockets of poverty tend to develop. Labour has been leaving each of the geographical areas mentioned above, but poverty has increased too. The reason is that the rate of exit has been slower than the rate of decline of the economic opportunities in the area. Indeed, the exit itself causes further decline, for when a family migrates all the locally provided goods and services that it once consumed suffer a reduction in demand, leading to a further decline in the demand for labour.

The modern non-market theories of wage determination suggest an additional force. According to these theories wages reflect the long-term value of labour to the firm but do not fluctuate with every change in labour's short-term value. This leaves employment and unemployment to do much of the short-term equilibrating. Assume, for example, a fairly rapid fall in the demand for labour in area A and a rise in demand in area B. If wages, being responsive to long-term considerations, do not respond quickly, employment will. There will be unemployment in region A and a labour shortage in region B. Labour may then move from A to B not in response to a wage differential but to a differential in the probability of obtaining employment. Indeed, there is some substantial evidence that at some times and places, differences in probability of finding a job motivates the movement of labour at least as much as differences in wage rates.

Marginal productivity theory and the macro-distribution of income

The theory of distribution discussed above concentrates on the pricing of factors in each of the many markets of the economy. The previous discussion has repeatedly shown that the theory does successfully predict the consequences for particular prices and quantities of changes that impinge on particular markets. But does the theory say anything about what determines the functional distribution of income among such broad classes of factors as land, labour and capital? What, for example, determines the share of total income going to labour as a class? What influences do unions and government policy have on this share? Questions of distribution at this level of aggregation are often referred to as questions about *macro-distribution* (as opposed to *micro-distribution*, which refers to such questions as what determines the share of total income going to some small group of labour operating in a single labour market).

Marginal analysis and macro-distribution

Questions of the macro-distribution of income among the great social classes of the society, labourers, landlords and capitalists, were of great concern to classical economists such as Ricardo, Malthus and Marx. With the development of marginal analysis in the last half of the nineteenth century emphasis shifted to the determination of factor prices and quantities in millions of individual markets. The theory that grew out of this development (often called marginal productivity theory after its demand half) offers few general predictions about the macro-distribution of income. It holds that to discover the effect of some change, say a tax or a new trade union, on the macro-distribution between wages, profits and rent, we would need to be able to discover what would happen in each individual market of the economy and then aggregate to find the macro-result. To do this we would need to know the degree of monopoly and monopsony in each market, we would need to be able to predict the effect on oligopolists' prices and outputs of changes in their costs, and we would need to have a theory of the outcome of collective bargaining in situations of monopoly and monopsony. We would also need to know how much factor substitution would occur in response to any resulting change in relative factor prices. Finally, we would need a general equilibrium theory linking all of these markets together. Clearly we are a long way from being able to do all this: with our present state of knowledge, marginal productivity theory provides few if any predictions about the effects on macro-distribution of such changes as shifts in total factor supplies, taxes on one factor, and the rise of trade unions.

This conclusion is not necessarily a criticism of the theory. It may well be that relative shares are determined by all the detailed interactions of all the markets in the economy, and that general predictions about the effects of various events on macro-distribution can be obtained only after we have enough knowledge to solve the general equilibrium problem outlined in the previous paragraph. Neither does this conclusion mean that we can never identify forces that will affect the macro-distribution in a predictable way. If some common cause were to act on most demands or supplies of labour in individual markets, the average return to all labour, and hence labour's share in total national income, could be significantly affected.

Many economists argue that we should not expect to get further than this. They hold that the great macro-questions on the scale of *labour versus capital* are largely unanswerable, and that, pedestrian though it may seem, the ability of the traditional theory to deal with micro-questions is a remarkable triumph. One reason advanced for the view that the great macro-distribution questions are unanswerable is that it only makes sense to talk about laws governing macro-distribution if labour, capital and land are each relatively homogeneous and each subject to a common set of influences not operating on the other two factors, whereas in fact (so goes the view) there is likely to be as much difference between two kinds of labour as between one kind of labour and one kind of machine. On the one hand, the micro-distribution of income can be thought of as subject to understandable influences because it deals with innumerable relatively homogeneous factors. On the other hand, macro-distribution is nothing more than the aggregate of the micro-distributions, and there is no more reason to expect that there should be simple laws governing the macro-distribution among land, labour and capital than to expect that there should be simple laws governing the macro-distribution between blondes and brunettes.[1]

Alternative theories of distribution

Many economists have been dissatisfied with the answer that there is no answer to the great question of macro-distribution. This dissatisfaction has lead to alternative theories which deal explicitly with macro-distribution problems.

Macro-marginal productivity theories An attempt that is in the tradition of marginal productivity theory is based on the postulated existence of a *macro-production function* for the whole economy. Assume that total national output can be treated as a simple composite commodity that varies in amount according to the inputs of three homogeneous factors: labour, land and capital. This allows us to write a single production function for the economy as a whole:

---

[1] In case it is not obvious to the reader trying to guard against the author's biases, I am in general agreement with this view (although, like most other economists who believe that their subject can explain some of what we see in society, I should be overjoyed if someone did succeed in getting a workable theory of macro-distribution that stood up to some serious empirical tests).

$$Y = Y(L, N, K),$$

where Y stands for output and L, N and K for inputs of land, labour and capital respectively. If the total supply of each factor is fixed at any one time, and if the economy is usually at, or near, full employment of all factors, then the inputs of L, N and K are determined and so, through the production function, is Y.

Each factor of production will have a marginal product – the change in output that would occur if the quantity of the factor were varied slightly, the quantity of the other factors being held constant – and this will determine the price of the factor. The total payment going to the factor measured in real terms will be the quantity of the factor multiplied by its marginal product. The macro-distribution of income is thus determined by the nature of the production function (which determines marginal products) and the total available supplies of the three factors. Although aggregate production functions of this sort are commonly used in theoretical models, there is little evidence that they are good descriptions of the behaviour of total output over long periods of time or that they isolate important forces that determine the macro-distribution of income.[1]

The degree-of-monopoly and Keynesian theories   A more radical departure from traditional theory was expounded by Michael Kalecki, who sought to explain labour's share by the economy's overall degree of monopoly. Mention should also be made of the many 'macro-theories' that followed from Keynes's general theory. Theories of this sort make use of the Keynesian aggregates that we shall not study until Part 8 so we will say no more about them here. We can observe, however, that, in spite of the obvious appeal of being able to relate distribution to only a few measurable variables, such theories have received no significant empirical support.

The Cambridge School   Finally, and perhaps most important in the list of dissenters from orthodox distribution theory, we should mention a group of radical dissenters at Cambridge University which includes such famous economists as Professors Joan Robinson, Pierro Sraffa and

---

[1] The Cobb-Douglas production function was an early attempt to explain labour's share. In the two-factor version, real national output (Y) is determined in inputs of labour (N) and capital (K), according to the single macro-production function applying to the whole economy:

$$Y = AN^{\alpha}K^{1-\alpha},$$

where A and α are positive constants and α is also less than unity. The real wage of labour (w) is its real marginal product which those who know calculus will recognise as the partial derivative of Y with respect to N:

$$w = \frac{\partial Y}{\partial N} = \alpha AN^{\alpha-1}K^{1-\alpha}.$$

The total wage bill is

$$wN = \frac{\partial Y}{\partial N} \cdot N = \alpha AN^{\alpha}K^{1-\alpha},$$

and the share of wages in the national product is

$$\frac{wN}{Y} = \frac{\alpha AN^{\alpha}K^{1-\alpha}}{AN^{\alpha}K^{1-\alpha}} = \alpha.$$

Thus the Cobb-Douglas national production function leads to the prediction that labour's share of the national product will be a constant, α, and will be independent of the size of the labour force.

Nicholas Kaldor. The most outspoken member of the group has been Professor Robinson, who has written numerous influential attacks on orthodox distribution theory. She has for many years propounded the view that distribution theory went off on the wrong track with the late nineteenth-century development of marginal productivity theory. In her view we need to go back to the classical theories of Ricardo and Marx and develop them into satisfactory theories of macro-distribution. It is impossible to do justice to Professor Robinson's view, to say nothing of criticizing it in depth, within the confines of this book. Rather than present a capsule summary that would inevitably be a caricature, it is probably fairer to refer interested readers to Professor Robinson's own writings in which she attacks the traditional theory of distribution and propounds her own 'classical' alternative.[1] Two specific criticisms of capital theory that are made by the Cambridge School should at least be mentioned. These concern the concept of the quantity of capital and the so-called reswitching problem.

The quantity of capital: In the simple development of the theory of capital and interest in Chapter 28 we talked of changes in 'the' quantity of capital and invoked the 'law' of diminishing returns to predict that the marginal efficiency of capital would decline as the stock of capital grew. But society's stock of capital is in fact a very heterogeneous collection of tools, factories, equipment, etc. How can we speak of 'the' stock of capital? How can we reduce this heterogeneous collection of capital goods to a single number so that we can say that the capital stock is increasing or decreasing?

The obvious way is to use a price. If we take the price of capital we can value all these diverse physical things and obtain the total value of the economy's capital stock. But if we then use this quantity of capital in combination with the *MEC* schedule to determine the price of capital (i.e., the pure return on capital which in equilibrium is equal to the pure rate of interest) we may be involved in circular reasoning: if we wish to use 'the' quantity of capital in conjunction with 'the' production function *to determine the price of capital* (and hence the share of total income going to the owners of capital) we cannot use the price of capital to determine the quantity of capital.

For over a decade a debate raged over the possibility of calculating a single measure of the quantity of capital that could, without circularity, be placed into a macro-production function to determine the price of capital. The outcome of the debate appears to be that this cannot be done.[2]

---

[1] See, in particular, Joan Robinson and John Eatwell, *An Introduction to Modern Economics* (McGraw-Hill, 1974). Cambridge critics are often unwilling to give any points at all to the 'marginal productivity theory'. It seems to me, however, that when new theories replace old ones they should save what is valid in the old theories as well as discard what is invalid. Traditional theory is very successful in explaining micro-distribution problems. If it were to be supplanted by new theories, it would be a serious blunder to throw away the baby of successful micro-applications along with the admittedly dirty bath water of unsuccessful macro-applications. Furthermore, it is not clear to me how Cambridge-style classical distribution theories can even be brought to bear on the sort of micro-distribution problems outlined earlier in this chapter. It seems only fair to add that I think Professor Robinson's 'classical alternative' says very little of a positive nature about the economy. Thus I do not so much think it is wrong but rather nearly empty of positive content.

[2] Note that the same problems exist with land and labour. The society's stock of land is a heterogeneous collection of good, bad and indifferent land, some suited for some crops and some for others. The society's stock of labour is a heterogeneous collection of human beings no two of whom are the same: if identical quantities of other factors are combined first with individual *A* and then with individual *B*, very different quantities of output may result. To talk about 'the' quantity of labour and 'the' quantity of land is just as heroic an oversimplification as to talk about 'the' quantity of capital. Furthermore, just as with capital, to obtain 'the' quantities of labour and land by aggregating their values (i.e., multiplying each kind of labour by its price and then aggregating, and similarly for land), and then to use these aggregate quantities to determine the price of land and labour is to engage in circular reasoning.

For the economist who wishes to combine marginal productivity theory with a macro-production function in order to deal with the macro-distribution of income, this is a serious matter. To the economist who accepts only the traditional micro-theory of distribution it is not so upsetting. Such an economist believes that there are thousands of distinct factors, which it may sometimes be convenient to group into such broad classes as land, labour and capital, but which get separately priced and which are more or less substitutable for each other. In this view there is no particular reason to believe that labour as a whole will be subject to one set of influences, land as a whole to another distinct set and capital as a whole to yet a third distinct set. Thus the inability to measure *the* quantity of capital (and *the* quantities of labour and land) is not a particularly serious matter.

Reswitching: A second controversy concerning capital theory revolves around the 'reswitching debate' that arose out of Professor Sraffa's famous book, *Production of Commodities by Means of Commodities*[1]. This debate is too technical to be discussed here, but its burden is the view by the Cambridge School that a smoothly declining *MEC* schedule cannot necessarily be derived. Once again this appears to be correct. The possibility of other situations has been established by numerical illustrations. The empirical relevance of the possibilities raised by the Cambridge School remains to be demonstrated.[2]

Conclusion

For the traditional theorist there are at least two distinct issues: 'Does a demand-and-supply model of factor pricing shed any light on micro-distribution problems? and 'Does marginal productivity theory adequately explain the demand for factors of production, particularly the demand for capital?' Some traditional theorists would answer 'yes' to both questions. Others would say that the answer to the second question may be 'no', particularly in respect to capital, but that the answer to the first question is surely 'yes'. They would hold that the questions of macro-distribution theory are not really interesting, whereas questions of micro-distribution concerning both functional shares among many factors and the size distribution among households are important and relevant to most government policies that attempt to change the distribution of income.

---

[1] (Cambridge University Press, 1975).

[2] An excellent summary and critique of the Cambridge School from the standpoint of orthodox theory is given by M. Blaug, *The Cambridge Revolution: Success or Failure?*, Hobart Paperback No. 6 (Institute of Economic Affairs, 1975).

Part six

International trading relations

30

International trade and protection

Production and distribution occur not only in the context of national economic decisions; they are also influenced by trading relations with foreign countries. Some of these complications concern us in this part.

The gains from trade

In Chapter 11 we studied a small economy faced with fixed international terms of trade. We saw that such an economy could gain by entering into trade because such trade expanded its consumption possibility set. In this chapter we look at trade from the point of view of the whole world. Does the small open economy achieve its gains from trade at the expense of the rest of the world? Or is it possible for all trading countries simultaneously to gain from trading with each other? What are the reasons why governments may seek to interfere with the free flow of international trade?

Interpersonal, interregional and international trade

Economists have long recognized that the principles governing the gains from trade apply equally well both to foreign and to domestic trade. Governments have always tended to regard the two aspects of trade in very different lights, but economists have been prominent in the fight for recognition that the causes and consequences of international trade were merely an extension of the principles governing domestic trade. Some of these principles were developed quite early, but it was not until the mid-nineteenth century that the British economist John Stuart Mill showed satisfactorily that international and domestic trade could be explained by exactly the same principles.

> **Economists now recognize that they are asking the same question when they ask what is the advantage of trade between two individuals, between two groups, between two regions or between two countries.**

The source of such gains is easiest to study by considering the differences between a world with trade and one without it.

First, consider trade among individuals. If there were none, each person would have to be self-sufficient, producing all the food, clothing, shelter, medical services and entertainment that he or she required. It does not take much imagination to realize that living standards would be very low in such a world of universal self-sufficiency. Trade among individuals allows people to specialize in things they can do well and to buy from others the things they cannot easily produce. Someone who is a bad carpenter but a good doctor can specialize in medicine, providing a physician's services not only for his or her own family but also for a person who is an excellent carpenter yet has neither the training nor the ability to practise medicine. Thus trade and specialization are intimately connected. With trade everyone can specialize in what he or she does well.

The same principles apply to regions. Without interregional trade, each region would have to be self-sufficient. With such trade, plains regions can specialize in growing grain, mountain regions in mining and lumbering, regions with abundant power sources in manufacturing, and so on. One would suspect – and soon we shall demonstrate – that living standards in all regions will be higher if the inhabitants of each specialize in those lines of production in which they have some natural or acquired advantage, obtaining other products by trade, than if each region is self-sufficient.

Identical remarks apply to nations. National boundaries tend to be arbitrary with respect to the advantages of regional specialization and trade. There is no reason, therefore, to expect that a national boundary will define an area that could be self-sufficient at little cost to itself. Thus nations, like regions or persons, can gain from specialization and the international trade that must accompany it.

This preliminary discussion suggests one important possible gain from trade:

> **With trade, each individual, region or nation is able to concentrate on producing things in which it has an advantage while trading to obtain things that it cannot produce efficiently itself.**

We are going to look in more detail at the source of mutual gains accruing to all trading nations. Before we do so, however, a word of warning is needed. In what follows we shall often speak of nations, e.g., the United Kingdom and the United States, trading various commodities. This convenient anthropomorphism should not cause you to overlook the fact that in market economies most of the decisions determining the size, content and direction of foreign trade are taken by households and firms. Firms may see an opportunity of selling goods abroad and arrange to have these goods exported; other firms may see an opportunity of selling foreign goods in the home market and arrange to have these goods imported. If households either at home or abroad find such goods attractive and purchase them, the ventures will be successful; if they do not, the goods will remain unsold and will no longer be imported or exported. Governments may, of course, try to influence this process: they may provide subsidies for exports, seeking to encourage foreign sales of domestically produced goods by making their prices more attractive; they may put tariffs on imports, seeking to discourage domestic sales of foreign-produced goods, by making their prices less attractive. None of this, however, should obscure the basic fact that in free-market economies foreign trade is determined just as is domestic trade, mainly by thousands of independent decisions taken by firms and households and co-ordinated – more or less effectively – by the price system.

A special case: reciprocal absolute advantage

The gains from specialization are clear if there is a simple situation involving reciprocal absolute advantage. ABSOLUTE ADVANTAGE relates to the quantities of a single product that can be produced with the same quantity of resources in two different regions. One region is said to have an absolute advantage over another in the production of commodity X if an equal quantity of resources can produce more X in the first region than in the second.

Suppose region A has an absolute advantage over region B in one commodity, while B has an absolute advantage over A in another. We refer to this as a case of *reciprocal absolute advantage*: each region has an absolute advantage in some commodity. In such a situation, total production of both can be increased (relative to a situation of self-sufficiency) if each region specializes in the commodity in which it has the absolute advantage. Table 30.1 provides a simple example on the

Table 30.1 World gains from specialization with reciprocal absolute advantage

| | One unit of resources can produce: | |
	Wheat (bushels)	Cloth (yards)
America	10	6
England	5	10

Changes resulting from the transfer of 1 unit of American resources into wheat production and 1 unit of English resources into cloth production:

	Wheat (bushels)	Cloth (yards)
America	+10	− 6
England	− 5	+10
World	+ 5	+ 4

assumption that, with a given quantity of resources, America can produce 10 bushels of wheat or 6 yards of cloth, while England (with the same quantity of resources) can produce 5 bushels of wheat or 10 yards of cloth. The top half of the table shows the production of wheat and cloth that can be achieved in each country by using one unit of resources. Suppose at first that America and England are both self-sufficient, each producing wheat and cloth for its home markets. Now assume that trade is opened between the two countries and America moves resources out of cloth into wheat, while England moves resources out of wheat into cloth. The gains and losses in each country are summarized in the table. There is an increase in world production of 5 bushels of wheat and 4 yards of cloth: worldwide there are gains from specialization. The total world production of both wheat and cloth increases when this reallocation of production takes place – as is shown by the fact that there is both more wheat and more cloth for the same use of resources.

When there is reciprocal absolute advantage, specialization makes it possible to produce more of both commodities.

These potential gains from *specialization* make possible gains from *trade*. England is producing more cloth and America more wheat than when they were self-sufficient. America is thus producing more wheat and less cloth than American consumers wish to buy, and England is producing more cloth and less wheat than English consumers wish to buy. If consumers in both countries are to get cloth and wheat in the proportions in which they desire them, it will be necessary for America to export wheat to England and to import cloth from that country.

International trade is necessary to achieve the gains that international specialization makes possible.

Because specialization and trade go hand in hand – no one would be motivated to achieve the gains from specialization without being able to trade the goods produced for goods desired – it is usual to use the term *gains from trade* to embrace them both.

A first general statement: Ricardian comparative advantage

When each country has an absolute advantage over the other in one commodity, the gains from trade are obvious: if each produces the commodity in the production of which it is more efficient than the other, world production will be higher than if each tries to be self-sufficient. But what if America can produce both wheat and cloth more efficiently than England? In essence, this was the question David Ricardo posed over 150 years ago, and his answer forms the basis of the theory of comparative advantage that is still accepted by economists as a valid statement of the potential gains from trade.

Assume that American efficiency increases above the levels recorded in the previous example, so that a unit of American resources can produce either 100 bushels of wheat or 60 yards of cloth, while English efficiency remains unchanged, so that a unit of English resources can produce either 5 bushels of wheat or 10 yards of cloth. Now surely America, which is better at producing both wheat and cloth than England, has nothing to gain by trading with this inefficient island country! It *does* have something to gain, however, and it is important to see why.

The gain from specialization in this case is illustrated in Table 30.2. The new figures make America 10 times as efficient as she was in the situation of Table 30.1. England no longer has an absolute advantage in producing either commodity. Total production of both commodities can nonetheless be increased by specialization. The movement of one-tenth of one unit of American resources out of cloth and into wheat and the opposite movement in England of one unit of resources causes world production of wheat to rise by 5 bushels and cloth by 4 yards. This shows that reciprocal absolute advantage is not necessary for gains from trade.

There is a gain from specialization because although America has an absolute advantage over England in the production of both wheat and cloth, its margin of advantage differs in the two commodities. America can produce 20 times as much wheat as can England using the same quantity of resources, but only 6 times as much cloth. America is said to have a COMPARATIVE ADVANTAGE in the production of wheat and a comparative disadvantage in the production of cloth. England has a comparative disadvantage in the production of wheat and a comparative advantage in the production of cloth.

One of the most important propositions in the theory of international trade is:

The gains from specialization and trade depend on the pattern of comparative, not absolute, advantage.

A comparison of Tables 30.1 and 30.2 shows that the absolute *levels* of efficiency of two areas do not affect the gains from specialization. What matters is that the margin of advantage that one area has over the other differs between commodities. When this is true, total world production can be increased if each area specializes in the production of the commodity in which it has a comparative advantage.

Table 30.2 World gains from specialization with comparative advantage

| | One unit of resources can produce: | |
	Wheat (bushels)	*Cloth* (yards)
America	100	60
England	5	10

Changes resulting from the transfer of $\frac{1}{10}$ of 1 unit of American resources into wheat production and 1 unit of English resources into cloth production:

	Wheat (bushels)	*Cloth* (yards)
America	+10	− 6
England	− 5	+10
World	+ 5	+ 4

Table 30.3 Absence of world gains from specialization where there is no comparative advantage

| | One unit of resources can produce: | |
	Wheat (bushels)	*Cloth* (yards)
America	100	60
England	10	6

Changes resulting from the transfer of 1 unit of American resources into wheat production and 10 units of English resources into cloth production:

	Wheat (bushels)	*Cloth* (yards)
America	+100	−60
England	−100	+60
World	0	0

Comparative advantage is not only sufficient for gains from trade, it is also necessary. This is illustrated by the example in Table 30.3, in which America has an absolute advantage in both commodities but neither country enjoys a comparative advantage over the other in the production of either commodity. America is 10 times as efficient as England in the production of wheat and also in the production of cloth. Now, try as you may, there is no way to increase the production of both wheat and cloth by reallocating resources within America and within England. The lower half of the table provides one example of this. You should try others. Absolute advantage without comparative advantage does not lead to gains from specialization.

> **Without comparative advantage, there is no reallocation of resources within each country that will increase the production of both commodities.**

A second general statement: opportunity costs

Much of the previous argument has made use of the concept of a unit of resources and has also assumed that units of resources can be equated across countries, so that such statements as 'America can produce 10 times as much wheat with the same quantity of resources as England' are meaningful. Measurement of the real-resource cost of producing commodities poses many difficulties. If, for example, England uses land, labour, and capital in proportions different from those used in America, it may not be clear which country gets more output 'per unit of resource input'. Fortunately, the proposition about the gains from trade can be restated without any reference to absolute efficiencies and in a way that should make even clearer the sources of gain in the previous examples.

To do this, return to the examples of Tables 30.1 and 30.2 and calculate the opportunity cost of wheat and cloth in the two countries. If resources are assumed to be fully employed, the only way to produce more of one commodity is to reallocate resources and thus produce less of the other commodity. Table 30.1 shows that a unit of resources in America can produce 10 bushels of wheat *or* 6 yards of cloth, from which it follows that the opportunity cost of producing a unit of wheat is 0·6 units of cloth, while the opportunity cost of producing a unit of cloth is 1·67 units of wheat. These data are summarized in Table 30.4. The table also shows that in England the opportunity cost of 1 unit of wheat is 2 units of cloth forgone, whereas the opportunity cost of a unit of cloth is 0·50 units of wheat. These opportunity costs can be obtained either from Table 30.1 or from Table 30.2. The English opportunity cost of one unit of wheat is obtained by dividing the cloth output of one unit of English resources by the wheat output. The resulting figure of 2 shows that 2 yards of cloth must be sacrificed for every extra unit of wheat produced by transferring English resources out of cloth production into wheat. The other three cost figures are obtained in a similar manner.

Comparative advantages can always be expressed in terms of opportunity costs that differ among countries.

Table 30.4 The opportunity cost of 1 unit of wheat and 1 unit of cloth in America and England

	Wheat	Cloth
America	0·6 yards cloth	1·67 bushels wheat
England	2·0 yards cloth	0·50 bushels wheat

Table 30.5 World gains from specialization when opportunity costs differ

Changes resulting from each country's producing one more unit of commodity in which it has the lower opportunity cost:

	Wheat (bushels)	Cloth (yards)
America	+1·0	−0·6
England	−0·5	+1·0
World	+0·5	+0·4

The sacrifice of cloth involved in producing wheat is much lower in America than in England, and world production can be increased if America rather than England produces wheat. Looking at cloth rather than wheat production, one can see that the loss of wheat involved in producing one unit of cloth is lower in England than in America. England is a lower (opportunity) cost producer of cloth than is America, and world production can be increased if England rather than America produces cloth. This situation is shown in Table 30.5.

Gains from trade arise from differing opportunity costs among countries.

The conclusions about the gains from trade in the hypothetical example of two countries and two commodities may be generalized as follows.

(1) One country has a comparative advantage over a second country in producing a commodity if the opportunity cost (in terms of some other commodity) of production in the first country is lower. This implies, however, that it has a comparative disadvantage in the other commodity.

(2) Opportunity costs depend on relative costs of producing two commodities, not on absolute costs. (To check this, notice that the data in both Tables 30.1 and 30.2 give rise to the opportunity costs in Table 30.4.)

(3) If opportunity costs are the same in all countries, there is no comparative advantage and no possibility of gains from specialization and trade. (You should illustrate this for yourself by calculating the opportunity costs implied by the data in Table 30.3.)

(4) If opportunity costs differ in any two countries, and both countries are producing both commodities, it is always possible to increase production of both commodities by a suitable reallocation of resources within each country.

Proposition (4) is illustrated in Table 30.5. The calculations in the table show that there are gains from specialization given the opportunity costs of Table 30.4. To produce one more bushel of wheat, America must sacrifice 0·6 yards of cloth. To produce one more yard of cloth, England must sacrifice 0·5 bushels of wheat. Making both changes raises world production of both wheat and cloth.[1]

Although we derived Table 30.4 from the data in Tables 30.1 and 30.2, the determination of opportunity cost does not require that we are able to compare output per unit of resources in various countries. The gains from trade require only that the sacrifice of one commodity needed to get one unit of a second commodity is different in the various countries. It does not matter how this difference comes about, nor do we have to be able to measure output per unit of resources; all that is needed is that, for any reason, opportunity costs do differ.

Nonetheless, the statement of the gains from trade in terms of comparative advantage is a great insight. It is commonly believed by the general public that absolute efficences can be measured and that inefficient countries cannot gainfully trade with efficient ones. The statement in terms of comparative advantage effectively refutes this belief. It shows that *if* the concept of absolute efficiency can be given any meaning, then there is potential for mutual gains from trade when absolutely efficient countries trade with absolutely inefficient ones – provided only that the *comparative* advantages exist.

> **If, but only if, opportunity costs differ among countries, specialization of each country in producing those commodities in which it has comparative advantages will make it possible to achieve gains from trade.**

Learning by doing: an additional source of the gains from trade

The theory of the gains from trade takes the production possibility curve as given. It then shows that there are gains from specialization and trade as long as there are interregional differences in opportunity costs. If costs are not given, additional sources of gain are possible. Classical economists placed great importance on a factor that is now called *learning by doing*. They felt that as regions specialized in particular tasks, the workers and managers would become more efficient in

---

[1] In practice the gains from specialization must be large enough to cover the real resource costs involved in transporting the goods between two countries. In this elementary treatment this minor complication is ignored.

performing them. As people acquire expertise, or know-how, costs tend to fall. A substantial body of modern empirical work suggests that this really does happen. If this is the case, then output of cloth per worker may rise in England as England becomes more specialized in that commodity, while the same may happen to output of wheat per worker in America. This is, of course, an additional gain to that which occurs if costs are constant.

Learning by doing suggests that the existing pattern of comparative advantage need not be taken as immutable. If a country can learn enough by doing things in which it currently is at a comparative disadvantage, it may gain in the long run by specializing in commodities in which it has a current comparative disadvantage as long as it learns enough to develop an eventual comparative advantage. We shall see later in this chapter that learning by doing provides an important weakening of the case for universal free trade with specialization based on the existing pattern of comparative advantage.

The distribution of the gains from trade

So far it has been shown that world production can be increased if America and England specialize in the production of the commodity in which they have a comparative advantage and that specialization requires trade. How will these gains from specialization and trade be shared between the two countries? The division of the gain depends on the terms at which trade takes place. The TERMS OF TRADE were defined in Chapter 11 as the quantity of domestic goods that must be given up to get a unit of imported goods. Thus the terms of trade are nothing more than the opportunity cost of obtaining goods through international trade rather than producing them directly.

In the example of Table 30.4, the American domestic opportunity cost of one unit of cloth is 1·67 bushels of wheat. If Americans can obtain cloth by international trade at terms of trade more favourable to them than 1·67 bushels of wheat, they will gain by doing so. Suppose that international prices are such that one yard of cloth exchanges for (i.e., is equal in value to) one bushel of wheat. At those prices, Americans can obtain cloth at a lower wheat opportunity cost by trade than by domestic production. Therefore the terms of trade favour selling wheat and buying cloth on international markets.

By a similar argument, English consumers in the example of Table 30.4 gain if they can obtain wheat abroad at any terms of trade more favourable than 2 yards of cloth per bushel of wheat, which is the English domestic opportunity cost. If the terms of trade are 1 bushel of wheat for 1 yard of cloth, the terms of trade favour English traders' buying wheat and selling cloth on international markets. Both England and America in this example gain from trade: each can obtain the commodity in which it has a comparative disadvantage at a lower opportunity cost through international trade than through domestic production.

Indeed both countries will gain from trade as long as the terms of trade lie between the domestic opportunity cost ratios of the two countries. Although we do not go into it here, it is possible to show that if the terms of trade lie in the range where one of the countries would lose from trade, the price system would cause that country not to trade.

Trade policy

Today, debates over trade policy are as heated as they were two hundred years ago when the theory of the gains from trade was still being worked out. Should a country permit the free flow of international trade, or should it seek to protect its local producers from foreign competition at least to some extent? PROTECTIONISM refers to the protection of domestic industries from foreign competition. Such protection may be achieved either by tariffs, that raise the price of foreign goods, or by such *non-tariff barriers* as quotas on imports and subsidies on goods produced for export that make importing difficult or impossible. FREE TRADE is a situation in which no protectionism is practised.

The case for free trade

We have seen that, where opportunity costs differ among countries, some degree of specialization with some consequent amount of trade will raise world standards of living. Free trade allows all countries to specialize in producing commodities in which they have comparative advantages. They can then produce (and consume) more of all commodities than would be available if specialization had not taken place.

> **Free trade makes it possible to maximize world production and makes it *possible* for every household in the world to consume more goods than it could without free trade.**

Yet this does not mean that everyone will be better off with free trade than without it. Protectionism could give some people a large enough share of a smaller world output so that they will benefit. If we ask if it is possible for free trade to be advantageous to everyone, the answer is 'yes'. But if we ask if free trade is in fact always mutually advantageous to everyone, the answer is 'not necessarily so'.

Yet free trade does maximize average world income. Indeed there is abundant evidence to show that significant differences in comparative costs exist, and that there are large potential gains from trade because of these differences. There is also ample evidence that trade occurs and that no nation tries to be self-sufficient or refuses to sell to foreigners the items it produces cheaply and well.

The case for free trade is powerful. What needs explanation is not the extent of trade but the fact that trade is not wholly free. Tariffs and non-tariff barriers to trade exist 200 years after Adam Smith stated the case for free trade. Do these interferences exist merely because policymakers are ignorant of the principles of comparative advantage, or are there reasons (not included in the case for free trade) that make it sensible for a nation to enact protectionist policies? Is there a valid case for protectionism? If there is, how does one find the balance between the advantages of more or less trade?

Methods of protectionism

There are basically three means by which a country can reduce its imports of some good. (1) It may place a tax on imported commodities, called a TARIFF. Such a tax shifts the supply curve of the foreign good upwards because it adds to the foreign producer's cost of every unit sold in the country imposing the tariff. (2) It may impose an IMPORT QUOTA that limits the quantity of the commodity that may be shipped into the country in a given period. Until the quota has been reached there is no change in supply, but once the quota has been reached, the effective supply curve becomes a vertical line. (3) It may adopt domestic policies that reduce its demand for the imported commodity. For example, it may require potential importers to acquire a special licence, or it may restrict the ability

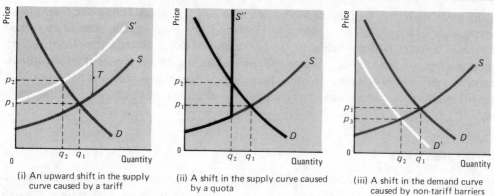

(i) An upward shift in the supply
curve caused by a tariff

(ii) A shift in the supply curve caused
by a quota

(iii) A shift in the demand curve
caused by non-tariff barriers

Fig. 30.1 Three ways of reducing imports

of its citizens to use their funds to purchase the foreign exchange needed to pay for the commodity. Such steps shift the demand curve for the import to the left.

The three parts of Figure 30.1 illustrate the three methods. In each diagram D and S represent the domestic market demand and foreign supply for some imported good not produced at home. Price p_1 and quantity q_1 are the equilibrium values. The government wishes to achieve some smaller quantity of imports, say q_2.

In part (i) of the Figure the government imposes a tariff of £T on each unit of the imported good. This shifts the supply curve vertically upwards by the amount of the tariff since, as well as meeting all other costs, suppliers must also pay the tariff. The new supply curve becomes S' and price and output change to p_2 and q_2. In part (ii) of the Figure the government imposes a quota allowing a maximum of q_2 units to be imported. This makes the supply curve into the heavy kinked line S''. Again price and quantity shift to q_2 and p_2. In part (iii) of the Figure the government shifts the demand curve to the left, from D to D', by using non-tariff barriers to trade. Once again the quantity imported falls to q_2 but this time price falls to p_3 rather than rising to p_2.

Although each means of restricting trade has some different effects, they all achieve the same reduction in the quantity of imports. In what follows we shall concentrate on tariffs, which are probably the single most important tool of trade restriction.

Tariffs come in two main forms. SPECIFIC TARIFFS are so much money per unit of the product. AD VALOREM TARIFFS are a percentage of the price of the product. Tariffs have two different and opposite purposes: for revenue and for protection. The latter use is more common, to raise the price of imported goods in order to discourage imports by offsetting (to some extent, at least) a cost advantage that foreign producers have over domestic producers of a particular product. The protective function of a tariff is opposed to the revenue function because the tariff will not yield much revenue if it is effective in cutting imports. This chapter concentrates on the protective feature of tariffs.

The case for protectionism

Two kinds of arguments for protection are common. The first concerns objectives other than maximizing output; the second concerns the difference between the welfare of a single nation and that of the world.

Objectives other than maximizing output   It is quite possible to accept the proposition that production is higher with free trade and yet rationally oppose free trade because of a concern with policy objectives other than maximizing real national income.

For example, comparative costs might dictate that a country should specialize in producing a narrow range of commodities. The government might decide, however, that there are distinct social advantages to encouraging a more diverse economy – one that would give citizens a wider range of occupations. The authorities might decide that the social and psychological advantages of a diverse economy more than compensate for a reduction in living standards by, say, 5 per cent below what they could be with complete specialization of production.

Specializing in the production of one or two commodities, although dictated by comparative advantage, may involve risks that a country's leaders do not wish to take. One such risk is a technological advance that renders its basic product obsolete. The quartz crystal badly damaged the Swiss watch industry in just this way; between 1974 and 1979 its share of the world market dropped from 40 to 30 per cent, and 30,000 jobs were lost.

Another risk is cyclical fluctuations in the prices of basic commodities; these may face depressed prices for years at a time, followed by periods of very high prices. The national income of a country specializing in the production of such commodities will be subject to wide fluctuations. Even though the average income level over a long period might be higher when there is specialization in the production of basic commodities, the serious social problems associated with a widely fluctuating national income may make the government decide to sacrifice some income in order to reduce fluctuations. Such a government might use protectionist policies to encourage the expansion of several cyclically stable industries.

Yet another reason for protectionism may be the desire to maintain national traditions. For example, many Canadians are passionately concerned with maintaining a separate nation with traditions that differ from those of the United States. Many believe that a tariff helps them to do this. They seem prepared, if necessary, to tolerate a 5 or 10 per cent differential in living standards in order to maintain this independence.

One frequently cited non-economic defence of protectionism concerns national defence. It has been argued, for example, that Britain needs an experienced merchant marine in case of war and that this industry should be fostered by protectionist policies, even though it is less efficient than the foreign competition.

There is nothing irrational in a decision to accept substantial costs in order to attain objectives other than maximizing living standards. Although most people would agree that, *ceteris paribus*, they prefer more income to less, economists cannot pronounce as irrational a nation whose leaders choose to sacrifice some income in order to achieve other goals. Economists can do three things when faced with such reasons for tariffs. First they can try to see if the proposed tariff really does achieve the ends suggested. Second they can calculate the cost of the tariff in terms of lost living standard. Third, they can check policy alternatives to see if there are other means that would achieve the stated goal at lower cost in terms of lost output.

Protectionism as a means to higher national living standards   The most important example in this category relates to economies of scale. It is usually called the INFANT INDUSTRY ARGUMENT. If an industry has large economies of scale, costs and prices will be high when the industry is small, but they will fall as the industry grows. In such an industry, the country first in the field has a tremendous advantage. A newly developing country may find that its industries are unable to compete in the early stages of their development with established foreign rivals. A tariff or import quota may protect these industries from foreign competition while they grow up. When they are large enough, they may be able to produce as cheaply as foreign rivals and thus compete without protection.

A similar argument in favour of protectionism concerns learning by doing. Giving a domestic industry protection from foreign competition may enable it to learn to be efficient and give the labour force the time needed to acquire necessary skills. If so, it may pay the government to protect the industry while the learning occurs.

The difficulty with tariff policies based on these considerations is being able to identify industries that will succeed in the long run. All too often the protected infant grows up to be a weak sister requiring permanent tariff protection for its continued existence, or the learning goes on at a slower rate than is occurring in similar industries in other countries where they are not protected from the chill winds of international competition, so that the anticipated comparative advantage never materializes.

How much protectionism?

So far we have seen that there is a strong case for allowing trade in order to realize the gains from trade and that there are also valid reasons for departing from completely free trade.

> **It is not necessary to choose between free trade on the one hand and absolute protectionism on the other; a country can have some trade and some protectionism too.**

Free trade versus no trade   It would undoubtedly be possible, by using greenhouses, to grow coffee beans, oranges, cotton, and other imported raw materials and foodstuffs in Britain. But the cost in terms of other commodities forgone would be huge, for artificial means of production require lavish inputs of factors of production. It would likewise be possible for a tropical country, currently producing foodstuffs, to set up industries to produce all the manufactured products that it consumes. The cost in terms of resources used, for a small country without natural advantages in industrial production, could be enormous. It is thus clear that there is a large gain to all countries in having specialization and trade. The real output and consumption of all countries would be very much lower if each had to produce domestically all the goods it consumed.

> **In an all-or-nothing choice, virtually all countries would choose free trade over no trade.**

Some trade versus no trade   Some tariffs in force today reflect protectionism, while others reflect a use of tariffs to raise revenue. It is clear that these tariffs are not sufficient to offset widely differing cost conditions, the most dramatic being those associated with climate. Even the most casual observation reveals major cost differences among countries. Thus there are significant gains from trading for commodities in which a country has a large comparative disadvantage. Careful empirical measurement might put an actual numerical value on the amount of the gains, but certainly production and consumption in the world, and in each major trading country, are higher with trade than they would be with no trade.

A little more trade versus a little less trade Today we have trade between nations, but that trade is not perfectly free. Would we be better off if today's barriers to trade were reduced or increased a little bit? It is quite a jump from the proposition that 'Some trade is better than no trade' to the proposition that 'A little more trade than we have at present is better than a little less trade.' Yet most arguments about commercial policy involve the latter sort of proposition, not the former. 'Should workers be given *some* increased protection against Japanese imports?' is the question debated today, not 'Should Japan be totally excluded from the European market?'

Most actual policy disagreements concern the relative merits of free trade versus controlled trade with tariffs on the order of, say, 5, 10 or 15 per cent. Such tariffs would not cut out imports of bananas, coffee, diamonds, bauxite, or any commodity in whose production Europe would be really inefficient. (Yet these are just the commodities that defenders of free trade sometimes use as examples when the hypothesis of the gains from trade is challenged.) When one accepts the hypothesis that some trade is better than no trade, it is not necessary to accept the hypothesis that free trade is better than controlled trade, with, say, 15 per cent tariffs; nor is one committed to saying that 9 per cent tariffs would be better than 10 per cen tariffs.

As a rule, tariffs are seldom advocated to protect industries that are extremely inefficient compared to foreign industries; they are usually advocated to protect industries that can very nearly compete, but not quite. As a simplified version of the sort of argument that really does take place over commercial policy, compare the effects of a 20 per cent uniform *ad valorem* tariff with those of free trade. How much would be gained by removing 20 per cent tariffs or how much lost by imposing 20 per cent tariffs in a situation of free trade?

Tariffs of 20 per cent will protect industries that are up to 20 per cent less efficient than foreign competitors. If the costs of the various tariff-protected industries were spread out evenly, some would be 20 per cent less efficient than their foreign competitors and others would be only 1 per cent less efficient. Their average inefficiency would be about half the tariff rate, so they would be on average about 10 per cent less efficient than their foreign competitors.

Suppose that as a result of tariffs, approximately 10 per cent of a country's resources are allocated to industries different from the ones to which they would be allocated if there were no tariffs. This means that about 10 per cent of a country's resources would be working in certain industries because of tariff protection. If the average protected industry is 10 per cent less efficient than its foreign rival, approximately 10 per cent of a country's resources are producing about 10 per cent less efficiently than they would be if there were no tariffs. This causes a reduction in national income of the order of 1 per cent as a result of tariff protection.

The above rough calculation is meant only to give some intuitive understanding of why the many careful measures of the cost of moderate tariffs keep producing figures closer to 1 than to 10 per cent of the levying country's national income.

> **The potential net gains from somewhat freer trade than there is today are not so large as to make it certain that the removal of all remaining barriers is desirable.**

Suppose the gains from free trade would be 1 per cent of national income. Is the sacrifice of national income implied by existing tariffs large or small? As a percentage it seems small, yet in 1980 prices it was £1·7 billion *per year* in the UK. That amount every year for ever could buy a lot of hospitals, schools, medical research, solar energy research – or even petrol.

Whether free trade is better than a policy of moderate protectionism depends on the policy goals that a country is trying to attain, the magnitude of the benefits, and the costs of the actions. Here is a highly important area for study and debate about trade and trade barriers.

There are also many claims that do not advance the debate; fallacious arguments are heard on both sides, and they colour much of the popular discussion. These arguments have been around for a long time, but their survival does not make them true.

Fallacious free trade arguments

Free trade always benefits all countries This is not necessarily so. The potential gains from trade might be offset by costs such as unemployment or economic instability or by the interference with policy objectives other than maximizing income. These factors may render some interference desirable.[1]

Infant industries never abandon their tariff protection It is argued that to grant protection on an infant-industry basis is a mistake because infant industries seldom admit to growing up and will cling to their protection even when they are fully grown. Even if this allegation were true, it would not be a sufficient reason for avoiding the protection of infant industries. When economies of scale are realized, the real costs of production are reduced and resources are freed for other uses. Whether or not the tariff or other trade barrier remains, a cost saving has been effected by the scale economies.

Fallacious protectionist arguments

The exploitation doctrine According to this view, one trading partner *must* always reap a gain at the other's expense. The principle of comparative advantage shows that it is possible for both parties to gain from trade and thus refutes the exploitation doctrine of trade. When opportunity cost ratios differ in two countries, specialization and the accompanying trade make it possible to produce more of all commodities and thus make it possible for both parties to get more goods as a result of trade than they could get in its absence.

Keep the money at home This argument says, If I buy a foreign good, I have the good and the foreigner has the money, whereas if I buy the same good locally, I have the good and our country has the money too.

This argument is based on a misconception. When British importers purchase Indian-made goods, they do not send pound notes abroad. They (or some financial agent) buy Indian rupees (or claims on them) and use them to pay the Indian producer. They purchase the rupees on the foreign-exchange market by giving up sterling to someone who wishes to use it for expenditure in Britain. Even if the money did go abroad physically – that is, if an Indian firm accepted a shipload of pound notes – it would do so because the firm (or someone to whom it could sell the sterling) wanted to spend it in the only country where it is legal tender, the UK.

---

[1] To see how sensitive the gains from trade are to other considerations, suppose that totally free trade led to an allocation of resources that was 1 per cent more efficient than an allocation resulting from 20 per cent tariffs, but led simultaneously to an average level of unemployment 1·2 per cent higher. In this case, free trade would bring losses rather than gains.

Currency ultimately does no one any good except as purchasing power. It would be miraculous if pieces of paper could be exported in return for real goods; after all, the central bank has the power to create as much new money as it wishes. It is only because the British paper money can buy British commodities and financial assets that others want it.

Protection against low-wage foreign labour   Surely, the argument says, the products of such low-wage countries as Taiwan or Hong Kong will drive our products from the market, and the high European standard of living will be dragged down to that of their poorer trading partners. Arguments of this sort have swayed many voters through the years.

As a prelude to considering them, stop and think what the argument would imply if taken out of the international context and put into a local one, where the same principles govern the gains from trade. Is it really impossible for a rich person to gain from trading with a poor person? Would the local millionaire be better off if he did all his own typing, gardening and cooking? No one believes that a rich person cannot gain from trading with those who are less rich. Why then must a rich group of people lose from trading with a poor group? It may then be argued that the poor group will price their goods 'too cheaply'. Does anyone believe that consumers lose from buying a given good at a low rather than a high price? If the Koreans pay low wages and sell their goods cheaply, *Korean* labour may suffer, but we will gain because we obtain their goods at a low cost in terms of the goods that we must export in return. The cheaper our imports are, the better off we are in terms of the goods and services available for domestic consumption.

Stated in more formal terms, the gains from trade depend on comparative, not absolute, advantages. World production is higher when any two areas, say the UK and Japan, specialize in the production of the goods for which they have a comparative advantage than when they both try to be self-sufficient.

Might it not be possible, however, that Japan, for example, will undersell the UK in all lines of production and thus appropriate all, or more than all, the gains for itself, leaving the UK no better off, or even worse off, than if it had remained self-sufficient? The answer is no. The reason for this depends on the behaviour of exchange rates, which we studied in Chapter 11. As we saw there, equality of demand and supply on the foreign-exchange market ensures that trade flows in both directions. Japanese imports can be obtained only by spending yen. Claims to foreign currency can only be obtained either by selling goods and services abroad or by borrowing. Thus, lending and borrowing aside, imports must equal exports; all trade must be in two directions; we can buy only if we can also sell.

In the long run, trade cannot hurt a country by causing it to import without exporting.

Trade, then, always provides scope for international specialization, with each country producing and exporting those goods for which it has a comparative advantage and importing those goods for which it does not.

Exports raise national income, imports lower it   Exports add to total demand for domestic output; imports subtract from it because they are the demand for some other country's output. Exports thus tend to increase national output and national income, *ceteris paribus*, while imports reduce them, *ceteris paribus*. Surely, then, it is desirable to encourage exports and discourage imports. This is an appealing argument, but it is incorrect.

Exports raise national income by adding to the value of domestic output, but they do not add to the value of domestic consumption. In fact, exports are goods produced at home and consumed abroad, while imports are goods produced abroad and consumed at home. The standard of living in a country depends on the goods and services available for *consumption*, not on what is produced.

If exports were really good and imports really bad, then a fully employed economy that managed to increase exports without a corresponding increase in imports ought to be better off. Such a change, however, would result in a reduction in current standards of living because when more goods are sent abroad and no more are brought in from abroad, the total goods available for domestic consumption must fall.

What happens when a country achieves a surplus of exports over imports for a considerable period of time? It will accumulate claims to foreign exchange for which there are three possible uses: to add to foreign-exchange reserves, to buy foreign goods, and to make investments abroad. Consider each of them.

(1) Some foreign-exchange reserves are required for the smooth functioning of the international payments system, as we shall see in Chapters 37 and 45. But the accumulation of reserves over and above those required serves no purpose. Permanent excess reserves represent claims on foreign output that are never used.

(2) Japanese yen and Indian rupees cannot be eaten, smoked, drunk, or worn. But they can be spent to buy Japanese and Indian goods that can be eaten, smoked, drunk, or worn. When such goods are imported and consumed, they add to British living standards. Indeed, the main purpose of foreign trade is to take advantage of international specialization: trade allows more consumption than would be possible if all goods were produced at home. From this point of view, the purpose of exporting is to allow the importation of goods that can be produced more cheaply abroad than at home.

(3) An excess of exports over imports may be used to purchase foreign assets. Such foreign investments add to living standards only when the interest and profits earned on them are used to buy imports, or when the investment is liquidated. The essence of any investment is to permit the investor to earn profits or interest that can then be used to buy goods. Foreign investments permit the later purchase of foreign goods.

> **The living standards of a country depend on the goods and services consumed in that country. The importance of exports is that they permit imports to be made. This two-way international exchange is valuable because more goods can be imported than could be obtained if the same goods were produced at home.**

Protectionism creates domestic jobs and reduces unemployment It is sometimes said that a country with substantial unemployment, such as the UK in the 1930s or in the early 1980s, provides an exception to the case for freer trade. Suppose that tariffs or import quotas cut the imports of Japanese cars, Korean textiles, Italian shoes and German beer. Surely, the argument maintains, this will create more employment for British car workers, textile manufacturers, shoe makers and brewers. The answer is that it will – initially. But the Japanese, Koreans, Italians, and Germans can buy from the UK only if they earn sterling by selling goods in the UK. The decline in their sales of cars, textiles, shoes and beer will decrease foreign purchases of British machinery, aircraft, banking services and holidays in London. Jobs will be lost in our export industries and gained in those industries that formerly faced competition from imports.

The long-term effect is that overall unemployment will not be reduced but merely redistributed among industries. There will now be less employment in those industries in which Britain has a comparative advantage and more employment in those industries where Britain has a comparative disadvantage. As a result total employment is unchanged but total output is reduced (because resources are now used less efficiently than they were previously). This explains why

industries and unions that compete with imports often favour protectionism while those with large exports favour freer trade. Most economists are highly sceptical about the government's ability to reduce overall unemployment by protectionism.

Subsidizing exports increases employment   Export industries do not necessarily favour free trade; they may argue instead that the government should subsidize them. This argument is closely related to the last point, though it is made by different groups. Assume that there is a rise in exports without a corresponding rise in imports, perhaps because the government pays producers a subsidy on every unit exported. The direct effect of this rise in exports will be an increase in employment. Surely, in times of unemployment, this is to be regarded as a good thing.

Two points may be made about such a policy. In the first place, the goods being produced by the newly employed workers in the export sector are not available for domestic consumption and so do not directly raise domestic standards of living. Surely it would be better if, instead of subsidizing exports, the central authorities subsidized the production of goods for the home market so that the goods produced by the newly employed workers would contribute to a rise in domestic living standards. Or, if there is objection to the government's subsidizing private firms, the government could create new employment by building more public goods such as roads, schools and research laboratories. Consequently income and employment would go up, but there would be something more tangible to show for it in the first instance than the smoke of ships disappearing over the horizon bearing the subsidized exports to foreign markets.

The second point to be made concerns the foreign effects of a policy that fosters exports and discourages imports in a situation of general world unemployment. Although the policy raises domestic employment, it will have the reverse effect abroad, where it creates unemployment. The foreign countries will suffer a rise in their unemployment because their exports will fall and their imports rise. Not surprisingly, they may be expected to retaliate; as we will see, this has been the historical experience. If all countries try a policy of expanding exports and discouraging imports, the net effect is likely to be a large drop in the volume of international trade without much change in the level of employment in any one country.

Trade policy

The above is what happened in the tariff wars of the 1930s. Faced with massive unemployment, each country sought to raise its own employment by restricting imports and encouraging exports. Everyone's efforts were self-cancelling, thus doomed to failure; the only result was reduced world trade as each country made more things at home inefficiently and exported less things that they could produce efficiently. World employment was not raised but world trade and world productivity were dealt serious blows.

After the Second World War, the major trading countries entered into the General Agreement on Tariffs and Trade (GATT). This organization is dedicated to further reducing tariffs and to making it difficult for individual countries to raise their existing tariffs. The very heavy worldwide unemployment in the early 1980s has led, however, to a strong revival of protectionist sentiments. Employers and employees in industries subject to heavy import competition push for higher tariffs to protect and create jobs in their industries. Governments are tempted to give in to these demands, forgetting that every restriction in volume of trade destroys jobs in the export sector just as it creates jobs in the import sector. There is no doubt that the GATT is a major force resisting the very strong protectionist pressures that have arisen in the wake of the most serious recession the world has known since the Great Depression of the 1930s.

Another institution pushing in the direction of free trade has been the European Economic Community. This association of nations is dedicated to the belief that the mutual prosperity of the countries of Western Europe depends on maintaining a high degree of trade among them. The Community has established and enforced free trade in manufactured goods throughout member countries and has encouraged trade in other sectors.[1]

While there are cases in which a restrictive policy has been pursued following a rational assessment of the approximate cost, it is hard to avoid the conclusion that, more often than not, such policies are pursued for flimsy objectives or on fallacious grounds, with little idea of the actual costs involved. The very high tariffs that marked the 1920s and 1930s are a conspicuous example. Clamour for the government to do something about the competition from Japan, Korea and other countries of the East may well be another. So may be the heavy pressures currently put on the governments of the world's major trading countries to 'solve' their serious unemployment problems by discouraging imports and encouraging exports.

---

[1] For further details of the GATT and the EEC see Harbury and Lipsey, Chapter 5.

31

Less developed and developing countries[1]

In the civilized and comfortable urban life of the highly developed countries, most people have lost sight of the fact that a very short time ago, *very* short in terms of the lifespan of the earth, man lived like any other animal, catching an existence as best he could from what nature threw his way. It has been less than 10,000 years since the agricultural revolution, when people changed from food gathering to food producing, and it has been only within the last century or two that a large proportion of the population of even the richest countries could look forward to anything but an endless struggle to wrest an existence from a reluctant nature. Most earlier civilizations were based on a civilized life for a privileged minority and unremitting toil for the vast majority.

The uneven pattern of development

There are over 4,000 million people alive today. The wealthy parts of the world, where people work no more than forty or fifty hours per week and enjoy substantial amounts of leisure and a consumption similar to that of Western Europe, contain only about 20 per cent of the world's population. Many of the rest struggle for subsistence. About 2,000 million people exist at a level at or below that enjoyed by peasants in the more advanced civilizations of 5,000 years ago.

If one were studying the effect of variations in rainfall from year to year in Great Britain or Holland, one would find that they were reflected in agricultural output and income: for each inch that rainfall fell below some critical amount, output and income would vary in a regular way. By stark contrast, in poorer countries such as China, India and Ethiopia, variations in rainfall are often reflected in the death rate. Many people in such countries have so few alternatives to living off their own current production that even slight fluctuations in their food supply bring death by starvation.

The fact that effects measured in money units in rich countries are often measured in lives in poor ones makes the problem of economic growth very much more urgent in poor countries. Reformers in poor countries, therefore, often feel a sense of urgency not felt by their counterparts in the developed world.

Table 31.1 shows how few countries have made the transition from poverty to relative comfort. The unequal distribution of the world's income is shown in columns 5 and 6. Groups I–III, with over 60 per cent of the world's population, earn only 9 per cent of world income. Groups VI–VII, with

---

[1] For factual background to this chapter see Harbury and Lipsey, Chapter 5.

Table 31.1 Income and population differences among groups of countries, 1980

Classification (based on GNP per capita in 1976 US dollars)[a]	Number of countries (1)	GNP (billions) (2)	Population (millions) (3)	GNP per capita (4)	Percentage of the world's GNP (5)	Percentage of the world's population (6)	Growth rate[b] (7)
I Less than $175	22	$ 130	968	$ 135	1·7	23·1	1·5
II $175–349	19	84	347	242	1·1	8·3	4·8
III $350–699	22	481	1,254	384	6·4	29·9	5·2
IV $700–1,399	25	478	442	1,081	6·4	10·5	4·0
V $1,400–2,799	19	416	183	2,276	5·4	4·4	4·7
VI $2,800–5,599	12	2,314	574	4,028	30·6	13·7	3·5
VII $5,600 or more	18	3,669	426	8,606	48·4	10·1	4·6
Totals	137	$7,572	4,194	$1,805	100·0	100·0	

Source: International Financial Statistics; Statistical Abstract.
[a] The groups represent arbitrary groupings in which real GNP per capita doubles with each progression.
[b] Average annual percentage rate of growth of real GNP per capita, 1970–80.

24 per cent of the world's population, earn 79 per cent of world income. Column 7 shows that the gap in income between rich and poor countries is not being closed.

Over half of the world's population live in poverty; many of the poorest people are in countries with the lowest growth rates, and thus fall ever farther behind.

Many terms have been used to describe the countries that are our concern in this chapter. They have variously been referred to as *underdeveloped, developing, emerging* and *less developed*. Fads and fashions grow up around particular terms, but none of them will be descriptive of all of the economies in question, for the very reason that their present characteristics and the problems they face differ. We shall mainly use the term *developing countries*. We do this with no value connotations and in full realization that it covers a great variety of countries with a great variety of levels and rates of growth of real national income. We may measure the development of an economy in dozens of different ways, among them: income per head; the percentage of resources unexploited; capital per head; savings per head; conduciveness to growth of the social system; conduciveness to growth of local religion; amount of 'social capital' (i.e., roads, railroads, schools, etc.); degree of education of the working classes, and so on.

Countries that are 'underdeveloped' or 'developing' in one of these ways may not be underdeveloped or developing in another. For example, one country may have a lower income per head than others, but have a higher percentage utilization of existing natural resources. For this reason we cannot have a unique ranking of the various countries in terms of degree of development. Furthermore, the problem of raising the income of a country that has low capital per head, much unemployed labour, but few unexploited natural resources is likely to be very different from that of raising the income of a country which is under-populated and has many unexploited natural resources. It is often thought, however, that an important first step in any study is to find the 'true' definition of underdevelopment and developing. Of course, different investigators may concern themselves with different groups of countries and different problems. One, for example, defines an underdeveloped country as one with a per capita national income of less than $700. Another confines his study to countries with substantial quantities of underdeveloped resources. Each of these groups of countries can be studied, and it is futile to argue which group is properly defined as 'underdeveloped'. Instead of trying to find the true meaning of 'underdevelopment' and 'development', and trying to isolate *the* problem of development, we shall look for some common problems in various groups of countries, being prepared to find major differences in both the problems and the solutions in whatever group of countries we study.

Barriers to economic development

If income per head is taken as an index of the level of economic development, a country may develop by any policies that cause its aggregate income to grow faster than its population. A growing population, a shortage of natural resources or inefficiency in resource use can all be important barriers to development.

Population growth

Population growth is a central problem of economic development. If population expands rapidly, a country may make a great effort to raise the quantity of capital only to find that a corresponding rise in population has occurred, so that the net effect of its 'growth policy' is a larger population now maintained at the original low standard of living. They will have made appreciable gains in income, but much of it will be eaten up (literally) by the increasing population.

Table 31.2 The relation of population growth to per capita GNP, 1970–80 (percentages)

Classification of countries (GNP per capita, 1976 US dollars)			Average annual rate of growth of			Population growth as a percentage of real GNP growth
Group[a]	Average income level	Percentage of population	Real GNP	Population	Real GNP per capita	
I	less than $175	23·1	4·0	2·6	1·4	65
II–IV	$175–1,399	48·7	6·8	2·1	4·7	30
V–VII	$1,400 or more	28·2	4·4	0·5	3·9	10

Source: Calculated from *International Financial Statistics*.
[a]Groups from Table 31.1.

This is illustrated in Table 31.2. The very poorest countries have *both* a relatively low growth rate of national income and a relatively high growth rate of population. The middle group shows rising living standards despite large population growth, by virtue of a high growth rate of national income. The wealthiest countries owe much of their growth in living standards to a low rate of population increase.

Growth in per capita real income depends upon the difference between growth rates of real national income and of population.

If population control in the poor countries is left to nature, nature often solves it in a cruel way. Population increases until many are forced to live at a subsistence level; further population growth is halted by famine, pestilence and plague. This grim situation was perceived early in the history of economics by Thomas Malthus. In some ways, the population problem is more severe today than it was even a generation ago because advances in medicine and in public health have brought sharp and sudden decreases in death rates. It is ironic that much of the compassion for the poor and underprivileged people of the world has traditionally taken the form of improving their health, thereby doing little to avert their poverty. Men laud the medical missionaries who brought modern medicine to the regions where it was previously unobtainable, but the elimination of malaria has doubled the rate of population growth in Ceylon. Cholera, once a killer, is now largely under control. No one would argue against controlling disease, but other things must also be done if the child who survives the infectious illnesses of infancy is not to die of starvation in early adulthood.

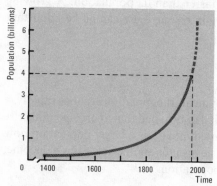

Fig. 31.1 World population growth. (The broken line gives projections of the population from 1980 to 2000.)

Figure 31.1 illustrates actual and projected population growth in the world today. It took about 40 to 50 thousand years after the emergence of modern Cro-Magnon Man for the world's population to reach 1,000 million. It took 100 years to add a second thousand million and 30 years to add the third thousand million. If present trends continue, the 1980 population of 4,000 million will be doubled in 30 years.

> **The growth of world population has been so explosive over the last two centuries that scientists can, with some realism, speak of the human animal as having reached the swarming stage.**

Economists sometimes speak of a 'critical minimum effort', by which they mean an increase in GNP sufficiently large to provide an appreciable increase in per capita living standards in spite of the rise in population. Experience suggests that when people become used to higher living standards they will seek to protect these by voluntarily limiting the sizes of their families. When and if this happens, the population 'problem' solves itself through voluntary individual decisions.

Resource limitations

Kuwait has one of the world's highest per capita incomes because of its good fortune in sitting on top of one of the world's largest oil fields. Lack of oil proved a devastating blow to many of the least developed countries when the OPEC cartel quadrupled oil prices during the early 1970s and then increased them sharply again at the end of the decade. Without oil their development efforts would be crippled; but to buy oil took too much of their scarce foreign exchange. Unlike many developed countries, which also bought oil, the least-developed countries were not markets in which the oil producers spent their new wealth.

It might seem obvious that development would be easier in a country lavishly endowed with natural resources than in a country poorly endowed. But as so often happens in development economics, propositions that seem obvious turn out to be suspect on closer attention. Kuwait and the United States are examples of countries that have developed on a base of plentiful natural resources – a single resource in one case and a multiplicity in the other. That natural resources are not sufficient is shown by the fact that the North American Indians lived with the American resources for centuries. Although they were well above the subsistence level and had civilizations of their own, there is no evidence that the Indians of North America had anything other than static living standards for many centuries. That natural resources are not necessary is shown by the long list of diverse economies that have developed without indigenous resources and sometimes in such hostile environments as malaria-ridden swamps. Consider, for example, Holland, Hong Kong, Japan, Singapore, Switzerland, Taiwan and Venice.

Financial capital Investment plays a vital role in economic growth. It may take as much as £10 of capital to increase national income by £1 per year. If this is so, it will take £66,000 million of capital to raise average income per year by £100 in a country of 66 million people such as Mexico. £66,000 million is a lot of money in any country, but it is not much less than the annual Mexican GNP.

One source of financial capital is the savings of households and firms. Banks and banking are particularly important in developing economies because if they do not function smoothly, the link between private saving and investment may be broken and the problem of finding funds for investment greatly intensified.

Reliance on deposit money and faith in bankers is limited to a small fraction of the world's economies. Many people in undeveloped economies do not trust banks, and they will therefore either not maintain deposits, or periodically panic, withdraw their money, and seek security in mattresses, in gold or in real estate. Thus savings do not become available for investment in productive capacity. If banks cannot count on their deposits being left in the banking system, they cannot readily lend money for investment purposes. Thus, distrust of banks, and of deposit money, may impede economic development even if private individuals are willing to refrain from current consumption.

Social-overhead capital The progress of economic development is reflected in the increasing flow of goods and services from a nation's farms and factories to its households. But the ability to sustain and expand these flows depends on many supporting services, particularly transportation and communications, which are sometimes called the 'infrastructure' of the economy. In the early stages of the development of Western industrial nations much of the infrastructure grew up slowly due to private enterprise. Today people usually look to the government to provide the infrastructure, but there is debate over the extent to which this is necessary. The absence, whatever the reason, of a dependable infrastructure can impose severe barriers to economic development.

Human capital A well-developed entrepreneurial class of persons motivated and trained to organize resources for efficient production is often lacking in underdeveloped countries. This lack may be a heritage of a colonial system that gave the local population no opportunity to develop[1]; it may result from the fact that managerial positions are awarded on the basis of family status or political patronage; it may reflect the presence of economic or cultural attitudes that do not favour the acquisition of wealth by organizing productive activities; or it may simply be due to a lack of the required education or training.

Poor health is another source of inadequate human resources. Less time is lost and more effective effort is expended when the labour force is in good health. The economic analysis of medical advances is a very young field, however, and there is a great deal to be learned about the quantitative importance of such gains.

Inefficiency in the use of resources

Low levels of income and slower than necessary growth rates may result from inefficient use of resources as well as from scarcity of key resources.

Allocative inefficiency and X-inefficiency It is useful to distinguish between two kinds of inefficiency. A man-hour of labour would be used inefficiently, for example, even though the labourer was working at top efficiency, if he was engaged in making a product that no one wanted. Using society's resources to make the wrong products is an example of ALLOCATIVE INEFFICIENCY. In terms of the production-possibility boundary encountered in Chapter 4, allocative inefficiency represents operation at the wrong place on the boundary. If 2 tons of coal and 50 man-hours of labour are being used to make steel in the most efficient way, this may, nevertheless, be inefficient if this coal and labour could be more productive making electric power to be used to make aluminium. Allocative inefficiency will arise if the signals to which people respond do not reflect opportunity costs – both monopoly and tariffs are commonly cited sources of distortions – or if market imperfections prevent resources moving to their best uses.

A second kind of inefficiency has come to be called X-inefficiency, following Professor Harvey Leibenstein. X-INEFFICIENCY arises whenever resources are used in such a way that even if they are making the right product, they are doing so less productively than is possible. If a labourer, for example, is debilitated by disease, unmotivated, or inhibited by taboos, an hour of his labour may be less productive than it could be, even in its best use. Similarly, land or coal may be poorly used because of ignorance, indifference or poor technology.

Sources of X-inefficiency Both inadequate education and poor health, discussed above, may be important sources of X-inefficiency. For example, as modern techniques are introduced, a large rise in the educational standards of the workforce is necessary. A man who cannot read or write or do simple calculations will be much less efficient in many jobs than one who can. A manager who is trained in modern methods of bookkeeping, inventory control and personnel management is likely to be much more effective in getting the most output from a given input than one who is ignorant of these techniques.

---

[1] Some did; some did not. For example, the British colonial system, whatever else can be said against it, was remarkable in encouraging education and skill development among many of the populations that it controlled.

Traditions, institutions and habitual ways of doing business vary among societies, and not all are equally conducive to productivity. Often personal considerations of family, of past favours, or of traditional friendship or enmity are more important than market signals in explaining behaviour. One may find a too-small firm struggling to survive against a larger rival and learn that the owner prefers to stay small rather than expand because expansion would require use of non-family capital or leadership. To avoid paying too harsh a competitive price for his built-in inefficiency, the firm's owner may then spend half his energies attempting to influence the government to prevent larger firms from being formed or trying to secure restrictions on the sale of output, and he may well succeed. Such behaviour is very likely to inhibit economic growth.

Do a society's customs reflect cherished values or only such things as the residual influences of a passing social system or a former oligarchical political structure? This is an important question to the policymakers who must decide whether or not the cost in terms of inefficiency should be paid to maintain the customs. In any case, cultural attitudes are not easily changed. If people believe that your father's background is more important than your present abilities, it may take a generation to persuade employers to change their attitudes and another generation to persuade workers that things have changed. Structuring incentives is a widely used form of policy action in market-oriented economies, but this may be harder to do in a traditional society than in a market economy. If people habitually bribe the tax collector instead of paying taxes, they will not be likely to respond to policies that are supposed to work by changing marginal tax incentives. All that will change is the size of the bribe.

Several empirical studies have shown large differences in productivity from country to country in particular industries using the same technologies of production. In some cases, great increases in productivity have been achieved simply by changing incentive systems. These facts suggest a large quantitative importance to X-inefficiency and a large payoff to overcoming it.

X-inefficiency, which refers to a lower level of productivity than could be achieved due to social attitudes and structures, seems to be a major cause of low levels and rates of growth of national income in many developing countries.

Fostering economic development

Economic development policy involves identifying the particular barriers to the level and kind of development desired and then devising policies to overcome them. Governments can seek funds for investment, and they can attempt to identify cultural, legal, social and psychological barriers to growth. They can undertake the programmes of education, legal reform, resource development, negotiation of trade treaties or actual investment that smooth the way to more rapid growth. All of this is more easily said than done. Further, as the dozens of 'development missions' sent out by the World Bank and other international, national and private agencies have discovered, the problems and strategies vary greatly from country to country. Economic development as a field of economic expertise is in its infancy. A few choices, however, seem to be pervasive and therefore worth mentioning here.

Planning or *laissez-faire*?

How much government control over the economy is necessary and desirable? Practically every shade of opinion has been seriously advocated, from 'The only way to grow is to get the government's dead hand out of everything' to 'The only way to grow is to get a fully-planned, centrally controlled economy.' Such extreme views are easily refuted by factual evidence. Many economies have grown with very little government assistance. Great Britain, the United States and Holland are important examples. Others, such as the Soviet Union and Hungary, have sustained growth with a high degree of centralized control. In still other countries, there is almost every conceivable mix of government and private initiative in the growth process.

What sense can be made of these apparently conflicting historical precedents? Probably the most satisfactory answer is that the appropriate action depends on the circumstances presently ruling in the country. In some cases, ineffective governments may have been interfering with the economy to the point of discouraging private initiative, in which case growth may well be enhanced by a reduction in government control over the economy. In other cases, where major quantities of social capital are needed or where existing institutional arrangements, such as land tenure, are harmful to growth, active intervention by the central authorities – 'planning', as it is called – may be essential. On the question of which is the best mix between state and private initiative at a particular time and in a particular place, there is likely to be much disagreement.

The case for planning The two major appeals of planning are that it can accelerate the pace of economic development and that it can significantly influence its direction. Any one of the barriers to development may be lowered by actions of the central authorities. Consider, for example, the way they might seek to mitigate a shortage of investment funds. In a fully employed free-market economy, investment is influenced by the quantity of savings households and firms make, and thus the division of resources between consumption and saving is one determinant of the rate of growth. When living standards are low, people have urgent uses for their current income. Left to individual determination, saving may be low, and this is an impediment to investment and growth. In a variety of ways, central authorities can intervene and force people to save more than they otherwise would. Such compulsory saving has been one of the main aims of most of the 'plans' of communist governments. The justification offered for this compulsory sacrifice of present living standards for future benefits is that without it growth would be slow or non-existent, inflicting a low living standard on all future generations.

The goal of the five-year plans of Russia, Poland and China was to raise savings and thus to lower current consumption below what it would be, given complete freedom of choice. Extra savings may be the subject of planning even in less centrally controlled societies, through tax incentives and monetary policies. The object is the same: to increase investment in order to increase growth, and thus to make future generations better off.

Central governments of an authoritarian sort can be particularly effective in overcoming some of the sources of X-inefficiency. A dictatorship may suppress social and even religious institutions that are barriers to growth, and hold on to power until a new generation grows up that did not know and does not value the old institutions. It is much more difficult for democratic government, which must command popular support at each election, to do currently unpopular things in the interests of long-term growth.

One of the reasons why authoritarian governments often have a large initial success in raising growth rates is their willingness and ability to sweep away some of the sources of X-inefficiency, often against the wishes of a large part of the society. The value judgement as to whether the growth gains are worth the social sacrifices is, of course, outside economics.

The case for the free market Most people would agree that government must play an important part in any development programme. The sectors of the economy that are reserved for public enterprise in most developed economies – education, transportation, and communication – are very important to development. But what of the sectors usually left to private enterprise in advanced capitalist countries?

The advocates of the free market in these sectors place great emphasis on human drive, initiative and inventiveness. Once the infrastructure is established, an army of entrepreneurs will do vastly more to develop the economy than will an army of civil servants. The market will provide opportunities and direct their efforts and individuals will act energetically within it once they are given a self-interest in doing so. People who seem irretrievably lethargic and unenterprising when held down by lack of incentives will show amazing bursts of energy when given sufficient self-interest in economic activity.

Furthermore, goes the argument, individual capitalists are far less wasteful than civil servants of the country's capital. An individual entrepreneur who risks his own capital will push investment in really productive directions. If he fails to do so, he loses his investment and thus his role in deciding on the allocation of the country's capital. A bureaucrat, however, investing capital that is not his own – possibly raised from the peasants by a state marketing board that buys cheap and sells dear – will behave very differently. His first thought may be to enhance his own prestige by spending too much money on cars, offices and secretaries, and too little on really productive activities. Even if he is genuinely interested in the country's well-being the incentive structure of a bureaucracy does not encourage creative risk-taking. If his ventures fail his own head is likely to roll; if they succeed he will not receive the profits anyway, and his superior may get the medal.

This is a brief suggestion of the case that is often argued for leaving much of the main thrust of development in the hands of private producers. It is a very emotive subject and readers are likely to have had strong reactions to it. Those with 'leftish' leanings are likely to have reacted to this case in a hostile fashion, and those with 'rightish' leanings in a favourable fashion. Clearly people have strong, divergent and often doctrinaire views on these matters; equally clearly, these are matters of life and death to millions in the developing countries who will suffer or die if their governments adopt an inappropriate road to development. Human welfare would be well served if these issues could be removed from the realm of emotion into that of precise statement and careful testing.

Educational policy

Most studies of underdeveloped countries suggest that under-education is a serious barrier to development and urge increased expenditures on education. This poses the choice of how to spend educational funds. Should they go to erasing illiteracy and increasing the level of mass education, or to training a small cadre of scientifically and technically trained specialists? The problem is serious, because education is very expensive and does not pay off quickly. Basic education requires a large investment in schools, in teacher training and in curriculum revision that may take decades to raise the level of education significantly, and even longer to produce a payoff in terms of greater labour-force productivity.

The opportunity cost of educational expenditures always seems high; yet it is essential to make them sometime because the gains will be critical to growth a generation later.

Many developing countries have put much of their education resources into training a few highly educated people because the tangible results of a few hundred doctors or engineers or PhDs are relatively more visible than the results from raising the school-leaving age by a year or two, say, from age 10 to age 12. It is not yet clear whether this policy pays off, but it is clear that there are some drawbacks to it. Many of this educated elite are recruited from the privileged classes on the basis of family position, not merit; many regard their education as the passport to a new aristocracy, rather than as a mandate to serve their fellow citizens; and, in addition, an appreciable fraction emigrate to countries where their newly acquired skills bring higher pay than at home. Of those who stay home, many seek the security of a government job and become part of the new establishment. Although the risks of waste may be large, so also are the gains from a successful specialist educational policy. Engineers, agronomists, economists and a host of other experts can be very productive when their talents are used successfully.

Population control

The race between population and income has been a dominant feature of many developing countries. There are two possible ways for a country to win this race. One is to create conditions that produce a growth rate well in excess of the rate of population growth. The second is to control population growth. The problem *can* be solved by restricting population growth. This is not a matter of serious debate, although the means of restricting population growth are, for considerations of religion, custom and education are involved.

Positive economics cannot decide whether population control is morally good or bad, but it can describe the consequences of any choice made. Economic development is much easier to achieve with population control than without it.

Both Sweden and Venezuela have death rates of about 10 per 1,000 population per year. The birth rate in Sweden is 12; in Venezuela it is 42. While the causes of variations in birth rates are complex, they have inescapable economic consequences. Thus, in Venezuela the net increase of population per year is 33 per 1,000 (3·3 per cent), but it is only 3 per 1,000 (0·3 per cent) in Sweden. If each country achieved an overall rate of growth of production of 3 per cent per year, Sweden would be increasing her living standards by 2·7 per cent per year, while Venezuela would be lowering hers by 0·3 per cent per year. In 1980 Sweden's income per capita was three and a half times as high as Venezuela's, and Venezuela was the wealthiest country in South and Central America. The gap will widen rapidly, if present population trends continue.

Acquiring capital

A country can acquire funds for investment in three distinct ways: from the savings (voluntary or forced) of its domestic households and firms, by loans or investment from abroad, or by contributions from foreigners.

Capital from domestic saving If capital is to be created at home by the country's own efforts, resources must be diverted from the production of goods for current consumption. This requires a cut in present living standards, which may be difficult to achieve if living standards are already low. At best, it will be possible to re-allocate only a small proportion of resources to the production of capital goods. Such a situation is often described as the *vicious circle of poverty*: because a country has little capital per head, it is poor; because it is poor, it can devote only a few resources to creating new capital rather than producing goods for immediate consumption; because little new capital can be produced, capital per head remains low; because capital per head remains low, the country remains poor.

The vicious circle can be made to seem an absolute constraint on growth rates. Of course it isn't, since if it were we would all be back at our original subsistence level. In any case some countries that count as underdeveloped now already have per capita GNPs that must be larger than were those of many early free-market economies when they began on a path of sustained economic growth. The grain of truth in the vicious circle argument is that some surplus must be available somewhere in the society to promote saving and investment. In a poor society with an even distribution of income, so that nearly everyone is on the subsistence level, saving may be very difficult. But this is not the common experience. Usually there will be at least a small middle class that can save and invest if opportunities for profitable uses of funds arise. Also, even in poor societies the average household is usually above the physical subsistence level. Even the poorest households will find that they can sacrifice some present living standards for a future gain. After all, presented with a profitable opportunity, Ghanaians planted cocoa plants at the turn of the century even though there was a seven-year growing period before any return could be expected!

This last example points to an important fact. Often in developing countries one resource that is *not* scarce is labour hours. Profitable home or village investment that requires mainly labour inputs may be made with relatively little sacrifice in current living standards. This is not the kind of investment, however, that may appeal to central authorities who are mesmerised by such large, spectacular, symbolic investments as dams, nuclear power stations and steel mills.

Imported capital Another way of accumulating capital needed for growth is to borrow it from abroad. If a poor country, *A*, borrows from a rich country, *B*, it can use the borrowed funds to purchase capital goods produced in *B*. Country *A* thus accumulates capital and needs to cut its current output of consumption goods only to pay interest on its loans. As the new capital begins to add to current production, it becomes easier to pay the interest on the loan and also to begin to repay the principal out of the increase in output. Thus, income can be raised immediately, and the major sacrifice postponed until later, when part of the increased income that might have been used to raise domestic consumption is used to pay off the loan. This method has the great advantage of allowing a poor country to have an initial increase in capital goods far greater than it could possibly have created by diverting its own resources from consumption industries.

Many countries, developed or undeveloped, are suspicious of foreign capital, lest the foreign investor gain control over their industries or their government. The extent of foreign control depends on the form that foreign capital takes. If the foreigners buy bonds in domestic companies, they do not own or control anything; if they buy common stocks, they own part or all of the company; if they subsidize a government, they may feel justified in exacting political commitments. Whether foreign ownership of one's industries carries political disadvantages is a subject of debate. In Canada, for example, there has been significant political opposition to having so much of Canadian industry owned by US nationals who are presumably more open to pressure from US central authorities than from Canadian authorities.

The economic choices are quite clear:

Accumulating a given amount of capital through domestic saving requires greater current sacrifice but later pays a higher return. Foreign financing requires small present sacrifices but involves holding down living standards later in order to make the interest payments to foreign investors and eventually to repay the principal.

When both ways of financing are equally possible, the choice between them raises an important intergenerational question: to what extent should the sacrifices required to pay for growth be met now rather than decades from now? One suspects that, political considerations aside, most people would prefer to postpone the cost by using borrowed capital.

Getting foreign capital is easier said than done in the early stages of development. America and Canada were once underdeveloped in the sense of being underpopulated, with many unused resources, but they were latent giants that promised rich returns to foreign investors. It is harder to see similar investment opportunities in Pakistan, say, where overpopulation has been a problem for centuries and where the soil has been severely damaged by centuries of irrigation without proper drainage. The ability of such a country to borrow from private sources is small. Foreign capital plays a role, but it is capital provided by foreign governments and international agencies, not by private investors.

Foreign capital may be imported and invested by private firms in which case its use is determined by the free market. It may also be imported and invested by the central authorities. This planning solution has been the one adopted by many developing countries in the 1970s and 1980s. Unfortunately, a truly vast number of the investments made by these central authorities have not paid off. There is no new production to show for the unsuccessful investments. The countries are now burdened with large foreign debts which will either be defaulted on – making further financing of development programmes more difficult – or will be a heavy burden on current and future generations who will have to save to service and pay off the foreign debt whose use contributed nothing to raising incomes. Of course, in those countries where the capital was invested productively the extra flow of output provides the stream of income from which the debt can be serviced and eventually repaid.

Contributed capital From the point of view of the receiving country, contributed capital in the form of foreign aid expenditures of individual countries and international institutions would seem to be ideal. It has the advantage of enabling the country to shift to more rapid growth without either sacrificing consumption now or having to repay later. There is significant resistance to accepting aid in some countries. The explanation lies in the country's suspicions of the motives of the givers and fear that hidden strings may be attached to the offer. Independent countries prize their independence and want to avoid either the fact or the appearance of being satellites. Pride – a desire to be beholden to no one – is also a factor. The economist cannot say that these fears and aspirations are either foolish or unworthy. He can only note that they do have a cost, for there is no doubt that economically it is better to receive than to give.

Patterns of development

To what extent should a developing country pursue a policy of BALANCED GROWTH, pushing expansion in all sectors of the economy, rather than one of UNBALANCED GROWTH, pushing specialization in certain sectors? How should it decide how much effort to devote to increasing agricultural production, needed to feed its masses, and how much to the industrialization that might change its role in the world economy? If it is to push industrialization, what commodities should it manufacture – those for which there is a large export market, or those which will free it from the need to import?

Comparative advantage: the case for unbalanced growth

The principle of comparative advantage provides the traditional case for the desirability of unbalanced growth. By specializing in those sectors in which it has the greatest comparative advantage, a country can achieve the most rapid growth in the short run. Its potential for growth is certainly not equal in all sectors of the economy. Balanced growth pursued to the extreme of equal growth in all sectors would be virtually sure to result in a lower living standard than would result from some degree of specialization accompanied by increased international trade.

These are cogent reasons in favour of *some* specialization. But specialization involves risks that may be worth avoiding even at the loss of some income. Specialization involves concentrating one's production in one or a few products. This makes the economy highly vulnerable to cyclical fluctuations in world demand and supply. Even more seriously, if technological or taste changes render a product partially or wholly obsolete, the country can face a major calamity for generations. Just as individual firms and regions may become overspecialized, so may countries.

> **Unplanned growth will usually tend to exploit the country's *present* comparative advantages; planners may choose a pattern of growth that involves changing the country's *future* comparative advantage.**

Many skills can be acquired, and the fostering of an apparently uneconomic domestic industry may, by changing the characteristics of the labour force, develop a comparative advantage in that line of production. The Japanese were in a feudal state and showed no visible comparative advantage in any industrial skill when their country was opened to Western influence in 1854, yet they became a major industrial power by the end of the century. Soviet planners in the 1920s and 1930s chose to create an industrial economy out of a predominantly agricultural one and succeeded in vastly changing the mix between agriculture and industry in a single generation. These illustrations should serve as cogent reminders that an excessive reliance on current comparative advantage may lead to an excessive defence of the status quo in the pattern of international specialization.

Agricultural development versus industrialization

India, Pakistan and Taiwan, along with other Asian countries, have achieved dramatic results by the application of new technology – and particularly new seed – to agricultural production. Increases of up to 50 per cent in grain production have been achieved, and it has been estimated that with adequate supplies of water, pesticides, fertilizers and modern equipment, production could be doubled or even trebled. This has been labelled the 'green revolution'. When the Nobel Prize Committee gave the 1970 Peace Prize to Norman Borlaug, it recognized the potential importance of these developments in alleviating, for at least a generation, the shortage of food that the population explosion was expected to bring. The possibilities of achieving such dramatic gains in agricultural output may seem almost irresistible at first glance, but many economists think they should be resisted and point to a series of problems.

One is that a vast amount of resources are required to irrigate land and mechanize production, and these resources alternatively could provide industrial development and industrial employment opportunities. Thus there is a clear opportunity cost. Critics of the agricultural strategy argue that the search for a generation free from starvation will provide at best only a temporary solution, because population will surely expand to meet the food supply. Instead, they argue, underdeveloped countries should start at once to reduce their dependence on agriculture. Let someone else grow the food; industrialization should not be delayed.

A second problem with the agricultural strategy is that the great increases in world production of wheat, rice and other agricultural commodities that the 'green revolution' makes possible could depress their prices and not lead to increased earnings from exports. What one agricultural country can do, so can others, and there may well be a glut on world markets.

A third problem has arisen (most acutely in India and Pakistan) where increasing agricultural output has been accompanied by decreasing labour requirements in agricultural production without a compensating increase in employment opportunities elsewhere. Millions of tenant farmers – and their bullocks – have been evicted from their tenant holdings by owners who are buying tractors to replace them. Many have found no other work. Where there is already large-scale unemployment, devoting resources to labour-saving innovations makes little sense unless at the same time new jobs are developed for the displaced labour.

Despite the worldwide need for food, the agriculture strategy of development has not proved to be a surefire path to economic development.

Industrialization for import substitution

In the period since the Second World War, industrialization of developing countries has largely taken the form of producing domestically goods that were previously imported, largely for sale in the home market. Because these countries characteristically suffered from a significant comparative disadvantage in such production, it proved necessary both to subsidize the home industry and to restrict imports. A study of such policies in seven countries – Argentina, Brazil, Mexico, India, Pakistan, the Philippines and Taiwan – concluded:

although there are arguments for giving special encouragement to industry, this encouragement could be provided in forms which would not discourage exports, including

agricultural exports, as present policies often do; which would promote greater efficiency in the use of resources; and which would create a less unequal distribution of income and higher levels of employment in both industry and agriculture.[1]

These conclusions are controversial, and critics point to the fact that Taiwan, for example, represents one of the great successes of economic development. Its income per capita has averaged a rate of increase of over 6 per cent during the whole of the last two decades.

Implementing an import substitution policy is relatively easy because it can be done by imposing import quotas and by raising tariffs. Such tariffs and other restrictions on imports provide incentives for the development of domestic industry by carving out a ready-made market and by providing a substantial price umbrella that promises high profits to succeessful local manufacturers and to foreign investors who might enter with both capital and know-how. Subsidies, governmental loans and other forms of encouragement have also been used in many cases.

Little, Scitovsky and Scott concluded that policies of industrialization accomplished by effective rates of protection that varied from 25 per cent for Mexico to over 200 per cent for Pakistan aggravated inequalities in the distribution of income by raising the prices of manufactured goods relative to agricultural goods and by favouring profits over wages. Moreover, they found that productivity increased more than employment opportunities, and that unemployment has grown because of the discouraging of such labour-using industries as textiles and the encouraging of the use of capital-intensive, labour-saving processes.

The argument against import-substituting industrialization policies is that they have given too much attention to the advantages of self-sufficiency and too little to comparative advantage.

Moreover, the opportunities for import substitution are limited. Once the country runs out of imports to substitute for, what then? Industrialization, these critics argue, ought to be encouraged, but along the lines where infant industry arguments are truly valid: where, once the development period is past, the country will have a reliable industry that can compete in world markets.

Industrialization for export

Obviously, if Tanzania or Burma could quickly develop steel, shipbuilding and manufacturing industries that operated as efficiently as those of Japan or West Germany, they, too, might share in the rapid economic growth that has been enjoyed by these industrial countries. Indeed, if a few decades of protectionism could give infant industries time to mature and to become efficient, the price might be worth paying. After all, both Japan and Russia were recently underdeveloped countries.

But the catch-up problem is a race against a moving target. Suppose one is committed to having a given industry competitive in 10 years. In such a situation, it is not sufficient to be making gains in productivity; they must be made at a fast enough rate to overcome a present disadvantage against an improving opponent. Suppose you must improve by 50 per cent to achieve the present level of a competitor who is improving at r per cent per year. If you want to catch him in 10 years you must

---

[1] Little, Scitovsky and Scott, *Industry and Trade in Some Developing Countries* (Oxford University Press, 1970), p. 1.

improve at $r+4$ per cent per year. If r is 6 per cent, you must achieve 10 per cent. To achieve 6 per cent or 7 per cent may be admirable, but you will lose the race just the same. Thus, while the industrialization route to development is available, it depends both on having required resources and on overcoming X-inefficiency. This often means devoting resources for a long period to education, training, development of an infrastructure, and overcoming the various cultural and social barriers to efficient production. All of this is difficult, although not impossible.

The greatest success in development has been achieved by nations that have succeeded in developing efficient industrial export industries.

Having recognized this fact, it is easy to be led astray by it. Developing countries sometimes pursue certain lines of production on a subsidized basis either for prestige purposes or because of a confusion between cause and effect. Because most wealthy nations have a steel industry, the leaders of many underdeveloped nations regard their countries as primitive until they develop a domestic steel industry. Because several developing countries have succeeded in producing consumer durables, many others assume that they should try to do so. However, if a country has a serious comparative disadvantage in steel or in making consumer durables, fostering such industries will make that country poor. Possibly such industries bring the country international prestige? It is doubtful, however, if a nation really gains international prestige by having an uneconomic steel industry, an unprofitable national airline or a sleek aeroplane that no airline can afford to operate even if it were given to them free. In the long run, prestige probably goes to the country that grows rich, rather than to the one that stays poor but produces, at high cost, a few prestigious commodities that its government regards as signs of wealth.

Commodity-price stabilization agreements

When all or most producers of a commodity can agree on price and output levels, they can achieve monopoly profits not available in competitive markets. Many developing economies are heavily committed to the production and export of one or a few basic commodities such as bananas, bauxite, cocoa, coffee, copper, cotton, iron ore, jute, manganese, meat, oil, phosphates, rubber, sugar, tea, tropical timber or tin. Why not get together and create an effective cartel that gives producers the monopoly profits that are potentially available? This has been tried many times in history; until OPEC, it has always failed. Yet everyone knows that OPEC's success transformed a handful of formerly poor economies into the wealthiest of nations.

OPEC's success has not been easy to copy because the special conditions of demand and supply that apply to oil do not apply to most other primary commodities. In the case of oil there are few large producing countries, supply is quite inelastic outside those countries, and demand is relatively inelastic in the short and middle run. Perhaps equally important, the largest producer – Saudi Arabia – has been prepared to put up with a good deal of cheating by its partners.

Wheat, coffee, cocoa, tin, rubber and copper have all been suggested as potential targets for similar joint marketing strategies, but none has the right combination of attributes, and only copper has supply and demand situations that are remotely similar to those of oil.

The New International Economic Order (NIEO)

In May 1974 the General Assembly of the United Nations adopted (over the objections of the developed countries) a Declaration on the Establishment of a New International Economic Order (NIEO). This represented an attempt on the part of the developing nations to utilize collective *political* power to achieve a larger share of the world's goods. The NIEO proposals are aimed basically at wealth transfers instead of wealth creations; they are concerned with a more equal distribution of existing wealth rather than economic development.[1]

The major proposals were threefold. First, establishment of marketing boards for primary products exported by the developing nations. These, modelled along the lines of OPEC, would reduce output, raise prices and thus create monopoly profits for producers. Second, exports of manufactured goods from developing countries should receive preferential treatment in the markets of developed countries. Third, the enormous debts of the developing countries, incurred partly to finance development projects and partly to finance the greatly increased cost of oil imports, should be partly forgiven and partly rescheduled to provide for longer repayment periods and easier terms of finance.

Thus far the major accomplishments of NIEO demands have been small. The issues and proposals have been discussed extensively, but little major redistribution of wealth has resulted. From an economic point of view NIEO has two major flaws. First, it focuses too much on redistribution and too little on seeking real growth in world output. Second, it puts its faith in bureaucratic allocations of wealth, trade, and natural resources rather than in market mechanisms. Nothing in the world's experience to date suggests that this will increase total world output. Many modern development economists would share the view of Professor McCulloch that the developed countries should be adopting policies to expand rather than contract world wealth. If that is so, the major proposals of NIEO will not prove attractive.

Some awkward issues

The speed of development

Reformers in underdeveloped countries often think in terms of transforming their economies within a generation or two. The sense of urgency is quite understandable but unless it is tempered by some sense of historical perspective, totally unreasonable aspirations may develop – only to be dashed all too predictably. Many underdeveloped countries are probably in a stage of development analogous to that of medieval England – they have not yet developed anything like the commercial sophistication of the Elizabethan era. It took 400 years for England to develop from that stage to its present one. To do the same elsewhere in half the time of 200 years would be a tremendous achievement; to aspire to do it in 25 or 50 years may be to court disaster.

Population policy

This view presented in this chapter is neo-Malthusian and constitutes the current conventional wisdom on underdevelopment. There are, however, opposing views.

---

[1] An excellent introduction to this development is Rachel McCulloch's *Economic and Political Issues in the NIEO* (International Institute for Economic Research, 1979).

The neo-Malthusian view gives no place for the value of children in parents' utility functions. Critics point out that the psychic value of children should be included as part of the living standards of their parents. They also point out that in rural societies even quite young children are a productive resource because of the work they can do; while fully grown children provide old-age security for their parents in societies where state help for the aged is negligible.

The neo-Malthusian theory is also criticized for asserting that people breed blindly like wild animals. Critics point out that traditional methods of limiting family size have been known and practised since the dawn of history. Thus they argue that large families in rural societies are a matter of choice. The population explosion came not through any change in 'breeding habits' but by medical advances that greatly extended life expectancy (which surely must be counted as a direct welfare gain for those affected). The critics argue that once an urban society develops, family size will be reduced voluntarily. This was certainly the experience of Western industrial countries and why, ask the critics, should it not be the experience of the now-developing countries?

The cost of creating capital

Is it true that developing countries must sacrifice current living standards if they wish to invest in future growth? Production of consumption and capital goods are substitutes for each other only if factor supplies are constant. But, say the critics, the development of a market economy will lead people to substitute work for leisure. For example, the arrival of Europeans with new goods to trade led the North American Indians to collect furs and other commodities needed for exchange. Until they were decimated by later generations of land-hungry settlers, the standard of living of the Indians rose steadily with no immediate sacrifice. They created the capital needed for their production – weapons and means of transport – in their abundant leisure time so that their consumption began to rise immediately. This too, the argument runs, could happen in underdeveloped countries if market transactions were allowed to evolve naturally. The spread of a market economy would lead locals to give up leisure in order to produce saleable output that would provide the money needed to purchase new goods that private traders were introducing from the outside world.

Other controversies exist but this discussion should be sufficient to suggest that in development economics, as in all other branches of the subject, established views should always be regarded as open to challenge from conflicting theories and awkward facts.

Part seven

Microeconomic policy

32

The case for and against the free-market system

An unkind critic of economics once said that economists have two great insights: *markets work* and *markets fail*. An unkind critic of politics once added that economics was thus a step ahead of both the political left and the political right, each of which accepts only one of these insights. Indeed economists try to take the critical step of showing when each of the insights applies and why. In this chapter we shall consider the questions of when and why markets do and do not work. Then in Chapter 33 we shall go on to consider government intervention in the working of the economy.

The general case for some reliance on free markets is that the system of decentralized decision-taking that they permit is vastly more efficient in a number of identifiable ways than is a system where all economic decisions are taken, and consciously co-ordinated, by a centralized planning body. This is a lesson that the governments of the USSR and the countries of Eastern Europe have learned the hard way. Pressure in these countries is now to decentralize some decision-taking through actual, or simulated, market processes while not losing centralized control over what are regarded as the key decisions.

The general case for some intervention is that almost no one wants to let the market decide everything about our economic affairs. Most people's moral and practical sense argues for some state intervention to mitigate the disastrous results that the market deals out to some. Most people believe that there are areas where the market does not function well and where state intervention could improve or replace its functioning, to the general social good. For such reasons no economy is known where the citizens have opted for complete *laissez faire* and against any kind of government intervention.

So the operative question is not unhampered free-market economies *versus* fully centralized, command economies, but what kind of a mix between markets and government intervention best suits our hopes and needs?

Characteristics of the free market

Before we study the arguments related to the question just posed, it is worthwhile reviewing some very basic characteristics of the market system. These are characteristics that we have studied throughout this book, so here we merely need to draw them together and summarize them.[1]

---

[1] I have discussed the issues in the first half of this chapter in more detail elsewhere. See R. G. Lipsey, *Can the Market Economy Survive?* (Fraser Institute, Vancouver B.C., 1983).

A social control system

A co-ordinator of decisions Every day millions of people make millions of independent decisions concerning production and consumption. Most of these decisions are not motivated by a desire to contribute to the social good, or to make the whole economy work well, but by fairly immediate considerations of personal or group self-interest. The price system co-ordinates these decentralized decisions, making the whole system respond to the wishes of the individuals who compose it.

The basic insight into how this system works is that decentralized private decision-takers, acting in their own interests, respond to such public signals as the prices of what they buy and sell. Economists have long emphasized price as the signaling agent. When a commodity such as oil becomes scarce, its free-market price rises. Firms and households that use it are led to economize on it and to look for alternatives. Firms that produce it are led to produce more of it. This system works best when price is determined on free markets where there are many buyers and many sellers. The signals about scarcities and surplus are then given to individuals through prices that are set by the impersonal aggregate forces of demand and supply.

Administered prices For many commodities, including most manufactured goods, however, there are relatively few producers and their prices do not change from day to day according to the conditions of demand and supply. We have called these *administered prices* since firms, rather than impersonal market forces, set them. In such cases the price system still works; but it works slightly differently (and possibly less efficiently) than when prices are determined on competitive markets. Let us see what happens in such circumstances. Manufacturing firms tend to respond to price signals on the input side since many of the materials they use do have prices that are determined on competitive markets. On the output side, however, these firms respond to quantity signals. For example, having set the prices of their cars, the big American automobile firms found not long ago that they could sell all the small cars they could produce, but that they were left with a glut of larger cars. The firms reacted by altering next year's plans, to produce more small cars and fewer large ones at existing administered prices. What matters is that when prices are administered the market system does still co-ordinate decisions. It does so, however, by having firms adjust their outputs as their sales and their inventories change, rather than as the prices of their products change.

Windfall profits The basic engine that drives the adaptation of the economy is what economists call quasi rents, and what the general public has come to know as *windfall profits*. This concept was first introduced on page 372. It refers to earnings above ('profits') or below ('losses') transfer earnings as a result of shifts in demand for a factor in a particular use. Quasi rents arise because the factor does not move among uses with infinite speed. In the long run they are eliminated by the movement of factors among alternative uses until net advantages are equalized.

A rise in demand or a fall in production costs creates windfall profits for that commodity's producers, while a fall in demand or a rise in production costs creates windfall losses. Windfall profits signal that there are too few resources devoted to that industry. In search of these profits, more resources will enter the industry, increasing output and driving down price, until the windfall profits are driven to zero. Windfall losses signal the reverse. Resources leave the industry until those left behind are no longer making losses.

If the government taxed away *all* windfall profits and replaced by subsidy *all* windfall losses, it would effectively destroy the market economy by removing its driving force. Because the economy is continuously adjusting to shocks, a snapshot of the economy at any moment of time reveals substantial positive windfall profits in some industries and substantial windfall losses in others. A similar snapshot at another moment in time will also reveal windfall profits and losses, but their locations will be different (because their existence sets up a set of decentralized decisions that have the effect of removing them).

An illustration of market co-ordination Say, for example, that every family in the Greater London area decides that it wants its own house with garden. This would be physically impossible because there is not nearly enough land in all of the Home Counties surrounding London to house its population at the low density consistent with single-family dwellings. If the entire populace tried to move to such dwellings, they would, on the one hand, vastly bid up the price of land and the price of existing housing, while, on the other hand, causing the rents of flats to plummet. Reacting to these signals, many people would decide that, although they preferred to live in single-family dwellings at the original prices, they preferred to live in multi-family units at the now relatively cheap rents. With a price system, no central administrator has to calculate scarcities and decide what proportion of the population must live in multi-family dwellings. Furthermore, no one has to have the unenviable task of saying who is allowed to live in each type of dwelling. If there is excess demand for one type and excess supply of the other, their relative prices will change. As this happens, some people will switch from demanding the type that is becoming more expensive to demanding the type that is now relatively cheaper. Once the excess demand and supply are eliminated, the relative prices of the two will be in equilibrium. If there is a change in tastes with respect to the two types of accommodation, their relative prices will again change, leading to adjustments in both demand and supply.

Lack of conscious direction

The market economy fulfils its function of co-ordinating decisions without anyone having to understand how it works. As Professor Tom Schelling puts it:[1]

The dairy farmer doesn't need to know how many people eat butter and how far away they are, how many other people raise cows, how many babies drink milk, or whether more money is spent on beer or milk. What he needs to know is the prices of different feeds, the characteristics of different cows, the different prices . . . for milk . . ., the relative cost of hired labor and electrical machinery, and what his net earnings might be if he sold his cows and raised pigs instead.

By responding to such public signals as the costs and prices of what he buys and sells, the dairy farmer helps to make the whole economy fit together, to produce more or less what people want and to provide it more or less where and when they want it.

It is, of course, an enormous advantage that all the citizens of a country can collectively make the system operate without any one of them having to understand how it works. This becomes a disadvantage, however, when they are asked, as voters or as legislators, to pass judgement on schemes for consciously intervening in the system in order to improve its operation. *Ignorance of how the system does work then becomes a drawback serious enough to invite real trouble.*

---

[1] T. C. Schelling, *Micromotives and Macrobehavior* (New York: Norton & Co., 1978).

The distribution of income

The third important characteristic of a market economy is that it determines a *distribution* of the total income that it generates. People whose services are in heavy demand relative to supply, such as TV comedians and football players, earn large incomes, while people whose services are not in heavy demand relative to supply, possibly because they have low IQs or poor muscular co-ordination, earn very little and sometimes nothing.

The distribution of income produced by the market can be looked at in equilibrium or in disequilibrium. In equilibrium, similar efforts by similar people will be similarly rewarded everywhere in the economy. But dissimilar people are dissimilarly rewarded. In disequilibrium, windfall profits and losses abound, so that similar people making similar efforts of work or investment will be very dissimilarly rewarded. People in declining industries, areas and occupations suffer the punishment of windfall losses for no fault of their own. Those in expanding sectors earn the reward of windfall gains for no extra effort of their own. These rewards and punishments serve an important function of causing decentralized decision-takers to respond appropriately to changes in consumers' demands and in production costs. The 'advantage' in such a system is that individuals can take their own decisions about how to alter their behaviour when market conditions change; the 'disadvantage' is that temporary rewards and punishments are dealt out as a result of changes in market conditions that are beyond the control of the individuals affected.

Thinkers who support the market economy's distribution of income from an ethical point of view usually rely on an argument that says something like the following. (1) No society can be made equitable from the point of view of results. Just as the good man may die of a lingering and painful disease at fifty while the evil one dies peacefully in his bed at ninety-two, so may the latter earn a higher income than the former. (2) Income inequalities serve a function in helping the market system to work effectively and thus to produce a high total income. (3) It is more realistic, therefore, to look for some rough justice in opportunity rather than in results; attempts should be made, so they argue, to reduce the inequalities in starting points in the economic race rather than the inequalities in rewards once the race is run.

The product cycle

The motto of the market economy could be 'nothing is permanent'. New products appear continually while others disappear. At the early stage of a new product, total demand is fairly low, costs of production are high and many small firms are each trying to get ahead of their competitors by finding the twist that appeals to consumers or the technique that slashes their costs. Sometimes new products never get beyond that phase. They prove to be passing fads, or else they remain as high-priced items catering to a small demand; others, however, do become items of mass consumption. Successful firms in growing industries buy up, merge with, or otherwise eliminate their less successful rivals. Simultaneously their costs fall, due to scale economies. Competition drives prices down along with costs. Eventually at the mature stage it is often, although not invariably, the case that a few giant firms control the industry. They become large, conspicuous and important parts of the nation's economy. Sooner or later further changes bring up new products that erode the position of the established giants. Demand falls off, and unemployment occurs as the few remaining firms run into financial difficulties. A large, sick, declining industry appears to many as a national failure and disgrace. At any moment of time, however, industries can be found in all phases, from small firms in new industries to giant firms in declining industries. Large declining industries are as much a natural part of a healthy changing economy as are small growing ones.

The case for the market system

In defending market economies, economists have used two types of argument. The first makes up what can be called the intuitive case. This case, which is at least as old as Adam Smith, is based on variations on, and ramifications of, the theme that the market system is a co-ordinator of decentralized decision-taking. The case is intuitive in the sense that it is not laid out in equations leading to some mathematical, maximizing result. But it does follow from some hard reasoning, and it has been subjected to some searching intellectual probing. We shall first consider this case in brief outline. (In writing what follows I try to *present* the intuitive case, *not* to evaluate it.)

The intuitive case

The best co-ordinator Here the case is that the market system co-ordinates decisions on production and consumption better than any known alternative. Compared with the alternatives, the decentralized market system is more flexible and leaves more scope for personal adaptation at any moment of time and for quick adjustment to change over time. If, for example, a scarcity of oil raises its price, one individual can elect to leave his heating up high and economize on his driving, while another may wish to do the reverse. In order to obtain the same overall effect by non-price rationing, the authorities must force the same reduction in heating and driving on both individuals independent of their tastes, doctor's advice or other perceived needs.

Furthermore, as conditions change over time, prices change and decentralized decision-takers can react continuously, while government quotas, allocations and rationing schemes are much more cumbrous to adjust. The great value of the market is in providing automatic signals *as a situation develops*, so that all of the changes consequent on some major economic change do not have to be anticipated and allowed for by a body of central planners. Millions of adaptations to millions of changes in tens of thousands of markets are required every year; and it would be a Herculean task to anticipate these and plan for them all.

A producer of growth The flexibility of the market system is very powerful in producing growth by having every avenue for cost reductions or profit-earning innovations explored by private capital and decentralized decision-takers. It also is very powerful in allowing adaptations to change. The outlook is for major changes in resource availabilities in all economies over the next decades. New products, new inputs and new techniques will have to be devised if we are to cope with those vast changes that can already be foreseen, such as the exhaustion both of fossil fuels and of the enormous prehistoric water reservoirs that currently irrigate much of the farm land of the world's largest exporter of agricultural produce, the United States. A decentralized economy will be more responsive and inventive in producing the necessary adaptations than will a bureaucratic, centrally planned economy, provided that its taxation system does not eliminate the profits that are the incentive for these adaptations.

Impersonal decisions Another important part of the case for a market economy is that it tends to decentralize power and thus involves less coercion than does any other type of economy. However, although markets tend to diffuse power, they do not do so completely because large firms and unions clearly do have substantial economic power. This is a point that many existing defences tend to ignore. Probably the best attempt to make a case for the market while recognizing the existence of market power was made by Joseph Schumpeter. He argued that the economic power of particular firms and labour groups would not persist indefinitely. High profits, earned by monopolistic firms and unions, are the spur for others to invent cheaper or better substitutes that allow their suppliers to gain some of these profits. He called this process *creative destruction*, and provided many illustrations where a seemingly well-entrenched position of economic power was eroded by the invention of new products and processes introduced to gain some of an existing monopoly's profits.

Planned or command economies tend to put larger and more permanent concentrations of power into the hands of the central authorities than market economies put into the hands of large firms and unions. If markets are not to deal with allocation of people to jobs and of outputs to consumers, then some centralized coercive power is *necessary* to do the same job. Such power creates major incentives for bribery, corruption, and allocation according to the tastes of the central administrators. If at the going prices and wages there are not enough apartments or plum jobs to go around, the local bureaucrat will often allocate some to those who pay the largest bribe, some to those with religious beliefs, hairstyles or political views that he likes, and only the rest to those whose names come up on the waiting list.

Prices are related to costs Competition tends to force prices to bear a close relation to costs (including capital costs). Assuming that private costs to firms reflect social costs to society, there is an advantage in having relative prices approximately reflect relative costs because market choices are then made in the light of social opportunity costs. Firms will not choose methods that use more resources over methods that use less, and households will not choose commodities that use more resources to produce over commodities that use less, unless they value them correspondingly more at the margin.

Having relative prices reflect relative costs tends to be efficient in that it encourages consumers to choose the alternative that uses fewer of the nation's resources. Producing any output with the fewest possible of a nation's scarce resources clearly raises average living standards because it allows the maximum output to be produced.

The formal case

Professional economists wanted to be more precise about just what the market economy did so well and about the circumstances that tended to contribute to its success. In dealing with these very interesting questions, they developed the proof that an idealization of the market economy called perfect competition would lead, in equilibrium, to an optimum allocation of resources. This is an equilibrium situation which is efficient in the sense that it is impossible to make anyone better off without simultaneously making someone else worse off. We do not make that formal case here; it belongs in a course on welfare economics. (We did however discuss it briefly when we mentioned the optimality of perfect competition in Chapter 23.) What we will do, however, is to mention some of the implications for political economy of using this defence of the price system.

Political economy The proof of the optimality of perfect competition is certainly an enormous intellectual triumph. But basing the practical case for the market system on the formal proof of the optimality of perfect competition had some serious consequences. While professional economists went on studying and refining the model, and their academically bound graduate students went on learning it, the great bulk of their students were sent out into the world with an intellectual defence of the market economy that would not stand up to five minutes' rough handling by anyone who knew anything about the actual behaviour of real markets.[1]

What was obvious to most non-economists who were exposed to the economists' model was, among other things, that the model of consumers' behaviour on which the theory is based[2] is a dubious theory for defining the 'social good', since most people's welfare depends in important ways on variables excluded from the theory; that the case is based on equilibrium properties but says nothing about what will exist in any snapshot of the economy as it adjusts to continuous shocks; that the assumptions of perfect competition are not even remotely fulfilled in the world in which we live; and that many who would have accepted the proposition that market economies were superior to other forms of economic organization were not willing to join Voltaire's Dr Pangloss in holding that, whatever misery and injustice it produced, the market economy was the best of all possible economic worlds (i.e., the only *optimal* economy).

---

[1] The intellectual Odyssey whereby economists got to being unable to say much about the case for anything but this unreal abstraction is an interesting one. In the early twentieth century, the theory of the optimality of perfect competition was worked out under the Utilitarian assumption of measurable, additive utility. It was shown that for a given supply of resources, a perfectly competitive economy would lead to a higher money value of national income (which could be thought of as the sum of all the utilities produced by the economy and available for consumption by its citizens) than would any other economic organization. Second- and third-best organizations could be evaluated by comparing the national incomes that each would produce for the same given set of resources.

Then in the 1930s, English-speaking economics underwent the 'ordinalist revolution'. Economists found that all their positive theory about consumer behaviour could be derived by replacing the dubious assumption that everyone's utility from consumption could be calculated and added up, with the much weaker assumption that each individual could order alternative consumption sets and say which he or she preferred to which. From the point of view of positive economics, which predicts how consumers will react to changing market situations, getting rid of measurable utility was pure gain. For welfare economics, which investigates the formal case for alternative economic systems, the ordinalist revolution had more serious consequences.

The new welfare economics (founded on the ordinalist theory of indifference curves) could prove that perfect competition led to an optimum allocation of fixed quantities of productive resources. All other forms of organizing production led to non-optimal allocations of resources (in the sense that it would be possible to reallocate resources.so as to make at least one person better off without making anyone worse off). Perfect competition was optimal, or efficient, and everything else was non-optimal, or inefficient. The non-optimal set included 'socialist' economies, market economies that contained monopolies and oligopolies, and any other form of organizing production that was not, or did not effectively duplicate, perfect competition. Although every organization in the non-optimal set was inferior to perfect competition, the economies in the non-optimal set could *not* be ranked against each other.

(Economists did go on a long search for a social welfare function, or a set of compensation criteria, that would allow the results of various sub-optimal market organizations to be compared. The outcome of this long search was, however, that as long as only ordinal assumptions are made about consumer behaviour, the outcomes of non-optimal states cannot in general be ranked against each other. The only exceptions are certain obvious cases – where one economy produces less of all goods than another or where some very restrictive and unrealistic assumptions are made about people's tastes.)

[2] This is indifference-preference theory where the only economic variables about which a household cares are the quantities of goods and services it consumes itself. According to this theory, households do *not* care about how much they have relative to their neighbours at home or on the job; householders do *not* want to force their moral judgements and tastes on others by passing laws concerning prostitution, drugs, child pornography, etc!

All of this left the field open to persons who had no trouble showing that the assumptions of perfect competition were utterly unrealistic and went on to conclude incorrectly that there was, therefore, no case in favour of actual free-market economies. Clearly, if there is such a case favouring *actual* free-market economies over more centrally controlled ones, it must rely on the general intuitive case rather than the formal case proving the optimality of perfect competition.[1]

Piecemeal efficiency advice Perfect competition leads to an optimal allocation of resources. Price is everywhere equal to marginal cost and, provided that the private marginal cost incurred by producers adequately reflects the public marginal cost incurred by the society, then no reallocation of resources can

(i) increase the output of any commodity without simultaneously reducing the output of some other commodity, or

(ii) make any household better off without simultaneously making some other household worse off.

Making the economy perfectly competitive cannot, however, be a goal of practical economic policy. Economies of large scale dictate that in many industries perfect competition is impossible. Production with many small firms would thus be inefficient because each would be operating well to the left of the lowest point on its long-run average cost curve. Large firms would have lower costs than small firms, and hence in a free market would be able to undersell them. Large firms would thus grow at the expense of small firms until the industry ended up with only a few large firms (possibly only one), who were able to produce at or near their least-cost output.

If actual economic policy cannot make the economy optimal or efficient in the sense of satisfying the two conditions listed above, what can it try for? PIECEMEAL EFFICIENCY POLICY seeks to *reduce* inefficiencies. This means instituting any change that would make it *possible* for more of all goods to be produced or for every household in the economy to be made better off. Some complicated, subtle and largely unresolved issues are involved here and they cannot be explored short of giving a full course in, and critique of, welfare economics. In practice, however, piecemeal efficiency advice boils down to the *act of faith* that the direct, measurable efficiency effects of some policy are larger in total than the sum of the large number of individually small, indirect effects that the policy has on the rest of the economy.[2] Given this act of faith, efficiency advice is really saying that anything that brings the economy closer to perfect competition must make things better, in the sense defined above, while anything that makes it less like perfect competition must make things worse.

There is a strong intuitive argument in favour of making prices bear some relation to costs (as given above), but the 'scientific argument' that prices in any sector the government can control should be made exactly equal to marginal costs is on very shaky ground indeed. It is the strong

---

[1] Yet I would hazard the guess that the vast majority of graduate students of economics who are taught in the English language today are, as a matter of course, put through a rigorous training in proving all the theorems about the optimality of perfect competition, and left with the view that that is the intellectual basis of the case for the market economy; they are seldom given help in core courses in thinking about the real questions of more or less intervention into existing oligopolistic and oligopsonistic market economies.

[2] Twenty-five years ago it was shown that this was nothing more than an act of faith (R.G. Lipsey and K.J. Lancaster, 'The General Theory of Second Best', *Review of Economic Studies*, 24, no. 63, 1956–7). In general, if government policy can alter the behaviour of only one sector of the economy (piecemeal policy), making that sector follow the perfectly competitive rule of price equals marginal cost may raise the economy's overall efficiency or lower it or leave it unchanged. The basic reason is that the policy affects not only the behaviour of that sector but of all other sectors as well and in each of the other sectors, where perfect competition does not rule, the changes can improve or worsen efficiency.

intuitive argument that prices should bear some close relation to costs that probably accounts for the general popularity of piecemeal efficiency policies. For example, when capital had no price in the Soviet Union, planners had to allocate it and they had no criteria to decide where its use would most contribute to household satisfaction. For another example, when an ordinary consumer good that is costly to produce is provided free, this is very probably inefficient since scarce resources are being used to provide goods to which everyone gives a zero value at the margin.[1] The intuitive case is one thing, but the belief that we can tell with any precision which piecemeal changes in specific policies will increase efficiency, and which will reduce efficiency, is nothing more than an heroic act of faith.

Thus most people, especially those with experience of other economic systems, will accept that prices should bear some reasonably close relation to costs. But exactly what that relation should be, given that we do not live in a perfectly competitive economy, cannot be established with any pretence of scientific objectivity and precision. In what follows we shall outline efficiency policies as they are. In many cases – such as taking some account of smoke emitted by factories – the intuitive case is strong. But the case for a precise policy – such as to estimate the marginal cost to society of the smoke and add it by way of a tax to the producer's costs – is much less secure.

The case for intervention – 1: efficiency considerations

We now consider a number of major reasons for government intervention into the working of free markets. No list can be exhaustive, of course, but most of the main considerations are discussed below. Whenever market performance is judged to be faulty, it is the practice to speak of MARKET FAILURE. The word 'failure' in this context probably conveys the wrong impression. *Market failure does not mean that nothing good has happened, only that the best attainable outcome has not been achieved.*

As a result of market failure, many people believe it desirable to modify, restructure, complement or supplement the unrestricted workings of the market. There are several major sources of market failure, and it is important to understand how they arise. As we have seen, there are two somewhat different senses in which the phrase is used. One is the failure of the market system to achieve efficiency in the allocation of society's resources, the other is its failure to serve social goals other than efficiency. We shall discuss both.

Externalities

Cost, as economists define it, concerns the value of resources used up in the process of production. According to the opportunity-cost principle, value is the benefit the resources would produce in the best alternative use. But who decides what resources are used and what is their opportunity cost? When a timber company buys a forest, it perhaps regards the alternative to cutting the trees this year as cutting them five years hence. But citizens in the area may value the forest as a nature sanctuary or a recreation area. The firm values the forest for the trees; the local residents may value the trees for the forest. The two values need not be the same.

These differences in point of view lead to the important distinction between private cost and

---

[1] Even this is not a certainty since it is easy to concoct examples where, given that the government cannot control all prices, the second-best price of a commodity the government can control is negative.

social cost. PRIVATE COST measures the value of the best alternative uses of the resources available to the producer.

As we noted in Chapter 17, private cost is usually measured by the market price of the resources that the firm uses. SOCIAL COST measures the value of the best alternative uses of the resources that is available to the whole society.

For some resources the best measure of the social cost may be exactly the same as the private cost: the price set by the market may well reflect the value of the resources in their best alternative use. For other resources, as will soon be clear, social cost may differ sharply from private cost. Discrepancies between private and social cost lead to market failure from the social point of view. The reason is that efficiency requires that prices cover social cost, but private producers, adjusting to private costs, will neglect those elements of social cost that are not included in private costs. When an element of (social) cost is not part of a private firm's profit and loss calculation, it is *external* to its decision-making process.

Discrepancies between social and private cost lead to EXTERNALITIES, which are the costs or benefits of a transaction that are incurred or received by members of the society but are not taken into account by the parties to the transaction. They are also called THIRD-PARTY EFFECTS because parties other than the two primary participants in the transaction (the buyer and the seller) are affected. Externalities arise in many different ways.

Some externalities are beneficial. When I paint my house, I enhance my neighbours' view and the value of their property. When an Einstein or a Rembrandt gives the world a discovery or a work of art whose worth is far in excess of what he is paid to produce it, he confers an external benefit. Educating my children may make them better citizens and thus benefit third parties, even if they do not prove to be latter-day Nightingales or Mozarts. Individuals will tend to engage in too little of activities that produce beneficial externalities because they bear all of the costs while others reap part of the benefits.

Other externalities are harmful. We consider several examples immediately below. In the meantime we observe that the unregulated market will generally lead to too much production of a good conferring a harmful externality because its producer will ignore these additional social costs.

Micro efficiency – macro inefficiency Labour markets have evolved bargaining arrangements that tend to hold wages rigid while allowing employment to fluctuate in the face of normal cyclical variations in aggregate demand. It has been argued that such arrangements may be optimal from the point of a single firm or group of workers. This is still subject to debate but, whatever the outcome of that micro-debate, it is clear that from a macro point of view such arrangements are inefficient. They give rise to large cyclical reductions in output and employment which are never efficient because, if they were removed, *everyone* could be better off.

Pollution A major source of differences between private cost and social cost occurs when firms use resources they do not regard as scarce. This is a characteristic of most examples of pollution. When a paper mill produces pulp for the world's newspapers, more people are affected than its suppliers, employees and customers. Its water-discharged effluent hurts the fishing boats that ply nearby waters, and its smog makes many areas less attractive, thereby reducing the tourist revenues that local hotel operators and boat renters can expect. The firm neglects these because its profits are not affected by the external effects of its actions, while they are affected by how much paper it produces.

This example, and hundreds more, concern the production of goods and services by private firms. They also concern the use of society's basic resources such as timber, coal, labour, iron ore, water and air. Much of the pollution connected with production is not an accidental event, as is the periodic breaking up of oil tankers off the world's beaches or the blowout of oil in the North Sea. It is the result of calculated decisions as to what, and how, to produce or consume.

Common-property resources The world's oceans once teemed with fish, but today a worldwide fish shortage is upon us. There seems to be no doubt that overfishing has caused the problem.

Fish are one example of what is called a COMMON-PROPERTY RESOURCE. No one owns the oceans' fish until they are caught. The world's international fishing grounds are common property for all fishermen. If by taking more fish one fisherman reduces the catch of other fishermen, he does not count this as a cost, but it is a cost to society.

Assume, as is true of most fishing grounds, that there is congestion. Not only does each additional boat that fishes the area catch less than each previous boat (declining marginal product), but each additional boat lowers the catch of all other boats (declining average product). A social planner adding boats to the fishing ground would go on increasing the size of the fleet until the value of the marginal product (the value of the net *addition* to the total catch) just equalled the cost of operating the marginal boat. Interestingly enough, this is also what a monopolist who owned the fishing ground would do. But the free market will not produce that result. Private fishermen will go on entering the area as long as they can show a profit, i.e., as long as the value of *their own catch* at least covers their cost of operation. Thus private boats will be added to the fleet until the value of the *average product* per boat has been driven to zero. As Figure 17.1 on page 213 shows, the quantity of resources devoted to an activity is larger when *AP* must be driven down to some particular level than when only *MP* must be driven to that level (to apply Figure 17.1 to the present case, read fishing boats instead of quantity of labour on the horizontal axis of the figures). *The free market always leads to the over-exploitation of a common property resource with many of the last units of productive resources used having a marginal product well below their cost.*

Congestion Collisions between private planes and commercial airliners are headline news when they occur. They cannot occur unless *both* planes are in the air; this is what creates the externality. Suppose that the probability of a mid-air plane crash is roughly proportional to the number of planes in the air. Suppose too that I have the choice of flying my own plane or taking a commercial airliner that has 100 of its 150 seats filled. In choosing to fly by myself, I decide that the slight extra risk to me of a mid-air collision is more than balanced by the extra convenience of my own plane.

What I have neglected is the social cost of my action: the increased risk for every other person in the air on my route of flight that results from one more plane in the air. Since I do not consider other travellers' increased risk, my private decision may have been the wrong social decision, wrong in the sense that if all travellers got together they would willingly pay me enough to persuade me to take the commercial trip and so reduce their risk. (Also if the plane has an empty seat the social cost of my filling it is very small – much less than what I will have to pay for my ticket, which is an added incentive for me to take the 'wrong' decision of travelling in my own plane.)

Neglect of future consequences of present actions When private producers ignore or undervalue future effects on others, they neglect an externality. A business facing bankruptcy tomorrow may be motivated to cheat on safety standards in order to cut costs today, even if it would hurt the firm's reputation in the long term and impose heavy future costs on others. It may also be motivated to exploit, for an immediate quick profit, a resource that would be worth much more tomorrow. It would not pay to do this if capital markets were perfect so that the resource could be sold to someone else for the present value of its future profit. But a businessman on the edge of bankruptcy may be too desperate, too ignorant or just not have enough time to do this.

Asymmetric information   The above discussion was based on possibilities – ignorance, desperation, lack of time – that are omitted from the classical theory of these issues where perfect knowledge and zero costs of making any transaction are generally assumed.

An important branch of recent research turns around the issues that are raised when buyers and sellers in some market have, of necessity, different information. There are still many unsettled issues in this research, and much doubt about which results are general and which are specific to some of the simple models studied. But it may be worthwhile outlining a few of the interesting cases that arise.

The market for lemons: Here a lemon refers not to a citrus fruit, but instead is Professor George Akerlof's term for a car of less than average quality. Any particular vintage of car will include a certain proportion of 'lemons'. Purchasers of new cars of a certain vintage take a chance on their car turning out to be a lemon. Those who are unlucky to get a lemon are more likely to resell their car early than are those who are lucky to get a quality car. Hence in the used-car market there will be a disproportionately large number of lemons for sale. Thus buyers of used cars are right to be suspicious of why the car is for sale while salespeople are quick to invent reasons. ('It was owned by a little old lady who only drove it on Sundays'.) Because it is very difficult for a buyer to identify a lemon before buying it, he or she will be prepared to buy a used car only at a price low enough to offset the increased probability that it is a lemon. This, Akerlof maintains, explains why one-year-old cars typically sell for a discount much larger than can be explained by the physical depreciation that occurs in one year. The prices at which these sales take place are not optimal in the sense that, if all buyers of used cars had the same knowledge as the sellers, a set of prices could be established where buyers and sellers were better off on average than they are at the actual market prices.

Moral hazard: Moral hazard arises whenever someone's superior knowledge leads him to behave differently than he or she would if knowledge were perfect. For example, people taking out insurance almost always know more about themselves as individual insurance risks than do their insurance companies. The company can try to identify the risk by setting up broad categories based on relevant variables such as age and occupation and then varying the rate charged across categories. But there must always be much variability of risk within any one category. Someone who knows he is a high risk within his category is offered a bargain and will be led to take out more car, health, life, fire, etc., insurance than he otherwise would. Someone who knows she is a low risk pays more than her own risk really warrants and she is motivated to take out less insurance than she otherwise would.

Principal-agent issues: Another series of intriguing problems arises out of the relations between a principal (e.g., an employer) and his agent (e.g., the employee). It is clear for example that owners would like their managers to maximize the firm's profits. It is also clear that managers have other motivation and there is some evidence that in large corporations they are as much concerned with their own consumption (of what the company accounts for as costs) as about the firm's profits. This is a failure of the market, and the issue is how can the agent be motivated to do what the principal wants him to do? (Profit-sharing schemes are an obvious possibility in this case.)

Market imperfections

A second major source of market failure is market imperfections. If actual markets always behave as do markets in the theory of perfect competition, the economic system would behave perfectly. Unfortunately, actual behaviour is often far from what would occur under perfect competition.

Imperfections affecting factor behaviour If factors are relatively immobile, the supply will tend to be inelastic in the short run, and even large increases in the price offered may induce only small factor movements. Unions can also put up substantial barriers to the movement of labour. For example, they can limit membership and simultaneously insist on closed shops.

Markets may also be poor allocators of labour among possible uses if labour is ignorant of the signals being provided by the market. Signals do not work if they are not received. Before dismissing this imperfection as trivial, ask yourself if you have any clear idea of the expected lifetime income of a person following the subject of study you have chosen and that of persons following the subject your friends have chosen. Also, do you know enough to be able to compare the lifetime earnings of the few people who are unusually successful with the earnings of those who have only average success in each of the occupations?

Imperfections affecting firm behaviour Profit-maximization in a world of perfect competition makes firms into passive adjusters who follow market signals without exerting any personal pressure on the outcome. When we depart from perfect competition and/or profit-maximizing behaviour, firms achieve the power to interfere with the behaviour of the market. Profit-maximizing monopoly presents one pure case. Monopoly power prevents resources from moving in response to market signals. A rise in demand for a monopolist's product will cause a rise in the monopolist's profits. In a perfectly competitive industry this would lead to an increase in resources allocated to the production of this good until profits fell to zero, but if the monopolist can restrict entry into his industry, no such resource reallocation will occur except as the monopolist finds it profitable to increase his own output.

If the firm is not concerned with profit-maximization, the market mechanism may not work as well as described by our theory. A rise in demand will not even necessarily be met by a rise in output of the existing monopolist if he is not a profit-maximizer.

Imperfections affecting consumer behaviour Economists usually do not pass judgement on the tastes of consumers. A market system is said to work if it responds to consumers' tastes whatever the nature of the tastes. But the market will not work effectively if consumers are misinformed about the products they buy. Lack of correct consumer information can be an important cause of market failure.

Collective consumption goods Certain goods or services, if they provide benefits to anyone, necessarily provide them to a large group of people. Such goods are called COLLECTIVE CONSUMPTION GOODS or PUBLIC GOODS. National defence is a prime example. If we have an adequate defence establishment, it protects us all. It protects you, even if you do not care to 'buy' any of it. The quantity of national defence to be provided must be decided collectively, and there is no market where you can buy more or less of it than your neighbour.

There are many other examples. The beautification of a city provides a service to all residents and visitors. A barrage that protects a city from a flood is also a collective consumption good, as is a storm-warning system. Another important example is police protection. If a police force reduces the number of crimes, everyone gains. In a market system, even if you did not pay to have the police watch your house, you would gain from the fact that your neighbour did.

In general, market systems cannot compel payment for a public good, since there is no way to prevent a person from receiving the services of the good if he refuses to pay for it. Only governments, through their power to tax, can compel payments by all. Indeed, it is the existence of collective consumption goods that necessitates putting some of our production into government hands and prevents the government from selling everything it produces on the free market just as any other firm does (and as the government does with postal services but does not, and cannot, do with military and police services).

The costs of collecting revenue A good that is not a collective consumption good will still not be produced privately if the cost of collecting revenue from individual consumers is prohibitive. Here it is not the nature of the good but the absence of a low-cost, private mechanism to collect revenue that leads to market failure.

Consider an example. Suppose motorists in a metropolitan area are willing to pay to have a high-speed urban motorway system leading into and out of town. Suppose that there are enough people willing to pay 6 pence a mile to cover the costs of building such a road system, but that different groups of them want to use different sections of the system. A private company would find it profitable to build and operate the road if it could collect 6 pence a mile from everybody willing to pay that much. But if it must build a toll house at every entrance and exit to the road in order to collect this money, the costs of the system would be increased and the venture might seem an unprofitable one. Intra-urban motorways with many access points and many short-journey travellers are often unsuitable for private ventures, because the cost of collecting tolls is too high. It is no accident that in countries where privately built toll roads are common, virtually all toll roads are *inter-urban* roads which require few access points and where the average journey is a long one.

The case for intervention – 2: distribution

The second major reason for government intervention to alter the outcome of free-market processes is because of concern over the distribution of income. General reasons are, first, a desire to put a minimum on everyone's income – to avoid extreme deprivation and even starvation – and, second, to narrow the overall range of inequality of income produced by the market. With the second reason, efficiency and equity considerations come into conflict and some compromise has to be struck. A strong case can be made on philosophical grounds that the only just distribution of income is an equal one. (Not everyone accepts this case but it is nonetheless a strong one.) But economic theory predicts and evidence confirms that, without an income incentive, people will not be motivated to take on harder, riskier or more unpleasant jobs. Communist states that tried to achieve more equality of income distribution, quickly found that they had to draw a line that stopped well short of full income equality in order to provide economic incentives for the efficient allocation of labour and capital.

A third reason is to pursue narrow sectoral lines of self-interest with the help of the state. Throughout history, various sectoral groups of either firms or workers have found that they could use the state to alter the distribution of income in their favour. Creating a monopoly or a monopsony of firms or workers' organizations, giving particularly favourable tax or regulatory treatment to that group or unfavourable treatment to its competition, are commonly used techniques for granting the government's favour to particular groups. These, and other similar policies, are abuses of the state's redistributive powers in the sense that the redistribution does not follow any generally accepted ideas of social justice but instead is just an expression of narrow self-interest on the part of the favoured groups. The reason for mentioning this third reason for redistributive policies is that it is clearly operative in all countries and observers need to guard against the fallacious belief that all state redistributive policies are in pursuit of generally accepted principles of social justice. Some are, but others represent nothing more than the pursuit of special gain by particular self-interest groups.

The case for intervention – 3: the protection of value systems

Exclusive reliance on markets, even if they perform efficiently with respect to allocation of resources among competing uses, may lead to the neglect of other goals that seem important to members of society. Individuals who value these other goals will consider their neglect by the market system as a case of market failure. Consider four examples.

The protection of the individual from the actions of others In economics the household is assumed to be the basic decision-taking unit. We must not forget that most households contain several persons and that the process of making a choice within the household is a political one. Whose desires are to be favoured and by how much in taking the purchasing decisions for the household? One example should suffice to show how important this point is. In an unhindered free market the adult members of the household will take decisions about how much education to buy, and thereby exert a profound effect on the lives of their children. A selfish parent may buy no education, while an egalitarian one may buy the same quantity for all his children. The central authorities may interfere in this choice both to protect the child and to ensure that some of the scarce educational resources are unequally distributed according to intelligence rather than wealth. Most governments force all households to educate their children and we provide strong inducements, through student grants, for the more able to consume much more education than either they or their parents might have voluntarily selected if they had to pay the whole cost themselves. The latter is done probably because of a divergence between social and private costs, but the former is done in the belief that the head of the household should not have perfect freedom to take decisions that affect the welfare of other members of the household, particularly when they are minors.

The protection of the individual from his or her own actions In the case of education, society interferes to protect children from possibly harmful decisions taken on their behalf by others. In other cases the state seeks to protect individuals against themselves. Laws prohibiting opium and other hard drugs and laws prescribing the wearing of seatbelts in motorcars protect individuals against their own ignorance or shortsightedness. Arguments for and against such policies go well beyond economics. Advocates of such laws say, for example, that this is one way of educating people about what is in their own best interests. Opponents often argue that it is a basic tenet of a free society that the individual must be assumed to be the best judge of his or her own interests and that the individual's right to do what he or she thinks best, even to take what may seem to others to be reckless risks of life and limb, should be interfered with only if the behaviour has serious adverse effects on others.[1]

Intervention by the government to protect the individual from himself or herself is called PATERNALISM. There is no question that much actual intervention into the market has paternalistic motives: the central authorities feel they know better than the individual citizen what is in that citizen's own best interest. There is great debate about the pros and cons of paternalistic intervention and the debate will be considered further in the next chapter.

The existence of social obligations　In a market system, if you can pay for something, you can have it. If you have to clean your house and if you can persuade someone else to do the job for you in return for £10, presumably both parties to the transaction are better off: you would prefer to part with £10 rather than clean the house yourself and your cleaner prefers £10 to not cleaning your house. Normally we do not interfere with people's ability to negotiate such mutually advantageous contracts.

Most people do not feel this way, however, about activities which are regarded as social obligations. A prime example is military service. At times and places in which military service is compulsory, contracts similar to the one between the housewife and her cleaner could also be struck. Some persons faced with the obligation to do military service could no doubt pay enough to persuade others to do their turn of service for them. By exactly the same argument as we used above, we can presume that both parties will be better off if they are allowed to negotiate such a trade. But such contracts are usually prohibited. Why? Because there are values other than those that can be expressed in a market. In times when it is necessary, military service by all healthy males is usually held to be an obligation independent of their tastes, wealth, influence or social position. It is felt that everyone *ought* to do this service, and trades between willing traders are prohibited.

Compassion　A free-market system rewards certain groups and penalizes others. The workings of the market may be stern, even cruel; consequently, it may seem humane to intervene. Should unproductive farmers be starved off the farm? Should men be forced to bear the full burden of their misfortune if, through no fault of their own, they lose their jobs? Indeed, even if they lose their jobs through their own fault, should they and their families have to bear the whole burden, which may include starvation? Should the ill and aged be thrown on the mercy of their families? What if they have no families? Should small businessmen have to compete with chain stores and discount houses? A great many government policies are concerned with modifying the distribution of income

---

[1] There are many other arguments. Advocates of seatbelts and other compulsory road-safety regulations claim that disabled survivors of 'unnecessary' accidents may become public charges and that this gives the state a right to prevent such injuries from occurring. Opponents reply that this slim possibility is not enough to justify governmental interference with individual freedom.

that results from such things as where one starts, how able one is, how lucky one is and how one fares in the free-market world.

Policies under this heading clearly affect the distribution of income, and, if we want, we can classify them as redistributive policies. But the motivation is sometimes different. For example, even if the distribution of income were unaffected, we might for social reasons want to encourage, or discourage, small shops or small farms as against large shops and large farms. Of course we care about the distribution of income but we also care about other aspects of our society, and we often intervene in its economic behaviour in pursuit of social goals other than the distribution of income.

Optimal intervention

We have seen that members of the society may be concerned with efficiency, income distribution and a host of other goals such as the preservation of particular ways of life and a concern to preserve the individual's freedom to act and to be responsible for his or her own actions. Multiple goals often involve conflicts, and require choices. The decision on when and where and to what extent to interfere with the free-market system must require value judgements about the relative values to be placed on alternative policy goals whenever they come into conflict. The decisions are likely to be better by almost any criterion if they are informed by a knowledge of their economic consequences.

The spirit of our times has led many to treat all problems of market failure, such as pollution, as a national scandal and perhaps even as an imminent crisis of survival. The problems in fact run the whole range from threats to human survival down to minor nuisances. Virtually all activity leaves some waste product behind it. To say that all pollution must be removed, whatever the cost, is certainly to try for the impossible and probably to get a vast commitment of society's scarce resources to some projects which will yield a low utility. If by emitting smoke a factory is appreciably lowering the life expectancy of those in surrounding communities, it is clearly worthwhile investing a great deal in purifying the effluent. But suppose that the smoke from another factory is not a health hazard, but does smell bad. Further assume that the 10,000 local residents affected by this pollution would be willing to pay on average no more than £10 a year to be rid of the smell. The social cost of the present smoke emission is thus £100,000 a year. Say that the firm was forced to adopt an alternative disposal method at a cost of £500,000 a year. This means that £500,000 worth of society's scarce resources will be used to create a result that the society values at only £100,000. Because these resources could have produced other goods valued at £500,000, there is an overall loss of £400,000.

This example points to an important problem: control of pollution and other externalities is costly; it makes sense where the benefits have a higher value than the cost. Pollution control, as with other services, may have great benefits at first and then run into diminishing returns. Instances of the need for external control where social costs are great (e.g., control of nuclear wastes) are obvious and dramatic; in other cases social costs are more nearly equal to private costs.

Which activities to prohibit and which to modify, which to clean up after and which to tolerate, are important choices. The economist can help those who have to make these choices by carefully designating costs and benefits. It is important to note that the choices made may vary among communities and over time. As a society grows wealthier, the value placed on improvements in the quality of life relative to material gains may rise. Poor communities may welcome new industries for the employment and tax revenues they bring, while richer communities may seek to remove these same industries in order to avoid the unpleasant externalities they bring.

33

Aims and objectives of government policy[1]

The central authorities play a major role in all of the world's economies. The nature and amount of intervention differ greatly from country to country. Britain is somewhere in the middle between the extremes to be found in such command economies as the USSR and China and in such relatively free-market economies as the USA and Brazil. Even in the latter countries, however, the economic activities of the central authorities are widespread, and many individual markets are largely controlled. In this chapter we shall take a brief look at government microeconomic policy, a topic that requires a whole book for adequate coverage. We shall look first at the major tools available to the central authorities and then at the goals of policy, relating the tools to the goals.

The tools of policy

The central authorities have three main tools with which to implement their economic policies: rules and regulations, taxation and expenditure. We shall consider each of these in turn.

Rules

Rules pervade economic activities. Shop hours and working conditions are regulated. Employees of British firms have the right under the 1978 Employment Protection Act to have a closed shop set up on their request. Discrimination between labour services provided by males and by females is illegal in the UK and in a large number of other countries. There is growing pressure in the US to make termination of employment solely on account of age illegal. Children cannot be served alcoholic drinks. They must attend school in most countries and be inoculated against certain communicable diseases in many. Laws prohibit people from selling or using certain drugs. Prostitution is prohibited in many societies, although it usually takes place between a willing buyer and a willing seller. In many countries you are forced to purchase insurance for the damage you might do to others with your private motorcar, even if you don't want to carry insurance. In some countries a person who offers goods for sale cannot refuse to sell them to someone just because he does not like the customer's colour or dress. There are rules against fraudulent advertising and the sale of sub-standard, adulterated or poisonous foods. In some countries, such as the United States, anyone who

---

[1] Factual and institutional background for this chapter can be found in Harbury and Lipsey, Chapter 6.

wants to can purchase a wide variety of firearms ranging from pistols to machine guns. In other countries, such as the United Kingdom, it is extremely difficult for a private citizen to obtain a gun.

Most business practices are controlled by rules and prohibitions. In many countries agreements among oligopolistic firms to fix prices or divide up markets are illegal. The mere existence of monopoly is also often outlawed; monopoly firms are then broken up into independent competing firms. When the cost advantages of monopoly resulting from scale economies are considerable, the prices a monopolistic firm can charge and the return it can earn on its capital investment are often regulated. The reality of such control is beyond question; its advisability and its effectiveness are subject to substantial debate.

Minimum-wage laws An interesting case of rule-setting occurs when governments legislate minimum and maximum prices at which goods and services can be sold on the open market. We studied many such cases in Chapter 10. Let us now expand that discussion to deal with one of the most important rules governing market prices, the setting of minimum wages.

For a large fraction of all employment covered by the law, the minimum wage is below the actual market wage. Where this is true, the wage is said to be not 'binding'. But many workers are in occupations or industries where the free-market wage rate would be below the legal minimum, and there the minimum wage is said to be binding, or effective. Whether minimum wages are effective is not always easy to determine. For example, one response of employers to minimum-wage legislation might be to reduce non-wage benefits so that total compensation remains constant.

Minimum wages are controversial. To the extent that they are effective, they raise the wages of employed workers. But, as our analysis in Chapter 10 indicated, an effective price floor may well lead to a market surplus – in this case, unemployment. Let us see to what extent this prediction applies to the minimum wage.

There are two main cases to consider. First, the minimum wage may be set in a market that is otherwise quite competitive, with many buyers and many sellers. Second, the wage may be set in a market where a few large buyers, who are able to exploit their monopsonistic position, buy from many unorganized sellers of labour services.

Effective minimum wages in a competitive market: Here the results are precisely the same as those for a union setting a wage in a competitive industry, as shown in Figure 27.3 on page 378:

> **The minimum wage will increase the wages of those employed, decrease employment, increase unemployment, and create incentives to evade the law by working below the legal minimum wage.**

Effective minimum wages in a monopsonistic market: Here the results are the same as those for a union setting a wage in a monopsonistic market, as shown in Figure 27.5 on page 379:

> **The minimum wage, when set at the competitive level, will raise both wages and employment.**

In this case the minimum wage can protect the unorganized worker against monopsony power in the same way that a union can. It is possible, however, that minimum wages will be set above the competitive level. If so, while wages of those employed will be raised, no prediction can be made as to whether employment will increase or decrease compared to the monopsony level. (It depends both on how high the wage is and on the shapes of the curves.)

Empirical knowledge: A great deal of empirical work has been done on the actual effect of minimum wages on employment. Some unemployment is caused by minimum wages, particularly among youths. It is also clear that some new employment is created in monopsonistic industries. Most studies show that on balance employment is lower and unemployment higher as a result of minimum wages.

The employment effect is, however, only one element in deciding whether, overall, minimum wages are beneficial or harmful. It is clear that minimum-wage laws raise the incomes of many workers at the very lowest levels of employment. Because union 'wage-structures' maintain differentials between skill classes, an increase in minimum wages also raises wages in a large number of occupations that are already above the minimum. The issue of possible harmful effects of wages that are too high is raised again in Chapter 46.

Taxation

Taxes are of major importance in the pursuit of many government policies. They provide the funds to finance expenditure, but they are also used as tools in their own right for a wide range of purposes including altering the distribution of income.

Direct and indirect taxes Taxes are divided into two broad groups depending on whether persons or things are taxed. DIRECT TAXES are levied directly on persons and vary with the status of the taxpayer. The most important direct tax is the income tax. The personal income tax falls sometimes on the income of households and sometimes separately on each member of the household. It varies with the size and source of the taxpayer's income and various other characteristics laid down by law, such as marital status and number of dependents. Joint stock companies also pay taxes on their income. This is a direct tax both in the legal sense that the company is an individual in the eyes of the law and in the economic sense that the company is owned by its shareholders so that a tax on the company is a tax on them. An expenditure tax (as advocated for the UK by the royal commission headed by Nobel-prize-winning economist James Meade) is also a direct tax. It is based on what a person spends, rather than on what he or she earns, and has exemptions that are specific to the individual taxpayer. A poll tax, which is simply a lump-sum tax levied on each person, is also a direct tax. Inheritance taxes, based on the amount of money an individual inherits from someone else's estate, are also direct taxes.

The rate of tax is the tax expressed as a percentage of the thing on which it is levied. The rate of income tax, for example, is a percentage of the income on which it is levied. It is important to distinguish between average and marginal rates. The AVERAGE RATE OF TAX paid by a person is that person's total tax divided by his or her income. The MARGINAL RATE OF TAX is the rate he or she would pay on another unit of taxable income.

An INDIRECT TAX is levied on a thing, and is paid by an individual by virtue of association with that thing. Local rates on property are indirect taxes. They vary with the value of the real estate and are paid by either the owner or the occupier of the real estate, independent of his or her circumstances. Taxes and stamp duties on the transfer of assets from one owner to another are also indirect taxes since they depend on the circumstances of the transaction, not on those of the person making it. Estate duties, which depend on the size of the estate and not on the circumstances of the beneficiaries, are an indirect tax. By far the most pervasive and important of the indirect taxes are taxes on the sale of currently produced commodities. These taxes are called excise taxes when they are levied on manufacturers, and sales taxes when they are levied on the sale of goods from retailer to consumer. The EEC countries levy a comprehensive tax of this sort on all transactions whether at the retail, wholesale or manufacturer's level. This tax is called the VALUE ADDED TAX (VAT).[1] It is an indirect tax because it depends on the value of what is made and sold, not on the wealth or income of the maker. Thus two self-employed fabric designers, each with a 'value added' of £8,000 in terms of designs produced and sold, would pay the same VAT even if one had no other source of income while the other was independently wealthy.

Indirect taxes may be levied in two basic ways. An AD VALOREM tax is a percentage of the value of the transaction on which it is levied. An 8 per cent retail sales tax would mean, for example, that the retail firm had to charge a tax of 8 per cent of the value of everything it sold. A SPECIFIC or PER UNIT TAX is a tax expressed as so much per unit, independently of its price. Taxes on cinema and theatre tickets, and on each gallon of petrol and alcohol independent of the price at which they are produced or sold, are specific taxes.

Shifting and incidence The INCIDENCE of a tax refers to who bears it. The SHIFTING of a tax refers to the passing of its incidence from the person who initially pays it to someone else. Consider an example in which a tax is placed on every new painting sold by its painter. If painters raise the prices of their paintings by the full amount of the tax and (miraculously) continue to sell as many paintings as before, the incidence of the tax shifts entirely from the painters to the collectors. More commonly, as we shall see, the final incidence of a tax falls partly on the person who initially pays it and partly on others.

To illustrate tax-shifting, we consider a tax placed on the sellers of a commodity that is sold in a competitive market. The tax must be paid by producers, so as far as they are concerned it adds to their costs: as well as paying all their factors of production they must also pay the tax to the government. The tax adds to each producer's costs and shifts its marginal cost curve upwards by the rate of tax. But if each producer's marginal cost curve shifts upwards by the amount of the tax, then the market supply curve, which is the sum of all firms' marginal cost curves, also shifts upwards by the amount of the tax. This is shown in Figure 33.1 by the shift upwards from S_1 to S_2 caused by a tax that is a proportion of each firm's costs. Although the supply curve shifts upwards by the full amount of the tax (shown by T in the Figure), the price rises by less, from p_1 to p_2 in the Figure. This is because the demand curve slopes downwards. If the price rose by T, the market would not clear because consumers would want to buy less, while sellers, who were passing the whole tax on through a higher price, would want to sell an unchanged amount.

Instead, therefore, the tax lowers the price sellers receive, by $p_1 - p_3$. So the tax is shared between them.

When the demand curve slopes downward and the supply curve slopes upward, the

---

[1] Value added is the difference between the value of factor services and materials that the firm purchases as inputs and the value of its output. It therefore represents the value that a firm adds by virtue of its own activities. See pages 510–11 for a more extended discussion of the concept.

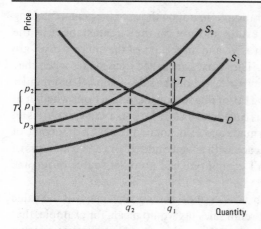

Fig. 33.1 The shifting and incidence of an indirect tax

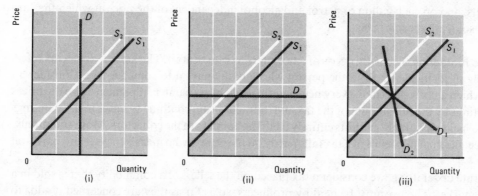

Fig. 33.2 The effect of a tax on price and quantity, given demand curves of various elasticities

imposition of a tax will raise the price paid by consumers and lower the price received by producers, in both cases by less than the amount of the tax.

Figure 33.2, like Figure 33.1, shows two supply curves, representing before-tax and after-tax situations. It combines them with different demand curves. Part (i) shows a perfectly inelastic demand curve, part (ii) a perfectly elastic one, and part (iii) two intermediate cases. In the case of the perfectly inelastic curve, the equilibrium price increases by the full amount of the tax; in the case of the perfecty elastic curve, the equilibrium price is unchanged in spite of the shift in the supply curve. In the intermediate cases we see that the steeper the demand curve, the more the price rises. This suggests the following general prediction:

The incidence of an indirect tax on a commodity sold in a competitive market falls more on buyers and less on sellers the more inelastic is the demand.

Consider the common sense of the above result. The more inelastic is the demand, the less willing are buyers to cut their purchases in response to a price rise. So the price rises until they are paying most of the tax and producers are motivated to sell almost as much as they were selling before the tax was levied.

Progressivity How does the amount of a tax vary with the taxpayers' incomes? The general term for the relation between income and the percentage of income paid by a tax is PROGRESSIVITY. A REGRESSIVE TAX takes a smaller percentage of people's incomes the larger is their income. A PROGRESSIVE TAX takes a larger percentage of people's incomes the larger is their income. A PROPORTIONAL TAX is the boundary case between the two: it takes the same percentage of income from everyone. Taxes on food, for example, tend to be regressive because the proportion of income spent on food tends to fall as income rises. Taxes on alcoholic spirits tend to be progressive since the proportion of income spent on spirits tends to rise with income. Taxes on beer, on the other hand, are regressive.

Progressivity can be defined for any one tax or for the tax system as a whole. Different taxes have different characteristics. Inevitably some will be progressive and some regressive. The impact of a tax system as a whole on high, middle and low-income groups is best judged by looking at the progressivity of the whole set of taxes taken together. For example, income taxes are progressive in all countries and steeply progressive in the UK and Sweden. The whole tax system is also progressive in these two countries, but much less so than one would guess from studying only the income-tax rates. This is because much revenue is raised by indirect taxes, all of which are less progressive than income taxes and some of which are regressive.

Expenditure

The value of total government expenditure on goods and services in the UK was just over 20 per cent of national income in 1980. If we include transfer payments, the figure was somewhat in excess of 40 per cent. In assessing the impact of government expenditure, this distinction is extremely important. Some government expenditures are in return for goods and services that count as part of current output – i.e., as part of the national product. They create a claim by the central authorities on the economy's factors of production. When the government purchases more factors of production to produce goods and services in the public sector of the economy, there are fewer factors available to produce output in the private sector. The remainder of government expenditure goes for TRANSFER PAYMENTS, which are payments *not* made in return for any contribution to current output. Old-age pensions, unemployment insurance benefits, welfare payments, disability payments and a host of other expenditures made by the modern welfare state are all transfer payments. They do not add to current marketable output; they merely transfer the power to purchase output from those who provide the money (usually taxpayers) to those who receive it. Transfer payments do not represent a claim by the government on real productive resources.[1] Revenue must nonetheless be raised to pay them.

---

[1] It does, of course, take resources to make the transfers, but the salaries of civil servants who do this are counted as an expenditure on current output. Thus *providing* transfer payments is a part of current national product, while the transfers themselves are not.

Goals of policy

Governments use the tools of economic policy to intervene in the markets of the economy for many reasons. The economist's traditional view of economic policy treats the government as a passive agent that intervenes only to correct clearly identified shortcomings of the market. More recently economists have become increasingly aware that this view of government leaves much observed behaviour unexplained. Theories are now being developed that allow governments their own objectives, analogous to those of firms and households. In a simple example of such a theory we might assume that households seek to maximize their utility, that firms seek to maximize their profits and governments seek to maximize the votes they get in the next election. In this theory, the government would favour a scheme that would reduce economic efficiency and lower standards of living in ten years' time but was popular with voters now.

This is no doubt a rather simplistic view, but it is less so than the old view that the central authorities have no utility function of their own but merely do whatever has been shown to be good for the economic well-being of the populace. Many economists now feel that the analysis of government behaviour will not be fully successful until a politician's utility[1] function is developed.

We shall, in the rest of this chapter, ask what economic rationale exists for government economic activity. This is as far as economics can take us now, but we must guard against the belief that in so doing we are explaining the real motives behind *all* government interventions in the economy.

Efficiency

Many of the economic reasons for government intervention come under the heading of increasing the efficiency of the market system. All of the 'market failures' discussed in the previous chapter provide such reasons.

The provision of collective consumption goods is one obvious way to improve the efficiency of the system since, if the government does not provide them, few will be provided.[2] Defence, police and fire protection, street lighting, the judicial system, regulatory bodies of all sorts, public parks and monuments, clean air and rivers, weather forecasting, and navigational aids are all goods and services which, once provided, are freely available to everyone and therefore would not be produced in a completely free-market economy. Commodities which are not strictly collective consumption goods, but are hard to market privately because of the high cost of raising revenue, present in practice a very similar case to genuine collective consumption goods. Urban roads and various kinds of information services are examples. Divergencies between private and social cost provide a major reason for intervention. The central authorities can levy taxes related to the excess of social costs over private costs and thus force the firm to take account of these costs. When the state does this, it is said to be INTERNALIZING AN EXTERNALITY. Taxes, regulations and prohibitions are all used in these cases. Firms that pollute are sometimes taxed an amount equal to the social costs of their pollution; firms are often forced by regulation to adopt alternative, more privately costly

---

[1] Household utility depends on the quantities of goods the household consumes; similarly, a government's utility might depend on several things including its position in the popularity polls and its chances of winning the next election, as well as more 'altruistic' motives such as the good it can do for its citizens.

[2] It would not be correct to say 'none', since private clubs can be formed to provide some such goods. For this to be practical, either the collective consumption must extend over a small range so that all the potential consumers can be included in the club or there must be a way to exclude non-club members from consuming the good.

technologies that are less polluting. Households are also regulated in their polluting activities by such controls as restrictions on the kinds of fuel that can be used in urban areas and emission standards for private cars.

The alleviation of market imperfections is another major goal of interventions. Where cost conditions make it possible, monopolies are broken up. Where cost conditions create natural monopolies, these are regulated as to the price they can charge and the profits they can earn (or else they are nationalized, as we shall see below). Labour mobility can be enhanced by providing information, by subsidizing relocation and by retraining. Many other policies, such as legislation for closed shops and the provision of council housing below cost but with long waiting lists, may inhibit labour mobility.

All kinds of intervention to set minimum standards of quality, to ensure correct information and to prevent fraud come under the general classification of compensating for market imperfections. The economic system is clearly not working efficiently if someone is poisoned by a tin of beans he thought was edible, or if someone else wants to know the calorie count on some particular product but cannot find out. Myriad government rules and regulations seek to protect consumers from forces beyond their control and provide them with reliable information on which to base their own utility-maximizing choices.

Paternalism

The above reasons for intervention are based on improving the efficiency with which the market responds to household demand. Accepting this as a policy goal depends on believing that the household is the best judge of its own interests. This is called INDIVIDUALISM. An alternative view that often leads to quite similar interventions is paternalism. It holds that the central authorities are a better judge of the household's self-interest than the household itself. Paternalistic intervention may take the form of downright prohibitions on the consumption of commodities such as certain drugs and gambling. In many countries, for example, off-track betting is illegal – as it was until the 1960s in the UK – on the grounds that the punter must be protected against him or herself. In Canada, for another example, pubs used to close for an hour from 5.30 to 6.30 on the grounds that this would force the man of the house to go home, where his wife could get her hands on some of his pay before he had spent it all on beer. Paternalism often takes more subtle forms of subsidizing certain commodities such as milk and housing on the grounds that it is in households' own interests to consume more of these commodities than its members would consume voluntarily if they were merely given an income transfer equal in value to the subsidy. (The individualistic view of such a policy is that if households are thought to be too poor they should be given a simple income supplement and left to spend it as they wish.)

The issue of individualism versus paternalism raises many fascinating issues concerning human freedom and social justice. Suffice it to say here that much existing economic policy is paternalistic in the sense that it is justified on the grounds that the central authorities understand the household's best interests better than does the household itself.[1]

---

[1] The distinction between individualism and paternalism would be much clearer than it actually is if all households contained only one member. Because households typically have many members, including minors, some apparently paternalistic interventions can be understood as protecting some members from the paternalism of others. This really replaces one form of paternalism with another. Difficult cases aside, however, influencing actions that primarily affect the person taking the action is clearly paternalistic.

The distribution of income and wealth

The central authorities attempt to change the distribution of income in countless ways. Some attempts are general in their effects, but some are quite specific and localized.

The functional distribution of income   Governments have many policies with respect to the functional distribution of income. For example, in the UK income arising from the provision of labour services (called *earned income*) is taxed at lower effective income tax rates than income that arises from the sale of the services of capital (called *unearned income*). This is done by levying a surtax of 15 per cent on investment income (over £6,250 in 1982). Few other Western industrial countries discriminate in this way among functional shares in their tax policies. This UK policy tends to redistribute income among the owners of factors away from those who provide capital and in favour of those who provide labour. Also, by reducing the return to invested capital, it may provide a disincentive to saving and investing, although this has not been conclusively demonstrated.

Governments also have policies affecting the distribution of income within the broad functional class of labour income. Labour governments may try to redistribute income from professional-managerial and other middle-class groups to skilled and unskilled workers who are members of the working class. Conservative governments may try to resist, or reverse, this redistribution.

Governments also change the distribution of income in favour of all sorts of relatively small special-interest groups. Special tax treatment, subsidies, legislation that restricts competition, and a host of other measures operate in many countries to turn the distribution of income in favour of various groups – small businessmen, farmers in general and poultry and milk producers in partic-ular, households with large numbers of children, certain professional groups, some groups of skilled workers and unmarried mothers, for example. The treatment afforded to many of these special-interest groups is often hard to explain on grounds of correcting inefficiencies or of changing the distribution of income according to any generally agreed canons of justice. Many economists believe many of these kinds of redistribution can be understood only in terms of the theory of the vote-maximizing government. Such a government would adopt policies that greatly help each member of a small identifiable group and slightly hurt each member of a large, diffuse, unorganized group.

In case this notion sounds scandalous, remember that the basic idea of democracy is that politicians are supposed to respond to the wishes of the people. The proof that they are doing so is their ability to get re-elected.

> **Economists have actually come late to the view of governments maximizing their own utility functions. They have done so only after repeated failures to explain and predict much government behaviour using a model in which the government sought solely to make the economy work efficiently and to alter the distribution of income in ways that satisfied generally accepted ideas of social justice.**

The size distribution of income   Governments try to alter the size distribution of income in some ways that are widely accepted as socially desirable. In looking at the size distribution of income, government is concerned with large and small incomes, irrespective of the source of income. Most governments seek to narrow the range of the distribution, reducing the incomes of those at the upper end and raising the incomes of those at the lower end. The more egalitarian the government, the more it seeks to do this, but all governments recognize a trade-off between equality and efficiency. Some jobs are more skilled, more difficult, more unpleasant or more risky than others and, unless the former are more highly paid than the latter, people will not be persuaded to do them. Even communist governments allow major inequalities in the size distribution of income in order to provide the incentives needed to make the economic system function relatively efficiently.

The disincentive of these very high marginal rates of tax is still a subject of debate. If we consider a 'closed economy' where there is no possibility of emigration, then there seems little evidence that rates of up to 50 per cent are a strong disincentive. Some people work less hard but others work harder in order to restore their after-tax income to what it would have been if tax rates were lower. Above 50 per cent there seems to be more disincentive effect, and clearly as rates approach 100 per cent the disincentive effect becomes absolute. Indeed, very high rates have other effects that reduce efficiency. People whose income is high for a few years and low thereafter pay very high taxes, and therefore suffer disincentives relative to others with the same lifetime income that is spread more evenly over the years. People with high incomes spend much time and expense on lawyers and accountants to shield their incomes from taxes. Such activities produce no other net output for the society. When taxes get high enough, downright evasion becomes common and tax yields are lower than they would have been if rates had been lower but the taxes were actually paid.

In an open society where emigration is possible, it is clear that very high marginal rates of tax can have major effects. Authors, artists, pop groups and others who 'strike it rich' are strongly tempted to emigrate to other countries that will allow them to keep a higher proportion of their incomes. The temptation is particularly strong when there are countries with common linguistic and cultural environments and substantially lower tax rates. Emigration of successful people of this type from the UK to the US and various even lower-tax countries has been significant. From the point of view of maximizing tax revenues and reducing tax burdens on middle- and lower-income groups, it would be better to have these successful people still in the country paying tax rates of 40–50 per cent than out of the country, totally avoiding higher tax rates.

It is possible to imagine for each income bracket a tax rate that would maximize the tax yields. Zero yields nothing. So does 100 per cent, since people would not continue to earn income if it were all to be paid in tax. Somewhere in between is the rate that maximizes the total tax yield.

> **If the tax rate is set too high, the yield will fall. Among other things, it will pay people to spend much money and effort on ways to avoid paying tax legally; some people will cheat under the incentive of very high tax rates; and some – particularly the very successful – will leave the country.**

The first prong of any government's attempt to change the size distribution of income is its tax policy. The idea is to have a tax system that is progressive when viewed as a whole. The second prong is its expenditure policy. If, to take an extreme case, government expenditure benefited people in proportion to the taxes they paid, the overall effect of the government would not be to redistribute income. What it took away with one hand it would give back with the other. An effective redistribution scheme requires that the tax system be more progressive than the expenditure system. (A proportional tax system and a regressive expenditure system would do.) Transfer payments help to fulfil this criterion since many of them are welfare payments to various classes of needy such as the aged, the incapacitated, the unemployed, the unemployable and the very young. For government payments for goods and services that are part of national income, and that are provided at a zero or a subsidized price, the case is not so clear. Education, for example, tends to be consumed more by higher than lower income groups, since the higher a household's income, the more likely it is that its children will stay on beyond the minimum school-leaving age. This kind of relation, which exists for other commodities as well, means that much of the non-transfer part of the expenditure system is progressive, with larger benefits being received the larger the household's income at least up to some middle range of income.

The distribution of wealth   It is sometimes argued that egalitarian economic policy should concern itself more with the distribution of wealth and less with income than it now does. Certainly wealth does confer economic power and, equally certainly, wealth is more unequally distributed than is income. Heavy estate duties in the UK have, however, caused a substantial reduction in the inequality of wealth distribution over this century.

There are two main ways in which the distribution of wealth can be made less unequal. The first is to levy taxes on wealth at the time that wealth is transferred, either by gift during the lifetime of the owner or by bequest after death, from one owner to another. In the UK such transfers are subject to a CAPITAL TRANSFER TAX. The rate of tax is progressive and rises to 75 per cent on taxable transfers in excess of £2 million. The second method is an annual tax on wealth held in the hands of its owners. A wealth tax of this sort has been under consideration since 1975 in the UK. It has aroused much controversy, and as yet there has been no agreement as to its provisions or its basic desirability. Certainly it poses some formidable difficulties and may cause some serious disincentive effects.

Distribution versus efficiency

A number of conflicts between advice given by economists and policy decisions taken by governments can be understood in terms of a difference in emphasis: efficiency considerations for economists and distribution considerations for the central authorities. There is little doubt that from a pure efficiency point of view the correct policy was to let domestic oil prices in all oil-importing countries rise along with the world price that was first raised dramatically by OPEC in 1973. Instead many governments held the price down – being concerned, among other things, with the effect of rising prices on the profits earned by large oil companies and on the welfare of poorer citizens. 'We just can't let the poor find their heating bills rise so much and so fast' was a typical consideration.

Here is a genuine conflict for which economics cannot provide a solution, for in the end the decision must rest on value judgements. Economics can, however, make the consequences of various choices apparent, and suggest policy alternatives. The consequences of holding down the price of oil because of concern about the effect on the poor was to lead to an inefficient use of the countries' resources. (The UK avoided much of this problem by ceasing to be a major oil-importer once North Sea oil came on line later in the decade.) This meant that total production was reduced and some new investment was misdirected into high- rather than low-cost methods of production. Thus in the long run average standards of living were reduced. Whether the reduction in the average was a reasonable price to pay for shielding the poor is an open question, but it is unlikely that the question was ever really posed or the calculations ever made.

> **Changes in prices and quantities always hurt someone. If the price system is not allowed to do its job because of effects on particular groups, then the society is effectively opting for some more centrally controlled form of resource allocation.**

An alternative is to let the price system do its job of signalling relative scarcities and costs, thus ensuring some efficiency in the allocation of resources, and then use the tax-expenditure system to ensure that the poor have some minimum living standard. This method does not seek to help the poor, or other under-privileged groups, by subsidizing oil or any other prices and thus presenting everyone with prices that do not reflect opportunity costs. It seeks rather to provide these groups with sufficient income by direct income transfers, and then leaves producers and consumers to respond to relative prices that approximately reflect relative opportunity costs. Advocates of this method argue that it is surer, more direct and less costly in its side-effects than the method of subsidizing the prices of particular goods. The price-subsidy method surely produces a somewhat haphazard method of distribution, since some who *are not* in the under-privileged group gain as well, and some who *are* in the under-privileged group – those who don't want or can't get the subsidized commodity – do not gain at all.

Opponents claim that certain commodities such as food, heat, medical care and housing are basic to a civilized life and should be provided to households cheaply whatever their real opportunity cost. They feel that the inefficiencies resulting from presenting people with prices that do not reflect opportunity costs are a small price to pay for ensuring that everyone can afford these basics. They reject the view that a minimum living standard can be provided simply by providing a minimum income and letting the recipients spend it at market-determined prices. They feel, possibly paternalistically, that some commodities should be provided cheaply to everyone.

As with all such issues, it is impossible to do justice to both sides of this one in a few pages. The purpose of this discussion is to make the reader aware of the question, in the hope that further discussion will bring to light many of the considerations omitted from this necessarily brief account.

A further consideration of government expenditure

So far we have considered government activity intended to increase the efficiency of the economic system and to change the distribution of income. Some government production of goods and services is hard to classify this way, although there may be an element of each type in them. It is convenient, therefore, to complete our discussion of government policy by considering the production of goods and services by the public sector as a topic in its own right.

Collective consumption goods

Much government production is of collective consumption goods. These are clearly meant to raise the efficiency of the economy in satisfying consumers' demands, and have thus been discussed already under earlier headings. The resource costs of this production must be met from general taxation since the very nature of the products imply that they cannot be sold to individual users.

The provision of commodities free or at a price below their cost of production

Collective consumption goods must, by their very nature, be paid for out of general tax revenue. Many other commodities that could be sold at a price that would cover costs, are in fact provided at a lower price (zero in the limit) with the shortfall between price and costs being made up out of tax revenue.

The opportunity cost of 'free' goods   Voters sometimes opt to have the government subsidize a product, or even provide it free, because it seems a good idea to avoid cost wherever this is possible. Such policies do not, however, remove the cost; they merely transfer it from one set of persons, the consumers, to another set, the taxpayers. The opportunity cost of using resources to produce one commodity is the other commodities that could have been produced with the resources instead of that commodity. The money equivalent of this is the market value of the resources being used. Whenever a commodity is provided free by the government, the costs are met by taxes.[1] The taxpayers thus forgo what they would have consumed by spending their tax money, and the free commodity is consumed by its users instead. Insofar as they are the same people, then the consumers merely pay in a different form: taxes rather than purchase prices. Insofar as they are different people, there is a transfer of income from taxpayers to the consumers of the free commodity.

> **Providing a commodity free does not remove the opportunity cost, it merely transfers it from consumers of the product to taxpayers.**

The case against free commodities   If a commodity is provided free and all demand is met, then households will go on consuming it until the last unit consumed has a zero marginal utility. As long as extra units consumed have a positive marginal utility (no matter how small) and a zero marginal private cost, households can raise their total utility by raising their consumption of the commodity. Thus, resources will have to be used up in producing units of the commodity which have zero marginal utility to each and every household. Since resources are scarce, they must be taken from the production of other goods that have positive marginal utilities for all households (i.e., households would like to have more of them). To use scarce resources to produce commodities with zero or even very low marginal utilities when the same resources could produce commodities with higher marginal utilities ensures that all households will have lower total utilities than they could have. If a price were charged for the commodity, its consumption would decline and resources would be freed to move to uses where their product would have a higher marginal utility.[2]

The quantitative extent of this problem depends on the shape of the marginal utility schedule. Commodity I in Figure 33.3 (i) has a very flat schedule and there is a great difference between the consumption of a when the market price is charged and the consumption of b when the commodity is free. Commodity II in part (ii) of the figure has a steep schedule, and the consumption of d at zero price is not much higher than the consumption of c when the market price is charged. The case against providing commodity I free is that this will absorb some of the nation's scarce resources in providing units of the commodity which have a very low marginal utility. The case against providing commodity II free is the same, but quantitatively it is much less serious.

We have already discussed the case of water (see pages 172–3). This is an example of a very weak case. Water undoubtedly has a flat marginal utility schedule of the sort illustrated in Figure 33.3 (i). Thus the no-price policy means that a great deal of the economy's scarce resources must be committed to producing units of water which have a very low marginal utility. Furthermore, water does not provide a case where there are obvious social gains from encouraging consumption beyond

---

[1] This assumes that government expenditure is financed by taxes. We shall see in Chapter 43 that there are other methods of finance. These do not, of course, avoid the cost; they merely shift it to other groups.

[2] This case against free goods can be maintained *without* having to admit any practical policy relevance of the proposition that perfect competition provides an optimal allocation of resources.

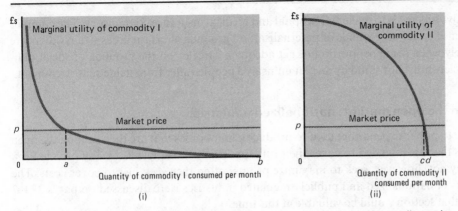

Fig. 33.3 (i) Providing the commodity free greatly increases the amount of resources allocated to producing it
(ii) Providing the commodity free increases only slightly the amount of resources allocated to producing it

what the individual would voluntarily choose. Indeed, if a commercially profitable market price were charged, there is little reason to believe there would be serious divergencies between social and private costs. Here is a case in which it is hard to see a rationale behind existing policy.

The case for free commodities The case for providing some commodities such as medical services and education at a price below cost (zero in the limit) rests partly on a divergence between social and private costs, partly on compassion and partly on more subtle welfare arguments.

Water may provide a weak case for a free good. The case for hospitals and schools, however, is somewhat different. First, there is some doubt that many people waste free hospital care in the way they are observed to waste free water. Studies suggest a low incidence of unnecessary hospitalization in a free-hospital system. In the case of education up to the statutory age, consumption is compulsory in any case.[1] Secondly, whereas the annual cost of necessary medical and hospital care can easily be in excess of a household's annual income, it is not a great burden for a household to pay a commercial rate for all the water that is necessary for a moderately civilized life. Charging a price that covers costs of production would deny medical and educational services to many. Thirdly, in both cases social and private costs and benefits are thought to diverge substantially: if I choose not to, or cannot afford to, buy a cure for an infectious disease, the effects are not felt by me alone. If all children are better educated, not only do they and their parents gain, but everyone gains from any rise in output that results from an increase in their labour productivity. Thus, there are arguments for reducing the private cost of these services below the market rate by means of a subsidy. There is debate, however, on whether the cost should merely be lowered or should actually be reduced to zero. Part of this argument concerns the positive question of the elasticity of demand for these services in the range between a moderate and a zero price. If this elasticity is high, then the difference between a modest and a zero price will be a large quantity of society's scarce resources producing services that provide households with only low marginal utilities.

---

[1] Indeed, there is some evidence that the consumption of 'free' education paid for by all taxpayers whether or not they are parents of school-age children leads to a lower consumption of education than would result from education paid for solely by the households that were consuming, and obviously benefiting from it.

The alternative scheme is to make full hospital and medical insurance compulsory. The compulsion can be justified either on grounds of paternalism; on grounds of externalities – that others are affected adversely when some people do not get adequate care; or on the grounds of social obligation – that society must not stand by and let uninsured people suffer from inadequate treatment.

Goods sold on the open market: nationalized industries

Finally we come to public expenditure used to produce commodities that are then sold on the open market at prices that are intended to cover their full opportunity cost, just as by any private firm. Public firms may not, however, seek to maximize profits; often they seek just to cover costs. The pricing problems of nationalized and publicly regulated industries were discussed on pages 324–7 and a review of that section would be valuable at this time.

Various reasons for nationalizing industries have been put forward and we can only give very brief mention to some of them.

(1) *To confiscate the return on capital for the welfare of the general public instead of the private capitalist.* This is the standard reason – stemming from both Marxian and Fabian socialist policies – for the production and sale of goods by government on the open market: the state should own the means of production (capital) and the return on it should go to the people rather than to a capitalist class privately owning the capital. After the experience of running planned economies, communists came to realize that capital had to be priced if it were to be allocated efficiently among its alternative uses. They continued to believe, however, that this price should not produce an income for a group of households in the economy. In this view the state – in the person of taxpayers – must provide the capital and receive the return on capital. This means that taxpayers are forced to save and invest in the nation's industries and then receive the return – in the sense that profits will be available to be spent by the state. This compares with private ownership, where those who wish to save and invest do so and then receive the return on capital as a reward.

There are two problems with this view as far as UK nationalized industries are concerned. First, as nationalized industries raise capital by reinvesting their own profits, by selling bonds to the public, or by borrowing from the government money that was originally raised by selling bonds to the public, their behaviour is indistinguishable from that of private firms. When money is raised by selling bonds to the public, the return on capital is paid to the bondholders, not to the state. Second, only a few of the nationalized industries in the UK have ever produced a surplus which they paid to the state as the return on capital going to the people rather than to private capitalists.

(2) *To get more co-ordination where private costs do not reflect social costs.* Nationalization of all forms of transport, for example, might be used to produce a single transport policy wherein decisions made by railways took into account the costs imposed on the road haulage industry and vice versa. Whatever the facts of such interrelationship, the British nationalized industries have up to now made little attempt to look beyond their own parochial boundaries when taking decisions.

(3) *To obtain a radically different pattern of production than would have been obtained under private enterprise.* If this were a goal, the nationalized industries would require a clear directive as to how their outputs and prices were to be determined. In fact they have usually been given the major task of trying to avoid losses, which requires that they make average revenue equal to average costs. In industries presently making losses, the attempt to cut losses is profit-maximizing behaviour. Thus behaviour in these industries is indistinguishable from what the private firm's behaviour would be.

In the case of a profitable industry, on the other hand, the directive 'cover costs' $(AR = ATC)$ will lead to higher output and a lower price than the directive 'maximize profits' $(MR = MC)$, as we saw in Chapter 23. But if more of something is produced, there must be less of something else, and the extra production caused by nationalized industries pricing at average costs represents a gain only if this production is valued higher than the production forgone elsewhere.

More recently, in an effort to reduce the total amount of public-sector borrowing in the UK, the nationalized industries have been directed to finance many capital requirements out of retained earnings. This means that the consumers of the products of those industries are forced to provide the funds needed to buy the capital that is then owned by the general public.

(4) *To control a natural monopoly.* Industries such as the postal, water, telephone, gas and electricity industries are natural monopolies. The alternatives here are public regulation of privately owned industry or public ownership. One of the main purposes set forth for nationalization is to secure effective control over such natural monopolies. All countries seem to accept this argument in the case of the post office, and many countries also accept it for the great public-utility industries such as gas and electricity. Those who believe that privately owned industries cannot be controlled effectively through regulation favour nationalization. It is difficult to believe that the price-output decisions of such public utility firms are very different when they are nationalized from when they are privately owned but under effective public regulation. The major difference is once again in the ownership of their capital. When they are privately owned, the capital is raised by people who voluntarily contribute it and who receive its return as their income. When such firms are publicly owned, they have a call on the taxpayer for capital, although in practice they often raise capital from private savers by selling bonds on the open market, or by borrowing money that the government has raised by selling bonds (which comes to the same thing since the return on capital is paid out as interest to bondholders). They also have a call on the taxpayer to meet operating deficits where current expenditures exceed current revenues.

Natural monopoly is a long-run concept, meaning that with the existing technology there is room for only one firm to operate profitably. In the very long run, technology changes. Not only does what was today's competitive industry become tomorrow's natural monopoly, but what was today's natural monopoly becomes tomorrow's competitive industry. A striking example is the telecommunications industry. A decade ago, message transmission was a natural monopoly. Now technological developments have made it highly competitive. In many countries an odd circumstance has now arisen. Nationalized industries seek to maintain their profitability by prohibiting entry into what would otherwise become a highly fluid and competitive industry.

> **One problem of nationalizing today's natural monopoly is that publicly owned industries can become conservative vested interests just as can privately owned monopolies.**

One difference is, however, that with the full force of legal sanctions behind it the public firm may be more successful than the privately owned firm in preserving its monopoly long after technological changes have destroyed its 'naturalness'.

(5) *To get greater efficiency and a more dynamic growth policy than under private industry.* The relative efficiency of private versus public production is still the subject of heated debate. Although universal agreement is not forthcoming, I would hazard the personal guess that the experience of nationalized industries in the United Kingdom suggests that they have been neither vastly better nor

vastly worse than their private predecessors in running their day-to-day affairs. There are, however, longer-term considerations. Are private industries unimaginative and unenterprising, ignoring existing possibilities to modernize and become profitable? Can public firms encourage innovation and very-long-run change as easily as private firms?

Coal mining – an example   The view that public control was needed to save an industry from the dead hand of third-rate, unenterprising, private owners was very commonly held about the British coal industry in the inter-war period, and was undoubtedly a factor leading to its nationalization in 1946. This view was clearly held by the Commission which reported in 1926 on the state of the coal industry:

> It would be possible to say without exaggeration of the miners' leaders that they were the stupidest men in England, if we had not had frequent occasion to meet the owners.[1]

On the other hand, the late Sir Roy Harrod argued that the run-down state of the industry in South Wales and Yorkshire and the advanced state of the pits in Nottinghamshire and Derbyshire represented the correct response of the owners to the signals of the market. He writes:

> The mines of Derbyshire and Nottinghamshire were rich, and it was worth sinking capital in them. If similar amounts of capital were not sunk in other parts of the country, this may not have been because the managements were inefficient, but simply because it was known that they were not worth these expenditures. Economic efficiency does not consist in always introducing the most up-to-date equipment that an engineer can think of but rather in the correct adaptation of the amount of new capital sunk to the earning capacity of the old asset. In not introducing new equipment, the managements may have been wise, not only from the point of view of their own interest, but from that of national interest, which requires the most profitable application of available capital ... it is right that as much should be extracted from the inferior mines as can be done by old-fashioned methods (i.e., with equipment already installed), and that they should gradually go out of action.[2]

Declining industries always present a sorry sight to the observer. Revenues have fallen below long-run total costs, and as a result new equipment is not brought in to replace old equipment as it wears out. The average age of equipment in use thus rises steadily. A declining industry will *always* display an old age-structure of capital and thus 'antiquated' methods. The superficial observer, seeing the industry's very real plight, is likely to blame the antiquated equipment, which is actually the effect, not the cause, of the industry's decline.

To modernize at high capital costs merely makes the plight worse, since output and costs will rise in the face of declining demand and prices. To nationalize a declining industry in order to install new plant and equipment which privately owned firms are unwilling to install is to use the nation's scarce resources where they will not lead to large increases in the value of output. Capital resources are scarce: if investment occurs in mines, there is less for engineering, schools, roads, computer research and a host of other things. To re-equip a declining undustry which cannot cover its capital costs is to use scarce resources where by the criterion of the market their product is much less valuable than what it would be in other industries. The correct response to a steadily declining demand is indeed

---

[1] Quoted in David Thomson, *England in the Twentieth Century* (Pelican Books, 1965), p. 110. But see also L. S. Amery's reply that the Commission had ignored the very strong claim of the government to be so considered. Some of the policies that gave the government that claim are discussed on pages 658–60.

[2] Roy Harrod, *The British Economy* (McGraw-Hill, 1963), p. 54.

not to replace old equipment, but to continue to operate what exists as long as it can cover its variable costs of production.

Innovation under private and public control One of the major issues concerning public versus private ownership concerns the relative incentive to innovate under each. Innovation of new products and techniques has been the source of the phenomenal economic growth that has transformed living standards throughout much of the world over the last two centuries. Innovation not only raises living standards under given environmental conditions, but it is the main hope for allowing the world to cope with such changing circumstances as the eventual exhaustion of fossil fuels.

The pro-public ownership argument is as follows. First, private firms, particularly very large ones, are conservative and unwilling to take risks. Indeed, there does seem to be some evidence that larger firms are more risk-averse than small firms. Second, the state has the willingness and the capital to take risks and innovate where private firms either will not or cannot. Third, the state is in a better position than private firms to assess the direction that research and innovation should take. Uncoordinated private activity will lead to much waste in 'going off in all directions at once' and a centrally co-ordinated effort will be much more effective. Fourth, the profits from innovation should go to the people, not to a private class of innovators.

The pro-private ownership view argues as follows. First, the incentive structure of public bueaucracies is even more unfavourable to risk-taking than that of large private firms. It is largeness, not 'privateness', that leads to risk aversion. Second, the state's record in ventures like the Concorde aircraft is disastrous (for understandable reasons, because political calculations becloud economic ones). In the private sector, even if existing firms are slow to innovate, the Schumpeterian process of creative destruction will cause new firms to arise whenever conditions are ripe for successful innovations. Nationalization, its critics argue, places the full coercive power of the state behind the preservation of the existing state monopoly and tends to frustrate the Schumpeterian process, which is the ultimate free-market protection against the inefficiencies of established monopolies. Third, it is argued, there is protection in diversity. Co-ordinated state action can throw all of the economy's resources down what subsequently turns out to be a blind alley. Private enterprise will cause every promising direction to be explored. Those who go down blind alleys lose their money; those who find successful routes prosper. Fourth, in such an inherently risky business as innovation it is better to risk the money voluntarily subscribed by private savers than the money forcibly extracted from taxpayers.

Conclusion

The tools available for government economic policy, and the major economic objectives that can be pursued, are fairly uncontroversial. To what extent the government pursues selfish, vote-maximizing objectives described by its own utility function is a matter of current controversy. There seems little doubt, however, that the model that gives the government no selfish objectives and makes it a mere selfless public servant has been refuted by evidence and is correctly rejected. Correct determination of the balance between selfishness and altruism awaits the formulation and testing of more elaborate models.

Another subject of current controversy is the cost of meeting various social objectives such as a more equal income distribution. There seems little doubt that this particular objective is pursued at a cost of more inefficiency in the economic system (which reduces the total output available for everyone). 'How much is lost?' and 'Is it worth it?' remain questions on which disagreement is rampant.

A major debate concerns the long-run and very-long-run behaviour of free-market and centralized economies. Since great flexibility will be needed to meet forthcoming crises such as the exhaustion of certain raw materials, increasing scarcity of fossil fuels, climate changes and population explosions, the long-run flexibility of various alternative systems is a matter of great significance today as well as for the generations to come. Here again, although there is evidence from the workings of various types of economies now and in the past, there is still room for vast differences in honestly held opinions.

Part eight

The determination of national income with a fixed interest rate and a fixed price level

34

Macroeconomic concepts and variables

From micro to macro economics

On page 55 of Chapter 4 we briefly noted that economics is divided into two main branches called microeconomics and macroeconomics. So far we have been studying microeconomics; now we shall study macroeconomics, and our first task is to distinguish between the two branches a little more fully than was necessary earlier.

The microeconomic view of the circular flow of income

In microeconomics, we start with households whose members have needs and desires for goods and services. They have resources – incomes, assets, time and energy – with which to satisfy their wants. But the limitations on their resources force them to make choices, and this they do through markets where they are offered many ways to spend their money, their energy and their time. The signals to which the households respond are market prices; given a set of prices, each household will make a given set of choices. In so doing they also, in the aggregate, affect those prices. The prices signal to firms what goods they may profitably provide. Given technology and the cost of factors, firms must choose among (i) the products they might produce, (ii) the ways of producing them, and (iii) the various quantities (and qualities) they can supply. In so doing, they affect prices. Firms demand factors of production, in quantities that depend on their output decisions, which in turn depend upon consumers' demands. These derived demands for factors affect the prices of land, labour and capital. The owners of factors respond to factor prices by deciding how much of their services to offer and where to offer them. These choices determine factor supplies. Payments by firms to factor owners provide factor incomes. The recipients of these incomes are members of households who have needs and desires for goods and services – and we have now come full circle.

The above passage describes a *circular flow of income*: money passes from housholds to firms in return for goods and services produced by firms, and money passes from firms to households in return for factor services provided by households. In microeconomics we study individual parts of this flow in microscopic detail.

The macroeconomic view of the circular flow of income

We now study the circular flow in a broad macroscopic view. We suppress the details and ask such

497

questions as: 'What determines the total amount of the flow?' and 'Why does this total flow vary over time?' Macroeconomics is a study of the characteristics and determinants of the circular flow looked at in the large with most of its interesting, but bewildering, detail suppressed.

Another useful way of putting the same distinction is to say that microeconomics deals with detailed or *disaggregated* data, while macroeconomics deals with *aggregated* data expressed in terms of large totals or averages. In microeconomics we are concerned, for example, with prices and quantities in thousands of individual markets for consumers' goods and services. In macro-economics we aggregate all of these markets and study both the single total flow of expenditure on all consumers' goods produced and sold in the economy and the single average price at which all sales of consumers' goods take place.

The distinction illustrated

There is no clear-cut dividing line between macroeconomics and microeconomics. Perhaps the best way of showing the scope of each is to list the most important sets of problems with which we shall be concerned in the remainder of this book, contrasting them with the related problems dealt with in micro-theory.

(1) Macroeconomics studies the total amount of employment of each of the major factors of production, with special attention to the total amount of labour employed. Microeconomics takes the total volume of employment of resources as given and studies how the employed resources are allocated among their alternative uses.

(2) Macroeconomics studies the total volume of output produced, and income earned, in the whole economy. Microeconomics studies the details of this output as determined in thousands of individual product markets as well as the details of the distribution of this income which is determined in thousands of individual factor markets.

(3) Macroeconomics studies the average level of prices in all product markets (called 'the' price level) and the average level of money wage rates in all labour markets (called 'the' level of money wages). Microeconomics takes these levels as given and studies the structure of *relative* product prices, as determined in all of the economy's individual markets for commodities, and the structure of *relative* wages, as determined in all of the economy's individual factor markets. In short, microeconomics is concerned with the structure of *relative* wages and prices, while macroeconomics is concerned with the average level of *absolute*, or money, wages and prices.

(4) Macroeconomics does study some allocation problems, but at a fairly high level of aggre-gation. For instance, macroeconomics is concerned with the allocation of total resources and of total expenditure between consumers' goods and capital goods. Microeconomics usually deals with the allocation of resources at a more disaggregated level, but there is no rigid division between what is microeconomics and what is macroeconomics in this respect.

(5) Macroeconomics deals with the problem of growth of the economy's total output, both actual and potential. (Potential output is what can be produced when all resources are fully employed.) Microeconomics takes a more disaggregated approach, dealing with changes in actual and potential output in individual sectors of the economy.

The division between macro and micro economics as illustrated by these contrasting problems is not a matter of right and wrong, but rather one of convenience. We employ the distinction because the problems differ, and also because the method of analysis differs, between these two branches.

The basic problem in microeconomics is the determination of the allocation of resources, and the basic theory is that of the determination of relative prices through demand and supply. The basic problem in macroeconomics is the determination of total employment, output and the price level, and the basic theory is that of the determination of national income through aggregate demand and aggregate supply.

A survey of some key macro variables[1]

In this part of the chapter we discuss some of the major macroeconomic variables that are of concern both to the economic policy-makers and to the general public. In the final part we discuss the details of how output and income variables are defined and related to each other. This latter topic takes us into what is called national income accounting.

Employment variables

Definitions   The EMPLOYED are those persons working for a wage or a salary, while the SELF-EMPLOYED are those who work for themselves. The UNEMPLOYED are those persons who are not employed but who, by some measure or another, are looking for a job. The WORKING POPULATION or LABOUR FORCE is the total of the employed, the self-employed and the unemployed, i.e., those who have, plus those who would like to have, work.

The unemployment figure is often expressed as a percentage of the labour force. We will use it in this form and will denote it by the symbol U where

$$U = \frac{\text{number unemployed}}{\text{working population}} \cdot 100\%.[2]$$

Why unemployment is a matter of concern   Keynes distinguished between voluntary and involuntary unemployment. Voluntary unemployment occurs when there is a job available but the unemployed person is not willing to accept it at the going wage rate. Involuntary unemployment occurs when a person is willing to accept a job at the going wage rate but no such job can be found. Clearly when we are concerned about the undesirable social effects of unemployment in terms of lost output and human suffering, it is involuntary unemployment that concerns us. When we use the word *unemployment*, hereafter, we mean involuntary unemployment.

The social and political importance of the figure that expresses the unemployment rate is enormous. It is widely reported in newspapers; the government is blamed when it is high and takes

---

[1] For factual background on these variables see Harbury and Lipsey, Chapter 1.

[2] A note on notation: Mathematics is no different from other subjects. It does not spring into fully developed existence by some act of immaculate conception; instead it evolves through the work of fallible people. As a result there is no fully agreed, mathematical notation for most operations. The notational problem that most concerns us in this book is how to indicate the simple operation of multiplication. Consider how the operation of multiplying x by y is variously denoted in mathematical literature: (i) $x \times y$, (ii) $(x)(y)$, (iii) $x.y$, (iv) xy. The convention adopted in this book is: (a) if there is no obvious ambiguity, to use method (iv) where juxtaposition indicates multiplication, and (b) where there is a possible ambiguity, e.g. with $\frac{a}{b}$ multiplied by $\frac{c}{d}$, to use a dot to indicate multiplication: $\frac{a}{b} \cdot \frac{c}{d}$.

credit when it is low; it is often a major issue in elections; and few macroeconomic policies are formed without some consideration of their effect on it. No other summary statistic, with the possible exception of the retail price index, carries as much weight as both a formal and an informal objective of policy as does the percentage of the labour force unemployed.

There are two main reasons for worrying about unemployment: it produces economic waste and it causes human suffering. The economic waste is fairly obvious. If a fully employed economy with a constant labour force has 30 million labour years available to it in some year, these must either be used in that year or wasted. If only 25·5 million are used because 15 per cent of the labour force is unemployed, the potential output of four and a half million labour years *is lost for ever*. In an economy characterized by scarcity, where there is not nearly enough output to meet everyone's needs, this waste of potential output is a serious matter.

In addition to economic waste, there is the human cost of unemployment. Severe hardship and misery can be caused by prolonged periods of unemployment. It is wrong, however, to think that if the number of unemployed rises by, say, 100,000, this means that 100,000 workers join the ranks of the permanently unemployed. Modern research has shown that short-term variations in the unemployment rate at or near the full-employment level are caused to a great extent by changes in the duration of short-term unemployment. Moreover, some people stay unemployed rather than accept a lower-level job than the one they lost because they feel the margin of difference between what they would earn and their unemployment benefits is too small. For such people unemployment is an alternative they choose.

When, however, a deep recession is followed by a slow recovery, as was the case in the mid 1970s and again in the early 1980s, long-term unemployment increases. This has more serious effects on the morale and the social outlook of the unemployed than do bouts of short-term unemployment. When a region develops heavy long-term unemployment, possibly due to the decline of a large industry, the economic and social effects are felt by everyone including those who remain employed or are in business for themselves. Furthermore, heavy and prolonged unemployment among members of some groups, such as youths or racial minorities, can cause major social unrest. Today there is the added phenomenon particularly among youth of those who collect unemployment benefits but who do part-time work for cash (on which they pay no taxes). They may well prefer a full-time steady job, but for them unemployment is not the same serious problem that it was for the unemployed worker of the 1930s who usually had no means of earning extra income.

Before a value judgement can be made about the human costs of a rise in unemployment, we need to know how that increase is distributed between long-term and short-term unemployment, between those for whom there is no work alternative and those for whom there is a non-preferred employment alternative, and between those who are able to earn some cash on the side and those who are not.

> **The costs in terms of human suffering will usually be much higher for long-term, or involuntary, than for short-term, or voluntary, unemployment.**

Experience of unemployment Figure 34.1 shows the behaviour of the UK unemployment rate since 1929. The postwar period has been, on average, significantly better in its unemployment performance than the interwar period, during which unemployment was rarely less than 10 per cent. Through the first quarter-century after the Second World War, unemployment was usually less than

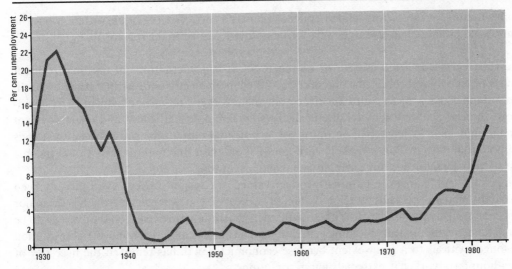

Fig. 34.1 Unemployment in Great Britain, 1929–1982.

3 per cent, and in the mid-1970s it exceeded 4 per cent for the first time since the 1930s. It rose steadily in the mid-1970s, reaching 7 per cent early in 1978. By 1981 the unemployment rate at 11·2 per cent had gone over 10 per cent for the first time since the 1930s and by October 1982 it had reached 13·8 per cent. Over the entire postwar period, unemployment has drifted up slowly but perceptibly, each peak in the trade cycle having more unemployment than the previous peak, and each trough having more than the previous trough.

There is marked inequality of unemployment rates among regions and among types of labour. Northern Ireland, Scotland and north-eastern England have tended to have rates three to four times as high as those in south-eastern England. Much of this is structural unemployment connected with the decline of the old staple industries concentrated in the north and the rise of new technologically based industries in the south-east. In recent years unemployment rates among youths and among males have been higher than female rates. The male–female relation in the UK is in striking contrast to that in the US and Canada, where unemployment among males from 25 to 65 years of age has typically been much lower than unemployment among females.

Output variables

Definitions The nation's total output, which is its GROSS DOMESTIC PRODUCT (GDP), is loosely described as its *national product* or its *national income*. Precise measures are discussed in the last half of this chapter. In the meantime, we notice that this total output may be valued at current market prices or at constant prices. When valued at current prices, changes in national product are a result of changes both in the quantities produced and the prices at which the goods are sold. When valued in constant prices, output for each year is valued at the prices ruling in one particular year. Changes in national product valued at constant prices must indicate changes in quantities produced. National product may also be expressed as a total or, by dividing by the country's population, as a per capita figure. An important related concept is POTENTIAL NATIONAL PRODUCT, what the economy could produce if all resources were fully employed; it is given the symbol Y_F.

Why output variables are a matter of concern   Short-run fluctuations of national product around its potential level reflect the ebb and flow of economic activity called the trade cycle. In periods of high activity, often called *booms*, employment is high and unemployment correspondingly low. In periods of low activity, often called *slumps*, employment is low, and unemployment correspondingly high. When actual output is below potential output, the gap between the two is wasted potential output. Policy-makers care about short-term fluctuations in national income because of their consequences for unemployment and lost output.

Long-run, trend changes in national product valued at constant prices have generally been positive in the modern era. Thus we refer to them as ECONOMIC GROWTH. Such growth is the major cause of changes in living standards. With growth, each generation can expect, on the average, to be substantially better off than all preceding generations. The horrors of the early industrial revolution are no longer with us to a great extent because economic growth has removed the necessity of fourteen-hour days worked in extremely harsh conditions.

Output experience   Figure 34.2 shows the growth of national product in the UK valued at constant prices. Slow British growth rates have moved Britain down the list of present EEC countries from the second highest per capita GNP in 1960 to the second lowest in 1982. If present growth rates persist to the end of this century, West Germany's per capita GNP will be six times Britain's. This is the same relative discrepancy as now exists between Britain and Guatemala.

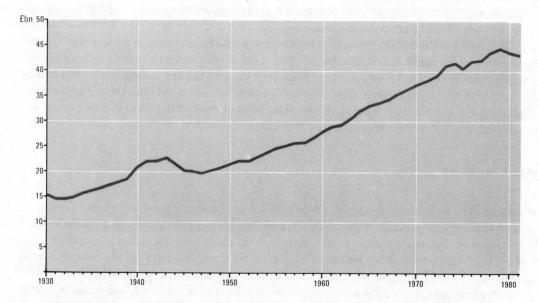

Fig. 34.2 UK constant GNP (1963 prices)
Sources: European Historical Statistics and World Bank tables.

Price-level variables

Definitions Macroeconomics uses the concept of the PRICE LEVEL. This is invariably an index number of relevant prices. (See the Appendix to Chapter 3 for a discussion of index numbers.) The most familiar index is the Retail Price Index (RPI), which measures the cost of purchasing a bundle of goods bought by a typical consumer, with the cost in the base period taken as 100. It is calculated from current price data using weights that reflect the relative importance of each item in the typical consumer's consumption bundle in the base period.

The most comprehensive index of the price level is the index derived from the national product calculated at current and at constant prices. It is called the IMPLIED GDP DEFLATOR and is calculated as

$$\frac{\text{GDP at current prices}}{\text{GDP at constant prices}} \cdot 100\%.$$

The logic behind this measure is that the difference between the nation's current output valued at current and at base-year prices must be the result of changes in prices between those two years. Since the deflator is based on the current year's output, the implied index has current-year quantity weights. It thus takes account of changes in the relative importances of different commodities between the base and the current year.

Why the price level is not a matter of concern By and large, governments do not have policies about the price level *per se*. No one feels that the price level ruling in Britain in 1770 was intrinsically better or worse than the one ruling in 1970. The *level* of prices of commodities and factors of production at which the economy's transactions occur is irrelevant to living standards. If, for example, all money incomes and all prices doubled overnight, the living standards of income earners

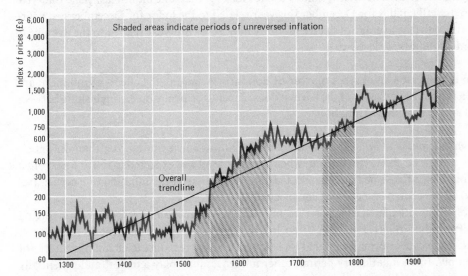

Fig. 34.3 Price index of consumables in southern England 1275–1970 (1451–75 = 100). The retail price index has been used to extend the series beyond 1959. Source: *Lloyds Bank Review,* No. 58, October 1960.

would be left unchanged. What does matter is what happens while the price level is changing; what matters, that is, is the process of inflation. Whatever the present level of prices, there will be many economic consequences if it rises sharply over the course of the next few years.

The experience of the price level   Figure 34.3 shows a remarkable price-level series calculated some time ago by Professor Henry Phelps-Brown of the London School of Economics. It is an index of prices of the basic items in a worker's budget of food, clothing and fuel. It pertains to southern England and extends from 1275 to 1959! The trend line shows that the average change in prices over the whole period was 0·5 per cent per year. The shaded areas indicate periods of major, unreversed inflation. The series also shows that the perspective of one century can be misleading in the broader view because long periods of stable or greatly falling prices tended to alternate with long periods of rising prices.

Inflation

For our present purposes an INFLATION may be defined as any rise in the price level and a DEFLATION as any fall – although we shall want to make some further distinctions later. An inflation refers to a rise in all prices including those of commodities and of factors of production. Thus, in an inflation, money incomes rise on average as fast as the money prices of commodities.

Definition   Inflation may be measured by

$$\frac{\text{present price index} - \text{previous price index}}{\text{previous price index}} \cdot 100\%.$$

When the annual rate of inflation is required, it will be this year's price index related to last year's index. It is common to relate this month's index to the index for the same month last year. End-year figures are also used (the index for December this year related to the index for December last year), as are annual averages (the average of twelve monthly indices for this year related to the average of the twelve monthly indices for last year).

Why changes in the price level are a matter of concern   Assessing the effects of inflation, and hence making a rational assessment of the harm it does, depends critically on distinguishing between an anticipated and unanticipated inflation.

The effects of unanticipated inflations: Unanticipated inflations cause more upset than do anticipated inflations. Contracts freely entered into when the price level was expected to rise at 6 per cent a year will yield hardships for some, and unexpected gains for others, if the inflation rate accelerates unexpectedly to 12 per cent, or decelerates unexpectedly to zero.

One effect of an unanticipated inflation is to influence the allocation of resources by changing relative prices (including relative wages), often in a haphazard fashion. In a market economy, changes in relative prices are normally a signal for resource shifts in response to changing patterns of demand and supply. In an inflationary period, other influences may play a major (and potentially distorting) role. For example, workers in occupations with strong unions will be able to keep their wages rising as fast as prices; they may even be able to do better than they would have done if prices had never risen. In other occupations, wages and salaries will be very slow to adjust. Employees in these occupations will lose substantially because of the inflation. Not only do these individuals suffer, but the change in relative wages will affect the allocation of resources.

A second effect of unanticipated inflations is to redistribute wealth from lenders to borrowers, whereas unanticipated deflations do the opposite. To see why this happens, suppose that A lends B £100 at 5 per cent interest for one year. If the price level rises by 10 per cent over the year, A will actually earn a negative rate of interest on the loan. The £105 A gets back from B will buy fewer goods than the £100 A originally parted with. A's loss, however, is B's gain. B did not even have to use the £100 in any productive business enterprise to show a gain. All he needed to do was to buy and hold goods whose prices rose merely by the average rate of inflation. At the end of the year B can sell the goods for £100, pay back the £100 he borrowed plus £5 interest, and show a gain of £5 for having done nothing more than hold goods instead of money. This type of inflationary redistribution occurs not just on borrowing and lending contracts but on any form of contract that is stated in terms of monetary units.

A third effect of inflation (whether anticipated or unanticipated) is to reduce the living standards of those on fixed incomes. Consider the case of a couple who invested in an annuity designed to provide them with a fixed annual money income after retirement. The couple saved enough throughout their working years to give themselves a satisfactory retirement income of £6,000 a year. If, however, the price level doubles just before the couple retires, the purchasing power of their money income will be halved. They will still get £6,000 a year, but it will buy only half as many goods as they had expected it to buy. Furthermore, if the price level continues to rise slowly, say at 3 per cent per year, the couple will have to cut their real purchases of goods and services by a steady 3 per cent each year. If they should live for 23 years after retirement, their living standard will have been halved once again. By that time they will be able to buy only as many goods per year as if they had saved just enough to provide themselves an income of £1,500 a year and prices had remained constant. Instead of having a modest but satisfactory living standard, the couple will have been made progressively worse off, until finally they will have been reduced to poverty.

This kind of example was not far from the experience of those who saved during the years before the Second World War and then retired into the creeping inflation of the 1950s and 1960s. And it understates the plight of retirees facing the sharp inflations that characterized the 1970s and early 1980s. Ten per cent inflation halves the purchasing power of a fixed money income every 7 years!

The reduction in the purchasing power of money savings is one of the most dramatic and obvious effects of an inflation. It helps to explain the hostility to inflation felt by anyone who has suffered seriously from one.

The effects of anticipated inflations: To the extent that inflations are anticipated, some of the haphazard effects can be avoided by allowing for the expected changes in prices when contracts are drawn up, or by 'indexing' that builds changes in average price levels into some wage and price contracts.

While some people may be able to avoid the effects of inflation when they see it coming, many people cannot do so. One of the most troubling aspects of the rapid increase in the inflation rate in the mid-1970s, and again in the early 1980s, was the unavailability to many ordinary people of 'inflation proof' havens for their savings. Thus many of those who correctly anticipated a continued inflation were unable to protect themselves against it.

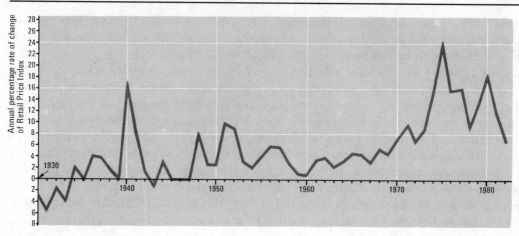

Fig. 34.4 Annual inflation rate, UK, 1930–81

Even a fully foreseen inflation has redistributional effects. Many practices – such as business accounting conventions, definitions of allowable expenses given in tax laws, and many private pension schemes – make use of money definitions that cannot be altered even in the face of an inflation that is fully foreseen. In addition, not everyone can find a way to adjust to an anticipated inflation without incurring substantial transactions costs, for example paying commissions for buying and selling property. These transactions costs may be particularly high for those with relatively small amounts to protect.

Saying that the main effects of inflation are redistributional does not imply that inflation is unimportant. Redistributions of income can be very important. Rapid inflations, particularly if they are unexpected, but even if they are expected, cause major, arbitrary, and sometimes socially destructive redistributions. The continual erosion of the purchasing power of fixed money incomes is tragic to those who suffer it, and such erosion is only one of the many serious redistributive effects of inflation.

The experience of inflation Figure 34.4 shows the inflation rate for each year since 1930. Throughout the 1950s and the 1960s the UK inflation rate, although low by current standards, was high enough in most years to worry policy-makers and voters. Indeed, the purchasing power of the pound was approximately cut in half over these two decades. Then in the late 1960s the United Kingdom followed the rest of the developed world into a period of accelerating inflation that is commonly thought to have been initiated in the United States. From 1967 to 1971 the inflation rate rose steadily. Then, after a slight deceleration in 1972, the rate of inflation accelerated to rates never before seen in the UK during peacetime. By 1975 the annual rate of inflation was approximately 25 per cent. This rate halves the purchasing power of money in just under three years! Had it persisted, it would have reduced any fixed money income to one-tenth of its original purchasing power within 10 years. The inflation rate did not, however, remain at that high level. Instead it fell steadily through 1978. But in 1979 it accelerated once again, which was all the more remarkable because this coincided with the election of a new government pledged to fight inflation with strict measures of monetary control. Since then, the rate has fallen again and at the end of 1982 was well below 10 per cent. The inflation rate over this extraordinary decade was such that a household retiring with a

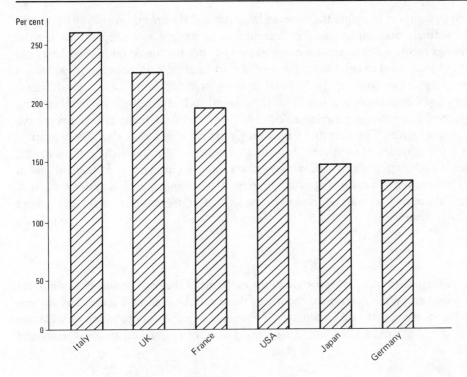

Fig. 34.5 Comparative inflation rates for selected countries: retail price indices in 1981 as a percentage of 1975. *Source:* NIESR *Economic Review*, 1982.

comfortable fixed income in 1972 saw 75 per cent of that income's purchasing power eroded over the ten years that followed. Figure 34.5 gives some international comparisons of inflation rates.

The balance of payments and exchange rates

The balance of payments and exchange rates have already been briefly discussed in Chapter 11, so we shall only quickly outline a few additional points that are relevant here. From 1945 to the early 1970s the major countries of the world operated a system of fixed exchange rates. When a government that was committed to maintaining a fixed exchange rate found its balance of payments in an unsatisfactory condition, achieving a satisfactory balance of payments in the long term and defending the current exchange rate by any available means in the short term became the overriding policy goals to which all others had to be subjugated.

With the breakdown of the system of fixed rates in the early 1970s, most major industrial countries allowed their exchange rates to fluctuate on free markets. As a result, obtaining a satisfactory balance of payments in order to defend the existing exchange rate ceased to be the dominant policy consideration. The adoption of floating exchange rates allowed macroeconomic policy-makers to turn their attentions to domestic rates of inflation, unemployment and growth, while leaving the balance of payments more or less to take care of itself. The free-market exchange rate was supposed to fluctuate to ensure that international payments were automatically balanced.

Unfortunately, freely fluctuating, market-determined exchange rates did not provide the unmitigated blessings predicted by their advocates. Exchange rates fluctuated far more than would have been dictated by the need to equilibrate flows of imports and exports. Short-term exchange-rate fluctuations were dominated by highly volatile movements of short-term capital. These fluctuations worried policy-makers because of their potential to interfere with trade by causing imports and exports to be temporarily under- or over-priced. As a result, many governments have adopted exchange-rate targets. This they do by operating what is called a *dirty float*. No attempt is made to defend a pre-announced fixed rate. Instead governments, through their central banks, intervene in foreign-exchange markets with a view to smoothing out short-term fluctuations in exchange rates. This intervention can be important in some circumstances, but it is minor compared with the overriding attention that must be given to the balance of payments when exchange rates are fixed at pre-announced par values.

Conclusion

These, then, are the main variables of macroeconomics and some of the reasons why policy-makers are concerned about them. What determines the size of these variables, and the scope that governments have to influence them, is the subject-matter of macroeconomic theory to which we will soon turn our attention. But first we must look in much more detail at the output and income variables of macroeconomics.

A closer look at output, income and expenditure variables: the national accounts[1]

Three important macroeconomic concepts are output, income and expenditure. Firms produce the goods and services which in total are the nation's output (O). Production requires factors of production whose owners are paid for services provided and it thus generates income (Y). When the nation's output is sold, people spend money to purchase it, the value of expenditure (E) being the amount required to purchase the nation's output.

The most important empirical measure of these variables is called GROSS DOMESTIC PRODUCT or GDP. This is the value of total output actually produced in the whole economy over some period, usually a year (although quarterly data are also available). Statisticians measure the GDP by measuring the incomes generated in producing it and by measuring the expenditure needed to purchase it. In doing this they define O, Y and E in such a way that they are the same thing, the value of total output. We shall review how this is done after we study the three approaches to measuring GDP.

The income approach

The first approach is to measure Y, the incomes generated by production. The main income items are shown for the UK in Table 34.2. It is worth noting that these categories do not exactly coincide

---

[1] For a parallel discussion, in somewhat less detail than what follows, see Harbury and Lipsey, Chapter 7.

Table 34.2 GNP and GDP of the UK, 1981 (current prices)

The Income Approach		The Output Approach		The Expenditure Approach	
(1) Income from employment	147,439	Agriculture, forestry and fishing	4,867	(1) Consumer expenditure	151,042
(2) Income from self-employment	18,569	Petroleum and natural gas	11,972	(2) General government final expenditure	55,151
(3) Income from rent	15,282	Other mining and quarrying	3,455	(3) Gross domestic fixed investment	39,377
(4) Gross trading profits of companies	27,101	Manufacturing	49,916	(4) Investment in stocks	−4,160
(5) Gross trading surplus of public enterprises	7,551	Construction	13,545	(5) Exports (goods and services)	67,854
(6) Imputed charge for consumption of non-trading capital	2,318	Services and distribution	141,183	(6) Total final expenditure (TFE), at market prices	309,264
(7) Total domestic income	218,260	Total Domestic Output	224,938	(7) Less imports (goods and services)	−60,866
(8) Less stock appreciation	−5,692	Adjustment for financial services	−12,370	(8) Less adjustment to factor costs	−37,610
(9) Gross Domestic Product at factor cost (from income)	212,568	GDP at factor cost (from output)	212,568	(9) GDP at factor cost	210,788
(10) Residual error	−1,780	Residual error	−1,780	(10) Net property income from abroad	1,004
(11) GDP at factor cost (from expenditure)	210,788	GDP at factor cost (from expenditure)	210,788	(11) Gross National Product (GNP), at factor cost	211,792

with the categories of returns to land, labour and capital as defined in microeconomics. Item (1) is straightforward: income from employment is wages and salaries. In microeconomics self-employed persons are treated as firms, so item (2) would be partly wages and partly a return on the capital belonging to self-employed persons. The income from rent, item (3), includes not only the rent of land but also the rent of buildings plus royalties earned from patents and copyrights; it is thus partly a return to land and partly a return to capital. The next two items, (4) and (5), are the major parts of the return on capital, item (4) for the private sector and item (5) for the public sector. Item (6) represents depreciation, which is that part of the value of output that is not earned by any factor but is the value of capital used up in the process of production. This depreciation is part of the gross return on capital.

Item (8) involves inventories, and requires some explanation. Goods produced by a firm but not sold are part of a firm's inventories. These are valued at their market price, i.e., the price they would currently fetch if they were sold. Thus the difference between their cost of production and their market price shows up in the profit figures. This means that a rise in market prices causes a rise in the value of existing inventories. Unless something was done, all of this increase in value would be recorded as a profit since the production costs of existing inventories have already been incurred. Thus with no change in physical inventories, an increase in GDP would be recorded if these inventory 'profits' were used. To avoid this distortion, a correction is made to eliminate changes in the value of inventories due to pure price changes. Thus inventory changes only contribute to changes in GDP when their physical quantity changes. The correction for the change in the value of existing inventories yields gross domestic product, valued at factor cost and calculated from the income side of the economy. The residual error will be mentioned below.

The phrase 'valued at factor cost' deserves notice. The value of output is the value of all factor services, including capital, that goes into making them. The GDP at factor cost does not value output in terms of market prices because these market prices include indirect taxes.

> **The income approach measures GDP in terms of the factor-income claims generated in the course of producing the total output.**

The output approach

The second method of measuring the GDP is to add up the outputs of each firm to get the total value of the nation's output.[1] The outputs can be grouped into more or less aggregated categories corresponding to industries, to sectors or to any other desired grouping. One such grouping is shown in Table 34.2.

Adding up the value of output presents two conceptual problems. The first concerns the valuation of inventories of goods produced but unsold. We have already seen that these are valued at market prices. This has the effect of recording as part of current output (and income) the profits that will only be received by the firm when, and if, the goods are sold.[2]

The second problem concerns what is called *double counting* and it requires further attention. So far in this book we have proceeded as if all firms made goods and services which they sold for final use. In this case, the value of output is the sum of the values of all sales made by firms. In reality, however, production of commodities is divided into stages, with particular firms and industries often specializing in one stage of production. For example, one set of firms may mine iron-ore; the ore may be sold to another set of firms for manufacturing into steel; the steel may be sold to another set of firms for use in making household tools; the manufacturer of the tools may sell them to a wholesaler, who sells them to a retailer, who in turn finally sells them to households.

Stages of production, and the consequent inter-firm sales, raise a problem for measuring national income. If we merely added up the market values of the outputs of all firms, we would obtain a total greatly in excess of the value of output actually available for use. Suppose we took the value of all farmers' outputs of wheat and added to it the value of all flour mills' outputs of flour, plus the value of the outputs of bakeries, plus the value of the sales of bread by all retail shops. The resulting total would be much larger than the value of the final product – bread – produced by the economy. We would have counted the value of the wheat four times, of the flour three times, of the bread produced by the bakery twice, and of the services of the retail shop once.

This is called the problem of DOUBLE COUNTING. *Multiple counting* would be a better term, since if we add up the values of all sales, the same output is counted *every time* it is sold from one firm to another. This problem is avoided by using the important concept of value added. Each firm's VALUE

---

[1] These output data can be measured independently from the annual Census of Industry.

[2] This convention can cause a serious distortion of profit figures during times of slump. Goods that are produced but cannot be sold because of a lack of demand still produce reported profits even though the firm has not now seen, and (if prices fall) may never see, these profits.

Exhibit 1
Value added through stages of production: an example

Because the output of one firm often becomes the input of other firms, the total value of goods sold by all firms greatly exceeds the value of the output of final goods. This general principle is illustrated by a simple example in which firm R starts from scratch and produces goods (raw materials) valued at £100; the firm's value added is £100. Firm I purchases raw materials valued at £100 and produces semi-manufactured goods that it sells for £130. Its value added is £30 because the value of the goods is increased by £30 as a result of the firm's activities. Firm F purchases the semi-manufactured goods for £130 and works them into a finished state, selling them for £180. Firm F's value added is £50. The value of final goods, £180, is found either by counting the sales of firm F or by taking the sum of the values added by each firm. This value is less than the £410 that we obtain by adding up the market value of the commodities sold by each firm. The following table summarizes the example.

Transactions between firms at three different stages of production

	Firm R	Firm I	Firm F	All firms
A. Purchases from other firms	£ 0	£100	£130	£230 = Total inter-firm sales
B. Purchase of factors of production (wages, rent, interest, profits)	100	30	50	180 = Value added
Total A + B = value of product	£100	£130	£180 = Value of final goods and services	£410 = Total value of all sales

ADDED is the value of its output *minus* the value of the inputs that it purchases from other firms. Thus a flour mill's value added is the value of its output *minus* the value of the grain it buys from the farmer and the values of any other inputs, such as electricity and fuel oil, that it buys from other firms. The relation between value added and total value of sales is illustrated in Exhibit 1.

> In macroeconomics a firm's *output* is defined as its value added; the sum of all values added must be the value, at factor cost, of all goods and services produced by the economy.

The concept of value added suggests an important distinction between intermediate and final products. INTERMEDIATE PRODUCTS are all goods and services used as inputs into a further stage of production. FINAL PRODUCTS are the outputs of the economy after eliminating all double counting. In the previous example, grain, flour, electricity and fuel oil were all intermediate products used at various stages in the process leading to the final product, bread. We look in detail at what constitutes final products in the next section.

> The output approach measures GDP in terms of the values added by each of the sectors of the economy.

The expenditure approach

The third way of calculating the GDP is from the expenditure side, the flows of expenditure needed to purchase the nation's output. The categories of expenditures are extremely important when we come to national-income theory, so we shall take some time on them here.

Consumption Consumption expenditure is all purchases by households of currently produced goods, except new houses. There are several points to notice here. First, private housing is the one exception to the general rule. It is counted as investment and hence considered below. Second, we are only interested in currently produced goods and services. For example, the purchase of a used car (produced in an earlier year) represents a transfer of an existing asset but does not represent current car production.[1] Third, the measurement is of purchases, not of actual use in consumption. With services and non-durable goods such as haircuts and eggs, there is no significant difference, since the point of consumption is very close in time to the point of purchase. With durables such as cars and TV sets, there is, however, a marked difference. Expenditure occurs in a lump when the good is purchased while consumption occurs as a flow over the lifetime of the good, which may be many years.

Investment The terms *investment* and *investment goods* are used in the same way in macro as in micro economics. INVESTMENT is defined as the act of producing goods that are not for immediate consumption; the goods themselves are called INVESTMENT GOODS.[2] They are produced by firms and they may be bought either by firms or by households. Three major components of investment goods are inventories, capital goods such as plant and equipment, and residential housing.

Investment in inventories: Virtually all firms hold inventories of their inputs and of their outputs. Inventories of inputs allow production to continue at the desired pace in spite of short-term fluctuations in the deliveries of inputs bought from other firms. Inventories of outputs allow firms to meet orders in spite of temporary, unexpected fluctuations in the rate of output or sales.

Inventories are an inevitable part of the productive process, and they require an investment of the firm's money since the firm has paid for them but has not yet sold them. An accumulation of inventories counts as current investment because it represents goods produced but not used for current consumption, while a drawing down – often called a decumulation – counts as negative investment or, as it is sometimes called, *dis*investment, because it is a reduction in the stock of goods produced in the past.

Intended and unintended inventory investment: Inventory investment may be either intentional or unintentional. If the firm produces and holds goods that it planned to use to build up its inventories, then its investment is intentional, or planned. If the firm produces goods that it plans to sell but does not sell because expected orders do not materialize, then its inventory investment is unintentional, or unplanned. Similarly, inventory disinvestment may be intentional or unintentional. If the firm plans to produce less than it sells, its inventory disinvestment is intentional; if sales are unexpectedly greater than output, the resulting inventory disinvestment is unintentional.

Investment in capital goods: Capital was discussed in detail in Chapter 28. The production of new capital goods is a part of total investment and is often called FIXED INVESTMENT (because the goods

---

[1] The part of the purchase price that is the markup of the car dealer will show up in GDP, since this is a payment for a service rendered this year. The part of the purchase price that goes to pay the former owner is, however, not current income.

[2] In common speech an individual speaks of 'investing' his money when he or she buys an equity or a bond. From the national-income point of view, this is a transfer of ownership of an existing asset; investment expenditure must be expenditure on currently produced investment goods.

created are usually fixed to a location, unlike inventories which are moveable). Such investment may either replace capital that has been used up in the process of production (or otherwise consumed) or make net additions to the stock of capital.

Investment in housing: A house is a very durable asset that yields its utility slowly over a long life. For this reason, housing construction is counted as investment expenditure rather than as consumption expenditure. This is done by assuming that the investment is made by the firm that builds the house, and that the sale to a user is a mere transfer of ownership that is not a part of national income. Behaviourally, however, investment in housing is different from investment in capital goods in that housing is built to be sold to households, while other capital goods are built to be sold to firms.

Total investment: The total investment that occurs in the economy is called GROSS INVESTMENT. The amount necessary for replacement is called the CAPITAL CONSUMPTION ALLOWANCE and is often referred to as DEPRECIATION; the remainder is called NET INVESTMENT. It is net investment that increases the economy's total stock of capital, while the replacement investment keeps the existing stock intact by replacing what has been worn out or otherwise used up. National-income accounts record total spending on investment as well as the breakdown into its various categories.

Government expenditure All government payments to factors of production in return for factor services rendered are counted as part of the GDP. All government activity is counted as producing output of goods or services without any attempt to judge whether or not the activities are in some sense worthwhile. Very often government expenditure produces no marketable product. Rather, as with the Foreign Office or the Department of the Environment, it produces a service for public consumption that is in the nature of a *public good* (see Chapter 32). The only feasible way to value these services, since they do not have a market price, is at cost. This does, however, have a curious consequence. If, due to a productivity increase, one civil servant now does what two used to do, and the displaced worker shifts to the private sector, the government's contribution to the GDP will register a decline. On the other hand, if two now do what one used to do, the government's contribution will rise. Both of these movements can occur in spite of the fact that what is actually done by the government is unchanged. This is an inevitable but curious consequence of measuring the value of the government's output by the value of the factors, mainly labour, used to produce it.

Government transfer payments, which make up about a half of the government budget, are not included because they are not made in return for any marketable production. Payments to those on welfare or the unemployment rolls or to the retired are transfers from taxpayers to the recipients and, however much they may fulfil our social goals, they do not of themselves create current production. (Transfer payments are further discussed on page 481.)

Exports Some domestic output is sold abroad. Although this represents expenditure by foreigners, it is expenditure on domestic output. Clearly, therefore, exports are a part of GDP and hence they are included in the GDP (item 5).

Total final expenditure The sum of the five items just discussed is called TOTAL FINAL EXPENDITURE (TFE). This represents the total expenditure required to purchase all the goods produced domestically when they are valued at market prices.

Imports Expenditure to purchase imports is part of total final expenditure since some of consumption, investment and government expenditure goes to imports. These imports are not, however, a part of total domestic production. Imports are the converse of exports: they represent expenditure by *domestic* purchasers on *foreign* production. They must, therefore, be deducted from TFE in order to move towards GDP (item 7).

Indirect taxes and subsidies Before we can get from TFE to GDP a second adjustment is required. Indirect taxes that are part of the sale price of commodities do not create income since they are paid to the government. The principal tax in this category in all the countries of the European Economic Community is the Value Added Tax (VAT). Such indirect taxes drive a wedge between the market value of commodities produced and the factor incomes generated by their production. Indirect taxes must, therefore, be *deducted* from expenditure to get to GDP at factor cost. Subsidies, however, are the reverse case. If a firm receives a subsidy, this creates income which will accrue as wages, rent or profits, but which is not generated by the sale of commodities. Subsidies must, therefore, be *added* to expenditure to get to GDP at factor cost. The second correction to TFE is, therefore, item (8), which is subsidies minus taxes and, since the latter usually exceeds the former, this correction is usually negative. The result is then GDP at factor cost (item 9).

Net property income A final adjustment takes us from GDP to what is called GROSS NATIONAL PRODUCT (GNP). This latter concept measures incomes earned in the UK in return for contributions to current production. To get from GDP to GNP we have to add receipts by British residents of dividends, interest and profits from assets that they own but which are located overseas. Clearly, this is part of the factor incomes earned by UK residents but it is not part of UK production. By the same token, dividends, interest and profits earned on assets located in the UK, but owned abroad, must be deducted from GDP if we wish to arrive at income earned in the UK in the course of contributing to UK production. Item (10) is the sum of these two corrections, and it takes us from GDP to GNP. Since the correction is usually quite small, we shall ignore it in what follows and treat gross domestic product as being the equivalent of gross national product.

> **The expenditure approach measures the GDP in terms of the categories of expenditure required to purchase the total production.**

Residual error Finally we note that the two calculations of GNP from income data and from expenditure data are genuinely independent measures and thus will not give an identical result. The residual error reconciles the two. It also gives some check on the accuracy of the overall measures.

Net national income Two other income measures deserve passing notice. The first is the NET NATIONAL PRODUCT (NNP). The GDP measures the value of output at factor cost. The income claims generated by the GNP are equal to the total value of output. The profit figure generated is, however, gross, in that it includes depreciation. To keep its capital intact each firm must deduct its capital consumption before arriving at net profits that can be either paid out to the firm's owners or saved on their behalf by the firm and then reinvested. The deduction of the capital consumption allowance from the economy's total output yields NNP. This is a measure of net output after deducting an amount needed to replace capital used up in the course of producing that output.

Disposable income

The remaining measure is the amount of income that households actually have available to spend or to save. This is called DISPOSABLE INCOME. To calculate disposable income, which is indicated by Y_d, several adjustments must be made to GNP. First, all those elements of the value of output that are not paid out to households must be *deducted*: business savings represent receipts by firms from the sale of output that are withheld by firms for their own uses, and corporation taxes are receipts that are paid over to the government. Second, personal income taxes must be *deducted* from the income paid to households in order to obtain the amount households actually have available to spend or save. Finally, it is necessary to *add* government transfer payments made to households. Although these are not themselves a part of GNP, they are made available to households to spend and save, and are thus a part of disposable income. To sum up:

> **Disposable income is GNP *minus* any part of it that is not actually paid over to households, *minus* the personal income taxes paid by households, *plus* transfer payments received by households.**

Real and nominal measures

In Chapter 13 we distinguished two concepts of income. The first values income in terms of its current money value and is variously called MONEY or NOMINAL income. The second measures income in terms of its purchasing power and is variously called REAL or CONSTANT PRICE income.

This distinction can be carried over to all the measures we have just discussed. Output, expenditure and income can be valued at current market prices in which case we speak, for example, of money or nominal NNP, or NNP valued at current prices. Changes from one year to another are then a compound of changes in physical quantities and prices. Output, expenditure and income can also be valued at the prices ruling in some base year. In this case, each year's quantity is priced at its base-year prices and then summed. We then speak, for example, of GDP at constant prices, or real GDP. These measures respond only to quantity changes. For example, this year's GDP valued at 1975 prices tells us what the value of output would have been this year if this year's quantities had been produced but prices had not changed since 1975.

> **Changes in constant-price GDP give a measure of real or quantity changes in total output.**

The identity of output, income and expenditure

In all national-income accounting the basic *overall* aggregate being measured is the total value of output at factor cost (either in constant or in current market prices). This can be looked at directly in terms of the output itself, O, or the income it generates, Y, or the expenditure required to purchase it, E. Although the details of each calculation give us independent information, the totals do not, since all three are defined so that they are identical:

$$Y \equiv O \equiv E \quad .$$

The reason for the identity of Y and O is that Y does not measure incomes actually paid out during the course of the year but, instead, measures the income claims generated by producing O. The identity of Y and O then follows from the accounting practice that all output must be matched by claims on that output: what is not wages, interest and rent becomes profits. Between them they must account for all output since someone must own the value that has been produced. Also, goods produced and not sold are valued at market prices, and the difference between their value and their cost of production is counted as part of profits.

The reason for the identity between O and E is that E does not measure actual expenditure but what *would have to be spent* to buy the output, O. This, of course, immediately makes E the same thing as O.

The interest in having all three measures lies not in their identical total but in the breakdown of each. In the case of O, this is by industry; in the case of E, it is by type of expenditure, such as consumption; in the case of Y, it is by type of income, such as wages and salaries.

35

National income in a two-sector model

We have seen that what happens to GDP affects everyone's welfare. The long-term trend in real GDP has been a rising one over the last century. This is the source of long-term growth that has made the material living standards of each generation higher than those of all preceding generations. The short-term behaviour of GDP has, however, been characterized by oscillations which give rise to some serious problems. Rapidly rising real GDP often causes labour shortages, balance-of-payments problems and severe inflations. Declining real GDP often causes bouts of heavy unemployment, static or falling living standards and pockets of severe poverty, conditions which were found, for example, in the UK in the early 1980s.

Why does GDP behave as it does? Can governments do anything to influence the course of GDP, employment and prices? In particular, can they do anything to prevent lapses from full employment and to restrain the inflations that often accompany periods of relatively full employment?

To deal with these and many related questions, we need to develop a theory of national income. We begin with preliminary definitions and assumptions; then, because it is easier to study complex things one at a time rather than all at once, we shall proceed in a series of small steps. In the present part we study the forces that determine the GDP under the extreme simplifying assumptions that both the rate of interest and the price level are exogenous variables. We do this, first, for the simplest model in which there are only two sectors, households and firms. Then we add a government and a foreign-trade sector. This allows us to study the basic forces that cause national income to change both when the rate of interest and the price level are fixed, as in this part, and when they are variable, as in later parts. In Part 9, we go on to integrate money into our theory. In the process we make the interest rate an endogenous variable. This allows us to get substantial insight into the interrelations between the economy's production and spending sector and its monetary and financial sector. When this has been done, we are at last ready, in Part 10, to make the price level endogenous so that we can study inflation and all of its related problems. This plan may seem to take a long time to get to one of the decade's key problems, the causes and control of inflation. But everything that we do along the way is needed for a study of the behaviour of an endogenously determined price level. In any case we are able, along the way, to gain some substantial insights into the macroeconomic behaviour of the economy.

Some preliminaries

First we need to introduce a few more definitions, some key concepts and some assumptions.

Further definitions

National income   In measuring national income, distinctions are made among such concepts as GNP, GDP and NNP. In their theories, economists usually use the generic concept of *national income* (indicated by the symbol Y). Usually Y may be thought of as interchangeable with constant-price GDP, i.e., total real output. Note, however, that this is almost the same, and on the assumption on page 514 is exactly the same, as constant-price GNP, i.e., total real incomes earned in the economy.

Equilibrium income   Equilibrium is a state of rest, usually brought about by a balance between opposing forces. National income is said to be in equilibrium when there is no tendency for it either to increase or to decrease. The actual national income achieved at equilibrium is referred to as the EQUILIBRIUM NATIONAL INCOME. In this chapter we begin our study of the forces that determine the size of equilibrium national income, which is often described as the problem of *the determination of national income.*

Autonomous and induced expenditure   Any expenditure that is taken as a constant, unaffected by the economic variables within our theory, is called AUTONOMOUS EXPENDITURE. Any expenditure that is determined by, and thus varies with, economic variables within our theory is called INDUCED EXPENDITURE. For example, in the simplest theory of the determination of national income, investment expenditure is assumed to be autonomous and consumption is assumed to be induced expenditure. (Note that, using the terminology introduced on page 28, autonomous and induced are the same, respectively, as exogenous and endogenous.)

The concept of the circular flow   In any economy both commodities and the services of factors of production are constantly being exchanged for money. To look at this circular flow in its simplest possible form we imagine an economy containing four households, A, B, C and D. Each household makes a different commodity and earns its income by selling it to other households. Assume that there is only one pound note in the economy and that the following transactions occur over one week: A makes commodities that it sells to B for £1; B does the same, selling to C; C does the same, selling to D; D in its turn makes commodities that it sells to A for £1. Each household has made and sold commodities for £1, which becomes that household's weekly income. Each household has also spent £1 on commodities made by some other household.

The transactions in this simple economy are shown in Figure 35.1. Commodity flows are shown with broken lines and money flows with solid lines. A single pound note has passed around the circle and has been used for four separate transactions. Each household has earned £1 as its income, and each has spent £1. If these are all the transactions over a week, then the total income earned by households in the economy in that week is £4. Note that the total income exceeds the quantity of money (£1) because the same pound note was used for more than one transaction. This illustrates an important fact: total income is not necessarily equal to the total quantity of money, because a single unit of money can create income each time it changes hands. (The relation between the stock of money and the flow of income is called the *velocity of circulation*, and is studied in detail in the Appendix to Chapter 44.)

In any real economy, each separate household does not earn its income by producing and selling

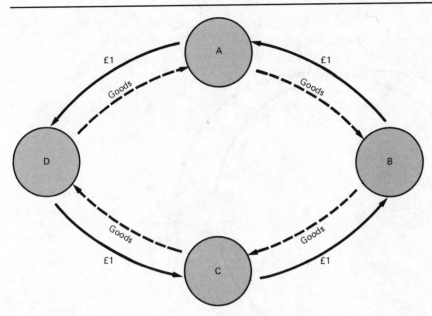

Fig. 35.1 Flows of commodities and money among four households

its own commodities. Instead, production is organized by firms. Firms obtain the services of factors of production from households – paying wages, rent, interest and profits in return – and then use these factors to make commodities that households consume. Households earn income by providing factor services to firms; they spend this income by buying commodities from firms.[1] We define the CIRCULAR FLOW OF INCOME as *the flow of payments and receipts for factor services and for currently produced output passing between domestic* (as opposed to foreign) *firms and domestic households*. In Figure 35.2, the flows of payments are shown by the solid lines, while the flows of goods and services, which are being paid for, are shown by the broken lines.

Basic assumptions

In constructing our theory of the determination of national income we start by making some simplifying assumptions. These assumptions are designed to isolate the main forces that determine national income. The consequences of dropping them are considered in later chapters.

(1) Potential national income is constant Because an economy's productive capacity changes slowly from year to year, potential national income (see p. 502) changes slowly. Thus, although cumulative effects of small annual changes in Y_F can be dramatic over several decades, the effects are relatively minor over a period of a year or two. As a result, assuming Y_F to be constant is not greatly unrealistic for short periods of time. In Chapter 42, we drop this assumption in order to study longer-term problems of growth in potential income. This assumption allows us to isolate some

---

[1] This is usually the case but not always. People in domestic service, for example, earn their incomes by selling their services directly to other households. In everything that follows we ignore this minor complication.

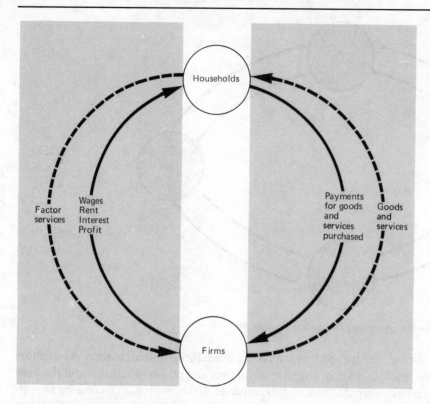

Fig. 35.2 Real and money flows between firms and households

forces that strongly influence national income over short periods of time. When Y_F is constant, real (constant-price) national income changes only because of changes in the employment of factors of production.

(2) There are unemployed supplies of all factors of production This assumption implies that output can be increased by using land, labour and capital that is currently unemployed. In subsequent chapters we shall study the behaviour of national income when unemployment has reached such a low level that it is difficult, if not impossible, to increase output by putting to work factors of production that are currently unemployed.

(3) The level of prices is constant Of course, we want to move on as quickly as possible to problems of inflation. Since it is vastly easier to do things one at a time rather than all at once, we seek first to understand the determination of income when prices are constant. In Part 10 we drop this assumption.

Armed with the three assumptions just stated, we can focus on the problem of what determines the equilibrium level of national income from the demand side. The procedure is to take a model of an economy and discover what determines its equilibrium national income. (We shall begin with the simplest possible model and then add complications one at a time.) But first it may be helpful to look in a little more detail at our assumption that prices are constant.

The aggregate supply curve of an economy with substantial unemployment

The microeconomic theory of competitive markets leads us to expect that prices will rise when there is excess demand and fall when there is excess supply. The state of the economy described in assumption (2) above is one of excess supply: firms would like to sell more than they are now selling at existing prices and unemployed workers would be willing to work at the existing wage. Why then do individual prices, and hence the whole price level, not fall? The basic microeconomic explanation is to be found on pages 276–82 of Chapter 21 and pages 387–90 of Chapter 27.

Assumption (2) above means that firms are producing below normal capacity. We saw in Chapter 21 that oligopolistic firms with flat cost curves and positive costs of changing prices will vary output (and hence employment of factors of production) at constant prices when demand fluctuates below normal-capacity output. But why does the price of labour not fall when there is heavy unemployment, thus reducing the cost curves of firms and causing them to cut prices? A possible answer is to be found in Chapter 27 where we saw that wages may not fluctuate so as to clear labour markets in response to short-term fluctuations in the demand for labour. Under these circumstances both product *and* labour markets adjust quantities rather than prices in the face of short-term reductions in demand. This means that the supply curves of firms are flat (perfectly elastic) at least up to capacity output. Under these conditions, individual firms produce whatever they can sell, i.e., their output is demand-determined.

What is true for each firm is also true for the economy, and we can illustrate this by drawing what is called an AGGREGATE SUPPLY CURVE which relates the economy's total output, Y, to the price level, P. If product and labour markets behave as just described, then the economy's aggregate supply curve will be perfectly elastic up to normal-capacity output. This is shown by the curve labelled SRAS, for short-run aggregate supply, in Figure 35.3. The curve tells us that, as far as the supply side is concerned, output can vary between 0 and Y_1 without any pressure for the price level to depart from its present level of P_1. Thus, for the economy as a whole, the output that is produced in the aggregate, i.e., the level of Y, is determined by total demand which is usually called aggregate demand.

At this stage of our study, income is demand-determined.

For the moment, we do not need to enquire into the slope of the aggregate supply curve to the

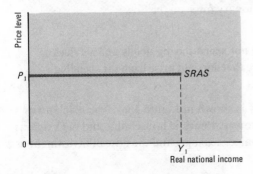

Fig. 35.3 A perfectly elastic short-run aggregate supply curve

right of Y_1 since for the time being our studies are confined to the unemployment case. We do this so that we can study the forces determining aggregate demand. Once this is done we can introduce the complications that arise if firms are not prepared to supply at existing prices everything that is demanded.

The determination of income in a two-sector economy

The basic model We first consider the simplest economy that will reveal the forces we wish to study. This economy contains only households and firms. It produces only two kinds of commodities, consumers' goods, sold by the firms that produce them to the households that consume them, and investment goods, sold by the firms that produce them to the firms that use them. To simplify matters at the outset, we assume that firms pay out all of their profits to the households that own them. This means that all national income is paid out to households and becomes their disposable income. They then decide how much of that income to spend for consumption purposes, C, and how much to save, S. Firms produce all of the consumption goods that households demand and all of the investment goods that firms demand. Investment goods are paid for by borrowing money either directly from households or from banks where households deposit some of their savings.

According to these simple assumptions, all savings decisions are taken by households and all investment decisions are taken by firms. This separation has one obvious, but very important, implication:

> **There is no reason why a change in the desire of households to save, or in the desire of firms to invest, should automatically be matched by a similar change on the part of the other group.**

The effects of saving and investment First consider the effects of saving on this simple economy's circular flow of income. Consumption expenditure is income that households receive from firms and then pass back to firms through their consumption purchases. Saving is income received by households that they do not pass back to firms through consumption expenditure. Saving thus represents a withdrawal, or a leakage, of expenditure from the circular flow of income between households and firms. Since savings are a leakage out of the circular flow, they tend to exert a contractionary force on the flow.

Now consider the effect of investment. Investment expenditure creates for the capital-goods-producing firms, and for the factors they employ, income that does not arise from the expenditure of households. Investment expenditure thus creates an addition to, or what is called an injection into, the circular flow of income. As such it exerts an expansionary force on the flow.

In summary:

> **Saving is income that households receive but do not spend buying goods and services from firms. Investment is income that firms receive that does not arise from the spending of households.**

The circular flow in the simple two-sector economy is shown in Figure 35.4. The black arrows show the circular flow of expenditure from domestic firms to domestic households and back again; the white arrows show the flow of saving as a withdrawal, or leakage, and the flow of investment as an injection.

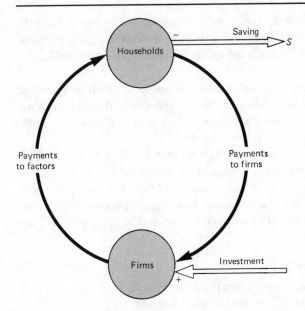

Fig. 35.4 The circular flow of income in the two-sector economy

Total demand: aggregate desired expenditure

Definitions According to the assumptions we have made, total output will be determined by the total demand to buy that output. In this simple model there are two elements of demand, what households want to spend on consumption goods, C, and what firms want to spend on investment goods, I. Since the term aggregate demand is reserved for a different concept, the term AGGREGATE DESIRED EXPENDITURE is used to refer to the total amount of purchases that all spending units in the economy wish to make. Using E for aggregate desired expenditure, we have

$$E \equiv C + I \tag{1}$$

where the three-bar identity sign emphasizes that this is merely a definition of aggregate desired expenditure.

Behavioural assumptions Next, to build our model, we make assumptions about the behaviour of the two elements of aggregate desired expenditure, investment and consumption.

Investment decisions: For the moment, it is convenient to study how the level of national income adjusts to a fixed level of investment. Thus, we assume that firms plan to spend a constant amount on investment in plant and equipment each year and that they plan to hold their inventories constant. This makes investment an autonomous expenditure flow (i.e., it is an exogenous variable). In Chapter 42 we drop these assumptions and study the behaviour of national income when investment is made an induced expenditure flow (i.e., an endogenous variable). In the meantime, we write our present assumption as

$$I = I^* \ , \tag{2}$$

which says that the desired amount of investment, I, is some constant amount which we call I^*. Depending on the size of the economy, I^* might be £1,000 million or £100,000 million per year. (When autonomous expenditure flows are given specific values, these are indicated by asterisks.)

The consumption-saving decision: Each household makes plans about how much to spend on consumption, C, and how much to save, S. These are not, however, independent decisions. Since saving is income not spent on consumption, it follows that households have to decide on a single division of their disposable income between saving and consumption.

How do households in the aggregate actually divide their income between C and S? This question is studied in detail in the Appendix to this Chapter. In the meantime we shall make the simple assumption that consumption and saving are constant fractions of income. If, for example, every household spends 80 per cent of its income and saves the remaining 20 per cent, then in this economy consumption will be 80 per cent of national income and savings will be 20 per cent. We can write this assumption

$$C = cY \ , \tag{3}$$

where c is a fraction greater than zero (positive consumption) and less than unity (positive saving). (The assumption of constancy is a 'first approximation' that we shall amend later.)

Since what is not spent on consumption is by definition saved, we can also express our single assumption about household spending behaviour as

$$S = sY \ , \tag{3'}$$

where s is a positive fraction such that[1]

$$s = 1 - c \ . \tag{4}$$

All this means is that if c pence out of every pound of disposable income is spent on consumption, then $1 - c$ pence must be saved.

Propensities to consume and save   To summarize the relation between consumption and income, Keynes developed two concepts. The AVERAGE PROPENSITY TO CONSUME (APC) is the average amount of all income spent on consumption, i.e., total consumption expenditure divided by total income. This is C/Y. Since in our simple model $C = cY$, the APC is $cY/Y = c$. The MARGINAL PROPENSITY TO CONSUME (MPC) is the proportion of each new increment of income that is spent on consumption. This is $\Delta C/\Delta Y$. Equation (3) shows that $\Delta C = c\Delta Y$, making the MPC equal to c. (Recall that Δ means a change in whatever it is attached to.)

All that these results summarize is the obvious property that, according to our simple consump-

---

[1] Since income is either spent on consumption or saved

$$Y \equiv C + S \ .$$

So if $\qquad C = cY$,

we have $\qquad Y = cY + S$

or $\qquad S = (1 - c)Y$.

So if $\qquad S = sY$,

then $\qquad s = 1 - c$,

which is the result given in the text.

tion function, households spend on consumption £c out of every £1 of income so that consumption as a fraction of income is c, and so also is the consumption out of every new £1 of income equal to £c.

The savings propensities are similarly defined. The AVERAGE PROPENSITY TO SAVE (APS) is total saving as a fraction of total income ($S/Y = s$ in our model). The MARGINAL PROPENSITY TO SAVE (MPS) is the fraction of any additional £1 of income that is saved ($\Delta S/\Delta Y = s$ in our model).

As an example, if $C = 0 \cdot 8 Y$ so that $S = 0 \cdot 2 Y$, total consumption will be 80 per cent of total income and 80p out of every new £1 of income will be consumed ($APC = MPC = 0 \cdot 8$); while total saving will be 20 per cent of total income and 20p out of every new £1 of income will be saved ($APS = MPS = 0 \cdot 2$).

The aggregate expenditure function If we substitute our behavioural equations (2) and (3) into the definition of aggregate expenditure in (1), we obtain what is called the aggregate expenditure function,

$$E = cY + I^* \quad , \tag{5}$$

which expresses E, in this case, as a function of the endogenous variable Y (and the constant I^*). In general, the AGGREGATE EXPENDITURE FUNCTION expresses desired expenditure, E, as a function of all the variables that determine it.

Equilibrium conditions

The model is completed by adding an equilibrium condition. This can be expressed in either of two equivalent ways, which we consider one at a time.

Expenditure equals income Recall the assumption that, because they are operating below normal-capacity output, firms will produce anything they can sell. This implies that total output, Y, will be equal to total desired expenditure because whatever people and firms try to buy will be produced for them by firms eager to sell all they can. Thus, our equilibrium condition is[1]

$$Y = E \quad . \tag{6}$$

Saving equals investment An alternative way of expressing the same equilibrium condition is in terms of the equality of desired saving and desired investment. We saw that all income is either saved or consumed, which can be expressed

$$Y \equiv C + S \quad . \tag{7}$$

From (1) we know that all expenditure is either for consumption or investment. Substituting (1) and (7) into the equilibrium condition (6) yields

$$C + S = C + I \quad .$$

Cancelling out the C, which is common to both sides, yields

$$S = I \tag{8}$$

[1] This equilibrium condition has nothing to do with the identity between expenditure and income in the national-income accounts. Here Y and E refer to actual GDP produced and to the amount spending units would actually like to spend.

as an alternative statement of the equilibrium condition in (6).

> **Equilibrium income occurs when demanders are just willing to purchase everything produced, $E = Y$, or equivalently, when the contractionary force exerted by saving is just equal to the expansionary force exerted by investment.**

The determination of equilibrium income

We must now see how equilibrium income is established in this model. Since much of the more complex analysis that follows uses these results, it is worthwhile studying them in detail in a model that is simple enough for its workings to be readily apparent.

A numerical example Assume for purposes of illustration that consumption is always 80 per cent of income and that investment is constant at £100 m. This makes the aggregate expenditure function

$$E = 0{\cdot}8Y + 100 \quad .$$

Combined with the equilibrium condition $E = Y$, this yields the solution of £500 m for equilibrium income.[1]

Table 35.1 shows some illustrative figures for this numerical example. It is clear from the table that if output were to be held at any level below £500 million, people would wish to buy more than

Table 35.1 Equilibrium national income in a numerical example (£m)

(1)	(2)	(3)	(4)	(5)	(6)
National income Y	Desired consumption[1] C	Desired saving[2] S	Desired investment I	Desired expenditure E	Excess of desired expenditure over actual output (5) – (1)
100	80	20	100	180	80
300	240	60	100	340	40
400	320	80	100	420	20
500	400	100	100	500	0
600	480	120	100	580	−20
700	560	140	100	660	−40
900	720	180	100	820	−80

[1] $C = 0{\cdot}8Y$.
[2] $S = 0{\cdot}2Y$.

---

[1] Putting (9) into (6) yields

$$Y = 0{\cdot}8Y + 100$$

or $$0.2\,Y = 100$$

and $$Y = 100/0{\cdot}2 = 500 \quad .$$

was being produced. Desired purchases would then exceed actual output. For example, if GDP were £400 m, desired expenditure would be £420 m. Since firms are assumed to produce to meet all demand, this is not a possible equilibrium position and output must rise.

On the other hand, if output is held above £500 m, desired expenditure would fall short of actual output. For example, if GDP is £700 m, desired expenditure would be only £660 m. Since firms could not sell all they were producing, output would fall until firms were just able to sell all they wished.

Clearly, the only possible equilibrium position in the table is at a GDP of £500 m. At this output, demand is just enough to buy what is produced, no more and no less. At that GDP, households spend £400 m on consumption and save £100 m. But firms spend £100 m to buy investment goods, so total demand is £500 m, which is just enough to buy the total output of £500 m.[1]

Notice also that, at the equilibrium level of income, desired saving is equal to desired investment (at a value of £100 m). Below the equilibrium, desired saving is less than desired investment, while above it desired saving exceeds desired investment. When saving and investment are the same, the addition to demand caused by investment expenditure just matches the subtraction from demand caused by households not spending all of their income. Desired expenditure is thus equal to GDP so that all output will just be bought.

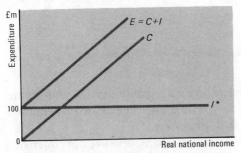

Fig. 35.5 The consumption, investment and aggregate expenditure functions

A graphical determination We now introduce some graphs that will be very useful in subsequent work, so it will pay to give them some attention now. Figure 35.5 graphs the behaviour relations from equations (2) and (3), first individually and then substituted into the definition of aggregate expenditure in (1). The line labelled I^* shows the flow of desired investment expenditure as a constant amount, equal in this example to £100 m. The line labelled C shows consumption as a constant percentage of income, 80 per cent in this case. The consumption line passes through the origin indicating zero consumption expenditure when income is zero and has a slope of 0·8 indicating that £0·80 out of every £1 of income is spent on consumption. The third line, labelled E, shows aggregate expenditure as the sum of consumption and investment expenditure, equation (5). (Graphically, therefore, E is the vertical summation of C and I^*.)

Figure 35.6 (i) replots the E line from Figure 35.5 and adds the so-called 45° line. This line shows all the points where expenditure equals income, $E = Y$. The 45° line is thus a graph of the equilib-

---

[1] Notice we have not said what would happen if the economy were temporarily at some disequilibrium level of income. To do this we would need to specify lags in the expenditure functions. All we have done is to argue that no other income except £500 m could be an equilibrium because if it were to be established demand would not equal output.

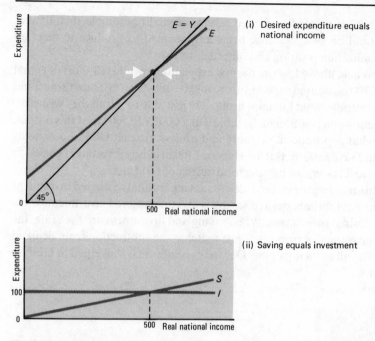

Fig. 35.6 Alternative equilibrium conditions to determine equilibrium national income in the two-sector model

rium condition of equation (6) which tells us that national income is in equilibrium when buyers are just prepared to buy (E) as much as is being produced (Y). Above the 45° line desired expenditure exceeds income, while below it desired expenditure falls short of income.

The equilibrium level of income (£500 m in this example) occurs where these two lines intersect: desired expenditure as shown by the E line is equal to actual income. For lower incomes, say £300 m, desired expenditure exceeds output. Since firms are assumed to meet all demand, this cannot be an equilibrium so income must rise. For higher incomes, say £800 m, desired expenditure falls short of actual income. Again this cannot be an equilibrium since desired expenditure now falls short of output. If this income were to be maintained, firms could not sell all of their output so sooner or later output would fall.

The graphical expression of the alternative view of the model is shown in Figure 35.6 (ii). The investment function shows a constant level of investment (at £100 m in this example), while the savings function shows saving at zero when income is zero and rising at a slope of 0·2 indicating £0·2 is saved out of every £1 of income. The intersection of these two lines represents the alternative equilibrium condition (equation (8)), where desired saving equals desired investment.

An algebraic determination[1] The model is so simple that its formal solution is a trivial matter. Quite a bit can, nonetheless, be learned from studying it, so let us first gather its equations together.

---

[1] At this point it would be very helpful to read the discussion on the use of algebra in macroeconomic models on pages xx and xxi at the beginning of the book.

Definitional Equation	$E \equiv C + I$	(1)
Behavioural Equations	$I = I^*$	(2)
	$C = cY \qquad 0 < c < 1$	(3)
Equilibrium Condition	$Y = E$	(6)

Equation (1) is what is called a definitional equation (or more properly a definitional identity), defining aggregate expenditure. Equations (2) and (3) are called behavioural equations. They tell us how investment behaves (it is a constant), and how consumption behaves (it varies with income). Equation (6) is what is called an equilibrium condition. It tells us what must hold in equilibrium: in this case desired expenditure must equal actual income.

Note that, as a matter of convention, the variables, whether autonomous or induced, are indicated by upper-case (i.e., capital) letters. Lower-case (i.e., non-capital) letters are reserved for what are called the behavioural parameters. These are the coefficients that describe decision-takers' behaviour in the model. In the present case, there is only one behavioural parameter, c. In general these parameters are usually only restricted in their signs, i.e., restricted to be positive or negative. The parameter c, however, is generally restricted to be positive and less than unity, indicating that the MPC is positive but less than unity. The restrictions on behavioural parameters are usually given to the right of the equation where they occur or, if there are too many of them, immediately below the list of equations. Specific examples and empirical applications arise by giving exact numerical values to these parameters (as well as to the exogenous variables). The numerical example used above arose from setting $c = 0.8$ and $I^* = 100$.

Now consider the model as set out above. Substituting (2) and (3) into (1) yields the two equations whose solution is illustrated in Figures 35.6(i):

$$E = cY + I^* \tag{5}$$

$$E = Y . \tag{6}$$

The algebraic solution is found by solving these two equations simultaneously to obtain[1]

$$Y = I^*/(1 - c) \tag{9}$$

We can also solve for equilibrium income using the saving equals investment condition. To do this we use the following equations

---

[1] Substituting (5) into (6): $\qquad Y = cY + I^*$.

Subtracting cY from both sides: $\qquad Y - cY = I^*$.

Factoring out the Y: $\qquad Y(1 - c) = I^*$.

Dividing through by $(1 - c)$ yields equation (9) in the text.

$$S = sY \tag{3'}$$

$$I = I^* \tag{2}$$

$$S = I \tag{8}$$

where (3') and (2) are behavioural equations and (8) is the equilibrium condition. Substitution easily produces[1]

$$Y = I^*/s \quad . \tag{10}$$

Since $s = 1 - c$ (equation (4)), it follows that (9) and (10) are equivalent; they are just two ways of discovering the single equilibrium income implied by the model.

A link between saving and investment?

Earlier in this chapter we stressed that saving and investment decisions were made by different groups, and that there was no necessary reason why households should decide to save the same amount that firms decide to invest. We have just concluded, however, that in this simple two-sector economy national income is in equilibrium when saving is equal to investment. Does this not mean that we have found a mechanism that ensures that households end up desiring to save an amount equal to what firms desire to invest? The answer is 'yes'. Is there not, then, a conflict between what we said at first and what we have now concluded? The answer is 'no'.

The explanation of the apparent conflict provides the key to the theory of the determination of national income in the simple two-sector case. There is no reason why the amount that households wish to save at a randomly selected level of national income should be equal to the amount that firms wish to invest at the same level of income. This is the meaning of the statement made at the outset. But when saving is not equal to investment, there are forces at work in the economy that cause national income to change until the two do become equal. This is the meaning of the latter statement.

The graphical expression of this is that the saving function does not everywhere coincide with the investment function in Figure 35.6(ii). Where it does not, desired saving does not equal desired investment at the indicated level of income. But the two functions do intersect somewhere, and the equilibrium level of income, in the simple two-sector economy, occurs at the intersection point. To recapitulate:

> **There is no reason why saving should equal investment at any randomly chosen level of income, but when they are not equal in the two-sector economy, national income will change until they are brought into equality.**

Changes in income in the two-sector model

Our next step is to study the forces that cause income to change in the simple two-sector economy.

---

[1] Substituting (3') and (2) into (8):

$$sY = I^* \quad .$$

Dividing through by s then produces equation (10) in the text.

As a preliminary to this study, recall the important distinction, first made with respect to demand and supply curves, between movements along curves and shifts of curves. We now apply this distinction to the curves used in macroeconomics.

If desired consumption expenditure rises, it makes a great deal of difference whether the rise is in response to a change in national income or to an increased desire to consume *at each level of national income* including the present one. The former change is represented by *a movement along* the aggregate consumption curve; it is the response of consumption to a change in income. The latter change is represented by *a shift* in the consumption curve that indicates a change in the proportion of income that households desire to consume. It is the second type of change that can itself disturb an existing equilibrium.

Figure 35.7 illustrates this important distinction. The lines in the figure conform to our assumptions about how consumption, savings and investment are related to national income. They are repeats of the same lines in Figure 35.5.

Movements along curves In part (i) of Figure 35.7, in response to an increase in income from Y_1 to Y_2, we must *move along* the I, C and S curves to determine the new flows of investment, consumption and savings, respectively. The change in income of ΔY leads to an increase in savings of ΔS and in consumption of ΔC. Investment does not change, i.e., ΔI equals zero, and cannot therefore be shown. The slopes of the curves show the ratios of these changes in the variables to the changes in income (i.e., the *responses* of those variables to changes in income). They are known as MARGINAL PROPENSITIES.

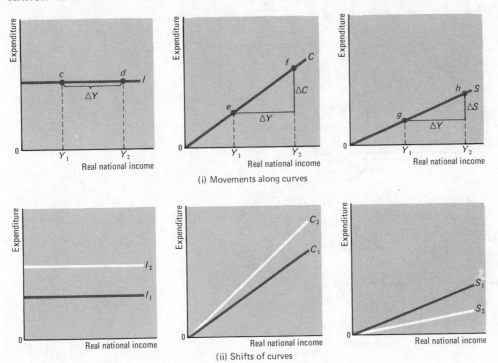

(i) Movements along curves

(ii) Shifts of curves

Fig. 35.7 Movements along and shifts of curves

The response of investment, consumption and savings to a change in income is indicated by a movement along the relevant curves and is shown graphically by the slope of the curve.

We have already encountered the MARGINAL PROPENSITY TO CONSUME (MPC) and the MARGINAL PROPENSITY TO SAVE (MPS). Since these marginal propensities are the fraction of any increase in income spent or saved, it follows that they are equal to c and s in the equations (3) and (3′) above and to the slopes of the C and S lines in Figure 35.7.

Marginal propensities relate to movements along curves and tell us how much particular flows respond to changes in income.

Shifts of curves Flows of expenditure or withdrawals can change for a second reason: the curves *themselves* may shift, indicating a new level of the relevant flow for *each* level of national income. Such shifts are illustrated in Figure 35.7(ii). In each panel of part (ii), the curve *shifts* to the white line. The change is not a consequence of a change in income but of a change in the whole relationship with income. The indicated shifts represent a rise in the investment function, a rise in the consumption function and a fall in the savings function.

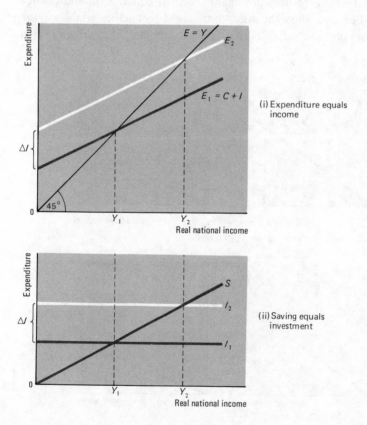

(i) Expenditure equals income

(ii) Saving equals investment

Fig. 35.8 A shift in investment expenditure changes equilibrium national income

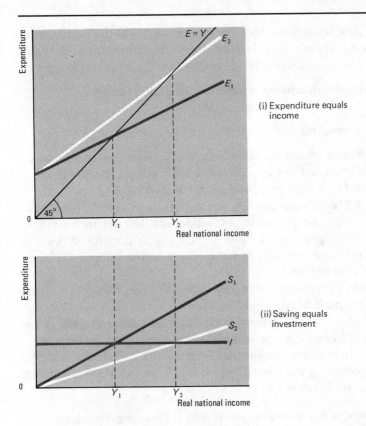

Fig. 35.9 A change in the marginal propensity to consume changes equilibrium national income

While the figure shows three shifts, the shift in consumption and the shift in savings are necessarily related. An upward shift in the consumption curve, for example, indicates an increase in the desired consumption expenditure that is associated with each level of income. In this case, desired household saving must fall at each level of income, since saving is all income not spent on consumption. Therefore, a rise in the consumption curve implies a fall in the savings curve. With this distinction in mind we can now pass to a study of the causes of changes in equilibrium income.

A shift in investment

Figure 35.8 shows the two ways to analyse the effects of a shift in investment. In part (i) the original expenditure function is E_1. A rise in investment of ΔI increases the total expenditure associated with each level of income by that amount. This shifts the expenditure function upwards to the new line E_2. At the old level of income, Y_1, desired expenditure now exceeds output and income will rise as firms expand production to meet the new demand. The new level of income is indicated by Y_2 where, given the new expenditure function, desired expenditure is once again exactly equal to total output.

A fall in investment expenditure can be shown by reversing the shift. Investment falls by ΔI, taking the expenditure line from E_2 to E_1 and equilibrium income from Y_2 to Y_1.

Part (ii) of the figure shows the same result in a saving-investment graph. The rise in investment takes the investment line from I_1 to I_2. At the original level of income, Y_1, desired investment now exceeds desired savings and national income rises until these two flows are again equal at income Y_2.

A rise in investment increases equilibrium national income, while a fall reduces it.

A change in the propensity to consume

Say that there is a rise in the proportion of income households wish to spend on consumption and a corresponding fall in the proportion of income saved. In our numerical example, the propensity to consume might go from 0·8 to, say, 0·9 taking the propensity to save from 0·2 to 0·1.

The effect is shown in Figure 35.9. The consumption function shifts from a slope of 0·8 to 0·9 and the expenditure function (which is merely the consumption function plus the constant amount of investment expenditure) does the same, going from E_1 to E_2. Clearly at the original level of equilibrium income, Y_1, desired expenditure now exceeds output. Firms will produce more to meet the new demand and equilibrium income will rise to Y_2.

A fall in consumption is illustrated by reversing the process. The E line goes from E_2 to E_1 and equilibrium income falls in response to the fall in demand.

The same analysis is shown in part (ii) of the Figure where the increased desire to spend pivots the savings function downwards from S_1 to S_2. At the original level of income, desired investment expenditure exceeds desired savings. In response, income rises from Y_1 to Y_2, where investment is once again equal to saving. The opposite case is analysed by pivoting the saving function upwards from S_2 to S_1 so that equilibrium income falls from Y_2 to Y_1.

An upward shift in the consumption function (a downward shift in the savings function) increases equilibrium national income. The opposite shifts have the reverse effect.

The interpretation of these results is further considered in the Chapter 43 in the section on The Paradox of Thrift. So far, our results have a very strong common-sense appeal since they follow from a model whose formal properties are really quite simple. Here are its characteristics in summary form.

(1) Firms are assumed to have perfectly elastic supply curves, so that output is demand-determined.
(2) Total demand exceeds output at zero income (by virtue of the constant investment assumption) and rises with income at a rate less than the rise in income (because the MPC is positive but less than unity).
(3) There exists, therefore, an equilibrium level of income at which total demand equals total output.
(4) Upward shifts in demand raise income as firms increase production to meet the extra demand; downward shifts in demand lower income as firms decrease production in response to the fall in sales.

How much does income change?: the multiplier

It remains to consider the magnitude of the changes that result from shifts in the expenditure function. Here we will concentrate on shifts in the investment function.

The definition of the multiplier A key prediction of national-income theory is that a change in expenditure, whatever its source, will cause a change in national income that is greater than the initial change in expenditure. The MULTIPLIER is defined as the ratio of the change in national income to the change in expenditure that brought it about. The change in expenditure might come, for example, from an increase in private investment. The importance of the multiplier in national-income theory makes it worthwhile to use more than one approach to developing it, and to showing why its value exceeds unity.

An intuitive statement What would you expect to happen to national income if there were a rise in investment expenditure of £1 billion *per year*, say on building new factories? Will national income rise by only £1 billion? The answer is 'no, national income will rise by more than £1 billion.' The impact of the initial rise will be felt by the construction industry and by all those industries that supply it. Income and the employment of factors used in these industries will rise by £1 billion as a result. But the newly employed factors will spend much of their new income buying food, clothing, shelter, holidays, cars, refrigerators and a host of other products. This is the induced rise in the consumption expenditure, and when output expands to meet this extra demand, employment will rise in all of the affected industries. When owners of factors that are newly employed in these industries spend their incomes, output and employment will rise further; more income will then be created and more expenditure induced. Indeed, at this stage we might begin to wonder if the increase in income will ever come to an end. The answer is that it will come to an end because every increase of £1 in income induces an increase in consumption expenditure of less than £1. Thus the multiplied expansion of income that ripples through the entire economy in response to the initial increase in income is a damped series where each repercussion is smaller than the one that preceded it.

This is as far as intuitive arguments can take us. Now we must look for a more formal demonstration of these propositions.

A numerical statement The multiplier is nothing more than the sum of a convergent series. In the earlier numerical example, a *permanent* flow of new investment expenditure initially raises income by £1 billion. With an *MPC* of 0·8 the first round of induced expenditure by those who earn the £1 billion of new income is £800 million. Those who receive this new income raise their expenditure by 80 per cent of it, which means £640 million of new expenditure. This in turns gives rise to £512 million of new expenditure, and so on, each of these new flows being added to the ones that preceded them. Thus, in total, we have $1 + 0·8 + (0·8)^2 + (0·8)^3 + \ldots$. As is well known from school mathematics, the sum of this series is $1/(1 - 0·8) = 1/0·2 = 5$. Thus the continued expenditure of £1 billion on new investment projects sets up a series of repercussions with each person who receives a new flow of income increasing his or her flow of expenditure by 80 per cent of the new income (and saving the extra 20 per cent) until national income has risen by £5 billion. In this case, therefore, the multiplier is *five*, since every £1 of new investment expenditure raises equilibrium income by £5.

Now let us drop the numerical example and consider an initial new investment of £1 and let c stand for the *MPC*. Let the initial increase in income be £1, so that the first induced round of the new expenditure is £c. The next is $cc = c^2$, and so on. The multiplier thus becomes the sum of the series $1 + c + c^2 + c^3 + \ldots$, which is $1/(1 - c)$, which by equation (4) above is $1/s$.

So we can see that the multiplier is larger, the larger is c (the smaller is s). This should not surprise us since the larger is c the greater is the spending that is induced by each new increment in income.

A graphical statement The multiplier is most easily illustrated graphically in a saving-investment diagram. Figure 35.10 repeats the S and I curves from Figure 35.9. When the investment function is I_1, equilibrium national income is Y_1, while when the investment function is I_2 equilibrium income is Y_2. The multiplier is defined as the ratio of the change in income to the change in autonomous expenditure that brought it about. In our present simple model, investment is the only autonomous expenditure flow, so letting K be the multiplier, we have $K = \Delta Y/\Delta I$. Figure 35.10 shows that the slope of the savings function, s, is $\Delta I/\Delta Y$. Thus the multiplier is the reciprocal of the slope of the savings function, $K = 1/s$.

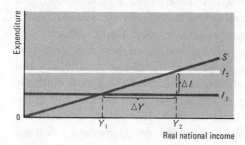

Fig. 35.10 The multiplier is the reciprocal of the slope of the savings function

An algebraic statement The solution for the equilibrium value of income derived earlier is

$$Y = I^*/(1-c) = I^*/s \ .$$

(See equations (9) and (10) above.) Taking first differences of these yields[1]

$$\Delta Y = \Delta I^*/(1-c) = \Delta I^*/s \ ,$$

or

$$K = \frac{\Delta Y}{\Delta I^*} = \frac{1}{1-c} = \frac{1}{s} \ . \tag{11}$$

> **The value of the multiplier is the reciprocal of the marginal propensity to save or, what is the same thing, the reciprocal of unity minus the marginal propensity to consume.**

Conclusion

Early national-income models used the two-sector model outlined in this chapter. With empirical savings propensities between 0·1 and 0·2 in most countries, multipliers were often thought to be between 5 and 10. Such values suggest extreme instability for free-market economies. Relatively small shifts in investment would produce very large changes in national income and employment. Fortunately, modern measures of most countries' multipliers are very much smaller than these figures. To see why, we need to build a somewhat more elaborate model, which is our task in the next chapter.

---

[1] The operation of first differencing is described in section (9) of the Appendix to Chapter 2.

Appendix to chapter 35

The consumption function

Consumption is by far the largest component of aggregate expenditure of all countries. In the UK it represents nearly half of total final expenditure. This makes the consumption function one of the most important functions in macroeconomics. If we are to predict the effects of shifts in government taxation and spending policies on the other elements of private expenditure, we need to know the shape of the consumption function. For as we saw in the discussion of the multiplier, when one function shifts the magnitude of the effects on income depends on the slope of the other function.

In this Appendix we go beyond the crude assumption used so far that households always consume a constant fraction of their income, and thus also save a constant fraction. First we shall look in more detail at the Keynesian theory of the consumption function, then we shall outline some modern theories that go beyond the basic Keynesian hypothesis that current consumption depends on current income.

The Keynesian theory of the consumption function

The basic hypothesis of the Keynesian theory of the consumption function is that current consumption is related to current income. To describe this relation Keynes coined the twin concepts of the average and the marginal propensities to consume, as we saw in Chapter 35. AVERAGE PROPENSITY TO CONSUME (APC) is the proportion of income spent on consumption. To calculate this value, take total consumption expenditure, C, and divide it by Y, total income, $APC = C/Y$. We can obtain an average propensity to consume by using either total income, Y, or disposable income, Y_d, as the divisor. Which of these concepts is being used is almost always obvious from the context.

The marginal propensity to consume, the MPC, measures the relation between changes in consumption, ΔC, and changes in income, ΔY. By dividing ΔY into ΔC, we measure how much of the last pound's worth of income is consumed; in symbols, $MPC = \Delta C/\Delta Y$.

Various Keynesian consumption functions

In the text we used the simple case of a constant proportion of income spent on consumption. This function is $C = cY$. On it $\Delta C/\Delta Y = C/Y = c$. Then the average and the marginal propensities are both equal to c.

Empirical consumption functions, that describe how household consumption varies as income varies from year to year over periods of a decade or two, tend to fit the data better if they contain a constant: $C = a_o + cY$. On this function the MPC is still c but the APC is $(a_o + cY)/Y = a_o/Y + c$. This makes the APC larger than the MPC and makes the APC approach the MPC from above as Y increases without limit.

Other Keynesian determinants

Several other variables appear to exert a strong influence on consumption. These can be thought of as parameters that shift the simple relation between C and Y.

Changes in income distribution If households have different MPCs, aggregate consumption depends not only on aggregate income but also on the distribution of this income among households. In this case, a change in the *distribution* of income will cause a change in the aggregate level of consumption expenditure associated with any given *level* of national income.

Since the distribution of income tends to change fairly slowly, such changes do not destroy stable consumption-income relationships. Nevertheless, such changes can occur, and they cause the consumption function to shift.

Changes in the terms of credit   Many durable consumer goods are purchased on credit, whose terms may range from a few months to pay for a radio, to two or three years to pay for a car. If credit becomes more difficult or more costly to obtain, many households may postpone their planned, credit-financed purchases. If the typical initial payment required for goods purchased on hire purchase was increased from 10 to 20 per cent, households that had just saved up 10 per cent of the purchase price of the goods they wished to consume would now find this sum inadequate, and would have to postpone their planned purchases until they saved 20 per cent of the purchase price. There would then be a temporary reduction in current consumption expenditures until these extra savings had been accumulated.

Monetary authorities can, by controlling the cost and availability of credit, shift the consumption function and thus affect aggregate demand.

Changes in existing stocks of durable goods   It is now recognized that any period in which durables are difficult or impossible to purchase and monetary savings are accumulated is likely to be followed by a sudden outburst of expenditure on durables. Such a flurry of spending will also follow a period of unemployment, during which many families may have refrained from buying durables.

The emphasis here is on durable goods (e.g., cars and refrigerators) because purchases of non-durable consumer goods (e.g., food and clothing) and of services (e.g., car repairs) cannot be long postponed. While expenditures on non-durables are relatively steady, purchases of durables are volatile and can lead to sharp shifts in the consumption function.

Changes in price expectations   If households expect an inflation to occur, they may be willing to purchase durable goods they would otherwise not have bought for another one or two years. In such circumstances, purchases made now yield a saving over purchases made in the future. By the same argument, an expected deflation may lead to postponing purchases of durables in hopes of purchasing them later at a lower price.

The permanent-income and life-cycle hypotheses

In the Keynesian theory of the consumption function, current consumption expenditure is related to current income – either current disposable income or current national income. In recent years, empirical observations have several times seemed to conflict with this Keynesian hypothesis. The attempt to reconcile the basic theory of the consumption function with existing evidence has led to a series of modified theories that relate consumption to some longer-term concept of income than the income that the household is currently earning.

The two most influential theories of this type are the PERMANENT-INCOME HYPOTHESIS (PIH), developed by Professor Milton Friedman, and the LIFE-CYCLE HYPOTHESIS (LCH), developed by Professor Franco Modigliani and Albert Ando and the late Professor Aldo Brumberg. For our purposes the similarities between these theories are more important than their differences, and they may be looked at together when studying their major characteristics.

Variables

The three important variables used in these theories are consumption, saving and income. These need to be considered carefully since they are defined somewhat differently than in Keynesian theory.

Consumption   Keynesian-type theories seek to explain the amounts that households spend on purchasing goods and services for consumption. This concept is called *consumption expenditure*. Permanent-income theories seek to explain the actual flows of consumption of the services that are provided by the commodities that households buy. This concept is called *actual consumption*.[1] With services and non-durable goods, expenditure and actual consumption occur more or less at the same time and the distinction between these two concepts is not important. The consumption of a haircut, for example, occurs at the time it is purchased, and an orange or a package of cornflakes is consumed soon after it is purchased. Thus, if we knew purchases of such goods and services at some time, say last year, we would also know last year's consumption of these goods and services. But this is not the case with durable consumer goods. A screwdriver is purchased at one point in time, but it yields up its services over a

---

[1] Because Keynes's followers did not always distinguish carefully between the concepts of consumption expenditure and actual consumption, the word 'consumption' is often used in both contexts. We follow this normal practice, but where there is any possible ambiguity in the term we will refer to 'consumption expenditure' and to 'actual consumption'.

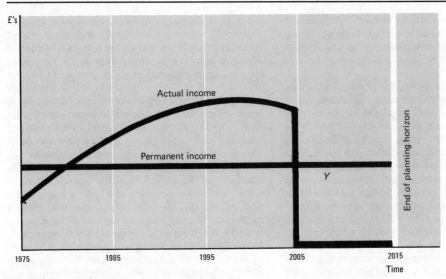

Fig. 35.11 Actual current income and permanent income

long time, possibly as long as the purchaser's lifetime. The same is true of a house and a watch and, over a shorter period of time, of a car and a dress. For such products, if we know purchases last year, we do not necessarily know last year's consumption of the services that the products yielded.

Thus one important characteristic of durable goods is that *expenditure* to purchase them is not synchronized with consumption of the stream of services that the goods provide. If in 1980 Mr Smith buys a car for £4,000, runs it for six years, and then discards it as worn out, his expenditure on automobiles is £4,000 in 1980 and zero for the next five years. His consumption of the services of automobiles, however, is spread out at an average annual rate of £666·66 for six years. If everyone followed Mr Smith's example by buying a new car in 1980 and replacing it in 1986, the automobile industry would undergo wild booms in 1980 and 1986, with five intervening years of slump even though the actual consumption of automobiles would be spread more or less evenly over time. This example is extreme, but it illustrates the possibilities, where consumers' durables are concerned, of quite different time-paths of *consumption expenditure*, which is the subject of Keynesian theories of the consumption function, and *actual consumption*, which is the subject of permanent-income type theories.

Saving Now consider saving. The change in emphasis from consumption expenditure to actual consumption implies a change in the definition of saving. Saving is no longer income minus consump-

tion expenditure; it is now income minus the value of actual consumption. When Mr Smith spent £4,000 on his car in 1980 but used only £666·66 worth of its services in that year he was actually consuming £666·66 and saving £3,333·34. The purchase of a consumers' durable is thus counted as saving, and only the value of its services actually consumed is counted as consumption.

Income The third important variable in this type of theory is the income variable. Instead of using current income, the theories use a concept of long-term income. The precise definition varies from one theory to another, but basically it is related to the household's expected income stream over a fairly long planning period. In the *LCH* it is the income that the household expects to earn over its lifetime.[1]

Every household is assumed to have a view of its expected lifetime earnings. This is not as unreasonable as it might seem. Students training to be doctors have a very different view of expected lifetime income than those training to become primary-school teachers. Both of these expected income streams – for a doctor and for a primary-school teacher – will be very different from that expected by an assembly-line worker or a professional athlete.

One such possible lifetime income stream is illustrated in Figure 35.11. The graph shows a

---

[1] In the *PIH* the household has an infinite time horizon and the relevant permanent-income concept is the amount the household could consume for ever without increasing or decreasing its present stock of wealth.

hypothetical expected income stream from work for a household whose planning horizon is 40 years from 1975. The current actual income rises to a peak, then falls slowly for a while, and then suddenly falls to zero on retirement.

The household's expected lifetime income can be converted into a single figure for *annual* PERMANENT INCOME. In the life-cycle hypothesis this permanent income is the maximum amount the household could spend on consumption each year without accumulating debts *that are passed on to future generations*. If a household were to consume a constant amount equal to its permanent income each year, it would add to its debt in years when current income was less than permanent income and reduce its debt or increase its assets in years when its current income exceeded its permanent income; however, over its whole lifetime it would just break even, leaving neither accumulated assets nor debts to its heirs. If the interest rate were zero, permanent income would be just the sum of all expected incomes divided by the number of expected years of life. With a positive interest rate, permanent income will diverge somewhat from this amount because of the costs of borrowing and the extra income that can be earned by investing savings.

Assumptions

The basic assumption of this type of theory, whether *PIH* or *LCH*, is that the household's actual consumption is related to its permanent rather than to its current income. Two households that have the same permanent income (and are similar in other relevant characteristics) will have the same consumption patterns even though their current incomes behave very differently.

Implications

The effect on consumption of changes in income
The major implication of these theories is that changes in a household's current income will affect its actual consumption only so far as they affect its

permanent income. Consider two income changes that could occur to a household with a permanent income of £5,000 per year and an expected lifetime of 30 more years. In the first, suppose the household receives an unexpected extra income of £1,000 *for this year only*. The increase in the household's permanent income is thus very small. If the rate of interest were zero, the household could consume an extra £33·33 per year for the rest of its expected lifespan; with a positive rate of interest the extra annual consumption would be more because money not spent this year could be invested and would earn interest.[1] In the second case, the household gets a totally unforeseen increase of £1,000 a year for the rest of its life. In this event the household's permanent income has risen by £1,000 because the household can actually consume £1,000 more every year without accumulating any new debts. Although in both cases current income rises by £1,000, the effects on permanent income are very different in the two cases.

Keynesian theory assumes that *consumption expenditure* is related to current income and therefore predicts the same change in this year's consumption expenditure in each of the above cases. Permanent-income theories relate *actual consumption* to permanent income and therefore predict very different changes in actual consumption in each of these cases. In the first case there would be only a small increase in actual consumption, while in the second case there would be a large increase.

In permanent-income theories, any change in current income that is thought to be temporary will have only a small effect on permanent income and hence on actual consumption.

The implication of these theories for the efficiency of government policy is discussed in Chapter 43.

---

[1] If the rate of interest were 7 per cent the household could invest the £1,000, consume an extra £80·50 per year, and just have nothing left at the end of 30 years.

36

National income in more elaborate models

In this chapter we shall see that the two-sector model of the determination of national income easily generalizes to deal with many sectors. As a first step we recall that the equilibrium condition for national income in the two-sector model can be stated in either of two ways.

(1) *Aggregate desired expenditure equals national income.* When this holds, desired expenditure is just sufficient to purchase the whole of the nation's output, and there is thus no tendency for output to change.

(2) *Saving equals investment.* When this holds, the contractionary force of income earned by households but not spent (saving) is just balanced by the expansionary force of income earned by firms that does not arise from household spending (investment). When these two forces are in balance, there will be no tendency for total output either to rise or to fall.

These results generalize with surprising ease to all circular-flow models. To see this, consider the two alternative equilibrium conditions one at a time.

The first applies, without amendment, to any circular-flow model.

> When aggregate desired expenditure is less than total income, national income will fall; when aggregate desired expenditure exceeds total income, national income will rise. Equilibrium national income occurs where aggregate desired expenditure is equal to national income.

In moving from one circular-flow model to another, all we need to do is to identify any new components of aggregate expenditure, and make assumptions about how each is related to national income.

The second equilibrium condition, saving equals investment, requires a slight but important reinterpretation before it can be extended to all circular-flow models. Saving and investment are examples of two more general categories of expenditure called withdrawals and injections. A WITHDRAWAL, which is also called a LEAKAGE, is any income that is not passed on in the circular flow. Thus if households earn income and do not spend it on domestically produced goods and services, this is a withdrawal from the circular flow. Similarly, if firms receive money from the sale of goods and do not distribute it as payments to factors, this is a withdrawal from the circular flow. An INJECTION is an addition to the income of domestic firms that does not arise from the expenditure of domestic households, or an addition to the income of domestic households that does not arise from the spending of domestic firms. If, for example, firms gain income by producing investment goods which they sell to other firms, this is an injection because the income of firms rises without households having increased their expenditure.

Now consider the effect of withdrawals on national income. If, for example, households decide to increase their saving and correspondingly reduce the amount they spend buying consumption goods, this reduces the income of firms and reduces the payments they will make to factors of production. Thus national income falls. *Withdrawals, by reducing expenditure, exert a contractionary force on national income.*

Next consider the effect of injections on national income. If, for example, firms increase their sales of machines to other firms, their incomes and their payments to households for factor services will rise without there having been an increase in household expenditure. Thus national income rises. *Injections, by raising expenditure, exert an expansionary force on national income.*

In the two-sector model, saving is the only withdrawal and investment is the only injection. Thus it makes no difference if we say that national income is in equilibrium when saving equals investment or when withdrawals equal injections. In more complex models, however, there are many withdrawals and many injections. In such models, national income will be in equilibrium when the aggregate contractionary force of all withdrawals is equal to the aggregate expansionary force of all injections.

> **When withdrawals exceed injections, national income will fall; when injections exceed withdrawals, national income will rise. Equilibrium national income occurs where withdrawals equal injections.**

Letting W and J stand for withdrawals and injections respectively, this gives us the equilibrium condition[1] $W = J$. All that is required to apply this theory to any particular model is to identify the withdrawals and injections in that model and to make assumptions about how each is related to national income.

National income in a three-sector model

We now add a government sector to our model as a preliminary to analysing various policy issues concerning fiscal policy. Following the discussion on page 513, we define G as government expenditure on currently produced goods and services, which is all government expenditure *minus* transfer payments. This is part of the economy's total expenditure, part of the total demand for goods and services. Second, we define Q as total government transfer payments. These are not part of national income but they do provide disposable income that is available to be spent. Third, we define T as the total tax revenues raised by the government. Fourth, the government's budget surplus is $T - (G + Q)$, positive when there is a surplus and negative when there is a deficit.

Behavioural assumptions

The government sector We assume that government expenditures on goods and services and on

---

[1] The general equivalence of $E = Y$ and $W = J$ is shown as follows. All income is either spent on consumption or withdrawn, $Y \equiv C + W$, and all expenditure is either consumption expenditure or injections, $E \equiv C + J$, so $E = Y$ immediately reduces to $W = J$.

transfer payments, Q, are held constant in real terms. Thus

$$G = G^* \qquad (1)$$

and $$Q = Q^* \quad . \qquad (2)$$

The justification is the same as with investment expenditure in the previous chapter: we first want to see how income responds to a constant rate of government expenditure and transfer payments, before going on to see how it reacts to changes in G and Q. For simplicity we assume that all transfer payments are made to households.

For simplicity we can also assume that all taxes are direct taxes on personal and company incomes and that they take a constant proportion of the national income. This gives us our tax function:

$$T = tY \qquad 0 < t < 1 \quad . \qquad (3)$$

The constant, t, is the AVERAGE PROPENSITY TO TAX (T/Y) and also the MARGINAL PROPENSITY TO TAX $(\Delta T/\Delta Y)$.

The firm sector We continue with our assumptions that firms supply all the goods that are demanded at the going price level and that planned investment expenditure by firms is a constant:

$$I = I^* \quad . \qquad (4)$$

The household sector In the two-sector model all of national income was paid out to households and was thus available for them to spend on consumption or to save. Direct taxes, however, place a wedge between GDP and households' disposable income. This disposable income is diminished by direct taxes and enhanced by transfer payments which give households income to spend that does not arise out of any contribution to current GDP.

Letting Y_d stand for the disposable income of households, we can write

$$Y_d = Y - T + Q \quad , \qquad (5)$$

which says that we must deduct total direct taxes from national income and add transfer payments in order to obtain households' disposable income.

We continue to assume that households spend a constant fraction c of their disposable income on consumption and save the rest:

$$C = cY_d \quad . \qquad (6)$$

From (3), (5), and (6) we can now derive a function relating consumption to national income:[1]

$$C = c(1 - t)Y + cQ \quad . \qquad (7)$$

---

[1] Substituting (3) into (5):

$$Y_d = Y - tY + Q$$
$$= Y(1 - t) + Q$$

and then substituting for Y_d in (6):

$$C = c[Y(1 - t) + Q] \quad .$$

Since t is the proportion of income that goes as taxes, $1-t$ is the proportion that goes to disposable income, and $c(1-t)$ is the proportion that gets spent. So $c(1-t)$ is the MPC out of national income. The other term cQ is the proportion of transfer payments that get spent. All together the relation in (7) describes a linear relation between C and Y with $c(1-t)$ as the slope coefficient and cQ as the constant.

Equilibrium income

In this model, aggregate desired expenditure has three components: consumption, investment and government expenditure

$$E \equiv C + I + G \tag{8}$$

The equilibrium level of national income is, as always, where desired expenditure equals income

$$E = Y \ . \tag{9}$$

Geometric The graphical solution, which is exactly the same as that shown in Figure 35.6, is given in Figure 36.1. The C line (which is the graph of equation (7) above) is now flatter since consumption is a smaller fraction of national income than previously because of the deduction of taxes, but it has a positive constant because of transfer payments (equal to cQ). This indicates that even if income falls

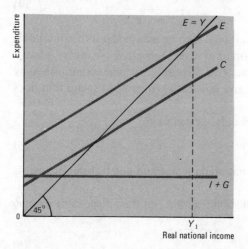

Fig. 36.1 Equilibrium national income in the three-sector model

to zero, transfer payments will allow consumption to remain positive. The expenditure function is augmented however by the new element, government expenditure. The equilibrium occurs where the expenditure function (equation (10) below) intersects the $E = Y$ equilibrium condition (equation (9)). Thus equilibrium national income is Y_1 in the Figure.

Algebraic The algebraic solution to the model is again simple. As a first step, let us gather together the equations of the model.

Definitions
$$E \equiv C + I + G \tag{8}$$
$$Y_d \equiv Y - T + Q \tag{5}$$

Behaviour	$G = G^*$		(1)
	$Q = Q^*$		(2)
	$T = tY$	$0 < t < 1$	(3)
	$I = I^*$		(4)
	$C = cY_d$	$0 < c < 1$	(6)
Equilibrium	$E = Y$		(9)

Substituting the definition of disposable income (5) into the consumption function (6) and then substituting all of the behavioural assumptions into the definition of aggregate expenditure reduces the above to the two equations that are graphed in Figure 36.1:

$$E = c[(1-t)Y + Q^*] + I^* + G^* \tag{10}$$
$$E = Y \tag{9}$$

Equation (10) is the aggregate expenditure function. The first term is the consumption function which we derived as equation (7) on page 543 and interpreted at the top of page 544. The other two terms merely express constant investment and government expenditure. Equation (9) is the equilibrium condition which graphs as the 45° line. Next, the two equations are solved by substituting (10) into (9) to yield[1]

$$Y = \frac{I^* + G^* + cQ^*}{1 - c(1-t)} . \tag{11}$$

This expresses equilibrium income as a function of autonomous expenditure flows, I^* and G^*, transfer payments, Q^*, and the behavioural parameters that determine how much national income becomes disposable income, t, and how much disposable income gets spent, c. It is the algebraic expression of Y_1 in Figure 36.1.

Changes in equilibrium income

Geometric Aside from changes in I and c, already analysed in Chapter 35, there are three new variables that can affect national income: G, Q and t. A change in G has exactly the same effect as a change in I. A rise in G is an increase in desired expenditure on goods and services. Output will expand to accommodate it and, because of the multiplier, the rise in equilibrium income will exceed the initial rise in G. This effect is shown in part (i) of Figure 36.2. Here the aggregate expenditure function shifts upwards from E_1 to E_2 because of an increase in I^* or an increase in G^*. As a result, equilibrium income rises from Y_1 to Y_2.

An increase in Q raises income but not by as much as the same increase in G. Why is this? When the government spends £1 more on goods and services this increases national income by £1 in the first instance, and the multiplier then magnifies this amount. When the government spends £1 more on transfer payments, however, this raises disposable income by £1 but the initial effect on national income depends only on that fraction, c, that is actually spent (the rest, $1-c$, is saved).

Note that these are *ceteris paribus* experiments. When G or Q are increased, t is not changed so

---

[1] Putting (10) into (9): $Y = c[(1-t)Y + Q^*] + I^* + G^*$. Multiplying out the c and the Y: $Y = cY - ctY + cQ^* + I^* + G^*$, or $Y - cY + ctY = I^* + G^* + cQ^*$. Now look just at the LHS for a moment. First factor out the Y: $Y(1 - c + ct)$, then factor out the c: $Y[1 - c(1-t)]$. Now divide through by $1 - c(1-t)$ to obtain equation (11).

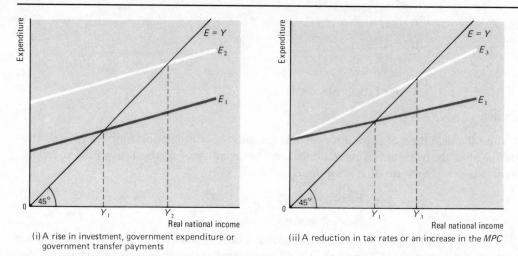

(i) A rise in investment, government expenditure or government transfer payments

(ii) A reduction in tax rates or an increase in the *MPC*

Fig. 36.2 Changes in equilibrium national income using the income-expenditure approach

the extra government expenditure on goods and services or on transfer payments causes an increase in the government's budget deficit.

Increases in government expenditure on goods and services or on transfer payments increase national income, reductions in expenditure do the reverse.

A change in tax rates has a slightly more complex effect and we must look at it in a little more detail. A reduction in tax rates means a larger amount of each £1 of GDP reaches households as disposable income. Hence, with a given propensity to consume out of disposable income, consumption rises as a proportion of national income. This causes an upward rotation of the line relating consumption to national income and hence increases equilibrium income. The same result is obvious by inspecting the consumption function in equation (7) above: a reduction in t clearly increases the slope of this function. This is illustrated in Figure 36.2 by the pivoting movement in the aggregate expenditure function from E_1 to E_3 raising equilibrium income from Y_1 to Y_3.

A rise in the tax rate has the opposite effect. A smaller fraction of each £1 of GDP will reach households as disposable income and with a given *MPC* out of disposable income, a smaller proportion of each £1 of GDP will be passed on through household consumption expenditure.

Note that a cut in tax rates has the same effect as a rise in c, the *MPC*. The proportion of national income devoted to consumption expenditure rises (i) because more of total income reaches households as disposable income when t falls and (ii) because more of a given total income is spent on consumption purchases when c falls.

A cut in tax rates shifts the consumption function upward and increases equilibrium national income. An increase in tax rates lowers the consumption function and lowers equilibrium national income.

Exactly the same results can be obtained by using the withdrawals-injections approach. In the three-sector economy there are two withdrawals, savings and taxes. These represent, in the case of taxes, national income that is not available to households to spend and, in the case of saving, disposable income that is not passed on through spending. There are three injections. Two of them are straightforward: investment, which we discussed in the previous chapter, and government purchases of goods and services, which is income for firms that does not arise from the spending of households. The third is transfer payments. We can if we wish regard all these as an injection and the part that is saved, sQ, as an immediate withdrawal. For a geometric treatment, however, that would be awkward since a change in transfer payments will then shift both the injections and the withdrawals functions. It is simpler, therefore, to regard injections as *national* income that arises from outside the circular flow. Then injections are only the fraction of transfer payments that gets spent. In this case injections that arise from transfer earnings are only cQ.[1] The equilibrium condition that withdrawals should equal injections thus becomes

$$S + T = I + G + cQ \quad .$$ (12)

Since S and T both rise with income while I and G are both assumed constant, we get the result shown in Figure 36.3. In both parts of the Figure the initial equilibrium is at Y_1 where the initial withdrawals and injections schedules, W_1 and J_1, intersect. Part (i) shows the effects of an increase in injections, I, G or cQ. The injection schedule shifts to J_2, increasing national income to Y_2. Part (ii) shows the effect of a decrease in the withdrawals propensities, s or t. The W schedule pivots downwards from W_1 to W_3 increasing national income from Y_1 to Y_3. This is merely an alternative derivation of the results given in the previous section.

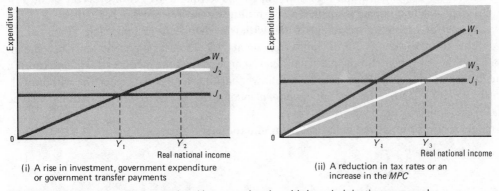

(i) A rise in investment, government expenditure or government transfer payments

(ii) A reduction in tax rates or an increase in the *MPC*

Fig. 36.3 Changes in equilibrium national income using the withdrawals-injections approach

Algebraic The equilibrium level of national income for this model is given by equation (11) above. To investigate the effect of changes in autonomous expenditure flows we merely first difference the equation to obtain the following expression where, for ease of interpretation, we list separately the elements of expenditure that all appear over a common denominator.

$$\Delta Y = \frac{\Delta I}{1 - c(1 - t)} + \frac{\Delta G}{1 - c(1 - t)} + \frac{c\Delta Q}{1 - c(1 - t)} \quad .$$ (13)

This tells us that the effect of a change in G is exactly the same as the effect of a change in I. This is not surprising since both types of expenditure increase GDP and those who secure the newly generated

---

[1] In this case an increase in transfer earnings increases the injections function by $c\Delta Q$. Clearly we get the same result if we say the increase shifts the injections function by ΔQ and the savings functon by $s\Delta Q$, which is that part of the transfer payments that never enters the income stream. In this latter case, the *net* increase in injections is $\Delta Q - s\Delta Q = (1-s)\Delta Q = c\Delta Q$ (since $1 - s = c$).

income set up the same chain reaction in which further expenditure breeds further income which breeds yet further expenditure. The value of the expenditure multiplier in this case is

$$K = \frac{\Delta Y}{\Delta I} = \frac{\Delta Y}{\Delta G} = \frac{1}{1 - c(1-t)} \ . \tag{14}$$

But the value of the transfer payments multiplier is smaller at

$$\frac{\Delta Y}{\Delta Q} = \frac{c}{1 - c(1-t)} \ . \tag{15}$$

A little examination will reveal a similarity of (14) with the multiplier from the two-sector model in Chapter 35, which was $1/(1-c)$. In that case the multiplier was the reciprocal of one minus the fraction of national income spent on consumption. In (14) the multiplier is also the reciprocal of one minus the fraction of national income spent on consumption, only now, because of taxes, that fraction is $c(1-t)$, rather than c.

The generalization of this result is:

> **The expenditure multiplier is the reciprocal of one minus the proportion of any new income that gets passed on in terms of new expenditure.**

This result holds for any expenditure whose first impact is to raise Y by £1 for every £1 spent. For transfer payments the first impact is smaller, so the multiplier is correspondingly smaller.

Now consider an algebraic treatment of the withdrawals-injections approach. Some care is needed on how to treat savings out of transfer payments, sQ. Transfer payments only become an injection when they are spent. So the part that is saved never enters the income stream and cannot, therefore, be regarded as a leakage from it. It follows that the savings that enter the withdrawals function are $S = s(Y - T)$, i.e., the amount of *national* income that is saved, which is national income minus taxes multiplied by the propensity to save.

The model is now summarized in the following equations.

Definitions	$W \equiv S + T$	(16)
	$J \equiv I + G + cQ$	(17)
Behaviour	$S = s(Y - T)$	(18)
	$T = tY$	(19)
	$Q = Q^*$	(20)
	$I = I^*$	(21)
	$G = G^*$	(22)
Equilibrium	$W = J$	(23)

Substituting (19) into (18) yields an expression for saving as a function of national income, $S = s(1-t)Y$. Then substituting this, and the rest of the behavioural equations, into (16) and (17) yields the equations of the withdrawals and the injections functions shown in Figure 36.3.

$$W = [s(1-t) + t]Y \tag{24}$$

$$J = I^* + G^* + cQ^* \ . \tag{25}$$

Notice that $s(1-t)$ is the amount of each £1 of GDP that is withdrawn through saving, while the second t is the amount that is withdrawn through taxes. Thus $s(1-t)+t$ is the fraction of each new £1 of national income that gets withdrawn, i.e., not passed on through consumption spending. This can be called the MARGINAL PROPENSITY TO WITHDRAW. Substituting (24) and (25) into the equilibrium condition (23) yields the solution

$$Y = \frac{I^*}{s(1-t)+t} + \frac{G^*}{s(1-t)+t} + \frac{cQ^*}{s(1-t)+t} \quad . \tag{26}$$

The multipliers for I and G are then obviously

$$K = \frac{\Delta Y}{\Delta I} = \frac{\Delta Y}{\Delta G} = \frac{1}{s(1-t)+t} \quad , \tag{27}$$

while the multiplier for transfer payments is

$$\frac{\Delta Y}{\Delta Q} = \frac{c}{s(1-t)+t} \quad . \tag{28}$$

This suggests the simple generalization that

> **The expenditure multiplier is the reciprocal of the marginal propensity to withdraw income from the circular flow.**

The effect of a change in the tax rates can be seen from equation (26) by regrouping the term $s(1-t)+t$ to read $s+t(1-s)$.[1] Since s, the MPS, is a positive fraction, $1-s$ is positive. Thus an increase in t increases the magnitude of the denominator and hence reduces the value of equilibrium income in (26) and the value of the multiplier in (27). This checks with the result stated earlier that an increase in tax rates lowers national income while a decrease raises it.[2]

Fiscal policy and demand management

Fiscal policy is considered in detail in Chapter 43. It is worth noting at this point, however, that the above section has developed the basic analytical framework of fiscal policy. A major aspect of fiscal policy is DEMAND MANAGEMENT, which is an attempt to influence the macro behaviour of the economy by influencing aggregate expenditure through alterations in the government's budget. We have seen that a *ceteris paribus* rise in government expenditure on goods and services or transfer payments, or a fall in tax rates, increases total demand in the economy. In the present model where firms produce all they can sell, it also increases total output and employment. A *ceteris paribus* fall in government expenditure on goods and services or transfer payments, or a rise in tax rates, reduces total demand. In the present model it reduces total output and employment.

> **Expansionary demand-management policies seek to raise total desired expenditure by increasing government expenditure on goods and services or on transfer payments or by lowering tax rates. Contractionary policies seek to do the reverse.**

---

[1] Multiply out $s(1-t)+t$ to get $s-st+t$ and factor the t out of the last two terms to get $s+t(1-s)$.

[2] The equivalence of the multiplier in (27) for the $W = J$ approach and the multiplier in (14) for the $E = Y$ approach is shown as follows. The denominator of (27) is $s(1-t)+t$ and, replacing s by $1-c$, this yields $(1-c)(1-t)+t$ which expands to $1-t-c+ct+t = 1-c+ct = 1-c(1-t)$, which is the denominator of (14).

A four-sector, open economy

Finally in this chapter we consider a four-sector model, the fourth sector being foreign trade. This addition changes our previously closed economy into an open economy.

Aggregate expenditure

Definitions   We now have to allow for two circumstances. First, part of the expenditure on domestically produced GDP comes from foreign sources. These are the country's exports, symbolized by X. Exports constitute demand for domestic output and, when the demand is met, exports create domestic employment. Second, part of the expenditure of domestic spending units goes on imports, symbolized by M. It is necessary to subtract this amount from total spending because it constitutes demand for the output of foreign firms and, when that demand is met, employment is created abroad. Thus we have for aggregate desired expenditure

$$E = C + I + G + (X - M) \quad . \tag{29}$$

The two amounts of X and M are customarily grouped together to show desired expenditure on what is called NET EXPORTS. This value is usually small in relation to the total value of either X or M. Thus, the correction to E when we move from a closed economy to an open economy will not usually be large. However, a change in either X or M, not matched by a change in the other, will cause E to change in the same way as would an equivalent change in C, I or G.

Behavioural assumptions   Noting our new definition of aggregate expenditure, all we now need to do is to add behavioural assumptions for X and M.

The amount of exports depends upon the domestic prices of these goods, on the exchange rate (which determines their foreign prices), on the prices of competing goods from other countries, and on foreign incomes. As with I and G, it is convenient to see how national income adjusts to a fixed level of exports before seeing how it reacts when exports change. Thus exports are assumed constant for the time being.

Imports, however, will rise as national income rises, both because domestic households spend a fraction of their consumption expenditure on imported consumers' goods, and because almost all domestic output has some import content of raw materials and semi-manufactured goods. Iron-ore, oil, paper and timber are but a few of the many examples.

This gives us two new behavioural equations:

$$X = X^* \tag{30}$$

$$M = mY \tag{31}$$

where m is the MARGINAL PROPENSITY TO IMPORT, the fraction of each additional £1 of income that goes to imported commodities.

Equilibrium income

As in all these models there are two ways of looking at the equilibrium conditions: either expenditure equals income, or withdrawals equals injections.

Expenditure equals income For the graphical solution all we need to do is note that the E function in Figures 36.1 and 36.2 now contains an added term, $X - M$. An increase in X or a fall in M shifts the E curve upwards while a reduction in X or a rise in M shifts it downwards.

> **Equilibrium income is increased by a rise in exports or by a fall in imports; it is reduced by a fall in exports or a rise in imports.**

Notice that this result follows from treating exports and imports as independent of each other. Under a fixed exchange rate this is possible, at least in the short term. Under a flexible exchange-rate regime, however, a significant change in either will affect the exchange rate, which will cause the other to change. Indeed if the only source of demands and supplies on the foreign-exchange market were exports and imports (no capital flows) and the exchange rate were left perfectly free, it would fluctuate so as to keep exports equal to imports at all times. Under these circumstances the net export term could be ignored. This matter is considered further in Chapter 37. In the meantime we are assuming that there is enough stabilization of the exchange rate, either through private capital flows or government intervention, that exports and imports can fluctuate independently of each other at least in the short term.

The algebraic solution is found by starting with the model on pages 544–5 and substituting the new definition of E and then adding the two new behavioural equations for X and M. Substitution then produces the new expenditure function

$$E = [c(1-t)-m]Y + I^* + G^* + X^* + cQ^* \tag{32}$$

which differs from the E function in the three-sector model only by the addition of X^* for exports and the subtraction of mY for imports. The solution, found by substituting into the equilibrium condition $E = Y$, is

$$Y = \frac{I^* + G^* + X^* + cQ^*}{1 - c(1-t) + m}, \tag{33}$$

which yields an expenditure multiplier of

$$K = \frac{\Delta Y}{\Delta I} = \frac{\Delta Y}{\Delta G} = \frac{\Delta Y}{\Delta X} = \frac{1}{1 - c(1-t) + m}. \tag{34}$$

The existence of m thus reduces the value of the multiplier because some of the spending induced by new income leaks out onto demand for foreign goods.

The multiplier in (34) follows a now-familiar pattern. The proportion of new income that gets passed on in domestic spending in this model is $c(1-t)-m$, i.e., the $c(1-t)$ of the closed economy model minus m, the fraction of the new spending that goes to imports. Thus the denominator of (34), which is $1 - [c(1-t)-m] = 1 - c(1-t) + m$, is one minus the proportion of new income that gets passed on. This illustrates once again the generalization stated in bold type on page 548.

Withdrawals equals injections Exports are clearly an injection since they create income for domestic producers that does not arise from the spending of domestic households. Imports are clearly a withdrawal since they are income not passed on in the domestic circular flow but which instead leaks out to foreign producers. Thus we now have

$$W = S + T + M \quad \text{and} \quad J = I + G + cQ + X.$$

The graphical solution comes by adding these two terms to Figure 36.3 and noting that an increase in X shifts up the injections line and thus raises equilibrium income, while an increase in m, the marginal propensity to import, pivots the withdrawal function upwards and thus reduces equilibrium income.

The algebraic solution follows from substituting the behavioural assumptions into the new definitions of W and J just given, and then substituting them into the equilibrium condition, $W = J$. This yields

$$Y = \frac{I^* + G^* + X^* + cQ}{s(1-t)+t+m} \tag{35}$$

and an expenditure multiplier:

$$K = \frac{1}{s(1-t)+t+m} . \tag{36}$$

Once again we see the multiplier as the sum of the proportions of each new £1 of income that are withdrawn from the circular flow for various reasons. The first term, $s(1-t)$, is the marginal propensity to save out of national income, the second term is the marginal propensity to tax and the third is the marginal propensity to import. All three are stated as propensities out of national income. This illustrates once again the first generalization stated in bold type on page 549.

Conclusion

In Chapter 35 we saw that multipliers for the two-sector model were quite large. For example, with an MPS of ·1 the multiplier in the two-sector economy is 10. In the four-sector model, however, the multiplier is much smaller. Assume, for example, the values $s = ·10$, $t = ·40$ and $m = ·25$, which are in the approximate range of the British figures. Substituting these into (34) or (36), yields a multiplier of 1·41. This suggests vastly smaller fluctuations in Y in response to changes in autonomous expenditure flows than did the multiplier for the two-sector model. In this example, a change of £1 in autonomous expenditure changes equilibrium national income by £1·41. The difference between the two models is that taxes and imports create large withdrawals from the circular flow. Thus a much smaller part of every £1 of new income gets spent on domestic consumption and hence passed on to create yet more new income.

> **For open economies with large government sectors, multipliers are typically between 1 and 2 rather than between 5 and 10 as they are in two-sector models.**

37

National income, international trade and the balance of payments

In Chapters 11 and 30 we focused on the microeconomic aspects of international trade: exports and imports arise out of the incentive to *specialize* in production in order to exploit comparative advantage. We now focus on some macroeconomic aspects of international trade. We saw in the previous chapter that exports are an important source of demand for domestically produced goods, while imports are a component of domestic expenditure that leaks out of the domestic circular flow of income. There we assumed that exports and imports were independent of each other. In this chapter we examine both the causes of trade imbalances and their implications for the domestic economy.

The BALANCE OF TRADE (or the trade balance) is the difference between the value of exports and imports in a given year. An excess of exports over imports is referred to as a *surplus*, and an excess of imports over exports as a *deficit*. A situation where exports are just equal in value to imports is a situation of balanced trade. Any balance-of-trade surplus, or deficit, requires financial flows between the countries involved. The relationship between trade imbalances and international financial flows is summarized in the balance-of-payments accounts, which we discuss at the end of this chapter.

National income and the balance of trade

International transmission of demand shocks

The export multiplier Exports are an important source of demand for domestically produced goods. A key determinant of exports is the level of activity in the country's major trading partners. When the United States experiences a boom, there is a large American demand for European exports. Then, via the multiplier process, the increase in European exports will cause an expansion in the national incomes of European countries. Similarly, when the United States experiences a recession, as it did in 1981–83, American demand for European goods will fall. Again, the fall in European exports causes a multiplier effect, this time leading to a reduction in European national incomes. As a result of the export multiplier, shifts in domestic demands in major trading countries are transmitted to their trading partners. (See in particular equation (34) in Chapter 36.)

> **Exports provide a key link between trading partners, so that their national incomes tend to move together.**

Imports and the multiplier As we saw in Chapter 36, imports and domestic national income are positively associated. Since expenditure on imports is a leakage from the domestic circular flow, imports reduce the value of the multiplier. This is apparent from the multiplier expression in equation (34) of Chapter 36. This reduces the impact on national income of fluctuations in such autonomous expenditure items as investment and exports. It also reduces the effectiveness of domestic policies that attempt to change the level of domestic income.

The net export function

The NET EXPORT FUNCTION relates the balance of trade, $X - M$, to national income. In Chapter 36 we saw that, assuming a fixed exchange rate, exports depend on foreign circumstances, such as foreign national income and prices, and on domestic prices. While we are holding the domestic price level constant, this makes exports depend only on foreign influences and hence makes them exogenous to the domestic economy: in the simple model of fixed exchange rates and a fixed domestic price level, exports are autonomous expenditure flows. Imports, however, fluctuate with national income: as we assumed in the last chapter, $M = mY$. This makes the net export function

$$N = X^* - mY \qquad (1)$$

where N stands for net exports, X^* is exogenous total exports and mY gives imports as a function of national income.

Part (i) of Figure 37.1 shows the export and import functions separately while part (ii) shows their difference, the net export function. Trade is in balance at income Y_1 where $X = M$ in part (i) and $X - M = 0$ in part (ii). From equation (1), Y_1 is equal to X^*/m.

A movement along the net export function means a change in the trade balance as a result of a change in income. A shift of the function means a change in the whole relation between net exports and national income. There are several possible causes of such a shift.

Foreign income A rise in foreign national income, *ceteris paribus*, will lead to a rise in the quantity of domestic goods demanded by foreign countries. This is shown in Figure 37.1. In part (i), a rise in foreign income causes the level of exports to rise from X^*_1 to X^*_2. The level of income at which there is balanced trade rises from Y_1 to Y_2, and in part (ii) the net export function shifts

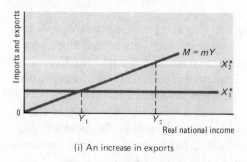

(i) An increase in exports

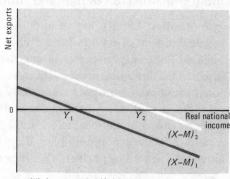

(ii) An upward shift in the net export function

Fig. 37.1 The effect on the trade balance of an exogenous increase in exports

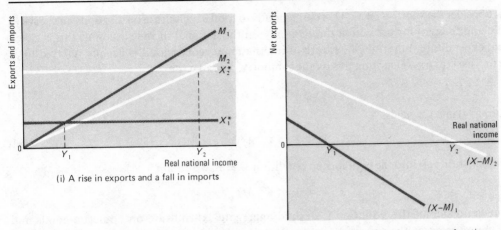

Fig. 37.2 The effect of a rise in foreign prices relative to domestic prices

upward from $X^*_1 - mY$, indicated on the figure as $(X-M)_1$, to $X^*_2 - mY$, indicated on the figure as $(X-M)_2$. The reverse case is shown by having exports fall from X^*_2 to X^*_1, shifting the net export function down from $(X-M)_2$ to $(X-M)_1$.

Relative prices If foreign prices rise relative to domestic prices, both imports and exports will change as shown in Figure 37.2. In part (i), the initial export and import functions are shown as the black lines X^*_1 and M_1. In part (ii), the corresponding net export function is the black line $(X-M)_1$.

A fall in the prices of domestic goods relative to foreign goods, whether due to foreign inflation, domestic deflation or a devaluation of the domestic currency, makes domestic goods more attractive relative to foreign goods. This causes exports to increase to the level of the white line X_2^* and the import function to fall to the level of the white line M_2. As a result, the level of income that corresponds to balanced trade rises from Y_1 to Y_2, and the net export function shifts upward to $(X-M)_2$ in part (ii).

A rise in the relative prices of domestic goods, whether due to domestic inflation, foreign deflation or an appreciation of the domestic currency, causes exports to fall, imports to rise and the net export function to shift downward, reversing the process just analysed.

> **A fall in domestic prices relative to foreign prices due to a slower inflation at home than abroad, or to a devaluation of the domestic currency, shifts the net export function upwards and raises the level of national income associated with balanced trade. A rise in domestic relative prices has the opposite effects.**

Net exports and domestic absorption

In the four-sector, open economy model the aggregate expenditure function is given by

$$E \equiv C + I + G + (X-M) \quad , \tag{2}$$

Now consider the sum $C+I+G$. This corresponds to total expenditure on all goods and services (domestic and foreign) for use within the economy. In the national-income accounts this is called total final expenditure, but in the literature of international economics it is usually referred to as DOMESTIC ABSORPTION. Denoting this by the symbol **A**, we can write

$$\mathbf{A} \equiv C+I+G \tag{3}$$

Substituting (4) into (2) yields

$$E = \mathbf{A}+(X-M) \quad . \tag{4}$$

If we now substitute (4) into the equilibrium condition $Y = E$, we obtain

$$Y = \mathbf{A}+(X-M) \quad . \tag{5}$$

The right-hand side of this equation is desired aggregate expenditure on domestic goods and services, represented as the sum of expenditure due to *internal* use (domestic absorption) plus expenditure due to *external* demand (net exports).

In an open economy, equilibrium national income equals domestic absorption plus net exports.

This is illustrated in Figure 37.3, where domestic absorption is given by the dashed line **A**, and aggregate desired expenditure by the line E. Note several things about this figure: (1) The absorption line, **A**, has a slope of less than unity because the MPC out of the national income is less than one while I and G are constants. Indeed equation (10) on page 545 gives the slope of the **A** line as $c(1-t)$. (2) The expenditure line, E, lies above the **A** line at zero income by the amount of export expenditure (which is an exogeneous constant). (3) The E function is flatter than the **A** function because it contains the effect of the additional leakage of imports. Indeed equation (32) on page 551 shows the slope of the E curve to be $c(1-t)-m$.

From these properties we see that, at low levels of income, domestic absorption is less than domestic expenditure; as income grows, absorption grows faster than expenditure until eventually the two are equal, i.e. net exports are zero.

In Figure 37.3 equilibrium income is Y_1 where the E line cuts the 45° line and, at that income, domestic absorption is less than national income so net exports are positive and equal to e_1-e_2.

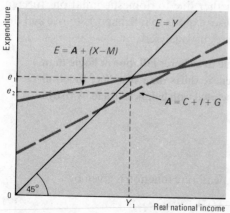

Fig. 37.3 Domestic absorption, aggregate expenditure and national income

Rearranging equation (5) by subtracting **A** from both sides, we get

$$Y - A = X - M \quad .$$

(6)

This shows that

> **positive net exports means that national income exceeds domestic absorption, that is, total demand for goods and services for domestic use is less than total domestic output of goods and services.**

Similarly, a domestic balance-of-trade deficit occurs when domestic absorption of goods and services exceeds national income.

Absorption versus component approaches to the trade balance

All of these relations between income, absorption and net exports are simply matters of definition. The relationship between net exports and the gap between national income and absorption does, however, suggest a useful way of grouping categories of expenditure in an open economy. Since the trade balance is also equal, by definition, to the sum of all exports minus the sum of all imports, it is tempting to try to *explain* changes or trends in the trade account by counting up the changes or trends in particular exports and imports. Since both this 'component' definition and the absorption definition are correct as *definitions* of the trade balance, either is valid as a framework that can be used to organize information in order to *analyse* the trade account. The component approach, however, tends to lead the analyst to ignore the interactions among the items included in the trade balance and other variables such as national income. The absorption approach has the advantage of drawing attention to such interactions.

In order to compare the approaches, consider the effect on the trade balance of an exogenous increase in the foreign demand for one particular domestic export. As we saw in Chapter 36, an increase in exports, *ceteris paribus*, will increase national income. But an increase in national income leads in turn to increased imports. If one takes the component approach to analysing the trade account, one could miss this induced effect. For example, if exports of Scotch whisky rise by £20 million in a given year, the component approach might suggest that the trade balance would improve by £20 million. But the increased exports will be reflected in higher incomes for whisky producers. They will spend some of their increased incomes on imports and some on domestic goods. The domestic expenditure will lead to a multiplier effect on national income which will result in further increases in imports.

Clearly, the net effect on the trade balance of the increased exports must include the induced increases in imports. By relating the trade balance to the difference between total income and total spending in the domestic economy, this is exactly what the absorption approach does.

The effects of a change in the exchange rate

We are now able to consider more fully the effects of a change in the value of domestic currency on the foreign-exchange market. We will study the case of a depreciation of sterling, noting that an appreciation has exactly opposite effects. Since we are assuming fixed exchange rates, we shall speak of a devaluation, but the same analysis applies to a depreciation under flexible rates.[1]

We first show that devaluation shifts the net export function upwards. We consider two models that use quite different mechanisms to yield this result.

A perfectly elastic aggregate supply

This is the model we have been considering so far in our discussion of macroeconomics: prices are fixed *in terms of domestic currency* and firms supply all that is demanded at those prices. A devaluation reduces the foreign-exchange value of the home currency and thereby also lowers the price of home goods *in terms of foreign currency*. Similarly, a devaluation raises the domestic price of imported goods. Hence, in this model, a devaluation is associated with a change in the *external terms of trade* (the relative price of exports to imports). It thus causes a shift of expenditure on the part of both domestic and foreign consumers away from the now relatively expensive foreign goods and towards the now relatively inexpensive domestic goods.

Now consider the effects of a devaluation on the trade balance in this model. More exports are sold at constant domestic prices, *so exports valued in domestic currency must rise.* Domestic residents buy fewer imports but at a higher domestic price, hence *imports valued in domestic currency fall only if domestic import demand is elastic.* The possibility of inelastic demand raises the potential for a devaluation to lead to a worsening of the trade balance, thus shifting the net export function downward. This occurs if import demand is sufficiently inelastic so that imports, valued in domestic currency, rise by more than exports, also valued in domestic currency. Such a possibility has been at the centre of a long-standing controversy about the effectiveness of devaluation. It can be shown that, if domestic prices are unaffected by variations in foreign demand, the perverse case can occur only if the *sum* of the domestic country's elasticity of demand for imports and the foreign demand for its exports is less than one. In other words, quite highly inelastic demands are required to produce this case. If this situation were commonly encountered, the case for freely fluctuating rates would be dealt a crippling blow because, far from improving matters, currency depreciations in the face of balance-of-payments deficits and currency appreciations in the face of surpluses would make matters worse. Most economists today dismiss the perverse case as a theoretical curio of little practical importance. For simplicity, we assume that the domestic demand for imports is elastic so that the devaluation raises the value of exports and lowers the value of imports. Thus devaluation shifts the net export function upwards.

The upward shift in the net export function, *ceteris paribus*, also means a shift in the aggregate expenditure function. Given a perfectly elastic aggregate supply function, the shift in aggregate expenditure leads to an increase in real national income with no change in domestic prices. Since there is no further change in the terms of trade, the response of the trade balance occurs as a movement along the *new* net export function. The effect of the devaluation on the trade account can be read off the new net export function at the new higher income level.

The devaluation raises foreign prices relative to domestic prices and so shifts the net export function from $(X-M)_1$ to $(X-M)_2$ in part (ii) of Figure 37.4. This leads to a shift in aggregate expenditure in part (i) from E_1 to E_2. Real national income rises both absolutely, as shown in part

---

[1] Under a fixed exchange rate the exchange value of domestic currency is said to be devalued or revalued; under a flexible exchange rate it is said to depreciate or appreciate.

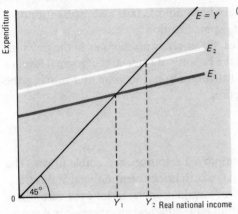

(i) The expenditure
function shifts upwards
as expenditure is
switched to domestic
goods

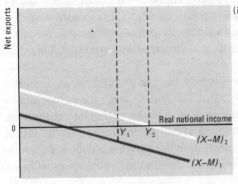

(ii) The net export function shifts
upwards as exports rise and
imports fall

Fig. 37.4 The effect of a devaluation

(i), and relative to domestic absorption. The combined effect is an increase in net exports. In the case illustrated, net exports were negative at the initial level of national income Y_1, while after the devaluation, net exports are zero at the new level of national income Y_2.

The non-tradeable goods model

A second model assumes a small open economy (SOE) with tradeable and non-tradeable goods. Recall from Chapter 11 that *tradeables* are bought and sold on world markets at world prices set in terms of foreign currency and beyond the power of the SOE to influence. Thus the external terms of trade are beyond the control of the SOE. *Non-tradeables* do not enter directly into international trade, either because they cannot be transported (e.g., services such as haircuts, maid services and restaurant meals) or because the cost of transport is prohibitively high (e.g., cement). The price of non-tradeable goods is determined not on world markets but by domestic supply and demand.

A devaluation causes the *domestic* price of traded goods to rise. The change in the relative prices of traded and non-traded goods is often referred to as a change in the *internal terms of trade*. Domestic production of traded goods rises because resources shift out of the lower-priced, non-traded goods sector. Domestic demand shifts away from traded goods and toward the lower-priced, non-traded goods. As we saw in Chapter 11, excess demand for imports falls and excess supply of exports rises. This gives rise to an upward shift in the net export function.

From here, as long as there are unemployed resources, the analysis proceeds as in the previous case: the net export function shifts upwards, improving the balance of trade at the original level of income, but the expenditure function also rises thus raising national income and moving the economy down to the right along its new net export function.

Full employment

So far we have confined our analysis to the case of unemployed resources and stable prices. The devaluation has a different effect at full employment and it is worth briefly mentioning it at this time.

Just for the moment, in order to round out our study of devaluation, let us take the case where the economy is at full employment: no increase in real output is possible and any increase in demand will merely bid up prices. The increase in the expenditure function implied by the devaluation causes no change in *real* national income but increases domestic prices instead. This in turn causes a downward shift in the net export function since a rise in domestic prices encourages domestic consumers to buy more tradeable goods whose prices are fixed on international markets. This shift in demand raises imports and lowers exports.

Thus, the devaluation shifts the net export function upwards, but the ensuing rise in domestic prices causes the net export function to shift downward again.[1] The remedy is for the authorities to accompany devaluation with tax increases or expenditure cuts to shift the aggregate expenditure function down again, leaving equilibrium income unchanged at full employment and the initial price level but leaving the upward shift in the net export function to improve the balance of trade.

The moral to this story is that there is no point increasing the demand for your exports if more exports cannot be produced.

> In an already fully employed economy, devaluations designed to improve the balance of trade must be accompanied by measures that reduce domestic absorption and thus free resources to produce more exports.

Balance-of-payments records[2]

In order to know what is happening to international payments, governments keep track of the actual transactions among countries. The record of such transactions is called the BALANCE-OF-PAYMENTS ACCOUNTS. Each transaction, such as a shipment of exports or the arrival of imported goods, is recorded and classified according to the payments or receipts that would typically arise from it.

> Any item that typically gives rise to a purchase of foreign currency is recorded as a debit item on the balance-of-payments accounts, and any item that typically gives rise to a sale of foreign currency is recorded as a credit item.

---

[1] Because, as we shall see, it also causes a reduction in domestic absorption, net exports remain slightly higher than they were initially. Domestic absorption falls, for reasons outlined in detail in Chapter 39. The rise in the price level raises the interest rate and this reduces those domestic expenditures that are sensitive to interest rates.

[2] For further details concerning these accounts see Harbury and Lipsey, Chapter 5.

If, for example, a British importer buys an American washing machine to sell in the United Kingdom, this appears as a debit in the UK balance of payments because when the machine is paid for, sterling will be sold and dollars purchased. On the other hand, if a US shipping firm insures with Lloyd's of London a cargo destined for Egypt, this represents a credit in the UK balance of payments, because when the insurance premium is paid, the shipping firm will have to buy sterling in order to pay Lloyd's.

The first thing that we need to notice about the record of international transactions is that the balance of payments always balances. Although it is possible for holders of sterling to want to purchase more dollars in exchange for pounds than holders of dollars want to sell in exchange for pounds, it is not possible for sterling holders actually to buy more dollars than dollar holders sell. Every dollar that is bought must be sold by someone, and every dollar that is sold must be bought by someone. Since the dollars actually bought must be equal to the dollars actually sold, the payments actually made among countries must balance, even though desired payments may not.

Although the total number of pounds bought on the foreign-exchange market must equal the total number sold, the value of purchases and sales for a particular purpose may not be equal. It is quite possible, for example, that more pounds were sold for the purpose of obtaining foreign currency to import foreign cars than were bought for the purpose of buying British cars for export to

Table 37.1 UK balance of payments 1980 (£ million)

Current Account	
Visibles:	
Exports	47,389
Imports	46,211
Balance	+1,178
Invisibles:	
Credits	25,764
Debits	23,736
Balance	+2,028
*Current balance	+3,206
Capital Account	
Overseas investment in the UK	+4,649
UK investment overseas	−7,016
Trade credit	−1,145
Foreign currency lending by UK banks	+2,024
Exchange reserves and other miscellaneous transactions	+13
*Balance	−1,475
*Allocation of SDRs	+180
Official Financing	
Net transactions with overseas monetary authorities	−140
Foreign-currency borrowing (net)	−941
Additions to official reserves	−291
*Total Official Financing	−1,372
*Balancing item	−539
Sum of starred items	0

Source: Annual Abstract of Statistics, 1982.

other countries. In such a case, we would say that the UK had a balance-of-payments deficit on the 'car account', meaning that the value of UK imports of cars exceeded the value of its exports of cars. For most purposes, we are not interested in the balance of payments for single commodities but only for larger groups. The major divisions of the balance of payments are illustrated in Table 37.1.

The current account The CURRENT ACCOUNT records all transactions in goods and services. VISIBLES are goods, i.e., things such as cars, pulpwood, aluminium, coffee, and iron-ore, that we can see when they cross international borders. INVISIBLES are services, i.e., those things that we cannot see, such as insurance and freight haulage and tourist expenditures. Another main invisible item on the current account is the receipt of interest and dividends on loans and investments in foreign countries. If, for example, British residents hold shares in the International Telephone and Telegraph Company (IT & T), they will receive dividend payments in US dollars. If they wish to spend these at home, they will have to exchange the dollars for pounds. Interest and dividends on foreign loans and investments thus provide foreign exchange and are entered as a credit item. (The literature of international-trade theory usually associates the $(X - M)$ encountered in the first part of this chapter with the balance of visible trade. There is no reason, however, why it should not be associated with the broader concept of the balance of payments on current account.)

The capital account The CAPITAL ACCOUNT records transactions related to movements of long- and short-term capital. Consider, for example, holders of sterling who wish to invest abroad. We say that they are exporting capital. Suppose, for example, they wish to buy bonds being sold in New York by expanding American firms. In order to do this, they need to obtain dollars. They are demanders of foreign exchange and suppliers of sterling. Their transactions are, therefore, debit items in the UK balance-of-payments account.

Capital movements may be divided in several ways. One important division is between direct and portfolio investment. DIRECT FOREIGN INVESTMENT occurs when firms themselves transfer funds in order to create new capital in foreign countries. If a UK firm decides, for example, to invest some of its sterling profits in building a new plant abroad, this is direct foreign investment. It is a debit item on the balance of payments because the UK firm will have to sell sterling and buy foreign money in order to obtain the funds to build its factory. PORTFOLIO INVESTMENT occurs when equities or bonds are purchased. If, for example, a UK saver buys a share issued by the American company IBM, this is a portfolio investment and it is a debit on the UK balance of payments.

Capital movements may also be classified according to their term. If a UK citizen buys a Brazilian tin-mining company's bond that will mature in 2005, this is a long-term capital outflow from the UK. If a British firm elects to transfer some of its working balances from London to its New York bank, this is an outflow of short-term capital, since the New York bank has the obligation to pay the deposit on demand. Short-term capital holdings arise in many ways. The mere fact of international trade forces traders to hold money balances. The funds can easily be moved from one currency to another in response to small changes in incentives. When this happens, purchases and sales of foreign exchange must occur.[1]

---

[1] Beginners sometimes find it confusing that the export of capital is a debit item and the export of a good is a credit item. The situation is, however, really very simple. The export of a good earns foreign exchange, and the export of capital uses foreign exchange. Therefore they have opposite effects on international payments. Another way of looking at it is that the capital transaction involves the purchase, and hence the *import* of a foreign bond or share; this has the same effect on the balance of payments as the purchase, and hence the import, of a foreign good. Both transactions use foreign exchange and are thus debit items in the UK balance of payments.

Official financing   The OFFICIAL FINANCING item represents transactions involving the central bank of the country whose balance of payments is being recorded; in this case, the Bank of England. There are three ways in which credit items may occur on the official financing account. First, the Bank of England may borrow from the IMF. This represents a capital inflow and is thus a credit item on the balance of payments. (Repayment of old IMF loans is a debit item.) Second, the Bank may borrow from other central banks through a network of arrangements built up in the 1960s to defend fixed exchange rates against speculative attacks. Such foreign borrowing by the Bank of England is a credit item on the balance of payments. Third, the Bank may run down its official reserves of gold and foreign exchange. This is a credit item because it gives rise to a sale of foreign exchange and a purchase of sterling. The running down of reserves occurs when the Bank of England is supporting the value of sterling on the foreign-exchange market. The Bank then enters the free market selling foreign exchange and buying sterling.

Good and bad items?   The discussion above should have made it obvious that there is nothing necessarily good about credit items or bad about debit items on the balance of payments. For example, investment by UK firms in foreign countries that will yield future profits for UK owners is a debit item; the running down of Bank of England reserves of foreign currencies is a credit item, as is the transfer of ownership of UK firms to foreigners.

The relation among the three main divisions   The relation among the three divisions of accounts follows simply from the fact that their sum must be zero:

$$C+K+F \equiv 0$$

where C, K and F are, respectively, the *balance* on current, capital and official settlement accounts.

> **A deficit on current account must be matched by a net surplus on capital plus official settlement accounts, which means borrowing abroad or running down exchange reserves. A surplus on current account implies a deficit on the sum of the other two accounts.**

To illustrate this relation, assume that in a given year the value of UK imports exceeds the value of UK exports, considering all current-account transactions. The foreign exchange needed to finance the imports that were in excess of exports had to come from somewhere. It must have been lent by someone or else provided out of the government's reserves of gold and foreign exchange. If foreigners are investing funds in the UK, they will be selling foreign currency and buying sterling in order to be able to buy equities and bonds issued by UK firms. Such foreign lending can provide the foreign exchange necessary to allow the UK to have an excess of imports over exports. The other possibility is that the Bank of England financed the current-account deficit either by selling some of its reserves of foreign exchange or by borrowing from the IMF or other central banks.

Now consider a situation in which the value of exports is in excess of the value of imports. This means that foreigners will have been unable to obtain all the sterling they need in order to buy UK goods from the UK sources who wish to supply sterling in return for foreign currency in order to buy foreign goods. The excess of exports over imports could only have been paid for if foreigners obtained sterling from other sources. There are several possibilities. First, sterling may be provided by UK investors wishing to obtain foreign currency so that they can buy foreign stocks and bonds.

In this case, the excess of exports over imports is balanced by UK loans and investments abroad. Second, the UK Government, rather than its firms or citizens, may have lent money to foreign governments to finance their purchases of British-produced goods or services. Third, the UK Government may have given money away as aid, particularly to underdeveloped countries. Such gifts allow these countries to purchase more from the UK than they sell to it. The fourth main possibility is that the Bank of England has added to its reserves of foreign exchange by selling sterling on the foreign-exchange market.

We have already noted that when we add up all the uses of foreign currency, and all the sources from which it came, these two amounts are necessarily equal, and thus the overall accounts of all international payments necessarily balance. What, then, do we mean when we say that payments are not in balance, that there is a deficit or a surplus on the balance of payments?

When we speak of a balance-of-payments deficit or surplus, we refer to the balance on some part of the accounts. Usually, we are referring to the balance on current plus capital account. A balance-of-payments deficit thus means that the reserves of the central bank are being run down or its foreign indebtedness is rising, while a surplus means the opposite.

Part nine

The determination of national income with a variable interest rate and a fixed price level: an integration of money into the theory of national income

38

The money supply [1]

The real and money parts of the economy

In some economic theories, the economy is conceptually divisible into a 'real part' and a 'monetary part'. The real part determines the allocation of resources through the forces of demand and supply. This allocation depends on the structure of *relative* prices. For example, how much beef is produced relative to pork depends on the relation between the prices of the two commodities. If the price of beef were higher than the price of pork and both commodities cost about the same to produce, the incentive would be to produce beef rather than pork. The incentive depends on the relationship between the prices of the two commodities, not on the money price of each. At 50p a pound for pork and £1·50 for beef, the *relative* incentive will be the same as it would be at £1 for pork and £3 for beef. The structure of relative prices is then determined by the 'real' forces of tastes, factor supplies and technology.

In such theories, the price *level* is determined in the monetary part of the economy. An increase in the money supply leads to an increase in the money prices at which all transactions take place. In the example above, an increase in the money supply might raise the price of pork from 50p to £1 a pound and the price of beef from £1·50 to £3. In equilibrium it would leave relative prices unchanged and hence would have no effect on the real part of the economy. In this example the real part of the economy refers to the amount of resources allocated to beef and to pork production. If the quantity of money were doubled, the prices of everything bought would double, but money income would also double, and everyone earning income would be made no better or worse off by the change. Thus, in equilibrium, the real and monetary parts of the economy have no effect on each other according to these theories.

Because early economists believed that the most important issues, such as How much does the economy produce? and What share of it does each group in the society get?, were settled in the real sector, they spoke of money as a 'veil' behind which occurred the real events that affected material well-being. The doctrine that the quantity of money influences the level of money prices but has no effect on the real part of the economy is referred to as the doctrine of the NEUTRALITY OF MONEY.

> **The doctrine of the neutrality of money concerns an economy that is in static equilibrium with full employment of all its resources and a stable price level.**

[1] For a more detailed discussion of some of the institutional aspects relevant to this chapter, see Harbury and Lipsey, Chapter 8.

When there is unemployment and/or a rising price level many theories allow for an interconnection between the monetary and the real parts of the economy. In this chapter we begin our study of just how money can affect national income and the price level. But first we must pause to study in some detail the very nature of money itself.

The nature of money

There is probably more folklore and general nonsense believed about money than about any other aspect of the economy. In the first part of this chapter the functions of money will be described and a brief history of money will be outlined. One purpose of this account is to remove some of these misconceptions. Also, the recent revival of interest in, and advocacy by some economists of a return to, the gold standard makes some discussion of this earlier monetary system of topical importance.

Traditionally in economics MONEY has been defined as any generally accepted medium of exchange – anything that will be accepted by virtually everyone in exchange for goods and services. In fact, money has several different functions: to act as a medium of exchange, as a store of value and as a unit of account. Different kinds of money vary in the degree of efficiency with which they fulfil these functions, so we shall consider the functions one at a time.

A medium of exchange Without money, our complicated economic system based on specialization and the division of labour would be impossible, and we would have to return to a very primitive form of production and exchange. Money frees us from the cumbrous system of barter in the manner described on pp. 59–60 of Chapter 5. For this reason it is not without justification that money has been called one of the great inventions contributing to human freedom.

To serve as an efficient medium of exchange, money must have a number of characteristics: it must be readily acceptable; it must have a high value for its weight, for it would otherwise be a nuisance to carry around; it must be divisible, for money that comes only in large denominations is useless for transactions having only a small value; and it must not be readily counterfeitable, for money that can be easily duplicated by individuals will quickly lose its value.

A store of value Money is a handy way to store purchasing power. In barter, you must take some other good in exchange immediately; with money, you can sell goods today and store the money. This means that you have a claim on someone else's goods that you can exercise at some future date. Separating the two sides of the barter transaction confers an obvious increase in freedom. To be a satisfactory store of purchasing power, however, money must have a stable value. If prices are stable, one knows how much command over real goods and services has been stored up when a certain sum of money has been accumulated. If prices change rapidly, one has little idea how many goods an accumulated sum of money will be able to command.

Notice that although money can serve as a perfectly satisfactory store of accumulated purchasing power for individuals, it cannot do so for society as a whole. If a single individual stores up money, she will, when she comes to spend it, be able to command the current output of some other individual. The whole society cannot do this. If everyone saved their money and all simultaneously retired to live on their savings, there would be no current production to purchase and consume. The society's ability to satisfy wants depends on goods and services being available; if want-satisfying capacity is to be stored up for the *whole society*, then goods that are currently produced must be left unconsumed and carried over to future periods.

A unit of account   Money may also be used purely for accounting purposes, without having any physical existence. For instance, a government shop in a Communist society might say that everyone had so many 'dollars' at his or her disposal each month. Goods could then be given prices and each consumer's purchases recorded, the consumer being allowed to buy all he or she wanted until the supply of 'dollars' was exhausted. The money would have no existence other than as entries in the shop's books, but it would be serving as a perfectly satisfactory unit of account (although it could serve as a medium of exchange only if the shop agreed to transfer credits from one customer to another at the customers' request).[1]

The origins of money

The origins of money are lost in antiquity. Most primitive tribes known today make use of some form of it; and its ability to free people from the cumbersome necessity of barter is a powerful incentive to do so.

Metallic money

All sorts of things have been used as money at one time or another, but precious metals must have gained ascendancy early as the most satisfactory media. They were in heavy and permanent demand for ornament and decoration, and they were in continuous supply (since they do not easily wear out). Thus they tended to have a high and stable value. They were easily recognized and generally known to be commodities which, because of their stable price, would be accepted by most people. They were also divisible into extremely small units (gold to a single grain, for example).

Precious metals thus came to circulate as money and to be used in many transactions. A sack of gold and a highly sensitive set of scales were thus the common equipment of the merchant and trader. 'Princes', to use Machiavelli's term for rulers, perceiving the inconvenience suffered by traders and merchants, decided to do the weighing for once and for all. They took a fixed quantity of precious metal for value, mixed it with some base metal for durability, and minted the mixture into a coin. An imprint of the prince's own seal was affixed, guaranteeing the coin's content of precious metal. This was clearly a great convenience, as long as traders knew that they could accept a coin at its 'face value'.

Abuse of metallic money   The prince's subjects, however, could not let a good opportunity pass. If the subject collected a coin stamped as containing half an ounce of gold, he could clip a thin slice off the edge and pass the coin off as still containing half an ounce. If he was successful, he would have made a profit equal to the market value of the clipped metal. If this practice became common, even the most myopic of traders would notice that things weren't what they used to be in the coinage world. Mistrust would grow, and it would once again be necessary to weigh each coin. To get around this problem, the prince began to mint his coins with a rough edge, which made it obvious if a coin had been clipped. The rough edge still survives on some coins of today as an interesting

---

[1] A fourth function of money is sometimes distinguished: that of a standard of deferred payments. Payments that are to be made in the future, on account of debts, etc., are reckoned in money terms. Money is then being used as a unit of account with an added dimension in time, for the account is not settled until some time in the future.

anachronism reminding us of times when the market value of the metal in a coin was equal to its face value, the coin itself being nothing more than a guaranteed amount of precious metal.

Debasement of metallic money Not to be outdone by the cunning of his subjects, the prince himself was quick to seize the chance of getting something for nothing. As the maker of the coins, he was in a very good position to work a *really* profitable fraud. When he found himself with accounts that he could neither settle nor repudiate, he would re-mint the coinage. The subjects would bring their coins to the mint to be melted down and coined afresh with a new stamp. Between the melting down and the recoining, however, the prince had only to toss some inexpensive base metal into the works to earn himself a handsome profit. If the coinage was debased by adding, say, one part base metal to every four parts of melted-down coins, then five new coins could be made for every four turned in. For every four coins reminted, the prince could have one left over for himself as profit. With these coins, he could pay his bills.

The result would be an inflation. The people would have the same number of coins as before and hence could demand the same number of goods. Once the prince paid his bills, however, his creditors could be expected to spend some or all of the extra coins. The extra demand would bid up prices. Debasing of coinage thus led pretty certainly to a rise in prices. Early economists, observing these processes in action, propounded the *quantity theory of money*. They argued that there was a relation between the average level of prices and the quantity of money in circulation, such that a change in the quantity of money would lead to a change in the price level in the same direction.

Gresham's law The early experience of currency debasement led to a famous economic 'law' that has many applications even today. The hypothesis, that has come to be known as GRESHAM'S LAW after the financial expert who first explained its workings to Queen Elizabeth the First, is that *bad money drives out good*.

Assume that the currency has been seriously debased so that there are gold sovereigns in circulation containing only half their alleged gold content. Assume that the ruler, wanting to make trade more secure, decides to improve the coinage by minting new sovereigns with the correct gold content and feeding them into circulation hoping eventually to replace the entire stock of debased sovereigns. What will happen is that the new sovereigns will disappear as fast as they are minted and the debased sovereigns will remain the only coinage in circulation. The bad money will have driven out the good. Why? The answer lies in the fact that the two kinds of sovereigns have the same face value but one has twice the precious-metal content of the other. Anyone who has both kinds will pay his bills with the debased coins and melt down the new ones, gaining enough metal to make two debased sovereigns.

Gresham's law is as valid today as it was when it was first propounded nearly four hundred years ago. A modern example concerns metallic coins in high-inflation countries over the last few decades. Ten or twenty years ago coins were typically made of copper, nickel and even silver, which had a significant market value but one that was less than the face value of the coins. There might, for example, have been 2 pesetas' worth of metal in a 10 peseta coin. Governments then printed vast amounts of paper money, and prices of everything, including the metal in the coins, rose. In the example just given, anything over a fivefold rise in prices would make the value of the metal in a coin worth more than the face value of the coin. As soon as this happened, paper money became 'bad money' and coins 'good money' in Gresham's sense of the terms. The coins were melted down and the metal sold, yielding more than the face value of the coins. In country after country where inflation rates were really high, the traditional metal coins disappeared when they became 'good money'. The coinage then had to be replaced using metals that were very much cheaper and hence worth much less than the face value of the coins that contained them. This is why in most high-inflation countries today the coins are made of very light, low-cost alloys rather than the traditional metals of silver, nickel and copper.

Paper money

The next important step in the history of money was the evolution of paper currency. Goldsmiths – craftsmen who worked with gold – naturally kept very secure safes in which to store their supplies.[1] The practice grew up among the public of storing their gold with a goldsmith for safe keeping. The goldsmith would give the depositor a receipt for the gold, promising to hand it over on demand. If the depositor wished to make a large purchase, he would go to the goldsmith, reclaim his gold, and hand it over to the seller of the goods. Chances were that the seller would not require the gold, but would carry it back to the goldsmith for safe keeping. Clearly, if people knew the goldsmith to be reliable, there was no need to go through the cumbersome and risky business of physically transfer-ring the gold. The buyer need only transfer the goldsmith's receipt to the seller, who could accept it secure in the knowledge that the goldsmith would pay over the gold whenever it was needed. Thus, the first paper money represented a promise to pay on demand so much gold.

Eventually the goldsmiths were replaced by banks. The paper money that was issued by banks was *backed* by precious metal and was *convertible* on demand into this metal. As long as these institutions were known to be reliable, this paper would be 'as good as gold'.

In the nineteenth century, paper money was commonly issued by banks; in Britain each bank issued its own notes, backed by its own reserves. Also, the Bank of England issued notes backed by the country's gold reserves, for, although it was nominally a private institution until 1947, the Bank always had close links with the government. Since these notes were convertible on demand into gold, the country was said to be on a GOLD STANDARD.

Fractionally backed notes For most transactions, individuals were content to use paper currency. This made it unnecessary, therefore, to keep an ounce of gold in the vaults for every claim to an ounce circulating as paper money. It was necessary to keep some gold on hand, because some holders of the bank notes would require gold for some purposes. On the other hand, some of the bank's customers would be receiving gold in various transactions and wanting to store it in the bank. They would accept promises to pay (i.e., bank notes) in return. At any one time, therefore, some of the bank's customers would be withdrawing gold, others would be depositing it, and the great majority would be carrying out their transactions using only the bank's paper notes. Thus each bank was able to issue more money redeemable in gold than it actually had gold in its vaults. This was a profitable thing to do, because the bank could invest its newly created money in interest-earning assets.

This discovery was made early on by the goldsmiths and, down to the present day, banks have

---

[1] All the basic ideas about paper money can be displayed by concentrating on the goldsmiths, although there were earlier sources of paper money in various negotiable evidences of debt.

had many more claims outstanding against them than they actually had reserves available. In such a situation, we say that the currency is *fractionally backed*. A rough rule of thumb is that a 10 per cent backing for these claims is more than sufficient: if a bank holds £10,000 worth of reserves and has issued £100,000 in notes, it will be perfectly safe in normal times and will be able to convert all of its notes that are presented for conversion.

The major problem with a fractionally backed gold standard is maintaining the currency's *convertibility* into gold. In the past, the imprudent bank that issued too much paper money found itself unable to redeem its currency in gold when the demand for gold was even slightly higher than usual. This bank would then have to suspend payments, and all holders of its notes would suddenly find them worthless. The prudent bank, which kept a reasonable relation between its note issue and its gold reserve, found that it could meet the normal, everyday demand for gold without any trouble. It was always the case with any fractionally backed currency, however, that, if all noteholders demanded gold at once, they could not be satisfied. Thus, if ever the public lost confidence and, *en masse*, demanded redemption of their currency, the banks would be unable to honour their pledges, and the holders of their notes would lose everything.

The development of fiat currencies As time went on, note issue by commercial banks became less common, and central banks took over a steadily increasing share of this responsibility. The paper currency was, as it always had been, freely convertible into gold. It was also only fractionally backed by gold. The commercial banks retained the power to create money, but this was no longer done by printing paper money; instead, deposit money was created.

During the period between the two World Wars, virtually all the countries of the world abandoned the gold standard. The result of abandoning the gold standard was that currency was no longer convertible into gold.

Was the gold standard better?

Today, paper money is valuable because, by habit, everyone accepts it as valuable. The fact that it can no longer be converted into anything has no effect on its functioning as a medium of exchange.

This fact, that present-day money is not convertible into anything – that is nothing but paper whose value derives from common acceptance through habit – often disturbs people who feel that money should be more substantial than mere pieces of paper. Once it is accepted that the value of money is based on nothing more than custom, habit and the need for some medium of exchange, the next question that comes to mind is: does it matter? Gold derived its value because it was scarce relative to the heavy demand for it. Tying a currency to gold meant that the quantity of money in a country was left to such chance occurrences as the discovery of new gold supplies. In early times this was not without advantage, the most important being that it provided a check on the prince's ability to cause inflation. Gold cannot be manufactured at will; paper currency can. There is little doubt that, if the money supply had been purely paper, many governments would have succumbed to the temptation to pay their bills by printing new money rather than by raising taxes. Such increases in the money supply would have led to inflation in just the same way as did the debasement of metallic currencies. Thus, the gold standard provided some check on inflation by making it difficult for governments to change the money supply. On the one hand, however, periods of major gold discoveries brought about inflations of their own. In the sixteenth century, for example, Spanish gold and silver flowed into Europe from the New World, bringing inflation in its wake. On the other hand, it is usually desirable to increase the money supply in a period of rising trade and income. On a gold standard, this cannot be done unless, by pure chance, gold is discovered at the same time.

The gold standard took discretionary power over the money supply out of the hands of the central authorities. Whether or not one thinks that this was a good thing depends on how one thinks the central authorities use this discretion. In general, a gold standard is probably better than having the currency managed by an ignorant or irresponsible government, but worse than having the currency supply adjusted by a well-informed, intelligent one. Better and worse in this context are judged by the criterion of having a money supply that varies adequately with the needs of the economy, but does not vary so as to cause violent inflations or deflations.

Modern money

Deposit money

In most countries today, the money supply consists of notes and coins issued by the government and the central bank, and deposit money. The inconvertible monies that we have already discussed are notes and coins. DEPOSIT MONEY is money that is created by the commercial banking system. *When the individual banks lost the right to issue notes of their own, the form of money creation changed but the substance did not.* Today, banks have money in their vaults (or on deposit with the central banks) just as they always did, only the money is no longer gold; it is the legal tender of the times, actual paper money or claims on it. Banks' customers sometimes deposit paper money with the banks for safe keeping just as, in former times, they deposited gold. The bank takes the money and gives the customer a promise to pay it back on demand. Instead of taking the form of a printed bank note, as in the past, this promise to pay is recorded as an entry of the customer's account. If the customer wishes to pay a bill, he may come to the bank and claim his money in pound notes; he may then pay the money over to another person, and this person may redeposit the money in a bank. Just as with the gold transfers, this is a cumbersome procedure, particularly for large payments, and it would be much more convenient if the bank's promise to pay cash could merely be transferred from one person to another. This is in fact done by means of a *cheque*. If individual A deposits £100 in a bank, the entry of a £100 credit in his account is the bank's promise to pay £100 cash on demand. If A pays B £100 by giving her a cheque that B then deposits in the same bank, the bank merely reduces A's deposit by £100 and increases B's by the same amount. Thus the bank still promises to pay out on demand the £100 originally deposited, but it now promises to pay it to B rather than to A.

Banks can create money by issuing more promises to pay than they actually have cash to pay out. Banks can grant loans by crediting customers' accounts with the amounts of the loans. If borrowers use their loans to pay accounts by cheque, then deposits are transferred from person to person. In most circumstances, any one bank can have liabilities greatly in excess of the amount of cash that it has in reserve. Since bank deposits are generally accepted means of exchange that can be transferred among persons by the medium of cheques, they are money. The great majority of transactions (by value) take place by cheque; only a small proportion involve notes and coins. Thus in the modern world, the greater proportion of the money supply is the deposit money that is created by commercial banks. The banks can, if they wish, contract the money supply by not creating deposits, or they can expand it by creating deposits up to the limit of prudence or law (so that there is just enough cash to meet either the normal demands of customers who do not wish to pay by cheque or the requirements set by law). It is, of course, in the banks' interest to expand deposits up to the allowable limit because every pound created can be used to acquire some income-earning asset.

The modern banking system of the UK[1]

The most visible units in the present-day banking system are the privately owned banks that deal with the ordinary public. These banks are variously called COMMERCIAL BANKS, LISTED BANKS or CLEARING BANKS. (The latter term covers most, but not all, of the commercial banks.) These banks are profit-seeking firms. They accept deposits, they transfer certain kinds of deposits among their customers and other banks when ordered to do so by cheque, they make loans to customers, called ADVANCES, charging them interest in return, and they invest some of their funds by purchasing interest-earning financial assets on the open market.

In the United Kingdom, commercial banks are called LISTED BANKS. The most important of these are the London clearing banks, located in England and Wales, and the clearing banks of Scotland and Northern Ireland. The four largest London clearing banks dominate the system in terms of value of deposits held. They have numerous branches throughout the country. For this reason the UK system is called a 'branch banking' system as opposed to the US system, which is a 'unit banking' system. In the US, banks are not allowed to have branches in more than one state and in some states there is a limit to the number of branches allowed. This means that the group of American commercial banks is composed of a large number of individual banks (over 15,000 in 1981), each with at most only a few branches.

The banks of the system require a mechanism to settle their interbank debts. If a depositor in Bank A writes a cheque to someone whose account is with Bank B, then a mere book transfer within Bank A will not do, because Bank A now owes money to Bank B. It is exactly the same as if one individual withdrew cash from Bank A and gave it to the second individual, who deposited it in Bank B. When the transaction is done by cheque, however, the banks rather than the individuals, transfer the money.

Multibank systems make use of a CLEARING HOUSE where interbank debts are cancelled. At the end of the day, all of the cheques drawn on Bank A's customers and deposited in Bank B are totalled, and set against the total of all the cheques drawn by Bank B's customers and deposited in Bank A. It is only necessary to settle the difference between these two sums. This is done for every pair of banks. The actual cheques are passed through the clearing house back to the bank on which they are drawn. The bank is then able to adjust each individual's account by a set of book entries; a flow of cash between banks is necessary only if there is a *net* transfer of deposits from the customers of one bank to those of another.

The second main element of the UK banking system is the DISCOUNT HOUSES. These specialized institutions, which are peculiar to the UK, borrow money at call (i.e., repayable on demand) or at very short notice from banks and other lending institutions. They then use this money to purchase such short-dated financial assets as treasury bills and local authority bills. Since they borrow money that is repayable on demand and lend it out for terms of up to a month or more (as they do when, for example, they buy a treasury bill that has 30 days to run to maturity), they are in the classic exposed

---

[1] This brief discussion is confined to essentials. More detail can be found in Harbury and Lipsey, Chapter 8.

position of borrowing short and lending (relatively) long.[1] The advantage to the regular banks of this arrangement is that they can earn interest on their cash reserves. (Loans to the discount houses are repayable at call and hence are as good as cash.)

The third main element of the banking system is the CENTRAL BANK. The central bank was itself a natural outcome of the evolutionary process described earlier in this chapter. Where were the commercial banks to keep their cash reserves? Where were they to turn if they had made good loans and investments that would mature in the future, but were in temporary need of reserves to meet an exceptional demand to withdraw gold by their depositors? If banks provided loans to the public against reasonable security, why should not some other institution provide loans to *them* against the same sort of security? Central banks evolved in response to these and other needs. At first they were private profit-making institutions, providing services to ordinary banks, but their potential to influence the behaviour of commercial banks and, through them, the behaviour of the whole economy led to the development of close ties with governments. In most European countries these ties eventually became formalized as central banks were taken over by governments.

Almost all advanced countries have central banks, and their functions are similar: to be banker to the government and the commercial banking system, to manage the public debt, to control the money supply and to regulate the country's monetary and credit system. The central bank is always an instrument of the central authorities, whether or not it is owned publicly. The Bank of England is one of the oldest and most famous of the central banks. It began to operate as the central bank of England in the seventeenth century, but was not officially nationalized until 1947. It operates in two self-contained sections, the issue department and the banking department, each of which publishes its own balance sheet. In the US the central bank is the Federal Reserve System, which was organized in 1913.

Most banking systems also have a variety of other specialized institutions. Some of these accept time deposits from the public and lend money out on a longer-term basis. Two British examples are finance houses and building societies. Finance houses grant loans to finance hire-purchase acquisitions of durable goods; building societies grant mortgages for the purchase of real estate. These institutions are often called FINANCIAL INTERMEDIARIES, since they stand between those who save money and those who ultimately borrow it.

From our point of view, the most important thing about the banking system is its control of the money supply through the creation and destruction of deposit money. We must now look at this process in a little more detail.

The creation of deposit money

Assume that, in a system with many banks, each bank obtains new deposits in cash. (This, as we shall see, is something that the central bank can engineer.) Say, for example, that the community contains ten banks of equal size and that each receives a new deposit of £100 in cash. Each bank now has on its books the new entries shown in Table 38.1. The banks are on a fractional reserve system and we assume that they hold 10 per cent reserves against all deposits. The deposit just received puts

---

[1] The discount houses provide a good example of the division of labour. They are specialists in the short-term money market. Institutions that specialize in other forms of loans do not find it worth their while to acquire detailed knowledge of the short-term market. They lend those funds that they can commit only for short terms to the discount houses who, guided by their specialist knowledge, can lend them profitably.

Table 38.1 A new deposit of £100 is made

Liabilities		Assets	
Deposit	£100	Cash	£100

each bank into disequilibrium since it has 100 per cent reserves against that new deposit.

First assume that only one of the banks begins to expand deposits by making new loans and buying bonds. Now when cheques are written on these deposits, the majority would be deposited in other banks. Thus the bank must expect much of its £100 in cash to be drained away to other banks as soon as it creates new deposits for its own customers.

If, for example, one bank has only 10 per cent of the total deposits held by the community, then on average 90 per cent of any new deposits it creates will end up in other banks. If other banks are not simultaneously creating new deposits, then this one bank will be severely restricted in its ability to expand deposits. The reason for the restriction is that the bank will suffer a major cash drain as cheques are written payable to individuals who deal with other banks.

> **One bank in a multibank system cannot produce a large multiple expansion of deposits based on an original accretion of cash, unless other banks also expand deposits.**

Now assume, however, that each bank begins to expand deposits based on the £100 of new reserves. On the one hand, since each bank does one-tenth of the total banking business, on average 90 per cent of the value of any newly created deposit will find its way into other banks as customers make payments by cheque to people in the community. This represents a cash drain to these other banks. On the other hand, 10 per cent of the new deposits created by each other bank should find its way into this bank. Thus, if all banks receive new cash and all start creating deposits simultaneously, no bank should suffer a significant cash drain to any other bank. All banks can go on expanding deposits without losing cash to each other; they need only worry about keeping enough cash to satisfy those depositors who occasionally require cash. Thus the expansion can go on, with each bank watching its own ratio of cash reserves to deposits, expanding deposits as long as the ratio exceeds 1:10 and ceasing when it reaches that figure. Assuming no cash drain to the public, the process will not come to a halt until each bank has created £900 in additional deposits, so that, for each initial £100 cash deposit, there is now £1,000 in deposits backed by £100 in cash. Now *each* of the banks will have new entries in its books similar to those shown in Table 38.2 (where the division between bonds and loans is arbitrary and for purposes of illustration only).

Table 38.2 £900 is invested in loans and bonds with no cash drain

Liabilities		Assets	
Deposits	£1,000	Cash	£100
		Loans	£500
		Bonds	£400

Table 38.3 Expansion of credit in expectation of a 90 per cent cash drain to other banks when no cash drain actually occurs

Liabilities		Assets	
Deposits	£190	Cash	£100
		Loans and bonds	£90
	£190		£190

It might help to think of this process as taking place in a series of hypothetical steps. In the first period, each bank gets £100 in new deposits and the books of each bank show new entries similar to those in Table 38.1. During the second period, each bank makes loans of £90 expecting that it will suffer a cash drain £81 on account of these loans. Indeed, 90 per cent of the new loans made by Bank A do find their way into other banks, but 10 per cent of the new loans made by each other bank find their way into Bank A. Thus, there is no net movement of cash among banks. Instead of finding itself with its surplus cash drained away, each bank's books at the end of the day will contain the entries shown in Table 38.3.

Cash is now just over 50 per cent of deposits, instead of only 10 per cent as desired. Thus each bank can continue to expand deposits in order to grant loans and to purchase income-earning assets. As long as all banks do this simultaneously, no bank will suffer any significant cash drain to any other bank, and the process can continue until each bank has created £900 worth of new deposits and then finds itself in the position shown in Table 38.2.

A multibank system creates deposit money when all banks with excess reserves expand their deposits in step with each other.

A complication: cash drain to the public So far we have ignored the fact that the public actually divides its money holdings in a fairly stable proportion between cash and deposits. This means that, when the banking system as a whole creates significant amounts of new deposit money, the whole system will suffer a cash drain as the public withdraws enough cash from the banks to maintain its desired ratio of cash to deposits.

An example: Assume, for example, that the public wishes to hold 10 per cent of its money in cash and 90 per cent in the form of deposits. Now when the commercial banks create new deposits, 90 per cent of the value will circulate in the form of cheques and so will stay with the banking system. The other 10 per cent, however, will be withdrawn as cash. This means that if banks receive new deposits of £100, the system cannot create as much as £900 of new deposits (assuming a 10 per cent reserve requirement). Banks will begin to expand deposits, but, as they do, they will all suffer a net cash drain. When their reserve ratios fall to 10 per cent of their deposits, their deposit expansion must cease. In the example, the results will be those shown in Table 38.4. The cash drain to the public is £52·63. This yields a ratio of cash held by the public to total money held (cash plus deposits) of $52\cdot63/(473\cdot68 + 52\cdot63) = 0\cdot10$. The banks are left with £47·37 of reserves which provide the necessary 10 per cent backing for deposits of £473·68.

A significant cash drain to the public greatly reduces the expansion of deposit money that can be supported by any new deposits accruing to the banking system.

Table 38.4 Equilibrium deposit expansion with a 10 per cent cash drain to the public

Liabilities		Assets	
Deposits	£473·68	Cash reserves	£47·37
		Loans and bonds	£426·31
	£473·68		£473·68

The general case: This argument is easily generalized using simple algebra. Let there be new deposits of £N reaching the banking system. Banks find themselves with reserves and deposits in this amount. When they expand deposits, some of their reserves will be lost as a cash drain, C, to the public and the rest will remain as reserves, R. Thus

$$C + R = N \quad . \tag{1}$$

Now assume that there is a required reserve ratio of α. This allows us to write

$$\alpha D = R \quad , \tag{2}$$

where D is the total deposits that will be created as a result of the new deposit of £N. Finally, assume that the public wishes to hold a fraction, β, of all its money in cash:

$$C = \beta(C + D) \quad . \tag{3}$$

Substituting the second and third equations into the first and solving for D yields:

$$D = \frac{1 - \beta}{\beta + \alpha - \alpha\beta} N \quad . \tag{4}$$

If, for example, you put into equation (4) a bank's required reserve ratio of 0·10 and a public's desired cash to money ratio of 0·10, and then substitute back through equations (1) to (3), you will be able to verify the numerical results given in Table 38.4.

Equation (4) shows if the public's desired cash ratio is zero, deposits rise by the reciprocal of the cash reserve ratio. A positive β, however, means that the resulting cash drain lowers the increase in deposits since it reduces the value of the numerator and raises that of the denominator in equation (4).

Kinds of deposit money

If a customer has a deposit in a bank, he can keep it in one of two forms: either as a sight or demand deposit (current account), or as a time deposit (savings or deposit account). The distinction between the two is commonly made throughout the world, although the terms applied to them vary.

The two main characteristics of SIGHT DEPOSITS or DEMAND DEPOSITS, as they are variously called, are first that the owner can withdraw cash on demand, and, second, that the bank agrees to transfer sight deposits from one person to another when ordered to do so by the writing of a cheque. The first characteristic makes the deposit a satisfactory store of value, since it is as good as cash. The second characteristic helps to make the sight deposit a medium of exchange. TIME DEPOSITS or DEPOSIT ACCOUNTS differ in both of these essential features. The owner of a time deposit must legally give notice of his intention to withdraw cash. Although banks often do not enforce this law, they could do so at any time if they wished. Furthermore, holders of deposit accounts cannot pay their bills by writing cheques ordering their banks to pay their creditors out of their deposits. Banks always pay a higher rate of interest on time deposits than on sight deposits. (Sight deposits frequently, although not invariably, carry a zero interest rate.)

Banks have recently created a number of new deposit instruments. The most important is the CERTIFICATE OF DEPOSIT (CD). With a CD, money is deposited for a fixed period ranging from a month to several years. It earns a higher rate of interest than when deposited in a saving account where in effect the money can be withdrawn at any time. Some CDs are negotiable, others are not.

Evolution of monetary instruments

Over the centuries what has been accepted as money has expanded from gold and silver coins to include, first, bank notes and then bank deposits subject to transfer by cheque. Until recently, most economists would have agreed that money stopped at that point. No such agreement exists today, and an important debate centres around the definition of money that is appropriate to the present world.

If we concentrate only on the medium-of-exchange function, money consists of notes, coins, and deposits subject to transfer by either cheque or by cheque-like instruments such as standing orders to transfer funds from one account to another. No other asset constitutes a generally accepted medium of exchange. The problem of deciding what is money arises because anything that can fulfil the medium-of-exchange function can also fulfil the store-of-value function, but many things that can fulfil the second do not fulfil the first.

Near money   The term NEAR MONEY refers to assets that adequately fulfil the store-of-value function, that are readily convertible into a medium of exchange but that are not themselves a medium of exchange.

As long as all sales and purchases do not occur at the same moment, everyone needs a temporary store of value between the act of selling and the act of buying. Whatever serves the function of a medium of exchange can be held and thus can also serve the function of a temporary store of value. But other assets can also be used for this store-of-value function. If, for example, you have a deposit account at a bank or a building society, you know exactly how much purchasing power you hold (at today's prices) and, given modern banking practices, you can turn your deposit into cash or a sight deposit at short notice. Additionally, your time deposit will earn some interest during the period that you hold it. Why then does not everybody keep their money in deposit accounts instead of in demand deposits or currency? The answer is that the inconvenience of continually shifting money back and forth may outweigh the interest that can be earned. One week's interest on £100 (at 12 per cent per year) is less than 25p, not enough to cover the time and money costs in transferring money needed in a week into an interest-earning account and back out again.

> **Whether it pays to convert cash or sight deposits into interest-earning deposits for a given period depends on the inconvenience and other transactions costs of shifting funds in and out, and on the amount of interest that can be earned.**

There is a wide spectrum of assets in the economy that yield an interest return and also serve as reasonably satisfactory temporary stores of value. The difference between these other assets and time deposits is that their capital values are not quite as certain as are those of time deposits. If I elect to store my purchasing power in the form of some financial asset that matures in 30 days, its price on the market may change between the time I buy it and the time I want to sell it – say 10 days later. If the price changes, I will suffer or enjoy a change in the purchasing power available to me. But because of the short horizon to maturity, the price will not change very much. (After all, its face value will be paid in a few weeks.) Such a security is, thus, a reasonably satisfactory short-run store of purchasing power. Indeed, any readily saleable capital asset whose value does not fluctuate significantly with the rate of interest can fulfil this short-term, store-of-value function.

Money substitutes Things that serve as a temporary medium of exchange but are not a store of value are sometimes called MONEY SUBSTITUTES. Credit cards are a good example. With a credit card many transactions can be made without either cash or a cheque. But the evidence of credit, in terms of the credit slip you sign, is not money because it cannot be used to effect further transactions. Furthermore, when your credit card company sends you a bill, you have to use money in (delayed) payment for the original transaction. The credit card serves the short-run function of a medium of exchange by allowing you to make purchases even though you have neither cash nor a positive bank balance currently in your possession. But this is only temporary; money remains the final medium of exchange for these transactions when the credit account is settled.

Definitions of money

What is an acceptable medium of exchange has changed and will continue to change over time. Furthermore, new monetary assets are continuously being developed to serve some, if not all, of the functions of money, and these are more or less readily convertible into money.

Economists now distinguish several concepts of money. In the UK the most important of these are:

M1: notes and coin plus sight deposits of the private sector, symbolized M1;
STERLING M3: M1 plus sterling time deposits of the private sector plus sterling time and sight deposits of the public sector, symbolized £M3;
M3: £M3 plus deposits of UK residents held in other currencies, symbolized M3.

(In the US the term M2 covers roughly what in the UK is called £M3.)

The first definition concentrates on the medium-of-exchange function. The second definition adds in time deposits with banks, which serve the temporary-store-of-value function and are in practice instantly convertible into a medium of exchange at a completely secure price that does not fluctuate with the rate of interest. The third adds in deposits held in foreign currencies that can quickly be converted into deposits held in sterling.

Economists use the terms SUPPLY OF MONEY and MONEY SUPPLY to refer to the economy's total amount of money (defined in one of the above ways). It is a relatively easy matter to collect statistics on the total amount of currency in circulation (since the currency is issued by the central bank) and the total of bank deposits (since banks must publish their balance sheets). Thus, we can know with a high degree of accuracy what the money supply is at any moment of time.

The Bank of England has the ultimate legal control over the supply of money in the UK. The supply can also be influenced, as we shall see, by the decisions of ordinary profit-seeking banks.

It is also very useful to distinguish the nominal from the real money supply. The NOMINAL MONEY SUPPLY is measured in monetary units. The REAL MONEY SUPPLY is measured in purchasing-power units and expressed in constant prices ruling in some base year. To obtain the real money supply, the nominal money supply is deflated by a price index. For example, the nominal money supply (M1) was £10,500 million in 1970 and £34,300 million in 1981. The real money supply, measured in 1970 prices, was £10,500 million in 1970 and £8,000 million in 1981. The latter figure is found by dividing the nominal money supply of £34,300 by the index of retail prices for 1981 of 430 (1970 = 100) and then multiplying by 100. Thus, although the nominal money supply increased by nearly three and a half times, the real money supply – the purchasing power of the existing money stock – actually fell over the period in question.

39

Monetary equilibrium

What determines how much money people hold in their purses and wallets and how much they keep in the bank? What happens when everyone discovers that they are holding more, or less, money than they believe they need to hold?

These turn out to be key questions for our study of the influence of money on national income. The answers will help us to establish a link between money supply and the aggregate expenditure function which is the major topic of the first half of this chapter.

Kinds of assets

At any moment in time, households have a given stock of wealth. This wealth is held in many forms. Some of it is held as money in the bank or in the wallet; some is held as short-term securities such as CDs and treasury bills; some is held as long-term bonds; and some as real capital, which may be held directly (in such forms as farms, houses and family businesses) or indirectly (in the form of equities that indicate part ownership of a company's assets).

All these ways of holding wealth may be grouped into three main categories: (1) assets that serve as a medium of exchange, that is, paper money, coins and bank chequing deposits; (2) other financial assets, such as bonds earning a fixed rate of interest, that will yield a fixed money value at some future *maturity* date and that can usually be sold before maturity for a price that fluctuates on the open market; and (3) claims on real capital, that is, physical objects such as factories and machines. To simplify our discussion, it is helpful to assume that only two kinds of financial assets exist: *money*, which is perfectly liquid but earns no interest, and *bonds*, which are less liquid but earn an interest return. Thus the term *bonds* stands for all interest-earning financial assets plus claims on real capital such as equities.[1]

The rate of interest and the price of bonds A bond is a promise by the issuer to pay a stated sum of money as interest each year and to repay the face value of the bond at some future 'redemption date', often many years distant. The time until the redemption date is called the TERM TO MATURITY or often simply the TERM of the bond. Some bonds, called perpetuities, pay interest for ever and never repay the principal.

---

[1] This simplification can take us quite a long way. For many problems, however, the simplest satisfactory model has three assets, money, debt (bonds) and real capital (equities).

The relationship between interest rates and bond prices was discussed in Chapter 28, pp. 404–6, and here we only need to recall the key conclusions that are important for present purposes:

(1) the price of any bond reflects the value of the stream of future payments that its owner will receive;

(2) the rate of interest and bond prices vary inversely with each other;

(3) the closer to the present date is the redemption date of a bond, the less the bond's value will change with a change in the rate of interest.

A full understanding of the reasoning behind these propositions is important for what follows, so if you are in any doubt about them you should review the discussion in Chapter 28 now.

Money demand and supply

The supply of money

As used in this chapter, the supply of money is M1: the total quantity of currency plus demand deposits. We saw in the preceding chapter that deposit money is created by banks, but only within limits set by their reserves. How the central bank seeks to influence the money supply is part of the theory of monetary policy which is discussed in Chapter 44. In the meantime we treat the money supply as an exogenous variable. This allows us to see how the economy adjusts to any given money supply; later we can study the reasons why the money supply changes.

The demand for money

There is a cost of holding any money balance: the money could have been used to purchase a bond which would have earned interest.

> **The opportunity cost of holding money is the rate of interest that could have been earned if the money had been used to purchase an income-earning asset.**

Thus money will be held only if it provides services to the holders that are at least as valuable as the opportunity cost of holding it.

The total amount of money balances that everyone wishes to hold for all purposes is called the DEMAND FOR MONEY. Notice that the quantity of money is a *stock* and that the demand for it is a demand for a stock: people wish to hold so much money in cash or deposits. This makes the demand for money to hold different from the demand for any commodity to consume. The demand for a consumption commodity is a flow demand and requires a time dimension to make it meaningful: so many units *per week*, *per month* or *per year*.

The transactions demand for money   Virtually all transactions in our economy require money. Money is passed from households to firms to pay for the goods and services produced by firms, and money is passed from firms to households to pay for the factor services supplied by households. Money balances that are held because of these flows are called TRANSACTIONS BALANCES, and the desire to hold balances to finance these flows is called the TRANSACTIONS MOTIVE. The quantity of transactions balances people want to hold is called the TRANSACTIONS DEMAND FOR MONEY.

In an unreal world where the receipts and disbursements of households and firms were perfectly synchronized, it would be unnecessary to hold transactions balances. If every time a household wished to spend £10 it received £10 as part payment of its income, no transactions balances would be needed. In the real world, however, receipts and disbursements are not perfectly synchronized.

Consider, for example, the balances held in order to make wage payments. The level of balances that must be held depends on the pay period and on the size of the wage bill. Assume, for purposes of illustration, that firms pay wages every Friday, that households spend all their wages on the purchase of goods and services, and that expenditure is spread out evenly over the week. Thus, on Friday morning, firms must hold balances equal to the weekly wage bill, while on Friday afternoon, households will hold these balances. Over the week, households' balances will run down as a result of purchasing goods and services. By the same token, the balances held by firms will build up as a result of selling goods and services until, on the following Friday morning, firms will again have amassed balances equal to the wage bill that must be met on that day. On the average over the week, firms will hold balances equal to half the wage bill and so will households. Total balances held between them will equal the weekly wage bill. Notice that although the balances circulate so that each group holds a varying balance over the week, the total demand for balances summed over both groups is constant and equal to the weekly wage bill.

As it is with the wage bill so it is with all receipts and payments of households and firms. Because their receipts and their disbursements are not fully synchronized, they must hold money balances to bridge the gap.

The transactions demand for money arises because of the non-synchronization of payments and receipts.

What determines the size of transactions balances to be held? It is clear that in the above example total transactions balances held vary with the value of the total wage bill. Say that the wage bill doubles either because twice as much labour is hired at the same wage rate or because the same amount of labour is hired at twice the wage rate. In either case, the weekly wage bill will double and the transactions balances held by firms and households on this account will also double. As it is with wages so it is with all other transactions: the size of the balances held is positively related to the value of the transactions.

Next we must ask how the total value of transactions is related to national income. Because of the 'double counting' problem first discussed on page 510, the value of all transactions exceeds the value of the economy's final output. When the flour mill buys wheat from the farmer and when the baker buys flour from the mill, both are transactions against which money balances must be held, although only the value added at each stage is part of national income. Typically, the total value of transactions tends to be five to ten times as large as the total value of final output which is national income.

We now make an added assumption that there is a stable relation between transactions and national income. If, for example, a 10 per cent rise in aggregate expenditure leads to a 10 per cent rise in national income, we assume that this will also lead to a 10 per cent rise in the total value of all transactions, and hence to an associated rise in the demand for transactions balances. This allows us to relate transactions balances to national income.

The larger the value of national income measured in current prices, the larger the value of transactions balances that will be held.[1]

The precautionary demand for money Uncertainty plays no role in the need for transactions balances. If there is uncertainty about the exact timing of receipts and payments, households and firms may wish to hold additional balances called PRECAUTIONARY BALANCES in response to the PRECAUTIONARY MOTIVE for holding money. Let us see how this demand arises.

Many goods and services are sold on credit, and the seller can never be quite certain when these goods will be paid for, whereas the buyer can never be quite certain of the day of delivery and thus of the day on which payment will fall due; nor can he be certain of the degree to which his suppliers will be pressing for prompt payment. In order to be able to continue in business during times in which receipts are abnormally low and/or disbursements are abnormally high, firms carry money balances. The larger such balances, the greater the degree of insurance against being unable to pay bills because of some temporary fluctuation in either receipts or disbursements. If the firm is pressed for cash or has other very profitable uses for its funds, it may run down these balances and take the risk of being caught by some temporary fluctuations in receipts and disbursements. How serious this risk is, depends on the penalties of being caught without sufficient reserves. A firm is unlikely to be pushed into insolvency, but it may have to incur considerable costs if it is forced to borrow money at high interest rates for short periods in order to meet such temporary crises. The cost depends on the lines of short-term credit open to the firm.

Whereas the transactions demand arises from the certainty of non-synchronization of payments and receipts, the precautionary demand arises from uncertainty about the degree of non-synchronization.

The precautionary motive arises, therefore, out of stochastic disturbances in the flows of payments and receipts.

The protection provided by any given stock of precautionary balances depends on the degree to which payments and receipts are subject to haphazard fluctuations and on the value of the payments and receipts. To provide the same degree of protection as the value of transactions rise, more money is necessary. Thus, the firm's demand for money can be expected to rise as its own sales rise. Aggregating over all firms and households, the total precautionary demand for money will rise as

---

[1] The modern theory of the transactions demand for money suggests that this demand also varies with the rate of interest. Consider, for example, a man who is paid monthly. He can hold all unspent income in a demand deposit at his bank, in which case he will have an average transactions balance equal to half his monthly salary. Or, dividing the month into four quarters, he could keep a quarter of his salary in cash at payday and invest the other three-quarters in bonds. At the start of the second quarter, he would cash in a third of these bonds and obtain enough cash to finance the second quarter's expenditure. He would do the same at the start of the third quarter, and at the start of the fourth quarter he would cash in the last of these bonds. In this way he reduces his *average transactions holding* to one-eighth of a month's income (at the start of each quarter of the month he has one-fourth of a month's income as a balance, and by the end of the quarter he is down to nothing) and correspondingly increases his average holding of interest-earning assets.

Similar calculations would show that if the same man made *daily* transfers of funds, he could reduce his transactions balances even further. Obviously, the sensible arrangement will depend on how much interest can be earned and how costly (in terms of trips to the bank, inconvenience and brokerage fees) it is to switch assets. Empirical evidence suggests substantial interest sensitivity at least for the very large transactions balances held by large firms: the higher the interest rate the more it is worth their while to economize on these balances.

national income rises. Firms can also be expected to hold more funds for precautionary purposes, the lower the opportunity cost of holding such funds, as measured by the market rate of interest.[1]

The precautionary demand for money is negatively related to the rate of interest as well as being positively related to the level of income.

The speculative demand for money Firms and households that hold bonds will have to sell some of them if a temporary excess of payments over receipts exhausts their current money holdings. At one extreme, if a household or firm held all of its wealth in bonds, it would earn interest on all that wealth, but it would have to sell some bonds the first time its payments exceeded its receipts. At the other extreme, if a household or firm held all its wealth in money, the money would earn no interest, but the household or firm would never have to sell bonds to meet temporary excesses of payments over current receipts. Wealth-holders usually do not adopt either extreme position; instead, they hold part of their wealth as money and part as bonds (which in our theory stand for all interest-earning assets).

Households and firms that hold bonds *and* money run the risk that an unexpected gap between their payments and receipts will force them to sell some bonds. If the price of bonds were fixed, there would be no risk in selling. But, instead, the price of bonds fluctuates from day to day. Therefore, a household or firm that may have to sell bonds to meet a temporary need for money, takes the risk that the price of bonds may be unexpectedly low at the time that it must sell them. Of course, if the household is lucky, the price may be unexpectedly high. But because no one knows in advance which way the price will go, firms and households must accept a risk whenever they hold, in the form of bonds, wealth that they may need to spend. Many firms and households do not like risk – economists say they are *risk-averse*. This leads them to hold more money than they otherwise would, in order to reduce the risk of having to sell bonds in the future at a price that cannot be predicted in advance.

The motive that leads firms to hold more money *in reaction to the risks inherent in a fluctuating price of bonds* was first analyzed by Keynes, who called it the SPECULATIVE MOTIVE. The modern analysis of this motive, sketched in the preceding paragraph, is the work of Professor James Tobin of Yale University, winner of the 1981 Nobel prize in economics.[2]

Firms and households tend to insure against this risk by holding some fraction of their wealth in money and the rest in earning assets. Thus the speculative demand for money depends on wealth and varies directly with wealth. For example, household A might elect to hold 5 per cent of its wealth in money and the other 95 per cent in bonds. If A's wealth is £50,000, its demand for money will be £2,500. If its wealth increases to £60,000, its demand for money will rise to £3,000. Although one household's wealth may rise or fall rapidly, the total wealth of a society changes only slowly. For the

---

[1] Institutional arrangements affect the precautionary demand. In the past, for example, a traveller would have to carry a substantial precautionary balance in cash, but today his credit card covers him against almost any unforeseen expenses that may arise on his travels.

[2] Keynes' theory was couched in terms of a normal, or expected, rate of interest and an actual rate that diverged from time to time from the normal rate, causing households to switch their assets between money and bonds. At any one time a firm or household held only money or only bonds but in aggregate both were held because different firms and households had different ideas about the 'normal' rate of interest. This theory has for a long time been accepted as unsatisfactory for reasons explained in Professor Tobin's famous paper, 'Liquidity Preference as Behaviour Toward Risk', published in 1958, which also spells out the theory briefly discussed in the above text.

analysis of short-term fluctuations in national income, the effects of changes in wealth are fairly small, and we shall ignore them for the present. (Over the long term, however, variations in wealth can have a major influence on the demand for money.)

An important force acting on the decision of how to divide wealth between bonds and money is the cost of holding money. Wealth held in cash earns no interest; hence the reduction in risk involved in holding more money also carries a cost in terms of interest earnings forgone.

> **The speculative motive leads households and firms to add to their money holdings until the reduction in risk obtained by the last £1 added is just balanced (in the wealth-holder's view) by the cost in terms of the interest forgone on that £1.**

Because the cost of holding money balances is the interest that could have been earned if wealth had been held in bonds instead, the demand to hold money will be negatively related to the interest rate. When the rate of interest falls, the cost of holding money falls. This leads to more money being held for the speculative motive, to reduce risks associated with fluctuations in the market price of bonds. When the rate of interest rises, the cost of holding money rises. This leads to less money being held for the speculative motive.

> **The speculative demand for money has its source in uncertainty about future bond prices. It is negatively related to the rate of interest and positively related to wealth.**

The total demand for money: recapitulation

The demand for money is defined as the total amount of money balances that everyone in the economy wishes to hold. The previous discussion about the motives for holding money can be summarized by listing three hypotheses.

(1) *The demand for money is positively related to national income valued in current prices.* Both transactions and precautionary motives lead to this hypothesis. The higher the level of income, the larger the amount of money needed for transactions purposes and the larger also is the amount required to provide a given level of security against unforeseen fluctuations in receipts and payments.

(2) *The demand for money is negatively related to the rate of interest.* The higher the rate of interest, the higher the opportunity cost of holding money and the less money will be held for precautionary purposes. The rate of interest also influences decisions as to whether to hold money for speculative purposes, since the higher the rate of interest the greater the cost of holding the money.

(3) *The demand for money is positively related to wealth.* If households and firms wish to hold some fraction of their wealth in money because of uncertainty over bond prices, the demand for money to hold will rise as wealth rises.

Note that although there are separately identifiable motives for holding money, money is not necessarily held in separate accounts labelled transactions, precautionary and speculative accounts. When households and firms decide how much of their monetary assets they will hold as money rather than as bonds, they are said to be exercising their preference for liquidity. LIQUIDITY PREFERENCE thus refers to the demand to hold wealth as money rather than as interest-earning assets.

We can now state the money demand function implied by the previous discussion. In doing so, however, we must be very careful to distinguish real from nominal values. First, let us consider the demand for money in real terms. Now by the demand for money we mean the number of units of purchasing power the public wishes to hold as money balances. In an imaginary one-product, wheat economy, this would be measured in the number of bushels of wheat that could be purchased with the money balances held. In a real economy it could be measured in terms of the number of weeks of national income. For example, the demand for money might be equal to one month's national income. Our previous discussion suggests that the demand for money measured in real, purchasing-power units is related to the real value of national income, the real value of wealth and the rate of interest.[1]

We let the function $L(Y, r, W)$ determine *the real demand for money measured in purchasing-power units* as a function of real national income, Y, the interest rate, r, and the real, purchasing-power value of wealth, W. The letter L, which stands for liquidity preference, indicates a functional relation that, given values for Y, r and W, determines the real demand for money, which we denote by M_D:

$$M_D = L(Y, r, W) \; . \tag{1}$$

Now we may determine the nominal demand for money merely by multiplying (1) through by the price level, P, which makes the nominal demand equal to $PL(Y, r, W)$. Thus the nominal demand for money varies in proportion to the price level, e.g., doubling the price level doubles nominal demand.

For short-term analysis, we can take the quantity of wealth as a constant, since it changes very slowly. For simplicity we assume the relation to be linear and write[2]

$$M_D = dY + er \qquad e < 0 < d \; , \tag{2}$$

where M_D is the real demand for money, Y is real national income, d is a positive constant indicating the fraction of annual income desired to be held in money balances, r is the market rate of interest, and e is a negative constant showing how responsive the demand for money is to changes in the market rate of interest.[3]

Figure 39.1 shows these three key relations graphically. Holding real national income and the price level constant, the demand for money is shown in part (i) to be negatively related to the rate of

[1] When the price level is changing continuously it is necessary to distinguish the real from the nominal rate of interest. This distinction will be introduced when it is needed. Right now, however, we are considering equilibrium situations where the price level is constant. There is no need to distinguish these two concepts of the interest rate since they are the same in these circumstances and are measured by the market rate of interest.

[2] Strictly speaking, this function should have a positive constant indicating the amount demanded as a result of the autonomous quantity of wealth. This constant, however, makes much of the subsequent algebraic manipulation much more sordid that it needs to be without adding any economic understanding. Thus it is simpler in an elementary treatment to ignore the constant. Anyone with a theoretical bent may find it interesting, however, to introduce a constant, a_2, into (2) indicating a constant real demand for money and carry it through subsequent manipulations. If you try this, and interpret your results in terms of economic behaviour, at all stages, you will encounter some quite interesting problems. These will illustrate once again that even trivial mathematics can reveal some quite subtle issues.

[3] In the previous chapters, we have reserved lower-case letters for behavioural parameters. Here we make one exception by using r for the endogenous variable, the rate of interest. Consistency would call for the use of R rather than r but the lower-case r for the rate of interest (or sometimes i) is so hallowed by use that it seems better to stick with standard usage by allowing this one endogenous variable to be indicated by a lower-case letter.

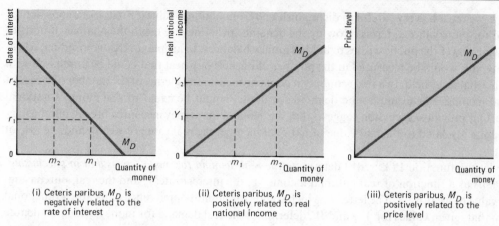

Fig. 39.1 The demand for money

interest. Holding the rate of interest and the price level constant, the demand for money is shown in part (ii) to be positively related to real national income. Holding real national income and the rate of interest constant, the demand for money is shown in part (iii) to be positively related to the price level.[1]

Asset equilibrium

Households and firms have a given amount of wealth and they must decide how much to hold in bonds and how much to hold in money. Since, in our simple model, these are the only two assets in which wealth can be held, there is only one decision to take: how to divide wealth between these two assets. The decision, for example, to hold 80 per cent of wealth in bonds *implies* a decision to hold the other 20 per cent in money. We will concentrate on the demand to hold money (recognizing that, with given wealth, a demand to hold money implies a demand to hold bonds).[2] To see what is involved in equilibrium between the demand for and supply of money it is best to start with disequilibrium situations.

An excess demand for money If a single firm or household is short of money balances, it can sell some of its bonds and immediately replenish its stock of money. It is not possible, however, for everyone to do this simultaneously if the total stocks of money and bonds are constant. Under these

---

[1] Note that, as is usual with demand functions, economists reverse the normal labling of the axes. The dependent variable, the quantity of money demanded, would on normal mathematical conventions be plotted on the vertical axis but economic convention dictates that it be plotted on the horizontal axis. (See footnote 1, page 76.)

[2] Since wealth can only be held as either money or bonds, we have (using B_D to indicate the demand to hold bonds):

$$M_D + B_D \equiv W \quad ,$$

from which it follows that

$$B_D \equiv W - M_D \quad .$$

If we have determined M_D we have also determined B_D.

circumstances, general attempts to turn bonds into money balances will only succeed in altering the price of bonds. When all firms and households are short of money they try to sell bonds to replenish their money holdings. This causes the price of bonds to fall which means, of course, a rise in the interest rate. As the interest rate rises, people will economize on cash holdings. Eventually, the rate will rise high enough so that people will no longer be trying to add to their cash balances by selling bonds. The quantity of money demanded will again equal its supply, and, since there will no longer be an excess supply of bonds, the interest rate will stop rising. The net effect of the original excess demand for money will have been an increase in the rate of interest.

An excess demand for money causes firms and households to try to sell bonds. This raises the interest rate until the quantity of money demanded equals its supply.

An excess supply of money Now consider a case in which firms and households hold larger money balances than they wish to hold. A single household would purchase bonds with its excess balances. It would thus reach the desired holdings of money by adjusting quantities of money and bonds at given prices. But what one household or firm can do, all cannot do. When all households and firms enter the bond market and try to purchase bonds with unwanted stocks of money, all they do is to bid up the price of existing bonds (i.e., bid down the rate of interest). As the rate of interest falls, households and firms are willing to hold larger quantities of money. This rise in the price of bonds continues until firms and households stop trying to convert money into bonds. Whereas a single wealth-holder reaches equilibrium by adjusting quantities of money and bonds at fixed prices, the whole society reaches equilibrium by having prices adjust so that people are willing to hold the existing, fixed quantities of money and bonds.

An excess supply of money causes firms and households to try to buy bonds. This lowers the interest rate until the quantity of money demanded equals its supply.

Demand equals supply We have seen that when the supplies of money and bonds are fixed, the rate of interest must vary until people are satisfied to hold bonds and money in their existing proportions. Now let us look at what must be true if the demand for money is to be equal to its supply.[1]

---

[1] Equilibrium between M_D and M_S implies equilibrium between the demand for bonds, B_D, and the supply of bonds, B_S. To see this, we reason as follows. The total quantity of wealth in this two-asset model is the total quantities of bonds, B_S, and money, M_S. These are the supplies available to be held:

$$W \equiv B_S + M_S \ . \tag{i}$$

In a two-asset model, there are only two ways in which wealth can be held, so the total demand to hold money, M_D, and the total demand to hold bonds, B_D, must sum to total wealth:

$$W \equiv B_D + M_D \ . \tag{ii}$$

Substituting (ii) into (i) yields

$$B_S + M_S \equiv B_D + M_D \ .$$

Rearranging:
$$B_S - B_D \equiv M_D - M_S \ .$$

So an excess supply of bonds, $B_S > B_D$, implies an excess demand for money, $M_D > M_S$, and equilibrium between the demand for and supply of either bonds or money implies equilibrium between the demand for and supply of the other asset.

We have assumed the supply of money to be a constant for the time being:

$$M_S = M^* \quad , \tag{3}$$

where M_S is the money supply and M^* is some constant *nominal quantity measured in monetary units*.

We now need an equilibrium condition to equate the demand for money with its supply. We have, however, defined M_D in real, purchasing-power units and M_S in nominal money units, and to relate them we need to measure them in comparable units. We start by multiplying the real demand by the price level to obtain the nominal demand for money as PM_D. This can then be equated to the nominal supply to yield the equilibrium condition[1]

$$PM_D = M_S \quad . \tag{4}$$

Alternatively we can divide (4) through by P to obtain

$$M_D = M_S/P \quad . \tag{5}$$

Equation (5) can be thought of as deflating the nominal money supply by the price level to express it in purchasing-power units and then equating it to the demand for money equivalantly expressed in purchasing-power units.

The LM curve

Next we take the real demand for money from (2) above, the nominal supply from (3), and substitute them into the equilibrium condition (5) to obtain

$$dY + er = M^*/P \quad . \tag{6}$$

This tells us that the real demand for money measured in purchasing-power units equals its real supply. We can now derive the famous relation called the *LM* curve. To do this we merely manipulate (6) to obtain[2]

$$r = \frac{M^*}{P} \cdot \frac{1}{e} - \frac{d}{e}Y \quad . \tag{7}$$

This relation is plotted in Figure 39.2. Notice that (7) describes a linear relation between Y and r where the slope is $-d/e$ and the constant is the real money supply multiplied by the reciprocal of e, the responsiveness of money demand to the rate of interest.

> **The *LM* curve is the locus of all *Y-r* combinations that yield equilibrium between the demand for and supply of money.**

Now consider the slope of this curve. Algebraically it is seen to be negative: d is positive, e is negative, so d/e is negative, but $-d/e$ is positive. The common sense is as follows. A rise in national income *increases* the quantity of money demanded. So, if the demand for money is to be equated to

---

[1] For example, in a simple, one-product, wheat economy, M_D might be 2m bushels and, if wheat cost £3 a bushel, the nominal demand for money, PM_D, would be £6m.

[2] (i) Subtract dY from both sides; (ii) divide through by e.

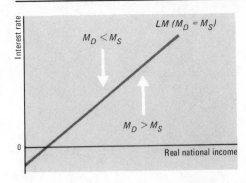

Fig. 39.2 The *LM* curve

an unchanged supply, the quantity demanded must be reduced by a rise in the rate of interest.

Consider an example. If national income were to increase say from Y_1 to Y_2 in part (ii) of Figure 39.1 on p. 588, demand for money would rise from m_1 to m_2 as a result. Firms and households who needed more transactions and precautionary balances would seek to obtain them by selling bonds. This would force the price of bonds down, i.e., drive the rate of interest up, until everyone was content to hold the same amount of money as they originally held. In part (i) of Figure 39.1, if the rate of interest was at r_1 originally, it would have to rise to r_2 so that the reduction in the demand for money on account of the rise in r exactly balanced the increase on account of the rise in Y.[1]

Along the *LM* curve, the quantity of money demanded equals its (fixed) supply. Below the *LM* curve, the quantity of money demanded exceeds its supply, as indicated on Figure 39.2. When decision-takers wish to hold more money than they now hold, they seek to sell bonds. This causes the rate of interest to rise (the price of bonds to fall). The rate goes on rising, thus reducing the quantity of money people wish to hold, until the excess demand money has been eliminated. This pressure for interest rates to rise whenever $M_D > M_S$ is shown by the upward-pointing arrow in the figure.

Above the *LM* curve, the quantity of money demanded is less than its supply, as indicated on Figure 39.2. When decision-takers hold more money than they wish to hold, they seek to buy bonds with the excess. This pushes the rate of interest down (the price of bonds up). The rate goes on falling, increasing the quantity of money demanded until the excess supply of money has been eliminated. This pressure for interest rates to fall whenever $M_D < M_S$ is shown by the downward-pointing arrow in the figure.

The demand for money, and for bonds, is equated to the fixed supplies of these assets through changes in the price of bonds (the rate of interest).

Shifts of the *LM* curve

A glance at the equation of the *LM* curve in (7) above shows that the only two exogenous variables it contains are the money supply, M, and the price level, P. Furthermore, since they appear as a simple

---

[1] The compensating nature of these changes can be seen by first differencing equation (6) to obtain $d\Delta Y + e\Delta r = \Delta(M/P)$. Since M and P are fixed, this yields $d\Delta Y + e\Delta r = 0$: since the real supply of money is constant, equilibrium requires that the quantity of money demanded does not change. Manipulation produces $\Delta r/\Delta Y = -d/e$, which is the slope of the *LM* curve: to hold M_D equal to the constant M_S, an increase in Y that increases M_D must be balanced by a rise in r that lowers M_D.

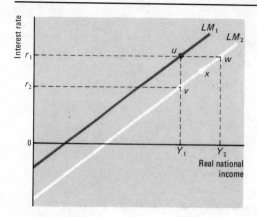

Fig. 39.3 A rise in the nominal quantity of money or a fall in the price level shifts the *LM* curve to the right

ratio they can be thought of as being a single exogenous variable, the *real* money supply, M/P. What happens to the *LM* curve if the real money supply changes? Say, for example, that it increases, either because M rises or P falls.

The mechanical result is simple. The constant on the *LM* curve in (7) above is $(M/P)(1/e)$ which is negative because e, the response of M_D to a change in r, is negative.[1] Increasing M/P makes the absolute size of the constant larger, i.e., it shifts the *LM* curve downwards as shown, for example, by the shift from LM_1 to LM_2 in Figure 39.3.

It is important to do more than just follow this algebraic result. We need to understand the market processes that are at work behind it. To see what is involved, imagine starting at the point u on the curve LM_1 in Figure 39.3. National income is Y_1, and, at the interest rate r_1, the demand for money is equal to its supply. Now assume that the real supply of money is increased, shifting the *LM* curve to LM_2. At u there must now be an excess supply of money since there is more money available with no change in the quantity demanded. To restore monetary equilibrium, changes in Y and/or r are needed. For illustration, assume that r is held constant at r_1. The only way to restore equilibrium is then to raise income to Y_2, taking the economy to the point w on the new *LM* curve. The increase in income $Y_2 - Y_1$ is just enough to induce people to absorb the additional money supply into their money holdings. Alternately, we can imagine the level of national income being held constant at Y_1, in which case the rate of interest must fall to r_2 taking the economy to the point v. The fall in the rate of interest is then just sufficient, by lowering the cost of holding money, to induce people to add the new money supply to their money balances. These are the two 'pure cases' where all of the adjustment is done either by Y or by r. Clearly, any suitable combination of Y and r will do the job. For example, a rise in Y and a fall in r that takes the economy to the point x will also restore monetary equilibrium.

A rise in the real money supply shifts the *LM* curve to the right, indicating that some combination of suitable changes in Y and r is needed to restore monetary equilibrium.

---

[1] The necessity of the negative constant arises because we have suppressed the positive term relating the demand for money to exogenous wealth. See note 2, page 587 above. As long as the *IS* and *LM* curve intersect in the positive quadrant, the sign of the constant on the *LM* curve is irrelevant. In a fuller treatment, however, we would assure it had a positive intercept by introducing, and then making suitable assumptions about, a constant on the demand-for-money function.

Not until the next chapter can we establish which of the possible Y-r combinations will actually be achieved. All we have done here is to show what combinations of changes in Y and r are needed *if* monetary equilibrium is to be restored. (Any combination that takes the economy from LM_1 to LM_2 will do the job in the above example.)

Asset equilibrium and portfolio balance

The theory developed in this chapter concerns the allocation of private-sector wealth among the assets in which wealth can be held. We have used the simplest case where 'money' means $M1$, and bonds means *all* income-earning assets (both of the debt and the equity type). At any moment of time, there is only so much wealth in existence. This must be held in some form or another: in the simple two-asset model, there are only two available forms, bonds and money.

At any point in time, the stocks of these two assets are fixed. Each wealth-holder's problem is then to allocate a fixed amount of wealth among the two available assets. When this has been done satisfactorily, the wealth-holder, whether a firm or a household, is in PORTFOLIO BALANCE: it is satisfied with the existing division of its wealth between money and bonds. For the society, ASSET EQUILIBRIUM occurs when all wealth-holders are in portfolio balance. Since the supplies of the wealth-holding assets (and the level of national income) are fixed at any moment of time, equilibrium must be achieved by price fluctuations – i.e., interest-rate fluctuations – alone.

(1) **The** LM **curve indicates those combinations of** Y **and** r **at which all wealth-holders are in portfolio balance; it thus describes** Y-r **combinations that leave the whole economy in asset equilibrium; the quantity demanded of each wealth-holding asset is equal to its given supply.**

(2) **The** LM **curve slopes upwards because the demand for money is positively associated with national income and negatively associated with the rate of interest.**

(3) **The** LM **curve is shifted to the right by an increase in the real money supply brought about either by an increase in the nominal money supply,** M, **or a decrease in the price level,** P. **It is shifted to the left by a decrease in the real money supply.**[1]

---

[1] For an alternative derivation of the LM curve and analysis of the causes of its shifts, see the appendix to Chapter 40.

40

The *IS-LM* model: the determination of national income and the interest rate with a fixed price level

Investment in national-income theory

We have seen how the rate of interest fluctuates to produce an asset equilibrium in which all decision units are in equilibrium with respect to their holdings of money and bonds. We now come to the critical link between the financial-asset side of the economy and the real expenditure side: not only does the rate of interest affect the demands for money and bonds, it also affects aggregate expenditure. To allow for this, we need to expand our earlier model of the determination of national income. Up to now we have treated investment as an exogenous constant. We now make this important element of aggregate expenditure endogenous.

The determinants of investment

In this section we discuss the influence of interest rates on the volume of desired investment expenditure. (Other determinants of investment are discussed in Chapter 42.)

Much investment is made with borrowed money. As we saw in Chapter 28, it pays a firm to borrow additional money to finance new investment projects as long as the marginal efficiency of its capital exceeds the rate of interest. Because the lower is the rate of interest the lower is the cost of borrowing money for investment purposes, it might seem natural to expect that the lower is the rate of interest the higher would be the amount of investment in new plant and equipment. Yet this possible relation between investment and the rate of interest has been, and still is, the subject of much controversy. We must now look at it more closely.

If we assume that capital is subject to diminishing returns, then the marginal efficiency of capital, the *MEC*, will fall as the stock of capital increases. This is illustrated by the curve in Figure 40.1. The capital stock will then be of equilibrium size when *MEC* equals the rate of interest. From this it follows that the equilibrium size of the capital stock is related negatively to the rate of interest. In particular, a fall in the rate of interest will lead to a rise in the desired capital stock; firms will all wish to add to their capital, which is to say they will wish to engage in positive net investment. In Figure 40.1, for example, a fall in the rate of interest from r_1 to r_2 causes an increase in the desired capital stock from K_1 to K_2. This requires $K_2 - K_1$ of new investment.

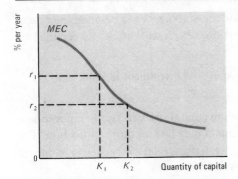

Fig. 40.1 The marginal efficiency of capital schedule

The rate of interest and investment in capital equipment A desired increase in the capital stock generates investment only while the increase is under way. Suppose, for example, that in response to a fall in interest rates there is an increase of £10 billion in the desired size of the capital stock. If the capital stock is raised by £10 billion within a year, net investment will rise for a year and then fall to zero. In this case a fall in the interest rate will lead to an increase in the amount of investment for only one year.

But the timing of investment may be more complicated than this; it may depend on how fast the stock of capital can be built up to its new desired level. The actual volume of investment in plant and equipment that takes place each year is limited by the capacities of the capital-goods and construction industries. Assume that all firms in the economy decide that they want a total of 3,000 newly built and equipped factories in operation next year, but that factories can only be built and equipped at the rate of 1,000 a year. Also assume that this situation has just been generated by a fall in the rate of interest. It will take three years before the desired addition to the capital stock is achieved. If, at the end of the first year, a rise in the rate of interest decreases the desired overall addition to the capital stock to 2,000 factories instead of 3,000, this new change will have no effect on investment in 'year two' because the capital-goods industries would still have to work to capacity to create the desired addition. Alternatively, if a fall in interest rates at the end of the first year raised the desired overall addition from 3,000 to 5,000 this, too, would not affect the rate of *current* investment, which is already at its maximum. The upper limit to annual investment in plant and equipment is set by the capacity of the capital-goods producing industries. Whenever the desired increase in the capital stock is more than can be produced in a year, there will be a backlog of orders. Thus, substantial variations in the interest rate may affect the length of the backlog more than the level of investment in a particular year. If so, these variations will affect the *duration* of an investment boom generated by changes in desired capital stock, but will have less effect on the *amount of investment* occurring in one year during that boom.

Of course this picture is over-simplified, since it is always possible to produce more capital by working overtime. This extra capital will usually be produced at higher cost and so will not be profitable unless there is a particularly urgent demand for new capital. The urgency will depend on the expected profitability of new investment, which will tend to be higher the lower the rate of interest.

For the reasons outlined above, major changes in interest rates are usually associated with changes in investment. If they lead to large changes in the relation between the present and the desired capital stock, they will usually lead to changes in the rate at which the capital stock is growing. But there is no reason in theory to expect a permanent, stable relation between the rate of interest and the amount of investment. The permanent relation, *ceteris paribus*, is between the rate of interest and the stock of capital.

A fall in the rate of interest will lead to temporary spurts of investment in plant and equipment.

Since it may take many years to move from one equilibrium capital stock to another in response to a change in interest rates, the 'temporary' spurt of investment may last for quite a long time. For this reason most studies show a discernible, but by no means perfect, relation between changes in the rate of interest and changes in the volume of investment in fixed capital.

The rate of interest and inventory investment The opportunity cost of holding inventories is what the firm could earn by selling the inventories and investing their value in something else. A measure of this is the interest rate, since the firm could certainly lend out its funds and earn the market rate of interest. A rise in the rate of interest raises the cost of holding inventories and causes firms to reduce their inventories until the advantage of the marginal unit of inventories is just equal to the rate of interest. Thus the desired stock of inventories tends to be negatively related to the rate of interest. But as with the stock of physical capital, inventory investment occurs only when inventories are being changed. Thus,

a fall in the rate of interest usually leads to a temporary spurt of inventory investment, while a rise usually leads to a temporary spurt of inventory disinvestment.

The rate of interest and investment in housing Interest payments are a large part of total mortgage payments. At an interest rate of 8 per cent, about half of the money paid on a twenty-year mortgage is interest, and only half is for repayment of principal. Because interest is such a large part of the total payments on a mortgage, small changes in the rate of interest cause relatively large changes in the annual payments For instance, a rise in the rate of interest from 8 to 10 per cent increases the monthly payments on a 20-year mortgage by nearly 15·4 per cent (from £8·37 to £9·66 per thousand pounds borrowed). Changes in interest rates can therefore have large effects on the demand for new housing.

A fall in the rate of interest will lead to a temporary spurt of investment in new housing. A rise will reduce the demand for new housing.

The rate of interest and total investment expenditure Although, for the reasons outlined above, investment does not necessarily bear a stable, permanent relation to the rate of interest, most econometric studies show some significant associations such that the higher the rate of interest, the lower the amount of investment expenditure. The extremely high world interest rates brought about by an attempt to cure inflation by restrictive monetary policy has given recent testimony to the power of interest rates to influence aggregate expenditure. Interest rates were driven to historically unprecedented highs in 1981–2 and, as a result, investment in new plant and equipment, inventories and housing plummeted to very low levels. The decline in aggregate expenditure produced throughout the world some of the largest declines in output and the highest unemployment figures to be registered since the Great Depression of the 1930s.

The effects of investment

The theory of income determination that we have studied so far takes the economy's technology and its supplies of factors of production – land, labour *and* capital – as given. This means that potential national income, Y_F, is given. The theory then looks to fluctuations in aggregate demand to determine the degree to which resources are utilized and hence, also, the size of national income. This is basically a short-run theory of national income. In the long run, investment causes the capital stock to increase and thus causes potential national income to change.

> **In the long run, the decisive effect of investment on national income is through its effects on the capital stock and hence on full-employment national income. In the short run, the important effect of investment is on aggregate demand, hence on the degree to which existing resources are employed, and through that on national income.**

Concentration on the short-run effects of investment on aggregate demand can lead to a neglect of these long-run supply influences of investment on potential income. Readers should therefore be clear that these long-run effects are of great importance. The effect of investment on growth of full-employment national income will be discussed in Chapter 42. In the meantime, we continue to study investment expenditure as a force influencing aggregate demand.

The financing of investment

To see the effects of making investment an endogenous variable we must now look at the financing of investment. In circular-flow models it is common to speak of withdrawals and injections in pairs: imports and exports, government expenditure and government revenue, and saving and investment. This pairing is no accident and, in the case of saving and investment, it reflects the fact that the savings of firms and households are the major source of finance for investment. If the volume of investment expenditure exceeds the volume of funds currently saved, where does the money come from? Basically there are two main sources: the money may come from funds accumulated in the past by firms or households, or it may be money *newly created* by the banking system. Since banks can, within very wide limits, create money, they can lend this money to firms for investment expenditure without there being any corresponding saving of funds on the part of households and firms. There is one more possibility: investment may fall short of saving. In this case the excess savings must take the form of additions to idle funds owned by households and firms and held either by them or by financial institutions on their behalf.

The *IS* curve

We are now ready to return to the simple model of Chapter 35 and make investment an endogenous variable. Aggregate desired expenditure is composed of consumption and investment expenditure, the former depending on income and the latter on the rate of interest. If we express those as linear relations for simplicity, we have[1]

---

[1] We have added a constant to the consumption function of Chapter 35 for the reasons explained in the Appendix to that chapter.

Definition	$E \equiv C + I$		(1)
Behaviour	$C = a_0 + cY$	$0 < c < 1. \quad 0 < a_0$	(2)
	$I = a_1 + br$	$b < 0 < a_1$	(3)
Equilibrium	$E = Y$		(4)

These relations concern the demand for, and the output of, goods and services in the economy. To distinguish this expenditure sector from the asset sector described by the *LM* curve, the above equations are often said to refer to 'the goods market'. To understand the principles involved, it is best to work with this simple model first. Later we will see that what we do generalizes in an almost trivial fashion to multi-sector models of both open and closed economies.

Equation (1) is a definition of aggregate expenditure. Equation (2) shows consumption depending on disposable income which, in this two-sector model, is equal to national income. The behavioural parameters are a positive constant, a_0, and an *MPC*, denoted by c, which is positive but less than unity. Equation (3) shows investment as a linear function of the rate of interest. To ensure positive investment, the constant a_1 must be positive, and to capture the behavioural assumption that investment falls as the interest rate rises, b is negative (b will in fact be a very large number because it gives the rise in investment expenditure caused by a one-point fall in the interest rate).

Derivation of the *IS* curve Substituting for C and I in equation (1), and then for E in the equilibrium condition of equation (4), yields:

$$Y = a_0 + cY + a_1 + br \quad . \tag{5}$$

These terms can then be rearranged to produce the equation (in linear form) of the famous *IS* curve[1]

$$r = \frac{1-c}{b}Y - \frac{A}{b} \quad , \tag{6}$$

where A stands for all exogenous expenditure and is equal in this case to $a_0 + a_1$.

Since equation (6) was obtained by substituting the behavioural equations into the equilibrium condition, $E = Y$, it follows that:[2]

> the *IS* relation gives all those combinations of national income, *Y*, and the rate of interest, *r*, that makes desired expenditure equal to national income.

Let us first look at its slope. Algebraically it is clear from (6) that the *IS* curve is negatively sloped. The coefficient c is the marginal propensity to consume. Since it is positive but less than unity, $1 - c$ is also positive. But b, which indicates the effect on aggregate expenditure of a rise in the interest rate, is negative, so $(1-c)/b$ is also negative.

Figure 40.2 shows a geometric derivation that may help in understanding how the *IS* and the aggregate expenditure curves are related. For a given interest rate, r_1, the aggregate expenditure

---

[1] The steps are (i) subtract cY, a_0 and a_1 from both sides, (ii) factor out the Y to obtain $Y(1-c)$, (iii) divide through by b, and (iv) write A for $a_0 + a_1$.

[2] It is called the *IS* curve because it was originally developed (by Sir John A. Hicks) to describe Keynes' model in which the equilibrium condition was stated in terms of withdrawals equals injections and there was only one withdrawal, saving, and one injection, investment. Thus the curve was thought of as the locus of *Y-r* combinations for which $I = S$, which is the same thing in the two-sector model as the locus of *Y-r* combinations where $Y = E$.

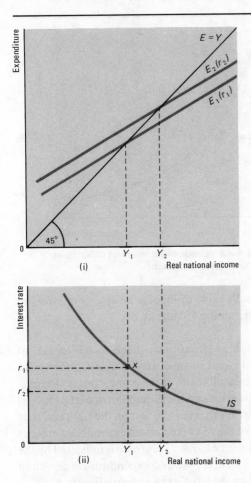

Fig. 40.2 The derivation of the *IS* curve from the aggregate expenditure curve

function is determined at some position, say $E_1(r_1)$, where the r_1 in parenthesis indicates that this E function is based on a given interest rate of r_1. The expenditure function determines equilibrium national income at Y_1, in the manner detailed in Chapter 35. Now *lower* the rate of interest to r_2. This shifts the aggregate expenditure function upwards to $E_2(r_2)$ (because the lower rate of interest raises investment expenditure) and raises equilibrium income to Y_2. Plotting Y_1 and r_1 as point x in part (ii) of the figure, and the higher income Y_2 and its associated lower interest rate r_2 as point y, yields two points on the *IS* curve. A similar procedure for every possible rate of interest yields the whole downward-sloping *IS* curve.

The common sense of the downward slope follows from the fact that the *IS* curve shows equilibrium positions where desired expenditure equals national income. If we increase national income by some amount, ΔY, we move along the E function, increasing desired expenditure but by less than ΔY (the marginal propensity to spend is less than unity). In order, therefore, to make the higher level of income an equilibrium income, it is necessary to do something to raise expenditure. This is done by lowering the rate of interest, shifting the E function upwards until the increased expenditure due to the rise in income *and* the fall in the interest rate is equal to the rise in income. Looking at part (i) of Figure 40.2, we start with the expenditure function (E_1) and equilibrium

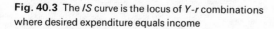

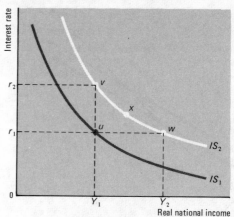

Fig. 40.3 The *IS* curve is the locus of *Y-r* combinations where desired expenditure equals income

Fig. 40.4 An increase in autonomous expenditure shifts the *IS* curve to the right

income Y_1. If we then raise income to Y_2, expenditure falls short of income unless r is cut to r_2 to shift the expenditure function upwards enough to make it cut the 45° line at Y_2.

Income-expenditure disequilibrium   Now let us look at situations off the *IS* curve, i.e., at situations where aggregate desired expenditure does not equal income. In Figure 40.2, start with income Y_1 and interest rate r_1 which puts the economy in equilibrium at the point x on its *IS* curve. Now consider some point to the left of x. Income is less than Y_1, and the E function in part (i) tells us that desired expenditure exceeds income. Similar exercises at other points, first on the right and then to the left of the curve, tell us that at any point to the left of the *IS* curve desired expenditure exceeds income. As analysed in Chapter 35, this causes national income to rise. This force is indicated by the right-facing arrow in Figure 40.3. To the right of the *IS* curve, desired expenditure is less than income. This causes national income to fall, as indicated by the left-facing arrow in Figure 40.3.

Shifts in the *IS* curve   A glance at equation (6) shows that the only exogenous variable in the *IS* curve is A, autonomous expenditure. In this model A is the sum of the constants on the consumption and investment functions, i.e., those parts of consumption and investment expenditure that do not vary with Y or r. In more general models, A includes all exogenous expenditure such as G and X.

In the present model, an increase in A must come from an increase in either a_0 or a_1 (or both) indicating either more consumption expenditure at every level of income or more investment expenditure at every level of the interest rate (or both). Inspection of (6) shows that an increase in A increases the positive constant in the *IS* curve and thus shifts the curve outwards, as shown in Figure 40.4 by the shift from IS_1 to IS_2. (Although b is negative, the negative sign on the whole term converts it into a positive number.)

The economic behaviour that lies behind this can be seen by starting at an equilibrium at point u on IS_1 in Figure 40.4, with income Y_1 and interest rate r_1. The increase in autonomous expenditure means that u is no longer an equilibrium. The *IS* curve shifts to IS_2. Equilibrium can be restored either at a constant interest rate of r_1 and a higher income of Y_2 (point w) or a constant income of Y_1, and a higher interest rate of r_2 (point v). In this latter case, the rise in r reduces aggregate expenditure

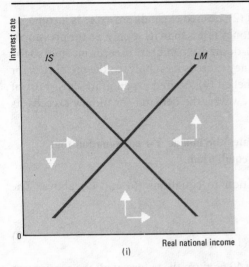 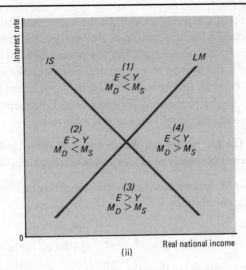

Fig. 40.5 Disequilibrium in the *IS-LM* model

just enough to offset the initial increase in autonomous expenditure and so leaves income unchanged. Clearly any suitable combination of Y and r changes can restore equilibrium. For example, a rise in Y and a rise in r that takes the economy to point x will restore the equality between income and desired expenditure.

The *IS-LM* model

We are now in a position to determine goods market equilibrium and portfolio equilibrium simultaneously. To do this we bring together the *IS* curve from equation (6) above and the *LM* curve from equation (7) of Chapter 39.

The IS-LM Model

IS curve:
$$r = \frac{1-c}{b}Y - \frac{A^*}{b} \tag{6}$$

LM curve:
$$r = -\frac{d}{e}Y + \frac{M^*}{P} \cdot \frac{1}{e} \tag{7}$$

For the graphic representation we merely put Figure 40.2(ii) together with Figure 39.2 to create the new Figure 40.5. This *IS* curve is the locus of all points that satisfy the goods-market equilibrium condition $E = Y$. When the economy is not on its *IS* curve, the pressure is for income to move towards the curve. The *LM* curve is the locus of all points that satisfy the asset-market equilibrium condition $M_D = M_S$. When the economy is not on its *LM* curve, the pressure is for the interest rate to move towards the curve. These two sets of pressures are shown by the arrows in Figure 40.5(i). The forces that give rise to them are displayed in part (ii) of the Figure and are described below.

The *IS* and *LM* curves divide the Figure into four segments and the characteristics of each are summarized in Figure 40.5(ii). In the segment labelled (1), desired expenditure is less than income, so the pressure is for income to fall. Also the demand for money is less than its supply, so the pressure is for interest rates to fall as well. In the segment labelled (2), desired expenditure exceeds income, so the pressure is for income to rise. But the demand for money is less than its supply, so the pressure is also for interest rates to fall. In the segment labelled (3), desired expenditure exceeds income, so the pressure is for income to rise. Also the demand for money exceeds its supply, so the pressure is for interest rates to rise as well. Finally in the segment labelled (4), desired expenditure falls short of income, so the pressure is for income to fall. Here, however, the demand for money exceeds its supply so the pressure is for interest rates to rise.

The intersection of the _IS_ and _LM_ curves indicates the unique _Y-r_ combination that simultaneously produces goods-market and asset equilibrium.

The _IS-LM_ intersection gives the simultaneous solution to equations (6) and (7) above. The algebraic solution for Y is[1]

$$Y = \frac{1}{(1-c)+bd/e}A^* + \frac{1}{d+e(1-c)/b}\cdot\frac{M^*}{P}\ . \tag{8}$$

This is nothing more than the solution for Y_1 in Figure 40.6, given the values of all the parameters that determine the location of IS_1 and LM_1 in that Figure.

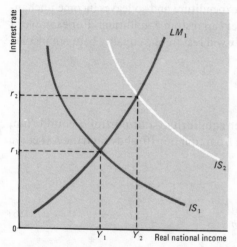

(i) _IS_ shifts cause changes in income and the interest rate to be positively associated with each other

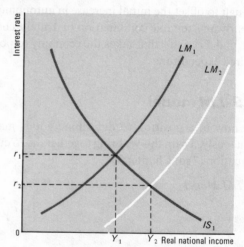

(ii) _LM_ shifts cause changes in income and the interest rate to be negatively associated with each other

Fig. 40.6 The effects of shifts in the _IS_ and _LM_ curves

[1] Straightforward manipulation of (6) and (7) produces the solution shown in (8). Anyone who can do O-Level algebra can do it. Try it. When you succeed, you will have gone a long way towards gaining self-confidence in formal proofs. Here are the steps: (i) eliminate r by equating the LHSs of (6) and (7); (ii) multiply through by bc; (iii) gather the two terms containing Y on the LHS and the other terms on the RHS; (iv) factor out the Y to obtain $Y[(1-c)e-db]$ on the LHS; (v) divide through by the coefficient of Y just given; (vi) clear the e from the numerator of the term containing A by dividing denominator and numerator by e; (vii) clear the b from the numerator of the M^*/P term by dividing numerator and denominator by b; this gives you equation (8). Similar manipulation of (6) and (7) shows the solution for r to be:

$$r = -\frac{1}{b+e(1-c)/d}A^* + \frac{1}{e+db(1-c)}\cdot\frac{M^*}{P}\ .$$

Comparative statics

We have seen in Figures 40.4 and 39.3, and their surrounding discussions, that changes in autonomous expenditure shift the *IS* curve while changes in the real money supply shift the *LM* curve. The effects on Y and r of each of these shifts is shown in Figure 40.6. Consider first a rightward shift in the *IS* curve. In part (i) of the figure the initial curves are IS_1 and LM_1, yielding equilibrium values of Y_1 and r_1 for income and the interest rate. An increase in autonomous expenditure now shifts the *IS* curve to IS_2. At the old equilibrium values there is now an excess of desired expenditure over desired income, which causes income to rise. The rise in income increases the quantity of money demanded and the shortage of money forces up the interest rate. At the new equilibrium, the values for income and interest rate are Y_2 and r_2. A reduction in autonomous expenditure reverses the process, shifting the *IS* curve from IS_2 to IS_1, which lowers income and interest rate from Y_2 and r_2 to Y_1 and r_1.

> **An increase in autonomous expenditure shifts the *IS* curve to the right and raises the equilibrium values of both national income and the interest rate. A decrease does the reverse.**

Second, consider the effects of changes in the real money supply that shifts the *LM* curve rightwards. Since we are still, for one more chapter, holding the price level constant, this must be done by increasing the nominal money supply. This means an increase in M in equation (7). As a result, the *LM* curve in part (ii) of the figure shifts from LM_1 to LM_2. At the original equilibrium values of Y_1 and r_1 there is now an excess supply of money. Decision units seek to buy bonds with their surplus funds and force the rate of interest down (price of bonds up). The fall in interest rates leads to more investment expenditure, which increases national income. Thus the pressure is for a fall in r and a rise in Y, which takes these variables to their new equilibrium values of Y_2 and r_2. A reduction in the money supply is analysed by letting the *LM* curve shift from LM_2 to LM_1, thus reducing income from Y_2 to Y_1 and raising the interest rate from r_2 to r_1.

> **An increase in the money supply shifts the *LM* curve right and lowers the equilibrium interest rate while raising the equilibrium level of national income. A decrease does the reverse.**

This analysis leads to the interesting result that, when income fluctuates due to fluctuations in aggregate expenditure, income and interest rates rise and fall together, while when income fluctuates due to the influence of monetary factors, income and interest rates move in opposite directions.

The *IS-LM* multiplier

In Chapter 35 on page 536 we developed a simple multiplier that took the form

$$\frac{\Delta Y}{\Delta A^*} = \frac{1}{1-c} , \tag{9}$$

where c is the marginal propensity to spend out of GDP. This multiplier is often called the *naive multiplier* or, more descriptively, the *interest-constant multiplier*. It tells us how national income changes in response to a change in autonomous expenditure on the assumption that income is the only force causing expenditure to change.[1]

Since we know that aggregate expenditure also responds to interest rates, the above multiplier can be understood to tell us what would happen if interest rates were held constant. This is illustrated in part (i) of Figure 40.7 where IS_1 and LM_1 produce an initial equilibrium at Y_1 and r_1. Now assume that an increase in autonomous expenditure takes the IS curve to IS_2. If the rate of interest were held constant at r_1, equilibrium income would rise from Y_1 to Y_2'. But instead, the expansion of income increases the amount of money demanded and, given a constant money

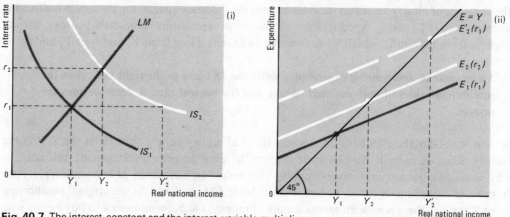

Fig. 40.7 The interest-constant and the interest-variable multipliers

supply, this forces up the rate of interest. This chokes off some of the expansion by reducing investment expenditure.

> **The interest-constant multiplier is shown by the horizontal shift in the IS curve in response to a shift in autonomous expenditure. The interest-variable IS-LM multiplier is always smaller than the interest-constant multiplier.**

This assumes that the IS curve is negatively sloped while the LM curve is positively sloped.

In Figure 40.7(i) we see that equilibrium income only rises to Y_2 instead of to Y_2'. The shortfall of Y_2 below Y_2' is due to the rise in interest rates which lowers investment expenditure. This reduction in equilibrium expenditure, and income, below what they would have been if interest rates had remained constant is called THE CROWDING-OUT EFFECT. Expenditure is crowded out due to the rise in interest rates that occurs when the demand for money rises because income rises.

Algebraically the crowding-out effect can be seen by first differencing equation (8), which is the equilibrium solution for Y. Doing this, and holding $\Delta M = \Delta P = 0$, i.e., holding the real money supply and hence the LM curve constant, yields

---

[1] In Chapter 36 the interest-constant multiplier for the four-sector model was shown to be

$$\frac{1}{1-c(1-t)+m} = \frac{1}{s(1-t)+t+m} .$$

In general, the interest-constant multipliers are always the reciprocal of the sum of marginal propensities to withdraw income from the circular flow. So the simple two-sector case in the text can be taken quite generally as long as c is understood to be the overall propensity to spend out of GDP and $1-c$ is understood to be the overall propensity not to spend, i.e., to withdraw.

$$\frac{\Delta Y}{\Delta A^*} = \frac{1}{(1-c)+bd/e} \quad . \tag{10}$$

This is the *IS-LM*, interest-variable multiplier. To understand it, assume first that expenditure is totally insensitive to interest rates, which means $b = 0$. The multiplier then becomes $1/(1-c)$, which is the interest-constant multiplier. This confirms that, if expenditure is completely insensitive to interest rates (or if interest rates do not change), the interest-constant multipliers give correct results. If, however, expenditure does respond to interest rates then b takes on a negative value. Now, since d and e, the responses of the demand for money to income and to interest rates, are respectively positive and negative, the whole term $(bd)/e$ is positive. The term then increases the value of the denominator in (10) and hence reduces the value of the whole expression. *The crowding-out term lowers the value of the multiplier.*

One way of looking at what is happening is shown in part (ii) of Figure 40.7. We start with interest rate r_1, and the expenditure function E_1, which generates equilibrium income Y_1. The rise in autonomous expenditure then shifts the E function to E_2'. If the rate of interest remains at r_1, equilibrium income would rise to Y_2'. Instead, however, the rate of interest rises to r_2, shifting the expenditure function downwards to E_2. As a result income only rises from Y_1 to Y_2 instead of to Y_2'.

The crowding-out of private-sector expenditure

Assume that to expand the economy back towards full employment the government greatly increases its public investment programme. This could be seen as shifting the *IS* curve from IS_1 to IS_2 in Figure 40.7 through an increase in government expenditure, G. If interest rates did remain constant, the rise in income from Y_1 to Y_2' would be made up of the initial increased autonomous expenditure, G, and an induced increase in consumption expenditure. As it is, however, interest rates rise and this crowds out interest-sensitive private expenditure, particularly private investment expenditure. Thus, although the expansionary fiscal policy does succeed in increasing total expenditure and total national income, it also leads to the crowding out of some private expenditure. Thus public expenditure is substituted for some private expenditure. This change in the balance between private- and public-sector investment expenditure is an inevitable, and to some undesirable, side-effect of increased expenditures that seek to bring about the otherwise desirable effect of raising national income, output and employment in times of economic slump.

An evaluation of the IS-LM model

The *IS-LM* model is the simplest possible model that integrates the monetary-asset side of the economy with the real-expenditure side. There is a strong reaction in some circles against its alleged naivity and crudity. It is worth noting, however, that this model is a prototype version of the demand side of the great majority of econometric models. More subtle models allow for much more detail, splitting aggregate expenditure into dozens of components, each with its own determinants, and splitting 'bonds' into many assets, each with its own demand and supply function. Nonetheless, all such models are elaborations on the basic *IS-LM* model which remains an intellectual prototype, or 'mark I Model', of all the more detailed expenditure-asset models of the demand side of the economy.

Appendix to chapter 40

An alternative derivation of the *LM* and *IS* curves

In Chapters 39 and 40 we derived the *LM* and *IS* curves using algebra, words and simple geometry. In many ways the simple algebraic derivation is most satisfactory. Many students, however, feel much more at home with geometry than with algebra. This appendix is designed for those who would like to see a more detailed geometric derivation where every individual relation that lies behind the *LM* and *IS* curves is displayed on its own graph. Those who are fully satisfied with the textual material in Chapters 39 and 40 can either skip this appendix or read it as a check on their understanding. Deep economic understanding takes a long time to develop, and the more times one goes through a given point from different approaches, the greater one's understanding becomes.

The *LM* curve

Derivation

To derive the *LM* (and the *IS*) curves geometrically we start by introducing the so-called four-quadrant diagram. This diagram measures positive quantities in four different directions from a common origin. The advantage is that four different but linked relations can be shown on the one diagram. The disadvantage is that you have to get used to seeing some relations upside down and/or back to front from the way they are displayed on the usual graph. For reference, we label the four quadrants geographically: SE (bottom right), SW (bottom left), NW (top left) and NE (top right).

Figure 40.8(i) shows the derivation of the *LM* curve. Our text discussion shows the demand for money depends on income and the rate of interest. These relations are depicted by the line $M_D(Y)$ in the SE quadrant, which shows the demand rising as Y rises, and by the line $M_D(r)$ in the NW quadrant, which shows the demand falling as r rises.

The line labelled 45° in the SW quadrant shows the equilibrium condition that the total demand for money (measured in real terms) should equal the real money supply M^*/P. The given real supply is measured along the two axes labelled M/P. Because these two distances are the same, the line joining the two M^*/P points has a slope of 45°. It is a characteristic of this line that any point on it represents two M/P values that sum to M^*/P.

Now, to derive the *LM* curve, start with any arbitrarily chosen level of real national income, say Y_1. The quantity of money demanded as a result of Y_1 is m_a. The 45° line in the SW quadrant then tells us that if the total demand for money is to equal its supply of M^*/P, then m_b must be demanded in addition to m_a. This occurs, according to the relation in the NW quadrant, if the interest rate is r_1. Now Y_1 and r_1 are projected into the NE quadrant to obtain the point x on the *LM* curve.

Next, pick another level of income, say Y_2. The demand for money, given Y_2, is now m_c. This means that to maintain equality of M_D and M_S a further m_d must be demanded. This in turn requires an interest rate of r_2. Extending Y_2 and r_2 into the NE quadrant yields a second point, z, on the *LM* curve.

If the procedure is repeated for every level of Y, the results plot out an upward-sloping *LM* curve in part (i) of the Figure. All we have done is to lay out geometrically the two relations that the demand for money varies positively with Y and negatively with r, and to show that if the quantity of money demanded is to equal a fixed supply, Y and r must vary directly with each other (an increase in Y raising quantity demanded and an increase in r lowering it).

Shifts in the *LM* curve

Figure 40.8(ii) repeats the curves from 40.8(i) and repeats the derivation of the point x on the *LM* curve. Now let the real money supply increase, either

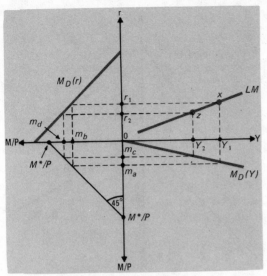

(i) The derivation of the *LM* curve

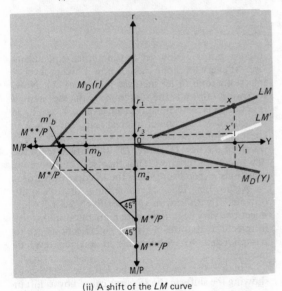

(ii) A shift of the *LM* curve

Fig. 40.8 A four-quadrant interpretation of the *LM* curve

because M increases or P falls. To be specific, assume that the nominal money supply increases from M^* to M^{**}. This shifts the 45° line in the SW quadrant outwards to its new intercepts on each axis of M^{**}/P. Now consider how to equate the demand for money with the newly increased supply at a level of income of Y_1. Following around the quadrants, we see that the original level of income is still associated with a demand for money of m_a. With the larger

supply of money, however, equality of M_D and M_S requires that a further m'_b now be demanded. This in turn requires a fall in the interest rate to r_3.

Now plotting Y_1 against r_3 yields the point x' on the new *LM* curve, *LM'*. What we have shown is that since the quantity of money demanded varies positively with Y and negatively with r, a rise in the supply of money requires, to restore the equality of demand and supply, a fall in the equilibrium rate of interest associated with each given level of national income.

The downward shift in the *LM* curve in Figure 40.8(ii) can be caused by a decrease in the amount of money demanded at each level of income or by a decrease in the amount demanded at each rate of interest. Readers can now work out for themselves the various possible shifts in the *LM* curve caused by various possible shifts in the behavioural relations which relate the quantity of money demanded to Y and r.

The *IS* curve

Derivation

Figure 40.9(i) shows the derivation of the *IS* curve. The diagram is now familiar and the techniques used are similar.

The graphical derivation is simpler, however, if we use the $W = J$ version rather than the $E = Y$ version, which we have learned are identical in any case. The *IS* curve in Chapter 40 is derived for the simple case of one injection, I, and one withdrawal, S. In more complex models, withdrawals are savings, taxes and imports, while injections are investment, government expenditure and exports. All that matters, however, is that withdrawals depend on income, so we write $W = \mathrm{W}(Y)$, and that injections depend partly on the rate of interest and are partly autonomous, so we write $J = \mathrm{J}(r) + A$.

The withdrawals-injections version of the model is shown in Figure 40.9(i). In the SE quadrant we have the withdrawals function, relating withdrawals positively to income. In the NW quadrant we have the injections function, relating injections negatively to the rate of interest and also showing the exogenous component, A. The SW quadrant shows the equilibrium condition that withdrawals should equal injections. This is the familiar 45° line, only it now goes off to the SW because of the quadrant in which it is plotted.

To construct the *IS* curve, pick an arbitrary level of income, Y_1. The withdrawals function tells us that, for this level of income, withdrawals are W_1.

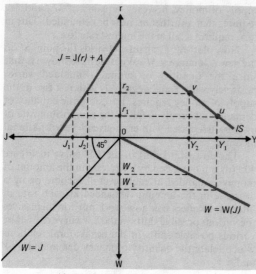

(i) The derivation of the *IS* curve

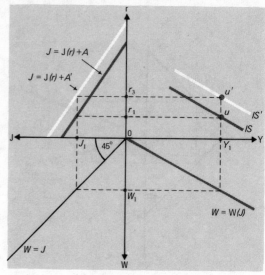

(ii) A shift of the *IS* curve

Fig. 40.9 A four-quadrant interpretation of the *IS* curve

Following around through the equilibrium condition in the SW quadrant tells us that this requires an interest rate of r_1. Plotting Y_1 against r_1 in the NE quadrant yields the point u on the *IS* curve.

Now pick a different level of income, say Y_2. This yields W_2 of withdrawals and, if injections are to equal withdrawals at J_2, then the interest rate must be r_2. Plotting Y_2 against r_2 in the NE quadrant yields a second point, v, on the *IS* curve. Repeating this procedure for every level of income yields a downward-sloping *IS* curve.

What this tells us is that, since withdrawals vary positively with income while injections vary negatively with the rate of interest, the two flows of withdrawals and injections can only be kept equal if Y and r vary inversely with each other.

Shifts in the *IS* curve

Part (ii) of Figure 40.9 repeats part (i) and shows the single equilibrium combination of income Y_1 and interest rate r_1. Now let autonomous expenditure rise. At every level of r there is now a higher level of injections (due to an increase in I, G or X). Now, following around the diagram with the new J function, it is clear that any given level of Y, say Y_1, is associated with a higher interest rate. The new Y, r combination is plotted by the point u', which is one point on the new *IS* curve, *IS′*, that arises from the new injections function. Thus the rise in autonomous injections' expenditure shifts the *IS* curve upwards.

Again this tells us something that is quite obvious. If withdrawals vary positively with Y while injections vary negatively with r, an autonomous rise in injections requires a rise in r if injections are to remain equal to withdrawals at a given level of income.

Finally, the reader can be left the exercise of showing the shifts in the *IS* curve caused by a shift in the withdrawals function: if there are more withdrawals associated with each level of income, the *IS* curve shifts downwards.

Part ten

The determination of national income with a variable interest rate and a variable price level

41

Closure version 1: aggregate demand and aggregate supply

In everything that has been done so far we have assumed we were on a perfectly elastic aggregate supply function (see page 521). All firms were assumed to be operating at less than normal capacity and so willing to sell whatever was demanded at the going price level. It is high time that we considered situations where the price level can rise. Fortunately, what we have already done is needed for our analysis of inflationary cases (otherwise it would not have been worth spending so much time on the case of a constant price level). Adding a relation to determine the price level is referred to as the problem of *closure*.

Let us now ask what would happen if an increase in national income, caused, say, by a shift in the *IS* curve, pushed firms beyond their normal-capacity outputs or possibly even to the upper limit of their ability to produce? Surely, in this case prices would rise. But if the increase in national income causes the price level to rise, this means that the price level is an *endogenous* variable: *it changes in response to changes in other variables*. This means that, in such circumstances, we cannot treat the price level as exogenous, as we have done so far.

This has serious consequences for the *IS-LM* model. Recall that as long as the rate of interest was an exogenous variable we were able to use the aggregate expenditure function to determine national income, as we did in Chapters 35 and 36. When the rate of interest was made endogenous, however, we could not use that function because as we moved along it, due to a change in income, the function itself shifted due to a change in the rate of interest. An analogous limitation now arises with the *LM* curve, which has M/P, the real money supply, as an exogenous variable in its equation. Now consider an outward shift in the *IS* curve which increases Y and r along a given *LM* curve. This is fine as long as we are on a perfectly elastic aggregate supply curve so that the price level stays constant as income changes. But if the price level rises as income rises, this reduces the real money supply, M/P, and shifts the *LM* curve. This curve then ceases to be a satisfactory tool for a complete analysis of any problem since as soon as we try to move along it, the curve itself shifts. The final outcome cannot be determined until we know by how much the *LM* curve shifts. (It is worth noting that this problem does not arise with the *IS* curve because all its variables are defined in real terms.)

To get around this problem we need some new functions that do not themselves shift when Y, r or P change. These are called aggregate demand and aggregate supply curves. In this chapter they allow us to deal with the comparative statics of shocks that cause *once-and-for-all changes* in national income, the interest rate *and* the price level. From this analysis we can learn quite a bit about inflation. Then in Chapter 47 we introduce one final tool that will allow us to study the process of *continuing* inflation.

The aggregate demand curve

We now wish to make the price level an endogenous variable. The first step towards doing this is to develop a new tool called the aggregate demand or AD curve. (To avoid some serious terminological confusions, it is important to read the section on the aggregate demand curve in the Note on Definitions that starts on p. xxi.)

The meaning of the AD curve

It is easy to derive this curve formally but a little harder to see what market behaviour lies behind the formal relation we discover.

Algebraic derivation   For the formal derivation we return to equation (8) on page 602. This equation gives the solution of the IS-LM model for equilibrium national income when autonomous expenditure, A, and the nominal money supply, M, and the price level, P, are all treated as exogenous variables. We repeat this equation below:

$$Y = \frac{1}{(1-c)+bd/e}A^* + \frac{1}{d+e(1-c)/b} \cdot \frac{M^*}{P} \ . \tag{1}$$

The Y so determined ensures simultaneous goods-market, or IS, equilibrium, $E = Y$, and asset-market, or LM, equilibrium, $M_D = M_S$.

To derive our new tool we merely treat the price level P as an endogenous variable. Equation (1), the IS-LM solution, is now one equation in two variables. It thus defines a locus of P, Y combinations. This locus is called the AGGREGATE DEMAND CURVE and it shows all those combinations of the price level, P, and real national income, Y, that satisfy the twin equilibrium conditions $E = Y$ and $M_D = M_S$.

Now consider the nature of the relation. Treating autonomous expenditure, A, and the money supply, M, as constants, the relation between Y and P boils down to a linear relation

$$Y = h_0 + h_1 \frac{1}{P} \ , \tag{2}$$

where the slope coefficient h_1 is

$$\frac{M^*}{d+e(1-c)/b} \ .$$

This is positive by the following argument: M is positive; $1-c$, the marginal propensity to save, is positive; b, the dependence of investment on the interest rate, is negative; d, the dependence of the demand for money on income, is positive; and e, the dependence of the demand for money on the interest rate, is negative; thus the entire term is positive.[1] *But since P appears as a reciprocal in (2), Y is negatively related to P, i.e., an increase in P results in a fall in Y.* The constant is positive by virtue of the fact that A, $(1-c)$ and bd/e are all positive (since b and e are *both* negative).

---

[1] To see this, lay out the sign pattern with signs of parameters and exogenous variables in parentheses:

$$\frac{(+)}{(+)+(-)(+)/(-)} = \frac{(+)}{(+)+(-)/(-)} = \frac{(+)}{(+)+(+)} = + \ .$$

The aggregate demand curve relates P and Y (although its equation is in terms of $1/P$ and Y). It is a negatively sloped curve with the equation

$$Y = \frac{A^*}{(1-c)+bd/e} + \frac{M^*}{d+e(1-c)/b} \cdot \frac{1}{P} \quad . \tag{3}$$

It shows that the price level is negatively associated with the equilibrium level of national income that follows from the *IS-LM* model.

This aggregate demand curve is plotted in Figure 41.1. Note that, following the Marshallian convention when price and quantity variables are involved, we plot price on the vertical and quantity on the horizontal axes.

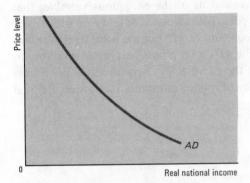

Fig. 41.1 An aggregate demand curve

Underlying market behaviour So much for pure mechanical derivation. As is so often the case with economic models, the real problem is to understand what market behaviour is going on behind the scenes to produce the relation in question.

The key in this case is the effect of a change in the price level on asset-market equilibrium. Recall from page 587 the two ways of expressing the equilibrium condition for portfolio balance:

$$M_D = M_S/P \quad , \tag{4}$$

$$PM_D = M_S \quad . \tag{5}$$

Equation (4) tells us that the real demand for money measured in purchasing-power units must equal the real supply, which is the nominal quantity of money divided by the price level. Equation (5) states that the nominal demand for money, the real demand *times* the price level, must equal the nominal supply. It is clear from either of these that *a rise in the price level creates excess demand for money*. In terms of equation (4), the rise in P lowers the real supply, leaving the real demand unchanged. In terms of equation (5) the rise in P raises the nominal demand for money (so as to hold the real quantity demanded constant), leaving the nominal supply unchanged. The reason why the excess demand develops is that a rise in the price level *ceteris paribus* raises the nominal value of transactions and firms require larger nominal money balances in order to finance these transactions. We have now established the key piece of behaviour needed to understand the *AD* curve:

A rise in the price level *ceteris paribus* creates excess demand for money.

The excess demand for money then starts up a now familiar chain of events: wealth-holders seek to add to their money balances by selling bonds and this pushes the interest rate up (bond prices down). The rise in the interest rate lowers total desired expenditure (i.e., the aggregate expenditure function shifts downwards). This in turn lowers equilibrium national income. In short the rise in the price level is associated with a fall in the equilibrium level of real national income, i.e., the aggregate demand curve that relates equilibrium income to the price level has a negative slope.

> **The excess demand for money caused by the rise in the price level pushes up the interest rate, which lowers desired aggregate expenditure, which in turn lowers equilibrium national income.**

Graphical derivation Figure 41.2 (i) shows an initial equilibrium real income of Y_1 and an interest rate of r_1 produced by the curves IS and LM_1. To remind us of the exogenous variables that influence the position of the LM curve, we indicate the particular values of M and P to which each LM curve relates. The nominal money supply is held constant at M^* but the price level varies as indicated in the Figure. To obtain the first point (u) on the AD curve, plot in part (ii) the equilibrium income Y_1 against the price level P_1 that gave rise to the curve LM_1. Now raise the price level arbitrarily from P_1 to P_2, holding the nominal quantity of money constant. This lowers the real

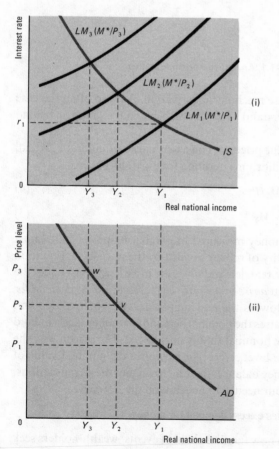

(i)

(ii)

Fig. 41.2 The derivation of the aggregate demand curve from IS and LM curves

quantity of money to M^*/P_2 and shifts the LM curve left to LM_2. The new equilibrium income is Y_2. This may now be plotted against P_2 in part (ii) of the Figure to obtain a second point, v, on the AD curve. Now raise the price level to P_3, shifting the LM curve to LM_3 and taking equilibrium income to Y_3. Plotting Y_3 against P_3 in part (ii) of the Figure yields a third point, w, on the AD curve. Repetition derives the whole curve.

> **The AD curve plots the locus of P-Y points that yeild goods- and asset-market equilibrium, with autonomous expenditure and the nominal money supply being held constant.**

Shifts in the *AD* curve

The equation of the aggregate demand curve contains the two exogenous variables, the money supply, M, and autonomous expenditure, A. Inspection of equation (3) also shows that an increase in either of these variables shifts the AD curve outwards: a rise in A increases the value of the constant term, while a rise in M increases the absolute value of the slope term (i.e., makes the curve flatter).

A shift in autonomous expenditure To see the economic behaviour involved, consider first a rise in autonomous expenditure. As we saw in Chapter 35, a rise in autonomous expenditure shifts the aggregate expenditure function upwards and raises the equilibrium level of national income associated with any given interest rate and price level. This change is shown by a rightward shift in the IS curve (each r is associated with a higher level of income than previously). The outward shift in the IS curve raises the equilibrium Y and r that would result if the price level remained constant (so the LM curve did not shift). This increase in the equilibrium value of Y from the IS-LM model for a given price level is shown by an outward shift in the aggregate demand curve.

The process is illustrated graphically in Figure 41.3A. The increase in autonomous expenditure shifts the expenditure function from E_1 to E_2' in part (i). If the interest rate were constant, equilibrium income would rise from Y_1 to Y_2'. This shifts the IS curve out parallel to itself to pass through the point r_1, Y_2'. But because the LM curve slopes upwards, equilibrium income, for a constant price level, only rises to Y_2. (The rise in the interest rate from r_1 to r_2 shifts the expenditure function down to E_2 where it cuts the 45° line at Y_2.) The rise in equilibrium income from Y_1 to Y_2 is shown by an outward shift in the AD curve in part (iii) of the figure so that it now passes through the point P_1, Y_2.

An increase in the nominal money supply Figure 41.3B shows the effects of an increase in the nominal money supply. Initially equilibrium is at Y_1 and r_1 as determined by IS and LM_1. The expenditure function is E_1 (r_1) and the aggregate demand curve is AD_1. Now with the price level constant at P_1, let the nominal money supply rise from M_1 to M_2. This shifts the LM curve to LM_2, lowering the interest rate to r_2 and raising equilibrium income to Y_2. In part (ii) the fall in the interest rate shifts the aggregate expenditure function upwards to $E_2(r_2)$. In part (iii) the AD curve shifts outwards from AD_1 to AD_2 showing a new equilibrium level of income, Y_2, associated with the original price level of P_1.

Any given increase in the real money supply, M/P, raises equilibrium income. When it is accomplished by a fall in P, this is shown as a movement along the AD curve (which relates Y and

P, as in Figure 41.2). When it is accomplished by a rise in *M*, this is shown by a shift in the *AD* curve (since the new equilibrium *Y* is associated with the same price level, as in Figure 41.3B).

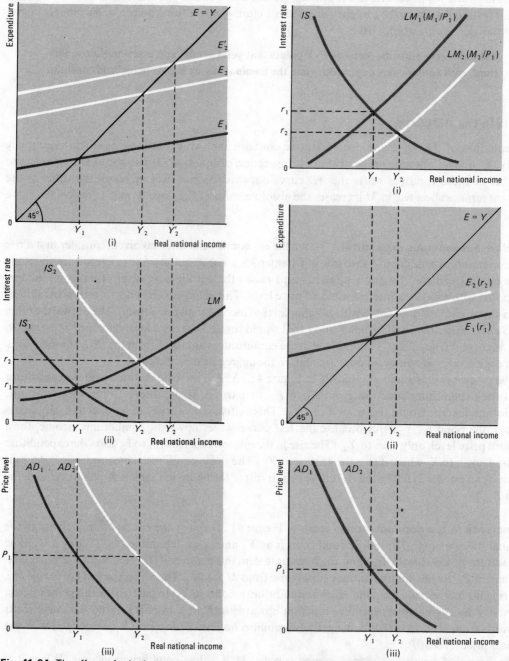

Fig. 41.3A The effects of a rise in autonomous expenditure traced through the $E = Y$, $IS\text{-}LM$ and AD relations

Fig. 41.3B The effects of a rise in the nominal money supply traced through the $IS\text{-}LM$, $E = Y$ and AD relations

A rise in either autonomous expenditure or the nominal money supply shifts the *AD* curve to the right. A fall in either of these two variables shifts the curve to the left.

Equilibrium of aggregate demand and aggregate supply

We now wish to see how our new concept of the aggregate demand curve interacts with the aggregate supply curve to determine the equilibrium real income and the equilibrium price level. First, we must pay a little more attention to the aggregate supply curve than we have done so far.

The aggregate supply curve: version 1

We first introduced the aggregate supply curve in Chapter 35 and since then we have been dealing with a very simple curve that described a situation in which output was demand-determined: firms had excess capacity and would supply at the going prices anything that was demanded. We now wish to look in more detail at the supply side of the economy. Recall first that *the aggregate supply curve shows the relation between the price level and the total GDP that will be produced in the economy.*

In the next section we shall see how the intersection of aggregate demand and aggregate supply can jointly determine national income and the price level. In this section, however, we must study the slope of the aggregate supply curve and to do that we make arbitrary changes in real national income and enquire into their effects on the price level.

It is common in textbooks, and even in some more advanced writings, to analyse the short-run behaviour of income and the price level using a short-run aggregate supply curve of the sort shown in Figure 41.4. Here the short-run aggregate supply curve, *SRAS*, is shown as continuously upward-sloping, rather flat below potential income, Y_F, and increasingly steep above it.

This *AS* curve catches one of the major characteristics of all Keynesian macro models: there is

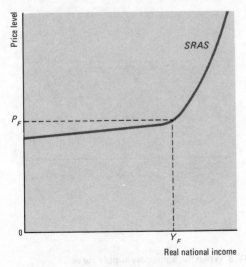

Fig. 41.4 A short-run aggregate supply curve with some properties that conflict with observed behaviour

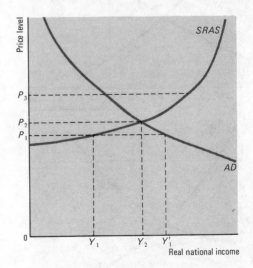

Fig. 41.5 The determination of national income and the price level by aggregate demand and aggregate supply

an asymmetry in the relation between price and quantity above and below potential income. We shall shortly argue that this curve is not fully satisfactory for all our purposes. But just for the moment it is convenient to use it to establish the interactions between aggregate demand and aggregate supply.

Equilibrium price level and real national income

Figure 41.5 brings the aggregate demand curve of Figure 41.1 together with the aggregate supply curve of Figure 41.4. The equilibrium level of real national income is Y_2 and the equilibrium price level is P_2 in this model. Only at this P-Y combination is aggregate demand equal to aggregate supply. To see what is involved, assume that the current price level is P_1. At P_1 aggregate demand is Y_1'. This means that the solution to the IS-LM part of the model, given a price level of P_1, is income Y_1'. But firms are only willing to supply Y_1 at a price level of P_1. And if firms only produced a total output of Y_1 we know from the demand side of the model that desired expenditure would exceed total output. The excess demand forces prices up. This causes the quantity firms are willing to supply to rise and the quantity demanded to fall (because the rise in P pushes the LM curve left and lowers equilibrium income as determined in the demand, IS-LM, side of the model).

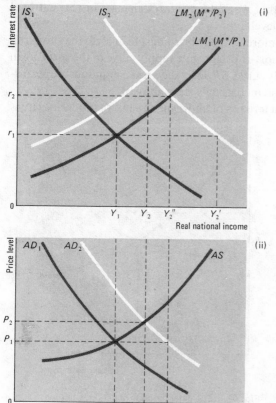

Fig. 41.6 When the aggregate supply curve slopes upwards some of the expansionary effect of the multiplier is dissipated in price increases

The multiplier once again Consider Figure 41.6 where the initial equilibrium values are r_1, Y_1, and P_1. An increase in exogenous expenditure shifts the IS curve from IS_1 to IS_2. The interest-constant multiplier would raise income to Y_2'. The rise in interest rates from r_1 to r_2 along the given LM curve LM_1 means, however, that equilibrium income only rises to Y_2''. What that means is that the aggregate demand curve shifts out to Y_2'' at the initial price level P_1. This would take equilibrium income to Y_2'' *if the price level remained constant*. What this interest-variable multiplier tells us is how much national income would rise, taking expenditure and asset effects into account, *if* firms were prepared to produce all that was demanded at the going price level. The upward-sloping AS curve in Figure 41.6(ii) tells us, however, that this supply-side assumption is incorrect: firms will only increase output if prices rise. The new AD-AS equilibrium is income Y_2 and price level P_2. In this case, the rise in prices dissipates part of the rise in desired expenditure so that the rise in real national income is less that it would have been if prices had been stable. Real income only rises to Y_2. (The rise in the price level shifts LM left to LM_2 to intersect IS_2 at Y_2 in part (ii) of the Figure.)

> **The variable-price multiplier, expressing the effect of a change in exogenous expenditure on equilibrium real national income, is less than the constant-price multiplier whenever an increase in income causes the price level to rise.**

Required aggregate-supply characteristics

Empirical evidence suggests three main characteristics that we would wish to be included in any relevant model of the aggregate supply of the economy. The first characteristic is displayed by the

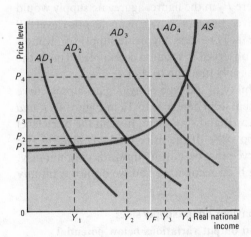

Fig. 41.7 The division of the effects of increases in aggregate demand between increases in real national income and increases in the price level

aggregate supply curve that we have just been using. Assume that we start in Figure 41.7 with AD_1 which produces price level P_1 and real income Y_1, which is well below potential income. Aggregate demand then shifts to AD_2, increasing income a lot from Y_1 to Y_2 and the price level only a bit from P_1 to P_2. Now assume that we start from AD_3 with price level P_3 and real income, Y_3, slightly in excess of potential income, Y_F. A rise in aggregate demand to AD_4 raises real income only a bit from Y_3 to Y_4 and the price level a lot from P_3 to P_4. (The microeconomic underpinning of this asymmetry is the theory of short-run oligopoly behaviour detailed on pp. 276–82.)

Increases in aggregate demand mainly affect quantities below potential income and mainly affect prices above potential income.

This proposition is so important that it may be called one of the fundamental Keynesian asymmetries. The asymmetry is between the reaction of Y and P to shifts in AD below and above potential income. The adjective Keynesian is meant to distinguish this type of behaviour from that assumed in the neo-Classical model of perfect competition where prices are equally flexible in both an upwards and downwards direction. In such a model the Keynesian asymmetry does not appear.

The aggregate supply curve in Figure 41.4 and 41.7, however, misses two other fundamental properties of observed supply-side behaviour. One is the nearly complete irreversibility of price-level increases. Assume, for example, that we start in Figure 41.7 at income Y_1 and an associated price level P_1. Aggregate demand then rises to AD_2, AD_3 and AD_4 and then falls back progressively to AD_1. This is a typical trade-cycle fluctuation of demand from slump to boom and back again. National income goes from Y_1 to Y_4 then falls back to Y_1. So far so good. The problem is, however, that according to the aggregate supply curve of Figure 41.7, the price level should rise from P_1 to P_2 to P_3 to P_4 and then fall progressively back to P_1. Thus the cycle would be accompanied by a burst of inflation during the expansion phase and *an equivalent burst of deflation* during the contraction phase.

The evidence is overwhelming, however, that if price levels fall at all, they fall only very slowly. Thus if a boom takes the price level from P_1 to P_4, reducing income back to Y_1 will not return the price level to P_1 but will leave it at, or near, P_4. Another way of putting the same point is to say that when showing the forces pushing towards equilibrium in Figure 41.5, we could not have started from a price level that was too high. If the price level were P_3 in the figure, aggregate supply would exceed aggregate demand. Equilibrium would *not*, however, be reached by having the price level fall to P_2. Such downward flexibility of the price level in the face of excess aggregate supply (or, what is the same thing, deficient aggregate demand) is just not observed in modern economies. This is the second basic characteristic that we want any aggregate supply function to show.

The third characteristic that we require is the instability of the type of aggregate supply curve that is shown in Figures 41.4 and 41.7. The evidence is that if income rose to Y_4 in Figure 41.7, *and were then held there*, the price level would *not* just rise to P_4 and stay there. Instead the price level would continue to rise as long as income remained above Y_F. If the price level *continues* to rise whenever income is above Y_F, the aggregate supply curve must be shifting upwards continuously. This instability of the aggregate supply curve has long been recognized and we do not want any supply relation that we use to deny it.

There are three key aspects to observed macro behaviour on the supply side:
(1) Variations in demand are mainly reflected in output variations below potential income and in price variations above potential income.
(2) Although the price level rises in the face of excess aggregate demand, it does not fall significantly in the face of excess aggregate supply.
(3) As long as output is held above its potential level, the price level will continue to rise.

The aggregate supply curve: version II

To analyse the short-term behaviour of the economy in the face of demand and supply shocks without contradicting any of these key behavioural characteristics, we use the short-run aggregate supply curves shown in Figure 41.8. This curve makes a sharp distinction between the behaviour of the economy at less than full employment where the price level is stable and output is variable, and at full employment where output is fixed by an absolute full-employment constraint but the price level is variable. We can get a long way in understanding the relation between real income and the price

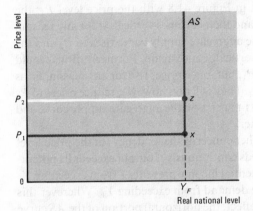

Fig. 41.8 A kinked aggregate supply curve with a ratchet effect on the price level

level using this curve and, when we run into problems that we can not handle with it, we shall introduce a more subtle supply-side relation that will capture aspects of macro behaviour that are ruled out of this simple supply-side model. Here are this curve's characteristics.

(1) To the left of Y_F, output will vary without any variations in the price level. This is the case of less than full employment of all resources that we dealt with in previous chapters. Its micro underpinnings were summarized in Chapter 35. They depend on the model of short-run pricing behaviour outlined in Chapter 21 and the theory of the lack of response of wage rates to cyclical fluctuations in demand briefly discussed at the end of Chapter 27.

Of course all prices are not completely inflexible downwards. The horizontal portion of the aggregate supply curve is not intended to be an exact description of any real economy. It is meant instead to capture in simple form the essential condition that has prevailed in every recession and depression since the 1930s: the price level does not fall significantly in the presence of those output gaps that the economy has actually experienced.

When the economy reaches its potential output of Y_F, an absolute capacity constraint is reached. No increase in real output is possible, so the aggregate supply curve is vertical. This assumption clearly suppresses the fact that it is always possible to squeeze a little more output from the economy by working overtime, extra shifts, etc. Recall that full-employment output rises when all factors are employed at their normal levels of utilization. Although there is no absolute full-employment ceiling to output, the vertical section of the AS curve catches the reality that under the usual conditions there is some level beyond which output will not respond greatly to further increases in aggregate demand. We get clarity in studying some problems by ignoring the grey area around potential output, where a little more output can be squeezed out but at rapidly rising cost. When we wish to study it explicitly, we shall change our aggregate supply assumptions accordingly.

The above properties of our aggregate supply curve catch, in extreme form, the first of the empirical characteristics listed earlier: a fall in output below Y_F is associated with little fall in prices (in this case none); and an attempt to raise output above Y_F causes a large rise in prices and only a small rise in output (in this case none). The aggregate supply curve in Figure 41.8 can be thought of as an extreme version of the *SRAS* curve in Figure 41.4, produced by flattening the curve's slope to zero to the left of Y_F and increasing the curve's slope to infinity at Y_F.

(2) The second key characteristic of the aggregate supply curve in Figure 41.8 is that although the price level can rise, it never falls. Anything that raises the current price level ratchets the horizontal section of *AS* up to that price level. Thus, if we start in Figure 41.8 with the price level P_1, the aggregate supply curve runs horizontally from P_1 to x and then becomes vertical. If for any reason, however, prices rise to P_2, the horizontal portion of the aggregate supply curve rises to P_2 and the new *AS* curve passes through P_2 and z and then rises vertically once again. Formerly, firms would supply anything demanded up to Y_F at a price level of P_1, but, once prices rise for any reason, firms will supply anything demanded at the new price level, P_2. They will not, however, reduce prices to P_1 in spite of excess capacity. This is the so-called RATCHET EFFECT on the aggregate supply curve and it catches the second macro characteristic outlined earlier.

(3) The third important macro characteristic listed earlier concerns the tendency for the price level and the short-run aggregate supply curve to shift upwards continuously if output exceeds its potential level. Although the absolute output constraint at potential income prevents Y from exceeding Y_F in this simple model, there is nothing to stop aggregate demand from exceeding Y_F. Wherever this occurs, the price level rises and, according to the rachet effect, the horizontal portion of the *AS* curve shifts upwards.

On all the above counts, therefore, the kinked aggregate supply curve of Figure 41.8 comes closer to short-run macroeconomic reality than does the smooth upward-sloping curve of Figure 41.4. Accordingly, we use this curve until, in Chapter 47, we find it necessary to introduce a more sophisticated relation that allows us to deal with the range around Y_F, where demand shocks are observed to have impact effects on both prices and output.

Shifts in aggregate supply

Figure 41.9 shows the two main ways in which our simple *AS* function can shift. In part (i) we start at

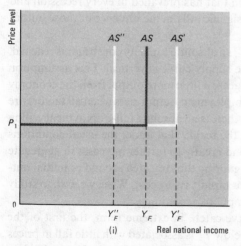

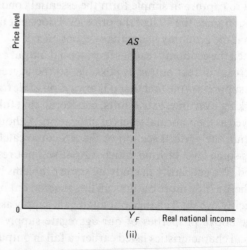

Fig. 41.9 Shifts in the aggregate supply curve

a potential income of Y_F. Economic growth that raises the level of potential income, say to Y_F', shifts the AS curve to AS'. A decline in resources caused, say, by not replacing capital as it wears out or by a reduction in the labour force, can shift the curve inwards to AS'' (potential income Y_F'').

In part (ii) of the figure, the horizontal portion of the AS curve shifts upwards. This indicates a rise in the prices at which firms are prepared to sell their output when operating at or below capacity output. This upward shift in AS will occur as a result of a rise in the costs of producing output. The most important reasons for such a rise in costs are listed below.

(1) The costs of imported materials rise.

(2) Excess demand for labour and other inputs force up wages and materials costs.

(3) Labour costs rise due to some 'cost-push' pressure from labour.

(4) Capital costs rise due to a large rise in interest rates which raise the cost of borrowed money.

(5) Indirect taxes raise the selling prices of commodities without any rise in their costs of production.

Comparative statics

What will happen to total output, and the price level, if one or both of the aggregate curves shift? Shifts in aggregate demand and aggregate supply are often called DEMAND SHOCKS and SUPPLY SHOCKS respectively.

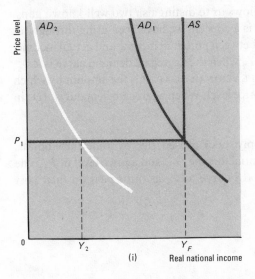
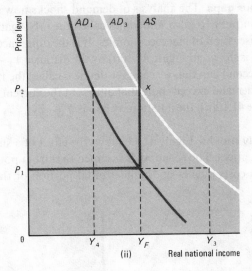

Fig. 41.10 Aggregate demand shocks

Demand shocks   Figure 41.10 shows the effects of demand shocks. In part (i), fluctuations in aggregate demand between AD_1 and AD_2 cause GDP to fluctuate between Y_F and Y_2 leaving the price level constant at P_1. In part (ii), we see that a rise in aggregate demand from AD_1 to AD_3 causes excess demand of $Y_3 - Y_F$ at the initial price level of P_1. (The IS-LM part of the economy now solves for an income of Y_3 as long as the price level is P_1.) The excess demand causes prices to rise until the price level is pulled up to P_2. At this point the excess demand has been removed and there is no further demand pressure on the price level. (The rise in the price level shifts the *LM* curve left until the new *LM* curve intersects the new *IS* curve at the initial income of Y_F.) This is a typical demand-shock inflation.

> **The basic asymmetry is that fluctuations in demand at or below full employment cause output to change, while increases that take aggregate demand above potential income cause the price level to rise.**

This asymmetrical behaviour of the economic system tends to give it an inflationary bias whenever demand is oscillating above and below full-employment income. To see this, assume that a slump takes aggregate demand from AD_1 to AD_2 in Figure 41.10(i). Income and employment fall and the price level stays constant at P_1. Now assume that a boom takes aggregate demand to AD_3 in part (ii) of the figure. Now income and employment hold steady at their full employment levels and the price level rises to P_2. Now assume that demand falls off to AD_1 in part (ii). The price level does not fall back to P_1; instead it stays constant at P_2 and output falls to Y_4 along the horizontal portion, P_2x, of the *AS* curve.

> **The asymmetrical behaviour tends to put an inflationary bias into an economy in which demand fluctuates around potential income, since prices tend to rise in booms while output tends to fall (with prices stable) in slumps.**

Various gaps The analysis of demand shocks now allows us to distinguish two well-known gaps. The output gap (also sometimes called the GNP gap) is a concept we have been using throughout our discussion of macroeconomics. It is the difference between potential income and actual income, and it is shown in Figure 41.10(i) by the distance $Y_F - Y_2$ when the aggregate demand curve is AD_2. The second gap that we can now define is called the INFLATIONARY GAP. It is the amount by which total demand exceeds potential output at the current price level. When aggregate demand is AD_3 in Figure 41.10(ii), the inflationary gap is $Y_3 - Y_F$.

Supply shocks Figure 41.11 shows the effect of a supply shock caused, say, by some autonomous rise in prices. The economy is assumed to start at potential income, Y_F, and a price level of P_1. The rise in costs pushes up the horizontal portion of the *AS* curve to P_2 as firms pass on their cost

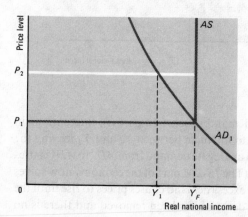

Fig. 41.11 Aggregate supply shocks

increases through increased product prices. Equilibrium national income falls, however, to Y_1. (The rise in the price level shifts the LM curve left and this raises the interest rate, curtailing real expenditure.) This is a typical supply-shock inflation: a rising price level combined with falling output.

With demand-shock inflations, a rising price level is associated with high employment and high output. With supply-shock inflations, a rising price level is associated with falling employment and falling output.

An illustration: 1972–3 was a time of a world-wide boom. Demand pressures were strong and prices rose in response. Then, in 1973–4, a severe recession occurred throughout much of the world as aggregate demand shifted leftwards. At that time, the world's economies were hit by some severe supply shocks. Serious crop failures combined with the sale of surplus North American wheat to the USSR raised food prices greatly. The newly active OPEC forced up not only the price of energy but the price of fertilizer, plastics, synthetic rubber and dozens of other products produced from petroleum. High prices and shortages of oil caused buyers to shift to such alternative energy sources as coal, and this in turn drove their prices up. All these forces pushed the aggregate supply curve upward because they increased costs of production and the price level.

The leftward shift in the AD curve combined with an upward shift in the AS curve brought about a serious stagflation: the world's major economies experienced simultaneously the twin problems of falling output and rising prices. The mid-1970s were the first time in the last half century that a major part of the explanation of the behaviour of prices and output lay in a rapidly upward-shifting aggregate supply curve. The public was so used to the behaviour of the economy under the impact of demand-side shocks that behaviour under severe supply-side shocks seemed incomprehensible. Even economists were so used to explaining observed events by demand-side shocks that many of them did not at first appreciate what was happening. Some announced the collapse of conventional macroeconomic theory; others claimed to see a complete change in all economic behaviour. Although plausible at the time, such reactions can now be seen to have been excessive, once the part played by aggregate supply is appreciated. All that was needed was to appreciate that although aggregate demand shocks tend to make real income and the price level positively correlated, aggregate supply shocks tend to make real income and the price level negatively correlated.

Stagflations are unfortunate events and we may not be clear on how to avoid them. But they are no mystery. Properly understood, they are fully comprehensible within the framework of standard Keynesian macroeconomic theory as the consequence of aggregate supply shocks.

42

Fluctuations and growth

So far our macroeconomic analysis has concentrated on comparative statics. This is very helpful in showing the forces causing national income, interest rates and the price level to change. Comparative-static equilibrium analysis is, however, limited to studying basically static behaviour whereas, in fact, the real world is constantly changing. The constant change of national income can be split into two basic movements: an up-and-down oscillatory movement called CYCLICAL FLUCTUATIONS, and a trend rate of change of real GDP, which in most cases over the last two centuries has been positive and so is spoken of as ECONOMIC GROWTH.

Fluctuations in national income

Output, employment and living standards have all shown an upward trend in advanced countries over the last two centuries. If you compare any year in the 1980s with any year in the first decade of this century, your overwhelming impression will be one of growth, even if you choose a recent year of low activity and compare it with a boom year from the 1900s.

If, however, you take each year of the 1970s and 1980s and compare it with the year following, you will find that economic activity proceeds in an irregular path, with forward spurts being followed by pauses and even relapses. These short-term fluctuations are commonly known as TRADE CYCLES in Britain and BUSINESS CYCLES in North America, the word 'cycle' suggesting an oscillation between good times and bad. At some times and places the patterns have been remarkably regular, at other times less so.

Some investigators have thought that they could discern several types of cycles in economic activity. One type, which is clearly observable in the nineteenth-century British data, had a duration of about nine years from peak to peak. This nine-year cycle was the one usually identified in the past as *the* trade cycle. A second type of cycle, for which there is considerable current evidence, is one of much shorter duration, lasting anywhere from 18 to 40 months. This cycle is sometimes associated with variations in inventories. Finally, some economists have thought that they could perceive a third, very long cycle, of about 50 years' duration, that was associated with, among other things, major fluctuations of investment activity following some fundamental innovation. Each burst of innovation was thought to be followed by eventual exploitation of all the obvious new lines, then by a long pause in innovative activity. Of all the 'cycles', this long-wave one is the most conjectural, and we shall say nothing further about it in this book except to notice that the depressed 1980s are five decades after the depressed 1930s!

Over the years, many different theories have been put forward to explain these fluctuations. In this chapter we can do little more than provide a very general introduction to this interesting and difficult subject.

The terminology of trade cycles

Although recurrent fluctuations in economic activity are neither smooth nor regular, a vocabulary has developed to denote their different stages. Figure 42.1 shows some stylized fluctuations that will serve to illustrate the most important terms.

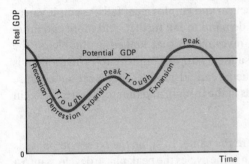

Fig. 42.1 Some stylized fluctuations

Trough The trough is, simply, the bottom. If the trough is sufficiently severe, it may be called a DEPRESSION. A trough is characterized by unemployment of labour and a level of consumer demand that is low in relation to the capacity of industry to produce goods for consumption. There is a substantial amount of unused industrial capacity. Business profits will generally be low, or negative. Confidence in the future will be lacking and, as a result, firms will be unwilling to take risks in making new investments. Banks and other financial institutions will have surplus cash that no one whom they consider to be a reasonable credit-risk wishes to borrow.

Expansion or recovery When something sets off a recovery, the lower turning point of the cycle has been reached. The symptoms of an expansion are many: worn-out machinery will be replaced; employment, income, and consumer spending all begin to rise; expectations become more favourable as a result of increases in production, sales and profits. Investments that once seemed risky may now be undertaken as the climate of business opinion begins to change from pessimism to optimism. As demand expands, production will be expanded with relative ease merely by re-employing the existing unused capacity and unemployed labour.

Peak The peak is the top of the cycle; it may be a sharp point between expansion and recession, or it may be a long plateau. At the peak there is a high degree of utilization of existing capacity, labour shortages begin to occur, particularly in certain key skill categories, and shortages of some key raw materials develop. Bottlenecks appear with increasing frequency. It now becomes difficult to increase output because the supply of unused resources is rapidly disappearing; output can be raised further only through investment that increases capacity. Because a lot of such investment expenditure is being attempted, investment funds will be in short supply. Because such investment takes time, further rises in demand are now met more by increases in prices than by increases in production. As shortages develop in more and more markets, a situation of general excess demand for factors develops. Costs rise but prices rise also, and business remains generally very profitable. Losses are infrequent because a money profit can be earned merely by holding on to goods whose prices are rising and selling them later at higher prices. Expectations of the future are favourable, and more investment may be made than is justified on the basis of current levels of prices and sales alone.

Recession   The end of the peak is called the UPPER TURNING POINT. Beyond that point, the economy turns downward. When the contraction is sustained, it is called a RECESSION. Suppose that for some reason demand falls off and, as a result, production and employment fall. As employment falls, so do households' incomes; falling income causes demand to fall further, and more and more firms get into difficulties. Prices and profits fall. New investments that looked profitable on the expectation of continuously rising demand and prices, suddenly appear unprofitable; investment is reduced to a low level, and it may not even be worth replacing capital goods as they wear out because unused capacity is increasing steadily. The recession ends in the trough, and the story starts up again where we began it.

The variety of cyclical fluctuations   No two cycles are the same. In some the recession phase is short; in others a full-scale period of stagnation sets in. In some cycles the peak phase develops into a severe inflation; in others the pressure of excess demand is hardly felt, and a new recession sets in before the economy has fully recovered from the last trough. Some cycles are of long duration, some are very short. Cycles differ from one another in terms of the origin and the magnitude of the initiating shock. Sometimes, but not always, economists can identify the initiating causes. (The causes of the Great Depression of the 1930s remain shrouded in controversy despite nearly four decades of study.) Inventories are believed by many economists, and housing by some, to lead to their own special patterns of fluctuation. Governments bent on re-election may affect the course of a cycle by timing expenditures or tax cuts in order to create a favourable economic climate at election time.

> **No two cycles are exactly the same. In some, the contraction is short and the resulting recession is not severe; in others, a full-scale period of depression sets in. In some cycles the boom phase develops into a severe inflation; in others, the pressure of excess demand is hardly felt.**

Causes of fluctuations

The shocks that can cause income and employment to rise and fall are numerous. Occasionally, there are sufficient shifts in the consumption function to raise or lower aggregate expenditure significantly and hence alter income and employment. Major shifts in government expenditure and tax policies can raise or lower aggregate expenditure sufficiently to affect income and employment. Monetary policy can also have a major influence. A tight monetary policy that shifts the *LM* curve to the left and forces up interest rates can reduce expenditure, income and employment. A lax monetary policy that lowers interest rates can do the reverse. Increases in exports, or decreases in imports that increase domestic production, can give a major upward push to aggregate expenditure, income and employment. All of these forces can give significant demand shocks to the economy. Possibly the most important factor from the demand side, however, is investment expenditure, and we shall look at it in more detail in the next section. To complete our preliminary list, however, we must add supply shocks. An upward shift in the aggregate supply function can, as we saw in the discussion surrounding Figure 41.11, cause a recession in which income falls in the face of inflation.

Investment

A major source of demand shocks in most industrial countries has been variations in investment expenditure. Asking what causes investment to change is really asking what are the determinants of investment in industrial countries. In Chapters 28 and 40 we saw that the rate of interest was a major determinant of investment. We now turn our attention to additional influences. While each pound's worth of investment has the same consequences for aggregate expenditure, different types of investment respond to different sets of causes. Thus it is useful to discuss separately the determinants of investment in plant and equipment, changes in inventories, and residential construction.

Investment in inventories[1] Inventory changes represent only a small proportion of private investment in a typical year. Their average size is not, however, an adequate measure of their importance because they are one of the more volatile elements of total investment and, therefore, contribute significantly to shifts in the investment schedule.

Firms characteristically hold substantial inventories of raw materials, work in progress, and goods already produced but unsold. It is almost impossible to imagine a manufacturing firm doing business successfully without some minimum holdings of inventories. In fact, most firms choose to hold inventories well above the necessary minimum level. They do this for many reasons; for one, it is usually cheaper to hold production constant in the face of daily, weekly or even monthly fluctuations in sales than to make continuous adjustments to the rate of production. Although many things can influence the desired size of a firm's inventory holdings, the two most important factors are the size of a firm's sales and the rate of interest.

Empirical studies show that the stock of inventories held tends to rise as a firm's rate of production and sales rises. But, while the size of inventories is related to level of sales, the *change* in inventories (which is a form of investment) is related to the *change* in the level of sales.

A firm might, for example, wish to hold inventories of 10 per cent of its sales: if sales are £100,000, it will wish to hold inventories of £10,000; if its sales increase to £110,000, it will want to hold inventories of £11,000. *Over the period during which the stock is being increased*, there will be a total of £1,000 new inventory investment.

> **The higher the level of production and sales, the larger the desired stock of inventories. Changes in the rate of production and sales cause temporary bouts of investment (or disinvestment) in inventories.**

---

[1] There are two kinds of changes in inventories. Intended changes are a *cause* of cyclical fluctuations and are discussed here. Unintended changes are a *consequence* of fluctuations, due (for example) to firms finding their inventories rising in a recession because they do not have customers for their current production and thus their goods pile up in warehouses.

Investment in residential construction Expenditures on residential structures are a significant part of all gross private investment. They also display substantial fluctuations from year to year. Because these expenditures are both large and variable, they exert a major impact on the economy.

To what does residential construction respond? Many of the influences on residential construction are non-economic, dependent on demographic or cultural forces such as new family formation. A rapidly expanding population will require more new construction than will a static population. Changes in marriage age also affect the demand for housing: if marriages are postponed, as during major wars, so too is family formation, and the demand for new housing units declines. Periods of high employment and high average family earnings tend to lead to increases in house-building, and unemployment and falling earnings to decreases in such building.

> **Expenditures for residential construction tend to be positively associated with changes in average income (as well as negatively associated with interest rates).**

Fixed investment by firms Investment in machinery, equipment and non-residential construction is a large component of domestic investment. Successful firms invest in plant and equipment because they want to sell at a profit the goods that the equipment can produce. But profitability, and thus the level of investment in plant and equipment, depends on a variety of economic variables. One is the rate of innovation. New innovations typically require new plant and equipment, and in some instances (e.g., the basic changes that followed the introduction of railways) innovation brings fundamental changes in the nature of the capital stock and leads to vast amounts of new investment.

The profitability of production, and hence the incentive to invest in new productive capacity, also depends on costs. High real wage rates and high taxes on company profits may reduce profit margins and so make investment seem less attractive. Buoyant conditions that allow profit margins to be raised may make investment seem more attractive.

Expectations also play a role. The decision to invest *now* is to a great extent an act of faith in the future. If the firms guess wrong, the penalties can be great. Many things can influence the firms other than the tastes of households. A new government may adopt different taxing and spending policies that affect a business profoundly. An increase in the price of oil can shift the demand for large and small cars, for coal, for skis, for stay-at-home recreational activities, and for a host of other goods and services. Particularly in the short run, expectations can have a decisive influence on the timing of investment. Business firms are unable or unwilling to borrow all the funds they require and so they may use their own funds to finance their investment projects. Profits thus become a key explanatory factor in investment because retained profits provide an important source of investable funds. Certainly retained profits are the largest source of investment funds for modern companies.

Some economists, and many business analysts, lay great stress on the effect of profits on investment. Business firms are unable or unwilling to borrow all the funds they require and so they may use their own funds to finance their investment projects. Profits thus become a key explanatory factor in investment because retained profits provide an important source of investable funds. Certainly profits are the largest source of investment funds for modern companies.

The accelerator: The need for plant and equipment is obviously derived from the demand for the goods the plant and equipment are designed to produce. If there is a demand that is expected to persist, and that cannot be met by increasing production with existing industrial capacity, then new plant and equipment will be needed.

Investment expenditure occurs while the new plant and equipment is being built and installed. If the desired stock of capital goods increases, there will be an investment boom while the new capital is being produced. But if nothing else changes, and even though business conditions continue to look rosy enough to justify the increased stock of capital, investment in new plant and equipment will cease once the larger capital stock is achieved. According to the theory of the ACCELERATOR, investment is related to the *rate of change* of national income. When national income is increasing, investment is needed in order to increase the capacity to produce consumption goods; when income is falling, it may not even be necessary to replace old capital as it wears out, let alone to invest in new capital.

The theory runs as follows. Let there be a simple relationship between the GDP and the amount of capital needed to produce it:

$$K = \alpha Y \ ,\tag{1}$$

where K is the required capital stock. The coefficient alpha is the capital-output ratio, $\alpha = K/Y$ and is also called the accelerator coefficient. First differencing (1) and noticing that investment is, by definition, the change in the capital stock, yields

$$I \equiv \Delta K = \alpha \Delta Y \ ,\tag{2}$$

i.e., investment is a constant proportion of the change in national income. This is called the simple, or sometimes the naive, accelerator.

The main insight which the accelerator theory provides is its emphasis on the role of net investment as a *disequilibrium* phenomenon – something that occurs when the stock of capital goods differs from what firms and households would like it to be. This gives the accelerator its particular importance in connection with *fluctuations* in national income. As we shall see, it can itself contribute to those fluctuations.

Taken literally, the accelerator posits a mechanical and rigid response of investment to changes in sales (and thus, aggregatively, to changes in national income). It does this by assuming a proportional relationship between changes in income and the size of the desired capital stock, and by assuming a fixed capital-output ratio. Each assumption is to some degree questionable.

Changes in sales that are thought to be temporary in their effect on demand will not necessarily lead to new investment. It is usually possible to increase the level of output from a given capital stock by working overtime or extra shifts. While this would be more expensive per unit of output in the long run, it will usually be preferable to making investments in the new plant and equipment that would lie idle after a temporary spurt of demand had subsided. Thus expectations about what is the required capital stock may lead to a much less mechanistic response of investment to income than the accelerator suggests.

A further limitation of the accelerator theory is its view of what constitutes investment. The fixed capital-output ratio emphasizes investment in capital widening, which we first encountered in Chapter 28 and which is investment in additional capacity that uses the same ratio of capital to labour as existing capacity. It does not explain capital deepening, which we also encountered in Chapter 28 and which is the kind of increase in the amount of capital per unit of labour that occurs in response to a fall in the rate of interest. Neither does the theory say anything about investments brought about as a result of new processes or new products. Furthermore, it does not allow for the fact that investment in any period is likely to be limited by the capacity of the capital-goods industry.

For these and other reasons, the accelerator does not by itself give anything like a complete explanation of variations in investment in plant and equipment, and it should not be surprising that a simple accelerator theory provides a relatively poor overall explanation of changes in investment. Yet accelerator-like influences do exist, and they play a role in the cyclical variability of investment.[1]

Theories of the cycle

There is no dearth of reasons to account for shocks that raise or lower national income. Supply shocks occur for all of the reasons itemized on page 623 of Chapter 41, and these lower income (while raising the price level). Demand shocks occur when any of the components of aggregate expenditure undergo a significant change: consumer expenditure may be unexpectedly high or low this year; government expenditure may be cut or raised; taxes, which affect disposable income and hence consumption, may be increased or decreased; private investment may rise or fall in response to a change in any of the factors that influence it; exports may rise or fall in response to changes in such influencing factors as the exchange rate, foreign income and the development of new products at home or abroad.

The existence of such shocks explains why the economy does not settle down in an unchanging position of static equilibrium. But do they explain why the economy shows a cyclical form of behaviour? If these shocks impinge on the economy in random sequence, why should the economy not itself exhibit a random sequence of ups and downs? Why, instead, does it show a wavelike motion, with each period's income and employment being related to last period's? It is a search for an explanation of the observed cyclical behaviour that has inspired most theorizing. Here we can do no more than mention a few possibilities.

Multiplier-accelerator theory The basic Keynesian theory of systematic cyclical fluctuations comes from a union of the multiplier theory of the expenditure-income relation and the accelerator theory of investment. This elementary theory is divided into three steps: first, a theory of cumulative upswings and downswings explains why, once started, movements tend to carry on in the same direction; second, a theory of floors and ceilings explains why upward and downward movements are eventually brought to a halt; and third, a theory of instability explains how, once a process of upward or downward movement is brought to a halt, it tends to reverse itself.

Cumulative movements: Why does a period of expansion or contraction, once begun, tend to develop its own momentum? First, the multiplier process tends to cause cumulative movements. As soon as a revival begins, some unemployed labourers find work again. These people, with their newly acquired income, can afford to make much-needed consumption expenditures. This new demand causes an increase in production and creates new jobs for other unemployed workers. As incomes rise, demand rises; as demand rises, incomes rise. Just the reverse happens in a downswing. Unemployment in one sector causes a fall in demand for the products of other sectors, which leads to a further fall in employment and a further fall in demand.

---

[1] In spite of decades of attempts to refute the accelerator empirically, *flexible accelerators* continue to provide significant explanation of much investment expenditure in many econometric models. (The flexible accelerator avoids some of the simple accelerator's mechanical rigidities referred to in the text.)

A second major factor is to be found in the accelerator theory. New investment is needed to expand existing productive capacity and to introduce new methods of production. When consumer demand is low and there is excess capacity, investment is likely to fall to a very low level; once income starts to rise and entrepreneurs come to expect further rises, investment expenditure may rise very rapidly. Furthermore, when full employment of existing capacity is reached, new investment becomes the only way available for firms to increase their output.

A third major explanation for cumulative movements may be found in the nature and importance of expectations. All production plans take time to fulfil. Current decisions to produce consumer goods and investment goods are very strongly influenced by business expectations. Such expectations can sometimes be volatile, and can sometimes be self-fulfilling. If enough people think, for example, that stock-market prices are going to rise, they will all buy stocks in anticipation of a price rise, and these purchases will themselves cause prices to rise. If, on the other hand, enough people think stock-market prices are going to fall, they will sell now at what they regard as a high price and thereby actually cause prices to fall. This is the phenomenon of *self-realizing expectations*. If enough managers think the future looks rosy and begin to invest in increasing capacity, this will create new employment and income in the capital-goods industries, and the resulting increase in demand will help to create the rosy conditions whose vision started the whole process. One cannot lay down simple rules about so complicated a psychological phenomenon as the formation of expectations, but they do occasionally show a sort of bandwagon effect. Once things begin to improve, people expect further improvements, and their actions, based on this expectation, help to cause yet further improvements. On the other hand, once things begin to worsen, people often expect further worsening, and their actions, based on this expectation, help to make things worse.

The multiplier-accelerator process combined with changes in expectations that cause expenditure functions to shift can explain the cumulative tendencies of recessions and recoveries.

Floors and ceilings: The next question that arises is: Why do these upward and downward processes ever come to an end?

A very rapid expansion can continue for some time, but it cannot go on for ever because eventually the economy will run into bottlenecks (or ceilings) in terms of some resources. For example, if investment funds become scarce, interest rates will rise. Firms will now find new investments more expensive than anticipated, and some will now appear unprofitable. In another case the expansion may be halted by exhaustion of the reservoir of unemployed labour. The full-employment ceiling guarantees that any sustained rapid growth rate of real income and employment will eventually be slowed. At this point the accelerator again comes into play. A slowing down in the rate of increase of production leads to a decrease in the investment required in new plant and equipment. This causes a fall in employment in the capital-goods industries and, through the multiplier, a fall in consumer demand. Once consumer demand begins to fall, investment in plant and equipment will be reduced to a low level because firms will already have more productive capacity than they can use. Unemployment begins to mount, and the upper turning point has been passed.

A rapid contraction, too, is eventually brought to an end. Consider the worst sort of depression imaginable, one in which every postponable expenditure of households, firms or governments has been postponed. Even then, aggregate demand will not fall to zero. Even if aggregate demand consisted only of consumption, it would not fall to zero because households can and will use up savings, or go into debt, to buy the necessities of life. Moreover, transfer payments to households in the form of unemployment compensation and welfare payments provide the funds to support minimum consumption expenditures.

Nor is consumption the only element of aggregate demand that will remain above zero. Much government expenditure is committed by statute and so must be sustained. Civil service salaries and defence expenditures will continue. Moreover, the political pressure for governments to increase their expenditures will surely grow and may be effective. Even business investment, in many ways the most easily postponed component of aggregate demand, will not fall to zero. In the industries providing food, basic clothing, and shelter, demand may remain fairly high in spite of quite large reductions in national income. These industries will certainly be carrying out some investment to replace equipment as it wears out, and they may even undertake some new investment. Furthermore, new innovations may provide opportunities for new investment even in the midst of a serious general depression. For example, even in the depths of the Great Depression, the electronics industries, based on such newly popular products as radios, underwent a boom that held unemployment low and investment high in south-east England.

Taken together, the minimum levels of consumption, investment and government expenditure will assure a minimum equilibrium level of national income that, although well below the full-employment level, will not be zero. This is the floor. (This may be small comfort to those affected. It is possible for the economy to settle into a period of heavy unemployment for a long time, and if it does, many people will suffer long-term unemployment.)

Turning points: The final aspect of the Keynesian theory of cycles seeks to explain why once floors and ceilings stop income from changing at a rapid rate, income does not stabilize at the high of the ceiling or the low of the floor, but instead tends to change direction.

We saw in the previous section that the accelerator theory of investment may help to explain the cumulative nature of upswings and downswings. It also can explain reversals of direction of expansions and contractions. We have seen that the accelerator makes the desired level of *new* (not replacement) investment depend upon the rate of change of income. If income is rising at a constant rate, then investment will be at a constant *level*. If the speed at which income is rising slackens, then the level of investment will decline. This means that a *levelling off* in income at the top of a cycle may lead to a *decline* in the level of investment. The accelerator thus provides a theory of the upper turning point. The decline in investment at the upper turning point will cause a decline in the level of income that will be intensified through the multiplier process.

What about the possible stabilization of income at a floor? Investment theory predicts that, sooner or later, an upturn will begin. If nothing else causes an expansion of business activity, there will eventually be a revival of replacement investment. As existing capital wears out, the capital stock will eventually fall to the level required to produce current output. At this stage new machines will be bought to replace those that subsequently wear out. The rise in the level of activity in the capital-goods industries will then cause, by way of the multiplier, a further rise in income. The economy has turned the corner. An expansion, once started, may trigger the sort of cumulative upward movement already discussed.

The theory of the inventory cycle A second theory of why the economy undergoes cyclical oscillations is related to inventories. All firms hold inventories of materials and finished goods, and these inventories fluctuate widely. Such sharp fluctuations are a major cause of the short-term variations in the level of activity. The theory of inventory cycles is similar to the accelerator mechanism, only now we emphasize investment in *inventories* rather than in plant and equipment.

Start by assuming that national income is in equilibrium at full employment. Now, in order to get the process started, assume that there is an autonomous rise in the propensity to save (a fall in the propensity to consume). The first result of the fall in demand will be a piling up of unsold goods on dealers' shelves. After some time, dealers will reduce their orders so as to prevent inventories from increasing indefinitely; retailers will reduce purchases from wholesalers; after wholesalers' stocks have risen, they in turn will reduce their purchases from manufacturers. Manufacturers may maintain production for a while, adding the unsold goods to inventories, in the hope that the fall in demand is only temporary. If this proves not to be the case, manufacturers will cut back on production, laying off some workers and reducing the hours worked by the remainder. Thus income and output will begin to fall; at this stage inventories will have risen to an abnormally high level. Once production falls to a level equal to the new (lower) level of consumer demand, there will be no further rise in inventories.

Unfortunately, however, matters will not remain at this point. Inventories will now be too high on two counts: first, because sales will be at a lower level than they were originally, and second, because inventories will have increased during the transitional process. In order to work off the excess, retailers will buy less from wholesalers than they are selling to consumers, wholesalers will buy less from manufacturers than they are selling to retailers, and manufacturers will produce less than they are selling to wholesalers. Thus the current level of output will fall below the current level of sales. The resulting fall in income will reduce the level of demand still further. As long as production can be held below the level of current sales, inventories will be falling even though the level of sales is itself falling.

Once inventories are reduced to the desired level, the retailers and wholesalers will increase their orders, so that their purchases are equal to their current sales. Their inventories will thus be held constant. Manufacturers will also increase the levels of their outputs until output is equal to the (increased) level of sales, thus keeping their own stocks at a constant level. But this means that production, and hence income earned by households, is increased. As this happens, the demand for goods will rise. The initial impact here will be on inventories, which will be run down as sales rise unexpectedly. Now the whole process is set into reverse. For a while, everyone's inventories will be run down, but then orders will increase, first from retailers, then from wholesalers. Finally, the output of manufacturers will increase. This means that income, and with it the level of demand, will rise even further. Once production is increased to the level of current sales, inventories will no longer be decreasing.

But now the level of inventories is too low for two reasons: first, because the level of sales is higher than it was when inventories were at the correct level, and second, because inventories have been run down during the transitional phase. In order now to build up their inventories, retailers will order more from wholesalers than they sell to consumers, wholesalers will buy more from manufacturers than they sell to retailers, and manufacturers will produce more than they sell to wholesalers. This rise in production will raise incomes, and thus the level of demand, still further. As long as production is kept above the level of sales, however, inventories will be rising in spite of the fact that sales are also rising. Once the inventories are brought up to the desired level, orders will fall off. Retailers and wholesalers will reduce orders to the level of current sales, and manufacturers will reduce output to that level as well. But this fall in output will reduce incomes and, with them, demand. For a while, inventories will pile up, but orders and output will be cut back, thus reducing the level of income and demand. Now the whole downward process is set in motion again. If you go back to the beginning of this section and start to read there, you can continue the process.

A theory relying on random events and long lags   The two theories outlined so far cover investment cycles both in capital equipment and in inventories. They look to oscillations in the spending of households and firms to explain oscillations in the economy's major macro-variables.

An alternative and quite different theory does not require cyclical behaviour from firms and households in order to generate cycles. This theory begins with lags. Most macro-models that are designed to fit the data have quite long lags in their behavioural relations. For example, if a fall in the rate of interest makes a new investment programme profitable, it may take six months to plan it, three months to let contracts, six more months before spending builds up to its top rate and another twenty-four to complete the project. This means that investment expenditure will be subject to a distributed time-lag: changes in the rate of interest will cause a reaction in investment expenditure that is distributed over quite a long period of time.

A pioneering study by two American economists, Irma and M. A. Adelman, established that, if occasional random shifts in exogenous expenditure disturb a system of expenditure-determining equations all of which contain long lags, a cycle is generated. Here the disturbing influences are random or erratic, but the consequences are a cyclical path to the major endogenous macro-variables such as national income and unemployment.

> **Each of the major components of aggregate expenditure have sometimes undergone shifts large enough to disturb the economic system significantly. The long lags in the expenditure function can then convert these shifts into cyclical oscillations in national income.**

A policy induced cycle   Government-induced demand shocks have sometimes caused cyclical fluctuations. But why should the government administer such potentially disturbing demand shocks? Several reasons have been suggested.

A political business cycle: As early as 1944, the Polish-born Keynesian economist Michael Kalecki warned that once governments had learned to manipulate the economy, they might engineer an election-geared business cycle. In pre-election periods they would raise spending and cut taxes. The resulting expansionary demand shock would create high employment and good business conditions that would bring voters' support for the government. But the resulting inflationary gap would lead to a rising price level. So, after the election was won, the government would depress demand to remove the inflationary gap, also providing some slack for expansion before the next election.

This theory invokes the image of a very cynical government manipulating employment and national income solely for electoral purposes. Few people believe that governments deliberately do this all the time, but the temptation to do it some of the time, particularly before close elections, may prove irresistible.

Alternating policy goals: A variant of the policy-induced cycle does not require a cynical government and an easily duped electorate. Instead both sides need only be rather short-sighted. In this theory, when there is a recession and relatively stable prices, the public and the government identify unemployment as the number-one economic problem. The government then engineers an expansionary demand shock. This, plus such natural cumulative forces as the multiplier and accelerator, expands the economy and cures unemployment. But as Y rises above Y_F, the price level begins to rise. At this point the unemployment problem is declared cured. Now inflation is seen as the nation's number-one economic problem and a contractionary policy shock is engineered. The natural cumulative forces again take over, reducing income to a low level. The inflation subsides but unemployment rises, setting the stage once again for an expansionary shock to cure the unemployment problem.

Many economists have criticized government policy over the last few decades for causing fluctuations by shortsightedly pursuing expansion to cure unemployment then contraction to cure inflation. This phenomenon has occurred often enough in the UK that it has been given a name: the STOP-GO POLICY CYCLE or more simply just *stop-go*.

Misguided stabilization policy: In a variant of the previous theory, the government tries to hold the economy at its potential level of national income by countering fluctuations in private-sector expenditure functions with offsetting changes in its own spending and taxes. This is the theory of *stabilization policy* which we shall cover in the next chapter. For now, we can observe that cycles in income and employment can be induced, or at least unwittingly exaggerated, by poorly conceived government policies. Unless the authorities are very sophisticated, bad timing may accentuate rather than dampen cyclical fluctuations. We return to this difficulty in the next chapter.

An exogenous theory of the cycle All of the theories considered so far look to forces within the economy as the cause of cycles. Of course the world as a whole is a closed economy, and cyclical movements in world national income and employment must have endogenous causes (although once upon a time a plausible theory was advanced linking trade cycles to cyclical activity in sun spots!). Small parts of the world, such as Britain or any one of the other EEC countries, are open economies. For these economies, cyclical fluctuations may have exogenous causes. Through the operation of the international trade multiplier, which we studied in Chapter 37, a foreign recession may be transmitted to the EEC countries through an induced fall in foreign demand for EEC exports.

The more open an economy, the more vulnerable it is to 'imported' cyclical fluctuations in its national income. Since exports are a larger part of the UK's total final expenditure than is investment expenditure, it is clear that the UK is open to such international effects and some sharp year-to-year changes in exports have occurred in both directions.

There is a second mechanism by which cycles have been transmitted internationally. Today there are large international flows of capital. A recession in a capital-exporting country that makes its firms and households less willing to invest abroad as well as at home, will show up to the capital-importing countries as exogenous falls in their investment expenditure.

A third mechanism concerns interest rates. The sharp rise in American interest rates caused by restrictive monetary policy in the US in 1981 and 1982 forced up interest rates in the rest of the world and helped to worsen their already serious recession.

There is some evidence that UK fluctuations since 1945 were partly domestic in origin. There can be no doubt, however, that they were also in some measure exogenous to the UK economy, being 'imported' through the links of international trade and capital flows.

Economic growth[1]

The theory of income determination developed so far is a short-run theory. It takes potential income as constant and concentrates on the effect of investment expenditure on aggregate demand. From this short-term viewpoint an increase in investment expenditure raises national income by shifting aggregate demand from, say, AD_1 to AD_2 in Figure 42.2, and taking equilibrium real income from Y_1 to Y_2.

Short-run national-income theory concentrates on the effects of investment on aggregate demand, and thus on variations of actual income around a given potential income.

In the long run, by adding to the nation's capital stock, investment raises potential income. This effect is shown by the outward shift of the AS curve from Y_F to Y_F' in Figure 42.2

The theory of economic growth is a long-run theory. It ignores short-run fluctuations of actual national income around potential income and concentrates on the effects of investment on raising potential income.

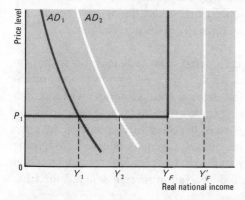

Fig. 42.2 The short-run and long-run effects of investment

Since the average output gap shows no long-term tendency to change, increases in actual income and living standards over the decades will be due mainly to long-term increases studied in the theory of growth, rather than to the short-term fluctuations in demand.

The contrast between the short- and long-run aspects of investments is worth emphasizing. From the short-run, income-generating point of view, any activity that puts income into people's hands will raise aggregate demand. Thus the short-run effect on national income is the same if a firm 'invests' in digging holes and refilling them or in building a new factory. From the growth point of view, however, we are concerned only with that part of investment that adds to a nation's productive capacity. The point is important because much of what is classified as investment in the national

[1] For further background material on economic growth see Harbury and Lipsey, Chapters 5 and 9.

income accounts, and that does add to aggregate demand, is really consumption expenditure. Assume, for example, that a firm discards an adequate but dingy office building and 'invests' in a lavish new head-office block with superior facilities for its staff. This will count as investment in the national-income data, and the expenditure will add to aggregate demand. From the growth point of view, however, it is really disguised consumption for the firm's staff.

Similar remarks apply to public-sector expenditure. Any expenditure will add to aggregate demand and raise national income if there are unemployed resources. Only some expenditure adds to the growth of full-employment income. Indeed some investment expenditure that shores up an industry that would otherwise be declining, in order to create employment, may have an anti-growth effect. It may prevent the reallocation of resources in response to shifts both in the pattern of world demand and in the country's comparative advantage. Thus in the long run the country's capacity to produce commodities that are demanded on open markets may be diminished.

The nature of economic growth

Economic growth has been one of the dominant forces in industrial nations over the last 200 years. It has been the source of some of industrialization's greatest triumphs: it has raised living standards to levels where leisure, travel and luxury goods are within the reach of ordinary people for the first time in human history. In industrial nations it has produced standards of living that are the envy of the peoples in much of the rest of the world, many of whom have striven – with varying degrees of success – to imitate that performance. Economic growth has also been the source of spectacular failures – including pollution of the air, water and land by chemicals, heat and noise.

Members of developed societies have come to accept growth. Even when they worry about such things as pollution, they ask 'How can we remove this or that side-effect of growth?' Only a few people ask 'How can we stop growth?' and even fewer take those few seriously. But growth, which seems inevitable to most of us, has not always been present, nor is it present everywhere today. There have been historical periods of increases in living standards followed by long periods of no change. One of the latter was documented by Professor Phelps-Brown, of the London School of Economics, who showed that there was no significant trend increase in the real incomes of English building-trade workers between 1215 and 1798, a period of almost six centuries. Peasants in many poor countries today enjoy a living standard little different from that of their ancestors 1,000 or more years ago.

Rapid growth, when it occurs, is impressive. For example, total world output doubled between 1960 and 1975. Despite dramatic population growth, output per person for the world as a whole has increased sharply also. It was twice as high in 1975 as in 1950!

Capacity versus utilization The growth in an economy's national income over three or four years reflects changes in either its productive capacity or its percentage utilization of that capacity, or both. Productive capacity is measured by potential national income, Y_F. Percentage utilization can be measured by expressing actual income, Y, as a percentage of potential income: $(Y/Y_F) \times 100$.

If there have been large changes in percentage utilization, very high rates of increase in actual national income will be observed, but such increases will not be sustainable once capacity is fully utilized. A great deal of confusion would be avoided if the term 'growth rate' were used to refer only to the growth of potential national income, and if comparisons of national-income figures for one country over several years were divided into two parts: changes due to the growth in productive capacity and changes due to variations in the employment of existing productive capacity.

Total versus per capita measures The economy's growth in real potential output is measured by its growth of constant-price potential output. This measure is relevant to such things as the nation's capacity to wage war and to influence other nations by giving foreign aid.

Growth in per capita output is growth in potential income per person. This is a measure of the economy's ability to produce output for each person in the society. Where population growth is rapid, countries often find their total output burgeoning while their output per person is static or growing only slowly. In these cases, growth in total output has been matched by growth in the number of mouths to feed, leaving the amount per person constant. Improvement in living standards is clearly more closely related to growth in per capita than in total output.

The cumulative nature of growth A growth rate of 2 per cent per year may seem rather insignificant, but if it is continued for a century it will lead to more than a sevenfold increase in real national income! To see the cumulative effect of what seem like very small differences in growth rates, notice that if one country grows faster than another, the gap in their living standards will widen progressively. If two countries start from the same level of income and country A grows at 3 per cent while B grows at 2 per cent per year, A's income per capita will be twice B's in 69 years. You may not think it matters much whether your economy grows at 2 per cent or 3 per cent, but your children and grandchildren will!

> **Small differences in growth rates make enormous differences in levels of potential national income over a few decades.**

The dramatic cumulative effects of small differences in growth rates are illustrated by the change in the UK's relative position among the EEC countries. In 1960 UK per capita income was second only to that of Luxembourg among the original six EEC countries. It was also well above the average for the nine countries who were EEC members by 1980. But the UK's growth rate at the time was one of the slowest in Europe. By the beginning of the 1980s its per capita income had fallen below the average of both 'the six' and 'the ten'. Indeed, it was higher only than Italy's and Greece's. Furthermore, in the 1970s the UK began to be overtaken in per capita GDP by the more prosperous of the Eastern European countries.

Benefits of growth

There is no doubt that growth confers many benefits. A few of the most important are discussed here.

Improved living standards A primary reason for desiring growth is to raise the general living standards of the population as measured by per capita national income. A country whose per capita GNP is growing at 3 per cent per year is doubling its living standards approximately every 24 years. (A helpful approximation device is the 'rule of 68'. Divide any growth rate into 68 and the resulting number approximates the number of years it will take for income to double.)

For those who share in it, growth is a powerful weapon against poverty. A family earning £6,000 today can expect to earn £7,600 within eight years (plus a further increase due to any inflation) if it just shares in a 3 per cent growth rate (compounded annually). The transformation of the lifestyle of the ordinary industrial worker over the present century is a notable example of the escape from poverty made possible by growth. Unfortunately, not everyone benefits equally from growth. Many of those who are poorest are not even in the labour force, and so will not enjoy the higher wages through which the gains from growth are generally distributed to the population.

Growth and income redistribution Economic growth makes many kinds of income redistribution easier to achieve. For example, a rapid rate of growth makes it much more feasible politically to alleviate poverty. If existing income is to be redistributed, someone's standard of living will actually have to be lowered. If, however, there is economic growth and the increment in income is redistributed (through government intervention), then it is possible to reduce income inequalities without actually having to lower anyone's income. It is much easier for a rapidly growing economy than for a static one to be generous toward its less fortunate citizens, or its neighbours.

Growth and lifestyle A family often finds that a big increase in its income leads to a major change in the pattern of its consumption – that extra money buys important amenities of life. In the same way, the members of society as a whole may find that some goods are increasingly attainable as income rises. For example, the households in a rapidly growing country find it desirable not only to demand more cars and highways but also more parks and recreational areas. Furthermore, once the basic needs of food, etc., have been met for a substantial majority of the population, the society may even begin to worry about the litter and pollution that comes with growth itself.

National defence and prestige If one country is competing with another for power or prestige, then rates of growth are important. If our national income is growing at 2 per cent, for instance, while the other country's is growing at three per cent, all the other country has to do is wait for our relative strength to dwindle. Also, the faster a nation's productivity is growing, the easier the expense of an arms or a space race will be to bear.

More subtly, but similarly, growth itself has become part of the currency of international prestige. Countries that are engaged in persuading other countries of the might or right of their economic and political systems frequently point to their rapid rates of growth as evidence of their achievements.

> **Growth is an enormous long-term force in raising living standards and it dwarfs anything that can be done by redistributive policies to raise the ordinary employed person's standard of living.**

Costs of growth

The benefits discussed above suggest that growth is a great blessing. It is surely true that, other things being equal, most people would regard a fast rate of growth as preferable to a slow one. But other things are seldom equal.

Social and personal costs of growth Industrialization, unless very carefully managed, causes deterioration of the environment. Unspoiled landscapes give way to highways and factories and billboards; air and water become polluted; unique and priceless relics of earlier ages – from flora and fauna to ancient ruins and works of art – disappear. With urbanization people move out of the simpler life of farming and small towns into the crowded, unhealthy life of an urban slum. Further growth may turn the urban area into a pleasant place in which to live a few generations later, but by that time many people will have lived and died there. The growth was 'worth it' for their descendants, but was it so for those who originally moved? When the original movement to cities occurs those who remain behind find that rural life, too, has changed because of large-scale farming, the decline of population and the migration of young people from the farm to the city. The faster tempo of life brings joy to some, but tragedy to others. Accidents, ulcers, crime rates, suicides, divorces and murder all tend to be higher in periods of rapid change and in more developed societies.

A growing economy is a changing economy. Innovation leaves obsolete machines in its wake, and also partially obsolete people. Rapid growth requires rapid adjustments, and these can cause upset and misery to the individuals affected. The decline in the number of unskilled jobs means that when an untrained worker loses his job, he may not find another, particularly if he is over 50. It is not only the unskilled who may suffer. No matter how well-equipped you are at 25, in another 25 years you are likely to be partially obsolete. This can happen to a doctor or an engineer as well as to a mechanic.

It is often argued that the costs of growth are a small price to pay for its great benefits. But some of these costs are not so small. Moreover, they are very unevenly borne; many of those for whom growth is most costly (in terms of jobs) share least in the fruits of growth. At the other extreme, it is foolish to see only the costs – to yearn for the good old days – while thriving on higher living standards that growth alone has made possible.

The opportunity cost of growth In a world of scarcity, almost nothing is free. Growth usually requires an investment of resources in capital goods, in education and in health. Such investments do not yeild any *immediate* return in terms of goods and services for consumption. Growth, which promises more goods tomorrow, is achieved by consuming fewer goods today because resources must be diverted to producing capital. For the economy as a whole, this is a primary cost of growth.

A hypothetical example will illustrate the basic choice involved: a more rapid rate of growth may be purchased at the expense of a lower rate of current consumption. Suppose a particular economy has full employment and is experiencing growth at the rate of 2 per cent per year. Its citizens are consuming 85 per cent of the GNP and investing 15 per cent. Suppose that if consumption were reduced to 77 per cent of GNP immediately, the country would produce more capital and that this would shift them at once to a 3 per cent growth rate, which could be maintained as long as saving and investment were held at 23 per cent of national income. Should this be done?

Table 42.1 illustrates the choice open to the society by showing two alternative growth paths of real consumption, C and C′. Path C is what will happen if resources are not reallocated. In year zero total income is 100, of which 15 is allocated to investment and 85 to consumption. This percentage division of resources is maintained so the output of investment and consumption goods continues to grow at 2 per cent per year. The alternative growth path of consumption is shown in the C′ column. In year zero national income is 100, but now the resources are reallocated so that output of investment goods is 23, while output of consumption goods falls to 77·0. Everything now starts to grow, however, at 3 per cent per annum. The economy holds this new percentage distribution of its

Table 42.1 The opportunity costs of growth

In year	The level of consumption	
	2% growth rate of consumption (C)	3% growth rate of consumption (C')
0	85·0	77·0
1	86·7	79·3
2	88·5	81·8
3	90·3	84·2
4	92·1	86·8
5	93·9	89·5
6	95·8	92·9
7	97·8	95·0
8	99·7	97·9
9	101·8	100·9
10	103·8	103·9
15	114·7	120·8
20	126·8	140·3
30	154·9	189·4
40	189·2	255·6

resources between consumption and investment output. Consumption now grows at 3 per cent per annum and follows the path shown by the column C'.

On the assumed figures, it takes 10 years for the actual level of consumption to catch up to what it would have been had no reallocation been made. But the cumulative losses in consumption must be made up before society can really be said to have broken even. It takes an additional 9 years before total consumption over the whole period is as large as it would have been if the economy had remained on the 2 per cent path. This comparison looks only at actual amounts of consumption. If future income is discounted at a positive rate of interest, so that a quantity of goods now is preferred to the same quantity in the future, it will take longer than 9 years to compensate consumers for the loss of goods during the first 10 years. But at some point after 20 years, the initial sacrifice yields bigger and bigger dividends.

Policies to raise growth rates by increasing investment always have this characteristic: present consumption is to be reduced so that future consumption can be raised. Many people will be unattracted by sacrifice whose payoff is 10 or 20 years away. The question of how much of our present living standards should be sacrificed to raise the living standards of our heirs, who are probably going to be richer in any case, is troublesome. As one sceptic put it: 'Why should we sacrifice for them? What have they ever done for us?'

Theories of economic growth

Economists have done a great deal of theorising about economic growth over the last thirty years. Although many elegant models have been built and many conceptual issues clarified, it is probably safe to say that such meagre advice as we can give to policy-makers in market economies as yet owes little to these modern theories. In what follows we shall discuss growth from the view of the relation between the stock of capital and opportunities for investment in new capital.

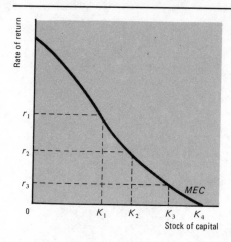

Fig. 42.3 The marginal efficiency of capital function

Growth in a world without learning Suppose that there is a known and fixed stock of projects that might be undertaken. Whenever the opportunity is ripe, some of them are undertaken, thus increasing the stock of capital goods and depleting the reservoir of unutilized investment opportunities. Of course, the most productive investments will be made first. Such a view of investment opportunities can be represented by a fixed marginal efficiency of capital function, of the kind met in Chapter 28. A function relating the stock of capital to the productivity of an additional unit of capital is drawn in Figure 42.3.

The downward slope of the *MEC* function indicates that increases in the stock of capital are assumed to bring smaller and smaller increases in output per £1 of investment. This shape is a prediction based on the 'law' of diminishing returns. If, with land, labour and knowledge constant, more and more capital is used, the net amount added by successive increments is predicted to diminish and possibly eventually to reach zero. Given this schedule, as capital is accumulated in a state of constant knowledge the society will move down its *MEC* function. Thus when the capital stock increases from K_1 to K_2 to K_3 the marginal return on capital falls from r_1 to r_2 to r_3. Eventually, when the capital stock is K_4, the marginal return reaches zero.

In such a 'non-learning' world, where new investment opportunities do not appear, growth occurs only as long as there are unutilized opportunities to use capital effectively to increase output. Growth is a transitory phenomenon that occurs because the society has a backlog of unutilized investment opportunities.[1]

So far we have discussed the marginal efficiency of capital. The average efficiency of capital refers to the average amount produced in the whole economy per unit of capital employed. It is measured by the ratio of total output to total capital; this is the OUTPUT/CAPITAL RATIO. Its inverse, the amount of capital divided by the amount of output, is the CAPITAL/OUTPUT RATIO.

Suppose, as is commonly believed, that both the average and the marginal efficiencies of capital are declining. In such an economy the output/capital ratio will be falling and the capital/output ratio will be rising as the capital stock grows.

---

[1] The argument has been conducted using concepts such as 'the' quantity of capital and 'the' productivity of capital. All that it requires is that there be a finite number of investment opportunities which can be arranged in descending order of the yield that they provide.

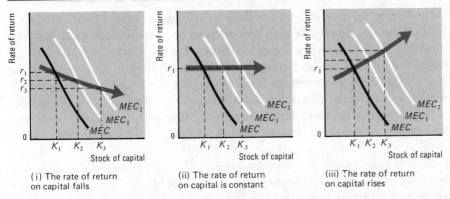

Fig. 42.4 Shifting investment opportunities and a growing capital stock: three cases

Two important implications of this theory of growth through capital accumulation with constant knowledge are the following:
(1) successive increases in capital accumulation will be less and less productive, and the capital/output ratio will be increasing; and
(2) the marginal efficiency of new capital will be decreasing and will eventually be pushed to zero as the backlog of investment opportunities is used up.

Growth with learning The steady depletion of the country's growth opportunities in the previous model resulted from the fact that new investment opportunities were never discovered or created. If, however, investment opportunities are created as well as used up by the passage of time, then the *MEC* function will shift outward period after period, and the effects of increasing the capital stock may be different. This is illustrated in Figure 42.4. Such outward shifts can be regarded as the consequences of 'learning' either about investment opportunities or about the techniques that create such opportunities. If learning occurs, it is next necessary to know how rapidly the *MEC* function will shift relative to the amount of capital investment being undertaken.

Three possibilities are shown in the Figure. In each case, the economy at period 1 has the *MEC* curve, a capital stock of K_1, and a rate of return of r_1. In period 2, the curve shifts to MEC_1 and there is new investment to increase the stock of capital to K_2. In period 3 the curve shifts to MEC_2 and there is new investment to increase the capital stock from K_2 to K_3. It is the relative size of the shift of the *MEC* curve and the additions to the capital stock that are important. In part (i), investment occurs more rapidly than increases in investment opportunities and the rate of return, r, must fall along the grey arrow. In (ii), investment occurs at exactly the same rate as investment opportunities and r is constant. In (iii), investment occurs less rapidly than increases in investment opportunities and r will rise.

In a world with rapid innovation:
(1) Successive increases in capital accumulation may prove highly productive, and the capital-output ratio may be constant or decreasing.
(2) In spite of large amounts of capital accumulation, the marginal efficiency of new capital may remain constant or even increase as new investment opportunities are created.

Gradual reduction in investment opportunities: the classical view: If, as in Figure 42.4(i), investment opportunities are created but at a slower rate than they are used up, there will be a tendency for a falling rate of return and an increasing ratio of capital to output. The predictions in this case are the same as those given above for the 'non-learning state'. This figure illustrates one version of the theory of growth held by the Classical economists. They saw the economic problem as one of fixed land, a rising population and a gradual exhaustion of investment opportunities. These things, they said, would ultimately force the economy into a static condition with no growth, very high capital/output ratios, and the marginal return on additional units of capital forced down to zero.

Constant or rising investment opportunities: one contemporary view: The Classical economists were pessimistic because they failed to appreciate the possibility of really rapid innovation – of technological progress that could push investment opportunities outward as rapidly as, or more rapidly than, they were used up. These two cases are shown in parts (ii) and (iii) of Figure 42.4. Because the facts (as will be seen in a moment) suggest that the economy generates new investment opportunities at least as rapidly as it uses up old ones, a general rethinking of the causes of growth has occurred. More attention is now devoted to understanding the *shifts* in the *MEC* curve over time than to its *shape*. The record shows that it is the shifts over time that have led to sustained growth.

Factors affecting growth Many factors affect economic growth, here we consider only a few.

Quantity of capital per worker: Man has always been a tool user, and it is still true today that more and more tools tend to lead to more and more output. As long as a society has unexploited investment opportunities, productive capacity can be increased by increasing the stock of capital. Capital accumulation has such a noticeable effect on output per person that it was once regarded as virtually the sole source of growth. If it were the only source of growth, however, it would lead to movement down the marginal efficiency curve and to the predictions printed on page 644. The evidence does not support these predictions.

> **The evidence suggests that investment opportunities have expanded at least as rapidly as investment in capital goods, so that the marginal efficiency of capital has not declined in spite of a great increase in the capital stock. Thus although capital accumulation has accounted for much observed growth, it cannot have been the only source of growth.**

Innovation: New knowledge and inventions can contribute markedly to the growth of potential national income. In order to see this, assume that a society devotes just enough of its resources to the production of capital goods to replace capital as it wears out. If the old capital is merely replaced in the same form, the capital stock will be constant and there will be no increase in the capacity to produce. Now assume that there is new knowledge, so that as old equipment wears out it is replaced by a different, more productive kind. National income will now be growing because of the increase in knowledge rather than because of the accumulation of more and more capital. This sort of increase in productive capacity is called EMBODIED TECHNICAL CHANGE because it inheres in the *form* of capital goods in use. Its historical importance is clearly visible.

The prevalence of the surnames Black and Smith in English-speaking countries (and their equivalents elsewhere) attests to the enormous proportion of human resources once devoted to the upkeep of horses, the main source of power a mere century ago. Nor was only labour involved. Over half of the world's arable land was devoted to growing feed for horses and other work animals. Vast investment opportunities were created when the horse was replaced by fossil fuels as a source of power. The freeing of resources to make other products also led to great improvements in living standards. The assembly line, and then automation, transformed the means of production. The aeroplane revolutionized transportation, and electronic devices have come to dominate communications. The silicon chip, which compresses thousands of electronic circuits in the space taken by one circuit 10 years ago, is making fundamental changes by computerizing many business and household activities. These innovations, plus less well-known but no less profound ones such as improvements in the strength of metals, the productivity of seeds and the techniques for recovering materials from the earth, have all tended to create new investment opportunities.

Less visible but nonetheless important changes occur through DISEMBODIED TECHNICAL CHANGE. These concern innovations that are not embodied in the form of the capital goods or raw materials used. One example is improved techniques of managerial control. Another follows from a better educated and healthier labour force.

The quality of human capital: 'Labour' is often talked about as if it were a homogenous input into production. But, clearly, a 'man-hour' is very different for a skilled mechanic, a scientist or a dustman, because what each of them produces in an hour is valued differently by the market.

The 'quality' of human capital has several aspects. One of these involves the health and longevity of the population. Improvements in these things are, of course, desired as ends in themselves, but they have consequences for production and productivity as well. There is no doubt that productivity per man-hour has been increased by cutting down on illness, accidents and absenteeism.

A second aspect of the quality of human capital concerns technical training, from learning to operate a machine to learning how to be a scientist. More subtly, there are often believed to be general social advantages to an educated population. It has been shown that productivity improves with literacy and that, in general, the better educated a person is the more adaptable he or she is to new challenges and thus, in the long run, the more productive.

The quantity of labour: Economies can be overpopulated or underpopulated economies, depending on whether the contribution to production of additional people would raise or lower the level of per capita income. Figure 42.5 relates population to per capita income and illustrates a case in which there is an optimum population for which living standards are at a maximum. The curve is drawn in

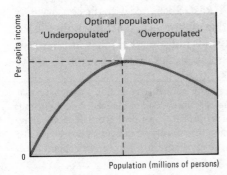

Fig. 42.5 One concept of the optimal population

the shape illustrated because resources and knowledge are assumed constant at any moment in time, and alternative populations are assumed to be exploiting them. After a certain size, the pressure of more and more population applying given techniques to a given quantity of resources will force diminishing returns into operation. Once output does not grow in proportion to additional population, output per person must fall.

Social and legal institutions: Social and religious habits can affect economic growth. In a society in which children are expected to stay in their fathers' occupations, it is more difficult for the labour force to change its characteristics and thus adapt to the requirements of growth than where upward mobility is itself a goal. Max Weber argued that the 'Protestant ethic' encourages the acquisition of wealth and is thus more likely to encourage growth than an ethic that directs activity away from the economic sphere.

Legal institutions may also affect growth. The pattern of ownership of land and natural resources, in affecting the way such resources are used, may affect their productivity. To take one example, if agricultural land is divided into very small parcels, one per family, it may be much more difficult to achieve the advantages of modern agriculture than if the land were available for large-scale farming. Many economists are thus concerned with patterns of land tenure.[1]

Policies to influence growth

Centrally controlled economies, in which growth is the overriding goal of policy, have often shown substantial initial successes in altering the growth rate. The main policy required is to engineer a massive and fairly abrupt shift of resources from current consumption to investment. There is usually such a backlog of obviously useful investment projects that, whether or not they are exploited wastefully, and whatever system of free enterprise or central control is used, the large-scale, new investment pays off in a more rapid growth rate for some considerable time.

Sustaining a high growth rate, even in an economy in which growth remains the overriding objective, may require things other than a high proportion of resources devoted to investment. Research and development of new ideas is important, and so are the entrepreneurial activities of innovating. Here there is much debate and little hard knowledge. Economists and historians will no doubt continue to debate the experience of Soviet Russia, India, China and other centrally planned economies for a long time to come. When they do, one of the basic questions will be: 'Is it possible for the bureaucracy of a centrally planned economy to sustain the risk-taking activities that are one of the basic components of the growth process in the same way that they are sustained by many private profit-seeking entrepreneurs in a free-market system?' Past experience with the conservative tendencies of bureaucratic systems must suggest that here is one of the most vulnerable points in the position taken by advocates of central planning. Conservatism is not something that just happens inexplicably in bureaucracies; it happens for the quite comprehensible reason that the incentive

---

[1] Economists are interested in such relationships for positive reasons, not for normative ones. If it is true that social, religious or legal patterns make growth more difficult, this does not mean that they are undesirable; instead, it means that the benefits of these institutions must now be weighed against the costs, of which their effect on growth is one. If people derive satisfaction from a religion whose beliefs inhibit growth, if they value a society in which everyone owns his own land and is more nearly self-sufficient than in another society, they may be quite willing to pay a price in terms of growth opportunities forgone.

system often discourages individuals from taking risks: punishment for failure is focused on a few individuals, while reward for success is diffused throughout the system.

In the mixed economies of Western Europe, North America and other industrially developed regions, growth is but one of a half a dozen or more of the key objectives of the central authorities. In such economies the problem is much more difficult than in the 'growth-dominated' economies referred to above. The policy-makers in these relatively advanced economies want more growth, but only if it does not conflict too much with other goals of policy. They may ask what tools are available to encourage a little more growth without fundamentally changing the present nature of the economy. They may attempt to influence each of the factors listed earlier as affecting growth. The problem, however, is that although we have some qualitative knowledge, we have little quantitative knowledge. If, for example, we spend £10 million more on education each year, what will be the quantitative effect on our growth rate and on other goals? (There will be £10 million less to spend on other projects.) Nonetheless, central authorities do have growth policies, and they do try to influence the factors thought to affect growth. One approach is to encourage investment by making it more profitable. There is a real fear felt by many that profits in European countries are so low that investment in industrial plant and equipment is severely discouraged. This issue is further discussed in Chapter 46. Profitability can be raised by income policies that try to keep real wages from consuming 'too much' of the profits, by direct subsidies to lower the cost of investment or by tax concessions to raise the profitability of investment-related activities.

Invention and innovation clearly play an important role in growth, but it is not so easy to turn them on and off. There is substantial faith that increases in research and development (R and D) do pay off in more rapid innovation. The government itself engages in a good deal of R and D, provides research grants to others, and in certain areas participates in joint projects with business firms. We are still uncertain about the quantitative importance of R and D in the growth process. Much current research is being devoted to estimating its importance.

Public expenditures on education at all levels, but particularly on higher education and training of scientific personnel, have recently come under pressure due to attempts to cut back government expenditure in many advanced countries. It is thought that these expenditures have fostered growth, both in the sense of positively promoting it by increasing the likelihood of discovering new and better techniques, and by avoiding barriers to it that arise if there are not enough competent people to operate the new machines that are invented. Serious empirical studies indicate that, at the present levels of education, further expenditures on education 'pay' in the sense of providing benefits in excess of all costs, including the output forgone during the educational period. Obviously for a society, as for an individual, a point can be reached beyond which further education is not wise, but the present evidence indicates that we have not yet reached that point.

Growth requires change. Labour and other factors of production must be reallocated from industries that are declining in terms of total employment and into industries that are expanding. If restrictive practices and union-enforced manning agreements prevent much of this reallocation from occurring, growth will be greatly slowed. Some potentially cost-saving innovations will not be introduced because their benefits cannot be reaped. Others will be adopted but their full effect on growth will not be felt because labour will be allocated to 'overmanning' the new machines rather than being reallocated to other industries where it could increase output. Thus measures to enhance labour mobility and to allow the potential cost reductions of new innovations actually to be achieved can greatly affect the growth rate.

This brief discussion must make it clear that we are not able to control the growth rate with the nice degree of precision with which we can control the level of total demand or even the balance of payments. Indeed, central authorities in Western countries do not have the ability to raise or to lower the growth rate by changing their policies, let alone to alter it by x per cent. We must conclude that, although we do know something about the growth process, we do not know nearly enough to give policy-makers in market economies the ability to exert *measurable* control over the rate of economic growth, at least over small ranges of variation.

Current controversies over economic growth

Current controversies over economic growth concern whether or not further sustained growth is either desirable or possible. The question of desirability can be reviewed by examining the cases that might be made by advocates and opponents of further economic growth.

An open letter to the ordinary citizen from a supporter of the Growth-Is-Good School

Dear Ordinary Citizen:

You live in the world's first civilization that is devoted principally to satisfying *your* needs rather than those of a privileged minority. Past civilizations have, without exception, been based on leisure and high consumption for a tiny upper class, a reasonable living standard for a numerically small middle class, and hard work with little more than subsistence consumption for the great mass of people. In the past, the average person saw little of the civilized and civilizing products of the economy, except when he or she was toiling to produce them.

What is unique about the continuing Industrial Revolution is that it is based on mass-produced goods for consumption by the ordinary citizen. It also ushered in a period of sustained economic growth that has raised the consumption standards of ordinary citizens to levels previously reserved throughout the entire history of civilization for a tiny privileged minority. Reflect on a few examples: travel, live and recorded music, art, good food, inexpensive books, universal literacy and a genuine chance to be educated if you want to be. Most important of all, there is enough leisure to provide time and energy to enjoy these and myriad other products of the modern industrial economy.

Would any ordinary citizen seriously doubt the benefits of growth and wish to be back in the world of 150 or 500 years ago, in his or her same relative social and economic position? Most surely the answer is no. But we cannot say the same for persons with incomes in the top 1 to 2 per cent of the income distribution. Economic growth has destroyed much of their privileged consumption position: they must now vie with the masses when visiting the world's beauty spots and be annoyed, while lounging on the terrace of their palatial mansions, by the sound of chartered jets carrying ordinary people to holidays in far places. Many of the rich resent their loss of exclusive rights to luxury consumption, and it is not surprising that they find their intellectual apologists.

Whether they know it or not, the anti-growth economists – such as John Kenneth Galbraith, Joan Robinson and Ed Mishan – are not the social revolutionaries they assume themselves to be. They are the counter-revolutionaries who would set back the clock of material progress for the ordinary person. They say that growth has produced pollution and wasteful consumption of trivia that contribute nothing to human happiness. But the democratic solution to pollution is not to reduce output to such a low level that pollution is trivial; it is to accept pollution as a transitional phase connected with the ushering in of mass consumption, to keep the mass consumption, and to learn to control the pollution.

It is only through further growth that the average citizen can enjoy consumption standards (of travel, culture, medical and health care, etc.) now available to people in the top 20 per cent of the income distribution – which includes the intellectuals who earn large royalties from the books they write denouncing growth. If you think that extra income confers little or no real benefit, ask that top 20 per cent of the income distribution to trade incomes with the average citizen.

Ordinary citizens, do not be deceived by disguised elitist doctrines. Remember that the very rich and the elite have much to gain by stopping growth – and even more by rolling it back – but you have everything to gain by letting it go forward.

Onward!

I. Growthman

An open letter to the ordinary citizen from a supporter of the Growth-Is-Bad School

Dear Ordinary Citizen:

You live in a world that is being despoiled by a mindless search for ever higher levels of consumption at the cost of all other values. Once upon a time, men and women knew how to enjoy creative work and to derive satisfaction from simple activities undertaken in scarce, and hence highly valued, leisure time. Today the ordinary worker is a mindless cog in an assembly-line process that turns out ever more goods that advertisers must work overtime to persuade people to consume.

Statisticians and politicians count the increasing flow of material output as a triumph of modern civilization. Consider not the flow of output in general, but the individual products that it contains. You arise from your electric-blanketed bed, clean your teeth with an electric toothbrush, open with an electric tin-opener a tin of the sad remains of a once-proud orange, you eat your bread baked from super-refined and chemically refortified flour, and you climb into your car to sit in vast traffic jams on exhaust-polluted motorways. And so the day goes, with endless consumption of high-technology products that give you no more real satisfaction than the simple products consumed by your grandfathers: soft woolly blankets, natural bristle toothbrushes, real oranges, old-fashioned and coarse but healthy bread, and public transport that moved on uncongested roads and gave its passengers time to chat with their neighbours, to read, or just to daydream.

The slick magazines of today tell you that by consuming more you are happier. But happiness lies not in increasing consumption but in increasing the ratio of *satisfaction of wants* to *total wants*. Since the more you consume the more the advertisers persuade you that you want to consume, you are almost certainly less happy than the average citizen in a small town in 1900, whom we can visualize sitting on the family porch, sipping beer or lemonade, and enjoying the antics of the children as they play with discarded barrel staves and home-made skipping ropes.

Today the landscape is dotted with countless factories producing the plastic trivia of the modern industrial society and drowning you in a cloud of noise, air, and water pollution. The countryside is despoiled by slag heaps and dangerous nuclear power stations that produce the energy that is devoured insatiably by modern factories and motor vehicles.

Worse still, our precious heritage of natural resources is fast being used up. Spaceship earth flies, captainless, in its senseless orgy of self-consuming consumption. Now is the time to stop this madness. We must stabilize production, reduce pollution, conserve our natural resources, and seek justice through a more equitable distribution of existing total income.

A long time ago Malthus taught us that if we do not limit population voluntarily, nature will do it for us in a cruel and savage manner. Today the same is true of output. If we do not halt its growth voluntarily, the halt will be imposed on us by a disastrous increase in pollution and a rapid exhaustion of natural resources.

Citizens, awake! Shake off the shackles of growth worship, learn to enjoy the bounty that is yours already, and eschew the endless, self-defeating search for increased happiness through ever-increasing consumption.

Upward!

A. Non-growthman

Both of these cases have real merit. Possibly a balanced judgement lies somewhere in between, although both extremes have their sincere supporters.

Are there limits to growth?

Those opposed to growth argue that sustained growth for another century is undesirable; some even argue that it is impossible. Of course all terrestrial things have an ultimate limit. Astronomers predict that the solar system itself will die as the sun burns out in another 6,000 million or so years. To be of practical concern, however, a limit must be within some reasonable planning horizon. Several books published in the 1970s predicted the imminence of a growth-induced doomsday. They predicted that living standards will reach a peak about the turn of the century and then, in the words of Professor Nordhaus, a leading critic of these models, will 'descend inexorably to the level of Neanderthal man'. Whatever the final verdict, there can be no doubt that the debate that raged about these so-called doomsday models has helped to give needed awareness of, and attention to, problems of population growth, pollution, and exhaustion of the supplies of specific natural resources. While there is debate, on many matters there is also substantial consensus.

The increasing pressure on natural resources The years since the Second World War have seen a rapid acceleration in the utilization of the world's resources, particularly the fossil fuels and the basic minerals. The world's population has increased from under 2·5 billion to over 4 billion in that period, which alone increases the demand for all of the world's resources. But the fact of population growth greatly understates the pressure on resources. Calculations by Professor Nathan Keyfitz and others focus on the resource use by the so-called middle class, defined roughly as those who can claim a lifestyle of the level enjoyed by 90 per cent of American families. This middle class, which today includes about one-sixth of the world's population, consumes 15 to 30 times as much oil per capita and, overall, at least five times as much of the earth's scarce resources per capita as do the other 'poor' five-sixths of the population.

The world's middle class has grown by nearly 4 per cent per year – twice the rate of population growth – over the post-war period. The resulting increases in demand in the last two decades have outstripped discovery of new supplies and caused crises in energy and mineral supplies as well as food shortages. Yet the 4 per cent growth rate of this middle class is too slow for the billions who live in underdeveloped countries and see the fruits of development all around them. Even if population growth is reduced, therefore, the pressure on our resources of energy, minerals, and food is likely to accelerate.

Another way to look at the problem of resource pressure is to note that present technology and resources could not possibly support the present population of the world at the standard of living of today's average West German, French or American middle-class family. Such a shift in level of living, if made overnight, would more than quadruple the world's demand for resources. The demand for oil would increase tenfold. Since these calculations (most unrealistically) assume no population growth anywhere in the world and no growth in living standards for the richest sixth of the world's population, the fact of insufficient resources is manifest. On all of this there is no serious disagreement among informed people.

Doomsday predictions Some people foresee imminent doom. The doomsday advocates combine the undoubted acceleration of resource utilization referred to above with a series of more questionable assumptions: first, that there is no technical progress; second, that no new resources are discovered or rendered usable by new techniques; and third, that there is no substitution of more plentiful resources for those that become scarce. Under these circumstances, exhaustion of one or more key resources is predictable. If, in addition, population growth continues at historical rates, this exhaustion will occur relatively quickly – certainly within the next century. And if the increasing production continues to pollute the atmosphere faster than the pollutants can be absorbed, the capacity to produce will be diminished and the quality of life further reduced.

These are the basic assumptions of the doomsday models. Doom can come in several ways (or in any combination of them): natural resources depletion, famine due to overpopulation, or an increasing and ultimately fatal pollution of the land, sea or air.

The many possible routes to disaster foreseen by doomsday advocates mean that no single restraint will suffice to prevent it. If both natural resource usage and pollution are controlled, doom results from overpopulation. Population control will prove self-defeating because it leads to an increase in the per capita food supply and in the standard of living – which in turn generates forces to trigger a resurgence in population growth. The only way to prevent disaster is to stop economic growth at once through a comprehensive plan, drastically curtailing natural resource use (by 75 per cent), pollution generation (by 50 per cent), investment (by 40 per cent), and the birth rate (by 30 per cent). Since the countries of the world are not likely, within the next forty years, to agree on the stern measures needed to meet these targets, a descent down the slippery slope of declining living standards during our own lifetimes is inevitable – and disaster looms for our grandchildren.

A reply to doomsday Critics reply that predictions of imminent doom are as old as human life itself and about as reliable as predictions of the arrival of universal peace and goodwill on earth. They recognize the pressures on the world's resources, and they concede that at present rates of utilization we would clearly run out of some specific resources in the foreseeable future. They argue, however, that the doomsday models can be faulted in several critical ways.

(1) The assumption of constant technology (the case of growth without learning is analysed on page

644) is nonsense in the light of past human history. Constant technology and a declining marginal efficiency of capital is sufficient by itself to reduce first the marginal and then the average product of capital to zero. The attempt to sustain growth in such a world must eventually produce zero per capita output! But, they argue, all of our economic history shows this key assumption of the doomsday models to be invalid. Nothing could be clearer than that technology is not constant and that people are ingenious in finding ways not only to economize on the use of scarce resources but also to substitute materials that are common for those that become scarce. Just as ample taconite replaced scarce iron-ore in making steel, just as ample coal replaced scarce charcoal in smelting steel, and just as synthetic rubber replaced natural rubber in making tyres, so it is reasonable to expect new energy sources to replace fossil fuels. The potential supplies of nuclear and solar energy are inexhaustible.

(2) The assumption of a fixed and relatively small supply of resources that are consumed by production of goods and services is nonsense. It defies the law of conservation of mass energy and denies the fact that in the earth's crust beneath the sea and further in towards the core there are vast supplies of mineral resources, some located and charted and others known to exist in a general way. As with assumption (1), this assumption is sufficient to produce disaster by itself. A finite supply of limited resources that is destroyed in the course of production must soon be exhausted if output increases exponentially.

(3) The model has no place for the co-ordinating effects of the price system. As a particular resource becomes scarce, its price rises and this has many effects: people are induced to try harder to discover new supplies, it becomes profitable to produce from known sources that were previously too costly, producers are induced to substitute other resources within already known technologies and a search for new substitutes and new technologies is encouraged. Such trends are observable in the pattern of use of most resources over the past centuries, yet the model makes no allowance for them.

The list has been extended to a score or more of similar points, all of which, say the critics, show the pitfalls ready to trap the person who approaches the economy without using the insights provided by a century of theory and observation of the operation of the price system. Thus, say the critics, the model only proves the consistency of logic: from silly assumptions one can only derive silly conclusions. Can it be doubted, ask the critics of doomsday models, that a society that has developed birth-control pills and explored Mars can solve the problems of over-population and pollution?

A tentative verdict Most economists agree that conjuring up absolute limits to growth based on the assumptions of constant technology and fixed exhaustible resources is not warranted. But this does not mean there is no cause for concern. Any barrier can perhaps be overcome by technological advances – but not in an instant, and not automatically. Clearly there is a problem of timing: how soon can we discover and put into practice the knowledge required to solve the problems that are made ever more imminent by growth in population, growth in affluence, and the desire for growth of many who now live at very low incomes. There is no guarantee at all that a whole generation will not be caught in transition, with enormous, if not cataclysmic, social and political consequences. The nightmare conjured up by the doomsday models may have served its purpose if it helps to focus our attention on these problems.

43

Demand management 1: fiscal policy[1]

There is no doubt that government can exert a significant influence on national income. During major wars, when governments throw fiscal caution to the winds and engage in massive military spending, both GDP and employment tend to rise to unprecedented heights. UK government expenditure rose dramatically in real terms and as a percentage of GDP from 1938 to 1944 as the UK converted from a peacetime to a wartime economy. At the same time the unemployment rate fell from 13 to less than 1 per cent. Economists agree that it was the increase in the government's aggregate expenditure that caused the rise in the GDP and the fall in unemployment. Most European countries had similar experiences during rearmament in the late 1930s or early 1940s. It is this ability of the government to influence the macroeconomic behaviour of the economy that gives rise to macroeconomic policies.

We can distinguish a hierarchy of macroeconomic policies. At the top is MACROECONOMIC POLICY itself, which includes any measure directed at influencing such macroeconomic variables as the overall levels of employment, unemployment, national income and prices. One branch of macroeconomic policy is DEMAND MANAGEMENT, which seeks to influence macroeconomic variables by working through aggregate demand. One branch of demand management is FISCAL POLICY, which seeks to influence aggregate demand by working through the *IS* curve. We study fiscal policy in this Chapter, while in Chapter 44 we study MONETARY POLICY, which, as the second main arm of demand management, seeks to influence aggregate demand by working through the *LM* curve.[2] The other branch of macroeconomic policies seeks to work through aggregate supply. Such policies have recently been dubbed 'supply-side economics', which is rather unfortunate because a strong emotional reaction, for or against, is usually evoked by this term. As positive economists we want to try, in so far as we can, to make a dispassionate assessment of supply-side issues. One final policy that we should mention is STABILIZATION POLICY. This is the attempt to reduce fluctuations in income and employment and, if possible, stabilize national income at its full-

---

[1] For background material for this chapter see Harbury and Lipsey, Chapter 9.

[2] The term demand management is sometimes reserved in Britain to mean only fiscal policy. This is an historical accident because fiscal policy was for decades the main tool of demand manipulation. The logic of the case clearly requires, however, that monetary policy is also a tool of demand management. Demand management seeks to shift the aggregate demand curve. Both monetary and fiscal policy shift that curve (and also shift the aggregate expenditure curve). They are both instruments for operating on the demand side of the economy and are distinct from the instruments of supply management that seek to operate on the aggregate supply curve.

employment level. The most commonly used tool of stabilization policy is demand management.

The theory of fiscal policy

Fiscal policy and the *IS* curve

Earlier we developed the IS–LM and the AD relations from the simple two-sector model of households and firms. Since fiscal policy works through the IS curve, our first task is to derive the IS curve for the three-sector model that includes government. The relations are the same as those given by equations (1) to (9) on pp. 543–5 of Chapter 36 (with the addition of a constant to the consumption function and a linear equation relating I to r following from the discussion in Chapter 40).

Definitions	$E \equiv C+I+G$	(1)
	$Y_d \equiv Y-T+Q$	(2)
Behaviour	$C = cY_d+a_0 \qquad 0<c<1, 0<a_0$	(3)
	$I = br+a_1 \qquad b<0<a_1$	(4)
	$T = tY \qquad 0<t<1$	(5)
	$G = G^*$	(6)
	$Q = Q^*$	(7)
Equilibrium condition	$E = Y$	(8)

Substitution then produces the equation for the IS curve:[1]

$$r = -\frac{G^*+A^*+cQ^*}{b} + \frac{1-c+ct}{b}Y \quad,$$

(9)

where $A^* = a_0+a_1$. This is a simple linear equation of the form

$$r = \alpha_0+\alpha_1 Y \quad.$$

(10)

Note that as usual all the elements of income-creating, autonomous expenditure enter additively. An autonomous increase in the G or I or C functions of £1 all have the same effect. Transfer payments, however, only matter in the proportion, c, in which they are spent to create national income. The slope coefficient $[1-c+ct]/b$ is negative (making α_1 negative in (10)) since both c and t are positive but less than unity while b is negative. This is as it should be, since it tells us that the IS curve slopes downwards. The minus sign outside of the term containing the autonomous expenditure constants converts their influence into a positive one (since they are divided by a negative constant, b). This makes α_0 positive in (10).

---

[1] Straight substitution into (8) with no further manipulation yields

$$Y = c(Y-tY+Q^*)+br+G^*+a_0+a_1$$
$$= cY-ctY+cQ^*+br+G^* +a_0+a_1 \quad.$$

Subtracting $cY-ctY$ from both sides and factoring out the Y:

$$Y(1-c+ct) = cQ^*+br+G^*+a_0+a_1 \quad.$$

Subtracting $cQ^*+G^*+a_0+a_1$ from both sides and dividing through by b yields equation (9) in the text.

Inspection of (9) tells us what we need to know formally about the effects of fiscal policy. An increase in G^* or Q^* increases the constant in the IS curve and this shifts the curve outwards parallel to itself as shown in Figure 43.1(i). To shift the IS curve from IS_1 to IS_2, a larger increase is needed in transfer payments than in government expenditure on goods and services, since all of the initial expenditure creates national income in the case of G, while only cQ of the initial transfer creates national income in the case of Q.

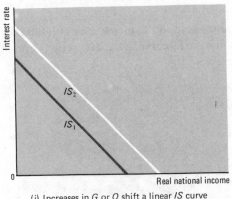
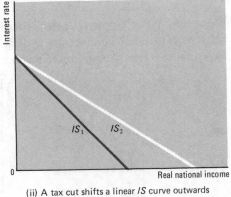

(i) Increases in G or Q shift a linear IS curve outwards parallel to itself

(ii) A tax cut shifts a linear IS curve outwards and flattens its slope

Fig. 43.1 The effects on the IS curve of increases in government expenditure on goods and services, increases in government transfer payments and decreases in tax rates

The effect of a change in tax rates is also clear by inspection. Consider a cut in t. This reduces the value of $1-c+ct$ and so lowers the absolute value of the slope coefficient, $(1-c+ct)/b$, which means raising its algebraic value (e.g. from -0.6 to -0.5).The IS curve thus gets flatter, as shown by the shift from IS_1 to IS_2 in Figure 43.1(ii). Raising t has the reverse effect. It lowers the algebraic value of the slope coefficient thus steepening the IS curve, e.g. from IS_2 to IS_1 in Figure 43.1(ii). The common sense of these results is as follows. Raising any element of autonomous expenditure has the same effect on expenditure whatever the initial equilibrium level of income. It therefore increases equilibrium income by the same amount whatever the starting point (i.e. the IS curve shifts parallel to itself). Cutting tax rates, however, has a proportionate effect on expenditure, so its absolute effect depends on the initial size of national income. Thus equilibrium income for any given interest rate increases in proportion to the initial equilibrium income (i.e. each point on the IS curve shifts out a constant percentage amount).

As we saw in Chapter 40 (see especially Figure 40.4, with its surrounding discussion), shifts in the IS curve, by increasing equilibrium income, cause the AD curve to shift in the same direction.

> **Increases in government expenditure on goods and services or on transfer payments, and also cuts in tax rates, shift the IS curve, and hence the aggregate demand curve, outwards to the right. Decreases in expenditure and increases in tax rates have the opposite effect.**

In subsequent sections we shall put some interpretive flesh on these bare analytical bones.

The 'paradox of thrift'

Not so many years ago it was generally accepted, and indeed many people still fervently believe, that a prudent government should always balance its budget. The argument is based on an analogy with what seems prudent for an individual: it is a foolish person whose current expenditure consistently exceeds his current revenue so that he gets steadily further into debt and, so went the argument, what is good for the individual must be good for the nation. The fallacy was exposed in the so-called 'paradox of thrift', which we now consider.

Household saving What happens if, *ceteris paribus*, all households try to increase the amount they save at each level of income? This increase in thriftiness shifts the *IS* curve to the left: at each level of income, expenditure is less, so equilibrium income is also less.

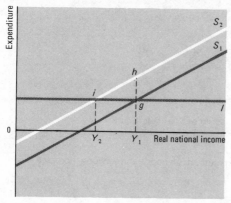 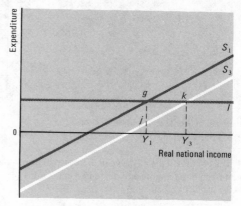

(i) An increase in the desire to save results in a fall in income and no increase in actual saving if autonomous expenditure remains constant

(ii) A reduction in the desire to save results in a rise in income and no reduction in actual saving if autonomous expenditure remains constant

Fig. 43.2 The paradox of thrift

We can see in a more intuitive way what is happening if we return to the simple two-sector model of Chapter 35, where interest rates are constant, and use the withdrawals and injections approach. The increase in the desire to save shifts the withdrawals function upwards, say from S_1 to S_2 in Figure 43.2(i). As long as income remains at its original equilibrium level Y_1, the volume of desired savings is increased by gh. But now income will fall until total saving has been reduced to its original level so that saving is again equal to investment. The effect on actual savings of the shift of the savings function from S_1 to S_2 is totally offset by a movement *along* the new S schedule from h to i.

Now consider an increase in households' desire to consume at each level of income. This means that less will be saved at each level of income so that the savings function will be shifted downwards, say from S_1 to S_3 in Figure 43.2(ii). Income will rise until saving is once again equal to the unchanged level of investment. In this case, the downward shift in the savings function from S_1 to S_3 raises national income from Y_1 to Y_3. It also leads to no change in the actual amount of savings because the effect of the attempt to reduce saving by gj is offset by the movement along the new curve to the point k.

We have now derived the prediction of the so-called PARADOX OF THRIFT. In our more complete model, the predictions are that, *ceteris paribus*, an increase in the desire to save shifts the aggregate demand function to the left while a decrease in the desire to save shifts the *AD* function to the right.

Other things being equal, the more thrifty households are, the lower will be the level of national income and total employment. The more spendthrift households are, the higher the level of national income and employment will be.

This, of course, is not a paradox in the formal sense. It is indeed a straightforward prediction of the theory of income determination. It is called a 'paradox' because it seems paradoxical to those people who expect good advice to a single household, which wishes to raise its wealth and its future income ('save, save and save some more'), to apply also to the economy as a whole.

Government taxing and spending The paradox of thrift applies to governments as well as to households. If governments decide to save more, they must raise taxes or cut expenditure. Both of these policies shift the *IS* curve leftwards and cause national income to fall. If governments decide to save less (i.e., to become more spendthrift), they lower taxes and/or raise spending. This shifts the *IS* curve rightwards and raises national income.

The paradox of thrift implies that substantial unemployment is corrected by encouraging governments, firms and households to spend rather than to save. In times of unemployment and depression, frugality will only make things worse. This prediction goes directly against our inclination to tighten our belts when times are tough. The idea that it is possible to spend one's way out of a depression offends the consciences of people who were reared in the belief that success is based on hard work and frugality, and not on prodigality. As a result, the suggestion very often provokes great hostility.

The paradox of thrift was not generally understood during the Great Depression of the 1930s. At that time, many mistaken policies were followed. One such is suggested in a message delivered by King George V to the House of Commons on 8 September 1931, on the occasion of the formation of a new National Government after the collapse of the Labour administration:

The present condition of the national finances, in the opinion of His Majesty's Ministers, calls for the imposition of additional taxation, and for the effecting of economies in public expenditure.

At the time, the unemployment rate stood at 21 per cent of the labour force! In the US, President Roosevelt, though he achieved the reputation of grappling vigorously with the problems of the decade while others shilly-shallied, showed no more appreciation of the real nature of the basic situation than did the British leaders. In his first inaugural address in 1933 he stated:

Our greatest primary task is to put people to work. . . . [This task] can be helped by insistence that the Federal, state and local governments act forthwith on the demand that their cost be drastically reduced. . . . There must be a strict supervision of all banking and credits and investment.

At the time, the American unemployment rate was 23 per cent!

National-income theory predicts that the correct response to the Great Depression of the 1930s was to encourage firms, households and governments to spend and not to save. Attempts to save or to cut government expenditure would only serve to lower national income and raise unemployment even further. The suffering and misery of that unhappy decade would have been greatly reduced had those in authority known even as much economics as is contained in this chapter. Another case which many people felt fitted the paradox was the attempt of the British government from 1979 to

1982 to reduce the public-sector borrowing requirement in the face of a very serious economic slump. There may have been good reasons for wishing to reduce government expenditure and borrowing as a long-term policy, but to do so at a time of slump was to exert a short-term downward pressure on expenditure and income at a time when a substantial output gap already existed.

Conditions necessary for the paradox to operate The striking prediction of the paradox of thrift depends critically on two key assumptions.

(1) There is a significant amount of unemployment of all resources, capital equipment as well as labour, so that the level of output depends solely on aggregate demand. In these circumstances anything that reduces aggregate demand reduces output and employment, and anything that increases AD increases output and employment.

(2) Desired investment is assumed to be completely independent of desired savings. There is no reason, according to the theory, why the amount that firms wish to spend on investment at any level of income should bear any particular relation to the amount that households wish to save.

First consider assumption (1). If the economy is at, or near, full employment of any important factor of production, then this assumption will not be correct. Where full employment already obtains, a decrease in household saving and an increase in consumption expenditure will not cause an increase in real output and employment. In such circumstances the effect of an increase in spending will probably be to cause the price level to rise. An increase in saving, however, with its accompanying decrease in spending, will tend to reduce output and employment.

Now consider assumption (2). If this assumption is not correct, the paradox of thrift will not apply. If, for example, the saving and investment functions are linked together in any way such that changes in desired household saving cause changes in investment, there will be offsetting shifts in *both* the savings and investment functions whenever the desire to save changes. Such offsetting shifts can leave the aggregate expenditure function, hence the *IS* curve, unchanged. An increase in the desire to save, for example, will shift the saving function upwards but, by permitting more investment, it may also shift up the investment function so that there is no downward pressure on national income.

This second key assumption of the paradox of thrift reveals a key difference that – then and now – separates extreme Keynesian models from extreme Classical models. Let us look at these extreme cases in more detail.

The Classical theory: The prevailing view about the working of the economy (at least among English-speaking economists) prior to the publication of Keynes's *General Theory* has come to be called 'Classical'. Historians are quick to point out that there were many disagreements among economists of the time, and that to talk of '*the* Classical theory' is to caricature a complex situation. Nonetheless, there was a more or less common view on many points and, for better or worse, the term 'Classical theory' or 'Classical model' has come to be used to express one consistent version of the views prevalent before Keynes. This book is not a treatise on the history of economics, and we would not bother to describe this view of investment and saving were it not for the fact that it has recently gained substantial support from a group of economists who believe that the profession was altogether too uncritical in accepting Keynesian theory and rejecting Classical theory.

The basic proposition of the 'Classical theory' is that changes in investment and saving cause changes only in the rate of interest. The theory, which is called the *loanable funds theory of interest*, can be summarized as follows: (1) the desired level of investment falls as the rate of interest rises; (2) the desired level of saving rises as the rate of interest rises; (3) the rate of interest changes smoothly and rapidly in such a way as to keep the volume of investment always equal to the volume of saving. As long as the rate of interest always keeps saving and investment equal, there is no reason for changes in either saving or investment to cause changes in income. This is illustrated in Figure 43.3, which shows a demand for investment and a supply of savings both plotted against the rate of interest. If desired savings exceed desired investment as they do by the amount $b-c$ at interest rate r_2 in the Figure, then the rate of interest will fall until savings and investment are equated (at the amount a and the interest rate r_1 in the Figure). According to this theory, the whole process happens quickly enough so that there is no significant fall in income generated during the time in which investment is less than saving.

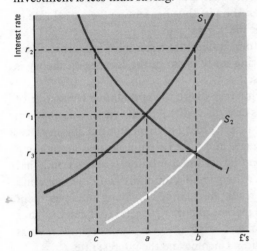

Fig. 43.3 The loanable funds theory of interest

Shifts in the desire to save and invest cause interest rates to change. Consider, for example, an increased desire to save that shifts the savings function from S_1 to S_2. At the original rate of interest, r_1, desired saving exceeds desired investment. But the surplus of funds for investment will quickly force the interest rate down to r_3 where desired savings are once again equal to desired investment.

> The Classical theory of saving, investment and interest is built on two important assumptions: (1) the investment schedule is sufficiently interest-elastic that suitable variations in the rate of interest can bring about investment sufficient to match any volume of saving that may be forthcoming; and (2) the rate of interest is perfectly free to vary, so as to bring saving and investment into equality.

Notice that this theory provides an automatic link between the most important withdrawal and the most important injection: it ensures that, except for temporary fluctuations, the volume of saving will be equal to the volume of investment. Thus as long as the central authorities pursue a balanced-budget policy ($G = T$), the volume of withdrawals can differ from the volume of injections only by the difference between imports and exports, which will generally be a trivial amount compared to the whole of national income.

In the Classical theory, the equilibrium level of national income was that which, with only temporary aberrations, produced full employment. It was believed that, if there was unemployed labour, wage rates would fall, and the demand for labour increase until full employment prevailed. This labour-market mechanism kept income at the full-employment level; it then did not matter how much people wished to save at this equilibrium level of income, because the interest rate would fluctuate until firms wished to invest exactly what households wished to save. This model of the economy is very close to that espoused by the modern group of economists called new classicists.

The Keynesian theory: The theory that the interest rate will fluctuate so as to equate saving and investment was challenged by Keynes' theory of interest rates. The extreme version of the Keynesian theory was that the interest rate was completely stabilized by the speculative actions of bond-holders: according to this theory, bondholders have an idea of the normal rate of interest, and whenever fluctuations in current savings and investment cause even small changes in the price of bonds, they will buy or sell from their existing stocks of bonds, thus preventing the actual rate of interest from diverging far from what they believe to be the normal rate.

If the interest rate is not free to vary, what will restore equilibrium when there is a large shift in either savings or investment? The equilibrium-restoring mechanism in the Keynesian theory is income fluctuations of the kind we have already analysed.

Although Keynes' liquidity preference theory of interest where the speculative behaviour of wealth-holders completely stabilized the interest rate is now discredited, the Keynesian mechanism whereby fluctuations in desired savings or investment cause fluctuations in income remains in place. The essence of Keynesian-style models is, first, that wages and prices are not flexible enough in a downwards direction to produce full employment automatically and continuously and, second, that the rate of interest fluctuates so that wealth-holders are willing to hold the entire *stock* of money and bonds that is in existence at any moment of time. As a result, fluctuations in saving and investment will, as we have seen in the *IS–LM* models, cause both income and interest rates to fluctuate. Thus the modern theory of income lies between the Classical and original Keynesian extremes: savings and investment are equated by fluctuations in both national income and the interest rate.

A major difference between the Keynesian and the Classical theory is that in the former, income fluctuates in order to bring saving and investment into equality, while in the latter the rate of interest does the same job.

The predictions of the paradox of thrift depend critically on the assumption that saving and investment decisions are taken to a great extent by different groups in society and that there is no mechanism whereby a change in desired savings at a particular level of income will cause an offsetting change in the investment at the same level of income.

This long digression on the paradox of thrift illustrates the importance of variations in aggregate demand in causing variations in income and employment during times of recession. We now look a little more generally at fiscal policy as a means of shifting the aggregate demand curve under any set of initial conditions.

The budget balance

The BUDGET BALANCE refers to the difference between all government revenue and all government expenditures. For this purpose government expenditure includes both purchases of currently produced goods and services, and transfer payments. There are three possibilities for the relations between these two flows. If current revenue is exactly equal to current expenditure, the government has a BALANCED BUDGET; if revenues exceed expenditures, there is a BUDGET SURPLUS; if revenues fall short of expenditures, there is a BUDGET DEFICIT. If the government raises its spending without raising taxes, its extra expenditure may be said to be *deficit-financed*. If the extra spending is accompanied by an equal increase in tax revenue, we speak of a *balanced-budget change in spending*.

The public-sector borrowing requirement   The importance of public-sector production by nationalized industries in Britain has caused attention to be focused on a larger concept of the deficit. This is called the PUBLIC-SECTOR BORROWING REQUIREMENT (PSBR), which is the combined excess of expenditure over revenue of the central government, the local authorities and public corporations. The PSBR is therefore the deficit of all branches of government plus the deficit of all publicly owned corporations. Once public corporations are included in any concept of the deficit, it becomes important to be clear on the concept of a deficit.

A deficit means more is spent than is taken in. But what if what is spent is for the purchase of capital? Any successful private enterprise knows it must often borrow now to pay for capital that will yield revenue in the future. For this reason budget deficits are common in expanding private industries that are borrowing for expansion. Thus a positive PSBR does not necessarily mean government prodigality. If the borrowing is to meet current expenditures such as transfer payments or civil service salaries, there may be real cause for concern, but if the borrowing is to cover capital expenses on, say, a new power station that will produce revenues sufficient to cover its capital costs, there may be no need for concern.

> **The PSBR records the excess of expenditures for current and capital purposes of governments and public corporations over all of their current revenues.**

Financial implications of budget deficits and surpluses   The difference between the public sector's expenditure and current revenue must show up as changes in the level of public-sector debt. An excess of expenditure over revenues requires additional borrowing, for which there are two main sources: the central bank, and private-sector financial institutions, firms and households. The public sector borrows money from these sources by selling treasury bills or bonds to them. An excess of revenues over expenditures allows the public sector to reduce its outstanding debt. Treasury bills and bonds may be redeemed from tax revenue when they fall due rather than from money raised by selling new bills and bonds.

When the public sector makes new loans from, or repays old loans to, the private sector, this action merely shifts funds between the two sectors. When the public sector 'borrows' from the central bank, however, the central bank creates new money. Since, unlike the private sector, the central bank can create as much money as it wishes, there is no limit to what the public sector can 'borrow' from the central bank.

Fiscal policy when private expenditure functions do not shift

A relatively easy problem faces policy-makers when private-sector expenditure functions for consumption, investment and net exports are given and unchanging. What is needed then is a once-and-for-all fiscal change that will make actual income equal to potential income if that is not already the case.

We saw earlier the fiscal changes required to remove an output gap: an increase in government expenditure on goods and services or transfer payments, or a cut in tax rates, sufficient to push the aggregate demand function out to potential national income.

Figure 43.4 illustrates the required fiscal policy. Initially, with IS_1, LM_1 and AD_1 equilibrium income is Y_1, yielding an output gap of $Y_F - Y_1$. Expansionary fiscal policies then push the IS curve to IS_2 and the aggregate demand curve to AD_2 thus eliminating the output gap, so that equilibrium income becomes Y_F.

An inflationary gap occurs if aggregate demand exceeds potential output at the current price level. Such a gap is removed by lowering G or Q or by raising t to shift the AD curve to the left until it intersects the AS curve at Y_F.

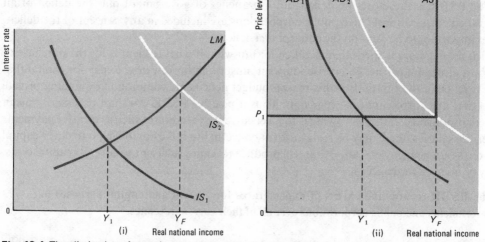

Fig. 43.4 The elimination of a persistent output gap by fiscal policy.

Balanced-budget changes in expenditure and tax rates The changes analysed so far would move government expenditure and tax rates in opposite directions. Another policy available to the government is to make a balanced-budget change in both expenditures and taxes.

Consider a balanced-budget increase in expenditure. Say the government increases personal income-tax rates enough to raise an extra £1 billion, which it then spends on purchasing goods and services. Aggregate expenditure will be unaffected by this change only if the £1 billion that the government takes from the private sector would have been spent by the private sector. If so, the government's policy will reduce private expenditure and raise its own expenditure both by £1 billion, and hence national income and employment will remain unchanged.

But this is not the usual case. When an extra £1 billion in taxes is taken away from households, they usually reduce their spending on domestically produced goods by less than £1 billion. If, say, the marginal propensity to consume out of disposable income is ·75, consumption expenditure will fall by only £750 million. If the government spends the entire £1 billion on domestically produced goods, aggregate expenditure will increase by £250 million. In this case the balanced-budget increase in government expenditure has an expansionary effect because it shifts the AD curve outwards.

> **A balanced-budget increase in government expenditure exerts expansionary pressure on national income, and a balanced-budget decrease exerts contradictionary pressure.**

The BALANCED-BUDGET MULTIPLIER measures these effects. It is the change in income divided by the balanced-budget change in government expenditure that brought it about. Thus, if the extra £1 billion of government spending financed by the extra £1 billion of taxes causes national income to rise by £500 million, the balanced-budget multiplier is ·5; if income rises by £1 billion, it is 1.

In general, the balanced-budget multiplier is much lower than the multiplier that relates the change in income to a deficit-financed increase in government expenditure with tax rates constant. For with a deficit-financed increase in expenditure, there is no decrease in consumption expenditure to offset the increase in government expenditure. With a balanced-budget increase in expenditure, however, the offsetting increase in taxes and decrease in consumption does occur.[1]

Fiscal policy when private expenditure functions are shifting

Thus far we have considered fiscal policy when the expenditure function is given (and unchanged by anything other than the fiscal policy itself). But as we saw in Chapter 42, private-sector expenditure functions change continually. This makes stabilization policy much more difficult than it would be if it were necessary only to identify a stable inflationary or output gap and then to take steps to eliminate it for once and for all.

What can the government reasonably expect to achieve by using fiscal policy when private expenditure functions are shifting continually? We can distinguish two objectives that differ in the scope of required policy intervention. The first objective is the more ambitious of the two. In this case, the authorities try to keep national income at exactly its full-employment level by trying to offset every fluctuation in the private investment, consumption or export expenditure functions that occurs. The second objective is much less ambitious. In this case the authorities accept fluctuations as inevitable. They recognize, however, that sometimes large and persistent inflationary or deflationary gaps (see pp.623–4) will develop. The task of demand management is then seen as offsetting these major gaps to prevent both deep and persistent recessions and long and rapid inflations.

Fine-tuning In the 1950s and 1960s many economists advocated the use of fiscal policy to remove even minor fluctuations in national income around the full-employment level. When this is attempted, fiscal policy is said to be used to FINE-TUNE the economy. Fiscal fine-tuning was popular in many countries during that period. British Chancellors of the Exchequer introduced budgets each year, sometimes more often, that varied taxes and expenditure in an attempt to influence aggregate demand. Careful assessment of the results, where such policies were followed, shows that their successes fell short of expectations.

---

[1] To derive the balanced-budget effect on the *IS* curve, return to equations (1)–(8) and add a new equation $G + Q = T$, and treat t as a variable. In other words, the rate of tax, t, is to be varied to ensure a balanced budget. Substitution then produces the following equation for the *IS* curve

$$r = \frac{1-c}{b} Y - \frac{(1-c)G + A}{b} \ .$$

The tax rate no longer appears as a parameter affecting behaviour since it is now no longer a policy parameter: it must be set so as to balance the budget. Notice that G still appears in the autonomous expenditure terms but now multiplied by $(1-c)$. This tells us that the impact of a balanced-budget increase in G is only that part, $1-c$, that would *not* have been spent if it had been left in private hands. The condition $G + Q = T$ used above assumes a globally balanced budget. For a balanced-budget *change* in expenditure, one must use the appropriate multiplier expression and add the condition $\Delta G + \Delta Q = \Delta T$.

All of the fiscal policies that seek to stabilize the economy create NEGATIVE FEEDBACK. Negative feedback is a technical term meaning that, when any system deviates from its target level, forces are set in motion that push the system back *towards* its target level.[1] Thus, when demand is too high, so that inflationary conditions prevail, demand is reduced; when demand is too low, so that unemployment prevails, demand is increased. Negative feedback is a necessary but not a sufficient condition for stability. If any control system operates with delays (lags) that are large relative to the period of fluctuations it is seeking to control, it can do the very opposite of stabilizing: the controls can actually accentuate rather than check fluctuations.[2]

The importance of time-lags: Controls operate with lags for many reasons. We mention two here. The first is called the DECISION LAG: it takes time to assess a situation and decide what corrective action should be taken. At a minimum it takes a month, and often very much longer, to gather data about current happenings. Our current information thus tells us not what is happening today, but what was happening anytime from a month to six months ago. The data must then be interpreted. Questions such as 'Is the downturn the beginning of a large potential slide or just a temporary aberration?' need to be answered. After the situation is assessed, alternative corrective actions need to be considered and finally a decision taken on what action is appropriate.

A second source of lag is called the EXECUTION LAG: it takes time to initiate corrective policies and for their full influence to be felt. For example, if the corrective action is a very large increase in G in the form of a new road-building programme, it may take months to make surveys, to hear objections from persons affected by chosen routes and to sign contracts. Once the government has done its work, it may take time before the effects on the private sector are felt. A strike in the cement industry may delay still further the flow of wage payments to construction workers that will raise disposable income and finally lead to an induced rise in consumption expenditure throughout the economy.

A simple explanation of the potentially destabilizing effects of lags on the outcome of fiscal policy can be developed along the following lines.[3] Consider an economy that is oscillating around a full-employment level of output as illustrated in Figure 43.5(i). Time is measured along the horizontal axis, and on the vertical axis we measure the difference between potential and actual income. The fluctuations are such that a boom in which aggregate expenditure exceeds full-employment output is followed by a slump in which aggregate expenditure falls short of full-employment output. Assume that the government plans to vary its own expenditure so as to exactly offset these fluctuations. The government wants its plan to have the impact shown by the solid line in Figure 43.5(ii). At first, it plans a surplus that will reduce aggregate expenditure; later, in period 3, it plans a deficit that will raise aggregate demand. If there are neither decision nor execution lags, then the addition of the solid lines in Figure 43.5(i) and 43.5(ii) will produce aggregate demand for the private plus the public sector, which is always equal to full-employment output. The government's deficit or surplus exactly counterbalances the difference between aggregate expenditure and full-

---

[1] The *system* may be anything from an economy to an aeroplane using an automatic pilot; the *target level* may be anything from full-employment national income to a compass course.

[2] We illustrated this point in the case of a single competitive market when discussing the cobweb theory in the Appendix to Chapter 10.

[3] This particular formulation of the problem is taken from A. W. Phillips, 'Employment, Inflation and Growth', *Economica*, February 1962.

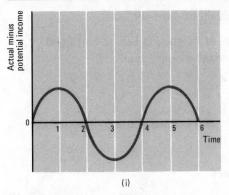 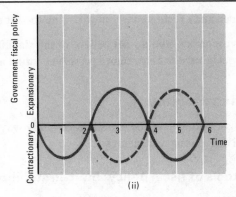

Fig. 43.5 Fluctuations in expenditure
(i) The private sector
(ii) The government sector

employment output in the private sector, so that its stabilization policy is completely successful.

Now assume that there are decision and execution lags. Further assume, to make the point as clear as possible, that the overall effect of these lags is equal to half the period of the cycle. Now the balanced budget planned at period zero will not occur until period 2; the maximum surplus planned for period 1 will not occur until period 3, when the economy is already in a slump; and the maximum deficit planned for period 3 will not occur until period 5, when the economy is already in a period of boom. Although planned government expenditure still follows the solid line in Figure 43.5(ii), actual government expenditure now follows the broken line. Instead of stabilizing the economy as intended, the policy will actually destabilize it. The combination of public and private demand will give rise to larger fluctuations than would have occurred if the government had done nothing!

This simple example is sufficient to show that the problem of controlling the economy is not so simple as comparative-static analysis can make it seem. Stabilization policies will have differing effects depending on the time-lags both in the actual working of the economy and in the functioning of the stabilization scheme.

The decline of fine-tuning as a goal of policy: Theoretical reasoning of the sort just described made an increasing number of economists suspicious of fine-tuning throughout the 1950s.[1] Then in the 1960s a series of applied studies suggested that stabilization policy had sometimes succeeded in destabilizing the economy, making fluctuations in income and employment larger than they would have been in the absence of any government intervention. As a result of this work, most economists and government policy-makers set much less ambitious objectives for fiscal policy in the 1970s and 1980s than they had done in the 1950s and 1960s.

The elimination of persistent gaps

The economy occasionally develops fairly severe and persistent inflationary or deflationary gaps. Such gaps last long enough for their major causes to be studied and for possible fiscal remedies to be

---

[1] Some of the basic theoretical work showing the difficulties of fine-tuning was done in the 1950s by the late Professor A. W. Phillips, the inventor of the famous Phillips curve that we shall study in Chapter 47.

carefully planned and executed without worrying too much about short-term lags.

Many economists who do not believe in the viability of fine-tuning believe that fiscal policy can be used to help remove persistent output and inflationary gaps.

Tools of fiscal policy

The tools of fiscal policy can be classified in many ways; one is based on the division between automatic and discretionary measures.

Automatic tools of fiscal policy : built-in stabilizers

Since the level of aggregate demand is continually fluctuating, stabilization policy for fine-tuning the economy requires a policy that is itself ever-changing. If such a conscious fine-tuning policy is impossible, because of time-lags, is there no room for fiscal policy to correct short-term fluctuations in the economy?

Fortunately, much of the job of adjusting fiscal policy to an ever-changing economic environment is done automatically by what are called built-in stabilizers. A BUILT-IN STABILIZER is anything that reduces the economy's cyclical fluctuations and that is activated without the need for a conscious governmental policy decision. Two major ways to achieve this are, first, to reduce the magnitude of destabilizing shifts in expenditure functions and, second, to reduce the size of the multiplier which determines the economy's response to such shifts.

Government expenditure   Government expenditure on goods and services tends to be relatively stable in the face of cyclical variations in national income. Much expenditure is already committed by earlier legislation, so only a small proportion can be varied at the government's discretion from one year to the next; and even this small part is slow to change. In contrast, private consumption and investment functions are subject to major autonomous shifts, increases tending to expand the economy and decreases to contract it.

The twentieth-century rise in the importance of government in the economy may have been a mixed blessing. One benefit, however, has been to transfer expenditure from the private sector, where it is subject to major disturbances, to the public sector, where it is not. Thus the absolute magnitude of *given percentage shifts* in the investment and consumption functions is reduced, because consumption and investment expenditures are of smaller absolute size than they would have been if the government sector had been substantially smaller than it now is.

Taxes   Direct taxes act as a built-in stabilizer because they reduce the marginal propensity to consume out of national income and thus reduce the value of the multiplier. Consider an example. If there were no taxes, every change in national income of £1 would cause a change in disposable income of nearly £1. With a marginal propensity to consume out of disposable income if, say, ·8, consumption would change by 80p. With a marginal direct-tax rate of, say, 35p in the £, disposable income only changes by 65p for every change in national income of £1. Thus with an MPC out of Y_d of ·8, consumption only changes by 52p in the £ for every change in national income of £1. By reducing the MPC out of national income, direct taxes act as a built-in stabilizer, reducing the value of the multiplier.

National insurance and welfare schemes So far we have treated government transfer payments as an exogenous constant, Q^*. In fact both unemployment payments and welfare benefits tend to vary counter-cyclically. In a slump, when employment is low, these payments are high; in a boom, when employment is high, these payments are low. Such transfer payments have the effect of partially stabilizing disposable income and, hence, of partially stabilizing consumption expenditure. For example, if when disposable income from income sources dropped by 65p transfer payments rose by 30p, then total disposable income would only drop by 35p. With an MPC out of disposable income of ·8, consumption expenditure would only drop by 28p. By partially stabilizing disposable income, national insurance and welfare payments reduce the value of the multiplier and thus reduce the magnitude of fluctuations in response to shifts in exogenous expenditure.

Agricultural-support policies When there is a slump in the economy, there is a general decline in the demand for all goods, including agricultural produce. The free-market price of agricultural goods tends to fall, and government agricultural supports come into play. This ensures that government support expenditure will rise as national income falls. This is as true of EEC agricultural-support policies as it is true of most policies in developed countries throughout the world.

If the supports take the form of purchasing surplus produce, then this element of government *expenditure* is rendered anti-cyclical. If the supports take the form of grants or subsidies, then this element of *transfer payments* is rendered anti-cyclical. Either way, the government policies reduce fluctuations by damping the multiplier process that would otherwise work through a drastic fall first in agricultural incomes and then in the consumption expenditure of the agricultural sector.

> **The shocks impinging on the economy are weaker, the larger is the (stable) government-expenditure sector and the smaller are the (less stable) consumption and private-investment sectors. The multiplied swings in income in response to expenditure shocks are smaller, the more are tax receipts pro-cyclical and transfer payments counter-cyclical.**

A formal analysis This section provides a formal analysis for those who would like to study it; others may skip immediately to the next section. Consider the equation of the *IS* curve on page 656:

$$r = -\frac{G^* + A^* + cQ^*}{b} + \frac{1 - c + ct}{b}Y . \tag{11}$$

Now take first differences to yield

$$\Delta r = -\Delta G^*/b - \Delta A^*/b - c\Delta Q^*/b + \Delta Y(1 - c + ct)/b. \tag{12}$$

We are interested in the horizontal shift in the *IS* curve. The larger is this shift, *ceteris paribus*, the larger is the increase in equilibrium income. The property of the *horizontal* shift of any point on the *IS* curve, when the whole curve shifts, is that the interest rate is held constant. Thus $\Delta r = 0$ in the above expression. Now we can, by setting the LHS at zero, write the constant-interest-rate multipliers (i.e., the horizontal shifts in the *IS* curve) as

$$\frac{\Delta Y}{\Delta G^*} = \frac{\Delta Y}{\Delta A^*} = \frac{\Delta Y}{c\Delta Q^*} = \frac{1}{1 - c + ct} . \tag{13}$$

Increasing the size of G lowers the size of A and hence the magnitude of the ΔA disturbances that impinge on the economy. (ΔA stands for $\Delta a_0 + \Delta a_1$ which are shifts in the consumption and investment functions.)

An increase in t, the proportion of national income that leaks out as taxes rather than becoming disposable income, clearly reduces the multiplier shown in (13) above.

Finally to show the effects of counter-cyclical transfer payments we replace equation (7) on page 656 with the following:

$$Q = q_0 + qY \qquad q < 0 < q_0 \tag{7'}$$

This makes some transfer payments, q_0, independent of national income while the rest varies negatively with income according to the coefficient q.

If you re-solve the IS curve, and the relations just given, using (7') instead of (7), you obtain an autonomous expenditure multiplier of

$$\frac{\Delta Y}{\Delta A^*} = \frac{2}{1 - c + ct - cq}.$$

Consider the new term $-cq$. Since c is positive while q is negative, $-cq$ is positive. The coefficient $-q$ gives the amount that transfer payments rise for every £1 fall in Y, and $-cq$ gives the amount that consumption rises as a result. Inspection of the above equation shows that the addition of a positive term to the denominator of the multiplier lowers the value of the multiplier. Hence counter-cyclical transfer payments are a built-in stabilizer.

The origin of built-in stabilizers Most of these built-in stabilizers are fairly new phenomena. Fifty years ago agricultural-stabilization policies, steeply progressive income taxes and large unemployment and other national-insurance payments were unknown in the UK. Each of these built-in stabilizers is the unforeseen by-product of policies originally adopted for other reasons. The progressive income tax arose out of concern to make the distribution of income less unequal. The growth of the government sector has been the result of many factors other than a desire for cyclical stability. Unemployment insurance and agricultural-support programmes were adopted more because of a concern with the welfare of the individuals and groups involved than to stabilize the economy. But, unforeseen or not, they work as stabilizers.

Discretionary fiscal policy

Short-term, minor fluctuations that are not removed by automatic built-in stabilizers cannot, with present knowledge and techniques, be removed by consciously fine-tuning the economy. When larger and more persistent gaps appear, however, there is time for the government to operate a DISCRETIONARY FISCAL POLICY, i.e., to institute changes in taxes and expenditures designed to offset gaps. To do this effectively the government needs to consciously change fiscal policy. There is often sharp debate on whether taxes or expenditures or both should be used to achieve those stabilizing changes that are generally agreed to be desirable. What issues are involved in these debates?

Location of effects The multiplier effects of an increase in aggregate demand tend to spread over the whole economy, causing a rising demand for virtually every commodity. If a slump is general, with widespread unemployment, this will be an advantage. If, however, a slump has severely localized characteristics, with a major depression in a particular industry (such as automobiles) or area (such as South Wales), then it may be desirable to achieve a disproportionate effect in the seriously depressed industry or area. In this case, raising expenditure has a distinct advantage over cutting taxes. The tax cut will have its initial impact on the entire economy, but by careful choice of projects much of the initial effect of extra expenditure can be channelled into the depressed sector.

If specific impact effects are important, expenditure has an advantage over tax changes.

The duration of the time-lag Long time-lags in fiscal policy are undesirable both because they delay the desired effects and because they introduce the possibility of destabilizing the economy. Tax cuts have a substantial advantage over expenditure increases in respect to the execution lag. Although the execution lag can be extremely long for a new road-building programme, it can be very short for changes in taxes and transfer payments. Only a matter of weeks after a tax cut has been legislated, wage-earners may find themselves with more take-home pay because their employers are withholding tax payments at a lower rate than before. Similarly, transfer payments can be changed only weeks after the enactment of the necessary legislation.

The reversibility of the policy Excessive concentration on comparative-static analysis can make one think in terms of policies to remove what would otherwise be permanent output gaps. In fact, as we saw in Chapter 42, the private sector undergoes continual oscillations in its expenditure. Even when a persistent gap develops, the one thing that is clear, at least if past experience is any guide, is that the gap will sooner or later change as a result of changes in private expenditure.

One of the most important principles of anti-cyclical fiscal policy is that the policy should be reversible.

On this count, tax policy seems superior both to government expenditure on goods and services and to transfer payments. Transfer payments are usually part of social policy, and it would seem callous to change the rates on such payments every time inflationary or output gaps developed. Government expenditures can be increased, but experience shows that they are not easy to cut since a very high proportion of such expenditures is committed through statutory programmes. Although they could no doubt be reduced over a decade by a really determined effort, the degree of discretion that any government has to reduce them rapidly is very small. Furthermore, a new line of expenditure following from a decision to increase G usually requires a new set of civil servants to administer it. These people become a vested interest who will resist any cuts in the expenditure flows that support them. This behaviour helps to explain why expenditure changes are not easy vehicles for anti-cyclical policies. Tax rates, on the other hand, do not suffer from this inertia. The civil servant apparatus required to administer income tax is independent of the rates being levied. Of course there may be voter resistance, but experience suggests that in practice tax rates are easier to vary in both directions as an anti-cyclical device than are expenditures.

The public's reaction to short-term changes An economist advising on how to stabilize a fluctuating economy through tax policy might advocate temporary tax increases to remove an inflationary gap and 'temporary tax reductions to remove a deflationary gap. These tax changes would cause changes in household disposable income, and, according to the Keynesian theory of the consumption function, the resulting changes in expenditure would tend to stabilize the economy. Consumption expenditure would increase as taxes were cut in times of deflationary gaps and decrease as taxes were raised in times of inflationary gaps.

This theory of the stabilizing effects of short-term tax changes relies on the assumption that household consumption expenditure depends on current disposable income. But many of the recent theories of the consumption function have emphasized households' expected *lifetime income* or *permanent income* as the major determinant of consumption. According to such theories, which we studied in the Appendix to Chapter 35, households have expectations about their lifetime incomes and they adjust their consumption to these expectations. Thus, when there is a purely temporary rise in income, households will save all the extra, and when there is a purely temporary fall in income, households maintain their long-term consumption plans by using up part of their wealth (accumulated through past savings) – at least so goes the modern theory of 'life-cycle' consumption.

To the extent that this kind of influence is at work, it has serious consequences for short-run fiscal stabilization policies. A temporary tax reduction raises household disposable income, but households, recognizing this as temporary, might not revise their expenditure plans and might save the money instead. The hoped-for increase in aggregate expenditure would then not materialize. Similarly, a temporary rise in taxes reduces disposable income, but it may merely cause a fall in saving, thus leaving total expenditure unchanged.

> **If household's consumption expenditure is more closely related to lifetime than to current income, then the effectiveness of fiscal measures that are known to be of short duration is uncertain.**

There remains, however, the important questions of what kind of assets households acquire when they save. According to these theories, households save and add to their wealth just as much when they buy consumer durables, such as washing machines and TV sets (which are consumed slowly over long periods of time) as when they buy financial assets such as local authority bonds or shares in ICI. But the effect on the economy is very different in the two cases. If households spend their temporary increases in income on financial assets such as shares and bonds, this will not add directly to aggregate demand for currently produced goods and services. (There may, however, be an indirect effect if the rate of interest is influenced by the increased household demand for financial assets.) If, however, households spend their temporary increase in income on consumer durables (which add to their present stock of wealth), this does add to aggregate demand for current output. Such spending will tend to raise both the GDP and total employment. What matters for the efficacy of short-term tax changes is whether households allow short-term fluctuations in income to affect their expenditures on current output of durables (including investment goods such as new housing), or whether such fluctuations affect only their expenditures on financial assets such as shares and bonds, building-society deposits and life insurance.

> **Changes in tax rates will have a weak effect on the economy if both of the following are true: households feel that the government-induced changes in their disposable income are transitory, and households allow transitory fluctuations in income to affect the rate at which they are accumulating financial assets rather than the rate at which they are spending to purchase currently produced output.**

Changes in tax rates will have a strong effect if either or both of the following are true: households regard the government-induced changes in disposable income as permanent, and households allow their fluctuations in income, whether regarded as permanent or temporary, to affect the rate at which they are prepared to spend on currently produced output.

Doubts about the possible efficacy of short-term variations in tax rates give a reason favouring government expenditure. Since government expenditure is itself a direct injection into the circular flow, its effect on income and expenditure is more reliable. It does not rely on giving money to others and then having the effect depend on what they elect to do with it.

Fiscal policy in practice

Keynesian economics in general, and fiscal policy in particular, has recently come under very severe criticism. It is not uncommon to hear it said that the Keynesian model is totally 'wrong' and its policy recommendations totally misguided. We will not go into these extreme views here. Suffice to say that the view that the *basic* theory of income determination is misguided is difficult to sustain. The concept of the circular flow of income long predates Keynes.[1] Almost every econometric model in existence today uses it. Of course certain behavioural relations used in particular models, and certain policy recommendations based on these models, may be open to criticism; but the view that the model itself, and all of the aggregates based on it, are useless just does not seem to stand up to careful analysis.

What can fiscal policy accomplish? In the United States, where fiscal policy was not seriously used until the 1960s, there is a school of extreme monetarists who argue that fiscal policy has no effect on the economy because the crowding-out effect is 100 per cent: every change of $1 in government expenditure causes a change in the opposite direction of $1 in private expenditure. The experience of Britain and other countries where fiscal policy has been used over the past 30 years makes it very hard to take this view seriously (indeed it does not command majority support among US economists).

The empirical evidence seems to provide overwhelming support for the theory that the government's deficit or surplus is the relation between its expenditure and its tax expenditures or tax rates.[2]

Judging the stance of fiscal policy

The 'stance' of fiscal policy refers to its expansionary or contractionary effects on the economy. An expansionary fiscal policy is one that increases national income; a contractionary fiscal policy

---

[1] A very clear statement is to be found in Chapter 1 of Schumpeter's great book, *The Theory of Economic Development: An Inquiry into Profits, Capital, Interest and the Business Cycle* (English translation, Harvard University Press, Cambridge, Mass., 1934). (First published in German, 1912.)

[2] Fiscal policy has gone through some extraordinary variations in the UK over the last two decades. There is substantial debate about the wisdom of some of these budgetary changes. Indeed, one well-known authority writing about the period referred to '... this extraordinary combination of self-inflicted errors and externally imposed misfortunes....' M. V. Posner writing in M. V. Posner (ed.), *Demand Management* (Heinemann, London, 1978). Saying that fiscal policy should not be used because its potent effects are often harmful is quite different from saying it should not be used because it is impotent.

reduces national income. How can we judge changes in the stance of fiscal policy from one year to the next?

In popular discussion, a change in the government's current budget deficit or, more broadly in the UK, in the PSBR, is often taken as an indicator. When the PSBR rises, this is widely taken as an indication of an expansionary change in fiscal policy. When the PSBR falls, this is widely taken to indicate a contractionary policy. This argument is based on a comparison of public-sector expenditure and tax revenue. But tax revenues are the result of the interaction of tax rates, which the government does set, and the level of national income, which is influenced by many forces that are beyond the government's control. Thus to judge changes in the stance of fiscal policy from changes in the government's budget deficit, or the PSBR, can be very misleading. It confuses endogenous changes in the deficit due to changes in national income with exogenous changes due to changes in the stance of fiscal policy.

The major tools of fiscal policy are government expenditure and tax *rates*. The government's deficit or surplus is the relation between its expenditure and its tax *revenues*.

The distinction between the two causes of changes in the budget balance is easily seen in what is called the public sector's BUDGET SURPLUS FUNCTION.[1] This function, which relates the surplus to national income, is graphed in Figure 43.6. Its equation is $tY - (G^* + Q^*)$. Endogenous changes in the government's budget balance due to changes in national income are shown by movements along a given surplus function. Changes in the budget balance due to policy-induced changes in government expenditure, G^*, transfer payments, Q^*, or in tax rates, t, are shown by shifts in the surplus function. Such shifts indicate a different budget balance at *each* level of national income.

When measuring changes in the stance of fiscal policy, it is common to calculate changes in the estimated budget balance at some base level of national income. Holding income constant ensures that measured shifts in the budget balance are due to policy-induced shifts of the surplus function rather than income-induced movements along the function. The base most commonly used is potential national income, and the measure calculated is called the HIGH-EMPLOYMENT SURPLUS (HES). This is an estimate of tax revenues minus expenditures, not as they actually are, but as they would be if full-employment national income had been achieved (i.e., if the output gap had been zero). In this usage, a high-employment budget deficit (expenditures exceed revenues) is regarded as a negative high-employment surplus.

Changes in the high-employment surplus are an indicator of changes in the stance of fiscal policy.[2]

Figure 43.6 analyses the use of the full-employment surplus, as well as the errors that can arise from use of the current surplus as an indicator of the stance of fiscal policy. The curve shown in (i) assumes that as national income fluctuates, tax revenues fluctuate more than public-sector expenditures. Thus deficits are associated with low levels of income and surpluses with high levels.

[1] In Britain this would include the government plus public enterprises; in other countries it may include only the government. The analytics are the same in either case.

[2] The high-employment surplus is the simplest adequate measure and it is vastly superior to the current surplus for estimating year-to-year changes in the stance of fiscal policy. More sophisticated measures exist and are often used in detailed empirical work. These use what is called the *weighted, standardized surplus*.

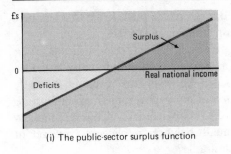

(i) The public-sector surplus function

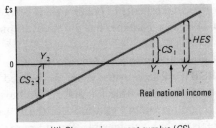
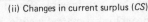

(ii) Changes in current surplus (CS)

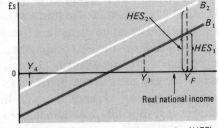

(iii) Changes in high-employment surplus (HES)

Fig. 43.6 The public-sector surplus function

In (ii) a fall in national income from Y_1 to Y_2 causes the budget to go from a current surplus of CS_1 to a current deficit of CS_2 with no change in expenditure or tax rates – that is, the fiscal policy stance is unchanged. The unchanged fiscal stance is correctly measured by the constant high-employment surplus that remains at HES when income falls from Y_1 to Y_2.

In (iii) there is a contractionary change in the stance of fiscal policy: a public-expenditure cut and/or a tax-rate increase shifts the surplus function from B_1 to B_2, indicating that there is a larger budget surplus at each level of national income. This change is correctly measured by the rise in the high-employment surplus from HES_1 to HES_2. The misleading effects of judging changes in the policy stance from changes in the *current* surplus can be seen by noting that if national income had fallen from Y_3 to Y_4 at the same time that the surplus function shifted from B_1 to B_2, the current balance would have gone from surplus to deficit in spite of the rise in the high-employment surplus.

The possibility just described was an actuality for many governments in the early 1980s. A major recession generated large budget deficits as governments were shifted to the left along given surplus functions. The deficits evoked major criticisms of government prodigality and, in response, tax rates were increased and expenditures curtailed in many countries. This shifted the surplus function upwards and tended to worsen the recession as the fiscal stance became more contractionary. Instead of being criticized for worsening the recession (by shifting the surplus function upwards), governments had in fact to withstand strong criticism of their unprecedented current deficits (caused by movements along the function).

> **Changes in national income cause changes in the current surplus by moving the economy along its surplus function; changes in the stance of fiscal policy shift the surplus function.**

Balanced-budget proposals

Concern over what some people feel is wastefully high government spending and over alleged inflationary pressures resulting from deficit-financed government spending has led to various proposals to force governments to balance their budgets. For example, in the UK the Conservative government of Margaret Thatcher has put great emphasis on reducing the PSBR.

An annually balanced budget Some people advocate as a policy goal an annually balanced budget, or a PSBR of zero every year. With fixed tax rates, however, tax revenues fluctuate endogenously as national income fluctuates. We have seen that much government expenditure is fixed by past commitments and that most of the rest is hard to change quickly. Thus an annually balanced budget is probably unfeasible. But suppose an annually balanced public-sector budget, or even something approaching it, were feasible. Would it be desirable?

We saw earlier that a large government sector whose expenditures on goods and services are not very sensitive to the cyclical variations in national income is a major built-in stabilizer. To insist that annual government expenditure be tied to annual tax receipts would be to abandon much of the built-in stability provided by the government. Government expenditure would then become a major destabilizing force. Tax revenues necessarily rise in booms and fall in slumps; an annually balanced budget would force government expenditure to do the same. Changes in national income would then cause induced changes not only in household consumption expenditure but also in government expenditure. This would greatly increase the economy's marginal propensity to spend and hence increase the value of the multiplier.[1]

> **An annually balanced budget would accentuate the swings in national income that accompany autonomous shifts in private-sector expenditure functions.**

A cyclically balanced budget Balanced-budget proposals are aimed at two major problems: first, they seek to avoid the alleged inflationary consequences of chronic budget deficits; second, they seek to prevent stabilization policy from leading to a long-term increase in the size of the public sector. The process creating the second problem would be as follows. During a slump, the government increases expenditures to stimulate the economy, but during a boom the government allows inflation to occur rather than cut expenditure; then in the next slump, government expenditure is raised once again. The greater willingness to follow an expansionary fiscal policy in slumps than to follow a contractionary policy in booms can lead to a long-term increase in the size of the government sector. The annually balanced budget would prevent this – but at the cost, as we have seen, of destabilizing the economy.

An alternative policy, one that would prevent continual deficits and could inhibit the growth in the size of the government sector, would be to balance the budget over a number of years, say over a five-year or a seven-year period. This would be more feasible than the annually balanced budget and would not make government expenditure a destabilizing force. The policies are illustrated in Figure 43.7. The flow of tax receipts is shown varying over the trade cycle, while government expenditure is shown at a constant rate.

In parts (i) and (ii), government expenditure is constant but tax revenue is fluctuating cyclically, being high in booms and low in slumps. In both situations the presence of government acts as a stablilizer against cyclical fluctuations because surpluses (dark areas) are highest in booms and deficits (white areas) are highest in slumps.

---

[1] To see this, solve the three-sector *IS-LM* model given on pp. 598–604 for Y, with the added equation $T = G$ (with G treated as a variable), and you will discover that the value of the multiplier is increased.

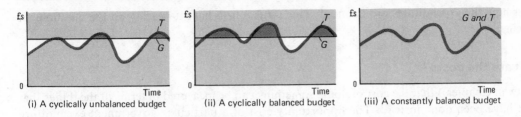

Fig. 43.7 Balanced and unbalanced budgets

In part (i) the average level of taxes is lower than in part (ii). Indeed in (i) surpluses are rare while deficits are common, so the average fiscal stance is expansionary. In (ii) tax rates have been increased so that surpluses are as common as deficits. The government's budget is still a cyclical stabilizer but now the average fiscal stance is neither expansionary nor contractionary.

In (iii) an annually balanced budget has been imposed. Deficits have been prevented, but government expenditure now varies over the trade cycle, tending to destabilize the economy by accentuating the cyclical swings in aggregate demand.

> **An annually balanced budget is a destabilizer; a cyclically balanced budget is a stabilizer.**

Although more attractive in principle than the annually balanced budget, a cyclically balanced budget would carry problems of its own. The government might well spend in excess of revenue just before an election, leaving the next government the obligation to spend less than current revenue in subsequent years. Clearly, however, the cyclically balanced budget is both more feasible and less undesirable than the annually balanced budget.

Yet there is serious doubt that the idea of a balanced budget over any time period is a sensible one. Many economists believe that a superior alternative to insisting on a precise balance is to pay attention to the balance without making a fetish of never adding to the public debt. After all, private firms borrow to finance capital expenditures; there seems no reason in principle why governments and public corporations should not do the same. To insist on a balanced public-sector budget is to insist that current taxpayers, and users of the output of public corporations, should pay for capital expenditures that will benefit future taxpayers and consumers. We shall see in the next section that there is no reason why a country cannot live satisfactorily for ever with a growing public-sector debt.

The costs of government activity

We have seen that the operation of fiscal policy may well entail government expenditure in excess of tax receipts. This implies increases in the public debt. In recent decades, increases have far outweighed decreases in most Western countries, so that the trend of the debt has been upward. Does an increasing debt matter? Would an ever-increasing debt lead to an ultimate collapse of market economies? Does the debt represent a burden we are passing on to our heirs? It is to these and related questions that we now turn. In discussing the significance of the debt, it is important to keep the costs of the *actual expenditure* distinct from the costs of the *method of financing* the expenditure. Both are important, but only the second is a 'cost of the debt'. Before discussing the particular consequences of debt financing, let us note certain costs of government expenditures that exist no matter how the expenditures are financed. This turns out to have a bearing on the questions of financing.

What are the costs?

We saw in Chapter 4 that the cost of doing something can be measured in terms of the things that might have been done instead. The opportunity cost of a particular government expenditure depends on what resources the government project will use and from where they are drawn. In times of heavy unemployment, most of the resources used in government activity might otherwise have remained unemployed. In this case there is no opportunity cost in employing them in the government activity because there is no alternative current production sacrificed by so doing. In contrast, if, in a fully employed economy, the government builds dams, roads, schools and nuclear submarines, the opportunity cost of these are the consumer goods and capital goods that would have been produced instead.

To the extent that the resources for the government activity were drawn away from the production of consumer goods and services, the opportunity cost is necessarily borne by the present generation in terms of a reduced consumption of goods produced by the private sector of the economy. To the extent that the resources are drawn away from the production of capital goods, the opportunity cost will be spread out over the future, because the current generation is giving up not consumption, but capital goods. This leads to a smaller stock of capital, and to a lower capacity to produce goods and services for consumption in the future, than there would have been had the government activity not taken place.

> **The opportunity cost of government activity is in terms of the commodities that would have been produced instead. This cost can approach zero in times of unemployment but it is always significant in times of full employment of any factor of production. To the extent that the commodities forgone are consumer's goods, the cost is all borne currently; to the extent that the commodities forgone are capital goods, the cost is spread out over the future.**

Alternative means of financing government activity

There are essentially three different ways in which a government can finance an expenditure: (1) it can raise the money by increasing taxes, thus transferring purchasing power from taxpayers to itself; (2) it can borrow the money from willing lenders, thus transferring current purchasing power from them to itself in return for the promise to repay future purchasing power; (3) it can (in effect) print enough money to permit itself to bid the resources it needs away from other potential users.

The major effect of the method of financing government expenditures is on *who* bears the costs, not on how much they are. Suppose the economy is at full employment, so that the government must incur real opportunity costs in order to produce its commodities. If the cost of a new government programme is met by increases in taxes, then the current taxpayers bear the cost by having their purchasing power reduced.

If the government expenditure is financed by borrowing from households and firms, the reduction in purchasing power for current consumption is incurred by those who lend their money to the government instead of spending it on currently produced goods and services. People who do not buy government bonds do not postpone current consumption and thus do not bear any of the real current cost of the government activity.

The third possibility is that the activity is financed by creating new money. (As we shall see later, the way this is done in the modern world is for the government to sell bonds to the central bank. In return, the central bank credits the government with a deposit on which the government can draw cheques to pay for its purchases.) Because the economy is already in a state of full employment, this method of finance must create an inflationary gap and thus cause a rise in the price level. Aggregate demand, already high enough to purchase all the output the economy is producing, becomes excessive as the government enters the market with its own new demand. The rise in prices will mean that households and firms will be able to buy less than they would otherwise have bought, and the government will be able to obtain resources for its own activities. Thus fewer resources will be available for private consumption and private capital formation. The result in the aggregate is the same as if the government had reduced private expenditure by taxation.

As far as distributing the opportunity cost is concerned, inflationary finance is similar to financing by taxes, although the identity of the groups forced to cut back on their own purchases is likely to be different in the two cases. By choosing which taxes to increase, the government using tax finance can exert a considerable influence on the distribution of the burden (although we must never forget that taxes may be shifted from the groups on which they are levied to other groups in surprising ways – see pages 479–80). Under inflationary finance, the government bids up prices and leaves it to the market to determine those groups that are to reduce their consumption and thus to pay the current cost. Retired persons and others on fixed incomes will bear much of the cost. Those whose incomes respond only slowly to changes in price levels will bear more of the cost than those whose incomes rise nearly as fast as prices. Some, indeed, will not pay any of the cost. Inflationary finance is usually regarded as a less just method of taxation than income taxes, because it places much of the burden on the economically weak, the unfortunate, and the uneducated, and the least burden on those who can adjust to rising prices, often the richest and most powerful groups.

The opportunity cost of government activity in terms of forgone alternatives is incurred whether the money to pay for the projects is raised by taxes, by borrowing from the public, or by creating new money. Methods of finance determine who bears the costs but do not necessarily affect the total cost.

Now consider what happens once the government project is finished. To the extent that it was financed by current taxes (or by inflationary creation of new money) the matter is finished once the government expenditure has been made. Resources can then be transferred back to the production of goods and services, and households' real disposable income can be allowed to rise by reducing taxes. But to the extent that the government activity was financed by borrowing from the private sector, the debt remains after the activity has been completed. It is necessary to pay interest each year to the bondholders and eventually to repay the bonds as they reach maturity. To the extent that interest payments and eventual redemption of the bonds are made from tax revenue, taxpayers now suffer a reduction in their consumption below what it would otherwise have been. The transfer is thus reversed. In return for bearing the original reduction in consumption, bondholders (or their heirs) now enjoy a rise in consumption and taxpayers who are not bondholders suffer a reduction. For the society, the cost in terms of forgone output was borne during the original activity. Once the activity is finished, total production goes back to normal. The opportunity cost could not be postponed, but individuals who did not buy bonds must now pay for their share of the cost of the activity by transferring some claims on current production to other individuals.

Worries about debt financing

Worries about public-sector deficits come under three heads. First they may cause inflations. This worry is better discussed in Chapter 47, where we develop a model of continuous inflation. Second, public-sector borrowing may crowd out private-sector investment. Third, the growing public-sector debt may cause a crisis of confidence as investors begin to doubt the government's ability to repay.

Crowding out To study the crowding-out argument we need to consider separately the cases of full employment and substantial unemployment. Figure 43.8 shows the case where, with LM_1, IS_1, and AD_1, the economy is initially in equilibrium at a national income of Y_1. If there is a balanced-budget increase in expenditure there will be a small rightward shift in IS because of the balanced-budget

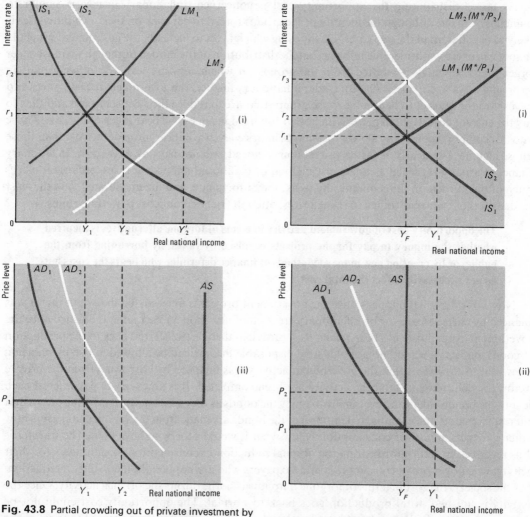

Fig. 43.8 Partial crowding out of private investment by debt-financed, public expenditure at less than full employment.

Fig. 43.9 Complete crowding out of private expenditure by debt-financed public expenditure at full employment.

multiplier. If, however, there is a debt-financed increase in government expenditure there will be a large shift in the IS curve, say to IS_2. If interest rates had remained constant, national income would have risen to Y'_2. Instead, however, interest rates rise from r_1 to r_2 and national income only rises to Y_2. The difference between Y'_2 and Y_2 represents private-sector investment (and other interest-sensitive private-sector expenditure) that is crowded out by the rise in interest rates.

Of course, in the situation shown here the avoidance of crowding out is a simple matter. All the government has to do is to increase the money supply in line with the increase in the quantity of money demanded so as to keep the rate of interest constant. If the LM curve in Figure 43.8 is shifted outwards to LM_2 by an increase in the money supply, then income rises to Y'_2 and there is no crowding out of private expenditure. What may inhibit the government from following this policy is the existence of some arbitrary monetary rule that has been adopted as an anti-inflationary device. Such rules will be considered in Chapter 47.

Now consider the full-employment case shown in Figure 43.9. Initially national income is at full-employment income, Y_F, with interest rate r_1 and price level P_1 (the relevant curves being IS_1, LM_1, AD_1 and AS). The government now makes a debt-financed increase in expenditure that shifts the IS curve to IS_2. Aggregate demand is now sufficient to purchase output of Y_1 but, because potential income in only Y_F, there is an inflationary gap of $Y_1 - Y_F$. The price level now starts to rise. This lowers the real money supply, shifting the LM curve leftward and taking the economy upward along its new aggregate demand curve, AD_2. When the price level has risen to P_2 the economy is once again at equilibrium with national income equal to expenditure at Y_F. Since total real expenditure is unchanged, the increase in government expenditure must have crowded out an exactly equivalent amount of private expenditure. The force causing the crowding-out is the rise in the interest rate from r_1 to r_3.

(1) When there are unemployed resources, a debt-financed increase in government expenditure combined with an increase in the money supply sufficient to hold interest rates constant causes no crowding out of private-sector expenditures.

(2) When there are unemployed resources, a debt-financed increase in government expenditure combined with a constant money supply will cause some crowding out of private-sector expenditure.

(3) When there is full employment of resources, any increase in government expenditure will crowd out exactly the same amount of real private expenditure through an increase in the price level and the rate of interest.

Worries about government solvency   Local authorities in the UK, and all those branches of governments in other countries that do not have their own captive central banks, must worry about their solvency. Their ability to service their debt depends on their taxing capacity. Such governments have, in the past, occasionally had to default on their debts.

Central governments, however, are in a different position. If they cannot raise enough tax revenue or borrow enough by selling bonds to the private sector, they can sell an unlimited quantity of bonds to their central banks. This is the so-called 'printing-press method of finance' because the central bank buys the government's bonds with newly created money. At full employment such finance is inevitably inflationary.

For central governments there can be no fear of ultimate insolvency; the fear is, rather, that if the government is forced to printing-press finance, the ensuing inflation will destroy much of the real purchasing power of government debt that is denominated in nominal money terms. Such worries would cause lenders to demand a substantial interest premium to protect themselves against the purchasing-power erosion coming from the anticipated inflation. Such concern only arises, however, when investors feel that the growth of debt is outstripping the future capacity to service it[1].

A non-Keynesian view of the national debt The view of the national debt that we have just discussed may be called the Keynesian view. Its basic points are: (1) within very broad limits, the size of the debt is of no great practical importance and (2) the debt should be increased or decreased according to the needs of stabilization policy.

An alternative view, which may be called *fiscal conservatism*, uses the theory of government behaviour first discussed on page 482. Its first premise is that governments are not passive agents doing what is necessary to create full employment and otherwise to maximize social welfare; instead they seek to maximize their own utility functions. This they do by spending as much as they can and by levying as few taxes as they can get away with. Spending is desirable to the central authorities because some of it, such as civil service salaries, expense accounts and pensions, is for the authorities' own consumption and because much of the rest benefits the public and thus helps gain votes and keep the present party (whichever it is) in power. Taxation is undesirable because heavy taxes tend to lose votes for the party in power and may also cause pressure for reductions in spending which may reduce the consumption of the central authorities themselves. In this view any government is a body that is rather irresponsible by economists' standards: it seeks to increase its own welfare by making its budget deficit as large as possible.

The non-Keynesian view takes a broad historical perspective. It says that in the eighteenth century spendthrift rulers habitually spent more than their tax revenues and created inflationary gaps. The resulting inflations were harmful to the economy because they reduced the purchasing power of everyone's savings and disrupted trade. All through that century a battle was fought between Parliament – advocating fiscal responsibility, and the rulers – practising fiscal irresponsibility. Parliament won the battle by imposing on the rulers the obligation to balance their budget.

Thus the balanced-budget doctrine was not the silly irrational doctrine that Keynes made it out to be. It was, instead, the symbol of the peoples' victory in a century of struggle to control the spendthrift proclivities of the nation's rulers. The doctrine that had been well established by the end of the nineteenth century was that a balanced budget is the citizens' only protection against profligate spending and wild inflation. The Keynesian revolution swept that view away. Budget deficits became, according to Keynesians, the tool by which a benign, enlightened set of central authorities sought to ensure full employment. But, say the anti-Keynesians, this let the tiger out of the cage; it took 100 years to get him in and the Keynesians let him out in a decade. Released from the nearly century-old constraint of balancing the budget, the central authorities went on a series of wild spending sprees. Inflationary gaps, deflationary gaps, or full employment notwithstanding,

---

[1] Lack of confidence in the government's ability to pay interest on the debt and to repay the principal on time should not be confused with an unwillingness to take up new debt at too low a money rate of interest in the face of inflationary expectations. Few investors would be willing, for example, to buy new government bonds yielding an 8 per cent nominal interest rate if they expected a 16 per cent annual rate of inflation. The inability to sell bonds on these terms has nothing to do with investors' confidence in the government's ability to meet its contractual obligations. The problem is rather that investors would not wish to make a perfectly safe loan to anyone on such unfavourable terms.

governments spent and spent. Deficits accumulated, the national debt rose, and inflation became the rule of the day. Inflation robbed the people of the real value of their savings by lowering the purchasing power of money saved. In the end the inflations even defeated the full-employment goal: when governments were finally forced to accept the need to reduce inflation, they imposed massive deflationary gaps in order to reduce the inflations that had developed an inertia of their own.[1] Today we see the legacy of these disastrous policies: the simultaneous occurrence of high inflation, high unemployment rates and large budget deficits.

> **According to fiscal conservatism the long, hard struggle to enforce a balanced-budget policy on the state was a victory for the common people against the forces of central-authority prodigality. Then, when Keynes swept the balanced-budget doctrine away, he released the selfish forces that would lead the central authorities back into a position of chronic deficit. This caused a chronic inflationary gap which inflicted suffering and misery on all those who could not protect themselves against the ensuing inflation.**

Here is an issue in political economy that is very important for our views on the functioning of the modern state. The interested student will want to pursue this matter further.[2]

---

[1] The nature of the inertia to which this view appeals is the expectations theory of inflation that is outlined in Chapter 47.

[2] The pro-Keynesian view can be found in almost any modern textbook on macroeconomics. The view of the fiscal conservatives is well expounded in J. M. Buchanan, J. Burton, and R. E. Wayne, *The Consequences of Mr. Keynes* (Institute of Economic Affairs, London, 1978).

44

Demand management 2: monetary policy[1]

A second major way in which the central authorities can seek to influence aggregate demand is through MONETARY POLICY, which may be defined as the attempt to influence macroeconomic variables by regulating supplies of monetary aggregates and the terms and availability of credit. In the first part of this chapter we look at the objectives of monetary policy on the assumption that the central bank can exercise exact control over the money supply. In the second part we consider how far from exact this control really is.

The theory of monetary policy

From the money supply to aggregate demand

The *LM* curve The equation of the *LM* curve that we derived in Chapter 39 was as follows:

$$r = \frac{M^*}{P} \cdot \frac{1}{e} - \frac{d}{e} Y \quad .$$ (1)

It is clear from inspection that an increase in M shifts the *LM* curve to the right, while a decrease shifts it to the left.

> At its simplest level, monetary policy consists in manipulating the nominal money supply so as to shift the *LM* curve and thus to shift the aggregate demand curve.

Shifts in the *LM* curve when there is an output gap Figure 44.1 shows an economy in equilibrium at Y_1, r_1 and P_1, given IS, LM_1 and AD_1. Equilibrium income, Y_1, is assumed to be less than potential income. An increase in the money supply shifts the *LM* curve to the right, say from LM_1 to LM_2. Equilibrium income rises to Y_2 while the interest rate falls to r_2. The rise in equilibrium income means an outward shift in the aggregate demand curve from AD_1 to AD_2. Given a perfectly elastic aggregate supply curve, equilibrium now occurs at Y_2 on the new aggregate demand curve AD_2.

---

[1] For factual and institutional background on this chapter, see Harbury and Lipsey, Chapter 8.

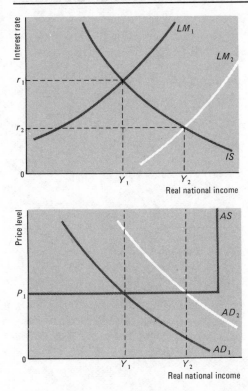

Fig. 44.1 Monetary policy operates on aggregate demand by shifting the *LM* curve

An increase in the quantity of money shifts the *LM* curve right, increases aggregate demand and, assuming the *AS* curve is perfectly elastic, it lowers the interest rate and raises real national income by the full amount of the increase in demand.

A reduction in the money supply has the opposite effects, shifting the aggregate demand curve to the left and, assuming a perfectly elastic *AS* curve, lowering income by the full amount of the decrease in demand and also raising the rate of interest.

Shifts in the *LM* curve when there is an inflationary gap The previous section looked at demand management when there were unemployed resources which resulted in a perfectly elastic aggregate supply curve. In this section we look at demand management when there is full employment and inflationary pressure. Assume that the economy starts in a disequilibrium position with inflationary pressure. The relevant curves are IS_1, LM_1, AS and AD_1 in Figure 44.2. The current price level is P_1 and, at full-employment income, there is excess demand of $Y_2 - Y_F$. We now consider three policies.
(1) Contract the money supply to shift the *LM* and *AD* curves to yield equilibrium at income Y_F and price level P_1. The *LM* curve is shifted to LM_2 by a change in M, and the *AD* curve shifted to pass through the point (P_1, Y_F). (The resulting *AD* curve is not shown in the figure.) This policy removes the excess demand by monetary contraction and leaves the price level at P_1.
(2) Hold the nominal money supply constant. The price rise then operates a *monetary adjustment mechanism*: the higher the price level, the greater the demand for money and so, with a fixed quantity

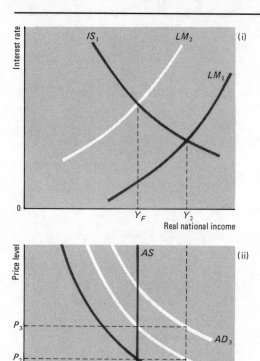

Fig. 44.2 The validation of an inflation by increases in the nominal money supply to hold the real money supply constant

of money, the higher must the rate of interest be if M_D is to equal M_S. The higher the rate of interest, the lower is aggregate expenditure and the lower the resulting equilibrium income.

The adjustment mechanism is illustrated in Figure 44.2. Given the aggregate demand curve AD_1, there is excess demand of $Y_2 - Y_F$ at the original price level of P_1. A demand inflation now ensues and the price level rises. The LM curve shifts left, and expenditure falls along the IS curve as interest rates rise. When the price level has risen to P_2, the excess demand has been completely removed. Aggregate demand equals aggregate supply at full-employment income Y_F in part (ii) and in part (i) the LM curve has been shifted to LM_2 by the fall in the real money supply caused by the rise in P.

> **The monetary adjustment mechanism removes the excess demand and eventually brings any demand inflation to a halt.**

(3) The central bank frustrates this adjustment mechanism by increasing the money supply at the same rate as the price level is rising. This keeps the real money supply constant and prevents the LM curve from shifting left in response to the increasing price level. Since no shortage of money develops, there is no rise in real interest rates to cut off demand. Thus real demand is not reduced by the inflation. By the time the price level has risen to P_2, which should have choked off the demand inflation, the rise in the money supply has shifted the aggregate demand curve out to AD_2, leaving

excess demand unchanged at $Y_2 - Y_F$. The demand inflation continues and, by the time the price level has risen to P_3, the AD curve has shifted out to AD_3, and so on. On the IS-LM diagram the same process shows up in the stability of the LM curve in spite of the rising price level. *Ceteris paribus*, the rise in the price level shifts the LM curve to the left; *ceteris paribus*, the rise in the nominal money supply shifts the LM curve to the right. If the rate of money growth is equal to the rate of price inflation, these two opposing forces just cancel each other out; the real money supply stays constant and the LM curve does not shift. The demand side of the model continues to call for an equilibrium level of income, Y_2, higher than full-capacity output, Y_F, so prices continue to rise.

> **A continuing excess demand inflation requires that the central bank frustrate the monetary adjustment mechanism by increasing the money supply as fast as prices are rising.**

A validated inflation When an inflation is allowed to carry on because the money supply is increased fast enough to frustrate the monetary adjustment mechanism, we say that the inflation is *validated* by monetary policy. When the money supply is not increased, we say the inflation is *non-validated*. Any non-validated inflation must be accompanied by a fall in equilibrium quantity of real GNP determined from the demand side (because the LM curve must be shifting leftward). A fully validated inflation, however, is not accompanied by any decline in the quantity of output demanded (the LM curve does not shift left because M and P increase at the same rate).

That central banks throughout the world have chosen to validate inflations for long periods of time is beyond dispute. Why they might adopt such a seemingly perverse policy is a matter we shall take up later.

Monetary *versus* fiscal policy

Properly understood, monetary and fiscal policy are complementary. Both are tools of demand management and an effective demand-management policy will normally rely sometimes more heavily on one and at other times more heavily on the other, but will generally rely on both.

There have, however, sometimes been disputes over the relative effectiveness of the two policies. Some economists have argued that fiscal policy is utterly ineffective. (Although how they explain the experience during the rearmament leading up to World War II, alluded to at the beginning of Chapter 43, must be a mystery.) It is worth noting, however, that there are circumstances in which either policy can lose much of its effectiveness.

The case of fiscal policy is shown in Figure 44.3. The initial IS curve, IS_1, intersects the LM curve at Y_1, r_1. A fiscal stimulus in the form of an expenditure increase, or a tax cut, then shifts the IS curve to IS_2. The most favourable case occurs with the perfectly elastic LM curve, LM'. Here we get the full interest-constant multiplier taking income to Y_2'. The least favourable case occurs with the vertical LM curve LM''', where income is unchanged but the interest rate rises to r_2'''. One intermediate case is shown by LM'' where income rises to Y_2'', and the interest rate rises to r_2''.

Inspection of the equation of the LM curve on page 684 shows that the slope of the curve is $-d/e$, where d is the effect on the demand for money of income and e is the effect of the interest rate. Given the dependence of the demand for money on income, the unfavourable case occurs if e is very small, and the favourable case if e is very large.

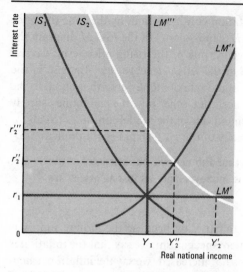

Fig. 44.3 A given fiscal stimulus has less effect on national income the steeper is the *LM* curve

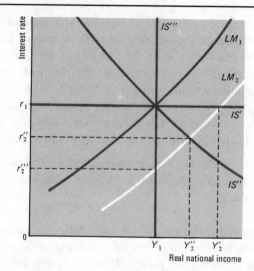

Fig. 44.4 A given monetary stimulus has less effect on national income the steeper is the *IS* curve

What is happening here is that the expansion of national income increases the quantity of money demanded, and this puts upward pressure on the interest rate. If the demand for money is highly sensitive to interest rates, then only a small rise in interest rates is sufficient to restore the quantity of money demanded to its original level. If there is only a small rise in interest rates, then there is only a small crowding-out effect to reduce the efficacy of the fiscal expansion. If, on the other hand, the demand for money is not very interest-sensitive, then a large rise in the interest rate is needed to restore the quantity of money demanded to its original level (and thus equal to the unchanged supply of money). In this case, there is a large crowding-out effect to reduce the efficacy of the fiscal expansion.

The less interest-sensitive is the demand for money, the steeper is the *LM* curve, and the smaller is the increase in equilibrium income, caused by any given expansionary fiscal stimulus.

Now let us consider a monetary policy designed to affect aggregate demand. In Figure 44.4, at the initial equilibrium of Y_1 and r_1, the curve LM_1 cuts the *IS* curve. An expansionary monetary policy now takes the *LM* curve to LM_2. The most favourable case is the horizontal *IS* curve which yields the interest-constant multiplier and takes real income to Y_2'. The least favourable case is the vertical *IS* curve, IS''', where income is constant and the interest rate falls to r_2'''. One intermediate case is shown by IS'' where income rises to Y_2'' while the interest rate falls to r_2''.

Inspection of the equation for the *IS* curve on page 656 shows its slope to be $(1-c+ct)/b$. Taking c and t as given, the slope varies with b, the sensitivity of investment expenditure to the interest rate. A large absolute value of b gives a flat *IS* curve, while a small absolute value gives a steep curve. What is happening here is that the expansive monetary policy pushes down the interest rate and works by having expenditure rise in response to the fall in interest. The more responsive is expenditure to interest rates, the larger is the increase in equilibrium income resulting from the monetary stimulus.

The less sensitive is aggregate expenditure to the interest rate, the steeper is the _IS_ curve, and the less is the increase in equilibrium income, resulting from any given monetary stimulus.

Not surprisingly, those who wish to favour monetary policy over fiscal policy have sought to show that variations in the interest rate have a large effect on aggregate expenditure and a small effect on the demand for money. Evidence suggests, however, that there is sufficient sensitivity of both expenditure _and_ money demand to interest rates, so that neither policy can be judged ineffective on these grounds.

Monetarists

There is a group of economists called monetarists whose intellectual leader is the American, Nobel prize-winning economist, Milton Friedman. These economists hold that the money supply is a key economic magnitude that exerts a strong influence on other macroeconomic variables. They believe that there is a close relation between the money supply on the one hand, and income, employment and the price level on the other hand. We shall discuss these economists' ideas in more detail in Chapter 48. In the meantime we can notice that nothing we have said so far would cast doubt on the idea that manipulation of the money supply is a potent tool for controlling the economy.

Problems arise however as soon as we move away from the pristine model where there are only two assets one of which, money, is under the precise control of the central authorities. It is to some of these practical problems that we must now turn.

The practice of monetary policy

The transmission mechanism

Starting from an equilibrium position, an increase in the supply of money creates an excess supply while a decrease creates an excess demand. Ever since the original quantity theory was formulated in the eighteenth century, theories of money have been in agreement that when an excess demand or supply of money develops, this will cause a change in the aggregate expenditure function. The mechanism by which excess demand or supply of money makes its effects felt on the aggregate expenditure function is called the TRANSMISSION MECHANISM. Views on the transmission mechanism have changed greatly over the years. The classical quantity theory emphasized a very direct link: if households had larger money balances than they required, they spend the excess on currently produced goods and services; if they had less than they required, they cut their expenditures below their incomes and used the resulting savings to add to their money balances. This theory is further discussed in the Appendix to this chapter.

Modern theories use a less direct link that emphasizes money as just one method of holding wealth. We have been using a simple version of these modern theories in which there are only two assets, money and bonds. To get a working picture of real links between money and aggregate demand we must allow for much more complexity in the spectrum of assets. Indeed there is a whole series of assets that are alternative ways of holding wealth – from currency and sight deposits, through time deposits, to treasury bills and short-term bonds, to very long-term bonds and equities.

With the exception of currency and demand deposits, each of these assets yields a return of interest or dividends and, with the exception of currency and all deposit money, each carries uncertainty as to its market price before its maturity date. The longer the term of the bond, the larger the fluctuations in the bond's current price for a given fluctuation in the rate of interest.

Thus financial assets can be thought of as a chain stretching from ones with the least uncertainty attached to their money prices to the ones with the most uncertainty. Money itself has the least uncertainty as to its money price (zero uncertainty); long-terms bonds have the most. Wealth-holders will typically hold a portfolio that includes some money and quantities of some, or all, of these other assets. If households and firms find themselves with larger money balances than they require, they will transfer some money into short-term bonds, and the extra demand will cause the prices of those bonds to rise. The rise in the price of short-term bonds will make longer-term bonds seem more attractive and households will move into them, making their price rise in turn. Eventually a whole chain of substitutions will occur, with short- and long-term interest rates changing as households try to hold less money and more of all the other interest-earning assets. The change in interest rates will in turn affect interest-sensitive expenditures.

The two-asset Keynesian model of money and bonds captures the essence of these substitutions. If firms and households have too much money relative to bonds, they seek to buy bonds. This pushes the price up, which means a fall in interest rates. If they have too little money, they seek to sell bonds, which drives their price down (interest rates rise). The first link in the transmission mechanism is from excess demand, or supply, of money to interest rates.

The second link is from interest rates to aggregate demand. We saw in Chapter 42 that expenditures on consumer durables, inventory accumulation, residential construction and on plant and equipment are all expected to respond to changes in the rate of interest. Other things being equal, a decrease in the rate of interest makes borrowing cheaper and also makes it less costly to have funds tied up in such non-interest-yielding assets as inventories, houses and consumer durables. Thus a decrease in interest rates is predicted to touch off bouts of new expenditure.

Empirical evidence seems to confirm that, overall, there is a negative relation between the rate of interest on the one hand, and investment and other interest-sensitive expenditure on the other.

> **The transmission mechanism works from excess demand or supply of money, to changes in the demand or supply of bonds, to changes in bond prices and interest rates, to changes in interest-sensitive expenditures.**

Central banks and the money supply

When we move from the pristine simplicity of the two-asset model to any real-world monetary system, we encounter, as we have just seen, a labyrinth of specialized assets and can quickly lose our bearings in our search for 'the' money supply. In the 1970s the authorities in many of the world's governments became converted to MONETARISM, the belief, first, that there is a stable relation between some monetary aggregate identified as 'the' money supply on the one hand, and the price level and real income on the other hand, and, second, that these relations are robust enough so that the important macro variables can be manipulated by manipulating the money supply. But such relationships have been difficult to identify and often much less stable than many had hoped they would be.

There are so many highly substitutable monetary assets that control of any one group of assets can often lead to DISINTERMEDIATION, as decision units slip into holding more of a similar but uncontrolled asset and less of the controlled one with little change in anyone's real behaviour.

Also a series of institutional changes in the 1970s have allowed firms and households to economize greatly on their holdings of typical transaction balances measured by M1. These financial innovations have occurred partly in response to inflation, which made it very costly to hold non-interest-earning assets, partly in response to exogenous innovations in the electronics industry, but may also have been partly in response to the very monetary control exercised by the central banks. If, for example, you hold fewer transactions balances because of a tight monetary policy, one response is to engage in a lower volume of transactions, as monetarists hoped would happen; but another may be to learn to handle the same volume of transactions with less money balances, which appears to have been what happened to some extent.

Many central banks started out controlling M1. Those who were successful, however, often found the simple statistical relation between M1 and those macro aggregates they sought to control breaking down. The public learned to do with assets not in M1, and the central banks then sought to control a wider monetary aggregate.

The search for the right monetary aggregate for central banks to control has led to the identification of a bewildering array of possible aggregates. In Britain these include the M1, £M3 and M3, which we have already identified; M2, a new measure not to be confused with an earlier M2 which went out of favour in the early 1970s; and PSL1 and PSL2 – private-sector liquidity, narrowly and broadly defined. Table 44.1 shows what each of these aggregates includes. If the 1980s is anything like the 1970s, new aggregates will continue to be defined and some of the older ones will fall into disfavour, rapidly rendering any table such at this one out of date. The table does serve, however, to illustrate the several monetary aggregates thought to be relevant at some point of time. Clearly, contol of the money supply has proven more elusive than was first suspected when central banks became converted to monetarism. What is the right magnitude to control? Can it be controlled? Will there prove to be an enduring relation between that monetary magnitude and the macro variables in which the Bank is interested once the Bank starts to control the aggregate? Such questions remain much-debated issues a decade or more after most of the world's banks set out to control 'the' money supply.

The controlling body: the central bank

The central bank is the agent of monetary policy. Banking institutions, and the instruments that central banks use to achieve their goals, vary substantially from country to country. These institutional details can have major effects on the workings of central-bank policy. In this introductory treatment we shall concentrate mainly on what can be said about central banks in general. First we shall discuss the major functions of central banks; then we shall consider how they give effect to their monetary policies.

Banker to the government Governments need to hold their funds in an account into which they can make deposits and against which they can draw cheques. Such government deposits are usually held by the central bank, although some governments attempt to spread their surplus deposits through the commercial banks while keeping only a minimum working balance at the central bank.

Table 44.1 The UK monetary aggregates

	M1	M2	£M3[1]	PSL1	PSL2
A. Notes and coin	x	x	x	x	x
B. Bank deposits					
1. Maturity and interest					
(a) Non-interest-bearing sight deposits	x	x	x	x	x
(b) Interest-bearing checkable deposits	x	x	x	x	x
(c) Other interest-bearing sight deposits	x		x	x	x
(d) Time deposits[2] of less than one month		x	x	x	x
(e) Time deposits[2] of one month to two years			x	x	x
(f) Time deposits[2] of over two years			x		
2. Sector of depositor					
(a) UK private sector	x	x	x	x	x
(b) UK public sector			x		
3. Size of deposit					
(a) Less than £100,000	x	x	x	x	x
(b) £100,000 and over	x		x	x	x
C. Other money market instruments[3]				x	x
D. Savings deposits and securities[4]					x

[1] M3 is the same as £M3, but includes foreign currency deposits of UK non-bank residents.
[2] Including Certificates of Deposit.
[3] Treasury Bills, Certificate of tax deposit, bank bills, deposits with local authorities and finance houses.
[4] Shares and deposits with building societies, National Savings Bank deposits, and National Savings securities, excluding all assets not realisable within a year without significant loss. Includes Trustee Savings Bank deposits to November 1981, but since then they have been reclassified as bank deposits within the new monetary sector.

Source: Lloyds Bank Economic Bulletin, No. 44, August 1982.

Manager of the public debt The central bank helps the government with its debt requirements. It smooths over the effects that might otherwise ensue from uneven borrowing and lending requirements. The Bank of England generally purchases any part of new issues of public debt that is not taken up by other lenders on the day of issue at what seems like a reasonable interest rate. If the Bank has judged the market correctly, it will be able to sell the remaining part of the new debt over the next week or so. If it has guessed incorrectly, it may end up holding some of the new debt indefinitely. The Bank also enters the market if there is a large issue of government debt due for early redemption. The central bank buys this issue up over a period of time, thus preventing a sudden large accretion of cash to the public on redemption date.

In its capacity as manager of the public debt, the central bank is motivated to keep interest rates, and thus the government's interest payments, as low as possible. If the public will not take up all of the government debt being offered at the going rate of interest, either interest rates can rise until all of the debt is taken up, or the bank can buy up whatever the public will not take at the present rate of interest. If banks choose the latter course, they are holding down interest rates. As we shall soon see, this leads to an expansion of the money supply.

Banker to commercial banks Commercial banks also require a banker: they need a place to deposit their funds, they need someone to transfer their funds among themselves, and they need someone to lend them money when they are short of cash. The central bank accepts deposits from commercial banks and will, on order, transfer these deposits among them. In this way the central bank provides the commercial banks with the equivalent of a chequing account, and with a means of settling debts among themselves. Commercial banks also hold their cash reserves against outstanding deposit liabilities in the form of their own deposits at the central bank.

Lender of last resort   Financial institutions often have sudden needs for cash, and one way of getting it is to borrow from the central bank. Historically, the central bank would lend money to financial firms with good investments but in temporary need of cash. In many countries, commercial banks borrow directly from the central bank.

In the UK, the discount houses stand between the clearing banks and the central bank. If the banks find themselves in need of cash, they recall some of their demand loans made to the discount houses. But the discount houses will have used their borrowed money to buy short-term financial assets. Thus they are not in a position to repay the banks out of their own cash reserves. If they cannot borrow money from private sources, they can always obtain the money by borrowing from the Bank of England. They must put up approved financial assets (mainly short-term treasury bills) as security. They pay interest on the loan at a rate that used to be set in advance by the Bank of England and was called the *minimum lending rate* (MLR), but which is now determined by the Bank from day to day.

One of the problems with the British banking system is that, unlike most other central banks which really are lenders of last resort, the Bank of England is closer to *a lender of first resort*. When the clearing banks want cash, the first thing they do is to call in loans from the discount houses and the discount houses are forced to repay their loans with money obtained from the Bank of England in the manner just described. This tends to make the whole system more liquid than are systems where the central bank really only makes loans as a last resort and then often at a penal rate.

There are two ways in which the central bank can provide assistance when the banking system is short of cash. First, it can lend money to the discount houses as described above. Second, it can buy bills and bonds directly. If clearing banks try to sell bills and bonds in large quantities, this will force down the price of these assets. But if the central bank enters the market and buys everything offered at the present prices, this allows any holder who is in need of cash to sell those financial assets and to obtain cash in return. The Bank of England now favours the latter method and no longer states a fixed rate at which it will lend money directly to the discount houses. The purpose of this change is to make the system more uncertain about the cost of having to look to the Bank to provide liquidity. This, it is hoped, may make the system more cautious when expanding credit.

Supporter of money markets   What is often referred to as the SUPPORT FUNCTION of the central bank arose from its operation as a lender of last resort to the commercial banks. Today the support function relates to the whole of the financial system. Many financial institutions borrow short and lend long. If their lending rates can only be raised slowly while their borrowing rates rise quickly (because their borrowing contracts are short-term ones while their lending contracts are long-term ones), then a rapid rise in interest rates may put them in danger of insolvency. Rather than let this happen, the central bank may try to slow down the rise in interest rates. To do this, the bank enters the open market and buys bonds, thus preventing their prices from falling as much as they otherwise would. In its efforts to control the level and speed of change of interest rates, in general support of the financial system, the central bank necessarily varies the money supply. The changes in the money supply required if the central bank is to pursue its support function may be very different from the changes in the money supply needed if it seeks to control aggregate demand with a view to removing inflationary and deflationary gaps.

Regulator of the money supply   In most countries the central bank has the sole power to issue paper money. In Britain this is done by the Issue Department of the Bank of England. No attempt is made, however, to control the overall money supply by controlling the quantity of banknotes in circulation. Suppose that the public wishes to increase the fraction of the total money supply it holds as notes and coin (as it does, for example, each Christmas season). Faced with a cash drain to the public, the commercial banks will withdraw deposits from the Bank of England and the Bank will print the necessary banknotes.[1]

The central bank leaves the public to decide how much of the total money supply they wish to hold in notes and coins, and provides these amounts to the system. It then tries to exert its control over the money supply by influencing the volume of credit money, deposits created by the banking system.

Control with a cash base

In many countries, the central bank requires banks to hold reserves against their deposit liabilities. These reserves are called the RESERVE BASE of the money supply. The liabilities against which reserves must be held are called ELIGIBLE LIABILITIES. The ratio of required reserves to eligible liabilities is called the REQUIRED RESERVE RATIO.

In most countries today, central banks enforce a reserve base in terms of cash. Where such reserves are required, the cash available to be held as reserves is called the CASH BASE of the money supply. The cash base is also then called HIGH POWERED MONEY. It consists of notes and coins in the hands of the public and cash held by the commercial banks on deposit at the central bank. A 10 per cent cash reserve ratio means that 10 per cent of the value of deposit liabilities of the banking system must be backed by deposits held to the credit of the banking system recorded on the books of the central bank. We saw earlier that the commercial banks' ability to create deposit money is limited by the amount of reserves available to them. If the central bank can control the size of these reserves, it can control the quantity of deposit money created by the commercial banks. Central banks that enforce a reserve ratio between the deposit liabilities of commercial banks and their cash reserves have two tools of control: they can alter the cash reserves available to the commercial banks, or they can alter the required ratio of deposits to cash reserves.

Changing the cash base   The central bank can change the cash reserves available to the banking system by OPEN-MARKET OPERATIONS. Assume, first, that the central bank enters the open market and buys bonds. To see the effect of such purchases let us follow through the transactions that they cause. The central bank buys a bond from some holder in the private sector. The bank pays for the

---

[1] The accounting would be kept straight by the banking department transferring financial assets to the currency department who would issue currency against these. Thus, if the commercial banks withdraw £X cash, the banking department reduces its deposit liabilities to commercial banks by £X and its holdings of interest-earning assets by the same amount. The currency department increases its holdings of interest-earning assets and increases its note issue (which is a liability) by £X.

bond by making out a cheque drawn on itself, payable to the seller. The seller deposits this cheque in his own bank. The commercial bank presents the cheque to the central bank for payment. The central bank makes a book entry increasing the deposit of the commercial bank at the central bank. At the end of these transactions, the central bank will have acquired a new asset in the form of a bond and a new liability in the form of a deposit by the commercial bank. The individual will have reduced his bond holdings and will have raised his cash holdings. The commercial bank will have a new deposit equal to the amount paid for the bond by the central bank. Thus the commercial bank will find its cash assets and its deposit liabilities increased by the same amount. The balance sheets of the three parties concerned will show the changes indicated in Table 44.2 after £100 worth of open-market purchases have been completed.

Table 44.2 Changes resulting from the purchase of a £100 bond by the central bank from a private household

Central Bank

Liabilities	Assets
Deposits of commercial banks +£100	Bond +£100

Commercial Banks

Liabilities	Assets
Deposit of households +£100	Deposits with central bank +£100

Private Households

Liabilities	Assets
No change	Bonds −£100
	Deposits with commercial banks +£100

Table 44.3 Changes resulting from the sale of a £100 bond by the central bank to a private household

Central Bank

Liabilities	Assets
Deposits of commercial banks −£100	Bond −£100

Commercial Banks

Liabilities	Assets
Deposits of households −£100	Deposits with central bank −£100

Private Households

Liabilities	Assets
No change	Bonds +£100
	Deposits with commercial banks −£100

The commercial banks are now in the position that was originally illustrated in Table 38.1 (page 576). They have received a new deposit of £100 against which they hold £100 of reserves on deposit with the central bank. Now they can engage in a multiple expansion of deposits of the kind already studied in Chapter 38. Notice that everything has been accomplished by a set of book transactions. The commercial banks have extra cash *to their credit on the books of the central bank*. No new notes or coins have been created. If the subsequent credit expansion causes some cash drain to the public, only then will the commercial banks withdraw some of their deposits from the central bank, and only then will new notes and coins have to be created by the central bank.

A central-bank purchase of any financial asset has the effect of increasing the cash reserves of the banking system.

Second, let the central bank enter the open market and sell bonds to the public. Now follow through the set of transactions caused by this sale. The central bank sells a bond to someone in the private sector. It hands over the bond and receives the buyer's cheque drawn against his deposit at his own bank. The central bank presents this cheque to the commercial bank for payment. The payment is made merely by a book entry reducing the commercial bank's deposit at the central bank.

Now the central bank has reduced its assets by the value of the bond it sold, and reduced its liabilities in the form of cash owed to commercial banks. The individual has increased his holding of bonds and reduced his cash on deposit with his own bank. The commercial bank has reduced its deposit liability to the individual and reduced its cash assets (on deposit with the central bank) by the same amount. Each of the asset changes is balanced by a liability change.

The balance sheets of the three parties concerned will initially show the changes indicated in Table 44.3 after £100 worth of open-market sales have been accomplished. This is not the end of the story, for the banks find that as a result of suffering an equal change in their cash assets and their deposit liabilities, their ratio of cash to deposits falls. If this ratio was previously at the minimum, the commercial banks will have to take steps to restore their cash ratio. The necessary reduction in deposits can be effected by not making new investments when old ones are redeemed (e.g., by not granting a new loan when old ones are repaid) or by selling existing investments (e.g., by selling bonds to the public and receiving payment in cheques, which reduces the deposits held by the public).

> **A central-bank sale of any financial asset has the effect of decreasing the cash reserves of the banking system.**

Any open-market purchase or sale by the central bank has the effects just analysed. If the Bank buys bills and bonds directly from the government, this also increases the cash base and allows a multiple expansion of deposit money. In the first instance it is the government's account with the central bank that gains the new credit balance. But as soon as the government spends the money, writing cheques to households and firms, the money finds its way into the commercial banks, which are once again in the position of securing new deposits that simultaneously increase both their cash assets and their deposit liabilities by an equal amount. This permits a multiple expansion of deposit money.

Furthermore, it does not matter *why* the central bank engages in open-market operations; the effect is the same whatever the purpose of the purchase or sale. The open-market operations might have been engaged in for the express purpose of changing the cash base, or for the purpose of assisting the government to float new loans, or to prevent an anticipated rise in short-term interest rates. Whatever the reason for a particular open-market operation, the effect on the cash base is unavoidable.

Varying the required cash-reserve ratio The other technique that the central bank can use, still working with the cash base, is to change the required cash-reserve ratio. A fall in this ratio can permit a multiple expansion of deposits. The effect is similar to open-market purchases by the central bank because both policies present the banking system with excess reserves – in one case because reserves rise, and in the other case because reserve requirements fall. Conversely, if the required cash-reserve ratio is raised, banks find themselves with inadequate reserves. They are then forced to initiate a multiple contraction of deposits in order to achieve the newly required ratio.

> **Open-market purchases by the central bank and/or reductions in the cash-reserve ratio permit a multiple expansion of deposit money by presenting the banking system with excess reserves. Open-market sales and/or increases in the cash-reserve ratio force a**

multiple contraction of deposit money by making the banking system's existing reserves inadequate.

The key aspect of a cash-reserve system is that bank reserves are under the full *de facto* control of the central bank. Assume, for example, that the commercial banks want more reserves than the central bank is willing to make available through its open-market operations. The only alternative source is the notes and coins held by the public. If the banks could persuade the public to hold less currency and use cheques instead, the public would deposit the excess currency and the banks would find their reserves replenished. But the public's demand for cash is highly stable and in practice the banks cannot replenish cash reserves by attracting cash from the public. Thus, when they are short of reserves, they must reduce their deposit liabilities.

Control of the money supply in Britain

In 1971 the Competition and Credit Control document introduced a *reserve-asset system* for the UK banks. A required ratio between *eligible liabilities* and what were called *reserve assets* was enforced. The reserve assets included 'normal' deposits of the banking system with the Bank of England (cash reserves), treasury bills, money loaned out at call to the discount houses and other similar institutions, UK local authority bills, British government stocks, and bonds of nationalized industries that were guaranteed by the government and had less than one year to run to maturity. This list makes it obvious that the total supply of assets held by the banks for their reserve base could not be controlled by the Bank of England. To see this, assume that the commercial banks want more reserves than the central bank is willing to supply. Their alternative is to persuade the public to hold less of the given total supply so that the banks can hold more. With the UK reserve-asset base, it was possible to persuade the public to do this. The reserve assets were similar to, and hence substitutable for, other assets that were not in the reserve base. Hence slight changes in prices of the assets, caused by the banks demanding more of them, made it possible for the banks to acquire more as people switched to other assets. Thus the reserve-asset system left the Bank of England unable to control the quantity of deposit money created by the banking system by controlling its reserve base.

It is not surprising, therefore, that the period following 1971 saw an unprecedented increase in the money supply as banks attracted reserve assets from the public and created deposit money on this base.

Faced with a need to control the rapid monetary expansion, the Bank fell back on the Special Deposit scheme that had been introduced in the 1960s. From time to time the Bank of England could require that the commercial banks make special, non-interest-earning deposits with it. This had the effect of increasing the required reserve ratio. At the end of 1973 a new variant of the scheme, which came to be called the 'corset', was introduced. The Bank of England announced a target for the expansion of deposit money, and if this target was exceeded, banks had to place amounts of money (determined on a sliding scale) into Special Deposits. This was intended to provide a disincentive against exceeding the target for growth in the money supply.

This system of control was abandoned in the early 1980s and a new set of measures was introduced.

(1) The required minimum reserve-asset ratio has been abolished.

(2) The MLR, the stated rate at which the Bank would supply funds to the system, was abandoned.

The intention was to make the banking system more uncertain about the terms on which the Bank would provide liquidity to the system and thus make the banks more cautious about expanding credit to the utmost limit dictated by financial prudence.

(3) All banks in the system must hold a small part (1 per cent when originally set up) of their eligible liabilities with the Bank (a required cash ratio). This is in addition to the working deposits held by the London clearing banks to settle their interbank transactions. Although this (small) cash reserve ratio is now required, the Bank of England did not, at the time, contemplate controlling the money supply through the cash base.

(4) The Bank will seek to keep interest rates within an *unannounced* band that will be changed whenever necessary to fulfil targets for money-supply growth. If there is a stable demand for money as a function of interest rates, then the Bank can control the money supply by intervening with open-market operations to fix the appropriate interest rate. This is illustrated in Figure 44.5. The Bank's target money supply is M_t, and it knows the demand to hold money as a function of the interest rate, the relation shown by M_D. It then indulges in open-market operations to stabilize the interest rate at r_1. This creates a perfectly elastic supply of money at r_1 and gives a quantity of money actually in existence equal to the target quantity. If the target changes, say to M'_t, then the Bank needs merely to stabilize the interest rate at r_2 to meet its money-supply target.

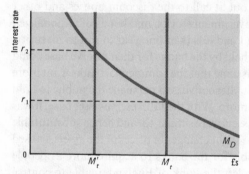

Fig. 44.5 Meeting money-supply targets by open-market operations fixing the required interest rate

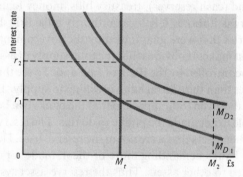

Fig. 44.6 Interest-rate stabilization versus monetary targets when the demand for money shifts

This system does not require adjusting the money stock to stabilize the interest rate at a target level. Rather the interest rate is adjusted to stabilize the money supply at a target level. Figure 44.6 illustrates the important difference between these two policies. At first the demand for money is M_{D1} and the money-supply target of M_t is met by stabilizing the interest rate at r_1. Now assume that an economic recovery shifts the demand-for-money function to M_{D2}. If the underlying policy were to stabilize the interest rate at r_1, the money supply would have to be increased to M_2. If, however, the underlying policy is to meet the money-supply target of M_t, then the interest rate must be allowed to rise to r_2 (choking off the extra demand for money until it is equal to the targeted supply of M_t). Clearly this system required that the demand for money bear a clear relation to the rate of interest and that the Bank have a pretty good estimate of what it is. Note also that the Bank is working through the partial relation between M_D and r. Since the demand for money is positively related to national income, changes in income will necessarily shift the relation between M_D and r to the right when income rises and to the left when income falls. Thus the Bank has to vary interest rates to meet its money-supply targets as income fluctuates.

Basically, because there is no cash-reserve base, there is no limit to the amount of money UK banks can create. In the end it is their own voluntary restraint that limits their money creation. Given their behaviour, the Bank of England then seeks to meet its money targets by open-market operations. Large sales of debt to mop up excess money does, however, affect bond prices. It tends to keep them down and hence interest rates up. This then gives rise to fears of excessive crowding out: high long-term interest rates may discourage private investment by raising the cost of borrowed money.

Milton Friedman and many other monetary economists have criticized the Bank of England's approach as yet another self-inflicted impediment to effective monetary control in the UK. They argue that a cash-base requirement would provide a more reliable structure for control.

Theories of the determination of the money supply

Two extreme situations concerning the determination of the money supply are imaginable. In the first, the money supply is determined precisely by the central bank. The supply neither expands nor contracts with the ebb and flow of business activity unless the central bank decides to allow it to do so. In such a case, economists speak of an EXOGENOUS MONEY SUPPLY. In the other extreme situation, the money supply is completely determined by forces such as the level of business activity and rates of interest, and is wholly out of the control of the central bank. In such a case, economists speak of an ENDOGENOUS MONEY SUPPLY, which means that the size of the money supply is not imposed from outside by the decisions of the central bank, but is determined by what is happening within the economy (just as is the production of steel plates or motorcars).

Exogenous theories

A required cash-reserve system such as is operated in many countries is the basis for the best-known exogenous theory. Here the money supply is related to the cash base by the so-called DEPOSIT MULTIPLIER, which relates deposits to reserves according to equation (2) below. The assumptions of the theory are (i) that the central bank fixes a minimum cash-reserve ratio, and (ii) that the profit incentive of commercial banks leads them to avoid holding excess reserves if at all possible. Idle cash reserves earn nothing for a bank, while loans and other investments always yield some interest income. Therefore banks will always try to be fully loaned up (i.e. have no excess reserves).

We can write assumption (i) as

$$\frac{R}{D} \geq \alpha \quad , \tag{1}$$

where R is cash reserves, D is deposit liabilities, α is the minimum required cash-reserve ratio and the sign '$\geq$' is read greater than or equal to. Assumption (ii) above allows us to replace the '$\geq$' sign with an '$=$' sign since banks are assumed never to carry significant amounts of excess reserves. Now rewrite the equation as follows:

$$D = \frac{R}{\alpha} \quad . \tag{2}$$

This gives us the quantity of deposit money expressed as a function of the cash base and the required cash-reserve ratio. If we allow for a cash drain to the public, the deposit multiplier becomes a little more complex. It is then given by the equation (4) in Chapter 38. (The difference between (2) and (4) occurs because with a cash drain all high powered money newly created by the central bank's open-market operations does not end up as reserves of the banking system since some is withdrawn and held as cash by the public.)

With or without a cash drain, this is a theory of an exogenous money supply, because the cash base is under the complete control of the central bank through its open-market operations. In practice the money supply is not completely exogenous in cash-base systems. Some reasons why are (i) banks do not always choose to be fully loaned up, so D may fluctuate below the upper limit set by R/α at the discretion of the banking system; (ii) sight and time deposits are often subject to different cash-reserve ratios and so a change in the proportions in which the public holds these can lead to different Ms emerging from a given cash base. In spite of these and other difficulties, a cash-base system seems to permit substantial control over the money supply by the central bank provided the bank is willing to pursue monetary targets to the exclusion of such other goals as stabilizing the interest rate or the exchange rate. We saw in Figure 44.6 that if the demand for money as a function of the rate of interest is fluctuating, then fulfilling a money-supply target requires substantial variations in the interest rate. We shall see in the next chapter that fulfilling a money-supply target may also require accepting substantial variations in the exchange rate.

Endogenous theories

There are many theories of how the money supply may become an endogenous variable. First, the central bank may be more concerned with the rate of interest than the quantity of money. If the bank is to engage in whatever open-market operations are needed to stabilize the price of bonds and other financial assets, then the change in the money supply will be determined by the necessary amount of open-market operations. If the price of bonds would otherwise be falling on the open market, the bank must buy bonds in order to hold their price up. (This, as we have seen, tends to expand the money supply.) If the price of bonds would be rising on the open market, the bank must sell bonds in order to hold their price down. (This, as we have seen, tends to contract the money supply.) If the bank behaves in this way, the money supply becomes endogenous.

Figure 44.7 illustrates this. In part (i), the IS curve fluctuates from a low or 'slump' level, IS_S, to a high or 'boom' level, IS_B. If the money supply is held constant, interest rates and national income fluctuate between r_S and r_B and Y_S and Y_B respectively. If, however, the central bank stabilizes the interest rate at $\bar{r}$ in part (ii) of Figure 44.7, the money supply must be altered to yield LM curves of LM_S and LM_B. The money supply now fluctuates pro-cyclically, and the variations in income are now from Y_S' to Y_B', larger than they were before. We now get the full interest-constant multiplier effect of the fluctuations in expenditure, since the policy of interest-rate stabilization stops the operation of the crowding-out effect which would otherwise operate as a built-in stablizer.

> **If the object of the central bank's open-market policy is to fix interest rates, the money supply becomes endogenous and cannot be fixed by the central bank at any particular predetermined level. Also cyclical swings in income are enlarged.**

A second way in which the money supply can become endogenous is if the bank sets a reserve base which the commercial banks themselves can control. This, as we have seen, was the UK system over the decade of the 1970s. Large quantities of these reserve assets were held by the non-banking private sector, and the banks could obtain more of them by purchasing them at a price favourable enough to persuade the public to sell them and hold other closely substitutable assets instead.

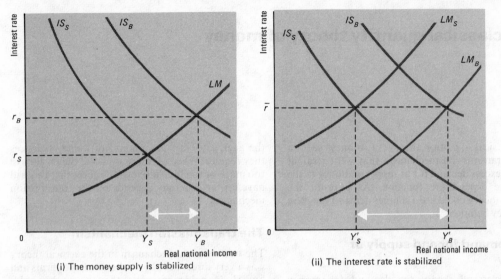

Fig. 44.7 The effect of *IS* fluctuations with a stable money supply and a stabilized interest rate

Mixed theories

In practice, the money supply of most countries is partly endogenous, because commercial banks can change it in response to economic incentives, and partly exogenous, because the central bank is able to exert some substantial control over it. When we treat the money supply as an exogenous variable in theoretical sections, we are studying the *tendencies* that can be imparted to economic behaviour by that degree of influence over the money supply that the central bank is able to exert.

Appendix to chapter 44

The classical quantity theory of money

The classical quantity theory of money used a simple transmission mechanism that went straight from an excess demand for or supply of money to the aggregate expenditure function. As a result the classical theory could use a simpler demand function for money balances.

The demand for and supply of money

In the classical theory the demand for money depends solely on the transactions motive. This demand, expressed in *nominal* money units, is written

$$M_d = kPY, \qquad (1)$$

where P is the price level and Y is real national income.[1] The value of k is the fraction of the annual value of national income that firms and households wish to hold as transactions balances – which is the only reason for holding money in this theory.

Next we express the assumption that the supply of money is a constant determined by the central authorities:

$$M_s = M^*, \qquad (2)$$

where M_s is the supply of money and M^* is some constant amount (measured in pounds sterling). Equation (2) merely says that the supply of money does not depend on any other factors in the economy; it is simply what the central authorities want it to be.

Finally we write a condition for equilibrium between the demand for money and the supply of it. This is written as

$$M_d = M_s. \qquad (3)$$

When (3) holds, households and firms will have, in

---

[1] Dividing through by P yields the money demand in real terms, M_d/P, that was used in the text and symbolized M_D.

the aggregate, just the amount of money balances they require. When (3) does not hold, they will have too much or too little money. The effect that this will have on the economy depends on the transmission mechanism.

The transmission mechanism

The transmission mechanism in the classical theory was a very direct one. If, on the one hand, firms and households hold more money than they wish to hold, there is excess supply of money. According to the classical theory, excess money balances are spent to purchase currently produced goods and services. If, on the other hand, firms and households hold smaller money balances than they would like to hold, then there is excess demand for money and they cut their expenditures below their incomes in an effort to build up their balances.

> Comparing the classical theory and the modern theories, the transmission mechanism differs but the final result is the same: excess demand for money reduces aggregate expenditure and excess supply increases it.

The quantity theory with full employment

To see how the quantity theory works, let us first assume that real national income is constant at its full-employment level, so that excess aggregate demand must cause the price level to rise. The equations of the quantity theory are summarized in Table 44.4. Substitution of (1) and (2) into the equilibrium condition (3) produces the basic relation between P and M^* as shown in the fourth equation, which merely states that the demand for money (kPY) should equal its supply (M^*).

Table 44.4 The equations of the quantity theory

(1)	Demand for money	$M_d = kPY$
(2)	Supply of money	$M_s = M^*$
(3)	Equilibrium condition	$M_d = M_s$
(4)	Equations (1), (2) and (3) give	$kPY = M^*$

or $P = \dfrac{1}{kY} \cdot M^*$

If k and Y are constant, P varies proportionately with M.

Table 44.5 From k to V

If the demand for money, kPY, equals the supply, M^*, we have, from Table 44.4,

(4) $kPY = M^*$

(5) Rewriting (4) gives $PY = M^* \dfrac{1}{k}$

(6) Letting V stand for $\dfrac{1}{k}$ gives $PY = M^* V$.

If we are dealing with inflationary-gap situations so that income is constant at its full-employment level and if k is constant, then the price level must rise in proportion to any increase in the quantity of money.

To see how this result comes about we must consider disequilibrium behaviour. Assume that the economy begins in a situation of full-employment equilibrium with the demand for money equal to its supply. Now assume that the central bank increases the supply of money in the hands of households and firms by 10 per cent. According to the behavioural hypothesis of the quantity theory, the firms and households try to convert this extra cash into goods and services but, since the economy is already at full employment, their efforts can only open up an inflationary gap. Indeed, the price level must rise until the demand for money is again equal to its supply. Since the demand for money is kPY, and since k is fixed by assumption, and since Y cannot change because the economy remains at the same level of full-employment output, the demand for money will increase by exactly 10 per cent when P increases by 10 per cent. Until that time the demand for money will be less than its supply, and the attempt to convert the excess money into currently produced goods and services will generate excess demand that will cause further inflation. Thus, equilibrium can be restored only when the price level rises by the same percentage as did the supply of money.

Often the quantity theory is presented and discussed using V (VELOCITY OF CIRCULATION) instead of k. V stands for the average number of times a unit of money turns over in the transactions that create GDP. It is defined as the reciprocal of k. Table 44.5 shows the effect of substituting symbols. Of course it makes no difference whether we work with k or V, as long as we are careful about the way we interpret these two variables.

The stock of money people wish to hold might, for example, be one-tenth of the annual value of national income. If k is 0.1, then V must be 10. This indicates that if the money supply is to be one-tenth of the value of national income, the average unit of money must change hands ten times in order to bring about an aggregate value of income ten times as large as the stock of money.

The quantity theory with unemployment

The quantity theory became a part of the classical model in which the *equilibrium* level of national income was always at full employment. Thus Y remained fixed at its full-employment value, and not only did P rise in proportion to a rise in the money supply, but P also *fell* in proportion to a *reduction* in the money supply. Thus Y was determined by its full-employment level and P was determined by the quantity of money. To adapt the classical quantity theory to situations in which actual income is less than potential income, we merely use our assumption that in this situation the price level is constant while national income varies with aggregate demand. This makes P a constant and Y a variable but preserves the link provided by the quantity theory between the excess demand for money and changes in aggregate demand.

To see what is implied we take the theory in the form:

$$kPY = M^*,$$

which is equation (4) in Table 44.4 and divide through by kP to obtain:

$$Y = \frac{1}{kP} M^*.$$

This tells us that:

If P is constant during periods of unemployment, national income (and

hence output and employment) will vary in proportion to the money supply.

The reason for this is analogous to the reasons given in the discussion of disequilibrium under inflationary conditions. If firms and households have too much money, they spend it and the resulting increase in aggregate demand raises output and employment. If firms and households have too little money, they lower their expenditures in an attempt to increase their money balances, and the resulting fall in aggregate demand lowers the equilibrium level of output.

The basic prediction of the quantity theory is that there will be a change in the *money value* of national income, in proportion to any change in the quantity of money. In some cases the change will be mainly a price change (a change in *P*); in others it will be a change in output and employment (a change in *Y*). In either case, control over the money supply becomes a potent method of controlling national income.

45

Macro policy in an open economy[1]

In the second half of this chapter we consider the serious complications brought to macroeconomic policy by the openness of an economy. As a prelude we consider in the first half of the chapter alternative exchange-rate regimes and, for this, a review of Chapter 11 would be advisable at this point.

Alternative exchange-rate regimes

Two extreme regimes may be distinguished. The first is a system where exchange rates are fixed at pre-announced 'par' values that are changed only occasionally when the existing rate can no longer be defended. This is the system which operated from the end of the Second World War until the early 1970s. The second is a system of freely fluctuating rates determined by private-sector demand and supply in the complete absence of government intervention. This is a system that some countries have occasionally come close to since 1971. A third, intermediate system, called a *dirty float*, is one where the central bank seeks to have some stabilizing influence on the rate without trying to fix it at a publicly announced par value. This system is really a combination of the other two. We first study the two extreme cases of fully fixed and freely fluctuating rates, both because understanding them is a prerequisite to understanding the dirty float and because many economists and policy-makers advocate returning to one or the other of the extreme systems.

Background

The onset of the Great Depression of the 1930s brought an end to the ancient stability of the gold standard and ushered in a period of experimentation in exchange regimes. Experiments were tried with both fixed and fluctuating rates. Often a rate would be allowed to fluctuate on the free market until it had reached what looked like equilibrium, and it would then be fixed at that level. Sometimes, as with the British pound, the rate was left to be determined by a free market throughout the whole period. Sometimes rates would be changed in an attempt to secure domestic full employment without any consideration of the state of the balance of payments.

The period of experimentation coincided with the Great Depression. This was a terrible period

---

[1] For background material see Harbury and Lipsey, Chapters 7 and 9.

of mass unemployment, and governments began to cast around for any measure, no matter how extreme, that might alleviate their domestic unemployment problem. One superficially plausible way of doing this was to cut back on imports and produce those goods domestically. If one country managed to reduce its imports, then its unemployment might be reduced because people would be put to work producing replacement goods at home. Other countries would, however, find their exports falling and unemployment rising as a consequence. Because such policies attempt to solve one country's problems by inflicting them on others, they are called BEGGAR-MY-NEIGHBOUR POLICIES.

If the policies worked, there would at least be selfish arguments in their favour. But they work only as long as other countries do not try to protect themselves. Once they find their exports falling and unemployment rising, these other countries may retaliate by reducing their own imports and producing the goods at home, and the first country will find its exports falling and unemployment rising as a result. The simultaneous attempts of all countries to cut imports without suffering a comparable cut in exports is bound to be self-defeating. The net effect of such measures is to decrease the volume of trade, thereby sacrificing the gains from trade without raising worldwide employment.

When unemployment is due to insufficient world aggregate demand, it cannot be cured by measures designed to redistribute, among nations, the fixed and inadequate total of demand.

Beggar-my-neighbour policies in the 1930s used such instruments of commercial policy as import duties, export subsidies, quotas, prohibitions, and, also, exchange-rate depreciation. If a country with a large portion of its labour force unemployed devalues its exchange rate, two effects can be expected: exports will rise, and domestic consumers will buy fewer imports and more domestically produced goods. Both of these changes will have the effect of lowering the amount of unemployment in the country. If other countries do nothing, the policy succeeds. But again, the volume of unemployment in other countries will have increased because exports to the devaluing country will have been reduced. If other countries try to restore their positions, they may devalue their currencies as well. If all countries devalue their currencies in the same proportion, they will all be right back where they started, with no change in the relative prices of goods from any country and, hence, no change in relative prices from the original situation. When all countries devalue their currencies in an attempt to gain a competitive advantage over one another, we speak of COMPETITIVE DEVALUATIONS.

The Bretton Woods system

The one lesson that everyone thought had been learned from the 1930s was that either a system of freely fluctuating exchange rates or a system of fixed rates with easily accomplished devaluations was the road to disaster. In order to achieve a system of orderly exchange rates that would be conducive to the free flow of trade following the Second World War, representatives of most countries that had participated in the alliance against Germany, Italy, and Japan met at Bretton Woods, New Hampshire, in 1944. The international monetary system that developed out of the agreements reached at Bretton Woods consisted of a large body of rules and understandings for the regulation of international transactions and payments imbalances.

It was the first and so far the only international payments system that was consciously designed and then implemented through international governmental co-operation. In the words of Charles Kindleberger of MIT, the Bretton Woods meeting was 'the biggest constitution-writing exercise ever to occur in international monetary relations'. The system lasted until the early 1970s, when it broke down and was replaced by the piecemeal adoption of free-market exchange rates.

The object of the Bretton Woods system was to create a set of rules that would maintain fixed exchange rates in the face of short-term fluctuations; to guarantee that changes in exchange rates would occur only in the face of long-term, persistent deficits or surpluses in the balance of payments; and to ensure that when such changes did occur they would not spark a series of competitive devaluations.

The basic characteristic of the Bretton Woods system was that US dollars held by foreign monetary authorities were made directly convertible into gold at a fixed price by the US government, while foreign governments fixed the prices at which their currencies were convertible into US dollars. It was this characteristic that made the system a GOLD EXCHANGE STANDARD: gold was the ultimate reserve, but other currencies were held as reserves because directly or indirectly they could be *exchanged* for gold.

The rate at which each country's currency was convertible into dollars was fixed within a narrow band on either side of a pre-announced par value or pegged rate. This rate could be changed from time to time in the face of a 'fundamental disequilibrium' in the balance of payments. A system with these two characteristics, a rate that is pegged against short-term fluctuations but that can be adjusted from time to time, is referred to as an ADJUSTABLE PEG SYSTEM.

In order to maintain convertibility of their currencies at fixed exchange rates, the monetary authorities of each country had to be ready to buy and sell their currency in the foreign-exchange markets. In order to be able to support the exchange market by buying domestic currency, the monetary authorities had to have stocks of acceptable foreign exchange to offer in return. In the Bretton Woods system, the authorities held reserves of gold and claims on key currencies – mainly the American dollar and the British pound. When a country's currency was in excess supply, their authorities would sell dollars, sterling, or gold. When a country's currency was in excess demand, their authorities would buy dollars or sterling. If they then wished to increase their gold reserves they would use the dollars to purchase gold from the Federal Reserve System (the US central bank, hereinafter called the 'Fed'), thus depleting the US gold stock. The problem for the United States was to have enough gold to maintain fixed-price convertibility of the dollar into gold as demanded by foreign monetary authorities. The problem for all other countries was to maintain convertibility (on a restricted or unrestricted basis, depending on the country in question) between their currency and the US dollar at a fixed rate of exchange.

> **The Bretton Woods international payments system was an adjustable peg, gold exchange standard where the ultimate international money was gold. Countries held much of their exchange reserves in the form of US dollars, which they could convert into gold, and British pounds, which they could convert into US dollars.**

The International Monetary Fund The most important institution created by the Bretton Woods system was the International Monetary Fund (also called the IMF or the Fund). The Fund had several tasks. First, it tried to ensure that countries held their exchange rates pegged in the short run. Second, it made loans – out of funds subscribed by member nations – to governments that needed them to support their exchange rates in the face of temporary payments deficits. Third, the Fund was supposed to consult with countries wishing to alter their exchange rates to ensure that the rate was really being changed to remove a persistent payments disequilibrium and that one devaluation did not set off a self-cancelling round of competitive devaluations. The importance of the Fund is attested by the fact that it has outlived the system that created it and is as active an instrument of international monetary co-operation today as it was under the Bretton Woods system.

Management of the fixed rates Figure 45.1 shows free-market demand and supply curves for dollars. Assume that the Bank of England fixes the exchange rate between the limits of 40⅓p and 42⅓p to the dollar and restricts demand, through an exchange control system of rationing and prohibitions, to the average level of demand at D'. By these means, the Bank keeps the demand for dollars lower than it otherwise would be. Even this restricted demand will, however, be subject to seasonal, cyclical and other fluctuations.

The Bank then controls the exchange rate by being ready to enter the market to prevent the rate from going outside the permitted band on either side of the par value. At the price of 42⅓p to the dollar, the Bank offers to sell dollars, for permitted purposes, in unlimited amounts; at the price of 40⅓p per dollar, the Bank offers to buy dollars in unlimited amounts. When the Bank must buy foreign exchange, its exchange reserves rise; when it must sell foreign exchange, its exchange reserves fall.

(1) If the demand curve cuts the supply curve in the range 40⅓p to 42⅓p, then the Bank need not touch its exchange reserves. The amount of dollars being supplied for pounds will be equal to the amount of dollars being demanded in exchange for pounds, and no intervention into the market is needed.

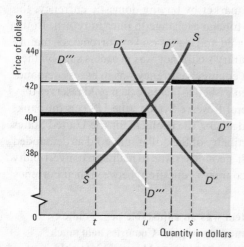

Fig. 45.1 The stabilization of the exchange rate through the intervention of the central authorities

(2) If the demand curve shifts to D'', then the Bank must sell dollars to the extent of rs in order to prevent the price of dollars from rising above 42⅓p. These dollars must be removed from its exchange reserves.

(3) If the demand curve shifts to D''', the Bank must buy dollars to the extent of tu and add them to the exchange reserves in order to prevent the price of dollars from falling below 40⅓p.

If the Bank has restricted demand sufficiently so that *on the average* the demand and supply curves intersect in the range 40⅓p to 42⅓p, then the exchange reserves will be relatively stable, with the Bank buying dollars when the demand is abnormally low and selling them when the demand is abnormally high. Over a long period, the average level of reserves will then be fairly stable.

If the Bank has guessed wrongly or if conditions change (e.g., there is a more rapid inflation in one country than in the other), the exchange reserves will rise or fall more or less continuously. Say that the average level of demand is D'' with fluctuations on either side of this level. Then the average drain on reserves will be rs per period. *This situation cannot continue indefinitely.* The Bank has two possibilities: it can change the controlled price so that the band of permissible prices straddles the equilibrium price. In other words, it can devalue. Or it can try to shift the curves so that the intersection is in the band 40⅓p to 42⅓p. To accomplish this, it must take further steps to restrict demand for foreign exchange: it can impose import quotas and foreign-travel restrictions, or it can seek to increase the supply of dollars by encouraging exports.

The Bank can also induce movements of short-term capital as part of its policy of keeping a fixed exchange rate in spite of fluctuations in the demand for and supply of foreign exchange. Let us see how a temporary deficit in the balance of payments may be alleviated by attracting short-term capital into the country. Assume that, in Figure 45.1, the demand for dollars is D'' and the supply S, so that there is a balance-of-payments deficit of rs per period. The Bank can raise the short-term rate of interest and attract short-term capital. People holding dollars now wish to obtain pounds in order to lend them out at the high British rates. Thus the supply of dollars shifts to the right. The horizontal distance between the new curve and the original curve S indicates the amount of dollars supplied on account of the movement of short-term capital into Britain. If the curve is shifted to cut D'' vertically above s, the inflow of short-term capital is rs per period and this just covers the deficit on current account, and the exchange reserves are not run down. *Provided the Bank guessed correctly* that the demand was *abnormally* high, the policy will work. If the demand now falls to an abnormally low level, say, D''', the Bank can stop the capital inflow, letting the supply curve return to S. It can then buy tu dollars per period and add them to exchange reserves. When the reserves have been built up, the Bank can allow the capital to flow back abroad. It does this by lowering short-term rates of interest so that people who have lent money in Britain would now prefer to lend it in, say, New York. There will be a demand on the part of these investors to turn pounds into dollars. The government can now sell tu dollars per period to these investors.

Short-term deficits in the balance of payments can be covered by attracting short-term capital into a country, but this policy will be successful only if an equivalent short-term surplus subsequently develops so that the capital can again be transferred out of the country.

Problems of an adjustable peg system Three major problems of the Bretton Woods system were (1) providing sufficient reserves to iron out short-term fluctuations in international receipts and payments while keeping exchange rates fixed; (2) making adjustments to long-term trends in receipts and payments, and (3) handling speculative crises. Since these problems would be present in any adjustable peg system that might be designed in the future, they are worth studying in detail in the forms in which they plagued the Bretton Woods system.

Reserves to accommodate short-term fluctuations: Reserves are needed to accommodate short-term balance-of-payments fluctuations arising from both the current and the capital accounts. On current account, normal trade is subject to many short-term variations, some systematic and some random. This means that even if the value of imports does equal the value of exports, taken on average over several years, there may be considerable imbalances over shorter periods.

On a free market, fluctuations in current and capital account payments would cause the exchange rate to fluctuate. To prevent such fluctuations when rates are fixed, the monetary authorities buy and sell foreign exchange as required, to keep the exchange rate pegged. These operations require that the authorities hold reserves of foreign exchange. If they run out of reserves, they cannot maintain the pegged rate, so they will want to hold some safety margin over the maximum they expect to use. It is generally felt that the absolute size of any gap they may have to fill with their own foreign-exchange sales increases as the volume of international payments increases. Since there was a strong upward trend in the volume of overall international payments, there was also a strong upward trend in the demand for foreign-exchange reserves.

The ultimate reserve in the Bretton Woods gold exchange standard was gold, which entailed two serious problems. First, the world's supply of monetary gold did not grow fast enough to provide adequate total reserves for an expanding volume of trade. The gold backing needed to maintain convertibility of currencies became increasingly inadequate throughout the 1960s. Second, the country whose currency is convertible into gold must maintain sufficient reserves to ensure convertibility. During the 1960s the United States lost substantial gold reserves to other countries that had acquired dollar claims through their balance-of-payments surpluses with the United States. By the late 1960s the loss of US reserves had been sufficiently large to undermine confidence in America's continued ability to maintain dollar convertibility. *By 1970 there was an inadequate world supply of gold for monetary uses, and the United States had too small a proportion of the supply that did exist.*

Under the Bretton Woods system, the supply of gold was augmented by reserves of key currencies, the US dollar and the British pound. Because the need for reserves expanded much more rapidly than the gold stock in the period since the Second World War, the system required nations to hold an increasing fraction of their reserves in dollars and sterling. Of course they would do this only as long as they had confidence in the convertibility of these currencies, and maintaining confidence was made difficult by a continually declining percentage of gold backing for the dollar.

Adjusting to long-term disequilibria: With fixed exchange rates, long-term disequilibria (what the IMF used to call *fundamental disequilibria*) can be expected to develop because of secular shifts in the demands for and supplies of foreign exchange. There are three important reasons for these. First, different trading countries have different rates of inflation. Chapter 11 discussed how these cause changes in the equilibrium rates of exchange and, if the rate is fixed, cause excess supply or excess demand to develop in each country's foreign-exchange market. Second, changes in the demands for and supplies of imports and exports are associated with long-term economic growth. Because different countries grow at different rates, their demands for imports and their supplies of exports would be expected to be shifting at different rates. Third, structural changes, such as major new innovations or the rise in the price of oil, cause major changes in imports and exports.

The associated shifts in demand and supply on the foreign-exchange market imply that, even starting from a current-account equilibrium with imports equal to exports at a given rate of exchange, there is no reason to believe that equilibrium will exist at the same rate of exchange 5 or 10 years later.

The rate of exchange that will lead to a balance-of-payments equilibrium will tend to change over time; over a decade the change can be substantial.

Governments may react to long-term disequilibria in at least three ways.

(1) The exchange rate can be changed whenever it is clear that a balance-of-payments deficit or surplus is a result of a long-term shift in the demands and supplies in the foreign-exchange market, rather than the result of some transient factor. During the period of the Bretton Woods system, there were three major rounds of exchange-rate adjustments.

(2) Domestic price levels can be allowed to change in an attempt to establish an equilibrium set of international prices. Changes in domestic price levels have all sorts of domestic repercussions (e.g., reductions in aggregate demand intended to lower the price level are more likely to raise unemployment than to lower prices), and one might have expected governments to be more willing to change exchange rates – which can be done by a stroke of a pen – than to try to change their price levels. A deflation is difficult to accomplish, while an inflation is thought to be accompanied by undesirable side-effects.

(3) Restrictions can be imposed on trade and foreign payments. Imports and foreign spending by tourists and governments can be restricted, and the export of capital can be slowed or even stopped. Surplus countries were often quick to criticize such restrictions on international trade and payments. As long as exchange rates were fixed and price levels proved difficult to manipulate, the deficit countries had little option but to restrict the quantity of foreign exchange their residents were permitted to obtain so as to equate it to the quantity available.

Handling speculative crises: When enough people begin to doubt the ability of the central authorities to maintain the current rate, speculative crises develop. The most important reason for such crises is that, over time, equilibrium exchange rates get further and further away from any given set of fixed rates. When the disequilibrium becomes obvious to everyone, traders and speculators come to believe that a realignment of rates cannot long be delayed. At such a time, there is a rush to buy currencies expected to be revalued and a rush to sell currencies expected to be devalued. Even if the authorities take drastic steps to remove the payments deficit, there may be doubt as to whether these measures will work before the exchange reserves are exhausted. Speculative flows of funds can reach very large proportions, and it may be impossible to avoid changing the exchange rate under such pressure.

Speculative crises were, and will always be, one of the most intractable problems of any adjustable peg system. The impact of such crises might be reduced if governments had more adequate reserves. If a speculative crisis precedes an exchange-rate adjustment, however, more adequate reserves may just mean that speculators will make larger profits since more of them will be able to sell the currency about to be devalued and to buy the currency about to be revalued before the monetary authorities are forced to act. During the Bretton Woods period, governments tended to resist changing their exchange rates until they had no alternative. This made the situation so obvious that speculators could hardly lose, and their actions set off the final crises that forced exchange-rate readjustments.

Under an adjustable peg system, speculators get an easy opportunity for making large profits since everyone knows which way an exchange rate will be changed if it is to be changed at all.

As the equilibrium value of a country's currency changes, possibly under the impact of a high rate of inflation, it becomes obvious to everyone that the central bank is having more and more difficulty holding the pegged rate. So when a crisis arises, speculators sell the country's currency. If it is devalued, they can buy it back at its now lower price to earn a profit. If it is not devalued they can buy it back at the price at which they sold it and lose only the commission costs on the deal. This asymmetry, speculators having a chance of large profits by risking only a small loss, was what eventually undid the system. As trade became more unsettled, as differences in inflation rates became greater and as exchange reserves became smaller, more frequent adjustments in the pegged rates were necessary. Seeing these coming, speculators sold currencies under pressure to be devalued, and bought currencies under pressure to be revalued. There were massive movements of speculative funds, which destabilized the system and which were one of the major causes of its abandonment in the early 1970s.

Flexible exchange rates

Under a system of flexible exchange rates, demand and supply determine the rates without any government intervention. Since the market always clears with demand equal to supply, the central authorities can turn their attention to domestic problems of inflation and unemployment leaving the balance of payments to take care of itself – at least so went the theory before flexible rates were introduced.

For reasons that we shall analyse later in this chapter, this optimistic picture did not materialize when the world went over to flexible exchange rates. Free-market fluctuations in rates were far greater – and hence more upsetting to trade – than many economists had anticipated. As a result, central banks have felt the need to intervene quite frequently, and heavily, to stabilize exchange rates at least against the more extreme short-term fluctuations. This has brought the world to the mixed regime of dirty floats.

Dirty floats

Although many of today's exchange rates are determined on the free market, there is nevertheless substantial intervention in these markets by central banks. The difference between the present system and Bretton Woods is that central banks no longer have publicly announced par values for exchange-rate values that they are committed in advance to defend even at heavy cost. Central banks are thus free to change their exchange-rate targets as circumstances change. Sometimes they leave the rate completely free to fluctuate, and at other times they interfere actively to alter the exchange rate from its free-market value. Such a system is called a MANAGED FLOAT or a DIRTY FLOAT.

To manage exchange rates, central banks must hold foreign-exchange reserves. One of the major forms in which reserves are held are US dollars; another, and one that is growing in importance, is the SPECIAL DRAWING RIGHTS (SDRs) held with the IMF. SDRs, first introduced in 1969, were designed to provide a supplement to existing reserve assets by setting up a Special Drawing Account kept separate from all other operations of the Fund. Each member country of the Fund was assigned an SDR quota that was guaranteed in terms of a fixed gold value and that it could use to acquire an equivalent amount of convertible currencies from other participants. SDRs could be used without prior consultation with the Fund, but only to cope with balance-of-payments difficulties.

An assessment of post World War II co-operation

One of the most impressive aspects of international payments history in the last thirty years has been the steady rise of effective international co-operation. When the gold standard broke down and the Great Depression overwhelmed the countries of the world, 'every man for himself' was the rule of the day. Rising tariffs, competitive exchange-rate devaluations and all forms of beggar-my-neighbour policies abounded.

After the Second World War, the countries of the world co-operated in bringing the Bretton Woods system and the IMF into being. The system itself was far from perfect, and it finally broke down as a result of its own internal contradictions. But the international co-operation that was necessary to set the system up survived the system itself. The collapse of Bretton Woods, therefore, did not plunge the world into the same chaos that followed the breakdown of the gold standard. The countries of the world were also able to cope with the terrible strains caused by the sharp rise in oil prices in the 1970s better than they could have earlier, although there still are, of course, enormous oil-related problems.

Whatever the problems of the future may be, it seems clear that the world has a better chance of coping with them – or even of just learning to live with them – when its countries co-operate through the IMF and other international organizations than when every country engages in a self-defeating pursuit of its own selfish solution without concern for the interests of others.

In 1981–2 the world fell into the deepest and most prolonged slump since the 1930s. Under the extreme pressures of this difficult economic situation, beggar-my-neighbour pressures surfaced and many governments found them hard to resist politically. American elections in November 1982 showed very strong support for advocates of increased tariffs to protect hard-pressed American import-competing industries. Many countries negotiated unofficial quotas restricting the importation of Japanese cars. European agricultural protectionism nearly wrecked the GATT negotiations in December 1982. Earlier in the year Sweden initiated what appeared to be a beggar-my-neighbour devaluation of the kroner. Less developed countries sought covert ways of protecting their own infant industries and complained, with some justice, that the developed nations gave lip-service rather than real action to the slogan of 'trade not aid'. It was clear that great pressure was being put on the whole postwar fabric designed to encourage trade and discourage beggar-my-neighbour policies. The longer the recession continued, the more alarming these pressures became.

Macroeconomic policy and the current account

Current-account problems arise when the exchange rate is pegged. Under a dirty float the same problems arise if the authorities wish to resist a tendency for the current exchange rate to change. It is easiest to analyse the problem from the point of view of a pegged exchange rate, but the analysis applies whenever the authorities seek to stop the exchange rate from changing freely in response to private-sector demands and supplies.

To concentrate on the current account for the moment, we assume that the central authorities desire neither major imports nor major exports of capital. They therefore regard their external objective as a state of zero balance on the current account.

The current account and domestic policy objectives

There is potential for conflict between the objectives of internal and external balance, where internal balance means full employment and external balance means a balanced current account. Policies used to achieve one objective will also affect the other and, because of this, the two objectives may well come into conflict. The conflict arises under a fixed exchange rate because the only instrument available to the government is to affect national income through demand-management policies. Two goals, internal and external balance, and only one policy instrument, demand management, create the potential for policy conflicts.

The use of monetary or fiscal policy to eliminate an inflationary or an output gap will change the balance of trade by causing a *movement along* the net export function. Whether there is a conflict between the objectives of internal and external balance depends on whether the initial situation is one of a surplus or a deficit in the trade account and whether there is an output or an inflationary gap. (See Chapter 37.)

1. A trade-account *deficit* combined with an *output gap* poses a conflict because the expansion of aggregate demand to eliminate the output gap leads to an increase in expenditures on imports and hence a worsening of the trade deficit.
2. A trade-account *deficit* combined with an *inflationary gap* poses no conflict because the contraction of aggregate demand to eliminate the inflationary gap leads to a reduction in imports and hence reduces the trade deficit.
3. A trade-account *surplus* combined with an *output gap* poses no conflict because the expansion of aggregate demand to eliminate the output gap increases imports and hence reduces the trade surplus.
4. A trade-account *surplus* combined with an *inflationary gap* poses a conflict because the contraction of aggregate demand to eliminate the inflationary gap leads to a reduction in imports and hence an increase in the trade surplus.

In case 1, the deficit calls for a decrease in national income but the output gap calls for an increase. In case 4 the surplus calls for an increase in national income but the inflationary gap calls for a decrease.

> **A conflict arises between the objectives of internal and external balance when the two call for opposite changes in the level of national income.**

The absorption approach outlined in Chapter 37 is useful in suggesting policies to deal with such conflicts. Basically, these conflicts arise from *movements along* the net export function; resolution of the conflicts arises from *shifts* in the net export function.

Expenditure-changing and expenditure-switching policies In Chapter 37 we saw that aggregate desired expenditure is equal to domestic absorption plus net exports. It is useful to distinguish between two types of policies that might be used to maintain internal and external balance. Policies that maintain the level of aggregate desired expenditure but influence its composition between domestic absorption and net exports are called EXPENDITURE-SWITCHING policies. Policies that change aggregate desired expenditure are called EXPENDITURE-CHANGING policies. Both types of policies operate by influencing domestic absorption. The conflicts between the objectives of internal and external balance discussed above arise from the use of expenditure-changing policies. These policies involve moving along a given net export function, so changes in the trade balance and national income must be negatively related. If the initial situation calls for them to move in the same direction, the use of expenditure-changing policies necessarily involves a conflict.

An expenditure-switching policy shifts the net export function. As shown in Figure 37.4, on page 559, this can lead to positively related changes in the trade balance and national income. Domestic inflation or deflation relative to foreign conditions, a devaluation or revaluation of the domestic currency, or restrictions on international trade such as tariffs or quotas, are all expenditure-switching policies.

To illustrate, let us look at the conflict given in case 1 above. If only expenditure-changing policies were available, either internal balance could be achieved by raising expenditure or external balance achieved by lowering expenditure. To achieve internal and external balance, therefore, a combination of policies is required. Expenditure-increasing policies can be used to achieve full employment, and expenditure-switching policies to achieve balanced trade. This is illustrated in Figure 45.2. Initial equilibrium is at Y_1 in (i) where the E_1 curve intersects the 45° line. In (ii) the net export function is the black line $(X - M)_1$. At the initial equilibrium, there is an output gap because Y_1 is less than Y_F, and a trade deficit because the net export function lies below the axis at Y_1.

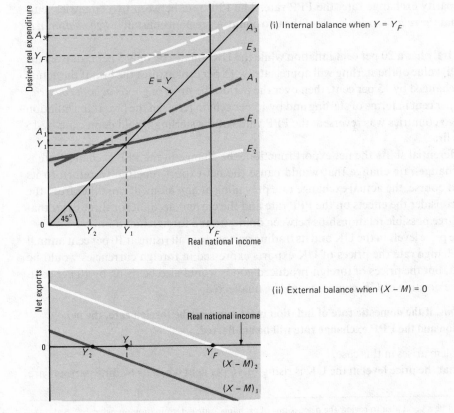

Fig. 45.2 Expenditure-changing and expenditure-switching policies

An expenditure-reducing policy aimed at eliminating the trade deficit shifts the expenditure function downward to E_2. (As net exports are zero at the new equilibrium level of income, Y_2, it is evident that the A_2 line would intersect E_2 at the new equilibrium level of income Y_2.) The conflict is apparent since net exports are zero but the output gap has increased.

An expenditure-increasing policy designed to eliminate the output gap shifts E_1 upward to E_3 by shifting the domestic absorption line to A_3. The conflict arises in this instance because the trade deficit increases.

Starting from equilibrium income of Y_1 and net export function of $(X - M)_1$, it is evident that two policy instruments are needed to achieve both internal and external balance. First, expenditure-changing policies (e.g. a tax cut) are needed to shift the expenditure function to E_3, creating equilibrium at Y_F. Second, expenditure-switching policies (e.g. a devaluation) are needed to shift the net export function up to $(X - M)_2$, thus making domestic absorption just equal to income at Y_F (i.e. the **A** line intersects the E line at Y_F).

Inflation, the current account and the PPP exchange rate[1]

Inflation differentials between trading partners have important implications for their exchange rates and their current accounts. In order to focus on the role of relative prices, we use the concept of the purchasing-power-parity exchange rate, the PPP rate. The PPP rate between two countries' currencies adjusts so that the *relative* price levels of the two countries remain constant *when measured in a common currency*.

For example, if Italy has a 20 per cent inflation while the UK inflates by only 5 per cent over the same period, the PPP value of the sterling will appreciate by 15 per cent against the lira. If the actual exchange rate also changed by 15 per cent, then over the period the price of goods *in both countries* will have risen by 5 per cent in terms of sterling and by 15 per cent in terms of the lira. If the inflation experience of the two countries was reversed, the PPP value of the sterling would depreciate by 15 per cent against the lira.

An inflation differential shifts the net export function; the change in the PPP exchange rate is defined as that exchange-rate change that would cause the net export function to return to its original position. Of course, the actual exchange rate prevailing at any moment can differ from the PPP rate. Here we consider the effects on the PPP rate and the current account for three cases that correspond to the three possible relationships between domestic and foreign inflation.

Suppose that the price levels in the UK and its trading partners are all rising at 10 per cent annual rate. At a given exchange rate the prices of UK exports expressed in foreign currencies would be rising by 10 per cent, but the prices of foreign-produced goods would also be rising by 10 per cent. Thus the competitive position of UK exports would be unaffected.

> **Ceteris paribus, if the domestic rate of inflation is the same as the foreign rate, the net export function and the PPP exchange rate will be unaffected.**

Thus no policy problem arises in this case.

Next, suppose that the price level in the UK is rising by 10 per cent while its trading partners are

---

[1] At this time it would be a good idea to review the discussions of exchange-rate determination on pages 142–6 and the role of relative prices in influencing the current account on page 555.

experiencing inflation at a 4 per cent rate. At a given exchange rate, domestic exports will fall and imports will rise.

> **If the domestic rate of inflation is higher than the foreign rate, the net export function will be shifting downward, so the PPP value of the domestic currency will be falling.**

Under these circumstances the UK would have basically two policy options. It could allow its currency to depreciate continuously at a rate of 6 per cent. This would keep the exchange rate at the equilibrium PPP level and stop the net export function from shifting. Alternatively, policies could be introduced to reduce inflation to an average annual rate of 4 per cent.

Suppose, finally, that the situation is reversed, that the inflation rate in the UK is 4 per cent compared with 10 per cent in the rest of the world. In this case the relative price of British goods will be falling, exports will rise, and imports will fall.

> **If the domestic rate of inflation is lower than the foreign rate, the net export function will be shifting upward and to the right, so the PPP value of the domestic currency will be rising.**

Here the policy option is either to allow sterling to appreciate or to *raise* the domestic rate of inflation to 10 per cent.

Macroeconomic policy and the capital account

The capital account of the balance of payments records international movements of investment funds, and its details were discussed in Chapter 37. The primary means by which capital flows can be influenced by the policy authorities is the manipulation of domestic interest rates.

In discussing the current account we did not distinguish between the effects of monetary and fiscal policy. However, capital flows respond to interest rates, and monetary and fiscal policies that have the same influence on income have opposite effects on interest rates. As we saw in Chapter 40, expansionary monetary policy exerts its influence on aggregate demand by *reducing* interest rates, while expansionary fiscal policy influences aggregate demand directly and, by raising national income, creates an excess demand for money, which causes interest rates to rise. In discussing capital flows it is necessary therefore to consider fiscal and monetary policies separately.

> **An expansionary fiscal policy will raise domestic interest rates and lead to an inflow of foreign capital, thereby moving the capital account towards a surplus position. A contractionary fiscal policy will have the opposite effect.**

> **An expansionary monetary policy will lower domestic interest rates and lead to an outflow of capital, thereby moving the capital account toward a deficit position. A contractionary monetary policy will have the opposite effect.**

An alternative concept of external balance

Earlier we used the term *external balance* to mean zero net exports. In many circumstances this is not appropriate; a country may have a target level other than zero for its capital account and hence also for its current account. It may be, for example, that it wishes to preserve its stock of international reserves. In that case, external balance would mean a zero balance on the combined current and capital accounts. Let us see how monetary and fiscal policy might be combined to achieve internal and external balance in this circumstance.

In principle, any short-term conflict between internal and external balance at a given exchange rate can be overcome by an appropriate combination of fiscal and monetary policy. This is illustrated in Figure 45.3 where initially the curves IS_1 and LM_1 intersect to produce the interest rate r_1 and national income of Y_1, which is assumed to be less than Y_F. If the authorities wish to raise

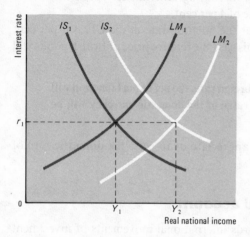

Fig. 45.3 Fiscal and monetary policy used together to achieve target levels of both national income and interest rates

income while keeping short-run capital flows unchanged, they can shift IS to IS_2 by an expansionary fiscal policy and LM to LM_2 by an expansionary monetary policy. This raises income to Y_2 while holding the rate of interest constant at r_1. If they wish to raise income and improve the balance of payments by increasing short-run capital inflows, they can shift IS to IS_2 by an expansionary fiscal policy while shifting the LM curve less far out than LM_2. This raises income and the rate of interest. Finally, if they wish to raise income while reducing a balance-of-payments surplus by reducing short-term capital inflows (or encouraging outflows), they can shift the LM curve to LM_2 by an expansionary monetary policy and shift the IS curve less far out than IS_2. This raises income and lowers the interest rate.

> **In principle it is possible to achieve any direction of change in income and the balance of payments, at least for the short term, by suitable combinations of monetary and fiscal policy.**

Although this strategy may be workable in the short run, it is unlikely to be a satisfactory solution to a persistent balance-of-payments problem. A country that is unable to maintain full employment because of a genuinely overvalued currency will find it increasingly difficult to maintain its exchange rate by importing short-term capital. If investors lose confidence in a country's ability to maintain its existing parity, capital inflows will fall in spite of the high local interest rates, and ultimately a devaluation will be required to reduce the deficit and restore confidence.

Macroeconomic policy under fixed exchange rates

The responsiveness of capital flows to interest rates has important implications for the ability of fiscal and monetary policy to achieve full employment. If the interest elasticity of capital flows is very high, the maintenance of a fixed exchange rate will make monetary policy less effective, and fiscal policy more effective, for the purposes of domestic stabilization. To see why this is so, it is useful to examine the relationship between the money supply and the balance-of-payments deficit.

The balance of payments and the money supply Suppose that the UK is experiencing a balance-of-payments deficit and that the Bank of England intervenes in the foreign-exchange market in order to maintain the value of sterling. The Bank will be selling foreign currency in exchange for sterling and thereby running down the stock of official reserves. This is an open-market operation by the Bank and it has exactly the same effect on the money supply as if the Bank sold domestic bonds. We have already analysed the effects of open-market operations in domestic assets. To see the effect of open-market operations in foreign exchange, all you need to do is to return to pages 693–5 and Tables 44.2 and 44.3, and change 'bond' to read 'foreign exchange'.

> **If the Bank is supporting the international value of sterling by buying sterling and selling foreign exchange (reducing exchange reserves), this leads to a fall in domestic money supply. If the Bank is holding sterling below its free-exchange value by selling sterling and buying foreign exchange (adding to foreign-exchange reserves), this leads to an expansion of the domestic money supply.**

The Bank does, however, have the option of undertaking other offsetting transactions. For example, a decrease in bank reserves can be offset by an open-market purchase of domestic bonds, which will have the effect of increasing bank reserves. This procedure of insulating the domestic money supply from the effects of balance-of-payments deficits or surpluses is known as STERILIZATION.

Monetary policy under fixed exchange rates To see the limitations of monetary policy under a fixed exchange rate, consider the following sequence of events. Suppose that interest rates in Britain are at levels similar to those in the rest of the world, and thus there is no inducement for large international movements of capital. Suppose now that the Bank of England, faced with a high domestic unemployment rate, seeks to stimulate demand through an expansionary monetary policy. The Bank buys bonds in the open market, thereby increasing both bank reserves and the money supply while reducing interest rates.

Lower interest rates stimulate an outflow of capital and thus cause a deficit on the capital account. To maintain the fixed exchange rate, the Bank will have to intervene in the foreign-exchange market and sell foreign exchange. *This will have the effect of reducing the money supply and thus reversing the increase brought about by the open-market operation.* If no other transactions are initiated by the Bank, the money supply will fall until it returns to its initial level and domestic interest rates will return to something close to their initial level. Thus the deficit will be self-correcting, and the Bank's expansionary policy will be nullified.

Suppose now that the Bank attempts to sterilize the impact on the money supply of the balance-of-payments deficit. The difficulty with this strategy is that it can be continued only as long as the

Bank has sufficient reserves of foreign exchange. If capital flows are highly sensitive to interest rates, as is usually the case, these reserves will be run down at a rapid rate and the Bank will be forced to abandon its expansionary policy.

> **Under a fixed exchange rate, there is little scope for the use of monetary policy for domestic stabilization purposes. Because of the sensitivity of international capital flows to interest rates, the central bank will be forced to maintain domestic interest rates close to the levels existing in the rest of the world. It will not, therefore, be able to bring about substantial changes in the domestic money supply.**

Fiscal policy under fixed exchange rates Consider now the effectiveness of fiscal policy under fixed exchange rates. Suppose again that British interest rates are in line with those of the rest of the world when an expansionary fiscal policy is introduced, aimed at reducing a high domestic unemployment rate. The fiscal expansion raises the level of domestic interest rates and national income.

Higher interest rates stimulate an inflow of capital, thereby leading to a surplus on the capital account. If the capital flows are large enough, as they are likely to be given the high degree of integration of international capital markets, the surplus on capital account will be larger than the current-account deficit arising from the increased national income. Hence there will be an overall balance-of-payments surplus.

To maintain the fixed exchange rate, the Bank of England will have to intervene in the foreign-exchange market and buy foreign currency. This will have the effect of increasing the money supply, *thus reinforcing the initial fiscal stimulus.*

> **Under a fixed exchange rate, interest-sensitive international capital flows tend to stabilize the domestic interest rate and enhance the effectiveness of fiscal policy by inducing a reinforcing monetary expansion.**

This can be illustrated by reinterpreting Figure 45.3. The initial curves are IS_1 and LM_1. The expansionary fiscal policy shifts IS to IS_2 and raises income and the interest rate. The higher interest rate induces a large inflow of capital, opening up a balance-of-payments surplus. To stop sterling from appreciating, the Bank buys foreign exchange thereby increasing the domestic money supply. This continues until LM shifts to LM_2, increasing income yet further to Y_2 but restoring the original interest rate and thereby removing the extra incentive for capital inflows.

Macroeconomic policy under flexible exchange rates

A major advantage of a flexible exchange rate is that it reduces any conflict between domestic stabilization objectives and the balance of payments, because deficits or surpluses tend to be automatically eliminated through movements in the exchange rate. In addition, a flexible exchange rate tends to cushion the domestic economy against cyclical variations in economic activity in other countries. If, for example, the US economy goes into a recession, the decline in US income will lead to a reduction in demand for goods exported from the UK. The fall in exports will reduce income in the UK through the multiplier effect, but if the value of sterling is allowed to respond to market forces, there will also be a depreciation. This fall in the external value of sterling will stimulate British exports and encourage the substitution of domestically produced goods for imports. Thus the depreciation will provide a stimulus to demand in the UK that will at least partially offset the depressing effect of the US recession.

Fiscal policy under flexible rates   Suppose the government seeks to remove an output gap by expansionary fiscal policy. An increase in government expenditures and/or a reduction in taxes will increase income through the multiplier effect and reduce the size of the gap. There will also be an increase in imports as a result of the increase in income, which will cause the domestic currency to depreciate. This will provide an additional stimulus to demand because it will increase demand for British exports and encourage the substitution of domestically produced goods for imports. Thus the effect of a flexible exchange rate operating through the current account is to add to the potency of fiscal policy. However, this is not the whole story, for there will also be repercussions on the capital account.

Expansionary fiscal policy causes domestic interest rates to rise. This causes interest-sensitive private expenditures to fall, thus partially offsetting the initial expansionary effect of the fiscal stimulus. This is the crowding-out effect once again. In an open economy, this crowding out will be magnified by the influence of interest rates on international capital flows. Higher domestic interest rates will induce a capital inflow and cause the domestic currency to appreciate. If capital flows are highly interest elastic, this effect will swamp the depreciation induced by the current-account effect so that on balance the external value of sterling is likely to rise substantially. This will depress aggregate demand by discouraging exports and encouraging the substitution of imports for domestically produced goods.

Thus under flexible exchange rates there will be a strong crowding-out effect that will greatly reduce the effectiveness of fiscal policy. It is possible, however, to eliminate the crowding-out effect by supporting the fiscal policy with an accommodating monetary policy. The central bank responds to the increase in demand for money induced by the fiscal expansion, by increasing the supply of money so as to maintain domestic interest rates at their initial level. There will then be no capital inflow and no tendency for the currency to appreciate. Income will expand by the multiplier process and there will be an additional stimulus from a depreciation of the currency.

> **The effectiveness of fiscal policy under flexible exchange rates depends on an accommodating monetary policy that permits the money supply to expand so as to prevent an increase in interest rates.**

Monetary policy under flexible rates   We have seen that there is little scope under fixed exchange rates for the use of monetary policy for domestic stabilization purposes. Under flexible exchange rates, the situation is reversed and monetary policy becomes a powerful tool.

Suppose the Bank of England seeks to stimulate demand through an expansionary monetary policy. The Bank buys bonds in the open market, thereby increasing the money supply and reducing interest rates. Lower interest rates will cause an outflow of capital from the UK and thus a deficit on the capital account.

Under a fixed exchange rate, the Bank may be forced to reverse its policy in order to stem the loss of foreign-exchange reserves. Under a flexible rate, however, sterling can be allowed to depreciate, and this will stimulate exports and discourage imports so that the deficit on the capital account will be offset by a surplus on the current account.

Domestic employment will be stimulated not only by the fall in interest rates but also by the increased demand for domestically produced goods brought about by a depreciation of the currency. The initial monetary expansion shifts the *LM* curve right while the resulting depreciation, by increasing net exports, also shifts *IS* to the right.

Under flexible exchange rates, monetary policy is a powerful tool of expansionary demand management because an initial monetary stimulus opens up a balance-of-payments deficit which depreciates the currency causing an increase in aggregate demand through an increase in net exports.

Finally, consider a contractionary monetary policy. If the Bank wants to contract aggregate demand it reduces the money supply, shifting the *LM* curve to the left. This raises domestic interest rates and causes an inflow of short-term capital. The inflow in turn appreciates sterling, making it harder to export and so reinforcing the contractionary process.

The theory of exchange-rate overshooting

Let us now consider this process in a little more detail. Assume that in pursuit of a restrictive monetary policy the Bank of England has forced British interest rates above those ruling in other major financial centres. A rush to lend money out at the profitable rates in London will lead to an appreciation of sterling. Where will this process stop? When will the short-term equilibrium be reached? The answer is that the rise in sterling's external value must be large enough so that investors expect it to fall in value subsequently, thus offsetting the interest premium from lending funds in the UK.

To illustrate this very important point, assume that interest rates are 4 percentage points higher in London than in New York due to a very restrictive monetary policy in the UK. Investors believe the PPP rate is $2·00 = £1, but as they rush to buy sterling they drive the rate to, say, $2·20. They do not believe this rate will be sustained and instead expect sterling to lose value at 4 per cent per year. Now foreign investors are indifferent between lending money in New York or London. The extra 4 per cent of interest they earn in London per year is exactly offset by the 4 per cent they expect to lose when they turn their money back into their own currency because they expect the external value of sterling to be falling (back towards its PPP) at that rate.

A restrictive monetary policy that raises domestic interest rates above world levels will lead to an inflow of capital that will appreciate the external value of the home currency so far that future expected depreciations just offset the interest differential.

If all the Bank wants to do is reduce aggregate demand, this added effect reduces it further, as the appreciation shifts the net export function downwards. But if the Bank is trying to achieve some long-run monetary target without causing too much short-term unemployment, these capital flows can be very disturbing. A central bank that is seeking to meet a monetary target must put up with some large fluctuations in the exchange rate. In particular, if a restrictive monetary policy is needed to hold the money supply on target, the resulting high interest rates may lead to a large overshooting of the external value of the currency above its PPP rate. This may put export and import-competing industries under temporary but very severe pressure from foreign competition. We shall return to this point in Chapter 47.

Part eleven

Some current issues in theory and policy

46

Employment and unemployment

In the early 1980s world-wide unemployment rose to very high levels, higher than during some of the years of the 1930s although not as high as the peak unemployment rates of that earlier 'Great Depression'. Not only was the overall level of unemployment wastefully large, the structure of unemployment was extremely varied – in Britain at the beginning of 1982 the unemployment rate was about 25 per cent among males under 25 and 5 per cent among women over 55. Regional disparities were significant, although not so large as they were a decade or two before. Currently the most serious problem of localized unemployment seemed to be the very high rates among the mainly unskilled residents of the decaying inner cores of large industrial cities.

Social policies instituted since the 1930s have no doubt made the short-term economic consequences of unemployment much less serious than they were in earlier times. This may be counted as a real success of economic policy. But the longer-term effects of current high unemployment rates, in terms of disillusioned groups who have given up trying to succeed within the system and who sow the seeds of future social unrest, should be a matter of serious concern to the 'haves' as well as to the 'have-nots'.

In the 1970s control of inflation emerged as a serious social problem. To cure inflation, governments induced the major world-wide recession of the early 1980s. Was the resulting unemployment worth it? What were its effects on individuals and on whole economies? Can the unemployment be reduced in the last half of the 1980s just as easily as it was induced in the late 1970s and early 1980s? It is to these and other urgent questions that we must now turn.

Kinds of unemployment

It is sometimes helpful to distinguish a number of kinds of unemployment.

Frictional unemployment

FRICTIONAL UNEMPLOYMENT is unemployment associated with the normal turnover of labour. People leave jobs for all sorts of reasons, and they take time to find new jobs; old persons leave the labour force and young persons enter it, but often new workers do not fill the jobs vacated by those who leave. Inevitably all of this movement takes time and gives rise to a pool of persons who are 'frictionally' unemployed while in the course of finding new jobs.

National-income theory seeks to explain the causes of, and cures for, unemployment in excess of unavoidable frictional unemployment. Indeed when we speak of 'full employment' we do not mean zero unemployment, but rather that all unemployment is frictional unemployment caused solely by the normal entry into and exit from, and job turnover within, the labour force.

Structural unemployment

Structural changes in the economy can be a cause of unemployment. As economic growth proceeds, the mix of required inputs changes, as do the proportions in which final goods are demanded. These changes require considerable economic readjustment. STRUCTURAL UNEMPLOYMENT occurs when the adjustments are not fast enough, so that severe pockets of unemployment occur in areas, industries and occupations in which the demand for factors of production is falling faster than is the supply. In Britain today, structural unemployment exists, for example, in Wales and in the motorcar industry.

Structural unemployment can increase because either the pace of change accelerates or the pace of adjustment to change slows down. Policies that discourage movement among regions, industries and occupations can raise structural unemployment. Policies that prevent firms from replacing some labour with new machines may protect employment in the short term. If, however, they lead to the decline of an industry because it cannot compete with more innovative foreign competitors, such policies can end up causing severe pockets of structural unemployment.

Structural unemployment may be said to exist when there is a mismatching between the unemployed and the available jobs in terms of regional location, required skills or any other relevant dimension.

As with many distinctions, the one between structural and frictional unemployment becomes blurred at the margin. In a sense, structural unemployment is really long-term frictional unemployment. For illustration, consider a change that requires a reallocation of labour. If the reallocation occurs quickly, we call the unemployment frictional while it lasts; if the reallocation occurs slowly – possibly only after the person who has lost a job dies or retires from the labour force and has been replaced by a new person with different and more marketable skills – we call the unemployment structural.

One useful measure of the total of frictional *plus* structural unemployment is the percentage of the labour force unemployed when the number of unfilled job vacancies is equal to the number of persons seeking jobs. When these two magnitudes are equal, there is some kind of job opening to match every person seeking a job and the unemployment that occurs must be either frictional or structural.

This measure is illustrated in Figure 46.1, which plots the number of unfilled vacancies (v) against the number of unplaced applicants (u). Observed uv relations are roughly hyperbolic, such as the curve shown by uv_1 in the Figure. The 45° line is the locus of points where $u = v$. On that line there is some job available to match every unemployed person, so there is no deficient-demand unemployment. In an economy with the relation uv_1, zero deficient-demand unemployment occurs at the point x and, at that point, frictional plus structural unemployment is given by the distance $0a$ measured on either axis. A boom takes the economy to some point such as y, where there are more vacancies than unemployed. A slump takes the economy to some point such as z, where there are fewer vacancies than unemployed. A change in structural plus frictional unemployment *shifts* the *uv* curve. In the diagram, a shift to uv_2 indicates a rise in frictional plus structural unemployment from $0a$ to $0b$.

On this measure, structural plus frictional unemployment has risen significantly in the UK over the last 10–15 years. The percentage of the labour force unemployed when aggregate unemployed equalled aggregate vacancies remained fairly constant up until 1966 and then began to rise for adult males. Now there is substantially more unemployment than there used to be at times when, in the aggregate, the number of unfilled jobs equals the number looking for jobs. Similar shifts have been observed in many other developed economies. Although the reasons are still subject to debate, the change is certainly consistent with a rise in structural unemployment among adult male workers.

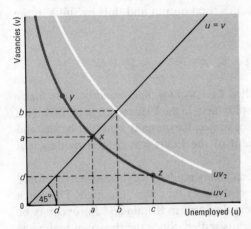

Fig. 46.1 The vacancies–unemployment relation

Deficient-demand unemployment

Unemployment that occurs because there is insufficient total demand to purchase all of the output that could be produced by a fully-employed labour force is called DEFICIENT-DEMAND UNEMPLOYMENT. It is common to measure this kind of unemployment as the difference between the number of persons seeking jobs and the number of unfilled job vacancies (i.e., total unemployment minus frictional and structural unemployment) expressed as a percentage of the labour force. This statistic shows the excess of the supply of workers looking for jobs over the number of jobs available. It will be positive when there is not enough total demand and negative when there is more than enough.

Figure 46.1 suggests, however, that this measure will provide an overstatement of deficient-demand unemployment. Assume the curve uv_1 applies and a severe recession has taken the economy to point z. The measure just described would estimate deficient-demand unemployment as $u - v = c - d$. But now let a recovery of aggregate demand occur that takes the economy back to point x where there is no longer any deficient-demand unemployment. The rise in aggregate demand has reduced unemployment by $c - a$, not by $c - d$.

This analysis suggests a second, more satisfactory measure: deficient-demand unemployment is total unemployment *minus* estimated frictional unemployment *plus* structural unemployment. This makes it the current u minus the u where the uv relation cuts the 45° line. This measure is $c - a$ in the Figure. Both measures, $c - a$ and $c - d$, agree that deficient-demand unemployment is zero at x but the first gives a larger total of deficient-demand unemployment than does the second in times of recession and it overstates the amount by which unemployment can be reduced by raising aggregate demand to move the economy back to the point at which $u = v$.

Deficient-demand unemployment may be measured by the number of unemployed in excess of the number that would be unemployed if unfilled vacancies were equal to the number of unemployed.

Deficient-demand unemployment is the main subject of national-income theory, which seeks to explain unemployment caused by variations in the nation's total output and thus by shifts in the derived demand for labour.

Real-wage unemployment

Unemployment due to too high a real wage is often called *Classical unemployment* because many economists, dubbed Classical by Keynes, held that unemployment in the 1930s was due to too high a real wage. Their remedy for unemployment was to reduce wages. Keynesians won that battle, and there is now general agreement that the unemployment of the 1930s was caused by deficient aggregate demand.

Because the battles of the 1930s aroused such emotions, many modern Keynesians have refused to believe that *any* unemployment could be caused by real wages that were too high. There is a growing concern, however, that some of the current unemployment in Britain and Europe may be traceable to high real-wage levels. The issue is by no means settled. Since the theory of real-wage unemployment is now well understood,[1] it is important that economists at least accept the possibility, keeping an open mind on its actual existence as further empirical research goes on. Because of the emotionally loaded nature of the phrase 'Classical unemployment', the term REAL-WAGE UNEMPLOYMENT, defined as unemployment due to the existing level of real wages, is probably the preferable term. We can distinguish two types of real-wage unemployment, one associated with relative wages among different groups of labour and one associated with wages in general.

A disequilibrium structure of relative wages Typical causes here are minimum wages, union agreements that narrow wage differentials, nationally agreed wage structures that take no account of local market conditions, and equal pay laws where employers perceive unequal marginal-value products among the groups concerned.

All of these can cause particular groups to lose employment because their relative wages are too high. Assume, for example, that an elderly person is prepared to work for £Y a week to be a caretaker of a block of flats, and the owner believes this person is capable of doing what is needed.

---

[1] The most important book on this issue is probably E. Malinvaud, *The Theory of Unemployment Reconsidered* (Basil Blackwell, Oxford, 1977). A more recent contribution by the same author is 'Wages and Unemployment', *The Economic Journal*, 92 (March 1982), pp. 1–12, which also contains a number of other valuable references.

Also assume that the minimum wage is £2Y. In the absence of the minimum wage, the elderly person would get the job. Given the minimum wage, however, the owner who has to pay twice as much as he needs to, hires someone who can provide him with more services than he needs. He reasons that, if he has to pay more, he might as well get something for it. Now consider an inexperienced school-leaver who would accept £X for his or her first job. A potential employer is willing to pay this, but the minimum wage is £1·5X. Once again the employer gets someone overqualified for the job on the grounds that, if he has to pay more than he needs to, he might as well get something extra in return.

Much empirical work supports the conclusion that wage structures such as the ones just discussed tend to transfer employment from those whose relative wages are raised by the intervention to those whose relative wages are lowered. But does it affect overall employment? That is a much more difficult question.

> **The imposition of non-equilibrium wage structures will generally reduce employment of those whose *relative* wages are raised thereby and increase employment of those whose *relative* wages are reduced thereby.**

A disequilibrium average real wage So far, by the real wage, we have meant the purchasing power of money wages. This can be measured by deflating the money wage by the retail price index. Now we introduce a second type of real wage: THE REAL PRODUCT WAGE, which is the real wage deflated by the price of the product that labour produces. Note also that, since it is *labour costs* in which we are interested, the wage is the full cost to the employer of hiring a unit of labour, which includes the pre-tax wage rate, any extra benefits such as pension plan contributions, and any government payroll taxes such as employers' contribution to national insurance. Too high a real wage can affect employment through forces operating both in the short run and in the long run.

Consider the short run first. As we saw in Chapter 19, technological change that is embodied in plant and equipment means that, at any moment in time, an industry will have an array of plants running from those that can do little more than cover their variable costs through to those that make a handsome return over variable costs. A rise in the real product wage of 10 per cent will mean that some plants can no longer cover their variable costs and they will close down. If, for example, a plant had wages of 64p and other direct costs of 30p in every sales £1, production would be worthwhile since 6p of every £1 of sales would be available as a return on already invested capital. If the product wage rose by 10 per cent to 70·4p in every £1 of sales, then the plant would immediately be shut down, since it would not even be covering its variable costs. The plant's employees would then lose their jobs.

If the rise in real product wages occurred across the whole economy, plants and firms that could no longer cover their variable costs would shut down and unemployment would rise throughout the country. In Figure 46.1, this change will show up, approximately, as a movement along the existing *uv* curve rather than as a shift of that curve. There will be a large rise in unemployment and a small fall in vacancies (which would otherwise have resulted from the normal turnover of labour in the now-closed plants).

> **A general rise in the real product wage can lead to a general rise in unemployment that looks like deficient-demand unemployment because there is a rise in unemployment with no corresponding rise (probably a fall) in unfilled vacancies.**

Now consider the long run. Much capital is what is called PUTTY-CLAY: at the design stage, more or less capital can be spread over the labour force, thus varying the capital-labour ratio but, once built, factor ratios are embodied in the equipment and cannot be significantly varied. For example, you can design highly automated or quite simple textile plants and so vary the capital-labour ratio continuously on the drawing board. Once an automated plant is built, however, you cannot vary the labour-capital ratio greatly by productively applying masses of labour to the automated machinery.

In such circumstances, unemployment caused by too high a real product wage would show up as a structural mismatching between the labour force and the capital stock. Given the size of the labour force, not enough capital may be built and what is built may be too labour-saving in its construction.

That a rise in the real product wage would lead to more capital-intensive methods of production (i.e., a substitution of capital for labour) is a direct consequence of the principle of substitution discussed in Chapter 17. When plants that are too labour-intensive are being replaced by plants that are more capital-intensive, we would expect unemployment to develop. But that is a transitional phase. Wouldn't more of these capital-intensive plants be built until all of the available labour force is put to work?

The answer depends on whether or not the real product wage is too high to encourage sufficient investment. General cases need to be distinguished. First, the real product wage may be raised so high that no new plants built with existing technology are profitable. Then old plants that cannot cover variable costs will be closed down, no new plants will be built and an alleviation of the unemployment (assuming the real wage is not lowered) must await the very long run when technologies that are profitable at existing input prices are invented. Second, capital-intensive plants may be profitable at existing prices, in which case some will be built. While older, more labour-intensive plants are being scrapped and new ones are being built, however, severe unemployment may develop, although the new plants will create some new employment. If the profitability of investment diminishes at the margin as the capital of stock grows, then new construction will stop when further units of capital are not sufficiently profitable. Whether or not this happens before the whole labour force is put back to work depends on the height of the real wage (and capital costs) and on the speed with which returns to investment decline at the margin as the capital stock grows. Since these are both empirical matters on which we currently have insufficient evidence, either answer is possible.

It is theoretically possible that too high a real wage is the cause of much unemployment. Whether or not this is so in practice is an unsettled empirical issue.

Notice that the failure to produce full employment comes because the real wage does not reflect labour-market conditions. If the Classical wage-adjustment mechanism worked, the unemployment could be cured by a combination of automatic wage adjustments, to produce a lower capital-labour ratio and conscious demand management to ensure that the expansion of capital capacity was not halted by demand deficiency before it was halted by full employment of the labour force.

Measured and non-measured unemployment

The number of persons unemployed in the UK is estimated from a monthly count of those who have registered at an Employment Office during the month and who are, on the day of the count, classified as 'capable of and available for' full-time work. The two main reasons for registering are to obtain unemployment benefits and to receive help in finding a job.[1]

There are reasons why this measured figure for unemployment may not reflect the number of people who are truly unemployed in the sense that they would accept the offer of a job for which they were qualified. On the one hand, the measured figure may understate involuntary unemployment by missing people who are genuinely willing to work at going wage rates. For example, some people who have worked in the past are not, or do not think themselves, eligible for unemployment benefits and, therefore, do not bother to register. Also, those who have not worked before are not eligible for benefits. School-leavers and housewives who would work if a booming economy offered them jobs, may never show up on the statistics as unemployed. On the other hand, the measured figure may overstate unemployment by including people who are not truly unemployed in the sense we have just defined. Some people defraud the system by registering as unemployed (and collecting unemployment benefits) when they are employed. Some people do not really wish to work because the difference between their unemployment benefits and what they can earn in work is not sufficient to compensate them for the disutility of work. These people have voluntarily withdrawn from the workforce, but they register as unemployed in order to collect their benefits. Others, for reasons of age or disability, are unemployable but register in order to receive benefits.

In the UK, estimates are available of the size of most of the important groups that contribute to under- and over-measurement of true employment. In the early 1970s, for example, it was estimated that 11 per cent of males and 18 per cent of females who were registered as unemployed were not, in fact, involuntarily unemployed. On the other hand, it has been estimated that between 10 and 20 per cent of male unemployment, and as much as 50 per cent of female unemployment, goes unregistered. The ratio of unregistered to registered unemployment seems to have a marked cyclical pattern, rising in the boom and falling in the slump in the UK. (The reverse cyclical pattern is evident in the US, for well-understood reasons connected with the institutional arrangement for unemployment benefits. This suggests that international comparisons of unemployment performance must be made with caution and only in the light of detailed knowledge of what the figures show.)

The coexistence of some sharp labour shortages and heavy general unemployment in the late 1970s and early 1980s led some observers to suggest that a higher proportion of registered unemployment may be voluntary than in the past. Very careful study is needed, however, to distinguish structural from voluntary unemployment, since both will give rise to the observation just mentioned.

Cures for unemployment

Frictional unemployment

The turnover which causes frictional unemployment is an inevitable part of the functioning of the economy. In so far as it is caused by ignorance, increasing the knowledge of labour-market

---

[1] In other countries such as the US and Canada, the number unemployed is estimated from a monthly sample survey to locate people who are without a job but say they have actively searched for one during the sample period. The two methods, a sample survey of job searches and a tally of those registered as unemployed, each have their own biases and will give different estimates of 'total unemployment'.

opportunities may help. But such measures have a cost, and it is not clear that there is much to be gained by further investment at the margin here. Some frictional unemployment is an inevitable part of the learning process. One reason why there is a high turnover rate, and hence high frictional unemployment, among the young is that one has to try jobs to see if they are suitable. New entrants typically try more than one job before settling into one that most satisfies, or least dissatisfies, them.

Structural unemployment

The changes that cause structural unemployment are an inevitable concomitant of economic growth (but that does not make structural unemployment any the less unpleasant for those who suffer it). Consider two ways commonly used to avoid structural unemployment. The first is manning agreements to prevent people from becoming structurally unemployed by new innovations. (For example, the replacement of coal by diesel in railway engines made firemen technically unnecessary, but existing firemen were kept on by agreement between British Rail and the firemen's union.) The second way is to support declining industry by public funds. If the market would support an output of X but subsidies are used to support an output of $2X$, then jobs are provided for, say, half of the industry's labour force who would otherwise first become unemployed and then have to find jobs elsewhere.

   Both of these policies may be attractive to the people who would otherwise become unemployed. It may be a long time before they can find another job and, when they do, their skills may not turn out to be highly valued in their new industries. But in the long term such policies are not viable. Manning agreements raise costs and hasten the decline of an industry threatened by competitive products. An industry that is declining due to economic change becomes an increasingly large charge on the public purse as economic forces become less and less favourable to its success. Sooner or later, public support is withdrawn and an often precipitous decline then ensues. In assessing these remedies for structural unemployment, it is important to realize that, although not viable in the long run for the economy, they may be the best alternative for the affected workers. Thus,

> **there is often a real conflict between those threatened by structural unemployment, whose interests lie in preserving their old jobs, and the general public, whose interests are served by economic growth that is the engine of rising living standards.**

   One way to reduce this conflict is to accept the decline of industries and the destruction of specific jobs that go with the economic change, and to try to reduce the cost of adjustment for those affected. Retraining and relocation grants make movement easier and reduce structural unemployment without inhibiting economic change and growth.

Deficient-demand unemployment

We do not need to say much more about this type of unemployment since its control is the subject of demand management which we have studied in several earlier chapters. A major recession that occurs due to natural causes can be countered by monetary and fiscal policy to reduce deficient-demand unemployment. There was, however, a new situation in the 1980s: policy-induced, deficient-demand unemployment. This results from a policy-induced recession designed to cut inflation. Deficient-demand unemployment is accepted as the price of reducing inflation. In this case the only way to reduce the unemployment is to find ways of first reducing inflation so that policy-makers will then be willing to raise aggregate demand.

Real-wage unemployment

If this type of unemployment exists, its cure is not an easy matter. Basically what is required is a fall in the real product wage, combined with measures to increase aggregate demand so as to create enough total employment. But the cure is a slow one, requiring enough time to build the new labour-using capital. The steps would run as follows.

(1) **The real product wage would be cut substantially, possibly by some form of incomes policy or 'social contract'.**
(2) **Since wages determine disposable income, and disposable income determines consumer demand, the cut in wages will tend to reduce aggregate demand and hence reduce equilibrium national income. This deflationary force would then be countered by fiscal and monetary policy that restored sufficient aggregate demand.**
(3) **But unemployment will remain high until new capital capacity is built to employ the surplus labour. Any attempt to push aggregate demand beyond the capacity output of current capital will re-create the conditions for an excess-demand inflation.**

Whether or not real-wage unemployment is a serious problem in Britain and Europe is a matter of current dispute. *But the answer is a matter of some major importance.* Advocates of the real-wage explanation argue that, for example, British real wages were some 10–15 per cent too high in 1982, and, as a result, significant amounts of capital were being scrapped. They also point out that the first sign of such a national disaster is a rise in recorded labour productivity. Since the least efficient plants are scrapped first, the average output per head of those remaining in employment will rise steadily. But a rise in productivity that resulted from destroying the capital that provided employment for a significant fraction of the labour fource in manufacturing would hardly be the first glimmerings of an economic sunrise; it would be closer to the first winds of an economic hurricane.

Economists of this persuasion argue that attacking the unemployment by demand-management techniques will cause the economy to hit capital constraints while there are still substantial amounts of unemployed labour. Further demand increases would then become inflationary long before unemployment fell to levels that would be regarded as satisfactory by historical standards.

Opponents argue that the great bulk of unemployment in 1982 was deficient-demand unemployment. They reject the idea of an incomes policy to reduce the real wage and they push for an end to very tight monetary policy followed by an expansionary demand-management policy to restore full employment.

We will learn more about this debate from the performance of the various EEC economies once some economic recovery begins. Very probably these words will be read by some who have much more evidence on this critical social issue than was available at the time of writing in January 1983.

47

Closure version 2: a core-augmented Phillips curve and inflation[1]

Earlier we studied the effects on the price level of once-and-for-all aggregate demand and aggregate supply shocks. Let us start by summarizing what we have already established.

(1) The level of equilibrium national income that satisfies the demand-side conditions ($E = Y$ and $M_D = M_S$) is negatively related to the price level. This is the result of the operation of the monetary adjustment mechanism: an increase in the price level reduces the real money supply, forces up interest rates, and reduces real expenditure and hence equilibrium national income. The graphical expression of this is the negative slope of the aggregate demand curve.

(2) Demand shocks that create an inflationary gap cause the price level to rise, and this brings the monetary adjustment mechanism into play and eventually eliminates the excess demand.

(3) Supply-shock inflations cause rising prices to be associated with falling output.

(4) The only way in which a demand inflation can persist indefinitely or a supply-shock inflation can avoid being associated with falling output is for the inflation to be *validated* by sufficient increases in the nominal money supply to frustrate the operation of the monetary adjustment mechanism. (This prevents the *LM* curve from shifting left and causes the *AD* curve to shift right as fast as the price level is rising). *This is the sense in which virtually everyone agrees that persistent inflation is a monetary phenomenon.* (See pages 685–6 for this very important result.)

In this chapter we study continuous rises in the price level in more detail. We also drop our assumption of a kinked aggregate supply curve so that we can study the grey area where there appears to be some trade-off between unemployment and inflation, at least in the short term. In the first half of the chapter we consider the theory; in the second half we deal with policy issues.

Closure with an inflation equation

So far we have closed the *IS–LM* model with a kinked aggregate supply curve that makes a strict break between the behaviour of the model at less than full employment – prices are fixed and output is variable – and its behaviour at full employment – output is fixed and prices are variable.

This closure has four inadequacies which we now need to repair.

(1) It makes potential output an absolute constraint. In fact, however, it is always possible to

---

[1] Factual background for the policy issues discussed in this chapter may be found in Harbury and Lipsey, Chapter 9.

squeeze a bit more output from the economy by such devices as working more overtime or extra shifts.

(2) It makes the price level completely inflexible downwards. In fact, although most oligopolistic prices do not fall in the face of normal cyclical declines in demand, some prices that are set on more competitive markets do fall, and major reductions in costs are usually reflected in reductions in oligopolistic prices.

(3) It makes a strict dichotomy between behaviour below and at full employment. In fact, the economy does not show an abrupt change in its behaviour when full employment is reached.

(4) There is nothing in the kinked AS curve to tell us about the behaviour of the price level if a demand inflation is validated so that the inflationary gap persists more or less indefinitely. We know that the price level will rise but the theory does not predict the speed or possible acceleration of the rate of inflation. This is a serious deficiency, since the last few decades have witnessed many validated inflations.

A Keynesian inflation equation

One way to remove these deficiencies is to employ the relation that is used to explain inflation in many macro models. These give rise to what may be called a 'Keynesian inflation equation'.[1]

This first step is to observe that any change in the price level can be decomposed (i.e., broken up) into three separate influences called demand inflation, core inflation and shock inflation:

$$\dot{P} = \dot{P}_c + \dot{P}_d + \dot{P}_s, \tag{1}$$

where $\dot{P}$ refers to the rate of price inflation, e.g., 10 per cent per year, $\dot{P}_c$ refers to core inflation, $\dot{P}_d$ to demand inflation and $\dot{P}_s$ to shock inflation. We must now look at these components one at a time.

Demand inflation This refers to the influence on the price level of inflationary and output gaps. Figure 47.1(i) isolates the demand component of inflation by drawing what may be called a price-Phillips curve. Notice that we now have *the rate of change* of the price level on the vertical axes. (The name comes from the pioneer of this type of closure of macro models, the late Professor A. W. Phillips, who developed his theories while at the London School of Economics.)[2] The curve allows income to rise above its potential level when there is excess demand just as it can fall below its potential level when there is deficient demand. (This removes the first deficiency stated above.) The curve also shows a small downward pressure on the price level when there is deficient demand, $Y < Y_F$. (This rectifies the second deficiency.) It also shows the rate of deflation decreasing to zero as Y approaches Y_F from below and then the rate of inflation accelerating as Y rises further and further above Y_F. Indeed the only income where there is no demand pressure on the price level in either direction is Y_F itself.

With the Phillips curve, the economy does not move abruptly from a situation of underemployment of resources and constant prices to a situation of full employment with rising prices and fixed

---

[1] This treatment follows Otto Eckstein's analysis in his excellent book *Core Inflation* (Prentice-Hall, New Jersey, 1981), but it is pretty standard stuff in the majority of econometric macro models these days (although not fifteen years ago).

[2] The Phillips curve was widely misunderstood, particularly in the US, as indicating a cost-push element of inflation. I have discussed this error and other related matters in R. G. Lipsey, 'The Place of the Phillips Curve in Macroeconomic Models', in A. R. Bergstrom (ed.), *Stability and Inflation: Essays in Honour of A. W. Phillips* (Wiley 1978).

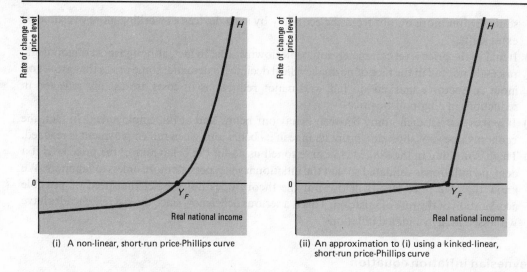

(i) A non-linear, short-run price-Phillips curve

(ii) An approximation to (i) using a kinked-linear,
short-run price-Phillips curve

Fig. 47.1 The demand component of inflation: how inflation is related to Y when core and shock inflation are zero

output; instead, it moves by degrees from one situation to the other. (This rectifies the third deficiency listed above.)

It is important to remember that the Phillips curve does not tell the whole story of inflation, it only describes the effects of demand. This effect displays what may be called the fundamental Keynesian asymmetry:

> **A growing inflationary gap (Y rising above Y_F) causes the *inflation rate* to rise rapidly. A growing output gap (Y falling below Y_F) causes the *deflation rate* to fall only slowly.**

In other words, the price-Phillips curve is steep above Y_F but flat below Y_F. For many purposes it is convenient to capture this asymmetrical behaviour by showing the demand component by two linear segments, one steep for $Y > Y_F$ and one flat for $Y < Y_F$. We shall employ this simplification, which is shown in Figure 47.1(ii).

The micro behaviour that lies behind the flat part of the curve to the left of Y_F is in two parts.[1] First there is the theory of short-run oligopoly pricing described in Chapter 21: firms absorb cyclical demand fluctuations by varying their outputs rather than their prices. Second, there is the theory that wage costs do not fall rapidly in the face of an excess supply of labour, although they can rise rapidly in the face of excess demand for labour.

Wage 'rigidity': The behaviour of wage rates is a key part of the Keynesian micro underpinnings and we must look at it in some considerable detail. The hypothesis is that wage rates are relatively insensitive to the cyclical emergence of excess supplies of labour. The question is – why? One answer

---

[1] I have discussed the micro underpinnings of the Keynesian macro model in some detail elsewhere. See R. G. Lipsey, 'The Understanding and Control of Inflation: Is There a Crisis in Macroeconomics?', *Canadian Journal of Economics*, XIV, No. 4, November 1981.

is suggested by the long-term, implicit contract theory of wage determination outlined on pp. 389–90.

An alternative explanation is rooted in the ideas of Keynes himself. In the neo-Classical model that we discussed in Chapter 27 (see especially pages 387–8) there is a single homogeneous supply of labour which sells its services for a real wage W/P, which is the money wage, W, divided by the price level, P. Rejecting this model, Keynes observed that there are many different kinds of labourers selling their services in many imperfectly linked labour markets. To this he added the hypothesis that workers care not only about their own real wage but also about their wage relative to other similar labour groups, a possibility ignored in the neo-Classical model where people care about their own levels of income and consumption but not about their neighbours'.

Keynes argued that, in a world of multiple labour markets, a 5 per cent fall in real wages accomplished by a cut in money wages would be very different in its transitional effects from the same fall accomplished by an increase in the price level. *The latter preserves wage relativities in the transition, the former does not.* Consider a disequilibrium requiring a fall in W/P. No one can be quite sure in advance how much the fall must be. Thus if one group's money wage falls too much, the affected workers will lose until the wage can be raised to its correct position. Also, those who adjust sooner will lose more than those who adjust later. Furthermore, before the full adjustment is accomplished, conditions may change once again, requiring, say, that real wages return to their initial levels. Then those who have not yet made the first adjustment will have lost nothing. For these, and many other reasons, it pays a person who has influence over his wage to resist its downward adjustment so that others adjust first. If, however, the adjustment is made through an increase in the price level, all wage relativities are preserved and all workers gain or lose equally from any temporary over- or undershooting of W/P.

In the neo-Classical model, where a single homogeneous factor called labour is sold on a perfectly competitive market, it is a sign of money illusion to resist a fall in W/P accomplished by a fall in W while accepting it when accomplished by a rise in P; in a set of disaggregated labour markets where transactions occur out of equilibrium for a long time, the real transitional effects of a fall in W/P accomplished by a fall in W are not the same as the real effects of the same fall in W/P accomplished by a rise in P, and it is not necessarily a sign of money illusion to accept the operation of the latter while fiercely resisting the former.

So the Keynesian theory makes wages relatively rigid downwards, owing to concern over relativities in a dynamic, uncertain, non-homogeneous world. Given constant input prices, marginal costs of producers are constant owing to the technology of goods production (see pp. 276–8). Given this situation output fluctuates cyclically with demand, while prices remain downwardly inflexible.

So the behaviour envisaged is as follows. When demand falls, firms reduce their outputs and their demands for labour, holding their mark-ups approximately constant. The unemployment does not force wage rates down significantly, so firms' costs, and hence their prices, stay fairly constant. This is the main force that is operating but there will be some downward pressure on wages (particularly in non-unionized markets) and on prices (particularly in more competitive markets), so there will be a slow downward drift of the price level. When demand rises above potential income, firms try to expand output by hiring more labour, and the intense labour shortages that develop cause wages to rise. As costs rise, firms pass these on in terms of higher prices. This is a *continuing process* that goes on as long as excess demand holds income above its full-employment level.

Core inflation The demand component cannot be the whole explanation of inflation since, if it were, inflation would only occur if Y exceeded Y_F and inflation could be quickly removed by forcing income back to Y_F. Indeed this demand component does not handle the fourth deficiency listed above, and to do this we must add the concept of core inflation. CORE INFLATION refers to the underlying trend in inflation. Several points need to be made about this concept.

First, it depends solely on costs which are mainly labour and capital costs, i.e., wages and interest rates. In the long haul, inflation must follow costs since, although net profit margins can vary, they cannot account for a sustained inflation. This is an important point so we must be sure it is understood. Say, for example, that profits count for 20p out of £1 of the market price of a good. If all other costs start to rise by 10 per cent per year then the inflation rate could be held to zero *for one year* if profits fall to 12p out of every £1, and to zero in the second year if profits fall to 3·2p in every £1. Such wild variations in the percentage of price accounted for by profits from 20 to 3·2 per cent never occur in practice, yet even these can only hold the price level constant in face of a 10 per cent rise in costs for 2 years. Now consider variations in the other direction. If we start with net profits of 20p in the sales pound, then a 10 per cent inflation in the face of constant costs would require that profits rise to 30p in the first year and to 41p in the second year. Such enormous changes in the mark-up over labour and capital costs (from $20/80 = 25$ per cent, to $30/80 = 37$ per cent, to $41/80 = 51$ per cent) never occur, so *sustained* inflations cannot be caused by increases in profit margins any more than they can be long held in check by decreases in profit margins.

> **Even over a few years, price inflation must follow cost inflation quite closely since variations in profit margins cannot cause a *sustained* divergence of the former from the latter.**

Core inflation is thus fully determined by costs. Since variations in net profit margins can and do occur, and can cause price inflation to diverge temporarily from cost inflation, such variations are included in shock inflation.

The second point is that core inflation is related to *expected future changes* in wage and capital costs since firms who plan to change prices only infrequently must price on the basis of their expected costs over their planning period. So to make our concept of core inflation operative, we need a theory of how firms form their expectations of the future movement of costs. Here we use the simple theory of extrapolative expectations (although later in the chapter we shall consider substituting what are called rational expectations). The theory of extrapolative expectations says that expectations are based on extrapolations of past behaviour and respond only slowly to what is currently happening to costs.[1] The rationale is that, unless a deviation from past trends persists, firms dismiss it as some transitory change and do not let it influence their long-term, price-setting behaviour.

The third key point about core inflation is that it changes only slowly; it has a lot of inertia to it. One explanation of that inertia is the one just discussed: that expectations are formed extrapolatively, they are a simple moving average of past actual costs. Another explanation concerns the inertia of wage costs themselves. This explanation arises from an extension of Keynes' view that workers would fiercely resist cuts in their money wages.

---

[1] At the level at which we are operating here, extrapolative expectations give similar results to *adaptive expectations* where expectations are formed on a moving average of past experience and changed more rapidly the further are expectations from actual realizations.

Keynes talked about downward rigidity in *money* wages because he was working in a non-inflationary world. The logic of his argument, however, easily extends to an inflationary world. If a group of workers expects an x per cent general wage inflation, they will be reluctant to allow their own wage to rise by less than x per cent.[1] Workers resist reductions in their relative wage, which means they resist *increases* in their own wage which are lower than expected increases in either the general wage level or else a closely associated set of particular wages.

This behaviour causes core inflation to have a great deal of inertia. The clearest modern statement of this line of reasoning is to be found in the writings of James Tobin. Tobin's theory is really Keynes' transferred to a modern setting. Tobin claims that wage-setters are concerned about their wages relative to other closely related rates. He adds that wage bargains are made only infrequently. Union wages are rarely negotiated more frequently than once a year and, in some countries, two- and three-year contracts are not uncommon. Thus when a particular wage is set, all other closely related wages are predetermined and, on average, for a period of one-half the length over which the wage in question is now to be set. Thus, independent of their expectations about the future rate of inflation, each group of workers will resist setting their wages at a level which will alter their relations to other existing relevant wages.

This theory of wage inertia makes any given inflation rate hard to change. We can also add to it an asymmetry between raising and lowering relative wages: workers do not mind getting ahead of other closely related groups, but they fiercely resist falling behind. Therefore, the wage stickiness is only on the down side of reducing inflation.

Shock inflation   This refers to once-and-for-all changes that give a temporary upward or downward jolt to inflation. These include changes in indirect taxes, changes in profit margins, changes in import prices and all kinds of other factors often referred to as supply shocks.

Summary

Putting all of this together, the current inflation rate depends on (i) $Y - Y_F$, demand inflation, (ii) a weighted average of past changes in labour and capital costs, core (or inertial) inflation, and (iii) a series of exogenous forces coming from the supply side, shock inflation.

The influence of the three components to inflation may be illustrated first numerically and second graphically. For a numerical example assume that, in the absence of any demand pressures, prices would rise by 10 per cent because firms expect underlying costs to rise by 10 per cent, that this price rise is moderated by 1 percentage point because, due to heavy unemployment, costs only rise by 9 per cent, but the price rise is augmented by 3 percentage points because large increases in indirect taxes force prices up. The final inflation is 12 per cent, made up of a positive 10 per cent on core, a negative 1 per cent on demand and a positive 3 per cent on shock.

Graphically the components of inflation are shown in Figure 47.2 for two illustrative cases. In the first case income is Y_1 and the actual inflation rate is $\dot{P}_1$. This is made up of a positive core rate of

---

[1] No doubt early Keynesians typically thought in terms of downward inflexibility of money *wages*. No doubt it was the monetarists who really jolted Keynesians into thinking about rates of change of individual prices relative to expected rates of change of all prices. But once that point was absorbed – and it took nearly half a decade for the absorption to happen fully – it became clear that the logic of Keynes' argument extends to this situation.

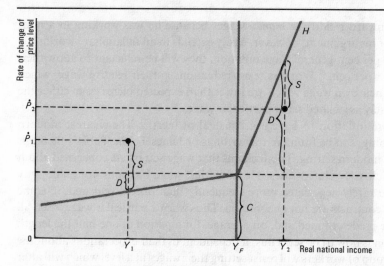

Fig. 47.2 Core, demand and shock inflation

inflation indicated by the brace 'C', a negative demand factor indicated by the brace 'D', and a large positive shock component indicated by the brace 'S'. In the second illustration, actual income and observed inflation are Y_2 and $\dot{P}_2$. This is made up of the same core rate 'C', a large positive demand component 'D' and a smaller negative shock component 'S'.

The curve H is the Phillips curve now raised above 0 at Y_F by the core inflation rate. Its height above the axis at Y_F indicates core inflation and its deviation from this core inflation, when Y does not equal Y_F, indicates how much the pressures of excess demand or excess supply cause the actual inflation rate to deviate from the core rate. Because this Phillips curve shifts upwards or downwards as the core rate of inflation rises or falls, the curve is called a SHORT-RUN PHILLIPS CURVE when it is drawn at any particular height above Y_F. Finally the amount by which actual inflation lies above or below the short-run Phillips curve shows the amount by which shocks cause the actual inflation rate to deviate from the sum of the core and the demand effects.

The curve shown in Figure 47.2 is called a 'core-augmented' Phillips curve. Originally the Phillips curve of Figure 47.1 was thought to provide the whole explanation of inflation. Later it was realized that the short-run Phillips curve shifted slowly upwards or downwards, and the core inflation concept was added to explain this. Hence the idea of a Phillips curve being *augmented* by a model of core inflation. We now summarize the key points about this theory and indicate where there is substantial agreement and where there is controversy with competing theories.

(1) *The inflation rate of prices must follow the trend inflation rate of costs quite closely.* There is little disagreement over this relation which defines the core, or underlying, rate of inflation. Notice however that it is just a matter of simple arithmetic that the major determinant of price inflation is cost inflation. This says nothing about causes. Costs could be rising because of the pressure of excess demand in factor markets or because of the exercise of arbitrary power on the part of unions. Whatever the causes of the behaviour of costs, prices must follow them fairly closely.

(2) *The core inflation rate changes very slowly because it is a moving average of past inflation in labour and capital costs.* There is substantial disagreement over this. Some economists believe the core rate can change quite rapidly, and this is a key difference underlying many differences in policy recommendations. We shall return to this point later.

(3) *The influence of demand on inflation is asymmetrical.* Inflationary gaps cause inflation to rise

well above the core rate while output gaps force the actual rate only slightly below the core rate. The evidence for this asymmetry is extremely strong[1] although some economists deny it.

(4) *Shocks caused by such influences as changes in indirect taxes, agricultural crop failures or increases in import prices temporarily affect the inflation rate.* This has not always been agreed and, at the time of the first OPEC oil-price shocks in 1974, some economists said that if oil-related prices rose, other prices would fall so as to keep the price level constant. As a result of the evidence of the OPEC shocks, most economists now accept that supply shocks affect the price level causing temporary deviations in the rate of inflation from what it would otherwise be. Another example of a clear supply-shock inflation was the rise in the price level that occurred in Britain in 1979–80 after income taxes were cut and value added taxes raised by the new Conservative government.

(5) *There is no permanent push coming from the aggregate supply side.* In the present theory, supply-side shocks are basically transitory. This is a much-debated point. Later in the chapter we shall consider the theory of an independent wage-cost push that is alleged to exert a continual upward pressure on wage costs and prices.

The expectations-augmented Phillips curve Many monetarists analyse inflation with what is called an expectations-augmented Phillips curve. That model has the same analytical structure as the core-augmented model considered above. Thus the core model is a framework for understanding both Keynesian and monetarist views on inflation. Major disagreements centre on the determinents of the three components of inflation: What determines the core or expected rate? How fast does the inflation rate respond to demand pressures? What shocks are capable of exerting a significant effect on the inflation rate?

It is also worth noting at this point that, as with any new concept, the core rate of inflation goes under several different names. Three of the most common are the core rate, the expected rate and the underlying rate of inflation.

Real and nominal interest rates

Before we can work with a model of continuous inflation we must reintroduce the distinction between the nominal and the real interest rates first encountered in Chapter 28 (see page 401). The nominal or market rate is the rate of interest actually paid. The real rate is the nominal rate minus the expected rate of inflation. In this calculation the expected rate of inflation is called the inflationary premium. Only after deducting the inflationary premium does the lender know if he has actually made any real return on his loan. Negative real rates are not uncommon in some inflationary situtations and they mean that the interest on the loan is lower than the rate at which the inflation is eroding the purchasing power of the principal of the loan.

A problem now arises with our *IS-LM* model. First, the *IS* curve depends on the real interest rate, which we may designate *r*. The theory of investment tells us that investment expenditure will be high or low depending on whether the real interest is high or low. The *LM* curve, however, depends on the nominal interest rate, which we may designate *i*. Wealth-holders, deciding how to divide their wealth holdings between money and bonds, respond to the opportunity cost of holding money, which is the difference between the rate of return on money and the rate of return on bonds. We can see that *i* rather than *r* is the relevant *LM* curve variable either by comparing nominal or by

---

[1] The asymmetrical behaviour of prices in the face of inflationary and output gaps has been extensively documented. See Phillip Cagan, *Persistent Inflation: Historical and Policy Essays* (New York: Columbia University Press, 1979).

comparing real rates on each asset. Consider nominal rates first. The nominal rate of return on money is zero while on bonds it is i. Therefore the opportunity cost of each £1 held in money balances is a forgone nominal return of i. Now consider real returns. The expected real rate of return on money balances held is not zero. Instead it is the negative of the expected inflation rate, $-\dot{P}^e$, since if you hold money during an inflation its purchasing power *depreciates* at the rate of inflation. The real rate of return on bonds is the nominal rate minus the expected inflation rate, $r = i - \dot{P}^e$. So the difference in the real return on bonds and on money is the $i - \dot{P}^e$ for bonds *minus* the $-\dot{P}^e$ for money, i.e., $i - \dot{P}^e - (-\dot{P}^e) = i$, the nominal rate of interest. Thus wealth-holders calculate that the opportunity cost to them of holding money rather than bonds is given by i, and the higher is i the less money and the more bonds will they wish to hold.

To illustrate, consider two situations. In the first, the inflation rate is zero and the real and the nominal interest rates are both 4 per cent; in the second, the inflation rate is 10 per cent and the nominal interest rate is 14 per cent, leaving the real interest rate at 4 per cent. *Ceteris paribus*, investment expenditure will be the same in both situations because the real cost of borrowing money is unchanged at 4 per cent per year. The proportion of wealth held in money balances should, however, be much smaller in the second situation because the opportunity cost of money held is 14 per cent per year compared to 4 per cent in the first situation.

Now consider the *IS-LM* equilibrium. Using linear versions of these curves, we have[1]

$$IS: \quad r = \alpha_0 + \alpha_1 Y \tag{2}$$

$$LM: \quad i = \beta_0 + \beta_1 Y \tag{3}$$

$$r = i - \dot{P}^e \tag{4}$$

Given an expected rate of inflation, which in the present model is the core inflation rate, the model solves just as it did before. Nothing new is involved except the determination of two interest rates *given* the inflation rate.[2]

The dynamic version of the model arises when we specify an equation for the evolution of $\dot{P}^e$. This, however, takes us into analytical techniques that are beyond the scope of this book.

Closure with the core-augmented curve

Demand inflation   Let us first assume that core and shock inflation are zero and study how the model would work if demand inflation were the only kind of inflation present. Consider Figure 47.3. Let the economy start in equilibrium with income Y_F given by IS_1 and LM_1 with a stable price level. Now let a demand shock take the IS curve to IS_2 and income to Y_1. The inflation rate rises to $\dot{P}_1$.

---

[1] The constants take on various forms depending on the model used. For example in the two-sector model, $\alpha_0 = -A/b$, $\alpha_1 = (1-c)/b$ from equation (6), and $\beta_0 = (M^*/P)(1/e)$, while $\beta_1 = -d/e$ from equation (7), both on p. 601.

[2] A problem does arise with how to graph the system. Probably the best way is to make the equilibrium occur not at the intersection of the *IS* and *LM* curves, but where the vertical gap between the two is equal to the expected rate of inflation, which makes $i = r + \dot{P}^e$. An alternative, and the one we use here, is to plot two scales on the interest axis, one for r and the other for $i - \dot{P}^e = r$. In other words, the i scale is shifted downward by $\dot{P}^e$ so that the *IS–LM* intersection still determines Y and r (and i by adding back the $\dot{P}^e$ constant). This allows the visually more familiar intersection to locate the equilibrium and poses no analytical problem as long as $\dot{P}^e$ is exogenously given.

This reduces the real money supply and shifts the *LM* curve to the left, as shown by the arrow. Equilibrium income falls back continuously towards Y_F and the inflation rate falls along the Phillips curve as shown by the arrow in part (ii). Static equilibrium is reached when the price level has risen sufficiently to shift the *LM* curve to LM_2. Income falls back to Y_F and the price level is stable at its new higher level.

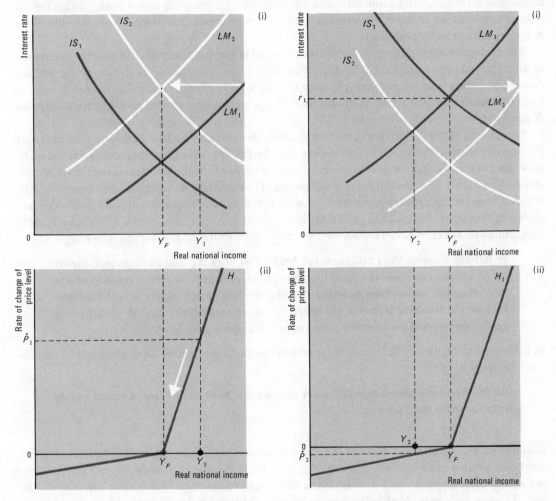

Fig. 47.3 An unvalidated demand inflation is brought to a halt by the leftward shift of the *LM* curve due to a rise in the price level

Fig. 47.4 Unemployment could eventually be removed by a rightward shift in the *LM* curve due to a fall in the price level

Now consider the contractionary shock shown in Figure 47.4. Once again, an equilibrium at Y_F and a stable price level is disturbed by a shift in the *IS* curve; this time, however, the curve shifts leftward to IS_2. Equilibrium income falls to Y_2 and the price level falls at a rate of $-\dot{P}_2$. Because of the flatness of the Phillips curve to the left of Y_F, the rate of price deflation is quite low. It might be no more than 1 per cent per year. The slow fall in the price level gradually raises the real money supply and shifts the LM curve right as shown by the arrow in part (i). Eventually, the deflation will shift the LM curve to LM_2 and restore full employment. But this can take a very long time. At a deflation rate of 1 per cent per annum, for example, it will take 10 years to increase the *real* money supply by 10 per cent. The same increase could be accomplished in a matter of months by the central bank's open-market operations that increased the *nominal* money supply. This observation has made many economists advocate active monetary policy to eliminate output gaps rather than waiting for the natural equilibrating forces of the economy which appear very weak, at least from the side of the monetary adjustment mechanism.

The horizontal aggregate supply curve that we used in previous chapters can now be understood as an empirical approximation. The downward drift in the price level (as shown by the Phillips curve) when there is an output gap is so slow that, as a first approximation that is close enough to reality for most practical policy purposes, the price level can be regarded as completely inflexible downwards.

Now, to relate the Phillips curve closure to the aggregate supply curve used earlier, let us ignore the slow deflation to the left of Y_F and *assume that the Phillips curve lies on the axis to the left of Y_F.* Now there is no monetary adjustment mechanism to restore full employment. If the curves are IS_2 and LM_1 in Figure 47.4, the output gap will persist. The monetary adjustment mechanism will still, however, remove inflationary gaps. As we saw earlier, if there is a once-and-for-all rise in demand caused by the curves shifting to IS_2 and LM_1 in Figure 47.3, output rises temporarily above Y_F but it then returns to Y_F as the monetary adjustment mechanism shifts the LM curve left to LM_2.

In full equilibrium, the Phillips curve[1] behaves as does the kinked aggregate supply curve: income can come to rest at less than full employment; it cannot come to rest at more than full employment provided that the nominal money supply is held constant, because the resulting inflation will lower aggregate expenditure until the inflationary gap is removed and the economy comes to rest at a stable price level.

But this is what happens when the price-level has reached equilibrium. Out of price-level equilibrium, however:

the Phillips curve allows an inflationary gap to cause both an increase in output and an inflation in the short term.

Demand plus core inflation Now let us add core inflation, still assuming shock inflation to be zero. Start with a stable-price-level equilibrium at Y_F with IS_1, LM_1 and H_1 (the short-run Phillips curve) in Figure 47.5. A demand shock now takes the IS curve to IS_2, income to Y_1 and inflation to $\dot{P}_1$. *This time, however, the central bank takes steps to validate the inflation by increasing the nominal money supply as fast as the price level is rising.* This frustrates the monetary adjustment mechanism and prevents the LM curve from shifting left as it did in Figure 47.3(i).

If the short-run Phillips curve stayed put at H_1, policy-makers could well conclude that they had achieved a pretty good trade-off. They would have gained a permanent increase in output of $Y_1 - Y_F$ at the cost of a permanent inflation of $\dot{P}_1$. But this is not the end of the story. Prices and costs are rising at $\dot{P}_1$ per year, and sooner or later firms will stop believing this is a transitory phenomenon.

---

[1] Where the slow downward pressure on the price level when $Y < Y_F$ is ignored.

They will come to expect some of this increase to persist. This will now become part of core inflation. Let us say that, after a passage of time, firms come to expect a core inflation at a rate of C_2 per annum in the Figure. The short-run Phillips curve now shifts up to H_2. Actual inflation rises to $\dot{P}_2$, of which C_2 is core inflation and $\dot{P}_2 - C_2$ is demand inflation. (It may be worth reiterating what is happening here: core inflation gives the rise in prices due to firms' expectations about the long-run trend in costs; the demand component – given by the height of the short-run Phillips curve above the core rate – gives the addition to inflation caused by cost increases due to what are thought to be transitory demand factors.) Now that the inflation rate has accelerated to $\dot{P}_2$, the central bank will have to raise its rate of monetary expansion if it is to validate the inflation completely and so prevent the LM curve from shifting left.

Notice, however, that in Figure 47.5 the actual inflation rate of $\dot{P}_2$ is still well above the core rate of C_2. Sooner or later this excess will come to be expected, the core rate will then rise, the short-run

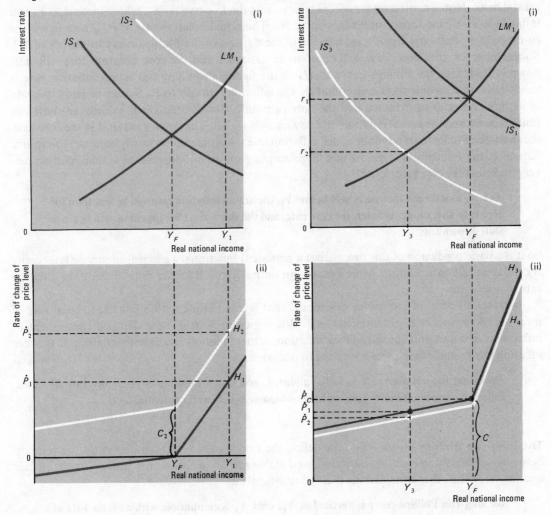

Fig. 47.5 An accelerating inflation rate   **Fig. 47.6** A decelerating inflation

Phillips curve will shift upwards and the rate of growth of the money supply will have to be increased in order to hold the LM curve at LM_1 and income at Y_1.

> **As long as national income is held above Y_F, the actual inflation rate will exceed the core rate and, as a result, the core rate, and the short-run Phillips curve, will sooner or later shift upwards.**

It follows that if the central bank validates any rate of inflation that results from Y being held above Y_F, first, the inflation rate will accelerate continuously and, second, there will also be an acceleration in the rate of monetary expansion required to frustrate the monetary adjustment mechanism by holding the real money supply constant.

Now consider a deflationary policy. Assume that the initial curves are IS_1, LM_1 and H_3 in Figure 47.6, giving an equilibrium income of Y_F and an inflation of $\dot{P}_c$ which is being validated by the central bank. Now a contractionary fiscal policy shifts the IS curve to IS_3, taking income to Y_3 and inflation to $\dot{P}_1$ on the short-run Phillips curve H_3. The actual inflation rate of $\dot{P}_1$ is now below the core rate of $\dot{P}_c$ (but only slightly so, because of the flatness of the Phillips curve to the left of Y_F). Sooner or later, this lower rate will come to be expected and the core inflation rate will shift downwards taking the Phillips curve to H_4 in the figure. Providing the actual inflation rate is validated so that income stays constant at Y_3, the inflation rate falls to $\dot{P}_2$. Sooner or later, this rate in its turn comes to be expected and the core rate shifts downwards again, taking the short-run Phillips curve and the actual inflation rate downwards with it. The downward shift in the core rate, the short-run Phillips curve and the actual inflation rate takes place quite slowly because the extreme flatness of the Phillips curve means that large output gaps do not depress the actual inflation rate very far below the core rate.

> **As long as national income is held below Y_F, the actual inflation rate will be less than the core rate and, sooner or later, the core rate, and the short-run Phillips curve, will begin to shift downwards.**

So it is a basic prediction of this theory that a persistent inflationary gap will sooner or later cause the inflation rate to accelerate, while a persistent output gap will sooner or later cause the inflation rate to decelerate.

Is there any level of income in this model that is compatible with a constant actual rate of inflation? The answer is potential income. When income is at Y_F, the demand component of inflation is zero and, still ignoring shock inflation, actual inflation equals core inflation. If the core inflation rate is stable then there is nothing to disturb it.

> **Providing the inflation rate is fully validated, and shock inflation is zero, any rate of inflation can persist indefinitely as long as income is held at its potential level.**

The long-run Phillips curve   We now define the LONG-RUN PHILLIPS CURVE as the relation between *national income*, on the one hand, and *stable rates of inflation* that neither accelerate nor decelerate, on the other hand. On the theory just described:

> **the long-run Phillips curve is vertical at Y_F; only Y_F is compatible with a stable rate of inflation, and any stable rate is, if fully validated, compatible with Y_F.**

The predictions from this method of closure are now summarized in Figure 47.7. Above Y_F, the actual rate of inflation, $\dot{P}$, exceeds the core rate, $\dot{P}_c$, and the inflation rate will be accelerating, $\ddot{P} > 0$, ($\ddot{P}$ means the rate at which the inflation rate itself is changing). Below Y_F, actual inflation is less than core inflation and the inflation rate is decelerating. At Y_F, actual inflation equals core inflation and the core rate need not change.

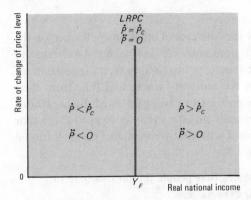

Fig. 47.7 The dynamics of core-augmented Phillips-curve inflations

Shock inflation It is important to realize that all of this analysis has been done on the assumption that shock inflation is zero. In today's world, many shocks hit the price level. What we see is a much less regular experience than the simple combination of core plus demand inflation. The inflation rate varies quite substantially from period to period due to the action of the many shocks that impinge on it.

Asymmetrical speeds of reaction The theory that the core rate of inflation is a moving average of past actual rates imparts substantial inertia to the inflationary process: the core rate changes only slowly. The asymmetry in the demand component, furthermore, makes it easier to raise the core rate then to lower it. The change in the core rate from period to period depends on the discrepancy between the actual rate and the core rate. The steepness of the short-run Phillips curve above Y_F means that it is easy to create a substantial gap between the actual rate and the core rate by increasing the inflationary gap. This will tend to drag the core rate up fairly quickly. The flatness of the short-run Phillips curve below Y_F means that only a small discrepancy between the actual and the core rates can be created by even a large output gap. Therefore, the core rate can be depressed only slowly by creating output gaps. For example, if holding Y a given amount above Y_F holds the actual inflation rate 4 percentage points *above the core rate*, then the core rate will eventually settle down to an *acceleration* of 4 percentage points per year. If, however, depressing Y below Y_F only forces the actual inflation rate one percentage point *below the core rate*, the core rate will begin to decelerate and finally settle at a *deceleration* of 1 percentage point per year. At this rate it would take $2\frac{1}{2}$ years to accelerate the core rate of inflation from 10 to 20 per cent but 10 years to decelerate it from 10 per cent to zero!

> **It is an important prediction of this theory that the core rate of inflation can accelerate fairly quickly but will decelerate only slowly.**

Some variations on a theme

In Chapter 48 we discuss some radically different theories. Here we consider some lesser variations that are nonetheless significant for current policy debates.

Rational expectations

In the theory just given, the expectations that determine the core rate of inflation are formed on the basis of past experience. In an obvious sense, such expectations are *backward looking*. An alternative is that people look to the government's current macroeconomic policy to form their expectations of future cost and price inflation. They understand how the economy works and they form their expectations rationally by predicting the outcome of the policies now being followed. In an obvious sense, such expectations are *forward looking*. They are usually called RATIONAL EXPECTATIONS, or sometimes *Muth rational expectations* after the economist who first wrote about them. Rational expectations are not necessarily always correct; instead,

> **the rational expectations hypothesis merely assumes that people do not continue to make persistent, systematic errors in forming their expectations.**

Thus, *if the system about which they are forming expectations remains stable,* their expectations will be correct *on average.* Any individual's expectations at any moment of time about next year's $\dot{P}$ can thus be thought of as the actual $\dot{P}$ that will occur next year, plus a random error term which has a mean of zero.

Rational expectations have the effect of speeding up the downward adjustment of inflation in the face of a deflationary demand policy. Instead of being an average of past inflation rates, core inflation is based on a correct anticipation of the outcome of existing policies. Notice, however, that by themselves rational expectations do *not* ensure that a deflationary policy that produces a large output gap will bring the inflation rate down very rapidly. To see this, take the extreme case where the short-run Phillips curve is horizontal for $Y < Y_F$ because wage costs do not respond in any way to an output gap with its associated unemployment. Now, when demand is depressed, the 'deflation' all comes as a fall in real income and none comes as a fall in the inflation rate. In this case, rationally formed expectations would predict no fall in inflation as a result of restrictive demand policies, and core inflation would remain unaffected by them. Few people believe this extreme case, but it shows that forward-looking expectations are not sufficient to get a rapid response of the inflation rate to demand restraint; what also matters is how wage and price-setting respond to the output gap.

Now, keeping the assumption of rational expectations, let us return to our basic assumption that the short-run Phillips curve is rather flat but not perfectly horizontal. A typical figure would be that a GNP gap resulting in 12 per cent unemployment gives a demand component between minus one and minus two percentage points. The reason for this small figure is that there is a lot of inertia in labour markets, so that 12 per cent unemployment typically reduces wage increases by no more than one to two percentage points below what they were last year. Assume that the government's demand policy moves the economy from full employment to 12 per cent unemployment. Inflation will then fall by one to two percentage points below its former stable value – say it was originally 10 per cent. Thus decision-makers will rationally expect costs to rise by 8 to 9 per cent next year and will increase prices by 8 to 9 per cent to cover the cost increases. The following year, if the high unemployment rate is maintained, they will rationally expect costs to rise by 6 to 8 per cent and their actions will cause a 6 to 8 per cent price inflation. Rational expectations have now got rid of the inflationary inertia caused by the core rate being an average of past actual rates. But we still have the inertia caused by the failure of wage-cost inflation to respond rapidly to even a large output gap.

There are two sources of inflationary inertia in the Keynesian model: first, the lag in adjusting expectations about future inflation rates to current conditions and, second, the sluggishness with which labour markets respond to current demand and supply forces. Rationally formed expectations eliminate the first source of inertia, but not the second.

Exogenous wage-push inflation

In the model presented earlier, there is no exogenous wage-push inflation. In an economy with no excess demand ($Y = Y_F$) and no shocks, a stable price level is possible. (See Figure 47.1 and its surrounding discussion.) There is wage-cost, *inertial* inflation in the sense that, once core inflation (which is largely wage-cost inflation) is positive, it is hard to get it back to zero by demand restraint. But this stubborn core inflation must have been the result of demand or shock inflation in the first place.

Many economists believe in an *independent* wage push that operates some, or all, of the time. This type of wage push is an upward pressure on wages not associated with demand or core pressures. In terms of the previous model, exogenous wage push would be another factor causing shock inflation but this time it would be a permanent rather than a transitory push. Supporters of this view point for an example to the wage explosion of 1968–9 where, for no obvious reason, there appeared to be an increase in union militancy and a resulting upward surge in wage settlements.

Since inflation rates are observed to vary greatly from year to year, a wage-cost-push theory needs to explain why the cost push varies from year to year. There are two possible routes here. The behaviour can either change arbitrarily from year to year or be related systematically to some other variable. In the former case, we have a theory that the price level is determined arbitrarily. This is unsatisfactory because it provides no explanation of systematic variations in the rate of inflation over time and across countries. In the latter case, we have a theory that the price level is determined by whatever variables determine the cost push. If the variable is aggregate demand, so that wage increases are related to $Y - Y_F$, then we are back to a demand-pull theory of the Phillips curve with just an added link from excess demand to unions to wages to prices. Thus, for the wage-cost theory to be different from the excess-demand theory, the cost push must vary with something other than aggregate demand.

One possible theory is that various groups' expectations of the share of national income each can expect add up to more than the total national income. One group tries to exercise its claims by obtaining a large wage increase, but this means less for others and they try to restore their shares by getting larger wage increases for themselves. After one complete round, all the wage increases cancel out. No group has increased its share but, in the process of trying, they have raised wage costs and, to cover these, firms have raised their prices. The stage is then set for another round where each group tries to increase its share and the self-defeating process of an all-around rise in money wages merely causes another round of price increases.

A second part of this argument relies on the theory of the firm. If firms sold their products in competitive markets they would be price-takers in product markets and could not yield to these 'unreasonable' wage demands for fear of bankruptcies. But, so goes the theory, most industries are oligopolistic and they administer their own prices. Thus they can grant large wage increases to avoid industrial disputes secure in the knowledge, first, that each can raise its price to pass on the wage increases and, second, that if all their competitors do the same, none of them will lose market shares as a result of getting prices out of line with each other. Supporters of exogenous wage-cost-push theory look to lack of competitive forces in factor and product markets to permit the wage-cost push to continue to generate inflation independent of aggregate demand.

This wage-cost-push theory has several implications. First, and most important, if it is true, the economic system has an inflationary bias that cannot be controlled by market forces. Let the economy start at Y_F in Figure 47.1. Exogenous wage push will then shock costs and prices upwards. As long as the push is either positive or zero, but never significantly negative, these shocks will drive the core inflation rate upwards and, therefore, be added to a rising core rate. Thus, the recorded inflation rate will drift upwards.

> The key prediction of the wage-push theory is that, even if we could impose a stable price level on the economy long enough to have everyone expect stable prices, the wage push would slowly push the economy back to positive, and ever-rising, rates of inflation.

Second, if the nominal money supply is held constant, a wage-cost push will lead to an ever-falling level of national income with its accompanying ever-rising level of unemployment. This is because an unvalidated inflation must shift the LM curve leftwards by the operation of the monetary adjustment mechanism. If, sooner or later, unions moderate their wage push in the face of high enough unemployment rates, then a wage-cost-push inflation with a constant money supply is self-correcting, but only at the level of unemployment at which unions are induced to stop their wage-cost push.

Third, if the government seeks to prevent the wage-cost-push inflation from raising unemployment, it can do so by validating the inflation. This frustrates the monetary adjustment mechanism and stops the LM curve from shifting leftwards. The inflation may then continue indefinitely.

Fourth, if the government wishes to control inflation without having the rise in unemployment required by the operation of the monetary adjustment mechanism, its only remaining policy is to operate on the strength of the wage-cost push itself. It may seek to restrain the consequences of wage-cost push by employing the legal sanctions of wage and price controls. It may also seek to change the unions' wage-cost-push behaviour by various forms of incomes policy or 'social contract'. These have the characteristic that they offer unions other things that they desire in return for a moderation of wage claims.

> Economists are divided over the existence of an independent wage-cost push. Its existence would greatly complicate the problem of controlling inflation and might make stable prices and full employment incompatible in a free-market society.

The independence of potential and actual income

The theory given at the outset of the chapter follows standard textbook lines and makes full-employment output a slowly evolving variable depending on long-term growth that is independent of short-term macro-stabilization policy. Critics, including many Keynesians, do not accept this separation between short-term stabilization and longer-term growth policy. They argue that investment is influenced by the level of income as well as by interest rates. If firms have substantial excess capacity, they will not be motivated to replace old capacity as it wears out, particularly at times when very high interest rates make investment funds very expensive.

Therefore, these economists argue, a prolonged period of holding Y below Y_F to reduce inflation will also reduce investment and cause Y_F itself to shrink. When the inflation is finally reduced, and demand reflated, full employment of plant and equipment may occur while there is still large-scale unemployment of labour because there is insufficient capital to employ all of the labour force. If this gloomy view turns out to be correct, governments will find that they cannot easily remove all of their heavy unemployment by expansionary demand-management policies once they have got their inflation rates down to satisfactory levels.

Policy issues

Should shock inflation be validated?

Assume an economy is operating at full-employment income and a stable rate of inflation of, say, 8 per cent as shown in Figure 47.8. For this position to persist, the central bank must be validating the inflation with increases in the money supply that hold the LM curve at LM_1. Now assume that some shock to the price level adds 8 percentage points to the rate of inflation for 12 months and then disappears. Assume the shock was fully recognized as a transitory factor and so does not affect the core inflation rate. Also assume that the central bank does not alter its rate of monetary expansion. The temporary burst of 16 per cent inflation for 12 months will raise the inflation rate above the rate of monetary expansion and so reduce the real money supply. This shifts the LM curve left, say to LM_2, and reduces income to Y_1. Once the shock passes, the inflation rate falls to what is dictated by the core rate plus demand forces. The rate, as is seen on this diagram, will now be slightly below the core rate, say 7 per cent per year.

The central bank now has two choices. First, it can increase the rate of growth of the nominal money supply to validate the shock inflation. It increases the money supply by the extra amount that the shock inflation added to the price level. This restores the real money supply to its pre-shock level, the LM curve to LM_1 and national income to Y_F. Second, it can maintain its rate of monetary expansion unchanged and wait for the real money supply to be restored to its pre-shock level by the fact that the price level is now rising at 1 per cent less than the rate of nominal money expansion. Monetary growth has been held at 8 per cent per year but, because of the negative demand component when income is Y_1, the inflation rate is below the core rate. This will shift the LM curve slowly rightward and gradually restore full employment. On the assumed figures it will, however, take more than 12 years for this monetary adjustment mechanism to restore full employment after the effects of just this one shock. Even if the assumed rate of adjustment were doubled, six years is a long time to wait for the monetary adjustment mechanism to remove the effects of one shock.

Fierce debate has often occurred over the last 15 years as to which of these policies a central bank should follow. Keynesians have generally advocated validating the supply-shock inflation to avoid what they predict to be the long period of unemployment that would follow from non-validation. Monetarists have generally favoured non-validation. Since in the model used here non-validation

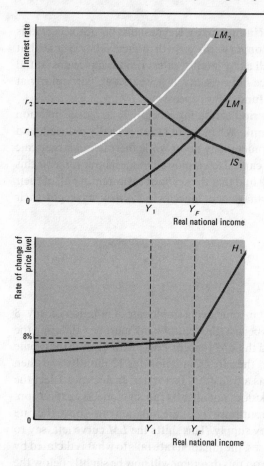

Fig. 47.8 Eliminating an entrenched inflation through restrictive monetary policy

seems so unreasonable, it is clear that these economists must have a different model which they think better describes reality. The major difference in this respect is that in many monetarist models the demand effect on the inflation rate is not flat to the left of Y_F. Their short-run Phillips curve is quite steep, and so a recession caused by non-validation would be quite short. For example, if the recession reduced the inflation rate 8 percentage points *below* the core rate, it would only have to last for 12 months to offset the effects of the earlier 12 months when the shock effects held the inflation rate 8 percentage points *above* the core rate.

Much of the policy disagreement turns, therefore, on the slope of the function describing the demand component of inflation. If it is steep, to the left of Y_F, as many monetarists believe, then the inflation rate can be reduced well below the core rate by even modest recessions, and, given a stable rate of monetary expansion, the monetary adjustment mechanism will restore full employment fairly quickly. If it is flat, as many Keynesians believe, the system does not adjust so flexibly in the downward direction.

Do budget deficits cause inflation?

The Conservative government elected in 1979 clearly took the view that reductions in the PSBR were a necessary condition for controlling inflation. There is still, however, much confusion and debate over this issue.

The predictions of our macro theory are quite clear on this matter: sometimes they may and sometimes they may not. If the government engages in a deficit-financed increase in government expenditure, this shifts the IS curve to the right and raises equilibrium income. Further effects depend on how the deficit is financed. If it is financed by selling bonds to the central bank, then the money supply goes on increasing as long as the deficit persists. This means that the LM curve shifts continuously to the right. Sooner or later this raises Y above Y_F and initiates a demand inflation. The inflation will then continue as long as the deficit persists in increasing the nominal money supply.[1]

If, however, the deficit is financed by the sale of bonds to the public, there is no monetary expansion and no rightward shift in the LM curve. Now the deficit either has no effect on the price level, if equilibrium Y remains below Y_F, or causes a once-and-for-all rise in the price level, and some crowding out of private expenditure, if the IS shift temporarily takes Y above Y_F.

> **Deficits cause permanent inflation if they are financed by monetary expansion. If they are financed by borrowing from the private sector, they cause no change in the price level if they leave Y below Y_F, or a once-and-for-all rise if they take Y temporarily above Y_F.**

Interest-rate policies

Can governments alter interest rates through their monetary policies? In particular can they bring about lower interest rates than would otherwise rule? Walter Eltis of Oxford University has accused Keynesians of spreading the myth that easy-money policies can lower interest rates. It is important therefore to see just what our macro theory does predict on this matter. To do so we need to distinguish three cases.

A once-and-for-all increase in the money supply with actual income below potential income

Consider Figure 40.6(ii) on page 602. The original curves are IS_1 and LM_1 yielding equilibrium values of r_1 and Y_1 where Y_1 is assumed to be less than Y_F. Now let the Bank increase the nominal money supply, shifting the LM curve to LM_2. Equilibrium income rises to Y_2 while the equilibrium interest rate *falls* to r_2. Providing Y_2 is still less than Y_F, that is the end of the story.

> **Starting from $Y < Y_F$ an increase in the money supply lowers the real and nominal interest rates.**

---

[1] In the UK a large increase in the PSBR usually implies an increase in the money supply, since it is understood that the discount houses will take up any residual of a new treasury bill issue that the public will not take up at the going interest rate and that the Bank will then provide the discount houses with enough cash to meet their liquidity needs. Previous governments worried mainly about the effect of the PSBR on aggregate expenditures. The Conservative government that took office in 1979 worried almost exclusively about its effects on the money supply. See Brian Tew, 'The Implementation of Monetary Policy in Post-war Britain', *Midland Bank Review*, Spring 1981.

A once-and-for-all increase in the money supply starting from potential income Starting with $Y = Y_F$, a once-and-for-all increase in the money supply shifts the LM curve right, lowers the real interest rate and moves the economy upwards along its Phillips curve where there is a demand inflation. The inflation lowers the real money supply, shifting the LM curve left until it comes back to its original position. At that point the price level stabilizes at a higher level, while Y returns to Y_F and the real and nominal interest rates return to their initial level.

> **Starting from potential income, a once-and-for-all increase in the money supply causes a transitory rise of Y above Y_F and a fall in the real interest rate. But when equilibrium is restored, income and the interest rate return to their initial level and only the price level rises.**

A continuous rise in the money supply to hold actual income above potential income Let the money supply be increased to shift the LM curve, taking equilibrium Y above Y_F and lowering the real rate of interest. A demand inflation then ensues and, to hold the real money supply constant (and hence maintain the higher Y and lower r), the money supply must be increased at the same rate as the price level is rising. As the actual rate of inflation passes into the core rate of inflation, the inflation rate accelerates and, to maintain the same real situation, the Bank must accelerate the rate of monetary expansion. As the inflation rate rises, the market rate of interest will rise along with it $(i = r + \dot{P}^e)$. Thus although the policy may succeed for a while in holding down the real rate of interest, the nominal or market rate of interest will accelerate continuously.

If the government were to try to stabilize the *market rate* of interest in the face of an accelerating inflation rate, this would require a falling real rate of interest. This would push equilibrium further out along the *IS* curve, create more and more excess demand and an ever-faster acceleration in the inflation rate.

> **Starting from potential income, the real rate of interest can be lowered for some time but at the cost of accelerating rates of inflation and nominal interest rates.**

Sooner or later governments cease to tolerate accelerating inflation rates and take steps to bring them under control. When this happens real interest rates must be allowed to rise. So sooner or later the policy of maintaining the lower interest rates breaks down.

Reducing an entrenched inflation

The trend inflation rate in OECD countries accelerated from the mid-1960s to the end of the 1970s. There were local aberrations, all sorts of world-wide shocks such as OPEC oil price increases, and a cyclical component imparted by demand fluctuations, but beneath all that the underlying trend was for core inflation to accelerate. Then in late 1970s and early 1980s, government after government became converted to the proposition that inflation was public enemy number one and had to be reduced at more or less any cost.

In order to reduce the inflation, many countries adopted policies to restrict demand. Typically, restrictive monetary policies were used, with the rate of monetary expansion being reduced below the rate of inflation. As long as this was done, the real money supply would shrink.[1] Thus the LM curve would shift further and further to the left. This would be accompanied, according to the model in this chapter, by rising interest rates (e.g., from r_1 to r_2 in Figure 47.8) and falling incomes (from Y_F to Y_1 in the Figure).

The actual inflation rate would be pushed slightly below the core rate, as shown in Figure 47.8 by the inflation rate associated with Y_1 being below the core rate of 8 per cent associated with Y_F. As a result the core rate itself would slowly fall. All of this is what actually happened, suggesting that the model is not a bad first approximation to the processes of a real economy.

A policy of breaking inflation through demand restraint alone would, according to the model of this chapter, call for a once-and-for-all demand restraint to open up a sufficient output gap (say $Y_F - Y_1$ in Figure 47.8) to put downward pressure on the inflation rate. After that the gradually falling inflation rate would be validated so as to hold the output gap constant.

Instead, the policies were guided by monetarist principles that the money supply itself was what mattered. Many countries adopted targets for the growth of their money supplies and quite a few of these were successful in meeting their targets.

> **The model in this chapter predicts that as long as the rate of monetary expansion is held below the inflation rate so that the real money supply continues to shrink, the output gap will *continue to grow* (unless of course, it is offset by shifts in expenditure functions).**

The consequences of money-supply rules in an open economy The key to meeting money-supply targets is that the authorities must *not* have targets with respect to the interest rate or the exchange rate. Instead, they must accept whatever fluctuations in these that the market dictates. We saw in Chapter 44 that when there is a shifting demand for money as a function of the interest rate, setting a money-supply target entails allowing the interest rate to vary widely. We also saw at the end of Chapter 45 that in a world of highly mobile capital, meeting monetary targets may have serious consequences for the exchange rate. Let us consider this point in more detail.

Consider a country that is following a money target. Assume that the demand for money as a function of the interest rate shifts to the right as a result of a rise in national income. To maintain its target for the money supply, the central bank must raise domestic interest rates. This causes an inflow of capital, which appreciates the external value of the country's currency. The value appreciates until investors come to expect a subsequent depreciation sufficient to wipe out the gain on the interest differential. (See page 722.)

While this process lasts, the appreciation of the currency switches expenditure from domestic to foreign goods. This shifts the IS curve further to the left and deepens the recession. Furthermore, when exports are sold in oligopolistic markets, lost market shares are not always easily regained once the currency depreciates back to its original level. Such a period of very high interest rates, high external value of the currency and difficulties for export industries occurred in the UK in 1979–80 and in the US in 1981–2. Their central banks were following tight, anti-inflationary, monetary

---

[1] For simplicity we have done everything in a non-growing economy. If the economy is growing, Y_F is shifting constantly to the right and a non-inflationary monetary policy would allow the real money supply to grow at the same rate as Y_F is growing. In this case a restrictive monetary policy might actually allow the real money supply to grow as long as it grew at a slower rate than Y_F.

policies that required forcing interest rates temporarily above those in most of the rest of the world.[1]

Additional policies to break an entrenched inflation

If curing an entrenched inflation by demand restraint alone is so costly in terms of unemployment and lost output, is there anything that can be done to speed up the process? Two commonly advocated measures are supply-side reforms and incomes policies.

Supply-side measures It is doubtful if supply-side measures could control inflation on their own, but since it is clear that many supply-side factors contribute to temporary bursts of inflation, reversing these may contribute to reducing inflation. Thus they could be a valid part of a package of policies designed to break an entrenched inflation. They could put once-and-for-all negative shock components into the inflation rate in the hope that these will contribute to reducing the core rate and thus breaking through inflationary inertias.

Here are a few: reductions in indirect taxes; alterations in wage-bargaining institutions to make wage rates a little more sensitive to current market conditions; policies to encourage competition, thus also making prices more sensitive to current market conditions; buffer stocks of agricultural goods and industrial raw materials to stabilize their prices against short-run fluctuations in demand and supply (see Chapter 10). By preventing upward shocks and encouraging downward ones, such policies might increase the speed with which inflation falls in response to restrictive demand-management policies.

Incomes policies to break an entrenched inflation Incomes policies run a whole gamut of measures from the government's setting of voluntary guidelines for wage and price increases, through consultation on wage and price norms between unions, management and government (more easily done, the more centralized are a country's wage- and price-setting mechanisms), through compulsory controls on wage, price and profit increases, to the so-called TIPs (tax-related incomes policies). The last is the only one of these that may not be self-evident. TIPs are meant to provide a tax incentive for management and labour to conform to government-established wage and price guidelines. Increases in wages and prices in excess of the guideline rates would be heavily taxed, thereby making firms and unions reluctant to engage in inflation-producing behaviour. TIPs have not yet been tried although they have been strongly advocated by many American economists.

> **TIPs would rely on tax incentives to secure voluntary conformity with the wage and price guidelines; wage and price controls try to force conformity by legal means.**

The great attractiveness of incomes policies in the situation of the early 1980s was that they suggested a possible way of breaking through the inflationary inertias and forcing the core rate of inflation down much faster than it would come down on its own. The policies would be used in conjunction with restrictive monetary policies reducing the rate of growth of the money supply down to what is compatible with the target rate of inflation, but then instead of waiting for a

---

[1] This gloomy view of the effects of exchange-rate fluctuations is not shared by all monetarists. Some of them hold that it is the result of the functioning of perfect markets and should be of no concern whatsoever. See, e.g., K. Phylaktis and G. Wood, 'Exchange-Rate Overshooting', *City University Annual Monetary Review*, No. 3, December 1981.

growing output gap and rising unemployment to curb wage and price inflation, incomes policies would be used. Say that starting from Y_F and an 8 per cent inflation in Figure 47.8 the rate of monetary expansion were cut from 8 to 4 to 0 per cent over three years and, at the same time, incomes policies would be used to force wage and price inflation down from 8 to 4 to 0 per cent over the same three years. In that case, the real money supply stays constant, so the LM curve does not shift left to create an output gap. The inflation is reduced by a combination of restrictive demand policy and an incomes policy. Once the target inflation rate is achieved and stabilized, the controls can be removed. If everyone then expects the new lower rate to persist, core inflation will have been broken without the recession required by the use of monetary restraint alone. *If* such a policy package had been tried and if it had worked in the early 1980s, the largest world recession since the 1930s, with all its consequent suffering and lost output, would have been avoided. Clearly there are large social stakes involved in the validity of these various theories.

Incomes policies further considered

We have spoken of incomes policies as part of a package to help break an entrenched inflation. Incomes policies have a long history in Britain and in Europe. They have been used in all sorts of circumstances; it may be of interest here to consider the alternative uses of such policies.

Such policies have sometimes been used in futile attempts to contain demand inflations. Assume for example there is an inflationary gap with income Y_1 and the curves IS_2 and LM_1 in Figure 47.3 (page 743). If wage-price controls are put on and if they are effective, they may succeed in forcing a zero inflation rate in spite of an inflationary gap of $Y_1 - Y_F$. If, however, nothing is done to remove the excess demand, so the IS and LM curves remain as IS_2 and LM_1, then the inflation will break as soon as the controls are removed.

Incomes policies can at best postpone, but cannot prevent, a demand inflation.

A second use of incomes policies is as a temporary supplement to demand restraint to help reduce an entrenched core inflation. This possible use was discussed in the previous section. It cannot be dismissed on theoretical grounds and many economists have advocated it as a way of avoiding the major recessions that accompany attempts to reduce stubborn inflations by demand restraint alone.

A third and quite different use of incomes policies is advocated by those who believe in the existence of a permanent inflationary bias caused by an exogenous wage push. Unlike wage inertia, this push will not go away merely because the inflation rate is forced to a low level for a year or two. Instead, inflationary pressure will always be present when the economy is anywhere near full employment. Economists who believe in exogenous wage push thus advocate *permanent* incomes policies as the only way to achieve anything approaching full employment and relatively stable prices.

Wage-price controls are poor tools for such long-term policies since there is substantial evidence that they severely distort incentives when applied for long periods of time. General 'social contract' type agreements between unions, management and governments seem more attractive for many for these long-term purposes. But such agreements, when they have been struck in the past, have proved notably fragile, usually lasting for only a few years (although occasionally for much longer). TIPS, if they could be made to work, have strong theoretical advantages since they leave decisions on wages and prices in the hands of labour and management and seek only to influence behaviour by altering the incentive system. Critics, however, argue that they would prove to be an administrative nightmare. Since incomes policies have had such a spotty record in the past, and since TIPs are the one really innovative idea to come into this field for a long time, it may be worth looking at them in a bit more detail.

Tax-based incomes policies (TIPs) were originally advanced in 1971 by American economists Henry Wallich and Sidney Weintraub. Though they have been advanced in numerous forms, all TIPs programmes are basically modifications of the original Wallich-Weintraub proposal.

The Wallich-Weintraub plan The original proposal called for the imposition of a surtax on any corporation that granted wage increases in excess of some national guideline. By biting into profits, such a plan would 'stiffen the backs of management' against granting 'excessive' wage settlements to workers. Although the basic TIP plan focused on wage restraint, it was not intended to penalize labour. Because real-wage growth is determined by productivity growth, the growth of money wages in excess of productivity growth leads to inflation, eroding any perceived gain by workers. Eventually the wage guidelines would be reduced until they matched the growth rate in national productivity, that is, to a non-inflationary rate of wage increase.

Extension to prices The effectiveness of the original plan depends critically on the assumption that most of the burden of the tax will be absorbed by firms and not shifted to consumers, that is, that firms will not exploit lower wage settlements to increase their profit margins. Advocates of TIPs have argued that competition from smaller firms not subject to the plan, and from imports, would keep price rises to a minimum. Historical evidence showing relatively constant price mark-ups over unit labour costs is also often cited as proof that firms will not use TIPs as an excuse to increase their profit margins.

It seems doubtful, however, that the constancy of mark-ups experienced during the pre-TIP period would still prevail after TIPs were imposed. This has led some economists to suggest that the plan be extended to include prices. This would involve tax penalties for those firms that raise prices in excess of the guidelines. A tax penalty that depends on *average* price increases for particular firms, however, raises such difficult measurement and index-number problems that most analysts are persuaded that this approach is impracticable.

Carrot or stick? Instead of merely punishing firms for failing to maintain the guidelines, rewards in the form of tax rebates could be given to those firms that grant wage increases that fall below the guidelines. Labour could also be involved by means of a payroll tax that places a surtax on workers who hold out for wage increases in excess of the guidelines and awards tax reductions to those who settle for less.

Under the penalty approach, a TIPs programme could be limited to, say, the large firms, which produce more than 50 per cent of GNP and provide most of the employment. These firms already have sophisticated accounting departments that could readily provide most of the information needed to implement such a plan. Few if any of the smaller firms would clamour to be included in the scheme if inclusion only raised the possibility of being penalized for granting excessive wage settlements. Under a penalty-reward approach, however, all firms, and possibly labour, would demand to be included because they stand to gain from reaching settlements that more than satisfy the wage guidelines. The administrative burden of implementing a penalty-reward scheme would be much greater than that of a penalty-only scheme.

Administrative problems Despite the apparent simplicity of a TIPs programme on paper, there are numerous practical problems that would have to be surmounted before such a policy could be implemented. Few if any of the supporters of TIPs have gone beyond a general description of how the system would operate.

For example, what should constitute the basic accounting unit over which wage increases are to be measured – the plant, the corporation, or the large vertically integrated industry? It may not be feasible to measure average wage increases for economic units in a manner appropriate for a tax-based penalty or subsidy. The unit for tax-accounting purposes often bears little resemblance to the unit that negotiates wages with its workers.

Another administrative detail not specifically addressed by most advocates is: How would non-monetary benefits fit into a TIP programme? Should pensions, unemployment insurance, private health insurance schemes, and other programmes contributed to by employers be included in the measurement of overall wage increases? Most economists would say yes, for to omit them would allow employers to evade the guidelines by increasing the size of the workers' benefits package. Yet measurement of these benefits can be administratively difficult. Separating increases in the wage rate from increases in overall labour income could be an administrative nightmare.

Of necessity, the rules governing wage-settlement behaviour would be arbitrary, yet the means to evade them are innumerable. It would be impossible to cover every eventuality under the rules, and to try to do so would only further increase the administrative burden. It is difficult to determine in detail how a particular TIP would work until someone has tried it. In the meantime, some believe that TIPs would be worth their cost because they would slow inflation. Others believe TIPs would be too costly because of the nightmarish web of rules and regulations they would eventually spin and because they would not in the end restrain inflation significantly.

Attempts to check inflation by restrictive demand-management policies have proved very costly for the world's economies. Those who believe that twentieth-century market economies are inflation-prone are actively looking for some extra-market control mechanism such as incomes policies. Those who blame inflation on past government mismanagement and who believe free-market economies are not inflation-prone argue that the price paid to break inflation, although heavy, was worth it. Once the inflationary inertias are removed and, given that there is now much more alertness to the signs of rising inflations, these economists feel that future inflation rates can be held at low levels. Only with the passage of time will further observations arise to test these theories. Was the world inflation from 1965 to 1983 a temporary aberration or is it a symptom of a basic built-in inflationary bias in unionized and oligopolistic market economies? Much of the future of twentieth-century mixed-market economies will depend on the answer finally given to this question.

48

Current issues in macroeconomic theory

Some of the most important debates over issues in political economy have taken place first between Keynesians and traditional monetarists, and then between Keynesians and the new-Classicists. The first of these two debates took place largely within the confines of the macro model presented in this book and concerned slopes of, and shifts in, the model's various functions. The second debate is between two very different models – a Keynesian, quantity-adjusting model and a new-Classical, perfectly competitive, flexible-price model. We shall first consider the debate between Keynesians and traditional monetarists and then that between Keynesians and new-Classicists.

Keynesians versus traditional monetarists

Models

The macroeconomic model presented in this book can loosely be described as neo-Keynesian. Its approach to income and expenditure flows and to quantity adjustments stems from the writings of Keynes (who, in his turn, built on many predecessors particularly the Swedish economists of his time). The approach has, however, been extended and developed as a result of countless more recent theoretical and empirical studies. Hence the qualification 'neo' to the term 'Keynesian'.

Although many monetarists tried to establish monetarism as a fundamentally different theory from Keynesianism, the attempt was never completely successful. In particular, after a decade of harsh criticism of Keynesian policies, the intellectual leader of the monetarists, Milton Friedman, accepted the challenge to lay out the underlying monetarist model. The result surprised and disappointed most observers. Friedman first specified an *IS-LM* model essentially the same as the one presented in Chapter 40 above. He then asserted that Keynesians closed it with a perfectly elastic aggregate supply curve, while monetarists closed it with a perfectly inelastic aggregate supply curve. On this count the model presented in this book comprehends both monetarism and Keynesianism.[1] It also implied that anyone who used an *IS-LM* model to analyse situations of full employment was a monetarist!

---

[1] Friedman's claim seemed bizarre. It could be argued that in the 1930s Keynesians did use a perfectly elastic *AS* curve (because they were concerned with situations of heavy unemployment). By the 1940s, however, Keynesians were commonly closing their models with the kinked, upward-ratcheting *AS* curve so that they could deal with full employment as well as unemployment. Then in the 1950s, ten years before Friedman's paper, the Phillips curve was integrated into Keynesian models, allowing them to deal with intermediate situations where both *P and Y* responded to aggregate demand shocks. So Friedman's claim about the Keynesian method of closure was several generations of models for closure evolution out of date. For Friedman's assertions see M. Friedman, 'A Theoretical Framework for Monetary Analysis', reprinted in R. J. Gordon, *Milton Friedman's Monetary Framework* (Univ. of Chicago Press, 1974).

In practice monetarists have used three 'models'. First, they often worked within the confines of the *IS-LM* model and sought to show that its characteristics were such as to favour their conclusions. Second, they sometimes used the quantity theory of money in the form $MV = PY$ (which we discussed in the Appendix to Chapter 44 and which needs to be read to understand this paragraph). Here V was derived from behavioural assumptions about the demand for money and was a function of such variables as the interest rate. M was 'the' quantity of money, which as we have seen is a tricky concept. If Y was fixed at Y_F, the theory determines the price level, P. If not, an aggregate supply relation is needed as well but was usually left unspecified. Third, they often used as their models single equations relating money income to monetary and expenditure variables that were fitted to the data econometrically to show the importance of monetary variables and the unimportance of expenditure variables. These 'models' invariably showed a strong relation between money national income, PY, and some measure of 'the' quantity of money. In the early days this was often M1; latterly it is more likely to be M3 or some even broader measure of 'the' money supply.[1]

General differences

Although traditional monetarists were unable to establish a well-articulated monetarist model that was fundamentally different from the neo-Keynesian model, they did argue for some basic differences in the behaviour of the economy that distinguished monetarists from Keynesian views.

Self-regulation Monetarists assert that the economy is inherently self-regulating around the full-employment level of income at a speed that does not require policy intervention. To justify this view, some amendment must be made in the macro model used so far in this book. The simplest amendment is to make the Phillips curve of Figure 47.1 (page 736) as steep to the left of Y_F as it is to the right. This denies the fundamental Keynesian asymmetry and allows the monetary adjustment mechanism to work just as quickly to remove an output gap as it does to remove an inflationary gap (when the money supply is held constant). Starting from potential income, shock the economy in either direction with a once-and-for-all *IS* or *LM* shift. If the shock is expansionary, Y will temporarily exceed Y_F but the resulting demand inflation will quickly shift the *LM* curve to the left until Y once again equals Y_F. If the shock is contractionary, Y will temporarily fall below Y_F and, given a steep Phillips curve to the left of Y_F, the price level will fall quickly, shifting *LM* rapidly to the right until the output gap is removed with Y once again equal to Y_F.

The neo-Keynesian model makes the Phillips curve very flat to the left of Y_F and hence this monetary adjustment mechanism works very slowly. Thus contractionary demand shocks can lead to persistent output gaps. This is a modification of the view that was propounded by Keynes himself in the *General Theory* and that so shocked the economics profession of his time. This was Keynes' theory of *underemployment equilibrium* (or *an equilibrium output gap*).

---

[1] These single-equation models are called 'quasi-reduced forms'. They are reduced-form equations such as our (11) on page 545 which shows an endogenous variable as a function of exogenous variables and behavioural parameters. But they are unsatisfactory because they are asserted rather than deduced from basic 'structural' equations in the way our (7) was from equations (1)–(6). This failure to do the underlying theory is unfortunate since it leaves one in doubt whether any particular reduced-form equation is or is not a valid deduction from the underlying theory. The most famous of these quasi-reduced-form models was the so-called St Louis model, which was used to 'demonstrate' the potency of monetary policy and the impotency of fiscal policy in the US. See, e.g., L. C. Anderson and K. M. Carlson in *The Econometrics of Price Determination* (Federal Reserve System, Washington D. C., 1972).

Underemployment equilibrium: This arises by making the Phillips curve horizontal to the left of Y_F, which means that although excess aggregate demand can raise the rate of inflation above its core rate, deficient aggregate demand will not lower it below the core rate. This gives us the perfectly elastic, upward-ratcheting *AS* curve. Now the economy can come to rest with $Y < Y_F$ and there is no monetary adjustment mechanism to propel the economy automatically back to full employment. Of course aggregate expenditure may recover sufficiently to reinstate full employment, but there is no monetary adjustment mechanism to guarantee it.

What if prices do fall?: Keynes also tried to argue that even if the price level did fall in the face of an output gap, this would not guarantee the restoration of full employment. The general verdict is that Keynes was wrong in this contention. A fall in the price level increases aggregate demand for two distinct reasons. The first is called the *Pigou effect*. All money and government bonds that are denominated in nominal monetary units increase in real value when the price level falls. Thus the private sector's wealth rises. As we saw in the Appendix to Chapter 35, wealth (or, as it is sometimes called, *permanent* income) is a term in the consumption function, and a rise in wealth is expected to lower saving and increase consumption expenditure. Therefore a fall in the price level, by raising private-sector wealth, increases consumption spending which means an upward shift in the aggregate expenditure function or, what is the same thing, a rightward shift in the *IS* curve. The second reason is our now familiar monetary adjustment mechanism. The fall in the price level raises the real value of the nominal money supply and leads wealth-holders to try to adjust their portfolios so as to hold less money and more bonds. This implies a rightward shift in the *LM* curve.

Summary: We may summarize these Keynesian positions on automatic stability as follows:
(1) Keynes argued that even if the price level fell when $Y < Y_F$, this would not necessarily restore full employment. The neo-Keynesian model of this book predicts that it would restore full employment as a result of the operation of both the Pigou effect and the monetary adjustment mechanism.
(2) The Keynesian model presented in this book will hold the price level constant in the face of an output gap as long as the Phillips curve is amended to be perfectly horizontal to the left of Y_F. In this case neither the Pigou effect nor the monetary adjustment mechanism are operative and there is *no* automatic mechanism to restore full employment. Underemployment equilibrium is possible.
(3) The Keynesian model as exactly presented in this book has a Phillips curve that, although quite flat, has some downward slope to the left of Y_F. In this case the monetary adjustment mechanism (and the Pigou effect) work to eliminate the output gap but their operation is very slow, too slow to be of interest for practical policy.

Equilibrium versus disequilibrium: Since forces tending to move the economy back to full employment probably do exist, it might be more accurate to describe a state of underemployment as a state of *underemployment disequilibrium* that is slowly moving towards full-employment equilibrium. But since these forces act very slowly, they are of little interest in the context of coping with a major depression and its accompanying heavy unemployment. For all practical purposes we may regard a situation where desired expenditure equals income at less than full-employment income as a short-run equilibrium which can be changed only by a further shift of the expenditure function. Those who, in the 1930s, were content to wait for long-run forces to produce full employment without government intervention could have been confronted with Keynes' famous words which he had in fact uttered earlier in another context: 'In the long run we are all dead.' Modern Keynesians might add that the Great Depression of the 1930s came to an abrupt end only after the Second World War forced the adoption of Keynesian remedies in the form of massive, deficit-financed government expenditures. They might well go on to conjecture that without these Keynesian remedies it might have taken another decade for full employment to have been produced by the economy's natural forces. Keynes did not, of course, hold that the economy would always settle in a position of underemployment equilibrium; only that it *could* settle there.

Keynesians versus monetarists: So on the issue of self-adjustment the difference between Keynesians and monetarists is now empirical – how steep is the Phillips curve to the left of Y_F? My reading of the evidence leaves me in no doubt that the price level responds quite slowly in a downward direction to output gaps. Some believe they see evidence of rapid downward response but their evidence is not well documented.[1]

Causes of fluctuations Monetarists tend to argue that the major causes of disturbances in the economy are monetary.[2] They accept that sometimes the commercial banks have been the cause of monetary shocks that, by shifting the *LM* curve, have caused fluctuations in national income. They also hold, however, that most of the severe depressions and inflations were caused by the perverse behaviour of policy-makers. Thus they believe that the monetary shocks that disturb the economy would be much less in total if central banks had absolutely passive monetary policies that did not try to exert any pressure on the short-run fluctuations of aggregate demand. Most monetarists also hold that expenditure fluctuations are not a major cause of serious deviations of national income from its full-employment level.

Neo-Keynesians stress expenditure shifts as major causes of trade-cycle fluctuations in the economy.[3] Keynesians do not rule out monetary shocks; it is merely that they believe expenditure shocks have been quantitatively important in the past, and probably will continue to be so in the future.

On this issue, differences between Keynesians and traditional monetarists are once again over empirical matters within the same general theoretical framework. Monetarists emphasize *LM* shifts as a cause of the trade cycle (some do so exclusively); Keynesians emphasize *IS* shifts (but few exclude *LM* shifts as of potential importance always and actual importance sometimes). No fundamental views on the underlying behaviour of the economy turn on the relative importance of *IS* and *LM* shifts and no one need be surprised if at different places, at different times and under different policy regimes the relative importance of the two have differed.

---

[1] For a really major piece of research documenting the relative downward insensitivity of the price level to the pressures of deficient demand, see Phillip Cagan, *Persistent Inflation: Historical and Policy Essays* (Columbia University Press, 1979).

[2] The view that fluctuations often have monetary causes is not new. The English economist R. G. Hawtrey, the Austrian Nobel laureate F. A. von Hayek and the Swedish economist Knut Wicksell are prominent among those who earlier gave monetary factors an important role in their explanations of the turning points in cycles and/or the tendency for expansions and contractions, once begun, to become cumulative and self-reinforcing. Modern monetarists carry on this tradition.

[3] Like the monetarists, the neo-Keynesians are modern advocates of some views that have a long history. The great Austrian (and later American) economist Joseph Schumpeter stressed such explanations early in the present century. The Swedish economist Wicksell and the German Speithoff both stressed this aspect of economic fluctuations before the emergence of the Keynesian school of thought.

Evidence

The major evidence that the monetarists quote in their favour is the high degree of correlation that can be found in most countries between money national income, PY, on the one hand and some measure of the money supply on the other hand. The most important piece of work in this connection was the monumental study by Milton Friedman and Anna Schwartz or the relation between money and business activity in the United States.[1] They established that there is a strong correlation between changes in the money supply and changes in the level of business activity. Major recessions are found to be associated with absolute declines in the money supply, and minor recessions with the slowing down of the rate of increase in the money supply below its long-term trend.[2]

The high correlation between PY and most monetary aggregates is accepted by most economists. Controversy occurs over how this correlation is to be interpreted. Monetarists believe first that the money supply is a mainly exogenous variable under the control of the central bank and, second, that variations in the money supply *cause* variations in money national income. For them the causal sequence is mainly from M to PY.

Criticisms of the evidence   Keynesians argue that the causal sequence is a two-way street. Although they accept that exogenous monetary shocks can cause major changes in PY, they also hold that the reverse has often happened: changes in PY have caused changes in M. When this happens the money supply becomes an endogenous variable and it is not correct to blame changes in PY on changes in the money supply.

In making this argument, Keynesians point to two facts. First, over the majority of the time between World War II and the present – the period when these correlations were established – central banks were seeking to stabilize interest rates rather than the money supply. When they do this they expand the money supply in booms (to prevent interest rates from rising) and they contract it in slumps (to prevent interest rates from falling). This was analysed in Figure 44.7(ii) on page 701 and it has the effect of making the money supply endogenous and positively correlated with the level of national income.

Second, commercial banks, even in a cash reserve system such as the US, let alone in the British system, have substantial power to vary their deposit liabilities, and hence the money supply, within very wide limits. In boom times, when demand to borrow is high, banks are likely to make as many loans as possible; in slumps, when demand to borrow is low, they may curtail their lending and carry some excess reserves. This behaviour also has the effect of making the money supply endogenous. The positive correlation between M and PY then occurs because fluctuations in PY cause fluctuations in M, not vice versa.

Policy debates

An inflation-output trade-off?   During the 1960s the naive Phillips curve was grafted onto many

---

[1] M. Friedman and A. Schwartz, *A Monetary History of the United States, 1867–1960* (Princeton Univ. Press, 1963).

[2] If this is evidence for the importance of money, it is also evidence that Friedman's attempt to distinguish Keynesian from monetarist theories on the basis of a horizontal and a vertical AS curve was inadequate. Here Friedman and Schwartz are explaining changes in Y by changes in M. Clearly monetarists who try to interpret the experience of actual economies need a theory to explain how the effect of demand shocks is split between changes in P and changes in Y.

Keynesian macro models. This made inflation depend *solely* on the gap $Y - Y_F$ as shown by Figure 47.1. This gave rise to the famous trade-off where, by validating an inflation, output could be held above Y_F at the cost of a constant, stable rate of inflation. Monetarists argued against this view and for the view, now fairly generally accepted, that if Y is held significantly above Y_F by validating the inflation, the inflation rate itself will accelerate so that more and more monetary validation of an ever-rising rate of inflation will be needed.

To make this argument, monetarists developed the theory of the expectations-augmented Phillips curve. In its macro behaviour this is the same as the core-augmented curve developed in Figure 47.2. Core inflation depends on expectations and so could just as well be called expectational inflation. The micro explanation is, however, somewhat different and we shall go into that when we discuss the aggregate supply curve of the new-Classicism.

The potency of monetary policy Monetarists believe that monetary shocks can have large effects on aggregate demand and hence on P and Y, but nonetheless they argue against the use of monetary policy as an active stabilizer. Their argument seems to be as follows: (1) monetary policy is a potent force of expansionary and contractionary pressures; (2) monetary policy works with lags that are both long and variable; and (3) throughout the world central banks are given to sudden and strong reversals of policy stances. Consequently monetary policy has usually had a destabilizing effect on the economy, the policy itself accentuating rather than dampening the economy's natural cyclical swings.

Monetarists argue from this position that the stability of the economy would be much improved if central banks stopped trying to stabilize it. What then should they do? Since growth of population and productivity leads to a rising level of output, the central banks ought to provide the extra money needed to allow the holding of additional transactions, precautionary, and speculative balances as real income and wealth rise over time.

According to the monetarists, central banks should expand the money supply year in and year out at a constant rate equal to the rate of growth of real income. When the growth rate shows signs of long-term change, the Bank could adjust its rate of monetary expansion, but it should not alter this rate with a view to stabilizing the economy against short-term fluctuations.

Early Keynesians often argued that monetary policy was relatively ineffective. They held this view because they believed that the *LM* curve was very flat, so that large horizontal shifts in the curve would have only a small effect on equilibrium income (i.e., shift the aggregate demand curve only slightly).

Empirical evidence has discredited this view and most Keynesian economists now hold that monetary shocks can have a significant effect on aggregate demand. Also as a result of experiences in the early 1980s most economists agree that, if it is sufficiently severe, monetary policy can have a major depressing effect on the economy. Provided the monetary authorities are willing to let interest rates rise high enough and restrict credit sufficiently, a really severe recession can be induced. Large enough doses of monetary medicine can be extremely powerful.

Keynesians do not agree, however, that active demand management, using monetary and/or fiscal policy, must always be destabilizing. Although they join most economists in being sceptical of fine-tuning, they believe that large and persistent inflationary or output gaps do sometimes develop. These gaps are large and persistent enough for stabilization policy to be called for and to be effective (for the discussion on this, see pp. 667–8).

The potency of fiscal policy One of the major tools of Keynesian macro-stabilization policy is fiscal policy, the changing of expenditures and tax rates with the purpose of shifting the aggregate demand function by shifting the *IS* curve. Monetarists have mounted a long-term attack on fiscal policy. They argue that the main effects of an expansionary fiscal policy will be to crowd out a more or less equivalent amount of private expenditure rather than to increase total expenditure. The crowding-out effect comes in three versions.

Crowding-out of the first kind: This is due to the slope of the *LM* curve. An expansionary fiscal policy forces up the interest rate and crowds out some private expenditure. As a result, the interest-variable multiplier is smaller than the interest-constant multiplier. We studied this version of the crowding-out effect on pages 687–9 and there observed that empirical estimates of the income elasticity of the demand for money suggested sufficient elasticity of the *LM* curve to leave plenty of scope for fiscal policy to shift the aggregate demand curve.

Crowding-out of the second kind: This type of crowding-out argument was first advanced by a set of economists centred at the Federal Reserve Bank of St Louis in the US. The main argument was that a bond-financed fiscal expansion would raise the ratio of bonds to money, B/M, and that this would induce portfolio adjustments among wealth-holders that would shift the *LM* curve in a perverse direction. We have not encountered this argument before but it is an extension of one already used. Earlier we argued that an increase in the nominal money supply would shift the *LM* curve to the right because wealth-holders would only be in portfolio equilibrium with the original bond supply and the new larger money supply if the interest rate fell, leaving them wanting to hold a higher proportion of their wealth in money. The new argument is that the increase in bonds consequent on a bond-financed increase in government expenditure shifts the *LM* curve to the *left*. This is because wealth-holders can only return to portfolio equilibrium with the original money supply and the new larger bond supply if the rate of interest rises, so increasing the proportion of their wealth they wish to hold as bonds.[1] According to this theory, a bond-financed fiscal expansion will shift the *LM* curve left and so raise interest rates even further than when the *LM* curve was fixed, crowd out even more private expenditure and lower the value of the multiplier even more. Keynesians had long been aware of the problem. They had usually sidestepped it by arguing that, although a government deficit could make a large percentage change in the money supply if it were financed by the central bank's creation of new money, it would make only a negligible percentage change in the bond supply if it were financed by the sale of bonds to the public. This is because the outstanding stock of bonds is very large relative to the existing stock of money. (Recall that 'bonds' stand for all financial assets other than M1.) There are many further problems related to this crowding-out argument[2] but all we

---

[1] This follows from Tobin's theory of the liquidity-preference demand for money which we studied briefly on pages 585–6. For a given level of income it makes the interest rate determine the *proportions* of their wealth that wealth-holders wish to hold in money and in bonds.

[2] For one thing, the argument ignores the fact that the supply of 'bonds' must be increasing in *any* macro equilibrium where investment is positive even if the government budget is balanced. For another, it ignores the effect of the change in wealth, due to changes in the quantity of bonds, on expenditure functions. Keynesians had avoided all of these issues by arguing that the effect of changes in the bond supply would be quantitatively insignificant because the outstanding stock of bonds was so large. Once monetarists raised them, however, they tried to apply them selectively to those aspects that would weaken fiscal policy. For a full analysis, see A. Blinder and R. Solow, *Analytical Fiscal Policy* (Brookings Institution, Washington D.C., 1977), and the references cited therein.

need to observe is that, even if the argument were correct, the additional crowding out could be avoided by financing a small amount of the deficit by money creation so that the ratio of M/B did not change (i.e., make $\Delta M/\Delta B$ due to the new deficit equal to M/B which is the ratio of the existing stocks of money and bonds). With an unchanged M/B ratio, wealth-holders would be in equilibrium at the old interest rate and the old level of income (i.e., the LM curve would not shift).

Crowding-out of the third kind: The third kind of crowding out was originally analysed by David Ricardo in the nineteenth century and as a result it is often referred to as the *Ricardo Invarience Principle*. Ricardo was showing what had to be true for fiscal policy to be impotent; he did not himself believe that these things were true of the real world.

The modern analysis is mainly due to an elegant paper by Robert Barro[1] in which he lays out a model of overlapping generations where fiscal policy has no effect on aggregate expenditure. Judging from the number of times it is cited in debates on the empirical efficacy of fiscal policy, it appears to have had a strong influence on some economists. Barro's model is beautifully formulated in abstract terms but its essence is as follows.

(1) The population consists of people of different ages, the young, the working and the retired.

(2) Each household has a plan for its life-time consumption and for a positive amount of net wealth that it wishes to pass on to its heirs.

(3) The government now introduces some new deficit-financed expenditure. Assume for illustration that it sells bonds on the open market and hands out the proceeds as extra unemployment benefits. If the recipients wished, they could spend the money and leave their heirs with the liability to pay the taxes that will have to be levied to redeem the bonds when they fall due. If they do this, the fiscal policy will have stimulated the economy by inducing extra expenditure on the part of the recipients of the government 'transfer' payments. But this violates the assumption that everyone has a rational plan that includes a target for net wealth to be handed on to their heirs. In order to fulfil this target, the present generation must save an amount equal to the new budget deficit and pass these new savings on to their heirs. This will exactly offset their heirs' extra tax liabilities to pay taxes to redeem the debt after it falls due. As a result, the new transfer payments induce no net increase in spending.[2]

It stretches credulity to breaking point to believe that all people behave in this way. Some people have no children, others, having educated their now-grown children, do not have a positive target for further net wealth that they wish to leave to them on death. Others who do, will not be paying close attention to the stock of national debt and trying to offset any increased tax liabilities their heirs incur as a result of the rise in the stock of debt.[3]

Some economists believe that this behaviour exists and renders fiscal policy impotent. No evidence to this effect has been gathered and, in the meantime, a general increase in saving by the unemployed following on a deficit-financed increase in unemployment benefits so that the unem-

---

[1] R. Barro, 'Are Government Bonds Net Wealth?', *Journal of Political Economy*, Nov./Dec. 1974.

[2] The people who receive the money do not have to do all of the offsetting saving. They must save enough to offset the extra tax liabilities of their own heirs. But everyone else now calculates that their own heirs have an additional tax liability and these people must make new savings so as to pass offsetting bonds on to their heirs. In total, since the new future tax liabilities must be equal to the new bonds created by the present increase in the deficit, total new saving must equal the total increase in the deficit. Thus there is no net increase in spending.

[3] For further, more detailed, criticisms see J. Tobin, *Asset Accumulation and Economic Activity* (Univ. of Chicago Press, 1980).

ployed could fulfil their targets to leave each of their heirs with a given net wealth position seems, to this observer at least, to be too bizarre to be taken really seriously.

Monetarist macro policy

Long term Monetarists see the economy as essentially self-regulating unless disturbed by mis-guided stabilization policy. Once transitional problems are overcome, their long-term macro policy calls for no stabilization policy. The fiscal levers should be set to give a balanced budget (at least on current account, although there is no general agreement on whether capital expenditure should also be financed out of current revenue). Since fiscal stimuli are generally impotent, it does not matter if the budget is balanced annually or over the cycle (in any case once governments abandon stabiliz-ation policy there won't be much of a cycle).

Monetary policy should be set to satisfy long-term monetary needs and to avoid any attempt at stabilization. This is done by taking all discretion away from central banks and by requiring that the rate of growth of the nominal money supply be equal to the rate of growth of real national income (assuming a unit income elasticity of demand for money). Thus, they argue, the supply of money will increase as fast as its demand, so output can grow without inflationary pressures.

Criticism: Keynesians argue that fluctuations in private-sector expenditure functions as well as supply shocks can cause substantial and sustained output and inflationary gaps to develop from time to time. They believe that in such circumstances corrective monetary and fiscal policy can be used to shift the aggregate demand function and eliminate the gaps far faster than the natural equilibrating forces of the economy can do the job.

They also argue that it is utterly naive to think that all discretion can be eliminated from monetary policy. Enormous technological changes in the banking system have occurred and will go on occurring. These will cause large changes in the demands for various monetary assets. (Over the last decade, firms have learned to economize greatly on their M1 balances thus reducing the demand for these assets.) So any given rule for the growth of a particular group of monetary assets called 'the money supply' will quickly become irrelevant. To cope with such changes in the demand for money even the most anti-inflationary central banks must exercise discretion over the rate at which various monetary assets are allowed to grow. The monetarists' strict money growth rule is a product of the classroom where there are only two assets, M and B; it has no application, so Keynesians argue, to the real world where there is a whole spectrum of monetary assets each with its own demand and supply function that shifts over the decades due to a host of changes in institutions and behaviour.

Eliminating an entrenched inflation By the late 1970s inflation had been proceeding at a rapid pace in most Western countries. The rate of inflation had been accelerating up to the mid-1970s. Then, although it receded slightly, it proved to be only slowly responsive to the excess supply pressures that built up in the recession of 1974–5. The slow recovery of the world's economies throughout the latter part of the 1970s was accompanied once again by a rise in inflation rates. Throughout the world, governments became frightened that not only had inflation become endemic, but the rate would ratchet up at the peak of booms to fall back only slightly during slumps.

Government after government declared inflation to be public enemy number one, and decided that it was worth paying a very heavy price to break the inflation. At the same time, many governments and central banks became converted to one version or another of monetarism. The basic tenets were as follows.

(1) The money supply can be controlled.

(2) Reduction of the rate of monetary expansion will bring immediate reductions in the rate of increase in money national income, PY. (In other words, the velocity of circulation, V, will prove to be stable.) For a short time the main effects may be felt on Y, then, however, a reduction in the rate of increase in P will occur (i.e., inflationary inertias are not strong because the Phillips curve is relatively steep to the left of Y_F).

(3) Target rates for monetary growth should be set and these should be reduced quite rapidly to reduce the rate of monetary expansion from that consistent with two-digit inflation to that consistent with a stable price level.

(4) These targets should be adhered to whatever the short-term consequences for the interest rate or for the exchange rate.

In most countries neo-Keynesians were sideline critics of this monetarist experiment. Their criticisms typically included the following points.

(1) It will be difficult, particularly in Britain, to control the chosen monetary aggregate.

(2) Even if it can be controlled, the effects on PY will be much less strong and much less certain than monetarists predict. This is because people will learn to economize on their holdings of the targeted set of monetary assets and will instead hold non-targeted assets which are very close substitutes. In other words, the simplicity of the monetarist message disappears as soon as we recognize the existence of a whole spectrum of highly substitutable monetary assets.

(3) Even if the desired effect on PY is obtained, a very high proportion of it will come out as a fall in Y rather than as a reduction in the rate of growth of P. In other words, the monetarist experiment risked throwing the world into a deep and prolonged recession. (This is because neo-Keynesians held that the core rate of inflation has a lot of inertia built into it and that the Phillips curve is very flat to the left of Y_F.)

In the event, the evidence was somewhat mixed, but the following conclusions seem fairly clear (although there will always be someone ready to debate any conclusion).

(i) Some countries, particularly those with cash-reserve systems, found that they could control their chosen monetary magnitude within reasonable limits. Because of its complex nature, the British banking sector's money creation proved less easy to control.

(ii) The relation between each country's chosen monetary aggregate and PY proved much less stable than had been hoped. The more successful was a country's central bank in controlling its chosen monetary aggregate, the more did its relation to PY change, as the private sector learned to use uncontrolled assets instead. The Bank of Canada, for example, was one of the most successful of the central banks in meeting gradually falling targets for the rate of growth of M1. But at the same time the rate of growth of uncontrolled M3 accelerated greatly as firms and households learned to use M3 assets as temporary stores of value (as a result, the velocity of circulation of M1, i.e. PY/M1, rose steadily, while the velocity of circulation of M3, i.e. PY/M3, held quite stable).[1]

---

[1] Between the writing of this section in late 1982 and the correction of the proofs in March 1983, the Bank of Canada, one of the most successful at following monetary targets, made a dramatic announcement completely abandoning monetary targeting. The reason given was that, in an ever-changing world, no single monetary magnitude bears a sufficiently stable relation to PY to make targeting a useful exercise.

(iii) Monetary policy certainly proved potent, although the more direct relation appeared to be between PY and r rather than between PY and M. Interest rates in the US soared to over 20 per cent and the US dollar appreciated strongly on the foreign-exchange market, encouraging imports and hurting exports. An extremely severe worldwide recession ensued. It was serious enough to put the whole fabric of postwar economic co-operation in jeopardy, as country after country sought beggar-my-neighbour solutions to their own domestic problems. Inflation fell, but at a rate that was very slow for those hoping to stick with monetarist rules although faster than the most pessimistic neo-Keynesians had predicted.

(iv) Exchange-rate and interest-rate fluctuations required to meet strict money-supply targets proved very large. Country after country moderated their strict money-supply rules in order to reduce some of the fluctuations in these other important variables.

(v) The whole experiment has been very costly in terms of unemployment and lost output, but it has succeeded in moderating inflation rates throughout the world. A critical test will come when the world's economies expand back towards full employment. If the monetarists, or the model presented in the first half of Chapter 47 are right, the lower rate of inflation should be sustainable provided that a serious inflationary gap is not allowed to develop. If those who believe in the autonomous wage push are right, the inflation rate will creep upwards as soon as national income approaches the full-employment range. In that case, the whole costly inflation-fighting experiment will have left no lasting effect. Then a burst of new idea formation will be necessary as economists seek to devise new methods of controlling endemic inflation other than by manipulating aggregate demand.

The new Classicism

Traditional monetarists tried very hard to establish a major difference in underlying theory between themselves and neo-Keynesians. In the main this was not successful and the Keynesian-monetarist debate was carried on mainly within the confines of the general model outlined in the present book.[1] Then, however, during the 1970s a radically different model was developed. This refined many monetarist views and took them to their logical conclusion. This so-called new-Classical model really was a different theoretical model from Keynesian-style macro models. Traditional monetarists were then forced to decide whether or not they would accept the new-Classical model. Some, such as Milton Friedman, did not. These economists then found the differences that divided them from the neo-Keynesians small relative to what divided them from the new-Classical model.[2] At this point Milton Friedman ceased to be the intellectual leader of the extreme monetarist school and the mantle passed to the leaders of the new-Classical school such as Robert Lucas of the University of Chicago.

The major characteristics of the new-Classical model are as follows.

(1) All markets behave as if they were perfectly competitive. In particular, price adjusts in all markets until there are neither unsatisfied buyers nor unsatisfied sellers. This means that involun-

---

[1] For a survey of these attempts, see D. Purvis, 'Monetarism: A Review', *Canadian Journal of Economics*, vol. XIII, No. 1, February 1980.

[2] For example, the reader is hard pressed to find really fundamental differences between the position taken by James Tobin, the leader of the American neo-Keynesians, and David Laidler, a monetarist who does not accept the new-Classicism, in their exchange in the *Economic Journal*, vol. 99, No. 361, March 1981. Probably their biggest difference is some implicit disagreement over the shape of the short-run Phillips curve when Y is less than Y_F.

tary unemployment does not occur, since this requires that there are unsatisfied sellers of labour who would like to work at the going wage rate but cannot find a job.

(2) Deviations from full-employment equilibrium occur only where people make mistakes. The really important mistake is the confusion of a change in the absolute price level with a change in relative prices. Booms and slumps are caused by employers and employees making mistakes.

(3) Since the theory of rational expectations implies that people do not make systematic mistakes, there is no systematic pressure for output and employment to diverge from its static equilibrium value.

The second point is illustrated in Figure 48.1 which shows a Classical labour market of the type discussed on pages 388–9 of Chapter 27. The demand and supply of labour are functions of the real wage rate, W/P. The market behaves as if it were perfectly competitive. Hence if no one is misinformed, equilibrium will be at q_F of employment and a real wage rate of $(W/P)_F$ with everyone who wishes to work at that wage actually being employed.

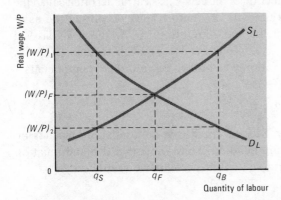

Fig. 48.1 Deviation from full employment due to asymmetric misperception of the real wage rate on the part of demanders and suppliers of labour

Now let us generate a boom. Assume that on 1 January an annual wage contract is signed, raising money wages, W, by 10 per cent. Further assume that workers anticipate a rise in the price level, P, of 5 per cent, so they believe the real wage they will receive this year will be $(W/P)_1$ and thus the quantity of labour supplied is q_B. Finally assume that employers anticipate a rise in the price level of 15 per cent, so they believe the real wage they will have to pay is $(W/P)_2$, so they demand q_B labour. Therefore there is a boom with employment rising above q_F to q_B, which is an equilibrium because employees anticipate a higher real wage than do employers over the planning period.

Now let us generate a slump. Assume that the same increase of 10 per cent in money wages occurs but that this time workers expect P to rise by 15 per cent while employers only expect it to rise by 5 per cent. Now workers expect a fall in their real wage to $(W/P)_2$ and so only offer q_S labour, while employers expect a rise in the real wage they must pay to $(W/P)_2$ and hence they only demand q_S of labour. Once again the labour market clears, with quantity demanded equalling quantity supplied and once again this is because demanders and suppliers have different, and mutually inconsistent, expectations about the inflation rate over their planning period.

In the new-Classical model all unemployment is voluntary. Employment falls below its static full-employment level because workers anticipate a fall in their real wage rate and voluntarily work less.

If the model is constructed carefully enough, either workers or employers can make the errors in predicting the actual real wage. All that matters is that in booms workers anticipate a higher real wage than do employers, while in slumps workers must anticipate a lower real wage than do employers.

For simplicity, however, we make the assumption, which is commonly used in these models, that employers always get their forecasts right, while workers may get them wrong. In this case where we have a slump, and a rise in unemployed labour, careful questioning should reveal that all unemployment is voluntary. Unemployed workers should all say that they voluntarily decided not to work because they overestimated the inflation rate which caused them to underestimate the real wage rate that they could have obtained if they had taken work.

The Lucas aggregate supply function

This analysis is the basis of the aggregate supply function of the new-Classical model often called the Lucas aggregate supply function after Robert Lucas, its originator. The causality in the basic Keynesian macro model runs from aggregate demand and output to prices. In the new-Classical model the causality is reversed, running from prices to output. Let us see how this occurs.

Recall that in equation (1) of Chapter 47 inflation was broken up into three components – demand, core and shock inflation:

$$\dot{P} = \dot{P}_d + \dot{P}_c + \dot{P}_s \quad . \tag{1}$$

First, assume zero shock inflation for simplicity. Second, recall that core inflation depends on expectations of future wage costs and hence future inflation. Third, note that demand inflation depends on Y-Y_F as shown in Figure 47.1. Taking all of this into account, we write (1) as

$$\dot{P}_t = \mathrm{F}(Y - Y_F)_t + \dot{P}^e_{t-1} \quad , \tag{2}$$

where $\dot{P}_t$ is this period's inflation rate, $(Y - Y_F)_t$ is this period's output or inflationary gap, F is the 'Phillips curve' function that translates the gap into demand inflation, and $\dot{P}^e_{t-1}$ is the expectation of inflation in period t formed in the previous period. This is the neo-Keynesian view where the inflation rate is the dependent variable which is determined by $Y - Y_F$ (which is in turn determined by the *IS-LM* part of the model) and by expectations of inflation (plus shocks, currently assumed to be zero for simplicity).

In the new-Classical model, as we have already seen, output deviates from its full-employment level when mistakes are made in predicting the price level. Thus in the new-Classical model the output gap is the dependent variable determined by the prediction errors on the inflation rate. To see how this occurs, we need to go beyond our earlier labour-market considerations. Assume that everyone, employers and employees, expect a rise in the price level of 10 per cent over their current planning period. Assume that prices actually rise by 15 per cent. Each firm sees its price rise by 15 per cent and mistakes this for a rise of 5 per cent in its own relative price (since each only expects the general price level to rise by 10 per cent). Each firm therefore decides to produce more. Similar considerations apply to labour. Thus when everyone is underpredicting the rate of inflation, they are misinterpreting their own price increase in excess of their expected rate of inflation as an increase in their relative price (when it is really just a part of the actual rate of inflation). Similar considerations suggest that if everyone is overpredicting the actual rate of inflation, each will be incorrectly believing their own relative price is falling. Assume for example that everyone expects a 10 per cent inflation but the actual rate is only 5 per cent. So they see their own price rise by 5 per cent and incorrectly think it has fallen relative to all other prices, which they expect to rise at 10 per cent.

For the above reasons, real output, Y, will exceed the equilibrium output Y_F if the actual rate of inflation exceeds the expected rate, while Y will fall below Y_F if actual inflation is less than the expected rate. This gives us

$$Y_t - Y_F = G(\dot{P}_t - \dot{P}^e_{t-1}) \qquad . \tag{3}$$

In other words the deviation of output from its 'full-employment' level depends on the deviation of actual from expected inflation. As a next step we introduce the rational expectations theory of inflationary expectations. As we saw in Chapter 47, this requires that people do not make systematic errors. Instead their prediction of what the inflation rate will be at time t, which they make at time $t-1$, will be equal to the actual inflation rate plus a random error term ε:

$$\dot{P}^e_{t-1} = \dot{P}_t + \varepsilon_t \qquad . \tag{4}$$

For some periods ε will be positive, indicating an overestimate of the inflation rate. In other periods it will be negative, indicating an underestimate. But on average over a large number of periods, ε will be zero, indicating no systematic, long-term tendency to over- or underestimate the inflation rate.

Substituting (4) into (3) yields

$$Y_t - Y_F = G(-\varepsilon_t) \tag{5}$$

But now we seem to have proved too much; there is no systematic business cycle; all departures of Y from Y_F are random. To avoid this obviously unrealistic prediction, the Lucas supply function introduces a lag so that

$$Y_t - Y_F = G(-\varepsilon_t) + \alpha(Y_{t-1} - Y_F) \qquad 0 < \alpha < 1 \qquad . \tag{6}$$

This introduces an inertia that makes income behave cyclically. But the disturbances which cause income to change are essentially random and if the disturbances were zero for a long time, the gap, $Y_t - Y_F$, would approach zero so that output would tend to settle down at Y_F.

In this model variations in output around its full-employment level are caused by errors in predicting the inflation. When combined with the theory of rational expectations, this makes the impulse for variations essentially random.

This model has been misnamed the rational expectations model. This is a misnomer, since rationally formed expectations can be used in any model. As we saw in Chapter 47, for example, rational expectations of the core rate of inflation can be used in the Keynesian model of inflation without altering its basic conclusions. The Lucas supply function depends on a new-Classical market-clearing model plus rationally formed expectations of the inflation rate. Hence 'the new-Classical model' is a better description of the model rather than 'the rational expectations model'.

Policy invariance

The model can be used to deduce the so-called policy invariance result which predicts that systematic stabilization policy has no effect on the economy! Start by assuming a crude form of monetarism that makes the rate of inflation simply equal to the rate of growth of the money supply:

$$\dot{P}_t = \dot{m}_{t-1} \quad . \tag{7}$$

Next assume that the central bank varies the rate of growth of the money supply, partly following some systematic rule of stabilization policy and partly randomly. Thus for the rate of change of the money supply, we have

$$\dot{m}_{t-1} = \dot{m}^r_{t-1} + \dot{m}^u_{t-1} \quad , \tag{8}$$

where $\dot{m}^r$ is that part of the monetary growth that follows a systematic rule, while $\dot{m}^u$ is that part that is unsystematic. Since $\dot{m}^u$ is unpredictable, it is always a surprise. It can be thought of as a random variable of mean zero. (If it were not random it would be systematic and hence would be a part of $\dot{m}^r$).

Now substitute the Bank's monetary rule from (8) into equation (7) that determines the inflation rate to obtain

$$\dot{P}_t = \dot{m}^r_{t-1} + \dot{m}^u_{t-1} \quad , \tag{9}$$

which merely says that inflation will have a systematic component as a result of the Bank's systematic monetary behaviour and a random component as a result of surprise variations in the money supply.

Next we must restate expectations formation according to the theory of rational expectations. We make the added assumption that when expectations about the inflation rate that will rule in period t are formed in period $t-1$, people know what the systematic component of $\dot{m}$ will be but they do not know what the random component will be. (The money-supply figures are available only with a lag, but the policy rule is known.) Thus we have

$$\dot{P}^e_{t-1} = \dot{m}^r_{t-1} + \varepsilon_t \quad , \tag{10}$$

which says that rational agents predict at $t-1$ what the inflation rate will be at t by a knowledge of the systematic rule the Bank is following and that their predictions are subject to an error that is a random variable of mean zero. (In other words, on average over a very long time their errors cancel out and do not have any systematic bias to over- or under-predict).

Next we return to the Lucas supply function in its full form. We have seen that this function explains deviations from potential income, $Y_t - Y_F$, in terms of errors in predicting the price level $G(\dot{P}_t - \dot{P}^e_{t-1})$ and a lagged adjustment back towards potential income, $\alpha(Y_{t-1} - Y_F)$. Writing this out in full gives us

$$Y_t - Y_F = G(\dot{P}_t - \dot{P}^e_{t-1}) + \alpha(Y_{t-1} - Y_F) \quad . \tag{11}$$

Now substitute the determinants of $\dot{P}_t$ from equation (9) and $\dot{P}^e_{t-1}$ from (10) to yield

$$Y_t - Y_F = G(\dot{m}^r_{t-1} + \dot{m}^u_{t-1} - \dot{m}^r_{t-1} - \varepsilon_t) + \alpha(Y_{t-1} - Y_F)$$

$$Y_t - Y_F = G(m^u_{t-1} - \varepsilon_t) + \alpha(Y_{t-1} - Y_F) \quad . \tag{12}$$

The systematic component of monetary policy $\dot{m}^r_{t-1}$ has disappeared, and deviations from potential income depend on the difference between two random variables $\dot{m}^u$ and ε and on the mechanical term that adjusts Y back towards Y_F whenever there are no other disturbances. This is the policy invariance result: systematic policy intervention has no effect on the economy.

Assessment It is important to understand that this policy invariance result stems from two critical characteristics of the new-Classical model. First, that deviations of Y from Y_F only occur because people make mistakes in predicting the inflation rate and, second, that according to the theory of rational expectations, people do not make systematic mistakes (which implies that they fully understand and act on anything systematic that the Bank does). It is also interesting to note that there is here a sharp difference of prediction between the new-Classical and traditional monetarists. Friedman and other traditional monetarists hold that monetary policy is such a powerful tool that it should not be used because it will do more harm than good. Lucas and other new-Classicists hold that monetary (and any other systematic) policy is such a useless tool that it should not be used. The, to my mind overwhelming, weight of empirical evidence supports Friedman's view that monetary policy is potent (and, often at least, destabilizes the economy) and conflicts with the new-Classical view that it is impotent.

In contrast, the neo-Keynesian model allows deviations of Y from Y_F where no one makes mistakes but which occur as a result of oligopolistic pricing policies and the working of the labour market. In these circumstances firms and workers can see a government policy coming and yet it will affect their behaviour because it will influence aggregate demand and total output. Assume, for example, that the Bank announces that one year from now it is going to contract the money supply by 20 per cent. According to the new-Classical model, people will correctly perceive that this will reduce the price level by 20 per cent and will all cut their own wages or prices by 20 per cent. As a result, relative prices will be unchanged and neither output nor employment will be affected. According to the neo-Keynesian model, even though people see the monetary shock coming, there is little they can do about it. Labour markets will not miraculously become perfectly competitive. Instead, money wages will be more or less unchanged, and as a result, oligopolistic prices will also be more or less unchanged. Thus when the monetary shock hits, output and employment will fall. The shock will have real effects.

The evidence seems to me to be overwhelmingly in favour of the neo-Keynesian model and specifically in showing that output deviates from its full-employment level not just because people make mistakes in predicting inflation. The underlying theoretical reason why neo-Keynesianism is right where the new-Classicism is wrong seems to me to be that the perfectly competitive model does not in any way describe the real-world behaviour of markets for labour or for most goods or services.

Micro and macro economics

One of the most valuable results of the criticisms of traditional monetarists and new-Classicists is that macro economists have been forced to examine in great detail the microeconomic underpinnings of assumed macroeconomic relations. We observed on page 67 that economics is about behaviour, the behaviour of households, firms and central authorities. Relations that cannot be traced back to the microeconomic behaviour of basic decision-taking units are a mystery. Scientists always have to live with some mysteries but they are never satisfied to leave them as mysteries. Progress comes by understanding what we observe in terms of our theoretical constructs so that it ceases to be a mystery (while always holding open the possibility that the theoretical construct, and hence the 'understanding' that builds on it, may be wrong).

The progress of economics

The operation of scientific method is not a simple matter in economics. We lack laboratory conditions. We cannot get the holders of opposing views to agree on critical tests and then repeat them over and over until everyone must agree on the results. The call that economics try to be a science is a plea that economists try to relate their theories to observations. If we hold that the truth of economic theories is totally independent of successful empirical applications, it is difficult to see how economics can claim to be in any way useful in interpreting the world around us.

In economics, general acceptance that theories should be tested by confronting their predictions with the available evidence is fairly new. At this point you should re-read the quotation from Lord Beveridge given at the beginning of this book (see pages xi and xii). The controversy that Beveridge was describing was the one that followed the publication in 1936 of Keynes' *General Theory of Employment, Interest and Money*. Keynes' work gave rise to the macroeconomics that we have developed in the macro part of this book. At many points, we have raised the question of how various parts of macroeconomic theory could be tested; we have also discussed some of the tests that have already been conducted. Reflect on the differences between this approach to the problem of accepting or rejecting theories and the one described by Beveridge.

There is no doubt that since economics first began, some progress, albeit irregular and halting, has been made in relating theory to evidence. This progress has been reflected in the superior ability of governments to achieve their policy objectives. The pathetic efforts of successive British governments to deal with the economic catastrophe that overwhelmed the country after the return to the gold standard in the 1920s and even more so during the Great Depression of the 1930s show measures adopted in all sincerity which in most cases actually served to make things worse. Across the Atlantic, President Roosevelt's attempts to reduce American unemployment in the same decade were greatly hampered by the failure of most economists to realize the critical importance of budget deficits in increasing aggregate demand and hence national income.

The debate between monetarists and neo-Keynesians is another illustration of the value of the rule of evidence. Monetarists have several times had to revise their positions in the face of evidence. For example, they no longer hold that the demand for money is completely interest-inelastic, nor that fiscal policy cannot affect aggregate expenditure. The monetarist anti-inflation experiments of the late 1970s and early 1980s have been closely watched and heavily documented. Already we have hard evidence on several issues on which economists could only conjecture 10 to 15 years ago. The debate between Nicholas Kaldor on the one hand and Anna Schwartz and Milton Friedman on the other hand that took place in *Lloyds Bank Review* in 1970 makes instructive re-reading. Several of the points that Kaldor could then only assert that he thought were right have now been shown by solid evidence to be right. Emotionally committed monetarists and neo-Keynesians will never abandon their basic positions, but through the testing of their specific positions, those who have open minds really do learn about the behaviour of the economy.

It is in such important policy areas as the curing of major depressions and the handling of major inflations that the general thrust of our theories is tested, even if all their specific predictions are not. In some general sense, then, economic theories have always been subjected to empirical tests. When they were wildly at variance with the facts, the ensuing disaster could not but be noticed, and the theories were discarded or amended in the light of what was learned.

What we do not know covers vast areas, which should give all economists a sense of humility.

But those who feel that we know nothing need only involve themselves in a policy-making situation with non-economists to lose some of their feelings of inferiority. First, we really do know positive things about the behaviour of the economy that help us to evaluate policy choices. Second, we have a method of looking at problems that is potentially enlightening to almost any problem whether or not it is conventionally described as economic.

The advance of economics in the last 50 years partly reflects a change in economists' attitudes towards empirical observation. Today, we are much less likely to dismiss theories just because we do not like them and to refuse to abandon theories just because we do like them. Today, we are more likely to try to base our theories as much as possible on empirical observation, and to accept empirical relevance as the ultimate arbiter of the value of those theories. As human beings, we suffer much anguish at the upsetting of a pet theory; as scientists, we should try to train ourselves to take pleasure in it because of the new knowledge we gain thereby. It has been said that one of the great tragedies of science is the continual slaying of beautiful theories by ugly facts. As economists, we are all too often swayed by aesthetic considerations. In the past, we have too often clung to our theories because they were beautiful or because we liked their political implications; as scientists, we must always remember that when theory and fact come into serious conflict, it is theory, not fact, that must eventually give way.

Index